UNSOLD TELEVISION PILOTS:
1955-1989

LEE GOLDBERG

PREFACE TO THE NEW EDITION

Unsold Television Pilots 1955-1989 was the first compendium of its kind. I began writing it when I was nine years old. By the time I finished it, I was in my early twenties and was far enough along in my TV career that one of my filmed, unsold pilots actually became an entry in this book (*If You Knew Sammy*, a potential spin-off from *Spenser: For Hire*). I appreciated the irony. It somehow seemed fitting.

The book was written in those dark ages when information couldn't be Googled.... when research meant spending thousands of hours in libraries, going through books, magazines, newspapers, and microfiches (remember those?) and digging through dusty file cabinets.

At the time, unsold pilots were a mystery, and there was no single resource for finding out information about them. This book became that resource. And to my shock, and delight, the book became a sensation when it was published, leading to scores of articles, national TV interviews, a paperback abridgement (since republished as *The Best TV Shows That Never Were*), and over the years not one, but two network TV specials, *The Greatest Shows You Never Saw* (which I produced) on CBS in 1996 and *The Best TV Shows That Never Were* (which I wrote and produced) on ABC in 2004. The biggest thrill for me, though, was sitting in the audience of *The Tonight Show* with my wife Valerie while Johnny Carson, a certified TV legend, held the book in his hand, talked about how much he liked it, and then did a comedy bit based on it.

Over the years, readers have alerted me to mistakes in the book... the most embarrassing of which were the inadvertent inclusion of a few pilots that actually *did* sell and became series. *Cringe.* I've deleted those entries from this edition but made note of them to preserve the integrity of the original index (the pilots are listed by entry numbers, not page numbers).

I've also received hundreds of letters and emails from many attentive readers, who corrected errors, gave me additional details on dozens of pilots and alerted me to some unsold pilots that I'd missed (a few of which I've added). I'd like to single out Barry I. Grauman and Bill Warren for their eagle eyes and keen knowledge of television.

I've corrected most of the errors in the book (I say *most*, because I did my best to get'em all but I'm sure I missed some) added some of the new details, and added a few of the unsold pilots that I failed to discover the first time around… but not all of them. Most of the other unsold pilots that I missed have since been noted in TV reference books that followed mine over the last twenty-five years.

Oh, who am I kidding? The truth is, I didn't add much new stuff because that would be the path to madness for me. I wouldn't be able to stop until I brought the book entirely up-to-date, adding all of the unsold pilots produced since 1989.

I'll share with you my dark secret. Since the day I finished this book, I've continued to compile information for a follow-up edition and possible new TV specials. I've transferred all my old VHS tapes of unsold pilots to DVD…and I grab any new unsold pilots I can get my hands on or that I can record off-the-air. I still clip, literally and virtually, every article that I see about pilots-in-development. But in this age when it's so easy to find information on the web, when everything is databased (including, probably, every word of this book), it becomes increasingly unlikely that I'll ever write a sequel to this book covering 1989-to-present.

And yet… I keep gathering the information. So why do I do it?

It could be because I'm mentally ill. Or maybe because it's a habit that I started when I was seven years old and I've never entirely grown up. I'm still that kid inexplicably fascinated by all those lost pilots, those would-be TV series that never were. And if you're reading this book, I guess that you are, too.

Lee Goldberg
May 1, 2015

PREFACE AND ACKNOWLEDGMENTS TO THE 1989 EDITION

This book would not have been possible without the help of Gloria Edwards of the Leo Burnett Agency—which has been reviewing pilots for its clients since 1955 and graciously made its files available to me.

I am indebted to Ms. Edwards, Leonard Reeg and all the people who have worked in the TV Program Department of the Leo Burnett Agency over the years preparing those invaluable reports.

The information in this book is culled from the Leo Burnett reports, network press releases, and personally conducted interviews, as well as listings, reviews, and articles from the entertainment industry publications *TV Guide, Variety, The Hollywood Reporter,* and *Electronic Media.*

All the information in this book was cross-checked against previously published material whenever possible. A bibliography of those works follows. I'd like especially to thank authors Vincent Terrace, Alvin H. Marill, James Robert Parish, Jeb Perry, and Larry James Gianakos for their definitive works.

During the years it took to research and write this book, many people shared their time, experience, guidance and patience with me – often more than I deserved. A special thanks to Burl Barer, William Rabkin, Adam Gold, Karen Bender, Stephen J. Cannell, Steven Bochco, Sherwood Schwartz, J. Bret Garwood, Roy Huggins, Harry Ackerman, David Gerber, Kelly Selvidge, Ron Givens, Janet Huck, Ron Alridge, David Klein, Richard Mahler, Morrie Gelman, David McDonnell, Lloyd Friedman, Elisa Williams, Megan Powell, Carol Fowler, Sean Hillier, Michael Carmack, and Peter Biskind.

Lee Goldberg
Los Angeles
March 21, 1989

TABLE OF CONTENTS

Preface to the New Edition   vii
Preface and Acknowledgments to the 1989 Edition   ix
How to Read This Book   xxiii
Original Introduction to the 1989 Edition   xxv

1956–1957   1
  ABC / Comedy   3
  ABC / Drama   3
  William Broidy Productions   4
  CBS / Comedy   5
  CBS / Drama   5
  Jack Chertok Productions   6
  Conne-Stephens Productions   6
  Ralph Edwards Productions   7
  Flying A Productions (Gene Autry)   7
  Four Star Productions   7
  Sam Gallu Productions   7
  Goodson-Todman Productions   7
  Gross-Krasne Productions   8
  Guild Films   8
  Sam Jaffe Productions   8
  Elliot Lewis Productions   8
  MCA   8
  McCadden Productions   9
  McGowan Productions   9
  NBC / Comedy   9
  NBC / Drama   11
  Roland Reed Productions   12
  Screen Gems Productions   12
  Studio City Productions – Republic Pictures   13

20th Century Fox Television	13
TPA	13
Warner Bros. Television	13
ZIV	13
Independent Productions	14
1957–1958	**15**
ABC / Comedy	17
ABC / Drama	17
Ashley Steiner Agency	17
Batjac (John Wayne Productions)	18
Irving Brecher Productions	18
CBS / Comedy	18
CBS / Drama	19
Frank Cooper and Associates	21
Desilu Productions	21
Dougfair Productions	22
Ralph Edwards Productions	22
Flying A Productions (Gene Autry)	22
Fordyce Productions	22
Four Star Productions	22
Ben Fox Productions	23
Goodson-Todman Productions	23
Guild Films	23
Mark VII Productions	23
MCA Productions	23
McCadden Productions	23
MGM Productions	24
NBC / Comedy	24
NBC / Drama	25
Official Films	25
RKO	25
Hal Roach Productions	26
Screen Gems Productions	26
TPA	27
20th Century Fox	27
Warner Bros. Television	27

1958–1959   **29**

  ABC / Comedy   31
  ABC / Drama   31
  BATJAC (John Wayne Productions)   31
  CBS / Comedy   31
  CBS / Drama   32
  Desilu   34
  Famous Artists   34
  Flying A Productions   34
  Four Star Productions   34
  Albert Gannaway   35
  General Teleradio   35
  Goldstone/Tobias Agency   35
  Bob Hope Enterprises   36
  MCA/Revue Productions   36
  MGM   36
  NBC / Comedy   37
  NBC / Drama   38
  Odyssey (Dougfair)   40
  Hal Roach Productions   40
  Screen Gems Productions   40
  Trendle/Campbell Productions   41
  20th Century Fox   41
  Warner Bros. Television   41
  William Morris Agency   41
  Independent Productions   42

1959–1960   **43**

  ABC / Comedy   45
  ABC / Drama   45
  Ashley Steiner Agency   46
  CBS / Comedy   47
  CBS / Drama   48
  Desilu Productions   50
  Film Masters   51
  Four Star Productions   51
  General Artists Corporation   51

Goodson-Todman Productions   52
Hal Hackett Productions/Official Films   52
Hecht Hill Lancaster   52
Sandy Howard and Associates   52
George Huskin and Associates   53
Independent Television Corporation   53
Mark VII Productions   54
MCA/Revue Productions   54
McCadden Productions   54
MGM   55
NBC / Comedy   55
NBC / Drama   57
Hal Roach Productions   58
Screen Gems Productions   59
Stagg Productions   60
20th Century Fox   60
United Artists   60
Warner Bros. Television   61
William Morris Agency   61
Young & Marcus Productions   61
Independent Producers   61

1960–1961   63
ABC / Comedy   65
ABC / Drama   65
Ashley Steiner Agency   66
CBS / Comedy   66
CBS / Drama   68
Frank Cooper and Associates   70
Film Masters   70
Four Star Productions   70
Goodson-Todman Productions   71
International Television Corporation   71
MCA Productions   71
MGM-TV   71
NBC / Comedy   72
NBC / Drama   73
Paramount   75

Roncom   76
Screen Gems Productions   76
20th Century Fox   76
Independent Producers   76

1961–1962   77
ABC / Comedy   79
ABC / Drama   79
Ardley Productions   79
Arrowhead Productions   80
Ashley Steiner Agency   80
Brogill Productions   80
California National   80
CBS / Comedy   80
CSB / Drama   82
Bing Crosby Productions   83
Desilu Productions   83
Ralph Edwards Productions   83
Don Fedderson Productions   83
Film Masters   84
Four Star Productions   84
Goodson-Todman Productions   84
Mark VII Productions   85
MCA Productions   85
MGM   86
NBC / Comedy   86
NBC / Drama   87
Redbill Productions   88
Roncom   88
Screen Gems Productions   89
Don Sharpe Productions   89
20th Century Fox   89
Warner Bros.   90
ZIV/United Artists   90

1962–1963   91
ABC / Comedy   93
ABC / Drama   94

Ashley Steiner Agency   95
CBS / Comedy   95
CBS / Drama   99
Desilu   101
Ralph Edwards Productions   101
Film Masters   102
Filmways   102
Four Star Productions   102
Goodson-Todman Productions   102
MCA/Revue Productions   103
MGM   103
NBC / Comedy   103
NBC / Drama   104
Southill Productions   106
20th Century Fox   106
United Artists   106
Independent Producers   106

1963–1964   **107**
ABC / Comedy   109
ABC / Drama   109
CBS / Comedy   112
MGM   112
NBC / Comedy   113
NBC / Drama   113
Paramount   115
Rand-Brooks Productions   115
Screen Gems Production   115
Stover Company   116
Time-Life Productions   116

1964–1965   **117**
ABC / Comedy   119
ABC / Drama   119
CBS / Comedy   122
CBS / Drama   124
NBC / Comedy   125
NBC / Drama   125

Independent Productions 126
Filmways 126
Four Star 127
Gannaway Productions 127
Green and Stone Productions 127
MCA/Revue 128
Screen Gems 128

1965–1966 **129**
ABC / Comedy 131
ABC / Drama 132
CBS / Comedy 133
CBS / Drama 137
NBC / Comedy 138
NBC / Drama 140
Independent Productions 142

1966–1967 **145**
ABC / Comedy 147
ABC / Drama 148
CBS / Comedy 151
CBS / Drama 153
NBC / Comedy 154
NBC / Drama 156
Independent Productions 159

1967–1968 **161**
ABC / Comedy 163
ABC / Drama 164
CBS / Comedy 164
CBS / Drama 166
NBC / Comedy 167
NBC / Drama 169
Independent Productions 170

1968–1969 **171**
ABC / Comedy 173
ABC / Drama 173

CBS / Comedy   174
CBS / Drama   175
NBC / Comedy   176
NBC / Drama   177

1969–1970   **179**
ABC / Comedy   181
ABC / Drama   182
CBS / Comedy   184
CBS / Drama   185
NBC / Comedy   186
NBC / Drama   187

1970–1971   **189**
ABC / Comedy   191
ABC / Drama   192
CBS / Comedy   193
CBS / Drama   194
NBC / Comedy   195
NBC / Drama   197

1971–1972   **199**
ABC / Comedy   201
ABC / Drama   202
CBS / Comedy   205
CBS / Drama   207
NBC / Comedy   208
NBC / Drama   211

1972–1973   **215**
ABC / Comedy   217
ABC / Drama   219
CBS / Comedy   225
CBS / Drama   227
NBC / Comedy   229
NBC / Drama   231

1973–1974   237
ABC / Comedy   239
ABC / Drama   241
CBS / Comedy   247
CBS / Drama   250
NBC / Comedy   252
NBC / Drama   255

1974–1975   261
ABC / Comedy   263
ABC / Drama   265
CBS / Comedy   272
CBS / Drama   276
NBC / Comedy   278
NBC / Drama   279

1975–1976   287
ABC / Comedy   289
ABC / Drama   291
CBS / Comedy   296
CBS / Drama   298
NBC / Comedy   301
NBC / Drama   302

1976–1977   309
ABC / Comedy   311
ABC / Drama   312
CBS / Comedy   318
CBS / Drama   321
NBC / Comedy   324
NBC / Drama   328

1977–1978   335
ABC / Comedy   337
ABC / Drama   339
CBS / Comedy   344

CBS / Drama 347
NBC / Comedy 352
NBC / Drama 358

1978–1979 **369**
ABC / Comedy 371
ABC / Drama 373
CBS / Comedy 375
CBS / Drama 381
NBC / Comedy 386
NBC / Drama 388

1979–1980 **397**
ABC / Comedy 399
ABC / Drama 402
CBS / Comedy 407
CBS / Drama 413
NBC / Comedy 420
NBC / Drama 427

1980–1981 **437**
ABC / Comedy 439
ABC / Drama 441
CBS / Comedy 444
CBS / Drama 449
NBC / Comedy 452
NBC / Drama 457

1981–1982 **465**
ABC / Comedy 467
ABC / Drama 470
CBS / Comedy 472
CBS / Drama 475
NBC / Comedy 478
NBC / Drama 483

1982–1983   489
   ABC / Comedy   491
   ABC / Drama   492
   CBS / Comedy   495
   CBS / Drama   499
   NBC / Comedy   503
   NBC / Drama   508

1983–1984   511
   ABC / Comedy   513
   ABC / Drama   515
   CBS / Comedy   517
   CBS / Drama   522
   NBC / Comedy   525
   NBC / Drama   529

1984–1985   533
   ABC / Comedy   535
   ABC / Drama   537
   CBS / Comedy   540
   CBS / Drama   543
   NBC / Comedy   546
   NBC / Drama   550

1985–1986   555
   ABC / Comedy   557
   ABC / Drama   560
   CBS / Comedy   566
   CBS / Drama   568
   NBC / Comedy   572
   NBC / Drama   575

1986–1987   579
   ABC / Comedy   581
   ABC / Drama   584

CBS / Comedy   591
CBS / Drama   594
NBC / Comedy   598
NBC / Drama   600

1987–1988   **605**
ABC / Comedy   607
ABC / Drama   609
CBS / Comedy   612
CBS / Drama   618
NBC / Comedy   622
NBC / Drama   625

1988–1989   **631**
ABC / Comedy   633
ABC / Drama   636
CBS / Comedy   640
CBS / Drama   645
NBC / Comedy   650
NBC / Drama   653

Bibliography   **659**

About the Author   **663**

Index   **665**

HOW TO READ THIS BOOK

If a pilot sold, and became a series, it is not included in this book. In some cases, there are pilots in this book that *did* lead to series – but only after substantial recasting or radical alterations in the concepts. Those few pilots are included because they are so different from the series they begat, and give us unique insight into the development process.

Each chapter represents a television season. For example, the flop pilots in the 1976-77 chapter were developed during the previous season for the 1976 fall schedule (or as replacement series).

As television entered its adolescence, control of programming gradually shifted from the advertisers to the networks. The early chapters (through about 1962 or 1963) are dominated by (and alphabetized by) production companies, all of which were trying to win sponsors and thereby a place on the network schedules. But several powerful forces changed all that (see Introduction).

Beginning in the early 1960s, producers pitched their series ideas directly to the networks, which commissioned the pilots and decided their fates, and that is how the system remains today. The pilots in the chapters from 1968–69 on are arranged exclusively by network (and further subdivided between comedy and drama); there were no active independents.

Only pilots for primetime, network television are examined here. Shows developed for daytime, or for syndication, are excluded. Variety shows and gameshows, with rare exceptions, are not covered.

The emphasis in this book, as in the networks themselves, is on the concepts, the continuing characters, and the star, who is sometimes more important than any other factor. The plot of the pilot story, while important, is not the chief concern of the networks or of the author. The same concepts can come back again and again, year after year. For that reason, many series ideas are listed even if the pilot was never produced and little, or no, other information is available about them.

Since the original publication of this book, several pilots listed have sold and others were incorrectly included. Those have been omitted, though the numerical order of the pilots from the previous edition has not been changed.

Of course, if you have any additional information about those shows, or about any other unsold pilots, we'd like to hear about it (that also goes for any errors you spot). Please write to the author in care of the publisher.

ORIGINAL INTRODUCTION
TO THE 1989 EDITION

A television pilot is a sample episode of a proposed weekly series. An unsold pilot is much, much more.

It's fresh faces and old favorites lining up for a one-night stand with the viewing public. It's producers, writers, directors and network executives scrambling to keep up with the changing trends in American taste. It's the betting stub you're left with after your horse has lost the race.

"When pilots work, they work well," says Perry Simon, NBC's head of comedy development. "And when they flop, they thud pretty loudly. There are a thousand ways it can go wrong and only one way it will go right."

Pilots sneak onto the airwaves disguised as television movies, specials, lavish miniseries, or even as an episode of your favorite show. Good or bad, pilots give viewers the rare opportunity to second guess the networks at their own game–judging which ideas have the potential to become hit series.

But it's more than a game. It's a business that eats up more than $30 million a year—at *each* network. That doesn't count the $20 million or more a studio invests. Each year a network is bombarded with thousands of ideas, from which it may buy 125 scripts, shoot 30 pilots, and pick up six or seven as fall series. Of those series, perhaps two will survive the season. In 1986, 103 pilots were made for the 1986–87 schedule, only 36 became series and of those, just 13 survived to celebrate their first birthdays.

With odds like that, why bother? Because if a pilot sells, and if the series can survive for a few seasons, untold riches could await the producers in syndication—perhaps well over the hundreds of millions of dollars M*A*S*H, *Magnum P.I.*, and *Cosby* have made.

A pilot is a way for networks to hedge their bets before risking millions of dollars for 22 episodes of a show that may look great on paper and turn out rotten when shot. For producers, pilot making is a multimillion dollar gamble that offers no hedging. Although the networks pay a fee for making the pilot, producers invariably spend more because they want the show to look great—because they want it to *sell*.

But unless the pilot evolves into a series, "we've got to absorb substantial deficits," says Dean Hargrove, producer of *Matlock*. "It's a big gamble and you'll probably never get your money back. Pilots are a waste of time and money. They don't make shows any more successful. At the end of every season, the streets are littered with canceled series."

Whether pilots are the best way to sell a series can be argued forever. The fact is, that's the way series have been sold since television began. What *has* changed is the buyer.

In its infancy, television was the bastard child of the entertainment industry. The new medium, modeled after radio, was shunned by the major Hollywood studios, which saw television as a threat to their bottom line. So, the programs came from aggressive, independent producers and the networks, all of whom pitched their series concepts directly to the advertising agencies, whose clients footed a big chunk of the pilot-production costs and ultimately decided which series would get on the air. Network television became picture radio, adopting many of the same series and carrying on the practice of single-sponsor shows.

That all changed around 1960, when several powerful forces wrestled control of television programming from the advertisers and gave it to the networks. The network chiefs had been anxious to change the power structure of commercial television for years. Sylvester "Pat" Weaver, NBC's president and a former advertising agency executive, believed networks should control programming and that sponsors should buy advertising time the same way they bought space in a magazine. And like a magazine, which chooses what articles it will print, a network should decide what series it will air.

Financial realities forced the advertisers to consider Weaver's vision whether they liked it or not. The high cost of production was making it impossible for any one advertiser to bankroll a program. With Weaver's magazine concept, several advertisers could share the burden and the rewards of sponsoring a show.

Meanwhile, Mickey Mouse was changing the movie moguls' minds about television. The enormous success of ABC's 1954 series *Disneyland*, produced for television by Walt Disney's studio, convinced the majors there was money in the medium. The experienced, deep-pocketed studios started cranking out programming, and they weren't about to let a bunch of advertisers tell them how to do it.

But it wasn't the big network honchos, the big price tags, or the big studios that finally forced advertisers out of the programming business. It was the revelation that the advertisers had rigged popular, primetime game shows, and the subsequent scandal which erupted, that dealt the final blow. The networks canceled the game shows and promised the American people *they* would control programming from now on.

The networks became the buyers, and frequently the originators, of series programming. Many influential advertising agency executives, like Lee Rich and Grant Tinker, left their jobs to join the networks or create their own production companies. A new system emerged. Independent producers and studios developed pilots specifically to suit a particular network's needs and personality.

The key to making any sale is the right product, at the right time, at the right price. A producer with a series idea makes a sales pitch to the networks. Having a major star, a prestigious writer or a well-known director already attached to the project can often turn an otherwise so-so concept into a quick sale. If the network likes the idea, it will commission a script, and if they like what they read, they will order a pilot. For a sitcom, that usually means a 30-minute sample episode. Dramatic series pilots are a different breed altogether.

By the early 70s, most dramatic pilots were two-hour or 90-minute television movies that cost a fortune and were designed to blow the network executives right out of their seats. The problem was, if the pilot sold, the studio had to "duplicate the pilot each week for a lot less money," says producer David Gerber, president of MGM Television. Often, the shows didn't fulfill the promise of their multimillion dollar pilots.

"If you dazzle 'em in your pilot with fancy footwork, spectacular car crashes, and European locales," says *Equalizer* producer James McAdams, "and then the first week that you're a series the hero chases someone through the backlot and tackles him, that's not a pilot, that's deceit."

That's the major reason why the networks currently are saving their pennies and ordering fewer movie-length pilots, opting instead for the so-called "typical hour-long episode" and other formats that don't cost so much. The networks feel a 60-minute pilot is more indicative of what a typical episode of the proposed series will be like. That's nice for the networks, but it makes pilots an even bigger risk for the studios. While a television movie pilot can recoup its production deficits in syndication, foreign theatrical release, and in home video sales, "what the hell can be done with a one-hour pilot that doesn't sell?" asks producer Stephanie Kowal, formerly Universal Television's dramatic development executive. "Nothing."

Producers also complain that the hour-long format forces them to cram too much information into the show, usually at the expense of character. And if the characters don't come across well, the pilot is dead. Greg Maday, CBS's vice president of dramatic development, believes a 60-minute pilot can still be "good entertainment if it's done correctly. We don't want the pilots to feel like a piece of engineering with no dramatic values, and they don't have to be." But they almost always are.

The pilot has to get across the series concept, the backgrounds and relationships of the characters and tell a compelling story, all in one show. That fact alone guarantees the pilot can never be like a typical episode of the proposed series, where the concept is a given, and the characters are already accepted by the viewers.

"The problem with one-hour pilots is you have to tell such a simple story that it's not interesting," says producer Stephen J. Cannell, the man behind such hits as *The Rockford Files* and *The A-Team*. "The network says 'make it like episode five.' Well, I'm sorry, you can't do that."

One way to avoid that problem has been to shoot the pilot as an episode of an existing series. It's also a lot cheaper, because if the pilot doesn't sell, the costs can be recouped when the host series goes into syndication. *Star Trek, Who's the Boss?, Kojak, Golden Girls, Magnum PI*, and *The Untouchables* are just a few of the many series that count unsold pilots among their episodes. Ann Daniel, ABC's vice president of dramatic development, thinks episodes-as-pilots are "a terrific way to do a pilot. It's more economically responsible." But episodes-as-pilots have their own artistic and financial pitfalls.

"You have to minimize your own protagonists to give the show to the pilot star. It makes for a bad episode of the show," says McAdams. "A good episode is where the hero of the series is the star, not the guest star. The hero is reduced to a book-end or a bystander." Some feel it's not worth the effort.

"They hardly ever work out. It's just a cheap way of knocking off a pilot," says Jeff Sagansky, head of TriStar Pictures and formerly NBC's vice president of series programming.

And what do the viewers think? "They probably hate it," Sagansky says. "The reason they watch the show is not to see pilots. But, if you only do it once a year, I guess it's okay."

Producers can get away with episodes-as-pilots much more often, and with a lot less grief, in anthology series. On shows like *Kraft Suspense Theatre, The Dick Powell Theatre*, and more recently with ABC's *Disney Sunday Movie*, nearly *all* the episodes were pilots.

With program costs and studio deficits skyrocketing, many producers believe that networks should junk pilots altogether and make series commitments to proven talent instead. "We are great believers that the best way to make the best series is to make commitments with the best possible people," says Stu Erwin, president of MTM Enterprises, which has sold several shows, including *St. Elsewhere* and *Mary*, that way.

"I understand networks' wanting to see what the new guys can do," says Kowal, "but when you're dealing with an established group, you don't need a pilot."

That philosophy worked with *Cheers, L.A. Law*, and *Hooperman*, but it can backfire, too. When *Hill Street Blues* producer Stephen Bochco pitched NBC on the serialized adventures of a baseball team, it sounded like a great idea. In 1983, NBC bought 13 episodes of *Bay City Blues* sight unseen but canceled it with half the episodes unaired. *Life with Lucy, Amazing Stories, AfterMASH, Jessie, Mr. Smith, Private Eye, Cassie and Company,* and *Partners in Crime* were also commitments—and disasters.

"It's the kind of deal everyone wants but it has its flaws," says producer Tom Mankiewicz, who sold *Gavilan* to NBC in 1982 without a pilot. It was canceled so fast even he has trouble remembering it. "You go on the air right away and everything that does and doesn't work about your character is rehearsed in front of the audience. But when you do a pilot, you can look at it and say 'It works great when he does X but it doesn't when he does Y.' You can fix it before the audience sees it."

Networks want pilots, but producers gripe about the high cost. Producers want commitments, but the networks want to see what they are buying. There's a possible compromise. Both networks and producers have long been experimenting with brief, 10–20 minute demonstration films rather than shooting a pilot. The practice has yet to take hold, and only a few series, like *Knightrider* and *Emerald Point, NAS* have sold that way.

"To get the point across, it works well," says producer Richard Chapman, who produced a demo film for CBS about a Ninja-trained female spy. "The 20-minute presentation is more eye-catching and gets the best of a shorter attention span." Chapman wrote an hour-long pilot script and from that culled the demo film, which was made up of three character scenes – one funny, one tense, and one showing warmth – and some Ninja combat. The series didn't sell.

CBS' Greg Maday thinks demos are useless. "They simply aren't indicative of what the series will be."

"It's a vicious circle," says veteran producer William Blinn, whose credits include *Our House, Fame,* and *Roots.* "You can't say demos are wrong because they have highlights and that two hours are wrong because the series won't deliver what the pilot did."

Selling the pilot, in whatever form, as a series is a feat every producer tries to achieve in April, when the networks huddle in New York in countless boardrooms, restaurants, hotel suites and limousines to devise their fall season strategy. And the producers are there to help them along—they are there for questions, drinks, dinners, plays and schmoozing, especially schmoozing. That ritual, too, is questioned by producers.

"It's all a nice convention, part of salesmanship, but I don't think wining and dining the executives is a decisive factor," says McAdams. "There might be a few borderline cliffhanger situations where it might help. But if I were a network executive, I would look at the producer's abilities and the pilot and not be influenced by a filet mignon."

"A producer's enthusiasm for his product is infectious, that's something the networks listen to," Sagansky admits. "Is it a deciding factor? In the end the program has to speak for itself." Yet most pilots die, whether it's in a scheduling meeting or over lobster at Sardi's.

"A lot of good scripts and pilots die because New York didn't understand it," laments David Gerber. "Or, everybody on the West Coast loved it but somewhere over the Rockies somebody with a Death Ray Beam hit the plane and the pilot show landed as dust in New York. You just sit there and wonder 'What happened to my film?'"

What happens to the flop pilot? Occasionally another network will pick one up. A few, like the disastrous *Marblehead Manor* and *She's the Sheriff*, get a second chance in first run syndication. And still others end up gathering dust at your local video store.

Those are the exceptions. Unsold pilots are rarely exhumed by anyone.

"It's dead, on my shelf, and late some night I might get stoned and I might look at it," says *Family Ties* producer Gary David Goldberg. "Or it will show up in one of those *Shame Theatres, Failure Playhouses*, or four-in-a-row specials when America doesn't know what hit 'em late one night."

By watching and studying flop pilots, we can feel like we "are in on the machinations of television," says Gerber. "There's a curiosity factor, maybe even a true perversity, in watching these things and asking 'why the hell did it ever get made?'"

And that's the fun of it. Do car companies share the new model designs they're thinking about? Does Yves St. Laurent pass out his sketches for everyone to see? Does Apple let IBM peek at their newest PC? Only television makes their developmental process public to their competitors—and to us.

The networks are in the entertainment business and, lucky for us consumers, even the business-behind-the business is entertainment. Pilots may be lunacy, but as long as they make them, as long as they sneak them into primetime, we can all pretend we can run a network.

1956–1957

ABC / COMEDY

1. **Publicity Girl.** Two pilots were made with Jan Sterling, in one she was a Hollywood publicity agent (which became the series *Publicity Girl*) and in the other she worked for the orange industry.

ABC / DRAMA

2. **Amazon Trader.** Production Company: Warner Bros. John Sutton would star as the title character in the proposed series, which would be shot on location in Uruguay.

3. **Arizona Ames.** Production Company: Four Star. The adventures of Zane Grey's western hero.

4. **Beauty Parlor.** Production Company: Screen Gems. The story of the woman who runs the beauty parlor in a typical American small town. And, in many ways, she runs the town as well.

5. **Big Foot Wallace.** Production Company: Conne-Stephens. Chuck Connors would star as a modern-day Davy Crockett.

6. **Command Performance.** 74 min. Production Company: Meridian Productions. Director: Don Weis. Executive Producer: William Self. Producer: John Gibbs. Writer: Milton Gelman. Music: Melvyn Lenard. Don Taylor, who starred in the pilot for the series *Richard Diamond*, plays an assistant to a slick publicist (Raymond Burr) who specializes in keeping his clients' indiscretions out of the papers in this pilot for a proposed anthology series. The pilot, which never aired, was released as the film *Ride the High Iron*, and costarred Sally Forrest, Otto Waldis, Nestor Paiva, Mae Clark, Maurice Marsac, Robert Johnson.

7. **The Forest Ranger.** 30 min. Production Company: 20th Century Fox Television. Director: Paul Landers. Executive Producer: Hal Roach, Jr. Producer: Ben Fox. Writers: Tom Blackburn and Ben Fox. Dick Foran stars as a forest ranger who, with his son, lives in the San Bernardino Mountains, where the series would have been shot on location. *Cast:* Dick Foran (as Will Roberts), Adam Kennedy (David Erickson), John Dehner (Frank Jennings), Dabbs Greer (Ted Borton), Willis Bouchey (Jody

Scott), Susan Cummings (Ann Loring), Bobby Clark (Jimmy Loring), Allen Jenkins (Harry Clark), Charles Smith (Chet Wiley), Chuch Robertson (Dan Talbot), Fred Krone (Hank Nixon).

8. **International Theatre.** Producer: Sheldon Reynolds. Host: Dan O'Herlihy. An anthology featuring stories of "international adventure."

9. **Knight of the South Seas.** Producers: Harry S. Rothschild and Leon Fromkess. This pilot is a reworking of *Ramar of the Jungle* (1952–53), which starred Jon Hall as a physician and scientist in Kenya. This time, Hall would play a similar hero working in the South Seas.

10. **The Landmark Show.** Production Company: Goodson-Todman Productions. Host: Bennett Cerf. Biographical stories adapted from the Landmark series of books. The pilot told the story of John Paul Jones.

11. **Latitude Zero.** Producer: Don Sharpe. Based on the science fiction/adventure radio program.

12. **Life Story.** Production Company: MCA. Producer: Ralph Edwards. This series would pick up where episodes of *This Is Your Life* left off. This anthology would dramatize the life stories of the *This Is Your Life* subjects.

13. **The Long Highway.** Production Company: Warner Bros. Television. Director: Lewis R. Foster. Writer: A. I. Bezzedires. J. Pat O'Malley starred as a truck dispatcher who introduced – in a host-like, narrator fashion – exciting tales about truck drivers. Based on the 1940 movie *The Drive by Night*, which was adapted from a book by A.I. Bezzerides.

14. **Marineland.** Production Company: Flying A Productions. Kenneth Brown, curator of the Marineland Aquarium in Palos Verdes, would tell the "little known stories" of "unusual fish."

15. **RFD USA.** Producer: Jerry Devine. True stories about "grass roots American life" that would be filmed on location.

16. **The Valley of Blue Mountain.** 60 min. Airdate: 3/11/61. Producer: Frank Wisbar. Aired as an episode of *Best of the Post*, this pilot starring Bonita Granville as a city-bred woman who owns a farm. The projected series would have been shot on Wisbar's ranch in Northern California.

WILLIAM BROIDY PRODUCTIONS

17. **Ride the Bugle.** Writer: James Warner Bellah. Adventures of a cavalry officer, to be played by Dennis O'Keefe.

CBS / COMEDY

18. **Adventures of a Model.** 60 min. Airdate: 8/19/58 (NBC) 9/6/60 (CBS). Production Company: Desilu Productions. Director: Norman Tokar. Creator/Producer: Sidney Sheldon. Joanne Dru starred as a professional model in this busted pilot that was made in 1956, aired as an episode of *Colgate Theatre* in 1958 and then offered again on CBS. Guest stars included Nancy Kulp, William Kendis, Rozanne Arland, Charles Waggenheim, Robert D. Jellison, Jimmy Cross, and Phil Arnold. *Cast:* Joanne Dru (as Marilyn Woods), John Emery (Ralph Carter), William Redfield (Dr. Roger Boone), Roland Winters (The Texan).

19. **Mr. Belvedere.** 60 min. Airdate: 4/18/56. Production Company: 20th Century Fox Television. Aired as an episode of *20th Century Fox Hour*. Reginald Gardiner starred as the quick-witted, intellectual butler Clifton Webb created in the movies. Costarred ZaSu Pitts, Eddie Bracken, Margaret Hayes.

20. **Time Out for Ginger.** 60 min. Airdate: 10/6/55. Director: Ralph Levy. Producer: Ralph Levy. Writers: Hugh Wedlock, Howard Snyder and Jack Tackaberry, from the play by Ronald Alexander. Aired as an episode of *Shower of Stars*. The misadventures of Ginger, a headstrong teenage girl who joins the high school football team to the consternation of everybody but her father. The play this pilot was based on would later serve as the basis for the 1965 comedy *Billie*, which Mr. Alexander wrote for Patty Duke. *Cast:* Jack Benny (as Howard Carol), Ruth Hussey (Agnes Carol), Janet Parker (Ginger Carol), Gary Crosby (Eddie Davis), Ronnie Burns (Tommy Carol), Edward Horton (Ed Hoffman), Fred Keating (WJ Archer), Mary Wickes (Lizzie).

21. **Waldo.** 30 min. Airdate: 9/19/60. Director: Arthur David Hilton. Executive Producer: Robert Maxwell. Producer: Rudy E. Abel. Writer: Sumner Long. Gil Stratton would star as an anthropologist sharing an apartment with an intelligent chimp named Waldo. Over twenty years later a similar concept—with a different animal—was tried out in *Ethel Is an Elephant*. Costars included Emory Parnell, Eleanor Odley, Virginia Wells, Frank Jenks and Robert Griffin.

CBS / DRAMA

22. **Assignment: Mexico.** Producer: Harry Ackerman. The adventures of a female CIA agent (Peggie Castle) who runs a travel agency in Mexico as her cover. The proposed series would be shot in color on location in Mexico.

23. **Cavalry Patrol.** 30 min. Director: Charles Marquis Warren. Producer: Charles Marquis Warren. Writer: John Champion, from a story by Charles Marquis Warren. Dewey Martin starred in this pilot, shot entirely on location in Utah, which was earmarked as a Friday night replacement series for *Our Miss Brooks* but got bumped by *Zane Grey Theatre.* The pilot opened with the narration, "This is the territory, Arizona, 1868. This is the fort, such as it is. These are the men. Ex-mutineers, deserters, confederate prisoners. But mixed in with these are a handful of the finest regulars on earth, all of them soldiers, at $13 a month. My name is Reardon." The show closed with these words: "16,000 miles of enemy frontier to be patrolled, a handful of men to do it. This is what had to be done." *Cast:* Dewey Martin (as Lt. Johnny Reardon), John Pickard (Sgt. Gilchrist), Sheb Wooley (Lank Clee), Harry Landers (Pvt. Danny Quintana), Charles Gray (Pvt. Reb Weeb), Royal Dano (Chattez), Paul Richards (Mango), Bing Russell (Jenner), Richard Golden (Pvt. Weldon).

24. **Hart of Honolulu.** A secret agent in the South Pacific. The proposed series would have been shot entirely on location. Warren Stevens starred.

25. **Plane-for-Hire.** Producer: Harry Ackerman. Writer: Art Cohn. The adventures of a charter airline pilot. Writer Art Cohn was later killed in a plane crash which also claimed the life of actor Michael Todd.

26. **The Trailblazer (aka Adventures of Fremont).** Producer: Harry Ackerman. A series based on the life of John C. Fremont, with Steve Cochran as the star. The episodes would include appearances by historical figures like Abraham Lincoln, Kit Carson, Jim Bridger and others.

JACK CHERTOK PRODUCTIONS

27. **The Family Tree.** Producer: Jack Chertok. A family tree would be presented each week and the episode would concern someone on that tree. Although an anthology, the concept is designed to get viewers interested in the clan. The series never made it but the concept proved its validity in the late 1970s with the success of *Roots.*

28. **Mr. Big.** Producer: Jack Chertok. A series about the life and adventures of a Hollywood tycoon. Walter Slezak and Gregory Ratoff were considered for the title role.

CONNE-STEPHENS PRODUCTIONS

29. **Boys' Town.** Writer: John Lee Mahin. The dramatization of true stories from the annals of Father Flanagan's juvenile center.

30. **Sheriff USA.** Keith Andes stars as a sheriff in a series that would be based on actual case files of various county sheriffs across the nation.

RALPH EDWARDS PRODUCTIONS

31. **The Professor and the Kids.** Bruce Kamman, who once was Koltenmeyer of *Koltenmeyer's Kindergarten*, teaches a class of kids, played by adult comedians like Artie Auerbach and Ben Lessey.

FLYING A PRODUCTIONS (GENE AUTRY)

32. **The Winning of the West.** Aimed at the audience of *Death Valley Days*, the producers offer an anthology with the same format but offering stories of "bigger scope."

FOUR STAR PRODUCTIONS

33. **The Joker.** The story of two comedy writers working for a great television comedian. The premise would be employed several years later for *The Dick Van Dyke Show*.
34. **Old Man Coffee.** Writer: Alan LeMay, based on his books. The title character is a "western Dr. Christian" who lives in the mountains and hunts lions with his pack of hounds and along the way, helps people in need or jeopardy. Chill Wills was set to star.
35. **The Salvage Master.** Stories of ocean salvage operations from the files of Merrit, Chapman and Scott, the largest salvage company in the world.
36. **The Stars and the State.** The story of a state, hosted by a famous actor from that state.

SAM GALLU PRODUCTIONS

37. The previously listed pilot **Border Patrol** became the series *U. S. Border Patrol*.
38. **Entry.** Producer: Sam Gallu. An anthology culled from the files of the U.S. Immigration and Naturalization Service.

GOODSON-TODMAN PRODUCTIONS

39. The previously listed pilot **The Gun and the Quill** became the series *Jefferson Drum*.
40. **Marvin.** Writer/Producer: Phil Leslie. A handyman who tries to help people and, although he screws things up, eventually comes out okay.

GROSS-KRASNE PRODUCTIONS

41. The previously listed pilot *O. Henry Playhouse* became the syndicated series of the same name.

42. **Test Pilot.** Preston Foster would star in the title role in a series that would explore a test pilot's work and family life.

GUILD FILMS

43. The previously listed pilot **Captain Grief** became the syndicated series *Capt. David Grief*

44. **Here Comes Tobor.** Producer: Richard Goldstone. The adventures of a boy (Tommy Terrell) and his mechanical man who, like Superman, arrives just in time to avert disaster and save the people in peril. Also starred Arthur Space. Aired as an episode of *Captain Video and his Video Rangers* and based on the 1954 film *Tobor the Great*.

SAM JAFFE PRODUCTIONS

45. **I, Mickey Spillane.** Host: Mickey Spillane. The creator of Mike Hammer hosts an anthology of action stories similar to his own.

46. **Flight Plan.** Dale Robertson stars in the adventures of an army flight surgeon.

47. **Stake Out.** A *Candid Camera* of crime. A camera would be hidden wherever the San Diego police get a tip that a robbery will occur. The actual crime will be filmed and aired along with a dramatization of the events leading up to the robbery. All this would be done with the criminal's subsequent permission.

ELLIOT LEWIS PRODUCTIONS

48. **Crime Classics.** Producer: Elliot Lewis. Great crime stories from history provide the episodes for this proposed anthology. The pilot script concerned the first woman to be hanged in the United States.

MCA

49. **Box 13.** The adventures of a newspaper man. Alan Ladd agreed to do 39 episodes.

50. **The City.** Mark Stevens was set to star and host the pilot for a series featuring true stories about the city of Manhattan.

51. **John Ford Presents.** Modeled after *Alfred Hitchcock Presents*, the famed director John Ford would host this action/adventure anthology and helm several episodes as well.

52. **The Teacher.** An anthology detailing the problems, frustrations and accomplishments of teachers. Greer Garson was being courted as the host and occasional star of the series.

53. **World's Greatest Letters.** Based on the Simon-Schuster book. The story behind each letter would serve as a story in this anthology. Producers suggested that Charles Laughton be the host.

MCCADDEN PRODUCTIONS

54. **Courage.** An anthology dramatizing the courageous acts of average people.

55. **The Delightful Imposter.** A modern Scarlet Pimpernel.

MCGOWAN PRODUCTIONS

56. **Snow Fire.** A *Lassie* clone about a wild white stallion who roams the range and befriends a rancher and his teenage daughter. The horse and girl can communicate psychically with one another.

NBC / COMEDY

57. **Alexander Botts.** Production Company: NBC Productions. The misadventures of a famous tractor salesman. They hoped the series would star either Eddie Mayehoff or Jonathan Winters.

58. **Baby Snooks.** 30 min. Executive Producer: Jess Oppenheimer. Based on the Fanny Brice radio program. Martha Raye plays a woman who is playing Baby Snooks on the radio and the problems she has raising her own children.

59. **Calling Terry Conway.** 30 min. Airdate: 8/14/56. Aired as an episode of *Sneak Preview*. The misadventures of a public affairs director at a Las Vegas casino. *Cast:* Ann Sheridan (as Terry Conway), Una Merkel (Pearl McGrath), Philip Ober (Stan).

60. **Carolyn.** 30 min. Airdate: 8/7/56. Aired as an episode of *Sneak Preview*. actress who, after her best friend is killed in an accident, becomes guardian to her three children.

It bore a striking resemblance to *Sis*, another NBC pilot, and the *Betty Hutton Show*, which aired on CBS 1959–60. *Cast:* Celeste Holm (as Carolyn Daniels), Patricia Morrow (Elizabeth), Susan Hawkins (Candy), Jimmy Hawkins (Buster), Jeanette Nolan (Mrs. Tuttle), Parley Baer (Smattering), Kay Walker (Reporter).

61. **The Darwin Family.** Production Company: William Morris. A spin-off from the *NBC Comedy Hour*. While monkeys frolic on the set, off-screen actors provide "their voices." Twenty years later, ABC would do a Saturday morning children's series entitled *Lancelot Link* based on the same notion.

62. **Johnny Come Lately. 30** min. Airdate: 8/8/60. Director: James V. Kern. Producer: Milt Josefsberg. Writers: Robert O'Brien and Irving Elison. Aired as an episode of *CBS Comedy Showcase*. Jack Carson plays a television commentator with "a nose for trouble" in this pilot that eventually aired on CBS. *Cast:* Jack Carson (as Johnny Martin), Marie Windsor (Angela Talbot), Dick Reeves (Eddie), Alvy Moore (Andy), Ernest Sarracino (Pardo), Tracy Morgan (Holly).

63. **Just Plain Folks.** 30 min. Airdate: 8/14/56. The misadventures of a husband (Cy Howard) and wife (Zsa Zsa Gabor) – he's a screenwriter and she's an actress.

64. **Life of Vernon Hathaway.** 30 min. Airdate: 11/9/55. Director: Norman McLeod. Writer: Barbara Merlin. Aired as an episode of *Screen Director's Playhouse*. Alan Young is a meek watch repairman who daydreams himself into exciting adventures a la *Walter Mitty*. Guest stars included Cloris Leachman, Douglas Dumbrillie, Raymond Bailey, Jay Novello, Herb Vigran, Beverly Jordan, Susan Morrow, and Percy Helton.

65. **Real George.** 30 min. Airdate: 7/24/56. George O'Hanlon plays a clutzy salesman in a large department store who works for an overbearing, authoritarian boss (Ray Collins) and has a crush on a sweet, adoring salesgirl (Gloria Henry).

66. **Sis.** 30 min. Executive Producer: Jess Oppenheimer. Nanette Fabray stars as a woman who suddenly finds herself with the obligation of raising two younger sisters. Betty Hutton was originally approached for the title role. She turned it down, but later starred in the series *The Betty Hutton Show* (1959–60, CBS) which featured her as a showgirl who inherits an estate from a lonely millionaire and becomes the guardian of his three kids.

67. **Tom and Jerry.** 30 min. Airdate: 10/22/55. Director: Leo McCarey. Writer: Leo McCarey. Peter Lawford and Nancy Gates are newlyweds in this pilot aired as an episode of *Screen Director's Playhouse*. Guest stars included Frank Fay, Marie Windsor, Charles Lane, Charles Herbert, Vernon Rich, Arthur Bryan, and Tommy Bernard.

NBC / DRAMA

68. **Arroyo.** 30 min. Airdate: 10/26/55. Director: George Waggoner. Writer: George Waggoner. Aired as an episode of *Screen Director's Playhouse*. Jack Carson is a judge trying to uphold law and order in Arroyo, New Mexico. *Cast:* Jack Carson (as Judge Kendall), Bob Steele (Deputy Dodd), Lynn Bari (Hattie Mae Warren), Lloyd Corrigan (Hank), William Schallert (Lawyer), Neville Brand (Bart Wheeler), Lola Albright (Nancy Wheeler), John Baer (Dude).

69. **Briefcase.** Producer: Tony Miner. Consultants: California State Bar Association. Dramatization of real-life court cases.

70. **Color Playhouse.** The network hoped to incorporate all the knowledge it acquired using color on *Matinee Theatre* on this proposed 30-minute anthology using a budget of $35,000 per episode.

71. **Fifty Grand Mystery.** Producer: John Guedel. Host: George Fenneman. A one-hour dramatization of a murder. Contestants must figure out "whodunit" to win $50,000.

72. **Johnny Moccasin.** Production Company: NBC Productions. Jody McCrea, son of Joel McCrea, stars as a white boy raised by Indians.

73. **Mystery Writer's Theatre.** Production Company: Screen Gems. Host: George Sanders. Loosely based on the radio series *The Whistler*, this anthology would have featured the host's omnipresent comments on the motives and thoughts of the character enacting the story.

74. **The Orson Welles Show.** 30 min. Airdate: 9/16/58. Production Company: Desilu Productions. Producer, Writer, Director: Orson Welles. Aired as an episode of *Colgate Theatre*. The series would have been comprised of dramatizations of classic tales, including books by Kipling and H.G. Wells, as well as episodes devoted to magic, interviews, readings and whatever else Welles wanted to do. For the pilot, Welles directed and narrated an adaptation of John Collier's *Fountain of Youth*, about a scientist who invents a secret elixir that keeps people young. Before the pilot was even completed, the proposed series was doomed. Welles went overbudget, took four weeks instead of the allotted ten days to shoot it, and threw an expensive wrap-party that he billed to Desilu. The pilot, though hailed by critics for its inventive directing and honored with the Peabody Award of Excellence, was rejected by the networks because they felt it was too sophisticated. It was, according to *Variety*, "unceremoniously dumped. Welles was never hired again to direct anything in

Hollywood." *Cast:* Orson Welles (as Dr. Humphrey Baxter), Joi Lansing (Caroline Coates), Rick Jason (Alan Broadie), Nancy Kulp (Stella Morgan), Billy House (Albert Morgan).

75. **Strategic Air Command.** 30 min. Airdate: 3/30/59. Production Company: Goodson-Todman Productions. Director: George Sherman. Producer: James Fonda. Writer: Frederic Frank. Consultant: General LeMay. An anthology based on the true-life adventures of the strategic air command. The pilot, aired as an episode of *Goodyear Theatre*, tells the story of an airplane on fire in the air and the Lieutenant who saves the day. *Cast:* Kerwin Matthews (as Lt. James Obenauf), Herbert Anderson (Major Joseph Mazwell), Douglas Odney (Major Jim Graves).

76. **The Third Commandment (aka The Ten Commandments).** 60 min. Airdate: 2/8/59. Director: Jack Smight. Producer: Jess Oppenheimer. Writer: Ben Hecht. Aired as an episode of *Kaleidoscope*. Charles Van Doren hosted this proposed anthology wherein the meaning of each commandment is told through a story set in modern times. NBC was hoping to entice writers like Ernest Hemingway to do the scripts. The pilot revolved around the third commandment and starred Arthur Kennedy, Anne Francis, Richard Erdman, Jack Weston, Simon Oakland, Fay Spain, John Hoyt and Regis Toomey.

ROLAND REED PRODUCTIONS

77. **Alarm.** Producer: Roland Reed. Host: Fred Waring. Two pilots were made for this proposed anthology series based on real cases handled by fire departments around the country.

78. **The Great Mouthpiece.** Producer: Roland Reed. Based on Gene Fowler's book about the adventures of a lawyer. Brian Donlevy starred.

79. **Julie Loves Rome.** Producer: Roland Reed. The adventures in Italy of a female tour-guide and her American boyfriend. Establishing shots would be done on location with principal photography done in Hollywood. Anna Maria Alberghetti was being courted to star.

SCREEN GEMS PRODUCTIONS

80. **Girls About Town.** The adventures of three girls sharing an apartment in New York. The brainy girl always seems to get the other two in trouble with her schemes.

81. **Uncle Charley's Showboat (aka Here Conies the Showboat).** Executive Producer: Irving Briskin. Rory Calhoun stars in the musical/action adventures of a Mississippi Riverboat captain in the 1870s. Negotiations were underway to use the title *Showboat* for the new series.

STUDIO CITY PRODUCTIONS – REPUBLIC PICTURES

82. **True Detective Stories.** An anthology based on stories published in the magazine of the same name.

20TH CENTURY FOX TELEVISION

83. **Cheaper by the Dozen.** Based on the movie and designed to star Irene Dunne.
84. **I Cover the Waterfront.** Based on the novel by Max Miller. An action hero who visits interesting waterfronts around the world.

TPA

85. **Digby.** Based on the *Saturday Evening Post* stories by Douglas Welch. William Demarest plays a newspaper photographer who solves crimes.
86. **The Mysterious Island.** Based on the novel by Jules Verne. Described as a blend of out and out adventure with science fiction. It would have been filmed entirely on location in Australia.
87. **One False Step.** Producer: John Guedel. An anthology based on the notion that criminals always make one false step that seals their fate.

WARNER BROS. TELEVISION

88. **98 William Street.** An ex – FBI agent, a young scientist, and a beautiful model team up to solve insurance fraud.
89. **Port of Call.** John Ireland would star as the skipper of a ship-for-hire in a series filmed on location in harbors around the world.

ZIV

90. The previously listed pilot **Annapolis** became the syndicated series *Men of Annapolis*.

91. **I Love a Mystery.** An anthology loosely based on Carleton's Morse's radio serial. This concept was tried again as a pilot shot in 1966 for NBC…but didn't air until 1973.

INDEPENDENT PRODUCTIONS

92. **African Drumbeat.** Producer: Edward Dukoff. Three pilots, filmed in Africa and England, were made starring Kevin McCarthy.

93. **For the Defense.** 30 min. Director: James Nielsen. Producer: Samuel Bishoff. Edward G. Robinson as a cop-turned-defense attorney. Guest stars were Glen Vernon, Ann Doran, John Hoyt, Robert Osteloh, Vic Perrin, Herbert Hayes, and Morris Ankrum.

94. **James Michener Presents a South Pacific Adventure.** Director: Orville Hampton. Producer: Orville Hampton. Writer: James Michener. Host: James Michener. A pilot about the adventures of a trading schooner captain (Lyle Bettger) who sails the South Pacific. In 1959 the concept was revived as *Adventures in Paradise*, starring Gardner McKay, and became a popular ABC series that ran for three years.

95. **Rescue.** Producers: Collier Young and Ida Lupino. The dramatizations of true-life cases of rescue.

96. **Rough Sketch.** Created by: Ted Sherdeman. Gerald Mohr played an American commercial artist traveling through Europe who stumbles into trouble wherever he goes. The pilot was shot on location in Sweden.

97. **The Young Reverend.** Producer: Robert Maxwell. From the producers of *Lassie*. The central character is an ex-football player, ex-army chaplain, and Korean War veteran who goes to a small American city to take over the pulpit of a Protestant church.

1957–1958

ABC / COMEDY

98. **The Ritz Brothers.** The network was looking for a concept that could best highlight the talents of this comedy team.

ABC / DRAMA

99. **Convicting the Innocent.** An anthology about how innocent people are proved not-guilty.
100. **Motorcycle Cop.** Production Company: Revue Productions. A series based on California Highway Patrol case files.
101. **One Man's Family.** A revival of the 1952 soap opera. This time, it's envisioned as a "Father Knows Best"–type sitcom.
102. **People.** 30 min. Airdate: 12/15/57. Production Company: Mark VII Productions. Director: George Stevens, Jr. Executive Producer: Jack Webb. Producer: Frank La Tourette. Ben Alexander interviews ordinary people on-the-street.
103. **Tales of the Barbary Coast.** Cesar Romero stars as a staid Nob Hill aristocrat whose friends include some of the waterfront's most colorful characters.
104. **Tokyo Police.** The series would revolve around an American detective on the Tokyo police department who, teamed with an old, wise-cracking Japanese cop, handles only those cases involving tourists from the U.S. and Europe.

ASHLEY STEINER AGENCY

105. **The Beebees Abroad.** Writer: Peg Lynch. The adventures of an American family traveling around the world.
106. **Cabin Boy.** Producer: Norman Blackburn. The adventures of a kid on the high seas.
107. **Cindy.** Producer: Hal Roach. Child actress Evelyn Rudie stars as the precocious young girl who goes to live with her uncle, a bachelor who works in an aircraft factory, after her parents are killed.
108. **Colonel North.** The adventures of the men who belong to the Army's G-2 section.

109. **My Old Man.** Production Company: Screen Gems Productions. Ed Wynn stars as the grandfather of a typical American family.

BATJAC (JOHN WAYNE PRODUCTIONS)

110. **Calamity Jane.** A pilot starring Elaine Rooney.

IRVING BRECHER PRODUCTIONS

111. **Big Time.** Ray Danton stars as an undercover agent who is also a famous singer. Plan was to blend action/adventure with music, a notion that was used to great success thirty years later on *Miami Vice*.

CBS / COMEDY

112. **Full Speed for Anywhere.** 30 min. Airdate: 9/13/60. Production Company: Four Star Productions. Director: Don Taylor. Producer: Charles Isaacs. Writers: Charles Isaacs and Jack Elinson. A musical comedy about a coast guard cutter traveling the world's seas, centering on Yeoman Stubby Kaye and Conrad Janis, in a character modeled on "Ensign Pulver." *Cast:* Stubby Kaye (as Yeoman Stubby Fox), Conrad Janis (Ensign Jones), George Dunn (Doc Clemens), Glen Turnbull (Slim Jackson), Jose Gonzales (Lew).

113. **It's Always Sunday.** 30 min. Airdate: 1/11/56. Production Company: CBS Productions. Director: Allan Dwan. Producer: Sidney Van Keuren. Writer: Allan Dwan. Aired as an episode of *Screen Directors Playhouse*. Dennis O'Keefe starred as a harried minister who, in the pilot, helps two bums who wander into town. *Cast:* Dennis O'Keefe (as the Rev. Charles Parker), Fay Wray (Mary Parker), Eileen Jensen (Nancy Parker), Sheldon Leonard (George), Chick Chandler (Eddie), Diane Jergens (Sue Stradler), Grant Withers (William Bracket, Sr.), Jimmy Hayes (William Bracket, Jr.).

114. **Junior Miss.** 30 min. Airdate: 12/20/57. Director: Ralph Nelson. Producer: Richard Levine. Writers: Joseph Stern and Will Glickman. Aired as an episode of *Schlitz Playhouse*. Carol Lynley is Judy Graves, a precocious girl who meddles in everyone's problems – and causes many of her own. Don Ameche and Joan Bennett are her parents, Jill St. John is her sister, and David Wayne is her uncle. Susanne Sidney, Paul Ford and Diana Lynn guest starred.

115. **Maggie.** 30 min. Airdate: 8/29/60. Production Company: McCadden Productions. Director: Rod Amateau. Executive Producer: George Burns. Producer: Bill Manhoff. Writer: Bill Manhoff. Margaret O'Brien stars as the precocious daughter of a couple of movie stars (Leon Ames and Fay Baker). In the pilot, they move from New York to Connecticut to begin a new life and clash with their neighbors. *Cast:* Margaret O'Brien (as Maggie Bradley), Leon Ames (Mark Bradley), Fay Baker (Annie Bradley), Jesslyn Fax (Miss Caldwell), also, Jeanne Tatum, Charles Cantor, Edwin Bruce, Michael Emmet, and Mona Knox.

116. **Magnificent Montague.** Producer: Nat Hiken. The comic adventures of a John Barrymore-type character. This was based on the 1950 NBC radio series that was written by Hiken and starred Monty Wooley, who did not appear in the pilot.

117. **Maisie.** 30 min. Airdate: 9/12/60. Production Company: MGM Television. Director: Edwin Ludwig. Executive Producer: Richard Maibaum. Producer: Tom McKnight. Writer: Mary R. McCall, from the novel by Wilson Collinson. Janis Paige stars as a Brooklyn show girl on the nightclub circuit in this pilot based on the Ann Sothern movies. In the pilot, Maisie wins the "Miss Guided Missile" pageant and has to go to a small town to help the Army recruiting program. Maibaum would later write the James Bond movies. *Cast:* Janis Paige (as Maisie Ravier), Lin McCarthy (Andy Clary), Joe Sawyer (Master Sgt. Blackenhorn), Olive Carey (Mrs. Clary), James Maloney (Mayor), Rudy Lee (Townsperson), Henry Kulky (Townsperson 2).

118. **McGarry and His Mouse (aka McGarry and Me).** 30 min. Airdate: 7/5/60. Production Company: Hal Roach Productions. Director: Norman Tokar. Executive Producer: Hal Roach, Jr. Producer: Stanley Shapiro. Writers: Stanley Shapiro and Maurice Richlin, from an article in *This Week* magazine. The life and adventures of a gentle beat cop and his wife in a large metropolitan city. *Cast:* Michael O'Shea (as Officer Dan McGarry), Virginia Mayo (Kitty McGarry), Les Tremayne (Captain), Richard Gaines (Officer).

119. **My Love Affair with the State of Maine.** A comedy revolving around two girls, one an outsider and one a Maine native, who buy a general store in Maine together.

CBS / DRAMA

120. **Blockade Runner.** Producer: Lindsay Parsons. The adventures of a ship-running blockade against Confederacy harbors.

121. **Chicago 212.** 30 min. Airdate: 4/30/57. Director: Norman Foster. Producers: Don Sharpe and Warren Lewis. Writer: William Rousseau. Aired as an episode of *Dupont Theatre*. Frank Lovejoy is Ed McCook, an inspector with the Chicago Fire Department who, in the pilot, searches for an arsonist, played by Roy Thinnes. Tomi Thurston and Frank McCormick also guest starred.

122. **Diplomat.** The adventures of an American career diplomat.

123. **The Firefighters.** Producer: Ed Byron. Anthology about true fire-fighting cases.

124. **Front Office.** Producer: Herbert Brodkin. Ralph Bellamy stars in a project designed to reap the drama inherent in American business.

125. **The Lonely Wizard.** 60 min. Airdate: 11/15/57. Production Company: MCA. Producer: Frank Rosenberg. Writer: Paul Monash. A spin-off from *Schlitz Playhouse of the Stars*, in which Rod Steiger portrayed Charles Proteus Steinmetz, an electronics genius who prefers solitude while he works. The episode garnered an Emmy for writer Monash and a nomination for its film editing. The proposed anthology, spotlighting great scientists of yesterday and today, would be hosted by Steiger. *Cast:* Rod Steiger (as Charles Steinmetz), Richard Anderson (Hayden), Diane Brewster (Marianne), Elsie Neff (Grandmother), Karl Swenson (Asmussen), Hugh Sanders (Inspectore), Ed Hinton (Official), Tom McKee (Kendall), Chet Stratton (Fowler), Kevin Hagen (Jacobi), Horst Elrardt (Quinn), Gene Harvey (Conrad), Faye Roope (Dr. Elliot), Rene Korper (Charles, Age 6), Phil Phillips (Joseph, Age 6), Sammy Ogg (Joseph, Age 16).

126. **The Marriage Broker.** 60 min. Airdate: 6/12/57. Production Company: 20th Century Fox. Director: Lewis Allen. Producer: Peter Packer. Writer: Joseph Calvelli. Based on the 1952 movie *The Model and the Marriage Broker*, starring Thelma Ritter as a woman, left by her husband, who now makes her living bringing people together. Glenda Farrell took over the role in the TV version, which would have been somewhat of an anthology, featuring a different couple or two every week and would shift in tone between comedy and drama. *Cast:* Glenda Farrell (as Mae Swasey), William Bishop (Matt Hornbeck), Kipp Hamilton (Christina Bradley), Harry Morgan (Mike Feeney), Jesse White (Doberman), Helen Walker (Shirley Larkin), Lee Patrick (Emmie Swasey), Lloyd Corrigan (Capt. Sam), Ellen Corby (Minerva Comstock), Roy Roberts (Don Chancelor), Parley Bear (George Wixted).

127. The previously listed pilot, **Melody Ranch**, became the syndicated series of the same name.

128. **Nancy Drew.** Producer: Bernie Proctor. The adventures of the teenage detective popularized in Carolyn Keene's books.

129. **Secrets of the Old Bailey.** 30 min. Airdate: 4/11/58. Production Company: MCA. Director: Don Weis. Producer: Allan Miller. Writers: Oscar Millard and John Kneubuhl, from a story by Ernest Dudley. Aired on *Schlitz Playhouse of the Stars.* Tom Hellmore stars as Tom Reid, a detective superintendent with Scotland Yard in this pilot filmed on location in London. *Cast:* Tom Hellmore (as Det. Superintendent Tom Reid), Edward Cast (George Chappel), Brian McDermott (Leo Willis), Naomi Chance (Jennie Elson), John Gill (Mr. Willis), Hugh Stribling (Richard Caldiwitt), Anthony Sheppard (P.C. Swopes).

130. **The Sergeant and the Lady.** An action show starring Peggie Castle and Jeff Lord as San Diego police officers who solve crimes when they aren't flirting with each other.

131. **The Sword.** 30 min. Airdate: 5/31/57. Director: Richard Irving. Producer: Richard Irving. Writer: Fenton Earnshaw. The adventures of Paul De La Force, A 17th century swashbuckler who, in the pilot, saves Cyrano De Bergerac from being beheaded as a spy. Aired as an episode of *Schlitz Playhouse of the Stars. Cast:* Jacques Sernas (as Paul De La Force), Fred Wayne (Cyrano De Bergerac), Nicola Michaels (Marion), John Doucette (Boudet), Henry Daniel (Count Malvern), Paul Frees (Bailiff).

132. **21st Precinct.** Producer: Bernie Proctor. A drama based on the radio series about the lives and cases of the cops who work at New York's 21st Precinct. Proctor would try again to sell this concept the follow season, with as little success.

133. **The World of White.** A hospital drama written by playwright Sidney Kingsley.

FRANK COOPER AND ASSOCIATES

134. **Rafferty's Angels.** A western to star Brian Keith and John Dehner.
135. **Rex Morgan, M.D.** A series based on the comic strip.

DESILU PRODUCTIONS

136. **A Night in Havana.** Producer: Fletcher Markle. Ricardo Montalban plays the father of a family living in Cuba.
137. **Sad Sack.** Tom Ewell would star in a comedy about army life.

DOUGFAIR PRODUCTIONS

138. The Gaucho. Based on the silent film starring Douglas Fairbanks, Sr., about the life of a pampas cowboy in Argentina. Carlos Reoas starred in the pilot, which was shot in Mexico.

RALPH EDWARDS PRODUCTIONS

139. The previously listed pilot, **End of the Rainbow**, became the series of the same name.

140. The Human Thing to Do. Contestants win by predicting what candidly photographed people will do (e.g., Will the man order a vanilla or chocolate shake?). Hosted by Tom Moore.

FLYING A PRODUCTIONS (GENE AUTRY)

141. Squad Car. Based on the radio series *Calling All Cars*.

142. Ticket of Fate. A dramatic anthology built around pawn tickets.

FORDYCE PRODUCTIONS

(Collier Young, Joseph Cotton and Larry Marcus)

143. The House of Seven Garbos. Seven would-be actresses who live together in a boarding house provide the action, comedy and romance this series would chronicle. Ida Lupino would be the special advisor to the series.

144. The Nowhere Boys. Writer: Charles Lederer. A comedy/western concept for David Wayne.

145. Rescue. An anthology based on true cases of rescue.

146. Wish You Were Here. Writer: Don Mankiewicz. A series that would follow an American adventurer as he travels around the world. Plans called for it to be filmed on location.

FOUR STAR PRODUCTIONS

147. Travel Agency. David Niven, Charles Boyer and Jane Powell would rotate as stars of this series about the adventuresome employees of a world-wide travel agency.

BEN FOX PRODUCTIONS

148. **Anchorage.** The adventures of a charter boat owner and his father, who runs a California yacht anchorage.
149. **Tension.** An anthology of mystery stories in the tradition of *Dial M for Murder*.

GOODSON-TODMAN PRODUCTIONS

150. **Stanley Kramer Presents.** An anthology hosted by Stanley Kramer.

GUILD FILMS

151. **Light of the World.** Based on the radio series of the same name which dramatized stories from the Bible. In the proposed TV version, stories would be filmed on location in foreign settings.
152. The previously listed pilot **The Michaels of Africa** became the series of the same name.

MARK VII PRODUCTIONS

153. **The Fighting Marines.** Producer: Jack Webb. A series culled from the experiences of the U.S. Marine Corps.

MCA PRODUCTIONS

154. **Charles Laughton Presents.** He would host an anthology series and star in at least 13 episodes.
155. **Fred Astaire Presents.** He would host an anthology series and star in at least 13 episodes. A Fred Astaire eventually hosted the ABC anthology series *Alcoa Premiere* from 1961-1963.

MCCADDEN PRODUCTIONS

This was actor George Burns' production company. The following two, unnumbered, unsold pilots were omitted from the previous edition of this book:

The Plumber and his Daughters. 30 minutes. A proposed spin-off from the *Burns & Allen Show* starring Howard McNear as Cusperd Jantzen, a befuddled plumber with four beautiful daughters. For star power in the pilot, Bob Cummings guest-starred as the photographer character he played in his series from *The Bob Cummings Show*. Cast: Howard McNear (Cusperd Jantzen), Jody Warner (Jean), Yvonne Lime (Joy), Darlene Albert (June) and Mary Ellen Kay (Joan), Bob Cummings (Bob Collins).

156. **The Carol Channing Show.** Producer: George Burns. A situation comedy designed for the singer/actress best known for *Hello Dolly*.
157. **The Fabulous Oliver Chantry.** Producer: George Burns. George Sanders stars in a situation comedy.
158. **The Hermione Gingold Show.** A situation comedy for the English comedienne who gained fame in *Gigi*.

MGM PRODUCTIONS

159. **The Feminine Touch.** The story of two women who run a beauty parlor.

NBC / COMEDY

160. **The Reluctant Eye.** Producer: Jack Chertok. A comedy with Bobby Van as a private eye.
161. **Snooks.** Starring Marthe Raye as a mother who plays a baby on the radio. A re-offering of the 1956 pilot, with more emphasis on the family life.
162. **You Know Me, Al.** Producers: Arthur Lewis and Abe Burroughs. Writer: Abe Burroughs, from the Ring Lardner stories. Dick York stars as a dim-witted pitcher for the Pittsburgh Pirates.

NBC / DRAMA

163. **The Lawless Years.** A series based on the book about policeman Barney Roditsky, who worked in New York during the 1920s.
164. **Midnight Mystery.** 60 min. Airdate: 6/5/57. Director: Lamont Johnson. Producer: Albert McCleery. Writers: Paula Fox and Marjorie Kellogg. A pilot for a proposed

mystery/suspense anthology. In the pilot, a psychopath terrorizes a woman who is alone in her home. Aired as an episode of *Matinee Theatre*. *Cast:* Peggy McCay (as Jane Wilson), Robert Morse (Larry), Theodore Newton (Mr. Wallace), Robert Karnes (Frank Wilson), Will J. White (Attendant), Barbara Drew (Bess Carlson), Ron Greenway (Harper).

165. **Pony Express.** A western starring James Best as a pony express rider.

OFFICIAL FILMS

166. **The Sixth Sense.** Based on the case history of Peter Harkess, a European psychic.
167. **Turnpike.** The adventures of commercial truck drivers in New York City.

RKO

168. **Charter Pilot.** Producer: Ben Fox. The stories of a family entrenched in the aviation world, from airplanes to rockets.

169. **El Coyote Rides.** 30 min. Director: Richard Talmadge. Producer: Ken Murray. Writers: Jean Holloway and Rudy Makoui. Creator: Ken Murray. Muriel Davis, the all-around girl gymnastics champion of the 1956 American Olympics team, stars as a Zorro-like avenger. In the original concept, she was the daughter of the local sheriff (Bill Elliott) and, whenever there was trouble, she'd disguise herself as a man, the infamous El Coyote, and help her father fight crime. In the pilot that was shot, the concept was basically the same – only now, she lives on a ranch run by her father, a former military man, near the California/Mexico border. *Cast:* Muriel Davis (as Jane Edwards), George Brent (Col. Bart Edwards), Billy Gilbert (Manuel), Paul Richards (Harvey Logan), Martin Garralaga (Father Gomez), Angela Greene (Claire), Michael Hinn (Sheriff), Loren Janes (Red), George Moreno (Lopez).

170. **Heidi.** Based on the series of books about a young girl with amazing strength. The proposed series would feature American actors and locations in the Bavarian Alps.

171. **Malolo of the South Seas.** Jon Hall stars as a trading schooner captain.

172. **Mr. Big.** Producer: Paul McNamara. Gregory Ratoff stars in this sitcom about a Hollywood mogul.

173. **Rails.** Producer: Ben Fox. RKO described this proposed series, about the adventures of a special agent for a railroad line, as the "On the Waterfront of the Railroad Industry."

HAL ROACH PRODUCTIONS

174. **Cavalry Surgeon.** The title explains itself. The episodes would focus on the off-beat, human interest angles of the story.

175. **Guns of Destiny.** A western anthology using "famous guns" as its launch pad for stories.

176. The previously listed pilot **Jacques and Jill** became the series *Love that Jill*.

177. **The Joe DiMaggio Show.** DiMaggio would host this anthology featuring dramatizations of little-known sports stories.

SCREEN GEMS PRODUCTIONS

178. **Beyond Tomorrow.** A science-fiction anthology featuring stories of life on earth in the near future.

179. **Combat Correspondent.** Lin McCarthy stars as a reporter covering Marine Corps missions.

180. **Florida Dragnet.** An action series based on files provided by the Florida State Police.

181. **Her Majesty, The Queen.** Producer: Carol Irwin. Myrna Loy would star in a family-oriented sitcom.

182. **Howe and Hummell.** The lives of two lawyers, one Jewish and one Irish, working in New York City in the 1890s. Starring Menasha Skulnik and Dennis King.

183. **Lady Law.** Barbara Stanwyck is a frontier heroine who inherits a stage line.

184. **The Secret Room.** The futuristic adventures of a secret government agency that dabbles in scientific research and espionage.

185. **Stage Coach.** Producer: Walter Wanger. Based on the movie. The series would chronicle the travels of a stage coach driver and his sidekick.

186. **This House Is Haunted.** An anthology featuring a different haunted house each week.

TPA

187. **Airline Hostess.** An adventure/romance that spends less time in the air than it does exploring exotic locales.

188. **Dude Ranch.** Producer: Irving Cummings, Jr. The daily life on a contemporary ranch in the American southwest.

189. **The Enchanted Forest.** Producer: Robert Maxwell. A family drama starring Charlotte Greenwood, Jay C. Flippen and Charles Herbert. Although a concept was still being developed, this was a viable pilot because of Maxwell's proven success with *Lassie*.

190. **Marshal of Manitoba.** Rory Calhoun as a lawman in the Canadian frontier.

191. **The Turning Point.** An anthology of fictionalized dramas based on the real winners of *The $64,000 Question*.

20TH CENTURY FOX

192. **Transatlantic.** This unsold pilot predates the successful *Love Boat* series by 20 years. This series would be an anthology, based on the movie, about romance and adventure on a passenger liner.

WARNER BROS. TELEVISION

193. **The Forty-Niners.** A western series about the Gold Rush.

194. **House of Wax.** The adventures of a wealthy bachelor whose hobby is exposing crooks who use the occult to hide their crimes and, by virtue of his expertise and his vast criminology library at his spooky mansion, he is called on by police departments worldwide.

195. **Las Vegas Story.** A sitcom about a family that lives in a house on the strip, adjacent to all the big casinos. Everyone wants their land but they won't sell. The son is county sheriff, the daughter is a showgirl, and the grandfather sits on the porch and sells dates.

1958–1959

ABC / COMEDY

196. Tin Pan Sally. Creator: Lou Edelman. A musical drama about a woman who inherits a music publishing business.

ABC / DRAMA

197. Johnny Pilgrim. William Bishop stars as a San Diego-based private eye.

BATJAC (JOHN WAYNE PRODUCTIONS)

198. Flight. A science fiction anthology about space travel.

CBS / COMEDY

199. Ben Blue's Brothers. 30 min. Airdate: 6/28/65. Production Company: Hal Roach Productions. Director: Norman McLeod. Producer: Jerry Stagg. Writers: Marion Hargrove and Russel Beggs. Comic Blue would portray four different brothers: an aristocrat, a bum, a vaudeville performer and an average joe. The only other character not portrayed by Blue was his mother, played by Ruth McDevitt. Costarred Barbara Heller, Robin Raymond, Lillian Culver, Yvette Vickers, Jane McGowan, Fred Easier.

200. Hey, Mack. 60 min. Airdate: 4/26/57. Production Company: MCA/Revue Productions. Aired as an episode of *Schlitz Playhouse of the Stars*. Gary Merrill stars as a widowed father raising a teenage daughter and running a roadside motel deep in the remote redwood country of Northern California. Also starred Sue George, Marion Marsh, and Gordon Gebert.

201. My Favorite Son. Peter Lind Hayes is a Congressman who moves with his wife, played by Mary Healy, and son to Washington, D.C., in this sitcom premise.

202. Papa Said No. 30 min. Airdate: 4/4/58. Director: Don Weis. Producer: Frank P. Rosenberg. Writers: Allen Rivkin and Edna Anhalt, from a story by Winifred Wolfe. Yvonne Craig is Suzanne Stacey, a woman constantly on the prowl for a suitable husband. In the pilot, aired as an episode of *Schlitz Playhouse of the Stars*, she falls for a photographer. *Cast:* Yvonne Craig (as Suzanne Stacey), Patrick Knowles (John Stacey), Jeanne Manet (Gabrielle Stacey), Scott Brady (Calvin Penny), Marjorie Bennett (Mrs. Ostericher), Harry Jackson (Policeman).

203. **Teenage Idol.** 30 min. Airdate: 7/8/58. Director: Ida Lupino. Producer: Howard Duff. Writer: Louella MacFarland. Aired as an episode of *Mr. Adams and Eve.* The pilot has the Howard and Eve Adams becoming involved in promoting Johnny Swivelhips' career. An "Elvis" spoof starring Darrell Howe as Swivelhips Jackson, America's newest teenage rock sensation. Patrick Wayne, Ida Lupino, Howard Duff, Olive Carsey, and Carolyn Craig guest starred.

204. **Tom, Dick and Harry.** 30 min. Airdate: 9/20/60. Production Company: Screen Gems. Director: Oscar Rudolph. Executive Producer: Fred Briskin. Producer: Ben Starr. Writer: Ben Starr. Gene Nelson, Joe Mantell and Marvin Kaplan are three warbuddies whose friendship is the basis for the comedy, which was made in 1958. Tom is a steelworker, Dick is a truck driver and Marvin is a mechanic. In the pilot, they open a restaurant. *Cast:* Gene Nelson (as Tom Fellows), Joe Mantell (Dick Rawlings), Marvin Kaplan (Harry Murphy), Cheryl Calloway (Shirley Fellows), Pamela Dean (Pamela Rawlings), Howard McNear (Owner), Hazel Shermet (Hazel), Irene Ryan (Customer #1), Mavis Davenport (Customer #2).

CBS / DRAMA

205. **The Adventures of Johnny Dollar.** Production Company: Screen Gems. Based on the radio serial about an insurance investigator working in San Francisco.

206. **Collectors Item.** 30 min. Production Companies: TCF Television Productions and CBS Productions. Director: Buzz Kulik. Producer: Herb Meadow. Writer: Herb Meadow. A detective pilot, subtitled *The Left Hand of David,* featuring Vincent Price as Henry Prentiss, an art gallery owner and Peter Lorre as Mr. Munsey, a forger with underworld ties who works for him. Guest stars included Whitney Blake, Thomas Gomez, Eduard Franz, Dick Ryan, Dick Winslow, Harvey Parry.

207. **Cool and Lam.** 30 min. Production Companies: CBS Productions and Paisano Productions. Director: Jacques Tourneur. Executive Producer: Gail Patrick Jackson. Producer: Edmund Hartman. Writer: Edmund Hartman, based on the books by A.A. Fair (Erle Stanley Gardner). The light-hearted adventures of private eyes Donald Lam, whom Erle Stanley Gardner describes as "the little thinking machine," and Bertha Cool, "his big, penny-pinching partner." Gardner, in a message to

would-be sponsors, said of this pilot: "To me, Billy Pearson is exactly right for the part of Donald and Benay Venuta is just what I wanted as Bertha. The Cool and Lam books have been successful for many years. I hope their TV series will be equally long-lived and successful." That, alas, was not to be. *Cast:* Billy Pearson (as Donald Lam), Benay Venuta (Bertha Cool), Maurice Manson (Dr. Listig), Maggie Mahoney (Marion Danton), Judith Bess Jones (Elsie Brand), Sheila Bromley (Flo Mortonson), Don Megowan (John Harbet), Movita (Carmen), Alison Hayes (Evaline Dell), John Mitchum (Bartender), Tristram Coffin (Thatcher), Alex Sharpe (Plainclothesman).

208. **Doc Holliday.** 30 min. Airdate: 3/14/58. Production Company: Four Star. Director: James Sheldon. Producer: Hal Hudson. Writer: Aaron Spelling. Music: Herschel Burke Gilbert. Aired as the "Man of Fear" episode of *Zane Grey Theatre.* Dewey Martin is frontier doctor/gunfighter Doc Holliday who, in the pilot, helps rid a town terrorized by a corrupt sheriff. *Cast:* Dewey Martin (as Doc Holliday), Arthur Franz (Lee Brand), Julie Adams (Julie Brand), Brett King (Sheriff).

209. The previously listed pilot **The Grey Ghost** became the series of the same name.

210. **Johnny Mayflower.** The adventures of an orphan boy who comes to America as a stowaway on the *Mayflower.*

211. **Johnny Nighthawk (aka Forced Landing).** 30 min. Airdate: 9/1/59. Production Company: Screen Gems. Director: Oscar Rudolph. Producer: Harold Greene. Writers: Sam H. Rolfe and Barney Slate, from a story by Lou Morheim. Aired as an episode of *Geritol Adventure Showcase.* Scott Brady is an adventurous, freelance pilot who likes to take on risky jobs. *Cast:* Scott Brady (as Johnny Night-hawk). Richard Erdman (Matt Brent), Maggie Mahoney (Lorna Kendiss), Joe DeSantis (Mac Ustich).

212. **Lone Woman.** 60 min. Airdate: 12/26/57. Producer: Ralph Levy. Writer: Al C. Ward. Aired as an episode of *Playhouse 90.* Kathryn Grayson stars as an Indian princess who marries a white trader in the 1870s. The cast included Raymond Burr, Vincent Price, Jack Lord and Scott Brady.

213. **Man from Denver.** 30 min. Airdate: 4/30/59. Director: John English. Producer: Hal Hudson. Writers: Nina Laemmle and William R. Cox, from a story by John Marsh. Aired as an episode of *Zane Grey Theatre.* Mark Miller is Ward Pendleton, an investigator for a chain of banks in the old West. Guest stars included James Whitmore, Marsha Hunt, Dabbs Greer, Richard Karlan, William Schallert, Howard Culver and Nan Peterson.

214. **New York's Finest.** Producer: Bernie Proctor. A series based on the radio program *21st Precinct.*

DESILU

215. The Abbotts. Husband and wife detectives cast in "The Thin Man" mold.

216. Black Arrow. A frontier schoolteacher by day is a masked avenger by night, ridding crime from the wild west.

217. The Last Marshal. Jim Davis stars as the last U.S. marshal to be appointed before the western territories all became states of the Union.

218. The previously listed pilot, **Official Detective**, became the syndicated series of the same name.

219. Personal Report. Producer: Lee Sholen. Wayne Morris and Mike Connors as two private eyes.

220. Ricky of the Islands. Thirteen-year-old Rick Vera plays a boy who is shipwrecked on a mystical tropical island in the East Indies. As he explores the island, he befriends unusual natives who help him in his adventures.

221. The Wildcatters. The exploits of two field mechanics in the international oil business.

FAMOUS ARTISTS

222. The Adventures of Hiawatha. The Indian boy immortalized in Longfellow's poem is the hero of this action series concept.

223. What Is a Man? A documentary/anthology hosted by producer Louis DeRochement that will examine important roles held by men. Each week they will ask a question, such as "What is a minister?" "What is a Cop," "What is a ballplayer?" "What is a bricklayer," etc.

FLYING A PRODUCTIONS

224. Winning of the West. Based on the radio series. An anthology covering all aspects of western development, from the cow-town days of Dodge City to the opening of the Erie Canal, up to the turn of the century.

FOUR STAR PRODUCTIONS

225. The Eddie Albert Show. A fantasy adventure series featuring Albert as a newspaper reporter who travels the nation, time and space in search of interesting, human stories.

226. **Flight Line.** The family operating a small airport and a restaurant in a mid-western American community get involved in the troubles of the people who pass through town.

227. **Indian Scout.** Casey Tibbs stars as an Indian scout, who is aided by a little boy and a dog.

ALBERT GANNAWAY

228. **Calamity Jane.** A series based on the radio program, which featured fictionalized stories about the famed Indian scout.

229. **The Judy Canova Show.** Canova is a travelling carnival entertainer. The series would focus on the difficulties of life on the road.

230. **Perils of Pinky.** Pinky Lee portrays a messenger boy with a nose for trouble in this comedy premise.

231. **Price of Peace.** Producer: Milton Geiger. An anthology about the development of the United States defense system. Robert Taylor and Van Heflin were signed for episodes if this went to series.

232. **The Story of a Star.** Joel McCrea hosts this anthology that features true stories about frontier sheriffs.

233. **Western Musketeers.** A government investigator travels with two singing cowboys. Starring Carl Smith, Webb Pierce and Marty Robbins.

234. **The Young Sheriff.** Faron Young, the singing star of radio and TV's *Grand Old Opry*, plays a 25-year-old who takes over as sheriff when his father retires.

GENERAL TELERADIO

235. The previously listed pilot **Aggie** became the syndicated series of the same name.

GOLDSTONE/TOBIAS AGENCY

236. **The Same, Old World.** Writer: Mary McCall. The adventures of a young boy growing up in Athens in 300 B.C. The series would attempt, by building stories around the Olympics, war, and philosophy, to draw parallels between the troubles of youth past and present.

237. **Cartoon Jesters.** A panel of celebrity guests put funny captions on cartoon drawings selected from the files of famous cartoonists.

BOB HOPE ENTERPRISES

238. **Police Hall of Fame.** Bob Hope would host this anthology that dramatizes true stories of police heroism.
239. **Jane Ahoy.** A female "Sgt. Bilko" in the Navy.
240. **Prince Valiant.** A series based on the comic strip character.

MCA/REVUE PRODUCTIONS

241. **Clue.** Producer: Alfred Hitchcock. Dennis O'Keefe stars as a criminology professor.
242. The previously listed pilot, **Chicago Beat**, became the series *M-Squad*.
243. **Chuck Goes to College.** 30 Minutes. Airdate: 2/28/57. Writer: Paul Henning. A proposed spin-off from *The Bob Cummings Show*. Dwayne Hickman's character Chuck MacDonald and his friend Jimmy (Jeff Silver) attend Gridley College for Men. Chuck's girlfriend Carol Henning (Olive Sturgess) is a student at the girl's college next door. Guest stars include Jody McCrea.
244. **Johnny Hawk.** Track and field star Floyd Simmons would play this modern-day sheriff who uses both a car and a horse in his efforts to fight crime.
245. **Portrait.** Ronald Colman would host, and star in 13 episodes, of this anthology of romantic tales.
246. **Six Shooter.** Based on the radio program, that starred Jimmy Stewart. John Payne takes over the role of a sharp-shooter who hates to use his skill to kill people – but ends up having to.
247. **The Trouble Shooter and Gunga Din.** Jack Kelly plays a European adventurer in the 1900s who travels with Gunga Din, a faithful hindu "with cousins in every port."

MGM

248. **The Adventures of Andy Hardy.** There was no concept or cast, just the title. Presumably, the series would be loosely based on the long string of movies starring Mickey Rooney about a teenager whose father is a judge.
249. **MGM Theatre.** An anthology series comprised of unproduced screenplays, plays and novels owned by the studio, including works by William Faulkner, Phillip Barry and Rebecca West.

NBC / COMEDY

250. **The Doctor Was a Lady.** 30 min. Airdate: 3/27/58. Production Company: MCA/Revue. Director: William Asher. Writer: Bill Manhoff. Aired as an episode of *Jane Wyman Theatre*. The comedic misadventures of a married couple – she's a doctor (Frances Bergen) and he's a real estate developer (Keith Andes). Guest starred Wendy Winkleman, Maudie Prickett, Shirley Mitchell, Eleanor Audley, Frank Wilcox, Ruthie Robinson and Milton Frome.

251. **Claudette Colbert Show (aka Welcome to Washington; aka Francy Goes to Washington).** 30 min. Airdates: 9/30/58 NBC and 8/23/60 CBS. Director: Norman Tokar. Producer: Norman Tokar. Writers: Inez Asher and Whitfield Cook. Initially aired as an episode of *Colgate Theatre* in 1958 and then offered on CBS as part of a showcase of flops entitled *Comedy Spot*. Claudette Colbert is elected to Congress, moves to Washington, D.C., with her family, and tries to cope.

252. **Follow That Man.** Producer: Sheldon Reynolds. A sitcom casting Milton Berle as a bumbling newspaper reporter.

253. **Joan of Arkansas.** 30 min. Production Companies: Joan Davis Enterprises and NBC Productions. Director: Philip Rapp. Producer: Robert Stillman. Writer: Philip Rapp. Joan Davis is Joan Jones as a dental technician selected by computer as the perfect person to be the first "man on the moon." John Emery is Dr. John Dolan, the scientist who trains the scatterbrained, good-natured clutz for her mission – and whom she falls in love with. Other stars included Whit Bissell, Ben Wright, Wilton Graff, Lee Patrick, Paul Frees, Bob Brubaker, Jolene Brand, and Olan Soule.

254. **June.** Producer: Jess Oppenheimer. Nanette Fabray stars in this sitcom about a young, aspiring novelist who owns a gift shop and sticks her nose into everybody's problems.

255. **Mr. Tutt (aka Strange Counsel).** 30 min. Airdate: 9/10/58. Director: Jerry Thorpe. Producer: Winston O'Keefe. Writers: Ellis Marcus and Harold Swanton, from the stories by Arthur Twain. Aired as an episode of *Colgate Theatre*. Walter Brennan is Mr. Tutt, a small-town lawyer whose backwoods charm hides a sharp intellect and is aided in his investigations by his detective Charlie and his secretary Olive. *Cast:* Walter Brennan (as Mr. Tutt), Olive Blakeney (Olive), Harry Harvey, Jr. (Charlie), Vera Miles (Judy Gregory), Don Shelton (Uncle Ben), Geraldine Carr (Aunt Sarah), Barbara Fuller (Mrs. Phillips), George Weise (Nate Phillips).

256. **Stage Father.** Producer: Elliot Lewis. Ed Wynn stars in this comedy about an old vaudevillian and his son, a contemporary actor.

257. **That's My Mom (aka Hey Mom).** Producer: Jess Oppenheimer. Betty Hutton stars as a widow with five children in this comedy inspired by *Mother Goose*.
They planned to do five of each 13 shows as musicals. A precursor to *Goldie* (aka *Betty Hutton Show*), wherein she played a manicurist who is suddenly named executor of a millionaire's estate…and guardian of his three kids.

258. **There Goes Calvin.** A comedy with Orson Bean as an orchestra leader living in France.

NBC / DRAMA

259. **The Black Knight.** Producer: Sheldon Reynolds. A jousting hero's adventures in medieval Europe.

260. **Expert Witness (aka Hide and Seek).** 30 min. Airdate: 5/22/58. Director: Harvey Foster. Writer: Robert Dennis. Aired as an episode of *Jane Wyman Theatre*. Everett Sloane is a criminologist who travels the country in a specially equipped crime lab helping people solve perplexing crimes. *Cast*: Everett Sloane (as Dan Wilder), Richard Erdman (Joe Sackett), Louis Jean Heydt (Joe McHale), James Westerfield (Sheriff).

261. **The Fox.** Anthony Dexter as a Robin Hood–like character.

262. **The Highwayman.** 30 min. Airdate: 8/17/58. Director: Robert Day. Producer: Sidney Cole. Writer: Anthony Haslett. Aired as the "Stand and Deliver" episode of NBC's *Decision*. Louis Hayward as an aristocrat/bandit in England in the mid-1700s, a role that bore a striking resemblance to "The Saint," the Leslie Charteris character Hayward was the first to assay on screen (he was replaced by George Sanders. In 1953, he played Simon Templar one last time in the disastrous *Saint's Girl Friday* before relinquishing the role to Roger Moore and the small screen). Shot on location in England. *Cast*: Louis Hayward (as James McDonald), Richard O'Sullivan (Luke), Adrienne Corri (Lady Sylvia), Sam Kydd (Jerry Bridger).

263. **If You Knew Tomorrow.** 30 min. Airdate: 10/7/58. Director: Thomas Carr. Producer: Vincent M. Fennelly. Writer: Palmer Thompson. Aired as an episode of *Colgate Theatre*. Bruce Gordon is a reporter whose teletype machine sends him news flashes from the future – and they usually aren't good. The series would have followed

him each week as he tries to save someone from certain peril. In the pilot, he saves a couple who will be hit by a train. Guest stars were Judith Ames, Dan Barton, Frances Bavier, Harry Harvey, Jr., Dick Ryan, Herb Vigran and Harry Cheshire.

264. **Indemnity.** 30 min. Director: Frank Telford. Producers: Joe Graham and Sam Grad. Writers: Milton Gelman and Stedman Coles. Richard Kiley as an investigator for an insurance company. *Cast:* Richard Kiley (as Paul Scott), Chuck Webster (Lt. Mike Kappell), George Chandler (George Thompson), Ruth Lee (Girl), Richard Healy (Thief).

265. **Johnny Risk.** 30 min. Airdate: 6/16/58. Production Company: Four Star. Director: Don McDougall. Producer: Vincent Fennelly. Writer: Fred Freiberger. Aired as an episode of *Alcoa Theatre.* Michael Landon starred as, he recalls, "a guy who owned a gambling ship in the Yukon in the late 1800s. I looked a solid 15 or 16 years old and wore a white lace shirt and tight, black pants. Alan Hale, Jr. was my sidekick and Lew Ayres was my brother. It was nothing but shots being fired. It just went on forever. Needless to say, it didn't go." Guest stars included DeForest Kelley, Forrest Lewis, Robert Griffin, and Bonnie Holding.

266. **Man Against Crime.** 30 min. Airdate: 9/21/58. Director: Richard L. Bare. Writer: Herb Meadow, from a story by Lawrence Klee. Darren McGavin is a young defense attorney in this pilot, aired as an episode of *Decision. Cast:* Darren McGavin (as Dan Garrett), David Opatoshu (Sam Mitschener), Stanley Peck (Bobbie Mitschener), Joe Sullivan (Voorhes), Terry Greene (Spotsy).

267. **MacGreedy's Woman.** 30 min. Airdate: 9/23/58. Production Company: Four Star. Director: Allen H. Miner. Producer: David Heilweil. Writers: Gloria Saunders and Dick Carr. Music: Billy May. Aired as an episode of *Colgate Theatre.* The adventures of a hostess (Jane Russell) working in a small San Francisco nightclub she inherited from her husband. Costarred Don Durant, Sean McClory, Jonathon Harris, Bill Erwin, and Ned Glass. It was rewritten, reshot, and recast with Julie London in 1959 but the new pilot, called *Maggie Malone,* still failed to generate any interest.

268. **Mike Shayne.** 30 min. Airdate: 9/28/58. Director: Mark Stevens. Producer: Mark Stevens. Writer: Steve Fisher, from the stories by Brett Halliday. Mark Stevens is private eye Mike Shayne. Aired as the "Man on Raft" episode of *Decision. Cast:* Mark Stevens (as Mike Shayne), Merry Anders (Lucy), Robert Brubaker (Tim Rourke), Diane Brewster (Ann Conway), Steve Mitchell (Turner), William Kendis (Ed Shelton), Mary Adams (Sara Redford).

269. **Special Agent.** The exploits of a contemporary, special police officer who works for a railroad line.

270. **Tarzan.** 74 min. (2) Director: H. Bruce Humberstone. Producer: Sol Lesser. Music: Paul Sawtell. Four pilots edited together and released as the feature films *Tarzan's Fight for Life* and *Tarzan and the Trappers* and starring Gordon Scott as the legendary "Lord of the Apes," Eve Brent as Jane, and Rickie Sorenson as Tartu, their adopted son. This was pitched again the following year with Denny Miller as Tarzan and Joanna Barnes as Jane – but didn't air until 1968, one year after the *Tarzan* series with Ron Ely was canceled.

271. **Tonight in Havana.** 30 min. Airdate: 9/2/58. Director: Fletcher Markle. Producers: Fletcher Markle and David Ahlers. Writer: David Ahlers, from a story by Burnham Carter. Aired as an episode of *Colgate Theatre*. The adventures of a restaurant owner (Ricardo Montalban) and his partner (Lita Milan) who get involved in people's problems. Guest starred James Gavin, Mari Aldon, Edward Colmans, Maria Munne, Luis Oquendo, Rogelio Hernandez, and Gustave Meler.

ODYSSEY (DOUGFAIR)

272. **Police Boat.** *Highway Patrol* on the water. This series would be culled from the files of the New York Harbor Police.

273. **Tramp Ship.** The travels of a steam ship captain and his crew.

HAL ROACH PRODUCTIONS

274. **Branding Irons.** A western anthology using various cattle brands as starting points for stories.

SCREEN GEMS PRODUCTIONS

275. **Johnny Wildlife.** The adventures of a wildlife cameraman and his young son.

276. **The Leathernecks.** This series, which would be produced in cooperation with the U.S. Marine Corps, would follow two "fighting leathernecks" on land and seas, in battle, in love, on leave and on special assignment.

TRENDLE/CAMPBELL PRODUCTIONS

277. **The Green Hornet.** A re-offering of a flop 1951 pilot, which was based on the comic book and radio adventures of Britt Reid, a newspaper reporter who has a secret identity as a nocturnal crime fighter. He has a super car, a unique gas-fighting gun, a secret laboratory, and a chauffeur/assistant named Kato.

20TH CENTURY FOX

278. **Anything, Inc.** Producer: Ben Feiner. An unskilled couple advertise they will do "anything for a dollar." They are so successful that they become rich and incorporate. The series will be about the people who come to them and the strange, odd, and risky jobs they propose. The pilot stars Kendell Scott.

279. **Mother Is a Freshman.** A widow goes back to school, where her son is a football star, to complete her education.

WARNER BROS. TELEVISION

280. **Billy the Kid.** The series would present the outlaw in a sympathetic light and deliberately stray from the character's true adventures.

WILLIAM MORRIS AGENCY

281. **The Celeste Holm Show.** Writer: Art Cohn, from the book *No Facilities for Women*. Holm would portray a reporter in this sitcom.

282. **Cowboy Hall of Fame.** An anthology series based on the famous cowboys honored by the National Cowboy Hall of Fame in Oklahoma City.

283. **The Great Muldoon.** Producer: John Sutherland. This is a comedy mixing live action with animation and follows the adventures of a cartoonist and his creation, "The Great Muldoon."

284. **The New Robinson Crusoe.** Dan O'Herlihy reprises his movie role as a castaway on an island. The series, however, would take place in modern day and would add other shipwrecked characters for him to interact with.

285. **The Scarlet Blade.** A Zorro-like character during Emperor Maximilian's reign in Mexico.

286. **Skippy.** A series based on the movie about a newspaper boy.
287. **The Vivian Blaine/George London Show.** Blaine, a Broadway musical star, and London, an opera singer, in a sitcom about husband and wife who have the same careers as these two stars.

INDEPENDENT PRODUCTIONS

288. **Primrose.** Producers: Frank La Tourette and James Mosher. Writer: Luke Short. A typical, frontier town is the setting for this western series concept.
289. **Rawhide Riley.** Producer: Sam White. Richard Arlen stars in this western anthology. The narrator is a frontier barber in Tucson, Arizona.

1959–1960

ABC / COMEDY

290. **Sissy.** Production Company: Screen Gems. Writer: Mac Hyman. A family living in the Ozarks. The stars were Molly Bee, Robert Easton and Roscoe Ates.

291. **Three of a Kind.** Tony Randall plays three identical brothers in this comedy about mistaken identity and the humor in romance.

292. **Where There's Smokey.** 30 min. Airdate: 3/1/66. Production Company: Desilu. Director: Rod Amateau. Producer: Sid Dorfman. Writers: Sid Dorfman and Rod Amateau. Gale Gordon is a fire chief who is constantly frustrated by his fireman nephew, Soupy Sales, and plots constantly to get him out of his house. This sat on a shelf for seven years. *Cast:* Soupy Sales (as Fireman Smokey), Gale Gordon (Warren Packard), Hollis Irving (Blossom Packard), Ricky Allen (Richie Packard), Louise Glenn (Maggie Dennison), Jack Weston (Fireman Hogan), Charles Tannen (Benson), Robert Nichols (Charlie).

293. **Willie.** Robert Morse stars in this comedy about a Brooklyn shipping clerk who dreams of being a star.

ABC / DRAMA

294. **The Astronaut.** Production Company: Screen Gems. Writer: Ted Sher-deman. An astronaut working in the 1970s.

295. **The Fat Man.** Production Company: Screen Gems. A series based on the Dashiell Hammett character that was the basis for the radio serial.

296. **The Frontier World of Doc Holiday.** 60 min. Airdate: 1959. Production Company: Warner Bros. Television. Director: Leslie H. Martinson. Producer: Roy Huggins. Aired as an episode of *Cheyenne* entitled "Birth of a Legend." Adam West, described by Warners as a "traditional western star. Tall and good looking, suggesting great strength and good breeding," played the title role. Warners planned to play down Holiday's tuberculosis but it would, nonetheless, provide the impetus for the series concept—a doctor tells Holiday he has six months to live. In the pilot episode, Holiday kills for the first time but doesn't care because he is doomed to die anyway. Adam West says "I played him as an alcoholic with

a consumptive cough. That isn't too attractive when you kiss your horse, and the horse dies. I don't think ABC, Warners, or Madison Avenue appreciated it at the time. And probably rightly so."

297. **The Long Green.** Production Company: Screen Gems. A man who will do anything as long as there is a reward for accomplishing it, though he is always on the side of goodness.

298. **Night People.** Real-life couple Tony Martin and Cyd Charisse play a modern-day crooner and his wife in this projected family drama.

299. **Night Stick (aka The Big Walk).** Production Company: Screen Gems. Producer: Gene Roddenberry. Writer: Gene Roddenberry. The adventures of Jim Ireland (Richard Shannon), a cop-on-the-beat in Greenwich Village. The never aired, pilot episode was entitled "Jim Ireland Meets the Giants." *Cast:* Richard Shannon (as Jim Ireland), Ann Robinson (Gail), Barry Neilson (Mr. Komansky).

300. **The Tapper.** Production Company: Screen Gems. A group of civilians team up to help the government in espionage operations. Based on a real organization that operated during World War II.

301. **Tarzan.** 60 min. Airdate: 2/23/68. Director: Joseph Newman. Producers: Al and Donald Zimbalist. Writer: Robert Hill. Music: Shorty Rogers. Aired as an episode of *Off the See the Wizard.* Denny Miller is Tarzan and Joanna Barnes is Jane in this unsold pilot that didn't air until a decade after it was made...and a year after the cancellation of the *Tarzan* TV series starring Ron Ely. The pilot guest stars included Cesare Danova, Robert Douglas and Thomas Yangha. It was released theatrically in 1959 in an 80-minute version.

302. **The Tiger of Sonora.** Creator: Russell Hayden. A Russian adventurer comes to the old west and becomes a pioneer Robin Hood.

ASHLEY STEINER AGENCY

303. **The Adventures of the U.S. Secret Service.** Producers: Peter Martin, Don Fairchild and Ted Granik. An anthology based on actual files that will chart the government's fight against crime at the turn-of-the-century.

304. **The Thoroughbreds.** Linda Darnell stars as a young mother and horse-trainer in California.

305. **The Wildcatters.** Production Company: Batjak. Claude Akins and Justice McQueen star as oil men. John Wayne, whose company produced the pilot, would narrate and his son, Pat, would occasionally guest star.

CBS / COMEDY

306. Bachelor Party. 30 min. Airdate: 6/5/59. Director: Richard Haydin. Producer: William Frye. Writers: Everett Greenbaum, Fritzell Greenbaum, and William Frye. Aired as "The Rumor" episode of *Schlitz Playhouse of the Stars*. Hal March, Whit Bissell, and Elliot Reid are three bachelors who work at the same insurance company. Guest starred Patricia Crowley, Richard Collier, Phillip Coolidge, Alice Backes and George Pirrone.

307. Ernestine (aka The Soft Touch). 30 min. Airdate: 7/3/62. Production Company: Desilu. Director: Sidney Salkow. Producer: William Harmon. Writers: Jay Sommers and Don Nelson. Marie Wilson, Charles Ruggles, Charlie Lane and Nancy Kulp star in this situation comedy modeled after Wilson's hit series *My Friend Irma* (CBS 1952–54). Ruggles owns a loan company and Wilson is his daughter, who inevitably gets involved in jams. Guest stars included Hayden Rorke, James Flavin, Claude Stroud and Jack Straw. Cast: Marie Wilson (Ernestine McDougal), Charlie Ruggles (Charles McDougal), Madge Blake (Mrs. Munson), Charles Lane (Mr. Martin), El Brendel (Mr. Hauser), Nancy Kulp (Woman).

308. Head of the Family. 30 min. Airdate: 7/19/60. Production Company: William Morris Agency. Director: Don Weis. Producers: Marty Poll and Stuart Rosenberg. Writer: Carl Reiner. Failing was the best thing that could have happened to this pilot, which starred Carl Reiner as Rob Petrie, a writer for the *Alan Sturdy* TV variety show, and Barbara Britton as his wife, Laura. Sound familiar? It was shot in New York with one camera and was financed by Joseph Kennedy and actor Peter Lawford. Although it wasn't picked up, Sheldon Leonard produced a new pilot, from a new script by Reiner, and brought in a new cast—and it became *The Dick Van Dyke Show. Cast:* Carl Reiner (as Rob Petrie), Barbara Britton (Laura Petrie), Gary Morgan (Richie Petrie), Morty Gunty (Buddy Sorrell), Sylvia Miles (Sally Rogers), Jack Wakefield (Alan Sturdy).

309. I Was a Bloodhound. 30 min. Airdate: 2/15/59. Director: Sidney Lanfield. Producer: Harry Tugend. Writers: Lawrence Marks and Milton Pascal. Aired as an episode of *GE Theatre*. Ernie Kovacs is a private eye who is great at sniffing out clues – literally – to baffling crimes. In the pilot, he finds a kidnapped baby elephant. *Cast:* Ernie Kovacs (as Barney Colby), Yvonne White (Eunice Colby), Shirley Mitchell (Jennie), Larry Dobkin (Singh), Bart Bradley (Prince Puranajab), Robert Nash (Walters), Joseph Mell (Joe), Michael Garrett (Charlie).

310. Ivy League. 30 min. Airdate: 3/13/59. Production Company: MCA/Revue Productions. Director: Richard Whorf. Executive Producer: Alan Ladd. Producer: Everett Freeman. Writer: Everett Freeman. This sitcom pilot aired as an episode of *Schlitz Playhouse of the Stars*. William Bendix is an ex–Marine sergeant who goes back to an eastern college as a student and faces the problems of re-adjustment to civilian and academic life. He befriends the son (Tim Hovey) of his landlady (Florence MacMichael) and the young man helps him to fit in. *Cast:* William Bendix (as Bull Mitchell), Tim Hovey (Timmy Parker), Florence MacMichael (Mamie Parker), Bartlett Robinson (Dean), Mary Tyler Moore (Student #1), Doug McClure (Student #2), Arte Johnson (Student #3), Sheila Bromley (Teacher #1), Kathleen Warren (Teacher #2).

311. You're Only Young Twice. 30 min. Airdate: 8/1/60. Production Company: Desilu. Director: Arthur Lubin. Executive Producer: Desi Arnaz. Producer: Ed Jurist. Writers: Bob Schiller, Bob Weiskopf, and Norman Tokar. Aired as an episode of *CBS New Comedy Showcase*. An insurance agent retires and suddenly he and his wife are plagued by the problems of their children and grandchildren. *Cast:* George Murphy (as Charles Tyler), Martha Scott (Kit Tyler), Sue Randall (Lois), Roger Perry (Arthur), Jane Darwell (Olga).

CBS / DRAMA

312. An American in Italy. Producer: Peter Vertel. Set in Rome, the series would focus on a freelance news photographer.

313. Ballad of the Bad Man. 60 min. Airdate: 1/26/59. Production Company: Desilu. A spin-off from *Desilu Playhouse* with Steve Forrest as a bounty hunter in the old west. Costarred Jane Russell, Jack Haley, Karen Sharpe and Mischa Auer.

314. Belle Starr (aka Way of the West). 30 min. Airdate: 6/6/58. Director: David Butler. Producer: Frank P. Rosenberg. Aired as an episode of *Schlitz Playhouse of the Stars*. Abby Dalton as a frontier "Simon Templar" – a woman with a criminal reputation who, however, always seems to apprehend bad guys and uphold the law. In the pilot, she helps a doctor fight a smallpox epidemic. *Cast:* Abby Dalton (as Belle Starr), John Forsythe (Dr. John Carter), Staats Cotsworth (Col. Taylor), K.L. Smith (Slim Enfield), Sheridan Comerate (Ed Coats), Claude Akins (Gus Garner), Mona Carrole (Elaine), Ciney Gray (Doreen), Michael Landon (Don Burns), Jack Bartell (Sentry), Robert Darin (Joe), John Bryant (Harry Ryan), Malcolm Atterbury (Johnson), Maudie Prickett (Miss Piper).

315. **Black Gold (aka Boom Town).** Production Company: Warner Bros. Television. Based on the movie *Boom Town*, this series would have featured stories about the oil industry. CBS was excited about the concept and had tentatively scheduled the series for Wednesdays at 7:30.

316. **Brock Callahan.** 30 min. Airdate: 8/11/59. Director: Don Siegel. Producer: James Fonda. Writer: Stirling Silliphant. Aired as an episode of *Geritol Adventure Showcase* as "The Silent Kill." The adventures of a football player-turned-Beverly Hills private eye. *Cast:* Ken Clark (as Brock Callahan), Randy Stewart (Jan Barrett), Richard Shannon (Lt. Larry Pascal), Barbara Darrow (Linda Hollander).

317. **The Caballero.** 30 min. Airdate: 4/13/59. Production Company: Desilu. Executive Producer: Desi Arnaz. Aired as an episode of *The Texan*. Cesar Romero is the chief of the Mexican Border Patrol in the old west. Guest stars included Whit Bissell, Mari Blanchard, Fred Graham, Abel Fernandez and Jim Hayward.

318. **Chez Rouge.** 60 min. Airdate: 2/16/59. Production Company: Desilu. Aired as an episode of *Desilu Playhouse*. Ray Danton, Abel Fernandez, Harry Guardino, Dan Blocker, Herbert Berghoff, Janis Paige, Kurt Kasznar. A beautiful woman runs a nightclub in Panama a la "Casablanca."

319. **Doctor Mike.** 30 min. Airdate: 8/18/59. Director: Oscar Rudolph. Producer: Harold Greene. Writer: John Kneubuhl. Keith Andes is a doctor in a sprawling, urban hospital who, in the pilot, clashes with a man who won't let the doctor operate on his wife. *Cast:* Keith Andes (as Dr. Michael Grant), Lewis Martin (Dr. Sam Talbert), Mary Adams (Mary Barker), Joe DeSantis (Alex Bartos), Greta Granstedt (Anna Bartos).

320. **Dog Face.** A true-story anthology about American soldiers.

321. **I Am a Lawyer.** Cameron Mitchell stars as a Texas lawyer who must "settle his problems with his fists as often as with his law books."

322. **Johnny Guitar.** 30 min. Airdate: 7/31/59. Director: Robert Leeds. Producer: Robert Carney. Writer: Otis Carney. Johnny (William Joyce) is a carefree, singing cowboy roaming the West and helping people in trouble. In the pilot, he's hired to sing at a wedding and discovers the groom is a killer who is forcing the bride to marry him. *Cast:* William Joyce (as Johnny Guitar), Fay Spain (Anna Carrick), Reg Parton (Harry Shay), Paul Burns (Gyte).

323. **Savage Is the Name.** Barry Sullivan and Pat O'Brien starred as two detectives working for an international airline.

324. **Silent Saber.** Producer: Leslie Harris. The adventures of a counterspy in the American Revolution who reports directly to General Washington.

325. **Six Guns for Donegan.** 60 min. Airdate: 10/16/59. Production Company: Desilu. Director: Douglas Heyes. Executive Producer: Desi Arnaz. Producer: Devry Freeman. Writer: John Mantley. Creators: John Mantley and Devry Freeman. A pilot from *Maverick* writer Heyes and *Gunsmoke* producer/writer Mantley that aired on *Desilu Playhouse*. The adventures of Sheriff Orville Darrow (Lloyd Nolan) and his five sharp-shooting sons as they fight to maintain the law in the city of Donegan. In the pilot, the Darrows must protect a cowardly man acquitted of killing one of the evil Clinton Brothers, who are out for revenge. Costars included Jean Hagen as Mrs. Darrow and James Franciscus and Barry Curtis as two of his sons. The pilot cast included Jack Elam, Harry Towns, Bill Erwin, Mickey Simpson, Hal Hopper, and Sherwood Price.

326. **War Correspondent.** 30 min. Airdate: 8/26/59. Director: Christian Nyby. Producers: Ray Singer and Dick Chevillat. Writer: Otis Carney. Aired as an episode of *Geritol Adventure Showcase*. Gene Barry is Sgt. Andy Pile, a war correspondent. Guest stars included Lin McCarthy, Eugene Iglesias, Didi Ramiti, Harry Dean Stanton, and William Bryant.

327. **The Woman in the Case.** An anthology modeled on the Loretta Young show. Maureen O'Hara would host and occasionally star in this series featuring stories about strong women.

328. **The Wonderful World of Little Julius.** Producer: Cy Howard. Eddie Hodges, popular for his role in Broadway's *The Music Man,* stars in this "family melodrama" along with Sam Levene and Gregory Ratoff.

329. **World of White.** Writer: Sidney Kingsley, based on his play *Men in White.* Dick York, Darryl Hickman and Robert Keith star as three doctors. James MacArthur guest starred in the pilot.

DESILU PRODUCTIONS

330. **Chick Bowdrie.** A spin-off from *The Texan* starring Chuck Wassil as a frontier gunfighter.

331. **The Man of Many Faces.** A detective who is, as the title suggests, a master of disguise.

332. **The Privateer.** Fernando Lamas is a sea-going Robin Hood in the 1700s.

333. **St. Louis Man.** A detective in 1870s St. Louis who uses the best in what was then considered modern technology.

FILM MASTERS

334. **Carter's Eye.** Producer: E. Jack Neuman. A tough private detective a la Phillip Marlowe or Mike Hammer.

335. **Shark Street.** The adventures of a "Jack Webb type" deep sea diver and adventurer living in San Pedro.

336. **Skagway.** A gold-mining western set in 1890s Alaska.

FOUR STAR PRODUCTIONS

337. **The Judy Canova Show.** Modeled after *The Real McCoys.* Canova plays an Arkansas mountain girl who is also owner and chief cook in a diner.

338. **The Outrider.** Producer: Vincent Fennelly. Aired as an episode of *Wanted: Dead or Alive.* The adventures of a man who hires himself out as protection to those traveling through dangerous western country. He works out of a hotel populated by other "outriders" and that is run by his love interest, an adventurous woman.

339. **Six Star Playhouse.** An anthology series featuring six big name stars.

340. **Stagecoach.** James Best stars as a stagecoach driver in this spin-off from *Wanted Dead or Alive.*

341. **The Trailman.** John Ericson stars as a cowboy traveling with a spoiled, 15-year-old "rich kid who has never roughed it before."

GENERAL ARTISTS CORPORATION

342. **Dangerous Dan McGrew.** Based on the poem by Robert Service, this western would be set in Alaska and chronicle the adventures of Dan, played by Scott Brady, and the "lady known as Lou."

343. **The Jimmy Rodgers Campus Show.** Rodgers and his orchestra would travel each week to a different college, perform and conduct a talent contest.

344. **Mayday.** Each episode of this series, based on the files of the Military Air Transport Command, would begin with a call for help. An American family, based in Japan, would come to the rescue.

345. **There's a Small Motel.** A situation comedy about a couple who run a small motel. Concept is designed to make the best use of guest stars. For instance, if Hoagy Carmichael shows up, there will be a piano for him to play in the lounge.

GOODSON-TODMAN PRODUCTIONS

346. **The Gimmick Man.** The adventures of a Hollywood public relations man who works out of the third booth at Romanoff's Restaurant. Whether he wants to or not, he always gets entangled in other people's often dangerous problems.

347. **Her Honor, The Mayor.** Producer/Writer: John Michael Hayes. An average, middle class housewife with three kids becomes mayor in this drama.

348. **The Joan Crawford Show.** A proposed 30-minute anthology. Crawford would host and star in 20 out of each 39 shows and occasionally endorse products.

HAL HACKETT PRODUCTIONS/OFFICIAL FILMS

349. **What Are the Odds?** Bob Warren would interview people from all over the world who have saved their lives – or someone else's – against incredible and almost unbelievable odds.

HECHT HILL LANCASTER

350. **Vera Cruz.** A series based on the Gary Cooper/Burt Lancaster film, a post-civil war adventure set after the Maximilian revolution.

SANDY HOWARD AND ASSOCIATES

351. The previously listed pilot **Congressional Investigator** became the syndicated series of the same name.

352. **Emergency Ward.** True cases of medical emergencies dramatized more as a procedural documentary than as drama.

353. **Fantastic.** Again, the same format as *Police Station* applied to cases of the supernatural. Carlton Young hosts and is joined by a panel of Duke University experts.

354. The previously listed pilot **Police Station** became the syndicated series of the same name.

355. **Spellbound.** Dramatizations of true psychiatric problems that are later reviewed by a panel of experts.

GEORGE HUSKIN AND ASSOCIATES

356. **The Files of the Tokyo Police.** Sessue Hayakawa stars as a Japanese detective.

357. **Fit as a Fiddle.** William Frawley, Eddie Foy, Jr., and Florence Halop (in a dual role) star as four partners who own a charm school, gymnasium and dance academy in this comedy.

358. **The Happy Time.** The dramatic lives of a San Joaquin Valley family of farmers. Aimed at capturing the style of the William Saroyan stories.

359. **Little America.** The story of a diplomat, his schoolteacher wife, and his family living abroad in Germany.

360. **Lord Joe.** The adventures of Joe Lord, "a Sunset Strip-type character," who moves to England.

361. **Merlin the Magician.** Writer: Phil Rapp. Dick Hearn stars in this "zany comedy" about the famed magician in King Arthur's court. The twist is he always conjures up such modern objects as gas ranges, cars and the like to solve his problems. The series is trying to capture the tone of Mark Twain in *A Connecticut Yankee in King Arthurs Court.*

362. **Tosti and Son.** Opera star Baccaloni and singer Frankie Laine play a father and son who run a New York restaurant catering to a show business clientele.

INDEPENDENT TELEVISION CORPORATION

363. **The Adventures of Tom Swift.** Producer: Jack Wrather. Based on the popular children's books about a brilliant, science-minded teenager. Gary Vinson stars.

364. **Centurian.** Producer: Jack Wrather. This is described only as a "Ben-Hur–type Roman western" shot in Europe.

365. **The Deputy Seraph.** Producer: Jack Wrather. Writer: Phil Rapp. A comedy starring Harpo and Chico Marx to be filmed in Europe.

366. **Emergency.** Producer: Arthur Lewis. Arthur Hill stars as a doctor working in an emergency ward of a "big city hospital." The series would have been shot on location in Manhattan.

367. **It Pays to Be Ignorant.** Producer: Jack Wrather. Lou Costello, who died in 1959, would have starred in this updated adaptation of the half-hour radio series.

368. **The Man from Lloyd's.** Producer: Jack Wrather. A half-hour adventure about an American insurance adjuster in London. A similar concept would be employed by Robert Wagner in 1985 in the short-lived *Lime Street*.

369. **Treasury Agent.** Producer: Jack Wrather. A self-explanatory series based on the book of the same title by Andrew Tully.

MARK VII PRODUCTIONS

370. **The Black Cat.** Producer: Jack Webb. John Hudson plays a San Francisco reporter. The title comes from the marble cat that is part of the SF Press Club decor.

371. **Series I.** Jack Webb would host this anthology series, which would encompass everything from mystery to fantasy to western, and would star in at least three episodes for every 13 shot.

MCA/REVUE PRODUCTIONS

372. **The Jan Clayton Show.** A sitcom based on the movie *Cheers for Miss Bishop*, with Clayton playing an English teacher in a mid-western college. This was later pitched to NBC in 1961.

373. **The Quiet Man.** Writer: Frank Gruber. Jack Lord stars as a western hero who is a man of few words. As a young man, he was outgoing and sharp with a gun. His father sends him to Harvard and when the boy returns, he's dedicated to living by his wits and not his gun. When his father and fiancée are murdered, he seeks revenge with his gun. His vengeance complete, he becomes a "quiet" but "deadly" man who uses his wits often and his gun sparingly. Gruber, the author of three dozen western novels, created *Wells Fargo* and *The Texan*.

MCCADDEN PRODUCTIONS

374. **Central Intelligence.** A half-hour series based on true cases in the files of the CIA. The hero would be a secret agent whose cover is a traveling salesman working for a large importing house.

375. The previously listed pilot **Ghost Squad of Scotland Yard** became the syndicated series *The Ghost Squad*.

376. Inspector General. A series based on files from the Inspector General's office in cooperation with the Air Force and the Department of Defense. The hero would be on roving assignment around the world and would work closely with the police and FBI.

377. The Women. "A Charles Boyer type host doing a Loretta Young type series," producers told advertisers.

MGM

378. Amigo. Gilbert Roland is a modern-day detective operating in the border town of El Paso. His closest friend will be a Mexican police officer working in Juarez. Very similar to a later pilot, *Border Town,* which appeared as an episode of *Stoney Burke* in 1963.

379. Johnny Eager. Producers: Wilbur Stark and Jerry Layton. Writer: Paul Monash. A detective who lives in Detroit and operates a fleet of taxi cabs. The pilot is based on the movie, which starred Robert Taylor.

380. You're Only Young Once. Producers: Richard Maibaum and Milo Frank. Dean Jones stars as an ex-GI who, with his wife, lives in a Quonset hut village in this half-hour comedy.

NBC / COMEDY

381. Another Day, Another Dollar. 30 min. Airdate: 9/21/59. Director: Walter Grauman. Producer: William Sackheim. Writer: Howard Rodman, from a story by Nate Monaster. Aired as an episode of *Alcoa/Goodyear Theatre.* The first of two pilots about the comedic trials and tribulations of a toy salesman and his family. The second, *How's Business,* aired a few months later. In this pilot, the toy salesman has to choose between seeing his son's art show at school or meeting an important client. Guest starred Ralph Gamble, Jeane Wood, Dorothy Crider and Lester Dorr. *Cast:* Jack Carson (as Augie Adams), Jean Gillespie (Joyce Adams), Flip Mark (Robbie Adams), Jesse White (John Burke).

382. Dear Mom, Dear Dad. 30 min. Airdate: 5/18/59. Production Company: Screen Gems. Director: Don Taylor. Producer: Winston O'Keefe. Writers: George W. George and Judith George. A sitcom about a teenager (Robert Trumbell) living away from home, attending college. His letter home to his parents each week will be the starting point of the episode and will "tell the tale." *Cast:* Robert Trumbell (as Bunty Perkins), Raymond Bailey (The Dean), Kathy Reed (Amy Porter), Bert Convy (Galen Lawrence), Jimmy Bates (Bill Davidson). Aired as an episode of *Alcoa / Goodyear Theatre*.

383. **Finch Finds a Way (aka Slightly Fallen Angel).** 30 min. Airdate: 5/4/59. Production Company: Screen Gems. Director: Robert Ellis Miller. Producer: William Sackheim. Writers: Sol Saks, William Cowley, and Peggy Chantler. Aired as an episode of *Alcoa/Goodyear Theatre*. Mr. Finch (Walter Slezak) is an angel who comes to earth to fix our human problems—but usually just makes the problems worse. This is a popular concept in television, a concept that would be pitched many times and become such series as *Good Heavens* and *Highway to Heaven*. Costarred Lee Bergere, David White, Elizabeth Watts, Jeffrey Roland, Paul Reed and Sid Raymond.

384. **Heave Ho Harrigan.** 30 min. Airdate: 9/22/61. Production Company: Goodson-Todman. Aired as an episode of *Westinghouse Preview Theater*. The comedic adventures of an ordinary enlisted man (Myron McCormick) on an aircraft carrier. He's likeable and anxious to do everything right but inevitably messes things up. *Cast:* Myron McCormick (as Heave Ho Harrigan), Allyn Joslyn (Capt. Towers), Darryl Hickman (Ensign Smithers).

385. **How's Business?** 30 min. Airdate: 12/28/59. Director: Walter Grauman. Producer: William Sackheim. Writer: Howard Rodman, from a story by Nate Monaster. The second pilot, aired as an episode of *Alcoa/Goodyear Theatre*, for *Another Day, Another Dollar* with the same regular cast. Guest stars were Norma Connolly, Scott Morrow, Timmy Cletro and Ronnie Dapo.

386. **I Remember Caviar.** 30 min. Airdate: 5/11/59. Director: Don Taylor. Producer: Winston O'Keefe. Writers: Nate Monaster and Norman Tokar. Aired as an episode of *Alcoa/Goodyear Theatre*. A wealthy family (Pat Crowley, Lurene Tuttle, Elliot Reid) lose their money in bad investments. A second pilot, pitching the same concept and cast, was made in 1960 and was entitled *All in the Family*.

387. **The Jacksons.** Producer: Jess Oppenheimer. Joan Blondell stars in this sitcom about a woman whose maternal instincts keep getting her in trouble – to the consternation of her retired husband and her adult children.

388. **The McGonigle.** 30 min. Airdates: 7/28/61 NBC and 7/11/64 CBS. Production Company: MGM. Director: Ralph Francis Murphy. Executive Producer: Harry Joe Brown. Producers: Ray Singer and Dick Chevillat. Writers: Ray Singer and Dick Chevillat, based on the *Saturday Evening Post* stories by Dan Gallery. The comedic misadventures of two seamen on the *U.S.S. Okinawa* who, in the pilot, try to arrange a honeymoon on the ship for a fellow shipmate and his bride. *Cast:*

Mickey Shaughnessy (as Mac McGonigle), Tom D'Andrea (Scuttlebutt Baines), Frank Gerstie (Capt. Amboy), Wally Cassell (Chief Petty Officer Jones), Charles Picerni (Bottleneck), Norman Grabowski (Hammerhead), Mark Damon (Artie Dale), Diane Jergens (Nina Dale).

389. **The Rowan and Martin Show.** Producer/Writer: Charles Isaacs. First of two sitcom pilots featuring the comedy team, which was under contract to NBC. They would later host *Laugh-In*, NBC's break-through comedy in 1968.

390. **The Secret Life of John Monroe (aka Secret Life of James Thurber).** 30 min. Airdate: 6/8/59. Production Company: Screen Gems. Director: James Sheldon. Producer: Jules Goldstone. Writer: Mel Shavelson, from the stories by James Thurber. Aired as the "Christabel" episode of *Alcoa/Goodyear Theatre*. Arthur O'Connell is magazine writer and cartoonist John Monroe who often escapes into the fantasy world of his drawings—which came alive through animation by UPA Pictures. In the pilot, Monroe's daughter dog Christabel dies. Although this didn't sell, another pilot was made in 1961 called *The Secret Life of James Thurber*, this time starring Orson Bean, and was aired on *The June Allyson Show*. It, too, failed to spawn a series. A decade later, however, Thurber's life and tales became the basis for *My World and Welcome To It*, starring William Windom as John Monroe, Joan Hotchkis as his wife Ellen, Lisa Gerritsen as daughter Lydia. The highly acclaimed series, produced by Sheldon Leonard and Danny Arnold, mixed animation and live action and survived for a single season. *Cast:* Arthur O'Connell (as John Monroe), Georgann Johnson (Ellen Monroe), Susan Gordon (Lydia Monroe), Charles Herbert (Charlie), Dabbs Greer (Policeman).

NBC / DRAMA

391. The previously listed pilot **Flight** became the series of the same name. However, the resulting anthology series included two unsold pilots that were not listed in the original edition of this book. Here are the details:

Warbirds. 30 minutes. Production Company: Filmways Productions. Director: Jean Yarbrough. Producers: Al Simon, George Burns. Writer: Leonard Heideman. The series would have focused on the adventures of U.S. Army pilots in France. Joe Maross starred.

Dawn Patrol. 30 Minutes. Production Company: Filmways Productions. Director: Tay Garnett. Producers: Al Simon, George Burns. Writers: Eliot Asinof & Sam

Neuman. A re-developed version of *Warbirds*, this CBS pilot featured Wayde Preston as the commander of a U.S. fighter squadron in France in 1917. Hoagy Carmichael played the owner of a club where the pilots hung out. Other Co-stars included William Wellman Jr. , Basil Rathbone, and Don Francks.

392. **Gentry's People.** 30 min. Airdate: 7/7/59. Director: Thomas Carr. Producer: Vincent Fennelly. Writer: John Robinson. Aired as an episode of *David Niven Theatre*. Keefe Brasselle is a newspaper reporter who helps people in trouble. *Cast:* Keefe Brasselle (as Gentry), James Best (Frank Simms), Virginia Gregg (Hazel), Jay C. Flippen (Sgt. Nelson), Jeanette Nolan (Mrs. Simms).

393. **High Noon.** A series based on the classic film, produced by Stanley Kramer.

394. **The Iron Horseman.** Producers: Lou Edelman and Walter Mirisch. Guy Williams stars as a railroad detective in the 1880s. Not to be confused with the 1966 series *Iron Horse,* starring Dale Robertson, on ABC.

395. **Justice of the Peace.** 30 min. Airdate: 6/30/59. Director: Don McDougall. Producer: Vincent M. Fennelly. Writer: John Robinson. Aired as an episode of *David Niven Theater*. Dan Duryea is Mark Johnston, the justice of the peace in a small town who, in the pilot, is terrorized by an escaped mental patient he put away. Dorothy Green is Johnston's wife, Adam Williams is the psycho. Guest stars included Robert Warga, Wright King, and Tol Avery.

396. **Maggie Malone.** 30 min. Airdate: 6/9/59. Production Company: Four Star. Director: Lewis Allen. Producer: Vincent M. Fennelly. Writers: John Robinson and Richard Carr. Aired as an episode of *David Niven Theatre*. A reworking of the 1958 pilot *Macgreedy's Woman*, which starred Jane Russell and was written by Gloria Saunders and Richard Carr. This time, Julie London is Maggie Malone, a singer at a nightclub she co-owns with Pete (Steve Brodie). Together, they get involved in the problems of their patrons. *Cast:* Julie London (as Maggie Malone), Steve Brodie (Pete), Stacy Harris (Frank Dennison), Regis Toomey (Detective Andy Cullen), John Wilder (Thug).

397. **Outpost of Space.** An adventure series which would tell "frontier stories of the old west and put them into the new frontier of space."

HAL ROACH PRODUCTIONS

398. **Desk Space.** Writer: Artie Stander. A woman who inherits a floor, complete with phones and desks, in an office building and rents out the space to different people by the hour, every week—bookies, salesmen, private eyes, etc.

399. **Fraternity Mother.** A situation comedy about a woman running a frat house.

400. **Grandparents.** A sitcom about two teenagers who go to live with their grandparents when their parents are killed. Walter Pidgeon stars as the grandfather.

401. **Hollywood Police Reporter.** An ex-police reporter becomes a Hollywood screenwriter who cannot seem to escape his past.

402. **Outpost.** Writer: Casey Robinson. A western about a woman who, with her young son, runs a small Arizona hotel that is an oasis and stopping-off place for the stagecoaches heading west. She insists on keeping this "outpost" free of problems – she will not tolerate racial or religious prejudices of any sort. The episodes would, of course, revolve around people who bring trouble and plight to this peaceful place.

SCREEN GEMS PRODUCTIONS

403. **The Blandings.** Airdate: 4/27/59. From the book and the movie, this pilot goes beyond the Blandings and their dream house. This series would begin after the dream house was built. Blandings, in the proposed series, would also have a job, a wife, and two teenage daughters. *The Blandings* aired as "A Light in the Fruit Closet" episode of *Alcoa-Goodyear Theater* on and starred Steve Dunne and Maggie Hayes.

404. **Cry Fraud.** A "modern-day" western about an insurance investigator.

405. **It's a Living.** Producer: William Sackheim. Sid Caesar stars in this sitcom as a traveling salesman who has a large family.

406. **Mom Is the Governor of Texas.** Helen Traubel stars as a woman who becomes governor when her husband dies and who is later re-elected. Based on the life story of Ma Ferguson.

407. **The Nancy Walker Show.** Writers: Ray Singer and Dick Chevillat. The problems of a couple living in a small town. This ultimately failed, but Walker – thanks to her success on *Rhoda* and *McMillan and Wife*—would get her "name" show in 1976 on ABC.

408. **Underworld.** Writers: Clarence Green and Russell Rouse. The adventures of an undercover cop who is so undercover, other cops don't even know he is a cop – so he can't count on the Force when he gets into trouble. He works only with the Mayor and the Police Chief. This concept was used in the 1987 series *Wiseguy*.

409. **Writer's Guild Theatre.** A half-hour anthology. The Writer's Guild had over 300 scripts for this show. A Guild Committee would choose the best 47 and then the agency would choose 39 from those 47. There would be no shortage of material for this series.

STAGG PRODUCTIONS

410. **Destination: Anywhere.** Producer: Jerry Stagg. Robert Stack and Jonah Crest star in this adventure about two importers who will do anything—travel anywhere—to get things to sell.

411. **Galaxy.** Producer: Jerry Stagg. A science fiction anthology from the pages of *Galaxy* magazine.

412. **Merrily We Go.** Producer: Jerry Stagg. Writer: Johnny Green. A comedy with Edie Adams as a movie star who gets into trouble, to the consternation of her mother, her kid brother, and her housekeeper.

413. **The Tender Years.** Producer: Jerry Stagg. A sitcom about a young lawyer and his wife during their first year of marriage. Michael Landon and Olive Sturgis starred.

20TH CENTURY FOX

414. **The Esther Williams Show.** A half-hour anthology with Esther Williams as hostess and star of at least half of the programs.

415. **Gunfighter.** The life and times of a reformed gunfighter.

416. **Helimarines.** Writer: Richard Tregaskis. A half-hour adventure about helicopter pilots who operate from aircraft carriers on the Pacific.

417. **The Last Frontier.** Writer: Art Napoleon. True stories about modern-day Alaska.

418. **Mr. Belvedere.** Hans Conried stars as the famed butler of the motion picture series. This character, repeatedly pitched by 20th Century Fox (last time in 1956 with Reginald Gardiner), wouldn't become a series until 1985.

419. **The Peggy Lee Show.** Peggy Lee stars in this sitcom as a music teacher of small children.

420. **Profile.** An anthology consisting of biographies of interesting people.

421. **Tales of Broadway.** Producer/Writer: Garson Kanin. An anthology of stories that take place in New York.

422. **Whodunit.** A murder is seen at the outset but the identity of the killer is withheld. Viewer figures out with the detective who done it.

UNITED ARTISTS

423. **Hudson Bay.** Producers: John Gibbs and Richard Steenberg. Barry Nelson and Gonzalez-Gonzalez star as cowboys in Canada during the 1800s.

WARNER BROS. TELEVISION

424. **Candy Cane.** Arlene Howell stars in this comedy about a hillbilly girl.

425. **Fraud.** A series about an insurance investigator. Stories would be culled from the files of the Insurance Underwriters of America.

426. **Public Enemies.** The saga of four crooks—who will rotate in episodes from week to week. The only actor signed was ex-football star Frank Gifford.

427. **Torrid Zone.** The adventures of a private eye who roams South America and will do just about anything for a buck—except kill.

WILLIAM MORRIS AGENCY

428. **Our Town.** Producer: Jerry Stagg. Burl Ives stars in a series concept based on the Thornton Wilder play.

YOUNG & MARCUS PRODUCTIONS

429. **The House of Seven Garbos.** Producers: Collier Young and Larry Marcus. A re-offering and recasting of the flop pilot about the life and times of young girls living in a boarding house while striving for stardom.

430. **Our Very Own.** Producers: Collier Young and Larry Marcus. Ex-President Harry Truman would host this anthology dramatizing the true stories of young Americans honored by the government for bravery and service.

431. **Virginia City.** Producers: Collier Young and Larry Marcus. Virginia City Enterprise Editor Lucious Beebe would host this series dramatizing true western adventures in the city, culled from the newspaper's files.

INDEPENDENT PRODUCERS

432. **The Adventures of Ali Baba.** Producer: Mitchell Gertz. Sabu stars in the fictional adventures of Ali Baba.

433. **Adventures of Duncan Maitland.** Producers: Wilbur Stark and Jerry Layton. The adventures of a blind private eye, played by Edward Arnold in the 1942 movie *Eyes in the Night*.

434. **Appointment with Fear.** Producer: Sheldon Reynolds. John Dehner stars as an American soldier-of-fortune who roams Europe. The pilot was shot in Berlin and,

shortly thereafter, Dehner was dropped in favor of Richard Burton – who would have starred had this gone to series.

435. **The Great Dane.** Producer: Alex Gottlieb. Opera star Lauritz Melchoir plays a retired singer who still occasionally belts out a tune when not coping with comedic family strife.

436. **Impulse.** Producer: Gross-Krasne Productions. Maria Palmer hosts this anthology examining why ordinary people suddenly commit crimes. The series would be produced with the cooperation of the American Psychiatric Society.

437. **Inquest.** Producer: George Draine. A series based on the true cases of private eyes who work for the San Diego County Coroner's office.

438. **Klondike Lou.** Producer: Robert Alexander. Mae West stars as an adventurous woman in the Alaskan gold country.

439. **Let's Make a Hit.** Producer: Martin Stone. A live program shot in a recording studio during the making of an album by a top performer.

440. **Mark Hellinger Theatre.** Producer: Arthur Leonard. An anthology based on Hellinger stories.

441. **The 33rd.** Producer: Jules Goldstone. Charles Bickford stars as a policeman.

442. **Trade Winds.** Producers: John Gibbs and Richard Steenberg. Michael Wilding stars as the operator of a vacation hotel in the West Indies.

443. **Zsa Zsa in Paris.** Producer: Alex Gottlieb. A comedy starring Zsa Zsa Gabor as an advice-to-the-lovelorn columnist who lives in Paris.

1960-1961

ABC / COMEDY

444. **Calvin and Clyde.** Producer: Jack Webb. A completed, 30-minute slapstick comedy starring Arthur Walsh and Ben Morris.

445. **Father of the Bride.** Jim Backus stars as a father who shoulders all the stress and aggravation of his daughter's marriage. The pilot, based on the book by Edward Streeter and the popular film was junked and was later reshot with Leon Ames, who would star in the 1961–62 CBS series.

ABC / DRAMA

446. **Bellevue Hospital.** Todd Andrews stars as a doctor in "America's best-known" hospital in this completed pilot.

447. **Johnny Fletcher.** Writer: Frank Gruber. John Goddard is Fletcher, and Read Morgan is his sidekick, in this completed pilot based on the radio series.

448. **Legend of Billy the Kid.** Producer: Jerry Schafer. William Murphy stars as the famed gunfighter in this completed pilot.

449. **Life Guard.** Producer: Vernon Clark. A Santa Monica lifeguard doubles as a private eye.

450. **Simon Lash.** 30 min. Production Company: ABC Productions. Director: Sidney Salkow. Producer: Sidney Salkow. Writers: George and Gertrude Fass. Creator: Frank Gruber. Jock Mahoney is a Phoenix-based private eye. *Cast:* Jock Mahoney (as Simon Lash), Elaine Edwards (Janie), Walter Sande (Slocum), Edward Kemmer (Joe), George Walcott (Lt. Wile), Warren Stevens (Paletti), Ann McCrea (Mavis), Murvyn Vye (Rocco), Vincent Barbi (Lou).

451. **The Yank.** 60 min. Production Company: Goodson-Todman. Director: Irvin Kerschner. Producer: Andrew J. Fenady. Writer: Andrew J. Fenady. James Drury stars as an ex-Union army surgeon wandering the West a decade after the war. John McIntire guest starred in the pilot.

ASHLEY STEINER AGENCY

452. Las Vegas Story. Writer: Jim Moser. There was no information on who starred in this pilot, which was shot on location and told the story of an ex-policeman who works for a casino as a private eye and overall troubleshooter. This is a concept that would work successfully for ABC in the 1970s as *Vega$*, starring Robert Urich.

453. Peter Novak's America. Producer: Norman Katkov. The adventures of a father and his four sons as they leave Czechoslovakia and head to the United States.

CBS / COMEDY

454. American in Paris (aka At Your Service). 30 min. Airdate: 8/3/64. Production Company: MCA. Director: Gene Kelly. Producer: Gene Kelly. Writer: Cynthia Lindsay. Music: George Gershwin. A comedy adventure starring Van Johnson as a young American who owns a travel agency in France and helps tourists in trouble. This pilot, shot on location and based on the 1951 movie starring Gene Kelly, sat on the shelf for four years before being aired. *Cast:* Van Johnson (as James Devlin), Marcel Dalio (Michel), Jan Sterling (Gloria Miles), Judi Meredith (Penny Miles).

455. Band of Gold. 30 min. Airdate: 3/19/61. Production Company: MCA. Director: Bud Yorkin. Producers: Norman Lear and Bud Yorkin. Writers: Dale and Katherine Eunson. Aired as an episode of *G.E. Theatre.* This was a pilot for a series of unrelated, 30 minute stories dealing with marriage and all starring James Franciscus and Suzanne Pleshette as a different couple each week. *Cast:* Suzanne Pleshette (as Renee Fontaine), James Franciscus (Bill Taylor), Jack Weston (Freddie Pringle), Fifi D'Orsay (Simone), J. Pat O'Malley (Cabbie), Mary Ellen Smith (Girl).

456. Barnaby (aka Mr. O'Malley). 30 min. Airdate: 12/20/59. Director: Sherman Marks. Producer: Stanley Rubin. Writer: Louis Pelletier. Aired as an episode of *G.E. Theatre.* A young boy (Ron Howard) wishes for a fairy godmother, and gets a cigar-smoking fairy godfather (Bert Lahr). *Cast:* Bert Lahr (as Mr. O'Malley), Ron Howard (Barnaby Baxter), June Dayton (Alice Baxter), William Redfield (George Baxter), Mel Blanc (The Leprechaun Voice), Don Beddoe (Dr. Harvey), Debbie Megowan (Janie).

457. Down Home. 30 min. Airdate: 9/10/65. Production Company: 20th Century Fox. Director: Hal Kanter. Producer: Hal Kanter. Writer: Milt Josefsberg. Pat Buttram stars as a small-town newspaper editor. The first two minutes of each show would be done live each week and feature Buttram in a topical monologue relating to the story about to be seen on film. The pilot didn't excite anyone and sat on the shelf for five years. *Cast:* Pat Buttram (as Hardy Madison), Sarah Haden (Emma Madison), Jack Orrinson (Warren Bullard), El Brendel (Late).

458. **Drumbeat.** Production Company: Frank Cooper and Associates. Producer: Ed Montagne. Writer: Bill Friedberg. Tony Randall stars as a press agent.

459. **For the Love of Mike.** 30 min. Airdate: 7/10/62. Production Company: Screen Gems. Writer: Stanley Shapiro. Shot in 1960 and aired as an episode of CBS' *Comedy Spot* two years later. Shirley Jones stars as a singer who, with her husband the struggling novelist copes with the comedic mishaps of married life – and making a living. *Cast:* Shirley Jones (as Betty Stevens), Burt Metcalfe (Mike Stevens), Jack Weston (Bill Broxton), Faye DeWitt (Fran Broxton), Gale Gordon (Emil Sinclair).

460. **High Time.** Producers: Cecil Barker and Seymour Berns. Stubby Kaye and Keefe Brasselle star as two social directors at a year-round resort in this comedy. *High Time* evolved into the series *Holiday Lodge*, but with Johnny Wayne and Frank Schuster replacing Stubby Kaye and Keefe Brasselle.

461. **The Incredible Jewel Robbery.** 30 min. Airdate: 3/8/59. Aired as an episode of *G.E. Theatre* and later of CBS' *Comedy Spot*. Harpo and Chico Marx portrayed two bumbling safecrackers named Harry and Nick.

462. **Meet the Girls.** 30 min. Airdate: 8/30/60. Director: Charles Barton. Producer: Harry Sauber. Writer: Roger Clay. Aired as an episode of *Comedy Spot*. The story of three girls in Hollywood – Maybelle "The Shape" Perkins (Mamie Van Doren), Lacey "The Face" Sinclair (Gale Robbins), and Charlotte "The Brain" Dunning (Virginia Field)—looking for fame and fortune.

463. **Mr. Bevis.** 30 min. Airdate: 6/3/60. Production Company: Cayuga Productions. Director: William Asher. Producer: Buck Houghton. Writer: Rod Serling. Creator: Rod Serling. A spin-off from *The Twilight Zone*. A fantasy-comedy about the problems of Mr. Bevis, who discovers his guardian angel J. Hardy Hempstead has come down to live with him. Burgess Meredith was originally envisioned as the angel but turned the role down. Serling would try this again as the "Cavender is Coming" episode of *The Twilight Zone* with Jesse White as the angel. *Cast:* Orson Bean (as Mr. Bevis), Henry Jones (J. Hardy Hempstead), Charles Lane (Mr. Peckin paugh), William Schallert (Policeman), House Peters, Jr. (Policeman), Colleen O'Sullivan (Lady), Horace McMahon (Bartender), Florence MacMichael (Margaret), Dorothy Neuman (Landlady), Vito Scotti (Peddler), Timmy Cletro (Little Boy).

464. **Slezak and Son.** 30 min. Airdate: 9/5/60. Director: John Rich. Producer: John Rich. Writer: Howard Teichman. Walter Slezak is Count Von Slezak, a slightly dishonest European nobleman trying to strike it rich in the U.S., and Leo Slezak is his son, Leo Von Slezak. Norman Lloyd and Neva Patterson guest star as hotel owners the Slezaks try to bilk.

465. **They Went Thataway.** 30 min. Airdate: 8/15/60. Director: Robert L. Friend. Producer: Robert J. Enders. Writers: Allan Sloane and Jack Schaefer. Aired as an episode of *New Comedy Showcase.* The story of Black Ace Burton (James Westerfield), a man striving to earn the title "Meanest Man in the West." Costarred Ron Hagerthy as Poison Pete and Wayne Morris as Sheriff Sam Cloggett.

466. **The Trouble with Richard.** 30 min. Airdate: 8/22/60. Production Company: Frank Cooper and Associates. Director: Al DeCaprio. Producer: George Wolfe. Writer: Aaron Ruben. Aired as an episode of *New Comedy Showcase.* Dick Van Dyke plays a meek, clutzy bank teller who always gets into trouble. *Cast:* Dick Van Dyke (Richard Abernathy), Parker Fennelly (Gramps), Howard Smith (Harold Martin), Doro Merande (Aunt Julia).

467. The previously listed pilot, **You're Only Young Twice** became the series of the same name.

CBS / DRAMA

468. **Call Me First.** Producer/Director: Paul Steward. A modern-day "Paladin" who runs a bookstore and "somehow gets involved in everybody's problems."

469. **Charley Paradise.** Producer: Herbert Brodkin. Ron Randell stars as the unofficial mayor of Greenwich Village who hangs around the local coffee house, solving people's problems in this completed pilot.

470. **Code of Jonathan West (aka Aftermath).** 30 min. Airdate: 4/17/60. Director: Jacques Tourneur. Producer: Harry Tattleman. Writer: John Paxton. Aired as an episode of *G.E. Theatre.* Fess Parker starred as a traveling preacher roaming the West after the Civil War. In the pilot, he helps a man falsely accused of murder. *Cast:* Fess Parker (as Jonathan West), James Best (Hardy Couter), Sammy Jackson (Galoot), John Hembreck (Gordon), Stephen Joyce (Murray), William Phipps (Hicks), Gina Gillespie (Young Girl).

471. **Confidentially Yours (aka Holiday Abroad).** 30 min. Airdate: 4/10/60. Production Company: MCA. Director: Richard Irving. Producer: Joseph Shaftel.

Writer: Ernest Pascal. Aired as an episode of *G.E. Theatre*. Dan Duryea stars as a newspaper columnist who, in the pilot, investigates a woman and her multi-million dollar business empire.

472. **Hard Case (aka The Sunday Man).** 60 min. Airdate: 2/25/60. Production Company: Four Star. Director: William Dario Faralla. Producer: William Hudson. Writers: Luke Short and Charles Wallace. Aired as an episode of *Zane Grey Theatre*. Dean Jones and Ross Elliot are brothers – and sheriffs. *Cast:* Ross Elliot (as Sheriff Walt Devlin), Dean Jones (Deputy Bill Devlin), Trudi Zizkind (Cassie), Brian Donlevy (Fred Childress), Leif Erickson (Cash Wilson).

473. **Hot Footage (aka Love and Wahr).** 30 min. Airdate: 5/15/60. Production Company: MCA. Aired as an episode of *G.E. Theatre*. Richard Greene and Robert Strauss star as two globetrotting correspondents for rival magazines. The pilot was shot in Mexico City.

474. **Jarrett of K Street.** Producer/Creator: Sam Gallu. Three pilots were shot starring Dean Jagger as a doctor who uses his medical laboratory to solve puzzling crimes.

475. **Jericho.** 30 min. Airdate: 5/18/61. Producer: Helen Ainsworth. Creator: Herb Meadows. Spin-off from *Zane Grey Theatre* starring Guy Madison and Beverly Garland.

476. **The Little Green Book.** Producers: Richard Sale and Al Scalpone. The series would follow the adventures of a boy whose father is killed by the FBI. When the boy becomes a man, he inherits his father's diary and discovers his father was a mobster. The hero then sets out to right his father's wrongs.

477. **Man on the Beach.** Producer: Al Scalpone. A 1959 pilot that was reshot with Dewey Martin as an adventurer who operates a beach patrol.

478. **Meeting in Apalachia.** 30 min. Airdate: 1/22/60. Production Company: Desilu. Director: Joseph M. Newman. Producer: Bert Granet. Writer: Adrian Spies. The adventures of a Chicago police sergeant, played by Frank Behrens. Aired as an episode of *Desilu Playhouse*. *Cast:* Frank Behrens (as Sgt. Ed Croswell), Joe Sullivan (Lt. Horlick), Cameron Mitchell (Gino Rospond), Cara Williams (Midge Rospond), Luther Adler (Sal Raimondo), Nicholas Georgiade (Tommy), Arthur Batanides (Vince), Edith Claire (Joan), Johnny Seven (Lou Varni).

479. **The Reno Brothers.** 30 min. Airdate: 2/25/60. Production Company: Four Star. Producer: Aaron Spelling. A spin-off from *Johnny Ringo*. Jim Cooper and Jim Best

star as two co-sheriffs in their early 20s who keep the peace in a small Texan town. Jacques Aubuchon guest starred.

480. **Rogue for Hire.** Producer: Phil Krasne. Jerry Thor as an airline pilot and adventurer in this completed pilot.

481. **Turnpike.** Producer: Frank LaTourette. Frank Gifford starred in this completed pilot based on the files of the New Jersey State Police Department.

FRANK COOPER AND ASSOCIATES

482. **Mountain Man.** 30 min. Director: Louis King. Producer: Norman Mac-Donnell. Writer: Kathleen Hite. Creators: Kathleen Hite and James Gunn. Music: Leah Stevens. Writer: Chris Knops. Peter Palmer of *Lil Abner* fame stars as a mountain man running a fur station in the Rockies circa 1840. *Cast:* Peter Palmer (as Critter Calhoun), Jack Weston (Stringer), Harry Shannon (Hoss Aggle), Crahan Denton (Gant), Conlan Carter (Webb), Ben Wright (Powder Price), Dawn Little Sky (Squaw), Robert Warwick (Bishop).

FILM MASTERS

483. **Jim Dandy (aka Man on the Road).** Producer: Nat Perrin. A spin-off of *Death Valley Days.* John Raitt stars as a dapper western dude who is a he-man underneath his fancy duds.

484. **The Little Trooper.** Producer: Nat Perrin. Spin-off from *Death Valley Days* inspired by Douglas MacArthur's childhood in the army. Stars Lennie Bremmer and Brian Russell.

FOUR STAR PRODUCTIONS

485. **The Eddie Hodges Show.** A sitcom about a widowed father and his young son, who would be played by Hodges.

486. **House of Four Keys.** Writer/creator: David Karp. Stewart Granger is the youngest of four brothers who run an art gallery and is a fool-hardy adventurer.

487. **JP.** Producer: Vincent Fennelly. Director: Don McDougall. Mark Stevens is a small-town justice-of-the-peace in this completed pilot. The stories would revolve around his family and his handsome assistant.

GOODSON-TODMAN PRODUCTIONS

488. One Performance Only. A live anthology hosted by Moss Hart, Dore Schary and Mervyn LeRoy that features prominent stars in roles not ordinarily associated with their careers. Examples: Red Skelton playing Disraeli, Milton Berle in a gangster drama, etc.

INTERNATIONAL TELEVISION CORPORATION

489. Emergency. Producer: Jack Wrather. Arthur Hill stars as a doctor in a major New York hospital in this completed pilot.

490. Calling CQ. Producer/Creator: Lindsay Parsons. Mark Damon and Dick Webb star as members of the U.S. Marine Corps who are assigned to a secret intelligence unit.

MCA PRODUCTIONS

491. The Brown Horse. Producer: Jack Chertok. Jan Clayton stars as a widow who works at a San Francisco restaurant called the Brown Horse so she can put her daughter through college.

492. The David Wayne Show. 30 min. Producer: Harry Tugend. Writers: Arthur Marx and Manny Manheim, based on Marx's short story "Not As a Crocodile." David Wayne starred in this pilot for a sitcom.

493. Double Hazard. Bob Cummings plays one of two brothers who will take on all kinds of dangerous missions. According to the 4/15/63 issue of *Newsweek*, the pilot was so bad, they tried adding a laugh track and selling it as a comedy. That didn't work, either.

494. Henry D. Producers/Writers: Bud Yorkin and Norman Lear. Charles Aidman is a small-time lawyer in the big city and Tex Ritter costars as a newspaper man in this completed pilot.

MGM-TV

495. Dr. Kildare. Producer: Collier Young. Writer: Larry Marcus, from the stories by Frederick Schiller Faust (aka Max Brand). Based on the movie series, which began in 1938. The pilot starred Joe Cronin as the young doctor and Lew Ayres as the elder physician who guided him. The pilot was re-cast with Richard Chamberlain and Raymond Massey and ran for five years on NBC. Another series, *Young Dr. Kildare*, was syndicated in 1972.

496. **The Paradise Kid.** Producer: Paul Monash. Richard Chamberlain stars as young man who leaves Harvard to manage a large Texas ranch which he has inherited.

NBC / COMEDY

497. **All in the Family (aka Togetherness).** 30 min. Airdate: 3/28/60. Production Company: Screen Gems. Director: Oscar Rudolph. Executive Producer: Harry Ackerman. Producer: Winston O'Keefe. Writers: Nate Monaster and Norman Tokar. Aired as an episode of *Alcoa Goodyear Theatre*. This follow-up to the 1959 pilot *I Remember Caviar* again revolves around a wealthy family that have lost all their money and must adjust to poverty. In this second pilot, they become interior decorators. *Cast:* Patricia Crowley (as Maggie Randall), Lurene Tuttle (Caroline Randall), Edward Mallory (Eric Randall), Henry Hull (Ansol Pryor), Adam West (David), Sue Ane Langdon (Kitty), Helen Heigh (Woman), Alma Murphy (Bertha).

498. **Call Me Annie (aka The Peggy Cass Show).** 30 min. Airdate: 4/10/61. Creator/Producer: Louis F. Edelman. A spin-off from *Barbara Stanwyck Theatre*. Cass stars as a babysitter.

499. **Happily Ever After.** 30 min. Airdate: 8/25/61. Production Company: Paramount Television. Director: Norman McLeod. Producer: Devry Freeman. Writers: John Green and Phil Shuken. Alice Sturgis and John Armstrong star as a young couple just out of law school and living with the bride's parents (Catherine MacLeod, James Gregory).

500. **Here Comes Melinda (aka The Sitter's Baby).** 30 min. Airdate: 5/9/60. Production Company: Screen Gems. Spin-off from *Alcoa Goodyear Theatre*. Spring Byington, Charles Ruggles and Roberta Shore star in a sitcom pilot.

501. **Miss Peters Speaking (aka Marked Down for Connie).** 30 min. Airdate: 4/25/60. Production Company: Screen Gems. Producer: Norman Krasna. Aired as an episode of *Alcoa Goodyear Theatre*. Starring Elinor Donahue and Troy Davis. A young couple, defying the rules of the department store where they work, get married and keep it a secret from their employers.

502. Three Wishes. 30 min. Airdate: 7/29/63. Director: Andrew McCullough. Executive Producer: Don Sharpe. Producer: Robert Welch. Writer: Robert Riley Crutcher. Although originally made for NBC, this pilot appeared on CBS three years later. Diane Jergens stars as a woman who finds an antique lamp, rubs it, and a male genie (George Gizzard) that only she can see appears to grant her and her friends wishes that will help them out of troubles.

NBC / DRAMA

503. The Avenger. 60 min. Airdate: 3/19/60. A spinoff from *Bonanza*. Vic Morrow starred as a young man who seeks revenge for the lynching of his father. Jean Allison costarred.

504. The Barbarians (aka Rivak the Barbarian). 60 min. Airdate: 10/4/60. Production Company: Mahin-Rackin. Director: Rudolph Mate. Producers: John Lee Mahin and Martin Rackin. Writers: Richard Mahlin and Martin Rahkin, from the book by F. Van Wyck Mason. Jack Palance starred as Rivak, a Roman gladiator, in this $750,000 pilot for a 90 minute series shot on location in Italy. Costars were Milly Vitale, Melody O'Brien, Richard Wyler, Guy Rolfe, and Austin Willie.

505. Big Jake. 30 min. Airdate: 6/5/61. Creator/Producer: Louis F. Edelman. A spinoff from *Barbara Stanwyck Theatre*. Andy Devine starred as a police officer, John Qualen costarred.

506. The previously listed pilot **The Blue and the Grey** became the series *The Americans*.

507. The Boston Terrier. 60 min. Airdate: 4/10/62. Production Company: Four Star. Director: Blake Edwards. Producers: Dick Powell and Blake Edwards. Writer: Lester Pine. Aired as an episode of *Dick Powell Theatre*. Robert Vaughn is a Harvard-educated private eye living in Boston in the first of two unsold pilots, the second of which was 30 minutes long and aired on ABC in 1963. *Cast:* Robert Vaughn (as Dunster Lowell), John McGiver (Professor Mumford), Robert J. Wilke (Lt. Duffy Cardoza), John Marley (Artie Pafco), Diana Millay (Sally Paine), Bennye Gatteys (Julia), Russell Collins (Otis Coots).

508. Doctor Cyrian. Production Company: California National. Producer: Tom McKnight. The doctor specializes in solving cases that puzzle everyone else.

509. The Elizabeth McQueeny Story. 60 min. Airdate: 10/28/59. Production Company: Universal Television. Director: Allen H. Miner. Producer: Howard Christie. Writer: Allen H. Miner. Aired as an episode of *Wagon Train*. Bette Davis stars as the leader of an all-female dance troupe that travels through the old West. The cast included Robert Strauss, Terry Wilson, Frank McGrath, Maggie Piece, John Wilder, Meg Wyllie, Marjorie Bennett, Daiele Aubry, Joseph Mell.

510. **The Frontiersman.** 60 min. Airdate: 3/2/60. Producer: Walter Mirisch. Aired as an episode of *Wichita Town*. Gene Evans and Frank Ferguson starred.

511. **The Hanging Judge.** 60 min. Airdate: 3/9/60. Producer: Walter Mirisch. Aired as an episode of *Wichita Town*. Frank Lovejoy and Carl Benton Reid starred.

512. **Hollywood Angel.** Writer/Producer: Dick Berg. Production Company: Ashley Steiner. Robert Webber stars as Christopher Angel, a suave Hollywood publicist who is also a private eye.

513. **The Iron Horse.** Guy Williams stars as a railroad agent in the 1800s in this completed pilot.

514. **Josephine Little (aka Little Joe).** 30 min. Producer: Louis F. Edelman. Barbara Stanwyck stars as the wealthy, tough owner of a Hong Kong import/export business in three flop pilots aired on her *Barbara Stanwyck Theatre*. They were:

515. **[Josephine Little #1] The Miraculous Journey of Tadpole Chan.** Airdate: 11/14/60. Little helps an orphan boy get to America. *Cast:* Barbara Stanwyck (as Josephine Little), Ralph Bellamy (Mr. Dobson), Dick Kay Hong (Tadpole Chan).

516. **[Josephine Little #2] Dragon by the Tail.** Airdate: 1/30/61. Little helps a U.S. secret agent find a killer. *Cast:* Barbara Stanwyck (as Josephine Little), Russell Arms (James Horn), Anna May Wong (Ahsing).

517. **[Josephine Little #3] Adventures in Happiness.** Airdate: 3/20/61. A doctor who can't get the medicines he needs turns to Little for help. *Cast:* Barbara Stanwyck (as Josephine Little), Lew Ayres (Dr. Paul Harris), Robert Culp (Archie Bishop).

518. **No Place Like Home.** 30 min. Airdate: 4/60. Director: William Asher. Producer/Writer: Ed James. A situation comedy starring Sheila and Gordon MacRae as a show business couple, Kelly Smith and Stephen Talbot as their kids (Laurie and Brad) and Louise Lorimer as their maid (Minnie). Andy Devine and William Frawley guest starred in the pilot.

519. **O'Conner's Ocean (aka The John Payne Show).** 60 min. Airdate: 12/13/60. Production Company: Ashley Steiner. Director: Earl Bellamy. Producer: John Payne. Writer: Tony Barrett. John Payne starred as O'Conner, a retired Los Angeles lawyer who wants to spend his time sailing but manages to get mixed up in people's problems. *Cast:* John Payne (as Torin O'Conner), Irene Harvey (Victoria Arden), Edward Andrews (Ben Matthews), Charles Cooper (Jason Chambers).

520. The Proud Earth. 30 min. Airdate: 5/23/60. Production Company: Screen Gems. Producer/Creator: Sam Rolfe. A spin-off from *Alcoa Goodyear Theatre*. John Larch and Vivi Janiss head a family that has settled in the old Western frontier.

521. The Renegade. 60 min. Airdate: 12/27/60. Production Company: MahinRackin. Steven Cochran and Richard Ney star in this Civil War adventure. *Cast:* Steve Cochran (as Rory O'Neill), Richard Ney (Burtram Smythe), Constance Powers (Felicia Post), Jack Weston (H.P. Daggett), Dayton Loomis (Capt. Flood), Robert Brubaker (Mr. Wilson).

522. Show Wagon. 30 min. Airdate: 2/29/60. Production Company: Screen Gems. Spin-off from *Alcoa Goodyear Theatre*. Luke Anthony, Connie Hines, and Jack Albertson are a theatrical group that travels throughout the wild West.

523. 333 Montgomery Street. 30 min. Airdate: 6/13/60. Production Company: Screen Gems. Director: Paul Wendkos. Executive Producer: Robert Sparks. Producer: Gene Roddenberry. Writer: Gene Roddenberry, from the book *Never Plead Guilty* by Jake Ehrlich. Aired as an episode of *Alcoa Goodyear Theatre*. DeForest Kelley starred as a criminal lawyer working in San Francisco. Kelley would later star in *Police Story*, another flop pilot by Roddenberry, who eventually hired Kelley to play Dr. McCoy in the classic series *Star Trek*. This pilot was later recast, reshot, and rewritten by a new production team and became the series *Sam Benedict*, starring Edmond O'Brien. *Cast:* DeForest Kelley (as Jake Brittin), Joanne Davis (Secretary), Tom Greenway (Captain), Joanna Barnes (Eva Fremont), Midge Ware (Liz), Steve Peck (Frank Piper).

524. Ways of the Peacemaker. Mike Road stars as a sheriff in Jackson Hole, Wyoming, in this completed pilot.

PARAMOUNT

525. The Joan Davis Show. Norman McLeod. Producer: Devry Freeman. Writers: John Green and Phil Shuken. Director: Norman McLeod. Davis runs a telephone answering service in her home on the Sunset Strip and manages to get involved in the comedic problems of her clients.

526. Man in the House. Writers: Phil Rapp and Phil Krasne. Teddy Rooney and his mother, Martha Vickers, and J. Pat O'Malley star in this completed "domestic family comedy."

527. Perils of Pauline. Writer: Larry Gilbert. Circa 1920. A young girl wins a beauty contest, comes to Hollywood and fails to find work. She lives in a boarding house and gets embroiled in many adventures while she tries to spark an acting career.

528. **Two for the Road.** Andy Williams and James Komack in a modern-day version of the Bob Hope–Bing Crosby "Road" pictures.

529. **The Weapon.** Burl Ives would host this anthology which uses a gun or knife or rope or any other weapon as a springboard for stories.

RONCOM

530. **Hometown.** Producers: Perry Como and Alvin Cooperman. Don De Fore stars as a P.E. teacher in a public high school and a father of four daughters in this completed pilot.

531. **What Is Harry's Business? (aka Uncle Harry).** 30 min. Airdate: 12/5/60 (Syndicated). Producers: Perry Como and Alvin Cooperman. Aired as an episode of *Play of the Month*. Ray Walston is a smalltown druggist and amateur photographer married to Elena Verdugo. The comedy series would try to use the *Our Town* story-telling technique.

SCREEN GEMS PRODUCTIONS

532. **Bringing Up Mother.** Three children help their widowed mother find a new husband.

20TH CENTURY FOX

533. **Untitled.** Luciana Paluzzi as a young housewife living in suburbia.

INDEPENDENT PRODUCERS

534. **Our Two Hundred Children.** Producer: James Kern. Writer: Frederick Hazlett Brennan. The adventures of a couple who take over an adoption home.

535. **The Ways of Love.** Producer: Collier Young. An anthology of television adaptations of famous love stories. Hosted by Joan Fontaine, Young's wife.

1961–1962

ABC / COMEDY

536. Edie Adams Show (aka Desk Space). Edie Adams stars in this sitcom about a woman who, when her employer goes bankrupt, buys the empty office space, and then starts renting the desks out to various clients. A comedy treatment of a dramatic concept offered a few seasons back.

537. Here's O'Hare. Producer: Whitney Ellsworth. Sheree North, dubbed by the producers as "the second Marilyn Monroe," stars as a private eye in this proposed tongue-in-cheek half-hour pilot.

538. La Femme. Patti Page stars in this 30-minute, comedy pilot as the editor of a women's magazine called *La Femme*.

ABC / DRAMA

539. Beverly Hills Is My Beat. Writer/Producer: Vernon Clark. Based on the book by Police Chief Howard Anderson.

540. Dr. Kate. Producer: Joseph Shaftel. Jane Wyman plays a country doctor, working at a hospital run by Rhys Williams, who gets involved in people's lives. The 60-minute pilot was shot on location at Lake Arrowhead. This pilot, based on the radio series, was pitched again in 62–63 and 63–64 without success.

541. The New Tightrope. Producers: Clarence Greene and Russell Rouse. An hour-long revamp of the half-hour CBS series. Mike Connors would again star as undercover agent Nick Stone. Quinn Reddecker would costar. They tried this again next season under the title *The Expendables*.

542. Unsolved. A half-hour series that would re-enact major unsolved crimes. Actor David Brian would host.

ARDLEY PRODUCTIONS

543. The Colonel's Lady. Producer: Stanley Roberts. Eve Arden plays a movie star who gives up her career to marry a soldier, her real-life husband Brooks West, in this sitcom pilot.

ARROWHEAD PRODUCTIONS

544. Joan Davis Show. Producer: Richard Bare. Davis stars in this comedy about a saleswoman in a department store.

ASHLEY STEINER AGENCY

545. Barnaby Monk. Barnaby is a newspaper reporter who travels around the country getting involved in people's troubles.

BROGILL PRODUCTIONS

546. Miss Brewster's Millions. Helen Traubel stars in this half-hour comedy about a widow who learns the vast wealth she inherited was earned by her husband through cons and frauds. She attempts to return the money to the suckers he bilked it from.

CALIFORNIA NATIONAL

547. Cottage 64. Producer: Sam Gallu. Richard Garland stars as an undercover agent pretending to be a wealthy San Diego playboy who loves nightlife, gambling, bull fighting, and horse-racing in this completed pilot.

548. Seven Cannery Row. Producer: Sam Gallu. Robert Knapp stars as a man who lives in an empty, waterfront cannery in San Francisco and who, for a price, protects any business connected with the ocean – fishing fleets, offshore drilling sites, lighthouses, freighters, etc. in this completed pilot.

CBS / COMEDY

549. The Alan King Show. 30 min. Airdate: 9/8/61. Director: Julio D. Benedetto. Producer: Julio D. Benedetto. Writers: Arnie Rosen and Coleman Jacoby. A suburban comedy with Alan King as the father, Denise Lor as his wife, and Rickey Sloan and Dennis Sturdevant as his children. Jan Chaney and Jack Fletcher guest starred.

550. Another April (aka Always April). 30 min. Airdate: 2/23/61. Production Company: Desilu. Director: Richard Whorf. Producer: Arthur Hoffe. Writer: Robert Van Scoyk. Aired as an episode of the *Ann Sothern Show*. Susan Silo as

April Fleming, a runaway with dreams of stardom who, in the pilot, stays at Katy's (Ann Sothern) hotel. The series would follow the young girl's attempts to become a star under the shadow of her parents, two famous celebrities. *Cast:* Susan Silo (as April Fleming), Constance Bennett (Guinevere Fleming), Marty Ingels (Erskine Wild), John Emery (David Fleming), Ann Sothern (Katy O'Connor), Leonid Kingskey (Instructor), Elmira Sessions (Nettie Parsons).

551. **Daddy O.** 30 min. Creator: Max Shulman. Don Defore stars as a handyman who is discovered by a producer and becomes the star of a popular TV show. The humor comes from his adjustment to sudden stardom.

552. **His Model Wife (aka Love and Kisses).** 30 min. Airdate: 9/4/62. Production Company: Screen Gems. Director: Norman Tokar. Producers: Tony Owen and Norman Tokar. Writer: Barbara Hammer. A situation comedy about a former model (Jeanne Crain), her magazine-publisher husband (John Vivyan) and their two children. Guest stars included Jimmy Gaines, Alice Frost, Jack Mullavey, Jerry Barclay, Frances Robinson, Annelle Hayes, Lorrie Thomas.

553. **Mickey and the Contessa.** 30 min. Airdate: 8/12/63. Production Company: Desilu. Director: William Asher. Producer: Cy Howard. Writers: William Davenport and Cy Howard. Eva Gabor stars as a dispossessed woman of nobility who comes to America and is hired as a housekeeper by Mickey Shaughnessy, a basketball coach with two kids who knows nothing about culture or high society. *Cast:* Mickey Shaughnessy (as Mickey Brennan), Eva Gabor (Contessa Czigoina), Ann Marshall (Sissy Brennan), Bill St. John (Mike Brennan), John Fiedler (Arney Tanner), Michael Green (Butch Gorkey).

554. **My Darling Judge.** 30 min. Airdate: 4/23/61. Director: Sidney Lanfield. Producer: Sidney Lanfield. Writer: Sara Locke. The misadventures of a Beverly Hills judge (Fred Clark), his wife (Audrey Totter), and their two daughters (Melinda Plowman, Anne Whitefield). Willie Tsang costarred as their gardener, and Wally Brown and Marjorie Bennett guest starred.

555. **Pandora (aka Pandora and Friends).** 30 min. Airdate: 3/16/61. Production Company: Desilu. Director: Richard Whorf. Producers: Arthur Hoffe and Richard Whorf. Writers: Benedict Freeman and John Fenton Murray. Aired as an episode of the *Ann Sothern Show.* The story of an actor (Guy Mitchell) and his secretary (Pat Carroll). *Cast:* Pat Carroll (as Pandora), Guy Mitchell (Anthony Bardot), Luke Anthony (Gabby), Fay Baker (Miss Norton), Ann Sothern (Katy O'Connor), Jeane Wood (Mrs. Dudley), Don Porter (Mr. Devery).

556. **The Rock.** 30 min. Creator: Jess Oppenheimer. Writer: Norman Jolley. Aldo Ray stars in this pilot as a professional athlete who writes for a sports magazine.

557. **Secret Life of James Thurber.** 60 min. Airdate: 3/20/61. Production Company: Four Star. Aired as an episode of *The June Allyson Show*. Orson Bean starred as James Thurber, a magazine writer and cartoonist who often slips into a fantasy world populated by his drawings, which come to life. Adolphe Menjou costarred. This was another attempt at adapting the Thurber stories and artwork to a television series. The first attempt, the 1959 pilot *Secret Life of John Monroe*, starred Arthur O'Connell. A series was eventually made, under the title *My World and Welcome to It*, in 1970 with William Windom as John Monroe.

CSB / DRAMA

558. **Baron Gus.** 30 min. Producer: John Hess. Ricardo Montalban is a Luxembourg aristocrat who tours America in a motorhome and writes about his adventures for a series of articles about our country.

559. **Beach Front.** 60 min. Keefe Brasselle would star as an adventurer hired by Miami to scare away the criminal element. The pilot was entitled *The Assassin* and guest starred Sammy Davis, Jr., Andy Clark, Pippa Scott, and Milton Selzer.

560. **Dr. Pygmalion.** A half-hour dramatic series that would be based on the life of plastic surgeon Maxwell Maltz.

561. **Durant (aka Barney's Bounty).** 30 min. Airdate: 3/29/61. Production Company: Four Star. Aired as the last original episode of *Wanted Dead or Alive* and starred Noah Beery and Jonathan Bolt. Costars in the episode were Jan Arvan, Bill Quinn, Vince Deadrick, Al Austin and William Hart.

562. **Hurricane Island.** Producer: Sam Rolfe. Special Effects: Jack Harris. A group of travelers are shipwrecked on an island that is populated by dinosaurs and other prehistoric terrors.

563. **Man from Everywhere.** 30 min. Airdate: 4/13/61. Producer: Hal Hudson. Writer: Fred S. Fox. Aired as an episode of *Zane Grey Theatre*. Burt Reynolds is a cowboy wandering through the west, picking up odd jobs as he goes. *Cast:* Burt Reynolds (as Branch Taylor), Cesar Romero (Tom Bowdry), King Calder (Sheriff Jed Morgan), Peter Whitney (Moose), Ruta Lee (Jenny Aldrich).

564. **Mr. Doc.** 30 min. Airdate: 4/29/62. Aired as an episode of *G.E. Theatre*. Dean Jagger stars as a small-town pharmacist working during the turn-of-the-century.

565. Our Man in Rome. 30 min. Airdate: 3/27/61. Production Company: Four Star. Producer: Dick Powell. Aired as episode of the *June Allyson Show*. Rosanno Brazzi and Eugenie Leontovich starred in this espionage-themed pilot.

566. The previously listed pilot **Ross of the Everglades** became the syndicated series **The Everglades**.

567. Russell. 30 min. Producer: Gordon Kaye. Fess Parker stars in this anthology of western dramas based on famous Russell paintings in this completed pilot.

BING CROSBY PRODUCTIONS

568. My Favorite Love Story. Writer/Producer: Richard Collins. Famous personalities would introduce adaptations of their favorite love stories in this proposed one-hour anthology.

DESILU PRODUCTIONS

569. The Man from Telegraph Hill. Dan Dailey as popular Bay Area columnist Herb Caen.

570. My Wife's Brother. Producer: Cy Howard. The comedy team of Dan Rowan and Dick Martin, along with actress Carole Cook, star in this sitcom about a brother living with his married brother-in-law.

571. You Can't Win Them All. Producer: Bernie Waitman. Based on the book *The Last Season*, this comedy would follow the life of a baseball player.

RALPH EDWARDS PRODUCTIONS

572. Aspen Hill. Producer: Hal Hudson. Jane Wyatt plays a big city doctor who moves to the mountains when her husband becomes gravely ill and needs to live in the country to convalesce. Once in the high sierras, she is in constant conflict with the mountain people's backward ways.

DON FEDDERSON PRODUCTIONS

573. Oh Johnny. Johnny Carson stars as the leader of an all-girl orchestra touring the world and the problems he gets into chaperoning them. Very similar to the short-lived 1963–64 comedy series *Harry's Girls*, which starred Larry Blyden as the leader of an all-girl Vaudeville company touring Europe.

574. **Tramp Ship.** Neville Brand as a steamer captain looking for adventure on the high seas.

FILM MASTERS

575. **Crawford's Key.** The adventures of the owner of a Florida hotel that caters to gangsters, movie stars, and other interesting people he can get involved with.

576. **Mike Angel.** Mike is an angel who appears wherever people need him. One week, he may be a construction worker, the next a cab driver.

FOUR STAR PRODUCTIONS

577. **Attorney General.** Producer: Jamie Del Valle. Adventure based on files form the California Attorney General's office.

578. **Frank Capra Comedy Theatre.** The director of such movies as *It Happened One Night* would direct each episode of this proposed 30-minute anthology.

579. **Ida Lupino Presents.** An anthology similar in tone to *Alfred Hitchcock Presents*.

580. **The Jimmy Durante/Eddie Hodges Show.** A comedy featuring the two stars as a grandpa/grandson show biz team.

581. **Three Star Theatre.** A half-hour anthology that would be hosted by Joan Crawford and would star her, with two other name stars, in each story.

GOODSON-TODMAN PRODUCTIONS

582. **Las Vegas Beat.** 60 min. Director: Bernard L. Kowalski. Production Companies: Fenady/Kowalski Corp., Goodson-Todman Productions, and NBC Productions. Executive Producers: Mark Goodson and Bill Todman. Producer: Andrew J. Fenady. Writer: Andrew J. Fenady. Creator: Andrew J. Fenady. Music: Richard Markowitz. Peter Graves is Bill Ballin, an ex-cop-turned-private eye who works for the casinos and occasionally helps out the police, through his friend, Lt. Bernard McFeety (Richard Bakalyan). He's aided by a wise-cracking assistant named Gopher (Jamie Farr) and a crusty, cynical reporter (William Bryant). This pilot wasn't cheap. It was shot on

location in Las Vegas, and featured a helicopter chase and a climax at Hoover Dam. The unusually violent story pitted Ballin against a gang plotting to rob an armored car loaded with casino cash. "I played a kind of public relations guy who also worked as a detective for some of the casinos," recalls Graves. "It was going to be a mystery but it would incorporate Las Vegas shows." The pilot ended with a sales pitch from Graves to would-be sponsors. "Well, that's it. The pilot. The Beginning. Now it's a well known fact for the great majority of pilots, the beginning and the ending are one in the same. Quite unashamedly, we don't think that's so for 'Las Vegas Beat.'...We think we have a chemistry that adds up to a tubeful of excitement." Of course, Graves was wrong. Today, he still doesn't know what happened. "We had a very hot line into NBC and then all of a sudden we weren't hearing anything anymore." *Cast:* Peter Graves (as Bill Ballin), Jamie Farr (Gopher), William Bryant (R.G. Joseph), Richard Bakalyan (Lt. Bernard McFeety), Diane Millay (Cynthia Raine), Lawrence Dobkin (Fredericks), Maggie Mahoney (Helen Leopold), Jay Adler (Duke Masters), Tom Drake (Leopold), Jim Sutton (Martin Scott), also, Harry Harvey, Jr., Ralph Moody, Beau Hickman, Jimmy Cavanaugh, Lisa Seagram, and Bill Couch.

583. **Medical Detective.** This would be a half-hour drama based on a series of articles in the *New Yorker* written by Burton Roueche. The stories would deal with efforts by the Public Health Service to combat plagues, epidemics and the like.

584. **Tigero.** Writer/Producer: Herman Julian Fields. Robert Culp as a "modern day Paladin."

585. **The Yank.** 30 min. Director: Irvin Kerschner. Producer: Andrew J. Fenady. Writer: Andrew J. Fenady. Once again, Goodson-Todman tried to sell the story of an ex-Union Army surgeon (James Drury) traveling through the west after the Civil War. This was last pitched in 1959.

MARK VII PRODUCTIONS

586. **Coffee, Tea or Milk.** Producer: Jack Webb. Barbara Nichols stars in this adventure about an airline hostess who travels the world.

MCA PRODUCTIONS

587. **Amos and Andy.** Writers: Joe Connelly and Bob Mosher. A cartoon version featuring animals written by 15 year veterans of the radio series.

588. **Mother Climbs Trees.** 30 min. Producer: Jack Chertok. Writer: Cynthia Lindsay. Jan Clayton stars in this comedy about an out-going mother of two kids and her weird friends.

589. **17 Battery Place.** Ron Randell as a U.S. Immigration Service agent.

590. **Uncle Elroy.** 30 min. Writer: Everett Freeman. George Gobel starred as a "Wally Mitty"-type character in this sitcom pilot.

MGM

591. **Cafe Bravo.** A private eye, the son of an American father and Mexican mother, who is at home on both sides of the U.S./Mexico border.

592. **Darrow the Defender.** 30 min. Producer: Norman Felton. Lloyd Nolan would star in this dramatic series based on the life of the famous attorney, though the stories would be almost entirely fictional.

593. **Hercule Poirot.** Jose Ferrer as Agatha Christie's famous French sleuth. Retried with Martin Gabel in 1962.

594. **Tangiers.** Rory Calhoun as an adventurer in North Africa.

NBC / COMEDY

595. **Five's a Family.** 30 min. Airdate: 7/14/61. Joe E. Brown is a retired private eye who moves in with his daughter (Hollis Irving), her husband (Dick Foran) and their son (Michael Petit) and, despite himself, always manages to get involved in crimesolving.

596. **Harry's Business.** 30 min. Airdate: 7/21/61. The misadventures of a Kansas-born girl (Elena Verdugo) as she adjusts to big-city, San Francisco life. Ray Walston, Michael Burns and Bill Mullikin guest starred.

597. **I Married a Dog.** 30 min. Airdate: 8/4/61. Hal March stars as a man who's constantly hampered by Noah, his wife's (Marcia Henderson) bothersome dog.

598. **Innocent Jones.** 30 min. Airdate: 8/11/61. Chris Warfield is Innocent Jones, a globetrotting, freelance writer who, in the pilot, visits Cannes. Guest stars included Merry Anders and Henry Corden.

599. **Miss Bishop (aka Cheers for Miss Bishop).** 30 min. Airdate: 9/1/61. Production Company: Paramount Television. A sitcom based on the 1941 movie *Cheers for Miss Bishop*, a drama which starred Martha Scott as a teacher at a midwestern college. This pilot, like the movie, was based on the book by Bess Streeter. Jan Clayton

starred in the pilot, in which Miss Bishop finds herself attracted to one of her students (Tom Helmore).

600. **Picture Window.** 30 min. Airdate: 9/8/61. Mary La Rouche and Charles Stewart are a young couple who move to suburbia to raise their son, played by Peter Oliphant.

601. **Shore Leave.** 30 min. Airdate: 8/18/61. Production Company: Screen Gems. The globetrotting adventures of two friends (Paul Gilbert and Peter Marshall) in the Navy who, in the pilot, lose a ring belonging to a shipmate (Henry Kulky). This pilot had been gathering dust since 1956, when it was shot.

NBC / DRAMA

602. **Along the Barbary Coast.** 60 min. Airdate: 2/27/61. Producer: Louis F. Edelman. Aired as an episode of *Barbara Stanwyck Theatre*. Jerome Thor played Pete Bishop, a private eye in San Francisco. Barbara Stanwyck and Richard Eastham guest starred.

603. **Amos Burke.** 60 min. Airdate: 9/26/61. Production Company: Four Star. Director: Robert Ellis Miller. Executive Producer: Dick Powell. Producers: Aaron Spelling and Richard Newton. Writer: Frank Gilroy. Music: Joseph Mullendore and Herschel Burke Gilbert. Aired as the "Who Killed Julie Greer?" episode of *The Dick Powell Show*. This cameo-laden, cliche-ridden pilot featured Powell in a wooden portrayal of Amos Burke, a millionaire by birth who works his way up police ranks to become a homicide inspector. Powell played the role with all the panache of Jack Webb as Sgt. Friday in this murder mystery that had him looking for the killer of a bed-hopping model named Julie Greer. The villain, through an absurd twist, turns out to be Burke's partner, Dean Jones. Someone at ABC, however, saw past the poor execution of this pilot and realized the possibilities of the concept, if done with some style and wit. Three years later, this NBC pilot was reworked as *Burke's Law*, with Gene Barry replacing Powell and Barry Kelly replacing Edward Platt as Lt. Joe Nolan. Leon Lontoc remained as Burke's faithful chauffeur Henry. *Cast*: Dick Powell (as Inspector Amos Burke), Dean Jones (Det. Phil Winslow), Leon Lontoc (Henry), Edward Platt (Det. Joe Nolan), Carolyn Jones (Julie Greer), Nick Adams (George Townsend), Ralph Bellamy (Judge Hansen), Edgar Bergen (Dr. Coombs), Jack Carson (Fairchild), Ronald Reagan (Rex Kent), Mickey Rooney (Mike Zampini), Kay Thompson (Mrs. Pierce), Joan Staley (Ann Farmer), Elaine

Devery (Miss Lawrence), Robert Burton (Policeman), Will J. White (Langsner), John Damser (Lester Hart), Alvy Moore (Reporter).

604. **The Jay Hawkers.** Production Company: 20th Century Fox. Producers: William Self and Roy Huggins. Jack Betts and Jock Gaynor are two wanderers from Kansas exploring the West in the pilot, which costarred Ann Blyth, Dan Dailey and Eddie Foy III.

605. **Monte Carlo (aka House on Rue Riviera).** 60 min. Airdate: 8/30/61. Production Company: 20th Century Fox. Producer: Roy Huggins. Writer: Douglas Heyes. Richard Anderson as an adventurer hired by the French Surete to keep a watchful eye on American tourists and keep them from falling into peril. Costarred John Ericson, Diana Trask and Jayne Mansfield.

606. **Panama.** Writer/Producer: John Larkin. The adventures of two good friends, one an American newspaper correspondent and the other a local shopowner, and their adventures.

607. **Sam Hill.** 60 min. Airdate: 6/3/61. Director: Robert Altman. Producer: David Dortort. Writer: David Dortort. Music: David Rose. Aired as an episode of *Bonanza.* Sam Hill (Claude Akins) is an exceptionally strong but kind-hearted blacksmith who roams the west. *Cast:* Claude Akins (as Sam Hill), Edgar Buchanan (John Henry Hill), Robert Ridgely (Billy Joe), Ford Rainey (Col. Tyson), Caroline Richter (Girl), Howard Wendell (Willis), Mickey Simpson (Bartender), Richard Bartell (Hathaway), Nelson Booth (Clerk).

608. **Three Men and a Girl.** Producer: Howard Erskine. A beautiful widow inherits a partnership in a Porto Fino hotel and shares the business with her husband's three best friends.

REDBILL PRODUCTIONS

609. **Loggers.** Producers: William Reynolds and Stanley Daugherty. Slim Pickens and Bing Russell star in this half-hour adventure pilot as loggers in the Pacific Northwest.

RONCOM

610. **Now Is Tomorrow.** A proposed half-hour anthology series hosted by Charles Bickford. *Cast:* Robert Culp (as Capt. Blair), Simon Scott (Col. Milyard), Sidney Pollack (Capt. Stein), Jack Hogan (Capt. Russell), Dan Wright (Doctor), John LaSalle (Capt. Nolan), Warren Vanders (Capt. Ward), David Garcia (Capt. O'Neill).

611. **Rio.** Producers: Perry Como and Alvin Cooperman. Writer: Roy Huggins. Creator: Roy Huggins. A "Maverick" clone with James Best and Adam West as two Americans living in South America. West says "I played a young banker who is nearly hit by a truck, and I see a travel poster for Rio and I go there as an adventurer. I got to go to Brazil for three weeks to shoot it."

612. **Two for the Road.** 30 min. Writer: Phil Schukin. A comedy pilot that starred Harvey Lembeck and Johnny O'Neill as two wartime buddies, one a singer and one a comic, who want to be stars.

SCREEN GEMS PRODUCTIONS

613. **Baron of Boston.** A half-hour series based on the novels by John Creasy that would be shot around the world.

614. **The Daring Deeds of Johnny Dru.** Producers: Clarence Greene and Russell Rouse. Scott Lane is a child Walter Mitty-type, with Del Moore and Jeff Donnell costarring.

615. **The Insider.** 60 min. Producer: William Sackheim. David Janssen plays a Hollywood press agent who gets involved in his clients' problems. In the pilot, he helps a fading star (Polly Bergen) in trouble with the mob. *Cast:* David Janssen (as Dan Castle), Polly Bergen (Belle Summers), Carroll O'Connor (Griffith), Jay Adler (Mr. Hiker).

616. **Man in the Middle.** Robert Sterling as the owner of a nightclub which is where the action is in the fictional city where this adventure takes place. The owner, who gets involved in people's problems, is protected by a huge dog that never leaves his side.

617. **The Venturers.** Producer: Herbert Leonard. The adventures of a three-manned sub and its crew. It starred Jim Brown and Johnny Seven.

DON SHARPE PRODUCTIONS

618. **K-Nine Patrol.** John Lupton and Jesse White as police officers in a series pilot based on the case histories of the canine squad of the Baltimore Police Department.

20TH CENTURY FOX

619. **The Hunters.** Writer/Producer: Robert Blees. Brett Halsey and Guy Stockwell as adventurers on safari.

WARNER BROS.

620. Las Vegas File. Producer: Jules Shermer. Peter Breck is a LVPD officer and Mike Road a county sheriff in this pilot about crime in the glitter city.

621. Solitaire. Ray Danton would star as a man roaming the world, living by his wits, and killing time playing solitaire. John Van Dreelen costarred.

ZLV/UNITED ARTISTS

622. Some Like It Hot. The adventures of two roving jazz musicians in the 1920s who, after witnessing a gangland hit, dress up as women to hide from the mob. Based on the movie starring Jack Lemmon and Tony Curtis.

1962–1963

623. **The Country Cousin.** 30 min. Production Company: Screen Gems. Producer: Tony Owen. A spin-off of *The Donna Reed Show* featuring Pat Breslin and William Windom as a young married couple from the city who move to the country with their kids.

624. **Hurrah for Love.** 30 min. Producer: Selig Seligman. Darryl Hickman stars as one of a group of college students who are married and live on a houseboat near the university in this pilot, which was reworked to become the CBS series *It's a Man's World* (CBS 1962–63) with Ted Bessell, Glenn Corbett and Randy Boone starring.

625. **Josie and Joe.** 30 min. Production Company: Four Star. Writer/Producer: Garson Kanin. Mort Sahl and Cloris Leachman star in pilot about the problems faced by a cabbie and his wife.

626. **Lum and Abner.** 30 min. Production Company: Four Star. Edgar Buchanan and Arthur Hunnicutt star as owners of a general store in Arkansas in this busted pilot based on the radio series.

627. **Medicine Men.** 30 min. Production Company: Screen Gems. Producer: Harry Ackerman. Creator: Joe Bigelow. Ernie Kovacs and Buster Keaton star in this pilot about a conman and his silent Indian partner roaming the West. The pilot was completed only a week before Kovacs' death and was never broadcast. *Cast:* Ernie Kovacs (as Doc), Buster Keaton (Junior), Kevin Brodie (Chris).

628. **Roberta Sherwood Show.** 30 min. Airdate: 5/3/62. Production Company: Screen Gems. Director: Jeffrey Hayden. Producer: Tony Owen. Writer: Sumner Long. A spin-off from *The Donna Reed Show.* Envisioned as a musical comedy for ABC starring Sherwood and Gale Gordon as a typical couple raising three children in a typical small town. The only untypical thing about them is that they break into song. Episode guest starred Robert Lansing.

629. **Wilber Wiggins.** 30 min. Producer: Tom Moore. Brian Russell and Frank McHugh star, along with Teddy Rooney and dozens of kids, in this pilot aimed at recapturing the fun of the old *Our Gang* comedies.

ABC / DRAMA

630. **All My Clients Are Innocent.** 30 min. Airdate: 4/17/62. Production Company: Ralph Edwards. Aired as an episode of *Alcoa Premiere*. Adventures of a criminal attorney in San Francisco. Starred Barry Morse, Joan Staley, Dick Davalos.

631. **The Barnstormers.** Production Company: Warner Bros. Television. Philip Carey stars in this pilot condensed from scenes from the motion picture.

632. **Chalk One Up for Johnny.** 60 min. Airdate: 4/8/62. Director: Leonard J. Horn. Producer: Ellis Kadison. Writer: Ellis Kadison. Aired as an episode of *Follow the Sun*. A retired California politician moves to Kauai with his wife and opens a hotel, where he helps people in trouble. *Cast:* Lee Tracy (as Johnny Pace), Rosemary DeCamp (Jeanette Pace), Joanne Gilbert (Jennifer), Lew Gallo (Theodore), Brett Halsey (Paul), Barry Cole (Ben), Gary Lockwood (Eric), Gigi Perreau (Kathy).

633. **Entre Nous.** Ray Danton stars as a flamboyant thief living on the Riviera. Based on the movie *To Catch a Thief*. Seven years later he would guest star in *It Takes a Thief*, a show loosely based on the same movie.

634. **The Expendables.** 60 min. Airdate: 9/27/62. Production Company: Screen Gems. Producers: Clarence Green and Russell Rouse. Yet another attempt to revive the old CBS series *Tightrope*, this time with original star Mike Connors and costars Zachary Scott and Dina Merrill.

635. **Lone Sierra (aka Timber Hall; aka Timber Lake).** Producer: Wilbur Stark. Art Lund stars in a one hour, adventure pilot as the leader of a family living in the mountains. Pilot was recut to 30 minutes.

636. **Misty.** Production Company: 20th Century Fox. Producer: Robert Radnitz. Director: John B. Clark. Writer: Lillie Hayward. Clips from the movie were edited together to form this 30-minute pilot about an elderly grandfather (Arthur O'Connell) raising his orphaned grandchildren (David Ladd and Pam Smith) on an island off the coast of Virginia that is populated by wild ponies – one of which is Misty.

637. **Perils of Pauline.** Production Company: Warner Bros. Television. A vehicle for Dorothy Provine.

638. **The Plainsman.** Production Company: MCA. Based on the movie. The adventures of Wild Bill Hickock, Buffalo Bill and Calamity Jane.

ASHLEY STEINER AGENCY

639. **The Alan King Show.** 30 min. A sitcom featuring King as both the central character and host/narrator in the pilot story that chronicled the comic problems of going on vacation with your family.

640. The previously listed pilot **Man of the World** became the syndicated series of the same name.

641. **Wake Up, Stupid.** 30 min. Producer: Herbert Brodkin. Larry Blyden as a college professor who used to be a prizefighter and can't stop day-dreaming about the old days.

CBS / COMEDY

642. **Acres and Pains.** 30 min. Airdate: 5/12/62. Production Company: ZIV/United Artists. Director: Perry Lafferty. Producer: Perry Lafferty. Writers: Harvey Yorkin and Dave Schwartz, based on material by S.J. Perelman. Aired as an episode of *G.E. Theatre*. A writer (Walter Matthau) and his wife (Anne Jackson) leave the big city to live in Bucks County, Pennsylvania. The house they rent turns out to be a wreck so they move into a motel/bowling alley full of strange tenants. Costarred Edward Andrews, Jerry Stiller, David Doyle and Alice Pearce. It was originally planned as a pilot for Tom Poston.

643. **Apartment in Rome.** 30 min. Airdate: 8/22/64. Production Company: Four Star. Director: Richard Kinon. Producer: Sol Sachs. Writer: Sol Sachs. Aired as an episode of *Summer Playhouse*. Alan Case is a successful artist who brings his wife (Susan Oliver), the daughter of a rich Connecticut family, to Italy where she has a hard time fitting in. The Leo Burnett Agency called the pilot, which they screened on 2/20/62, "expensive production but dull entertainment." Marie Windsor guest starred. *Cast:* Susan Oliver (as Debbie Adams), Allen Case (Steve Adams), Howard St. John (Uncle Howard), Lurene Tuttle (Aunt Ethel), also, Marie Windsor.

644. **Charlie Angelo.** 30 min. Airdate: 8/26/62. Director: Don McGuire. Producer: Jackie Cooper. Writer: Don McGuire. Music: Sonny Burke. James Komack is an angel who tries to convince people not to do evil things – bad deeds encouraged by Dan Devin aka The Devil (Larry Storch). In the pilot, Charlie tries to convince a debt-ridden nightclub owner (Bernard Kates) not to set his building aflame to collect the insurance money.

645. **Come a 'Runnin'.** 30 min. Airdate: 9/16/63. Production Company: Bing Crosby Productions. Director: Montgomery Pittman. Producer: Harry Tatelman. Writer: Jerome Poe. Theme: "Come A 'Runnin'," sung by Bing Crosby. The adventures of a

big city doctor (Linden Chiles) who moves his practice to a small town. Stu Erwin was the town druggist and Ruth Hussey was the doctor's nurse. *Cast:* Linden Chiles (as Dr. David Latham), Ruth Hussey (Edie), Sherry Jackson (Alie Watson), Andrew Prine (David Watson), Reta Shaw (Aunt Josie), Alan Hale, Jr. (Ernie Watson), Stu Erwin (Pharmacist), Susan Seaforth (Susan).

646. **The First Hundred Years.** 30 min. Airdate: 5/27/62. Director: Earl Bellamy. Producers: Everett Freeman and John Forsythe. Writers: Everett Freeman and Howard Leeds. The exploits of Ben Duncan (Roger Perry), a married engineering student who works nights in a supermarket to stay afloat. *Cast:* Roger Perry (as Ben Duncan), Joyce Bulifant (Connie Duncan), Nick Adams (Richard Martin), Barbara Bostock (Dina Martin), Barry McGuire (Buster Krause), Elvia Allman (Woman).

647. **The Free Wheelers.** 30 min. Airdate: 2/18/62. Production Company: MCA/ Revue. Director: Sherman Marks. Producer: Stanley Rubin. Writers: Robert Riley Crutcher and Sherman Marks. Aired as an episode of *G.E. Theatre.* Patricia Barry plays an American married to a writer, played by Tommy Noonan, living in Europe. Both of them get comically entangled with a secret agent, played by Jacques Bergerac. Guest stars included Elvia Allman, Kathleen Freeman, Nancy Kulp, Reggis Nadler, Gaylord Cavallero, Fritz Feld and Louis Mercer.

648. **His Model Wife.** 30 min. Airdate: 9/4/62. Director: Norman Tokar. Producer: Norman Tokar. Writer: Barbara Hamner. The lives of John Lauran, a magazine publisher (John Vivyan), his wife Jean, a model (Jeanne Crain), their two children (Jimmy Gaines and Jerry Barclay), and their housekeeper (Alice Frost). Jack Mullavey, Frances Robinson, Annelle Hayes and Lorrie Thomas guest starred.

649. **Howie.** 30 min. Producer/Director: William Asher. A sitcom pilot based on the play. Will Hutchins stars as a lovable, intellectual bum, with Mary Mitchell as his wife and Paul Lynde and Peggy Knudsen as his in-laws. This pilot was re-developed ten years later as the basis for the short-lived sitcom *The Paul Lynde Show.* John Calvin and Elizabeth Allen replaced Will Hutchins and Peggy Knudsen in the series. William Asher returned as producer.

650. **I Love My Doctor.** 30 min. Airdate: 8/14/62. Director: David Butler. Producer: Everett Freeman. Writer: Everett Freeman. Yet another pilot about an urban family – this time a doctor, his wife, and their two kids, who move to a small town. CBS would finally get it right with *Green Acres* in 1965. *Cast:* Don Porter (as Dr. Jim Barkley), Phyllis Avery (Connie Barkley), Terry Burnham (Liz Barkley), Ricky Kelman (Albert Barkley).

651. **Life with Virginia.** 30 min. Airdate: 9/18/62. Director: Ronald Alexander. Producer: Lewis Rackmil. Writer: Ronald Alexander. Aired as a segment of *Comedy Spot.* A

sitcom pilot starring Candy Moore as a teenage girl who tries to solve everyone's problems. Writer/director Alexander wrote the Broadway play *Time Out for Ginger* which later became a flop pilot and an unsuccessful film and was also about a precocious teenager. *Cast:* Candy Moore (as Virginia Carol), Maggie Hayes (Agnes Carol), Karl Swenson (Harold Carol), Roberta Shore (Joan Carol), Margaret Hamilton (Maggie).

652. **Little Amy.** 30 min. Director: Sidney Lanfield. Producer: George Cahan. A pilot about a nine-year-old girl (Debbie McGowan) a la *Dennis the Menace* and the parents (Bill Leslie and Shari Marshall) who try to cope with her. The Leo Burnett Agency called it "unbelievably bad."

653. **Low Man on the Totem Pole.** 30 min. Airdate: 8/8/64. Production Company: Four Star. Director: John Newland. Producer: Collier Young. Writer: Bill Manhoff. Dan Dailey stars as real-life writer H. Allen Smith who, with his wife (Diana Lynn), lives in Greenwich Village and struggles to get his books published, in this comedy pilot based on Smith's work. *Cast:* Dan Dailey (as H. Allen Smith), Diana Lynn (Nelle Smith), John McGiver (Mr. Turnbull), Pedro Gonzales-Gonzalez (Pepe Martinez), Cliff Norton (Manager), Irene Tedrow (Woman), Gloria Pall (Girl), John Haveron (Man).

654. **Maggie Brown.** 30 min. Production Companies: Desilu and Cy Howard Productions. Airdate: 9/23/63. Director: David Alexander. Producer: Jerry Thorpe. Writer: Bill Manhoff. Creators: Cy Howard and Arthur Julian. Ethel Merman is Maggie Brown, a widow who is raising a daughter (Susan Watson) and running a nightclub near a Marine base. *Cast:* Ethel Merman (as Maggie Brown), Susan Watson (Jeannie Brown), Walter Burke (McHesney), Roy Roberts (John Farragut), Mark Goddard (Joe Beckett), Marvin Kaplan (Marvin).

655. **Mighty O.** 30 min. Airdate: 8/21/62. Craig Stevens and Alan Hale, Jr. are two petty officers aboard the Coast Guard cargo ship "Ortega," aka "The Mighty O." *Cast:* Craig Stevens (as Chief Joe Slattery), Alan Hale, Jr. (Chief Barney Blaney), Richard Jaeckel (Chief Muldoon), Lola Albright (Mary), Jane Easton (Girl), Jack Prine (Man).

656. **Octavius and Me.** 30 min. Airdate: 7/17/62. Director: Don Taylor. Producer: Don Taylor. Writer: George Tibbles. The comedic adventures of a retired couple (Dub Taylor, Lois Bridge) who travel the country in their mobile home. In the pilot, they stop at a trailer court and help a couple patch up their crumbling marriage. *Cast:* Dub Taylor (as Octavius Todd), Lois Bridge (Hattie Todd), Grace Albertson (Blanche Hannigan), George O'Hanlon (George Hannigan), James Douglas (John Drake), Kaye Elhardt (Bess Drake).

657. **Poor Mr. Campbell.** 30 min. Airdate: 6/7/62. Director: David Swift. Producer: William Sackheim. Writer: David Swift. The misadventures of a man (Edward

Andrews) saddled with a nagging, whining wife (Agnes Moorehead). The character of Grindl was later adapted by David Swift into his 1963 NBC sitcom *Grindl* starring Imogene Coca. *Cast:* Edward Andrews (as Harley Campbell), Agnes Moorehead (Adrice Campbell), Ruta Lee (Priscilla Edwards), Mary Grace Canfield (Grindl), Barbara Pepper (Mrs. Dumphy), Harry Landers (Eric).

658. The pilot **The Soft Touch, #307,** was previously duplicated here in error.

659. **Swingin' Together.** 30 min. Airdate: 8/26/63. Production Company: Desilu. Director: Gene Reynolds. Producer: Jerry Thorpe. Writer: Howard Leeds. The misadventures of Bobby Day and the Four Knights, a group trying to make it big. *Cast:* Bobby Rydell (as Bobby Day), Peter Brooks (Yogi), Ben Bryant (Skoobydoo), Larry Merrill (Steve), Art Metrano (Big D), James Dunn (P.J. Cunningham), Stefanie Powers (Linda Craig), Dennis Crosby, Lindsay Crosby, Philip Crosby (Singers).

660. **The Two of Us.** 30 min. Airdate: 8/29/66. Production Company: Desilu. Director: Claudio Guzman. Producers: Elliot Lewis and Arthur Julian. Writer: Arthur Julian. This pilot, which mixed live action with animation, sat on the shelf for three years before being aired. It starred Billy Mumy as a boy who likes cartoon characters his widowed mother (Pat Crowley) creates for her children's books more than most people he meets. *Cast:* Billy Mumy (as Chris Williams), Pat Crowley (Elizabeth Williams), Mary Jane Croft (Helen), Barry Livingston (Roger), Russ Brown (Capt. Gibson).

661. **Young Men in a Hurry.** Producers: Andy White and Frank Pitman. The Kingston Trio portray musicians living and working around Phoenix in this hourlong comedy pilot shot on location.

662. **You're Only Young Once.** 30 min. Airdate: 9/11/62. Director: Richard L. Bare. Producer: Richard L. Bare. Writer: Norman Riley. The comedic exploits of newlyweds Casey (Jim Hutton) and Liz (Patricia Blair) McDermott, who live in a student dormitory while attending USC. *Cast:* Jim Hutton (as Casey McDermott), Patricia Blair (Liz McDermott), Dorothy Provine (Mildred Offenbach), Charlie Briggs (Piggy Burke), Lynn Alden (Midge Burke), Frank Killmond (Randall Fletcher), Ann Morgan Gilbert (Connie Fletcher), Gary Hunley (Tiger), Phillip O'Hanlon (Mopy Burke).

663. **Zelda.** Production Company: 20th Century Fox. Director/Producer: Rod Amateau. Sheila James stars as Zelda Gilroy in this spin-off pilot from the CBS *Dobie Gillis* series on which the character was a regular. Zelda is a teenager

interested in only one thing: boys. She may not be a stunning beauty, but she has the highest IQ in Central High School and is a champion dancer. In the pilot, she tries to get Bimbo, a photography buff, to fall in love with her. Her family (Joe Flynn, Jean Byron) lives over the garage where her father works.

CBS / DRAMA

664. **APO 923.** 60 min. Production Company: Screen Gems. Director: George Sherman. Producer: William Sackheim. Writer: Gene Roddenberry. Advisor: Richard Tregaskis. A World War II adventure, entitled *Operation Shangri La,* followed three buddies, a Signal Corps lieutenant (Ralph Taeger), a naval lieutenant (Pat Harrington, Jr.) and an Air Force captain (James Stacey) who battle the Japanese in the South Pacific. The pilot, which was shot on location in Hawaii, was criticized by the Leo Burnett Agency for being "in extremely bad taste. It's badly written and conceived." In 1963, Roddenberry would produce a similar series set in peacetime entitled *The Lieutenant* for NBC.

665. **Call to Danger.** 30 min. Airdate: 12/10/61. Producer: Perry Lafferty. Aired as an episode of *G.E. Theatre.* This was a concept that Perry Lafferty, later a CBS executive, championed for many years – the notion of a government agent recruiting ordinary people to help him in extraordinary situations. In this, the initial incarnation, Lloyd Nolan is a U.S. Treasury agent who recruits a locksmith (Larry Blyden) to help him find stolen plates. The concept was tried twice more, in 1968 and 1973, under the same title and with Peter Graves as the star. The concept finally made it to series television as *Masquerade,* with Rod Taylor in the 1980s, and lasted just a few short weeks. *Cast:* Lloyd Nolan (as Robert Hale), Larry Blyden (Johnny Henderson), Grace Lee Whitney (Audrey Henderson), Edward Andrews (Andre Kellman), Paul Mazursky (Joseph Kane), Frank Behrens (Reynolds), Ed Peck (Paul Wilkins), Forrest Compton (Charles Peake), Stacy Graham (Joan Lawrence).

666. **Defiance County.** 60 min. Production Company: Screen Gems/Green-Rouse Productions. Producers: Clarence Green and Russell Rouse. Writer/Creator: Gene Roddenberry. David Gardner as a district attorney in the "Perry Mason" mold fighting crime in San Francisco, where the pilot was shot. Frank Overton costarred as the sheriff. It resurfaced in the 1963–64 selling season as *Ty Cooper.* Both pilots bare a striking resemblance to Screen Gems' 333 *Montgomery Street,* Roddenberry's 1960 NBC pilot starring DeForest Kelly as a San Francisco attorney, which later evolved into *Sam Benedict,* a 1963 NBC series with Edmond O'Brien.

667. Hercule Poirot. 30 min. Airdate: 4/1/62. Production Company: MGM. Producer: Buck Houghton. Aired as an episode of *G.E. Theatre*. Martin Gabel replaces Jose Ferrer in this second pilot for a series about the adventures of Agatha Christie's famous Belgian detective. *Cast:* Martin Gabel (as Hercule Poirot), Nina Foch (Mrs. Davenham), Philip Ober (Chief Davenham), James Callahan (Detective Floyd), John Harding (Billy Kellett).

668. Johnny Dollar. 30 min. Production Company: MCA/Revue. Producer: Blake Edwards. William Bryant stars as the insurance investigator popularized in the radio series.

669. Patrick Stone. 30 min. Airdate: 7/16/65. Production Company: Four Star. Director: Sheldon Leonard. Producer: Sheldon Leonard. Writer: Sheldon Leonard. Music: Earle Hagen. Jeff Davis stars as a wise-cracking private eye. *Cast:* Jeff Davis (as Patrick Stone), Joanna Barnes (Janine D'Arcy), Keenan Wynn (Big Bill Tanner).

670. The Side of the Angels (aka Cavender Is Coming). 30 min. Airdate: 5/25/62. Production Company: Cayuga Productions. Director: Christian Nyby. Producer: Buck Houghton. Writer: Rod Serling. "Submitted for your approval: the case of one Agnes Grep, put on earth with two left feet, an overabundance of thumbs and a propensity for falling down manholes. In a moment she will be up to her jaw in miracles, wrought by apprentice angel Harmon Cavender, intent on winning his wings. And, though it's a fact both of them should have stayed in bed, they will tempt all the fates by moving into the cold, gray dawn of *The Twilight Zone*. Sound familiar? It should. *Cavender Is Coming* is Serling's second attempt to sell the concept he showcased in *Mr. Bevis*, which was also aired as a *Twilight Zone*. Though it didn't come across like a comedy, this had a laugh track. Cavender is a hapless angel who must earn his wings by helping chronically unemployed and clumsy Agnes Grep (Carol Burnett) support herself. Although he botches the assignment, the end result is a happy one and his boss, Mr. Polk, decides perhaps Cavender can help other mortals in distress (in the first pilot, Mr. Bevis was the angel's permanent assignment). Although it didn't sell, ten years later others with the similar notion were a little more successful—*Out of the Blue*, about an angel who helps a family, and *Good Heavens*, about an angel who helps people in need, both became series... and lasted less than a month. "A word to the wise now to any and all who might suddenly feel the presence of a cigar-smoking helpmate who takes bankbooks out of thin air. If you're suddenly aware of such celestial aids, it means that you're under the beneficent care of one Harmon Cavender, guardian angel. And this message from the Twilight Zone: lotsa luck!" *Cast:* Carol Burnett (as Agnes Grep), Jesse White (Harmon Cavender), Howard Smith (Mr. Polk), William O'Connell (Field

Rep), Pitt Herbert (Field Rep), John Fielder (Field Rep), G. Stanley Jones (Field Rep), Frank Behrens (Stout), Albert Carrier (French Man), Roy Sickner (Bus Driver), Norma Shattuc (Little Girl), Rory O'Brien (Little Boy), Sandra Gould (Woman), Adrienne Marden (Woman), Jack Younger (Truck Driver), Danny Kulick (Child), Donna Douglas (Woman), Maurice Dallimore (Man), Barbara Morrison (Woman).

DESILU

671. **Blue Fox.** Duncan McLain stars as a blind detective working out of the famous San Francisco restaurant in this concept which reached the script-writing stage.

672. **The Victor Borge Comedy Theatre.** Producers: Elliot Lewis and Claudio Guzman. This unaired pilot for a comedy anthology, which included a sketch with Gale Gordon and Lucille Ball about a woman who has never flown before (the material was later used in a 1967 *Lucy Show* episode), served as a showcase for two unsold pilots:

673. **[Victor Borge Pilot #1] Suzuki Beane.** Director: Jerry Thorpe. Producers: Elliot Lewis and Claudio Guzman. Writer: Richard M. Powell. Music: Walter Scharf. Katie Sweet played Suzuki, the young daughter of a beat poet and avant-garde sculptress in Greenwich Village. The show offers the pet peeves of Suzuki and her friends ("Like, school's so square; it's a like a total drag"). The Leo Burnett Agency described this pilot as "what an average family would be like if they were beatniks and zen buddhists." *Cast:* Katie Sweet (as Suzuki), Jimmy Garrett (Henry, a student), Dean Stanton (Hugh), Merlene Marrow (Marcia), Elmira Sessions (Miss Shoemaker).

674. **[Victor Borge Pilot #2] The Sound and the Fidelity.** Director: Jerry Thorpe. Producers: Elliot Lewis and Claudio Guzman. Writer: Arthur Julian. Music: Walter Scharf. A couple (Tom Ewell and Sarah Marshall) battle the warlike sounds of their neighbor's hi-fi system. Guest starred Fred Clark.

675. **Working Girls.** Producer: Desi Arnaz. Comedy project featuring Tuesday Weld as one of four working girls living in New York City.

RALPH EDWARDS PRODUCTIONS

676. **Counter Point.** A British criminologist comes to the United States and lives the high life of a glamorous bachelor when not solving crimes.

677. **Waterways.** An action concept about two men who own a small boat and travel the world, looking for adventure.

FILM MASTERS

678. Mr. In-Between. 30 min. Red Buttons stars in this sitcom as a married man who pals around with his bachelor friend next door and finds himself torn between the pleasures of married life and the attraction of bachelorhood.

FILMWAYS

In addition the numbered pilot listed below, the following unsold pilot was omitted from the previous edition of this book:

My Cousin Davey. 30 minutes. Airdate: 1/7/62 & 10/18/62 Aired as two episodes of *Mr. Ed*…"The Wrestler" and "The Bashful Clipper." The sitcom would have followed the misadventures of a professional dancer-turned-wrestler played by Ricki Starr. According to the book *George Burns Television Productions: The Series and Pilots*, a standalone pilot was also shot, written by Danny Simon and director by Arthur Lubin, but the details are unknown.

679. The William Bendix Show (aka Pine Lake Lodge). 30 min. Airdate: 6/61. Director: John Rich. Executive Producer: Al Simon. Producers: Arthur Lubin and Herbert W. Bower. Writers: Lou Derman and Bill Davenport. Music: Raoul Kraushaar. A spin-off of *Mr. Ed*. Bendix stars as the operator of a small mountain resort who sticks his nose in everybody's business. The Leo Burnett Agency called this "a terrible waste of good talent, trite and tiresome." Cast: William Bendix (Bill Parker), Coleen Gray (Ann), Nancy Kulp (Martha), Will Wright (JF Thompson).

FOUR STAR PRODUCTIONS

680. Sea Rover. Producer: Art Napoleon. A proposed adventure series about a widower and his teenage son riding the high seas.

GOODSON-TODMAN PRODUCTIONS

681. Count Your Chickens. Writer: Ernest Kinoy. A comedy project to showcase the talents of Ray Milland.

682. Sun Valley. Producer: Doug Morrow. The adventures of the general manager of a ski resort and his guests.

MCA/REVUE PRODUCTIONS

683. **Uncle Elroy.** Last year's George Gobel pilot was offered again, though MCA planned to recast the supporting players if it was picked up.

684. **Whatever You Do, Don't Panic.** Producer: Hubbell Robinson. Dana Wynter stars in this comedy about a New York fashion model.

MGM

685. **Boone Bay Harbor.** A proposed sitcom starring Russell Nype as a Maine minister. No pilot was made, but there was a script and 26 outlines.

686. **Buttons.** Producer: Robert Maxwell. The story of a teenage girl (Linda Evans) living on a modern ranch in the high sierras. Also starred Jim Davis and Big Boy Williams. Evans and Davis, twenty years later, would star in the competing primetime soaps *Dynasty* and *Dallas*.

687. **Designer Gal.** Producer: Norman Felton. The life of a fashion designer married to a newspaper reporter.

688. **Grand Slam.** Producer: Norman Felton. Dan Duryea would host this half-hour anthology about sports.

689. **House of Seven.** An action series concept devised by Blake Edwards for Charles Bickford.

NBC / COMEDY

690. **Amy.** 30 min. Director: Don Weis. Producer: Bob Hope. Sharon Farrell stars as a zany adolescent girl who gives her parents, played by Donald Woods and Irene Harvey, all sorts of comic aggravation in this sitcom pilot.

691. **The Big Brain.** 30 min. Airdate: 8/19/63. Production Company: Famous Artists. Director: Paul Stanley. Producer: Jess Oppenheimer. Writers: Sam Taylor and Jess Oppenheimer. The misadventures of absent-minded scientist Lester Belstrip, played by Frank Aletter. In the pilot, he creates a machine that makes people tell the truth. *Cast:* Frank Aletter (as Lester Belstrip), Ellen McRae (Ellen), George Niese (Seymour), Evelyn Ward (Adele Weston).

692. **The Big Wheel.** Production Company: Famous Artists. A sitcom about two elderly people living in Florida and sharing a home with their unmarried son, who is a high school teacher.

693. **Kings of Broadway.** 30 min. Production Company: Bob Banner and Associates. Airdate: 1962. Director: Buzz Kulik. Producer: Bob Banner. Writer: David Shaw. Creator: Herb Baker. David Wayne stars as the patriarch of a vaudeville family which includes wife Georgann Johnson and kids Kathy Dunn and Michael Carter. Writer Baker was the son of vaudeville star Belle Baker, who would supply her son with many of the storylines. This pilot was considered again in 1963–64 as a possible NBC show for 10:00 Wednesdays.

694. **The Milton Berle Show.** NBC was developing a 30-minute sitcom starring Mr. Television in stories based on his life. It was planned as a spin-off of *Mrs. G. Goes to College.*

NBC / DRAMA

695. **Adam McKenzie.** 60 min. Airdate: 3/27/63. Production Company: MCA/ Revue. Producer: Howard Christie. Writer: Norman Jolley. A spin-off of *Wagon Train.* Michael Ansara stars as a doctor roaming the wild West who, in the pilot, helps a girl who has been accused of being a witch. *Cast:* Michael Ansara (as Dr. Adam McKenzie), Peter Brown (Benedict O'Brien), Lois Roberts (Juana Perez), Danny Bravo (Felipe Perez), William Mims (Esteban Perez), John McIntire (Chris Hale), Frank McGrath (Charlie Wooster).

696. **African Queen (aka Safari).** 60 min. Airdate: 4/3/62. Production Company: Four Star. Executive Producer: Dick Powell. Writer: Juarez Roberts. James Coburn and Glynis Johns recreate the roles of Charlie Allnot, a ragged riverboat captain, and Rosie Sayer, an African missionary, made famous by Humphrey Bogart and Katharine Hepburn in the motion picture *The African Queen.* This pilot was aired as an episode of *Dick Powell Theatre* and had the two heroes sabotaging the German war effort in World War I. Costarred Juan Hernandez, Oscar Beregi, and Ellen Corby.

697. **The Attorney General (aka The Hook).** 60 min. Airdate: 3/6/62. Production Company: Four Star. Executive Producer: Dick Powell. A spin-off from *Dick Powell Theatre* starring Robert Loggia. Costars included Ed Begley, Ray Danton, David Lewis, Ted De Corsia, Joan Taylor and Anthony Caruso.

698. **Doctor on Horseback (aka G.P.).** 60 min. Airdate: 5/19/62. Production Company: MCA/Revue. Director: Ed Montagne. Spin-off from *The Tall Man.* Stars Ed Nelson as a doctor in a small western town who must battle the prejudices and superstitions of the ignorant locals. Guest starred Mabel Anderson and

Barry Sullivan. The Leo Burnett Agency thought it was "abominally directed and clicheridden—a saddlesore Dr. Kildare."

699. **Ghostbreakers.** 60 min. Airdate: 9/8/67. Production Company: Four Star. Director: Don Medford. Executive Producer: Dick Powell. Producer: Norman Felton. Writers: Peter Stone and Sherman Mellin. This pilot, set to air on *The Dick Powell Theatre*, sat on the shelf for five years and initially was designed to star David Farrar as a man whose hobby is investigating haunted houses. Instead, it starred Kerwin Matthews as a professor who, with his assistant Cassandra (Diana Van Der Vlis) investigates the occult and solves murders. Matthews would again play an occult investigator in *In the Dead of Night* several years later. *Cast:* Kerwin Matthews (as Dr. Barnaby Cross), Diana Van Der Vlis (Cassandra), Norman Fell (Lt. P.J. Hartunian), Larry Blyden (Waldo Kent), Richard Anderson (Timothy Selfridge), Michael Constantine (Oscar Jensen), Margaret Hamilton (Ivy Rumson), Kevin McCarthy (Cameron Witherspoon), Anne Jeffreys (Florence Blackstone), Richard Ney (Bunky Norris).

700. **Medicine Lance.** Production Company: MCA/Revue. A spin-off from *Wagon Train*. A young Indian who is sent to medical school returns to the tribe as a doctor.

701. **Outpost.** 60 min. Airdate: 3/22/62. Director: John Florea. Producer: Frank Telford. Aired as an episode of *The Outlaws*. The adventures of three cavalry scouts – Claude Akins, Jay Lanin and Christopher King.

702. **The Search.** 60 min. Airdate: 2/1/62. Production Company: MCA/Revue. A spin-off from *Dr. Kildare* starring Jeremy Slate as a doctor for the U.S. Public Health Service. Costarred Pippa Scott.

703. **Squadron.** 60 min. Airdate: 1/30/62. Production Company: Four Star. Director: Walter Doniger. Executive Producer: Dick Powell. Producer: William Froug. Writer: Walter Doniger. Aired as an episode of *The Dick Powell Theatre*. Powell stars as the commander of an Air Force squadron in World War II. *Cast:* Dick Powell (as Col. Luke Harper), Herschel Bernardi (Major Abrams), Pat Conway (Lt. Bert Evans), Joanna Moore (Jeannie), Robert Boon (Col. Klauber).

704. **330 Independence Southwest.** 60 min. Airdate: 3/20/62. Production Company: Four Star. Director: Samuel Fuller. Executive Producer: Dick Powell. Producer: Manny Rosenberg. Writer: Allan Sloane. Music: Herschel Burke Gilbert. A spin-off from *Dick Powell Theatre*, starring William Bendix as an agent working for the U.S. Public Health Service. The pilot was reworked as *The Robert Taylor Show* and four never-telecast episodes were made. *Cast:* William Bendix (as Jim Corcoran), Julie Adams (Robin), David McLean (Guts Finney), Alan Reed (Guy Vista), Yale

Sommers (Jeff), Ed Kemmer (Mac), Lee Damon (Mr. Somers), Adrienne Ellis (Connie), Norman Alden (Gooby), Michael Harvey (Bill), Bert Freed (Joe Vista).

SOUTHILL PRODUCTIONS

705. **Bachelors' Quarters.** Producer: Dick Linkroum. A comedy about a man, who dreams of writing quality novels, working for a cheap paperback publisher and living in a brownstone apartment with his two younger brothers.

20TH CENTURY FOX

706. **The Commuters.** An anthology with rotating stars loosely linked by the fact they take the same commuter train into town. No pilot was planned.

707. **Dateline (aka San Francisco Beat).** 60 min. Director: Jules Bricken. Producer: Jules Bricken. Writers: Ivan Goff and Ben Roberts. An attempt to reboot the cancelled series *Hong Kong*, which starred Rod Taylor as reporter Glenn Evans. Now Evans is working in San Francisco as a newspaper columnist. In this episode, entitled "Return to the City," the publisher's (Larry Gates) daughter (Barbara Rush) thinks she's killed someone and asks Taylor for help. According to a 1963 *Newsweek* article, this $200,000 pilot failed to sell, Fox executives said, because it got to New York too late to make it for consideration for the new season.

UNITED ARTISTS

708. **Pilot Showcase.** A panel of celebrities and contestants would pass judgment and comment on seven-minute versions of unseen pilots and try to match others' predictions about the saleability of the concepts in an effort to win money and prizes.

INDEPENDENT PRODUCERS

709. **The Moon Is Blue.** Writers: Frank and Doris Hursley, from the play by F. Hugh Herbert. A comedy based in Washington about the 15-year-old daughter of a congressman.

710. **R.B. and Mymalene.** 30 min. Production Company: Procter & Gamble Productions. Producer: Don Fedderson. Ann B. Davis and Aldo Ray are two people who meet in a boarding house.

1963–1964

ABC / COMEDY

711. Butterball Jones. 30 min. Production Company: MCA/Revue. The comic misadventures of a baseball team headed by a "Sgt. Bilko"-type manager.

712. The Fun Makers. 30 min. Producer: Robert Alan Arthur. A pilot was completed about young people who live in Greenwich Village and work off-Broadway.

713. Lollipop Louie. 30 min. Airdate: 1/10/63. Director: Don Weis. Producer: Fred Finklehoff. Writer: Fred Frinklehoff. Aired as an episode of *Alcoa Premiere*. Aldo Ray as a California fisherman who travels to New York. Guest stars included Barbara Turner, Paul Comi, and Ralph Manza.

714. September Jones. A comedy about an outlandish talent promoter a la Col. Parker.

ABC / DRAMA

715. Blow High, Blow Clear. 60 min. Airdate: 2/14/63. Pilot aired as an episode of *Alcoa Premiere*. It starred Jane Wyatt, Tommy Sands, Dan Duryea, Chris Robinson and John Anderson.

716. Border Town (aka Border Patrol). 60 min. Airdate: 3/4/63. Production Company: Daystar Productions. Producer: Leslie Stevens. Writer: Leslie Stevens. Aired as an episode of *Stoney Burke*. This was a pilot for a would-be adventure series about a sheriff (Bill Smith) and his Mexican counterpart (Cesare Danova) just over the border. Guest stars included Antoinette Bower, Stefan Gierasch, Ben Wright, and Jack Lord as "Stoney Burke."

717. Boston Terrier. 30 min. Airdate: 6/11/63. Production Company: Four Star. Director: Walter Grauman. Executive Producer: Blake Edwards. Producer: Tom Waldman. Writers: Frank Waldman and Tony Waldman. Music: Henry Mancini. A second attempt to sell the adventures of Harvard-educated private eye Dunster Lowell, played by Robert Vaughn, assaying a role he first assumed in the 1962 NBC pilot. The collaboration of Blake Edwards, Tom and Frank Waldman and Henry Mancini began with the series *Peter Gunn* and carried on through the *Pink Panther* comedies and such recent pilots as *The Ferret*. *Cast:* Robert Vaughn (A. Dunster Lowell), Elizabeth Montgomery (Millie Curtain), Stanley Adams (Lt.

Clarence McKenzie), John Hoyt (Judge Josiah Bowditch), Paul Comi (Lt. Foley), Helen Wallace (Mrs. Dee), Frank Killmond (Alf Carter).

718. Captain Horatio Hornblower. 60 min. Airdate: 2/28/63. Director: John Newland. Producers: Julian Plowden and Collier Young. Writer: Donald Wilson, from the stories by C.S. Forester. Aired as an episode of *Alcoa Premiere*. David Buck is Capt. Horatio Hornblower (a role played by Gregory Peck in the 1951 feature film), a British warship captain during the war between France and England in the early 1800s. Shot on location in England. *Cast:* David Buck (as Capt. Horatio Hornblower), Terence Longdon (Lt. Bush), Peter Arne (Nathaniel Sweet), Nigel Green (Brown), Sean Kelly (Lt. Carlon), Jeremy Bulloch (Midshipman Bowser).

719. The Hat of Sergeant Martin. 60 min. Airdate: 2/7/63. Aired as an episode of *Alcoa Premiere*. Claude Akins and Roger Perry are two U.S. Marines stationed in Latin America in the 1930s.

720. The Leathernecks. 60 min. Airdate: 2/2/63. Aired as an episode of *The Gallant Men*. Philip Carey, Van Williams, Armand Alzamora and George Murdock are a group of Marines fighting in World War II.

721. Postmark: Jim Adam (aka Postmark: Jim Fletcher). 30 min. Production Company: Goodson-Todman. Director: Bernard McEveety. Producer: Andrew J. Fenady. Writer: Andrew J. Fenady. James MacArthur plays a young magazine writer who travels around the country looking for stories. Guest stars included Noah Beery, Jr. and Harry Dean Stanton.

722. [The Seekers Pilot #1] Elegy. 60 min. Airdate: 11/20/62. Production Company: Desilu. Director: Robert Butler. Producers: Jerry Thorpe and Leonard Freeman. Writers: Herman Groves and Harold Gast. Creator: Leonard Freeman. Music: Nelson Riddle. Barbara Stanwyck starred as detective in the missing persons bureau of the Chicago Police Department in two pilots aired as episodes of *The Untouchables*. In the first pilot, titled "Elegy," she looks for a missing woman whose father is a gangster. *Cast:* Barbara Stanwyck (as Lt. Agatha Stewart), Robert Stack (Elliot Ness), Bill Sargent (Lt. Harrison), Peggy Ann Garner (Margaret), John Larch (Charlie Radick).

723. [The Seekers Pilot #2] Search for a Dead Man. 60 min. Airdate: 1/1/63. Production Company: Desilu. Director: Robert Butler. Executive Producer: Leonard Freeman. Producer: Alvin Cooperman. Writers: Herman Groves and Harold Gast. Creator: Leonard Freeman. Music: Nelson Riddle. Lt. Stewart tries to uncover the identity of a corpse floating in Lake Michigan. *Cast:* Barbara Stanwyck (as Lt. Agatha

Stewart), Robert Stack (Elliot Ness), Edward Asner (Benson), Jerry Douglas (Officer Harrison), Virginia Capers (June), Alan Dexter (Feeney), Tom Reese (Sonny Dale), Sheree North (Claire Simmons), Anthony Carbone (Rudy Portuguese), Gerald Gordon (Walter Rimer), Grant Richards (Arnie Retzik).

724. **Tack Reynolds.** 60 min. Airdate: 10/29/62. Production Company: Daystar Productions. Director: Leslie Stevens. Producer: Leslie Stevens. Writer: Leslie Stevens. Aired as an episode of *Stoney Burke*. Michael Parks is a stock car racer who roams the country, vying in competitions and helping people in trouble. *Cast:* Michael Parks (as Tack Reynolds), Jack Lord (Stoney Burke), Gene Lyons (Clyde Lambert), Bill Gunn (Bud Sutter), Ford Rainey (Frank Hughes), Denise Alexander (Arlette Hughes).

725. **Weapons Man.** 60 min. Airdate: 4/8/63. Production Company: Daystar Productions. Director: Leslie Stevens. Producer: Leslie Stevens. Writer: Leslie Stevens. Aired as an episode of *Stoney Burke*. J.D. Cannon stars as a weapons expert who helps law enforcement agencies solve crimes involving unusual weapons. Henry Silva guest starred.

726. **Which Way Did They Go?** 30 min. Airdate: 4/1/63. Production Company: Four Star. Director: Arnold Laven. Producers: Arthur Gardner, Arnold Laven, and Jules Levy. Writer: Arthur Browne, Jr. Music: Herschel Burke Gilbert. Aired as an episode of *The Rifleman*. A broke, widowed farmer and his three sons head west, where they stumble on a small town in desperate need of a sheriff. The widower (Peter Whitney) takes the job – and discovers it's anything but easy. *Cast:* Peter Whitney (as Neb Jackson), Mickey Manners (Moss Jackson), Conlan Carter (Haslam Jackson), John Craig (Bo Jackson), Vito Scotti (Marcello Carbini), Beatrice Kay (Miss Goldie Drain), Dale McKennon (Judge Moze), Leo Gordon (Stack Wade), Chuck Connors (Lucas McCain), Johnny Crawford (Mark McCain).

727. **The World of Floyd Gibbons (aka Floyd Gibbons: Reporter).** 30 min. Airdate: 12/11/62. Production Company: Desilu. Producer: Leonard Freeman. Music: Nelson Riddle. Scott Brady stars in the fictionalized adventures of real-life globe-trotting newspaper reporter Floyd Gibbons in this spin-off from *The Untouchables*. Actual Gibbons' adventures (during 1916–1939) include being captured by Pancho Villa and losing an eye in the Battle of the Marne. The pilot was presented again during the 1964–65 selling season. *Cast:* Scott Brady (as Floyd Gibbons), Stu Erwin (Barney Rich), Dorothy Malone (Kitty Edmonds), Paul Langton (Carleton Edmonds), Robert Stack (Elliot Ness).

CBS / COMEDY

728. All About Barbara. 30 min. Airdate: 9/2/63. Director: Jack Donohue. Producer: Quinn Martin. Writers: Madelyn Davis, Bob Carroll, Jr., and F.D. Smith. Barbara Nichols is an actress who gives up her career to marry a small town college professor (William Bishop). *Cast:* Barbara Nichols (Barbara Adams), William Bishop (James Hadley), Willard Waterman (Coach Ray Biddle), Larry Keating (Dean Albert Murdock), Bea Benaderet (Sybil Murdock), Shirley Mitchell (Shirley Biddle).

729. Hooray for Love. 30 min. Airdate: 9/9/63. Director: Jerry Hopper. Producer: Bob Fisher. Writers: Alan Lipscott and Bob Fisher. Darryl Hickman and Yvonne Craig are two newlyweds who are still in college. *Cast:* Darryl Hickman (as Schuyler "Sky" Young), Yvonne Craig (Abby Young), Beverly Willis (Clare Boone), Don Edmonds (Gillis Boone), Alvy Moore (Otis Platt), Cheryl Lee (Samantha Soo).

730. A Love Affair Just for Three (aka The Ginger Rogers Show). 30 min. Airdate: 7/22/63. Executive Producer: William Self. Producers: Sidney Sheldon and Ron Higgins. Writer: Norman McLeod. Ginger Rogers plays identical twin sisters – one a model and one a magazine writer – and Charles Ruggles costars as her befuddled uncle. Cesare Danova guest starred and Gardner McKay appeared as himself. Rogers designed her own wardrobe for this pilot, which had been in the works since the 1961–62 season.

731. The Miss and the Missiles. 30 min. Airdate: 7/25/64. Director: Peter Tewksbury. Producer: Jack Chertok. Writer: Everett Freeman. The comedic adventures of a magazine writer (Gisele MacKenzie) in love with an Air Force test pilot (John Forsythe). *Cast:* Gisele MacKenzie (as Connie Marlowe), John Forsythe (Bill Adams), Gordon Gerbert (Buzz Marlowe), Kathleen Freeman (Emma), John McGiver (John P. McBain), Michael J. Pollard (Spider), Jocelyn Brando (Girl).

MGM

732. Grand Slam. 30 min. Director: Buzz Kulik. Producer: Norman Felton. Murray Hamilton stars as Pete Dailey, a sports columnist who gets involved in people's problems in this sitcom pilot. In this story, Albert Salmi guest starred as a catcher who blows his shot at the major leagues, returns to the minors, and faces adjustment problems with himself and his young son. Other guests included Donald

Losby and Pat Breslin. The Leo Burnett Agency thought this was "a medium grade piece of schmaltz with a low-budget look" while producer Felton was quoted in magazine articles as considering this one of his best pilots.

NBC / COMEDY

733. **Last of the Private Eyes.** 60 min. Airdate: 4/30/63. Production Company: Four Star. Director: Marc Daniels. Producer: Aaron Spelling. Writers: Richard Carr and Robert L. Jacks. Music: Herschel Burke Gilbert. Aired as an episode of *Dick Powell Theatre*. Bob Cummings stars as a bumbling private eye who accidentally solves crimes. The pilot featured cameo appearances by Keenan Wynn, Eddie "Rochester" Anderson, Sebastian Cabot and Jay C. Flippen. *Cast:* Bob Cummings (J.F. Kelly), Linda Christian (Susan Lane), Jeanne Crain (Elsie), MacDonald Carey (Lt. Duff Peterson), Arnold Stang (Donald Joe), Lawrence Dobkin (The Butler), Janis Paige (Laverne), William Bendix (George Lane), William Laudigan (Frank Jeffers).

734. **Outlaws.** 60 min. Airdate: 2/20/63. Production Company: MCA/Revue. Producer: Howard Christie. Aired as an episode of *Wagon Train*. The misadventures of a hillbilly outlaw (Jeanette Nolan), her two inept sons (L.Q. Jones, Morgan Woodward) and their bungled attempts at crime.

NBC / DRAMA

735. **Colossus.** 60 min. Airdate: 3/12/63. Production Company: Four Star. Director: Don Medford. Producers: Dick Powell and Richard Alan Simmons. Writer: Richard Alan Simmons. Music: Herschel Burke Gilbert. Aired as an episode of *Dick Powell Theatre*. William Shatner and Robert Brown are two immigrants in turn-of-the-century California trying to make new lives for themselves. Guest stars included Frank Overton, Geraldine Brooks, and Joan Staley.

736. **The Judge.** 60 min. Airdate: 2/5/63. Production Company: Four Star. Director: Bernard Kowalski. Producers: Bernard Kowalski and Bruce Geller. Writers: Bruce Geller and Harry Mark Petrakis. Aired as an episode of *Dick Powell Show*. Richard Basehart is a newly appointed Superior Court judge. *Cast:* Richard Basehart (Judge Daniel Zachary), Otto Kruger (Chief Justice Caleb Cooke), Mary Murphy (Karen Holm), Edward Binns (Matthew Connors).

737. **The Losers.** 60 min. Airdate: 1/15/63. Production Company: Four Star. Director: Sam Peckinpah. Executive Producer: Dick Powell. Producers: Sam Peckinpah, Bruce Geller, and Bernard L. Kowalski. Associate Producer: Stanley Kallis. Writer: Bruce Geller, from a story by Geller and Sam Peckinpah. Creator: Sam Peckinpah. Music: Herschel Burke Gilbert. Aired as an episode of *Dick Powell Theatre*, which was guest hosted by Charles Boyer. An attempt to update and revive Pechinpah's short-lived series *The Westerner,* which survived for a mere 13 episodes in 1960. The original series starred Brian Keith as Dave Blassingame, a cowboy who wandered the old West with his dog Brown and – sometimes – cowardly conman Burgundy Smith (John Dehner). It's become something of a cult-classic, its demise blamed on its violence and "adult" attitude. The same production team that produced the series was responsible for this pilot, which was set in the present and sought a light tone reminiscent of *Maverick.* Lee Marvin was Dave Blassingame, a drifter who wanders the country accompanied by his dog Brown and conman Burgundy Smith, played by Keenan Wynn. In the pilot, they are pursued by thugs they bilked in a poker game. The two drifters befriend a blind gospel singer and his orphan companion and hide out with an ornery farmer and his shy daughter. *Cast:* Lee Marvin (as Dave Blassingame), Keenan Wynn (Burgundy Smith), Rosemary Clooney (Melissa), Adam Lazarre (Blind Johnny), Michael Davis (Tim), Mike Mazurki (Mr. Anston), Dub Taylor (Gregory), Carmen Phillips (Jeen), Elaine Walker (Diedre), Jack Perkins (Farr), Charles Horvath (Mulana), Paul Stader (Monroe), Kelly Thordsen (Frank Davis), Russ Brown (Isaiah).

738. **Luxury Liner.** 60 min. Airdate: 2/12/63. Production Company: Four Star. Executive Producer: Dick Powell. Producer: Aaron Spelling. Music: Herschel Burke Gilbert. Aired as an episode of *Dick Powell Theatre.* An anthology/drama, which would be hosted by James Stewart, about the lives of the people who travel on a cruise ship commanded by Rory Calhoun, who would be the only regular. Over a decade later, producer Aaron Spelling would later take the same concept, add a touch of *Love American Style,* and title it *The Love Boat. Cast:* Rory Calhoun (as Capt. Victor Kihlgren), Jan Sterling (Selena Royce), Michael Davis (Digo), Carroll O'Connor (Dr. Lyman Savage), Ludwig Donath (Jan Veltman), Ed Kemmer (Sam Barrett), Oscar Beregi (La Guerne), Danny Scholl (Mr. Marion).

739. **The Old Man and the City.** 60 min. Airdate: 4/23/63. Production Company: Four Star. Director: William A. Graham. Executive Producer: Dick Powell. Writer: John Pickard. Aired as an episode of *Dick Powell Theatre.* Charlie Ruggles stars as

a judge in the small town of Adamsburg, which relies on a factory run by Charles Bickford for its livelihood. Guest stars included Kenneth Tobey, Gene Raymond, John Larkin, and Edward Binns.

PARAMOUNT

740. The previously listed pilot **Funny Funny Films** became the series *Your Funny Funny Films.*

RAND-BROOKS PRODUCTIONS

741. Bear Heart. 30 min. Director: Randy Brooks. Producer: Robert Huddleston. Two half-hour pilots were shot in Big Bear, California, starring Marshall Reed as a widower who brings his two teenage children to a trading post he recently bought in the high sierras, where they befriend a wild German Shepherd named Bear Heart. The first story shows how Bear Heart was mistreated by his owner, the former manager of the Trading Post, and became wild. The second story shows how he became a part of this new family.

SCREEN GEMS PRODUCTION

742. Gulliver. Producer: Charles Schneer. Based on the story by Jonathan Swift. Adapted from the movie *Three Worlds of Gulliver*, made in 1960 by Schneer and effects wizard Ray Harryhausen. John Cairny steps in for Kerwin Matthews as Gulliver, the sailor who lands on the Lilliput, an island populated by miniature people. In this retelling, he lands with his girlfriend, played by Christina Gregg. Filmed in *Dynamation*, Harryhausen's animation process. NBC was reportedly interested.

743. Rockabye the Infantry. 30 min. Production Company: Screen Gems. Director: Don Taylor. Executive Producer: Harry Ackerman. Producer: Winston O'Keefe. Writer: Budd Grossman. Creator: Budd Grossman. Music: Stu Phillips. Bobby Rydell is a young version of "Sgt. Bilko," a conscientious but scheming soldier who runs a babysitting service on the base, among other commercial enterprises, to the consternation of his father, the base commander (Fred Clark). *Cast:* Bobby Rydell (Pvt. Gifford Tyler), William Bendix (Sgt. Mahoney), Fred Clark (Col. Tyler),

Nancy Carroll (Hortense Tyler), Florence Sundstrum (Alice Mahoney), Lynda Day (Connie Mahoney), Jimmy Bates (Dudley), Joey Walsh (Augie), Bill Mullikin (Toothpick), Keg Johnson (Wally), Jan Conaway (Max), Roy Roberts (General), Gene Blakely (Capt. Becker), Anne Bellamy (Mrs. Becker), Michael Pataki (Sgt. Webb), B.G. Norman (Ben Loo).

STOVER COMPANY

744. The Charlie McCarthy Show. Director: Don Shay. Producer: Glen Hall Taylor. A demo film was shot mixing live action and animation featuring Edgar Bergen's puppets Charlie McCarthy, Mortimer Snerd and Effie Klinker. Costarred Doug Lambert, Jerome Cowan and Paula Winslow. The Leo Burnett Agency called it "humorless, badly produced. It's difficult to believe professionals have involved themselves in this fiasco."

TIME-LIFE PRODUCTIONS

745. Crises. Producer: Robert Drew. A proposed documentery series that focuses on interesting people each week. The pilot featured Eddie Sachs, a race car driver, as he competed in two different races.

1964–1965

ABC / COMEDY

746. **Inside Danny Baker.** 30 min. Production Company: United Artists. Director: Arthur Hiller. Producer: Richard Brill. Writer: Mel Brooks. ABC initially planned to schedule this as a Friday evening series. Danny is a precocious boy who decides he wants a motor boat but his father, a dentist, tells him to earn the money himself. When Danny sees "modern art" selling for a fortune, he decides to turn the family ping pong table into a "chef d'oeuvre." Roger Mobley is Danny. Paul O'Keefer and Frank McHugh costarred.

747. The previously listed pilot **The Mickey Rooney Show** became the series *Mickey*.

748. **Pioneer Go Home (aka Kwimpers of New Jersey).** 30 min. Producer: Robert Alan Arthur. Sitcom starring Tom Ewell and Mr. and Mrs. Ernest Truex. Shot on location in Florida.

749. **Take Me to Your Leader.** 30 min. Production Company: MGM. The story of two aliens from Venus who come to earth, meet an inventor, and go into business with him selling products created for another planet to unknowing earthlings.

ABC / DRAMA

750. **Alexander the Great.** 60 min. Airdate: 1/26/68. Production Company: Selmur Productions. Director: Phil Karlson. Producer: Albert McCleery. Writers: William Robert Yates and Robert Pirosh. Aired as an episode of *Off to See the Wizard*. William Shatner starred in the title role in this dramatization of the Battle of Issus between the Greeks and the Persians. Costar Adam West recalls: "We did it in the desert outside St. George, Utah. I played Alexander's associate, General Cleander, the wine, women, and song General, who rode his Arabian stallion across the desert dressed in a loin cloth. Man it was cold. It just didn't work. The audience and Madison Avenue just weren't ready for orgies with Shatner and West lying there on their backs eating grapes with belly dancers beside them." No loss. Shatner says "the nine months I spent working on *Alexander the Great* came in handy for *Star Trek*. Capt. Kirk is, in many ways, the quintessential hero and the Greek heroes in literature have many of the same qualities I wanted to explore." *Cast:* William Shatner (as Alexander), John Cassavetes (General Karonos), Joseph Cotten (General Antigonus), Simon Oakland (Attalos), Cliff Osmond (General Memnon), Ziva Rodann (Ada), Adam West (Cleander).

751. **The Dog Troop.** 60 min. Airdate: 3/9/64. Director: Herschel Daughterty. Producer: Howard Christie. Writer: Norman Jolley. Aired as an episode of *Wagon Train.* Ron Hayes leads a group of frontier soldiers who try to maintain order in the unruly West. *Cast:* Ron Hayes (as Lt. Duncan McIvor), Chris Robinson (Lt. Carter), John Larkin (Col. Lipton), Gene Evans (Sgt. Jake Orly), Joanna Moore (Lucinda Cater), James Griffith (Garrett).

752. **Great Bible Adventures.** 60 min. Airdate: 9/11/66. Production Company: MGM. Aired as an episode of *Preview Tonight.* A proposed anthology of biblical tales. The pilot episode, "Seven Rich Years and Seven Lean" starred Hugh O'Brian as Joseph and followed him from bondage to becoming the pharaoh's minister. *Cast:* Hugh O'Brian (as Joseph), Joseph Wiseman (Pharaoh), Eduardo Ciannelli (Aton), Torin Thatcher (Potiphar), Katharine Ross (Asenath), John Abbott (Butler), Paul Mantee (Greek), Sorrell Booke (Baker), Anthony Caruso (Captain of the Guard).

753. **Kincaid.** 60 min. Airdate: 4/22/63. Production Company: Daystar Productions. Director: Leonard J. Horn. Producer: Bob Barbash. Writer: Bob Barbash. Aired as an episode of *Stoney Burke.* Dick Clark is a detective specializing in juvenile cases. *Cast:* Dick Clark (as Sgt. Andy Kincaid), Jack Lord (Stoney Burke), Sarah Marshall (Diane Banner), David Macklin (Frankie Sommers), David Winters (Lip), Gerald Trump (Zero), Craig Curtis (Tommy).

754. **Mr. Kingston.** 60 min. Production Companies: Daystar Productions and United Artists. Director: Leslie Stevens. Producer: Leslie Stevens. Writer: Leslie Stevens. Music: Dominic Frontiere. Peter Graves is Mr. Kingston, the executive officer of the *S.S. Atlantis,* a luxury liner on which adventure, drama and intrigue are always happening. Walter Pidgeon played the Captain. "It was wonderful," recalls Peter Graves. "But nobody liked it. The ad guys told me 'what a piece of crap, who wants to see something on a ship? We got Buddy Ebsen in *Beverly Hillbillies.* That's what everybody wants to see.' It was a real shame." In the pilot, titled "Trouble in Paradise," Ina Balin guest starred as a Princess in danger.

755. **Operation Secret.** 60 min. Airdate: 2/16/63. Production Company: Warner Bros. Television. Aired as an episode of *Gallant Men.* Ray Danton and Bart Hammond starred as O.S.S. agents operating in the Mediterranean during World War II. In

the pilot, told as a flashback, they have to go behind German lines and pin down a Panzer unit so that it cannot defend the beach at Salerno when the Army lands.

756. **Ready for the People.** 60 min. Production Company: Warner Bros. Television. Director: Buzz Kulik. Executive Producer: William Orr. Producer: Anthony Spinner. Writers: E.M. Parsons and Sy Salkowitz, from a story by Eleanor Lipsky. The story of three assistant D.A.'s and the cases they handle. In the pilot, shot on location in Brooklyn, Simon Oakland is torn between his job and the gut feeling the accused is innocent. In the end, however, the criminal is justly proven guilty but thanks Oakland for thinking well of him. The Leo Burnett Agency thought this pilot, then tentatively scheduled on ABC Tuesday as an 8:30–9:30 series, was "five years behind the times." It was subsequently released theatrically. *Cast:* Simon Oakland (as Murray Brock), Karl Held (Dave Ryan), Simon Scott (The D.A.), Everett Sloane (Paul Boyer), Connie Helm (Connie Zelenko), Richard Jordan (Eddie Dickson), Bartlett Robinson (John McGrane), Louis Guss (Joe Damico), Harold Gould (Arnie Tompkins), Don Keefer (Dr. Michaels), Jo Helton (Karen Brock), William Bramley (Nick Williams), Robert Lieb (Judge), King Calder (Chaplain).

757. **Tempo (aka Five, Six Pick Up Sticks; aka The Music Maker).** 60 min. Airdate: 1/24/63. Production Company: Revue. Director: Robert Ellis Miller. Producer: Dick Berg. Writer: John T. Kelly. Spin-off from *Alcoa Premiere*. John Forsythe stars as a record company executive. In the pilot, Forsythe tries to reunite a popular band for one more album. Mickey Rooney plays an alcoholic, many-married drummer who had an affair with the dead bandleader's wife fifteen years earlier. The drummer's guilt is responsible for his plight and threatens the reunion album. Also starred Barbara Nichols, John Lupton, Geraldine Brooks and Bibi Osterwald.

758. **The Unknown.** 60 min. Airdate: 5/4/64. Production Company: Daystar Productions. Director: Gerd Oswald. Producer: Joseph Stefano. Writer: Joseph Stefano. Creator: Joseph Stefano. Music: Dominic Frontiere. Aired as the "Forms of Things Unknown" episode of *The Outer Limits*. This was a pilot for a proposed anthology story of eerie tales. David McCallum played a mad scientist who can manipulate time – as well as life and death. The pilot version of this episode had a different ending in which guest star Vera Miles guns down McCallum who, in "The Outer Limits" episode escapes in his machine. Frontiere's score was later used for the TV series *The Invaders*. Guest stars included Scott Marlowe, Barbara Rush, and Sir Cedric Hardwicke.

759. **The Yellow Bird.** 30 min. Production Company: Selmur Productions. Director: Richard Donner. Executive Producer: Selig Seligman. Producer: Ivan Tors. Robert Brown and Carroll O'Connor are reluctant American spies in this comedic adventure that was shot on location in Nassau. Pat Harrington Jr. was one of the guest-stars. In *Gangway Lord: The Here Comes The Brides Book*, Brown says: "We were shooting for months. It was one of the most expensive pilots, cost millions. For a pilot, that was unheard of at the time. Carroll wanted the script changed. Since they wouldn't do that, he gave his notice. He said 'Of course I'll do the pilot, but I won't do the series. You'll have to find a replacement.' And it flopped."

CBS / COMEDY

760. **The Apartment House.** 30 min. Airdate: 9/5/64. Director: Sidney Miller. Producer: Joseph Shaftel. Writer: George Tibbles. George Gobel is the harried manager of an apartment house who tries his best to help his tenants – a tendency that always gets him into trouble. In the pilot, he takes care of a tenant's pet monkey. Sue Ane Langdon was his wife, Jane Withers was his maid, and Steve Allen and Fred MacMurray made cameo appearances as themselves. Woodrow Parfrey, Reginald Gardner and Christine Nielson guest starred.

761. **The Eve Arden Show (aka Take Him – He's Yours).** 30 min. Airdate: 7/20/64. Director: Don Taylor. Executive Producer: Harry Ackerman. Producer: Walter Shenson. Writers: Sy Gomberg and Al Lewis. Eve Arden is Claudia Cooper, a New York widow raising her teenage daughter (Cindy Carol) and working at a global travel agency. In the pilot, Cooper is transferred to London, where the owner's (Howard Smith) inept nephew (Jeremy Lloyd) has opened a branch office. Shot on location in London. *Cast:* Eve Arden (Claudia Cooper), Cindy Carol (Marsha Cooper), Howard I. Smith (J.T. Gittings), Jeremy Lloyd (Bertie Barrington), also, Ambrosia Philpots, Katy Greenwood, Nicholas Parsons, Derek Bond, Roger Avon.

762. **Hey Teacher.** 30 min. Airdate: 6/15/64. Director: Bob Sweeney. Producer: Bob Sweeney. Writers: Hannibal Coons and Harry Winkler. Dwayne Hickman is the only male teacher in an elementary school.

763. **Hooray for Hollywood.** 30 min. Airdate: 6/22/64. Director: Barry Shear. Executive Producer: Warren Lewis. Producer: Barry Shear. Writer: Sheldon Keller. Herschel Bernardi is Jerome P. Baggley, the Louis B. Mayer-esque head of World Goliath Studios, who is always at odds with Albert P. Leviathan (John

Litel), head of Leviathan Pictures, in this sitcom pilot set in the 1930s. *Cast:* Herschel Bernardi (as Jerome P. Baggley), Joyce Jameson (Wanda Renee), Joan Blondell (Miss Zilke), John Litel (Albert P. Leviathan), Ruby Keeler (Ruby), Bobby Troup (Gardner), George Sidney (Executive), Marvin Kaplan (Marvin).

764. **The Human Comedy.** 30 min. Airdate: 9/19/64. Production Company: MGM. Director: Robert Ellis Miller. Producer: Rudy E. Abel. The story of a widow (Phyllis Avery) and her two sons (Timmy Rooney, Jimmy Honer) and their eccentric neighbor, Mr. Grogan (Arthur O'Connell). In the pilot, Timmy breaks an antique tea pot belonging to a neighbor. Based on characters created by William Saroyan, which led to the 1943 movie starring Mickey Rooney.

765. **I and Claudie. 30 min.** Airdate: 7/2/64. Director: Gene Nelson. Executive Producer: Warren Lewis. Producer: Frank O'Conner. Writer: Michael Fessier. Aired as an episode of *Vacation Playhouse.* Clint Hightower (Jerry Lanning) and Claudie Hughes (Ross Martin) are two roving conmen in this pilot, which guest starred Barbara Stuart, Jennifer Billingsley, Jay Novello, Jess Kirkpatrick, Bella Bruck, Frank Gerstie and Eddie Quinlan.

766. **The Jimmy Durante Show.** 30 min. Airdate: 7/18/64. Director: Hy Averback. Producer: Hy Averback. Writers: Billy Friedberg, Mel Diamond, and Mel Tolkin. Jimmy Durante is Jimmy Banister, an entertainer who wants his son (Eddie Hodges) to follow in his footsteps – problem is, his son doesn't want to. *Cast:* Jimmy Durante (as Jimmy Banister), Eddie Hodges (Eddie Banister), Audrey Christie (Rosie Banister), John McIntire (Mr. Duveen), Ralph Bell (Chet Hanson), Daryl Richard (Frank Peterson), Kevin O'Neal (Boy), Barry Gordon (Kid), Dorothy Konrad (Woman).

767. **Kibbie Hates Fitch. 30 min.** Airdate: 8/2/65. Production Company: United Artists. Director: Stanley Prager. Producer: Robert Alan Arthur. Writer: Neil Simon. Don Rickles starred as Kibbee and Lou Jacobi as Fitch, two bickering firemen who share a duplex and whose wives are sisters. This was revived and reworked by Paramount for NBC in 1973 by producer Robert Stambler and writers Fred Freeman and Lawrence J. Cohen. It starred Michael Bell as Kibbee and Chuck McCann as Fitch. *Cast:* Don Rickles (as Don Kibbee), Lou Jacobi (Lou Fitch), Nancy Andrews (Amy Kibbee), Pert Kelton (Martha Fitch).

768. **Mimi.** 30 min. Airdate: 8/29/64. Director: Philip Rapp. Producer: Philip Rapp. Writer: Philip Rapp. The comedic mishaps of Mimi, a dietician at the Garden of Eden health spa, and her friend Phil, a therapist who also works there. *Cast:* Mimi

Hines (as Mimi), Phil Ford (Phil), Dan Tobin (Peavey), Thomas Gomez (M. Quibideaux), Yoneo Iquchi (Jockey), Lee Patrick (Miss Birch), Roger Etlienne (Grisha), Lili Garner (Giselle), Lloyd Kino (Council).

769. **Papa G.I.** 30 min. Airdate: 6/29/64. Director: Sherman Marks. Producer: Edward H. Feldman. Writer: James Brewer. Dan Dailey is a U.S. army entertainer who adopts two Korean orphans while on tour and makes them part of his show. *Cast:* Dan Dailey (as Sgt. Mike Parker), Cherylene Lee (Kim Chi), Douglas Moe (Quang Due), Noam Pitlik (Soldier #1), Billy Halop (Soldier #2).

770. **Satan's Waitin'.** 30 min. Airdate: 9/12/64. Director: Charle Haas. Producer: Joel Malone. Writers: Joel Malone and Tom Tomlinson. Ray Walston is The Stranger, actually Satan, who each week would try to muddle someone's life by tempting them to indulge in avarice, jealousy, greed and vice. Walston also played The Devil in *Damn Yankees Cast:* Ray Walston (as The Stranger), Jo Van Fleet (Velma Clarke), Lee Phillips (Walter Leighton), Sue Randall (Linda), Tom Greenway (Police Lieutenant), Simon Twigg (Minister).

CBS / DRAMA

771. **Calhoun.** 60 min. Production Companies: United Artists and Jackie Cooper Productions. Director: Stuart Rosenberg. Executive Producer: Robert Alan Arthur. Producers: Everett Chambers and Norman Kahn. Writer: Merle Miller. The making of this pilot was the focus of *Only You, Dick Daring!*, a bestseller Miller cowrote with Evan Rhodes in 1964. Jackie Cooper starred as county agent Everett Calhoun, Barbara Stanwyck played his boss. Howard Duff, Barbara Luna, and Diana Hyland guest starred. In the pilot, Calhoun races against time, and faces pressure from panicked ranchers, to stop a parasite that infests an orange grove from threatening other ranches.

772. **Diagnosis, Danger.** 60 min. Airdate: 3/1/63. Production Company: Universal Television. Director: Sydney Pollack. Producers: Roland Kibbee and Gordon Hessler. Writer: Roland Kibbee. Music: Lyn Murray. A spin-off from *Alfred Hitchcock Presents* starring Michael Parks as Dr. Don Dana and Charles McGraw as Dr. Simon Oliver, two doctors with the Los Angeles Department of Health desperately trying to stop an anthrax outbreak, which they trace to a set of bongos purchased in Mexico by a man now dead. Berkeley Harris costars as a police sergeant. *Cast:* Michael Parks (as Dr. Daniel Dana), Charles McGraw (Dr. Simon Oliver), Rupert Crosse (Dr. Paul

Mackey), Allen Joseph (Dr. Norman Abrams), Berkeley Harris (Deputy Sheriff Judd), Dee J. Thompson (Miss Nelson), Douglas Henderson (Huntziger), Helen Wescott (Mrs. Fletcher), Marc Cavell (Alf Coldin), Gus Trikonis (Gordie Sikes), Marc Rambeau (Dough Lynch), Clarke Gordon (Dr. Miller), Al Ruscio (Dr. Taylor), Celia Lovsky (Mrs. Jatouba), Irene A. Martin (Mrs. Benson), Howard Wendell (Doctor), Audrey Swanson (Nurse), Stefan Gierasch (Sgt. Boyle).

773. **Magnificent Seven.** Producer: Leslie Stevens. A concept aimed at bringing the popular movie to television as a weekly series.

NBC / COMEDY

774. **The Seven Little Foys.** 60 min. Airdate: 1/24/64. Production Company: Universal Television. Director: Jack Laird. Executive Producer: Gordon Oliver. Aired as an episode of *Bob Hope Chrysler Theatre* and based on the 1955 movie which starred Bob Hope as widower Eddie Foy, a vaudevillian raising seven performing kids, and James Cagney as George M. Cohan. In the pilot, Eddie Foy, Jr. plays his real-life father and Mickey Rooney plays Cohan, with the Osmonds portraying the Foy sons. *Cast:* Eddie Foy, Jr. (as Eddie Foy), Mickey Rooney (George M. Cohan), George Tobias (Barney Green), Naomi Stevens (Aunt Clara), Christy Jordan (Mary Foy), Alan Osmond (Bryan Foy), Wayne Osmond (Charley Foy), Merrill Osmond (Richard Foy), Donny Osmond (Irving Foy), Jay Osmond (Eddie Foy, Jr.), Elaine Edwards (Miss Williams).

NBC / DRAMA

775. **Corridor 400.** 60 min. Airdate: 12/27/63. Production Company: Universal Television. Aired as an episode of *Bob Hope Chrysler Theatre*. Suzanne Pleshette is an undercover agent for the F.B.I. *Cast:* Suzanne Pleshette (as Anita King), Theodore Bikel (Ralph Traven), Andrew Duggan (Donald Guthrie), Joseph Campanella (Frank Mancini), Frank Overton (Gene Farrell).

776. **Double Indemnity (aka Shadow of a Man).** 60 min. Airdate: 6/19/63. Production Company: Universal Television. Director: David Lowell Rich. Writer: Frank Fenton, from a story by James Patrick. Aired as an episode of *Kraft Mystery Theatre*. Jack Kelly and Broderick Crawford as insurance investigators. Costarred Bradford Dillman, Ed Begley and Beverly Owen.

777. **Grand Hotel.** 60 min. Production Company: MGM. Executive Producer: Alan Courtney. Producer: Leonard Freeman. Writer: Leonard Freeman. Barry Sullivan stars as the manager of a San Francisco Hotel. Chad Everett played his assistant, who was jokingly modeled after a network executive then at NBC.

778. **Rifle Service.** 60 min. Production Company: MGM. The adventures of a private eye named Rifle who runs an insurance investigation service.

779. **The Robert Taylor Show.** 60 min. Production Company: Four Star. Director: Bernard Kowalski. Producer: Dick Powell. Writer: Bruce Geller. Robert Taylor stars as Assistant Chief of the U.S. Dept. of Health, Education and Welfare and Robert Loggia as his aide. In the pilot, they fly to Los Angeles to find a man who is carrying a dangerous plague. Three more episodes were made for this proposed series, based on the 1962 pilot *330 Independence S. W.* starring William Bendix, and were never aired. George Segal replaced Loggia in the subsequent episodes, which were written by Christopher Knopf, Tom Seller, and Lawrence Edward Watkin and directed by Kowalski and Bernard Girard. Guest stars included William Shatner, Michael Parks, Joanna Moore, and Luana Anders.

780. **13th Gate.** 60 min. Airdate: 7/20/65. Writer: Robert Barbash. David Opatoshu and Carl Held starred in this pilot about a secret agent in a science-fiction setting.

781. **The Watchman.** 60 min. Airdate: 5/14/64. Director: Sydney Pollack. Producer: Jack Laird. Writer: David Rayfield. Music: Lalo Schifrin. Aired as an episode of *Kraft Suspense Theatre.* Jack Warden is a novelist modeled after Ernest Hemingway who travels the world meeting people and exploring different ways of life. *Cast:* Jack Warden (as Jack Fleming), Tol Avery (Publisher), Victoria Shaw (Helena), Telly Savalas (Ramon Castillo), Carlos Rivas (Irregular), Peter Mamakos (Chauffeur), Arthur Batanides (Detective), Sam Gilman (Man), Eddy Williams (Enes), Frank DeKova (Edward).

782. **The Whistling Shrimp.** 60 min. Airdate: 11/20/63. Aired as an episode of *Espionage.* Arthur Kennedy as Fogue, an enterprising reporter. Costarred Earl Hyman, Nancy Wickwire, and Larry Gates.

INDEPENDENT PRODUCTIONS

Filmways

The following two, unnumbered, unsold pilots were omitted from the previous edition of this book:

Trials and Tribulations of Emmy Lou Harper. 30 Minutes. Director: Arthur Lubin. Writers: Ben Starr & Robert O'Brien. Aired as the "Ed the Matchmaker" episode of *Mr. Ed* and based on a cartoon strip by Marty Links. Noanna Dix stars as love-crazed teenager. The cast included Peter Brooks, George O'Hanlon, and Jeff Donnell.

Moko and Tatti. 30 minutes. Airdate: 5/17/64. Director: Arthur Lubin. Writers: Norman Paul & Willy Burns. Aired as the "Moko" episode of *Mr. Ed*. Moko and Tatti are two tiny animated cartoon martians (voiced by Richard Deacon and Dave Willock) interacting with live-action characters. The tiny aliens fly into people's ears and make them lose their inhibitions, making them do crazy things, and hilarity ensues.

Four Star

783. **The Dean Jones Show.** 30 min. Dean Jones stars as a bachelor who owns an apartment building and gets involved with his tenants' lives.

784. **Focus on Adventure.** Producer: Martin Manulis. Creator: James Michener. An international adventure series fashioned for Robert Wagner. When this failed to sell, Four Star fashioned another concept for Wagner for the following season.

785. **Royal Bay.** 60 min. Producer: Richard Alan Simmons. Writer: Richard Alan Simmons. Life and times of a family living in a small California coastal community. Paul Burke, Charles Bickford, Joan Crawford and Richard Carlson starred.

Gannaway Productions

786. **Holiday for Hire.** 30 min. Creator: Albert Gannaway. Producer/Director: Gerald Mohr. An adventure pilot shot in Acapulco and starring Gerald Mohr as the manager of a worldwide travel agency with offices everywhere. In the pilot, he looks for the runaway daughter of an American millionaire.

Green and Stone Productions

787. **Hollywood Yesterday.** Director: Don Reardon. Writer: Arthur Houseman. George Jessel is the host of this documentary/anthology. The show, as envisioned in the pilot, begins with Jessel arriving by limo at Grauman's Chinese Theatre. He enters the empty theatre and reminisces and sees a montage of stills tracing the career, life

and work of two famous personalities which were, in the pilot, Carole Lombard and Tyrone Power.

MCA/Revue

788. Ma and Pa Kettle. 30 min. Producer: Howard Christie. Writers: Al Lewin and Bud Styler. An attempt to turn the movie series into a TV series.

Screen Gems

789. The Turning Point. 60 min. Producers/Writers: Clarence Green and Russell Rouse. Mike Connors plays a young teacher, Charles Bickford the principal, in this pilot for a series set in a high school. In the pilot, a student steals exam questions to get a passing grade so he can enter college and win respect of his Dad. Connors solves everything. The show was endorsed by the National Education Association who wrote advertisers in support of the series.

1965–1966

ABC / COMEDY

790. Baby Makes Three (aka Baby Crazy). 30 min. Airdate: 9/19/66. Production Company: Bing Crosby Productions. Director: Richard Crenna. Producer: Richard Crenna. Writers: Harriet Frank and Irving Ravetch. The adventures of a young pediatrician (James Stacy) who tells everyone how to handle kids and yet, being single, has none of his own. Joan Blondell was his nurse. This pilot was written by the folks behind *Hud* and *Murphy's Romance*, among other feature films. *Cast:* James Stacy (as Dr. Peter Cooper), Joan Blondell (Joan Terry), Lynn Loring (Jennie Winston), Gavin MacLeod (Dr. Charles Norwood), Ronnie Dapo (Jimmy), Craig Hundley (Andy), Madge Blake (Grandmother), Pamelyn Ferdin (Linda Jayne), Dennis Rush (Buddy), Johnnie Whitaker (Freddy).

791. Bette Davis Show. 30 min. Production Company: Four Star. Producer: Aaron Spelling. Bette Davis is an interior decorator who lives with her clients in order to fit her designs to their personalities – which she usually adjusts by helping them with their problems.

792. Frank Merriwell. 30 min. Airdate: 7/25/66. Production Company: Desilu. Director: Allen F. Miller. Producer: Leslie Stevens. Writer: Leslie Stevens. A camp comedy starring Jeff Cooper as a Yale-educated renaissance man at the turn of the century who delights in competing with his nemesis Brandon Drood (Beau Bridges). In the pilot, they enter a car race. *Cast:* Jeff Cooper (as Frank Merriwell), Tisha Sterling (Elsie Stanhope), Bruce Hyde (Binkie Stubbs), Beau Bridges (Brandon Drood), Murvyn Vye (Bart Farge), Harry Dean Stanton (Dayton Skagg), James Flavin (Fire Chief), Joe Corey (Fireman #1), Lee Miller (Fireman #2), Jay Della (Aeronaut).

793. My Island Family. 30 min. Production Company: 20th Century Fox. Producer: Gene Rodney. Director: Henry Foster. Pat Boone stars as an engineer who goes to a remote Pacific island to work on a waterway, falls in love with a missionary's daughter and gets into trouble with a local tribal chief who makes his living selling water.

794. The previously listed pilot **My Man St. John"** became the series *O. K. Crackerby*.

795. Shirley Temple Show. 30 min. Production Company: 20th Century Fox. Producer: Vincent Sherman. Director: Vincent Sherman. Shirley Temple stars as a San Francisco social worker who gets involved with the people she works with.

796. Take Her, She's Mine. 30 min. Production Company: 20th Century Fox. Producer: Richard Murphy. Van Johnson is a widower trying to raise his mischievous daughter, a college freshman, who always has one scheme after another—and gets her Dad involved in all of them. Based on the play – and subsequent 1963 Jimmy Stewart movie – by Henry and Phoebe Ephron.

797. Thompson's Ghost. 30 min. Airdate: 8/6/66. Production Company: Bing Crosby Productions. Producer: Elliot Lewis. Writers: Richard Donovan and Lorenzo Semple, Jr. Bert Lahr is a ghost who haunts a California housing tract and must remain there to do good deeds and help those in trouble to make up for his checkered mortal life. In the pilot, he befriends 10-year-old Annabelle Thompson (Pamela Dapo), his descendent. *Cast:* Bert Lahr (as Henry Thompson), Pamela Dapo (Annabelle Thompson), Phyllis Coates (Milly Thompson), Robert Rockwell (Sam Thompson), Tim Matheson (Eddie Thompson), Willard Waterman (Dr. Wheeler), Barry Kelly (Chief Watson), Trudy Howard (Nurse).

798. Two's Company. 30 min. Production Company: Universal Television. Executive Producer: David Levy. Producer: Peter Tewksbury. Comedy about two newlyweds, a trial attorney (Paul Lynde) and his wife, a fashion model.

799. Vacation with Pay. 30 min. Production Company: Desilu. Writer: Robert Blees. Based on the book about inmates in a German P.O.W. camp who convert their cellblock into a resort. In the pilot, they make cognac out of grape juice and serve old rooster as "pheasant under glass."

ABC / DRAMA

800. Boom Town. 60 min. Production Company: MGM. Producer: Burt Kennedy. Based on the movie starring Clark Gable and Spencer Tracy. The life of a frontier oil town in the southwest at the turn of the century.

801. Diamond Jim. 60 min. Production Company: Selmer Productions. Producer: Andy White. Writer: Harry Brown. Dale Robertson is Diamond Jim, an adventurer living in New York in this completed pilot loosely based on the real person.

802. Hell Cats. 60 min. Airdate: 11/24/67. Production Company: Four Star. Director: Don Taylor. Executive Producer: Aaron Spelling. Writers: W.R. Burnett and Tony

Barrett. This pilot, shot in 1964, aired as part of the 1967 anthology *Off to See the Wizard*. George Hamilton was an aerial daredevil who traveled the country in a World War I biplane doing stunts and getting involved in people's problems. Costarred Warren Berlinger, Nehemiah Persoff, John Craig and Barbara Eden.

803. **Hercules (aka Hercules and the Sea Monster).** 60 min. Airdate: 9/12/65. Production Company: Embassy Pictures. Producer: Joseph Levine. Writers: Larry Forrester and Hugo Liberatore. Music: Fred Steiner. Narrator: Everett Sloane. Shot in Italy and Yugoslavia with Gordon Scott as Hercules, who does battle in the pilot with a sea monster to save the city of Troy. *Cast*: Gordon Scott (as Hercules), Paul Stevens (Diogenes), Mart Hulswit (Ulysses), Diana Hyland (Diana), Steve Garrett (Petra), Giorgio Ardisson (Leander).

804. **Will Banner.** 30 min. Production Company: Quinn Martin Productions. Producer: Quinn Martin. Writer: Harold Jack Bloom. Steve Forrest is an ex-prizefighter-turned-Sheriff who can't stop wondering why he lost the championship bout in this completed pilot that costarred Robert Middleton, Lola Albright.

CBS / COMEDY

805. **The Barbara Rush Show (aka Barbara Warren).** 30 min. Airdate: 8/9/65. Production Companies: Paramount Television and General Foods. Director: Fred DeCordova. Producer: Tony Owen. Writers: Paul West and Barbara Avedon. Barbara Rush is a mother of two who works part-time as a stenographer to help her husband through medical school. *Cast*: Barbara Rush (as Barbara Warren), Bob Fortier (Matt Warren), Alan Napier (Marsden).

806. **Captain Ahab.** 30 min. Airdate: 9/3/65. Director: Richard Crenna. Producer: Hal Kanter. Writers: Hal Kanter and Michael Fessier. Two distant cousins—a naive southern girl (Judy Canova) and a streetwise Las Vegas showgirl (Jaye P. Morgan)—inherit their uncle's New York townhouse, a lot of money, and Captain Ahab, a 90-year-old talking parrot. To keep the money, the two cousins have to live together and care for the smart-mouth parrot. *Cast*: Judy Canova (as Tillie Meeks), Jaye P. Morgan (Maggie Feeney), Don Porter (Battersea), Sid Gould (Angelo), Francine York (Miss Langdon), Eddie Quillan (Emcee), Larry Blake (Hardhat), Tom Lound (Chauffeur), Maury Hill (Cop), Tommy Alende (Delivery Boy).

807. **Coogan's Reward.** 30 min. Airdate: 8/20/65. Director: Don Taylor. Producer: Winston O'Keefe. Writers: David Swift, William Crowley, and Peggy Chantler.

Tony Randall is a reluctant correspondent covering World War II on the front lines—when he'd much rather be somewhere a lot safer. Costars included Alan Carney, Robert Gist and Roxanne Berall.

808. **The Dean Jones Show (aka Alec Tate).** 30 min. Airdate: 7/2/65. Production Companies: Four Star and General Foods. Director: Richard Kinon. Producers: Hank Garson and Ed Beloin. Writers: Hank Garson and Ed Beloin. Dean Jones is a young La Jolla scientist who, when his parents die, raises his teenage sister with the help of a computer he developed that is supposed to have the answer to every human problem and behavior. *Cast:* Dean Jones (as Alec Tate), Robyn Millan (Bunny Tate), Jay C. Flippen (Cappy Skidmore), Diane McBain (Sherry), Robert Middleton (Homer Ferguson), Ann Jillian (Bev Ferguson), Christine White (Miss Malloy).

809. **The Donald O'Connor Show.** 30 min. Production Company: Universal Television. Producer: Dick Wesson. Writers: Dick Wesson and Joel Kane. Donald O'Connor is a scientist working with animals in this completed pilot based on Universal's feature *Fluffy.* Also starred Sharon Farrell, Frank Faylen, Parley Baer and Fluffy the Lion. After this failed, O'Connor played a scientist in another Universal pilot, *Brilliant Benjamin Boggs*, on NBC in 1966.

810. **Dream Wife (aka Happily Ever After).** 30 min. Production Company: MGM. Director: Don Taylor. Executive Producer: Stanley Chase. Writers: Stanley Chase and Robert Kaufman. Shirley Jones is a mind reader/psychic, Donald May is her exasperated husband in this *Bewitched* clone.

811. **Eve Arden Show.** 30 min. Production Company: Universal Television. Director: Mitch Leisen. Producer: Lester Colodny. Eve Arden was a flamboyant, Manhattan widow who caused problems whenever she descended on her family and friends. Steve Franken costarred as her son-in-law in this completed pilot.

812. **Heaven Help Us.** 30 min. Airdate: 8/14/67. Production Company: 20th Century Fox. Director: Richard Whorf. Executive Producer: William Dozier. Producer: Stan Shpetner. Writer: Sol Sachs. Barry Nelson is a widower whose romantic life is frustrated by the ghost of his dead wife, who has a mean jealous streak and loves to interfere with his love life. Costarred Joanna Moore. *Cast:* Barry Nelson (as Dick Cameron), Joanna Moore (Marge Cameron), Mary Grace Canfield (Mildred), Bert Freed (Mr. Walker), Skip Ward (Collins), Sue Randall (Ruth), Sandra Warner (Linda).

813. **Hello Dere.** 30 min. Airdate: 8/9/65. Director: Jean Yarbrough. Executive Producer: Al Brodax. Producer: Ed Jurist. Writers: William Raynor and Myles

Wilder. Marty Allen and Steve Rossi play two bumbling television reporters. Roland Winters played their boss. Guest stars were Nina Shipman, Lisa Pera, Henry Corden and Nestor Paiva.

814. **Luke and the Tenderfoot.** 30 min. Airdates: 8/6/65 and 8/13/65. Directors: Montgomery Pittman (#1) and Herman Hoffman (#2). Producer: Steve Fisher. Writer: Steve Fisher. Two pilots were made starring Edgar Buchanan as a crooked peddler riding the west in his rickety wagon with his young apprentice, Carleton Carpenter. *Cast:* Edgar Buchanan (as Luke Herkimer), Carleton Carpenter (Pete Queen), Michael Landon (8/6/65) (Tough), Charles Bronson (8/13/65) (John Wesley Hardin), Richard Jaeckel (8/13/65) (Man).

815. **My Lucky Penny.** 30 min. Airdate: 8/8/66. Production Company: Desilu. Director: Theodore Flicker. Producers: Arne Sultan and Marvin Worth. Writer: Arne Sultan. Brenda Vaccaro stars as a naive woman married to a dental student (Richard Benjamin) and who works as a secretary for a man she only knows through tape-recorded instructions. *Cast:* Brenda Vaccaro (as Jenny Penny), Richard Benjamin (Ted Penny), Joel Grey (Freddy Rockefeller), Luana Anders (Sybil Rockefeller), Larry Storch (Commodore), David Moss (Frederick), Jonathan Harris (Money Collector).

816. **Legal Eagle (aka The Lawyer).** 30 min. Production Company: Goodson-Todman. Producer: Cece Barker. Writers: Jack Weinstock and Millie Gilbert. Will Hutchins stars as a dumb lawyer who works in his rich uncle's law firm and somehow manages to outwit truly smart attorneys. Costarred Chris Noel.

817. **McGhee.** 30 min. Airdate: 6/28/65. Director: Don McGuire. Producer: Don McGuire. Writer: Don McGuire. Jeremy Slate is a nearly bankrupt artist living in the Bronx who inherits a small California town, populated by 200 people, when a distant relative dies. *Cast:* Jeremy Slate (as Willie McGhee), Karen Steele (Ann Dorsey), George Chandler (Sheriff George), Connie Sawyer (Hilda).

818. **Meet Me in St. Louis.** 30 min. Airdate: 9/2/66. Production Company: MGM. Executive Producer: Alan Courtney. Producer: Paul West. Writer: Sally Benson, based on her story. Based on the 1944 Judy Garland musical set during the turn of the century at the world's fair. The pilot starred Shelley Fabares as Esther, a girl from Missouri who has just arrived in New York. It was ultimately rejected, says Courtney, when a network executive decided "he didn't want anything on his network with an ice wagon rattling down the street." *Cast:* Shelley Fabares (as Esther Smith), Celeste Holm (Anne Smith), Larry Merrill (Glenn Smith), Judy Land (Faye Morse), Reta Shaw (Katie), also, Suzanne Cupito and Tammy Locke.

819. **My Son, the Doctor.** 30 min. Airdate: 8/22/66. Production Company: Desilu. Director: Don Richardson. Producer: Jack Donohue. Writers: Hal Goodman and Larry Klein. About a mother (Kay Medford) who still treats her son (Jefferson Davis) like a child, even though he's a doctor and married (to Julie Gregg). *Cast:* Jefferson Davis (as Dr. Peter Piper), Julie Gregg (Barbara Piper), Dick Patterson (Dr. Jeffrey Berry), Patsy Kelly (Miss Primrose), Lee Meriwether (Doris), Cliff Norton (Phil), Dave Willock (Gilmore), William Lanteau (Dr. Hopkins).

820. **Polly Bergen Show.** 30 min. Production Company: Jack Webb Productions. Producer: Jack Webb. Polly Bergen would have starred in this television series based on the Selena Mead stories by Patricia McGerr.

821. **Sally and Sam.** 30 min. Airdate: 7/5/65. Production Companies: 20th Century Fox and General Foods. Director: Vincent Sherman. Producer: Vincent Sherman. Writer: Hal Kanter. Gary Lockwood and Cynthia Pepper as newlyweds planning to marry despite problems that often seem insurmountable. *Cast:* Cynthia Pepper (as Sally Marten), Gary Lockwood (Sam Cody), Bernie Kopell (Glen), Nancy Jeris (Joy), John Qualen (Picket), Jay Strong (Phil), Phyllis Douglas (Nurse).

822. **Sybil.** 30 min. Airdate: 6/25/65. Director: Hy Averback. Producer: Hy Averback. Writers: Jerry Davis, James Fritzell, and Everett Greenbaum. Suzy Parker is an angel who helps mortals in trouble, Wilfred Hyde-White is her heavenly mentor, and John Ericson is her charge in the pilot.

823. **This Is a Hospital.** 30 min. Production Company: Screen Gems. Executive Producer: Harry Ackerman. Producer: William Sackheim. Shecky Greene as hospital orderly who means well but always screws up. Dorothy Louden is the nurse who keeps him out of trouble.

824. **Who Goes There?** 30 min. Production Company: CBS Productions. Director: Jack Arnold. Producer: Stanley Kallis. Two troublesome ghosts haunting a southern California tract home materialize as General Custer (Pat Hingle) and Indian Chief Running Dog (Ben Blue) because pictures of those historical figures are on the wall, and roam the neighborhood.

825. **Young at Heart.** 30 min. Airdate: 8/16/65. Director: Fletcher Markle. Producer: Fletcher Markle. Writer: Whitfield Cook. Mercedes McCambridge stars as the housemother for a sorority. *Cast:* Mercedes McCambridge (as Margaret Malloy), Barbara Bain (Gerry Hart), Kay Stewart (Dean Winters), Lin Foster (Ted Halsey), Nancy Marshall (Liz Prescott), Charles Watt (Charles Prescott), Carolyn Kearney (Student).

826. You're Only Young Twice (aka Prof. Huberty Abernathy). 30 min. Airdate: 7/3/67. Production Company: 20th Century Fox. Director: Don Taylor. Executive Producer: William Dozier. Producer: Stan Shpetner. Writers: Stanley Drehen and Lorenzo Semple, Jr. Ed Wynn is a science teacher who creates a pill that can temporarily make people several years younger. In the pilot, he helps a depressed housewife by offering to make her young again. *Cast:* Ed Wynn (as Prof. Huberty Abernathy), Ethel Waters (Carrie), Kathryn Hays (Betsy Fleming), Andrew Duggan (George Fleming), Steve Dunne (Charlie), Andy Devine (Andy), Jerry Van Dyke (George), Dwayne Hickman (Lennie), Patricia Crowley (Joan).

CBS / DRAMA

827. Bravo Duke. 30 min. Airdate: 7/30/65. Director: Douglas Heyes. Producer: Douglas Heyes. Writer: Douglas Heyes. The adventures of Duke (Gerald Mohr), owner of a cantina/casino in a small Mexican town who helps tourists who get into trouble. Guest stars included Kathleen Crowley, Sebastian Cabot and Jay Novello.

828. Haunted. 60 min. Production Company: United Artists. Directors: Robert Stevens and Joseph Stefano. Producer: Joseph Stefano. Writer: Joseph Stefano. Martin Landau stars as a parapsychologist who investigates hauntings, most of which turn out to be frauds but sometimes end up being horrifyingly real. He's assisted by his housekeeper, played by Nellie Burke. Guest stars included John Drew Barrymore, Diane Baker, and Dame Judith Anderson. "It was a wonderful, wonderful pilot," recalls Landau. "My character had a very interesting, ethereal, poetic quality. His actual profession was the restoration of old Victorian homes. His subvocation, or hobby, was psychic research. Robert Stevens started to direct it, got sick, and Joe ultimately directed it." The pilot never aired in the United States but was, according to Landau, broadcast in England in the late 70s and it "knocked audiences out. It scared the shit out of them."

829. Mark Dolphin. 60 min. Production Company: United Artists. Producer: Robert Alan Arthur. Writer: Robert Nash. According to the *Saturday Evening Post* (3/26/66), "the only result of all this effort and expense was the name 'Mark Dolphin' has since become synonymous with total disaster in show business idiom: 'For God's sake, let's not have another Mark Dolphin on our hands,' or 'Don't try to pull a Mark Dolphin on me sweetheart.'" In 1963, CBS approached Robert

Horton, who was then starring in Nash's Broadway play *110 in the Shade*, to star in this Nash-written pilot. "It was just the kind of role I had been looking for after years in Westerns," Horton said. "The hero was a suave New York multimillionaire living in a Park Avenue penthouse. He involved himself in people's problems and solved them for them. Dolphin had a charming, off-beat personality, so I signed to do the pilot. It was a great deal." Because the play was a hit, they delayed making the pilot until 1964 for the 65–66 season. Then the problems began. The producer, Horton claimed, rewrote the script so that Dolphin was now "a tough Humphrey Bogart character who owns an antique shop in New York. Putting me in a role like that would be like asking Mickey Rooney to play a pro-football tackle. I phoned my agent and said 'Get me out of this.' He said, 'I can't. If you don't do the pilot now, CBS can sue you for everything you own.'" Costarred Michael Rennie, Shirley Knight, and Lew Ayres.

830. **Starr, First Baseman (aka Joe Starr; aka Starr of the Yankees).** 30 min. Airdate: 7/23/65. Production Company: ZIV. Director: Arthur Hiller. Producer: Vernon E. Clark. Writer: Freeman Dean. Martin Milner recalls this as a "pilot made for the syndication market back in 1957 or 1958. I played a first rookie first baseman for the Yankees who has problems after he's hit by a baseball." *Cast:* Martin Milner (as Joe Starr), Stuart Whitman (Coach Freddie Gordon), David Thursby (Eddie Ryan).

NBC / COMEDY

831. **The Alan King Show.** 30 min. Production Company: Universal Television. Director: Dick Weston. Producer: Max Shulman. The adventures of a New York taxi driver who doubles as a chauffeur for a rich Park Avenue family. The series would have starred Alan King, Dean Miller and Sybil Bowen.

832. **Campo 44.** 30 min. Airdate: 9/9/67. Production Company: NBC Productions. Director: Buzz Kulik. Producer: Buzz Kulik. Writer: David Westheimer. The comedic adventures of prisoners of war in an Italian concentration camp during World War II in a pilot that bears remarkable similarity to *Hogan's Heroes*. *Cast:* Philip Abbott (as Flickinger), Vito Scotti (Barracutti), Dino Fazio (Bergamo), Fred Smoot (Berry), Jim Dawson (Wellington), also, Danielle DeMetz.

833. **Good Old Days.** 30 min. Airdate: 7/11/66. Production Company: Desilu. Director: Howard Morris. Producer: Hal Goodman and Larry Klein. Writers:

Hal Goodman and Larry Klein. A comedy about the problems of a prehistoric family a la *The Flintstones*. In the pilot, teenage caveman Rok (Darryl Hickman) meets beautiful cavegirl Pantha (Chris Noel). *Cast:* Darryl Hickman (as Rok), Kathleen Freeman (Mom), Ned Glass (Dad), Chris Noel (Pantha), Dodo Denny (Ugh), Beverly Adams (Cavegirl), Dean Moray (Kid), Jacques Aubuchon (Soc), Joe Bova (Kook), Bruce Yarnall (Slag), Charles Horvath (Brute).

834. **Kissin' Cousins.** 30 min. Production Company: MGM. Director: Don Weis. Producer: Sam Katzman. Based on the movie starring Elvis Presley. Edd Byrnes plays an Army officer from the Ozarks who goes back to the mountains to scout a location for a missile site. The locals are suspicious and untrusting of him, so he uses his "kissin' cousins" to help him out. Stanley Adams costarred in this completed pilot.

835. **Li'l Abner.** Production Company: United Artists. Producer: Rod Amateau. A concept based on the Al Capp comic about the backwoods town of Dogpatch and the hillbillies who live there.

836. **See Here, Private Hargrove.** 30 min. Production Company: MGM. Producer: Marion Hargrove. Director: Jerry Thorpe. Writer: Marion Hargrove. Based on the book, play and film about a shy army officer. Starred Peter Helm, Tommy Rettig, Jimmy Hawkins and Shirley Mitchell.

837. **Steptoe and Son.** 30 min. Production Company: J. Levine Productions. Producers: Clarence Green and Russell Rouse. An American version of the English sitcom about a widower and his son who sell junk, starring Aldo Ray and Lee Tracy. Although this completed pilot didn't sell, producers Bud Yorkin and Norman Lear later adapted the British series for the NBC sitcom *Sanford and Son*.

838. **Take Five.** 30 min. Production Company: Paramount Television. Producer: Leonard Stern. Writer: Leonard Stern. Three Army musicians in Europe during WWII who are always bucking authority and it's up to their friend, a U.S.O. girl, to get them out of trouble.

839. **Tell Aggie.** 30 min. Production Company: Four Star. Producer: Everett Chambers. Writers: Ben Roberts and Ivan Goff. Marlyn Mason is a TV advice show host who always gets too involved in her viewers' problems. Costarred Lee Phelps.

840. **The Willies.** 30 min. Production Company: Universal Television. Producer: Frank Price. George Gobel is a man who lives in a haunted house and can't get his neighbors, who blame all the supernatural weirdness they witness on him, to believe his stories.

NBC / DRAMA

841. **Aftermath.** 60 min. Airdate: 1/14 & 21/1965. Production Company: Universal Television. Producer: Raymond Wagner. Aired as a two-part episode of *Kraft Suspense Theater* entitled "In Darkness, Waiting." This proposed anthology would introduce a set of characters one week, set them up in an unusual situation, and then next week visit those same characters ten years later.

842. **Bend in the River.** 60 min. Airdate: 5/2/65. Production Company: Universal Television. Director: Leo Sherman. Producer: Howard Christie. Rory Calhoun leads a frontier family attempting to establish their homestead. The pilot, which costarred Tom Simcox, Arthur Hunnicutt and Lee Philips, aired as the last episode of ABC's *Wagon Train*, entitled "The Jarbo Pierce Story."

843. **The Fliers.** 60 min. Airdate: 2/5/65. Production Company: Universal Television. Director: Sydney Pollack. Producer: Dick Berg. Writers: David Rayfield and Lorenzo Semple, Jr. Music: Cyril Mockridge. Aired as an episode of *Bob Hope Chrysler Theatre*. The adventures of a pilot (John Cassavetes) with the Lafayette Airial Escadrille in France before U.S. entered WWI. *Cast:* John Cassavetes (Sgt. Lee Harmon), Chester Morris (Major Whitman), Carol Lynley (Irene Ayers), Alfred Ryder (Boz), Tom Simcox (Lt. Walter Matthew).

844. The pilot **Ghostbreakers, #699,** was previously duplicated here in error because the pilot was, once again, under consideration.

845. **The Green Felt Jungle.** 60 min. Airdate: 4/1/65. Production Company: Universal Television. Director: William Graham. Executive Producer: Roy Huggins. Producer: Joe Swerling, Jr. Writer: Howard Browne. Aired as an episode of *Kraft Suspense Theatre*. Leslie Nielsen is a small-town district attorney whose wife is killed by a bomb meant for him – so he wages a relentless one-man war on crime to avenge her death. *Cast:* Leslie Nielsen (as Paul Maytric), MacDonald Carey (Pike), Richard Conte (Jack Sallas), Larry Pennell (Sgt. Phil Scanlon), Inez Pedrosa (Conchita Rivero), Indus Arthur (Elizabeth Pike), Michael Pate (Johnny Slato), Nick Alexander (Marty), William Edward Phillips (Frank), Walker Edmiston (George Baird), Ivan Bonar (Monroe), Ken Lynch (Larry Henderson), Roland LaStarza (Bugs), Harold Fong (Bert), Webb Pierce (Prescott).

846. **Guilty or Not Guilty (aka Indictment).** 60 min. Airdate: 3/9/66. Production Company: Universal Television. Director: David Lowell Rich. Producer: Richard Lewis. Writers: Guthrie Lamb and Roland Kibbee. Here's another pilot starring

Leslie Nielsen, this time as a New York assistant district attorney. Aired as an episode of *Bob Hope Chrysler Theatre*. Also starring were Robert Ryan, Richard Beymer, Pippa Scott, Leif Erickson, Robert Duvall, Diana Hyland, Pamela Toll, Bill McNally, Don Gazzaniga, Phil Fagan, Luke Saucier, Richard Venture, Lincoln Kilpatrick, William Bryant, Harvey C. Dunn, Laura Mason, Elsie Baker, Sandra Williams, Elizabeth Lawrence, Frank Campanella, Alfred Knickley, John Cecil Holme, William Zuckert, and Louis Criscuolo.

847. **Knight's Gambit.** 60 min. Airdate: 3/26/64. Production Company: Universal Television. Director: Walter E. Grauman. Executive Producer: Roy Huggins. Producer: Robert Blees. Writers: Lorenzo Semple, Jr. and Halsted Welles, from a story by Robert Blees. Creator: Robert Blees. Music: John Williams. Aired as an episode of *Kraft Suspense Theatre*. Roger Smith, formerly of *77 Sunset Strip*, is playboy reporter Anthony Knight. *Cast:* Roger Smith (as Anthony Griswald Knight), Eleanor Parker (Dorian Smith), Chester Morris (Blaine Davis), Murray Matheson (Douglas Henderson), Erika Peters (Bijou), Vito Scotti (Tout).

848. **Last Clear Chance.** 60 min. Airdate: 3/11/65. Production Company: Universal Television. Director: Sydney Pollack. Producer: Mort Abrams. Writer: Abraham Polonsky. Aired as an episode of *Kraft Suspense Theatre*. Glenn Corbett starred as an O.S.S. officer working behind German lines. Costarred Bruce Bennett, Barry Sullivan, Suzanne Cramer, and Ben Wright.

849. **The Mayor.** 60 min. Production Company: MGM. Director: Richard Donner. Producer: E. Jack Neuman. Robert Colbert is a young mayor who often makes mistakes but has the best intentions. The series would have focused on his conflicts with city hall, family and business people. Costarred K.T. Stevens, Ronald Hayes, Hilde Brawner, and Chad Everett.

850. **Panama (aka Jungle of Fear).** 60 min. Airdate: 4/22/65. Production Company: Universal Television. Director: John McGreevey. Producer: Howard Christie. Aired as an episode of *Kraft Suspense Theatre*. Set in the 1840s, this pilot told the story of a jungle hotel and its guests, struggling gold seekers trying to walk across the Isthmus of Panama in order to catch boats to California. Starred Robert Fuller, Robert Loggia, Richard Anderson, Warren Stevens, Tony Davis, Suzanne Cramer, Charles Briggs, Harold Sakata, and Ann Blyth.

851. **Pay the Piper (aka Double Jeopardy).** 60 min. Airdate: 1/8/65. Production Company: Universal Television. Producer: Richard Lewis. Aired as an episode of *Bob Hope Chrysler Theatre*. Jack Kelly as a high paid P.I. who only works on cases no

one else can solve. Guest starred Lauren Bacall, Zsa Zsa Gabor, Tom Poston, Jean Hale, Nobu McCarthy, Diane McBain, and Lee Meriwether.

852. **P.O.W. (aka The War and Eric Kurtz).** 60 min. Airdate: 3/5/65. Production Company: Universal Television. Director: Tom Gries. Producer: Roy Huggins. Aired as an episode of *Bob Hope Chrysler Theatre*. The dramatic adventures of prisoners at a German P.O.W. camp as seen through the eyes of the prisoner-elected officers, the camp commander, the chief medical officer and the man chosen to supervise fair distribution of the food. "I'm not sure how serious an attempt it was at a pilot," recalls star Martin Milner. "But it was a pretty good show." It also starred Lloyd Bochner, Jack Ging, and Warren Oates.

853. **Won't It Ever Be Morning?** 60 min. 3/18/65. Production Company: Universal Television. Director: David Lowell Rich. Executive Producer: Frank P. Rosenberg. Producer: Raymond Wagner. Writer: Larry Marcus. Aired as an episode of *Kraft Suspense Theatre*. John Cassavetes stars in the adventures of lawyer Paul Chandler. *Cast*: John Cassavetes (as Paul Chandler), Gena Rowlands (Lois Baxter), Jack Klugman (Ozzie Keefer), John Anderson (Rankin), Douglas Henderson (Sam Grayson), Carla Doherty (Shirley Rankin), Jimmy Joyce (Piano man), Barry Brooks (Court Reporter), John Hale (M.E.), Stanford Jolley (Mr. Shamley).

854. **Area Code 212.** Production Company: Four Star. Producer: Tom McDermott. Writer: Sheldon Reynolds. Robert Wagner as a suave, New York private eye who doesn't take himself too seriously.

INDEPENDENT PRODUCTIONS

855. **Barnaby.** 30 min. Production Companies: Yorkin and Lear. Producers: Bud Yorkin and Norman Lear. Writer: George Tibbles. A completed pilot based on the comic strip about a little boy named Barnaby who has an imaginary friend named Mr. O'Malley, who resembles W.C. Fields, that only he can see. Starred Sorrell Brooke, Allan Melvin, Jan Shutan, and Frankie Kabott.

856. **Barney.** 30 min. Production Company: Screen Gems. Director: Hy Averback. Producer: Hy Averback. Writer: Shelly Berman. Jim Hutton is a traveling salesman roaming the midwest whose young wife, Pat Smith, spends a lot of time alone – and a lot of time being hit on by men.

857. **Man Named McGee.** 30 min. Production Companies: United Artists and General Foods. Producer: Don McGuire. Writer: Don McGuire. Jeremy Slate plays a man who inherits a tropical island.

858. **Marty.** Production Company: Screen Gems. Executive Producer: Harold Hecht. Producer: Tom Sackheim. Based on Paddy Chayefsky's 1953 episode of *Kraft Television Theatre*, which starred Rod Steiger, and the subsequent movie starring Ernest Borgnine, which won Oscars for best screenplay, best direction and best actor. The proposed series would be the story of a lonely butcher who finds himself getting into trouble whenever he reaches out for affection. Starred Tom Bosley, Dick Balduzzi and Abigail Shelton.

859. **Meet Maggie Mulligan.** 30 min. Production Companies: United Artists and General Foods. Producer: Don McGuire. Director: Don McGuire. Janet Leigh is a New York commercial artist.

860. **Mr. Belvedere. 30 min.** Airdate: 7/12/65. Production Companies: 20th Century Fox and General Foods. Director: Fred De Cordova. Producer: Richard Sale. Writer: Richard Sale. Yet another attempt to translate the Clifton Webb movies about a wise-cracking butler to television. Victor Buono stars this time, and Mr. Belvedere is now an elderly gentleman who babysits for a young couple. The kids love him because he seems to know everything. *Cast:* Victor Buono (as Lynn Belvedere), Debbie Paine (Lily Van Cleve), Louise Troy (Mrs. Van Cleve), Harry Bellaver (Harry), Pamela Truman (Miss Briggs), Marty Brill (Mooney).

861. **The Shady Acres Mob.** 30 min. Production Company: Universal Television. Producer: Ed Montagne. Director: Ed Montagne. Writer: Roland Kibbee. Inspired by the movie *The Lavender Hill Mob.* A bunch of elderly people try to prove life is still interesting and get into trouble. Starred John McIntire, Andrew Prine, Spring Byington, Jeanette Nolan, and Jack La Rue as himself.

862. The previously listed pilot *The Smothers Brothers* became the series of the same name.

863. The pilot **Sybil, #822,** was previously duplicated here in error.

864. **Which Way to the Mecca, Jack?** 30 min. Writer: William Peter Blatty. Producer: Harry Ackerman. Based on Blatty's book about a Middle East king who is a swinger and uses American aid to build his harem to the consternation of the U.S. emissary who is supposed to control the money.

1966–1967

865. **Ace of the Mounties.** Production Company: Four Star. Ron Hussman stars as a bumbling mountie whose dog always makes sure he doesn't screw things up too bad. Joan Blondell costars as the mountie's girlfriend.

866. **The Clumbsies.** Production Company: Universal Television. Producer: Frank Rosenberg. Joan Staley stars as the chief clutz in a family of clutzes.

867. **Friends, Romans and Countrymen.** Production Company: United Artists. Creators: Wayne and Schuster. Producer: Bob Sweeney. Jack Carter stars in this sitcom set in ancient Rome and inspired by *A Funny Thing Happened on the Way to the Forum.*

868. **Jan and Dean Show.** Production Company: 20th Century Fox. Producer: William Asher. The two popular singers play two college students who, with their female manager, go on a nationwide concert tour in a pilot inspired by *A Hard Day's Night.*

869. **Little Leatherneck.** 30 min. Airdate: 7/20/66. Production Company: Paramount Television. Creator: Bob Finkel. Theme: "Little Leatherneck" by Donna Butterworth. Aired as episode of *Summer Fun.* Scott Brady stars as a widowed Marine Sergeant raising his tomboy daughter, played by Donna Butterworth. *Cast:* Donna Butterworth (as Cindy Fenton), Scott Brady (Sgt. Mike Fenton), Sue Ane Langdon (Delores), Jean Innes (Miss Raymond), Ned Glass (Mess Sergeant).

870. **McNab's Lab.** 30 min. Airdate: 7/22/66. Production Company: United Artists. Director: John Rich. Producer: George Burns. Writers: Norman Paul and William Burns. Aired as episode of *Summer Fun.* Cliff Arquette stars as Andrew McNab, a mild mannered druggist who creates weird inventions at night—inventions that always get the widower and his kids (Sherry Alberoni, David Bailey) in trouble. *Cast:* Cliff Arquette (as Andrew McNab), Sherry Alberoni (Ellen McNab), David Bailey (Timmy McNab), Paul Smith (Harvey Baxter), Elisha Cook (Coach), Jan Crawford (Steve Wilson), Eleanor Audley (Mother-in-law), Jonathon Hole (Nichols), Peter Lazer (Robert Harrison), Art Passarella (Umpire), Dee Carroll (Martha), Gary Owens (Henry).

871. **The Pirates of Flounder Bay.** 30 min. Airdate: 8/26/66. Production Company: Selmur Productions. Producer: William Wright. The misadventures of bumbling pirate Barnaby Kidd (William Cort) and his crew of idiots. *Cast:* William Cort

(as Barnaby Kidd), Basil Rathbone (Governor), Keenan Wynn (Capt. Jack Slash), Harold Peary (Mayor Abner Bunker), Bridget Hanley (Molly Bunker), Jack Soo (Sidney), Charles Dierkop (Taggert), Burt Mustin (Flint), Jim Connell (Wimple), Peter Bonerz (Chips), Jim Begg (Lookout).

872. **Sedgewick Hawk-Styles: Prince of Danger.** 30 min. Production Company: Ashmont Productions. Executive Producer: William Asher. Writers: Larry Cohen and Bud Freeman. Paul Lynde stars as a bumbling Sherlock Holmes-ish detective in Victorian England. Costarred Hermione Baddeley, Liam Redmond, and Maurice Ballimore.

873. **The Surfers.** Production Company: Filmways. Director: Barry Shear. Producer: Al Simon. Inspired by the popular "Beach Party" films, this sitcom pilot would revolve around a group of teenagers who spend all their time at the beach.

874. **Yankee Stay Here.** Production Company: MGM. Executive Producer: Alan Courtney. Producer: Jerry Thorpe. Writer: Arne Sultan. Jeremy Slate, in a role originally tailored for Chad Everett, is an American air force officer who leads a group of inept Italian partisans behind enemy lines during World War II. Courtney remembers screening it for ABC executives. "From the uproarious laughter, I knew I had a hit in the first few minutes," he recalls. "By the middle, I knew I could raise the price. When the lights came up, the executives had tears in their eyes. One of 'em told me 'it's the best pilot I've seen in years.' I was thrilled. Then he said 'shame we can't use it. We got savaged by Italians who didn't like the way they were portrayed in *The Untouchables*. We don't want to go through that again. Great pilot though, a riot.'"

ABC / DRAMA

875. **Attack.** 60 min. Production Company: Selmur Productions. Producer: Gene Leavitt. Gary Conway and Warren Oates star as Marines in the South Pacific during World War II.

876. **The Cliff Dwellers.** 60 min. Airdate: 8/26/66. Production Company: Bing Crosby Productions. Director: Boris Sagal. Producer: Irving Elman. Writer: David W. Rintels. Music: Lalo Schifrin. Bert Convy, Hal Holbrook, Carol Rossen, Beverlee McKinsey, Lee Allen, James Beck, Robert Hooks, and Terence Logan star in this precursor to *The Big Chill*. This is an urban social drama that picks up the lives of several college chums ten years after graduation as they mourn the suicide of one of their friends.

877. **Dangerous Days of Kiowa Jones.** 83 min. Airdate: 12/25/66. Production Company: MGM. Director: Alex March. Producers: David Karr, Max E. Youngstein, and Hank Moonjean. Writers: Frank Fenton and Robert E. Thompson, from the novel by Clifford Adams. Music: Samuel Matlovsky. Theme: Larry Kolber and Steve Karliski, performed by Hank Williams, Jr. Robert Horton is a drifter deputized by a dying lawman to take two killers to prison. *Cast:* Robert Horton (as Kiowa Jones), Diane Baker (Amilia Rathmore), Sal Mineo (Bobby Jack Wilkes), Nehemiah Persoff (Skoda), Gary Merrill (Marshall Duncan), Robert Harris (Dobie), Lonny Chapman (Roy), Royal Dano (Otto), Zalman King (Jesse), Harry Dean Stanton (Jelly), Val Avery (Morgan).

878. **From Here to Eternity.** 30 min. Production Company: Screen Gems. Producer: Matthew Rapf. Darren McGavin and Sally Kellerman star in this pilot for a twice-weekly serial based on the James Jones novel and the hit movie. Though this didn't sell, a decade later NBC tried it as a series—and failed. *Cast:* Darren McGavin (as Sgt. Milt Warden), Roger Davis (Pvt. Robert E. Lee Prewitt), Edmund Gilbert (Capt. Holmes), Tom Nardini (Pvt. Angelo Maggio), also, Sally Kellerman.

879. **The Happeners.** 60 min. Airdate: 3/17/67. Production Company: Plautus Productions. Director: David Green. Producer: Herbert Brodkin. Creator/Writer: Ernest Kinoy. Music: Bob Bowers, J. Butler. According to *Variety* (3/23/66), then-ABC President Tom Moore passed on this sitcom, which *Variety* described as "three folk-rock youngsters on the Greenwich Village expresso circuit…in a style much like a Richard Lester 'Beatles' flick," because it was just "too hip." *Variety* said "not in any of video's big years of sausage production has anything so hip and contemporary reached the network audition circuit." It starred Craig Smith, Chris Ducey and Susannah Jordan and guest starred Lou Jacobi, Lou Gossett and the Dick Clark Five. ABC spent $400,000 on this pilot, *Variety* said, "and bought itself the unseen hit of the year." It eventually showed up in syndication but failed to stir up any attention.

880. **House of Wax (aka Chamber of Horrors).** 99 min. Production Company: Warner Bros. Television. Director: Hy Averback. Producer: Hy Averback. Writer: Stephen Kandel. Music: William Lava. Wilfred Hyde-White starred in this pilot based on the 1953 motion picture that, once it was rejected as a series, was also released as a feature film, where it fared no better. Despite such cinematic gimmicks as the "Horror Horn and Fear Flasher," it was quickly (and justifiably) forgotten. Steven Scheuer says in *Movies on TV* that viewers will "laugh in the wrong places"

and that "Patrick O'Neal rolls his eyes a great deal as the notorious madman" killing people in Baltimore circa 1880. It also starred Jeanette Nolan, Laura Devon, Suzy Parker, Cesare Danova, Patrice Wymore, Marie Windsor and special guest star, Tony Curtis.

881. **The Long Hunt of April Savage.** 30 min. Production Company: Desilu. Producer: Gene Roddenberry. Creator/Writer: Sam Rolfe. Robert Lansing as a vigilante in the old West searching for the desperados who murdered his family. This was set for ABC's 1966 schedule but was yanked at the last minute and replaced it with *The Man Who Never Was*...which also starred Robert Lansing.

882. **Mr. Paracelsus, Who Are You?** Production Company: Screen Gems. Creator: Peter Tewksbury. A dramatic vehicle for Michael Rennie that would feature both comedy and suspense.

883. **One-Eyed Jacks Are Wild.** 60 min. Production Company: Plautus Productions. Director: Frank Schaffner. Producer: Herbert Brodkin. Writers: Albert Ruben and David Shaw. George Grizzard starred as an American who looks just like the king of a fictional European kingdom. When the king is assassinated, the American is asked to impersonate him. Shot on location in England.

884. **Roaring Camp.** 60 min. Airdate: 9/4/66. Production Company: Bing Crosby Productions. Producer: Lamont Johnson. Aired as an episode of *Preview Tonight*, a series that began with opening: "Each year many of the new shows developed for television fail to make the network grade even though they are entertaining and well produced. *Tonight's* pilot film is one of these. We invite you behind-the-scenes to see what you think of 'Roaring Camp' on *Preview Tonight*." The adventures of a widow who runs a Colorado frontier town during the Gold Rush with the help of the U.S. Marshall and a gunslinger. *Cast:* Katherine Justice (as Rachel), Richard Bradford (Marshall Walker), Jim McMullan (Cain), Ian Hendry (Angus), Bibi Osterwald (Mary), Mike Wagner (Brady), Donald Contreras (Boy).

885. **Search, Pursue, Destroy (aka Pursue and Destroy).** 60 min. Airdate: 8/14/66. Production Company: Four Star. Director: Don Taylor. Executive Producer: Thomas J. McDermott. Producers: Ivan Goff and Ben Roberts. Writers: Ivan Goff, Ben Roberts. Creators: Ivan Goff and Ben Roberts. Van Williams as a submarine commander in World War II who, in the pilot, tries to prove faulty torpedoes, and not his men, are to blame for a botched mission. *Cast:* Van Williams (as Commander Russ Enright), Paul Comi (Lt. Barney Redesko), Jessica Walter (Vivien Scott), David Thorpe (Lt. James Ford), Dame Edith Evans (Iris Milbanke),

Ward Wood (Chief Alex Jacobs), Henry Wilcoxon (Admiral Rockland), Dee Pollack (Chip Malloy), Thad Williams (Lonnie Cole).

886. **Silver Springs (aka Mike and the Mermaid).** 30 min. Airdate: 1/5/68. Production Company: Robert Maxwell Productions. Producer: Rudy Abel. Aired as an episode of *Off to See the Wizard*. A boy, living with his parents and his grandfather, meets a mermaid who followed a school of fish into Florida waters and now can't find her way home. *Cast:* Kevin Brodie (as Mike Malone), Jerri Lynn Fraser (Mermaid), Med Flory (Jim Malone), Rachel Ames (Nellie Malone), also, Dan Tompkins.

CBS / COMEDY

887. **Daphne.** 30 min. Production Company: CBS Productions. Producer: Morton De Costa. Maureen O'Hara is an "Aunt Mame type" who barges into her children's New Jersey home and refuses to leave.

888. **Green for Danger (aka Green for Action).** 30 min. Production Company: Universal Television. Producer: Don Weis. Larry Blyden is a bumbling insurance investigator who always gets into trouble but, despite his clumsiness, manages to get the job done.

889. **The Help (aka At Your Service).** 30 min. Production Company: Universal. Producer: Sherwood Schwartz. The wacky adventures of servants working for a wealthy family. Comedy would strike a similar vein as Schwartz's *Gilligans Island*. Godfrey Cambridge and Phil Silvers were among the stars.

890. **The Hoofer.** 30 min. Airdate: 8/15/66. Director: Jack Donohue. Producer: Jack Donohue. Writer: Ed Jurist. Donald O'Connor must have really been aching for a series. This flop pilot, one of several he did in this period, paired O'Connor with Soupy Sales as two singing-and-dancing performers on the vaudeville circuit in the 1920s. *Cast:* Donald O'Connor (as Donald Dugan), Soupy Sales (Fred Brady), Jerome Cowan (Brainsley Gordon), Jackie Coogan (Finnegan), Cliff Norton (Wake), Jolene Brand (Wanda), Carole Cook (Nurse), Ray Kellogg (Orderly), Ned Glass (Professor).

891. **Kelly's Kingdom.** 30 min. Production Company: Universal Television. Producer: Ed Montagne. Shecky Green stars as a Missouri butcher who discovers he owns some land that, through a loophole in the old Louisiana Purchase, is not governed by the U.S. He declares his own nation, sends an ambassador to Washington, a delegate to the United Nations, and fancies himself a world power.

892. **The Mouse That Roared.** 30 min. Production Company: Screen Gems. Producer: Jack Arnold. Sid Caesar plays three different roles in this pilot based on the 1959 Peter Sellers movie and the Leonard Wibberly novel about a mythical kingdom declaring war on the United States in order to lose – and then receive foreign aid. Arnold directed the original movie version. Costars included Joyce Jameson and Richard Deacon.

893. **Off We Go.** 30 min. Airdate: 9/5/66. Production Company: Official Productions. Director: Don Weis. Producer: Robert Blees. Writers: Bob Kaufman and William P. Fox. Aired as an episode of *Vacation Playhouse*. Michael Burns is a sixteen-year-old who, through various mishaps and confusions, becomes a Colonel in World War II. *Cast:* Michael Burns (as Rod Ryan), Dick Foran (Jefferson Dale), Nancy Kovack (Lt. Sue Chamberlin), Ann Jillian (Debbie Trowbridge), Dick Curtis (Capt. Julian Imbro), Alan Sues (Lt. Col. Jefferson Dale), Monroe Arnold (Major Stivers), Elisabeth Fraser (Josie Ryan), Dave Willock (Carl Ryan), Berkeley Harris (Lt. Staley).

894. **Operation Razzle-Dazzle (aka Somewhere in Italy, Company B).** 60 min. Airdate: 8/21/66. Production Company: Screen Gems. Director/Producer/Writer: Danny Arnold. Robert Reed heads a group of American soldiers who get trapped behind German lines in Italy during World War II who enlist the local folks to help them battle the enemy. *Cast:* Robert Reed (as Lt. John Leahy), Harold J. Stone (Sgt. Wilkie Krantz), Vassili Lambrinos (Paulo Pietri), Barbara Shelley (Selena), also, John Van Dreelen, Renzo Cesana, Richard Evans, Tim O'Kelley, Jack Colvin, and Frank Puglia.

895. **Penelope Beware.** 30 min. Production Company: Talent Associates. Producer: David Susskind. Writer: Arne Sultan. Nina Foch is a rich girl whose fortune will go to her servants if she dies of natural causes – and the butlers, maids, and groundskeepers try to help nature along.

896. **Perils of Pauline.** 99 min. Production Company: CBS Productions. Producer: Herbert Leonard. Directors: Herbert B. Leonard and Joshua Shelley. Pat Boone is a millionaire who travels the world searching for Pamela Austin, a girl he knew in the orphanage, who is being chased by evil Terry-Thomas. When this got nowhere as a series, it was expanded and released as a feature, where it met a similar response. Edward Everett Horton and Hamilton Camp guest starred. Pamela Austin and the concept were pitched again next season as a demo film and, the season after that, in a whole new pilot.

897. The Recruiters. 30 min. Production Company: Desilu. Dick Curtis, Elliot Reid, and Dick Patterson are Army, Navy, and Air Force recruiters who share a tiny booth on Times Square.

898. Separate Lives. 30 min. Production Company: MGM. Producer: Norman Felton. The lives of a young man and young woman in adjoining Greenwich Village apartments. Shelley Fabares starred.

899. Sidekicks. 30 min. Production Company: Screen Gems. Producer: Peter Tewskbury. Creator: Richard Alan Simmons. A comedy western starring Burr de Benning as one of two cowboys roaming the West.

900. Three on an Island. 30 min. Airdate: 8/27/65. Director: Vincent Sherman. Producer: Hal Kanter. Writer: Hal Kanter. Aired on *Vacation Playhouse*. Three girls on the "island of Manhattan" become part owner of a prizefighter's (Jody McCrea) contract and try to manage his career. *Cast:* Pamela Tiffin (as Taffy Warren), Julie Newmar (Kris Meeker), Monica Moran (Andrea Franks), Jody McCrea (Julius "Bulldog" Sweetley), Sheila Bromley (Martha Sweetley), Rhodes Reason (Perry), Ned Glass (Riley), Ron Husman (Glen).

901. Where's Everett? 30 min. Airdate: 4/18/66. Production Companies: Screen Gems and Proctor & Gamble Productions. Director: Gene Nelson. Producer: Ed Simmons. Writer: Ed Simmons. Music: Frank De Vol. Alan Alda is a young father who goes to get the morning paper and finds that an invisible baby has been left on his doorstep by an alien family, which his wife and kids gladly adopt and name Everett. *Cast:* Alan Alda (as Arnold Barker), Patricia Smith (Sylvia Barker), Doreen Miller (Lizzie Barker), Nicholas Coster (Dr. Paul Jellico), Frank De Vol (Murdock), Robert Cleaves (Milkman).

CBS / DRAMA

902. The Uninvited (aka The Black Cloak; aka Dark Intruder). 59 min. Production Company: Universal Television. Director: Harvey Hart. Producer: Jack Laird. Writer: Barre Lyndon. A pilot for a proposed series called *The Black Cloak*, this was shot as an episode of *Alfred Hitchcock Presents* initially called "The Uninvited," which was retitled "Dark Intruder" and released theatrically, despite its short running time, in 1965. Leslie Nielsen starred as an occult expert helping the S.F.P.D. nab a psycho killer. The pilot also starred Peter Mark Richman, Werner Klemperer, Gilbert Green, Charles Bolender, and Judi Meredith. Critic Leonard Maltin, in his compilation of movie reviews, praised it as "a near flawless supernatural thriller...a one-of-a-kind movie."

903. **The Insider.** 60 min. Production Company: United Artists. Producer: Irving Gitlin. Ralph Meeker and Sean Garrison are two undercover agents working for a secret government agency.

904. **The Iron Man.** 60 min. Producer: Jack Chertok. The adventures of two railroad men (Tom Simcox and Mike Whitney) in the old West.

905. **Walk in the Night (aka Nightmare in Chicago; aka Nightwatch).** 60 min. Airdate: 7/15/68. Production Company: CBS Productions. Director: Robert Altman. Producers: Robert Altman and Raymond Wagner. Writers: Brian McKay and Robert Eggenweiler, from a story by Robert Altman. Aired as episode of *Premiere.* Carroll O'Connor and Andrew Duggan are private eyes working for G.L.I.B. (Great Lakes Interstate Bureau) who look for a Swedish crewman in Chicago who jumped ship – without knowing that his suitcase contains a bomb that will explode in a few hours. This film was shot entirely at night on location. *Cast:* Andrew Duggan (as Owen Kerr), Carroll O'Connor (James Van Ducci), Michael Murphy (William Smith), Jacqueline Betton (Ellie Van Ducci), Gunnar Helstrom (Granstrom), Albert Paulsen (Linde), Karl Swenson (Erickson), Linda Wallenberg (Kathryn), Jim Lantz (McGrago), Don Mask (Sgt. Ford).

NBC / COMEDY

906. **Brilliant Benjamin Boggs.** 30 min. Airdate: 3/30/66. Production Company: Universal Television. Producer: Jack Laird. Writer: Nathaniel Curtis. Aired as an episode of *Bob Hope Chrysler Theatre.* Donald O'Connor is a brilliant but unlucky scientist who always gets into trouble. *Cast:* Donald O'Connor (as Benjamin Boggs), Emily Banks (Julie Thayer), Broderick Crawford (Bill Thayer), Susan Silo (Nancy Prentice), Eddie Mayehoff (Fred Thompson), Dick Sargent (Dick O'Hara).

907. **15 Blocks.** 30 min. Producer: Sheldon Leonard. Two episodes of this sitcom were shot starring Dean Jones as a beat cop who encounters interesting and unusual people. Apparently, NBC had a 13 episode commitment to this project – but backed out of it. Originally proposed to the networks in 1964 with Jan Murray as the star.

908. **Groober Hill.** 30 min. Production Company: Screen Gems. Creator/Producer: Ed Simmons. Kaye Stevens stars as a would-be actress who goes to work for a small-town TV station. Stubby Kaye costarred.

909. **Li'l Abner.** 30 min. Airdate: 9/5/67. Director: Coby Ruskin. Producer: Howard Leeds. Writer: Al Capp, from his comic strip. The antics of the hillbilly citizens of Dogpatch, U.S.A. *Cast:* Sammy Jackson (as Li'l Abner), Judy Canova (Mammy Yokum), Robert Reed (Senator Cod), Jerry Lester (Pappy Yokum), Jean-nine Riley (Daisy Mae).

910. **Paleface.** Production Company: Universal Television. Producer: Howard Christie. Based on the Bob Hope film, this pilot featuring folk singers Chad and Jeremy as British theatrical agents roaming the old West, was envisioned as a spin-off of *Laredo.*

911. **Pet Set.** 30 min. Production Company: Warner Bros. Television. Barbara Rush is a veterinarian who treats her patients at home, causing all kinds of chaos and confusion with her family – especially for her husband, a straight-laced lawyer.

912. **Ready and Willing (aka Kicks; aka Ready, Willing, and Pamela).** 60 and 30 min. Airdates: 10/13/68 (NBC/long) and 4/22/74 (CBS/short). Production Company: Universal Television. Director: Dick Wesson. Producer: Jack Laird. Writer: Lawrence Marks. Music: Hal Mooney. Originally aired as a 60-minute episode of *Bob Hope Chrysler Theatre*, this was reworked and edited down to 30 minutes for the pilot, which aired six years later on *Three in One*, a CBS flop pilot showcase. The pilot featured Melodie Johnson as a rich girl with a criminology degree and Jack Weston and Joe Flynn as two incompetent big-city cops who stumble through cases with her. The original pilot featured Don Gordon, Mickey Rooney, and Harold J. Stone as well. *Cast:* Joe Flynn (as Sgt. Joe Ready), Jack Weston (Sgt. Herbert Willing), Melodie Johnson (Pamela Stevens), John Zaremba (Lt. Perkins), Susan Saint James (Julia Prescott), Lola Albright (Wilma O'Brien), Kathleen Freeman (Mrs. Jonas), Fabian Dean (Archie), Ned Glass (Sammy), Larry Watson (Chauffeur), Harry Swoger (Bartender), Lloyd Kino (Houseboy), Drew Harmon (Kirby), Tiger Joe Marsh (Truck Driver).

913. **Run, Jack, Run.** 30 min. Airdate: 7/20/70. Production Company: Universal Television. Producer: Ed Montagne. David Astor and Adam Keefe star in this *Fugitive* spoof as two men who are framed for an attempted mafia murder and would spend the series running from mob killers and police. This flop pilot is nearly identical to the CBS 66–67 pilot *Run, Buddy, Run*, which became a series starring Jack Sheldon – as a man who overhears plans for a mafia murder and spends his time running away from mobsters. This flop pilot eventually aired on NBC. *Cast:* David Astor (as Jack Perry), Adam Keefe (Chester Blinsol),

Robert Middleton (Smiley John Grazioni), Anthony Caruso (Lefty), Marilyn Hanold (Girl).

914. **The Unpardonables (aka Plotkin Prison, We Love You).** 30 min. Production Company: NBC Productions. Director: Barry Shear. Don Rickles heads a group of inmates who, although eligible for parole, do all they can to stay in prison – where they enjoy the easy life.

915. **Weekend.** 30 min. Airdate: 9/9/67. Production Company: United Artists. Director: Rod Amateau. Producer: Rod Amateau. Writers: David Davis and Rod Amateau. A comedy about high school kids who spend their weekends at the beach. *Cast:* Tim Matheson (as Randy), Rick Kellman (Eldon), Lorie Martin (Eunice), Tony Dow (Norm).

916. **We'll Take Manhattan.** 30 min. Airdate: 4/30/67. Production Companies: Hanna Barbera Productions and Procter & Gamble Productions. Director: James Neilson. Executive Producers: William Hanna and Joseph Barbera. Producer: Chuck Stewart. Writers: Larry Markes and Michael Morris. Dwayne Hickman stars as a naive attorney who helps a 140-year-old Indian chief and his family regain their lost legal rights to downtown Manhattan. *Cast:* Dwayne Hickman (as Lucas Greystone), Allan Melvin (Eagle Eye), Ben Blue (Chief Irontail), Leslie Perkins (Laughing Brook), Walter Wolf King (Harrison Conroy).

NBC / DRAMA

917. **Holloway's Daughters.** 60 min. Airdate: 5/11/66. Director: Ida Lupino. Aired as an episode of *Bob Hope Chrysler Theatre*. Robert Young is Nick Holloway, a private eye who comes out of retirement because he doesn't like the way his son George (David Wayne) is running the business. So now Nick is driving George nuts – and solving crimes again with the able assistance of his two granddaughters (Brooke Bundy and Barbara Hershey). Marion Moses plays George's wife, and Ellen Corby is George's secretary. Guest stars included Bruce Gordon and Meg Wyllie.

918. **Jigsaw (aka The Faceless Man).** 60 min. Airdate: 5/4/66. Production Company: Universal Television. Producer: Stanley Chase. Director: Stuart Rosenberg. Aired as an episode of *Bob Hope Chrysler Theatre*. Jack Lord stars as an undercover secret agent. Co-starred Charles Drake, Shirley Knight, and Jack Weston.

919. **Journey Into Fear.** 60 min. Production Company: Greenway Productions. Executive Producer: William Dozier. Producer: Joan Harrison. Writer: Eric Ambler, from his novel. Jeffrey Hunter stars as a scientist who is forced into working for the C.I.A. The novel was also the basis for the 1942 film written by, and starring, Orson Welles and Joseph Cotten.

920. **Pay the Piper (aka One Embezzlement and Two Margaritas).** 60 min. Airdate: 5/18/66. Production Company: Universal Television. Director: Robert Ellis Miller. Producer: Frank Rosenberg. Writer: Luthor Davis, from a story by Howard Brown. Aired as an episode of *Bob Hope's Chrysler Theatre*. This is yet another attempt to sell Jack Kelly as an insurance investigator/private eye. Costarred Michael Rennie, Antoinette Bower, Jocelyn Lane, Karen Jensen, Matt Clark, John Holland, Nico Minardos, and Michael St. Clair.

921. **Police Story.** 30 min. Airdate: 9/8/67. Production Company: Desilu. Director: Vincent McEveety. Producer/Writer: Gene Roddenberry. Steve Ihnat, Rafer Johnson and Gary Clark are three cops who work on special assignment for the police commissioner. Grace Lee Whitney and DeForest Kelly guest starred in the pilot and both later appeared in Roddenberry's *Star Trek*. Questor, the name of Clark's character, became the title of a Roddenberry pilot in the mid-70s. *Cast:* Steve Ihnat (as Capt. James Paige), Rafer Johnson (Lt. Roy Haggerty), Gary Clark (Questor), Malachi Throne (Garrison), DeForest Kelley (Lab Chief), Ann Atmore (Dorian), Justin Smith (Bennett), Grace Lee Whitney (Sgt. Lilly Monroe), Les Brown, Jr. (Folsom).

922. **Pursuit (aka Don't Wait for Tomorrow).** 60 min. Airdate: 4/19/67. Production Company: Universal Television. Director: Harvey Hart. Executive Producer: Roy Huggins. Producer: Jo Swerling, Jr. Writer: Frank Fenton, from a story by John Thomas James. Aired as an episode of *Bob Hope Chrysler Theatre*. A reporter is hired to roam the world seeking a villain who always seems one step ahead of him. The pilot starred Rossano Brazzi, Juliet Mills, Donnelly Rhodes, Eva Soreny, Lily Valenty, Telly Savalas, and Will Kuluva.

923. **The Savages.** 60 min. Production Company: Four Star. Producer: Collier Young. Robert Pickering stars as a young attorney who returns to his small-town home to start his practice. Costarred Jeanette Nolan, John McIntire, and Warren Stevens.

924. **The Sheriff.** 30 min. Production Company: Arcola Productions. Creator/Producer: Aaron Rosenberg. Writer: Paul King. Gilbert Roland is the sheriff of a

small beach community who, with the help of his young deputy (James Stacy), tries to work within the surfer subculture that thrives there.

925. **Stranded.** 60 min. Production Company: Universal Television. Director: Leon Benson. Executive Producer: Frank Price. Producer: Frank P. Rosenberg. Writer: Dick Nelson, from a story by Dick Nelson and Larry Marcus. Music: Jack Elliott. Richard Egan leads a group of plane crash survivors, lost in the Andes amid ancient Inca ruins, who must form their own civilization until they are rescued. Costars included Fernando Lamas as a murderer being escorted back to Bolivia by a cop; Peter Graves as a writer and big-game hunter; Karen Sharpe as a stewardess; Joby Baker as a famous singer and actor; Harry Guardino as an ex-alcoholic comic on the way to his big comeback gig; Julie Adams as a shy school teacher; Leonard Nimoy as a Miami lawyer, and Otis Young as a black doctor. Producer Price loved this concept, and would revive it in several dramatic and comedic incarnations in following years, including *Lost Flight* (1969) with Lloyd Bridges and *Stranded* (1976) with Kevin Dobson. The pilot was released theatrically as *Valley of Mystery* with 40 minutes of extra footage that includes entirely new scenes with Lois Nettleton and ends with the castaways getting rescued. The film credits the screenplay to Richard Neal and Lowell Barrington, from a story by Neal and Larry Marcus. Joseph Leyteys is credited as the director of the film, Harry Tattelman as the producer. *Cast:* Richard Egan (as Wade Cochran), Peter Graves (Ben Barstow), Karen Sharpe (Connie Lane), Joby Baker (Pete Patton), Harry Guardino (Joey O'Neill), Julie Adams (Joan Simon), Fernando Lamas (Francisco Rivera), Lee Patterson (Dino Doretti), Leonard Nimoy (Spence Atherton), Otis Young (Dr. John Quincy), Lisa Gaye (Margo Yorke).

926. **Sullivan's Place (aka Sullivan's Empire).** 60 min. and 85 min. Production Company: Universal Television. Directors: Harvey Hart and Thomas Carr. Producer: Frank Price. Writer: Frank Chase. Three brothers (Martin Milner, Don Quine, and Linden Chiles) go to South America to look for their father (Arch Johnson), who abandoned them when they were children and who now has disappeared in a jungle plane crash. While searching for him, the brothers build a ranch and settle there. Clu Gulager, Bernie Hamilton, and Karen Jensen guest starred. Additional footage was shot and tacked onto the 60 minute pilot, which was subsequently retitled and released as a feature film.

927. **The Sweet Life (aka Who's Watching the Fleshpot?)** 60 min. Airdate: 3/7/66. Production Companies: Universal Television and Public Arts. Executive Producer:

Roy Huggins. Producer: Jo Swerling, Jr. Writer: John Thomas James. A spin-off of *Run for Your Life*. Bobby Darin is an American who opens a travel agency on the French Riviera and manages to get involved in all kinds of adventure. Costarred Eve Arden, Jeff Corey, and Davey Davison.

928. **Tarzan.** 60 min. Production Company: Weintraub Productions. Mike Henry, the "Tarzan" of the movies, would star in this series aimed at "contemporizing" the man of the jungle. In this version, Tarzan is a well-educated "man of today" who hates city life and opts for life in the jungle.

929. **This Gun for Hire (aka Above the Law).** 60 min. Airdate: 1/13/66. Production Company: Universal Television. A spin-off from *Laredo*. Jack Lord stars as a tough gunslinger in the old West. Costarred Lola Albright and John Kellogg.

930. **Three Coins in the Fountain.** 30 min. Airdate: 8/10/70. Production Companies: 20th Century Fox and General Foods. Director: Hal Kanter. Executive Producer: Hal Kanter. Producer: Robert L. Jacks. Writers: Hal Kanter and Mel Shavelson. Music: Jeff Alexander. This pilot, based on the film, sat on the shelf for four years before being aired. Cynthia Pepper, Joanna Moore, and Yvonne Craig star as three American girls living in Rome. *Cast:* Cynthia Pepper (as Maggie Wilson), Yvonne Craig (Dorothy), Joanna Moore (Ruth), Antony Alda (Gino), Nino Castelnuovo (Count Giorgio).

931. **Three for Danger.** 60 min. Airdate: 9/8/67. Production Company: Four Star. Director: William A. Graham. Producer: Warren Duff. Writers: Ivan Goff, Ben Roberts, and Warren Duff. Larry Pennell, Alejandro Rey, and Charles Carlson are three soldiers-of-fortune roaming the world on a schooner. *Cast:* Larry Pennell (as Chris), Alejandro Rey (Alan), Charles Carlson (Simon), Joanna Pettet (Serena), Jason Evers (Kirk), John Van Drelen (Lassiter).

932. **The Wonderful Years (aka New Doctor in Town).** 60 min. Airdate: 4/5/66. Production Companies: MGM and Arena Productions. Executive Producer: Norman Felton. Producer: Douglas Benton. A spin-off from *Dr. Kildare*. This series would have featured 16 regular characters, the hero being a young doctor who returns to his small-town home to start his practice. Audrey Totter and Sidney Blackmer were signed for the series.

INDEPENDENT PRODUCTIONS

933. **High Noon.** 30 min. Production Companies: Four Star and General Foods. Writers: James Warner Bellah and Robert Enders. Based on the 1952 film starring

Gary Cooper, though his character was not used in this pilot. Instead, Peter Fonda played the character's adult son. Katy Jurado costarred.

934. Rambling Wreck from Discotheque aka **Man in the Square Suit.** 30 min. Airdate: 4/22/66. Production Companies: Jack Chertok Productions and Bristol-Meyers. Producer: Jack Chertok. Writers: Frank Peppiatt and John Aylesworth. Paul Dooley plays a TV writer who reluctantly agrees to produce a rock-and-roll show for teenagers. Cast: Paul Dooley (Frank Johnson), Jan Shutan (Marilyn Johnson), Diane Sherry (Nancy Johnson), Astrid Warner (Maxine), Michael Blodgett (Gary Young).

1967-1968

935. **Dilby.** 30 min. Production Company: Selmer Productions. Producer: Marc Merson. Writers: Ben Joelson and Art Baer. Paul Ford plays the owner of a Manhattan repair shop who can fix machines better than he can the problems of his land-lady (Mabel Albertson), her daughter (Carole Demas) and her son-in-law (Bruce Hyde) and, of course, the problems of his own.

936. **Manley and the Mob.** 30 min. Production Company: Four Star. Producer: Fred De Cordova. Writers: Gerald Gardner and Dee Caruso. Paul Lynde is a dim-witted private eye. Costarred Nehemiah Persoff.

937. **The Medicine Men.** 30 min. Production Company: Screen Gems. Producer: Lester Colodny. Creator: Ed Simmons. The comedic adventures of six interns at an urban hospital. Starred Peter Haskell, E.J. Peaker, Stanley Beck, Fred Smoot, and Cathy Lewis.

938. **Mrs. Thursday.** 30 min. Production Company: Nepenthe Productions/Richard Crenna. Creator/Producer: Richard Crenna. Actor Richard Crenna devised this sitcom starring Joan Blondell as a maid who inherits a fortune and must learn to run a multi-million dollar business empire.

939. **Peace in the Family.** 30 min. Production Company: Screen Gems. Producer: Lester Colodny. Creator: Ed Simmons. Jack Albertson and Bibi Osterwald star as a couple who run a hardware story.

940. **The Pickle Brothers.** 30 min. Production Company: Four Star. Producers/Writers: Gerald Gardner and Dee Caruso. A vehicle for the comedy team The Uncalled for Three, whose members were Michael Mislov, Peter Lee, and Ronald Prince. The series would have portrayed them in modern-day antics modeled after the Marx Brothers movies.

941. **Rhubarb.** 30 min. Production Company: Goodson-Todman. Based on the novel by H. Allen Smith, which also inspired the 1951 movie starring Ray Milland. Groucho Marx is billionaire J. Paul Greedy, the richest man in the world and Sammy Jackson is his befuddled banker. In the pilot, Greedy has his will changed so that he will leave $2 million to an alley cat that he has befriended.

942. **Tay-Gar.** 30 min. Production Company: Screen Gems. Executive Producer: Harry Ackerman. Producer: Bob Claver. A *Tarzan* spoof starring former King of the Jungle Mike Henry.

943. **Three's a Crowd.** 30 min. Production Company: Screen Gems. Creators/Producers: Burt Schneider and Bob Rafelson. Bill Bixby stars as a man married to two women, neither of whom know he is two-timing them.

ABC / DRAMA

944. **Hannibal's Boy.** 60 min. Production Company: Banner Productions. Producer: Sy Weintraub. The adventures of a teenage boy who lives on an African game preserve with his father, Jason Evers, the game warden.

945. **Island of the Lost.** 60 min. Airdates: 11/10/67 and 11/17/67. Production Company: Ivan Tors. Director: John Floria. Executive Producer: Ivan Tors. Producer: John Floria. Aired as an episode of *Off to See the Wizard*. Richard Greene starred as a scientist who discovers a prehistoric world – not dinosaurs, but saber tooth tigers and the like which are cheaper to create and easier to shoot. Robin Mattson costarred as his ten-year-old daughter. Loosely based on the feature film.

946. **The Outside Man.** Production Company: Quinn Martin. This was a concept about a man imprisoned for a crime he didn't commit who, when released, devotes his life to helping others who are unjustly accused.

947. **Paul Pine.** Production Company: Quinn Martin. Based on the stories by Howard Brown, this concept features a private eye whose adventures would be more cerebral than most gumshoes on TV.

948. **Perils of Pauline.** 10 min. Production Company: Herbert Leonard Productions. Producer: Herbert Leonard. Writer: Mel Tolkin. Rising from the ashes of last season's flop *Pauline* pilot on CBS, this demonstration film showcases Pamela Austin in what would have been a contemporary reworking of the classic serial and another take on last year's flop pilot, which became the basis of a flop feature film. This project would resurface yet again next season, with a new 30 minute pilot, again starring Pamela Austin.

CBS / COMEDY

949. **Alfred of the Amazon.** 30 min. Airdate: 7/31/67. Production Company: Desilu. Director: Charles R. Rondeau. Producers: Herbert Solow and Arnie Rosen. Writer: Arnie Rosen. Wally Cox stars as the wimpish son of an American business tycoon, who

sends his spineless offspring to the Amazon to run a rubber plantation and prove himself as a man. *Cast:* Wally Cox (as Alfred), Allan Melvin (Willie), Mako (Simba), Susan Oden (Jennifer), Paul Hartman (Dr. Schwimmer), Leon Askin (Herr Futterman).

950. **Carol Channing Show.** 30 min. Production Company: Desilu/General Foods. Creators/Writers: Bob Carroll, Jr. and Madelyne Pugh Davis. Carol Channing is a small-town television show hostess who moves to New York, marries a mountie and looks for stardom.

951. **Doc.** 30 min. Production Company: Filmways. Producer: Jay Sommers. Writer: Jay Sommers. Creator: Jay Sommers. John McIntire is an old doctor in a small town who, planning to retire, takes in a young doctor (Eldon Quick) – and then keeps delaying his retirement. Regulars included Stu Erwin and Marilyn Devin. This was picked up by the network, yet never materialized. A recast, new pilot was done the following season on NBC.

952. **Eddie (aka Eddie Skinner; aka The Phil Silvers Show; aka Bel Air Patrol).** 30 min. Airdate: 8/5/71. Production Company: CBS. Director: Hy Averback. Producer: Irving Pincus. Creator/Writer: Larry Gelbart. Phil Silvers played a private patrolman working for the wealthy, the elite, and the famous who live in posh Bel Air. *Cast:* Phil Silvers (as Eddie Skinner), Fred Clark (Chief Pike), Frank Faylen (Patrolman Callahan), Edward Andrews (Mr. Milburn), Joanna Barnes (Sylvia), Patricia Barry (Mrs. Milburn), Nora Marlowe (Cook).

953. **My Boy Googie.** 30 min. Airdate: 7/24/67. Director: Ralph Levy. Producer: Herbert W. Browar. Writer: Bill Manhoff. Teddy Eccles is Googie, a precocious 12-year-old boy who constantly frustrates his parents (Jerry Van Dyke, Jeanne Ranier) and his sister (Pamela Dapo). Alice Pearce guest starred as Googie's music teacher.

954. **Operation Greasepaint.** 30 min. Airdate: 8/12/68. Production Company: MGM. Director: Bud Yorkin. Producer: Bud Yorkin. Writers: Johnny Wayne and Frank Schuster. Comics Jack Burns and Avery Schreiber costar as two entertainers-come-soldiers during World War II who are always bucking authority and getting into trouble. *Cast:* Avery Schrieber (as Spivak), Jack Burns (Minihane), Fred Willard (Bower), Johnny Haymer (Brown), Robert Fitch (Keller), Rex Allen, Jr. (Soldier), Ben Astar (General), Roger Newman (Wasserman), Karl Sadler (Guard), Bill Giorgio (Corporal), Chuck Privney (Chaplain), Robert Kaliban (Horton), Sam Capuano (DeGiullo), Arthur Adelson (Wilson).

955. **Out of the Blue.** 30 min. Airdate: 8/12/68. Production Company: CBS. Director: Sherman Marks. Producer: Sol Saks. Writer: Sol Saks. Shirley Jones, Barry Dennen, Carl Ballantine, and Marvin Kaplan are aliens from an over-populated planet who

come to earth to see whether or not they should move some of their people here. They befriend a physics professor living in Hollywood (John McMartin), who helps them understand our often confusing world. *Cast:* Shirley Jones (as Dr. Aphrodite), John McMartin (Professor Josh Enders), Carl Ballantine (Claude), Marvin Kaplan (Ethel), Barry Dennen (Solly), Richard Erdman (Murphy), Nydia Westman (Woman), Richard Jury (Man), John Hubbard (Captain), Rick Richards (Private).

956. **Shoestring Safari.** 30 min. Production Company: Van-Bernard Productions/Red Skelton. Producers: Dick Dorso and Bob Sweeney. Creator: Phil Sharp. Andy Devis and Kelly Jean Peters are a father and daughter who run a safari club in Africa where they swindle tourists by filling guns with blanks, filling the jungle with prerecorded animal noises, and pursuing a tame, elderly lion and billing the animal as a ferocious savage.

CBS / DRAMA

957. **Braddock.** 60 min. Airdate: 7/22/68. Production Company: 20th Century Fox. Director: Walter Doniger. Producer: Paul Monash. Writer: Paul Monash. A science-fiction/adventure about a private eye, played by Tom Simcox, who works in Los Angeles in 1977 and uses such futuristic devices as a Viewphone. It was shot on location at U.C.L.A. *Cast:* Tom Simcox (as Braddock), Stephen McNally (Tratner), Karen Steele (Louise Tratner), Lloyd Bochner (Lawrence), Kathy Kersh (Marie), Tom Reese (Mongol), John Doucette (Lt. McMillan), Colette Jackson (Beverly), Arthur Adams (Hitchess), Don Marshall (Gilmore), Laura Lindsay (Victoria), Robert Sampson (Policeman), Charles Macauley (Man).

958. **Call to Danger.** 60 min. Airdate: 7/1/68. Production Company: CBS Productions. Director: Lamont Johnson. Producer: Lamont Johnson. Writer: David P. Harmon. Peter Graves played the leader of the Office of National Resources, a secret government group that takes on cases that stump all other law enforcement agencies. "It was a good pilot," says Graves, "but came along at the same time there was change happening in *Mission Impossible* (Steven Hill was quitting) and, rather than go with *Call to Danger*, they decided they'd rather have me go into *Mission Impossible*." When *Mission Impossible* came to an end in 1973, he did another *Call to Danger* pilot, playing a resourceful Justice Department agent who recruits outsiders to help him fight crime. "I really didn't want to do that one, which was a new version of the old one by Larry Heath," he says. "CBS was determined to get that concept on the air as a series." A similar show, *Masquerade*, had a short run on ABC in 1984 with Rod Taylor as a secret agent who recruits civilians to help him with his espionage tasks. *Cast:* Peter Graves (as Jim Kingsley), James

Gregory (Paul Wilkins), Daniel J. Travanti (John Hinderson), Albert Paulsen (Andre Kellman), William Smithers (Joseph Kane), Forrest Lewis (Silver), Brad Trumbull (Tom), Henry Allin (Eddie), Laurel Goodwin (Rita Henderson).

959. Dhondo. Production Company: Warner Bros. Producer: Leon Benson. Gerald Michenaud is a ten-year-old elephant boy in India.

960. The Freebooters (aka Lost Treasure). 60 min. Airdate: 6/28/71. Production Company: Herbert Leonard Productions. Director: Richard Sarafian. Executive Producer: Herbert Leonard. Producer: Leo Davis. Writer: James M. Miller. Music: Mimis Flessas. Shot on location in Crete and aired as part of CBS' *Premiere* pilot showcase. The adventures of three globetrotting treasure-seekers. *Cast:* James Stacy (as Andrew Bass), Ben Cooper (Arleigh Marley), Bo Svenson (Milovan Drumm), Tige Andrews (Albert Sanchez), Roger C. Carmel (Egasto), Fritz Weaver (Niklaus), Danielle DeMetz (Mika).

961. Lassiter. 60 min. Airdate: 7/8/68. Production Company: Filmways. Director: Sam Wanamaker. Producer: Richard Alan Simmons. Writer: Richard Alan Simmons. Burt Reynolds played a freelance writer who specializes in exposing underworld crime for *Contrast* magazine. This pilot was often repeated, airing again on 7/5/71, 7/17/71, and then another network, NBC, repeated it on 11/6/80. *Cast:* Burt Reynolds (as Pete Lassiter), Cameron Mitchell (Stan Marchek), Sharon Farrell (Joan Mears), James MacArthur (Russ Faine), Nicholas Colasanto (Charlie Leaf), Stanley Waxman (Pat), Lloyd Haines (Kramer), Lawrence Haddon (Jerry Burns).

962. Sindbad. 15 min. Production Company: MGM/King Brothers. A demonstration film, based on the 1963 movie *Captain Sindbad* that starred Guy Williams, was made starring Michael Stefani, Abraham Safaer and Sammy Ross.

NBC / COMEDY

963. Li'l Abner. 30 min. Production Company: NBC. Based on the comic strip by Al Capp. A recasting of the project, which NBC tried to sell sponsors last season with Sammy Jackson. Again, no sale.

964. Mad Mad Scientist (aka Guess What I Did Today?). 30 min. Airdate: 9/10/68. Production Company: Screen Gems. Executive Producer: Lester Colodny. Creators: Norman Lieberman and Ed Hass. Almost a carbon copy of last season's flop ABC pilot *McNab's Lab.* Fred Gwynne stars as a widower who lives with his daughter and spends all his time in the basement, creating outlandish inventions. *Cast:* Fred Gwynne (as Warren Springer), Bridget Hanley (Bonnie Springer), Pamelyn Ferdin (Sally Springer), Reta Shaw (Phoebe).

965. **Make More Room for Daddy.** 60 min. Airdate: 11/6/67. Director: Sheldon Leonard. Producer: Danny Thomas. Writers: Jack Elinson and Norman Paul. Music: Earle Hagen. Aired as an episode of *The Danny Thomas Hour*. A pilot for a proposed continuation of the hit series *Make Room for Daddy* for the one network the show had never run on – NBC. The original series ran on ABC from 1953–57, then jumped to CBS, where it stayed until 1964. In this pilot, Danny Thomas returned as nightclub entertainer Danny Williams and Marjorie Lord again played his second wife, Kathy. Danny's son Rusty (Rusty Hamer) gets married to the daughter (Jana Taylor) of an Army Colonel while Kathy's daughter Linda (Angela Cartwright) begins college. Oddly, two years after this pilot was junked, Thomas did another pilot for a continuation for CBS, which passed on it as a series. A year later, though, the series turned up on ABC (with Sherry Jackson returning as daughter Terry, a role she played on the original series for the first few seasons) as *Make Room for Granddaddy* and managed to limp through one season. *Cast:* Danny Thomas (as Danny Williams), Marjorie Lord (Kathy Williams), Rusty Hamer (Rusty Williams), Angela Cartwright (Linda Williams), Jana Taylor (Susan McAdams Williams), Sid Melton (Charlie Halper), Amanda Randolph (Louise), Edward Andrews (Col. McAdams).

966. **Me and Benjie.** 30 min. Production Company: Universal. Producer: Joe Connelly. Writers: Dale and Katherine Eunson. The story of two 9-year-old boys, one black (Kevin Herron) and one white (Tony Fraser) and their parents, played by Bernie and Kim Hamilton and John Lupton and Pat Breslin. This was recast, with the exception of Bernie Hamilton, and rewritten for CBS in 1969 and aired in 1970.

967. **Return of the Original Yellow Tornado.** 30 min. Production Company: Universal. Creator: Jack Laird. Writers: George Balzar, Hal Goldman, and Al Gordon. In the year 1987, two famous superheroes have retired. Then, the Yellow Tornado, their arch enemy whom they put in prison in 1967, is set free – and vows to wreak havoc on the world. Mickey Rooney and Eddie Mayehoff played the elderly good-guys.

968. **Sheriff Who.** 30 min. Airdate: 9/5/67. Production Company: Mirisch-Rich Productions. Director: Jerry Paris. Producers/Creators/Writers: Garry Marshall and Jerry Belson. The heroes are a gang of villains, headed by John Astin as Roy Slade, that would defeat the new sheriff brought into the town in each episode of the proposed series. "It was ahead of its time," says Lee Rich, "it was the funniest, funniest pilot I ever saw. I knew how good it was, every network told me how good it was, but I still couldn't sell it. I was never so disappointed in my entire life." Dick Shawn,

Jeannine Riley, Dick Stahl, Hal Smith, Irene Tedrow, and Dub Taylor costarred in this pilot, which was offered a second time in 1969. It was revived a third time in 1972, again starring Astin and written by Marshall and Belson, as two new one-hour pilots strung into one, two-hour TV movie entitled *Evil Roy Slade*.

969. **Signed: Anxious.** 30 min. Production Company: Screen Gems. Producers: Harry Ackerman and William Sackheim. Stuart Margolin, Dave Barry, and Angus Duncan are three reporters who team up as one fictional person to write an advice column.

NBC / DRAMA

970. **Dick Tracy.** Production Company: 20th Century Fox. Producers: William Dozier and James Fonda. Music: Billy May, Theme: The Ventures. Ray McDonnell plays the iconic cop from the Dick Tracy comics created by Chester Gould. Cast: Ray McDonnell (Dick Tracy), Davey Davison (Tess Trueheart Tracy), Eve Plumb (Bonny Braids), Jay Blood (Junior Tracy), Ken Mayer (Chief Patton), Monroe Arnole (Sam Catchem), Liz Shutan (Detective Liz).

971. **The Hardy Boys.** 60 min. Airdate: 9/8/67. Production Company: 20th Century Fox. Director: Larry Peerce. Executive Producer: Richard Murphy. Producer: Larry Peerce. Writer: Richard Murphy. Aired as an episode of NBC's *Danny Thomas Hour*. Rick Gates and Tim Matheson star as the teenage detectives popularized in a series of books by Franklin W. Dixon. *Cast:* Tim Matheson (as Joe Hardy), Rick Gates (Frank Hardy), Richard Anderson (Fenton Hardy), Portia Nelson (Aunt Gertrude), Brian Fong (Jim Foy), Edward Andrews (Dr. Montrose), James Shigeta (George Ti-Ming), Emile Meyer (Burke), Stephen John (Chet), Malcolm Atterbury (Clams Daggett).

972. **I Love a Mystery.** 120 min. Airdate: 2/27/73. Production Company: Universal. Director: Leslie Stevens. Producer: Frank Price. Writer: Leslie Stevens, from the radio series by Carleton Morse. Music: Oliver Nelson. Originally planned as a 60 minute pilot, this sat on the shelf for six years before being aired as a two-hour movie. David Hartman, Hagger Beggs and Les Crane starred as three neophyte insurance investigators. *Cast:* Les Crane (as Jack Packard), David Hartman (Doc Long), Hagger Beggs (Reggie York), Ida Lupino (Randy Cheyne), Jack Weston (Joe Cheyne), Terry-Thomas (Gordon Elliot), Don Knotts (Alexander Archer), Karen Jensen (Faith), Deanna Lund (Hope), Melodie Johnson (Charity).

973. **Land's End.** 60 min. Airdate: 4/21/68. Production Companies: Desilu and Proctor & Gamble Productions. Executive Producers: Desi Arnaz and Mort

Briskin. Director: Desi Arnaz. Associate Producer: Dann Cahn. Writer: Mort Briskin. Rory Calhoun is the owner of a waterfront hotel and Gilbert Roland is the local sheriff in a Mexican village. Together, they fight crime and help people in trouble. Sonny Tufts and Martin Milner costarred.

The pilot was shot on location in Texas. In the book *Desilu: The Story of Lucille Ball & Desi Arnaz*, Cahn says that director Arnaz began improvising changes to the script during production. The project was supposed to be a 30 minute pilot, but Arnaz delivered a forty-five minute cut that he refused to trim, demanding instead that the proposed series be upped to hour-long episodes. That was a problem, considering there were only half-hour slots left in the network's schedule and, as Cahn says, the pilot "wasn't great."

974. Time of Flight. 60 min. Airdate: 9/21/66. Production Company: Universal. Writer: Richard Matheson. Creators: Stanley Chase and Richard Matheson. A science-fiction/adventure that aired as an episode of *Bob Hope's Chrysler Theatre* which starred Jack Kelly, Jack Klugman, Juliet Mills, Woodrow Parfrey, and Jeanette Nolan.

975. Two Young Men and a Girl in a Meat Grinder. 60 min. Production Company: Arena Productions. Director: Allen Baron. Producer: Norman Felton. The personal and professional lives of three lawyers, one white, one black, and one female. James McMullen starred.

INDEPENDENT PRODUCTIONS

976. I Married a Bear. 30 min. Production Company: Four Star/General Foods. Creators/Producers: Allan Burns and Chris Hayward. Michele Lee starred as a woman married to a baseball player, played by Stephen Young. Ron Rich was the husband's buddy.

977. My Husbands, Tom and John. 30 min. Production Company: Talent Associates/ R.J. Reynolds. Producers: Leonard Stern, Don Melnick, and David Susskind. A concept that never dies, though the pilots using it often do: A widow (Julie Sommars) marries a man (Peter Duryea) and the ghost of her dead first husband (Robert Reed) shows up and causes problems.

978. Walter of the Jungle. 15 min. Production Company: Universal. Producer: Joe Connelly. A "Tarzan" spoof starring Jonathan Daly as an American adventurer living in a jungle treehouse with his mother (Rose Marie). Bernard Fox, Nipsey Russell, and Vicki Harrington costarred in this demonstration film.

1968–1969

ABC / COMEDY

979. Billy Boy! 30 min. Production Company: Screen Gems. Producer/Creator: Cy Howard. Loosely based on the 1960s TV series *Fair Exchange*. Dan Dailey is an American business man who lets the 17-year-old son (Roy Holder) of one of his British friends live with his family for awhile – and brings with him all the trappings of England's "mod generation."

980. The Princess and Me. 30 min. Production Company: Screen Gems. Director: E.W. Swackhamer. Executive Producer: Harry Ackerman. Producer: E.W. Swackhamer. Writer: Bernard Slade. Barbara Hershey is a princess who comes to America to study democracy. She travels, under the guise of a normal European tourist, with a State Department official (Jeremy Slate) who doesn't particularly relish the assignment. Eventually, however, a romance would develop between them if this had gone to series.

ABC / DRAMA

981. The Hustler. Production Company: 20th Century Fox. The adventures of an international gambler.

982. Nick Quarry. 30 min. Production Company: 20th Century Fox. Producer: Aaron Rosenberg. Director: Walter Grauman. Modeled after the Frank Sinatra movie *Tony Rome*. This pilot, for a projected 60 minute series, stars Tony Scotti as a private eye.

983. The Specialists. Producer: Quinn Martin. The adventures of three mercenaries roaming America after the Civil War.

984. Tales of the Unknown. Production Company: 20th Century Fox. Producer: James Carerras. Hammer Films, famous for their horror movies, would produce this adult horror anthology in England.

985. United States—It Can't Happen Here (aka Shadow Over the Land). 2 hours. Airdate: 12/4/68. Production Companies: Screen Gems and Columbia Television. Director: Richard C. Sarafian. Producer: Matthew Rapf. Writers: Nedrick Young. Music: Sol Kaplan. A science fiction drama with Mark Strange and Michael Margotta as two resistance fighters trying to overthrow the totalitarian government that now controls the United States and return the land to democracy. John

Forsythe played the dictator and Jackie Cooper was slated for a recurring role. *Cast:* Mark Strange (as Major Shepherd McCloud), Janice Rule (Capt. Everett), Michael Margotta (Timothy Willing), Jackie Cooper (Lt. Col. Andy Davis), John Forsythe (General Wendell Bruce), Gene Hackman (Reverend Thomas Davis), Carol Lynley (Abigail Tyler), Bill Walker (Arnold), Scott Thomas (Felting), Myron Healey (General Hempstead), Frederic Downs (Drucker), Jonathon Lippe (Lt. Allen), Mickey Sholdar (Paul), Ronnie Eckstein (David), Ken Swofford (Ben).

986. **What's in It for Harry?** 2 hours. Production Company: Roger Corman Productions. Producers: Roger and Gene Corman. Vic Morrow stars as a tough, "likeable rogue" working in the French Riviera, where this pilot was shot on location.

CBS / COMEDY

987. **Harry and David.** 30 min. Production Companies: Kayro Productions and Universal Television. Producer: Joe Connelly. Writer: Bob Mosher. Based on the film *The Little Kidnappers.* Two orphans (Michael Wixted, Frankie Kabott) come to live on their grandfather's (John Anderson) farm in Canada after their parents are killed in the Civil War. Six more scripts were commissioned by CBS.

988. **Higher and Higher.** 60 min. Airdate: 9/9/68. Production Company: Clovis Productions. Director: Paul Bogart. Producers: Tony Ford and Jacqueline Babbin. Writer: Irving Gaynor Nieman. This "whodunit" comedy, modeled after *The Thin Man*, would be shot in New York and would chronicle the adventures of a husband and wife attorney team (Sally Kellerman and John McMartin) who solve murders. *Cast:* Sally Kellerman (as Liz Higher), John McMartin (John Higher), Dustin Hoffman (Arthur Greene), Robert Forster (Doug Payson), Alan Alda (Frank St. John), Barry Morse (Colin St. John), Ruth White (Ellen St. John), Marie Masters (Paula), George Wallace (Charlie), Billy Dee Williams (David Arnold), Gunilla Hutton (Astrid), Eugene Roche (McElheny).

989. **Missy's Men.** 30 min. Production Company: CBS Productions. Executive Producer/ Creator: Hank Garson. Producers/Writers: Ed Beloin and Hank Garson. Three American soldiers in Korea (Jack Sheldon, Dwayne Hickman, and Daniel J. Travanti) bring an orphaned girl back to San Francisco and team up to raise her.

990. **Rome, Sweet Rome.** 30 min. Production Compnay: Ed Sullivan. Producer: Howard Gottfried. Writers: Wayne and Schuster. Shot on video tape in New York, this sitcom featured Bill Bixby as an American in Rome. Costarred Jules Munshin and David Burns.

991. Stanley Against the System. 30 min. Production Company: Arvin Productions. Executive Producer: Martin Melcher. Producers: Bob Sweeney and Dick Dorso. Creators/Writers: Garry Marshall and Jerry Belson. Larry Hovis starred as a meek guy who lives in the suburbs with his wife, played by Penny Gaston, and every day sets out to do battle with the world around him. David Ketchum costarred.

CBS / DRAMA

992. The Big Prize (aka The Challengers). 2 hours. Airdate: 2/20/70. Production Company: Universal Television. Director: Leslie Martinson. Producer: Roy Huggins. Writer: Dick Nelson, from the story by John Thomas James and Robert Hamner. Music: Pete Rugolo. Sean Garrison and Nico Minardos would star as international race car drivers. In the pilot, shot in March 1968 and pre-empted from its original 3/28/69 airdate by Dwight Eisenhower's death, the racers compete for the Grand Prix trophy – and the same girl. The TV movie was critically assailed for being overly predictable. *Cast:* Darren McGavin (as Jim McCabe), Sean Garrison (Cody Scanlon), Nico Minardos (Paco), Anne Baxter (Stephanie York), Richard Conte (Ritchie), Farley Granger (Nealy), Juliet Mills (Mary McCabe), Sal Mineo (Angel de Angelo), Susan Clark (Catherine Burroughs), William Sylvester (Brad York), John Holland (Ambrose), Alan Caillou (Bryan Toomey).

993. European Eye (aka The Search). 60 min. Airdate: 7/29/68. Production Companies: 20th Century Fox and ITC Entertainment. Director: Lamont Johnson. Producer: Stanley Rubin. Writer: Robert Shaw. The adventures of an American private eye, played by Mark Miller, who works in England helping American visitors who get into trouble. His friend on the force is Barry Foster. Shot in the U.S. and London. *Cast:* Mark Miller (as Paul Cannon), Michael Rennie (Martin Purcell), Barry Foster (Inspector Sheppard), Julie Sommars (Molly), Irene Handi (Miss Dancy), Ryan O'Neal (Ingersoll).

994. Kona Coast. 93 min. Production Companies: Warner Bros. Television and Seven Arts. Director: Lamont Johnson. Producer: Richard Boone. Writer: Gilbert Ralston, John D. MacDonald, based on MacDonald's short story *Bimini Gal.* Music: Jack Marshall. This pilot, shot on location in Hawaii, for a 60 minute series was released as a feature film and starred Boone as a fishing boat skipper looking for his daugher's killer. The series would have focused on his adventures traveling on the high seas. Science fiction novelist & screenwriter Harlan Ellison was originally hired to expand MacDonald's outline into a script, but he reportedly clashed with Richard Boone and left the project. Supposedly the only work of Ellison's that survives is the opening scene. Cast: Richard Boone (Capt. Sam Morgan) Vera Miles (Melissa Hyde) Joan Blondell (Kitibelle Lightfoot) Steve Ihnat (Kryder) Chips Rafferty (Charlie Lightfoot) Kent Smith (Akamai), Sam Kapu, Jr. (Kimo), Gina Villines (Mim Lowry), Duane Eddy (Tiger Cat), Scott Thomas (Tate Packer).

995. **Man from the 25th Century.** 20 min. Production Company: 20th Century Fox. Producer: Irwin Allen. A demonstration film (completed 2/15/68) inspired by *The Day the Earth Stood Still* and starring James Darren as an alien who, for reasons unknown, Irwin Allen chose to call "The Man from the 25th Century." Costars included John Napier, John Crawford, and Ford Rainey. From John Gregory Dunne's book *The Studio* comes this description, by Irwin Allen, of the series: "A one hour weekly television series of science fiction, high adventure and action. It is the eerily horrifying tale of Andro, our nearest planetary neighbor, whose source of power is being used far more quickly than it can be created and whose need to attack earth and replenish such power is of the highest priority. An earthling, kidnapped in infancy and transported to Andro for indoctrination, is returned to earth to start its downfall. He is repelled by his assignment and defects to the earthlings. Each week the non-humans from Andro arrive in flying saucers and create havoc on earth. Each week the earthlings, aided by The Man from the 25th Century and his weaponry, succeed in dissuading the enemy." Allen, in Dunne's book, also went on to describe the leading character as "24, dark, handsome, six feet, three inches tall… he is the most unusual of men. Graduate of the sciences of Nali, the great technological studies offered by the scientists of the planet Andro. Brilliant, trained to kill, and a master in the art of self defense. Hidden deep within is a warm, friendly nature. But, so penetrating was his indoctrination, even he is unaware of his second personality." Originally planned as a spin-off of *Lost in Space*, this presentation film never aired.

996. **Operation Red.** Production Company: CBC Productions. An American CIA agent is teamed with a Canadian mountie to solve crimes along the border.

NBC / COMEDY

997. **Doc.** 30 min. Airdate: 7/28/69. Production Company: Filmways. Producers: Jay Sommers. Music: Vic Mizzy. A reworking of last season's CBS pilot. An older doctor (Forrest Tucker) in the small town of Stubbville plans to retire, so he brings a young

doctor (Rick Lenz) in to assume his practice – and then decides to stick around after all. *Cast:* Forrest Tucker (as Dr. Jason Fillmore), Rick Lenz (Dr. Orville Truebody), Margaret Ann Peterson (Amy Fillmore), Mary Green (Tillie), J. Pat O'Malley (Will), John Qualen (Luke), Guy Raymond (Sheriff Bart), Parley Baer (Conductor), Roland Winters (Watkins), Norma Varden (Mrs. Dobson), Bob Steele (Toby).

998. **Perils of Pauline.** 30 min. Production Company: Universal Television. Producer: Joe Connelly. A pilot that refuses to die. Yet another new show was shot, again starring Pamela Austin. This time, though, she is no longer an orphan pursued by an old lover and threatened by an evil villain. Now she's a reporter in the 1920s who travels the country with her photographer (Bruce Hyde). Her perpetual nemesis was played by Larry Storch.

999. **Walt's Girls.** 30 min. Production Company: Paramount Television. Creator/Producer: Sidney Sheldon. Craig Stevens stars as a New York advertising executive trying to raise three daughters, ages 18, 15, and 9, none of whom he can understand. The project was re-developed for CBS as *The Best Years* the following year, but failed there as well.

NBC / DRAMA

1000. **Assignment: Earth.** 60 min. Airdate: 3/29/68. Production Company: Desilu. Director: Marc Daniels. Producer: Gene Roddenberry. Associate Producer: Robert H. Justman. Writer: Art Wallace, from a story by Art Wallace and Gene Roddenberry. Music: Alexander Courage. Aired as an episode of *Star Trek*. Robert Lansing is Gary Seven, a benevolent alien who comes to earth to protect us from destroying ourselves. He's aided by scatterbrained Roberta Lincoln (Teri Garr) and a magical cat named Isis. He also brings with him a wide array of strange devices and his own version of a "transporter room." In the pilot, he tries to stop the launching of a satellite-come-nuclear bomb and clashes with the crew of the *U.S.S. Enterprise*, which has journeyed into the past on a routine historic research mission. At the end of the episode, Captain Kirk (William Shatner) and Mr. Spock (Leonard Nimoy) examine their computer's history banks and tell Gary Seven and Roberta Lincoln that they have "some interesting experiences" awaiting them. Unfortunately, TV viewers never got to see them. *Cast:* Robert Lansing (as Gary Seven), Teri Garr (Roberta Lincoln), James Keefer (Cromwell), Morgan Jones (Col. Nesvig), Paul Baxley (Security Chief), Bruce Mars (First Policewoman), Ted Gehring (Second Policeman).

1001. City Beneath the Sea. 20 min. Production Company: 20th Century Fox. Producer: Irwin Allen. A demonstration film for a proposed series about life in an undersea, prototype community. Glenn Corbett, Francine York and Lloyd Bochner starred. Allen later expanded and recast this pilot in 1971 as a two-hour television movie starring Stuart Whitman.

1002. The Big Train (aka Express to Danger; aka Istanbul Express). 94 min. Airdate: 10/22/68. Production Company: Universal Television. Producer/Director: Richard Irving. Associate Producer: Jerrold Freedman. Writers: Richard Levinson and William Link. Music: Oliver Nelson. Shot on location in France, Switzerland, Italy, and Turkey. Gene Barry starred as a secret agent who, while searching for a dead scientist's secret papers, poses as an art dealer heading for Turkey aboard the Orient Express. Costars John Saxon as the railroad security officer. *Cast:* Gene Barry (as Michael London), John Saxon (Cheval), Senta Berger (Mila Darvos), Tom Simcox (LeLand Coopersmith), Mary Ann Mobley (Peggy Coopersmith), Werner Peters (Dr. Lenz), Donald Woods (Shepherd), Jack Kruschen (Capt. Granicek), John Marley (Kapel), Philip Bourneuf (Claude), Norman Varden (English Woman), Emile Genest (Henri the Conductor).

1003. Joaquin Murietta. 15 min. Production Company: 20th Century Fox. Producer: Aaron Rosenberg. Director: Walter Grauman. A demonstration film featuring Ricardo Montalban as a Robin Hood–type hero during the early days of Spanish California settlement. Had this gone to series, Rosie Grier, James McMullan and Slim Pickens would have been regulars. The demonstration film was expanded into a two-hour pilot and offered again in 1969.

The following is an unsold pilot that was omitted from the previous edition of this book:

The Lonely Profession – 90 minutes. Airdate: 1/1/69. Production Company: Universal Television. Director: Douglas Heyes. Producers: Roy Huggins, Jo Swerling Jr. Music: Pete Rugolo. Writer: Douglas Heyes, based on his novel "The Twelfth of Never." Harry Guardino stars as a San Francisco private eye who looks for the murderer of a tycoon's mistress…and becomes a suspect himself. Cast: Harry Guardino (Lee Gordon), Dean Jagger (Charles Van Cleve), Barbara McNair (Donna Travers), Joseph Cotten (Martin Banister), Ina Balin (Karen Menardos), Dina Merrill (Beatrice Savarona), Jack Carter (Freddie Farber), Troy Donahue (Julian Thatcher), Stephen McNally (Lt. Webber), Fernando Lamas (Dominic Savarona)

1969–1970

1004. Gidget Grows Up. 90 min. Airdate: 12/30/69. Production Company: Screen Gems. Director: James Sheldon. Producer: Jerome Courtland. Writer: John McGreevey, from the book *Gidget Goes to New York* by Frederick Kohner. Music: Shorty Rogers. Karen Valentine replaces Sally Field as TV's Gidget, who has graduated from beach party politics to international relations – in the pilot, the surfer chick moves to New York and becomes a United Nations guide. She's still got the hots for Jeff "Moondoggie" Griffin (Paul Peterson), who has traded his surfboard for a fighter plane – he's become an Air Force officer stationed in Greenland. First of several attempts to revive *Gidget*, which eventually became a first-run, syndicated sitcom in 1987. *Cast:* Karen Valentine (as Frances "Gidget" Lawrence), Paul Peterson (Jeff "Moondoggie" Griffin), Paul Lynde (Louis B. Latimer), Bob Cummings (Russell Lawrence), Edward Mulhare (Alex MacLaughlin), Nina Foch (Bibi Crosby), Warner Anderson (Ambassador Postl), Susan Batson (Diana), Hal Frederick (Lee), Michael Lembeck (Arnold), Gunilla Knudson (Katrine), Doreen Lang (Mrs. Willard), Margot Jane (Rae Ellen), Donald Symington (Clerk), Harlen Carraher (Ben), Helen Funai (Minnie), Mario Aniov (Abdul).

1005. A Guide for the Married Man. 30 min. Production Company: 20th Century Fox. Director: James Frawley. Executive Producer: Frank Tarloff. Producer: Frank McCarthy. Writer: Frank Tarloff. Based on the motion picture. Episodes would explore such topics as how to hire a secretary, how to explain an old girlfriend and how to be a girl-watcher. The characters included a conservative, 35-year-old, recently married man and his friend Ed, who has been married for six years. This starred Hal Buckley, Anthony Roberts, Pat Delaney, and Sally Ann Richards.

1006. Holly Golightly. 30 min. Production Company: 20th Century Fox. Producer/ Director: James Frawley. Writer: Jim Henerson. Based on the Paramount film *Breakfast at Tiffany's*. In the pilot, Holly (Stefanie Powers) moves into a new apartment – and accidentally sparks an all-night party filled with dozens of strange people doing weird things. Costarred George Furth, Jack Kruschen, and Jean Pierre Aumont.

ABC / DRAMA

1007. Corporal Crocker (aka The Ballad of Andy Crocker). 73 min. Airdate: 11/18/69. Production Company: Thomas/Spelling Productions. Director: George McGowan. Executive Producers: Aaron Spelling and Danny Thomas. Producer: Stuart Margolin. Writer: Stuart Margolin. Music: Billy May. Theme: Stuart Margolin and Murray MacLeod. The troubles faced by a Vietnam veteran (Lee Majors) when he returns home – and finds his girlfriend married and his motorcycle repair business ruined. *Cast:* Lee Majors (as Andy Crocker), Joey Heatherton (Lisa), Jimmy Dean (Mack), Bobby Hatfield (Joe Bob), Marvin Gaye (David Owens), Agnes Moorehead (Mother), Pat Hingle (Earl Crocker), Jill Haworth (Karen), Peter Haskell (Nelson), Claudia Bryar (Emily Crocker), Lee LeBroux (Johnson), Charlie Briggs (Mr. Paisley), Lisa Todd (Cora Mae), Jackie Russell (Kitty), Barbara Leigh (Mia), Joel Higgins (Mr. Bedecker), Harry Harvey, Sr. (Mr. Kirkaby), Warren Peterson (Jimmy).

1008. In Name Only. 75 min. Airdate: 11/25/69. Production Company: Screen Gems. Director: E.W. Swackhamer. Executive Producer: Harry Ackerman. Producer: E.W. Swackhamer. Writer: Bernard Slade. Two marriage counselors (Michael Callan and Ann Prentiss) discover several marriages they performed were not legal and set out to find the couples, whose comic reactions to the news are the heart of this pilot. *Cast:* Michael Callan (as Steve Braden), Ann Prentiss (Jill Willis), Eve Arden (Aunt Theda), Ruth Buzzi (Ruth Clayton), Christopher Connelly (Tony Caruso), Bill Daily (Peter Garrity), Elinor Donahue (Ethel Garrity), Herb Edleman (Bert Clayton), Paul Ford (Elwy Pertwhistle), Elsa Lanchester (Mrs. Caruso), Herbert Voland (Sgt. Mulligan), Alan Reed (Phil Haskell), Heather Young (Debbie Caruso), Barbara Bostwick (Agnes), Ivor Francis (Father), Adrienne Marden (Mother), Jeannie Berlin (Heather), Chanin Hale (Barbara), William Long, Jr. (Uncle Fred), Vincent Perry (Justice of the Peace), Celeste Yarnall (Anne), Mary Wilcox (Receptionist), Lee Weaver (Bartender), Lindsay Workman (J.P. Robinson), Art Metrano (Joe), Jill Foster (Shirley), Merle Earle (Granny), Duane Grey (Uncle Larry).

1009. In the Dead of Night. 60 min. Airdate: 8/30/69. Director: Dan Curtis. Producer: Dan Curtis. Writer: Dan Curtis. Music: Robert Cobert. Kerwin Matthews plays supernatural investigator Jonathon Fletcher, not unlike the character played in the 1967 NBC pilot *Ghostbreaker*. Cal Bellini plays his assistant. Dan Curtis (of *Dark Shadows* fame) was seemingly obsessed with this concept, trying it again with *The Norliss Tapes* and, most successfully, with *The Night Stalker* and *The Night Strangler*, which became the TV series *Kolchak: The Night Stalker*. *Cast:* Kerwin

iver (Thelma Dwyer) John Saxon (Dave Poohler), Diana Lynn
s), Terry Carter (Jaffie) Robert Middleton (Owen Brady).

Y

Company. 30 min. Airdate: 5/12/69. Production Company: 20th
Director: Gene Reynolds. Producer: Gene Reynolds Writer: Jean
reator: Jean Holloway. A comedy set in New York at the turn-of-the-
Gwynne is the manager of one of the first department stores, the father
uly children, and the husband to a very bewildered wife (Abby Dalton).
Gwynne (as Marshall Anderson), Abby Dalton (Augusta Anderson),
Eilbacher (Amanda Anderson), Heather Harrison (Alfa Anderson),
ccles (Adienne Anderson), Nick Beauvy (Anstruther Anderson), Ray
Amory Anderson), Teddy Eccles (Ansford Anderson), Sean Kelly (Artanza
on), Leig Nervik (Apollo Anderson), Renie Riano (Miss Slight).

st Years. 30 min. Airdate: 8/4/69. Craig Stevens is the widowed father of
girls – Brooke Bundy, Robyn Millan, and Susan Joyce. A reworked version
e NBC pilot *Walt's Girls*, also written and created by Sidney Sheldon, the
ous season.

Flim-Flam Man. 30 min. Airdate: 9/1/69. Production Company: 20th
ntury Fox. Director: Alan Rafkin. Executive Producer: Lawrence Turman.
oducer: Herman Saunders. Writer: James Bridges. Music: Don Scardino. Based
n the motion picture. Forrest Tucker is Mordecai Jones, a conman roaming the
ackwoods of the North and deep South with his able assistant, Curley Treadway
(Don Scardino). Together, they swindle the greedy, the dishonest, the gullible –
but never an honest man. *Cast:* Forrest Tucker (as Mordecai Jones), Don Scardino
(Curley Treadway), James Gregory (Packard), Elena Verdugo (Mrs. Packard), Gene
Evans (Sheriff Slade), Dub Taylor (Weehunt), Lada Edmond, Jr. (Bonnie Lee), Guy
Raymond (Buck), Bob Hastings (Meeshaw), Hope Summers (Debbie Packard).

5. Hastings Corner (aka The Shameful Secrets of Hastings Corner). 30 min. Airdate:
1/14/70. Production Company: Screen Gems. Director: Bob Claver. Executive
Producer: Harry Ackerman. Producers: Lawrence J. Cohen and Fred Freeman.
Writers: Lawrence J. Cohen and Fred Freeman. Music: George Duning. A spoof of
soap operas revolving around the clash between the Honker and Fandango families.
Cast: Alan Oppenheimer (as Dr. Byron Dorman, the psychiatrist), Woodrow Parfrey
(Ta Ta Honker), Hal Linden (D.A. Corey Honker/Morey Honker), Karen Black

Matthews (as Jonathon Fletcher), Cal Bellini (Sajeed Rau), Marj Dusay (Angela
Marten), Thayer David (Seth Blakely), Louis Edmonds (Commodore Blaise).

1010. **The Monk.** 73 min. Airdate: 10/21/69. Production Company: Thomas/Spelling
Productions. Director: George McGowan. Executive Producers: Aaron Spelling
and Danny Thomas. Producers: Tony Barrett, Shelley Hull, and Ronald Jacobs.
Writer: Blake Edwards, from story by Tony Barrett. Creator: Blake Edwards.
Music: Earle Hagen. The adventures of San Francisco private eye Gus Monk were
panned by critics ("embarrassing dialogue, predictable resolution, unbelievable vil-
lains"). In the pilot, a crooked lawyer who entrusts Monk with a letter that incrim-
inates a mobster is murdered – and Monk is the prime suspect. *Cast:* George
Maharis (as Gus Monk), Janet Leigh (Janice Barnes), Rick Jason (Wideman),
Carl Betz (Danny Gouzenko), Jack Albertson (Tinker), Raymond St. Jacques (Lt.
Ed Heritage), William Smithers (Leo Barnes), Jack Soo (Hip Guy), Linda Marsh
(Lisa Daniels), Edward G. Robinson, Jr. (Trapp), Mary Wickes (Mrs. Medford),
Joe Besser (Herbie), George Burrafato (Stranger), Walter Reed (Director),
George Saurel (Sgt. Mawson), John Hancock (Charlie), Bob Nash (Doorman).

1011. **Shadow Man.** Production Company: Universal Television. Writers: Dean
Reisner and Robert Soderberg. A college professor, who is inadvertently responsible for the accidental death of his wife and child, agrees to have plastic surgery
and assume the identity of a "Howard Hughes"–type billionaire. He uses the billionaire's vast wealth to assuage his guilt and do good deeds around the world.

1012. **Under the Yum Yum Tree.** 60 min. Airdate: 9/2/69. Production Company:
Screen Gems. Director: E.W. Swackhamer. Executive Producer: Harry Ackerman.
Producer: E.W. Swackhamer. Writer: Bernard Slade. Music: Johnny Mandel. Jack
Sheldon is an unsuccessful writer who manages the Yum Yum Tree apartment com-
plex and, while toiling on his novels, manages to get involved in his tenants' lives. The
pilot story involves a pregnant woman who refuses to marry her lover. This was pre-
ceded by both a play an a movie version. Costarred Bobo Lewis and Dick Balduzzi.
Guest stars were Ryan O'Neal, Nita Talbot, Harold Gould, and Leigh Taylor-Young.

1013. **Until Proven Guilty.** Production Company: Universal Television. Executive
Producer: William Dozier. Producer: Stan Shpetner. Writer: Harry Kronman.
The heroine is a brilliant trial attorney in her late 30s who shares a law practice
with her lover. When her lover is murdered, she becomes the prime suspect –
and is defended by her lover's son, a neophyte trial attorney. Once cleared of the
murder charge, she continues the practice with her lover's son, and the proposed
series would chronicle their cases and personal conflicts.

CBS / COMEDY

1014. Barefoot in the Park. 30 min. Airdate: 11/24/69. Production Company: Paramount Television. Director: Jerry Paris. Executive Producers: Garry Marshall and Jerry Belson. Producer: Charles Shyer. Writers: Garry Marshall and Jerry Belson. After being rejected by CBS, this busted pilot was aired on *Love American Style* as the episode "Love and the Good Deal." This pilot was based on the Neil Simon play and the subsequent film starring Robert Redford and Jane Fonda about a young couple living on the top floor of a run-down Manhattan walk-up. The pilot episode dealt with the problems the couple had with a cheap bed they bought. The proposed series, which would have starred Skye Aubrey, Norman Fell, Hans Conried, Phil Clarke, Jane Wyatt, and Harvey Lembeck, would have featured stories in which the wife's blind faith and naivete would get her into trouble that the husband must patiently work out. The flop pilot was recast with all-black actors, reshot, and eventually aired as "The Bed" episode of the ABC series, which lasted 12 weeks. Marshall and Belson, who successfully brought Simon's *The Odd Couple* to TV, would later recast *that* for ABC with all-black actors (featuring Demond Wilson and Ron Glass) and redub it *The New Odd Couple*. That series lasted 13 weeks.

1015. Houseboat. 30 min. Production Company: Paramount Television. Director: William Asher. Producer: William Asher. Writers: James Parker and Arnold Margolin. Based on the motion picture. Arthur Hill starred as a widowed San Francisco newspaper reporter living on a houseboat in Marin with his three children – and a young housekeeper who, unbeknownst to the family, is actually the daughter of a wealthy Italian nobleman. Costarred Danielle Demetz, Audrey Christie, Jimmy Bracken, Gabbie Grammer, Ted Foulkes, Vito Scotti, and Barbara Pepper.

1016. Me and Benjie. 30 min. Airdate: 7/27/70. Production Companies: Kayro Productions and Universal Television. Director: Norman Tokar. Producer: Joe Connelly. Writer: Bob Mosher. A rewritten, recast version of the 1967 pilot. It's the story of two children, one black (Logan Harbough) and one white (Mark Brown) and their "Leave It to Beaver"–type adventures. Costarred Bernie Hamilton (who was in the original pilot), Anita Corsaut, Charles Bateman, and Kimberly Beck.

1017. The Minnie Pearl Show. 30 min. Production Company: 20th Century Fox. Director: Coby Ruskin. Producers: Jack Elinson and Norman Paul. Writers: Jack Elinson and Norman Paul. Country music personality Minnie Pearl played the owner of a rural boarding house populated by musicians, writers, actors, and even

---

inventors. Costan...
Dick Gautier, and ...

1018. Vernon's Volunteers.
Charles Barton. Produ...
ventures of the willing, b...
of Vernon. Joe Flynn playe...
the fire chief. Other cast me...

CBS / DRAMA

1019. Cutter's Trail. 2 hours. Air... Productions. Director: Vincent ... Paul Savage. Music: John Parker. Jo... his hometown, discovers it has been ... an 11-year-old boy and his mother in ... more scripts were ordered but no serie... Cutter), Manuel Padilla, Jr. (Paco Avila), ... Garland (Maggie Collyer), Joseph Cotten (C... (Santillo), J. Carrol Naish (Froteras), Shug F... Wooten), Victor French (Alex Bowen), Rober... Totten (Thather), Tom Brown (Orville Mason).

1020. Lost Flight. 105 min. Airdate: 1970. Production C... Director: Leonard Horn. Executive Producer: ... Donnelly. Writer/Creator: Dean Reisner. Price's s... "people lost on uncharted island and must create own ... time, it's an airliner that crashlands on a mid–Pacific isla... the captain and the leader of the survivors and Bobby Va... Shot on location in Hawaii with costars Billy Dee Williams, ... Meeker, Andrew Prine, and Michael James.

1021. The Protectors. 2 hours. Production Company: Universal Te... Jerry Thorpe. Executive Producer: E. Jack Neuman. Producer: ... Writers: E. Jack Neuman. Released as the feature film *Compan*... adventures of a harried police captain (Van Johnson) and his friend (... a newspaper reporter who covers the police beat and, sometimes, mu... of the captain. Cast: Van Johnson (Sam Cahill) Ray Milland (George... Brian Kelly (Nick Andros), Fritz Weaver (John Shankalien), Clu Gulag...

Quinn) Susan O...
(Edwina DeSalle...

NBC / COMED...

1022. Anderson an...
Century Fox...
Holloway. C...
century. Fred...
of eight un...
Cast: Fred...
Cynthia ...
Robin E...
Dimas (...
Anders...

1023. The B...
three ...
of th...
prev...

1024. The...
Ce...
P...
o...

(Jenny Honker), Ann Willis (Charlotte Honker), Hoke Howell (Pa Fandango), Peter Brocco (Brett Fandango), Stefani Warren (Tina Fandango), Barry Williams (Jr. Fandango), Madge Blake (Frieda Bindel), Robyn Millan (Stacy Bindel).

1026. **Pioneer Spirit.** 30 min. Airdate: 7/21/69. Director: Richard Bare. Producer: Jay Sommers. Writers: Jay Sommers and Dick Chevillat. Music: Vic Mizzy. Theme singer: Roy Clark. From the production team responsible for *Green Acres*. This pilot shares the same basic concept of urban people moving to a rural environment—this time it's three California couples (Rich Little and Marcia Rodd, Roy Clark and Donna Jean Young, and Craig Huebling and Francine York) who move to a remote Alaska valley to live like "pioneers."

1027. **The Swingles.** 30 min. Production Company: Schallter-Friendly Productions. Director: Bill Foster. Executive Producers: George Schlatter and Ed Friendly. Writers: Mike Marmer and Stan Burns. A comedy-variety show set in an actual "singles apartment building" where the unmarried folks gather around the pool and barbeque to trade one-liners and engage in *Laugh-In* style vignettes. Starred Marvin Kaplan, Barbara Minkus, and Linda Scott.

NBC / DRAMA

1028. **Bedeviled (aka Fear No Evil).** 98 min. Airdate: 3/3/69. Production Company: Universal Television. Director: Paul Wendkos. Producers: Richard Alan Simmons and David Levinson. Writer: Richard Alan Simmons, from the story by Guy Endore. Music: Billy Goldenberg. The first of two critically acclaimed, truly chilling pilots featuring Louis Jourdan as psychiatrist and occult expert Dr. David Sorrell and Wilfred Hyde-White as Harry Snowden. One of Sorrell's patients says she's brought her husband back from the dead through an antique mirror. And she has. Universal continued to dabble with this concept until they finally sold *The Sixth Sense*—about a parapsychologist—to NBC in 1972, which only lasted a few months and utilized some of the score from *Ritual of Evil*, the sequel to this pilot. *Cast:* Louis Jourdan (as Dr. David Sorrell), Carroll O'Connor (Myles Donovan), Bradford Dillman (Paul Varney), Lynda Day (Barbara Varney), Marsha Hunt (Mrs. Varney), Wilfred Hyde-White (Harry Snowden), Kate Woodville (Ingrid Dorne), Harry Davis (Wyant).

1029. **Forefront (aka The New Doctors).** 20 min. Airdate: 9/26/68. Production Company: Universal Television. Director: Leonard J. Horn. Executive Producer: Cy Chermak. Writer: Dick Nelson (from scenes written by Don M. Mankiewicz and

Sy Salkowitz). A demonstration film culled from *Split Second to Epitaph*, the second *Ironside* pilot. Joseph Cotten stars as Dr. Ben Stern as a research surgeon at the Institute of New Medicine and the adjacent St. Mary's Hospital. *Cast:* Joseph Cotten (as Dr. Ben Stern), Troy Donahue (Father Dugan), Lilia Skala (Sister Agatha).

1030. **Joaquin Murietta (aka Desperate Mission).** 2 hours. Airdate: 12/3/71. Production Companies: V-R Productions, Montalban Enterprises, and 20th Century Fox. Director: Earl Bellamy. Executive Producer: Aaron Rosenberg. Producers: David Silver and Joseph Silver. Writers: Jack Guss and Richard Collins. Music: Robert Drasnin. A new pilot based on last season's demonstration film. Ricardo Montalban played Murietta, a Mexican bandit who, with three others, fought those who preyed upon innocent ranchers and pioneers in the 1840s. *Cast:* Ricardo Montalban (as Joaquin Murietta), Slim Pickens (ThreeFinger Jack), Rosie Grier (Morgan), Jim McMullen (Arkansas), Earl Holliman (Shad Clay), Ina Balin (Otilia), Miriam Colon (Claudina), Armando Silvestre (Diego Campos), Robert J. Wilke (Gant), Anthony Caruso (Don Miquel Reuiz), Charles Horvath (Yuma), Allen Pinson (Croncracker), Ben Archibek (Frankie), Eddra Gale (Dolores).

1031. **The Scavengers (aka How to Steal an Airplane; aka Only One Day Left Before Tomorrow).** 2 hours. Airdate: 12/10/72. Production Companies: Public Arts and Universal Television. Director: Leslie H. Martinson. Executive Producer: Roy Huggins. Producers: Jo Swerling, Jr. and Carl Pingitore. Writers: Robert Foster and Phil DeGuere. Music: Pete Rugolo. Two adventurers reclaim goods taken by others and that the law can't return to the rightful owners. In the pilot, they steal a jet hijacked by a South American dictator. *Cast:* Peter Deuel (as Sam Rollins), Clintin Gryn (Evan Brice), Sal Mineo (Luis Ortega), Claudine Longet (Michell Chivot), Katherine Crawford (Jan), Julie Sommars (Dorothy), Don Diamond (Sgt. Sam).

1032. **Tiger, Tiger.** 60 min. Airdate: 6/18/69. Production Company: Ivan Tors Productions. Director: Herbert Kenwith. Executive Producer: Ivan Tors. Producer: Andy White. Writer: Earl Hamner. Music: Harry Sukman and Frances Sukman. The story of a young veterinarian (Peter Jason) and his wife (Marilyn Devin) who live in the Allegheny Mountains with a huge tiger and a pair of orangutans and draw parallels between the animals' behavior and common, human problems. Guest stars included J. Pat O'Malley, Carl Swenson, Phil Dean, and Otis Day.

Matthews (as Jonathon Fletcher), Cal Bellini (Sajeed Rau), Marj Dusay (Angela Marten), Thayer David (Seth Blakely), Louis Edmonds (Commodore Blaise).

1010. **The Monk.** 73 min. Airdate: 10/21/69. Production Company: Thomas/Spelling Productions. Director: George McGowan. Executive Producers: Aaron Spelling and Danny Thomas. Producers: Tony Barrett, Shelley Hull, and Ronald Jacobs. Writer: Blake Edwards, from story by Tony Barrett. Creator: Blake Edwards. Music: Earle Hagen. The adventures of San Francisco private eye Gus Monk were panned by critics ("embarrassing dialogue, predictable resolution, unbelievable villains"). In the pilot, a crooked lawyer who entrusts Monk with a letter that incriminates a mobster is murdered – and Monk is the prime suspect. *Cast:* George Maharis (as Gus Monk), Janet Leigh (Janice Barnes), Rick Jason (Wideman), Carl Betz (Danny Gouzenko), Jack Albertson (Tinker), Raymond St. Jacques (Lt. Ed Heritage), William Smithers (Leo Barnes), Jack Soo (Hip Guy), Linda Marsh (Lisa Daniels), Edward G. Robinson, Jr. (Trapp), Mary Wickes (Mrs. Medford), Joe Besser (Herbie), George Burrafato (Stranger), Walter Reed (Director), George Saurel (Sgt. Mawson), John Hancock (Charlie), Bob Nash (Doorman).

1011. **Shadow Man.** Production Company: Universal Television. Writers: Dean Reisner and Robert Soderberg. A college professor, who is inadvertently responsible for the accidental death of his wife and child, agrees to have plastic surgery and assume the identity of a "Howard Hughes"–type billionaire. He uses the billionaire's vast wealth to assuage his guilt and do good deeds around the world.

1012. **Under the Yum Yum Tree.** 60 min. Airdate: 9/2/69. Production Company: Screen Gems. Director: E.W. Swackhamer. Executive Producer: Harry Ackerman. Producer: E.W. Swackhamer. Writer: Bernard Slade. Music: Johnny Mandel. Jack Sheldon is an unsuccessful writer who manages the Yum Yum Tree apartment complex and, while toiling on his novels, manages to get involved in his tenants' lives. The pilot story involves a pregnant woman who refuses to marry her lover. This was preceded by both a play an a movie version. Costarred Bobo Lewis and Dick Balduzzi. Guest stars were Ryan O'Neal, Nita Talbot, Harold Gould, and Leigh Taylor-Young.

1013. **Until Proven Guilty.** Production Company: Universal Television. Executive Producer: William Dozier. Producer: Stan Shpetner. Writer: Harry Kronman. The heroine is a brilliant trial attorney in her late 30s who shares a law practice with her lover. When her lover is murdered, she becomes the prime suspect – and is defended by her lover's son, a neophyte trial attorney. Once cleared of the murder charge, she continues the practice with her lover's son, and the proposed series would chronicle their cases and personal conflicts.

CBS / COMEDY

1014. Barefoot in the Park. 30 min. Airdate: 11/24/69. Production Company: Paramount Television. Director: Jerry Paris. Executive Producers: Garry Marshall and Jerry Belson. Producer: Charles Shyer. Writers: Garry Marshall and Jerry Belson. After being rejected by CBS, this busted pilot was aired on *Love American Style* as the episode "Love and the Good Deal." This pilot was based on the Neil Simon play and the subsequent film starring Robert Redford and Jane Fonda about a young couple living on the top floor of a run-down Manhattan walk-up. The pilot episode dealt with the problems the couple had with a cheap bed they bought. The proposed series, which would have starred Skye Aubrey, Norman Fell, Hans Conried, Phil Clarke, Jane Wyatt, and Harvey Lembeck, would have featured stories in which the wife's blind faith and naivete would get her into trouble that the husband must patiently work out. The flop pilot was recast with all-black actors, reshot, and eventually aired as "The Bed" episode of the ABC series, which lasted 12 weeks. Marshall and Belson, who successfully brought Simon's *The Odd Couple* to TV, would later recast *that* for ABC with all-black actors (featuring Demond Wilson and Ron Glass) and redub it *The New Odd Couple*. That series lasted 13 weeks.

1015. Houseboat. 30 min. Production Company: Paramount Television. Director: William Asher. Producer: William Asher. Writers: James Parker and Arnold Margolin. Based on the motion picture. Arthur Hill starred as a widowed San Francisco newspaper reporter living on a houseboat in Marin with his three children – and a young housekeeper who, unbeknownst to the family, is actually the daughter of a wealthy Italian nobleman. Costarred Danielle Demetz, Audrey Christie, Jimmy Bracken, Gabbie Grammer, Ted Foulkes, Vito Scotti, and Barbara Pepper.

1016. Me and Benjie. 30 min. Airdate: 7/27/70. Production Companies: Kayro Productions and Universal Television. Director: Norman Tokar. Producer: Joe Connelly. Writer: Bob Mosher. A rewritten, recast version of the 1967 pilot. It's the story of two children, one black (Logan Harbough) and one white (Mark Brown) and their "Leave It to Beaver"–type adventures. Costarred Bernie Hamilton (who was in the original pilot), Anita Corsaut, Charles Bateman, and Kimberly Beck.

1017. The Minnie Pearl Show. 30 min. Production Company: 20th Century Fox. Director: Coby Ruskin. Producers: Jack Elinson and Norman Paul. Writers: Jack Elinson and Norman Paul. Country music personality Minnie Pearl played the owner of a rural boarding house populated by musicians, writers, actors, and even inventors. Costarred Stubby Kaye, Dabbs Greer, Pamela Rodgers, Jeff Donnell, Dick Gautier, and Sid Melton.

1018. **Vernon's Volunteers.** 30 min. Production Company: CBS Productions. Director: Charles Barton. Producer: Si Rose. Writer/Creator: Walter Kempley. The misadventures of the willing, but inept, volunteer fire department in the small, rural town of Vernon. Joe Flynn played the chairman of the town council and Paul Winchell was the fire chief. Other cast members included Mickey Shaughnessy and Cliff Norton.

CBS / DRAMA

1019. **Cutter's Trail.** 2 hours. Airdate: 2/10/70. Production Company: CBS Productions. Director: Vincent McEveety. Producer: John Mantley. Writer: Paul Savage. Music: John Parker. John Gavin is a U.S. marshall who returns to his hometown, discovers it has been decimated by a Mexican gang and, with an 11-year-old boy and his mother in tow, vows to track down the killers. Six more scripts were ordered but no series materialized. *Cast:* John Gavin (Ben Cutter), Manuel Padilla, Jr. (Paco Avila), Marisa Pavan (Amelita Avila), Beverly Garland (Maggie Collyer), Joseph Cotten (General Spalding), Nehemiah Persoff (Santillo), J. Carrol Naish (Froteras), Shug Fisher (Tuttle), Ken Swofford (Clay Wooten), Victor French (Alex Bowen), Robert Random (Kyle Bowen), Robert Totten (Thather), Tom Brown (Orville Mason).

1020. **Lost Flight.** 105 min. Airdate: 1970. Production Company: Universal Television. Director: Leonard Horn. Executive Producer: Frank Price. Producer: Paul Donnelly. Writer/Creator: Dean Reisner. Price's second attempt to sell the "people lost on uncharted island and must create own civilization" concept. This time, it's an airliner that crashlands on a mid–Pacific island with Lloyd Bridges as the captain and the leader of the survivors and Bobby Van as the troublemaker. Shot on location in Hawaii with costars Billy Dee Williams, Anne Francis, Ralph Meeker, Andrew Prine, and Michael James.

1021. **The Protectors.** 2 hours. Production Company: Universal Television. Director: Jerry Thorpe. Executive Producer: E. Jack Neuman. Producer: Lloyd Richards. Writers: E. Jack Neuman. Released as the feature film *Company of Killers.* The adventures of a harried police captain (Van Johnson) and his friend (Clu Gulager), a newspaper reporter who covers the police beat and, sometimes, must be critical of the captain. Cast: Van Johnson (Sam Cahill) Ray Milland (George DeSalles), Brian Kelly (Nick Andros), Fritz Weaver (John Shankalien), Clu Gulager (Frank

Quinn) Susan Oliver (Thelma Dwyer) John Saxon (Dave Poohler), Diana Lynn (Edwina DeSalles), Terry Carter (Jaffie) Robert Middleton (Owen Brady).

NBC / COMEDY

1022. Anderson and Company. 30 min. Airdate: 5/12/69. Production Company: 20th Century Fox. Director: Gene Reynolds. Producer: Gene Reynolds Writer: Jean Holloway. Creator: Jean Holloway. A comedy set in New York at the turn-of-the-century. Fred Gwynne is the manager of one of the first department stores, the father of eight unruly children, and the husband to a very bewildered wife (Abby Dalton). *Cast:* Fred Gwynne (as Marshall Anderson), Abby Dalton (Augusta Anderson), Cynthia Eilbacher (Amanda Anderson), Heather Harrison (Alfa Anderson), Robin Eccles (Adienne Anderson), Nick Beauvy (Anstruther Anderson), Ray Dimas (Amory Anderson), Teddy Eccles (Ansford Anderson), Sean Kelly (Artanza Anderson), Leig Nervik (Apollo Anderson), Renie Riano (Miss Slight).

1023. The Best Years. 30 min. Airdate: 8/4/69. Craig Stevens is the widowed father of three girls – Brooke Bundy, Robyn Millan, and Susan Joyce. A reworked version of the NBC pilot *Walt's Girls,* also written and created by Sidney Sheldon, the previous season.

1024. The Flim-Flam Man. 30 min. Airdate: 9/1/69. Production Company: 20th Century Fox. Director: Alan Rafkin. Executive Producer: Lawrence Turman. Producer: Herman Saunders. Writer: James Bridges. Music: Don Scardino. Based on the motion picture. Forrest Tucker is Mordecai Jones, a conman roaming the backwoods of the North and deep South with his able assistant, Curley Treadway (Don Scardino). Together, they swindle the greedy, the dishonest, the gullible – but never an honest man. *Cast:* Forrest Tucker (as Mordecai Jones), Don Scardino (Curley Treadway), James Gregory (Packard), Elena Verdugo (Mrs. Packard), Gene Evans (Sheriff Slade), Dub Taylor (Weehunt), Lada Edmond, Jr. (Bonnie Lee), Guy Raymond (Buck), Bob Hastings (Meeshaw), Hope Summers (Debbie Packard).

1025. Hastings Corner (aka The Shameful Secrets of Hastings Corner). 30 min. Airdate: 1/14/70. Production Company: Screen Gems. Director: Bob Claver. Executive Producer: Harry Ackerman. Producers: Lawrence J. Cohen and Fred Freeman. Writers: Lawrence J. Cohen and Fred Freeman. Music: George Duning. A spoof of soap operas revolving around the clash between the Honker and Fandango families. *Cast:* Alan Oppenheimer (as Dr. Byron Dorman, the psychiatrist), Woodrow Parfrey (Ta Ta Honker), Hal Linden (D.A. Corey Honker/Morey Honker), Karen Black

1970–1971

ABC / COMEDY

1033. **The Connie Stevens Show.** 30 min. Production Company: Screen Gems. Stevens plays a woman who, with several other women, runs a business that does odd jobs of all kinds in this completed pilot. Although this didn't sell, ABC remained high on Connie Stevens and the following season cast her in a 90 minute pilot entitled *Call Her Mom.*

1034. **The Don Rickles Show.** 60 min. Production Company: ABC Productions. Producers: Bud Yorkin and Norman Lear. A musical/variety special which included a "Honeymooners"-type sketch that was meant as a spin-off pilot for a proposed series.

1035. **The Murdocks and the McClays.** 30 min. Airdate: 9/2/70. Production Company: Paramount Television. Director: Charles R. Rondeau. Executive Producers: Jerry Belson and Garry Marshall. Producer: Jerry Davis. Writers: Jerry Belson and Garry Marshall. Creators: Jerry Belson and Garry Marshall. Noah Beery and Dub Taylor are the patriarchs of two feuding hillbilly families in a rural town who try to stop their children – Kathy Davis and John Carson – from falling in love. *Cast:* Dub Taylor (as Angus McClay), Kathy Davis (Julianna McClay), Noah Beery (Calvin Murdock), John Carson (Calvin Murdock, Jr.), Judy Canova (Ira Murdock), William Fawcett (Grandpa Murdock), Nydia Westman (Grandma Murdock), James Westerfield (Sheriff Bates), George C. Fisher (Turkey).

1036. **Prudence and the Chief.** 30 min. Airdate: 8/26/70. Production Company: 20th Century Fox. Director: Marc Daniels. Producer: David Gerber. Writer: Jean Holloway. Creator: Jean Holloway. From the creator of *The Ghost and Mrs. Muir* comes this comedy/western about a widow/missionary/teacher who, with the support of her two children and her mother, moves out West and starts a school in uncivilized Cheyenne territory and immediately clashes with the Indian chief. This love/hate relationship would form the central conflict. *Cast:* Sally Ann Howes (as Prudence MacKenzie), Rick Jason (Chief Snow Eagle), Kathryn Givney (Letitia MacKenzie), Teddy Quinn (Gavin MacKenzie), Johnny Lee (Fergus MacKenzie), Rhodes Reason (Major O'Toole), Mac Krell (Lt. Burns), Troy Melton (Sergeant).

1037. **Three for Tahiti.** 30 min. Airdate: 8/19/70. Production Company: Screen Gems. Director: E.W. Swackhamer. Producers: Bill Persky and Ken Kragen. Writer: Bill Persky. Music: Jack Elliot and Allyn Ferguson. Based on the true story of three men who escaped the pressures of urban life by purchasing a broken-down hotel in Tahiti, sight unseen. Shot on location. *Cast:* Robert Hogan (as Kelly), Bob Einstein (Mark), Steve Franken (Jay), Alan Oppenheimer (Cecil Barrett), Marcel Hillaire (Police Chief Longet).

ABC / DRAMA

1038. **McBride.** Production Company: MGM. Producer: Stan Shpetner. Alex Dreier stars as a famed trial attorney modeled after F. Lee Bailey.

1039. **Mister Jericho.** 85 min. Airdate: 3/3/70. Production Company: ITC Entertainment. Director: Sidney Hayers. Producer: Julian Wintle. Writer: Philip Levine, from a story by David T. Chandler. Music: George Martin. Theme: George Martin and Don Black, sung by Lulu. Patrick MacNee is a smooth conman who, in the pilot, teams up with Connie Stevens to swindle a dastardly millionaire out of his priceless diamond. Shot in Europe. *Cast:* Patrick Macnee (as Dudley Jericho), Marty Allen (Wally), Connie Stevens (Susan Gray), Herbert Lom (Victor Russo), Leonardo Pieroni (Angelo), Bruce Boa (George Nolan), Joanne Dainton (Merle Nolan), Paul Darrow (Hotel Clerk), Jasmina Hilton (Maid), Peter Yapp (Felipe), June Cooper (Stewardess #1), Nancy Egerton (Stewardess #2), Anne Godfrey (Elegant Lady).

1040. **The Over-the-Hill Gang.** 90 min. Airdate: 10/7/69. Production Company: Spelling/Thomas Productions. Director: Jean Yarbrough. Executive Producers: Aaron Spelling and Danny Thomas. Producer: Shelley Hull. Writer: Jameson Brewer. Music: Hugo Friedhofer. A group of aged, retired Texas rangers band together again to clean up a corrupt town. The show's sole saving grace was the opportunity to see some familiar faces again. This marked the first TV movie appearance of Gypsy Rose Lee and her last acting stint. *Cast:* Pat O'Brien (as Capt. Oren Hayes), Walter Brennan (Nash Crawford), Chill Wills (Gentleman George Agnew), Edgar Buchanan (Jason Fitch), Andy Devine (Judge Amos Polk), Gypsy Rose Lee (Cassie), Jack Elam (Sheriff Clyde Barnes), Edward Andrews (Mayor Nard Lundy), Rick Nelson (Jeff Rose), Kris Nelson (Hannah Rose), William Smith (Amos).

1041. **The Over-the-Hill Gang Rides Again.** 90 min. Airdate: 11/17/70. Production Company: Spelling/Thomas Productions. Director: George McCowan.

Executive Producers: Aaron Spelling and Danny Thomas. Producers: Shelley Hull and Andrew Brennan. Writer: Richard Carr. Music: David Raksin. Fred Astaire, as an ex–Texas ranger-turned-no-good-drunk, joins the gang after they sober him up and help him restore his tarnished reputation. A second shot at the *Over-the-Hill* concept featuring the same core cast as the first (with the exception of Pat O'Brien). *Additional Cast:* Fred Astaire (as The Baltimore Kid), Paul Richards (Sam Braham), Lana Wood (Katie), Parley Baer (The Mayor), Walter Burke (Stableman), Lillian Bronson (Mrs. Murphy), Jonathon Hole (Parson), Burt Mustin (Best Man), Don Wilbanks (Cowboy), Pepper Martin (Drifter).

1042. **The Wileys.** 60 min. Production Company: Paramount Television. Producers: Arnold Margolin and James Parker. Writers: Arnold Margolin and James Parker. Gary Collins and Penny Fuller are a husband and wife detective team reminiscent of Mr. and Mrs. North in this comedy/adventure shot on the backlot.

1043. **The Young Country.** 90 min. Airdate: 3/17/70. Production Companies: Public Arts and Universal Television. Director: Roy Huggins. Executive Producer: Roy Huggins. Producers: Carl Pingitore and Steve Heilpern. Writer: Roy Huggins. Creator: Roy Huggins. Music: Pete Rugolo. The adventures of gambler Stephen Foster Moody (Roger Davis) who, in the pilot, tracks down the rightful heir to $38,000 that belonged to a mysterious gunman, played by Wally Cox. Peter Deuel, as a shady drifter, would have costarred in the series. *Cast:* Roger Davis (as Stephen Foster Moody), Peter Deuel (Honest John Smith), Walter Brennan (Sheriff Matt Fenley), Joan Hackett (Clementine Hale), Wally Cox (Aaron Grimes/Ira Greebe), Skip Young (Hotel Manager), Steve Sandor (Parker), Walter Driscoll Miller (Harvey Fat Chance), Richard Van Fleet (Randy Willis).

CBS / COMEDY

1044. **Man in the Middle.** 30 min. Airdate: 4/14/72. Production Company: CBS Productions. Director: Herbert Kenwith. Producers: Harvey Bullock and Ray Allen. Writers: Harvey Bullock and Ray Allen. Creators: Harvey Bullock and Ray Allen. Music: Jerry Fielding. Van Johnson stars as a conservative father suffering the conflicts and confusion wrought by his wife (Nancy Malone), his son (Michael Brandon), his left-wing daughter (Heather Menzies), his right wing mother (Ruth McDevitt), and his middle-aged partner (Allan Melvin).

1045. **Maureen.** 30 min. Production Company: Andomar Productions. Producer: Aaron Ruben. Creator: Aaron Ruben. Maureen Arthur stars as a sweet, honest real estate agent who works for a less-than-honest boss (Pat Harrington) in this completed pilot.

1046. **Shepherd's Flock.** 30 min. Airdates: 8/29/71 and 8/11/72. Production Company: Talent Associates. Director: Peter Tewksbury. Executive Producer: Leonard Stern. Producer: David Davis. Writers: Allan Burns and Chris Hayward. Aired as an episode of *CBS Comedy Playhouse.* Jack Shepherd (Kenneth Mars) is an ex-football player who marries a fashion model (Jill Jaress), becomes a minister, and moves back to his hometown. Costarred Don Ameche as the Bishop.

CBS / DRAMA

1047. **Crisis Clinic (aka Crisis).** 60 min. Airdate: 4/16/70. Production Company: Quinn Martin Productions. Director: Paul Wendkos. Executive Producer: Quinn Martin. Producer: Adrian Samish. Writer: Anthony Spinner. Carl Betz heads a crack team of psychiatrists, doctors, and detectives who work with all city departments to predict and stop dangerous events before they happen. In the pilot, he tracks down a killer who calls in clues to the police. *Cast:* Carl Betz (as Dr. Frank Chandler), Susan Strasberg (Lisa Edwards), Billy Dee Williams (Dan Gardner), Roger Perry (Jerry Taylor), Robert Drivas (Art Winters), Ruth Roman (Mrs. Winters), Davey Davison (June Fielding), Joan Karr (Phyllis Edwards).

1048. **Hunter.** 90 min. Airdate: 1/9/73. Production Company: CBS Productions. Director: Leonard J. Horn. Producer: Bruce Geller. Writer: Cliff Gould. Creator: Bruce Geller. Music: Lalo Schifrin. John Vernon, usually cast as a villain, portrays an intelligence agent named Hunter (perhaps the most common name of a spy or law enforcement official on television) who, in the pilot, assumes the identity of a fellow agent brainwashed by unknown enemies into releasing a virus that could kill half the U.S. population. *Cast:* John Vernon (as David Hunter), Steve Ihnat (Alain Praetorius), Sabrina Scharf (Anne Novak), Edward Binns (Owen Larkdale), Fritz Weaver (Cirrak), Ramon Bieri (Mishani), John Schuck (McDaniel), Barbara Rhoades (Girl), Roger Bowen (Alfred Blunt), Woodrow Parfrey (Tyson), Lonny Chapman (Albert Treadway), Ed Flanders (Dr. Miles), Sheldon Allman (Dr. Abrams), Dary Jones (Lubbock), Tony Van Bridge (Griggs), Lawrence Cook (Donnelly), Walter Stocker (Gunner).

1049. **Juvenile Hall.** Production Company: CBS Productions. Producer: Ellis Marcus. A proposed summer replacement series which, had it been made, would have served as the prototype for a regular season show revolving around three separate probation officers and their cases. A "name" actor would play each officer and would alternate as the lead each week.

NBC / COMEDY

1050. **Arnold's Closet Revue.** 30 min. Airdate: 8/30/71. Production Company: Schlatter-Friendly Productions. Director: Alan J. Levi. Executive Producer: George Schlatter. Producer: Carolyn Raskin. Writers: Chris Bearde and Coslough Johnson. Music: Ian Bernard. A comedy showcase developed for Arte Johnson and utilizing the characters he made popular on Schlatter's *Laugh-In* in a selection of skits and blackouts. The supporting players included Bonnie Boland, Joyce Bulifant, Jim Connell, Joan Gerber, Harvey Jason, Chuck McCann, Carol Robinson, Fred Smoot, and Frank Welker.

1051. **Cat Ballou [Pilot #1].** 30 min. Airdate: 9/5/71. Production Company: Screen Gems. Director: Jerry Paris. Executive Producer: Harry Ackerman. Producer: Aaron Ruben. Writer: Aaron Ruben. The first of two pilots based on the movie that starred Jane Fonda as a ranch owner who hires Lee Marvin, in his Oscar-winning role as an ex-gunslinger. In the pilot, Cat (Lesley Ann Warren) hires Kid Shelleen (Jack Elam) and his friends Jackson Two Bears (Tom Nardini) and Clay (Bo Hopkins) to help her set up a school and protect her ranch. This pilot, shot for the 1970–71 season, was rejected and wasn't aired until the 1971–72 season, when the second pilot was offered to NBC. *Cast:* Lesley Ann Warren (as Cat Ballou), Jack Elam (Kid Shelleen), Tom Nardini (Jackson Two Bears), Joel Higgins (The Sheriff), Laurie Main (Land Developer), Bo Hopkins (Clay).

1052. **Cat Ballou [Pilot #2].** 30 min. Airdate: 9/6/71. Production Company: Screen Gems. Director: Bob Claver. Executive Producer: Bob Claver. Producer: Jon Epstein. Writer: William Blinn. An utterly revamped attempt to translate the film to TV and, aired the day after the first, was a sharp contrast that probably confused viewers who thought they'd be seeing more of the same. This time Forrest Tucker is Kid Shelleen, a drunk ex-gunfighter who is hired by ranch owner Cat Ballou (Jo Ann Harris) to help her protect her recently inherited ranch, where she lives with her adopted, 12-year-old Indian boy, Jackson Two Bears (Lee Casey). Though listed here for convenience, this was actually made for consideration in the 1971–72 season. *Cast:* Jo Ann Harris (as Cat Ballou), Forrest Tucker (Kid Shelleen), Lee J. Casey (Jackson Two Bears), Harry Morgan (The Rancher), Bryan Montgomery (Clay), Jim Luisi (Spider Levinsky), Bill Calloway (Loopy), Jay Silverheels (Indian Chief).

1053. **Harper Valley, USA.** 60 min. Airdate: 8/11/69. Production Company: Talent Associates. Director: Jonathan Lucas. Producer: Don Van Atta. Writers: Al Rogers, Rich Eustis, and Bernard Rothman. A "Hee-Haw" style comedy/variety show, inspired by the song "Harper Valley PTA" by Jeannie C. Riley, which revolved around the wacky residents of the fictional town of Harper Valley. The pilot was co-hosted by Riley and country singer Jerry Reed and guest starred Mel Tillis and Tom T. Hall. The pilot is included in this volume for sheer trivia—the song would later serve as the inspiration for the theatrical film *Harper Valley PTA* and the short-lived NBC sitcom of the late 70s, both of which starred Barbara Eden.

1054. **The Kowboys.** 30 min. Airdate: 7/13/70. Production Company: 20th Century Fox. Director: Ernest Pintoff. Producers: Ernest Pintoff and Don Kirshner. Creators: Ernest Pintoff and Don Kirshner. Music: Don Kirshner and Jeff Barry. A frontier version of *The Monkees* by the same folks who created it. The adventures of the Kowboys, five singers roaming the old West in the 1870s. In the pilot, they attempt to save the town of Civilization from an evil rancher. Ruth Buzzi would have had a recurring role in the proposed series. *Cast:* Boomer Castleman (as Matthew), Michael Martin Murphy (Zak), Jamie Carr (Sweetwater), Joy Bang (Smitty), Edward Andrews (Capt. Walker), Frank Welker (Clem).

1055. **Southern Fried. 30 min.** Airdate: 8/3/70. Production Company: 20th Century Fox. Director: Gene Reynolds. Producer: Gene Reynolds. Writer: William Fox, from his novel. The story of a small, rural town in South Carolina. The stars were Doria Cook, John Neilson, Ramon Bieri, and Jerry Lanning.

1056. **Two Boys.** 30 min. Airdate: 7/6/70. Production Company: Paramount Television. Producers: James Parker and Arnold Margolin. Writers: James Parker and Arnold Margolin. The comedic misadventures of two 13-year-old boys living in a small, Wisconsin town. *Cast:* Mitch Vogel (as Jud Thomas), Mark Kearney (Billy Beckett), William Schallert (William Beckett), Dabbs Greer (Mr. Landers).

NBC / DRAMA

1057. The Aquarians (aka Deep Lab). 2 hours. Airdate: 10/24/70. Production Companies: Ivan Tors Productions and Universal Television. Director: Don McDougall. Producer: Ivan Tors. Writers: Leslie Stevens and Winston Miller, from a story by Alan Caillou and Ivan Tors. Music: Lalo Schifrin. Ricardo Montalban plays a cross between Jacques Cousteau and Mannix, a deep sea scientist/explorer who, in the pilot, takes his team in a nuclear submarine and tries to salvage a sunken vessel full of nerve gas – before it seeps out and pollutes the ocean and before a villain can get his hands on it. Shot in Florida and the Bahamas. *Cast:* Ricardo Montalban (as Luis Delgado), Jose Ferrer (Alfred Vreeland), Leslie Nielsen (Official), Kate Woodville (Barbara Brand), Lawrence Casey (Bob Exeter), Tom Simcox (Jerry Hollis), Chris Robinson (Ledring), Curt Lowens (Ehrlich), Elisa Ingram (Jean Hollis), Joan Murphy (Norma), Austin Stoker (Bogan), Napoleon Reed (Aganda Official), Henry Mortimer (Bellboy), Phil Philbin (First Technician), Dan Chandler (Sonar), Ted Swanson (Aide), William Evenson (Jim Morgan), Ken Harris (Second Technician), Roger Phillips (Third Technician), Myron Natwick (First Reporter), Harlan Warde (Second Reporter).

1058. The Berlin Affair (aka Info C-3). 2 hours. Airdate: 11/2/70. Production Company: Universal Television. Director: David Lowell Rich. Producers: E. Jack Neuman and Paul Donnelly. Writer: Richard Alan Simmons, from a story by Elliot West. Creator: E. Jack Neuman. Music: Francis Lai. Darren McGavin is exspy Paul Killian who, in the pilot, is forced by a secret counter-intelligence organization to hunt down his best friend, an espionage agent gone sour. Shot on location in Europe. *Cast:* Darren McGavin (as Paul Killian), Fritz Weaver (Mallicent), Brian Kelly (Strand), Claude Dauphin (Lanquin), Pascale Petit (Wendi), Christian Roberts (Albert), Derren Nesbitt (Galt), Kathie Browne (Andrea), Marian Collier (Juliet), Reinhard Kolldehoff (Klaus), Heidren Hankammer (Mildred), Gitta Schubert (Copy Girl), Manfred Meurer (Vendor), Isabelle Ervens (Blonde).

1059. Drive Hard, Drive Fast. 2 hours. Airdate: 9/11/73. Production Company: Universal Television. Director: Douglas Heyes. Executive Producer: Roy Huggins. Producers: Jo Swerling, Jr., Steve Heilpern, and Carl Pingitore. Writer: Matthew Howard, from a story by John Thomas James. Music: Pete Rugolo. Shot in 1969, this projected series would have explored the adventurous life of race car driver/adventurer Mark Driscoll (*Flipper's* Brian Kelly) who, the pilot, is hired to drive a wealthy woman (Joan Collins) from Mexico City to New Orleans in her husband's (Joseph Campanella) sports car, which is bugged by a machete-wielding killer (Henry Silva) who is following them. *Cast:* Brian Kelly (as Mark Driscoll), Joan Collins (Carole Bradley), Joseph Campanella (Eric Bradley), Henry Silva (Richard La Costa), Karen Huston (Ellen), Todd Martin (William Fielder), Charles H. Gray (Blond Man), Patrick Whyte (Cartier), John Trayne (Gerald Ives), Jacques Denbeaux (Mechanic), Frank Ramirez (Commandante Morales), Budd Allbright (First Man), Michael Carr (Second Man), Socorro Serrano (Maria), Abel Franco (Mexican Cop), Luis Delgado (Handyman), Ref Sanchez (Mestizo).

1060. **The Mask of Sheba (aka Quest).** 2 hours. Airdate: 3/9/70. Production Company: MGM Television. Director: David Lowell Rich. Producer: Sam H. Rolfe. Writer: Sam H. Rolfe. Music: Lalo Schifrin. The story of three adventurers, played by Eric Braeden, Stephen Young, and Corinne Comacho, who take on all kinds of unusual, and usually scientific or archeological, challenges. In the pilot, they hunt for a priceless mask and a missing safari in deepest Ethiopia. Shot on location in Mexico. *Cast:* Eric Braeden (as Dr. Roan Morgan), Stephen Young (Travis Comanche), Corinne Comacho (Dr. Joanna Glenville), Walter Pidgeon (Dr. Max Van Condon), Inger Stevens (Sarah Kramer), Joseph Wiseman (Fandil Bondalok), William Marshall (Capt. Condor Sekallie), Christopher Carey (Peter Drake), Lincoln Kilpatrick (Ben Takahene).

1061. **They Call It Murder (aka Doug Selby).** 2 hours. Airdate: 12/17/71. Production Company: 20th Century Fox. Director: Walter Grauman. Executive Producer: Cornwell Jackson. Producers: Walter Grauman and William Kayden. Writer: Sam Rolfe, from *The D.A. Draws a Circle* by Erle Stanley Gardner. Creator/Consultant: Erie Stanley Gardner. Music: Robert Drasnin. Jim Hutton, as Santa Barbara, California, district attorney Doug Selby, tries to link a corpse in a swimming pool to a car accident and a large insurance claim. *Cast:* Jim Hutton (as Doug Selby), Lloyd Bochner (A.B. Carr), Jessica Walter (Jane Antrim), Nita Talbot (Rona Corbin), Jo Ann Pflug (Sylvia Martin), Edward Asner (Chief Otto Larkin), Carmen Mathews (Doris Kane), Leslie Nielsen (Frank Antrim), Robert J. Wilke (Sheriff Brandon), Bill Elliot (Deputy Bob Terry), Miriam Cohen (Anita Nogales), Vic Tayback (Jeffrey Poland), Harry Townes (Dr. Garrett), Michael Pataki (Pete Cardiff), Vaughn Taylor (Dr. Harry Maxwell), Normann Burton (Movie Director), Helen Kleeb (Ellen Saxe), Val DeVargas (Alex Cordoba), Buck Young (Charlie), Dan White (Judge Faraday), Dina Harmsen (Wardrobe Woman).

1971-1972

ABC / COMEDY

1062. Annie. Production Company: ABC Productions. Producer: Joe Cates. Writers: Joe Bologna and Renee Taylor. Anne Meara stars as a single woman, still living with her parents, trying to find a niche for herself in New York.

1063. Big Man, Little Lady. 30 min. Production Company: Warner Bros. Television. Producer: James Lee Barrett. Writer: James Lee Barrett. The setting is the mid-1800s. Claude Akins is a mountain man who reluctantly agrees at his best friend's deathbed to take Willie, the man's teenage daughter, to California. Michelle Nichols played the girl in this pilot modeled after *True Grit*.

1064. Captain Newman, M.D. 30 min. Airdate: 8/19/72. Production Company: Thomas/Crenna Productions. Producers: Danny Thomas and Richard Crenna. Writer: Frank Tarloff. Creator: Frank Tarloff. Jim Hutton starred as an unorthodox Air Force psychiatrist. Joan Van Ark and Bill Fiore costarred in this pilot based on the movie, which starred Gregory Peck.

1065. God Bless Mr. Ferguson. 30 min. Airdate: 10/29/71. Production Company: Paramount Television. Producers: Bill D'Angelo and Carl Kleinschmitt. Director: Alan Rafkin. A spin-off of the *Love, American Style* segment entitled "Love and the Young Unmarrieds." The comedic adventures of a minister (John McMartin) and his wife (Mary Ann Mobley). In the pilot, the minister tries to convince a couple that are living together to get married.

1066. Jamison's Kids. Production Company: Universal Television. Producer: Frank Price. Writer: Steve Pritzker. This proposed series would mix comedy and drama as Gary Collins, a counselor at an adoption bureau, helps work out the problems faced by orphans, foster parents, and adopted children.

1067. Li'l Abner. 60 min. Airdate: 4/26/71. Production Company: Blye-Bearde Productions. Director: Gordon Wiles. Producers: Chris Bearde and Allan Blye. Writers: Coslough Johnson, Ted Zeigler, Allan Blye, and Chris Bearde, from the comic strip by Al Capp. Music: Earl Brown and Jimmy Dale. A comedy-variety show about the residents of a hillbilly town. *Cast*: Ray Young (as Li'l Abner), Nancee Parkinson (Daisy Mae), Billy Hayes (Mammy Yokum), Billy Bletcher (Pappy Yokum), Bobo Lewis (Nightmare Alice).

1068. The Neighbors. 30 min. Production Company: 20th Century Fox. Producer: Gene Reynolds. Creator: William Woods. Writer: Gene Reynolds. Guess what happens when a liberal family with a 17-year-old son moves next door to a conservative family with a 17-year-old daughter? That's right, the kids fall in love. Eugene Troobnick is a liberal college professor, Darrel Larsen is his son. Jack Burns is a conservative construction worker and Cindy Williams is his daughter.

1069. S.A.M. Production Company: MGM. Producer/Writer: James Komack. The title means "Stories About Men." It's also the first name of the hero, a guy in the Public Works Department at City Hall who arbitrates the opinionated battles between his co-workers, neighbors, and people on the street. Paul Sand stars.

1070. Thunderguys. Production Company: Paramount Television. Producer: Albert Ruddy. The adventures of two L.A. County deputy sheriffs, a Texan (Richard Van Fleet) and a Mexican-American (Jonathon Lippe), who are adept at motorcycle riding, scuba diving, and other heroic acts.

1071. We Love You, Miss Merkle. 30 min. Production Company: Screen Gems. Producer: Paul Junger Witt. Creator/Writer: Bernard Slade. Julie Sommars stars as Miss Merkle, a famous Broadway singer/actress who had to retire after a throat operation. She becomes a small-town elementary school teacher and the series would focus on her adjustment and her interactions with the children and faculty.

ABC / DRAMA

1072. The Bravos. 100 min. Airdate: 1/9/72. Production Company: Universal Television. Director: Ted Post. Executive Producer: David Victor. Producer: Norman Lloyd. Writers: Christopher Knopf and Ted Post, from a story by Christopher Knopf, David Victor, and Douglas Benton. Creator: David Victor. Music: Leonard Rosenman. A western, shot on location in Arizona, about a U.S. Cavalry commander (George Peppard) trying to raise his 12-year-old son (Vincent Van Patten) in an outpost right in the heart of Indian country. The series would have dealt with the conflicts between the cavalry and Indians, with the problems of the settlers who stop at the fort on their way to California, and with the relationship between the commander and his son. In the pilot, his son is abducted by Indians. *Cast:* George Peppard (as Major John Harkness), Vincent Van Patten (Peter Harkness), Pernell Roberts (Jackson Buckley), Belinda J. Montgomery (Heller Chase), L.Q. Jones (Ben Lawler), George Murdock (Capt.

MacDowall), Barry Brown (Garrett Chase), Dana Elcar (Capt. Detroville), John Kellogg (Sgt. Maroy), Bo Svenson (Raeder), Joaquin Martinez (Santana), Kate McKeown (Kate), Randolph Mantooth (Corp. Lewis), Michael Bow (Sgt. Boyd).

1073. **Earth II.** 100 min. Airdate: 11/28/71. Production Company: MGM. Director: Tom Gries. Producers: Allan Balter and William Read Woodfield. Writers: Allan Balter and William Read Woodfield. Music: Lalo Schifrin. The day-to-day operations and soap opera machinations of 2000 people in a space station orbiting earth. The pilot was shot under the guidance of NASA and the Rockwell Corporation and was about as dramatically interesting as one of their industrial films. *Cast:* Gary Lockwood (as David Seville), Tony Franciosa (Frank Karger), Scott Hylands (Jim Capa), Hari Rhodes (Dr. Loren Huxley), Lew Ayres (President Charles Carter Durant), Mariette Hartley (Lisa Karger), Gary Merrill (Walter Dietrich), Inga Swenson (Ilyana Kovalefskii), Brian Dewey (Matt Karger), Edward Bell (Anton Kovalefskii), Diana Webster (Hannah Young), Bart Burns (Steiner), John Carter (Hazlitt), Herbert Nelson (Chairman).

1074. **Escape.** 73 min. Airdate: 4/6/71. Production Company: Paramount Television. Director: John Llewellyn Moxey. Producer: Bruce Lansbury. Writer: Paul Playdon. Creator: Paul Playdon. Music: Lalo Schifrin. Christopher George is an escape artist who, with his faithful sidekick Avery Shrieber, helps those who are wrongly imprisoned to escape their captors. In the pilot, he rescues a kidnapped scientist from a meglomaniac villain and saves the world. *Cast:* Christopher George (as Cameron Steele), Avery Schrieber (Nicholas Slye), William Windom (Dr. Henry Walding), Marlyn Mason (Susan Walding), John Vernon (Charles Walding), Gloria Grahame (Evelyn Harrison), William Schallert (Lewis Harrison), Huntz Hall (Gilbert), Mark Tapscott (Dan), George Clifton (Roger), Lucille Benson (Trudy), Lisa Moore (Vicki), Chuck Hicks (Carter), Ed Gail (Customer), Lester Fletcher (Designer), Merriana Henrig (Model), Caroline Ross (Photographer).

1075. **In Search of America.** 90 min. Airdate: 3/23/71. Production Company: Four Star. Director: Paul Bogart. Executive Producer: Richard M. Rosenbloom. Producer: William Froug. Writer: Lewis John Carlino. Music: Fred Myrow. When a family's 19-year-old son drops out of college because he's disenchanted with American society – and believes real human values are disappearing—the father buys a Greyhound bus and takes his clan on a cross-country trek to explore our nation and its people. *Cast:* Carl Betz (as Ben Olson), Vera Miles (Jenny Olson), Jeff Bridges (Mike Olson), Ruth McDevitt (Grandma Rose), Renne

Jarrett (Kathy), Howard Dugg (Ray Chandler), Kim Hunter (Cora Chandler), Michael Anderson, Jr. (J.J.), Sal Mineo (Nick), Tyne Daly (Anne), Glynn Turman (Bodhi), George Wallace (Clarence), Mary Gail Hobbs (Claire), Ken Syck (Skipper), Tom Baker (Doctor), Jeff Siggins (Announcer).

1076. **Incident in San Francisco.** 100 min. Airdate: 2/28/71. Production Company: Quinn Martin Productions. Director: Don Medford. Executive Producer: Quinn Martin. Producers: Adrian Samish and Arthur Fellows. Writer: Robert Dozier, from the book *Incident at 125th Street* by J.E. Brown. Music: Patrick Williams. The adventures of San Francisco newspaper reporter Christopher Connelly, city editor Tim O'Connor and managing editor Dean Jagger. In the pilot, the reporter tries to clear a man (Richard Kiley) falsely accused of murder. *Cast:* Christopher Connelly (Jeff Marshall), Dean Jagger (Sam Baldwin), Tim O'Connor (Arthur Andrews), Richard Kiley (Robert Harmon), Leslie Nielsen (Lt. Brubaker), John Marley (Mario Cianelli), Phyllis Thaxter (Lois Harmon), Ruth Roman (Sophia Cianelli), David Opatoshu (Herschel Rosen), Claudia McNeil (Odessa Carter), Tracy Reed (Penny Carter), Julius Hariss (Henry Carter), Tom Nardini (Alfred Cianelli), Richard O'Brien (Jasper Mahoney), Ken Lynch (Detective Hanson).

1077. **River of Gold.** 72 min. Airdate: 3/9/71. Production Company: Aaron Spelling Productions. Director: David Friedkin. Executive Producer: Aaron Spelling. Producers: David Friedkin and Mort Fine. Writer: Salvatore C. Puedes. Music: Fred Steiner. Two divers, who made a quick financial killing after finding oil, travel the world looking for romance and adventure. In the pilot, they go to Acapulco, where they find sunken treasure. *Cast:* Roger Davis (as Marcus McAllister), Dack Rambo (Riley Briggs), Ray Milland (Rose), Suzanne Pleshette (Anna), Melissa Newman (Julie), Jorge Luke (Tomas), Pedro Armendariz, Jr. (Angel), Jose Chavez (Rodrigo), Eduardo Lopez Rojas (Cepeda), Teddy Stauffer (Jay Marstron), Barbara Angeli (Tine Marstron), Francisco Cordova (Priest).

1078. **The Sheriff.** 73 min. Airdate: 3/30/71. Production Companies: Screen Gems and Columbia Pictures Television. Director: David Lowell Rich. Executive Producer: Marvin Worth. Producer: Jon Epstein. Writer: Arnold Perl. Creator: Arnold Perl. Music: Dominic Frontiere. The story of a black county sheriff (Ossie Davis) who, with his white deputy (Kaz Garas), works in a remote California town on the eastern slope of the Sierra Nevadas. The series would revolve around both their police cases and their family lives. In the pilot, similar to the feature film

Tick, Tick, Tick (1970), the rape of a black coed causes racial conflict. *Cast:* Ossie Davis (as Sheriff James Lucas), Kaz Garas (Deputy Harve Gregory), Ruby Dee (Sue-Anne Lucas), Kyle Johnson (Vance Lucas), Lynda Day (Aimy Gregory), John Marley (Kinsella), Ross Martin (Larry Walters), Edward Binns (Paulsen), Moses Gunn (Cliff Wilder), Brenda Sykes (Janet Wilder), Joel Fluellen (Charley Dobey), Austin Willis (Judge), Parley Baer (Braden), Bill Quinn (Doctor), David Moses (Sopes), Lynette Piernas (Wilma).

1079. **Yuma.** 73 min. Airdate: 3/2/71. Production Company: Aaron Spelling Productions. Director: Ted Post. Producer: Aaron Spelling. Writer: Charles Wallace. Creator: Aaron Spelling. Music: George Duning. Clint Walker stars as U.S. Marshall David Harmon, a tough lawman who eludes a killer, foils a plot to discredit him, and brings the law to a frontier town controlled by all sorts of Western-genre vermin. Katherine Hayes would have had a recurring role in the projected series. *Cast:* Clint Walker (as Marshall David Harmon), Katherine Hayes (Julie Williams), Barry Sullivan (Nels Decker), Edgar Buchanan (Mules McNeil), Morgan Woodward (Arch King), Peter Mark Richman (Major Lucas), John Kerr (Capt. White), Robert Phillips (Sanders), Miquel Alejandro (Anders), Neil Russell (Rol King), Bruce Glover (Sam King).

CBS / COMEDY

1080. **After the Honeymoon.** 30 min. Airdate: 3/20/71. Production Company: Don Fedderson Productions. Director: Fred DeCordova. Executive Producer: Don Fedderson. Producer: Edmund Hartman. Creator: Edmund Hartman. Aired as a spin-off from *My Three Sons*. Robbie (Don Grady) and Katie (Tina Cole) and their triplets move to a San Francisco apartment, where the manager (Pat Carroll) loves to take in stray animals and kids and her husband (Richard X. Slattery) whines about it. Mike Minor played their nextdoor neighbor, a bachelor.

1081. **Amateur's Guide to Love.** 30 min. Airdate: 8/8/71. Production Company: Filmways. Director: Gordon Wiles. Executive Producers: Merrill Heatter and Robert Quigley. Producer: Ed Simmons. Writers: Ed Simmons, Warren Murray, and Ed Haas. *Hollywood Squares* producers Heatter and Quigley created this *Candid Camera* of awkward romantic situations and gags. Hosted by Joe Flynn and guest starring Dick Martin, Rose Marie, Michael Landon, and Peter Marshall. This became a CBS daytime series in 1972.

1082. The Blonde (aka Carol). 30 min. Airdate: 2/1/67. Production Company: Filmways. Director: Bruce Bilson. Executive Producer: Paul Henning. Producer: Jay Sommers. Writers: Jay Sommers and Dick Chevillat. Music: Vic Mizzy. Aired as the "Ex-Secretary" episode of *Green Acres*. In the pilot, Oliver's (Eddie Albert) ex-secretary Carol (Elaine Joyce) is now working in a real estate office and constantly frustrates and confounds her boss, played by Richard Deacon. Emmaline Henry played her sister and Cliff Norton was her brother-in-law.

1083. The Elke Sommer Show (aka Elke). 30 min. Airdate: 8/22/71. Production Companies: Warner Bros. Television and Arwin Productions. Producers: Danny Arnold and Mel Shavelson. Writers: Danny Arnold and Mel Shavelson. Aired as an episode of *CBS Comedy Playhouse*. A shy, young American doctor (Peter Bonerz) on vacation in Switzerland meets a glamorous woman (Elke Sommers), marries her, and brings her back to America. The comedy would arise from the clash between his conservative personality and her outgoing one. *Cast:* Elke Sommers (as Elke Stefan), Peter Bonerz (Peter Stefan), Kay Medford (Mrs. Stefan), Debi Storm (Dodie Stefan), Paul Peterson (Charlie Stefan).

1084. Hawaiian Honeymoon (aka Pam). 30 min. Airdate: 3/16/71. Production Company: Filmways. Director: Richard L. Bare. Producers: Jay Sommers and Dick Chevillat. Writers: Jay Sommers and Dick Chevillat. Aired as an episode of *Green Acres*. Oliver (Eddie Albert) and Lisa (Eva Gabor) take a fifth honeymoon at the Moana Rexford Hotel, run by a widower (Don Porter) and his precocious, troublesome daughter (Pamela Franklin) – the would-be regulars of the would-be series.

1085. Me and Joe. 30 min. Production Company: Paramount Television. Director: Hal Cooper. Executive Producer: Jerry Davis. Producer: Tom August. Kenneth Mars becomes the guardian of a precocious boy, played by Scott Kolden. Costarred James Gregory and Ann Prentiss.

1086. My Wives Jane. 30 min. Airdate: 8/1/71. Director: Edward H. Feldman. Producer: Edward H. Feldman. Writer: Larry Gelbart. Janet Leigh stars as an actress who is married to a doctor (Barry Nelson) in real life and plays a doctor's wife in a soap opera. John Dehner is her TV husband and McLean Stevenson is her producer. *Cast:* Janet Leigh (as Jane Franklin), Barry Nelson (Dr. Nat Franklin), John Dehner (Vic Semple), McLean Stevenson (Dick Bennett), Mia Bendixsen (Molly), Nora Marlowe (Magda).

1087. **Scared Stiff.** 30 min. Production Company: Paramount Television. Producers: Gary Marshall and Jerry Belson. Writers: Gary Marshall and Jerry Belson. The adventures of two bumbling detectives, played by Bob Denver and Warren Berlinger.

1088. **Young Love.** 30 min. Airdate: 5/24/74. Production Company: Arwin Productions. Producer: Norman Tokar. Writers: Bruce Sand and Robert Stanton. This was originally intended to air as the last *Doris Day Show* episode of 1971. Because this pilot was designed to generate a series that would explore the special problems of young newlyweds today (through the lives of a couple played by Meredith Birney and Michael Burns), the producer hired two writers in their early 20s.

CBS / DRAMA

1089. **Crosscurrent (aka Cable Car Murder).** 2 hours. Airdate: 11/19/71. Production Company: Warner Bros. Television. Director: Jerry Thorpe. Executive Producer: E. Jack Neuman. Producer: Lloyd Richards. Writer: Herman Miller. Creator: E. Jack Neuman. Music: Jerry Goldsmith. Not unlike the ABC pilot *The Sheriff*, this features a black lawman, a homicide lieutenant played by Robert Hooks, and his white partner, played by Jeremy Slate. Simon Oakland costarred in what has become his typical role, that of the harried boss. In the pilot, telecast initially as 90 minutes and later syndicated in its full 2-hour form, a shipping tycoon's son is assassinated in broad daylight on a cable car. The cops hunt for the hitman and the man who hired him. Guest star Robert Wagner also guest starred in the pilot for a similar cop show, *Streets of San Francisco*. Cast: Robert Hooks (as Lt. Lou Van Alsdale), Jeremy Slate (Sgt. Pat Cassidy), Simon Oakland (Captain E.J. Goodlad), Robert Wagner (Howard McBride), Carol Lynley (Kathy Copper), Jose Ferrer (Dr. Charles Bedford), John Randolph (Frederick D. Cooper), Don Pedro Colley (Fred Tench), Joyce Jameson (Lulu), Wesley Lau (Inspector Poole), James McEachin (Don Cope), Lawrence Cook (Harold Britten), H.B. Haggerty (J.P. Moose), Milton Stewart (Ernie Deeds), Mario Van Peebles (Rafael), Fred Carson (Victor Shoddy), Marian Collier (Surgical Nurse), Ta-Ronce Allen (Lilly), Jarroo Wong (Ben).

1090. **Travis Logan, D.A.** 100 min. Airdate: 3/11/71. Production Company: Quinn Martin Productions. Director: Paul Wendkos. Executive Producer: Quinn

Martin. Producers: Adrian Samish and Arthur Fellows. Writers: Andrew Lewis and Arthur Fellows. Music: Patrick Williams. When a clever man (Hal Holbrook) kills his wife, and then fools a psychiatrist into believing he was temporarily insane, tough district attorney Vic Morrow struggles to prove him guilty of murder. *Cast:* Vic Morrow (as Travis Logan), Chris Robinson (Mark), James Callahan (Jerry), Hal Holbrook (Matthew Sand), Brooke Bundy (Eve), Brenda Vaccaro (Lucille Sand), George Grizzard (Chuck Bentley), Scott Marlowe (George Carnera), Edward Andrews (Judge Rose), Michael Strong (Dr. Reichart), Josephine Hutchinson (Mrs. Tice), James Chandler (Reporter), Richard Angarola (Tony Carnera).

NBC / COMEDY

1091. **Allan.** 30 min. Airdate: 8/23/71. Production Company: Warner Bros. Television. Producers: Danny Arnold and Mel Shavelson. Writers: Danny Arnold and Mel Shavelson. Mark Jenkins is a college graduate who still doesn't know what he wants to do or who he is so he sets out to find himself, dragging his parents (Florence Halop and Lou Jacobi) and his girlfriend (Barbara Press) along on the quest. In the pilot, his father wants him to work in the family hardware store and he wants to join a commune. *Cast:* Mark Jenkins (as Allan Fisher), Lou Jacobi (Harold Fisher), Florence Halop (Blanche Fisher), Barbara Press (Doris), Victor Brandt (Ted), Brioni Farrell (Alice), Connie Sawyer (Franny).

1092. **Bobby Parker and Company.** 30 min. Airdate: 4/22/74. Production Company: Universal Television. Director: Bill Persky. Executive Producer: Charles Engel. Producers: Bill Persky and Gerald S. Shepard. Writer: Bill Persky. Music: Jack Elliot and Allyn Ferguson. Ted Bessell is a man whose neurosis and troubles take on human form. This, along with *Doctor Dan* and the pilot for *The Partners* was supposed to air as a 90-minute *World Premiere* TV movie. Instead, a busted 1966 pilot for *Ready and Willing* was substituted for *The Partners* (which sold and became a short-lived series) and the three flops aired three years later under the title *Three-In-One. Cast:* Ted Bessell (as Bobby Parker), Marj Dusay (His Wife), Joan Blondell (His Mother), Tom D'Andrea (His Father), Tom Poston (His Psychiatrist), Noam Pitlik (The Policeman), Eric Shea (Nine-year-old Bobby), Chuck Bail (Burglary Suspect), Harvey Gardner (Wanted Man), Tony Giorgio (Burglary Suspect).

1093. Doctor Dan. 30 min. Airdate: 4/22/74. Production Company: Universal Television. Director: Jackie Cooper. Executive Producer: Charles Engel. Producer: Bob Finkel. Writer: Ed Weinberger. Music: David Shire. Jackie Cooper is a U.C.L.A. psychiatrist who also is a part-time counselor at Beverly Hills High School but can't seem to handle his own kids. In the pilot, he helps reform a 10-year-old thief and cope with his 16-year-old daughter, who is dating a college student. Barbara Stewart costarred as his wife, Heather Menzies played his daughter, and Willie Aames and Robert Reiser were his sons. *Cast:* Jackie Cooper (as Dr. Dan Morgan), Barbara Stuart (Elaine Morgan), Heather Menzies (Joyce Morgan), Willie Aames (Adam Morgan), Robert Reiser (Chris Morgan), Madeline Sherwood (Dr. Viola Nickerson), Ron Pinkard (Scott), Mitzi Hoag (Mrs. Wallace), Lee H. Montgomery (Jimmy Wallace), Patti Cohoon (Lisa), M. Emmet Walsh (Mr. Wallace), Noble Nelson (Alvin), Judy March (Woman), Nevada Spencer (Girl), Mary Lou Barnett (Pretty Girl).

1094. Inside O.U.T. 30 min. Airdate: 3/22/71. Production Company: Screen Gems. Director: Reza S. Badiyi. Executive Producer: Harry Ackerman. Producers: Lawrence J. Cohen and Fred Freeman. Writers: Lawrence J. Cohen and Fred Freeman. Creators: Lawrence J. Cohen and Fred Freeman. Music: Jerry Fielding. The story of the Office of Unusual Tactics, a secret government organization that cleans up other departments' screw-ups. Farrah Fawcett, Bill Daily, Alan Oppenheimer, and Mike Henry are the O.U.T. agents. This pilot was rebroadcast in May 1977 to capitalize on the popularity of Fawcett in *Charlie's Angels.* *Cast:* Bill Daily (as Ron Hart), Farrah Fawcett (Pat Boulion), Alan Oppenheimer (Edgar Winston), Mike Henry (Chuck Dandy), Edward Andrews (Director of Finance), Val Bisoglio (Bendix), Herb Vigran (Harry), James B. Sikking (Patrolman), Paul Smith (Chicken Man), Jim Begg (Student), Cliff Emmich (Coffee Vendor), Larry Fleishman (Majestic Man), Barney Phillips (First Man), Stack Pierce (Second Man).

1095. Is There a Doctor in the House? 30 min. Airdate: 3/22/71. Production Company: Screen Gems. Executive Producer: Harry Ackerman. Producer: Lawrence J. Cohen. Writer: Bernard Slade. Creator: Bernard Slade. William Windom is an overworked doctor in a small, New England town who hires a sharp, attractive woman just out of medical school as his assistant. Their love/hate relationship would have been the underlying source of comedy in the proposed series. *Cast:* William Windom (as Dr. Tim Newly), Rosemary Forsyth (Dr. Michael Griffin), Margaret Hamilton (Emma Proctor).

1096. **The Magic Carpet.** 2 hours. Airdate: 11/6/72. Production Companies: Westwood Productions and Universal Television. Director: William A. Graham. Producer: Randall MacDougall. Writer: Randall MacDougall. Music: Lyn Murray. Envisioned as a 30-minute sitcom or a 60-minute comedy/drama. Susan Saint James would star as an American tourguide in Rome who helps vacationers in trouble. Jim Backus and Nanette Fabray would costar. *Cast:* Susan Saint James (as Timothea Lamb), Jim Backus (George Benson), Nanette Fabray (Virginia Wolfe), Robert Pratt (Josh Tracy), Cliff Potts (Roger Warden), Enzo Carusico (Renato Caruso), Henny Backus (Edna Benson), Abby Dalton (Lucy Kane), Wally Cox (Harold Kane), Selma Diamond (Mrs. Vogel), John Larch (Mr. Tracy), Clint Kimbrough (John Doolittle), Burke Jamie MacDougall (Jamie), Michael Lerner (Michael Glassman), Barbara Pilaven (Clara Burke), Casey MacDonald (Mrs. Tracy).

1097. **The Powder Room.** 30 min. Airdate: 8/26/71. Director: Jonathan Lucas. Executive Producer: Greg Garrison. Producer: Rod Parker. Writers: Robert Hilliard, George Bloom, and Rod Parker. Dean Martin hosted this proposed comedy anthology that featured Jack Cassidy in three vignettes that look at love from a woman's point of view—with Joey Heatherton as a student who wants to seduce her professor, Jeanine Burnier as a woman trying to spark her husband's dormant libido and Elaine Stritch as a widow on the prowl for a new husband.

1098. **Year One (aka Marriage: Year One).** 2 hours. Airdate: 10/15/71. Production Company: Universal Television. Director: William A. Graham. Executive Producer: Norman Felton. Producer: Stephen Karpf. Writers: Elinor Karpf and Stephen Karpf. Music: David Shire. The proposed series was envisioned as either a 30-minute sitcom or 60-minute comedy/drama about the joys and problems of beginning a marriage. The husband (Robert Pratt) was raised on a mid-western farm and goes to medical school in Chicago. His wife (Sally Field) is the daughter of a wealthy, eastern family. They live together in a cramped apartment in a poor Chicago neighborhood – a situation the wife isn't at all prepared for. *Cast:* Sally Field (as Jane Duden), Robert Pratt (L.T. Mellons), William Windom (Warren Duden), Agnes Moorehead (Grandma Duden), Neville Brand (Golonkas), Bob Balaban (Bernie), Lonny Chapman (Phil), Michael Lerner (Lemberg), Susan Silo (Shirley Lemberg), Cicely Tyson (Emma Teasley), Randolph Mantooth

(Dan), Robert Lipton (Luke), Mantan Moreland (Mechanic), Essex Smith (Cal), Alison Rose (Connie), Lorri Davis (Lottie), Stanley Clay (Bobby), Annazette Chase (Loretta), Carol Swenson (Lillian), Paulene Myers (Mrs. Evans), Charles Steel (Mathews), Stuart Nisbet (Judge).

NBC / DRAMA

1099. **The Catcher.** 2 hours. Airdate: 6/2/72. Production Companies: Herbert Leonard Productions and Screen Gems. Director: Allen H. Miner. Executive Producer: Stanley Neufield. Producer: Herbert Leonard. Writer: David Freeman. Music: Bill Walker. Songs: "Half Moon, Half Son," written and performed by Jackie DeShannon, "Not For Long," written and performed by Kiel Martin. The adventures of an ex-agent for the Seattle Bureau of Missing Persons who, with a young Harvard graduate as his assistant, now operates as a private eye who specializes in finding missing people. Guest star Kiel Martin, who also performed one of the songs, later gained fame as a regular on *Hill Street Blues*. Cast: Michael Witney (as Noah Hendrix), Jan-Michael Vincent (Sam), Tony Franciosa (Joe Cade), Catherine Burns (Sara), David Wayne (Armand Faber), Mike Kellin (Capt. Mike Keller), Anne Baxter (Kate), Kiel Martin (Wes Watkins), Jackie DeShannon (Amy Lee), Andy Robinson (Andy), Marshall Efron (Shooting Gallery Attendant), Piano Red (Himself), Naomi Thornton (Woman), Jacqueline Bertrand (Jewelry Saleslady), David Williams (Young Clerk), Eugene Ray Katz (Arcade Manager), Louis Criscuolo (Fruit Vendor), Reuben Figueroa (Billy Figueroa), Reggie Baff (Car Rental Girl), Rehn Scofield (Record Producer), Kay Mason (Memphis Tourist).

1100. **Charlie Chan (aka Happiness Is a Warm Clue; aka Return of Charlie Chan).** 2 hours. Airdate: 7/17/79. Production Company: Universal Television. Director: Daryl Duke. Executive Producer: John J. Cole. Producer: Jack Laird. Writer: Gene Kearney, from a story by Gene Kearney and Simon Last, based on the character created by Earl Biggers. Music: Robert Prince. Although released theatrically in Europe in July 1973, this unsold pilot sat on the shelf for eight years before quietly being broadcast on ABC's late, late show. This time the Asian sleuth, horribly portrayed by caucasian Ross Martin, is an ex–Honolulu cop who has retired to run a pineapple plantation. He's called out of retirement to solve the murder of a Greek shipping tycoon killed on a yacht. Filmed on location in

Vancouver, British Columbia. The updating of the Charlie Chan character was initially going to be done by author Robert Joseph. Some reference works incorrectly cite Leslie Martinson as the pilot's director. *Cast:* Ross Martin (as Charlie Chan), Rocky Gunn (Peter Chan), Virginia Lee (Doreen Chan), Soon-Teck Oh (Stephen Chan), Ernest Harada (Oliver Chan), Pearl Hong (Jan Chan), Adele Yoshioda (Mai-Ling Chan), Richard Haydn (Andrew Kidder), Louise Sorel (Ariane Hadrachi), Joseph Hindy (Paul Hadrachi), Kathleen Widdoes (Irene Hadrachi), Don Gordon (Lambert), Peter Donat (Noel Adamson), Leslie Nielsen (Alexander Hadrachi), William Nunn (Fielding), Pat Gage (Sylvia Grombach), Ted Greenhalgh (Dr. Howard Jamison), Graham Campbell (Inspector Mckenzie), Neil Dainard (Richard Lovell), Otto Lowy (Anton Grombach), John Guiliani (Giancarlo Tui).

1101. **City Beneath the Sea.** 2 hours. Airdate: 1/25/71. Production Company: 20th Century Fox. Director: Irwin Allen. Producer: Irwin Allen. Writer: John Meredyth Lucas, from a story by Irwin Allen. Music: Richard LaSalle. A recast, revamped, feature-length pilot based on the demonstration film of several seasons back and that played like a long episode of *Voyage to the Bottom of the Sea.* Even Richard Basehart showed up, but as the President and not heroic Admiral Nelson. The heroism was up to Stuart Whitman as the leader and designer of Pacifica, an undersea city besieged by terrorists, environmental dangers, and bad dialogue. Robert Colbert, James Darren, and Whit Bissell, once stars of Allen's *Time Tunnel* were also on hand as costars. *Cast:* Stuart Whitman (as Admiral Michael Matthews), Robert Wagner (Brett Matthews), Rosemary Forsyth (Lia Holmes), Robert Colbert (Commander Woody Paterson), Susanna Miranda (Elena), Burr De Benning (Dr. Aguila), Richard Basehart (The President), Joseph Cotten (Dr. Zeigler), James Darren (Dr. Talty), Paul Stewart (Mr. Barton), Sugar Ray Robinson (Captain Hunter), Whit Bissell (Professor Holmes), Larry Pennell (Bill Holmes), Tom Drake (General Putnam), Charles Dierkop (Quinn), William Bryant (Capt. Lunderson), Bob Dowdell (Officer), Edward G. Robinson, Jr. (Dr. Burkson), Johnny Scott Lee (Tony), Glenna Sergent (Sally), Ray Disbury (Security Guard), Erik Nelson (Triton Controller), Sheila Matthews (The Blonde).

1102. **Ellery Queen (aka Ellery Queen: Don't Look Behind You).** 100 min. Airdate: 11/19/71. Production Company: Universal Television. Director: Barry Shear. Executive Producer: Edward J. Montagne. Producer: Leonard J. Ackerman.

Writer: Ted Leighton, from the novel *Cat of Many Tales* by Ellery Queen (Frederick Dannay and Manfred Lee). Music: Jerry Fielding. Writer/Producers Richard Levinson and William Link were involved in the conception of this unsold pilot which featured Peter Lawford as a suave detective writer who helps his father, a police inspector (Harry Morgan), solve baffling murder mysteries. Universal, Levinson, and Link tried again in 1975, taking a lighter approach (with Jim Hutton and Harry Morgan) and setting it in the 30s. They succeeded in selling a series that, although it lasted only a season, was critically praised and had a loyal following. *Cast:* Peter Lawford (as Ellery Queen), Harry Morgan (Inspector Queen), E.G. Marshall (Dr. Cazalis), Skye Aubrey (Christy), Stefanie Powers (Celeste), Coleen Gray (Mrs. Cazalis), Morgan Sterne (Commissioner), Bill Zuckert (Sergeant Velie), Bob Hastings (Hal Hunter), Than Wyenn (Registrar).

1103. Lock, Stock and Barrel. 90 min. Airdate: 9/24/71. Production Company: Universal Television. Director: Jerry Thorpe. Producer: Richard Alan Simmons. Writer: Richard Alan Simmons. Music: Patrick Williams. A western, set in the 1880s, about a couple (Belinda J. Montgomery and Tim Matheson) who elope and head west, pursued by the bride's disgruntled father and her brothers. Another pilot, *Hitched*, was aired in 1973, with Sally Field replacing Montgomery. *Cast:* Tim Matheson (as Clarence Bridgeman), Belinda J. Montgomery (Roselle Bridgeman), Claude Akins (Punch Logan), Jack Albertson (Brucker), Neville Brand (Sgt. Markey), Burgess Meredith (Reverend Willie Pursle), Robert Emhardt (Sam Hatwig), John Beck (Micah Brucker), Charles Dierkop (Corp. Fowler), Joe DiReda (Kane), Timothy Scott (Deville), Mills Watson (Plye), Dan Jenkins (Butcher), Marlene Tracy (Jean).

1104. McCormack (aka Impatient Heart). 103 min. Airdate: 10/8/71. Production Company: Universal Television. Director: John Badham. Producer: William Sackheim. Writer: Alvin Sargent. Creator: Alvin Sargent. Music: David Shire. Carrie Snodgress is a gung-ho social worker who has trouble solving her problems with her lover. *Cast:* Carrie Snodgress (as Grace McCormack), Michael Brandon (Frank Pescadero), Michael Constantine (Murray Kane), Marian Hailey (Nellie Santchi), Hector Elizondo (Mr. Hernandez), Brad David (Brewster Crowley), Harry Davis (Mr. Pescadero), Victor Millan (Felix Mandez), Penny Santon (Mrs. Esposito), Anna Navarro (Mrs. Hernandez).

1105. Sam Hill: Who Killed the Mysterious Mr. Foster? 100 min. Airdate: 2/1/71. Production Companies: Universal Television and Public Arts. Director: Fielder

Cook. Executive Producer: Roy Huggins. Producer: Jo Swerling, Jr. Writers: Richard Levinson and William Link. Music: Pete Rugolo. Ernest Borgnine is a dopey, alcoholic drifter who becomes sheriff of a small town and then, with the help of an adolescent thief (Stephen Hudis) has to solve the murder of a preacher who was collecting $10,000 for a new church. *Cast:* Ernest Borgnine (as Sam Hill), Stephen Hudis (Jethro), Judy Geeson (Jody Kenyon), Will Geer (Simon Anderson), J.D. Cannon (Mai Yeager), Woodrow Parfrey (Doc Waters), G.D. Spardlin (Reverend Foster), Bruce Dern (Deputy Doyle Pickett), Carmen Mathews (Abigail Booth), Sam Jaffe (Toby), John McGiver (Judge Hathaway), Jay C. Flippen (Sheriff Ben), George Furth (Fletcher), Dub Taylor (Lawyer Reed), Milton Selzer (Banker George Murdock), Ted Gehring (Lucas), Dennis Fimple (Hotel Clerk), Robert Gooden (Telegraph Operator).

1972–1973

ABC / COMEDY

1106. The Bar. 30 min. Production Company: Alan King Productions. Producer: Alan King. Writer/Creator: Alan Owns. Fred Gwynne stars as a bartender who meddles in his customers' problems. Producer Alan King recrafted the idea for actor Gabriel Dell, and it became the ABC 1972 summer series *The Corner Bar*. The concept was reworked again a year later, this time starring Anne Meara and Eugene Roche as co-owners of the bar.

1107. The Burtons Abroad. 30 min. Production Company: Universal Television. Producers: Jim Parker and Arnold Margolin. Earl Holliman is a successful American businessman who takes his wife and three teenage kids on a long European vacation.

1108. Call Her Mom. 90 min. Airdate: 2/15/72. Production Company: Screen Gems. Director: Jerry Paris. Executive Producer: Douglas S. Cramer. Producer: Herb Wallerstein. Writers: Gail Parent and Kenny Solms. Theme: Ross Bagdasarian and William Saroyan, sung by Connie Stevens. Connie Stevens is a waitress who becomes housemother at a wild fraternity house at a small-town college, run by Van Johnson. *Cast*: Connie Stevens (as Angela Bianco), Van Johnson (Chester Hardgrove), Gloria DeHaven (Helen Hardgrove), Charles Nelson Reilly (Dean Walden), Jim Hutton (Prof. Calder), Thelma Carpenter (Ida), Steve Vinovich (Randall Feigelbaum), John David Carson (Woody Guiness III), Mike Evans (Wilson), William Tepper (Roscoe), Alfie Wise (Jeremy), William Benedict (Mr. Feigelbaum), Thelma Palish (Mrs. Feigelbaum), Kathleen Freeman (Woman), Herbert Rudley (Mr. Guiness), Corbett Monica (Bruno), Fritz Feld (Waiter), Mike Malmbourg (Chip).

1109. The Class of '55. 30 min. Production Company: 20th Century Fox. Producer: James L. Brooks. An anthology that, in each episode, would show us what has happened to people since graduating from college in 1955. Louise Lasser and Alan Alda starred in the pilot.

1110. Gidget Gets Married. 90 min. Airdate: 1/4/72. Production Company: Screen Gems. Director: E.W. Swackhamer. Executive Producer: Harry Ackerman. Producer: E.W. Swackhamer. Writer: John McGreevey. Creator: Frederick

Kohner. Music: Mike Post and Peter Carpenter. This time Monie Ellis is Gidget, the precocious beach girl who was the focal point of several movies and the Sally Field TV series. In this second pilot, Gidget marries her long-time boyfriend Jeff "Moondoggie" Stevens (Michael Burns) and moves to Maryland, where she clashes with the bosses at the engineering company where he works. *Cast:* Monie Ellis (as Frances "Gidget" Lawrence), Michael Burns (Jeff "Moondoggie" Stevens), MacDonald Carey (Russell Lawrence), Don Ameche (Otis Ramsey), Joan Bennett (Claire Ramsey), Paul Lynde (Louis B. Latimer), Elinor Donahue (Medley Blaine), Corinne Camacho (Nancy Lewis), Roger Perry (Tom Blaine), Larry Gelman (Anatole), Burke Byrnes (Minister), Dennis Fimple (Policeman), Rademas Pera (Bob Ramsey), Tiger Williams (Richie).

1111. **Help, Inc.** 30 min. Production Company: Screen Gems. Producer: Douglas Cramer. Writers: Dee Caruso and Gerry Gardner. Creator: Bud Baumes. Avery Schrieber, Kenneth Gilman, and Anthony Holland are three hapless friends who work together doing odd jobs for anybody.

1112. **Melvin Danger, Private Eye.** 30 min. Production Company: Hanna-Barbera Productions. Producers: Joseph Barbera and William Hanna. Writers/Creators: Harvey Bullock and Ray Allen. Aired as the "Love and the Private Eye" episode of *Love American Style*, this pilot tried to sell ABC on a primetime, adult animated comedy about a private eye who is a master of disguise, so good that he can fool people into thinking he's a vacuum, a lamp post or a mail box. His beautiful female secretary, who makes no secret of her love for him, usually solves the cases, though.

1113. **The Out-of-Towners.** Production Company: Paramount Television. Producer: Howard Koch. Writers: Garry Marshall and Jerry Belson, from the Neil Simon play. A pilot script was written but no pilot was planned for this proposed series based on the movie, which starred Jack Lemmon and Sandy Dennis as a young married couple from the midwest who move to New York. The husband works for a newspaper and writes a column in which he views Manhattan through the wide, naive eyes of a small-town boy.

1114. **We Love Annie.** 30 min. Airdate: 3/1/72. Production Company: MGM. Producer: James Komack. Writer: James Komack. Aired as the "Thy Neighbor Loves Thee" episode of *Courtship of Eddie's Father*. The husband-and-wife comedy team of Anne Meara and Jerry Stiller stars in this pilot inspired by the movie *Bells Are Ringing*. Meara is an operator with a telephone answering service, run by Stiller, who gets herself involved with her callers' lives, and not always to their betterment.

ABC / DRAMA

1115. Biography (aka Portrait: Dupont Cavalcade of Television. 60 min. Production Company: Universal Television. Directors: Various. Executive Producer: David Victor. Producers: Various. Writers: Various. Four pilots were made in this proposed weekly anthology series dramatizing true events in the lives of fascinating, real people. In addition to the filmed pilots, producer Jack Laird was planning a segment on Houdini and producer Herbert Hirschman envisioned an episode about the wartime death of Joseph Kennedy, II.

1116. [Biography Pilot #1] **The Woman I Love.** Airdate: 12/17/72. Director: Paul Wendkos. Producer: David J. O'Connell. Writer: John McGreevey. The romance of King Edward VIII and Mrs. Simpson. *Cast*: Richard Chamberlain (as King Edward VIII), Faye Dunaway (Mrs. Wallis Warfield Simpson), Patrick MacNee (Lord Brownlow), Eileen Herlie (Queen Mary), Henry Oliver (Winston Churchill), Robert Douglas (Prime Minister Stanley Baldwin), Murray Matheson (Walter Monckton).

1117. [Biography Pilot #2] **A Man Whose Name Was John.** Airdate: 4/22/73. Director: Buzz Kulik. Producer: David J. O'Connell. Writer: John McGreevey. Raymond Burr stars as Archbishop Angelo Roncalli, the man who eventually became Pope John XXIII. *Cast*: Raymond Burr (as Angelo Roncalli), Don Galloway (Monsignor Thomas Ryan), David Opatoshu (Rabbi Isaac Herzog), John Colicos (Under Secretary Numan Menemengioglu), Henry Darrow (Minister Calheiros De Menezes), Eric Braeden (Col. Gunter Kroll), Scott Hylands (Capt. Melech Ben Zvi), Alizia Gur (Rachael Friedman), Gil Anov (Joseph Kahn), Penny Santon (Maria Roncalli), Peter Von Zerneck (Ambassador Franz Von Pappen), Diana Ferziger (Marta), Clete Roberts (Himself).

1118. [Biography Pilot #3] **Legend in Granite.** Airdate: 12/14/73. The adventures of football star Vince Lombardi as he led the Green Bay Packers to an NFL playoff. *Cast*: Ernest Borgnine (as Vince Lombardi), Colleen Dewhurst (Marie Lombardi), James Olson (Max McGee), John Calvin (Paul Hornung), John McLiam (Dom Olejnickzak), Alex Rocco (Tony Canadeo).

1119. [Biography Pilot #4] **The Man from Independence.** Airdate 3/11/74. Director: Jack Smight. Producer: Jon Epstein. Writer: Edward DeBlasio. The life of Harry Truman as a judge in Independence, Missouri, in 1929. *Cast*: Robert Vaughn (as Harry S. Truman), Arthur Kennedy (Tom Pendergast), Martha Scott (Mamma Truman), June Dayton (Bess Truman), Russell Johnson (Linaver), Ronne Troup

(Constance), Alan Fudge (Mooney), Tasha Lee (Margaret Truman), James Luisi (Stranger), Lou Frizzell (Quilling), Leonard Stone (Werner), Michael Vandever (Dayton), Alice Backes (Teacher), Jay Virela (Pete).

1120. Cassidy and Torres. 30 min. Production Company: Herbert Leonard Productions. Producer: Herbert Leonard. Writer/Creator: Pete Hamill. Shot on location in New York and based on Hamill's experiences as a columnist for the *New York Post*. Mitchell Ryan is Cassidy, a police beat reporter and Reni Santoni is Torres, a homicide detective, in this pilot that chronicles their adventures.

1121. Code 3. 30 min. Production Company: Screen Gems. Producer: Douglas Cramer. Writer: Bud Baumes. The adventures of a team of emergency room medics (Jim McMullen, Jon Cypher, and Craig Littler), the chief admitting nurse (Barbara Barrie) and Val Bisoglio, a cop. "Code 3" was also the title of a syndicated, 1956 series about the adventures of an L.A. County sheriff, played by Richard Travis.

1122. The Eyes of Charles Sand. 90 min. Airdate: 2/29/72. Production Company: Warner Bros. Television. Director: Reza S. Badiyi. Producer: Hugh Benson. Writers: Henry Farrell and Stanford Whitmore, from a story by Henry Farrell. Creator: Henry Farrell. Music (Uncredited): Henry Mancini. Charles Sand is a man who can see, very unclearly, the future. In the pilot, he helps a woman prove her brother was murdered. A composer's strike prevented Warner Bros. from commissioning an original score and instead they pirated Mancini's soundtrack for *Wait Until Dark*. Cast: Peter Haskell (as Charles Sand), Joan Bennett (Aunt Alexandra), Barbara Rush (Katherine Winslow), Sharon Farrell (Emily Parkhurst), Bradford Dillman (Jeffrey Winslow), Adam West (Dr. Paul Scott), Gary Clarke (Raymond), Ivor Francis (Dr. Ballard), Owen Bush (Gardner), Donald Barry (Trainer), Larry Levine (Groom).

1123. Fireball Forward. 2 hours. Airdate: 3/5/72. Production Company: 20th Century Fox. Director: Marvin J. Chomsky. Producer: Frank McCarthy. Writer: Edmund H. North. Music: Lionel Newman. Theme: "The Longest Day" sung by Paul Anka. From the producer (McCarthy) and co-writer (North) of *Patton* comes this adventure about fictional, Pattonesque World War II General Joe Barrett who takes on the toughest assignments. In the pilot, which utilized footage from *Patton*, Barrett commands a division at the front and looks for a traitor in his ranks. Cast: Ben Gazzara (as Major General Joe Barrett), Ricardo Montalban (Jean Duval), Anne Francis (Helen Sawyer), Dana Elcar (Col. Talbot), Edward Binns (Corps Commander), Morgan Paull (Sgt. Andrew Collins), Curt Lowens (Capt. Bauer),

L.Q. Jones (Maj. Larkin), Eddie Albert (Col. Douglas Graham), Robert Patton (Col. Avery), Richard Yniquez (Capt. Tony Sanchez), Kenneth Tobey (General Dawson), Don Eitner (Sgt. Brock), John Gruber (Doctor), Stanley Beck (M.P. Sgt.), Dick Valentine (Col. Fowler), Joseph Perry (First G.I.), Hank Jones (M.P. Private), Jerry Fogel (Signal Corpsman), Neil Schwartz (Cook), Henry Brown, Jr. (Wounded Soldier), Lair Bybee (First Lt.), James Secrest (Signal Corps Sgt.), Brent Davis (Second Lt.), Ilze Taurins (Mme. Accard), Bob Golden (Sergeant), Buck Holland (Second G.I.), Dan Keough (Supply Sgt.).

Great Detectives. Production Company: Universal Television. Executive Producer: Richard Irving. The umbrella title for three rotating series based on famous detective heroes. A pilot was made for each of the proposed series in the mix and they aired separately. They were:

1124. **[Great Detectives Pilot #1] Sherlock Holmes (aka Hound of the Baskervilles).** 90 min. Airdate: 2/12/72. Director: Barry Chase. Producers: Stanley Kallis and Arthur O. Hilton. Writer: Robert E. Thompson, from the book by Sir Arthur Conan Doyle. A universally panned retelling of the Doyle classic, with Stewart Granger as Holmes and Bernard Fox as Watson. *Cast:* Stewart Granger (as Sherlock Holmes), Bernard Fox (Dr. Watson), William Shatner (George Stapleton), Sally Ann Howes (Laura Frankland), John Williams (Arthur Frankland), Anthony Zerbe (Dr. Mortimer), Jane Merrow (Beryl Stapleton), Billy Bowles (Cartwright), Brendon Dillon (Barrymore), Arline Anderson (Eliza Barrymore), Alan Caillou (Inspector Lestrade), Chuck Hicks (Seldon), Karen Kondon (Mrs. Mortimer), Liam Dunn (Messenger), Michael St. Clair (Constable), Barry Bernard (Manager), Constance Cavenoish (Eel Monger), Arthur Malet (Higgins), Elaine Church (Maid), Jennifer Shaw (Peasant), Terence Pushman (Chestnut Salesman), Eric Brotherson (Porter).

1125. **[Great Detectives Pilot #2] Hildegarde Withers (aka A Very Missing Person).** 90 minutes. Airdate: 3/4/72. Director: Russ Mayberry. Producer: Edward J. Montagne. Writer: Philip Reisman, Jr., from the book *Hildegard Withers Makes the Scene* by Stuart Palmer. Music: Vic Mizzy. Eve Arden stars as Hildegard Withers, the Greenwich Village schoolteacher turned elderly detective popularized in the 1930s RKO films by Edna May Oliver. She still irritates N.Y.P.D. Inspector Oscar Piper (James Gregory) but, in this adaptation, she is aided by a motorcy-cle-riding assistant (Dennis Rucker). *Cast:* Eve Arden (as Hildegarde Withers), James Gregory (Inspector Oscar Piper), Dennis Rucker (Al Fister), Julie Newmar

(Aletha Westering), Ray Danton (Capt. Westering), Skye Aubrey (Sister Isobel/ Leonore Gregory), Robert Easton (Onofre), Woodrow Parfrey (Eberhardt), Bob Hastings (James Malloy), Pat Morita (Delmar Faulkenstein), Ezra Stone (Judge), Linda Gillin (Bernadine Toller), Dwan Smith (Ora), Peter Morrison Jacobs (Dr. Singer), Savannah Bentley (Mrs. Singer), Udana Power (Mariette).

1126. **[Great Detectives Pilot #3] The Adventures of Nick Carter.** 90 min. Director: Paul Krasny. Producers: Stanley Kallis and Arthur O. Hilton. Writer: Ken Pettus. Music: John Tartaglia. Robert Conrad stars as Nick Carter, a private eye working in the turn-of-the-century. Based on the hero popularized in literally 1000s of books and short stories by dozens of uncredited authors. In the pilot, he investigates the murder of another private eye and looks for the missing wife of a rich playboy. Today, Nick Carter lives on in paperbacks as a superspy. *Cast:* Robert Conrad (as Nick Carter), Shelley Winters (Bess Tucker), Broderick Crawford (Otis Duncan), Neville Brand (Captain Dan Keller), Pernell Roberts (Neal Duncan), Pat O'Brien (Hallelujah Harry), Sean Garrison (Lloyd Deams), Laraine Stephens (Joyce Jordan), Brooke Bundy (Roxy O'Rourke), Jaye P. Morgan (Singer), Sorrell Booke (Dr. Zimmerman), Ned Glass (Maxie), Joseph Maross (Archer), Arlene Martel (Flo), Byron Morrow (Sam Bates), Arthur Peterson (Coroner), Booth Colman (Parsons), Warren Parker (Butler), Larry Watson (Desk Sergeant), Leon Lontoc (Desk Clerk), James McCallion (Manager), Charles Davis (Minister), William Benedict (Newsboy), Elizabeth Harrower (Sister Effie), Deidre Hudson (Ivy Duncan).

1127. **Madame Sin.** 2 hours. Airdate: 1/15/72. Production Company: ITC Entertainment. Director: David Greene. Executive Producer: Robert Wagner. Producers: Lou Morheim and Julian Wintle. Writer: Barry Oringer. Creators: Barry Shear and Lou Morheim. Music: Michael Gibbs. A strange pilot that stars Bette Davis as an all-powerful dragon lady who kidnaps a former C.I.A. agent (Robert Wagner), brainwashes him with a special ray gun, and enlists him in her high-tech global intelligence agency that operates out of her Scottish castle. In the pilot, she uses him to steal a polaris submarine. Shot in England though, had it gone to series, it would have been produced in Hollywood. *Cast:* Bette Davis (as Madame Sin), Robert Wagner (Tony Lawrence), Denholm Elliot (Sin's Aide), Gordon Jackson (Commander Ted Cavendish), Dudley Sutton (Monk), Catherine Schell (Barbara), Paul Maxwell (Connors), Pik-Sen Lim (Nikko), David Healy (Braden), Alan Dobie (White), Roy Kinnear (Holidaymaker), Al Mancini (Fisherman), Charles Lloyd Park (Willoughby), Arnold Diamond (Lengett), Frank Middlemass (Dr.

Henriquez), Burt Kwouk (Scarred Operator), Paul Young (Naval Officer), Jack Weir (Chief Petty Officer), Gerard Norman (Lt. Brady), Stuart Hoyle (Naval Officer), Stuart McGugan (Sailor), Gabriella Ligudi (Nun), Vanessa Kempeter (Nun), John Orchard (Revolutionary), John Slavid (Revolutionary), Barry Moreland (Musician).

1128. **The New Healers (aka Med-Ex).** 60 min. Airdate: 3/27/72. Production Company: Paramount Television. Director: Bernard L. Kowalski. Producer: Stirling Silliphant. Writer: Stirling Silliphant. Creator: Stirling Silliphant. Music: Kenyon Hopkins. Leif Erickson stars as the chief doctor at a rural community hospital in the fictional town of Hope, California. He's aided by his son (Robert Foxworth), a paramedic and Vietnam vet; an ex–Navy nurse (Kate Jackson) and a young administrator (Jonathon Lippe). Writer Stirling Silliphant told *Newsweek* that he intended to go after "the good ole boy bullshit of the AMA" and tried to make the point that "the human touch is often more effective than surgery. Not always, but certainly sometimes. Hospitals have bad vibes, karmas stink. The networks would call this 'an action medical show.' Little does ABC know what I have in mind." Perhaps they did, because they didn't pick it up to series. *Cast:* Leif Erickson (as Dr. Victor Briggs), Robert Foxworth (Dr. Calvin Briggs), Kate Jackson (Nurse Michelle Johnson), Jonathon Lippe (Dr. Jimmy Martin), Burgess Meredith (Dr. Simmons), William Windom (Mr. Farrigan), Karl Swenson (Mr. Fisherman), Susan Moffitt (Terri), Barbara Baldwin (Mrs. Spencer), William Bryant (Mr. McDermott).

1129. **The People.** 90 min. Airdate: 1/22/72. Production Companies: Metromedia Producers Corp. and American Zoetrope. Director: John Korty. Executive Producer: Francis Ford Coppola. Producer: Gerald I. Isenberg. Writer: James M. Miller, from the novel *Pilgrimage* by Zenna Henderson. Music: Carmine Coppola. A slow-moving, low-key pilot which casts Kim Darby as a schoolteacher who goes to an isolated California community and is puzzled by students that don't behave like kids at all–and have some unusual abilities. What she eventually discovers is that they, along with William Shatner and Diane Varsi, are the last descendants of a peaceful alien race that possesses awesome psychic powers. *Cast:* Kim Darby (as Melodye Amerson), William Shatner (Dr. Curtis), Diane Varsi (Valency), Dan O'Herlihy (Sol Diemus), Laurie Walters (Karen Dingus), Chris Valentine (Francker), Johanna Baer (Bethie), Stephanie Valentine (Tabitha), Jack Dallgren (Kish), Andrew Chrichton (Thann), David Petch (Matt), Dorothy Drady (Dita), Mary Rose McMaster (Maras), Anne Walters (Obla), Tony Dario (Bram).

1130. RX for the Defense. 60 min. Airdate: 4/15/73. Production Companies: Herbert Brodkin Productions and 20th Century Fox. Director: Ted Kotcheff. Executive Producer: Herbert Brodkin. Producer: Robert Buzz Berger. Writer: Ernest Kinoy. Creator: Ernest Kinoy. The adventures of lawyer Zack Clinton, who is also an M.D. and tackles cases involving the world of health care (though the intended series would not have focused very often–if at all–on malpractice). In the pilot, Clinton tries to free a famous psychiatrist from a sanitarium, where he has been committed after an alleged suicide attempt. *Cast:* Tim O'Connor (as Zack Clinton), Nancy Malone (Laura Masters), Ronny Cox (Al Moore), Fritz Weaver (Dr. Daniel Kemper), Kathryn Walker (Hilda Kempter), Milton Selzer (Dr. Schwartz), Kevin Conway (Dr. Packer), Charles Durning (D.A. Horn), Marge Elliot (Marge).

1131. Second Chance. 90 min. Airdate: 2/8/72. Production Companies: Metromedia Producers Corp. and Danny Thomas Productions. Director: Peter Tewksbury. Executive Producer: Danny Thomas. Producer: Harold Cohen. Writer: Michael Morris. An over-worked stockbroker (Brian Keith) buys a Nevada ghost town, renames it Second Chance, and makes it a haven for people who want a second chance at life. This semi-anthology would focus on the lives of the people who come to Second Chance. Shot on location in Arizona. Guest star Kenneth Mars would later play Brian Keith's brother in a 1986 episode of *Hardcastle and McCormick*. *Cast:* Brian Keith (as Geoff Smith), Elizabeth Ashley (Ellie Smith), Brad Savage (Johnny Smith), Kenneth Mars (Dr. Julius Roth), William Windom (Stan Petryk), Pat Carroll (Gloria Petryk), Juliet Prowse (Martha Foster), Avery Schreiber (Robert Grazzari), Rosie Grier (Maxie Hill), Ann Morgan Guilbert (Charlene), Emily Yancy (Stella Hill), Vernon Weddle (Lester Fern), Bret Parker (Hardin), Bob Nichols (Dr. Strick), Olive Dunbar (Dr. Willard).

1132. Two for the Money. 90 min. Airdate: 2/26/72. Production Company: Aaron Spelling Productions. Director: Bernard Kowalski. Producer: Aaron Spelling. Writer: Howard Rodman. Creator: Howard Rodman. Robert Hooks is a black L.A.P.D. detective who, after he's injured in the line of duty, quits the force and becomes a bounty hunter. Stephen Brooks is his white partner on the force who quits to join him in tracking down wanted criminals who have prices on their heads. In the pilot, they look for a killer who has eluded police for a decade. *Cast:* Robert Hooks (as Larry Dean), Stephen Brooks (Chip Bronx), Walter Brennan (Cody Guilford), Catherine Burns (Judith Gap), Neville Brand (Sheriff Harley), Shelley Fabares (Bethany Hagen), Ann Rever (Mrs. Gap), Mercedes

McCambridge (Mrs. Castle), Richard Dreyfuss (Morris Gap), Skip Homier (Doctor), Michael Fox (Hospital Administrator), Mady Maguire (Waitress).

1133. Wheeler and Murdock. 60 min. Airdate: 5/9/73. Production Company: Paramount Television. Director: Joseph Sargent. Executive Producers: Eric Bercovici and Jerry Ludwig. Producer: Joseph Sargent. Writers: Eric Bercovici and Jerry Ludwig. Music: Robert Drasnin. Jack Warden is a private eye who, when his partner is killed, takes in his partner's son (Christopher Stone) as his associate. In the pilot, they try to solve a mafia murder. Shot entirely on location in Seattle. *Cast:* Jack Warden (as Sam Wheeler), Christopher Stone (Terry Murdock), Van Johnson (Buddy Shore), Diane Baker (Karen), Charles Cioffi (DeNisco), Jane Powell (Dorcie), Dewey Martin (Travanty), Robert Ellenstein (Galvin), Woodrow Parfrey (Weston), Michael Conrad (Turk).

CBS / COMEDY

1134. Bobby Jo and the Big Apple Good Time Band. 30 min. Airdate: 3/31/72. Production Company: Screen Gems. Director: Hal Cooper. Producer: Paul Junger Witt. Writer: Bernard Slade. Music: Jerry Fuller and Michael Murphy. A variation on Witt's *Partridge Family* series. Season Hubley is Bobby Jo, the 23-year-old lead singer of the "Big Apple Good Time Band," which is comprised of four young men. Forrest Tucker is their manager. *Cast:* Season Hubley (as Bobby Jo), Forrest Tucker (Cousin Jack), Robert Walden (Augie), John Bennett Perry (Jeff), Ed Begley, Jr. (Virgil), Michael Gray (Brian), Tom Bosley (Mayor).

1135. The Councilman. 30 min. Airdate: 3/4/72. Production Company: MTM Enterprises. Director: Jay Sandrich. Producer: David Davis. Writers: Arnold Margolin and Jim Parker. Music: Patrick Williams. Aired as the "His Two Right Arms" episode of the *Mary Tyler Moore Show* wherein Mary tries to make an incompetent councilman look good when he appears on WJM. The series would have focused on two secretaries, one white (Carol Androsky) and one black (Janet MacLachlan), who are constantly pulling the councilman (Bill Daily) out of the messes he makes.

1136. Keep the Faith. 30 min. Airdate: 4/14/72. Production Company: CBS Productions. Director: Jackie Cooper. Producer: Ed Simmons. Writer: Ed Simmons. The story of two New York rabbis, one old (Howard Da Silva) and one young (Bert Convy), who are always at odds with each other. This was recast and reworked the following season. *Cast:* Bert Convy (as Rabbi Miller), Howard

Da Silva (Rabbi Mossman), Henry Corden (Rosenthal), Milton Selzer (Pink), Nancy Walker (Sophie), Linda March (Judy).

1137. **The Living End.** 30 min. Airdate: 3/17/72. Production Company: Ilson-Chambers Productions. Director: Peter Baldwin. Producers: Saul Ilson and Ernest Chambers. Writers: Saul Ilson and Ernest Chambers. Aired as one segment of *CBS Comedy Trio*, a collection of busted pilots. Lou Gossett stars as a professional football player who tries to juggle the demands of his two loves—his team, and his wife, played by Diana Sands. This pilot was revamped the following year for ABC as *Two's Company*, with John Amos replacing Gossett and Sands returning as the football player's wife. *Cast:* Lou Gossett (as Doug Newman), Diana Sands (Nancy Newman), Dick O'Neill (Bullets), Paul Cavonis (Mickey), Don Sherman (Stan), Roger Mosley (Henry), John Calvin (Richie).

1138. **The Lucie Arnaz Show.** 30 min. Airdate: 2/28/72. Production Companies: Lucille Ball Productions and CBS Productions. Producer: Gary Morton. Aired as the "Kim Finally Cuts You-Know-Who's Apron Strings" episode of *Here's Lucy*. Kim Carter (Lucie Arnaz) and her friend (Susan Tolsky) move into a Marina Del Rey apartment and meddle in everyone's business, to the consternation of landlord Alan Oppenheimer. Lucille Ball and Desi Arnaz, Jr. would have been recurring characters.

1139. **Miss Stewart, Sir.** 30 min. Airdate: 3/31/72. Production Company: MGM. Director: Peter Tewksbury. Producer: Peter Tewksbury. Writer: A.J. Carothers. Based on the movie *Her Twelve Men*. Joanna Pettet is the first woman to teach at a boy's private boarding school who, in addition to running a fourth grade class, is also a dorm mother and coaches the football team. *Cast:* Joanna Pettet (as Kate Stewart), Gary Vinson (Buzz), Michael Witney (Joe), Murray Matheson (Principal Prentis), Nora Marlowe (Hannah), Don Clarke (George), Lee Hollingshead (Mike).

1140. **My Sister Hank.** 30 min. Airdate: 3/31/72. Production Company: CBS Productions. Director: Norman Tokar. Producer: Norman Tokar. Writer: Ben Starr. Jodie Foster is a likeable tomboy named Hank who, like "Dennis the Menace" before her, causes problems for her mother (Pippa Scott), her father (Jack Ging) and her grandfather (Edgar Bergen). Tod Glass is her best friend, the boy-next-door. *Cast:* Jodie Foster (as Henrietta "Hank" Bennett), Pippa Scott (Eunice Bennett), Jack Ging (Willis Bennett), Edgar Bergen (Grandpa Bennett), Suzanne Hillard (Dianne Bennett), Tod Glass (Arthur).

1141. **Oh, Nurse!** 30 min. Airdate: 3/17/72. Production Company: 20th Century Fox. Director: Bob Sweeney. Executive Producer: David Gerber. Producer: Charles B.

Fitzsimons. Writers: Stan Hart, Larry Siegel, and Treva Silverman. Aired as the second program in the *CBS Comedy Trio* playoff of busted pilots. The comedic misadventures of four student nurses (Lori Saunders, Heather Young, Judy Pace, and Susan Foster) living in a dorm run by Norman Grabowski. Pat Carroll played the head nurse and Stephen Young guest starred.

1142. **The Singles.** 30 min. Airdate: 3/17/72. Production Company: Sheldon Leonard Productions. Director: Sheldon Leonard. Producer: Sheldon Leonard. Writers: Ron Clark and Sam Bobrick. This was the final flop pilot in the *CBS Comedy Trio* special. Michele Lee and Ruth Buzzi are two co-workers at a greeting card factory who share an apartment in this feminine "Odd Couple." Costarred John Byner, Henry Jones, and Jerry Fogel.

1143. **This Week in Nemtim.** 30 min. Airdate: 4/14/72. Production Company: CBS Productions. Director: Bill Foster. Producers/Writers: Saul Turteltaub, Bernie Orenstein, Sam Bobrick, and Ron Clark. An attempt to satirize our society by looking at the events of the day in the fictional land of Nemtim, as seen through the reports of newscaster Alex Dreier and the eyes of wiseman Carl Reiner.

CBS / DRAMA

1144. **Doctor Grainger.** 60 min. Airdate: 2/9/72. Production Company: CBS Productions. Executive Producer: Frank Glicksman. Producer: AlC. Ward. Writer: Lee Segal. Creator: Lee Segal. Music: Lalo Schifrin. Aired as "The Choice" episode of *Medical Center*. Monte Markham stars as a doctor at a major, urban hospital who chooses between a top administrative post and a small practice in a community in desperate need of medical specialists – naturally he chooses the latter. The proposed series would have dealt with his uncomfortable transition as well as the problems of his patients. Costarred Tyne Daly and Clu Gulager.

1145. **Fitzgerald and Pride (aka Heat of Anger).** 90 min. Airdate: 3/3/72. Production Companies: Metromedia Producers Corp. and Stonehenge Productions. Director: Don Taylor. Executive Producer: Dick Berg. Producer: Ron Roth. Writer: Fay Kanin. Susan Hayward plays a lawyer who defends people prosecuted on the basis of circumstantial evidence; James Stacy is her detective. In the pilot, she defends a rich contractor who is accused of killing a man – by pushing him off the 21st floor of an uncompleted building—who was having an affair with his daughter. Originally, Barbara Stanwyck was going to star but had to bow out when she took ill. When this pilot didn't spark a series, Kanin and Berg revamped it and pitched it unsuccessfully the following year, without Stacy, to ABC (as well as another project starring Hayward). *Cast:* Susan Hayward (as Jessica Fitzgerald), James Stacy (Gus Pride), Lee J. Cobb (Frank Galvin), Bettye Ackerman (Stella Galvin), Jennifer Penny (Chris Galvin), Fritz Weaver (Vincent Kagel), Tyne Daly (Jean Carson), Mills Watson (Obie), Lynnette Mettey (Fran), Ray Sims (Roy Carson), Ron Masak (Police Sergeant).

1146. **Lost Flight.** 105 min. Airdate: 1973 (ABC). Production Company: Universal Television. Director: Leonard Horn. Executive Producer: Frank Price. Producer: Paul Donnelly. Writer: Dean Reisner. Creator: Dean Reisner. Shot on location in Hawaii in 1969 for CBS, which shelved it. ABC eventually aired it in 1973 and CBS became interested again in its series possibilities. Lloyd Bridges stars as the pilot of a commercial jet that crashlands on an uncharted isle in the mid–Pacific. Andrew Duggan, Bobby Van, Ralph Meeker, and Anne Francis are among the passengers who establish their own society – and soap opera entanglements—on the island.

1147. **Man on a String.** 90 min. Airdate: 2/18/72. Production Company: Screen Gems. Director: Joseph Sargent. Producers: Douglas Cramer and Joseph Goodson. Writer: Ben Maddows. A revamped version of Screen Gems' *Tightrope*, a short-lived 1960 series the production company won't let die. They tried reviving it several times (see *The New Tightrope* and *The Expendables*) in the two or three seasons that followed the cancellation and then let it lie – until 1972. Christopher George is a super-secret undercover agent working for William Schallert, the leader of a super-secret government organization. *Cast:* Christopher George (as Pete King), William Schallert (William Connaught), Michael Baselson (Mickey Brown), Keith Carradine (Danny Brown), Joel Grey (Big Joe Brown), Kitty Winn (Angela Canyon), Paul Hampton (Cowboy), Jack Warden (Jake Moniker), J. Duke Russo (Carlo Buglione), Jack Bernardi (Counterman), Lincoln Demyan (Billy Prescott), Bob Golden (Motor Officer), Jerome Guardino (Scarred Man), Byron Morrow (Judge), Carolyn Nelson (Anita), James Sikking (Pipe Smoker), Richard Yniquez (Officer Jack), Garry Walberg (Sergeant).

1148. **Stat!** 30 min. Airdate: 7/31/73. Production Company: CBS Productions. Director: Richard Donner. Producer: E. Jack Neuman. Writer: E. Jack Neuman. Frank Converse stars as a doctor in the emergency ward of a major metropolitan hospital. *Cast:* Frank Converse (as Dr. Ben Voorhees), Michael Delano (Dr. Nick Candros), Marian Collier (Nurse Ellen Quayle), Casey MacDonald (Dr.

Jan Cavanaugh), Henry Brown (Dr. Neil Patricks), Monika Henreid (Mary Ann Murphy), Peggy Rea (Doris Runyon), Marcy Lafferty (Dolores Payne).

NBC / COMEDY

1149. The Bear and I. 30 min. Production Companies: Apjac Productions and 20th Century Fox. Executive Producer: Arthur P. Jacobs. Producers: Chris Bearde and Allan Blye. Writers: Chris Bearde and Allan Blye. A spin-off of the "Cookie Bear" sketch on the *Andy Williams Show.* Soupy Sales stars as a guy who co-hosts a children's show with a talking bear that everyone thinks is a guy in a suit—but isn't. Joe Flynn is the harried station manager and Janos Prohaska, billed as a European animal impersonator, plays the bear.

1150. Call Holme. 30 min. Airdate: 4/24/72. Production Company: Screen Gems. Director: Gary Nelson. Executive Producer: Douglas S. Cramer. Producer: William Baumes. Writer: Gerald Gardner. Creator: William Baumes. Developed by: Larry Cohen and Fred Freeman. Music: Johnny Mandel. Arte Johnson is a bumbling detective who is a master of disguise. Aired as a segment of NBC's *Triple Play '72* flop pilot showcase and later rebroadcast in 1984 on CBS. *Cast:* Arte Johnson (as Holme), Arlene Golonka (Miss Musky), Jim Hutton (Lt. Frank Hayward), Linda Crystal (Phadera Hayes), Helmut Dantine (Freidrich Von Klug), Rosemary De Camp (Miss Paperman), Noel Harrison (Lester Faulkner), Hermione Baddeley (Nora Benedict), Vic Tayback (Avery Crest), Jim Connell (Jonathon Livermore), Pat Delaney (Cynthia Morganstern), Reta Shaw (Woman), Danny Bonaduce (Boy), Lord Basil Hyde-Smith, Dave Ketchum (Sgt. Dobbs), Ivor Barry (Butler), Tommy Lee (Epstein).

1151. Evil Roy Slade. 2 hours. Airdate: 2/18/72. Production Company: Universal Television. Director: Jerry Paris. Producers: Garry Marshall and Jerry Belson. Writers: Garry Marshall and Jerry Belson. Creators: Garry Marshall and Jerry Belson. Music: Stuart Margolin, Murray McLeod, and Jerry Riopelle. Two revamped versions of a busted pilot from several seasons back (see *Sheriff Who?*) strung together as a TV movie. John Astin once again stars as Evil Roy Slade (which stands for Sneaking, Lying, Arrogance, Dirtiness, and Evil), an orphan-turned-crook who leads an outlaw gang that runs every lawman that tries to stop them right out of town. In the first pilot, Slade battles Marshall Bing Bell, the "singing cowboy." In the second pilot, he fights the attempts of a pretty school teacher to reform him to a life of goodness – so she can marry him. *Cast:* John Astin (as Evil Roy Slade), Mickey Rooney (Nelson L. Stool), Pamela Austin (Betsy Potter), Dick Shawn (Marshall Bing Bell), Henry Gibson (Clifford Stool), Edie Adams (Flossie), Robert Lieberman (Preacher), Larry Hankin (Smith), Edmund Cambridge (Snake), Pat Morita (Turhan), Milton Berle (Harry Fern), Luana Anders (Alice Fern), Dom DeLuise (Logan Delp), Penny Marshall (Bank Teller), John Ritter (Minister), Jerry Paris (Souvenir Salesman).

1152. **Going Places.** 30 min. Airdate: 3/19/73. Production Companies: MTM Enterprises and 20th Century Fox. Director: Lee Phillips. Executive Producer: Grant Tinker. Producers: Arnold Margolin and Jim Parker. Writers: James L. Brooks and Michael Zagor. Music: Charles Fox. Aired as a segment of NBC's *Triple Play '73* showcase of flop pilots. Todd Susman is a novelist from Ohio who moves to New York when it looks as though his book is about to be published – but it isn't, and he has to go looking for a job in this strange new city. This is the first of many busted pilots for Susman, who never has landed a continuing role in a series that lasts more than a season—if that. Among his flop series was MTM's *The Bob Crane Show* (aka *Second Start*) for NBC. *Cast:* Todd Susman (as Wes Tucker), Jill Clayburgh (Gloria), Norman Fell (Mr. Shaw), Jed Allen (Steve), Judith DeHart (Ellen).

1153. **Here Comes the Judge (aka Father on Trial).** 30 min. Airdate: 9/3/72. Production Company: Warner Bros. Television. Director: Mel Shavelson. Producer: Mel Shavelson. Writer: Mel Shavelson. Music: Walter Marks. Darren McGavin stars as a widowed judge who presides, with the help of a younger nightclub singer he marries (Barbara Feldon), over his two precocious children – Moosie Drier and Kieran Mullaney. Joan Tompkins played the judge's secretary.

1154. **Keeping Up with the Joneses.** 30 min. Airdate: 4/24/72. Production Company: Screen Gems. Director: Jerry Paris. Executive Producer: Douglas S. Cramer. Producers: Gordon Farr and Arnold Kane. Writers: Gordon Farr and Arnold Kane. Creators: Gordon Farr and Arnold Kane. Aired as the second segment of NBC's *Triple Play '72* flop pilot special. Two couples, one black (John Amos and Teresa Graves) and one white (Warren Berlinger and Pat Finley) and both named Jones, remodel a San Fernando Valley home into a two-family household with a shared kitchen and rec room. The white man is a factory worker, the black is a cop. Rebroadcast on CBS in 1984.

1155. **Topper Returns.** 30 min. Airdate: 3/19/73. Production Companies: Ap-jac Productions and 20th Century Fox. Director: Hy Averback. Executive Producer:

Arthur P. Jacobs. Producer: Walter Bien. Writer: A.J. Carothers. Music: Pat Williams. A sequel to the old series, with Roddy McDowall taking over where Leo G. Carroll left off. Topper is a man frustrated by the ghosts of his uncle's dead niece and nephew, who only he can see and hear—the twist being they were killed in an auto accident 40 years ago and are utterly out-of-step with the society of the 70s. Stefanie Powers (who starred in *Girl from UNCLE*, which was spun off from the Carroll series *Man from UNCLE*) and John Fink are the ghostly couple portrayed in the original series by Robert Sterling and Anne Jeffreys. Kate Jackson and Andrew Stevens would later play the roles in another flop pilot. *Cast:* Roddy McDowall (as Cosmo Topper, Jr.), Stefanie Powers (Marian Kerby), John Fink (George Kerby), Reginald Owen (Jones), also, John Randolph and Jeanne Bates.

1156. **Wednesday Night Out.** 30 min. Airdate: 4/24/72. Production Company: Screen Gems. Director: Jerry Paris. Executive Producer: Douglas S. Cramer. Producer: Larry Rosen. Writer: Garry Marshall. Creator: Garry Marshall. Music: Jerry Fielding. A group of friends meet each week at a different home to play cards—but usually engage in a lively debate on issues of the day and problems in their lives. The couples are diverse – a conservative couple (Jim Hutton and Kathleen Nolan), Italian immigrants successful in business (Pat Harrington, Jr. and Brenda Benet), a Jewish doctor and his wife (Greg Mullavey and Marcia Strassman), and a divorcee (Gloria DeHaven) who brings a different boyfriend each week. When games are played at the conservative couple's home, the bigoted grandfather (John Qualen) who lives with them sits in. Guest stars were Cicely Tyson and Robert Sampson as the "boyfriend." This pilot, rebroadcast on CBS in 1984, was recast, revamped, and offered again in 1973 as *The Friday Night Group.*

NBC / DRAMA

1157. **Amanda Fallon.** 60 min. Airdate: 3/5/72. Production Company: Universal Television. Director: Don Taylor. Producer: Jack Laird. Writer: Robert Malcolm Young. Creator: Robert Malcolm Young. Music: Richard Clements. Aired as the "Discovery at 14" episode of "The Doctors" segment of *The Bold Ones*. Jane Wyman stars as a widowed pediatrician running a children's clinic in La Jolla, California. Other series regulars would have included Mike Farrell and Lillian Lehman. In the pilot, Dr. Fallon helps a boy suffering from bleeding ulcers. This was reworked the following year for a new one-hour pilot, this time with Wyatt as a general practitioner. *Cast:* Jane Wyman (as Dr. Amanda Fallon), Mike Farrell (Dr. Vic Wheelwright), Lillian Lehman (Nurse Crawford), Lynnette Mettey (Dee Merlino), Jim Davis (Peter Merlino), Ron Howard (Cory Merlino), Robert Hogan (Jack Merlino), Jill Banner (Girl), Michael Laird (Jonathon).

1158. **Baffled.** 2 hours. Airdate: 1/30/73. Production Companies: Arena Productions and ITC Entertainment. Director: Philip Leacock. Executive Producer: Norman Felton. Producers: Philip Leacock and John Oldknow. Writer: Theodore Apstein. Music: Richard Hill. Leonard Nimoy stars as a race car driver who, after being injured in a crash, acquires amazing psychic ability and is called upon to help police and government agencies. He's helped by a female psychiatrist who specializes in the occult and Hopkins, his chauffeur. Although shot in England, had this gone to series, it would have been produced in Hollywood. *Cast:* Leonard Nimoy (as Tom Kovack), Susan Hampshire (Michelle Brent), Ewan Roberts (Hopkins), Rachel Roberts (Mrs. Farraday), Vera Miles (Andrea Glenn), Jewel Blanch (Jennifer Glenn), Valeria Taylor (Louise Sanford), Ray Brookes (George Tracewell), Angharad Rees (Peggy Tracewell), Christopher Benjamin (Verelli), Mike Murray (Parrish), Milton Johns (Dr. Reed), Al Mancini (TV Interviewer), John Rae (Theater Doorman), Patsy Smart (Cleaning Woman), Shane Rimmer (Track Announcer), Roland Brand (Track Mechanic), Bill Hutchinson (Doctor), Michael Sloan (Ambulance Man), Dan Meaden (Policeman).

1159. **Brock's Last Case.** 2 hours. Airdate: 3/5/73. Production Company: Universal Television. Director: David Lowell Rich. Executive Producer: Leonard B. Stern. Producer: Roland Kibbee. Writers: Alex Gordon and Martin Donaldson. Music: Charles Gross. *McCloud* in reverse. Richard Widmark is a tough New York homicide lieutenant who retires and moves to a small, California town to grow oranges – but ends up becoming sheriff when he tries to clear his Indian ranch hand of murdering the current sheriff. Once Brook becomes the local law, he discovers his big-city ways just don't seem to work. *Cast:* Richard Widmark (as Lt. Max Brock), Henry Darrow (Arthur Goldencorn), Beth Brickell (Ellen Ashley), Will Geer (Smiley Crenshaw), John Anderson (Joe Cuspie), Michael Burns (Stretch Willis), David Huddleston (Jack Dawson), Henry Beckman (Jake Hinkley), Pat Morita (Sam Wong).

1160. **Cutter.** 90 min. Airdate: 1/26/72. Production Company: Universal Television. Director: Richard Irving. Executive Producer: Richard Irving. Producer: Dean Hargrove. Writer: Dean Hargrove. Music: Hal Mooney. The adventures of a black private eye in Chicago who, in the pilot for a proposed *Mystery Movie* segment, searches for a missing pro-quarterback. Filmed on location. *Cast:* Peter DeAnda (as Frank Cutter), Cameron Mitchell (Riggs), Barbara Rush (Linda), Gabriel Dell (Leone), Robert Webber (Meredith), Marlene Warfield (Susan Macklin), Archie Moore (Ray Brown), Herbert Jefferson, Jr. (Macklin), Anna Navarro (Miss Aquilera), Stepin Fetchit (Shineman), Karen Carlson (Janice), John Alexander, Jr. (Billy), Arlene Banas (Arlene French), Thomas Erhart (Benedict).

1161. **The Dark Side.** 60 min. Production Company: NBC Productions. Producer: Robert Markell. A video-taped pilot for a proposed suspense anthology that would not deal with occult or the supernatural. David Wayne and Geraldine Brooks starred in the pilot.

1162. **Elisha Cooper (aka Climb an Angry Mountain).** 2 hours. Airdate: 12/23/72. Production Company: Warner Bros. Television. Director: Leonard J. Horn. Producer: Herbert J. Solow. Writers: Joseph Calvelli and Sam H. Rolfe. Creators: Joseph Calvelli and Sam H. Rolfe. Fess Parker is a widowed, modern-day U.S. Marshall, who is raising his teenage children on his ranch near Mt. Shasta. In the pilot, he locks horns with a New York cop chasing a fugitive, who has fled to the mountain. *Cast:* Fess Parker (as Elisha Cooper), Clay O'Brien (Michael Cooper), Jewel Blanch (Christina Cooper), Marj Dusay (May Franklin), Arthur Hunnicutt (Sunny), Barry Nelson (Lt. Frank Bryant), Joe Kapp (Joey Chilko), Stella Stevens (Shiela Chilko), Richard Brian Harris (Javis Dwiggins), Casey Tibbs (Buck Moto), Kenneth Washington (Huggins), J.C. McElroy (Minister).

1163. **Hitched.** 90 min. Airdate: 3/31/73. Production Company: Universal Television. Director: Boris Sagal. Producer: Richard Alan Simmons. Writer: Richard Alan Simmons. Music: Patrick Williams. The second pilot aimed at telling the adventures of two newlyweds in the old West (see *Lock, Stock and Barrel,* 9/24/71). Tim Matheson returns, with Sally Field replacing Belinda J. Montgomery. In this pilot, they are accidentally separated and, while attempting to find one another, she gets involved with some nasty railroad workers and some unfriendly Indians while he gets mistaken for an outlaw and is almost hanged. *Cast:* Tim Matheson (as Clare Bridgeman), Sally Field (Roselle Bridgeman), Henry Jones (Barnstable), Neville Brand (Banjo Riley), John Anderson (Jomer Cruett), Slim Pickens (The Dawson Brothers), John Fiedler (Henry), John McLiam (P. Hunter), Don Knight (Reese), Charles Lane (Round Tree), Kathleen Freeman (Rainbow McLeod), Bo Svenson (Jay Appleby).

1164. The Judge and Jake Wyler. 2 hours. Airdate: 12/2/72. Production Company: Universal Television. Director: David Lowell Rich. Executive Producers: Richard Levinson and William Link. Producer: Jay Benson. Writers: Richard Levinson and William Link. Music: Gil Melle. Bette Davis stars as a retired judge who becomes a private eye. She is assisted in her investigations by Doug McClure, an ex-con serving his probation with her. In the pilot, they help a girl prove her father's suicide was actually murder. Davis was previously committed to *Madame Sin*, and could only star in a series based on this if the ABC pilot failed. As it turned out, both pilots died – though this one didn't go quietly. It was pitched again the following year as *Partners in Crime*, starring Lee Grant as a judge who goes into the private detective business with an ex-con, played by Lou Antonio, as her legman. *Cast:* Bette Davis (as Judge Meredith), Doug McClure (Jake Wyler), Eric Braeden (Anton Granicek), Joan Van Ark (Alicia Dodd), Gary Conway (Frank Morrison), Lou Jacobi (Lt. Wolfson), James McEachin (Quint), Lisabeth Hush (Caroline Dodd), Kent Smith (Robert Dodd), Barbara Rhoades (Chloe Jones), John Randolph (James Rockmore), Milt Kamen (Mr. Gilbert), John Lupton (Senator Joseph Pritchard), Michael Fox (Dr. Simon), Eddie Quillan (Billy Lambert), Celeste Yarnall (Ballerina), Ray Ballard (Harvey Zikoff), Virginia Capers (Mabel Cobb), Myron Natwick (Lyle Jefferson), Harriet E. MacGibbon (Hostess), Stuart Nisbet (Doctor), Rosanna Huffman (Receptionist), Steven Peck (Paul), Don Diamond (Workman), Margarita Cordova (Woman), Khalil Ben Bezaleel (African Diplomat).

1165. Lights Out. 60 min. Airdate: 1/15/72. Production Companies: Herbert Brodkin Productions and 20th Century Fox. Producer: Herbert Brodkin. Writer: Alvin Boretz. Creator: Arch Oboler. Based on the radio horror anthology and shot on tape in New York. Laurence Luckinbill, Joan Hackett, Louisa Morton, Kathryn Walker, and Michael McGuire starred in the pilot, entitled *When Widows Weep*, about a dollmaker whose dolls kill.

1166. Movin' On. 60 min. Airdate: 7/24/72. Production Company: Screen Gems. Director: E.W. Swackhamer. Executive Producer: Douglas S. Cramer. Producer: Jerome Courtland. Writer: Stirling Silliphant. Creator: Stirling Silliphant. Music: Dominic Frontiere. Lyrics: Sally Stevens. This pilot, not to be confused with the subsequent NBC series starring Claude Akins and Frank Converse as truck drivers, is a reworked version of *Route 66*. The adventures of a race car driver (Patrick Wayne) and a motorcycle racer (Geoffrey Deuel), who travel around the country meeting interesting people and getting involved in their lives. *Cast:* Patrick Wayne (as Clint Daniels), Geoffrey Deuel (Johnny Lake), Kate Jackson (Cory), David Soul (Jeff), Meg Wyllie (Mrs. Lake), Walter Barnes (Mr. Daniels).

1167. The Prosecutors (aka Incident on a Dark Street). 2 hours. Airdate: 1/13/73. Production Company: 20th Century Fox. Director: Buzz Kulik. Executive Producer: David Gerber. Producer: E. Jack Neuman. Writer: E. Jack Neuman. Creator: E. Jack Neuman. Music: Elmer Bernstein. The story of two lawyers (David Canary and Robert Pine), fresh out of law school, who go to work in the U.S. Attorney's office in New York. James Olson costars as their boss. In the pilot, they investigate the murder of a hood about to expose the dirty-doings of a mafia chieftain. *Cast:* James Olson (as Joseph Dubbs), David Canary (Pete Gallagher), Robert Pine (Paul Hamilton), Richard Castellano (Frank Romeo), William Shatner (Deaver Wallace), Murray Hamilton (Edmund), Gilbert Roland (Dominic Leopold), Kathleen Lloyd (Louise Trenier), Wesley Lau (John Pine), Donald Barry (Miles Henderson), David Doyle (Luke Burgess), Gordon Pinsent (Mayor), James Davidson (Arthur Trenier).

1168. Rex Harrison Presents Short Stories of Love (aka Short Story; aka Three Faces of Love). 2 hours. Airdate: 5/1/74. Production Company: Universal Television. Executive Producer: William Sackheim. Producers: Herbert Hirschman and Rita Dillon. A two-hour pilot for a proposed one-hour anthology of 30-minute love stories hosted by Rex Harrison. The segments of the pilot were:

#1. Epicac. Director: John Badham. Writer: Liam O'Brien, from the story by Kurt Vonnegut, Jr. A computer falls in love with its programmer. Badham would later do a movie along the same lines called *Short Circuit* (1986), about a woman who falls in love with a robot. *Cast:* Julie Sommars (as Patricia), Bill Bixby (William), Roscoe Lee Brown (Mr. Secretary), Soon-Teck Oh (Mr. Kim), David Sheiner (Ed).

#2. Kiss Me Again, Stranger. Director: Arnold Laven. Writer: Arthur Dales, from the story by Daphne du Maurier. A World War II vet (Leonard Nimoy) falls in love with a beautiful murderer (Juliet Mills). *Cast:* Leonard Nimoy (as Mick), Juliet Mills (Usherette), Donald Moffat (Fred), Diana Webster (Doria).

#3. The Fortunate Painter. Writer: John T. Kelley, from a story by Somerset Maugham. A man who helps his daughter marry a broke painter. It starred Lorne Greene, Agnes Moorehead, Jess Walton, Lawrence Casey, Claude

Woolman, Fred Holliday, Robert Emhardt, Lloyd Bochner, Colby Chester, and Alan Hale, Jr.

1169. **Savage.** 90 min. Airdate: 3/31/73. Production Company: Universal Television. Director: Steven Spielberg. Executive Producers: Richard Levinson and William Link. Producer: Paul Mason. Writers: Mark Rodgers, Richard Levinson, and William Link. Creators: Richard Levinson and William Link. Music: Gil Mille. Martin Landau was Savage, an investigative reporter with his own television show that examines the political world. Landau's then-wife Barbara Bain played his producer. In the pilot, they investigate a scandal involving a Supreme Court nominee. This was the last TV movie Spielberg directed before going into motion pictures and becoming an industry unto himself. "It needed work, no question about it, but it was a good beginning," Landau says. "It was ahead of its time. That show was a platform to do intelligent television. It was television doing television and it was innovative as hell and we got shot down for the wrong reasons. It was clearly political. The network news department took exception to our show. I got a call from (Universal President) Sid Sheinberg and he said 'it's the best thing we've got, NBC is crazy about it, it's on-the-air.' And it went from there to being buried in a week's time." *Cast:* Martin Landau (as Paul Savage), Barbara Bain (Gail Abbott), Will Geer (Joel Ryker), Paul Richards (Phillip Brooks), Michele Carey (Allison Baker), Barry Sullivan (Judge Daniel Stern), Louise Latham (Marion Stern), Dabney Coleman (Ted Seligson), Pat Harrington, Jr. (Russell), Susan Howard (Lee Reynolds), Jack Bender (Jerry).

1170. **A Time for Love (aka A New Kind of Love).** 2 hours. Airdate: 3/3/73. Production Company: Paramount Television. Director: Stirling Silliphant. Producer: Stirling Silliphant. Writer: Stirling Silliphant. Music: Patrick Williams. Two hour-long pilots strung together into a two-hour movie that was meant to lead to a one-hour anthology of love stories. In the first, John Davidson stars as a conservative executive who falls in love with a freewheeling woman, played by Lauren Hutton. In the second, Bonnie Bedelia is a shy school teacher who falls in love with a rock star. *Cast:* (Pilot One): John Davidson (as Larry), Lauren Hutton (Darleen), Jack Cassidy (Tom Pierson); (Pilot Two): Bonnie Bedelia (as Kitty), Chris Mitchum (Mark), Jennifer Leak (Patricia), Malachi Throne (Jamison May), Joanna Cameron (Mini), Joseph Hardy (Seabrook).

1973–1974

1171. Andy Capp. 30 min. Production Company: Tomorrow Entertainment. Director: Hy Averback. Producer: Hy Averback. Writer: Don Nicholl, from the comic strip by Reg Smythe. Pat Henry as a crusty, manipulative bar fly and Valorie Johnson as his frustrated wife Flo. Unlike the comic strip, this took place in Boston, not England.

1172. The Barbara Eden Show. 30 min. Airdate: 5/21/73. Production Company: 20th Century Fox. Director: Jerry Davis. Executive Producer: Ann Marcus. Producer: Jerry Davis. Writer: Jerry Davis. Creator: Ann Marcus. Barbara Eden stars as a widow who works as the head writer on a long-running soap opera and is raising a teenage son (Moosie Drier). Roger Perry is her boyfriend, Lyle Waggoner is the obnoxious soap opera star, and Joe Flynn is her harried producer. Pat Morita guest starred. Marcus, who created *All My Children*, *Ryan's Hope*, and other authentic hit soaps, oversaw the production of this pilot.

1173. The Boomtown Band and Cattle Company. 30 min. Production Company: 20th Century Fox. Producer: Bill D'Angelo. Writer: James Lee Barrett. Creator: Bill D'Angelo. Raymond St. Jacques stars as an ex-slave who becomes foster father to three orphans – a 17-year-old boy (David Holmes), a 15-year-old girl (Tanis Montgomery), and a 7-year-old boy (Dion Overstreet) – teaches them to sing and, under his guidance, they become a successful roaming song-and-dance troupe in the old West.

1174. Catch 22. 30 min. Airdate: 5/21/73. Production Company: Paramount Television. Director: Richard Quine. Producer: Richard Bluel. Writer: Hal Dresden. Based on the book by Joseph Heller and inspired by the film, directed by Mike Nichols and written by Buck Henry. Richard Dreyfuss plays Yossarian, assayed by Alan Arkin in the film, who in this pilot is a brash World War II Air Force flyer who finishes his tour of duty but, instead of returning home as he should, his rotation papers are lost and he ends up on a rear echelon base in the Mediterranean. Everywhere he turns he is confronted by insanity and no matter how he schemes to get home, his plans always fail. *Cast:* Richard Dreyfuss (as Capt. Yossarian), Dana Elcar (Col. Cathcart), Stewart Moss (Lt. Col. Kern),

Andy Jarrell (Milo Minderbinder), Frank Welker (Lt. McWatt), Susan Zenor (Nurse Duckett).

1175. **Day by Day.** 30 min. Production Company: Warner Bros. Television. Producers: Bruce Johnson and E. Duke Vincent. Writers: Burt and Adele Styler. A sitcom tailored for Harry Guardino, who would star as an insurance broker whose wife plays golf and does charity work all day and whose two teenage sons are philosophical opposites of each other and their father.

1176. **Ernie, Madge and Artie.** 30 min. Airdate: 8/15/74. Production Company: Screen Gems. Executive Producer: David Gerber. Producer: Jerry Paris. Writer: Bernard Slade. Once again, the comedic misadventures of a middle-aged couple (Cloris Leachman and Dick Van Patten) plagued by the ghost of the wife's dead husband (Frank Sutton). Susan Sennett and William Molloy guest starred.

1177. **The Furst Family of Washington.** 30 min. Airdate: 9/11/73. Production Company: Screen Gems. Director: Norman Campbell. Producer: Norman Campbell. Writer: Stanley Ralph Ross. Creators: Dan Bradley and Alan Rice. Godfrey Cambridge plays Oscar Furst, a black barber whose shop serves as watering hole for the neighborhood men, who include a numbers runner, the owner of an auto supply company, and a postman who knows everything about everyone. Oscar has a religious, pushy mother who pokes her nose into everyone's lives—especially her son's. This was later reworked by a bevy of producers (Allan Blye, Chris Bearde, Walter N. Bien, Gene Farmer, David Pollock) and reshot as *That's My Mama*, which won a short-lived berth on ABC's 1974–75 schedule. The only holdovers were Theresa Merritt as Mama and Theodore Wilson as the postman; Clifton Davis assumed the starring role. In 1987, Columbia Pictures Television (which absorbed Screen Gems in the 70s) tried to resurrect the project yet again, in first-run syndication, as a spin-off of *What's Happening Now!*—which was itself a revival of an off-network show. The proposed series would have starred Ted Lange as a lawyer who converts the barber shop into his office and hires Mama (Theresa Merritt) as his secretary. It was called, of course, *That's My Mama Now!* Cast: Godfrey Cambridge (as Oscar Furst), Theresa Merritt (Eloise "Mama" Furst), Theodore Wilson (Earl Jefferson), Eddy C. Dyer (King Osbourne), Dewayne Jessie (Low Lead), Eric Laneuville (Junior).

1178. **J.T.** 30 min. Production Company: Viacom. Producer: Chip Schultz. Writer: Jane Wagner. Robert Grant is J.T., a 12-year-old black boy in Harlem who befriends a 12-year-old boy (Sydney Sheriff) who has just moved there from a rural area of Georgia. Gilbert Lewis and Beverly Todd portray J.T.'s parents. Shot in New York.

1179. **The Karen Valentine Show.** 30 min. Production Company: 20th Century Fox. Producer: Bill D'Angelo. Writers: Jerry Rannow and Greg Strangis. Creators: Jerry Rannow and Greg Strangis. Valentine plays a public relations executive who is at odds with her older, outspoken, male boss. Her best friends are a teenage girl who always seeks her advice, and a salesman who is no good at his job.

ABC / DRAMA

1180. **The Bait.** 90 min. Airdate: 3/13/73. Production Company: ABC Circle Films. Director: Leonard J. Horn. Executive Producers: Aaron Spelling and Leonard Goldberg. Producer: Peter Nelson. Writers: Don M. Mankiewicz and Gordon Cotler, from the book by Dorothy Uhnak. Music: Allyn Ferguson and Jack Elliot. Donna Mills is an undercover policewoman who is constantly at odds with the precinct captain (Michael Constantine), who thinks she'd do herself and the department more good behind a desk. In the pilot, she's "the bait" to flush out a homicidal rapist. Guest star Noam Pitlik would later abandon acting in favor of directing, and subsequently worked for several seasons behind the camera on *Barney Miller*. Cast: Donna Mills (as Tracy Fleming), Michael Constantine (Capt. Gus Maryk), William Devane (Earl Stokey), June Lockhart (Nora), Arlene Golonka (Liz Fowler), Noam Pitlik (Solomon), Thalmus Rasulala (Eddie Nugent), Gianni Russo (Gianni Ruggeri), Xenia Gratsos (Denise), Brad Savage (Mickey), Timothy Carey (Big Mike), Don Keefer (Newsdealer), Mitzi Hoag (Nancy).

1181. **Chelsea D.H.O. (aka D.H.O.).** 60 min. Airdate: 6/17/73. Production Company: Herman Rush and Associates. Director: John Trent. Executive Producers: Herman Rush and Ted Bergman. Producer: William Finnegan. Writer: Alvin Boretz. Creator: Alvin Boretz. Frank Converse stars as the conscientious doctor who runs the District Health Office in the Chelsea section of Philadelphia and gets personally involved in his patients' lives. The pilot was filmed on location and was based on true case histories (as the series would have been). Producer Herman Rush would later become president of Columbia Pictures Television. Cast: Frank Converse (as Dr. Sam Delaney), Luther Adler (Dr. Levine, M.E.), Ruby Dee (Dr. Bianca Pearson), Ed Grover (Axel Thorson), Jack Weston (Mr. Randall), Richard Gere (Milo).

1182. **The Connection.** 90 min. Airdate: 2/27/73. Production Company: D'Antoni Productions. Director: Tom Gries. Executive Producer: Philip D'Antoni. Producer: Jacqueline Babbin. Writer: Albert Ruben. Creator: Philip D'Antoni. Music: John Murtaugh. The adventures of a police reporter (Charles Durning) who has made friends both in the underworld and with the police and often finds himself caught in the middle of the two worlds. *Cast:* Charles Durning (as Frank Devlin), Ronny Cox (Everett Hutchneker), Zohra Lampert (Hannah), Dennis Cole (Sy McGruder), Heather MacRae (June McGruder), Mike Kellin (Pillo), Dana Wynter (Eleanor Warren), Tom Rosqui (Det. Phaelen), Richard Bright (B.J.), Joe Keyes, Jr. (Dewey), also, Howard Cosell.

1183. **Crime (aka The Alpha Caper; aka Inside Job).** 90 min. Airdate: 10/6/73. Production Company: Universal Television. Director: Robert Michael Lewis. Executive Producer: Harve Bennett. Producers: Aubrey Schenck and Arnold Turner. Writers: Elroy Schwartz and Steven Bochco. Music: Oliver Nelson. A pilot for a proposed anthology that would track a crime from its initial conception on through the meticulous planning and finally, its flawed execution. In the pilot, Henry Fonda is a probation officer who recruits a team of ex-cons and masterminds the faultless hijacking of a gold shipment—only to get caught when their truck stalls and splits open on the highway. This pilot benefited from the talents of four people who would work together again on highly successful projects. Steven Bochco would later create, write and produce *Hill Street Blues*, which featured James B. Sikking. Harve Bennett later worked as both producer and writer on the *Star Trek* movies, which featured Leonard Nimoy as both actor and director. *Cast:* Henry Fonda (as Mark Forbes), Leonard Nimoy (Mitch), James McEachin (Scat), Elena Verdugo (Hilda), John Marley (Lee Saunders), Larry Hagman (Tudor), Noah Beery (Harry Balsam), Tom Troupe (Harlan Moss), Woodrow Parfrey (Minister), Vic Tayback (Policeman), Kenneth Tobey (Police Capt.), Paul Kent (John Woodbury), James B. Sikking (Henry Kellner), Paul Sorenson (Tow Truck Driver), Wally Taylor (Sergeant).

1184. **Egan.** 30 min. Airdate: 9/18/73. Production Company: Paramount Television. Director: Jud Taylor. Producers: Tom Miller and Ed Milkis. Writer: Abram S. Ginnes. Music: Lalo Schifrin. A pilot based on the true exploits of N.Y.P.D. detective Eddie Egan, whose adventures were dramatized in the Oscar-winning movie *The French Connection*. Gene Hackman won an Oscar for his portrayal of Egan, whose name was changed to Popeye Doyle in the film. Egan later began an acting career of his own, appearing in such series as *Eischied* and *Police Story*. This time Eugene Roche is Egan, now an L.A.P.D. detective who defies authority and does things his way. The Egan character was revived again in 1986 as *Popeye Doyle*, with Ed O'Neill starring. *Cast:* Eugene Roche (as Eddie Egan), Dabney Coleman (Capt. Jones), Glenn Corbett (Det. Burke), John Anderson (J.R. King), John Carlin (Deveaux), Marian Geller (Woman), Michael Bell (Bobby), Fred Holliday (Clerk), Ian Sander (Cab Driver).

1185. **The Fabulous Doctor Fable.** 60 min. Airdate: 6/17/73. Production Company: Tomorrow Entertainment. Director: Bernard Girard. Producers: Robert Christiansen and Rick Rosenberg. Writer: George Wells. Dr. Fable (William Brydon) is an eccentric professor of medicine at a small college who uses his diagnostic skills to uncover "medical" crime – sickness and death that seem natural or accidental but are actually premeditated criminal actions. His renowned wizardry at this unique niche of detective work frequently brings the police, in the person of Jack Ging, to his door. His dealings with the police – and the fact that he's married a woman (Jane Elliot) who's not much older than his daughter (Cynthia Hull) – make some of his colleagues at the university leery of him. *Cast:* William Brydon (as Dr. Justin Fable), Jane Elliot (June Fable), Cynthia Hall (Marilla), Jack Ging (Lt. DeLusso), William Daniels (Elliot Borden).

1186. **The Fuzz Brothers.** 60 min. Airdate: 3/5/73. Production Company: MGM. Director: Don Medford. Producers: Joel D. Freeman and John D.F. Black. Writer: John D.F. Black. Music: J.J. Johnson. Lou Gossett and Felton Perry are brothers Francis and Luther Fuzz, two L.A.P.D. cops working in a downtown precinct. *Cast:* Lou Gossett (as Francis Fuzz), Felton Perry (Luther Fuzz), Jeff Corey (Capt. Lean), Don Porter (Flowers), William Smith (Sonny), Nita Barab (Trina), Mario Roccuzzo (Andy), Mitchell Ryan (Ben).

1187. **Indict and Convict.** 2 hours. Airdate: 1/6/74. Production Company: Universal Television. Director: Boris Sagal. Executive Producer: David Victor. Producer: Winston Miller. Writer: Winston Miller, from the book by Bill Davidson. Music: Jerry Goldsmith. The adventures of three attorneys with the Los Angeles department of the state Attorney General's office. George Grizzard is the chief investigator and prosecuting attorney, Ed Flanders is the state's attorney, and Reni Santoni is a criminal investigator. In the pilot, William Shatner is a deputy district attorney accused of murdering his wife and her lover even though he was 150 miles away when the crime occurred. Myrna Loy is the judge.

Cast: George Grizzard (as Bob Mathews), Reni Santoni (Mike Belano), Ed Flanders (Timothy Fitzgerald), Susan Howard (Joanna Garrett), Eli Wallach (DeWitt Foster), William Shatner (Sam Belden), Myrna Loy (Judge Christine Taylor), Harry Guardino (Mel Thomas), Kip Niven (Norman Hastings), Ruta Lee (Phyllis Dorfman), Del Russell (Frank Rogers), Marie Cheatham (Barbara Mathews), Alfred Ryder (Dr. Frank Larsen), Eunice Christopher (Muriel Fitzgerald), Arlene Martel (Mrs. Ann Lansing), Henry Beckman (Max Theisen).

1188. Intertect. 60 min. Airdate: 3/11/73. Production Company: Quinn Martin Productions. Director: Lawrence Dobkin. Executive Producer: Quinn Martin. Producer: Philip Saltzman. Writer: Philip Saltzman. Creator: Philip Saltzman. Stuart Whitman is a wealthy, former spy with worldwide contacts and homes in London, Paris, New York, and Washington D.C. who establishes an international detective agency called Intertect. In the pilot, he tries to free an industralist's wife and son from the clutches of kidnappers who are demanding a $1 million ransom. Guest star Robert Reed would later star in the Quinn Martin series *Operation: Runaway.* *Cast:* Stuart Whitman (as John McKennon), Pamela Franklin (Amanda Hollister), David Soul (Curt Lowens), Bernard Fox (Barrett), Eric Braeden (Emhardt), Robert Reed (Blake Hollister), Sherry Alberoni (Sylvia Doyle).

1189. The Letters. 90 min. Airdate: 3/6/73. Production Company: Spelling/Goldberg Productions. Directors: Gene Nelson and Paul Krasny. Executive Producers: Aaron Spelling and Leonard Goldberg. Producers: Paul Junger Witt and Tony Thomas. Writers: Ellis Marcus, Hal Sitowitz, and James G. Hirish. Creator: Paul Junger Witt. Music: Pete Rugolo. A precursor to Spelling's subsequent "Love Boat"–brand of anthology series and pilots (*Fantasy Island, Hotel, Airport, Finder of Lost Loves*, etc.) and the first of two failed pilots about what happens to people when they receive letters that have been delayed by one year (they were lost in a plane crash and recently recovered). Henry Jones stars as the postman, bringer of sadness, happiness, and danger.

"The Andersons: Dear Elaine." *Cast:* John Forsythe (as Paul Anderson), Jane Powell (Elaine Anderson), Lesley Ann Warren (Laura Reynolds), Trish Mahoney (Stewardess), Gary Dubin (Paul Anderson, Jr.), Mia Bendixsen (Lisa).

"The Parkingtons: Dear Penelope." *Cast:* Dina Merrill (as Penelope Parkington), Leslie Nielsen (Derek Childs), Barbara Stanwyck (Geraldine Parkinton), Gil Stuart (Michael), Orville Sherman (Minister).

"The Forresters: Dear Karen." *Cast:* Pamela Franklin (as Karen Forrester), Ida Lupino (Mrs. Forrester), Ben Murphy (Joe Randolph), Shelly Novack (Sonny), Frederick Herrick (Billy), Ann Noland (Sally), Brick Huston (Officer), Charles Picerni (First Man).

1190. **Letters from Three Lovers (The Letter II).** 90 min. Airdate: 10/3/73. Production Company: Spelling/Goldberg Productions. Director: John Erman. Executive Producers: Aaron Spelling and Leonard Goldberg. Producer: Parke Perine. Writers: Ann Marcus ("Dear Vincent" and "Dear Maggie") and Jerome Kass ("Dear Monica"). Creator: Paul Junger Witt. Music: Pete Rugolo. The same concept as the previous pilot, with one slight alteration – the long-delayed letters are from lovers. Henry Jones again plays the postman.

"Dear Vincent." *Cast:* Belinda J. Montgomery (as Angie), Martin Sheen (Vincent), Logan Ramsey (Wilson), Lou Frizzell (Eddie), James McCallion (Al), Claudia Bryar (Manager), J. Duke Russo (Harry), Frank Whiteman (Officer).

"Dear Monica." *Cast:* June Allyson (as Monica), Robert Sterling (Bob), Barry Sullivan (Joshua), June Dayton (Jeanne), Roger Til (Maitre'd), Amaentha Dymally (Maid), Howard Morton (Desk Clerk).

"Dear Maggie." *Cast:* Ken Berry (as Jack), Juliet Mills (Maggie), Lyle Waggoner (Sam), Dan Tobin (Thompson), Ellen Weston (Donna), Kathy Baumann (Girl), Navis Neal (Jewelry Clerk), Bill McClean (Irate Man), Ed Fury (Man at Pool).

1191. **The Lottery.** Production Company: Palomar Productions. Producer: Ed Scherick. Writer: David Shaw. An anthology about people who win millions in the lottery and how it changes their lives. Not to be confused with the 1983 ABC series *Lottery*, which had a similar storyline and two regular characters—actor Ben Murphy as a lottery official and Marshall Colt as an IRS agent.

1192. **Nightside.** 60 min. Airdate: 4/15/73. Production Company: Henry Jaffe Enterprises. Director: Richard Donner. Producer: Herbert Leonard. Writer: Pete Hamill. Creator: Pete Hamill. The adventures of Carmine Kelly (John Cassavettes), a press agent, nightclub owner Smitty (Alexis Smith) and Aram Bessoyggian (Michael Kellin), a private eye and the people they befriend in the night. In the pilot, Kelly saves Smitty's from being torn down and helps a has-been movie star making her comeback in a terrible movie. Had the pilot gone to series, the three characters would alternate as the star of the episode. *Cast:* John Cassavettes (as Carmine Kelly), Alexis Smith (Smitty), Michael Kellin (Aram

Bessoyggian), June Havoc (Vantura Davis), Joseph Wiseman (Grudin), Richard Jordan (Gable), Seymouur Cassell (Ralph), Joe Santos (Jabbo), Seth Allen (Shane), F. Murray Abraham (Acky), Dick Cavett (Himself).

1193. **Operation Hang-Ten.** 30 min. Production Company: Viacom. Producer: Herbert Solow. Writer: Gene Coons. Creator: Gene Coons. Christopher Stone is an athletic, one man "Mod Squad"—a 23-year-old federal agent who mixes with the younger generation (at car races, surfing contests, skindiving expeditions, ski weekends) and ferrets out crime that preys on the incredibly active youth of America. Victor French portrays Stone's boss.

1194. **Pomroy's People.** 60 min. Production Company: Lorimar Productions. Executive Producer: Lee Rich. Producers: Earl Hamner, Jr. and Robert L. Jacks. Writer: Earl Hamner, Jr. The story of a black minister (Brock Peters) of a small Kentucky town and his girlfriend, a school teacher (Marlene Warfield).

1195. **Stone.** 30 min. Production Company: Spelling/Goldberg Productions. Director: Sutton Rolley. Executive Producers: Aaron Spelling and Leonard Goldberg. Producer: Everett Chambers. Writers: Richard Carr and Tony Barrett. Creators: Richard Carr and Tony Barrett. Robert Hooks is a high-priced, black private eye working in Santa Monica who is choosy about his cases. Tracy Reed was his supportive girlfriend, Bernie Hamilton was his father, and Robert Hogan was his friend on the force. Shot in January 1973.

1196. **The Susan Hayward Show.** Production Companies: Stonehenge Productions and Metromedia Producers Corp. Executive Producer: Dick Berg. The network was considering two series ideas tailored for Susan Hayward. They were:

#1. Fitzgerald. Writer: Fay Kanin. A reworking of the flop CBS pilot *Fitzgerald and Pride* aka *Heat of Anger*. Hayward plays a lawyer who defends people charged on circumstantial evidence. The part of her investigator, played by James Stacey in the first pilot, was uncast.

#2. Grant's Beat. Writer: Margaret Armen. Hayward portrays an experienced policewoman.

1197. **Weekend Nun.** 90 min. Airdate: 12/20/72. Production Company: Paramount Television. Director: Jeannot Szwarc. Producers: Tom Miller and Edward Milkis. Writer: Ken Trevey. Music: Charles Fox. Joanna Pettet is a nun who doubles as a probation officer in this pilot based on the real-life exploits of Joyce Duco. *Cast:* Joanna Pettet (as Sister Mary Damian/Marjorie Walker), Vic Morrow (Chuck Jardine), Ann Sothern (Mother Bonaventure), James Gregory (Sid Richardson), Beverly Garland

(Bobby Sue Prewitt), Kay Lenz (Audree Prewitt), Michael Clark (Rick Seiden), Tina Andrews (Bernetta), Judson Pratt (Priest), Barbara Werle (Sister Gratia), Lynn Borden (Connie), Marion Ross (Mrs. Crowe), Stephen Rogers (Arlen Crowe), Ann Summers (Administrator).

CBS / COMEDY

1198. **Bachelor-at-Law.** 30 min. Airdate: 6/5/73. Production Company: MTM Enterprises. Director: Jay Sandrich. Producer: Ed Weinberger. Writer: Ed Weinberger. MTM's first outright pilot since the inception of *The Mary Tyler Moore Show*. John Ritter is a young, naive, idealistic attorney who is hired by an older, seasoned lawyer (Harold Gould). When trouble erupts, it's the elder lawyer's daughter (Sarah Kennedy) who steps in between them. Richard Schaal costars as an inept investigator who thinks he's the savviest P.I. around. *Cast:* John Ritter (as Ben Sykes), Harold Gould (Matthew Brandon), Sarah Kennedy (Ellen Brandon), Richard Schaal (Lester), Betsy von Furstenburg (Gloria Farrell), Bill Zuckert (Mr. Woodward), Kathleen O'Malley (Mrs. Woodward), Craig T. Nelson (Mr. Pierce), David Frank (Prison Guard), Curt Conway (Judge), Richard Gittings (Bailiff), Wayne Heffley (Convict), Ron Rifkin (Assistant D.A.).

1199. **Big Daddy.** 30 min. Airdate: 6/19/73. Production Companies: Norman Tokar Productions and CBS Productions. Director: Norman Tokar. Producer: Norman Tokar. Writers: Perry Grant and Dick Bensfield. Creator: Lennie Horn. Music: H. B. Barnum. Vocals: O.C. Smith. Rosie Grier, ex-lineman for the Los Angeles Rams, plays a former football player and widower with two teenage daughters (Shari Frees and Deirdre Smith) who becomes a cooking show host to the consternation of his mother, played by Helen Martin. Patti Deutsch plays the show's producer. Edward Winter, Lennie Weinrib, and Nick Stewart guest starred.

1200. **Cops.** 30 min. Airdate: 6/5/73. Production Company: Cherokee Productions. Director: Jerry Belson. Executive Producer: Meta Rosenberg. Producers: Charles Shyer and Alan Mandel. Writer: Jerry Belson. Creator: Jerry Belson. The misadventures of several policemen in a precinct situated in a suburban, low-crime area. The comedy arises from the clash between the hardnosed, weary police captain (Vincent Gardenia) and his idealistic young detective (Bruce Davison) and the unusual cases they take on. *Cast:* Vincent Gardenia (as Capt. Sonny Miglio), Bruce Davison (Det. Dennis Till), Scoey Mitchlll (cq) (Sgt. Monroe Dupree),

Britt Leach (Det. Ed Carter), Pat Morita (Capt. Irving Ho), Ruth Roman (Wanda Burke), Stuart Margolin (Benny the Squealer), Vic Tayback (Coach), Little Dion (Winston), Betty Aidman (Donna Jo), Royce Wallace (Mrs. Wilcox).

1201. Daddy's Girl. 30 min. Airdate: 6/19/73. Production Company: Filmways. Director: Alan Rafkin. Producers: Jay Sommers and Dick Chevillat. Writers: Jay Sommers and Dick Chevillat. Music: Vic Mizzy. Eddie Albert is a Boston newspaper columnist and widower trying to raise a precocious eight-year-old daughter (Dawnyn) in a home he shares with his wife's sister (Helen Camp). Della Reese is his next-door neighbor and Alan Oppenheimer is his best friend.

1202. The Five Hundred Pound Jerk. 30 min. Production Company: David Wolper Productions. Director: William Kronick. Executive Producer: David Wolper. Producer: Stan Marguilies. Writer: James Henerson. Creator: James Henerson. Music: Neal Hefti. In this pilot, a combination of scenes from the 90 minute TV movie (which aired 1/2/73) and new footage, Alex Karras stars as a hulking hillbilly who goes to the Olympics, wins a gold medal for weight-lifting, and falls in love with a Soviet gymnast (Claudia Butenuth), who defects, marries him, and moves with him to Los Angeles. He goes to work with the park service and she tries to adjust to American life while they both try to avoid their international fame.

1203. Keep an Eye on Denise. 30 min. Airdate: 6/19/73. Production Company: Screen Gems. Director: Hy Averback. Executive Producer: Harry Ackerman. Writer: Stanley Roberts. Jackie Cooper plays a man who, while a flier in the Korean War, became close friends with a British flier (Richard Dawson). Many years later, the British flier's 18-year-old sister (Lynn Frederick) goes off to explore America – and her worried brother calls Cooper and asks him to "keep an eye on her." Cooper discovers it isn't that easy, and that is the central conflict of this proposed sitcom. Guest stars included Rae Allen, Ernie Anderson, Carmen Zapata, Barney Phillips, Joshua Shelley, and Elaine Church.

1204. Keep the Faith. 30 min. Production Company: CBS Productions. Producer: Ed Simmons. Writer: Ed Simmons. A complete revamping of last year's flop pilot. Now, when an elder rabbi (Jack Kruschen) retires, a younger rabbi (Todd Susman) takes his place – and the congregation has a hard time accepting his new ways. Marge Redmond costars as the young rabbi's friend.

1205. Starring: Nancy Clancy (aka The Nancy Dussault Show). 30 min. Airdate: 5/8/73. Production Company: Cave Creek Productions. Director: Dick Van

Dyke. Producer: Byron Paul. Writer: Carl Reiner. Creator: Carl Reiner. Aired as one segment of *CBS Triple Play*, a run-off of busted pilots. Nancy Dussault plays an actress who has been the understudy to the star of a long-running Broadway show. In the pilot, she impulsively marries a man she has known for one day (Lawrence Pressman) and has the chance to become a star when the leading lady (finally) gets sick. Dussault later co-hosted ABC's newsmagazine *Good Morning, America* and costarred in *Too Close for Comfort*.

1206. **The Ted Bessell Show.** 30 min. Airdate: 5/8/73. Production Company: Rollins-Joffe-Bessell Productions. Producers: Jack Rollins and Charles H. Joffe. Writer: Bruce Jay Friedman. Aired as part of *CBS Triple Play* pilot special. Bessell is a co-owner and co-editor with Robert Walden of a magazine and is also a newly-wed, having just married Barra Grant. The comedy comes from his struggle with married life and keeping his magazine afloat. Beth Howland costars as Grant's best friend. Joffe (who, with Rollins, produces Woody Allen's movies) and Bessell would later team up on *Good Time Harry*, an acclaimed 1980 NBC sitcom that lasted a scant five weeks. It also dealt with journalism – Bessell played a womanizing sportswriter.

1207. **To Sir, With Love.** 30 min. Airdate: 4/19/74. Production Companies: David Gerber Productions and Screen Gems. Director: Jay Sandrich. Executive Producer: David Gerber. Producer: Ronald Rubin. Writers: Ronald Rubin and Michael Zagor, from the screenplay by James Clavell, based on the book by E.R. Braithwaite. Based on the movie starring Sidney Poitier as a black high school teacher who, as part of a foreign exchange program, ends up in a school in London. Hari Rhodes assumes the role in the pilot. *Cast:* Hari Rhodes (as Paul Cameron), James Grout (Headmaster Hawthorne), Rosemary Leach (Philippa), Roddy Maude-Roxby (Walter), Jane Anthony (Cheryl), Jane Carr (Ruby), Marc Harris (Trevor), Leonard Brockwell (Terry), Brinsley Forde (Charles), Paul Eddington (Moran).

1208. **Two's Company.** 30 min. Airdate: 5/8/73. Production Company: Lison-Chambers Productions. Producers: Saul Lison and Ernest Chambers. Writers: Saul Lison and Ernest Chambers. A recasting of the flop CBS pilot *The Living End* from last season. John Amos is now the baseball player who tries to balance his married life (with Diana Sands) and his professional life.

1209. **We Two.** 30 min. Production Companies: Alan Landsburg Productions and Tomorrow Entertainment. Producers: Alan Landsburg and Laurence D.

Savadove. Writer: Rod Serling. Creator: Rod Serling. Herschel Bernardi is the widowed owner of a deli in upstate New York who lost his only son in World War II. He meets a 12-year-old black orphan (Damon Ketchens), whose only relative was killed in Vietnam, and they adopt one another. Together, they work to overcome their bitterness and loneliness, age and racial gaps, to be happy once again.

CBS / DRAMA

1210. **Call to Danger.** 90 min. Airdate: 2/27/73. Production Company: Paramount Television. Director: Tom Gries. Producer: Laurence Heath. Writer: Laurence Heath. Creator: Laurence Heath. Music: Laurence Rosenthal. A reworking of the 1968 pilot of the same title, which also starred Peter Graves (and is inaccurately billed in many reference works as the pilot for *Mission Impossible*). This pilot, a variation of the *Mission Impossible* theme, casts Graves as a federal agent who, with the aid of a sophisticated computer, selects civilians who are uniquely qualified to help him snare his prey and gives them a "call to danger." What's unusual about this pilot is that Graves did it while *Mission Impossible* was still on the air—a back-up in case his long-running series was canceled. It was. But his *Call to Danger* went unanswered. Graves continued to do pilots over the years, but to date, none have sold. *Cast:* Peter Graves (as Douglas Warfield), Diana Muldaur (Carrie Donovan), John Anderson (Edward McClure), Clu Gulager (Emmett Jergens), Tina Louise (April Tierney), Stephen McNally (Joe Barker), Ina Balin (Marla Hayes), Michael Ansara (Frank Mulvey), Roy Jensen (Dave Falk), William Jordan (Tony Boyd), Edward Bell (Reed), Paul Mantee (Adams), Wesley Lau (Police Sergeant), Victor Campos (Danny), Lesley Woods (Rosalind), Bart Barnes (Chairman), Dan Frazer (Reynolds).

1211. **Crime Club.** 90 min. Airdate: 3/6/73. Production Company: CBS Productions. Director: David Lowell Rich. Executive Producer: Frank Glicksman. Producer: Charles Larson. Writer: Charles Larson. Music: George Romanis. The Crime Club is an organization of lawyers, detectives, judges, and cops dedicated to fighting crime. The proposed series would revolve around the adventures of a private eye, an agent in the Department of Justice, a cop, and a judge. The only parts cast were those of the private eye (Lloyd Bridges) and the judge (Victor Buono) and the pilot concentrated on their efforts to find the killer of a club member. CBS gave Universal Television the assignment of crafting another pilot on the same theme in 1975 – and that failed, too. *Cast:* Lloyd Bridges (as Paul Cord), Victor Buono (Judge Roger Knight), Paul Burke (Robert London), Barbara Rush (Denise London), William Devane (Jack Kilburn), David Hedison (Nick Kelton), Cloris Leachman (Hilary Kelton), Belinda J. Montgomery (Anne Dryden), Martin Sheen (Deputy Wade Wilson), Mills Watson (Joe Parrish), Frank Marth (Sheriff Art Baird), Eugene Peterson (Roy Evens), Richard Hatch (Hugh London), Joan Tompkins (Phone Supervisor), Stephen Coit (Frederick), Alan Napier (John), Claiborne Cary (Clerk), James McCallion (Cabbie).

1212. **Genesis II.** 90 min. Airdate: 3/23/73. Production Company: Warner Bros. Television. Director: John Llewellyn Moxey. Producer: Gene Roddenberry. Writer: Gene Roddenberry. Creator: Gene Roddenberry. Music: Harry Sukman. Alex Cord is Dylan Hunt, a scientist experimenting with suspended animation in a secret base in Carlsbad Caverns when an earthquake buries him – and leaves him trapped in suspended animation. He is found – and revived – 150 years later by the few civilized people left in our post-apocalypse world. Together with Isiah (Ted Cassidy), Isaac Kimbridge (Percy Rodriquez), Primus (Majel Barrett) and Smythe (Lynne Marta), Dylan Hunt traveled on a subterranean bullet train bringing peace, knowledge, and order to this futuristic world. The pilot lost out to *Planet of the Apes* at CBS and was abandoned, although several scripts were commissioned. One of those scripts became the pilot *Planet Earth* for ABC the following season, with John Saxon replacing Cord. When that failed, Warner Bros. developed, without Roddenberry's participation, *Strange New World* for ABC. Saxon starred as one of a team of astronauts who, after floating through space in suspended animation, return to earth 150 years later and find a—you guessed it—*Strange New World*. It flopped, too. *Cast:* Alex Cord (as Dylan Hunt), Ted Cassidy (Isiah), Lynne Marta (Harper-Smythe), Linda Grant (Astrid), Percy Rodriques (Primus Isaac Kimbridge), Majel Barrett (Primus Dominic), Mariette Hartley (Lyra-a), Harvey Jason (Singh), Titos Vandis (Yuloff), Tom Pace (Brian), Leon Askin (Overseer), Liam Dunn (Janus), Harry Raybould (Slan-u), Beulah Quo (Lu-Chan), Ray Young (Tyranian Teacher), Ed Ashley (Weh-r), Dennis Young (General), Robert Hathaway (Shuttle Dispatcher), Bill Striglos (Dr. Kellum), David Westburg (Station Operator), Tammi Bula (Teenager), Terry Wills (Cardiologist), Didi Conn (TV Actress).

1213. **Murdock's Gang.** 90 min. Airdate: 3/20/73. Production Company: Don Fedderson Productions. Director: Charles S. Dubin. Executive Producer: Don

Fedderson. Producer: Edward H. Feldman. Writer: Edmund H. North. Creator: Edmund H. North. Music: Frank DeVol. Alex Dreier plays a famous trial attorney, disbarred and sent to prison for a crime he didn't commit, who becomes a private eye and hires a team of ex-cons to help him out. *Cast:* Alex Dreier (as Bartley James Murdock), Janet Leigh (Laura Talbot), Murray Hamilton (Harold Talbot), William Daniels (Roger Bates), Harold Gould (Dave Ryker), Don Knight (Glenn Dixon), Walter Burke (Bert Collins), Colby Chester (Larry DeVans), Donna Benz (Terry), Norman Alden (Red Harris), Ed Bernard (Ed Lyman), Charles Dierkop (Denver Briggs), Dave Morick (Mickey Carr), Milton Selzer (Frank Winston), Frank Campanella (Barney Pirelli), Fred Sadoff (Dr. Barkis), Eddie Firestone (Hellstrom), William Fletcher (George), Karen Arthur (Secretary), Larry McCormick (Reporter), Diana Chesney (Nurse Supervisor), Gerri Dean (Nurse).

NBC / COMEDY

1214. **The Friday Night Group.** 30 min. Production Companies: Douglas S. Cramer Productions and Screen Gems. Director: Jerry Paris. Executive Producer: Douglas S. Cramer. Producer: Garry Marshall. Writer: Garry Marshall. A reworking of last season's *Wednesday Night Group.* Now, a group of suburban couples (less affluent than those depicted in the last pilot) with diverse backgrounds gather on weekends – and clash over a variety of things. Stars include Pat Harrington, Dick Sargent, Steven Franken, Brenda Benet, Mitzi McCall, Ann Elder, and Timothy Blake.

1215. **Grandpa, Mom, Dad and Richie.** 30 min. Airdate: 5/15/74. Production Company: Metromedia Producers Corp. Executive Producer: Charles Fries. Writer: Robert Kaufman. Creator: Robert Kaufman. John Marley tries to mold his grandson (Scott Jacoby) in his own aggressive image, to the frustration of the boy's stockbroker father (Charles Adrian) and his mother (Abby Dalton).

1216. **Hello Mother, Goodbye!** 30 min. Airdate: 5/15/74. Production Company: MGM. Producers: Bud Freeman and Jack Sher. Writers: Bud Freeman and Jack Sher. Creators: Bud Freeman and Jack Sher. Kenneth Mars is an aerospace engineer who, bored with his job, resigns, starts his own mail-order business, and moves back home to his overbearing mother (Bette Davis), who thinks he'll go broke and wants him to return to his profession—where his brother is doing tremendously well.

1217. Kibbee Hates Fitch. 30 min. Production Company: Paramount Television. Producer: Robert Stambler. Writers: Fred Freeman and Lawrence J. Cohen. Creator: Neil Simon. Based on the 1965 pilot of the same name, which starred Don Rickles and Lou Jacobi. Two sisters marry two firemen and move into the same duplex. The two firemen (Chuck McCann and Michael Bell) constantly argue, to the frustration of their captain (Alan Oppenheimer) and their wives.

1218. Koska and His Family. 60 min. Airdate: 12/31/73. Production Company: Talent Associates. Director: Dan Dailey. Executive Producer: Leonard B. Stern. Producer: Ted Rich. Writer: Roger Price. Koska (Herb Edelman) is an unemployed engineer who decides to work as an inventor at his home, where he's distracted by his wife (Barbara Barrie), a PE teacher; his son, a basketball player (Jack David Walker); a daughter who visits from college (Ellen Sherman); his senile grandfather (Liam Dunn); and his old army buddy (Albert Henderson) who moves in to help out.

1219. Lady Luck. 30 min. Airdate: 9/12/73. Production Company: Universal Television. Director: James Komack. Producer: James Komack. Writers: Dean Hargrove, Charles Shyer, and Alex Mandel. Creator: Hunt Stromberg, Jr. Music: Hal Mooney. Valerie Perrine is a beautiful—perhaps supernatural—woman who helps people in trouble. *Cast:* Valerie Perrine (as Lady Luck), Paul Sand (Roger), Bert Convy (Clay), Sallie Shockley (Penny), J.D. Cannon (Walter), Carole Cook (Fran).

1220. Lily. 30 min. Airdate: 6/12/74. Production Company: Cooper-Finkel Productions. Producers: Jackie Cooper and Bob Finkel. Writers: Ed Weinberger and Stan Daniel. Creators: Ed Weinberger and Stan Daniel. Brenda Vaccaro is Lily, a single woman who works as an assistant to the deputy mayor of a major metropolitan city. Eileen Heckart is Lily's conservative mother.

1221. Patsy. 30 min. Production Company: Viacom. Executive Producers: Bernie Brillstein and Irv Wilson. Producers: E. Duke Vincent and Bruce Johnson. Creators: E. Duke Vincent and Bruce Johnson. Pat Cooper is "the patsy," the son who runs his close-knit Italian-American family's restaurant that he lives above. His family includes his mother (Penny Santon), his sister, her Irish husband (Dave Ketchum), their teenage daughter, and old Uncle Viduche (Joe DeSantis).

1222. Poor Devil. 90 min. Airdate: 2/14/73. Production Company: Paramount Television. Director: Robert Scheerer. Executive Producers: Arne Sultan and

Earl Barret. Producer: Robert Stambler. Writers: Arne Sultan, Earl Barret, and Richard Baer. Creators: Arne Sultan and Earl Barret. Music: Morton Stevens. Sammy Davis, Jr. stars as an inept disciple of the devil (Christopher Lee) who constantly fails to win over souls in this long-form pilot for a half-hour sitcom. *Cast:* Sammy Davis, Jr. (as Sammy), Christopher Lee (Lucifer), Jack Klugman (Burnett Emerson), Adam West (Crawford), Gino Conforti (Bligh), Emily Yancy (Chelsea), Madlyn Rue (Frances Emerson), Alan Manson (Mr. Moriarty), Ken Lynch (Desk Sergeant), Byron Webster (Blackbeard), Buddy Lester (Al Capone), Owen Bush (Tom), Nick Georgiade (Bob Younger), Don Ross (Eddie), Lila Teigh (Woman), Stephen Colt (Father-in-law), Joe DeWinter (Secretary), George Kramer (Cole Younger), Clyde Ventura (Clyde Barrow), Nancy Reichert (Bonnie), Tom Wize (John Younger), David Young (James Younger).

1223. **Shakespeare Loves Rembrandt.** 30 min. Airdate: 6/12/74. Production Company: Warner Bros. Television. Producer: Chris Hayward. Writer: Chris Hayward. Creator: Chris Hayward. The misadventures of a writer (Bert Convy) and his wife, a painter (Jo Ann Pflug), who move to Big Sur to escape the pressures of the big city. To earn a living while they explore their creative pursuits, he writes greeting cards and she illustrates them for a large greeting card company.

1224. **Sin, American Style (aka The Wonderful World of Sin; aka Fools, Females and Fun).** 90 min. Airdate: 9/4/74. Production Company: Universal Television. Director: Lou Antonio. Executive Producer: Glen A. Larson. Producer: Michael Gleason. Writers: Glen A. Larson and Michael Gleason. Creators: Glen A. Larson and Michael Gleason. Music: Glen A. Larson, Lee Holdridge, and Jerry Fielding. A proposed half-hour or one-hour anthology series that would explore greed, selfishness, lust and the like with a satirical and humorous eye. The three pilot stories involved a nightclub singer who falls for a chorus girl, a married man who has an affair with his wife's friend, and a banker who embezzles money to impress a woman.

"I've Got to Be Me." *Cast:* Jack Cassidy (as Danny Holliday), Julie Sommars (Alice Shoemaker), Dennis Rucker (Young Man), Bob Golden (Stage Manager).

"Is There a Doctor in the House?" *Cast:* Barry Nelson (as Dr. David Markham), Barbara Rush (Karen Markham), Jaclyn Smith (Susan Cole), Sam Melville (Stephen Cole), Maxine Stuart (Miss Bickley), Byron Morrow (Waiter), George McDaniel (Tailor).

"What About That One?" *Cast:* Dick Sargent (as Roger Morris), Brooke Bundy (Joanie Morris), Julie Newmar (Carla Dean), Robert Hogan (J.C. Tyler),

Leonard Beatty (Jack Manning), Booth Colman (Wally), Bill Quinn (Judge), Rommey Taylor (Patti Cubbison).

1225. **Where's Momma?** 30 min. Production Company: Lorimar Productions. Director: Carl Reiner. Executive Producer: Lee Rich. Producer: Carl Reiner. Writer: Muriel Resnick. Creator: Muriel Resnick. Yet another rehash of the dead spouse-from-beyond-returns premise. This time, it's Richard Mulligan as a widowed real estate agent having a hard time juggling work and the responsibility of raising his two five-year-old twin boys – so his wife (Michele Carey) returns from the grave to help him out. Only he, of course, can see her.

NBC / DRAMA

1226. **Amanda Fallon.** 60 min. Airdate: 5/4/73. Production Company: Universal Television. Director: Jack Laird. Executive Producer: William Frye. Producer: Jack Laird. Writers: Mark Rogers and Frank Pierson. Creator: Robert Malcolm Young. Music: Dave Grusin. A reworking of last season's flop pilot. Again, Jane Wyman is a doctor, this time a general practitioner instead of a pediatrician. In this new pilot, which aired as a *Bold Ones: The New Doctors* episode entitled *And Other Things I May Not Be*, Dr. Fallon helps a pregnant girl sort out her troubled life. *Cast:* Jane Wyman (as Dr. Amanda Fallon), Laurie Prange (Joyce Cummings), Katherine Nolan (Carol Steadman), Leslie Nielsen (Mr. Cummings), Pat O'Brien (Emory), David Fresco (Hertz), Miko Mayama (Irene Watanabe), Eric Chase (Washburn).

1227. **Hernandez (aka Hernandez: Houston P.D.).** 60 min. Airdate: 1/16/73. Production Company: Universal Television. Director: Richard Donner. Producer: David Levinson. Writer: Robert Van Scoyk. Creator: Robert Van Scoyk. Henry Darrow is a Mexican-American detective who, when he is not fighting crime in Houston, is dealing with the problems of his mother (Amapola Del Vando) and his younger brother. *Cast:* Henry Darrow (Detective Juan Hernandez), Desmond Dhooge (Sgt. Lukas), Dana Elcar (Jackman), Ronny Cox (Roper), G.D. Spradlin (Penner), Amapola Del Vando (Mama).

1228. **If I Had a Million.** 60 min. Airdate: 12/31/73. Production Company: Universal Television. Director: Daryl Duke. Executive Producer: David Levinson. Producer: James McAdams. Writer: Various. Based on the 1932 movie of the same name. Peter Kastner is a wealthy man who goes to the local library, randomly chooses a phone book from some American city, flips the pages, and picks a name. Then he anonymously gives that person a million dollars. The pilot was divided into four short stories about four different recipients.

#1. The Good Boy. Writers: Lionel E. Siegel and Herbert Wright, from a story by Lionel E. Siegel. *Cast:* John Schuck, Louis Zorich, Val Biscoglio, and Doolie Brown.

#2. The Searchers. Writer: Robert Van Scoyk. *Cast:* Joseph Wiseman, Ruth McDevitt, Gerald Hiken, and Rae Allen.

#3. Three. Writer: M. Charles Cohen. *Cast:* Kenneth Mars, Elayne HelVeil, Melendy Britt.

#4. First the Tube, and Now You, Darling. Writer: Oliver Hailey. *Cast:* Brett Somers, Ted Gehring.

1229. **Jarrett.** 90 min. Airdate: 8/11/73. Production Companies: Screen Gems and David Gerber Productions. Director: Barry Shear. Executive Producer: David Gerber. Producer: Richard Maibaum. Writer: Richard Maibaum. Creator: Richard Maibaum. Music: Jeff McDuff. Glenn Ford is an ex-prize fighter-turned-private eye specializing in cases associated with the arts. His constant nemesis is Bassett Cosgrove (Anthony Quayle), an eccentric, villainous art collector. Richard Maibaum, writer of most of the 007 scripts, says he created the character for a younger, more physical actor and that casting Glenn Ford was the pilot's death knell. *Cast:* Glenn Ford (as Sam Jarrett), Anthony Quayle (Bassett Cosgrove), Forrest Tucker (as Reverend Vocal Simpson), Laraine Stephens (Sigrid Larsen), Yvonne Craig (Luluwa), Richard Anderson (Spenser Loomis), Herb Jeffries (Karoufi), Elliot Montgomery (Dr. Carey), Lee Kolima (Kara George), Joseph Paul Herrara (I Knooh), Bob Schott (Gordon), Peter Brocco (Arnheim), Jody Gilbert (Sawyer), Robert Easton (Toby), Stack Pierce (Prison Guard), Read Morgan (Casimin), Ted White (Arthur), Frank Arno (Motor Man).

1230. **Key West.** 2 hours. Airdate: 12/10/73. Production Companies: Warner Bros. Television and Relyea-Petitclerk Productions. Director: Philip Leacock. Producers: Robert Relyea and Denne Bart Petitclerc. Writer: Denne Bart Petitclerc. Music: Frank De Vol. Stephen Boyd is a retired secret agent who runs a charter boat service in Key West, Florida – although what he does most of the time is behave like a private eye, ably assisted by Woody Strode as his buddy, Candy Rhodes. Shot on location. Other reference works credit Anthony S. Martin as producer and writer. The pilot was originally scheduled to air on

3/3/73. NBC production materials give the information reflected here. *Cast:* Stephen Boyd (as Steve Cutler), Woody Strode (Candy Rhodes), Tiffany Bolling (Ruth Frazier), Simon Oakland (General Tom Luker), William Prince (Senator Scott), Ford Rainey (Prescott Webb), Don Collier (Chief Jim Miller), George Fisher (Sam Olsen), Sheree North (Brandi), Earl Hindman (Rick), Stephen Mendillo (George), Virginia Kiser (Carol Luker), Tony Giorgio (Joseph Canto), Milton Selzer (Stauffer), Dick Sabol (Bodie), Courtney Brown (Ryder), Bud Owen (Elmo Gant), Earl Widener (Albert).

1231. **Mr. Inside/Mr. Outside.** 90 min. Airdate: 3/14/73. Production Companies: Metromedia Producers Corp. and D'Antoni Productions. Director: William A. Graham. Executive Producer: Philip D'Antoni. Producer: George Goodman. Writer: Jerome Coopersmith. Creator: Sonny Grosso. Music: Charles Gross. Hal Linden and Tony Lo Bianco were two Manhattan detectives who worked successfully together for many years—until Lo Bianco was shot and lost an arm, forcing him to leave the force. But that is not the end of their crimefighting partnership. Linden remains on the force – and Lo Bianco remains his partner, though on an unofficial basis as a private citizen. Shot on location in New York. *Cast:* Tony Lo Bianco (as Det. Rick Massi), Hal Linden (Det. Lou Isaacs), Paul Benjamin (Lt. Valentine), Marcia Jean Kurtz (Renee Isaacs), Stefan Schnabel (Luber), Philip Bruns (Brack), Arnold Soboloff (Gun Seller), Melody Santangelo (Hooker), Ed Van Nuys (Frederick Wakeman), Robert Risel (Sergeant), Sam Coppola (First Cop), Joe Girillo (Second Cop), Robert Levine (Desk Sergeant), Matt Russo (Foreman), Larry Sherman (Clerical Officer), Kevin Conway (First Fence), Randy Jergenson (Detective), Tony Palmer (First Detective), Sonny Grosso (Detective), Jacques Sandulescu (Bulier).

1232. **The Norliss Tapes.** 90 min. Airdate: 2/21/73. Production Companies: Metromedia Producers Corp. and Dan Curtis Productions. Director: Dan Curtis. Executive Producer: Charles Fries. Producer: Dan Curtis. Writer: William F. Nolan, from a story by Fred Mustard Stewart. Music: Robert Cobert. Dan Curtis' *The Night Stalker* done straight. Roy Thinnes is an investigative reporter who chases down the supernatural which, in the pilot, takes on the form walking corpses. Like Darren McGavin's Carl Kolchak before him, Thinnes'; David Norliss records his thoughts into a tape recorder. Curtis tried a similar concept, even before *The Night Stalker,* a few seasons back with Kerwin Matthews. The underlying premise of the Norliss series would be that the reporter had disappeared and that his publisher (Don Porter) was trying to find out what happened to him by listening to the various tapes – which would unfold as the episodes. The ultimate fate of Norliss would have remained unknown. *Cast:* Roy Thinnes (as David Norliss), Don Porter (Sanford Evans), Angie Dickinson (Ellen Sterns Cort), Claude Akins (Sheriff Tom Hartley), Michele Carey (Marsha Sterns), Vonetta McGee (Madame Jeckial), Nick Dimitri (James Cort), Hurd Hatfield (Charles Langdon), Robert Mandan (George Rosen), Bob Schott (The Demon), Edmund Gilbert (Sid Phelps), Jane Dulo (Sara Dobkins).

1233. **Partners in Crime.** 90 min. Airdate: 3/24/73. Production Company: Universal Television. Director: Jack Smight. Executive Producers: Richard Levinson and William Link. Producer: Jon Epstein. Writer: David Shaw. Music: Gil Melle. A reworking for last season's pilot *The Judge and Jake Wyler*, which starred Bette Davis as an ex-judge who teams up with an ex-con, played by Doug McClure, and opens a private eye agency. This time, it's Lee Grant and Lou Antonio. *Cast:* Lee Grant (as Judge Meredith Leland), Lou Antonio (Sam Hitch), Bob Cummings (Ralph Elsworth), Harry Guardino (Walt Connors), Richard Jaeckel (Frank Gordon), Charles Drake (Lt. Fred Hartnett), John Randolph (Judge Charles Leland), Richard Anderson (Roger Goldsmith), William Schallert (Oscar), Lorraine Gary (Margaret Jordan), Donald Barry (Bartender), Gary Crosby (Trooper), Maxine Stewart (Mrs. Harris).

1234. **Questor (aka The Questor Tapes).** 100 min. Airdate: 1/23/74. Production Company: Universal Television. Director: Richard A. Colla. Executive Producer: Gene Roddenberry. Producer: Howie Hurwitz. Writers: Gene L. Coon and Gene Roddenberry. Creator: Gene Roddenberry. Music: Gil Melle. Gene Roddenberry's second post–*Stor Trek* pilot. Robert Foxworth is an android searching the globe for the missing scientist—perhaps from another planet—who created him. Mike Farrell is the human scientist who accompanies him in his search, which brings them into contact with people in trouble. In the process, Questor's exposed to the constantly perplexing emotions of human beings. A humanoid robot would play a central role in Roddenberry's 1987 syndicated series *Star Trek: The Next Generation*. *Cast:* Robert Foxworth (as Questor), Mike Farrell (Jerry Robinson), John Vernon (Geoffrey Darro), Lew Ayres (Vaslovik), James Shigeta (Dr. Chen), Robert Douglas (Dr. Michaels), Ellen Weston (Allison Sample), Majel Barrett (Dr. Bradley), Reuben Singer (Dr. Gorlov), Walter Koenig (Administrative Assistant), Fred Sadoff (Dr. Audret), Gerald Sanderson (Randolph), Alan

Caillou (Immigration Officer), Eydse Girard (Stewardess), Lal Baum (Col. Henderson), Patti Cibbison (Secretary).

1235. **The Stranger.** 100 min. Airdate: 2/26/73. Production Company: Bing Crosby Productions. Director: Lee H. Katzin. Executive Producer: Andrew J. Fenady. Producer: Alan A. Armer and Gerald Sanford. Writer: Gerald Sanford. Creator: Gerald Sanford. Music: Richard Markowitz. Glenn Corbett is Stryker, an astronaut on a deep-space probe who crashlands on Earth – only to find out it isn't Earth, but rather a "parallel world" called Terra hidden behind the sun. They have everything we have (including Chryslers), except freedom. This alternate Earth is run by an evil dictatorship…that wants Stryker dead because he preaches free speech and other rights that he had on Earth. The series would depict Stryker's efforts to elude death (wielded by Cameron Mitchell), escape Terra and return home. *Cast:* Glenn Corbett (as Neil Stryker), Cameron Mitchell (George Benedict), Sharon Acker (Dr. Bettina Cooke), Lew Ayres (Prof. Dylan MacAuley), George Coulouris (Max Greene), Steve Franken (Henry Maitland), Dean Jagger (Carl Webster), Tim O'Connor (Dr. Revere), Jerry Douglas (Steve Perry), Arch Whiting (Mike Frome), H.M. Wynant (Eric Sconer), Virginia Gregg (Secretary), Buck Young (Tom Nelson), William Bryant (Trucker).

1974–1975

1236. Ann in Blue. 30 min. Airdate: 8/8/74. Production Companies: Viacom and Palomar Productions. Producer: Edgar J. Scherick. Writers: Norman Steinberg, Alan Uger, and Marshall Brickman. Creator: Norman Steinberg, Alan Uger, and Marshall Brickman. Penny Fuller is Ann, a policewoman who oversees the four other officers (Mary Elaine Monte, Mary-Beth Hurt, and Hattie Winston) in her neighborhood police team, which works with local merchants, families, and schools to prevent crime before it happens. She reports to Capt. Mulholland (John Randolph), an old-fashioned officer who still isn't comfortable having women on the force.

1237. Everything Money Can't Buy. 30 min. Production Company: Screen Gems. Producer: Bernard Slade. Writer: Bernard Slade. Creator: Bernard Slade. It's a concept that never seems to die – the adventures of an angel (Jose Ferrer) who grants wishes and helps people in trouble. The twist in this concept is that the angel can only grant wishes that money can't buy. This proposed comedy anthology was shot but never aired. It was later reworked by Carl Reiner, who also replaced Ferrer in the lead role, and was retitled *Good Heavens*, which sold and limped through 13 episodes as a midseason replacement in 1976.

1238. The Fireman's Ball (aka Where's the Fire?) 30 min. (2) Airdate: #1 unaired, #2 5/17/75. Production Company: Spelling-Goldberg Productions. Director: Jerry Paris. Executive Producers: Aaron Spelling and Leonard Goldberg. Producer: Douglas S. Cramer. Writers: Dee Caruso and Gerald Gardner. Creators: Dee Caruso and Gerald Gardner. The misadventures of six firemen in a suburban San Francisco firehouse. The cast for the first pilot were David Ketchum, Richard Yarmy, Cliff Gorman, Fred Grandy, Mark Thompson, Sam Kennedy, Johnny Brown, and Ted Knight. The second pilot starred Ketchum, Brown, Roger Bowen, Gregory Sierra, John Fink, and Danny Fortus. Guest stars were J. Pat O'Malley, Edward Andrews, Carl Ballantine, and Leigh French.

1239. The Karen Valentine Show. 30 min. Production Company: 20th Century Fox. Producers: David Davis and Lorenzo Music. Writers: David Davis and Lorenzo Music. Creators: David Davis and Lorenzo Music. From the team behind *The Bob Newhart Show*. Karen Valentine is a recently divorced woman who gets a job as a law clerk and tries to start a new life. She's dogged by her boyish ex-husband (Archie Hahn), pursued by the attractive minor league baseball player next door (Vern Rowe), and doted on by her parents (Garry Walberg and Dena Dietrich). Although this didn't sell, ABC remained hot on Valentine. She finally landed a series (playing an idealistic staffer for a Washington, D.C. lobbying group) in January 1975. The series costarred Dietrich and only lasted 13 weeks.

1240. **Kelly's Kids.** 30 min. Airdate: 1/4/74. Production Company: Paramount Television. Director: Richard Michaels. Executive Producer: Sherwood Schwartz. Producers: Howard Leeds and Lloyd J. Schwartz. Writer: Sherwood Schwartz. Creator: Sherwood Schwartz. Music: Frank DeVol. Aired as an episode of *The Brady Bunch* and intended as a possible replacement for the ailing sitcom. Ken Berry and Brooke Bundy are a show business couple who adopt three seven-year-old boys—one Asian, one white, and one black. ABC rejected it, but Sherwood Schwartz never lost faith. For 12 years he continued pitching the concept to the networks. "I am, if nothing else, persistent," he says. "It was an idea that was ahead of its time." In 1986, it seems, time finally caught up with the idea. CBS bought it, brought in writer Michael Jacobs and producer Al Burton, and it became *Together We Stand*, a series about a basketball coach (Elliot Gould) and his wife (Dee Wallace Stone) who adopt a white girl, then have a boy child naturally, and a decade later take in a 12-year-old Asian boy and a black girl. The series was on the air just a few weeks when it was yanked from the schedule. Gould was dropped, the title was changed to *Nothing Is Easy*, and survived another few weeks. *Cast:* Ken Berry (as Ken Kelly), Brooke Bundy (Kathy Kelly), Todd Lookinland (Matt Kelly), Carey Wong (Steve Kelly), William Attmore (Dwayne Kelly), Molly Dodd (Mrs. Payne).

1241. **The Muppet Show.** 30 min. Airdate: 1/30/74. Production Company: IFA. Executive Producer: Bernie Brillstein. Producer: Jim Henson. Creator: Jim Henson. Mia Farrow guest hosted this pilot featuring The Muppets, the cute puppet characters created by Jim Henson that won fame on *Sesame Street*. The comedy anthology/variety show would tackle and satirize a different aspect of American life each week. The network passed. But ABC's mistake became first-run syndication's gain. In 1976, a slightly different series, produced in England and bearing the same name as the pilot, premiered in syndication. It featured the Muppets in a variety show hosted by a different guest star each week. The series ran until 1981.

1242. **Only in America.** 30 min. Production Company: 20th Century Fox. Director: Fielder Cook. Producer: Fielder Cook. Writer: Stanley Shapiro. Creator: Stanley

Shapiro. Topol plays a carpenter who heads an immigrant family living in the lower east side of New York in 1912. Kathleen Widdoes is his wife, Ricky Powell is his American-born son, and Sam Jaffe is a rabbi.

1243. **Shirts/Skins.** 30 min. Production Company: MGM. Director: Bruce Paltrow. Producer: Bruce Paltrow. Writer: Bruce Paltrow. A sitcom pilot based on the TV movie of the same title, which aired on 10/9/73 and was written and produced by Bruce Paltrow. The proposed sitcom, like the TV movie, would focus on the lives of six businessmen who have gotten together each week for the last ten years to play basketball. Inevitably, something happens that involves them all in some wild scheme. Leonard Frey was the only actor that resumed his role from the TV movie, which also starred Rene Auberjonois, Bill Bixby, Doug McClure, McLean Stevenson, and Robert Walden in parts now played by Alan Oppenheimer, Oliver Clark, John Pleshette, William DeVane, and Robert Sampson.

1244. **The Toy Game.** 30 min. Production Company: Lorimar Productions. Executive Producer: Lee Rich. Producer: Danny Arnold. Creator: Danny Arnold. Barbara Eden is a single woman who creates toys for boss Nehemiah Persoff and lives with her widower father, James Gregory, and her widowed grandmother, Ruth McDevitt.

ABC / DRAMA

1245. **The Chadwick Family.** 90 min. Airdate: 4/17/74. Production Company: Universal Television. Director: David Lowell Rich. Executive Producer: David Victor. Producer: David J. O'Connell. Writer: John Gay, from a story by David Victor and John Gay. Creator: David Victor. Music: Hal Mooney. Fred Mac-Murray is the publisher of a small newspaper on an island off the coast of California who, with his wife Kathleen Maguire, has to deal with the pressures of leading a large and out-going family. The Chadwicks have four children – three daughters and a son. One daughter is a widow raising a child, another is married to a school-teacher and raising a family, and the other is a college student engaged to a Chinese-American boy. The son is still in high school. *Cast:* Fred MacMurray (as Ned Chadwick), Kathleen Maguire (Valerie Chadwick), Lara Parker (Eileen Chadwick Hawthorne), Darleen Carr (Joan Chadwick McTaggert), Jane Actman (Lisa Chadwick), Stephen Nathan (Tim Chadwick), Alan Fudge (Alex Hawthorne), Barry Bostwick (Duffy McTaggert), Carlene Gower (Cindy

Hawthorne), Kim Durso (Sari Hawthorne), Eben George (Jimmy Hawthorne), Frank Michael-Liu (Lee), John Larch (Fargo), Bruce Boxleitner (Danny), Pat Li (Madame Wu), Margaret Lindsay (Elly), Walter Brooke (Dr. Simon), Judson Morgan (Garvey), Elliot Montgomery (Mr. Villars), Ray Ballard (Taxi Driver), Sharon Cintron (Nurse), Carl Benson (Dr. Eisenberg), Morton Lewis (Herbie).

1246. The Champions (aka Mercy or Murder). 90 min. Airdate: 4/10/74. Production Company: Quinn Martin Productions. Director: Harvey Hart. Executive Producer: Quinn Martin. Producer: Adrian Samish. Writer: Douglas Day Stewart. Creators: Douglas Day Stewart and Cliff Gould. Music: Patrick Williams. The adventures of a 70-year-old defense attorney (Denver Pyle) and his partner, his 40-year-old son (Bradford Dillman), who work out of an innocuous office in Nashville and only take on cases of fundamental constitutional or moral importance. *Cast:* Bradford Dillman (as Sam Champion), Denver Pyle (Amos Champion), Melvyn Douglas (Dr. Paul Harelson), Mildred Dunnock (Lois Harelson), Don Porter (Henry Balin), David Birney (Dr. Peter Peterson), Robert Webber (Dr. Eric Stone-man), Betty Ackerman (Nurse Cantelli), Kent Smith (Judge), Bonnie Bartlett (Elena Champion), Arthur Franz (Dr. Raymond Eckworth), Regis J. Cordic (Arraignment Judge), Lindsay Workman (Bailiff), Warren Parker (Dr. Chadway), Stephen Colt (Coroner).

1247. Cro-Magnon (aka The Tribe). 90 min. Airdate: 12/11/74. Production Company: Universal Television. Director: Richard A. Colla. Producer: George Eckstein. Writer: Lane Slate. Creator: Lane Slate. Music: Hal Mooney. The adventures of a Cro-Magnon family fighting for survival—and against Neanderthals—in Europe at the end of the last Ice Age. Victor French played the leader of the family, Adriana Shaw was his wife, Mark Gruner his son, and Henry Wilcoxen was the wise elder. Shot in Beaumont, California. *Cast:* Victor French (as Mathis), Adriana Shaw (Jen), Henry Wilcoxen (Gana), Warren Vanders (Gorin), Stewart Moss (Gato), Sam Gilman (Rouse), Tani Phelps Guthrie (Sarish), Mark Gruner (Perron), Meg Wyllie (Hertha), Nancy Elliot (Ardis), Jeannine Brown (Orda), Dominique Pinassi (Kiska), Jack Scalici (The Neanderthal), Paul Richards (Narrator).

1248. The Douglas Family (aka A Dream for Christmas). 2 hours. Airdate: 12/24/73. Production Company: Lorimar Productions. Director: Ralph Senensky. Executive Producer: Lee Rich. Producer: Walter Coblenz. Writers: John McGreevey and Max Hodge, from a story by Earl Hamner, Jr. Creators:

Ricardo Montalban (Capt. Esteban), Gilbert Roland (Don Alejandro Vega), Yvonne DeCarlo (Isabella Vega), Louise Sorel (Inez Quintero), Robert Middleton (Don Luis Quintero), Anne Archer (Teresa), Tom Lacy (Filippe), George Cervera (Sgt. Gonzales), Inez Perez (Duenna Maria), John Rose (Rodrigo), Jay Hammer (Antonio), Alfonso Tafoya (Miquel), Robert Carricart (Duck Worker).

1254. **McNeill (aka The Winter Kill).** 2 hours. Airdate: 4/15/74. Production Company: MGM. Director: Jud Taylor. Executive Producer: Richard O. Linke. Producer: Burt Nodella. Writer: John Michael Hayes, adapted by David Karb, from the motion picture *They Only Kill Their Masters*, written by Lane Slate. Music: Jerry Goldsmith. A pilot inspired by the 1972 movie *They Only Kill Their Masters* starring James Garner. Andy Griffith assumes the role of a ski resort sheriff who solves baffling crimes. Producer Richard O. Linke and Griffith tried to sell the concept again and again – in two more pilots called *Adams of Eagle Lake* (8/23/75, 8/30/75) and two others (with Griffith as Sheriff Marsh) entitled *Girl in the Empty Grave* (9/20/77) and *The Deadly Game* (12/3/77). To further complicate things, these pilots were all preceded by the TV movie *Isn't It Shocking?* (10/2/73), which was directed by John Badham, and written by Slate. It starred Alan Alda as Police Chief Dan Barnes solving murders in a small New England town. It, too, was based on *They Only Kill Their Masters*, but was not a pilot. Perhaps it might have been considered as a pilot for a series if Alda wasn't already tied up starring in *M*A*S*H*. Cast: Andy Griffith (as Sheriff Sam McNeill), John Larch (Dr. Bill Hammond), Tim O'Connor (Bill Carter), Lawrence Pressman (Peter Lockhard), Eugene Roche (Mayor Clinton Bickford), Charles Tyner (Charley Eastman), Joyce Van Patten (Grace Lockhard), Sheree North (Betty), John Calvin (Deputy Jerry Troy), Louise Latham (Doris), Robert F. Simon (Harvey), Elayne Heilveil (Cynthia Howe), Nick Nolte (Dave Michaels), Ruth McDevitt (Mildred Young), Walter Brooke (Ben), Devra Korwin (Elaine Carter), David Frankham (Reverend Phillips), Vaughn Taylor (Frank).

1255. **Melvin Purvis, G-Man.** 90 min. Airdate: 4/9/74. Production Companies: Dan Curtis Productions and American International Pictures. Director: Dan Curtis. Executive Producer: Paul R. Picard. Producer: Dan Curtis. Writers: William F. Nolan and John Milius, from a story by John Milius. Music: Robert Cobert. Dale Robertson stars in the fictionalized drama based on the life of FBI agent Melvin Purvis, who captured or killed the ten most wanted men of the 1930s, including John Dillinger and Machine Gun Kelly. A second pilot, *The Kansas City Massacre*, followed and John Karlen replaced Steve Kanaly as Sam Cowley, Purvis' assistant. *Cast:* Dale Robertson (as Melvin Purvis), Steve Kanaly (Sam Cowley), Harris Yulin (Machine Gun Kelly), Maggie Blye (Katherine Ryan Kelly), Matt Clark (Charles Parimetter), Dick Sargent (Thatcher Covington), John Karlen (Anthony Redecci), David Canary (Eugene Farber), Woodrow Parfrey (Nash Covington), Jim Hill (Jim Langaker), Don McGowan (Hamburger Stand Man), Max Kleven (Driver), Eddie Quillan (Clerk).

1256. **Men of the Dragon.** 90 min. Airdate: 3/20/74. Production Company: David Wolper Productions. Director: Harry Falk. Executive Producer: Stan Margulies. Producer: Barney Rosenweig. Writer: Denne Bart Petitclerc. Creator: Denne Bart Petitclerc. Music: Elmer Bernstein. Jared Martin and Katie Saylor starred as an American brother and sister who are experts in the martial arts and, with an Asian friend (Robert Ito), open a self-defense school in Hong Kong. But, inevitably, they are called on to use their special skills to help people in trouble. Shot on location in Hong Kong. Martin and Saylor would later costar in the short-lived NBC series *Fantastic Journey. Cast:* Jared Martin (as Jan Kimbro), Katie Saylor (Lisa Kimbro), Robert Ito (Li-Teh), Joseph Wiseman (Balashev), Lee Tit War (Sato), Hsai Ho Lan (Madame Wu), Nang Sheen Chiou (O-Lan), Bill Jarvis (Inspector Endicott), Bobby To (K'Ang), Victor Kan (Chok), Herman Chan (Bellboy), David Chow (Tao).

1257. **Mrs. Sundance.** 90 min. Airdate: 1/15/74. Production Company: 20th Century Fox. Director: Marvin J. Chomsky. Producer: Stan Hough. Writer: Christopher Knopf. Music: Patrick Williams. A sequel to the movie *Butch Cassidy and the Sundance Kid.* Elizabeth Montgomery takes over for Katherine Ross as Etta Place, the fugitive lover of the outlaw Sundance Kid—who, she thinks, may still be alive. She's relentlessly pursued by Charles Siringo, a Pinkerton agent (L.Q. Jones). Katherine Ross returned to the role in a subsequent pilot from producer Stan Hough, *Wanted: The Sundance Woman,* in 1976 in which she still chased the Pinkerton man—played by Steve Forrest—and became a gunrunner for Pancho Villa. *Cast:* Elizabeth Montgomery (as Etta Place), Robert Foxworth (Jack Maddox), L.Q. Jones (Charles Siringo), Arthur Hunnicutt (Walt Putney), Lorna Thayer (Fanny Porter), Lurene Tuttle (Mrs. Lee), Claudette Nevins (Mary Lant), Byron Mabe (Merkle), Robert Donner (Ben Lant), Dean Smith (Avery), Jack Williams (Davis), Todd Shelhorse (David).

1258. **Parsons (aka The Gun and the Pulpit).** 90 min. Airdate: 4/3/74. Production Company: Danny Thomas Productions. Director: Daniel Petrie. Executive

Producer: Paul Junger Witt. Producers: Paul Maslansky and Tony Thomas. Writer: William Bowers, from the book by Jack Ehrlieh. Creator: William Bowers. Music: George Tipton. Evangelist-turned-actor Marjoe Gortner plays a gunfighter masquerading as an evangelist to escape a trumped up murder charge. As he wanders the West, he helps people in trouble. Filmed on location in Arizona. *Cast:* Marjoe Gortner (as Ernie Parsons), Slim Pickens (Billy One-Eye), David Huddleston (Mr. Ross), Geoffrey Lewis (Jason McCoy), Estelle Parsons (Sadie Underwood), Pamela Sue Martin (Sally Underwood), Jeff Corey (Head of Posse), Karl Swenson (Adams), Jon Lormer (Luther), Robert Phillips (Tom Underwood), Larry Ward (Max), Joan Goodfellow (Dixie), Walter Barnes (Oaf), Melanie Fullerton (Emma Underwood), Steve Tackett (Tommy Underwood), Jason Clark (Luke).

1259. Pioneer Woman. 90 min. Airdate: 12/19/73. Production Company: Filmways. Director: Buzz Kulik. Executive Producer: Edward H. Feldman. Producer: Richard M. Rosenbloom. Writer: Suzanne Clausen. Creator: Suzanne Clausen. Music: Al DeLory. Joanna Pettet plays a "pioneer woman" in the 1860s who leads her two children to California after her husband is killed. *Cast:* Joanna Pettet (as Maggie Sergeant), William Shatner (John Sergeant), Helen Hunt (Sarah Sergeant), Russell Baer (Jeremy Sergeant), David Janssen (Robert Douglas), Lance LeGault (Joe Wormser), Linda Kupacek (Phillipa Wormser), Lloyd Berry (Slim Hall), Bob Koons (William Seymour), Agatha Mercer (Trudy Seymour), John Scott (Jake), Les Kimber (Jordan Seymour), John Murrell (Henry Seymour), Frank Edge (Frank), Una Pulson (Mrs. Hill).

1260. Planet Earth. 90 min. Airdate: 4/23/74. Production Company: Warner Bros. Television. Director: Marc Daniels. Executive Producer: Gene Roddenberry. Producer: Robert H. Justman. Writers: Gene Roddenberry and Juanita Bartlett, from a story by Gene Roddenberry. Creator: Gene Roddenberry. Music: Harry Sukman. A reworking of the flop CBS pilot *Genesis II.* This time, John Saxon stars as Dylan Hunt, a 20th Century scientist frozen in suspended animation who awakens in the post-apocalyptic world of 2133. The title narration explained it like this: "This is the 22nd Century, the land renewed, the air and water pure again. The conflicts of the past are gone. It is a new Earth, with new peoples and new customs. In some places, bizarre savagery, in others, advanced cities. Everywhere, new challenge and new adventure. This is also the story of Dylan Hunt, lost in 1979 in a suspended animation accident. Over a century and a half later, in the year 2133, he was found and awakened by the people of this city called PAX, peace. The one place on Earth that escaped the final conflict of the 20th Century. The one place on earth where civilization did not perish. Dylan Hunt is one of them now, leader of a PAX science team exploring a much changed world, part of the PAX dream of rebuilding a new and wiser civilization. Their mission is mankind, rebirth of Planet Earth." They travel in superspeed shuttles through underground tubes that honeycomb the earth. In the pilot, Dylan Hunt is captured by a society run by women and enslaved. *Cast:* John Saxon (as Dylan Hunt), Janet Margolin (Harper-Smythe), Ted Cassidy (Isiah), Christopher Cary (Baylock), Diana Muldaur (Marg), Jo De Winter (Villar), Majel Barrett (Yuloff), Jim Antonio (Dr. Jonathon Connor), Sally Kemp (Treece), Claire Brennan (Delba), Corinne Comacho (Bronta), Sarah Chattin (Thetis), John Quade (Kreeg Commandant), Patricia Smith (Skylar), Raymond Sutton (Kreeg Captain), Rai Tasco (Paytre Kimbridge), Aron Kincaird (Gorda), James Bacon (Partha), Joan Crosby (Ayla), Lew Brown (Merlo), Craig Hundley (Harpsichordist).

1261. **Wonder Woman.** 90 min. Airdate: 3/12/74. Production Company: Warner Bros. Television. Director: Vincent McEveety. Executive Producer: John D.F. Black. Producer: John G. Stephens. Writer: John D.F. Black, based on the comic strip by Charles Moulton. Music: Artie Butler. Set in the 1970s, and dead serious, this initial pilot for *Wonder Woman* starred Cathy Lee Crosby as a female "Superman" working, unknown to all, disguised as a mild-mannered secretary at a government intelligence agency. In 1975, Warner Bros. brought in a new production team, new stars (Lynda Carter and Lyle Waggoner), set the story in the 1940s, and took a camp approach. Ironically, when the series died after 14 episodes, it jumped to CBS – and jumped forward to the 1970s and a more serious approach. *Cast:* Cathy Lee Crosby (as Diana Prince/Wonder Woman), Kaz Garas (Agent Steve Trevor), Ricardo Montalban (Abner Smith), Andrew Prine (George Calvin), Anitra Ford (Ahnjayla), Charlene Holt (Hippolyte), Robert Porter (Joe), Jordan Rhodes (Bob), Richard X. Slattery (Col. Henkins), Beverly Gill (Dia), Sandy Gaviola (Ting), Roberta Brahm (Zoe), Donna Garrett (Cass), Thom Carney (Fred), Ed McCready (Wesley).

CBS / COMEDY

1262. **Aces Up.** 30 min. Airdate: 3/29/74. Production Companies: Sheldon Leonard Productions and Metromedia Producers Corp. Director: Sheldon Leonard.

Producers: Sheldon Leonard and Danny Arnold. Writer: Robert Klane. Creators: Robert Klane and Lawrence Marks. Music: Earle Hagen. Jose Perez is a would-be race car driver and Raul Julia is his friend, a would-be race car designer. Together, they are building a car that they dream of one day racing in professional competition. To earn the money they need to build their dream car, they operate the Ace Moving and Hauling Service. Paul Michael Glaser guest starred.

1263. **Another April.** 30 min. Airdate: 3/7/74. Production Company: CBS Productions. Director: Alan Rafkin. Executive Producer: Lawrence Kasha. Producer: Lew Gallo. Writer: Lila Garrett. Leslie Charleson is a liberal divorcee, raising a young son, who goes back to living in Seattle with her understanding mother and conservative, argumentative father. *Cast:* Leslie Charleson (as April Weston Moss), Barnard Hughes (Marion Weston), Elizabeth Wilson (Ruth Weston), Brad Savage (Eric Moss), Howard Hesseman (Dennis Webber), Will MacKenzie (Howard Sanders).

1264. **The Boys.** 30 min. Airdate: 5/16/74. Production Company: Concept II Productions. Director: Bill Persky. Producers: Bill Persky and Sam Denoff. Writers: Bill Persky and Sam Denoff. Creators: Bill Persky and Sam Denoff. Eddie (Tim Conway) and Harry (Herb Edelman) are two television comedy writers who lead dramatically different personal lives. Eddie is married for a second time and is constantly nagged by his first wife. Harry is a swinging bachelor. *Cast:* Tim Conway (as Eddie Ryan), Herb Edelman (Harry Rufkin), Esther Sutherland (Cassie Ryan), Gwynne Gilford (Alice Ryan), Phyllis Davis (Vicki), Richard Stahl (Dr. Ferguson), Jack Berle (Captain), Alex Wilson (Man in Sauna).

1265. **Change at 125th Street.** 30 min. Airdate: 3/28/74. Production Company: Sullivan Productions. Producer: Robert Precht. Writer: Ernest Kinoy. Creator: Ernest Kinoy. Music: Ashford and Simpson. Ron Glass is a Harvard-educated broker at an all-white Wall Street firm who lives in Harlem with his mother (Roxie Roker), his activist sister (Chip Fields), and his tap dancing uncle (Vernon Washington). Frank Cover plays the boss of the Wall Street firm. Terry Kiser and Garrett Morris guest starred. Shot in New York.

1266. **Dominic's Dream.** 30 min. Airdate: 3/28/74. Production Company: Henderson Productions. Director: Garry Marshall. Executive Producers: William P. D'Angelo and Garry Marshall. Producer: Tony Marshall. Writer: Garry Marshall. Creator: Garry Marshall. Music: Buz Cohan. The misadventures of a New York couple and their teenage daughter who, after living all their lives in an Italian neighborhood, move to suburban Southern California. *Cast:* Joseph Mascolo (as Dominic Bente), Rita Moreno (Anita Bente), Toni Kalem (Marie Bente), Marjorie Battles (Crystal Hendrickson), Burt Heyman (Jess Hendrickson), Dennis Kort (Mark Hendrickson), Tom Pedi (Uncle Willie), Dee Gardner (Ginger), Peggy Doyle (Sister), Georgia Schmidt (Old Lady).

1267. **Evel Knievel.** 30 min. Airdate: 3/29/74. Production Company: Viacom. Director: Michael O'Herlihy. Executive Producer: Robert E. Relyea. Producer: John Strong. Writer: Richard Adams. Music: Gil Melle. A comedy/adventure adaptation of the movie of the same name, which starred George Hamilton as real-life motorcycle daredevil Evel Knievel. Sam Elliott assumes the role for the pilot, in which he is pitted against a female stunt cyclist. *Cast:* Sam Elliott (as Evel Knievel), Gary Barton (Gene Ray Stone), Noble Wallingham (Jack Decataur), Karen Phillip (Tracy Butler), Michael Anderson, Jr. (Darrell Pettet), Herbie Faye (Hymie), Edward Ansara (Reporter).

1268. **The Fess Parker Show.** 30 min. Airdate: 3/28/74. Production Company: Don Fedderson Productions. Director: Don Weis. Executive Producer: Don Fedderson. Producer: George Tibbles. Writer: John McGreevey. Music: Frank DeVol. Fess Parker plays a widowed construction worker raising three precocious daughters and whose best friend, played by Norman Alden, is a widower raising three sons. Florence Lake plays a maid who helps him handle his daughters. *Cast:* Fess Parker (as Fess Hamilton), Cynthia Eilbacher (Susie Hamilton), Dawn Lyn (Beth Hamilton), Michelle Stacy (Holly Hamilton), Florence Lake (Esther Crowe), Linda Dano (Julie Weston), Woodrow Parfrey (Mr. Johnson), Norman Alden (Boomer Landis).

1269. **If I Love You, Am I Trapped Forever?** 30 min. Airdate: 3/22/74. Production Company: 20th Century Fox. Director: Gene Reynolds. Producers: Gene Reynolds and Larry Gelbart. Writer: Larry Gelbart, from the book by M.E. Kerr. A comedy/drama about five teenagers in the *M*A *S*H* mold by the folks who did it–Gene Reynolds and Larry Gelbart. There are two twin sisters, one who is nice (and has an all-American boyfriend) and one who isn't. There's also a hypochondriac who is sure he won't live to be an adult and his friend, the class intellectual. Stars included Teddy Eccles, Bob Berger, Paul Clemens, Tanis Montgomery, Denise Nickerson, Vicky Hustable, Michael Talbott, Liam Dunn, Joe DiReda, and Elinor Donahue.

1270. **Jerry.** 30 min. Airdate: 5/15/74. Production Company: Warner Bros. Television. Director: Hal Cooper. Producer: Edward H. Feldman. Writer: Hal Dresner.

Creator: Hal Dresner. Robert Walden is a 30-year-old banker going through the ups-and-downs of bachelorhood. He's helped along the way by the wacky divorcee (Linda Lavin) and the married couple (Bob Hastings and Beatrice Colen) next door. *Cast:* Robert Walden (as Jerry Edwards), Linda Lavin (Nina Pope), Norman Alden (Winston Barlow), Bob Hastings (Frank Fuller), Beatrice Colen (Gloria Fuller), Keone Young (Morree Wu), Dian Parkinson (Girl).

1271. **Ma and Pa.** 30 min. Airdate: 3/7/74. Production Company: Warner Bros. Television. Director: Jerry London. Executive Producer: Phillip Mendelker. Producers: Bernie Kukoff and Jeff Harris. Writer: George Furth, from his play *Twigs.* Creator: George Furth. Music: Marvin Hamlisch. In the Broadway play *Twigs,* actress Sada Thompson played four roles – a strong-willed woman and her three very different daughters. Now, in the sitcom adaptation, the roles are given to four different actresses. Mary Wickes is the opinionated mother, who wants to live with her quiet husband (Arthur Space) but is constantly called on to help her daughters solve their problems. Dorothy Louden is Dorothy, the eldest, happily married; Marian Hailey is Celia, married, but bewildered and uncertain about life; and Barbara Sharma is Emily, a woman going through her second divorce and determined not to screw up a third time. Bruce Davison guest starred.

1272. **The Michele Lee Show.** 30 min. Airdate: 4/5/74. Production Company: Metromedia Producers Corp. Director: Peter Baldwin. Executive Producer: Charles Fries. Producer: Fred Coe. Writer: Robert Klane. Creator: Robert Klane. Music: Stephen Lawrence, theme sung by Michele Lee. Michele Lee is a clerk in a hotel newsstand who has the uncanny ability of bringing out people's inner-most feelings and getting them to realize things about themselves they never knew before. In the pilot, she dates an intern who, through her, discovers he doesn't really want to be a doctor after all. *Cast:* Michele Lee (as Michele Burton), Herbie Fay (Mr. Zelensky), Joyce Bulifant (Gladys Gooch), Stephen Collins (Dr. Steven Mayhill), Sidney Clute (Customer).

1273. **Moe and Joe.** 30 min. Airdate: 3/7/74. Production Company: Jed Productions. Director: Hy Averback. Executive Producer: Marc Merson. Producer: Joe Manetta. Writer: Bob Randall. Creator: Bob Randall. A sitcom-sequel to Bob Randall's broadway play *6 Rms Riv Vu.* Louise Lasser and Michael Tolan are a married couple who, at age 35 and with two kids, are worried that they are losing touch with their youth. This conflict is exacerbated by watching the life led by the college girl (Judith Kahan) who lives with them and watches the kids. The cast included Adam Arkin, Andrea McCardle, Matthew Anto, Marvin Lichterman, and Nina Wilcox.

1274. **Pete 'n' Tillie.** 30 min. Airdate: 3/28/74. Production Company: Universal Television. Director: Jerry Belson. Producer: Carl Kleinschmitt. Writer: Carl Kleinschmitt, based on the novel *Witch's Milk* by Peter de Vries. Based on the 1972 movie, which starred Walter Matthau as a 48-year-old school teacher who marries a 38-year-old social worker, played by Carol Burnett. It's the first marriage for both, and adjusting to living with someone else after such a long single life gets some getting used to. Carmine Caridi and Cloris Leachman were the couple in this sitcom adaptation. *Cast:* Cloris Leachman (as Tillie Schaefer), Carmine Caridi (Pete Schaefer), Mabel Albertson (Norma Jean Ryerson), Dick Balduzzi (Alan Kipeck).

1275. **Slither.** 30 min. Airdate: 3/21/74. Production Company: MGM. Director: Daryl Duke. Producer: Jack Shea. Writer: W.D. Richter. Creator: W.D. Richter. Based on the 1973 film, which starred James Caan as Dick Kanipsia, a friendly, slightly hapless ex-con who has a tendency to meet strange people and get in over his head in outlandish schemes. Barry Bostwick stars in this sitcom version. *Cast:* Barry Bostwick (as Dick Kanipsia), Patti Deutsch (Ruthie), Cliff Emmich (Fat Stranger), Michael C. Gwynne (Stranger), Seaman Glass (Farmer), Louis Quinn (Seller), Robert Stiles (Seller #2), John Delgado (Driver).

1276. **Sonny Boy.** 30 min. Airdate: 5/16/74. Production Company: Sullivan Productions. Director: Rob Reiner. Executive Producer: Robert Precht. Producers: Phil Mishkin and Rob Reiner. Writers: Phil Mishkin and Rob Reiner. Creators: Phil Mishkin and Rob Reiner. Allen Garfield is the prosperous owner of a toy store chain who lives in a building he owns with his doting mother (Florence Stanley) and has dated the same woman (Yvonne Wilder) for 15 years. *Cast:* Allen Garfield (as Sonny Boy Walker), Florence Stanley (Marjorie Walker), Yvonne Wilder (Lorraine), Joshua Shelley (Uncle Ralph), Beverly Carter (Doris).

CBS / DRAMA

1277. **Big Rose (aka Double Trouble).** 90 min. Airdate: 3/26/74. Production Company: 20th Century Fox. Director: Paul Krasny. Producer: Joel Rogosin. Writer: Andy Lewis. Creator: Andy Lewis. Music: Robert Prince. Shelley Winters is streetwise private eye Rose Winters who takes on a young, inexperienced investigator (Barry

Primus) who sees humor in things she takes quite seriously – like life or death situations. *Cast:* Shelley Winters (as Rose Winters), Barry Primus (Ed Mills), Lonnie Chapman (Lt. John Moore), Michael Constantine (Gunther), Joan Van Ark (Nina), Paul Mantee (Troy), Paul Picerni (Blass), Peggy Walton (Marian), Yale Summers (James Mayhew), Lenore Kasdorf (Waitress).

1278. **Dr. Max.** 90 min. Airdate: 4/4/74. Production Company: CBS Productions. Director: James Goldstone. Producers: James Goldstone and Cliff Gould. Writer: Robert L. Joseph. Creator: Robert L. Joseph. Music: Billy Goldenberg. Lee J. Cobb is Dr. Max, a dedicated, curmudgeonly medical practitioner who works out of his two-story Baltimore brownstone with his wife (Janet Ward), who is a nurse, while his son (Robert Lipton) struggles through law school. *Cast:* Lee J. Cobb (as Dr. Max Gordon), Janet Ward (Gloria Gordon), Robert Lipton (Alex Gordon), David Sheiner (Lester Opel), Katherine Helmond (Libby Opel), Sorrell Booke (Dr. Scott Herndon), Miriam Colon (Mrs. Camacho), Panchito Gomez (Rafael Camacho), John Lehne (Dr. Jules Grogin), Della Thomas (Jean), Caesar Cordova (Luis Camacho), Granville Van Dusen (Dr. John Poole), Henry Strosier (Ralph Larson), Alice Rodriquez (Pediatric Nurse), Erin Connor (Student).

1279. **The Family Kovack.** 90 min. Airdate: 4/5/74. Production Company: Playboy Productions. Director: Ralph Senensky. Executive Producer: Edward L. Rissien. Producer: Ron Roth. Writer: Adrian Spies. Music: Harry Sukman. A family saga revolving around widowed Ma Kovack (Sarah Cunningham), who runs a Chicago diner; her eldest sons (James Sloyan, Andy Robinson) who operate a barely viable trucking company; her youngest son (Richard Gilliland), who is studying law; and her daughter (Tammi Bula), who is studying to be a nurse. *Cast:* Sarah Cunningham (as Ma), James Sloyan (Vinnie Kovack), Andy Robinson (Butch Kovack), Tammi Bula (Karen Kovack), Richard Gilliland (Lennie Kovack), Renne Jarrett (Jill), Mary LaRoche (Mrs. Linsen), Philip Burns (Jo-Jo Linsen), Paul Bryar (Charlie), Peter Brocco (Mr. Manzak), Baruch Lumet (Mr. Czablinski), Norma Thayer (Thelma), James Jeter (Albert), Dorothy Mayer (Nurse).

1280. **Mr. and Mrs. Cop.** 30 min. Airdate: 5/3/74. Production Company: Viacom. Director: Harvey Hart. Producer: Leonard B. Kaufman. Writer: Howard Rodman. Creator: Howard Rodman. Music: Peter Matz. Anthony Costello and Marianne McAndrew are husband-and-wife. They are also uniformed police officers. They don't ride together, but they do bring the pressures and conflicts of work into their new marriage, making the adjustment to life together even more difficult. A similar concept, also titled *Mr. and Mrs. Cop* but later changed to *MacGruder and Loud*, was tried briefly in 1985 by producer Aaron Spelling with disastrous results. *Cast:* Anthony Costello (as Paul Roscommon), Marianne McAndrew (Nancy Roscommon), Richard Angarola (Lt. Ocala), William Campbell (Sgt. Baum), Redmond Gleason (Officer Irv Pyle), Tom Falk (Al Johnson), Howard Platt (Chester), Max Gail (Albanel), Holly Near (Mrs. Salmon), Alan Dexter (Minister), Gerald Ray (Sgt. Plantanos), Dan Spelling (Krunkle), Norma Connolly (Mother).

1281. **Nicky's World.** 30 min. Production Company: Tomorrow Entertainment. Executive Producer: Robert Markell. Producer: Joe Manduke. Writers: William Katz and Ed Adler. Creators: William Katz and Ed Adler. The life and times of a Greek family that operates a Manhattan bakery, as seen through the eyes of teenager Nick (Mark Shera). Charles Cioffi is the father, Olympia Dukakis is the mother, Despo is the grandmother, and George Voskovec is the grandfather. Shot on location in New York.

1282. **Sidekicks (aka The Skin Game).** 90 min. Airdate: 3/21/74. Production Company: Warner Bros. Television. Director: Burt Kennedy. Producer: Burt Kennedy. Writer: William Bowers. Creator: Richard Alan Simmons. Music: David Shire. A television sequel to the 1972 movie *Skin Game*, which starred James Garner and Lou Gossett as two conmen roaming the pre–Civil War West posing as master and slave. Larry Hagman steps in for Garner in the pilot, which aimed for a style reminiscent of the old *Maverick* series. Unfortunately the charm of both *Skin Game* and *Maverick* was Garner, and he's missing from this. *Cast:* Larry Hagman (as Quince), Lou Gossett (Jason), Blythe Danner (Prudy), Jack Elam (Boss), Harry Morgan (Sheriff Jenkins), Gene Evans (Sam), Noah Beery (Tom), Hal Williams (Max), Dick Peabody (Ed), Denver Pyle (Drunk), John Beck (Luke), Dick Haynes (Man), Tyler McVey (Jones), Billy Shannon (Carl).

NBC / COMEDY

1283. **For Better, For Worse.** 30 min. Production Company: Aaron Ruben Productions. Producer: Aaron Ruben. Writer: Aaron Ruben. Creator: Aaron Ruben. Marge Redmond and Jack Weston play a husband and wife who bicker constantly and have, for two decades, threatened divorce.

1284. Moose. 30 min. Production Company: Lorimar Productions. Director: Jack Shea. Producer: Jack Shea. Writer: Dan Greenberg. Creator: Dan Greenberg. The misadventures of three teenagers in pre–World War II, small-town America. Scott Jacobi is Moose, Bill Madden is his best friend and George O'Hanlon is the joker of the bunch.

1285. My Wife Next Door. 30 min. Production Company: Concept II Productions. Producers: Bill Persky and Sam Denoff. Writer: Jerry Davis. A divorced couple (James Farentino and Julie Sommers) coincidentally move into adjoining apartments on the beach.

1286. The Owl and the Pussycat. 30 min. Production Company: Screen Gems. Director: Paul Bogart. Producer: Marc Neufeld. Writer: Buck Henry. A sitcom adaptation of the motion picture starring George Segal and Barbra Streisand. Buck Henry and Bernadette Peters take over the roles of a frustrated writer and frustrated actress who become friends.

1287. Someone to Watch Over Me. 30 min. Production Company: Playboy Productions. Producer: Jerry Davis. Writers: Jerry Davis and Arthur Ross. Creators: Jerry Davis and Arthur Ross. The adventures of a married Beverly Hills couple with very different careers – he's (Laurence Luckinbill) a successful banker and she's (Jane Alexander) a parole officer—that they frequently bring home with them in one way or another.

1288. What Do You Feel Like Doing Tonight? 30 min. Production Company: Simcha Productions. Producer: Howard Gottfried. Writers: Paddy Chayef-sky, Elias Davis, and David Pollock. The problems facing a middle-aged man (James Coco) who suddenly finds himself alone in Manhattan and separated from his two children.

NBC / DRAMA

1289. Dr. Domingo. 60 min. Airdate: 3/14/74. Production Companies: Harbour Productions and Universal Television. Director: Don Weis. Producer: Cy Chermak. Aired as the "Riddle at 24,000" episode of *Ironside*. Desi Arnaz is Dr. Domingo, an unmarried doctor in a rural California community who dabbles in crime-solving, to the consternation of his nurse (Linda Foster) and the local police chief (L.Q. Jones). *Cast:* Desi Arnaz, Sr. (as Dr. Domingo), Linda Foster (Sue), L.Q. Jones (Lt. Mark Carter), Patricia Smith (Laura Blaine), Ralph Meeker (Westcott), Dolores Dorn (Mrs. Westcott).

1290. Fraud. 30 min. Airdate: 3/13/74. Production Companies: Mark VII Productions and Universal Television. Director: Jack Webb. Executive Producer: Jack Webb. Producer: Robert H. Forward. Writer: Joseph Calvelli. Aired as the "Clinic on Angel Street" episode of *Adam-12*. Ed Nelson stars as deputy district attorney who leads a special investigative unit dedicated to stopping fraud. Sharon Gless and Frank Sinatra, Jr. are his agents. *Cast:* Ed Nelson (as Abe Strayhorn), Sharon Gless (Lynn Carmichael), Frank Sinatra, Jr. (Gino Bardi), Dick Haynes (Dr. Elroy Guntham), Kenneth Tobey (Don Bates), Virginia Vincent (Marian Fenton).

1291. The Girl on the Late Late Show. 90 min. Airdate: 4/1/74. Production Companies: Columbia Pictures Television, Screen Gems, and David Gerber Productions. Director: Gary Nelson. Executive Producer: David Gerber. Producer: Christopher Morgan. Writer: Mark Rodgers. Music: Richard Markowitz. Don Murray is an intrepid producer and off-camera reporter for a network news show who, in the pilot, looks into the life of a famed movie queen and a series of murders. *Cast:* Don Murray (as William Martin), Bert Convy (F.J. Allen), Yvonne De Carlo (Lorraine), Gloria Graham (Carolyn Parker), Van Johnson (Johnny Leverett), Ralph Meeker (Inspector DeBiesse), Cameron Mitchell (Norman Wilder), Mary Ann Mobley (Librarian), Joe Santos (Sgt. Scott), Laraine Stephens (Paula), John Ireland (Bruno Walters), Walter Pidgeon (John Pahlman), Sherry Jackson (Pat Clauson), Felice Orlandi (Detective), Frankie Darro (Studio Guard).

1292. The Healers. 2 hours. Airdate: 5/22/74. Production Company: Warner Bros. Television. Director: Tom Gries. Executive Producer: Jerry Thorpe. Producer: John Furia, Jr. Writers: Howard Dimsdale and John Furia, Jr. Creator: Howard Dimsdale. Music: David Shire. John Forsythe heads a group of dedicated medical researchers in a California medical center and faces nothing but problems—with patients, with funding, with research, and with his family. *Cast:* John Forsythe (as Dr. Robert Kier), Pat Harrington (Joe Tate), Kate Woodville (Claire Parlini), Season Hubley (Ann Kilmer), Anthony Zerbe (Dr. Albert Scanlon), Beverly Garland (Laura Kier), John McIntire (Dr. Ernest Wilson), Lance Kerwin (Kennedy Brown), Michael C. Gwynne (Dr. Anton Balinkowski), Shelly Juttner (Nikki Kier), Christian Juttner (Vince Kier), Ellen Weston (Barbara), Liam Dunn (Mrs. Addison), Bill McKinney (Mr. Brown).

1293. Honky Tonk. 90 min. Airdate: 4/1/74. Production Company: MGM. Director: Don Taylor. Executive Producer: Douglas Heyes. Producer: Hugh Benson. Writer: Douglas Heyes. Music: Jerry Fielding. An attempt to turn the 1941 movie *Honky Tonk*, starring Clark Gable and Lana Turner, into a TV series. Richard Crenna is now Candy Johnson, a conman in the old West, and Margot Kidder is Lucy Cotton, his partner, a judge's daughter. Producer/Writer Douglas Heyes knows how to write western conmen – he did it best for several years on *Maverick*. *Cast:* Richard Crenna (as Candy Johnson), Margot Kidder (Lucy Cotton), Stella Stevens (Gold Dust), Will Geer (Judge Cotton), John Dehner (Brazos), Geoffrey Lewis (Roper), Gregory Sierra (Slade).

1294. The Impostor. 90 min. Airdate: 3/18/75. Production Company: Warner Bros. Television. Director: Edward Abrams. Executive Producer: Richard Bluel. Producer: Robert Stambler. Writers: Jerome Coopersmith and Jon Sevorg. Creators: Jerome Coopersmith and Jon Sevorg. Music: Gil Melle. Paul Hecht is a retired spy for the U.S. military who works as an actor off-broadway to hide his real vocation – a professional imposter used to ferret out crime. *Cast:* Paul Hecht (as Joe Tyler), Nancy Kelly (Victoria Kent), Meredith Baxter (Julie Watson), Jack Ging (Carl Rennick), Barbara Baxley (Margaret Elliot), John Vernon (Sheriff Turner), Edward Asner (Barney West), Paul Jenkins (Teddy Durham), Joseph Gallison (Dwight Elliot), Victor Campos (Del Gazzo), Bruce Glover (Jennings), Sherwood Price (Reager), Charlotte Stewart (Jean Durham), Suzanne Denor (April), Ronnie Schell (Dance Director), George Murdock (Glover).

1295. Log of the Black Pearl. 2 hours. Production Companies: Mark VII Productions and Universal Television. Executive Producers: Jack Webb and Robert A. Cinader. Producer: William Stark. Writer: Harold Jack Bloom. Kiel Martin is a stock broker who inherits his grandfather's yacht, gives up his career, and sets sail looking for adventure – and work. He hires Ralph Bellamy as his captain and Jack Krushen as the first-mate. *Cast:* Ralph Bellamy (as Capt. Fitzsimmons), Kiel Martin (Christopher Sand), Jack Kruschen (Jocko Roper), Glenn Corbett (Michael Devlin), Anne Archer (Lila Bristol), Henry Wilcoxon (Alexander Sand), John Alderson (Eric Kort), Edward Faulkner (Fenner), Pedro Armendariz, Jr. (Archie Hector), Jose Angel Espinosa (Benjamin Velasquez), Dale Johnson (Stock Broker).

1296. Punch and Jody. 90 min. Airdate: 11/26/74. Production Companies: Metromedia Producers Corp. and Stonehenge Productions. Director: Barry Shear. Executive Producer: Charles Fries. Producer: Douglas Benton. Writer: John McGreevey. Creator: John McGreevey. Music: Fred Karlin. Glenn Ford stars as Peter "Punch" Travers, a multi-talented performer who, for the last dozen years, has run a traveling circus owned by Lil Charney (Ruth Roman). In the pilot, he meets Jody (Pam Griffin), a 16-year-old daughter he never knew he had. The series, had it ensued, would have traced their travels and the conflicts involved in getting to know one another. *Cast:* Glenn Ford (as Peter "Punch" Travers), Pam Griffin (Jody Travers), Ruth Roman (Lil Charney), Kathleen Widdoes (Margaret Howell Grant), Parley Baer (Dan Baxter), Susan Brown (Aunt Jen Kingsley), Donald Barry (Delbert Butz), Billy Barty (Stilts), Mel Stewart (Woody), Cynthia Hayward (Aurora), Patty Maloney (Mrs. Stilts), Pat Morita (Takahasi), Peter Ford (Bus Driver), Read Morgan (Tom Poorbear), Barbara Rhoades (Barbara), Billie Jean Beach (Waitress).

1297. **Remember When.** 2 hours. Airdate: 3/23/74. Production Company: Danny Thomas Productions. Director: Buzz Kulik. Executive Producer: Danny Thomas. Producer: Paul Junger Witt. Writer: Herman Raucher. Creator: Herman Raucher. Music: George Aliceson Tipton. The pressures of World War II as experienced by a family in Hartford, Connecticut. Writer Raucher is best-known for his book, and subsequent movie, *Summer of '42. Cast:* Jack Warden (as Joe Hodges), William Schallert (Dick Hodges), Jamie Smith Jackson (Joanna), Robbie Benson (Frankie Hodges), Margaret Willock (Beverly), Nan Martin (Annie Hodges), Tim Matheson (Warren Thompson), Robert Middleton (Kraus), Muriel Landers (Shirley), Burton Gilliam (Zack), Frank Delfino (Wesso), Charles Haid (Jimmy).

1298. **Target Risk.** 90 min. Airdate: 1/6/75. Production Companies: Roy Huggins Productions and Universal Television. Director: Robert Sheerer. Executive Producer: Jo Swerling, Jr. Producer: Robert F. O'Neill. Writer: Don Carlos Dunaway. Bo Svenson is a bonded courier working out of Rome, who transports valuable objects of all kinds – secret formulas, wills, letters, contracts, diamonds, computer programs and people – any where in the world. He is an expert in mar-tial arts, espionage, disguise, and foreign languages. Roy Huggins and Jo Swerling, Jr. would try this again for the same network two years later with *The 3,000 Mile Chase,* starring Cliff DeYoung. I was beginning to think there were only four jobs held by television heroes – doctor, lawyer, cop an cowboy," Huggins says. "Then one day I received a book by Giles Tippette based on the adventures of a bonded courier. Now here was a fascinating character. I felt it was a fresh, new idea with great potential. *Cast:* Bo Svenson (as Lee Driscoll), Meredith Baxter (Linda Flayly), Keenan Wynn (Simon Cusack), John P. Ryan (Ralph Sloan), Robert

Coote (Julian Ulrich), Philip Bruns (Marty), Charles Shull (Bill Terek), Lee Paul (Harry), Jack Bender (Joe Cordova), William Hansen (Frederick), Regis J. Cordic (Mr. Ryan), Joey Aresco (Junkie), Cliff Carnell (Nick), Arthur Malet (Shoeshine Boy), Luis De Cordova (Berruezo), George Skaff (Maitre d').

1299. A Tree Grows in Brooklyn. 90 min. Airdate: 3/27/74. Production Companies: Norman Rosemont Productions and 20th Century Fox. Director: Joel Hardy. Producer: Norman Rosemont. Writers: Blanche Hanalis and Frank Davis, from the novel by Betty Smith. Music: Jerry Goldsmith. A television adaptation of the book, play, and Academy Award-winning 1945 Elia Kazan movie. This grim tale of family life in a poor Brooklyn neighborhood in the early 1900s starred Cliff Robertson as an alcoholic waiter, Diane Baker as a widow who marries a cop-on-the-beat (James Olson), and Nancy Malone as her married sister with a reputation for being "easy." *Cast:* Cliff Robertson (as Johnny Nolan), Diane Baker (Katie Nolan), James Olson (McShane), Pamela Ferdin (Francie Nolan), Nancy Malone (Sissy), Michael James Wixted (Neely Nolan), Liam Dunn (Barker), Anne Seymour (Miss Tilford), Allyn Ann McLerie (Miss Martin), Booth Colman (Doctor).

1300. Twice in a Lifetime (aka Flo's Place). 90 min. Airdate: 3/16/74. Production Company: Martin Rackin Productions. Director: Herschel Daugherty. Producer: Martin Rackin. Writers: Martin Rackin and Robert Pirosh. Creators: Martin Rackin and Robert Pirosh. Ernest Borgnine stars as a San Pedro, California, tugboat captain who lives in a boarding house and restaurant called Flo's Place, which is run by a salty widow (Della Reese), her son (Eric Laneuville) and a weary bartender (Vito Scotti). This was pitched again without Borgnine – as a sitcom called *Flo's Place* with Della Reese and Eric Laneuville – in 1976. *Cast:* Ernest Borgnine (as Vince Boselli), Della Reese (Flo), Eric Laneuville (Lewis), Vito Scotti (Carlos), Slim Pickens (Pete Lazich), Herb Jeffries (Hank Davis), Warren Vanders (Kipp), Arte Johnson (Ron Talley).

1301. The Underground Man (aka Lew Archer). 2 hours. Production Companies: Paramount Television and Aries Films. Director: Paul Wendkos. Executive Producer: Howard Koch. Producer: Phillip Parslow. Writers: Daniel Taradash and Douglas Heyes, from the book by Ross MacDonald. Music: Richard Hazard. Peter Graves stars as private eye Lew Archer, hero of Ross MacDonald's popular mystery novels and the basis for the Paul Newman movie *Harper*. This didn't sell, but a new version with Brian Keith was sold to NBC – and lasted three weeks in 1974. *Cast:* Peter Graves (as Lew Archer), Sharon Farrell (Marty Nickerson), Celeste Holm (Beatrice Broadhurst), Jim Hutton (Stanley Broadhurst), Kay Lenz (Sue Crandall), Biff McGuire (Cassidy), Vera Miles (Eleanor Strome), Jo Ann Pflug (Jean Broadhurst), Dame Judith Anderson (Mrs. Snow), Jack Klugman (Sheriff Tremaine), Arch Johnson (Joe Kelsey), Bill McKinney (Willy Coggins), Lee Paul (Fritz Snow), Ian John Tanza (Jerry Kilpatrick), Judson Morgan (Dr. Platt), Bill Stout (Newscaster), Maxine Stuart (Librarian), Jay Varela (Dr. Silcox), Brick Hines (Ronny Broadhurst).

1302. **Vector (aka The Specialists).** 90 min. Airdate: 1/6/75. Production Companies: Mark VII Productions and Universal Television. Director: Richard Quine. Producer: Robert A. Cinader. Writers: Robert A. Cinader and Preston Wood. Robert Urich, Jack Hogan, and Maureen Reagan are a Bureau of Epidemic Control team of scientists that tackles extremely contagious diseases before they can spread and unravels tricky medical mysteries afflicting any community anywhere in the nation. Rather than focusing on one story each episode, the projected series would have had the team involved in several cases each week, much like *Emergency* or *Adam-12*. *Cast:* Robert Urich (as Dr. William Nugent), Maureen Reagan (Dr. Christine Scofield), Jack Hogan (Dr. Edward Grey), Jed Allen (Dick Rowdon), Alfred Ryder (Dr. Alan Masdan), Harry Townes (Dr. Burkhart), Lillian Lehman (Doctor), Corinne Comacho (Ruth Conoyer), Anne Whitfield (Eileen), Jackie Coogan (Roger), David Lewis (Dave), Tom Scott (Leonard Pitt), Chris Anders (Erich), John Erich (Officer), Sidney Miller (Bartender), Priscilla Morrill (Mrs. Stinnett), Dolores Quinton (Pat Lathrop), Walter Stocker (Ernest Lathrop), Walter Altzman (Telescope Man), Kyle Anderson (Sylvia).

1303. **Where Have All the People Gone?** 90 min. Airdate: 10/8/74. Production Companies: Metromedia Producers Corp. and The Jozak Company. Director: John Llewellyn Moxey. Executive Producer: Charles Fries. Producer: Gerald I. Isenberg. Writers: Lewis John Carlino and Sandor Stern. Creator: Lewis John Carlino. Peter Graves is an archeologist who, with his children, is one of the few survivors of a nuclear holocaust in this pilot by novelist and screenwriter Lewis John Carlino. *Cast:* Peter Graves (as Steven Anders), Verna Bloom (Jenny), George O'Hanlon, Jr. (David Anders), Kathleen Quinlan (Deborah Anders), Michael James Wixted (Michael), Noble Willingham (Jim Clancy), Doug Chapin (Tom Clancy), Ken Sansom (Jack McFadden).

The following is an unsold pilot that was omitted from the previous edition of this book:

Hickok aka **This is the West That Was.** 90 Minutes. Airdate: 12/17/74. Production Company: Universal Television. Director: Fielder Cook. Producers: Roy Huggins, Jo Swerling Jr., Music: Dick DeBenedictis. Writer: Sam Rolfe. A comedic western that would have followed the exploits of Wild Bill Hickok, Calamity Jane and Buffalo Bill Cody. Producer Swerling, in a book about Roy Huggins, said of this pilot: "It was an attempt to spoof, and thereby expose, some of the legends of the old west." Swerling says the director and cast did an excellent job but, "when it was all strung together, it didn't make much sense." He says the screening of the pilot for network executives was a disaster. "It was one of the most humiliating experiences of my life. To a man, they absolutely hated it." Cast: Ben Murphy (Wild Bill Hickok), Kim Darby (Calamity Jane), Jane Alexander (Sarah Shaw), Tony Franciosa (JW McCanles), Stuart Margolin (Blind Pete), Stefan Gierasch (Carmedly), Matt Clark (Buffalo Bill Cody), Bill McKinney (Drago Wellman)

1975–1976

1304. Charo (aka Charo and the Sergeant). 30 min. Airdate: 8/24/76. Production Company: Andomar Productions. Director: John Rich. Producers: Aaron Ruben and John Rich. Creator/Writer: Aaron Ruben. Charo, the Latin American singer, dancer and frequent talkshow guest, plays an entertainer who marries a U.S. Marine sergeant and tries to adapt to life in Washington, D.C. *Cast:* Charo (as Charo Palmer), Tom Lester (Sgt. Hank Palmer), Noam Pitlik (Sgt. Turkel), Dick Van Patten (Chaplain).

1305. Dad's Army. Production Companies: Herman Rush Associates and David Wolper Productions. Producer: Herman Rush. Writer: Arthur Julian. An Americanized version of a hit BBC sitcom about civilians protecting the home-front during World War II. In this version, the locale is Long Island, the year is 1942, and these hapless folks are certain espionage is afoot and an enemy attack is imminent.

1306. Father O Father! 30 min. (x2) Airdate: 6/26/76. Production Company: The Fours Company. Directors: Peter Bonerz and Lee H. Bernhardi. Executive Producer: Jerry Weintraub. Producers: Rich Eustis, Al Rogers, and Ron Clarke. Writers: Rich Eustis and Al Rogers. These two 30-minute pilots followed the comedic conflicts between an old, conservative priest and a younger, liberal priest raised in the ghetto as they help their parish. *Cast:* Iggie Wolfington (as Father Flicker), Dennis Dugan (Father Morgan), Richard Stahl (Parishioner).

1307. Guess Who's Coming to Dinner. 30 min. Airdate: 5/28/75. Production Company: Columbia Pictures Television. Director: Stanley Kramer. Producer: Stanley Kramer. Writers: Dick DeRoy and Bill Idelson, based on the motion picture. A situation comedy, inspired by the film that starred Katherine Hepburn, Spencer Tracy, and Sidney Poitier, revolving around what happens when a white girl marries a black man and the two families become one. *Cast:* Leslie Charleson (as Joanna Prentiss), Bill Overton (John Prentiss), Eleanor Parker (Christine Drayton), Richard Dysart (Matt Drayton), Lee Weaver (Ralph Prentiss), Madge

Sinclair (Sarah Prentiss), Rosetta Le Noir (Tillie), William Calloway (Joe Delaney), Joseph R. Sicari (Orville Peacock).

1308. Home Cookin. 30 min. Airdate: 7/11/75. Production Company: Larry Gordon Productions. Director: Herbert Kenwith. Executive Producer: Lawrence Gordon. Producer: Don Van Atta. Writer: Tom Rickman. The comic antics of a husband and wife who run a roadside diner outside Nashville and the truck drivers they serve. Sue Ane Langdon, the original star of the pilot, was replaced by Fannie Flagg. In the pilot, the husband hires a sexy new waitress and sparks his wife's jealousy. *Cast:* Fannie Flagg (as Adelle), Wynn Irwin (Ernie), Nancy Fox (Dinette the Waitress), Burton Gilliam (Jammer), Walker Edmiston (Trooper), Bill McLean (Shorty).

1309. How to Succeed in Business Without Really Trying. 30 min. Airdate: 6/27/75. Production Company: ABC. Director: Burt Brinkerhoff. Producer: Abe Burrows. Writer: Abe Burrows, based on his play and the motion picture. A wily young man works his way up in a huge conglomerate where nobody quite knows what anybody else in the company is doing—but won't dare admit it. *Cast:* Alan Birsky (as J. Pierpoint Finch), Susan Blanchard (Rosemary), Marcella Lowry (Smitty), Larry Haines (Bratt), Max Showalter (J.B. Biggley), Jim Jansen (Frump), Polly Rowles (Miss Jones), Sam Smith (Twimble), Alan Resin (Peterson).

1310. The Last Detail. 30 min. Production Company: Columbia Pictures Television. Director: Jackie Cooper. Producer: Gerry Ayres. Writers: Gerry Ayres and Bill Kirby. This is a sitcom version of the movie, which starred Jack Nicholson and Otis Young. Robert F. Lyons and Charles Robinson now portray the two career men in the peacetime Navy who, as much as they may like civilian life, can't seem to fit in and really need the dull routine of the military to be happy.

1311. Mac. Production Company: Cave Creek Productions. Executive Producer: Byron Paul. Creator/Producer: Lila Garrett. Writers: George Bloom and Lila Garrett. Dick Van Dyke is a single cartoonist working for a big-city newspaper and living with 12-year-old Jimmy Baio, the son of his widowed best friend, a foreign correspondent who is never home. More often than not, the 12-year-old is the more adult of the two.

1312. Mason. 30 min. Airdate: 7/4/77. Production Company: Filmways. Director: Jack Shea. Producer: Ira Barmak. Creators/Writers: Austin and Irma Kalish. Ten-year-old Mason Reese, the precocious star of a series of sandwich spread commercials, was an overnight sensation that disappeared just as fast. During that brief moment of glory, however, he shot this pilot (that sat on the shelf for two years) about a boy genius and his befuddled parents. *Cast:* Mason Reese (as Mason Bennett), Barry Nelson (Howard Bennett), Barbara Stuart (Peggy Bennett), Lee Lawson (Joyce Bennett).

1313. **Muppets No-Nonsense Show.** 30 min. Airdate: 3/19/75. Producer/Creator: Jim Hensen. Music: Joe Raposa. This comedy/variety pilot, featuring the puppets popularized on PBS' *Sesame Street.* Although rejected by ABC, the series was eventually produced in London and became a smash hit in syndication.

1314. **The Orphan and the Dude.** 30 min. Airdate: 7/18/75. Production Company: MGM. Director: James Frawley. Producers: Jim Parker and Arnold Margolin. Writers: Jim Parker and Arnold Margolin. Creator: Joseph Goodson. Two eccentrics – a black, flashy, streetwise huckster and a white garage mechanic who grew up as an orphan—share an apartment in Culver City, California. *Cast:* Oliver Clark (as Oliver "The Orphan" Smith), Art Evans (Curtis "The Dude" Brown), Todd Bridges (Leonard Brown), Ed Barth (Sam Brodsky), Lynne Holmes (Amber), Frank McRae (Fast Freddie), David Moody (Dan).

ABC / DRAMA

1315. **Adams of Eagle Lake.** 60 min. (x2) Airdates: 8/23/75 and 8/30/75. Directors: Walter Grauman (#1) and Lawrence Dobkin (#2). Executive Producer: Richard O. Linke. Producers: Walter Grauman and Lawrence Dobkin. Writers: Charles Stewart, Jonathan Daly, and John Michael Hayes. Creator: Lane Slate, from his motion picture *They Only Kill Their Masters.* Music: Jerry Goldsmith. Andy Griffith is the sheriff of a resort community in two new pilots reworking a concept first proposed in the 1974 pilot *McNeill.* Despite the failure of these pilots, this concept wouldn't die. Producer Linke and Griffith brought it back again as *Abel Marsh* in 1977, and a similar format was proposed in 1978 called *Stedman.* *Cast:* Andy Griffith (as Sheriff Sam Adams), Abby Dalton (Margaret Kelly), Nick Nolte (Officer Jerry Troy), Iggie Wolfington (Officer Jubal Hammond), Paul Winchell (Monty), Sheldon Allman (Quinn), Eldon Quick (Leonard), William Mims (Lucas).

1316. **Best Years of Our Lives (aka Returning Home).** 90 min. Airdate: 4/29/75. Production Companies: Samuel Goldwyn Productions and Lorimar

Productions. Director: Dan Petrie. Executive Producer: Lee Rich. Producer: Herbert Hirschman. Writers: Bill Svanoe and John McGreevey, from the feature film. A TV-movie pilot based on the Academy Award-winning tale of three World War II soldiers – a married banker with two children, an airforce hero with a newlywed wife he hardly knows, and an infantryman who lost both his arms (played by Fredric March, Dana Andrews, and Harold Russell in the film) – who return home to a small town and try to adjust to civilian life. Dabney Coleman is the banker, Tom Selleck the flying ace, and newcomer James Miller, handicapped in Vietnam, plays the permanently scarred soldier. *Cast:* Dabney Coleman (as Al Stephenson), Tom Selleck (Fred Derry), James Miller (Homer Parrish), Whitney Blake (Millie Stephenson), Joan Goodfellow (Peggy Stephenson), Sherry Jackson (Marie Derry), Laurie Walters (Wilma Parish), James A. Watson, Jr. (Capt. Will Tobey), Lenka Peterson (Mrs. Parrish), Patricia Smith (Mrs. Cameron), Booth Colman (Vern Milton), Lou Frizzell (Butch Cavendish), Jim Antonio (Avery Novak), Don Keefer (Mr. Parrish), James Beach (Henry "Wimpy" Jergens), Paul Lambert (Mike Harris), Tom Blank (Dave), Joseph DiReda (ATC Sgt.), Ed Call (Hank), Allen Price (Rob Stephenson), Eileen McDonough (Luella).

1317. **Brenda Starr.** 90 min. Airdate: 5/8/76. Production Company: David Wolper Productions. Director: Mel Stuart. Executive Producer: Paul Mason. Producer: Robert Larson. Writer: George Kirgo, from a story by Ira Barmak, based on the comic strip by Dale Messick. Music: Lalo Schifrin. Jill St. John is Brenda Starr, the female newspaper reporter popularized in comic strips, who goes to Brazil to find a reclusive billionaire and expose a voodoo cult. A pilot for a syndicated, 30 minute *Brenda Starr* series, this one starring Sherry Jackson, aired in 1979 and also failed to generate any interest. *Cast:* Jill St. John (as Brenda Starr), Sorrell Brooke (A.J. Livwright), Jed Allan (Roger Randall), Tabi Cooper (Hank O'Hare), Victor Buono (Lance O'Toole), Joel Fabiani (Carlos Vargas), Barbara Luna (Luisa Santamaria), Marcia Strassman (Kentucky Smith), Torin Thatcher (Willis Lassiter), Arthur Roberts (Dax), Roy Applegate (Tommy), Judith Wright (Susan Lynn), Harold Oblong (Photographer).

1318. **Bridger.** 2 hours. Airdate: 9/10/76. Production Company: Universal Television. Director: David Lowell Rich. Producer: David Lowell Rich. Writer: Merwin Gerard. Music: Elliot Kaplan. Based on the true life of Jim Bridger, explorer, scout, and trader who was known as the Daniel Boone of the Rockies. Universal and ABC hoped he could be the Daniel Boone of television, too. In the pilot, Bridger and his sidekick Meek are ordered by President Jackson to blaze a trail from Wyoming to California in just 40 days...or Senator Daniel Webster will rally Congress to give the Northwest to England in exchange for fishing rights in Newfoundland. Shot on location in Sonora and Lone Pine, California. *Cast:* James Wainwright (as Jim Bridger), Dirk Blocker (Joe Meek), Ben Murphy (Kit Carson), Sally Field (Jennifer Melford), William Windom (Senator Webster), John Anderson (President Jackson), Claudio Martinez (David Bridger), Margarita Cordova (Shoshone Woman), Tom Middleton (Doctor), Robert Miano (Modoc Leader), Skeeter Vaughn (Paiute Chief), X Brands (Crow Chief).

1319. **The Daughters of Joshua Cabe Return.** 90 min. Airdate: 1/28/75. Production Company: Spelling/Goldberg Productions. Director: David Lowell Rich. Executive Producer: Aaron Spelling and Leonard Goldberg. Producer: Richard F. Lyons. Writer: Kathleen Hite. Creator: Paul Savage. The second attempt at a Joshua Cabe series, this time starring Dan Dailey as a fur trapper who convinces three women – a pickpocket, a hooker and a dance hall hostess – to pose as his daughters so that he can claim more acres in the West from the government for his homestead. In the pilot, one of the "daughters" is kidnapped by her real father and held for ransom. *Cast:* Dan Dailey (as Joshua Cabe), Ronne Troup (Ada), Brooke Adams (Mae), Christina Hart (Charity), Dub Taylor (Bitterroot), Kathleen Freeman (Essie), Carl Betz (Will), Arthur Hunnicutt (Miner), Randall Carver (Jim Finch), Terry Wilson (Sgt. Maxwell), Jane Alice Brandon (Jenny Finch), Robert Burton (Claver), Greg Leydig (Vickers).

1320. **First 36 Hours of Dr. Durant (aka A Small Step Forward).** 90 min. Airdate: 5/13/75. Production Company: Columbia Pictures Television. Director: Alexander Singer. Executive Producer: Stirling Silliphant. Producer: James H. Brown. Writer: Stirling Silliphant. Music: Leonard Rosenman. Scott Hylands stars as an overly idealistic young doctor who has to confront the frustrating realities of his residency in an urban hospital. He frequently clashes with his chief of staff—or anyone else who doesn't live in the same idealistic dreamworld he does. *Cast:* Scott Hylands (as Dr. Chris Durant), Lawrence Pressman (Dr. Konrad Zane), Katherine Helmond (Nurse Katherine Gunther), Karen Carlson (Nurse Clive Olin), Renne Jarrett (Dr. Lynn Peterson), Alex Hentelhoff (Dr. Alex Keefer), Dana Andrews (Dr. Hutchins), Michael Conrad (Graham), Peter Donat (Dr. Bryce), David Doyle (Dr. Atkinson), James Naughton (Dr. Baxter), Dennis

Patrick (Mr. Wesco), Joyce Jameson (Mr. Graham), Davis Roberts (Dr. Dorsett), Janet Brandt (Surgical Secretary).

1321. Friendly Persuasion (aka Except for Me and Thee). 2 hours. Airdate: 5/18/75. Production Companies: ITC Entertainment and Allied Artists. Director: Joseph Sargent. Executive Producers: Emmanuel Wolf and Herbert B. Leonard. Producer: Joseph Sargent. Writer: William Wood, from the books by Jessamyn West and the motion picture. Music: John Cacavas. Theme: Dimitri Tiomkin. Richard Kiley and Shirley Knight (assuming the roles played by Gary Cooper and Dorothy McGuire) are Quaker farmers who, during the Civil War, help runaway slaves reach freedom. Real-life brothers Michael and Kevin O'Keefe portray the Quaker's eldest sons. *Cast:* Richard Kiley (as Jess Birdwell), Shirley Knight (Eliza Birdwell), Michael O'Keefe (Josh Birdwell), Kevin O'Keefe (Labe Birdwell), Tracie Savage (Mattie Birdwell), Sparky Marcus (Little Jess Birdwell), Clifton James (Sam Jordon), Paul Benjamin (Swan Stebeney), Erik Holland (Enoch), Maria Grimm (Lily Truscott), Bob Minor (Burk).

1322. New Orleans Force (aka Dead Man on the Run). 90 min. Airdate: 4/2/75. Production Company: Sweeney-Finnegan Productions. Director: Bruce Bilson. Executive Producer: Bob Sweeney. Producer: Bill Finnegan. Writer: Ken Pettus. Creators: Bob Sweeney and Bill Finnegan. From the producers of *Hawaii Five-0* comes this pilot about an elite crime-fighting force, headed by Peter Graves, working out of New Orleans. Like *Hawaii Five-0*, the busted pilot was shot on location and used the exotic locale as the major star. *Cast:* Peter Graves (as Jim Gideon), Katherine Justice (Libby Stockton), Pernell Roberts (Brock Dillon), John Anderson (Jason Monroe), Diana Douglas (Meg), Mills Watson (Father Sebastian), Tom Rosqui (Fletcher), Jack Knight (Rocky Flanagan), Joe E. Tata (Bobby DiMosco), Hank Brandt (Alan Stockton), Stocker Fontelieu (Hollander), Don Hood (Sam Daggett), Eugene Autry (Antoine LeClerc), William J. Koolsber (Andre Foche), Pat McNamara (Mercer), Chuch Couch (Chaney), George Wilbur (Benet).

1323. The Oath (aka 33 Hours in the Life of God). 60 min. Airdate: 8/24/76. Production Company: Spelling/Goldberg Productions. Director: Glenn Jordan. Producers: Aaron Spelling and Leonard Goldberg. Writer: Hal Sitowitz. Two pilots were made in an attempt to sell a proposed medical anthology. In the first pilot, a cardiologist comes to the realization that his marriage and his medical ability are crumbling. *Cast:* Hal Holbrook (as Dr. Simon Abbott), Carol Rossen

(Alison Abbott), Hume Cronyn (Dr. Jaffe), Louise Latham (Nurse Levitt), John Devlin (Dr. Watt), Michael O'Keefe (Freddie), Doris Roberts (Paula Handy).

1324. The Oath [Pilot #2] Sad and Lonely Sundays. 60 min. Airdate: 8/26/76. Director: James Goldstone. Producers: Aaron Spelling and Leonard Goldberg. Writer: Rod Serling. An elderly doctor takes a refresher course at a big, metropolitan hospital and begins having second doubts about his abilities. Costar Ed Flanders would later star in the critically acclaimed medical series *St. Elsewhere*. *Cast:* Jack Albertson (as Dr. Sorenson), Will Geer (Lucas Wembly), Ed Flanders (Dr. Frankman), Eddie Firestone (Bainbridge), Sam Jaffe (Dr. Sweeny), Doreen Lang (Hester), Dorothy Tristan (Gloria Evans), Jeff Corey (Dean Miller), Dori Brenner (Sandy), Bert Remsen (Mort Cooper).

1325. Return of Melvin Purvis, G-Man (aka Kansas City Massacre). 2 hours. Airdate: 9/19/75. Production Company: ABC Circle Films. Director: Dan Curtis. Executive Producer: Dan Curtis. Producer: Robert Singer. Writers: Bronson Howitzer and William F. Nolan. Music: Robert Cobert. The second busted pilot about the exploits of bigger-than-life FBI agent Melvin Purvis and his associate Sam Cowley, this time portrayed by John Karlen. In this pilot, he takes on Pretty Boy Floyd, John Dillinger, and Baby Face Nelson. *Cast:* Dale Robertson (as Melvin Purvis), John Karlen (Sam Cowley), Bo Hopkins (Pretty Boy Floyd), Robert Walden (Adam Richetti), Mills Watson (Frank Nash), Scott Brady (Hubert Tucker McElway), Matt Clark (Verne Miller), Lynn Loring (Vi Morland), Elliot Street (Baby Face Nelson), Harris Yulin (Johnny Lazia), Philip Bruns (Capt. Jackson), Sally Kirkland (Wilma Floyd), William Jordan (John Dillinger), Morgan Pauli (Alvin Karpus), James Storm (Larry DeVol), Lester Maddox (Gov. Garfield Burns).

1326. Search for the Gods. 2 hours. Airdate: 3/9/75. Production Companies: Warner Bros. Television and Douglas S. Cramer Company. Director: Jud Taylor. Executive Producer: Douglas S. Cramer. Producer: Wilfred Lloyd Baumes. Writer: Ken Pettus, from a story by Herman Miller. Music: Billy Goldenberg. Silly, tedious pilot about two adventurers who have a piece of an alien "rosetta stone" and are looking for its missing parts which, once put together, could unlock the mysteries of the universe uncovered by an extraterrestrial race that visited us thousands of years ago. Inspired by the hype surrounding Erich von Däniken's nonfiction book *Chariots of the Gods?* and its sequels. *Cast:* Kurt Russell (as Shan Mullins), Stephen McHattie (Willie Longfellow), Ralph Bellamy (Dr. Henderson),

Victoria Racimo (Genera Juantez), Raymond St. Jacques (Raymond Stryker), Albert Paulson (Tarkanian), John War Eagle (Lucio), Carmen Argenziano (Wheeler), Joe David Marcus (Elder), Joe Marcus, Jr. (Council Indian), Larry Blake (Jailer), Jackson D. Kane (Glenn).

1327. **Sounder.** Production Company: Robert Radnitz-Mattel Productions. Producer: Robert Radnitz. Writer: Lonne Elder, based on her motion picture screenplay. The folks who brought you the film *Sounder* adapted it as a one-hour television drama about a black family living in depression-oppressed Louisiana. Harold Sylvester, Eboney Wright, Darryl Young, Ronnie Bolden, and Ericha Young star.

1328. **Strange New World.** 2 hours. Airdate: 7/13/75. Production Company: Warner Bros. Television. Director: Robert Butler. Executive Producers: Ronald F. Graham and Walon Green. Producer: Robert E. Larson. Writers: Al Ramrus, Ronald F. Graham, and Walon Green. Music: Elliot Kaplan and Richard Clements. A re-working of the flop pilot *Planet Earth* (a sequel to the failed pilot *Genesis II*) which starred John Saxon as a scientist who wakes up several hundred years after being placed in suspended animation. This time, producer Gene Roddenberry is not involved and the concept has been altered. Now Saxon, Kathleen Miller, and Keene Curtis are three astronauts who return to post-apocalypse earth after floating in space in suspended animation for 200 years. Director Robert Butler made the original *Star Trek* pilot ten years earlier. *Cast:* John Saxon (as Capt. Anthony Vico), Kathleen Miller (Dr. Allison Crowley), Keene Curtis (Dr. William Scott), James Olson (The Surgeon), Martine Beswick (Tana), Reb Brown (Sprang), Ford Rainey (Sirus), Bill McKinney (Badger), Gerritt Graham (Daniel), Cynthia Wood (Araba), Catherine Bach (Lara), Norland Benson (Hide), Richard Farnsworth (Elder).

CBS / COMEDY

1329. **Black Bart.** 30 min. Airdate: 4/4/75. Production Company: Warner Bros. Television. Director: Robert Butler. Executive Producer: Mark Tuttle. Producers: Michael Elias, Frank Shaw, and Robert Butler. Writers: Michael Elias and Frank Shaw. Creator: Mel Brooks. Based on the motion picture *Blazing Saddles*. The adventures of a black sheriff and his quick-drawing deputy working in a small, bigoted Arizona town. Lou Gossett and Steve Landesberg played the roles originated by Cleavon Little and Gene Wilder. *Cast:* Lou Gossett (as Black Bart),

Steve Landesberg (Reb Jordan), Millie Slavin (Belle Buzzer), Noble Willingham (Mayor Fern B. Malaga), Rueben Moreno (Moonwolf), Ted Lehmann (Mr. Swenson), Gerritt Graham (Curley), Brooke Adams (Jennifer).

1330. **Grandpa Max.** 30 min. Airdate: 3/28/75. Production Company: Rich-Ruben Productions. Director: John Rich. Producers: Aaron Ruben and John Rich. Writer: Aaron Ruben. Grandpa Max is a widowed New Yorker who moves west to live with his son, his wife, and his eight-year-old grandson. Max is an active, outgoing dreamer who thinks he's still young even though his overly protective son and daughter-in-law keep reminding him how old he is – and encouraging him to take it easy. The only one who truly understands Max is his grandson. *Cast:* Larry Best (as Max), Michael Lerner (Paul Sherman), Suzanne Astor (Liz Sherman), Brad Savage (Michael Sherman), Shimen Ruskin (Louis Yates), Dick Van Patten (Mr. Unger), Susan Alpern (Betty).

1331. **Harry and Maggie.** 30 min. Airdate: 4/25/75. Production Company: MGM. Director: Jay Sandrich. Producers: James Parker and Arnold Margolin. Writers: James Parker and Arnold Margolin. Creator: Joseph Goodson. Harry is a widower living in a slow-paced rural town and raising his 15-year-old daughter. Maggie is his sister-in-law, a five-times-divorced Manhattanite who believes Harry is a slow-minded idiot incapable of raising her niece – so she forces her way into Harry's home to make sure he doesn't screw up. Although Harry tries every scheme in the world short of murder, Maggie just won't leave. *Cast:* Don Knotts (as Harry Kellogg), Eve Arden (Maggie Sturdivant), Kathy Davis (Clovis Kellogg), Tom Poston (Arlo Wilson), Lucille Benson (Thelma), Eddie Quillan (Max Lovechild).

1332. **Rosenthal and Jones.** 30 min. Airdate: 4/11/75. Production Company: Filmways. Director: H. Wesley Kenney. Executive Producer: Ira Barmak. Producers: Lawrence Kasha and Robert Williams. Writer: Robert Klane. Music: Al Kasha and Joel Hirschhorn. Theme: "All Kinds of People" by Phyllis McGuire. Two old men – one a swinging, retired black mailman, the other a conservative, religious Jewish tailor—meet on a park bench and decide to live together so they can escape living with their respective children and grandchildren and enjoy greater independence. This irks the children, but the grandchildren understand. The hardest thing, though, is for the two men to just get along with each other. *Cast:* Ned Glass (as Nate Rosenthal), George Kirby (Henry Jones), Jerry Fogel (David Rosenthal), Nedra Deen (Marge Rosenthal), Dee Timberlake (Lucille Jones).

1333. Salt and Pepe. 30 min. Airdate: 4/18/75. Production Company: Warner Bros. Television. Director: Jack Shea. Executive Producer: E. Duke Vincent. Producer: Frank Gertz. Writers: E. Duke Vincent and Bob Arnott. Based on the British series *Simon and Gluckstein.* Salt is the black owner of a window washing firm who reluctantly hires his daughter's Puerto Rican husband Pepe and lets them live in his home. *Cast:* Mel Stuart (as Jeremiah Salt), Frank La Loggia (Pepe), Dorothy Meyer (Abigail Salt), Diane Sommerfield (Yolanda Salt), Clarice Taylor (Millie), Sharon Brown (Nadine Salt).

1334. Wives. 30 min. Airdate: 4/21/75. Production Company: Paramount Television. Director: Jay Sandrich. Executive Producer: Garry Marshall. Producer: Tony Marshall. Creator/Writer: Garry Marshall. Music: Buzz Kohen. This sitcom revolves around five wives who gather each week to play poker or canasta, mull one of the wives' problems and solve it. In the pilot, one wife is certain her husband is having an affair. The husbands would not be seen in the proposed series. *Cast:* Penny Marshall (as Connie), Phyllis Elizabeth Davis (Doris), Janie Sell (Frannie), Candice Azzara (Mary Margaret), Jacque Lynn Colton (Lillian), Barbara Luna (Miss Chin), Pat Morita (Waiter), Billy Sands (Man).

CBS / DRAMA

1335. Adventures of the Queen. 2 hours. Airdate: 2/14/75. Production Companies: Irwin Allen Productions and 20th Century Fox. Director: David Lowell Rich. Producer: Irwin Allen. Writer: John Gay, from a story by Irwin Allen. Creator: Irwin Allen. Music: Richard LaSalle. The adventures of a luxurious cruise ship, its crew, and its passengers. In the pilot, a villain threatens to blow up the ship as part of a vendetta against a billionaire who is a passenger. Episodes envisioned for the proposed series, which (like the pilot) would be shot aboard the Queen Mary in Long Beach, included stories about a jewel theft, a murder, and a sailor who swims from a passing foreign ship and pleads for political asylum. *Cast:* Robert Stack (as Capt. James Morgan), David Hedison (Dr. Peter Brooks), Ralph Bellamy (J.L. Dundeen), Bradford Dillman (Martin Reed), Sorrell Brooke (Robert Dwight), Burr DeBenning (Ted Trevor), John Randolph (John Howe), Ellen Weston (Ann Trevor), Linden Chiles (Matthew Evans), Sheila Matthews (Claudine Lennart), Mills Watson (Jim Greer), Frank Marth (Phillips), Richard X. Slattery (Riley), Francine York (Betsy Schuster),

Vito Scotti (Bill Schuster), Russell Johnson (Forbes), Elizabeth Rogers (Irene McKay), Lara Parker (Barbara), Paul Carr (Walter Fletcher), Than Wyenn (Fedderson).

1336. **Crime Club.** 90 min. Airdate: 4/3/75. Production Company: Universal Television. Director: Jeannot Szwarc. Executive Producer: Matthew Rapf. Producer: James McAdams. Writer: Gene R. Kierney. Music: Gil Melle. This is the second time CBS has pondered the *Crime Club* idea (see 1973) and considered this one as a possible replacement for their *Friday Night Movie*. In the tradition of *Name of the Game*, each week the series would feature either the detective (Scott Thomas), the newspaper reporter (Eugene Roche), or the criminal lawyer (Robert Lansing), each of whom is among the members of The Crime Club, a society devoted to stopping lawlessness. The club maintains a clubhouse – complete with gymnasium, law library, crime lab and dining rooms – in the heart of New York City. The pilot revolves around the detective who, with the aid of his fellow members, tries to solve a series of brutal ice pick murders. *Cast:* Scott Thomas (as Jake Keesey), Eugene Roche (Daniel Lawrence), Robert Lansing (Alex Norton), Biff McGuire (Byron Craine), Barbara Rhoades (Angela Swoboda), Michael Christofer (Frank Swobodal). David Clennon (Peter Karpf), Martine Beswick (Dr. Sonia Schroeder), M. Emmet Walsh (Lt. Jack Doyle), Kathleen Beller (Pam Agostino), Jennifer Shaw (Mary Jo Karp), Carl Gottlieb (Jorge Gamos), Regis J. Cordic (Judge Jack Dowd), Rosanna Huffman (Martha), Dolores Quinlan (Gloria), John Durren (Philip Considine), Robert Burton (Gorden Dent).

1337. **Force Five.** 90 min. Airdate: 3/28/75. Production Company: Universal Television. Director: Walter Grauman. Writers/Producers: Michael Gleason and David Levinson. Music: James DiPasquale. A dim-witted attempt at meshing *Mod Squad* with *The Dirty Dozen*. A police lieutenant assembles a special squad of paroled convicts – a swindler, a former vice-squad officer fired for being on the take, a second-story man, and a skilled driver—to battle crime. *Cast:* Gerald Gordon (as Lt. Roy Kessler), Nicholas Pryor (James T. O'Neil), William Lucking (Vic Bauer), James Hampton (Lester White), Roy Jenson (Arnie Kogan), David Spielberg (Norman Ellsworth), Leif Erickson (Cal Newkirk), Norman Burton (Arthur Haberman), Bradford Dillman (Michael Dominick), Victor Argo (Frankie Hatcher), Lee Paul (Steve Ritchie), George Loros (Detective Fletcher), Rod Haase (Reggie Brinkle), Claire Brennan (Shirley Cole), Nancy Belle Fuller (Patty).

1338. The Keegans. 90 min. Airdate: 5/3/76. Production Company: Universal Television. Director: John Badham. Producer: George Eckstein. Creator/Writer: Dean Riesner. Music: Paul Chihara. The serialized saga of the Keegan family. The father works on the docks, one son is a professional football player, one son is an investigative reporter, and one daughter, who is married to a low-level mobster, is a model with dreams of going to Hollywood. In the pilot, Larry, the reporter, proves that his brother Pat, the football star, didn't kill his sister's attacker. *Cast:* Adam Rourke (as Larry Keegan), Spencer Milligan (Pat Keegan), Heather Menzies (Brandy Keegan), Tom Clancy (Tim Keegan), Joan Leslie (Mary Keegan), Paul Shenar (Rudi Portinari), Priscilla Pointer (Helen Hunter McVey), Janit Baldwin (Tracy McVey), Penelope Windust (Penny Voorhees Keegan), Judd Hirsch (Lt. Marco Ciardi), Robert Yiro (Vinnie Cavell), Smith Evans (Angie Carechal), Anna Navarro (Martha Carechal), George Skaff (Don Guido Carechal), Michael McGuire (Bill Richardson), James Louis Watkins (Slim Montana).

1339. Shell Game. 90 min. Airdate: 5/9/75. Production Company: Thoroughbred Productions. Director: Glenn Jordan. Creator/Producer/Writer: Harold Jack Bloom. Music: Lenny Stack. John Davidson is an ex-convict conman who works as an investigator for his brother's criminal law practice and uses elaborate stings to capture the bad guys. In the pilot, he nabs the head of a charity fund who has been embezzling money to cover his gambling losses. *Cast:* John Davidson (as Max Castle), Tom Atkins (Stoker Frye), Robert Sampson (Stephen Castle), Marie O'Brien (Lola Ramirez), Jack Kehoe (Lyle Rettig), Joan Van Ark (Shirley), Louise Latham (Mrs. Margolin), Karen Machon (Susan), Robert Symonds (Carruthers), Gary Sandy (Bellhop), Cliff Emmich (Carmichael), Lancy Taylor, Sr. (Sammy), Gary Pagett (Tim Carson), Pete Gonneau (Louis), Signe Hasso (Countess), Deborah Sherman (Bonnie), Jason Wingreen (Klein).

1340. The Supercops. 30 min. Airdate: 3/21/75. Production Company: MGM. Director: Bernard L. Kowalski. Executive Producer: Bruce Geller. Producers: James David Buchannon and Ronald Austin. Writers: Austin Kalish and Irma Kalish. Music: Jack Urbont. Based on the true-life exploits of N.Y.P.D. cops Greenberg and Hantz. Known on the force and on the streets as "Batman and Robin," their adventures filled two books and were dramatized in the movie *Supercops*, starring Ron Liebman and David Selby. In the pilot, cut from 60 minutes, these unorthodox officers hunt down a brutal thief. *Cast:* Steven Keats (as

Dave Greenberg), Alan Feinstein (Bobby Hantz), Dick O'Neill (Capt. McLain), Peggy Rea (Bessie), Byron Morrow (Lt. Gorney), Tony Brande (Lt. Vanesian), Lou Tiano (Sgt. Falcone), George Loros (Delgado).

NBC / COMEDY

1341. Adventurizing with the Chopper. 30 min. Airdate: 8/7/76. Production Company: Paramount Television. Director: Hy Averback. Executive Producers: Bernie Kukoff and Jeff Harris. Producer: Norman Steinberg. Writers: Bernie Kukoff and Jeff Harris. Chopper Jackson is a black detective in the "Inspector Clouseau"/"Maxwell Smart" mold – a stumbling clod who thinks he's a supercool supersleuth and karate expert. He has an assistant who idolizes him, a secretary who loves him, and a friend-on-the-force who watches out for him. *Cast:* Harrison Page (as Arnold "The Chopper" Jackson), Antonio Fargas (Leonard Jones), Ketty Lester (Cousin Bea), Larry Cook (Lt. Hoover).

1342. Barbara and Phillip. 30 min. Production Companies: Talent Associates and Universal Television. Director: Leonard Stern. Executive Producer: Leonard Stern. Producer: Jerry Mayer. Writer: Jerry Mayer. Patty Duke and then-real-life husband John Astin play a married team of television comedy writers.

1343. The Cheerleaders. 30 min. Airdate: 8/2/76. Production Company: 20th Century Fox. Director: Richard Crenna. Producers: Jerry Zeitman and Robert Kaufman. Writer: Monica McGowan Johnson, from the novel by Ruth Doan MacDougall. Music: Earle Hagen. The story of three teenage girls in a small-town high school in California during the 1950s. *Cast:* Kathleen Cody (as Snowy), Debbie Zipp (B.J.), Theresa Medaris (Beverly), Mary Kay Place (Margie), Darel Glaser (Howard), Susan Quick (Mrs. Snow), George Wallace (Mr. Snow), Ruth McDevitt (Grandmother Snow), Ronald Roy (Joe King), Robin Mattson (Terry Sears).

1344. Flannery and Quilt. 30 min. Airdate: 2/1/76. Production Company: Carl Reiner Productions. Director: Carl Reiner. Producer: Carl Reiner. Creators/ Writers: Marty Feldman and Carl Reiner. A geriatric "Odd Couple"—Flannery, an argumentative ex-longshoreman, ex-cabbie, and ex-prizefighter who shares an apartment with Quilt, a sensitive calligrapher. *Cast:* Red Buttons (as Luke Flannery), Harold Gould (Sam Quilt), Pat Finley (Rose Flannery Caselli), Howard Storm (Kevin Caselli), Michael Lembeck (Quilt's grandson).

1345. Flo's Place. 30 min. Airdate: 8/9/76. Production Company: MGM. Director: Don Weis. Executive Producer: Martin Rackin. Producer: Lary Kasha. Writer: Stanley Ralph Ross. A comedic reworking of last year's flop pilot *Twice in a Lifetime.* This pilot, shot on location in San Pedro, focuses on the people who live and work in Flo's Place, a waterfront boarding house and cafe run by a widow, her young son, and an ex-jockey-turned-bartender. *Cast:* Della Reese (as Flo), Eric Laneuville (Her Son, Louie), Art Metrano (Beito), Johnny Silver (Eddie, the Bartender), Danny Wells (Abner), Michael Bell (Al Held), Bernie Kopell (Hoffman).

1346. Hickey (aka Hickey vs Anybody). 30 min. Airdate: 9/19/76. Production Company: Helix Productions. Director: Alan Alda. Producer: Marc Merson. Writer: Alan Alda. Creator: Alan Alda. Jack Weston is a hustling lawyer who hasn't quite stooped to chasing ambulances—yet. He hires a female attorney, played by Liberty Williams, to help him bring in cases and discovers that she is a real do-gooder, out to help all the downtrodden, and isn't the least bit motivated by profit. Beverly Sanders is his secretary, Malcolm Atterbury is an understanding colleague. *Cast:* Jack Weston (as Julius V. Hickey), Liberty Williams (Phyllis), Beverly Sanders (Netty), Malcolm Atterbury (Willie), Jack Gilford (Dr. McCaffery), Alan Manson (Taggert), Jesamine Milner (Mrs. Neilson).

NBC / DRAMA

1347. Aero Squad (aka Sky Hei$t). 2 hours. Airdate: 5/26/75. Production Companies: Warner Bros. Television and A.J. Fenady & Associate. Director: Lee H. Katzin. Executive Producer: Andrew J. Fenady. Producer: Rick Rosner. Writers: Rick Rosner, William F. Nolan, and Stanley Ralph Ross. Music: Leonard Rosenman. A flying team of L.A.P.D. special agents who use any aircraft that comes in handy in the war against crime. In the pilot, they battle thieves who stage a phony hijacking of a police chopper to divert authorities from a gold bullion heist. Producer Rick Rosner and actor Larry Wilcox would work in the series *Chips* for NBC. *Cast:* Don Meredith (as Sgt. Doug Trumbell), Joseph Campanella (Capt. Monty Ballard), Larry Wilcox (Deputy Jack Schiller), Ken Swofford (Deputy Pat Connelly), Stefanie Powers (Terry Hardings), Frank Gorshin (Ben Hardings), Shelley Fabares (Lisa), Ray Vitte (Deputy Rich Busby), Nancy Belle Fuller (Nan

Paige), James Daris (Lt. Bill Hammon), John Davey (Deputy Freedman), R.B. Sorko-Ram (Deputy Pearson), James Chandler (Convair Pilot), Alex Colon (Deputy Rodriquez), Stan Barrett (Aero Squad Mechanic), Steve Franken (Traffic Controller), Steven Marlo (Gunman), Ed McReady (Gunman).

1348. **Delaney Street (aka Delaney Street: The Crisis Within).** 90 min. Airdate: 4/19/75. Production Companies: Culzean Corporation, Emmet G. Lavery Productions, and Paramount Television. Director: James Frawley. Executive Producer: Emmet G. Lavery, Jr. Producers: Anthony Wilson and Robert Foster. Writer: Robert Foster. Music: Lalo Schifrin. Based on the real-life story of ex-con John Maher, founder of San Francisco's Delancey Street half-way house/rehabilitation center for ex-cons, junkies, runaways, battered wives, and other people in need. Almost a decade after this TV movie aired, Maher became an alcoholic and, when he couldn't overcome his own addiction, was forced out of the rehab program he created and he fled to New York, where he died in 1988. *Cast:* Walter McGinn (as John McCann), Michael Conrad (Robert Holtzman), Lou Gossett, Jr. (Otis James), Mark Hamill (Philip Donaldson), Barbara Babcock (Mrs. Donaldson), Barbara Cason (Ms. Sommerville), Anthony Charnota (Tony), Hector Elias (Rudolfo), John Karlen (Richard Copell), John Ragin (Jeff Donaldson), Jeri Woods (Suzie Franklin), Joseph X. Flaherty (George Miles), Sylvia Soares (Ruby James), Leigh French (Mary), Bart Cardinelli (Dixon), David Moody (Slim Jim), Bill Toliver (T.D.).

1349. **Delaney (aka Last Hours Before Morning).** 90 min. Airdate: 4/19/75. Production Companies: Charles Fries Productions and MGM. Director: Joseph Hardy. Executive Producer: Charles Fries. Producer: Malcolm Stuart. Writers: George Yanok and Robert Garland. Music: Pete Rugolo. Ed Lauter is Bud Delaney, a crimefighter in the 1940s. Delaney was a cop until some mystery man made it look like he was on-the-take. He's fired and becomes a house detective for an apartment complex, where he works while looking for the people who framed him. In the pilot, he tries to find jewel thieves who robbed a beautiful movie star and find the killers of an arrogant mobster. *Cast:* Ed Lauter (as Delaney), Thalmus Rasulala (Justice Sullivan), George Murdock (Sgt. Hagen), Rhonda Fleming (Vivian Pace), Robert Alda (Lucky English), Kaz Garas (Ty Randolph), Don Porter (Mr. Pace), Victoria Principal (Yolanda Marquez), Peter Donat (Peter Helms), Michael Baselson (Bruna Gant), William Finley (Elmo), Art Lund (Buck Smith), George DiCenzo (Owings), John Harkins (Cashman),

John Quade (Korbett), Philip Burns (Max), Michael Stearns (Muscle Man), Redmond Gleeson (Hopkins).

1350. Enter Horowitz (aka Horowitz and Horowitz; aka Conspiracy of Terror). 90 min. Airdate: 12/29/75. Production Company: Lorimar Productions. Director: John Llewellyn Moxey. Executive Producer: Lee Rich. Producer: Charles B. Fitzsimons. Writer: Howard Rodman, from the book by David Delman. Music: Neal Hefti. This pilot had a concept that could easily be reworked as a comedy. Jacob and Helen Horowitz are married police detectives looking into a suburban satanic cult and dealing with Jacob's family, who still are angry he married a Catholic. It wasn't a comedy. That didn't stop anyone from laughing, though. *Cast:* Michael Constantine (as Jacob Horowitz), Barbara Rhoades (Helen Horowitz), David Opatoshu (Arthur Horowitz), Jed Allan (David Horowitz), Arlene Martel (Leslie Horowitz), Mariclare Costello (Barbara Warnall), Roger Perry (Fred Warnall), Logan Ramsey (Mr. Dale), Jon Lormer (Mr. Slate), Norman Burton (Lt. Rossos), Eric Olson (Roger Logan Gordon), Stewart Moss (Rabbi Sinvale), Ken Sansom (Medical Examiner), John Finnegan (Sgt. Carroll), Bruce Kirby (Sgt. Brisbane), Murray MacLeod (Buyer), Paul Smith (Pound Supervisor), Shelley Morrison (Mrs. Kojova), Bob Hastings (Mr. Kojova), Ricky Powell (Steve Kojova).

1351. The Lives of Jenny Dolan. 2 hours. Airdate: 10/27/75. Production Company: Ross Hunter Productions. Director: Jerry Jameson. Executive Producer: Ross Hunter. Producer: Jacques Mapes. Writers: James Lee Barrett and Richard Alan Simmons. Music: Patrick Williams. Shirley Jones is an investigative reporter who marries a wealthy businessman. When he inexplicably dies, she suspects murder—though no one else does. She becomes a journalist once again and starts investigating. Although she exposes a political assassination plot, the truth behind her husband's death is still a mystery—a mystery that would have been explored weekly, amidst her journalistic investigations for the *News World Journal,* had this gone to series. *Cast:* Shirley Jones (as Jenny Dolan), Stephen Boyd (Joe Rossiter), David Hedison (Dr. Wes Dolan), Lynn Carlin (Nancy Royce), James Darren (Orlando), Dana Wynter (Andrea Hardesty), Farley Granger (Dave Ames), Stephen McNally (Lt. Nesbitt), George Gizzard (Ralph Stantlow), Pernell Roberts (Store Owner), Ian McShane (Sanders), Jess Oppenheimer (Springfield), Paul Carr (Eddie Owens), Percy Rodriquez (Dr. Laurence Mallen), Collin Wilcox-Horne (Mrs. Owens), Hayde Rourke (E. Norris Wilde).

1352. Mrs. R. (aka Death Among Friends). 90 min. Airdate: 5/20/75. Production Companies: Douglas S. Cramer Company and Warner Bros. Television. Director: Paul Wendkos. Executive Producers: Douglas S. Cramer and Wilford Lloyd Baumes. Producer: Alex Beaton. Writer: Stanley Ralph Ross. Music: Jim Helms. A grandmotherly widow working as an L.A.P.D. Homicide Detective whose motherly image hides a shrewd deductive mind a la "Columbo." What she lacks in brute force she makes up for with her driver, who keeps a watchful eye out for her. *Cast:* Kate Reid (as Mrs. Shirley Ridgeway), John Anderson (Capt. Lewis), A Martinez (Manny Reyes, Her Driver), Martin Balsam (Buckner), Jack Cassidy (Chico Donovan), Paul Henreid (Otto Schiller), Pamela Hensley (Connie), William Smith (Sheldon Casey), Lynda Day George (Lisa Manning), Denver Pyle (Morgan), Robyn Hilton (Nancy), Katherine Baumann (Carol).

1353. Nevada Smith. 90 min. Airdate: 5/3/75. Production Company: MGM. Director: Gordon Douglas. Creators, Writers, Producers: John Michael Hayes and Martin Rackin, based on character created by Harold Robbins. Music: Lamont Dozier. This western pilot has a long lineage. It's based on Harold Robbins' book *The Carpetbaggers,* the movie of the same name, and the celluloid sequel *Nevada Smith.* Cliff Potts and Lorne Greene star as Nevada Smith, a half-breed gunslinger, and his mentor Jonas Cord, roles portrayed earlier by Steve McQueen and Brian Keith, who carried on where Alan Ladd and Leif Erickson had left off. In the pilot, Cord and his family open the first munitions factory in the West and hire Smith to help run the operation and escort a shipment of explosives to Utah. Filmed on location in Durango, Mexico, this marks the return of Adam West to the genre in which he made his name prior to "Batman." *Cast:* Cliff Potts (as Nevada Smith), Lorne Greene (Jonas Cord), Adam West (Frank Hartlee), Warren Vanders (Red Fickett), Jorge Luke (Two Moon), Jerry Gatlin (Brill), Eric Cord (Davey), John McKee (McLane), Roger Cudney (Perkins), Alan George (MacBaren), Lorraine Chanel (Belva).

1354. 905-WILD. 60 min. Airdate: 3/1/75. Production Companies: Mark VII Productions and Universal Television. Executive Producer: Jack Webb. Producer: William Stark. Writers: Buddy Atkinson and Dick Connaway. This pilot for a proposed 30-minute series aired as an episode of *Emergency!* The adventures of two officers (Mark Harmon and Albert Popwell) working for the Los Angeles Bureau of Animal Control who have to deal with mountain lions who wander into suburbia, seals who sneak into beach homes, skunks who stink up restaurants and other bothersome beasts. David Huddleston is the staff veterinarian, Gary Crosby of *Adam-12* is their boss, and Roseanne Zecher is the unit secretary/clerk.

1355. **The River Men (aka Runaway Barge).** 90 min. Airdate: 3/24/75. Production Company: Lorimar Productions. Director: Boris Sagal. Executive Producer: Lee Rich. Producer: Boris Sagal. Writer: Stanford Whitmore. Creator: Sara Macon. Music: Nelson Riddle. Songs ("River King"): Al Kasha and Joel Hirschborn, performed by Johnny Rodriquez. The adventures of a Mississippi tugboat and its crew – the grizzled captain, his experienced mate, a cook, and two deck hands, a college dropout and a man who grew up on the Mississippi shores. Filmed entirely on location. In the pilot, they help thwart a hijacking scheme. *Cast:* Jim Davis (as Capt. Buckshot Bates), James Best (Mate Bingo Washington), Lucille Benson (Cooke Madge Henshaw), Tim Matheson (Deckhand Danny Worth), Bo Hopkins (Deckhand Ezel Owens), Nick Nolte (Ray Blount), Devon Ericson (June Bug Dobbs), Christina Hart (Reba Washburn), Clifton James (Sooey), Don Plumley (Whispering Wally), Beau Gibson (Rouge LeBlanc), G.W. Bailey (Booker), David Carlton (Supply Boat Captain), Joneal Joplin (Pilot Virgil Henderson), Chuck Gunkel (Arkansas Stupid).

1356. **Roman Grey (aka Art of Crime).** 90 min. Airdate: 12/3/75. Production Company: Universal Television. Director: Richard Irving. Executive Producer: Richard Irving. Producer: Jules Irving. Writers: Bill Davidson and Martin Smith, based on the novel *Gypsy in Amber* by Martin Smith. Music: Gil Melle. Ron Leibman stars as gypsy Roman Grey, an antique dealer who dabbles in crime solving and walks the thin line between the posh Fifth Avenue culture he's a part of and the underground gypsy world he came from. Shot on location in New York. *Cast:* Ron Leibman (as Roman Grey), Jill Clayburgh (Danny), Eugene Roche (Sgt. Harry Isadore), Tally Brown (Gypsy Queen), David Hedison (Parker Sharon), Jose Ferrer (Beckwith Sloan), Diane Kagan (Hillary), Cliff Osmond (Nanoosh), Dimitria Arliss (Madame Vera), Mike Kellin (Kore), Louis Guss (Dodo).

1357. **Rossi (aka Crossfire).** 90 min. Airdate: 3/24/75. Production Company: Quinn Martin Productions. Director: William Hale. Executive Producer: Quinn Martin. Producer: Philip Saltzman. Writer: Philip Saltzman. Music: Patrick Williams. James Farentino is Vince Rossi, an L.A.P.D. detective whose dead brother used to work for the mob. Rossi volunteers for an unusual undercover assignment—a permanent one. The L.A.P.D. fires him for gross misconduct on charges that only Rossi, the Commissioner, his boss Capt. McCardle, are fake. Now seemingly a crook, Rossi infiltrates the mob and works against them from within. In the pilot, Rossi tries to uncover a plot to corrupt city officials. *Cast:* James Farentino (as Vince Rossi), Ramon Bieri (Capt. McCardle), John Saxon (Dave Ambrose), Patrick O'Neal (Lane Fielding), Pamela Franklin (Sheila Fielding), Herb Edelman (Bert Ganz), Lou Frizzell (Arthur Peabody), Joseph Hindy (Jimmy), Ned Glass (Bartender), Fred de Kova (Albert Ambrose).

1358. **Shamus (aka A Matter of Wife and Death).** 90 min. Airdate: 4/10/76. Production Company: Columbia Pictures Television. Director: Marvin J. Chomsky. Executive Producer: David Gerber. Producer: Robert M. Weitman. Writer: Don Ingalls. Music: Richard Shores. Rod Taylor is the womanizing, free-wheeling private eye Burt Reynolds played in producer Robert Weitman's movie *Shamus.* Convenient name. He's lucky his name wasn't "Bricklayer." Shamus works out of a pool hall run by Dick Butkus and has a friend-on-the-force (Shamus *is* a lucky guy) played by Joe Santos, who became James Garner's friend-on-the-force in *The Rockford Files.* In the pilot, Shamus investigates the murder of a small-time private eye whose office was bombed. *Cast:* Rod Taylor (as Shamus), Joe Santos (Lt. Vince Promuto), Eddie Firestone (Blinky), Luke Askew (Snell), John Colicos (Joe Ruby), Tom Drake (Paulie Baker), Anita Gillette (Helen Baker), Charles Picerni (Bruno), Anne Archer (Carol), Larry Block (Springy), Dick Butkus (Heavy), Marc Alaimo (Angie), Cesare Danova (Dottore), Lynda Carter (Zelda).

1359. **Strike Force.** 90 min. Airdate: 4/12/75. Production Company: D'Antoni-Weitz Productions. Director: Barry Shear. Producers: Barry Weitz and Philip D'Antoni. Writer: Roger O. Hirson, from a story by Sonny Grosso. Music: John Murtaugh. Three representatives from three major law enforcement agencies – the N.Y.P.D., the F.B.I., and the state police – team up to become a crack investigative unit that cuts across bureaucratic lines and stops imminent crime before it happens. Costar Richard Gere would later gain international fame in the motion pictures *American Gigolo* and *Officer and a Gentleman,* among others. In the pilot, they bust a narcotics operation. *Cast:* Cliff Gorman (as Det. Joe Gentry), Donald Blakely (Agent Jerome Ripley), Richard Gere (Trooper Walter Spenser), Edward Grover (Capt. Pearson), Joe Spinell (Sol Terranova), Marilyn Chris (Faye Stone), Mimi Cecchini (Mrs. Morelli), Allan Rich (Police Commissioner).

1976–1977

1360. Cousins. 30 min. Airdate: 8/10/76. Production Company: First Artists. Director: Tony Mordente. Executive Producer: Robert Ellison. Producers: Pat Nardo and Gloria Banta. Writers: Pat Nardo and Gloria Banta. An impressionable young girl moves from Pittsburgh to share an apartment in New York with her cousin and join her as a secretary at the advertising agency where her cousin works. *Cast:* Deedee Rescher (as Gail Raymond), Lisa Mordente (Barbara Donohue), David Ogden Stiers (Leonard Mandroff), Ray Buktenica (Alan Peters).

1361. Flatbush Avenue. 30 min. Airdate: 8/24/76. Production Company: Davidson/ Verona Productions. Director: Martin Davidson. Executive Producers: Martin Davidson and Stephen Verona. Producer: Lee Miller. Writer: Martin Davidson, based on his film *Lords of Flatbush.* The story of two men who grew up together as members of a Long Island gang called Flatbush and now, as adults, still live together on the same block. One is a cop married to his high school sweetheart, the other a mechanic who is in love with the cop's wife's best friend, a beautician. *Cast:* Paul Sylvan (as Stanley Rosello), Brooke Adams (Frannie Rosello), Jamie Donnelly (Annie Yukaminelli), Paul Jabara (Wimpy Morzallo).

1362. Freeman. 30 min. Airdate: 6/19/76. Production Company: Harry Stoones, Inc. Director: Hal Cooper. Executive Producers: Bernie Kukoff, Jeff Harris, and Paul Mooney. Writer: Paul Mooney. Freeman is a black ghost inhabiting a colonial mansion a wealthy white family is moving into. Neither is willing to leave and it's from this conflict that the laughter was supposed to come. It didn't. *Cast:* Stu Gilliam (as Freeman), Linden Chiles (Dwight Wainright), Beverly Sanders (Helen Wainright), Jimmy Baio (Timmy Wainright), Melinda Dillon (Madam Arkadina).

1363. The New Lorenzo Music Show. 30 min. Airdate: 8/10/76. Production Company: MTM Enterprises. Director: Tony Mordente. Executive Producer: Lorenzo Music. Producer: Carl Gottlieb. Writers: Lorenzo Music, Carl Gottlieb, James L. Brooks, Jerry Davis, and Allan Burns. This flop pilot was the seed for the disastrous syndicated *Lorenzo and Henrietta Music Show.* Lorenzo Music, once a comedy/music performer with his wife Henrietta, was an MTM producer/ writer who worked on *The Bob Newhart Show* and later became the voice of

311

Carlton the Doorman on *Rhoda*. In this pilot, he plays himself and auditions for a talk show of his own. Although this and the subsequent syndicated series flopped, Music would return for an animated *Carlton Your Doorman* pilot and become the voice of Garfield the Cat in a series of CBS animated specials. *Cast:* Lorenzo and Henrietta Music, David Ogden Stiers, Jack Eagle, Steve Anderson, Roz Kelly, Lewis Arquette, and the Bandini Brothers.

1364. **The Rita Moreno Show.** 30 min. Airdate: 3/29/76. Production Company: John Rich Productions. Producer: John Rich. Writers: Ian LaFrenais and Dick Clement. This aired as an episode of the prison comedy *On the Rocks*. Moreno played an ex-stage actress who borrows money from an inmate to travel to Hollywood, where she meets up with a former actress (Yvonne Wilder) who now runs a dry cleaning business. Together, they try to become stars. Hamilton Camp is their agent.

1365. **Walkin' Walter.** 30 min. Airdate: 6/13/77. Production Companies: Miller Milkis Productions, Henderson Productions, and Paramount Television. Director: Arnold Margolin. Executive Producers: Garry Marshall, Edward Milkis, and Thomas L. Miller. Producers: Tony Marshall and Arnold Margolin. Writers: Lowell Ganz and Mark Rothman. Walter is an ex-vaudevillian who lives with his long-lost brother's wife and their two foster children. Guest star Theodore Wilson would later play star in *Sanford Arms*, a ridiculous attempt to keep *Sanford and Son* going without Sanford or Son. *Cast:* Spo-De-Odee (as Walkin' Walter), Madge Sinclair (Mama), Christoff St. John (Booker Brown), Denise Marcia (Jackie Onassis Orlando), David Yanez (Loud Leon), Jack Dodson (Wendell Henderson), Theodore Wilson (Reverend Tooley).

1366. **Zero Intelligence.** 30 min. Airdate: 8/10/76. Production Company: II-son Chambers Productions. Director: Jack Shea. Executive Producers: Saul Ilson and Ernest Chambers. Writer: Lee Kalcheim. The show featured the antics of an Army intelligence unit stationed in the North Pole during the cold war. *Cast:* Don Galloway (as Higgins), Sorrell Brooke (Deerfield), Tom Rosqui (Fred), Michael Huddleston (Arnold), Chu Chu Malave (Ruben), Clyde Kusatsu (Mo).

ABC / DRAMA

1367. **Crunch.** 90 min. Production Company: Frankovich/Self Productions. Executive Producer: William Self. Producer: Robert Jacks. Writers: Cliff Gould and

Charles Larson, from the novel and motion picture *Report to the Commissioner.* A proposed series based on the exploits of a real New York City undercover cop named Crunch, played in the movie and in this pilot by Yaphet Kotto. In the pilot, he is partnered with a young detective (Stephen Nathan) and works for a tough Lieutenant (Richard Venture).

1368. The D.A. (aka Street Killing). 90 min. Airdate: 9/12/76. Production Company: ABC Circle Films. Director: Harvey Hart. Executive Producer: Everett Chambers. Producer: Richard M. Rosenbloom. Writer: William Driskill. Music: J.J. Johnson. Andy Griffith stars as a New York City prosecutor who plays legal hardball with the mafia and local politicians. In the pilot, he tries to pin a fatal mugging on a mafia boss and a crooked politician. *Cast:* Andy Griffith (as Gus Brenner), Sandy Faison (Susan Brenner), Gigi Simone (Kitty Brenner), Bradford Dillman (Howard Bronstein), Harry Guardino (Al Lanier), Robert Loggia (Louis Spillane), Don Gordon (Sgt. Bud Schiffman), Adam Wade (J.D. Johnson), Anna Berger (Louise), Deborah White (Darlene Lawrence), John O'Connell (Wally Barnes), Fred Sadoff (Leonard), Paul Hecht (D.A. Carelli), Gerritt Graham (Dr. Vinton), Stan Shaw (Mitchell Small), Raymond Singer (Dr. Najukian), Randi Martin (Ace Hendricks), Jack Bannon (Richard Hager).

1369. D.A.'s Investigator (aka Kiss Me, Kill Me). 90 min. Airdate: 5/8/76. Production Companies: Stanley Kallis Productions and Columbia Pictures Television. Director: Michael O'Herlihy. Executive Producer: Stanley Kallis. Writer: Robert E. Thompson. Music: Richard Markowitz. The adventures of a former policewoman turned investigator with the Los Angeles District Attorney's office. In the pilot story, the D.A. thinks he has a solid case against an ex-con for a schoolteacher's murder, but investigator Stella Stafford (Stella Stevens) uncovers the victim's secret past—and a lot of likelier suspects. *Cast:* Stella Stevens (as Stella Stafford), Robert Vaughn (Edward Fuller), Dabney Coleman (Captain Logan), Michael Anderson, Jr. (Dan Hodges), Claude Akins (Harry Gant), Bruce Boxleitner (Douglas Lane), Alan Fudge (Lt. Dagget), Bruce Glover (Sgt. Hovak), Morgan Paull (James Deukmajian), Tisha Sterling (Maureen Coyle), Charles Weldon (Leonard Hicks), Steve Franken (Murry Tesco), Helena Carroll (Mrs. Harris), Pat O'Brien (Jimmy).

1370. The Four of Us. 60 min. Airdate: 7/18/77. Production Company: Titus Productions. Director: James Cellan Jones. Executive Producer: Herbert Brodkin. Producer: Robert Berger. Associate Producer: Dorothy J. Giobus.

Writer: Reginald Rose. Music: Morton Gould. This was envisioned as an early evening, hour-long, comedy drama about the efforts of a widow to raise her three children while working a nine-to-five job as a clerk in New York. *Cast:* Barbara Feldon (as Julie Matthews), Heather MacRae (Annie Ray), K. Callan (Marie), Vicki Dawson (Chrissa Matthews), Will McMillan (Andy Matthews), Sudie Bond (Mrs. Reilly), Lawrence Keith (Walter), Peter Maloney (Hardy), Marcia Jean Kurtz (Estelle Robinson), Sam Schacht (Harry Robinson).

1371. **Gemini (aka Twin Detectives).** 90 min. Airdate: 5/1/76. Production Company: Charles Fries Productions. Director: Robert Day. Executive Producer: Charles Fries. Producer: Everett Chambers. Creator: Don Sharpe. Writer: Robert Specht, from a story by Everett Chambers, Robert Carrington, and Robert Specht. Music: Tom Scott. Songs: "Spinning the Wheel" and "Hard on Me" by the Hudson Brothers. Country singers Jim and Jon Hager, who became famous on *Hee Haw,* starred in this pilot for a series about identical twins who pretend to be a single private eye, thereby using their ability to be in two places at once as an edge in crimefighting. In the pilot, they unmask a phony psychic, solve a murder, and recover stolen money through their twin ruse. Lillian Gish made her TV movie debut in this flop pilot. *Cast:* Jim Hager (as Tony Thomas), Jon Hager (Shep Thomas), Lillian Gish (Billy Jo Haskins), Patrick O'Neal (Leonard Rainer), Michael Constantine (Ben Sampson), Otis Young (Cartwright), Barbara Rhoades (Sheila Rainer), David White (Marvin Telford), Fred Bier (Dr. Hudson), Lynda Day George (Nancy Pendleton), Randy Oakes (Jennie), James Victor (Lt. Martinez), Frank London (Hutchins), Billy Barty (Bartender).

1372. **Jean Lafitte.** 60 min. Airdates: 2/1/76 and 2/8/76. Production Companies: Irwin Allen Productions and 20th Century Fox. Executive Producer: Irwin Allen. Writer: Anthony Lawrence. This aired as two episodes of *Swiss Family Robinson.* Frank Langella stars as the famous French swashbuckler who lived in the Louisiana bayous and helped the U.S. beat the British in the battle of 1815.

1373. **Lester Hodges and Dr. Fong.** 60 min. Airdate: 3/18/76. Production Company: Warner Bros. Television. Director: Jerry Thorpe. Executive Producer: Jerry Thorpe. Producers: Alex Beaton and Robert Dozier. Writer: Robert Dozier. This was an attempt to spin-off two of the recurring characters on *Harry O,* of which this was an episode. Keye Luke is a professional technician in a crime lab and Les Lannom is a wealthy, cheerful lad who likes to dabble in detective work, to the consternation of ex-cop-turned-private eye Harry Orwell (David Janssen). In this episode, Fong and Lester become partners in a private investigation firm. Anne Archer and Barry Atwater guest starred.

1374. **The New Daughters of Joshua Cabe.** 90 min. Airdate: 5/29/76. Production Company: Spelling/Goldberg Productions. Director: Bruce Bilson. Executive Producers: Aaron Spelling and Leonard Goldberg. Producer: Paul Savage. Writer: Paul Savage, from the story by Margaret Armen. Music: Jeff Alexander. Yet another attempt at a western series about a rascally old fur trader who has three women pose as his daughters in order to get more land for his dream homestead. In this, the third and final unsold proposal, Cabe is a part-time sheriff and ends up framed for a murder. His "daughters" try to save him from being hanged. John McIntire replaces Dan Dailey and Buddy Ebsen as Cabe. Other projected series regulars included Jack Elam as Cabe's old buddy and Jeanette Nolan as the owner of a boarding house. *Cast:* John McIntire (as Joshua Cabe), Jack Elam (Bitterroot), Jeanette Nolan (Essie Cargo), Liberty Williams (The Daughter, Charity), Renne Jarrett (The Daughter, Ada), Lezlie Dalton (The Daughter, Mae), John Dehner (Warden Manning), Geoffrey Lewis (Dutton), Sean McClory (Codge Collier), Joel Fabiani (Matt Cobley), Ford Rainey (The Judge), Larry Hovis (Clel Tonkins), James Lydon (Jim Pickett), Randall Carver (Billy Linaker).

1375. **Nunundaga.** 90 min. Production Companies: Palomar Productions and 20th Century Fox. Producer: Ed Scherick. Writer: I.C. Rapoport. This pilot, shot on location in the southwest, starred Ned Romero, Victoria Regimo, and John War Eagle as tribal Indians living on the Great Plains before the arrival of the white man.

1376. **Ohanion (aka The Killer Who Wouldn't Die).** 2 hours. Airdate: 4/4/76. Production Company: Paramount Television. Director: William Hale. Producers: Ivan Goff and Ben Roberts. Writer: Cliff Gould, from a story by Ben Roberts, Cliff Gould, and Ivan Goff. Music: George Garvarentz. Mike Connors plays Ohanion (Connors' real name), an Armenian cop who leaves the force after his wife is killed in an unsolved murder. Ohanion operates a charter boat service with his Uncle Ara, but his reputation as a cop led people to ask him to solve crimes. In the pilot, one of Ohanion's close friends, a spy, is killed in Hawaii by a ruthless assassin. *Cast:* Mike Connors (as Kirk Ohanion), Gregoire Aslan (Ara), Samantha Eggar (Anne Roland), Patrick O'Neal (Commissioner Pat Moore), Clu Gulager (Harry Keller), James Shigeta (David Lao), Mariette Hartley (Heather McDougall), Robert Colbert (Doug McDougall), Tony Becker (Steve

McDougall), Robert Hooks (Commissioner Frank Wharton), Lucy Benson (Flo), Kwana Hi Lim (Chew), Phili Ahn (Soong).

1377. **Our Man Flint (aka Our Man Flint: Dead on Target).** 90 min. Airdate: 3/17/76. Production Company: 20th Century Fox. Director: Joseph Scanlon. Executive Producer: Stanley Colbert. Producer: R.H. Anderson. Writer: Norman Klenman. Ray Danton takes over as superspy Derek Flint, originally portrayed by James Coburn in the 007 spoofs *Our Man Flint* and *In Like Flint*. This time Flint, an agent for Z.O.W.I.E. (Zonal Organization for World Intelligence and Espionage) searches for a kidnapped scientist. *Cast:* Ray Danton (as Derek Flint), Sharon Acker (Sandra), Gaye Rowan (Benita), Donnelly Rhodes (LaHood), Lawrence Dane (Runzler), Fran Russell (Della Cieza).

1378. **Panache.** 90 min. Airdate: 5/15/76. Production Company: Warner Bros. Television. Director: Gary Nelson. Executive Producer: E. Duke Vincent. Producer: Robert E. Relyea. Writer: E. Duke Vincent. Music: Frank DeVol. This lighthearted adventure was set in the 17th century and followed the exploits of Panache, a poet, romanticist, and the best swordsman in France, and his muske-teers, the overzealous and comically inexperienced Alain and the wise companion Donat. Together they battle the evil minions of Cardinal Richelieu and protect the crown. *Cast:* Rene Auberjonois (as Panache), David Healy (Donat), Charles Frank (Alain), Charles Siebert (Rochefort), John Doucette (Treville), Amy Irving (Anne), Harvey Solin (Louis), Joseph Ruskin (Cardinal Richelieu), Liam Dunn (M. Durant/Pere Joseph), Peggy Walton (Laval), Michael O'Keefe (Horseman), Marjorie Battles (Chevreuse), Judith Brown (Montvallier).

1379. **Quiller (aka Quiller: Price of Violence).** 90 min. Airdate: 12/3/75. Director: Peter Graham Scott. Producer: Peter Graham Scott. Writer: Michael J. Bird. Creator: Adam Hall. The first of two pilots based on the *Quiller* spy thrillers by Adam Hall, which also served as the basis for the 1966 movie starring George Segal. This time Michael Jayston is secret agent Quiller who, in the pilot, is pro-tecting a scientist from a killer. Shot in England. *Cast:* Michael Jayston (as Quiller), Moray Watson (Angus Kinloch), Sinead Cusack (Rosalind), Ed Bishop (Frank Ilroy), Peter Tuddenham (Erling Norgaard), Marc Zuber (Colonel Zodak), Judy Liebert (Deborah).

1380. **[Pilot #2] Night of the Father.** 90 min. Airdate: 12/10/75. Director: Viktors Ritelis. Producer: Peter Graham Scott. Quiller investigates the murder of another agent. *Cast:* Michael Jayston (as Quiller), Moray Watson (Angus Kinloch),

Sinead Cusack (Rosalind), Julian Glover (Schroder), Peter Arne (Neumann), Hans Mayer (Major Hardtmann), Patricia Hodge (Kate), Jim Norton (Lake), Gideon Kolb (Gunter), Margot Feld (Caroline).

1381. **The Quinns.** 90 min. Airdate: 7/1/77. Production Company: Danny Wilson Productions. Director: Dan Petrie. Producer: Danny Wilson. Writer: Sidney Carroll, from an idea by Fran Sears and Phyllis Minoff. Music: John Scott. This pilot follows three generations of an Irish-American family of firefighters living in New York City. *Cast:* Peter Masterson (as Michael Quinn), Barry Bostwick (Bill Quinn), William Swetland (Tom Quinn), Geraldine Fitzgerald (Peggy Quinn), Susan Browning (Elizabeth Quinn), Penny Peyser (Laurie Quinn), Liam Dunn (Sean Quinn, Sr.), Patricia Elliott (Rita Quinn O'Neill), Virginia Vestoff (Renee Carmody), Pat Corley (Eugene Carmody), Blair Brown (Millicent Priestly).

1382. **Time Travelers.** 90 min. Airdate: 3/19/76. Production Companies: Irwin Allen Productions and 20th Century Fox. Director: Alexander Singer. Producer: Irwin Allen. Writer: Jackson Gillis, from a story by Rod Serling and Irwin Allen. Music: Morton Stevens. Rod Serling lent his creativity to this reworking of Irwin Allen's old *Time Tunnel* series. This time, the stories would revolve around a doctor and a research scientist who go backward in time for the good of mankind. In the pilot, a dangerous epidemic is spreading across the country. Scientists believe a cure was once found for the disease, but the antidote and the man who developed it perished in the great Chicago fire over 100 years ago. The heroes go back to the days just before the fire in hopes of finding the antidote before everything goes up in flames. The pilot utilized the 20th Century Fox backlot sets remaining from *Hello, Dolly* and footage from the 1938 film *In Old Chicago. Cast:* Sam Groom (as Dr. Clint Earnshaw), Tom Hallick (Jeff Adams), Richard Basehart (Dr. Joshua Henderson), Trish Stewart (Jane Henderson), Booth Colman (Dr. Cummings), Francine York (Dr. Helen Sanders), Walter Burke (Dr. Stafford), Baynes Barron (Chief Williams), Dort Clark (Sharkey).

1383. **The Troubleshooters (aka High Risk).** 90 min. Airdate: 5/15/76. Production Companies: Danny Thomas Productions and MGM. Director: Sam O'Steen. Executive Producer: Paul Junger Witt. Producer: Robert E. Relyea. Writer: Robert Carrington. Music: Billy Goldenberg. Six former circus performers team up to solve crimes and help people in need. They aren't altruistic, they just love the sheer challenge of it—and the money. In the pilot, they use all their Big Top experience to steal a priceless golden mask. Proposed series regular JoAnna

Cameron was also starring as the superheroine *Isis* in the CBS Saturday morning show. *Cast:* Victor Buono (as Sebastian), Joseph Sirola (Guthrie), Don Stroud (Walter-T), JoAnna Cameron (Sandra), Ronne Troup (Daisy), Wolf Roth (Erik), Rene Enriquez (Ambassador Henriques), John Fink (Quincy), George Skaff (Aide), William Beckley (Butler).

CBS / COMEDY

1384. **At Ease.** 30 min. Airdate: 9/7/76. Production Company: Paramount Television. Director: Bob Claver. Executive Producer: Jay Benson. Producers: Bob Shayne, Eric Cohen, and Norm Gray. Writers: Bob Shayne and Eric Cohen. The story of opinionated, conservative, inflexible Sgt. Harry Rumsey, a 27-year-veteran of the army who finds himself overwhelmed everywhere he turns by young people and their new ways of doing things. The humor arises when Rumsey tries to cope with his teenage daughter, a superior officer just out of college, and the flood of young recruits he must face everyday. *Cast:* Richard O'Neill (as Sgt. Henry Rumsey), Peg Shirley (Agnes Rumsey), Kathleen Beller (Stacy Rumsey), Danny Goldman (Cpl. Harvey Green), Ken Gilman (Lt. Block), Roy Applegate (Pvt. Albert Franklin), Rod McCary (M.P.), Amanda Jones (W.A.C. Carol), Kenneth Martinez (Soldier), Rita Conde (Soldier's Mother), Roxanna Bonilla-Giannini (Soldier's Bride).

1385. **Best Friends.** 30 min. Airdate: 7/19/77. Production Company: Warner Bros. Television. Director: Jerry Paris. Producer: Alan Sacks. Writers: Stanley Ralph Ross and Peter Meyerson. Creator: Stanley Ralph Ross. CBS described this pilot as "the adventures of a zany group of Chicago teenagers." Apparently not enough zany teenagers were interested. The zany Chicago teenagers included a cheerleader, a hulking hillbilly, a precocious black boy, a supermarket box boy, and a gypsy. Just your typical American kids. *Cast:* James Canning (as Nick), Bill Henry Douglas (Arthur), Gary Epp (Mountain Man), Barry Pearl (Gypsy), Sherry Hersey (Kathy), Gloria LeRoy (Maggie), Cliff Osmond (Ouspensky), Ray Sharkey (Lionel "Big 0" Lapidus).

1386. **Don't Call Us.** 30 min. Airdate: 8/13/76. Production Company: MTM Enterprises. Director: Robert Moore. Producers: Ed Weinberger and Stan Daniels. Writer: David Lloyd. Creators: Ed Weinberger, Stan Daniels, and David Lloyd. Music: Pat Williams. The creative team behind *The Mary Tyler Moore Show* created this pilot to showcase the talents of Jack Gilford. He plays Larry

King, a struggling Philadelphia talent agent with a love for odd-ball acts, old-timers, and quirky people. Unfortunately, he has no idea how to run an organized, profitable business. That's where his brother and partner Marty comes in. Marty is all business and little affection – or patience – for Larry's weird array of clients. *Cast:* Jack Gilford (as Larry King), Allan Miller (Marty King), Leland Palmer (Receptionist Rene Patterson), Richard Narita (Jackie Nakamura), Patty Maloney (Sylvia), Billy Barty (Lloyd), Tina Louise (Tolanda Gelman), James Luisi (Gus DeMarco), Don Davis (One Man Band).

1387. **Duffy.** 30 min. Airdate: 5/6/77. Production Company: Universal Television. Director: Bruce Bilson. Producer: George Eckstein. Writer: Richard DeRoy. Duffy was the canine mascot of an elementary school. Everyone likes good old Duffy except the principal, the typical, red-cheeked, stuffy TV stereotype. *Cast:* Duffy (as Himself), Fred Grandy (Cliff Sellers), Lane Binkley (Marty Carter), Roger Bowen (Thomas N. Tibbles), George Wyner (Happy Jack), Jane Lambert (Mrs. Dreifuss), Dick Yarmy (Postman), John Sheldon (Nick), Jarrod Johnson (Danny), John Herbsleb (Craig), Stephen Manley (Josh), Robert E. Ball (Hobo), Jane Dulo (Neighbor).

1388. **Ernie and Joan.** 30 min. Production Company: Paramount Television. Executive Producers: Jacques Mapes and Ross Hunter. Producer: Norman Steinberg. Writers: Norman Steinberg and Elliot Shoenman. A 45-year-old widower and factory foreman who lives with his 20-year-old daughter and 12-year-old marries a 23-year-old nurse. The humor would come from the conflicts they have under one roof. *Cast:* Milt Kogan (as Ernie), Candy Azzara (Joan), Kit McDonough (His Daughter), Stephen Manley (His Son).

1389. **Heck's Angels.** 30 min. Airdate: 8/31/76. Production Company: Yongestreet Productions. Director: Richard Kinon. Executive Producers: Frank Peppiatt and John Aylesworth. Producer: Lew Gallo. Writers: Frank Peppiatt, John Aylesworth, and Jay Burton. Creators: Frank Peppiatt and John Aylesworth. Music: Frank Peppiatt and John Aylesworth. The comic adventures of a group of airmen stationed in France during World War I. The leader, Col. Heck, is in love with a French girl who is actually a German spy and has an airman who, unbeknownst to him, is actually a woman in disguise. The squadron cook is a former New York gourmet chef and the best flier is a lounge lizard with a wild array of clothes. *Cast:* William Windom (as Col. Gregory Heck), Joe Barrett (Lt. David Webb), Christopher Allport (Lt. Billy Bowling), Jillian Kasner (Lt. "George" MacIntosh),

Susan Silo (Odette), Henry Polic, II (Pierre Ritz), Chip Zien (Lt. Eddy Almont), Arnold Soboloff (Ludwig Von Stratter).

1390. Maureen. 30 min. Airdate: 8/24/76. Production Company: Viacom Enterprises. Director: Jay Sandrich. Executive Producer: Mark Carliner. Producer: Marty Cohan. Writer: Marty Cohan. Music: Arthur Rubinstein. Maureen is a widow who supports her cantankerous mother and herself by working as a lingerie clerk in a department store. She leads a drab, but comfortable life that her best friend, who works in the jewelry department, is always trying to liven up. In the pilot, Maureen is cajoled into going on a cruise. *Cast:* Joyce Van Patten (as Maureen), Sylvia Sidney (Ruth), Karen Morrow (Alice), Alan Oppenheimer (Mr. Frederick), Jack Bannon (Damon), Leigh French (Trudy), Ron Roy (Harvey), Timothy Blake (Jackie).

1391. Side by Side. 30 min. Airdate: 7/27/76. Production Company: CBS Productions. Director: H. Wesley Kenney. Executive Producer: Darryl Hickman. Producer: George Choderker. Writer: Richard Kimmel Smith. Creator: Richard Kimmel Smith. Title Song: Stephen Schwartz. A serialized sitcom about four couples, each with very different backgrounds, living on a dead-end street in adjoining homes. Charlie Ryan is a retired cop living with his wife. The Riveras are a Puerto Rican couple trying to understand American suburban life. Dick Stern is a liberal Jewish writer; his wife Sally is the buyer for a department store. And the fourth couple, the Pearsons, are a rural couple from the deep South. In the pilot, they all meet at a dinner party—and start arguing. *Cast:* Stubby Kaye (as Charlie Ryan), Peggy Pope (Connie Ryan), Barbara Luna (Carmine Rivera), Luis Avalos (Luis Rivera), Janie Sell (Sally Stern), Keith Charles (Dick Stern), Diane Stilwell (Hadley Pearson), Don Scardino (Billy Joe Pearson).

1392. This Better Be It. 30 min. Airdate: 8/10/76. Production Company: Charles Fries Productions. Director: Richard Kinon. Executive Producer: Charles Fries. Producer: Lila Garrett. Writers: Lila Garrett and Lynn Roth. Music: David Shire. A divorced dentist, who has a pint-sized 14-year-old son who reads the *Wall Street Journal* religiously and a married daughter, marries a divorcee who has a precocious 14-year-old daughter. *Cast:* Anne Meara (as Annie Bell), Alex Rocco (Harry Bell), Baille Gersten (Diana Bell, His Daughter), Linda Conrad (Flower), David Pollock (Paul).

1393. Three Times Daley. 30 min. Airdate: 8/3/76. Production Companies: Heyday Productions and Universal Television. Director: Jay Sandrich. Executive

Producer: Leonard B. Stern. Creator/Producer/Writer: John Rappaport. Music: Don Costa. The story of Bob Daley, a divorced newspaper columnist who lives with his son and his father. *Cast:* Don Adams (as Bob Daley), Liam Dunn (Alex Daley), Jerry Houser (Wes Daley), Bibi Besch (Stacy), Ayn Ruyman (Jenny).

1394. **You're Just Like Your Father.** 30 min. Airdate: 8/13/76. Production Company: Lorimar Productions. Director: Noam Pitlik. Executive Producers: Lee Rich and Lawrence Marks. Producers: Alan J. Levi and Gene Marcione. Writer: Alan J. Levi. Creator: Alan J. Levi, developed by Lawrence Marks. Music: Harry Geller. Dick Shawn is a likeable schlep who lives with his son, a psychology student, and daughter-in-law, who supports them both as an insurance agent, and avoids normal work in favor of hatching absurd get-rich-quick schemes. More often than not, the dreamer is able to lure his son into his helping him out, to the exasperation of his daughter-in-law and his girlfriend Claudine. *Cast:* Dick Shawn (as Harry Toffler, Sr.), Barry Gordon (Harry Toffler, Jr.), Nellie Bellflower (Cheryl Toffler), Maureen Arthur (Claudine).

CBS / DRAMA

1395. **Angel's Nest.** 60 min. Airdate: 3/1/76. Production Companies: Alfra Productions and MGM. Producers: Frank Glicksman and Al C. Ward. Writer: Al C. Ward. This was aired as an episode of *Medical Center.* This series would follow the adventures of two doctors, one white and one black, serving their residencies at a struggling private hospital in a racially mixed San Francisco neighborhood. Scott Hylands is the white doctor, Phillip Michael Thomas the black. Supporting cast would include Pepe Serna, William Redfield and Mary McCarthy. Hylands played a doctor in another unsold series pilot, *First 36 Hours of Dr. Durant,* last season.

1396. **Hazard's People.** 60 min. Airdate: 4/9/76. Production Companies: Roy Huggins-Public Arts and Universal Television. Director: Jeannot Szwarc. Executive Producer: Jo Swerling, Jr. Producer: Roy Huggins. Writers: Heywood Gould, Roy Huggins, and Jo Swerling, Jr. Creator: Roy Huggins. Music: John Cacavas. John Houseman, who so memorably portrayed law Prof. Kingsfield in the film *The Paper Chase* and the subsequent series, stars as a renowned criminal lawyer who works with a staff of neophyte attorneys—a magna cum laude graduate and former basketball star, a wealthy man who is a former Harvard Law

School *Law Review Editor* editor, and a feminist woman who graduated from Hastings College of Law in San Francisco. Together Houseman and this *Mod Squad* of the bar defend a doctor accused of murdering his girlfriend. *Cast:* John Houseman (as John Hazard), John Elerick (Michael Crowder), Jesse Welles (Trish Corelli), Roger Hill (Ernest Clay), Doreen Lang (Sylvia Freed), Stefan Gierasch (D.A. Robert F. Powell), Michael Tolan (Dr. Carl DeLacy), Hope Lange (Mrs. DeLacy), Cliff Emmich (Sam Colby), Richard Herd (Howard Frederickstein), R.A. Sirianni (Court Clerk), James Whitmore, Jr. (David Stock).

1397. **Jeremiah of Jacob's Neck.** 30 min. Airdate: 8/13/76. Production Companies: Palomar Productions and 20th Century Fox. Director: Ralph Senensky. Producers: Art Stolnitz and Ed Scherick. Creator/Writer: Peter Benchley. Music: Harry Sukman. The author of the novel *Jaws* created this 30 minute pilot for an envisioned 60 minute comedy/drama about a police chief and his family that move into a New England mansion inhabited by the ghost of a smuggler. *Cast:* Keenan Wynn (as Jeremiah the Ghost), Ron Masak (Chief Tom Rankin), Arlene Golonka (Anne Rankin), Brandon Cruz (Clay Rankin), Quinn Cummings (Tracy Rankin), Elliot Street (Deputy Wilbur Swift), Pitt Herbert (Mayor Dick Barker), Amzie Strickland (Abby Penrose), Alex Hentelhoff (Leonard), Les Lannom (Max), Tom Palmer (Crabtree), Don Burleson (Bob Peabody).

1398. **Land of Hope.** 60 min. Airdate: 5/13/76. Production Company: Titus Productions. Director: George Schaefer. Executive Producer: Herbert Brodkin. Producer: Robert Berger. Creator/Writer: Rose Leiman Goldberg. A turn-of-the-century drama about four immigrant families – one Jewish, one Irish, one German and one Italian – living in a tenement in the lower east side of New York. *Cast:* Marian Winters (as Reva Barsky), Phil Fisher (Isaac Barsky), Roberta Wallach (Devvie Barsky), Richard Liberman (Herschel Barsky), Joseph Miller (Benji Barsky), Ariane Munker (Gerda Gottschalk), Roy Poole (Gustav Gottschalk), Carol Williard (Kathi Gottschalk), Donald Warfield (Ernst Gottschalk), Anthony Cannon (Rafe Paolini), Colin Duffy (Kevin Dwyer), Maria Tucci (Lea Gianni), Michael Lombard (Labe Ravitz).

1399. **The P.I. (aka The Vigilante).** 60 min. Airdate: 3/28/76. Production Company: MGM. Executive Producer: Bruce Geller. Producer: Leigh Vance. Writer: Robert Lenski. Creators: Bruce Geller and Leigh Vance. Aired as an episode of *Bronk*. Vic Morrow starred as a secret agent who, while saving the life of a foreign diplomat, inadvertently causes the deaths of five innocent people. He quits, moves to an apartment above the famed Santa Monica Pier Merry-Go-Round, and occasionally fights crimes when friends or friends of friends are in need.

1400. Risko. 60 min. Airdate: 9/11/76. Production Companies: Larry White Productions and Columbia Pictures Television. Director: Bernard Kowalski. Executive Producer: Larry White. Producer: Robert Stambler. Writers: Adrian Spies and William Driskill. Gabriel Dell plays Risko, an ex-con with a law degree from a correspondence school who works as an investigator for an attorney while waiting for the American Bar Association to decide whether or not to let him take the bar exam. Although Risko looks like a sloppy itinerant, he is actually extremely intelligent and very sharp a la "Columbo." In the pilot, he helps his employer defend a race car driver accused of picking up a woman in a single's bar and murdering her. *Cast:* Gabriel Dell (as Joe Risko), Joel Fabiani (Attorney Allen Burnett), Peter Haskell (Lewis Pollack), Norman Fell (Max), Joyce DeWitt (Sharon), Karen McMahon (Marie), Hilary Thompson (Maggie), Barbara Sharma (Jenny), Jack Knight (Bartender), Paul Hampton (Tom Grainger), Laraine Stephens (Susan Grainger), John Durren (Frank Harkavy).

1401. Royce. 60 min. Airdate: 5/21/76. Production Company: MTM Enterprises. Director: Andrew V. McLaglen. Executive Producer: Jim Byrnes. Producer: William T. Phillips. Writer: Jim Byrnes. Music: Jerrold Immel. MTM's first dramatic pilot features Robert Forster as Royce, a western hero cast from the same mold as Clint Eastwood's Man with No Name. Royce, who was raised by Co-manches, says little, prefers to be alone, and doesn't carry a gun. Although this could easily have been an economy-sized Sergio Leone epic, action director McLaglen kept the violence to a minimum and played "family hour" values to a maximum. In the pilot, Royce escorts a female puppeteer, her daughter and her son to California, where her husband set out to find them a homestead and never was heard from again. Shot on location in Arizona. *Cast:* Robert Forster (as Royce), Mary Beth Hurt (Susan Mabry), Moosie Drier (Stephen Mabry), Teri Lynn Wood (Heather Mabry), Michael Parks (Blair Mabry), Eddie Little Sky (White Bull), Dave Cass (Dent).

1402. Salathiel Harms (aka Bad Dude). 60 min. Airdate: 1/25/76. Production Company: Universal Television. Executive Producer: Matthew Rapf. Producer: James McAdams. Aired as an episode of *Kojak*. Rosie Grier is a bounty hunter from California in the first of two unsold pilots. Costars include Roger Robinson, Bill Duke, Charles Weldon, and Dee Timberlake.

1403. State Fair. 60 min. Airdate: 5/14/76. Production Company: 20th Century Fox. Director: David Lowell Rich. Executive Producers: M.J. Frankovich and William Self. Producer: Robert L. Jacks. Writers: Richard Fielder and Dick DeRoy, based on the novel by Phillip Strong and the three feature films it inspired. Music: Laurence Rosenthal. Songs: "Carousel Love," "Wind in the Trees," by Harriet Schock; "Everything Reminds Me of You," by Mitch Vogel. The story of a family – a mother and father with a divorced daughter raising her child, a daughter studying to be a veterinarian and a son in high school who dreams of being a country music star—living on a dairy farm set against the backdrop of the annual State Fair that is the big event in their lives. This pilot was designed to launch a "family hour" series. *Cast:* Vera Miles (as Melissa Bryant), Tom O'Connor (Jim Bryant), Mitch Vogel (Wayne Bryant), Julie Cobb (Karen Bryant Miller), Dennis Redfield (Chuck Bryant), Linda Purl (Bobby Jean Shaw), Jeff Colter (Tommy Miller), W.T. Zacha (Catfish McKay), Jack Garner (Mr. Grant), Virginia Gregg (Miss Detweiler), Harry Moses (Ben Roper), Joel Stedman (David Clemmans), Dina K. Ousley (Marnie), Ranee Howard (Deputy), Ivor Francis (Judge).

1404. Stranded. 60 min. Airdate: 4/30/76. Production Company: Universal Television. Director: Earl Bellamy. Executive Producer: David Victor. Producer: Howie Horowitz. Writer: Anthony Lawrence. Music: Gordon Jenkins. A straight "Gilligan's Island" that was tried once before as *Lost Flight.* An Australia-bound airliner crashlands on a uncharted South Pacific island and the survivors, led by a New York cop, create their own civilization. Characters include a streetwise ghetto child who was a stowaway, the criminal the cop was taking back to Australia, a retired construction worker who is revitalized by building the island community, a woman who was on her way to get married in Australia, and a brother and sister whose parents are killed in the crash. *Cast:* Kevin Dobson (as Sgt. Rafe Harder), Lara Parker (Crystal Norton), Marie Windsor (Rose Orselli), Devon Ericson (Julie Blake), Jimmy McNichol (Tim Blake), Rex Everhart (John Rados), Erin Blunt (Ali Baba), Lal Baum (Burt Hansen), James Cromwell (Jerry Holmes), John Fujioka (Charley Lee).

NBC / COMEDY

1405. Ace. 30 min. Airdate: 7/26/76. Production Companies: Larry White Productions and Columbia Pictures Television. Director: Gary Nelson. Executive Producer:

Larry White. Producer: Jerry Davis. Writer: Jerry Davis. Creator: Jerry Davis. Music: Pat Williams. Ace is an inept private eye who thinks he's brilliant, not unlike Peter Seller's Inspector Clouseau, and if it weren't for his efficient secretary Gloria, he'd probably go bankrupt. In the pilot, he looks for a corporate spy. *Cast:* Bob Dishy (as Edward R. Ace), Rae Allen (Gloria Ross), Barbara Brownell (Janet Slade), Ruth Manning (Alice Slade), Dick Van Patten (Mr. Mason), Liam Dunn (Mr. Strutt).

1406. Bell, Book and Candle. 30 min. Airdate: 9/8/76. Production Company: Columbia Pictures Television. Director: Hy Averback. Executive Producer: Bruce Lansbury. Writer: Dick DeRoy, from John Van Druten's play and the 1958 feature film. The story of Gillian Holroyd, a young witch who'd like to forget her supernatural abilities and just work in her art gallery with her bumbling Aunt Enid. Unfortunately, she is constantly hampered by her warlock brother Nicky and his get rich quick schemes – all of which depend on her superior ability at witchcraft to succeed. To make matters worse, Alex, a New York editor, moves into the apartment above the gallery—and falls in love with Gillian. *Cast:* Yvette Mimieux (as Gillian Holroyd), Doris Roberts (Aunt Enid), Michael Murphy (Alex Brandt), John Pleshette (Nicky), Bridget Hanley (Lois), Susan Sullivan (Rosemary), Edward Andrews (Bishop Fairbarn), Dori Whittaker (Melissa).

1407. The Bellinis. 30 min. Production Companies: Albert S. Ruddy Productions and Universal Television. Director: Stuart Margolin. Executive Producer: Albert S. Ruddy. Producer: Alan Horowitz. Writers: Fred Freeman, Lawrence Cohen, Alan Mandell, and Charles Shyer. The comic story of a widower and how he copes with his dead wife's Italian-American family, which was once involved on the fringes of organized crime but now, with the popularity of *The Godfather*, likes to believe they were big time mafiosos. The hero's son buys into it but not the hero's daughter. The family members are Carmine Caridi, Michael Valente, Diana Canova, and Jay Novello.

1408. The Bureau. 30 min. Airdate: 7/26/76. Production Company: Jozak Productions. Director: Hy Averback. Executive Producer: Gerald I. Isenberg. Producer: Gerald W. Abrams. Creators/Writers: Charles Sailor and Eric Kalder. Music: Peter Matz. The adventures of two government agents, weary veteran Butterfield and his over-zealous partner Browning. Butterfield would like to transfer to Hawaii and lead the easy life, while Browning makes their boss Davlin happy by tirelessly working day and night in the service of his country. *Cast:* John Lawlor (as Agent Butterfield), Richard

Gilliland (Agent Browning), Henry Gibson (Chief Davlin), Barbara Rhoades (Agent Peterson), Arnold Stang (Charlie Sunglasses), Beeson Carroll (Combat Cummings), Dick Yarmy (Prentiss), Stanley Brock (Manny), Pearl Shear (Bus Driver), Phil Leeds (Repairman).

1409. **Four the Hard Way (aka Making It).** 30 min. Airdate: 8/30/76. Production Company: Lorimar Productions. Director: Peter Baldwin. Executive Producer: Lee Rich. Producer: Burt Metcalfe. Writer: John Riger. Creator: Ben Starr. The comedic adventures of four undergrads – one is an ROTC student from a rural community, one is a Chinese-American who loves to cook, one is described as a "Woody Allen"–type, and one sees himself as a natural leader of men – who are saving up for law school and live together in an apartment run by a woman who has been married three times. *Cast:* Ed Begley, Jr. (as Steve), Ben Masters (Pete), Alvin Kupperman (Jay), Evan Kim (Greg), Jeane Arnold (Cloris), Sandy Faison (Janice).

1410. **Local 306.** 30 min. Airdate: 8/23/76. Production Company: Viacom Enterprises. Director: Alan Rafkin. Executive Producer: Mark Carliner. Producer: Stanley Ralph Ross. Writer: Stanley Ralph Ross. The comedic mishaps of Harvey Gordon, the plumber who heads Local 306 of the Plumbers Union. His racially mixed, outspoken local meets in the Union Hall next door to the apartment he shares with his wife and daughter. In the pilot, he has to overcome his fear of flying to attend an out-of-town union meeting. *Cast:* Eugene Roche (as Harvey Gordon), Miriam Byrd Nethery (Rose Gordon), Susan Sennett (Helene Gordon), Milton Parsons (Hutchings), Roy Stewart (Rocco).

1411. **Newman's Drugstore.** 30 min. Airdate: 8/30/76. Production Companies: Playboy Productions and Paramount Television. Director: Hy Averback. Executive Producers: Robert Lovenheim and Mitchell Brower. Producer: Hy Averback. Writers: Lila Garrett and Sandy Krinski. Creators: Lila Garrett and Sandy Krinski. Music: Charles Fox. Newman is a widower raising a 12-year-old son and running a midwestern drugstore during the Great Depression. His store is the town's social center and Newman, despite his efforts, is always dragged into everyone else's problems. *Cast:* Herschel Bernardi (as Charlie Newman), Michael LeClair (Woody Newman), Allan Rich (Leon Rossoff), June Gable (Shirley Tinker), Robert Lussier (Murray Tinker), Fritzi Burr (Dora Goldman), Dominique Pinassi (Marcy Goldman).

1412. Over and Out. 30 min. Airdate: 8/11/76. Production Company: Viacom Enterprises. Director: Bob Claver. Executive Producer: Mark Carliner. Producer: Bob Claver. Writer: Linda Bloodworth. Music: Peter Matz. Five female communications officers bound for Australia crash land on an all-male, South Pacific army base during World War II and end up staying—to the consternation of the egotistical base commander who believes war is a man's job. *Cast:* Ken Berry (as Capt. Paddy Patterson), Michele Lee (Capt. Betty Jack Daniels), Susan Lanier (Sgt. Cookie Dobson), Pat Finley (Lt. Paula Rabinowitz), Alice Playten (Sgt. Lizard Gossamer), Mary Joe Catlett (Sgt. Alice Pierson), Stewart Moss (Sgt. Travis).

1413. Roxy (aka Roxy Page). 30 min. Airdate: 9/6/76. Production Companies: TAT Communications and Don Kirshner Productions. Director: Jack Shea. Executive Producers: Allan Mannings and Don Kirshner. Producer: Jack Shea. Writers: Ethel and Mel Brez and Allan Mannings. Creators: Ethel and Mel Brez. Roxy is an aspiring actress dreaming of Broadway stardom who lives with her Armenian-American parents and her kid sister and works in the local movie theatre. *Cast:* Janice Lynde (as Roxy Hagopian), Leslie Ackerman (Sylvia Hagopian), Rhoda Gimignani (Anna Hagopian), Jeff Corey (Alex Hagopian), Jim Catusi (Charlie Martin), Ken Olafson (Broadway Director).

1414. Second Time Around (aka Wild About Harry). 30 min. Airdate: 5/26/78. Production Companies: Heyday Productions and Universal Television. Director: Robert Moore. Producers: Leonard Stern and George Eckstein. Writer: Richard Waring. Efrem Zimbalist, Jr. starred in this Americanized version of a British situation comedy about a divorcé who marries a 20-year-old girl and faces disapproval from his ex-wife, his 15-year-old daughter and his old friends. This flop pilot was finally aired three years after it was made. *Cast:* Efrem Zimbalist, Jr. (as Harry Baxter), Andrea Howard (Vickie Knowles), Bernie Kopell (Don), Elaine Giftos (Maggie), Stephanie Zimbalist (Jennie), Reva Rose (Delia), Ruth Manning (Sophie), Gloria Stroock (Sheila Marshall), George Sperdakos (Larry Marshall), Dick Yarmy (Frank Knowles), Emmaline Henry (Molly Knowles).

1415. Shaughnessey. 30 min. Airdate: 9/6/76. Production Company: Bob Hope Enterprises. Director: Hy Averback. Executive Producer: Elliot Kozak. Producer: Lee Miller. Writers: Pat McCormick and Bob Hilliard. Eddie Shaughnessey is the harried dispatcher at a Chicago cab company who works for an inveterate gambler (who often bets and loses his cabs) and oversees a motley crew of drivers, which includes a pack-rat who hoards everything, a former lifeguard on the French Riviera, a loud-mouthed jerk, and the first female cabbie ever in the company. *Cast:* Pat McCormack (as Eddie Shaughnessey), Nita Talbot (Doris Shaughnessey), Sally Kirkland (Mona Phillips), Warren Berlinger (Banners), Jack Mullaney (Steve Williams), Ralph Wilcox (Phil Jenkins), David Doyle (Mr. Morgan).

1416. **Snafu.** 30 min. Airdate: 8/23/76. Production Companies: Heyday Productions and Universal Television. Director: Jackie Cooper. Executive Producer: Leonard B. Stern. Producer: Arnie Rosen. Writers: Arnie Rosen and Leonard B. Stern. The adventures of 23-year-old Lieutenant Hauser, who commands an American infantry company mired in the mud of war-torn Italy. His cohorts are Cpl. Conroy, a streetwise New Yorker, and Sgt. Kaminsky, a gregarious Southerner. *Cast:* Kip Niven (as Lt. Hemsley Hauser), Tony Roberts (Cpl. Mike Conroy), James Cromwell (Sgt. Billy Kaminsky).

1417. **Snip!** 30 min. Production Company: Komack Company. Executive Producer: James Komack. Producer: Stan Coner. Writer: Stan Coner. Creator: James Komack. This pilot, inspired by the success of the movie *Shampoo*, was actually bought and announced as part of NBC's 1976–77 season. But after three episodes were shot, NBC abruptly pulled the project from their schedule and never aired the episodes. Comic David Brenner starred as a part-time hair stylist who spends half his time courting his ex-wife, who has a beauty salon on Cape Cod, and being a dad to his 10-year-old daughter. Leslie Ann Warren was his wife; Kim Soloman played his daughter.

NBC / DRAMA

1418. **Alias Sherlock Holmes (aka Return of the World's Greatest Detective).** 90 min. Airdate: 6/16/76. Production Company: Universal Television. Director: Dean Hargrove. Producers: Dean Hargrove and Roland Kibbee. Writers: Dean Hargrove and Roland Kibbee. Music: Dick DeBenedictis. A motorcycle cop with a love for Sherlock Holmes is in an accident and, when he recovers, believes he actually is the famous detective. Now, with the help of a psychiatrist named Watson, he solves cases and badgers his former L.A.P.D. lieutenant. *Cast:* Larry Hagman (as Sherman Holmes), Jenny O'Hara (Dr. Watson), Nicholas Colasanto (Lt. Tinker), Woodrow Parfrey (Himmel), Helen Verbit (Landlady), Ivor Francis (Spiner), Charles Macauley (Judge Harley), Ron Silver (Dr. Collins), Sid Haig

(Vince Cooley), Booth Colman (Psychiatrist), Lieuz Dressier (Mrs. Slater), Benny Rubin (Klinger), Fuddle Bagley (Detective).

1419. Banjo Hackett (aka Banjo Hackett: Roamin' Free). 2 hours. Airdate: 9/1/76. Production Companies: Bruce Lansbury Productions and Columbia Pictures Television. Director: Andrew V. McLaglen. Producer: Bruce Lansbury. Creator/ Writer: Ken Trevey. Music: Morton Stevens. Banjo Hackett is a horsetrader roaming the West in the 1880s with his orphaned, nine-year-old nephew and occasionally visiting a ranch run by Molly, the woman he won't admit he loves. In the pilot, Banjo and his nephew look for the boy's Arabian mare, which was stolen by a ruthless bounty hunter when the boy's widowed mother died. Ike Eisenmann, who plays the nephew, would later star in Lansbury's short-lived and much maligned sci-fi series *Fantastic Journey*. *Cast:* Don Meredith (as Banjo Hackett), Ike Eisenmann (Jubal Winner), Jennifer Warren (Molly Brannen), Chuck Connors (Sam Ivory), Dan O'Herlihy (Tip Conaker), Jeff Corey (Judge Janeway), Gloria DeHaven (Lady Jane Gray), L.Q. Jones (Sheriff Tadlock), Jan Murray (Jethro Swain), Slim Pickens (Lijah Tuttle), David Young (Elmore Mintore), Richard Young (Luke Mintore), Stan Haze (Blacksmith), John O'Leary (Mr. Creed), Jeff Morris (Jack O'Spades), John Anderson (Moose Matlock), Kenneth O'Brien (Wiley Pegram), Elizabeth Perry (Grace Nye), Faith Quabuis (Ruttles).

1420. Brahmin (aka Invasion of Johnson County). 2 hours. Airdate: 7/31/76. Production Companies: Roy Huggins-Public Arts and Universal Television. Director: Jerry Jameson. Executive Producer: Jo Swerling, Jr. Producer/Creator: Roy Huggins. Writer: Nicholas E. Baehr. Music: Mike Post and Pete Carpenter. This pilot is eerily reminiscent of "War of the Silver Kings," the episode that launched Huggins' *Maverick* series. A Boston gambler, the blacksheep of his wealthy family, teams up with a Wyoming cowboy to battle a land baron who has hired a private army of gunslingers to wipe out the homesteaders who oppose him. The historical episode on which this story is based later provided the basis for Michael Cimino's disastrous *Heaven's Gate*. *Cast:* Bill Bixby (as Sam Lowell), Bo Hopkins (George Dunning), John Hillerman (Major Walcott), Billy Green Bush (Frank Canton), Stephen Elliott (Col. Van Horn), Lee DeBroux (Richard Allen), M. Emmet Walsh (Irvine), Mills Watson (Sheriff Angus), Alan Fudge (Teschmacher), Luke Askew (Deputy Sheriff Brooks), Edward Winter (Major Edward Fershay).

1421. **The Deputies (aka Law of the Land).** 2 hours. Airdate: 4/29/76. Production Company: Quinn Martin Productions. Director: Virgil W. Vogel. Executive Producer: Quinn Martin. Producers: John Wilder and Russell Stoneham. Writers: John Wilder and Sam H. Rolfe. Creator: John Wilder. Music: John Parker. The story of a frontier sheriff and his three deputies – one an Indian law school graduate, one an Iowa farm boy, and the other a skilled cowboy—as they watch Denver turn from sagebrush to metropolis during the late 1880s. In the pilot, they hunt for a lunatic who is killing hookers. What is unique about this pilot is that most of the cast would move onto fame in later years either in hit series or films (i.e. Jim Davis in *Dallas*, Don Johnson in *Miami Vice*, Charles Martin Smith in *Never Cry Wolf*, etc.), which is probably why this program is now available in home video. *Cast:* Jim Davis (as Sheriff Pat Lambrose), Don Johnson (Deputy Quirt), Cal Bellini (Deputy Tom Condor), Nicholas Hammond (Deputy Brad Jensen), Darleen Carr (Selina Jensen), Barbara Perkins (Jane Adams), Andrew Prine (Travis Carrington), Glenn Corbett (Andy Hill), Charles Martin Smith (Dudley), Dana Elcar (Rev. Endicott), Ward Costello (E.J. Barnes), Paul Stevens (Dwight Canaday), Barney Phillips (Doctor), Patti Jerome (Dutch Annie), Regis J. Cor die (Judge), Georganne LaPiere (Lila), Grant Goodeve (Soldier), Murray MacLeod (Cowboy).

1422. **The Hancocks (aka Dark Side of Innocence).** 90 min. Airdate: 5/20/76. Production Company: Warner Bros. Television. Director: Jerry Thorpe. Executive Producer: Jerry Thorpe. Producer: Philip Mandelker. Writer: Barbara Turner. Music: Peter Matz. The saga of the Hancock family, their children, and the lumber business they own. The elder Hancocks have five children, the youngest is a teenager girl who still lives at home. The oldest son is a doctor who married a doctor and has a daughter who is a divorced, frustrated model raising a five-year-old son. The middle daughter is married to a lawyer and has two sons. The youngest son is single and works at the family lumberyard. If the family business was oil, maybe this would have worked. *Cast:* Joanna Pettet (as Jesse Breton), Lawrence Casey (Skip Breton), Kristopher Marquis (Rodney Breton), Tiger Williams (Kim Breton), Anne Archer (Nora Hancock Mulligan), John Anderson (Stephen Hancock), Kim Hunter (Kathleen Hancock), Claudette Nevins (Maggie Hancock), Robert Sampson (Jason Hancock), James Houghton (Dennis Hancock), Ethelin Block (Rebecca Hancock), Denise Nickerson (Gabriela Hancock), Dennis Bowen (Michael

Hancock), Gail Strickland (Heather), Geoffrey Scott (Tony), Shane Butterworth (Topher Mulligan).

1423. **Just Another Polish Wedding (aka Gandolf and Fitch).** 60 min. Airdate: 2/18/77. Production Companies: Universal Television and Public Arts. Director: William Wiard. Executive Producer: Meta Rosenberg. Producers: Stephen J. Cannell, Charles Floyd Johnson, David Chase, and Juanita Bartlett. Writer: Stephen J. Cannell. Creator: Stephen J. Cannell. Music: Mike Post and Pete Carpenter. Aired as an episode of *The Rockford Files*. Lou Gossett is a slick conman, Isaac Hayes is a hard-headed ex-con. Together, they become private eyes. The character of Gandalf, played by Hayes, was introduced in the "Hammer of C Block" episode on 1/9/76.

1424. **Law and Order.** 3 hours. Airdate: 8/28/76. Production Company: Paramount Television. Director: Marvin J. Chomsky. Executive Producer: E. Jack Neuman. Producer: Richard Rosetti. Writer: E. Jack Neuman, from the novel by Dorothy Uhnak. Music: Richard Hazard. This three hour adaptation of Uhnak's best-selling novel also served as a pilot for a proposed series that follows three generations of an Irish American family of N.Y.P.D. officers. The focal point of the envisioned series would be the Deputy Chief of Public Affairs who is in constant conflict with his son, a Vietnam veteran-turned-beat cop who opposes his father's way of achieving law and order. *Cast:* Darren McGavin (as Deputy Chief Brian O'Malley), Jeanette Nolan (Margaret O'Malley), Art Hindle (Patrick O'Malley), Scott Brady (Sgt. Brian O'Malley, Sr.), Paul Jenkins (Lt. Kevin O'Malley), Redmond Gleeson (Rev. Martin O'Malley), Keir Dullea (Johnny Morrison), Robert Reed (Aaron Levine), James Olson (Inspector Ed Shea), Suzanne Pleshette (Karen Day), Teri Garr (Rita Wusinsky), Biff McGuire (Lt. Lenihan), Will Geer (Pat Crowley), Alan Arbus (Arthur Pollack), Whitney Blake (Mary-Ellen Crowley), Tom Clancy (Hennessey), James Whitmore, Jr. (Pete Caputo), James Flavin (Cpt. Toomey), Robert Hegyes (Angelo), Beverly Hope Atkinson (Lola), Brad Dexter (Patrolman Tiernay), Jack Knight (Lt. Fitzgerald), Patrick O'Moore (Father Damian), Marian Collier (Sister Providencia), Fred Wayne (Sgt. Haran), Paul Lichtman (Rabbi Schulman).

1425. **Mallory (aka Mallory: Circumstantial Evidence).** 2 hours. Airdate: 2/8/76. Production Companies: Crescendo Productions, R.B. Productions, and Universal Television. Director: Boris Sagal. Executive Producer: William Sackheim. Producer: Stuart Cohen. Writers: Joel Oliansky and Joseph Polizzi, from a story by Tom Greene. Music: James DiPasquale. Raymond Burr, in the first of his *post–ironside* pilots, plays a once-famous lawyer whose career floundered after being unjustly accused of coercing a client to commit perjury. Though cleared by the Bar, his reputation is still tarnished. In the pilot, Mallory defends a jailed criminal accused of killing a fellow prisoner. *Cast:* Raymond Burr (as Arthur Mallory), Mark Hamill (Joe Celli), Robert Loggia (Angelo Ronello), A Martinez (Robert Ruiz), Vic Mohica (Tony Garcia), Stanley Kamel (Cole), Bill Lucking (Georgie), Walter Lott (Hanigan), Armando Federico (Martinez), Roger Robinson (Clifford Wilson), Eugene Roche (Bob Latimer), Peter Mark Richman (John Shields), Allan Rich (Judge Paul Pieter), Alexander Courtney (Richardson), Karen Somerville (Sandy).

1426. Scott Free. 90 min. Airdate: 9/13/76. Production Companies: Cherokee Productions and Universal Television. Director: William Wiard. Executive Producers: Meta Rosenberg and Stephen J. Cannell. Producer: Alex Beaton. Creator/Writer: Stephen J. Cannell. Music: Mike Post and Pete Carpenter. What we have here is another classic example of the old con-the-conman-into-working-as-a-cop premise. Our hero is Tony Scott, a smooth-talking hustler who is blackmailed into helping Federal agents expose the dirty-doings of a mafia boss. Creator Stephen Cannell knows why this pilot failed: "It needed James Garner and we didn't have him." Garner was busy with the *Rockford Files*, though this pilot came from his production company. *Cast:* Michael Brandon (as Tony Scott), Susan Saint James (Holly), Ken Swofford (Ed McGraw), Cal Bellini (Tom Little Lion), Robert Loggia (Donaldson), Michael Lerner (Santini), Dehl Berti (George Running Bear), Peter Brocco (Rossa), Stephen Nathan (Kevin Southerland), Allan Rich (Max).

1427. Shark Kill. 90 min. Airdate: 5/20/76. Production Company: D'Antoni-Weitz Productions. Director: William A. Graham. Executive Producer: Philip D'Antoni. Producers: Barry Weitz and Robert Dijoux. Writer: Sandor Stern. Music: George Romanis. This pilot was originally conceived as a two-part, spin-off episode of the short-lived series *Movin On* but aired as a TV movie instead. Richard Yniquez and Philip Clark star as mariners-for-hire—one an inexperienced seaman and the other a trained oceanographer—who will do anything from finding lost treasure, searching for missing persons, or, as they do in the pilot, search for great white sharks. *Cast:* Richard Yniquez (as Cabo Mendoza), Philip Clark (Rick Daynor), Jennifer Warren (Carolyn), Elizabeth Gill (Bonnie), Victor Campos (Luis), David Huddleston

(Bearde), Carmen Zapata (Helena Mendoza), Jim B. Smith (Franey), Roxanna Bonilla Giannini (Maria), Richard Foronjy (Banducci).

1428. **Some People We Know (aka People Like Us).** 60 min. Airdate: 4/19/76. Production Company: Lorimar Productions. Director: Gene Reynolds. Executive Producer: Lee Rich. Producers: Gene Reynolds and Burt Metcalfe. Writer: Howard Rodman. The story of a blue-collar family—a steelworker, his wife, their unemployed son and rebellious daughter and their poor grandmother—as they struggle against economic hardship and the emotional troubles of life. *Cast:* Eugene Roche (as Davy Allman), Katherine Helmond (Irene Allman), Eileen McDonough (Sharon Allman), Grant Goodeve (Lennie Allman), Irene Tedrow (Anna Allman), Stock Pierce (Elgin), Richard Foronjy (Ray), William Flatley (Sesser).

1429. **Stonestreet (aka Stonestreet: Who Killed the Centerfold Model?).** 90 min. Airdate: 1/16/77. Production Company: Universal Television. Director: Russ Mayberry. Executive Producer: David J. O'Connell. Producer: Leslie Stevens. Writer: Leslie Stevens. Music: Pat Williams. Barbara Eden joined the endless list of formula private eyes as Liz Stonestreet (no relation to "Longstreet"), the widow of a detective killed on duty. She becomes a private eye to keep her husband's ideals of law and order alive – as well as herself. In the pilot, she poses as a porno actress and prowls the X-rated theatres of Santa Monica looking for a woman who has disappeared. *Cast:* Barbara Eden (as Liz Stonestreet), Joseph Mascolo (Max Pierce), Joan Hackett (Jessica Hilliard), Richard Basehart (Elliot Osborn), Louise Latham (Mrs. Schroeder), Elaine Giftos (Arlene), James Ingersoll (Eddie Schroeder), Sally Kirkland (Della Bianco), Val Avery (Chuck Voit), Robert Burton (Dale Anderson), Gino Comforti (Davis), LaWanda Page (Erna), Ryan MacDonald (Watch Commander), Ann Dusenberry (Amory Osborn).

1430. **Task Force.** 60 min. Airdates: 3/2/76 and 3/9/76. Production Companies: David Gerber Productions and Columbia Pictures Television. Executive Producer: David Gerber. Producer: Douglas Benton. Writers: Douglas Benton and Ed DeBlasio. Creator: David Levy. This pilot aired as a two-part episode of *Police Woman.* The adventures of an L.A.P.D. motorcycle task force comprised of three men and one woman (James Watson, James Darren, Don Stroud, and Cynthia Sikes) and their commanding officer (Dane Clark).

1977–1978

1431. Big George Diamond. 30 min. Production Company: EF-OH-EX-EX Productions. Producer: Norman Abbott. Writer: Jerry Ross. Creator: Jerry Ross. Redd Foxx is a maitre d' in a ritzy Las Vegas eatery who chucks it all in favor of owning his own highway diner, where he lives with his loving wife and his aggravating mother-in-law. Originally conceived for comic George Kirby.

1432. Bumpers. 30 min. Airdate: 5/16/77. Production Company: MTM Enterprises. Director: James Burrows. Producers: David Davis and Charlotte Brown. Writers: David Davis and Charlotte Brown. Creators: David Davis and Charlotte Brown. The lives of a group of assembly line workers in a Detroit auto plant. *Cast:* Richard Masur (as Joey Webber), Stephanie Faracy (Rozzie Webber), Jack Riley (Murphy), Michael McManus (Andy), Tim Reid (Jay), Zane Buzby (Jennifer), Ray Buktenica (Mr. Dickey), Brian Dennehy (Ernie Stapp).

1433. The Chopped Liver Brothers. 30 min. Airdate: 5/6/77. Production Company: MGM Enterprises. Director: Hugh Wilson. Executive Producers: Tom Patchett and Jay Tarses. Producer: Michael Zinberg. Writers: Tom Patchett, Jay Tarses, and Hugh Wilson. Creators: Tom Patchett and Jay Tarses. Music: Patrick Williams. Writer/Producer Tom Patchett and Jay Tarses star in this autobiographical pilot about a pair of nightclub comics hoping to some day strike it big. This flopped, but everyone behind the camera went on to bigger things. *Cast:* Tom Patchett (as Tom Van Brocklin), Jay Tarses (Jay Luckman), Gwynne Gilford (Sally Van Brocklin), Philip Bruns (Mr. Ruth), Robert Enhardt (Duffy), Michael Pataki (Kelso), Phil Roth (Nathan Brailoff), Madeline Fisher (Receptionist), Rick Podell (Impressionist), Donna Ponterotto (Michelle Rosen).

1434. Great Day. 30 min. Airdate: 5/23/77. Production Company: Aaron Ruben Productions. Director: Peter Baldwin. Executive Producer: Aaron Ruben. Producer: Gene Marcione. Writer: Aaron Ruben. Creator: Aaron Ruben. Music: Peter Matz. This pilot was supposed to illustrate how fun life is as a skid row bum in New York's bowery. It failed. *Cast:* Al Molinario (as Peavey), Dub Taylor (Doc), Guy Marks (Boomer), Spo-De-Odee (Jabbo), Joseph Elie (Moose), Billy

Barty (Billy), Pat Crenshaw (Pop), Alice Nunn (Molly), Audrey Christie (Mrs. Graham), Dorothy Konrad (Woman).

1435. **McNamara's Band.** 60 min. Airdate: 5/11/77. Production Company: Boiney Stoones Productions. Director: Hal Cooper. Executive Producers: Jeff Harris and Bernie Kukoff. Producer: Darrell Hallenbeck. Writers: Jeff Harris and Berme Kukoff. Creators: Jeff Harris and Bernie Kukoff. John Byner leads an inept band of criminals given the choice of going to jail or working as undercover military agents in World War II. Of course, they become spies. The first of two pilots. In this one, they have to silence a DJ sending secret messages to German U-boats. *Cast:* John Byner (as Johnny McNamara), Bruce Kirby, Sr. (Gaffney), Sid Haig (Zoltan), Joseph Sicarri (Milgrim), Lefty Pedroski (Aggie), Denise Galik (Hedy), Henry Polic, II (Schnell), Joe Mell (Dr. Fuchtenstein), Ben Wright (Gen. Grosshtecker).

1436. **[Pilot #2] McNamara's Band.** 30 min. Airdate: 9/5/77. Production Company: Boiney Stoones Productions. Director: Roger Duchowny. Executive Producers: Jeff Harris and Bernie Kukoff. Producers: Darrell Hallenbeck and Harry Colomby. Writers: Harry Colomby and Bob Sand. Creators: Jeff Harris and Bernie Kukoff. The band has to stop a renegade general. *Cast:* John Byner (as Johnny McNamara), Sid Haig (Zoltan), Bruce Kirby, Sr. (Gaffney), Steve Doubet (Aggie), Joe Pantoliano (Frankie), Albert Paulsen (General Zimhoff), Laurette Sprang (Helga Zimhoff), Ron Soble (Schlesser), Bruce Glover (Diegel), Joe Medalis (Kroger), Kate Murtaugh (Hildegard Hochmusser).

1437. **Mixed Nuts.** 30 min. Airdate: 5/12/77. Production Companies: Mark Carliner Productions and Viacom Enterprises. Directors: Peter H. Hunt and Jerry Belson. Executive Producer: Mark Carliner. Producer: Michael Leeson. Writers: Jerry Belson and Michael Leeson. Creator: Jerry Belson. The lives of the doctors and psychiatric patients at the Willow Center Hospital. In the pilot, the staff lets the patients choose where to go on a field trip—and they pick a singles bar. *Cast:* Zohra Lampert (as Dr. Sarah Allgood), Emory Bass (Dr. Folder), Dan Barrows (Bugs), Richard Karron (Logan), Morey Amsterdam (Moe), James Victor (Gato), Ed Begley, Jr. (Jamie), Conchata Ferrell (Nurse Cassidy).

1438. **The Primary English Class.** 30 min. Airdate: 8/15/77. Production Company: ABC Circle Films. Directors: Roger Beatty and Tim Conway. Executive Producer: Joe Hamilton. Writers: Arnie Kogan and Roger Beatty. Music: Peter Matz. Based on the broadway play. Valerie Curtin is an earnest teacher of a primary English class for foreign students. *Cast:* Valerie Curtin (as Sandy Lambert), Murphy Dunne (Hal), Harvey Jason (Yosef Ari), Maria O'Brien (Lupe), Joe Bennett (Sergio), Bob Holt (Wilhelm Ritterman), Suesie Elene (Yoko), Freeman King (Chuma).

1439. **Stick Around.** 30 min. Airdate: 5/30/77. Production Companies: Humble Productions and T.A.T. Communications. Director: Bill Hobin. Producers: Fred Freeman and Lawrence J. Cohen. Writers: Fred Freeman and Lawrence J. Cohen. An attempt at a live-action *Jetsons.* Fred McCarren and Nancy New as a typical married couple in the year 2055. In the pilot, they fight over whether to trade in their out-dated robot Andy (Andy Kaufman) for a new one. *Cast:* Nancy New (as Elaine Keefer), Fred McCarren (Vance Keefer), Andy Kaufman (Andy), Cliff Norton (Joe Burkus), Craig Richard Nelson (Earl), Jeffrey Kramer), Liberty Williams (Lisa).

1440. The pilot **Walking Walter, #1365,** was previously duplicated here in error.

ABC / DRAMA

1441. **Behind the Lines (aka Keefer).** 2 hours. Airdate: 3/16/78. Production Companies: David Gerber Productions and Columbia Pictures Television. Director: Barry Shear. Executive Producers: Bill Driskill and David Gerber. Producer: James H. Brown. Writers: Bill Driskill and Simon Muntner. Creator: Bill Driskill. Music: Duane Tatro. This pilot, set in World War II, casts William Conrad as the portly owner of a Lisbon bar, which is actually a cover for his secret activities as the leader of an elite undercover squad. *Cast:* William Conrad (as Keefer), Michael O'Hare (Benny), Cathy Lee Crosby (Angel), Kate Woodville (Amy), Brioni Farrell (Beaujolais), Jeremy Kemp (Kleist), Marcel Hillaire (Maureau), Bill Fletcher (Hegel), Ian Abercrombie (Rudy), Jack Ging (Benson), Richard Sanders (Bemmel), Norbert Weisser (Vorst), William H. Bassett (Sergeant), Steve Zacharias (Duval), Natalie Gore (Madame Cerral), Alain Patrick (Jacques), Andre Landzaat (Folger).

1442. **The Bionic Boy.** 2 hours. Airdate: 11/7/76. Production Company: Universal Television. Director: Phil Bondelli. Writers: Lionel E. Siegel & Tom Greene. Aired as an episode of *The Six Million Dollar Man.* Vincent Van Patten is a paralyzed, wheel-chair-bound boy who regains the feeling in his legs thanks to bionics. In 1987, Universal and NBC would mount a revival of both the *Six Million Dollar Man* and *The Bionic Woman* that would focus on the adventures of Steve

Austin's bionic son. *Cast:* Vincent Van Patten (as Andy Sheffield), Joan Van Ark (Valerie Sheffield), Carol Jones (Judy), Kerry Sherman (Coline), Greg Evigan (Joe Hamilton), Dick Erdman (Vernon), Dick Van Patten (Palmer), Nick David (Charlie), Lee Majors (Steve Austin), Richard Anderson (Oscar Goldman), Martin E. Brooks (Rudy Wells).

1442a. The Ultimate Imposter. 60 mins. Airdate: 1/2/77. Production Company: Universal Television. Director: Paul Stanley. Executive Producer: Harve Bennett. Writers: Lionel E. Siegel & W.T. Zacha. Aired as an episode of *The Six Million Dollar Man* and was based on the novel "Capricorn Man" by William Zacha. Stephen Macht stars as Joe Patton, an old friend of Steve's, who has a computer implanted in his brain that allows him to "download" specialized knowledge he can use undercover in new identities. The pilot was re-worked and re-cast in 1979 as a TV movie. Cast: Stephen Macht (Joe Patton) Pamela Hensley (Jenny), Martin E. Brooks (Dr. Rudy Wells), Kim Basinger (Lorraine Stenger)

1443. Delta County, U.S.A. 2 hours. Airdate: 5/20/77. Production Company: Leonard Goldberg Productions. Director: Glen Jordan. Executive Producer: Leonard Goldberg. Producers: Frank Von Zerneck and Robert Greenwald. Writer: Tom Rickman. A serial set in the rural South that traces the lives of three families. Joe Penny and Tisch Raye were billed in the ABC print ads as "the young rebels who find each other as their families fight for control of the county" while Jeff Conaway "likes girls and girls like him, perhaps too much." *Cast:* Doney Oatman (as McCain), Peter Donat (John, Jr.), Jim Antonio (Jack the Bear), Jeff Conaway (Terry), Joe Penny (Joe Ed), Tisch Raye (Robbie Jean), Peter Masterson (Billy Wingate), Joanna Miles (Kate McCain Nicholas), John McLiam (Cap McCain), Morgan Brittany (Doris Anne), Leigh Christian (Vonda), James Crittenden (Bevo), Robert Hays (Bo).

1444. The Gathering. 2 hours. Airdate: 12/4/77. Production Company: Hanna-Barbera Productions. Director: Randall Kleiser. Executive Producer: Joseph Barbera. Producer: Harry R. Sherman. Writer: James Poe. Music: John Barry. A Christmas drama about a dying businessman (Ed Asner) who tries to reunite his estranged family for one last celebration. This TV movie won an Emmy award for best drama and Maureen Stapleton, as his wife, earned a nomination. Although this did not inspire a series, a sequel was done for NBC in 1979. *Cast:* Edward Asner (as Adam Thornton), Maureen Stapleton (Kate Thornton), Rebecca Balding (Julie Pelham), Sarah Cunningham (Clara), Bruce Davison (George

Pelham), Veronica Hamel (Helen Thornton), Gregory Harrison (Bud Thornton), James Karen (Bob Block), Lawrence Pressman (Tom Thornton), John Randolph (Dr. John Hodges), Gail Strickland (Peggy Thornton), Edward Winter (Roger), Stephanie Zimbalist (Toni Thornton), John Hubbard (Reverend Powell), Mary Bradley Marable (Mary), Maureen Readinger (Tiffany), Ronald Readinger (Joey).

1445. **Go West, Young Girl!** 2 hours. Airdate: 4/27/78. Production Companies: Columbia Pictures Television and Bennett-Katleman Productions. Director: Alan J. Levi. Executive Producers: Harris Katleman and Harve Bennett. Producer: George Yanok. Writer: George Yanok. Music: Jerrold Immel. Karen Valentine is a naive, foolhardy Eastern reporter wandering the old West in search of Billy the Kid. She's joined in this effort by Billy's rugged, western sister (Sandra Will) who doesn't believe her brother is dead. *Cast:* Karen Valentine (as Netty Booth), Sandra Will (Gilda), Stuart Whitman (Deputy Shreeve), Richard Jaeckel (Billy the Kid), David Duke (Reverend Crane), Charles Frank (Capt. Anson), Richard Kelton (Griff), Gregg Palmer (Payne).

1446. **Good Against Evil (aka Time of the Devil).** 90 min. Airdate: 5/22/77. Production Companies: 20th Century Fox and Frankel-Bolen Productions. Director: Paul Wendkos. Executive Producers: Ernie Frankel and Lin Bolen. Writer: Jimmy Sangster. Music: Lalo Schifrin. Dack Rambo is Andy Stuart, a writer with the great misfortune of falling in love with Satan's girlfriend (Elyssa Davalos). When she is unceremoniously spirited away from him by a group of devil-worshippers, led by the evil Rimmin (Richard Lynch), Stuart enlists the aid of an exorcist (Dan O'Herlihy). Stuart and the exorcist search for her and rid the world of evil as they go. *Cast:* Dack Rambo (as Andy Stuart), Elyssa Davalos (Jessica Gordon), Dan O'Herlihy (Father Kemschler), Richard Lynch (Rimmin), John Harkins (Father Wheatley), Jenny O'Hara (The Woman), Lelia Goldoni (Sister Monica), Peggy McCay (Irene), Peter Brandon (Dr. Price), Kim Cattrall (Lindsay Isley), Natasha Ryan (Cindy Isley), Richard Sanders (The Doctor), Lillian Adams (Beatrice), Erica Yohn (Agnes), Richard Stahl (Brown), Sandy Ward (Lt. Taggert), Isaac Goz (Merlin).

1447. **Huggy Bear and the Turkey.** 60 min. Airdate: 2/19/77. Production Company: Spelling-Goldberg Productions. Director: Claude Ennis Starrett, Jr. Executive Producers: Aaron Spelling and Leonard Goldberg. Producers: Joseph T. Naar and Michael Hiatt. Writer: Ron Friedman. Creator: Ron Friedman, from characters created by William Blinn. Music: Tom Scott. Aired as an episode of *Starsky and Hutch*. Snitch Huggy Bear (Antonio Fargas) teams up with a strait-laced J.D. "Turkey" Turquet (Dale Robinette) and opens his own detective agency. In the pilot, Foxy Baker (Emily Yancy) asks Starsky (Paul Michael Glaser) and Hutch (David Soul) to find her missing husband, and they refer her to the private eyes. This pilot went nowhere, and the situation it set up was ignored in subsequent episodes of *Starsky and Hutch*—Huggy Bear showed up as a snitch again (as if nothing ever happened) and J.D. disappeared for good. *Cast:* Antonio Fargas (as Huggy Bear), Dale Robinette (J.D. "Turkey" Turquet), Emily Yancy (Foxy Baker), Richard Romanus (Sonny), Carole Cook (Scorchy), Blackie Dammett (Sugar), Mickey Morton (Moon), Stan Shaw (Leotis), LaWanda Page (Lady Bessie), R.G. Armstrong (Dad Watson), Fuddie Bagley (Walter T. Baker), Joe La Due (Yank), Darryl Zwerling (Man), Titus Napolean (Milo), Eddie Lo Russo (Doc Rafferty), Robyn Hilton (Miss O'Toole).

1448. **The New Maverick.** 90 min. Airdate: 9/3/78. Production Companies: Warner Bros. Television and Cherokee Productions. Director: Hy Averback. Executive Producer: Meta Rosenberg. Producer: Bob Foster. Writer: Juanita Bartlett, based on characters created by Roy Huggins. A revival of ABC's old *Maverick* series, which ran from 1957–1962 and featured James Garner and Jack Kelly as two gamblers roaming the West in the 1880s. Both are on hand to introduce young Ben Maverick (Charles Frank), the Harvard-educated son of their Cousin Beau (played by Roger Moore in the original series). In the pilot, the Mavericks become involved in a plot by a larcenous judge to steal a shipment of rifles. ABC turned it down, but CBS later reworked the concept as *Young Maverick* and commissioned a new pilot, which spawned a disastrously short-lived series. That didn't stop NBC from trying its own *Maverick* sequel—*Bret Maverick*, which starred James Garner and lasted one season. *Cast:* Charles Frank (as Ben Maverick), Susan Blanchard (Nell McGarrahan), James Garner (Bret Maverick), Jack Kelly (Bart Maverick), Eugene Roche (Judge Crupper), Susan Sullivan (Porker Alice), Jack Garner (Homer), Graham Jarvis (Lambert).

1449. **The Quinns.** 90 min. Airdate: 7/1/77. Production Company: Daniel Wilson Productions. Director: Daniel Petrie. Producer: Daniel Wilson. Writer: Sidney Carroll, from an idea by Fran Sears and Phyllis Minoff. Music: John Scott. A drama about four generations of a family of New York firefighters. *Cast:* William Swetland (as Tom), Geraldine Fitzgerald (Peggy), Barry Bostwick (Bill), Pat

Elliott (Rita), Peter Masterson (Michael), Liam Dunn (Sean), Susan Browning (Elizabeth), Virginia Vestoff (Rene Carmody), Pat Corley (Eugene Carmody), Blair Brown (Millicent Priestley).

1450. Roger and Harry (aka The Mitera Target; aka Love for Ransom; aka The Quentin Method). 90 min. Airdate: 5/2/77. Production Companies: Bruce Lansbury Productions and Columbia Pictures Television. Director: Jack Starrett. Executive Producer: Bruce Lansbury. Producer: Anthony Spinner. Writer: Alvin Sapinsley. Music: Allyn Ferguson and Jack Elliott. John Davidson and Barry Primus are two private eyes who recover stolen valuables. In the pilot, they go after a billionaire's missing daughter (Anne Randall Stewart), uncover a kidnapping plot, and decide they like her so much, they consider making her part of their team. Cast: John Davidson (as Roger Quentin), Barry Primus (Harry Jaworsky), Anne Randall Stewart (Joanna March), Carole Mallory (Kate Wilson), Richard Lynch (Curt Blair), Harris Yulin (Arthur Pennington), Susan Sullivan (Cindy St. Claire), Titos Vandis (Claude Du Cloche), Biff McGuire (Sylvester March), Alan McRae (David Peterson), Vaughn Armstrong (Heller), Henry Sutton (Cutts), James O'Connell (Mankowitz), Robert DoQui (Lt. Shelley), Fred Holliday (Reporter).

1451. Shack (aka Dr. Scorpion). 90 min. Airdate: 2/24/78. Production Company: Stephen J. Cannell Productions. Director: Richard Lang. Executive Producer: Stephen J. Cannell. Producer: Alex Beaton. Writer: Stephen J. Cannell. Creator: Stephen J. Cannell. Music: Mike Post and Pete Carpenter. When ABC asked producer Stephen J. Cannell for "James Bond as a 10 p.m. show," this is what he gave them—the adventures of Jonathan Shackelford, aka Shack, a secret agent he describes as being "in a high state of paranoia." When Cannell had troubles finding a star, ABC recommended Nick Mancuso for the role, a man Cannell believed was "totally wrong for the part. I couldn't find an actor worse for it." And Mancuso agreed. They went ahead with the pilot anyway, shooting it entirely on location in Hawaii. It was considered too violent by ABC and was rejected. Seven years later, Cannell created *Stingray*, an NBC series about a mysterious stranger with an espionage background who helps people in distress. He hired Nick Mancuso to play him. Cast: Nick Mancuso (as Jonathan Shackelford), Sandra Kerns (Sharon Shackelford), Christine Lahti (Tania Reston), Roscoe Lee Browne (Dr. Cresus), Richard Herd (Bill Worthington), Denny Miller (The Dane), Michael Cavanaugh (Whitey Ulman), Granville Van Dusen (Terry Batliner), Philip

Sterling (Admiral Gunwilder), Joseph Ruskin (Lt. Reed), Lincoln Kilpatrick (Eddie), James Murtaugh (Dave Steel), Zitto Kazann (Arubella), James Hong (Ho Chin), Eric Server (Agent Shelby), Bob Minor (Jean Claude), Richmond Hoxie (Morrison), Harvey Fisher (Tony).

CBS / COMEDY

1452. **The Banana Company.** 30 min. Airdate: 8/25/77. Production Company: Carnan/Becker Productions. Director: Bruce Bilson. Executive Producer: Carroll O'Connor. Producer: Ronald Rubin. Writers: Robert Klane, Ronald Rubin, and Bernard Kahn. Creator: Milton Sperling. The misadventures of a motley crew of war correspondents in the South Pacific during World War II. There's the by-the-book commander (Ted Gehring), the cynical *ex-New York Times* reporter (John Reilly), a gambling radio announcer (Ron Masak), a womanizing director (Sam Chew) and a kleptomaniac artist (Eddie Quillan). *Cast:* Ted Gehring (as Major Platt), John Reilly (Capt. Harry Gill), Gailard Sartain (Peebles), Sam Chew (Segal), Ron Masak (Muldoon), Bob Brown (Front Line Turner).

1453. **Best Friends.** 30 min. Airdate: 7/19/77. Director: Jerry Paris. Producer: Alan Sacks. Writers: Stanley Ralph Ross and Peter Meyerson. The misadventures of a group of "zany" Chicago teenagers. *Cast:* James Canning (as Nick), Bill Henry Douglas (Arthur), Gary Epp (Mountain Man), Barry Pearl (Gypsy), Shery Hursey (Kathy), Glorie DeRoy (Aunt Maggie).

1454. **Eddie and Herbert.** 30 min. Airdate: 5/30/77. Production Company: Filmways. Director: Robert Sheerer. Executive Producer: Perry Lafferty. Producers: E. Duke Vincent and Richard M. Rosenbloom. Writer: Sam Bobrick. Creator: E. Duke Vincent. Music: Ray Charles. The lives of loud-mouth Eddie (Jeffrey Tambor) and his friend Herbert (James Cromwell), who worships him. They are both meter-readers for the Department of Water and Power and are married—Eddie to a very practical woman (Candy Azzara) and Herbert to an over-protective manicurist (Marilyn Meyers). *Cast:* Jeffrey Tambor (as Eddie Scanlon), James Cromwell (Herbert Draper), Candy Azzara (Madge Scanlon), Marilyn Meyers (Dorine Draper).

1455. **Everything Is Coming Up Roses (aka You're Gonna Love It Here).** 30 min. Airdate: 6/1/77. Production Companies: S/K Productions and Warner Bros. Television. Director: Bruce Paltrow. Executive Producer: Frank Königsberg.

Producer: Mel Färber. Writer: Bruce Paltrow. Music: Peter Matz. Singer: Ethel Merman. The adventures of an out-of-work broadway star (Ethel Merman), her son the talent agent (Austin Pendleton), and her wise-cracking, 11-year-old grandson (Chris Barnes). *Cast:* Ethel Merman (as Lolly Rogers), Chris Barnes (Peter Rogers), Austin Pendleton (Harry Rogers), Dianne Kirksey (Neighbor).

1456. **Halfway House.** 30 min. Production Company: Taylor-Bologna Productions. A single woman gives up her law practice to open a halfway house of ex-cons, to the consternation of her mother.

1457. **Handle with Care (aka Nurses; aka Nurses in Korea).** 30 min. Airdate: 5/9/77. Production Company: 20th Century Fox. Director: Alan Rafkin. Executive Producer: Nancy Malone. Producer: Lew Gallo. Writers: Woody Kling, Dawn Alredge, Marion Freeman, and James Parker. Creator: Woody Kling. The female *M*A*5*H* centering on the misadventures of nurses working in the Korean war. *Cast:* Marlyn Mason (as Liz Baker), Didi Conn (Jackie Morse), Mary Jo Catlett (Major Kinkley), Bob Lussier (Corp. Karp), Betsy Slade (Shirley Nichols), Jeannie Wilson (Turk), Brian Dennehy (Col. Marvin Richardson), David Dukes (Dr. O'Brien), Okay Miller (Dr. Roberts), Howard George (Dr. Rogers), Ted Wass (Corp. Tillingham), Dick Yarmy (Soldier).

1458. **Hanging Out.** 30 min. Production Company: Ralph Bakshi Productions. Director: Ralph Bakshi. Producer: Ralph Bakshi. Writers: Don Reo and Allan Katz. Creator: Ralph Bakshi. The adventures of three teenagers living in the big city—the twist is the stars are animated and everything else is live action. The characters are Russo, a sharp-minded wheeler-dealer; Kanoff, a fat, animal-loving kid with dozens of pets; and Fogel, a short, intelligent kid who worships Russo.

1459. **Off Campus.** 30 min. Airdate: 6/6/77. Production Company: Jogadi/ Elephant Productions. Director: Burt Brinckerhoff. Producer: Gilbert Gates. Writer: Marshall Brickman. The misadventures of students living in a coed boarding house. It bares a remarkable resemblance to another flop pilot this season, NBC's *Off the Wall.* Peter Reigert would later appear in the movie *Animal House,* which was adapted into a short-lived TV series that featured Josh Mostel. *Cast:* Marilu Henner (as Janet), Josh Mostel (Steve), Peter Reigert (Stanley), Chip Zien (Josh), Joe Bova (Weineke), Ann Risley (Bonnie), Alexa Kenin (Stacy), Robert Hitt (Leon).

1460. **Sheila (aka Sheila Levine Is Dead and Living in New York).** 30 min. Airdate: 8/29/77. Production Company: Paramount Television. Director: Peter Bonerz.

Executive Producer: Gail Parent. Producer: Martin Cohan. Writers: Gail Parent and Kenny Solms, from the book by Gail Parent. Creator: Gail Parent. Based on the movie *Sheila Levine Is Dead and Living in New York*, which was adapted from the book of the same name about a single woman (Dori Brenner) who lives with a model (Barbara Trentham) and works for a Broadway agent (Milton Berle). *Cast:* Dori Brenner (as Sheila Levine), Milton Berle (Marty Rose), Barbara Trentham (Kate), George Wyner (Stewart Rose), Larry Breeding (Joshua), Phillip R. Allen (Brad Wooley).

1461. **Steubenville.** 30 min. Production Company: John Rich Productions. Director: John Rich. Producer: John Rich. Writers: Ian La Frenais and Dick Clement. Based on the BBC sitcom *Likely Lads*. The lives of an opinionated widower (Jack Grimes) and his two sons—one dependable hardworker (Rick Hurst) and the other a lazy shlump (Charles Murphy)—who work in a steel plant in Steubenville, Pennsylvania. The hardworker is engaged to a woman (Andrea Adler) whose mother (Mary Gregory) is against the marriage.

1462. **27 Joy Street.** 30 min. Production Company: King-Hitzig Productions. Director: Bill Persky. Executive Producer: Alan King. Producer: Rupert Hitzig. Writer: Peter Stone. Based on the BBC series *Rising Damp*. Jack Weston is the landlord of a Cambridge, Massachusetts, rooming house who reluctantly gets involved in the lives of his eccentric tenants, including two medical students from Africa, a professional wrestler, and a nude model.

1463. **There's Always Room.** 30 min. Airdate: 4/24/77. Director: Robert Moore. Executive Producers: Robert W. Christiansen and Rick Rosenberg. Producer: Michael Leeson. Writer: Michael Leeson. Music: Bill Conti. This shares the same format as *27 Joy Street*. Maureen Stapleton is a kindly landlady who rents out the rooms in her home. Her tenants include a wanna-be rollerskating queen and a cowboy with a pet turkey. *Cast:* Maureen Stapleton (as Madelyn Fairchild), Conrad Janis (Steward Dennis), Debbie Zipp (Annette Enderby), Barry Nelson (Bob End-erby), Leland Palmer (Valerie), Royce Applegate (Buck Burke), Woody Chambliss (McRaven).

1464. **T.R. McCoy.** 30 min. Writer: Peter Stone. The adventures of an aspiring country-western group—a woman and four men—struggling in Nashville.

1465. **Whatever Happened to Dobie Gillis?** 30 min. Airdate: 5/10/77. Production Company: Komack Company. Directors: James Komack and Gary Shimokawa. Executive Producers: James Komack and Paul Mason. Producer: Michael

Manheim. Writers: Peter Meyerson and Nick Arnold. Creator: Max Shulman. A sequel to the 1950s sitcom *Dobie Gillis*. Dobie (Dwayne Hickman) has married Zelda (Sheila James), has a 16-year-old son (Steven Paul) and runs his father's (Frank Feylen) grocery store. Maynard (Bob Denver) is now a successful entrepreneur and Chatsworth (Steve Franken) has become town banker. Another revival, entitled *Bring Me the Head of Dobie Gillis* was mounted for CBS in 1987. *Cast:* Dwayne Hickman (as Dobie Gillis), Bob Denver (Maynard G. Krebs), Sheila James (Zelda Gilroy), Frank Feylen (Herbert T. Gillis), Steven Franken (Chatsworth Osbourne), Steven Paul (Georgie Gillis), Lorenzo Lamas (Lucky), Irwin Wynn (Hen-shaw), Alice Backes (Mrs. Lazlo), Susan Davis (Mrs. Tucker).

CBS / DRAMA

1466. **The African Queen.** 60 min. Airdate: 3/18/77. Production Company: Viacom Enterprises. Director: Richard Sarafian. Executive Producer: Mark Carliner. Producer: Len Kaufman. Writer: Irving Gaynor Neiman. Music: John Murtaugh. The second attempt, the first was in the early 1960s, to turn the popular 1951 Humphrey Bogart and Katherine Hepburn movie into a TV series. Warren Oates plays a steamboat captain to Mariette Hartley's missionary in an adventure set in World War I Africa. Shot on location in the Florida Everglades. *Cast:* Warren Oates (as Charlie Allnot), Mariette Hartley (Rosie Sayer), Johnny Sekka (Jogana), Wolf Roth (Lt. Biedemeyer), Albert Paulsen (Major Strauss), Frank Schuller (Heinke), Clarence Thomas (Sgt. Abuto), Tyrone Jackson (Kaninu).

1467. **Bravo Two.** 30 min. Airdate: 3/25/77. Production Company: Lorimar Productions. Director: Ernest Pintoff. Executive Producers: Lee Rich and Philip Capice. Producers: Robert Stambler and Guerdon Trueblood. Writers: Leo V. Gordon and Guerdon Trueblood. Creator: Guerdon Trueblood. An *Adam-12* on the sea. The adventures of two police officers (Bruce Fairbairn and David Gilliam) patroling the waters off San Pedro and Playa Del Rey for the Los Angeles Harbor Police. *Cast:* Bruce Fairbairn (as Wiley Starrett), David Gilliam (Bud Wizer), James Hampton (Lt. O'Brien), Cooper Hackabee (T.J. Phillips), Don Matheson (Mr. Morgan), Lynn Carlin (Mrs. Morgan), Lucy Saroyan (Lucy), Matthew Laborteaux (Eddie Morgan).

1468. **The Cabot Connection.** 60 min. Airdate: 5/10/77. Production Companies: Barry Weitz Productions and Columbia Pictures Television. Director: E.W.

Swackhamer. Executive Producer: Barry Weitz. Producer: Robert Mintz. Writer: George Kirgo. Creator: Barry Weitz. Music: Morton Stevens. Craig Stevens is a former aristocrat who, with his two daughters, ferrets out crimes among the rich. The Cabots weren't always crimefighters. The once-wealthy family has fallen on hard times and now the government—in return for the Cabots' services and to sustain their "cover"—secretly pays the tab for the fancy clothes, luxurious mansion, and the Rolls Royce, which is driven by the secret agent sent to keep an eye on them. *Cast:* Craig Stevens (as Marcus Cabot), Jane Actman (Muffin Cabot), Catherine Shirriff (Olivia Cabot), Chris Robinson (Stephen Kordiak), Warren Kemmerling (Harold O'Hara), Matilda Calnan (Essie), Gloria DeHaven (Dolly Foxworth), Alf Kjellin (Heinz Vogel), Curt Lowens (Victor Kreindler), Dirk Benedict (Brom Loomis), James Luisi (Bozuffi), Frank Downing (Rosenfeld), Ivor Barry (Wendell), Lynn Storer (Clerk), Glenn Wilder (Wharfman).

1469. **Down Home (aka Just an Old Sweet Song).** 90 min. Airdate: 9/14/76. Production Company: MGM Enterprises. Director: Robert Ellis Miller. Executive Producer: Lionel Ephraim. Producer: Phillip Barry. Writer: Melvin Van Peebles. Music: Peter Matz. Theme Song: Melvin Van Peebles, sung by Ira Hawkins. Aired as a presentation of *General Electric Theatre*. The first of three pilots about a black family, headed by Robert Hooks and Cicely Tyson, that moves from urban Detroit to the rural South. *Cast:* Robert Hooks (as Nate Simmons), Cicely Tyson (Priscilla Simmons), Tia Rance (Darlene Simmons), Kevin Hooks (Nate Simmons, Jr.), Eric Hooks (Highpockets Simmons), Beah Richards (Grandma), Minnie Gentry (Aunt Velvet), Lincoln Kilpatrick (Joe Mayfield), Mary Alice (Helen Mayfield), Sonny Jim Gaines (Trunk), Anne Seymour (Sarah Claypool), Walt Guthrie (Winston), Deena Crowder (Julie Mayfield), Edward Binns (Abner Claypool), Emily Bell (Mrs. Claypool), Lou Walker (R. Stone), Johnny Popwell (J.T. Dunbar), Tia Ranee (Darlene), Phillip Wende (Sheriff), Ernest Dixon (Doorman).

1470. **[Pilot #2] [Down Home] Kinfolks.** 60 min. Production Company: MTM Enterprises. Director: Fielder Cook. Producer: Phillip Barry. Writer: Melvin Van Peebles. Creator: Melvin Van Peebles. The unaired, second pilot for the "Down Home" concept. Robert Hooks is back as the father, but Madge Sinclair replaces Cicely Tyson as his wife and Beah Richards, the dying grandmother of the first pilot, returns now as Aunt Velvet. And, once again, Hook's real-life kids play his fictional kids. In this pilot, a family reunion of Simmonses becomes racially strained when a heretofore unknown group of white Simmonses shows up.

1471. **[Pilot #3] Down Home.** 60 min. Airdate: 8/16/78. Production Company: MTM Enterprises. Director: Fielder Cook. Producer: Phillip Barry. Writer: Melvin Van Peebles. Creator: Melvin Van Peebles. Music: Patrick Williams. The third attempt at selling CBS on *Down Home.* In this pilot, Hooks' white business partner is murdered by a radical redneck. *Cast:* Robert Hooks (as Nate Simmons), Madge Sinclair (Priscilla Simmons), Tia Ranee (Darlene Simmons), Kevin Hooks (Nate Simmons, Jr.), Eric Hooks (Highpockets Simmons), Beau Richards (Aunt Velvet), Lincoln Kilpatrick (Joe Mayfield), Beverly Hope Atkinson (Helen Mayfield), Sonny Jim Gaines (Trunk), Anne Seymour (Sarah Claypool), Norma Connelly (Mrs. Winston), Deena Crowder (Julie Mayfield), Edward Binns (Abner Claypool), William Watson (as Burt Pritchard), Timothy Scott (Benjamin Pritchard), Woodrow Parfrey (Bobby Pritchard), Boyd Bodwell (Frank Simmons), Mickey Jones (Billy Joe Pritchard), John Gilgreen (Jeeter Simmons), George McDaniel (Dr. Johnson), Andrew Duggan (Sheriff).

1472. **Enigma (aka The Enigma People).** 60 min. Airdate: 5/29/77. Production Company: 20th Century Fox. Director: Michael O'Herlihy. Producer: Sam H. Rolfe. Writer: Sam H. Rolfe. Creator: Sam H. Rolfe. Music: Harry Sukman. Enigma is a super-secret, worldwide intelligence agency located beneath a tropical island in the Bermuda Triangle. The top operative is Andrew Icarus (Scott Hylands) who, in the pilot, is ordered by The Baron (Guy Doleman) to stop a Nazi organization in California. *Cast:* Scott Hylands (as Andrew Icarus), Guy Doleman (Baron Mayrice Mockcastle), Barbara 0. Jones (Princess Miranda Larawa), Soon-Teck Oh (Mei San Gow), Melinda Dillon (Dora Harren), Peter Coffield (Peter McCauley), Percy Rodriquez (Idi Ben Youref), Sherry Jackson (Kate Valentine), Jim Davis (Col. Valentine), Bill Fletcher (Wolf), Morgan Farley (Ben Harren), Melodie Johnson (Beverly Golden), Marsha Brown (Judith).

1473. **Martinelli: The Outside Man.** 60 min. Airdate: 4/8/77. Production Company: MGM Enterprises. Director: Russ Mayberry. Executive Producer: Paul Magistretti. Producer: William T. Phillips. Writer: Paul Magistretti. Creator: Paul Magistretti. Music: Tom Scott. Ron Liebman is an undercover agent who infiltrates the criminal underworld to bring bad guys to justice. When he isn't doing that, he runs a one-man delivery service in San Francisco as a cover. *Cast:* Ron Liebman (as Rich Martinelli), Woody Strode (Shaker Thompson), Janet

Margolin (Rosalie), Nicholas Colasanto (Stalio), Al Ruscio (Sal), Pepper Martin (Leo), Robert Donner (Armand), Pat Corley (Sally), Fred Stuthman (Bank Manager), Nicholas Pryor (Ellsworth), William Wintersole (Morgan), Michael Frost (Roger Elks).

1474. **The Mask of Alexander.** 60 min. Production Companies: A.J. Fenady Productions and MGM Television. Director: Bernard McEveety. Producer: Andrew J. Fenady. Writer: Paul Playdon. Creator: Andrew J. Fenady. Alexander Cross is the leader of an international criminal organization who, unbeknownst to even his closest associates, is killed in an accident. Interpol quickly finds Cross' exact lookalike—a hunter in Africa—and trains him to *be* Cross. Paul Shenar stars and Barbara Bach costars as his assistant, an Interpol agent.

1475. **McLaren's Riders.** 30 min. Airdate: 5/17/77. Production Companies: Herbert F. Solow Productions and Taft Broadcasting. Director: Lee Katzin. Producer: Herbert F. Solow. Writer: Cliff Gould. Music: Fred Karlin. The adventures of two plainclothes motorcycle cops—a New Yorker (George DiCenzo) and a Texan (Ted Neeley)—who travel the country helping police departments that need help. In the pilot, they investigate cattle rustling and murder. *Cast:* George DiCenzo (as Sam Downing), Ted Neeley (T. Wood), Harry Morgan (Billy Willett), Hilary Thompson (Kate), Brad Davis (Bobby John), James Best (Skinner), Kate Goodfellow (Wanda), Geno Silva (Pete Sunfighter).

1476. **Mobile Medics.** 30 min. Airdate: 5/10/77. Production Companies: Bruce Lansbury Productions and Columbia Pictures Television. Director: Paul Krasny. Executive Producer: Bruce Lansbury. Producer: Robert Hamilton. Writer: Robert Hamilton. Ben Masters and Jack Stauffer are two doctors who ride around in a van converted into a high-tech "operating room on wheels" that comes complete with a talking computer (called Lorelei) that can diagnose patients. Jaime Tirelli is the driver, and Ellen Weston is the doctor/hospital administrator in charge of the project. *Cast:* Ellen Weston (as Dr. Liz Rheiner), Jack Stauffer (Dr. Robb Spencer), Ben Masters (Dr. Craig Bryant), Jaime Tirelli (Pete Vasguez), Robert DuQui (Foreman), Julie Cobb (Cheryl), Maggie Malooly (Nurse), John Pikard (Fire Captain).

1477. **Relentless.** 90 min. Airdate: 9/14/77. Production Company: CBS Productions. Director: Lee H. Katzin. Producer: Fred Baum. Writer: Sam H. Rolfe, from the novel by Brian Garfield. Music: John Cacavas. Will Sampson is a "relentless" state trooper who, in the pilot, pursues escaped felons. *Cast:* Will Sampson (as Sam

Watchman), Monte Markham (Pal Vickers), John Hillerman (Major Leo Hargit), Marianna Hill (Annie Lansford), Larry Wilcox (Buck), Anthony Ponzini (Jack Hanratty), John Lawlor (Walker), Ted Markland (Lt. Dan Barraclough), David Pendleton (Dwayne Terry), Ron Foster (Sgt. Ed Kleber), Don Starr (Cal), Danny Zapien (Jasper Simalee), Steve Schemmel (Doctor), Richard Kennedy (Trooper), Pat Bolt (Waitress), Earl Smith (Deputy), Melvin Todd (Proprietor), Dick Armstrong (Reporter), Carroll Reynolds (Winthrop).

1478. **Salathiel Harms (aka The Black Thorn).** 60 min. Airdate: 12/5/76. Production Company: Universal Television. Executive Producer: Matthew Rapf. Producer: Chester Krumholz. Writers: Leon Tokatyan and Chester Krumholz. Creator: Joe Gores. Aired as an episode of *Kojak*. A second attempt to spin-off a series starring Rosie Grier as a California bounty hunter. The first pilot aired in 1976. *Cast:* Rosie Grier (as Salathiel Harms), Barry Snider (Anthony Meara), Swoosie Kurtz (Julie), John D. Reilly (Robert Whelan), Danny Aiello (Mattie), Leonardo Cimino (Mr. C.), Telly Savalas (Lt. Kojak), Kevin Dobson (Crocker), Dan Frazer (McNeil), George Savalas (Stavros), Mark Russell (Saperstein), Vince Conti (Rizo).

1479. **Sparrow.** 60 min. Airdate: 1/12/78. Production Company: Tori Productions. Director: Stuart Hagman. Executive Producer: Herbert Leonard. Producers: Sam Manners and Charles Russell. Writers: Walter Bernstein, Lawrence J. Cohen, and Paul Bauman. The first of two pilots about neophyte detective Jerry Sparrow (Randy Herman), a 20-year-old errand boy in a New Orleans detective agency. *Cast:* Randy Herman (as Jerry Sparrow), Don Gordon (Mr. Medwick), Beverly Sanders (Tammy), Karen Sedgeley (Harriet), Dori Brenner (Karen), Jeff Holland (Bruce), Jack Wallace (Bennett), Lenny Baker (Marty).

1480. **Winner Take All.** 60 min. Airdate: 4/1/77. Production Company: Quinn Martin Productions. Director: Robert Day. Executive Producer: Quinn Martin. Producer: John Wilder. Writer: Cliff Gould. Creator: Cliff Gould. Music: John Elizalde. Michael Murphy is a police lieutenant in the robbery division in love with Joanna Pettet, a freelance insurance investigator who makes nearly ten times as much as he does doing roughly the same thing. They often work on the same cases and, while they are very competitive, it doesn't lessen their attraction to one another. *Cast:* Michael Murphy (as Charlie Quiqley), Joanna Pettet (Allison Nash), Clive Revill (Woodhouse), Mark Gordon (Mo Rellis), David Huddleston (Hiram Yerby), Alain Patrick (Villemont), James Hong (Clarence

Woo), Martine Beswick (Solange Dupree), John Fiedler (Room Clerk), James McCallion (Hank), Dorothy Meyer (Mae Burt).

1481. Woman on the Run. 60 min. Airdate: 9/7/77. Production Company: Paramount Television. Director: Harvey Hart. Producer: Frank Glicksman. Writer: Charles Larson. Creator: Charles Larson. Donna Mills discovers that her husband (Edward Winter) is a hitman for a foreign country. She tries to tell authorities, but no one believes her—that's because the organization her husband works for has forged records that say she has a mental illness. She is forced to flee, pursued by her hitman husband and his secret organization. *Cast:* Donna Mills (Laura), Edward Winter (Daniel), Bo Hopkins (Owen), Dan O'Herlihy (Crandell), David Opatoshu (Ed Miles).

1482. World of Darkness. 60 min. Airdate: 4/17/77. Production Company: Talent Associates. Director: Jerry London. Executive Producer: David Susskind. Producer: Diana Karew. Writer: Art Wallace. Creator: Art Wallace. Music: Fred Karlin. The first of two pilots about a sportswriter (Granville Van Dusen) who, after a serious accident, "dies" for two minutes on the operating table and awakens with a supernatural, psychic tie to "the world beyond" (which, incidentally, is the title of the second pilot). Voices from beyond the grave send him on missions to help people facing supernatural dangers. *Cast:* Granville Van Dusen (Paul Taylor), Tovah Feldshuh (Clara Sanford), Beatrice Straight (Joanna Sanford), Gary Merrill (Dr. Thomas Madsen), James Austin (John Sanford), Shawn McCann (Matty Barker), Jaune Eastwood (Helen), Al Bernardo (Max).

NBC / COMEDY

1483. The Bay City Amusement Company. 30 min. Airdate: 7/25/77. Production Company: Universal Television. Director: Norman Steinberg. Executive Producer: Norman Steinberg. Producer: Robert Kaprall. Writers: Ken Levine and David Isaacs. The comedy revolving around the people who produce a local variety show on a San Francisco television station owned by Ted Gehring, an ultraconservative former cowboy star (a thinly disguised spoof of Gene Autry, who once owned KTLA in Los Angeles). Other regulars include Terry Kiser as the workaholic producer; Jim Scott as a comedian who dreams of being a dramatic actor; Pat McCormick as the seasoned writer; and Dennis Howard and Barrie Youngfellow as a married couple who perform on the show. *Cast:* Barrie Youngfellow (as Ann),

Dennis Howard (Alan), Ted Gehring (Bradshaw), Pat McCormick (Howie), Terry Kiser (Clifford), June Gable (Gail), Jim Scott (Warren).

1484. Calling Dr. Storm, M.D. 30 min. Airdate: 8/25/77. Production Companies: Silliphant/Konigsberg Productions and Warner Bros. Television. Director: James Burrows. Executive Producers: Stirling Silliphant and Frank Konigsberg. Writers: Lawrence J. Cohen and Fred Freeman. Larry Linville's first post-M*A*S*H role is once again that of a doctor—Dr. Jim Storm, chief of surgery at All Fellows Hospital. Dr. Storm is more concerned with his patients than with the financial well-being of the hospital, which puts him in constant conflict with the chairman (Bruce Gordon), who even put a revolving restaurant/nightclub on the roof to help cash flow. Such dedication leaves little time for Dr. Storm to spend with his wife (Sharon Spelman), a police officer who works odd hours herself. *Cast:* Larry Linville (as Dr. Jim Storm), Sharon Spelman (Patti Storm), Stephen Farr (Paul Storm), Bruce Gordon (Dr. Stendak), Mary Louise Weller (Vanessa Stendak), Richard Libertini (Dr. Nate Nateman), James B. Sikking (Bart Burton), Marian Mercer (Maggie Barbour), P.J. Soles (Sarah Baynes), Robert Hogan (Glenn Puber).

1485. Daughters. 30 min. Airdate: 7/20/77. Production Company: Witt/Thomas/ Harris Productions. Director: Bob Claver. Executive Producers: Paul Junger Witt and Tony Thomas. Producer: Susan Harris. Writer: Susan Harris. Creator: Susan Harris. Michael Constantine is a widowed police chief trying to raise his three daughters in a Chicago suburb. *Cast:* Michael Constantine (as Dominick), Olivia Barash (Diane), Judy Landers (Cookie), Robin Groves (Terry), Julie Bovasso (Aunt Rose).

1486. Father Knows Best Reunion. 90 min. Airdate: 5/15/77. Production Company: Columbia Pictures Television. Director: Norman Abbott. Producer: Hugh Benson. Writer: Paul West. Jim and Margaret Anderson (Robert Young and Jane Wyatt) mark their 35th anniversary and everyone comes back together for the celebration. Betty (Elinor Donahue) is now a widow with two kids; Bud (Billy Gray) is a married motorcycle racer with a young son; and Kathy (Lauren Chapin) is single but dating a doctor who is ten years older than she is. Two more pilots followed this one. *Cast:* Robert Young (as Jim Anderson), Jane Wyatt (Margaret Anderson), Elinor Donahue (Betty Anderson), Billy Gray (Bud Anderson), Lauren Chapin (Kathy Anderson), Hal England (Dr. Jason Harper), Jim McMullan (Frank Carlson), Susan Adams (Jeanne), Cari Anne Warder

(Jenny), Christopher Gardner (Robbie Anderson), Kyle Richards (Ellen), Nellie Bellflower (Mary Beth), Noel Conlon (Reverend Lockwood).

1487. **[Pilot #2] Father Knows Best: Home for Christmas.** 90 min. Airdate: 12/18/77. Production Company: Columbia Pictures Television. Director: Marc Daniels. Executive Producer: Rene Valentee. Producer: Hugh Benson. Writer: Paul West. Jim and Margaret Anderson are depressed about having to spend Christmas alone, and the possibility they may have to sell their home. *Cast:* Robert Young (as Jim Anderson), Jane Wyatt (Margaret Anderson), Elinor Donahue (Betty), Lauren Chapin (Kathy), Billy Gray (Bud), Hal England (Dr. Jason Harper), Jim McMullan (Frank Carlson), Susan Adams (Jeanne), Cari Anne Warder (Jenny), Christopher Gardner (Robbie Anderson), Kyle Richards (Ellen), Stuart Lancaster (George Newman), June Whitly Taylor (Jan Newman), Priscilla Morrill (Louise).

1488. **Good Penny.** 30 min. Airdate: 9/1/77. Production Company: Price Gabriel Productions. Director: Richard Harwood. Executive Producers: Renee Taylor and Joseph Bologna. Producer: Bryan Hickox. Writers: Renee Taylor and Joseph Bologna. Creators: Renee Taylor and Joseph Bologna. Renee Taylor is a pregnant woman with two children who has just been deserted by her husband. She gets a helping hand from her mother, her brother, her therapy group, and sometimes even her wayward husband drops by. *Cast:* Renee Taylor (as Penny), Scott Brady (Al), Gloria LaRoy (Pauline), Carmine Caridi (Jerry), Roger Bowen (Dr. Frosman), Bobby Alto (Herb), Fredric Franklyn (Mr. Grazer), Lila Teigh (Receptionist).

1489. **Hearts of the West (aka Riding High).** 30 min. Airdate: 8/25/77. Production Company: MGM. Director: Lee Phillips. Producer: Marc Merson. Writer: Larry Gelbart. Based on the movie *Hearts of the West,* which was set in the 1930s and starred Beau Bridges as a would-be western writer who works as an extra in cowboy serials. Charles Frank takes over in the pilot, which also stars Lonny Chapman as a has-been star who is now an extra; Allan Miller as the cheap producer; Allen Case as the western star; and Wendy Phillips as a production assistant. *Cast:* Charles Frank (as Lewis Tater), Wendy Phillips (Wendy Trout), Lonny Chapman (Howard Pike), Allan Miller (Bert Kessler), Don Calfa (Sid), Bill Hart (Wally), Allen Case (Lyle Montana), Pat Crenshaw (Bear).

1490. **Hollywood High.** 30 min. Airdate: 5/19/77. Production Companies: Jozak Productions and Paramount Television. Director: Gerald Abrams. Executive

Producer: Gerald I. Isenberg. Producer: Peter Baldwin. Writer: Michael Weinberger. The first of three pilots. In this one, the proposed series would follow the adventures of Phoebe (Annie Potts) and Dawn (Kim Lankford), two high school students who, in the pilot, accept dates and then change their minds. *Cast:* Annie Potts (as Phoebe), Kim Lankford (Dawn), Sam Kwasman (Dr. Bad), John Megna (Icky), Chris Pina (Wheeler), Rory Stevens (Bill).

1491. **[Pilot #2] Hollywood High.** 30 min. Airdate: 7/21/77. Production Companies: Jozak Productions and Paramount Television. Director: Burt Brinckerhoff. Executive Producers: Gerald I. Isenberg and Gerald W. Abrams. Producers: Elias Davis and David Pollock. Writers: David Pollock, Elias Davis, and Lloyd Garver. Annie Potts is now Paula, a high school journalist who dreams of being a big city reporter. Roberta Wallach is her smart but unattractive best friend; John Guerrasio is a photographer who only wants to shoot pretty girls; Darren O'Conner is the dictatorial editor; and Dick O'Neill is the journalism advisor. In this story, the journalists have to spend a night together in a motel room. *Cast:* Annie Potts (as Paula), Darren O'Conner (Eugene), Roberta Wallach (Allison), Beverly Sanders (Judith), Janet Wood (Janet), John Guerrasio (Stu), Dick O'Neill (Blaine).

1492. **[Pilot #3] Hollywood High.** 30 min. Airdate: 7/21/77. Production Companies: Jozak Productions and Paramount Television. Director: Burt Brinckerhoff. Executive Producers: Gerald I. Isenberg and Gerald W. Abrams. Producers: Elias Davis and David Pollock. Writers: David Pollock, Elias Davis, and Lloyd Garver. An insecure boy gets a date with the class beauty by agreeing to write her term paper. *Cast:* Annie Potts (as Paula), Darren O'Conner (Eugene), Roberta Wallach (Allison), Beverly Sanders (Judith), Janet Wood (Janet), John Guerrasio (Stu), Dick O'Neill (Blaine).

1493. **Instant Family.** 30 min. Airdate: 7/28/77. Production Companies: Lila Garrett Productions and 20th Century Fox. Director: Russ Petranto. Executive Producer: Lila Garrett. Producer: Mort Lachman. Writers: Lila Garrett, Mort Lachman, and Ray Brenner. William Daniels is a divorced piano teacher with three kids whose family shares a house with Lou Criscuolo, a widowed high school basketball coach with his two kids. *Cast:* William Daniels (as Clifford Beane), Lou Criscuolo (Frank Boyle), Wendy Fredericks (Lisa Boyle), Brad Wilkin (Robbie Boyle), Jeff Harlan (Kevin Beane), Robbie Rist (Ernie Beane), Sparky Marcus (Alexander Bean).

1494. Last Chance. 30 min. Production Company: Lorimar Productions. Director: Bob Moore. Executive Producers: Lee Rich and Philip Capice. Producer: Lew Gallo. Writer: Hal Dresner. The misadventures of a group of teenagers who have broken the law and been sent to a rehabilitation center called Bunkhouse D. The stars are Steve Guttenberg as a spoiled rich kid, Jason Walker as a hip guy who is not as tough as he thinks he is, Alvin Kupperman as a scientific genius, Will McKenzie as a social worker; Lauren Frost as a psychologist, and Sorrell Brooke as the man who runs the ranch.

1495. Look Out World. 30 min. Airdate: 7/27/77. Production Company: Filmways. Director: Hy Averback. Executive Producer: Perry Lafferty. Producer: Richard Rosenbloom. Writers: E. Duke Vincent, Hal Goldman, and Al Gordon. The misadventures of the folks who work at a car wash. The stars include Steve Doubet as a singing cowboy; Bart Braverman as a pick-pocket; Justin Lord as an aspiring comic; Arnold Soboloff and Maureen Arthur as the couple who run the business and Michael Huddleston as their dumb nephew. *Cast:* Michael Huddleston (as Cannonball), Justin Lord (Benny), Bart Braverman (Delfi), Steve Doubet (Beau), Arnold Soboloff (Gus), Maureen Arthur (Darcy), Damon Raskin (Byron), Susan Bay (Byron's Mother).

1496. The Natural Look. 30 min. Airdate: 7/6/77. Production Company: MTM Enterprises. Director: Robert Moore. Executive Producer: Lillian Gallo. Producers: Leonora Thuna and Pamela Chais. Writer: Leonora Thuna. Music: Charles Fox. The life of a newlywed couple—Edie (Barbara Feldon), a cosmetics executive, and Bud (Bill Bixby), a pediatrician. The cosmetics agency is owned by a Countess (Brenda Forbes) whose son (Michael MacRae) is the merchandizing director. *Cast:* Barbara Feldon (as Edie Harrison), Bill Bixby (Dr. Bud Harrison), Caren Kaye (Jane), Brenda Forbes (Countess), Sandy Sprung (Edna), Michael MacRae (Arthur).

1497. Off the Wall. 30 min. Airdate: 5/7/77. Production Companies: Universal Television and Franklin Barton Production. Director: Bob LaHendro. Executive Producer: Franklin Barton. Producers: George Tricker and Neil Rosen. Writers: George Tricker and Neil Rosen. Creators: George Tricker and Neil Rosen. Music: Mike Post and Pete Carpenter. This pilot, which revolved around the wacky lives of midwestern college students living in a coed dorm, was actually sold and slated for 8 p.m. Sundays on NBC's fall schedule. But NBC backed off later, despite Universal's plan to recast some of the key roles. *Cast:* Todd Susman (as Matt

Bozeman), Dana House (Jeannie), Harry Gold (Flash), Hal Williams (Mother), Cindy Heiberg (Lennie), Sean Roche (Gordon), Sandy Heiberg (Melvin), Frank Heiberg (Arthur).

1498. **The Rubber Gun Squad.** 30 min. Airdate: 9/1/77. Production Company: D'Antoni Productions. Director: Hy Averback. Executive Producer: Phil D'Antoni. Producer: Sonny Grosso. Writers: Simon Muntner and Sid Dorfman. The so-called Rubber Gun Squad is a group of misfit cops who have fouled up on duty and have been banished to Central Park. *Cast:* Andy Romano (as Chopper), Lenny Baker (Eddie), Tom Signorelli (Sgt. O'Leary), Betty Buckley (Rosie), Alan Weeks (Jerome), Paul Jabara (Austin), Frank Simpson (Dewey), Kenneth McMillan (Capt. Egan), Don Scardino (Mooney), William Robertson (Mr. Griffin).

1499. **Say Uncle.** 30 min. Production Company: Don Kirshner Productions. Director: Burt Brinckerhoff. Executive Producer: Don Kirshner. Producers: Ron Friedman and Gene Marclone. Writer: Ron Friedman. Creator: Ron Friedman. Dennis Cooley is Billy, a talented and easy-going singer who is constantly arguing with his outspoken and flamboyant uncle/manager, Col. Jack Whacker, played by Richard B. Shull.

1500. **Space Force.** 30 min. Airdate: 4/28/77. Production Companies: Len Rosenberg Productions and Columbia Pictures Television. Director: Peter Baldwin. Producers: John Boni and Norman Stiles. Writers: John Boni and Norman Stiles. Creators: John Boni and Norman Stiles. The misadventures of the officers aboard a massive army base floating in the cosmos. The stars included William Phipps as the incompetent commanding officer, Fred Willard as the wild leader of the pilots, and Maureen Mooney as the weapons expert. *Cast:* William Edward Phipps (as Capt. Irving Hinkley), Fred Willard (Capt. Thomas Woods), Larry Block (Pvt. Arnold Fleck), Jimmy Boyd (Capt. Leon Stoner), Hilly Hicks (Capt. Robert Milford), Maureen Mooney (Sgt. Eve Bailey), Joe Medalis (Lt. Kabar), Richard Paul (DORK).

1501. **The Sunshine Boys.** 60 min. Airdate: 6/9/77. Production Company: MGM. Director: Robert Moore. Executive Producer: Michael Leves. Producer: Sam Denoff. Writer: Neil Simon. Creator: Neil Simon, from his play. Playwright Neil Simon scripted this adaptation of his play, which became a hit movie starring Walter Matthau and George Burns as Willie Clark and A1 Lewis, two ex-vaudevillians who dislike each other but, deep down, have a great deal of affection for one another. In the proposed TV series version, they are a geriatric odd couple forced by circumstances to share an apartment together. Michael Durrell is Willie's nephew and agent, Sarina Grant is Willie's nurse, Barra Grant is Al's daughter and George Wyner is his son-in-law. *Cast:* Red Buttons (as Willie Clark), Lionel Stander (A1 Lewis), Michael Durrell (Ben Clark), Bobbie Mitchell (Myrna Navazio), Sarina Grant (Muriel Green), George Wyner (Ray Banks), Barra Grant (Sylvia Banks), Philip Tanzini (Gary Banks), Danny Mora (Julio), Bella Bruck (Mrs. Kraise), Ann Cooper (Anita DeVane).

1502. **Susan and Sam.** 30 min. Airdate: 7/13/77. Production Company: Helix Productions. Director: Jay Sandrich. Producers: Alan Alda and Marc Merson. Writer: Alan Alda. Creator: Alan Alda. Susan (Christine Belford) and Sam (Robert Foxworth) are lovers and reporters for Worldweek Magazine, but their competition for hot stories, and their conflicting lifestyles (she's quiet and restrained, he's hard- boiled and loud) make life difficult. *Cast:* Christine Belford (as Susan Foster), Robert Foxworth (Sam Denton), Lee Bergere (Doug Braden), Jack Bannon (Percy), Rod McCary (Lionel), Alan Oppenheimer (Hilly), Christina Hart (Barbara), Dick Balduzzi (Waiter), Maurice Sneed (Felix).

NBC / DRAMA

1503. **Abel Marsh (aka Girl in the Empty Grave). 2** hours. Airdate: 9/20/77. Production Company: MGM. Director: Lou Antonio. Executive Producer: Richard 0. Linke. Producers: Gordon A. Webb and Lane Slate. Writer: Lane Slate. Creator: Lane Slate. The fourth attempt, and the first of two *Abel Marsh* pilots, to turn the 1972 James Garner movie *They Only Kill Their Masters* into a TV series for Andy Griffith. The first three tries, starring Griffith as a resort town sheriff, were for ABC. *Cast:* Andy Griffith (as Abel Marsh), Mitzi Hoag (Gloria), James Cromwell (Deputy Malcolm Rossiter, Jr.), Claude Earl Jones (Deputy Fred), Sharon Spelman (Dr. Susan Glasgow), Hunter Von Leer (Deputy John), Jonathan Banks (Courtland Gates), Edward Winter (Dr. Peter Cabe), George Gaynes (David Allen), Byron Morrow (MacAlwee), Mary Robin Redd (Gilda), Robert F. Simon (Jedediah Partridge), Leonard J. Stone (Harry).

1504. **[Pilot #2] [Abel Marsh] The Deadly Game. 2** hours. Airdate: 12/3/77. Production Company: MGM. Director: Lane Slate. Executive Producer: Richard 0. Linke. Producer: Gordon A. Webb. Writer: Lane Slate. Creator: Lane

Slate. Marsh investigates a military cover-up involving a chemical spill. *Cast:* Andy Griffith (as Abel Marsh), Mitzi Hoag (Gloria), James Cromwell (Deputy Malcolm Rossiter, Jr.), Claude Earl Jones (Deputy Fred), Sharon Spelman (Dr. Susan Glasgow), Hunter Von Leer (Deputy John), Rebecca Balding (Amy Franklin), Eddie Foy, Jr. (Whit), Med Flory (Sgt. Redman), John Perak (Jake), Steve Zacharias (Vernon), Ellen Blake (Barkeep), Dan O'Herlihy (Col. Stryker), Fran Ryan (Mrs. Beezly), Miriam-Byrd Nethery (Polly), Christopher Tenney (Jeff).

1505. **Adventures of Freddy (aka The Magnificent Magical Magnet of Santa Mesa).** 90 min. Airdate: 6/19/77. Production Companies: David Gerber Productions and Columbia Pictures Television. Director: Hy Averback. Executive Producer: David Gerber. Producers: Hy Averback and James Brown. Writers: Dee Caruso and Gerald Gardner. Music: Allyn Ferguson and Jack Elliott. The misadventures of Freddy, a brilliant, good-hearted, but naive inventor whose creations, while always showing the promise of being worth millions to the company he works for, eventually cause nothing but problems—like the world's most powerful magnet. *Cast:* Michael Burns (Freddy Griffith), Bruce Kimmel (Cat Bixby), Susan Blanchard (Marcie Hamilton), Jane Connell (Mrs. Griffith), Keene Curtis (Undershaft), Conrad Janis (Kreel), Tom Poston (Bensinger), Susan Sullivan (McCaulley), Harry Morgan (Strange), Loni Anderson (Miss Daroon).

1506. **Benny & Barney: Las Vegas Undercover.** 90 min. Airdate: 1/9/77. Production Companies: Glen Larson Productions and Universal Television. Director: Ron Satlof. Executive Producer: Glen A. Larson. Producer: Ron Satlof. Writer: Glen A. Larson. Creator: Glen A. Larson. Music: Stu Phillips and Glen A. Larson. The adventures of two Las Vegas cops (Terry Kiser and Tim Thomerson) who double as night club performers. *Cast:* Terry Kiser (as Benny Kowalski), Tim Thomerson (Barney Hill), Jack Colvin (Lt. Callan), Jane Seymour (Margie Parks), Hugh O'Brien (Jack Davis), Jack Cassidy (Jules Rosen), Pat Harrington (Joey Gallion), Rodney Dangerfield (Manager), Marty Allen (Higgie), George Gobel (Drunk), Bobby Troup (Paul Mizener), Michael Pataki (Sgt. Ross), Dick Gautier (Will Dawson), Ted Cassidy (Jake Tuttle), Don Marshall (Detective Vincent), Rosalind Miles (Alice), Dorothy Konrad (Landlady), Larry Levine (Pit Boss), Dennis Levine (Gambler).

1507. **Bunco.** 60 min. Airdate: 1/13/77. Production Company: Lorimar Productions. Director: Alexander Singer. Executive Producers: Lee Rich and Philip Capice.

Producer: Jerry Ludwig. Writer: Jerry Ludwig. Creator: Jerry Ludwig. Music: John Parker. Tom Selleck (without his mustache) and Robert Urich may not have won over the network as a pair of Bunco cops trying to close down a school for swindlers, but they'd each later become popular private eyes—Selleck on *Magnum P.I.* and Urich on *Vega$* and *Spenser: For Hire. Cast:* Tom Selleck (as Ben Gordean), Robert Urich (Ed Walker), Donna Mills (Frankie Dawson), Milt Kogan (Lt. Hyatt), Alan Feinstein (Sonny), Michael Sacks (Dixon), Will Geer (Winky), Arte Johnson (Yousha), Bobby Van (Victim).

1508. **The Busters (aka Ransom for Alice).** 60 min. Airdate: 6/2/77. Production Company: Universal Television. Director: David Lowell Rich. Producer: Franklin Barton. Writer: Jim Byrnes. Music: David Rose. Gil Gerard is Brennan and Yvette Mimieux is Casey, two U.S. Marshalls working undercover in 1880s Seattle. Their names were later changed to Clint Kirby and Jenny Cullen. In the pilot, they look for a 19-year-old girl kidnapped by white slavers. *Cast:* Gil Gerard (as Brennan/Clint Kirby), Yvette Mimieux (Casey/Jenny Cullen), Charles Napier (Pete Phelan), Laurie Prange (Alice Halliday), Barnard Hughes (Jess Halliday), Gavin MacLeod (Yankee Sullivan), Gene Barry (Harry Darew), Harris Yulin (Isaac Pratt), Mills Watson (Toby), John Dennan (Johnson), Robert Hogan (Whitaker Halli- day).

1509. **Charlie Cobb: Nice Night for a Hanging.** 2 hours. Airdate: 6/9/77. Production Company: Universal Television. Director: Richard Michaels. Executive Producers: Richard Levinson and William Link. Producer: Peter S. Fischer. Writer: Peter S. Fischer. Creators: Richard Levinson and William Link. Music: Mike Post and Pete Carpenter. Clu Gulager is a private eye in the Old West who, in the pilot, is hired to find a wealthy rancher's long-lost daughter who was kidnapped many years ago. *Cast:* Clu Gulager (as Charlie Cobb), Blair Brown (Charity), Ralph Bellamy (McVea), Stella Stevens (Martha McVea), Tricia O'Neil (Angelica Adams), Pernell Roberts (Sheriff Yates), George Firth (Conroy), Christopher Connelly (Waco), Carmen Mathews (Miss Cumberland), Josh Taylor (Virg).

1510. **Code Name: Diamond Head.** 90 min. Airdate: 5/3/77. Production Company: Quinn Martin Productions. Director: Jeannot Szwarc. Executive Producer: Quinn Martin. Producer: Paul King. Writer: Paul King. Creator: Paul King. Music: Morton Stevens. Roy Thinnes is Johnny Paul, a Hawaii-based secret agent who has to stop a spy (Ian McShane) from stealing a poisonous gas. Code-named "Diamond Head," Paul's cover is that of a womanizing, beachcombing gambler. When he's on assignment, he works closely with Zulu (played by Zulu) and Tso- Tsing (France Nuyen), a nightclub owner with well-placed connections in island society. Morton Stevens, who did the music for *Hawaii Five-0*, did the score for this pilot. *Cast:* Roy Thinnes (as Johnny Paul), France Nuyen (Tso-Tsing), Zulu (himself), Ian McShane (Sean Donavan/Father Horton/ Col. Butler), Ward Costello (Capt. Macintosh), Don Knight (H.K. Muldoon), Eric Braeden (Ernest Graeber), Dennis Patrick (Commander Yarnell), Alex Henteloff (Edward Sherman), Frank Michael Liu (Sakai), Ernest Harada (Hero Yamamoto), Lee Stetson (Tanner), Harry Endo (Dr. En-Ping), Eric Christmas (Father Murphy).

1511. Corey: For the People (aka A.D.A.). 90 min. Airdate: 6/12/77. Production Companies: Jenni Productions and Columbia Pictures Television. Director: Buzz Kulik. Producer: Buzz Kulik. Writer: Alvin Boretz. Creator: Alvin Boretz. John Rubinstein is a Nassau County, N.Y., assistant district attorney who doesn't believe an apparently battered wife killed her husband in self-defense. Eugene Roche is his boss, the district attorney. *Cast:* John Rubinstein (as Dan Corey), Eugene Roche (Patrick Shannon), Carol Rossen (Harriet Morgan), Wynn Irwin (Detective Gilman), Ronny Cox (Dr. Hanley), Ann Sweeny (Laurie Casey), Steve Pearlman (Nick Wolf), Frank Campanella (Judge Taylor), Joan Pringle (Katie Ryan), Arnold Soboloff (Fen- niger), Lana Wood (Janet Hanley), Kip Niven (Andy Hansen), Bill Quinn (Justin Milford), Richard Venture (Spence Holland), Stephen Burleigh (Sam Myers), Deborah Ryan (Judy Corey), Yale McClosket (Mollie Schultz), Pitt Herbert (Judge Stone), Betty Carvalo (Gloria), Bob Gunner (Dr. Richard Morgan).

1512. Cover Girls. 90 min. Airdate: 5/18/77. Production Company: Columbia Pictures Television. Director: Jerry London. Executive Producer: David Gerber. Producers: Charles B. Fitzsimons and Mark Rodgers. Writer: Mark Rodgers. Music: Richard Shores. Cornelia Sharpe and Jayne Kennedy are globetrotting fashion models who are actually secret agents working for stone-faced Don Galloway. George Lazenby, who once played James Bond, guest stars. *Cast:* Cornelia Sharpe (as Linda Allen), Jayne Kennedy (Monique Lawrence), Don Galloway (James Andrews), George Lazenby (Michael), Vince Edwards (Russell Bradner), Jerry Douglas (Fritz Porter), Michael Baselson (Paul Reynolds), Don Johnson (Johnny Wilson), Ellen Travolta (Ziggy), Sean Garrison (Sven), Bill Overton (Football Player), Ellen Travolta (Photographer).

1513. **Deadly Triangle (aka Stedman).** 90 min. Airdate: 5/19/77. Production Company: Columbia Pictures Television. Director: Charles S. Dubin. Executive Producer: Bruce Weitz. Producer: Robert Stambler. Writer: Carl Gottlieb. Yet another attempt to sell the series concept pitched in numerous flop pilots starring Andy Griffith as a crimesolving ski resort sheriff (*McNeill—Winter Kill, Adams of Eagle Lake, Abel Marsh*, etc.). This time, a new studio, production team and cast tackled the concept. Dale Robinette is Stedman, a former international skier who's elected sheriff of a small resort community. Geoffrey Lewis is head of the ski patrol and Linda Scruggs Bogart runs a local hotel. This was the first of three more unsuccessful pilots. This time, Stedman finds the killer of a skier. *Crisis in Sun Valley*, a compilation of two one-hour pilots entitled *Outward Bound* and *The Vanishing Kind* followed in March 1978. *Cast:* Dale Robinette (as Sheriff Bill Stedman), Taylor Lacher (Deputy Archie Sykes), Linda Scruggs Bogart (Joanne Price), Robert Lansing (Chuck Cole), Diana Muldaur (Edith Cole), Geoffrey Lewis (Red Bayliss), Maggie Wellman (Mary Leonard).

1514. **Exoman.** 2 hours. Airdate: 6/18/77. Production Company: Universal Television. Director: Richard Irving. Executive Producer: Richard Irving. Producer: Lionel E. Siegel. Writers: Martin Caidin, Howard Rodman, and Lionel E. Siegel, from a story by Martin Caidin and Henri Simoun. Creator: Martin Caidin. Music: Dana Kaproff. Created by Martin Caidin, the man who devised *The Six Million Dollar Man*. David Ackroyd is a psychics professor who, after he apprehends a bank robber, is gunned down by hitmen. Crippled, he creates a supersuit that revital- izes his limbs and gives him superhuman strength—and enables him to not only catch the hitman, but wage a continuing battle against crime. Caidin says the pilot "was destroyed by the marketing people at Universal. They said 'You have to build the suit this way, so it'll be easier to mass-produce toys.' They killed the damn thing, turned it into cardboard. We had a great show planned, but execution was *pffft.*" *Cast:* David Ackroyd (as Nick Conrad), Anne Schedeen (Emily Frost), A. Martinez (Raphael), Jose Ferrer (Kermit Haas), Harry Morgan (Travis), Kevin McCarthy (Kamensky), Jack Colvin (Martin), Jonathan Segal (Rubenstein), Richard Narita (Yamaguchi), John Moio (Dominic Leandro).

1515. **Flight to Holocaust.** 2 hours. Airdate: 3/27/77. Production Companies: Aycee Productions and First Artists. Director: Bernard Kowalski. Producer: A.C. Lyles. Writers: Anthony Lawrence and Robert Heverly. Creator: A.C. Lyles. Music: Paul Williams. Patrick Wayne, Chris Mitchum, and Fawne Harriman are an elite rescue team that helps save the passengers of an airplane that crashed into a skyscraper—and remains precariously lodged in the 20th floor of the damaged building. When this pilot aired, NBC took out an advertisement that read: "*She was a circus performer . . . they were combat veterans . . . together* they made the darn- dest rescue team—ever!" Then, in small print, it said: "To the Viewer: How would you feel about a series based on tonight's program? Your answer on the coupon below will be appreciated. Thank you." The coupon asked viewers if "the idea of making a series based on 'Flight to Holocaust' is a) terrific, b) good, c) Ho-hum." Guess what the answer was. *Cast:* Chris Mitchum (as Mark Gates), Patrick Wayne (Les Taggart), Fawne Harriman (Scotty March), Desi Arnaz, Jr. (Rick Benter), Paul Williams (Colorado Davis), Sid Caesar (Sid Beam), Anne Schedeen (Linda Michaels), Lloyd Nolan (Wilten Benter), Greg Morris (Dr. Jeff Davis), Rory Calhoun (Ed Davis), Robert Patten (Gordon Stokes), Katherine Bowman (Sheila Waters), Shirley O'Hara (Mrs. Benter), Louis Elias (Ernie Roberts), Robert Gooden (George Balford).

1516. **The Hunted Lady.** 2 hours. Airdate: 11/28/77. Production Company: Quinn Martin Productions. Director: Richard Lang. Executive Producer: Quinn Martin. Producer: William Robert Yates. Writer: William Robert Yates. Music: Laurence Rosenthal. Once again, Donna Mills is "on the run." She was a woman chased by her hitman husband in CBS' *Woman on the Run* this season, now she's an undercover policewoman framed for a murder she didn't commit—and pursued by the police and mafia hitmen. *Cast:* Donna Mills (as Susan Reilly), Andrew Duggan (Capt. John Shannon), Lawrence Casey (Robert Armstrong), Alan Feinstein (Sgt. Stanley Arizzio), Geoffrey Lewis (Mr. Eckert), Michael McGuire (Lt. Henry Jacks), Jenny O'Hara (Carol Arizzio), Quinn Redecker (Max Devine), Robert Reed (Dr. Arthur Sills), Will Sampson (Uncle George), Mario Roccuzzo (Angie), Richard Yniquez (David Todd), David Darlow (James Radford), Panchito Gomez (Johnny Ute), Mark Miller (Senator Roger Clements), Patti Kohoon (Cathy Clements), Robert Nathan (Lewis Clements), Hank Brandt (Marvin Roister), Taylor Lacher (Sheriff Clancy).

1517. **The Man with the Power.** 90 min. Airdate: 5/24/77. Production Company: Universal Television. Director: Nicholas Sgarro. Producer: Alan Balter. Writer: Alan Balter. Music: Pat Williams. Robert Neill is a high school teacher, but not an ordinary high school teacher. He's actually the child of an alien being an earth woman—and he uses his incredible psychic powers as a part-time secret agent who, on this mission, protects a visiting princess from killers. *Cast:* Bob Neill (as Eric Smith), Persis Khambatta (Princess Siri), Vic Morrow (Paul), Noel DeSouza (Shanda), Rene Assa (Sajid), Tim O'Connor (Agent Bloom), Roger Perry (Farnsworth), Jason Wingreen (Klein).

1518. Murder in Peyton Place. 2 hours. Airdate: 10/3/77. Production Company: 20th Century Fox. Director: Peter Katz Productions. Producer: Bruce Kessler. Writer: Richard DeRoy. Creator: Grace Metalious. Music: Laurence Rosenthal. An attempt to revive the 1964–1969 serial. In this pilot, Rodney Harrington (played originally by Ryan O'Neal) and Alison MacKenzie (Mia Farrow in clips from the original series) are killed. Another attempt was made to continue the series in 1986's *Peyton Place: The Next Generation. Cast:* Christopher Connelly (as Norman), Tim O'Connor (Elliot Carson), Ed Nelson (Dr. Rossi), Dorothy Malone (Constance), Joyce Jillson (Jill), Janet Margolin (Betty), David Hedison (Steven Cord), Stella Stevens (Stella Chernak), Marj Dusay (Ellen), James Booth (Crimpton), Jonathan Goldsmith (Stan), Charlotte Stewart (Denise Haley), Kaz Garas (Springer), Linda Gray (Carla Cord), Kimberly Beck (Bonnie Buehler), Royal Dano (Bo Buehler), Priscilla Morrill (Mae Buehler), David Kyle (Billie Kaiserman), Norman Burton (Jay Kamens), Charles Siebert (Kaiserman), Chris Nelson (Andy Considine), Robert Deman (Tristan), Gale Sladstone (Ruth), Catherine Bach (Linda), Edward Bell (David Roerich).

1519. Nowhere to Hide (aka Scanlon). 90 min. Airdate: 1/5/77. Production Company: Viacom Enterprises. Director: Jack Starrett. Executive Producer: Mark Carliner. Producers: Edward Anhalt and Rift Fournier. Writer: Edward Anhalt, from a story by Edward Anhalt and Rift Fournier. Creator: Edward Anhalt. Music: Ray Ellis. Lee Van Cleef is a stony U.S. Marshall who, in the pilot, protects hitman Tony Musante from getting killed before he can testify in a mob trial. Writer Anhalt and director Starrett both appeared in the movie, as did one of producer Fournier's relatives. This pilot was based on the life of U.S. Marshall John Partington. *Cast:* Lee Van Cleef (Ike Scanlon), Tony Musante (Joey Faber), Lelia Goldoni (Linda Faber), Noel Fournier (Frankie Faber), Charlie Robinson (Willoughby), Edward Anhalt (Alberto Amarici), John Alderman (Vittorio), David Proval (Rick), Clay Tanner (Lee), John Randolph (Narrator), Richard Narita (Lou), Stafford Morgan (Ken), Blackie Dammett (John), Bud Davis (Rudy), Vince Di Paolo (Frederico), John Stefano (Pilot #1), Bill Yeager (Co-pilot), Jack Starrett (Gus), Brian Cutler (Gaynes), Isaac Ruiz

(Hernandez), Ric Dano (Torn), Gene Massey (Coxswain), Araceli Rey (Mrs. Amarrei), Hugette Pateraude (Deputy Rowan).

1520. Panic in Echo Park (aka Michael Stoner, M.D.). 90 min. Airdate: 6/23/77. Production Company: Edgar Scherick & Associates. Director: John Llewellyn Moxey. Producers: Edgar Scherick and Daniel H. Blatt. Associate Producer: Robert Greenhut. Writer: Dalene Young. Music: Johnnie Spence. Sung by: Dorian Hare wood. Dorian Harewood is a black resident physician at a hospital located in the Echo Park district of Los Angeles where he grew up. His girlfriend (Kate Adams) has very different roots—she's white, and comes from an upper-class Beverly Hills family. In the pilot, he investigates what seems like an epidemic striking low-income families in a slum apartment building. *Cast:* Dorian Harewood (as Dr. Michael Stoner), Robin Gammell (Dr. Tishman), Kate Adams (Cynthia), Norman Bartold (Harold Dickerson), Ramon Bieri (Fallen Reilly), Regis J. Cordic (Dr. Gavin O'Connor), Vernon Weddle (Mason), George Brenlin (Tony Lamberti), Tamu (Angie), Jane Elliot (Ebony), James Hong (Larrly Lee).

1521. The Possessed. 90 min. Airdate: 5/1/77. Production Company: Warner Bros. Television. Director: Jerry Thorpe. Executive Producer: Jerry Thorpe. Producer: Philip Mandelker. Writer: John Sacret Young. Music: Leonard Rosenman. James Farentino is a defrocked cleric (for adultery and alcoholism) who, after a serious car accident, is "saved" in order to battle supernatural evil wherever it lurks. In the pilot, it lurks at a girls' school. *Cast:* James Farentino (Kevin Leahy), Joan Hackett (Louise Gelson), Claudette Nevins (Ellen Sumner), Eugene Roche (Sgt. Taplinger), Ann Dusenberry (Weezie), Harrison Ford (Paul Winjam), Diana Scar- wid (Lane), P.J. Soles (Marty), Susan Walden (Sandy), Dinah Manoff (Celia), Ethelinn Block (Barry).

1522. Quail Lake (aka Pine Canyon Is Burning). 90 min. Airdate: 5/18/77. Production Company: Universal Television. Director: Christian Nyby, III. Executive Producer: R.A. Cinader. Producers: Gino Grimaldi and Hannah Shearer. Writer: R.A. Cinader. Music: Lee Holdridge. Kent McCord is Capt. William Stone, a widower who lives with his two children in Quail Lake, a wilderness area in the northern edge of Los Angeles County. Stone operates a one-man fire station that's not only a 24-hour job, but serves as home to his family. *Cast:* Kent McCord (as Capt. William Stone), Shane Sinutko (Michael Stone), Megan McCord (Margaret Stone), Diana Muldaur (Sandra), Andrew Duggan

(Capt. Ed Wilson), Dick Bakalyan (Charlie Edison), Brit Lind (Anne Walker), Curtis Credel (Whitney Olson), Sandy McPeak (Pete Madison), Larry Delaney (Captain), Joan Roberts (Woman).

1523. **Racket Squad.** 60 min. Airdate: 3/8/77. Production Companies: David Gerber Productions and Columbia Pictures Television. Executive Producer: David Gerber. Producers: Ed DeBlasio and Douglas Benton. Writer: Ed De Blasio. Aired as the "Silky Chamberlain" episode of *Police Woman*. Cheryl Ladd is an undercover cop who, partnered with a veteran Bunco officer played by Philip Clark, con the conmen and bring them to justice. In the pilot, they tried to con swindler William Windom. Other guest stars included Vito Scotti and Tom Ligon.

1524. **Spectre.** 2 hours. Airdate: 5/21/77. Production Companies: Norway Productions and 20th Century Fox. Director: Clive Donner. Executive Producer: Gene Roddenberry. Producer: Gordon Scott. Writers: Gene Roddenberry and Samuel A. Peeples, from a story by Gene Roddenberry. Creator: Gene Roddenberry. Music: John Cameron. An entertaining pilot which cast Robert Culp and Gig Young as a pair of ghost-hunters reminiscent of Sherlock Holmes and Watson. Culp is Sebastian, a flamboyant occult expert and the victim of a voodoo spell which could prove fatal. Young is Hamm, his alcoholic doctor, friend, and aide. Young committed suicide in 1978. *Cast:* Robert Culp (as William Sebastian), Gig Young (Dr. "Hamm" Hamilton), James Villiers (Sir Geoffrey Cyon), John Hirt (Mitri Cyon), Jenny Runacre (Synda), Gordon Jackson (Inspector Cabell), Ann Bell (Anitra Cyon), Majel Barrett (Lilith).

1525. **Target Risk (aka The Three Thousand Mile Chase).** 2 hours. Airdate: 6/16/77. Production Companies: Public Arts and Universal Television. Director: Russ Mayberry. Executive Producer: Roy Huggins. Producer: Jo Swerling, Jr. Writer: Phil DeGuere, from a story by Roy Huggins. Creator: Roy Huggins. Music: Elmer Bernstein. A second unsuccessful attempt by Roy Huggins to sell his 1974 concept *Target Risk*, about the adventures of a bonded courier. This time, Cliff De Young is the hero (replacing Bo Svenson), who has to escort a witness (Glenn Ford) to a murder trial. *Cast:* Cliff De Young (as Matt), Glenn Ford (Dvorak), Blair Brown (Rachel Kane), Priscilla Pointer (Emma Dvorak), David Spielberg (Frank Oberon), Brendon Dillon (Ambrose Finn), Lane Allan (Livingston), Michael Mancini (Quinn), Carmen Argenziano (Santeen), Don Maxwell (Seiden), John Zenda (Inspector), Tom Bower (Richette), Roger Aaron Brown (Prosecutor),

Titos Vandis (Vince Leone), Marc Alaimo (Burrell), Michael J. London (Jacoby), Stephen Coit (Steinhardt), Abraham Alvarez (Bathes), Tanya Swerling (Princess Y), Hugh Gillin (Jimbo), June Whitly Taylor (Mrs. Campbell), George Shug Fisher (Biker), Richard LePore (D.A.), Michael Don Wagner (Judge).

1526. Terraces. 90 min. Airdate: 6/27/77. Production Companies: Charles Fries Productions and Worldvision. Director: Lila Garrett. Executive Producer: Charles Fries. Producer: Lila Garrett. Writers: George Kirgo and Lila Garrett. Music: Pete Matz. A proposed serial revolving around the tenants of a swank high- rise apartment in Santa Monica, California. *Cast:* Kit McDonough (as Julie), Bill Gerber (Greg Loomis), Eliza Garrett (Beth Loomis), Jane Dulo (Roberta Robbins), Arny Freeman (Martin Robbins), Lloyd Bochner (Dr. Roger Cabe), James Phillips (Alex), Julie Newmar (Chalane), Lola Albright (Dorothea Cabe), Tim Thomerson (Steve), Allan Rich (Vogel), Ralph Manza (Doorman).

1978–1979

1527. Chateau Suavely (aka Suavely). 30 min. Airdate: 6/24/78. Production Company: Viacom Enterprises. Director: Hal Cooper. Producers: Roland Kibbee and Dean Hargrove. Writers: Roland Kibbee and Dean Hargrove. Creators: John Cleese and Connie Booth. Based on the BBC series *Fawlty Towers*, which starred husband and wife John Cleese and Connie Booth, who also wrote all the episodes. The Americanized version is almost identical in concept—the misadventures of an obnoxious, inept, loud-mouthed, perpetually frustrated man (Harvey Korman) who manages an off-the-highway hotel in Middle America with his wife (Betty White), who rules over him with an iron fist. Their staff includes a bellhop who barely understands English (Frank LaLoggia) and a bright college student working as a waitress (Deborah Zon). ABC reworked the concept, with Bea Arthur as star, for the short-lived 1983 series *Amandas*. *Cast:* Harvey Korman (as Henry Snavely), Betty White (Gladys Snavely), Deborah Zon (Connie), Frank LaLoggia (Petro), Ivor Francis (Chief), Jack Dodson (Mr. Bishop), George Pentecost (Mr. Foley).

1528. Fast Lane Blues. 30 min. Production Company: Viacom Enterprises. Producers: William Blinn and Jerry Thorpe. Writers: William Blinn and Jerry Thorpe. Creators: William Blinn and Jerry Thorpe. A huge oil company sponsors a cross-country scavenger hunt that has a wide variety of people racing in cars to 12 consecutive American cities in turn to search for hidden gold stars. The driver who passes through all the cities and finds the most stars wins $1 million. The performers are Talia Balsam, Tony Danza, Richard Herd, Gary Pendergast, and Sharon Ullrick.

1529. Jackie and Darlene. 30 min. Airdate: 7/8/78. Production Company: Aaron Ruben Productions. Director: Russ Petranto. Executive Producer: Aaron Ruben. Producer: Gene Marcione. Writer: Aaron Ruben. Creator: Aaron Ruben. The adventures of two black women—Jackie, a rookie police officer (Sarina Grant) and Darlene, a clerical worker (Anna Pagan)—who work at the same suburban police precinct and are also roommates. Lou Frizzell is the Sgt. Guthrie, their boss, and Nathaniel Taylor, Jr. is Jackie's boyfriend.

1530. **Mother, Juggs and Speed.** 30 min. Airdate: 8/17/78. Production Company: 20th Century Fox. Director: John Rich. Producer: Bruce Geller. Writer: Tom Mankiewicz. Creator: Tom Mankiewicz. Based on the movie, which starred Raquel Welch, Bill Cosby, Harvey Keitel and was written by Tom Mankiewicz. The proposed series, like the movie, is about the reckless paramedic team driving a rundown ambulance for a ramshackle company. *Cast:* Ray Vitte (as Mother), Joanne Nail (Jennifer "Juggs" Juggston), Joe Penny (Speed), Harvey Lembeck (Harry Fishbine), Shay Duffin (Whiplash Moran), Barbara Minkus (Mrs. Fishbine), Rod McCary (Murdock), Jan Shutan (Mrs. Barry), Charlotte Stewart (Iris), Marcus Smythe (Tom).

1531. **Sister Terri.** 30 min. Airdate: 5/27/78. Production Company: Paramount Television. Director: Jerry Paris. Executive Producers: Bob Brunner and Arthur Silver. Producer: Jeff Ganz. Writers: Bob Brunner and Arthur Silver. Creators: Bob Brunner and Arthur Silver. Music: Don Peake. Pam Dawber is Sister Terri, a nun in an inner-city parish elementary school where she doubles as a gym coach. She's also raising her teenage sister (Robbie Lee) in the apartment they share near the convent. Scott Colomby is her sister's boyfriend. *Cast:* Pam Dawber (as Sister Terri), Allyn Ann McLerie (Mother Superior), Amy Johnson (Sister Agatha), Robbie Lee (Samantha), Scott Colomby (Angel), Kimberly La Page (Jenny).

1532. **Three on a Date.** Production Company: ABC Circle Films. No production staff was aligned with this half-hour sitcom concept, which was lifted from the two-hour TV movie of the same name, which aired on 2/17/78 and was based on a book by Stephanie Buffington. The movie focused on four winning couples from *The Dating Game* and their Hawaiian vacation "dates." The proposed sitcom would star Forbesy Russell as the gameshow's beautiful female chaperone, based in a luxurious Hawaiian hotel, who would escort couples from the mainland on their exciting vacation. Sometimes this would lead to conflicts with her often puzzled boyfriend and the stuffy hotel manager, who thinks being involved with the gameshow is a mistake.

1533. **What's Up, Doc?** 30 min. Airdate: 5/27/78. Production Company: Warner Bros. Television. Director: E.W. Swackhamer. Executive Producer: Hal Kanter. Producers: Charles B. Fitzsimons and Michael Norell. Writer: Michael Norell. Based on the movie, which starred Ryan O'Neal as a stiff and uptight geology professor who, although engaged to a shrewish woman (Madeline Kahn), falls in love with a wild, carefree, fun-loving incarnation of Bugs Bunny (Barbra Streisand) while on a trip to San Francisco. In the pilot version, Barry Van Dyke is the professor, Caroline McWilliams is his former fiancée, and Harriet Hall is his new love. *Cast:* Barry Van Dyke (as Howard Bannister), Harriet Hall (Judy Maxwell), Caroline McWilliams (Claudia), Don Porter (Urban Wyatt), Neva Patterson (Amanda Wyatt), Jeffrey Kramer (Fabian Leek).

ABC / DRAMA

1534. Kate Bliss and the Ticker Tape Kid. 2 hours. Airdate: 5/26/78. Production Company: Aaron Spelling Productions. Director: Burt Kennedy. Executive Producers: Aaron Spelling and Douglas S. Cramer. Producers: Richard E. Lyons and E. Duke Vincent. Writer: William Bowers. Music: Jeff Alexander. Suzanne Pleshette is an investigator in the old West who, in the pilot, helps out a land baron being harassed by a stock broker turned outlaw. *Cast:* Suzanne Pleshette (as Kate Bliss), Don Meredith (Clint Allison), Harry Morgan (Hugo Peavey), David Huddleston (Sheriff), Tony Randall (Lord Seymour Devery), Burgess Meredith (William Blackstone), Buck Taylor (Joe), Jerry Hardin (Bud Dozier), Gene Evans (Fred Williker), Don Collier (Tim), Alice Hirson (Beth Dozier), Harry Carey, Jr. (Deputy Luke), Richard Herd (Donovan), James Brewer (Ben), Blair Burrows (Tad), George Dunn (Jim Haggerty), Alice Backes (Miss Grantland), Ned Wertimer (Preacher).

1535. Lassie: A New Beginning. 2 hours. Airdates: 9/17/78 and 9/24/78. Production Company: McDermott/Wrather Productions. Director: Don Chaffey. Executive Producer: Tom McDermott. Producers: Jack Miller and William Beaudine, Jr. Writer: Jack Miller. Creator: Jack Miller. Music: Jerrold Immel. This attempt to fashion a new *Lassie* series has a complicated back-story. There were two brothers in love with the same woman—and she chose one of them. The other moves west and cuts himself off from his family. Now, years later, the couple is killed in an accident, leaving their 14-year-old son (Shane Sinutko), nine-year-old daughter (Sally Boyden), and their pet dog Lassie orphaned. The grandmother takes the two kids and their pet to live with their bachelor uncle (John Reilly), editor of a small town newspaper, but she dies on the way. *Cast:* John Reilly (as Stuart Stratton), Sally Boyden (Sally Stratton), Shane Sinutko (Chip Stratton), Lee Bryant (Kathy McKen- drick), David Wayne (Dr. Amos Rheams), Gene Evans (Sheriff Marsh), Jeff Harlan (Buzz McKendrick), Jeanette Nolan (Ada Stratton),

John McIntire (Dr. Spreckles), Charles Tyner (Asa Bluel), Jim Antonio (Mr. Waldrop), Gwen Van Dam (Mrs. Waldrop), Woody Chambliss (Victor Turley), Lucille Benson (Juno), Logan Ramsey (Flannagan), Helen Page Camp (Miss Tremayne).

1536. **True Grit (aka True Grit: A Further Adventure).** 2 hours. Airdate: 5/19/78. Production Company: Paramount Television. Director: Richard T. Heffron. Producer: Sandor Stern. Writer: Sandor Stern, from characters created by Charles Portis. Music: Earle Hagen. Based on the book *True Grit*, a western which inspired the 1969 movie of the same name, and the 1975 sequel *Rooster Cogburn*, both of which starred John Wayne as a rough, grizzled, hard-drinking, one-eyed U.S. Marshall. Warren Oates, who last season had the unenviable task of stepping into Bogart's shoes for *The African Queen*, has the equally uncomfortable task of sitting in the Duke's saddle (Wayne won an Oscar in the role). In the pilot, Cogburn agrees to take an orphaned teenage girl (Lisa Pelikan) from Arkansas to her relatives in California. The proposed series would follow their adventures along the way. *Cast:* Warren Oates (as Rooster Cogburn), Lisa Pelikan (Mattie Ross), Lee Meriwether (Annie Sumner), James Stephens (Joshua Sumner), Jeff Osterhage (Chris Sumner), Lee Montgomery (Daniel Sumner), Ramon Bieri (Sheriff Ambrose), Jack Fletcher (Clerk), Parley Baer (Rollins), Lee DeBroux (Skorby), Fredric Cook (Chaka), Redmond Gleeson (Harrison), Gregg Palmer (Slatter), Derrel Maury (Creed), Roger Frazier (Moses Turk), John Perak (Tom Lacey), Dom Spencer (Doc Wade), Burt Douglas (Bast), Simon Tyme (Udall), Charles Burke (Hopkins).

1537. **The Two-Five.** 90 min. Airdate: 4/14/78. Production Company: Universal Television. Director: Bruce Kessler. Executive Producer: R.A. Cinader. Producers: Gian R. Grimaldi and Hannah L. Shearer. Writers: Joseph Polizzi and R.A. Cinader. Creators: Joseph Polizzi and R.A. Cinader. Music: Peter Matz. The first of two light-hearted pilots focusing on the misadventures of two irreverent undercover cops (Don Johnson and Joe Bennett) who are transferred to the "Siberia" of precincts—the 25th Precinct, aka the Two-Five—after they inadvertently arrest the mayor's mother. George Murdock is their commander, who is biding his time until retirement and wants nothing in his precinct to attract the attention of his superiors or the press. *Cast:* Don Johnson (as Charlie Morgan), Joe Bennett (Frank Sarno), George Murdock (Commander Malloy), Michael Durrell (Vinnie Lombardo), John Crawford (Capt. Paul Carter), Carlene Watkins (Dale

Von Krieg), Tara Buckman (Angel), Jacques Aubuchon (Pierre Menoir), Marty Zagon (Waldo), Richard O'Brien (Chief), Sandy McPeak (Ralston), Curtis Credei (Cliff Roberts), Henry Olek (Bandit).

1538. [Pilot #2] The Two-Five. 60 min. Airdate: 1/7/79. Production Company: Universal Television. Director: Jules Irving. Executive Producer: R.A. Cinader. Producer: Gino Grimaldi. Writer: R.A. Cinader, from a story by R.A. Cinader and Joseph Polizzi. Creators: R.A. Cinader and Joseph Polizzi. Detectives Morgan and Sarno scramble to use a mob accountant's detailed printout of a crime syndicate's operation bring down the bad guys before other lawmen beat them to it. Cast: Don Johnson (as Charlie Morgan), Joe Bennett (Frank Sarno), John Crawford (Capt. Carter), George Murdock (Commander Malloy), Michael Durrell (Vinnie Lombardo), Shelly Berman (J. Edward Ward).

1539. Wild and Wooly. 2 hours. Airdate: 2/20/78. Production Company: Aaron Spelling Productions. Director: Philip Leacock. Executive Producers: Aaron Spelling and Douglas S. Cramer. Producers: Earl W. Wallace and E. Duke Vincent. Writer: Earl W. Wallace. Music: Charles Bernstein. A frontier *Charlie's Angels* with Christine DeLisle, Susan Bigelow, and Elyssa Davalos as three ex-cons who, in the pilot, try to stop Teddy Roosevelt from being killed. Cast: Christine DeLisle (as Lacey Sommers), Susan Bigelow (Liz Hannah), Elyssa Davalos (Shiloh), Jessica Walter (Megan), Paul Burke (Tobias Singleton), Doug McClure (Delaney Burke), David Doyle (Teddy Roosevelt), Ross Martin (Otis Bergen), Vic Morrow (Warden Willis), Sherry Bain (Jessica), Charles Siebert (Sean), Med Flory (Burgie), Robert L. Wilkie (Demas Scott), Kenneth Tobey (Mark Hannah), Eugene Butler (Perty), Joan Crosby (Sophie), Wayne Grace (O'Rourke), Jim Lough (McHenry), Bill Smilie (Foreman), Borah Silver (Cooke), Marc Winters (Will), Joe Rainer (Capt. Merritt), Stephen Blood (Sheriff).

CBS / COMEDY

1540. Annie Flynn. 30 min. Airdate: 1/21/78. Production Company: Columbia Pictures Television. Director: Robert Moore. Producers: Coleman Mitchell and Geoffrey Neigher. Writers: Coleman Mitchell and Geoffrey Neigher. Creators: Coleman Mitchell and Geoffrey Neigher. The life of Annie Flynn (Barrie Young- fellow), a bright medical school student. She becomes good friends with a Chicano student (Carol Potter) who lives in the same building Annie does,which is managed by a pessimistic landlord (Louis Guss). Harvey Lewis is a brilliant, 18-year-old, first- year student and Annie's constant irritant. *Cast:* Barrie Youngfellow (as Annie Flynn), Carol Potter (C.C.), Harvey Lewis (Elliott Hoag), Louis Guss (Hoyt Hosloff), Charles Frank (Paul Lucas), Jack Fletcher (Mr. Braden), Lisa Loring (Sherry), Josh Grenrock (Marty Trellis), Rene Lippin (Stephanie).

1541. **Beane's of Boston.** 30 min. Airdate: 5/5/79. Production Company: Paramount Television. Director: Jerry Paris. Executive Producers: Garry Marshall and Tony Marshall. Producers: Bill Idelson and Sheldon Bull. Writers: Jeremy Lloyd, David Croft, Bill Idelson, and Sheldon Bull. Creators: Jeremy Lloyd and David Croft. Music: Don Peake. Writers Jeremy Lloyd and David Croft adapted their British series *Are You Being Served?* for American television with the help of sitcom king Garry Marshall. This proposed series would concentrate on the rivalry between the clerks and salespeople in the men's and women's clothing floor of a Boston department store. *Cast:* Tom Poston (as Mr. Beane), John Hillerman (John Peacock), Charlotte Rae (Mae Slocombe), George O'Hanlon, Jr. (Frank Beane), Lorna Patterson (Shirley Brahme), Alan Sues (George Humphreys), Morgan Farley (Mr. Granger), Larry Bishop (Mr. Lucas), Don Bexley (Mr. Johnson), Dana House (Ingrid).

1542. **Big City Boys.** 30 min. Airdate: 4/11/78. Production Companies: Warner Bros. Television and Silliphant/Konigsberg Productions. Director: Bill Per- sky. Executive Producer: Frank Königsberg. Producers: Bruce Paltrow and Stephanie Sills. Writer: Robert De Laurentis. A reworking of the flop 1977 CBS pilot *You're Gonna Love It Here.* Ethel Merman has been dropped, but otherwise the concept is pretty much the same. Austin Pendleton is a disorganized, flamboyant New York press agent who, when his brother and sister-in-law are imprisoned for tax evasion, takes in his organized, wise-cracking teenage nephew (Chris Barnes). *Cast:* Austin Pendleton (as Harry Buckman), Chris Barnes (Peter), Laurie Heinemann (Emily), Francesca Bill (Susan), David Yanez (Pancho).

1543. **Danny and the Mermaid.** 30 min. Airdate: 5/17/78. Production Company: Ivan Tors Productions. Director: Norman Abbott. Executive Producer: Ivan Tors. Producer: Budd Grossman. Writer: Budd Grossman. Creator: Ivan Tors. Danny is an oceanography student having troubles with his studies. He secretly befriends a mermaid, her dolphin, and her sea lion, all of whom help him explore the ocean. *Cast:* Harlee McBride (as Aqua), Patrick Collins (Danny Stevens), Ray Walston

(Prof. Stoneman), Rick Fazel (Turtle), Conrad Janis (Psychiatrist), Ancel Cook (Pilot).

1544. Fighting Nightingales. 30 min. Airdate: 1/16/78. Production Company: 20th Century Fox. Director: George Tyne. Producers: Barry Sand and Alan Unger. Writers: Barry Sand and Alan Unger. Creators: Barry Sand and Alan Unger. Music: Steve Kagan. From the studio that brought you *M*A *S*H*, comes this sitcom about army nurses stationed at a field hospital during the Korean War. Adrienne Barbeau stars as the easy-going, dedicated head nurse; Erica Yohn is the by-the- book career nurse; Stephanie Faracy is the ditzy model-turned-nurse; and Livia Genise is a street-smart Brooklyn native who is rough but competent. Kenneth Mars is the base commander, and Rod McCary is an accordion-playing, southern Baptist preacher. *Cast:* Adrienne Barbeau (as Major Kate Steele), Kenneth Mars (Col. H. Jonas Boyette), Livia Genise (Lt. Angie Finelli), Erica Yohn (Capt. Margaret McCall), Stephanie Faracy (Lt. Hope Philips), Randy Stumpf (Pvt. Tyrone Vallone), George Whiteman (Sgt. George Baker), Jerry Houser (Capt. Jules Meyer), Rod McCary (Billy Joe Lee), Jonathan Banks (Patient), Frank Whiteman (Driver), Kim Kahana (Soldier).

1545. Friends. 30 min. Airdate: 8/19/78. Production Company: Universal Television. Director: Hy Averback. Producers: Lorenzo Music and Steve Pritzker. Writers: Lorenzo Music and Steve Pritzker. Creators: Lorenzo Music and Steve Pritzker. Teddy (Michael Tucci) and Scott (Darrell Fetty) are two has-been folk singers who give up performing and become staff song writers for a big record company, run by a 21-year-old whiz kid (Larry Cedar). Teddy is a chubby bachelor who dreams of going back on the road but Scott likes songwriting since it's stable, and keeps him at home with his wife (Susan Buckner) and son (Stephen Mond). *Cast:* Michael Tucci (as Teddy Serano), Darrell Fetty (Scott Rollins), Susan Buckner (Susan Rollins), Stephen Mond (Kevin Rollin), Larry Cedar (Gordon Bass), Brian Cutler (J.B. Henderson), Dori Brenner (Leslie Frankel), George Wyner (Mike), Rae Dawn Chong (Diane Miller).

1546. Goober and the Trucker's Paradise. 30 min. Airdate: 5/17/78. Production Company: Rich Eustin Productions. Director: Rich Eustis. Producer: Rich Eustis. Writers: Rich Eustis, George Lindsey, and April Kelly. Music: Ray Stevens. George Lindsey returns as Goober Pyle, the dim-witted but good-hearted mechanic he played on *The Andy Griffith Show*, *Mayberry, RFD*, and *Hee Haw*. In this proposed sitcom, he moves to a small town outside Altanta to operate a truck stop garage and cafe with his oldest sister (Leigh French), her rebellious daughter (Audrey Landers), a sexy female mechanic (Lindsay Bloom), and a knock-out waitress (Sandie Newton). *Cast:* George Lindsey (as Goober Pyle), Leigh French (Pearl Pyle), Sandi Newton (Charlene), Audrey Landers (Becky Pyle), Lindsay Bloom (Toni), John Chappell (Deputy Eagle Keyes), Bill Medley (Bible Bill), Brion James (T-Bone), Bruce Fisher (Catfish), Robert Towers (Elwood), Mickey Jones (Troll), Ken Johnson (Bud).

1547. Hangin' Out. 30 min. Production Company: Ralph Bakshi Productions. Producer: Ralph Bakshi. Writer: Larry Parr. Creator: Ralph Bakshi. A reworking of last season's concept, which proposed mixing animation with live action. Now, there's a new script and it's a strictly animated affair. It's now about a group of kids who live near Coney Island Amusement Park because that's where their fathers work. The characters are Russo, the handsome leader; Stinkfish, who lives near an open fish market; Kanoff, an incredibly strong boy who loves animals and has every pet imaginable; and finally there's Norman, who worships Russo and does everything he tells him.

1548. John 'n' Willie T. 30 min. Production Company: King-Hitzig Productions. Director: Alan Rafkin. Executive Producer: Alan King. Producer: Rupert Hitzig. Writer: Richard Wesley. Creator: Richard Wesley. Josh (Reginald Vel Johnson) and Willie (Ralph Wilcox) are two black cabbies who form an all-black cab company serving the Bedford Stuyvesant area of Brooklyn. Josh is a conservative family man while Willie is a single man apt to take outrageous chances.

1549. King of the Road. 30 min. Airdate: 5/10/78. Director: Hal Cooper. Executive Producers: Norman Lear and Jerry Weintraub. Producers: Rod Parker and Hal Cooper. Writer: Rod Parker. Roger Miller is a country-western singer who runs a motel in Alabama. John Davidson guest starred as himself. *Cast:* Roger Miller (as Cotton Grimes), Lee Crawford (Maureen Kenney), Larry Haines (Sam Braffman), Marian Mercer (Mildred Braffman), R.G. Brown (Billy Dee Huff), Rick Carrott (Rick), Nedra Volz (Mrs. Hickey), Eddie Foy, Jr. (Eddie), Karen Specht (Karen Kleegle), Beth Specht (Beth Kleegle), Jenny Neumann (Jenny Kleegle), also, John Davidson.

1550. Leonard. 30 min. Production Companies: Warner Bros. Television and Silliphant/Konigsberg Productions. Executive Producer: Frank Königsberg. Producers: Lawrence J. Cohen and Fred Freeman. Writers: Lawrence J. Cohen and Fred Freeman. Creators: Lawrence J. Cohen and Fred Freeman. The misadventures of

Leonard (Leonard Frey) a harried lawyer who, in addition to fighting court cases, has to fend off a rival attorney trying to steal his clients (George Pentecost), pacify the friends his father (Nicholas Collasanto) sends in for free advice, and helps out his lazy ex-partner (John Lawlor). Marilu Henner is his secretary, who helps juggle his various responsibilities.

1551. **The Plant Family.** 30 min. Airdate: 9/2/78. Production Companies: Paramount Television, Bud Austin Productions, and Ne Productions. Director: James Burrows. Executive Producers: Robert Wood and Bud Austin. Producer: Monica Johnson. Writers: Monica Johnson and Jordan Tabat. The Plant family are all trying to cook up get-rich-quick schemes from their home in conservative Orange County, California. While Augie (Norman Alden) works on wax figures in the basement (in hopes of turning his house into a famous wax museum), his wife Lyla (Joyce Van Patten) and their maid (Jo Marie Payton) are getting involved in capers that will get the whole family in trouble. *Cast:* Joyce Van Patten (Lyla Plant), Norman Alden (Augie Plant), Kay Heberle (Ava), Larry Hankin (Art), Jo Marie Payton (Geneva), Jesse White (Leo Harrell), DeWayne Hessie (Homer Jay), Peter Elbling (Aerillo), Willie Tjan (Patty), Anthony Sirico (Eddie).

1552. **The Rita Moreno Show.** 30 min. Airdate: 5/2/78. Production Company: Paramount Television. Director: Tony Mordente. Producers: Mark Rothman and Lowell Ganz. Writers: Mark Rothman and Lowell Ganz. Creators: Mark Rothman and Lowell Ganz. Music: Peter Matz. Rita Moreno is a showgirl who, when her career nosedives, takes a job as social director at a rundown Pocono Mountains hotel which, when the owner dies, she unexpectedly inherits. *Cast:* Rita Moreno (as Marie Costanza), Victor Buono (Leo), Louis Nye (Mr. Gladstone), Kathy Bendett (Carol Costanza), Bert Rosario (Esteban), Kit McDonough (Miss Forbush), Ron Ver- nan (Mr. Leopold), Shirley Mitchell (Doris), Lee Bryant (Mrs. Kleppner).

1553. **Ship-Shape.** 30 min. Airdate: 8/1/78. Production Company: The Komack Company. Directors: James Komack and Gary Shimokawa. Producers: A1 Gordon and Jack Mendelsohn. Writers: James Komack, A1 Gordon, Jack Mendelsohn, Stan Cutler, Neil Rosen, George Tricker, and Gary Belkin. Deborah Ryan is a gorgeous Navy officer who dreams of commanding her own ship while she's busy trying to train an undisciplined, eccentric group of misfit sailors for new assignments. The sailors are an incorrigible ladies' man, a trumpet playing black, a practical-joking demolitions expert who plants bombs all over the base, and a technological genius who is afraid of electricity. *Cast:* Deborah Ryan (as Ensign Leslie O'Hara), Earl Boen (Captain Latch), Lorenzo Lamas (Lorenzo), Andrew Block (Beltzman), Gary Veney (Watkins), Demetre Phillips (Kozak), Shell Kepler (Capt. Rita Sweetzer), Ted Hartley (Congressman Nelson), Kristin Larkin (Mrs. Nelson).

1554. **Side by Side.** 30 min. Production Company: N/R/W Productions. Director: Jack Shea. Producers: Don Nicholl, Michael Ross, and Bernie West. Writers: Roger Schulman and John Baskin. Jeff (Steven Anderson) is a department store manager who is in love with Kim (Ginger Flick), a reader for a publishing company, but is afraid of marriage because of his parents' disastrous marriage and painful divorce. So, the young couple decide to live together, to the consternation of Kim's conservative parents (Macon McCalman and Barbara Perry).

1555. **Three-Way Love (aka Handle with Care; aka Citizen's Band).** 30 min. Production Company: Paramount Television. Producer: Gail Parent. Writer: Gail Parent. Creator: Paul Brickman. Based on the movie *Handle with Care*, which was originally released as *Citizens Band*. Ann Wedgeworth and Marcia Rodd recreate their roles as two women, one from Texas and one from South Dakota, who discover that they are married to the same man when he is hurt in an auto accident in Portland, Oregon. He deserts them both so, pooling their resources and their children (Robbie Rist, Shannon Terhune, and Poindexter), they decide to live together. Alix Elias reprises his role as their neighbor and friend.

1556. **What Are Friends For?** 30 min. Production Company: TTC Productions. Executive Producer: Ted Bergman. Producer: Alan J. Levi. Writer: Alan J. Levi. Based on the British sitcom *Cuckoo Waltz*. The misadventures of a frugal married couple (Paul Sand and Anne Schedeen) who share their home with the husband's swinging, free-spending bachelor friend (Ted Shackelford).

1557. **Wilder and Wilder.** 30 min. Airdate: 8/26/78. Production Company: Viacom Enterprises. Director: Peter H. Hunt. Executive Producer: Mark Carliner. Producers: Austin Kalish and Irma Kalish. Writers: Austin Kalish and Irma Kalish. Greg Mullavey and his real-life wife Meredith MacRae play a husband-and-wife team of television comedy writers who work at their home, which they share with her younger sister (Susan Lanier). *Cast:* Greg Mullavey (as Sam Wilder), Meredith MacRae (Steffi Wilder), Susan Lanier (Tina Chambers), Lou Criscuolo (Al Meredith), T.K. Carter (Jason), Lonnie Shorr (Roger Bacon), Warren Burton (Phil Crawford), Vaughn Armstrong (Joel).

1558. Your Place or Mine. 30 min. Airdate: 5/27/78. Production Company: MTM Enterprises. Director: James Burrows. Executive Producer: Bob Ellison. Producers: David Lloyd and Dale McRaven. Writers: Bob Ellison and David Lloyd. Creators: Bob Ellison and David Lloyd. This comedy would focus on the awkward relationship between a Manhattan-based freelance writer (Stuart Gillard) who wants to live in the country and a magazine editor (Jane Actman) who lives in Long Island with her parents but who dreams of living in the city. These two meet, fall in love, and agree to switch places with one another—she sublets his apartment, and befriends his taxi driver neighbor (Judy Graubart), and he moves in with her parents (Alice Hirson, Peter Hobbs). *Cast:* Jane Actman (as Kelly Barnes), Stuart Gillard (Jeff Burrell), Alice Hirson (Frances Barnes), Peter Hobbs (Ernie Barnes), Judy Graubart (Linda Heller), Elizabeth Kerr (Mrs. Hicks), Elizabeth Halliday (Carol), George Pentecost (Harold).

CBS / DRAMA

1559. The Busters. 60 min. Airdate: 5/28/78. Production Company: MTM Enterprises. Director: Vincent McEveety. Executive Producer: Stu Erwin. Producer: Jim Brynes. Writer: Jim Brynes. Creator: Jim Brynes. Music: Jerrold Immel. The misadventures of two roving cowboys—Chad (Bo Hopkins), a once-famous bull rider, and Albie (Brian Kerwin), an energetic and eager upstart—on the national rodeo circuit who live on a ranch near Lake Tahoe that's run by Slim Pickens. *Cast:* Bo Hopkins (as Chad Kimbrough), Brian Kerwin (Albie McRae), Slim Pickens (Kane), Devon Ericson (Marty Hamilton), Buck Taylor (Billy Burnett), Susan Howard (Joanna Bailey), Chris Robinson (Nick Carroll), Lance Le Gault (Mel Drew).

1560. Colorado C-I. 60 min. Airdate: 5/26/78. Production Company: Quinn Martin Productions. Director: Virgil W. Vogel. Executive Producer: Philip Saltzman. Producer: Christopher Morgan. Writer: Robert W. Lenski. Music: Dave Grusin. The adventures of two brothers—one Ivy League-educated (John Elerick) and the other a rugged cowboy (Marshall Colt)—who work as crack detectives for the elite Colorado Criminal Investigation Squad, The C.I. When they aren't busting bad guys, they're on their ranch, where their ex-cop father (L.Q. Jones) lives and works. Shot on location. *Cast:* John Elerick (as Mark Gunnison), Marshall Colt (Pete Gunnison), L.Q. Jones (Hoyt Gunnison), Laurette Sprang (Chris

Morrison), Christine Belford (Carla Winters), David Hedison (David Royce), William Lucking (Niles), Christine DeLisle (Piper Collins), Van Williams (Capt. Cochran), Randolph Powell (Stan Cusek), Lou Frizzell (Frank Bannock), John Karlen (Kessler), George D. Wallace (George Hopkins), Joan Roberts (Operator), Anne H. Bradley (Hazel Bicker).

1561. Donaldson and Street. 60 min. Airdate: 1/12/78. Production Company: Quinn Martin Productions. Director: Walter Grauman. Executive Producer: Quinn Martin. Producer: Philip Saltzman. Writer: Gerald Sanford. Aired as the "A Ransom in Diamonds" episode of *Barnaby Jones*. A lighthearted adventure that teams up a white private eye (Sam Weisman) with a black lawyer (Felton Perry). They shared a foxhole in Vietnam and now share a shabby office in Los Angeles. Both men are barely making a living, don't carry guns, and still have a lot to learn about their chosen professions. In the pilot, Barnaby Jones (Buddy Ebsen) helps them solve a kidnapping. *Cast:* Sam Weisman (as Stan Donaldson), Felton Perry (Alexander Street), Dennis Patrick (Warren Christy), Vincent Baggetta (David Harmon), Carl Weintraub (Bo Harper), Fawne Harriman (Andrea Christie), Chip Fields (Kelly Johnson), Byron Morrow (Keith Milland), Rozelle Gayle (Rambo), Buddy Ebsen (Barnaby Jones), Mark Shera (Jedediah Jones), Lee Meriwether (Betty Jones), Jim Bohan (Pete Gramis), Sharon Thomas (Barbara), Gayle Gannes (Gloria), Doug Hume (Doorman).

1562. Dr. Strange. 134 min. Airdate: 9/6/78. Production Company: Universal Television. Director: Philip DeGuere. Executive Producer: Philip DeGuere. Producer: Alex Beaton. Writer: Philip DeGuere. Creator: Stan Lee, based on the Marvel Comics book. In the Marvel comic, Dr. Steven Strange, Master of the Mystic Arts, was a moody, mysterious sorcerer who fought to save the Earth from demons, monsters and the bizarre denizens of other astral planes. In this pilot, Strange was a wisecracking psychiatrist who learned the "Hermedic arts"—the ability to control the elements of the universe—from an aging sorcerer just in time to fight Arthurian villainess Morgan Le Fay. The pilot keeps some elements of the comic book origin—the original Strange was a surgeon before losing his hands in an accident and becoming the disciple of the "Ancient One"—but substituted a campy, "comic-booky" tone for Stan Lee's dense, serious comic book style. *Cast:* Peter Hooten (as Dr. Strange), Clyde Kusatsu (Wong), John Mills (Thomas Lindmer), Jessica Walter (Morgan Le Fay), Philip Sterling (Dr. Frank Taylor), David Hooks (The Nameless One), Michael Ansara (Voice of the Ancient One), Eddie Benton (Clea Lake), June Barrett (Sarah), Diane Webster (Head Nurse), Harry Anderson (Magician), Michael Clark (Taxi Driver), Bob Delegall (Intern), Inez Pedroza (Agnes Carson).

1563. Escapade. 60 min. Airdate: 5/19/78. Production Company: Quinn Martin Productions. Director: Jerry London. Executive Producer: Quinn Martin. Producer: Philip Saltzman. Writer: Brian Clemens. Creator: Brian Clemens. Music: Patrick Williams. This was an attempt to do an Americanized version of *The Avengers,* an outlandish, stylized spoof of spy movies, which was made in England and ran on ABC from 1966–1969, becoming a cult classic. It starred Patrick MacNee as debonair spy John Steed and Diana Rigg as his sexy, and dangerous, partner Emma Peel (and later Linda Thorson as Tara King). Brian Clemens, who created, wrote, and produced *The Avengers,* penned this light-hearted pilot, about two San Francisco-based spies (Granville Van Dusen and Morgan Fairchild) who take their orders from an uppity computer. This pilot was made shortly after Clemens finished producing 26 episodes of a European-produced revival called *The New Avengers,* which starred MacNee, Joanna Lumley, and Gareth Hunt, and aired at 11:30 p.m. on CBS during the 1978–79 season. *Cast:* Granville Van Dusen (as Joshua Rand), Morgan Fairchild (Susie), Len Birman (Arnold Tulliver), Janice Lynde (Paula), Alex Heteloff (Wences), Gregory Walcott (Seaman), Dennis Rucker (Charlie Webster).

1564. The Gypsy Warriors. 60 min. Airdate: 5/12/78. Production Company: Universal Television. Director: Lou Antonio. Executive Producer: Stephen J. Cannell. Producer: Alex Beaton. Writers: Stephen J. Cannell and Phil DeGuere. Creators: Stephen J. Cannell and Phil DeGuere. Music: Mike Post and Pete Carpenter. The first of two unsold pilots Cannell developed to showcase the talents of James Whitmore Jr. and Tom Selleck for CBS. This time, they play two espionage agents, posing as gypsies roaming France and Germany, who take on unusual missions during World War II. The relationship between Cannell, Whitmore and Selleck pre-dated this pilot, and lasted long afterward. Whitmore and Selleck had both previously appeared frequently on *The Rockford Files,* and Whitmore would later have roles in Cannell's *Black Sheep Squadron* and *Hunter,* as well as Selleck's *Magnum P.I.,* on which even Cannell showed up as a guest star. *Cast:* James Whitmore, Jr. (as Capt. Shelley Alhern), Tom Selleck (Capt. Ted Brinkerhoff), James Bushkin (Ganault), Lina Raymond (Lola), Michael Lane (Androck), Albert Paulsen (Bruno Schlagel), Kenneth Tigar (Shulman), William

Westley (Ramon Pierre Cammus), Hubert Noel (Henry), Kathryn Leigh Scott (Lady Britt Austin Forbes).

1565. **The Islander.** 2 hours. Airdate: 9/16/78. Production Companies: Glen Larson Productions and Universal Television. Director: Paul Krasny. Producer: Glen A. Larson. Writer: Glen A. Larson. Creator: Glen A. Larson. Music: John Andrew Tartaglia. Singer: Shelby Flint. Dennis Weaver is a retired Los Angeles lawyer who buys a rundown Honolulu hotel, then finds himself constantly called on to help people solve their problems and solve baffling crimes. *Cast:* Dennis Weaver (as Gable McQueen), Sharon Gless (Shauna Cooke), Peter Mark Richman (Lt. Larkin), Bernadette Peters (Trudy Engels), Robert Vaughn (Senator Gerald Stratton), John S. Ragin (Bishop Hatch), Dick Jensen (Al Kahala), Ed Ka'ahea (Kimo), Sheldon Leonard (Paul Lazarro), George Wyner (Simms), Zitto Kazann (Paco), Glenn Cannon (Wallace), Jimmy Borges (Sgt. Chow), Danny Kamekona (Sgt. Rojo).

1566. **The New Millionaire.** 2 hours. Airdate: 12/19/78. Production Company: Don Fedderson Productions. Director: Don Weis. Producer: Don Fedderson. Writer: John McGreevey. Creator: Don Fedderson. Music: Frank DeVol. An attempted revival of *The Millionaire* (1955–60) with Robert Quarry taking over Marvin Miller's role as Michael Anthony, the executive secretary who delivers million dollar cashier's checks to unsuspecting people picked at random by the unseen, mysterious tycoon John Beresford Tipton. This pilot, like the original series, shows what happens to people once they get a million tax-free dollars. *Cast:* Robert Quarry (as Michael Anthony), Marti Balsam (Arthur Haines), Edward Albert (Paul Matthews), Bill Hudson (Eddie Reardon), Mark Hudson (Mike Reardon), Brett Hudson (Harold Reardon), Pat Crowley (Maggie), Pamela Toll (Kate), Allan Rich (George Jelks), John Ireland (Marshall Wayburn), Ralph Bellamy (George Matthews), Jane Wyatt (Mrs. Matthews), William Demarest (Oscar Pugh), Talia Balsam (Doreen), Michael Minor (Clark), Milt Kogan (Parker), Sally Kemp (Judge), Patricia Hindy (Dorothy), P.R. Paul (Alan), Ann Greer (Cory).

1567. **Outside Chance (aka Jackson County Jail).** 2 hours. Airdate: 12/2/78. Production Company: New World Productions. Director: Michael Miller. Executive Producer: Roger Corman. Producer: Jeff Begun. Writers: Michael Miller, Gaby Wilson, and Matt Crowley. Creator: Donald Stewart. A remake of the 1976 movie *Jackson County Jail.* Yvette Mimieux reprises her role as an advertising executive wrongly imprisoned by a small town sheriff, whom she later kills in self- defense when he tries to rape her. She escapes from jail and, in the proposed series, would have many exciting adventures on the run. Fredric Cook, Howard Hesseman, and Severn Darden also reprise their roles from the movie. *Cast:* Yvette Mimieux (as Dinah Hunter), Royce D. Applegate (Larry O'Brien), Beverly Hope Atkinson (Clair), Susan Batson (Mavis), Babett Bram (Miss Hopkins), Fredric Cook (Deputy Holme), Severn Darden (Sheriff Dempsey), Howard Hesseman (David), Lee Fergus (Doctor), John Lawlor (Bill Hill), Betty Thomas (Katherine), Britt Leach (Alfred), Charles Young (Luther), Ira Miller (Dale), Nancy Noble (Lola), Robin Sherwood (Tootie), Dick Armstrong (Arnold Bradfield), Janina D. White (Matron), Jerry Hamlin (Jimmy), Nan Martin (Allison), William Malloy (Deputy Lyle Peters), Larry Hankin (Deputy), Amparo Mimieuz (Woman), John Ross (Bailiff), Allen Wood (Judge), Janice Hamlin (Nurse), John Abbott (Coroner), H. Curley Moore (Sheriff).

1568. **Sparrow.** 60 min. Airdate: 8/11/78. Production Company: Tori Productions. Director: Jack Sold. Executive Producer: Herbert B. Leonard. Producer: Walter Bernstein. Writer: Walter Bernstein. Music: Paul Williams. A reworking of last season's flop *Sparrow* pilot. Once again, Randy Herman is neophyte detective Sparrow, now an operative with a New Orleans detective agency. Gerald S. O'Loughlin replaces Don Gordon as Mr. Medwick, Sparrow's boss. *Cast:* Randy Herman (as Jerry Sparrow), Gerald S. O'Loughlin (Mr. Medwick), Catherine Hicks (Valerie), Lillian Gish (Mrs. Benet), Jonelle Allen (Dory), Kurt Knudson (Rhino), Dolph Sweet (Landon).

1569. **Tom and Joanne.** 60 min. Airdate: 7/5/78. Production Company: Time-Life/ David Susskind Productions. Director: Delbert Mann. Executive Producer: David Susskind. Producer: Diana Kerew. Writer: Loring Mandel. It's been a year since Tom and Joanne ended their 16-year marriage and they are now friends again. The proposed series would explore how they, and their children, cope with their new relationship and their new single lives. *Cast:* Joel Fabiani (as Tom), Elizabeth Ashley (Joanne), Jennifer Cooke (Amy), Colin McKenna (T.C.), Bibi Besch (Lou), David Ackroyd (Gabe), Marie McCann (Beth), Tim Okon (Kenny), Brenda Donahue (Helene), Louis Del Grande (Norman).

1570. **War of the Worlds.** 20 min. Production Company: Paramount Television. Producer: Frank Cordea. Writer: George Schenck. A short demonstration aimed at selling the network on a science fiction series starring Jeff Osterhage and Morgan Fairchild as two secret agents working for "the good guys" in a war between two distant planets settled by earthlings. In 1988, Paramount aired a syndicated, first run series entitled *War of the Worlds* that lasted for two seasons…though it as not based on this pilot.

1571. **The Wilds of Ten Thousand Islands.** 60 min. Airdate: 2/24/78. Production Company: Lorimar Productions. Director: Charles S. Dubin. Executive Producers: Lee Rich and Philip Capice. Producer: Andy White. Writers: Andy White and Paul West. Music: Dominic Frontiere. The adventures of the Wild family—an animal behaviorist (Chris Robinson), his wife (Julie Gregg), his son (John Kauffman) and his daughter (Mary Ellen McKeon)—who move to a remote corner of the Florida Everglades to study wildlife.

1572. **The World Beyond.** 60 min. Airdate: 1/27/78. Production Company: Talent Associates. Director: Noel Black. Executive Producer: David Susskind. Producer: Frederick Brogger. Writer: Art Wallace. Creator: Art Wallace. Music: Fred Carlin. A second attempt to sell Granville Van Dusen as a sportswriter who nearly dies on the operating table and now gets messages from "beyond" to help people in supernatural danger. This was pitched last season as *The World of Darkness. Cast:* JoBeth Williams (as Marian Faber), Barnard Hughes (Frank Faber), Jan Van Evers (Sam Barker).

NBC / COMEDY

1573. **The Arrangement.** 30 min. Production Company: Tandem Productions. Producers: Brad Buckner and Eugene Ross Leming. Writers: Brad Buckner and Eugene Ross Leming. This proposed sitcom would chart the rocky romantic road traveled by a 26-year-old man and his 18-year-old girlfriend. He wants to get married, she'd rather they live together for awhile and, despite her father's strong opposition, they do.

1574. **California Girls.** 30 min. Production Company: First Artists. Executive Producer: Peter Engel. Producer: Bruce Johnson. Writers: Marc Sotkin, Judy Erwin, and Chris Thompson. P.J. Soles and Robin Dearden are two girls, one from New York and the other from Malibu, who want to be lifeguards, but are thwarted by the sexist director of lifeguards (William Boyett), even though his assistant (John Calvin) does all he can to help them. They also get a lot of encouragement in their dream from a beachbum (Richard Young).

1575. Clappers. Producer: Pat Nardo. Writers: Pat Nardo and Harvey Miller. The misadventures of two secretaries at Clappers, a fictional Philadelphia department store. One girl is a realist, the other an eternal optimist, and it's from this conflict in personalities that the comedy would spring.

1576. Coast-to-Coast. 60 min. Production Company: T.O.Y. Productions. Director: Bud Yorkin. Executive Producer: Bud Yorkin. Producers: Saul Turtel- taub and Bernie Orenstein. Writers: Saul Turteltaub and Bernie Orenstein. The misadventures of the staff of a New York-to-Los Angeles airline on both coasts. In Los Angeles, the story follows two stewardesses who share an apartment in the same building as the bumbling flight engineer and the slick PR man. In New York, the action shifts to a husband-and-wife who operate a bar at JFK, a cab driver who works the airport, and other undeveloped regulars. Of course, whether the emphasis is on east or west coast, the passengers will play an important role in each week's story.

1577. Good Ol' Boys. 30 min. Airdate: 6/7/79. Production Company: Filmways. Director: Harry Falk. Executive Producer: Perry Lafferty. Producers: Ted Bergman and William Ferguson. Writers: Ted Bergman and William Ferguson. Jerry Reed and Lane Caudell are two aspiring country-western singers who work as vending machine servicemen in Nashville while waiting to make it big. Mel Stewart is their boss, and Mo Malone and Linda Thompson are their girlfriends. The pilot was shot in Nashville.

1578. Many Loves of Arthur (aka Arthur Among the Animals). 60 min. Airdate: 5/23/78. Production Company: MTM Enterprises. Director: Bill Bixby. Producer: Philip Barry. Writer: Gerald DiPego. Music: Patrick Williams. Richard Masur is Arthur, a veterinarian who is very emotionally attached to the animals he treats at various zoos. Often, this attachment helps him better understand his own relationships and to sympathize with the people around him. *Cast:* Richard Masur (as Arthur), Carolina McWilliams (Gail Corbett), Constance McCashin (Karen), Silvana Gallardo (Mendoza), David Dukes (Dr. Chase), Linda Lukens (Michelle), Patti Edwards (Peg), Lee Bryant (Nancy), Ralph Ridgely (Jake).

1579. The Paul Williams Show. 30 min. Airdate: 6/27/79. Production Company: First Artists. Director: Dennis Steinmetz. Executive Producer: Peter Engel. Producer: Dennis M. Bond. Writer: Bruce Kane. Music: Paul Williams. Aired as a segment of *The Battle of the Generations*, a TV movie compilation of four flop sitcom pilots. Paul Hamilton (Paul Williams) is Marvin the Martian, the second banana on a kids' show on a Denver television station. When the host dies, Hamilton takes over—and thousands of children fall in love with him. In the pilot, he decides to tell his audience where babies come from—to the horror of his station director (Amanda McBroom). Sandra Kearns is his girlfriend and Rick Podell is his best friend, a lawyer. *Cast:* Paul Williams (as Paul Hamilton), Rick Podell (Denny Morton), Dana Hill (Debbie), Amanda McBroom (Victoria Woodbridge), Sandra Kearns (Barbara), Earl Doen (Virgil Weeks), Rex Riley (J. Edgar Remington, III).

1580. **Starting Fresh.** 30 min. Airdate: 6/27/79. Production Company: Danny Thomas Productions. Director: Bob Claver. Executive Producers: Ronald Jacobs and Danny Thomas. Producers: Pamela Chais and Leonora Thuna. Writer: Pamela Chais. Aired as a segment of *Battle of the Generations*, a compilation of busted pilots. Delores Harvey (Lynnette Mettey) is a 36-year-old divorcee who decides to go back to college—the one her 17-year-old daughter Stefanie (Kimberly Beck) is also attending and the one where her "swinging single" best friend (Janie Sell) is now Dean of Admissions. In the pilot, Delores won't let her daughter go to Aspen for a ski weekend with the campus playboy. *Cast:* Lynnette Mettey (as Delores Harvey), Kimberly Beck (Stephanie Harvey), Janie Sell (Phoebe Johnson), Susan Duvall (Judy), Ike Eisenmann (Cliffie), Michael MacRae (Roger), Jeffrey Byron (John).

1581. **The Three Wives of David Wheeler.** 30 min. Airdate: 8/1/79. Production Company: Filmways. Director: Burt Brinckerhoff. Executive Producers: Perry Lafferty and Norman S. Powell. Producer: Jay Folb. Writer: Jay Folb. Music: Jack Elliott and Allyn Ferguson. David Wheeler's (Art Hindle) marriage to Julia (Nancy Grigor) is complicated by the constant presence of his two ex-wives—his partner in his graphic arts business (Cathy Lee Crosby), his resident model (Sherrill Lynn Katzman). *Cast:* Art Hindle (as David Wheeler), Nancy Grigor (Julia Wheeler), Cathy Lee Crosby (Ginger Wheeler), Sherrill Lynn Katzman (Bibi Wheeler), Archie Hahn (Vinnie), Susan Tolsky (Debbie).

NBC / DRAMA

1582. **Big Bob Johnson's Fantastic Speed Circus.** 2 hours. Airdate: 6/27/78. Production Companies: Playboy Productions and Paramount Television. Director: Jack Starrett. Executive Producers: Edward L. Rissien and R.W.

Goodwin. Producer: Joseph Gantman. Writers: Bob Comfort and Rick Kellard. Music: Mark Snow. Three stunt car drivers (Charles Napier, Maud Adams, and Constance Forslund) and their PR man (Robert Stoneman) who, wherever they go, end up helping people solve their problems. *Cast:* Charles Napier (as Big Bob Johnson), Maud Adams (Vikki Lee Sanchez), Constance Forslund (Julie Hunsacker), Robert Stoneman (W.G. Blazer), William Daniels (Lawrence Stepwell), Burton Gilliam (Half-Moon Muldoon), Rick Hurst (Timothy Stepwell), Tom McFadden (Alfie), Clay Turner (Earl), James Bond, III (Jesse).

1583. **Clone Master.** 2 hours. Airdate: 9/14/78. Production Companies: Mel Ferber Productions and Paramount Television. Director: Don Medford. Executive Producer: Mel Ferber. Producer: John D.F. Black. Writer: John D.F. Black. Art Hindle is a government scientist who makes 13 clones of himself, each sent out to fight evil and each of whom would become the focus of a different episode of the proposed series. If the series had continued past 13 weeks, presumably the scientist would clone 13 more of himself. *Cast:* Art Hindle (as Dr. Simon Shane), Robyn Douglass (Gussie), John Van Dreelen (Salt), Ed Lauter (Bender), Mario Roccuzzo (Harry Tiezer), Ralph Bellamy (Ezra Louthin), Stacey Keach, Sr. (Admiral Millus), Lew Brown (Fire Chief), Bill Sorrells (Reporter), Robert Karnes (Trankus), Betty Lou Robinson (Alba Toussaint), Vernon Weddle (Pine), Steve Eastin (Huberman), Philip Pine (Commander Tiller), Kirk Duncan (General), Ian Sullivan (Pat Singer), Trent Dolan (Schnerlich), James O'Connell (Sands).

1584. **The Cops and Robin.** 90 min. Airdate: 3/28/78. Production Companies: Culzen Corporation and Paramount Television. Director: Allen Reisner. Executive Producers: Anthony Wilson and Gary Damsker. Producer: William Kayden. Writers: Brad Radnitz, Dawning Forsythe, and John T. Dugan. Creator: Anthony Wilson. Music: Charles Bernstein. A bewildering attempt to revive the flop 1977 ABC series *Future Cop*, which lasted six episodes and told the story of two veteran street cops (Ernest Borgnine and John Amos) teamed with a humanoid robot (Michael Shannon). The series was the center of a successful lawsuit filed by authors Harlan Ellison and Ben Bova, who contended that the series was taken from their short story *Brillo*. *Cast:* Ernest Borgnine (as Officer Joe Cleaver), Michael Shannon (Officer John Haven), Natasha Ryan (Robin Loren), Carol Lynley (Dr. Alice Alcott), Terry Kiser (Wayne Dutton), Phillip Abbott (Garfield), Richard Bright (Richards), James York (Richard),

Gene Rutherford (Carl Tyler), J. Kenneth Campbell (Detective Furie), Ivan Bonnar (Judge Wheeler), Jeff David (Jim Loren), Elizabeth Farley (Marge Loren), Linda Scott (Laura).

1585. The Courage and the Passion (aka Joshua Tree). 2 hours. Airdate: 5/27/78. Production Companies: David Gerber Productions and Columbia Pictures Television. Director: John Llewellyn Moxey. Executive Producers: David Gerber and Vince Edwards. Producer: Jay Daniel. Writer: Richard Fielder. Music: Richard Shores. Joshua Tree Air Force Base is the setting of this proposed series, which would star Vince Edwards as J.R. Agajanian, the head of the base, and Trish Noble and Desi Arnaz, Jr. as his assistants. *Cast:* Vince Edwards (as Col. J.R. Agajanian), Desi Arnaz, Jr. (Sgt. Tom Wade), Trish Noble (Lt. Lisa Rydell), Linda Foster (Capt. Cathy Wood), Robert Ginty (Airman Donald Berkle), Robert Hooks (Major Stalney Norton), Paul Shenar (Nick Silcox), Laraine Stephens (Brett Gardener), Don Meredith (Col. Jim Gardener), Monty Hall (General Sam Brewster), Melody Rogers (Janet Sayers), Irene Yah-Ling (Tuyet Berkle), Donna Wilkes (Tracy), Ellen Travolta (Emily), Wes Parker (Lt. Hogan).

1586. Critical List. 2 hours. Airdate: 9/12/78. Production Company: MTM Enterprises. Director: Lou Antonio. Executive Producer: Stu Erwin. Producer: Jerry McNeely. Writer: Jerry McNeely, from the novels *Skeletons* and *Critical List*, by Marshall Goldberg, M.D. This was originally conceived as three two-hour movies—fashioned for Lloyd Bridges and his sons Beau and Jeff—that charted the professional and personal life of Dr. Dan J. Lassiter, the physician and administrator of the fictional Los Angeles Hospital. Jeff would have starred in the first movie, Beau in the second, and Lloyd in the final one. When the sons bowed out, the project was scaled down into two loosely connected pilots starring Lloyd Bridges as doctor, administrator, father, and part-time detective. *Cast:* Lloyd Bridges (as Dr. Dan J. Lassiter), Melinda Dillon (Dr. Kris Lassiter), Buddy Ebsen (Charles Sprague), Barbara Parkins (Angela Adams), Robert Wagner (Dr. Nick Sloan), Ken Howard (Nels Freiberg), Winwood McCarthy (Ned Josephson), James Whitmore, Jr. (Dr. Jack Hermanson), Robert Hogan (Jordon Donnelly), Scott Marlowe (Dr. Albert Dubron), Felton Perry (Dr. Hill), Pat Harrington (Jimmy Regosi), Will Hare (Edmonds), Mel Gallagher (Bednarik), Sybil Scotford (Joanne Larwin), Joan Tompkins (Judge Morton), Brad David (Andrew Vivienne), Julie Bridges (Gale Taylor), William Joyce (Bill Shramm),

Wright King (Peter Kenderly), Russ Martin (Ed Moorhead), Eugene Peterson (Sidney Hammons), Janice Carroll (Nurse), Janice Karman (Cathy), Ron Trice (Larry Harrison).

1587. **[Pilot #2] Critical List.** 2 hours. Airdate: 9/13/78. Production Company: MTM Enterprises. Director: Lou Antonio. Executive Producer: Stu Erwin. Producer: Jerry McNeely. Writer: Jerry McNeely, from the novels *Skeletons* and *Critical List*, by Marshall Goldberg, M.D. See previous listing. *Cast:* Lloyd Bridges (as Dr. Dan J. Lassiter), Melinda Dillon (Dr. Kris Lassiter), Ken Howard (Nels Freiberg), Winwood McCarthy (Ned Josephson), James Whitmore, Jr. (Dr. Jack Hermanson), Robert Hogan (Jordon Donnelly), Felton Perry (Dr. Hill), Pat Harrington (Jimmy Regosi), Louis Gossett, Jr. (Lem Harper), Richard Basehart (Matt Kinsella), Ben Piazza (Dr. Henry De Jong), Joanne Linville (Nan Forrester), Eugene Peterson (Sidney Hammond), Jim Antonio (Detweiler), John Larch (Sprony), Wright King (Dr. Kenderly), Noble Willingham (Charlie), Steve Gravers (Senator), Jesse Dizon (Baker), Wayne Heffley (Sheriff), George Reynolds (Andy Simms), John Petlock (Ferris), Janice Kerman (Cathy), Hanna Hertelendy (Hilde), Jerry McNeely (Tom Neubeck), George Boyd (McBride), Marlyn Coleman (Nurse).

1588. **Hunters of the Reef (aka Peter Benchley's Mysteries of the Deep).** 2 hours. Airdate: 5/20/78. Production Companies: Writers Company Productions and Paramount Television. Director: Alexander Singer. Executive Producer: Stanley Kallis. Producer: Ben Chapman. Writer: Eric Bercovici. Creator: Peter Benchley. Music: Richard Markowitz. The adventures of charter boat captain Jim Spanner (Michael Parks) and his 12-year-old half-brother (Moosie Drier), who live on a tiny island off Florida in an abandoned, 200-year-old Spanish chapel. Spanner has leased a marine biology lab to the Navy, and it's operated by Tracy Russell (Mary Louis Weller), who carries out experiments. *Cast:* Michael Parks (as Jim Spanner), Mary Louise Weller (Tracey Russell), William Windom (Panama Cassidy), Felton Perry (Winston St. Andrew), Moosie Drier (Mike Spanner), Stephen Macht (La Salle), Katy Kurtzman (Kris La Salle).

1589. **Kate and the Mississippi Queen (aka Lacy and the Mississippi Queen).** 2 hours. Airdate: 5/17/78. Production Company: Paramount Television. Director: Robert Butler. Executive Producer: Lawrence Gordon. Producers: Robert Singer and Lew Gallo. Writers: Madeline DiMaggio and Kate Donnell. Music: Barry DeVorzon. Cool-headed cowgirl Kate Lacy (Kathleen Lloyd) and her poker-playing, gun-toting, half-sister Queenie (Debra Feuer) are ranchers who moonlight as frontier detectives for the Union Pacific Railroad. *Cast:* Kathleen Lloyd (as Kate Lacy), Debra Feuer (Queenie), Edward Andrews (Isaac Harrison), Jack Elam (Willie Red Fire), James Keach (Parker), Matt Clark (Reynolds), Les Lannom (Webber), Christopher Lloyd (Jennings), Anthony Palmer (Sam Lacy), David Byrd (Bixby), Alvy Moore (Reverend), Sandy Ward (Mitchell Beacon), Elizabeth Rogers (Madam Josephine), David Comfort (Lord Percival Winchester).

1590. **Killing Stone.** 2 hours. Airdate: 5/2/78. Production Company: Universal Television. Director: Michael Landon. Producer: Michael Landon. Writer: Michael Landon. Music: David Rose. Gil Gerard is an ex-con who becomes a freelance writer and roams the nation, helping people in distress and solving crimes. *Cast:* Gil Gerard (as Gil Stone), J.D. Cannon (Sheriff Harkey), Jim Davis (Senator Barry Tyler), Matthew Laborteaux (Christopher Stone), Corinne Michaels (Ellen Rizzi), Joshua Bryant (Harold Rizzi), Nehemiah Persoff (Earl Stone), Dick Decoit (Daniel Tyler), Valentina Quinn (Cindy), Ken Johnson (Barney Dawes), Dan McBride (Bobby Joe).

1591. **Mandrake the Magician (aka Mandrake).** 2 hours. Airdate: 1/24/79. Production Company: Universal Television. Director: Harry Falk. Producer: Rick Husky. Writer: Rick Husky. Music: Morton Stevens. As a young boy, Mandrake (Anthony Herrara) was the sole survivor of a plane crash in the Himalayas. Raised by Tibetan monks, he was taught the ancient magic of wizard Theron (James Hong) and given a magic amulet that endows him with special psychic powers which he now uses to fight crime. He's assisted by Lothar (Ji-Tu Cumbuka) and Stacy (Simone Griffeth) in his battle against evil. *Cast:* Anthony Herrara (as Mandrake), Simone Griffeth (Stacy), Ji-Tu Cumbuka (Lothar), Hank Brandt (Alex Gordon), Gretchen Corbett (Jennifer Lindsay), Peter Haskell (William Romero), Robert Reed (Arka- dian), David Hooks (Dr. Malcolm Lindsay), Harry Blackstone, Jr. (Dr. Nolan), James Hong (Theron), Donna Benz (Cindy), David Hollander (Young Mandrake), Alan Hunt (Walter Kevan).

1592. **Mark Twain's America (aka The Incredible Rocky Mountain Race).** 2 hours. Airdate: 12/17/77. Production Company: Sunn Classic Films. Director: James L. Conway. Executive Producer: Charles E. Sellier, Jr. Producer: Robert Stambler. Writers: David O'Malley and Tom Chapman. First in a proposed anthology of light-hearted frontier stories "hosted" by Mark Twain (Christopher

Connelly) and sometimes starring him as well. In the pilot, Twain challenges riverman Mike Fink (Forrest Tucker) to a race from Missouri to the Pacific Ocean. *Cast:* Christopher Connelly (as Mark Twain), Forrest Tucker (Mike Fink), Jack Kruschen (Jim Bridger), Mike Muzurki (Chief Crazy Horse), Larry Storch (Eagle Feather), Bill Zuckert (Mayor), Whit Bissell (Simon Hollaway), Dan Haggerty (Sheriff Benedict), Parley Baer (Farley Demond), William Kazaele (Burton), John Hansen (Bill Cody), Sam Edwards (Milford Petrie), Sandy Gibbon (Sheriff).

1593. **Sea Gypsies.** 90 min. Airdate: 1/7/79. Production Companies: Simpson Raffil Productions and Warner Bros. Television. Director: Stuart Raffill. Producer: Peter Simpson. Writer: Stuart Raffill. Robert Logan is a widower who sets sail from Seattle on a round-the-world cruise with his two daughters (Heather Rattray and Shannon Saylor) a female photographer/reporter (Mikki Jamison-Olsen), a 10-year- old black stowaway (Cjon Damitri Patterson), and the family dog. They end up getting stranded on an uncharted Alaskan island and must learn to survive. At least that was the story of the pilot, which was released as a feature film. The intended series would have focused on their adventures as they traveled the high seas all over the world.

1594. **Starfire (aka Indians; aka Born to the Wind).** 60 min. Airdates: 8/19/82, 8/26/82, 9/2/82, and 9/9/82. Production Company: Warner Bros. Television. Directors: Charles S. Dubin, I.C. Rapoport, and Philip Leacock. Executive Producers: Ed Scherick and Dan Blatt. Producer: I.C. Rapoport. Writers: Sue Milburn, William Keys, I.C. Rapoport, and Del Reisman. These four pilots for a proposed series about the Plains Indians, as seen through the eyes of the Chief's (Will Sampson) daughter Starfire (Rose Portillo), were shot in 1978 but languished for four years before being broadcast. Guillermo San Juan was Starfire's brother, Dehl Berti was the medicine man, and Emilio Delgado was the Chiefs advisor. *Cast:* Rose Portillo (as Starfire), Will Sampson (Painted Bear), A Martinez (Low Wolf), Dehl Berti (One Feather), Emilio Delgado (White Bull), Linda Redfearn (Prairie Woman), Guillermo San Juan (Two Hawks), Ned Romero (Broken Foot), Cynthia Avila (Arrow Woman), Sandra Griego (Red Stone), Claudio Martinez (Night Eyes), Manu Tupou (Cold Maker), Silvana Gallardo (Digger Woman), Nick Ramus (Grey Cloud), James Cromwell (Fish Belly), Rudy Dias (Red Leggins), Geraldine Keams (Wind Woman), Eric Greene (Lame Elk).

1595. Stedman (aka Crisis in Sunvalley). 2 hours. Airdate: 3/29/78. Production Company: Columbia Pictures Television. Director: Paul Stanley. Executive Producer: Barry Weitz. Producer: Robert Stambler. Writers: Carl Gottlieb and Alvin Boretz. Two one-hour pilots comprise this second—and final—attempt to fashion a series around a sheriff of a ski resort community, a concept the networks seemed enamored with. Just last season, NBC tried both *Abel Marsh* with Andy Griffith and the first *Stedman* pilot with Dale Robinette. These loosely strung-together Stedman pilot episodes—*Outward Bound* and *The Vanishing Kind*—put the concept to rest. Robinette later gave up acting to sell doggie treats. *Cast:* Dale Robinette (as Sheriff Stedman), Taylor Lac her (Deputy Archie Sykes), Bo Hopkins (Buchanan), Tracy Brooks Swope (Stella), Ken Swofford (Thorndyke), Paul Brinegar (Poole), Jason Johnson (Derry), John McIntire (Hubbard), Susan Adams (Eva), Julie Parsons (Jenny), Larry Jenkins (Lester), Max Kleven (Adler), Tony Jefferson (Scott), Deborah Winters (Sandy), Wayne Heffley (Baker), Grant Owens (Reynolds), Mark Simson (Michael), Lorraine Curtis (Marie), Mickey Livingston (Deputy Hank), Bill Quinn (Deputy Willard), Marcia Stringer (Hazen).

1596. Top Secret. 2 hours. Airdate: 6/4/78. Production Company: Sheldon Leonard Productions. Director: Paul Leaf. Executive Producer: Sheldon Leonard. Producer: David Levinson. Writer: David Levinson. Music: Teo Macero and Stu Gardner. Bill Cosby and Tracy Reed are spies trying to find stolen plutonium and the terrorists who stole it. Sheldon Leonard created and produced the hit espionage series *I Spy*, which starred Cosby and Robert Culp. *Cast:* Bill Cosby (as Aaron Strickland), Tracy Reed (McGee), Sheldon Leonard (Carl Vitali), Gloria Foster (Judith), George Breslin (Murphy), Paolo Turco (Gino), Luciano Bartoli (Pietro), Marisa Merlini (Rosa), Craig Hill (Zeeger), Leonard Treviglio (Tomas), Byron Rostram (Christian), Walter Williams (Macaferri), Nat Bush (Sergeant), Paul Leaf (Painter).

1597. When Every Day Was the Fourth of July. 2 hours. Airdate: 3/12/78. Production Company: Dan Curtis Productions. Director: Dan Curtis. Producer: Dan Curtis. Writer: Lee Hutson, from a story by Dan Curtis and Lee Hutson. First of two sentimental pilots—the second, *Long Days of Summer*, came two years later—about the lives of attorney Ed Cooper (Dean Jones) and his family in Bridgeport, Connecticut, during the 1930s. In the pilot, Cooper's 10-year-old daughter convinces him to defend a deaf-mute charged with murder. *Cast:* Dean Jones (as Ed

Cooper), Louise Sorel (Millie Cooper), Chris Peterson (Daniel Cooper), Katy Kurtzman (Sarah Cooper), Harris Yulin (Joseph T. Antonelli), Geoffrey Lewis (Albert Cavanaugh), Scott Brady (Officer Mike Doyle), Ronnie Claire Edwards (Mrs. Najarian), Ben Piazza (Herman Gasser), Henry Wilcoxon (Judge Henry J. Wheeler), Eric Shea (Red Doyle), Michael Pataki (Robert Najarian), Woodrow Parfrey (Dr. Alexander Moss), H.B. Haggerty (Bartender), Moosie Drier (Howie), Tiger Williams (Skipper), Charles Aidman (Narrator).

1979–1980

ABC / COMEDY

1598. America 2100. 30 min. Airdate: 7/24/79. Production Companies: Rothman/ Ganz Productions and Paramount Television. Director: Joel Zwick. Executive Producers: Austin Kalish and Irma Kalish. Producer: Gary Menteer. Writers: Austin Kalish and Irma Kalish. Creators: Mark Rothman and Lowell Ganz. Two nightclub comics (Jon Cutler and Mark King) are accidentally put into suspended animation and wake up in the year 2100, in a world now run by a friendly computer named Max (Sid Caesar), and are befriended by a female scientist (Karen Valentine).

1599. Camp Grizzly. 30 min. Airdate: 6/30/80. Production Company: Nick Vanoff Productions. Director: Steven Stern. Executive Producer: Nick Vanoff. Producer: Robert Klane. Writer: Robert Klane. Creator: Robert Klane. The misadventures of Nick (Richard Cox), an irreverent counselor at penny-pinching Uncle Barney's (Carl Ballantine) summer camp for kids. Nick's rival is the militaristic counselor Furman (Demetre Phillips) and the object of his affections is Missy (Hilary Thompson), another counselor. *Cast:* Richard Cox (as Nick), Carl Ballantine (Uncle Barney), Hilary Thompson (Missy), Demetre Phillips (Furman), Jay Fenichel (Garafala), Joey Coleman (Joey), Charlie Wilhite (Charlie), Bryan Scott (Brian), Timothy Roesch (Timmy), Steve Pollick (Steve), Jeannette Arnette (Jean), Donna Mason (Donna), Christine Richards (Chris), John Robert Yates (John), Dennis Dooder (Dennis).

1600. I Do, I Don't. 30 min. Production Company: Joe Hamilton Productions. Executive Producer: Joe Hamilton. Producers: Larry Freeman and Larry Cohen. Writers: Larry Freeman and Larry Cohen. This proposed sitcom would focus on the conflict between a novelist and long-time bachelor (John Considine) who marries a divorcee (Jo Ann Pflug) and moves in with her college-student son (David Elliot) and her rich-and-snooty daughter (Jennifer Perito), who just returned from living with her wealthy father in Paris. When the novelist needs help, he turns to his still-a-bachelor friend (Robert Hogan) for advice.

1601. Marie. 30 min. Airdate: 12/1/79. Production Company: The Osmond Company. Director: Richard Crenna. Executive Producers: Norman Paul and

Joseph Bonaduce. Producer: Dennis Johnson. Writer: Joseph Bonaduce. Marie (Marie Osmond) is a naive, traditional, midwestern girl who moves to New York to chase her dream of becoming a Broadway dancer. It isn't easy adjusting to big city life, but she gets some help from her two streetwise female roommates (Telma Hopkins and Zan Charisse). *Cast:* Marie Osmond (as Marie), Ellen Travolta (Carla Coburn), Telma Hopkins (K.C. Jones), Zan Charisse (Sandra), Tony Ramirez (Pancho), Bruce Kirby, Sr. (Edgar Merton), Stephen Shortridge (Detective Driscoll), Cliff Pellow (Sgt. Dryer).

1602. **Maxx.** 30 min. Production Company: The Komack Company. Director: James Komack. Producer: James Komack. Writer: James Komack. Tim Thomerson is divorced, the owner of a successful New York travel agency, and a happy-go-lucky bachelor when one day his 10-year-old daughter Maxx (Melissa Michaelson) shows up at his doorstep. Her mother, whom he had left because he knew he couldn't handle the responsibility of fatherhood, has gone away and left Maxx for him to handle. The comedy would come from his attempts to be a responsible parent, and her doubts that he really wants her around. Although ABC turned this pilot down, NBC was interested. A new pilot was shot and the concept was altered. Thomerson was dropped in favor of Joe Santos, who played the womanizing owner of the Empire Ticket Agency who is suddenly appointed guardian of the 11-year-old daughter he rarely sees and hardly knows. The subsequent series, *Me and Maxx*, lasted for nine weeks in 1980.

1603. **Mookie and Sheryl.** Production Company: Paramount Television. Writers: Austin Kalish and Irma Kalish. The misadventures of a young married couple—he's an actor, she's a fashion designer—living in New York.

1604. **My Buddy.** 30 min. Airdate: 7/3/79. Director: Garren Keith. Executive Producer: Redd Foxx. Producer: Norman Hopps. Writer: Redd Foxx. Creators: Redd Foxx, Michael O'Daniel, Christopher (cq) Joy, and Leon Isaac Kennedy. Woodrow "Buddy" Wilson (Redd Foxx) is a bar-and-grill owner who unexpectedly inherits a fortune and control of a multinational corporation from one of his customers—but to keep it all, he must live in the mansion with his late friend's snobbish sister (Pamela Mason) and money-hungry brother-in-law (Basil Hoffman). *Cast:* Redd Foxx (as Woodrow "Buddy" Johnson), Pamela Mason (Catherine Worth), Basil Hoffman (Bernard Billings-Worth), Irwin C. Watson (Sumpter), Slappy White (Melvin the Bartender), Iron Jaw Wilson (Messenger).

1605. Second Time Around. 30 min. Airdate: 7/24/79. Production Companies: Jerry Tokofksy Productions and 20th Century Fox Television. Director: Robert Drivas. Executive Producer: Jerry Tokofsky. Producer: Elliot Schoenman. Writer: Elliot Schoenman. Mariette Hartley and Edward Winter are two marriage counselors who are able to patch up other people's relationships but not their own. They are separated, but still live and work out of the same home, which they share with their 11-year-old son (Brad Savage). *Cast:* Mariette Hartley (as Dr. Joanne Norman), Edward Winter (Dr. David Norman), Brad Savage (Mark Norman), Simone Griffeth (Robin), Jim Staahl (Bert).

1606. Where's Poppa? 30 min. Airdate: 7/17/79. Production Company: Marvin Worth Productions. Director: Richard Benjamin. Producers: Marvin Worth and Robert Klane. Writer: Robert Klane. Creator: Robert Klane. Based on director Carl Reiner's 1970 feature *Where's Poppa*, which screenwriter Robert Klane adapted from his book about a New York lawyer (Steven Keats) constantly nagged by his selfish, over-protective mother (Elsa Lanchester), who demands . and gets . . . more of his time than his clients do. When all else fails, she pretends to be senile and helpless just to get him to do her bidding. And as much as he begs his older, married brother (Allan Miller) for help, he never gets any. George Segal, Ruth Gordon, and Ron Leibman played the roles in the motion picture. *Cast:* Elsa Lanchester (as Momma Hockheiser), Steven Keats (Gordon Hockheiser), Judith Marie Bergan (Louise Hamelin), Allan Miller (Sid Hockheiser).

1607. Who's On Call? 30 min. Airdate: 12/16/79. Director: Tony Mordente. Producers: Coleman Mitchell and Geoffrey Neigher. Writer: Laura Levine. The comedy misadventures of medical students at a Manhattan hospital. *Cast:* Forbesy Russell (as Dr. Liz Spencer), Jim McKrell (Dr. Leland Forsythe), Fran Ryan (Nurse Bremmer), Melissa Steinberg (Marsha Stone), Matt Landers (Eddie Grado), Frank Covsentino (Neil Goggini).

1608. Young Guy Christian. 30 min. Airdate: 5/24/79. Production Company: Viacom. Director: Stuart Margolin. Producers: Jerry Belson and Michael Leeson. Writers: Jerry Belson and Michael Leeson. Music: Murray MacLeod and J.A.C. Redford. Barry Bostwick is Young Guy Christian, a hero who fights evil with the help of brilliant scientist Professor Mishugi (Pat Morita), Mishugi's daughter (Shelley Long), and the professor's bionic creation Junkman (Richard Karron), a person with a radio in his head and a laser in his finger. In the pilot, an evil Dr. Gasss

(Charles Tyner) kidnaps six "Miss Planet" contestants and demands a hydrogen bomb as ransom. *Cast:* Barry Bostwick (as Young Guy Christian), Shelley Long (Mia Mishugi), Pat Morita (Professor Mishugi), Richard Karron (Junkman), Charles Tyner (Dr. Gasss), Linda Lawrence (Ava), Alfie Wise (Guard), Mitchell Group (Gang Member).

ABC / DRAMA

1609. Beach Patrol. 90 min. Airdate: 4/30/79. Production Company: Spelling/ Goldberg Productions. Director: Bob Kelljan. Executive Producers: Aaron Spelling and Leonard Goldberg. Producer: Philip Fehrle. Writers: James D. Buchanan and Ronald Austin. Music: Barry DeVorzon. A female narcotics cop (Robin Strand) is transferred to an elite police squad of three cops (Christine De- Lisle, Richard Hill, and Jonathan Frakes) that patrols the California beaches and, in the pilot, she is targeted for assassination after spotting a fugitive mafioso. *Cast:* Robin Strand (as Russ Patrick), Jonathan Frakes (Marty Green), Christine DeLisle (Jan Plummer), Richard Hill (Earl "Hack" Hackman), Michael Gregory (Sgt. Lou Markowski), Paul Burke (Wes Dobbs), Michael V. Gazzo (Banker), Panchito Gomez (Wild Boy), Mimi Maynard (Wanda), Princess O'Malley (Tall Girl).

1610. The Bible. 60 min. Airdate: 11/18/79. Production Company: Universal Television. Director: Leo Penn. Executive Producer: David Victor. Writer: Norman Hudis. Music: Morton Stevens. Raymond Burr narrated this tale, "The 13th Day: The Story of Esther," the pilot for a proposed hour-long weekly anthology of Bible stories. *Cast:* Olivia Hussey (as Esther), Tony Musante (King), Harris Yulin (Haman), Nehemiah Persoff (Mordecai), Ted Wass (Simon), Erica Yohn (Sura), Kario Salem (Dalphon).

1611. The Billion Dollar Threat. 2 hours. Airdate: 4/15/79. Production Companies: David Gerber Production and Columbia Pictures Television. Director: Barry Shear. Executive Producer: David Gerber. Producer: Jay Daniel. Writer: Jimmy Sangster. Music: Richard Shores. A lame attempt to copy 007 for television. Dale Robinette is secret agent Robert Sands, who is ordered (by Ralph Bellamy) to stop a megalomaniac villain (Patrick MacNee) threatening to destroy the ozone layer unless he is given $1 billion. Harold Sakata, Oddjob in *Goldfinger*, makes a cameo. The production team behind this flop would try again, with new characters, in 1980s *Once Upon a Spy* with similarly disastrous results. *Cast:* Dale Robinette (as Robert Sands), Ralph Bellamy (Miles Larson), Keenan Wynn (Ely), Stephen Keep (Harry Darling), Ronnie Carol (Marcia Buttercup), Patrick Macnee (Horatio Black), Beth Specht (Holly), Karen Specht (Ivy), William Bryant (Harry), Marianne Marks (Ming), Read Morgan (Charlie).

1612. **Casino.** 2 hours. Airdate: 8/1/80. Production Companies: Aaron Spelling Productions and Trellis Productions. Director: Don Chaffey. Executive Producers: Aaron Spelling and Blake Edwards. Producer: E. Duke Vincent. Writer: Richard Carr. Music: Mark Snow. Mike Connors is Nick, a suave, former CIA agent who now operates a floating casino in international waters. The proposed series would mingle romance, humor, and intrigue against the backdrop of highstakes gambling and the open sea. Barry Van Dyke is Nick's aide, and Hedley Mattingly is the wise, old English bartender. In the pilot, someone is trying to sink his ship—it turns out to be his financier, who is controlled by the mob. *People* magazine said "to get an idea of this TV film's flashy tone and byzantine plot, imagine 'Mr. Lucky' taking a 'Love Boat' cruise to 'Vega$.'" It's no coincidence. Blake Edwards produced the 1959 TV version of *Mr. Lucky* (as well as the similarly themed 1960 series *Dante's Inferno*) and Aaron Spelling produced *The Love Boat* and *Vega$*. *Cast:* Mike Connors (as Nick), Lynda Day George (Carol), Barry Sullivan (Sam Fletcher), Bo Hopkins (Stoney Jackson), Robert Reed (Darius), Gary Burghoff (Bill Taylor), Barry Van Dyke (Edge), Gene Evans (Captain Fitzgerald), Hedley Mattingly (Foxworth), Robert Loggia (Karl), Joseph Cotten (Ed Booker), Harry Townes (Harry), Neil Flanagan (Andre), James Murtaugh (Andrews), Sherry Jackson (Jennifer), Conrad Roberts (Faber), Austin Willis (Packard).

1613. **For Heaven's Sake.** 60 min. Production Companies: Blinn/Thorpe Productions and Viacom. Executive Producers: William Blinn and Jerry Thorpe. Writer: William Blinn. Creator: William Blinn. Ray Bolger stars as an angel sent to Earth to help people who are in trouble.

1614. **Grant Goodeve Project.** 2 hours. Production Company: Lorimar Productions. Director: Harry Harris. Executive Producers: Lee Rich and Phil Capice. Producer: Gary Adelson. Writer: Greg Strangis. A proposed spin-off from *Eight Is Enough*. David Bradford (Grant Goodeve) breaks up with his girlfriend Janet (Joan Prather) and decides to travel around the country to get himself back together again. A divorced friend of Janet's (Forbesy Russell), an aspiring journalist, agrees to go with him and share expenses so she can develop as a reporter. The relationship between them, as they tour America in his van and get involved with the people they meet, begins as strictly platonic, but might change as time went on—and had ABC commissioned the series, which it didn't.

1615. **The Man with the Power (aka The Power Within; aka The Power; aka The Power Man).** 90 min. Airdate: 5/11/79. Production Company: Aaron Spelling Productions. Director: John Llewellyn Moxey. Executive Producers: Aaron Spelling and Douglas S. Cramer. Producers: Alan Godfrey and E. Duke Vincent. Writer: William Clark. Creator: Ed Lasko. Music: John Addison. This pilot went through many titles, but under any name it would still be the same old story about a man who, thanks to a freak accident, acquires superpowers which he then uses to fight crime. Art Hindle is a decorated Vietnam hero who is struck by lightning, emerges with X-ray vision and the power to shoot electric bolts from his fingers, and takes on secret missions for his father (Edward Binns), an Air Force General. *Cast:* Art Hindle (as Chris Darrow), Edward Binns (General Tom Darrow), Joe Rassulo (Bill), Dick Sargent (Capt. Ed Holman), Susan Howard (Dr. Joanna Mills), Karen Lamm (Marvalee), Eric Braeden (Stephens), David Hedison (Danton), Isabell Mac- Closkey (Grandma), Chris Wallace (First Guard), John Dennis (Rancher).

1616. **The Night Rider.** 90 min. Airdate: 5/11/79. Production Companies: Stephen J. Cannell Productions and Universal Television. Director: Hy Averback. Executive Producers: Stephen J. Cannell and Alex Beaton. Producers: J. Rickley Dumm and William F. Phillips. Writer: Stephen J. Cannell. Creator: Stephen J. Cannell. Music: Mike Post and Pete Carpenter. Yet another reworking of *Zorro*. This time it's a western with David Selby as Thomas Earl, a New Orleans aristocrat by day and the infamous, masked crimefighter "Night Rider" by night. *Cast:* David Selby (as Thomas Earl), Percy Rodriquez (Robert), Kim Cattrall (Regina Kenton), George Grizzard (Dan Kenton), Anthony Herrara (Sheridan), Anna Lee (Lady Earl), Pernell Roberts (Alex Sheridan), Michael Sharrett (Chock Hollister), Harris Yulin (Billy Baines), Hildy Brooks (Marie Hollister), Curt Lowens (Hans Klaus), Van Williams (Jim Hollister), Stuart Nisbet (Doc Ellis), Gary Allen (Donald White), Sydney Penny (Melissa Hollister), Ed Knight (Paul), Maria Diane (Mrs. Klaus), Susan Davis (Deri Kenton), Hugh Gillin (Zack Bodine).

1617. **Nightside.** 90 min. Airdate: 6/8/80. Production Companies: Universal Television, Stephen J. Cannell Productions, and Glen A. Larson Productions.

Director: Bernard Kowalski. Executive Producers: Stephen J. Cannell and Glen A. Larson. Producer: Alex Beaton. Writers: Stephen J. Cannell and Glen A. Larson. Creators: Stephen J. Cannell and Glen A. Larson. Music: John Andrew Tartaglia. It looked great on paper: teaming up two of the most successful and respected producers of action/adventure shows on one series that they would devise and supervise together. "But Glen does what he does and I do what I do, and putting us together isn't going to make it twice as good," says Cannell. In fact, he says the pilot "wasn't any good at all. It was funnier than hell, but it just didn't work." He describes the show as a "comedy reality" pilot that focused on "off-beat characters functioning in a different world, a world that lives at night. The heroes are these two cops (Doug McClure and Michael Corneliuson). One is a fucking crazy man who's been on the nightshift too long, the other is a living computer. There are also these two jive-ass guys (Michael D. Roberts and Michael Winslow) that have an ambulance that is a total wreck and who race other ambulance companies to the scene of accidents." *Cast:* Doug McClure (as Officer Danny Dandoy), Michael Corneilson (Officer Ed Macey), John DeLancie (Dr. Willy Pitts), Roy Jenson (Sgt. Duckman), Jason Kincaid (Dr. Samuel Hicks), Melinda Naud (Jane Moody), Michael D. Roberts (Green-light), Michael Winslow (Redlight), Danny Wells (Eddie Kopeck), Joe Spinell (Michael Vincent), Wayne Heffley (Sgt. Treetorn), Vincent Schiavelli (Tom Adams), Timothy Agoglia Carey (Slowboy), Sondra Blake (Margie), Janice Lynde (Lily), Michael Alldredge (Tellinger), Larry Cedar (LaSalle), Peter Kowalski (Terry), Doug Cox (Bones), Patch MacKenzie (Redhead), Susan Plumb (Sharon), Karen Newell (Rusty), Louie Ellis (Vanilla), Sid Conrad (President), Doug Hume (Smitty).

1618. **Return of the Mod Squad.** 2 hours. Airdate: 5/18/79. Production Company: Spelling/Thomas Productions. Director: George McCowan. Executive Producers: Aaron Spelling and Danny Thomas. Producer: Lynn Loring. Writer: Robert Janes. Music: Mark Snow, Shorty Rogers, and Earle Hagen. An attempt at reviving the 1968–73 ABC series *The Mod Squad,* which followed the adventures of Pete Cochran (Michael Cole), Julie Barnes (Peggy Lipton), and Line Hayes (Clarence Williams III)—three young people who are arrested and drafted into a special unit of the police department, headed by a no-nonsense cop Adam Greer (Tige Andrews), that infiltrates hippie organizations. Now businessman Pete, housewife and mother Julie, and school teacher Line reunite to find a hitman who is after Greer, who is now Deputy Police Commissioner. *Cast:* Michael Cole (as Pete Cochran), Peggy Lipton (Julie Barnes-Bennett), Clarence Williams, III (Line Hayes), Tige Andrews (Deputy Commissioner Greer), Simon Scott (Commissioner Metcalf), Roy Thinnes (Dan Bennett), Todd Bridges (Jason Hayes), Ross Martin (Buck Prescott), Victor Buono (Johnny Starr), Mark Slade (Richie Webber), Tom Bosley (Frank Webber), Tom Ewell (Cook), John Karlen (Marty), Jess Walton (Kate Kelsey), Taylor Lacher (Jake), Rafael Campos (Johnny Sorella), Byron Stewart (Bingo), Hope Holliday (Willie).

1619. **Samurai.** 90 min. Airdate: 4/30/79. Production Companies: Danny Thomas Productions, Lamas Corporation, and Universal Television. Director: Lee H. Katzin. Executive Producers: Fernando Lamas and Danny Thomas. Producers: Allan Balter and Ronald Jacobs. Writer: Jerry Ludwig. Music: Fred Karlin. This ludicrous and unintentionally funny pilot starred caucasian Joe Penny as half-American/half-Asian Lee Cantrall, a San Francisco district attorney by day and sword-wielding Samurai warrior by night. In the pilot, the Samurai D.A. tackles a meglomaniac villain who uses an "earthquake machine" to scare people into selling their property to him at a cut rate. *Cast:* Joe Penny (as Lee Cantrall), Danny Elcar (Frank Boyd), James Shigeta (Takeo Chrisato), Beulah Quo (Hannah Mitsubishi Cantrall), Norman Alden (Lt. Al DeNisco), Charles Cioffi (Amory Bryson), Geoffrey Lewis (Harold Tigner), Morgan Brittany (Cathy Berman), Ralph Manza (Irving Berman), Sinutko (Tommy), Michael Pataki (Peter Lacey), James McEachin (Richardson), Philip Baker Hall (Professor Gordon Owens), Randolph Roberts (Phil Mercer), Diana Webster (Professor Helen Martell), Don Keefer (Norman Jonas), Michael Danahy (Harry Keller), Bob Minor (Zane), Fred Lerner (Powers), Tom Lupo (Frazier), Greg Barnett (Colfax), Jo McDonnell (Marianne).

1620. **Topper.** 2 hours. Airdate: 11/9/79. Production Companies: Cosmo Productions and Robert Papazian Productions. Director: Charles S. Dubin. Executive Producers: Andrew Stevens and Kate Jackson. Producer: Robert A. Papazian. Writers: George Kirgo, Mary Anne Kascia and Michael Scheff, from the novel by Thorne Smith. Music: Fred Karlin. An attempt to update *Topper* for television. This time, Kate Jackson and her then-husband Andrew Stevens are Marion and George Kerby, two carefree ghosts who haunt their lawyer Cosmo Topper (Jack Warden) to bring some fun into his life. *Cast:* Kate Jackson (as Marion Kerby), Andrew Stevens (George Kerby), Jack Warden (Cosmo Topper), Rue McClanahan (Clara Topper), James Karen (Fred Korbel), Macon McCalman

(Wilkins), Charles Siebert (Stan Oglivy), Larry Gelman (Mechanic), Gloria LeRoy (Saleswoman), Lois Areno (Charlene), Jane Wood (Nurse), Mary Peters (Marsha), Marsha Ray (Mrs. Quincy), Gregory Chase (Steve), Ellen Marsh (Hostess), Marshall Teague (Man at Disco), Tom Spratley (Jailer).

1621. **Vampire.** 2 hours. Airdate: 10/7/79. Production Companies: MTM Enterprises and Company Four. Director: E.W. Swackhamer. Executive Producer: Steven Bochco. Producer: Gregory Hoblit. Writers: Michael Kozoll and Steven Bochco. Creators: Steven Bochco and Michael Kozoll. Music: Fred Karlin. This off-beat pilot comes from the same production team that would later be responsible for *Hill Street Blues.* Architect John Rawlins (Jason Miller) builds a San Francisco church and unknowingly offends a vampire (Richard Lynch). When the enraged, centuries-old vampire kills Rawlin's girlfriend for vengeance, the architect teams up with a retired cop (E.G. Marshall) to pursue and destroy the blood-sucking beast. "The pilot was a longshot," says Bochco. "In a sense, it was a cop show with a little bit of the *Night Stalker.* It was fun. But making pilots *is* fun. It's what happens after they sell where it gets ugly." *Cast:* Jason Miller (John Rawlins), Richard Lynch (Anton Voytek), E.G. Marshall (Jarry Kilcoyne), Kathryn Harrold (Leslie Rawlins), Barrie Youngfellow (Andrea Parker), Michael Tucker (Christopher Bell), Jonelle Allen (Brandy), Jessica Walter (Nicole DeCamp), Adam Starr (Tommy Parker), Wendy Cutler (Iris), Scott Paulin (Father Hanley), David Hooks (Casket Salesman), Brendon Dillon (Father Devlin), Joe Spinell (Captain Desher), Byron Webster (Selby), Ray K. Gorman (Detective), Nicholas Gunn (Dance Instructor), Herb Braha (Felon), Tony Perez (Cop).

CBS / COMEDY

1622. **The Circus Is Coming, the Circus Is Coming.** 30 min. Production Companies: Skorpios Productions and Quinn Martin Productions. Director: Alan Myerson. Executive Producers: Jim Mulligan and Ron Landry. Producers: Rich Eustis and Harry Waterson. Writers: Jim Mulligan and Ron Landry. Creators: Jim Mulligan and Ron Landry. Richard Libertini is Jingo, a divorced clown in a rundown traveling circus whose 15-year-old daughter lives with him. The cast includes Marya Small, Corky Hubbert, Andrea Bell, Vic Dunlop, Gordon Connell, Joseph Burke, and Michelle Tobin.

1623. The Dooley Brothers. 30 min. Airdate: 6/12/79. Production Companies: Arnold Margolin Productions and Bud Austin Productions. Director: Don Weis. Producer: Arnold Margolin. Writer: Arnold Margolin. Creators: Arnold Margolin and Jim Parker. Long before Col. Sanders decided to franchise his Kentucky Fried Chicken, frontier entrepreneur Jack Black (John Myhers) created and franchised two legendary lawmen, whom he dubbed *The Dooley Brothers*. There are eight pairs of "Dooley Brothers" roaming the West, maintaining law and order, when inept cowboys George (Garrett Brown) and Billy (Robert Peirce) join their ranks by landing the Arizona franchise. Despite their utter stupidity and lack of talent, the boys still manage to save the day and live up to the "Dooley Brothers" legend. In the pilot, they help a nearly blind sheriff (Dub Taylor) and his niece (Shelley Long) battle the evil Simon Gang. Shot on location in Old Tucson, Arizona. *Cast:* Garrett Brown (as George Dooley), Robert Peirce (cq) (Billy Dooley), John Myhers (Jack Black), Dub Taylor (Cool Sam Bennett), Shelley Long (Lucy Bennett), Peter Schrum (Bear Breath), Rusty Lee (Zeke), Grizzly Green (Zack), Charles Julian (Gilbert), Allen Wood (Doctor).

1624. Featherstone's Nest. 30 min. Airdate: 8/1/79. Production Company: Danny Thomas Productions. Director: Jim Drake. Executive Producers: Danny Thomas and Ronald Jacobs. Producer: Michael Norell. Writer: Michael Norell. Music: Earle Hagen. Charlie (Ken Berry) is a pediatrician who has to raise his two teenage daughters (Dana Hill and Susan Swift) when his wife deserts him to study law. He hires a wisecracking maid (Virginia Capers) to help him out, and relies on his friends Dr. John DeMott (Fred Morsell), who is a black dentist, and Everett Buhl (Phil Leeds), who runs a temporary employment service, for moral support. *Cast:* Ken Berry (as Dr. Charlie Featherstone), Susan Swift (Kelly Featherstone), Dana Hill (Courtney Featherstone), Virginia Capers (Bella Beauchamp), Fred Morsell (Dr. John DeMott), Phil Leeds (Everett Buhl), Kate Zentall (Hedwig), Shane Sinutko (Thurgood), Anita Jodelsohn (Dee Dee), Rhonda Foxx (Sue Sue).

1625. Fix-It City. 30 min. Production Companies: Rothman/Wohl Productions and Universal Television. Director: John Astin. Executive Producers: Bernie Rothman and Jack Wohl. Producers: Peter Grad and Bernie Kahn. Writers: Bernie Rothman and Jack Wohl. Creators: Bernie Rothman and Jack Wohl. The misadventures of mechanic Joey Bellino (John Aprea), and the other mechanics he employs at his Fix-It City Car Repair Shop. Costars include Mary Ann Chinn,

Chip Zien, Ralph Wilcox, Jaime Tirelli, Richard Foronjy, Mickey Jones, Severn Darden, and Jerry Hardin.

1626. The 416th. 30 min. Airdate: 8/25/79. Production Company: Warner Bros. Television. Director: Buddy Tyne. Executive Producer: Rick Bernstein. Producers: Eric Cohen and Peter Engel. Writer: Eric Cohen. Music: Mike Post and Pete Carpenter. Yet another *M*A *H*-inspired war comedy, this one set during the Vietnam war and focusing on a group of Army reserve officers who are called into active duty and sent to Fort Dix, where they comprise the innocuous 416th Medical Detachment, Supply Distribution Team. The four men are a talent agent who joined the reserve to avoid the draft (Richard Lewis), an accountant (Bo Kaprall), a tough street-gang member (Donald Petrie) and a naive mid-westerner (Richard Dimitri). Raymond St. Jacques runs the base, and John Larroquette is his nasty Lieutenant. *Cast:* Richard Lewis (as Pvt. Rick Michaels), Richard Dimitri (Pvt. Carmine Pompinece), Donald Petrie (Pvt. Billy Henderson), Bo Kaprall (Pvt. Myron Kowalski), Raymond St. Jacques (Col. Davis), John Larroquette (Lt. Jackson Mac- Calvey), Joan Hotchkis (Iris Michaels), Louise Hovan (Phyllis Shankman), Susan Lanier (Heather Hanley).

1627. Getting There. 60 min. Airdate: 2/12/80. Production Companies: Lila Garrett Productions and Metromedia Corporation. Director: John Astin. Executive Producer: Lila Garrett. Producer: John Whittle. Writers: Lila Garrett and Sandy Krinski. Creators: Lila Garrett and Sandy Krinski. Music: Jeff Barry. A comedy anthology about the misadventures of people who rent cars from bickering Harry and Rose Miller (George S. Irving and Brett Somers). Although an hour-long pilot was produced, it was sliced in half for broadcast, sacrificing the contributions of guest stars Hermoine Baddeley and Imogene Coca. *Cast:* George S. Irving (as Harry Miller), Brett Somers (Rose Miller), Cathryn Damon (Mary), Norman Fell (Jim), Todd Susman (Jerome), Dub Taylor (Ben), Tim Thomerson (Lester), Diane Venora (Melanie), Kelly Mohre (Tricia), Stephen Mond (Joey), Kristi Jill Wood (Julie), Hermoine Baddeley (Agatha), Imogene Coca (Emily), Jane Connell (Grandma).

1628. The Good News. 30 min. Production Company: Quinn Martin Productions. Executive Producer: Quinn Martin. Producers: Allan Katz and Don Reo. Writers: Allan Katz and Don Reo. Creators: Allan Katz and Don Reo. Michael Lembeck plays a gag writer hired by a San Diego television station to jazz up the feature reporting done by the news staff. He's at odds with the gruff news director, an idiotic sports reporter, and a pretty-faced, man-and-woman news team. When he goes home, he's got to deal with his "zany" neighbors—a custodian at the zoo and a scatter-brained, but beautiful woman. Costars include Victoria Carroll, Barbara Deutsch, Norman Bartold, Michael McManus, Dave Landsberg, and Allan Rich.

1629. **Just Us Kids.** 30 min. Production Company: Universal Television. Executive Producers: Tamara Asseyev and Alex Rose. Producers: Harvey Miller and Nancy Meyer. Writers: Harvey Miller and Nancy Meyer. Creators: Harvey Miller and Nancy Meyer. The misadventures of six high school students growing up in the mid-60s. The stars include Helaine Lembeck, Dawn Dunlop, Jean Rasey, Gary Im- hoff, Peter Gallagher, and Eddie Deezen.

1630. **The Love Birds.** 7/18/79. Production Company: Paramount Television. Director: Peter Baldwin. Executive Producers: Mark Rothman and Lowell Ganz. Producer: Leslie Fritz. Writers: Mark Rothman and Lowell Ganz. Music: Peter Matz. Theme: "The Love Birds," sung by Bobby Van. This proposed series centers on the continual conflict between two married couples who live next-door to one another. Al Burley (Louis Welch) is a conservative, traditional man who works as manager of a supermarket produce department. His wife Janine (Lorna Patterson) is happy staying at home and doing the chores, the cooking, and whatever else has to be done. The Waxelblatts are the exact opposite. Patricia (Ellen Regan) is a buyer for a department store and an opinionated liberal, and her husband (Eugene Levy) is a professional writer. *Cast:* Lorna Patterson (Janine Burley), Louis Welch (Al Burley), Ellen Regan (Patricia Wexelblatt), Eugene Levy (Fred Wexelblatt).

1631. **Madame Sheriff.** 30 min. Production Companies: Allan Carr Enterprises, Columbia Pictures Television, and Asa Maynor Enterprises. Director: Nancy Walker. Executive Producers: Allan Carr and Asa Maynor. Producer: Gene Marcione. Writer: Laura Levine. Creator: Laura Levine. Conchata Farrell stars as an out-going woman who is elected sheriff and lives at home with her two brothers, a burly truck driver (Rick Hurst) and a swinging single (Grant Wilson). She works with two deputies, one who is strongly opposed to the idea of a female sheriff (David Landsberg) and one who isn't (James Cromwell).

1632. **My Brother's Keeper.** 30 min. Production Company: King/Hitzig Productions. Director: Peter H. Hunt. Executive Producer: Alan King. Producer: Rupert Hitzig. Writers: Alan Uger and Michael Kagan. Based on the BBC sitcom. Bo

(Fred Lehne) and Mike (William Winkler) are fraternal twins who are fiercely devoted to their mother (Bo Bo Lewis), but the similarities between them end there. Mike is a clean-cut, conservative cop while Bo is an undisciplined, out-spoken liberal. And they fight about everything. Rex Everhart costars as Sgt. Dugan, Mike's boss.

1633. **Never Say Never.** 30 min. Airdate: 7/11/79. Production Companies: Four R Productions and Warner Bros. Television. Director: Charles Dubin. Executive Producers: Leonard A. Rosenberg and Elliot Shoenman. Producer: Lee Miller. Writer: Elliot Shoenman. Creator: Leonard A. Rosenberg. Music: Danny Wells. George Kennedy is Harry, a hard-nosed widower who runs a plumbing company and falls in love with a younger woman, a fiercely independent pediatrician (Anne Schedeen). When he proposes marriage, she proposes living together for awhile first, and he reluctantly agrees. Other regulars include his son (Bruce Kim- mell) and his former mother-in-law (Irene Tedrow). *Cast:* George Kennedy (as (Harry Walter), Anne Sehedeen (Dr. Sarah Keaton), Irene Tedrow (Florence), Bruce Kimmel (Paul Walter), Rick Podell (Ronnie Marks), Ric Mancini (Demarco), Jan Jorden (First Mother), Rochelle Richelin (Second Mother), Danny Wells (French Waiter), Maidie Norman (Nurse), Danny Gellis (Little Boy), Jayson Naylor (Jimmy), Gary Allen (First Singing Waiter), Bill Grant (Second Singing Waiter).

1634. **Nosey and the Kid.** Production Companies: Quinn Martin Productions and A1 Rogers Productions. Executive Producer: Quinn Martin. Producer: A1 Rogers. Writers: David Chambers, Doug Gilmore, and A1 Rogers. This proposed comedy, presented in a demonstration film, would focus on a talking, singing porpoise named Nosey that befriends a young girl and her family. Cindy Baines plays the young girl, and John Byner gives Nosey his voice.

1635. **On Ice.** 30 min. Production Company: TAT Communications. Producers: Eugenie Ross Leming and Brad Bruckner. Writers: Eugenie Ross Leming and Brad Bruckner. Julie Cobb stars as Peggy Fleming, a young woman who inherits the Wild Walrus Saloon, which is located in the remote Alaskan frontier. She moves to Alaska to run the saloon and falls in love with the environmentalist U.S. Marshall (Alex Cord), befriends a trapper (Pete Schrum), and hires a tough lady bartender (Melanie Noble) who also dabbles at piano-playing. The proposed sitcom would focus on efforts to adjust to her new life-style and on the relationships she has with her various customers.

1636. Pottsville. 60 min. Airdate: 2/27/80. Production Company: Elmar Productions. Director: Hal Cooper. Executive Producers: Hal Cooper and Rod Parker. Producer: Gene Marcione. Writer: Rod Parker. Creator: Rod Parker. Music: Larry Camsler. Theme: Hal Cooper and Rod Parker. This hour-long comedy would follow life in the factory town of Pottsville, Pennsylvania, home of the Faraday Sandpaper Corporation, run by a wealthy matriarch (Nina Foch) and her sons (John Lawlor and Jimmy Samuels). Between the factory and the workers there is the union, which is presided over by Bulldog (Forrest Tucker), who lives in town with his wife (Jan Miner) and his son (George O'Hanlon). It is the conflict between these two camps that most of the stories would spring. *Cast:* Forrest Tucker (as Bulldog O'Halloran), Jan Miner (Grace O'Halloran), George O'Hanlon (Tinker O'Halloran), Richard Brestoff (Bill Gentry), John Lawlor (Holden Farraday), Nina Foch (Gardy Farra- day), Jimmy Samuels (Ted Farraday), Hamilton Camp (Snell), Jane Daly (Randy), Heidi Gold (Pippa), Edie McClurg (Helen), Lynn Thigpen (Sue), Rory Calhoun (Sundance Ewbanks), Christopher Murney (Benny), James Cromwell (Frank), Luke Andreas (Guido).

1637. Rendezvous Hotel. 2 hours. Airdate: 7/11/79. Production Company: Mark Carliner Productions. Director: Peter H. Hunt. Executive Producers: Austin Kalish and Irma Kalish. Producer: Mark Carliner. Writers: Austin Kalish, Clayton Baxter, and Irma Kalish. Music: Jonathan Tunick. Bill Daily, as the owner/operator of a Santa Barbara resort hotel, presides over this shameless rip-off of *The Love Boat*—one of many, many attempts over the years to clone the long-running ABC hit. Bobbie Mitchell is the bubbly social director, Jeff Redford is the wacky desk clerk, and Theodore Wilson is the black cook. Sound vaguely familiar? *Cast:* Bill Daily (as Walter Grainer), Jeff J. Redford (Jerry Greenwood), Theodore Wilson (Cleveland Jennings), Bobbie Mitchell (Barbara Claiborn), Talya Ferro (Concetta Jennings), Edward Winter (Jim Becker), Carole Cook (Lucille Greenwood), Severn Darden (Albert Church), Kathryn Witt (Anne Jones), Nellie Bellflower (Sherry Leonard), Emory Bass (Edward Daley), Dolph Sweet (Harvey Greenwood), Bruce French (Frank Leonard), Sean Garrison (Guy), Jeff Donnell (Mrs. Williams), Jane Abbot (Waitress), Jack O'Leary (Mr. Corman), Diane Lander (Dr. Coleman), Brooke Kaplan (Kiki), Jack English (Stuart).

1638. Starstruck. 30 min. Airdate: 6/9/79. Production Company: Herbert B. Leonard Productions. Director: A1 Viola. Executive Producer: Herbert B. Leonard.

Producer: Bob Kiger. Writer: Arthur Kopit. Creator: Arthur Kopit. The misadventures of a family operating an orbiting space station restaurant—the only place in the galaxy that still makes apple pie. The family includes widower Ebeneezer McCallister (Beeson Carroll), whose ancestors helped settle California; his stoic mother Abigail (Elvia Allman); his 172-year-old great-great-great-great grandfather Ezra (Guy Raymond); and his three children (Tania Myren, Meegan King, and Kevin Brando). There are also two robots, Hudson and Bridges, who are in love with each other. The envisioned series would focus on the family and the bizarre assortment of aliens who visit their galactic diner. *Cast:* Beeson Carroll (as Ebeneezer McCallister), Tania Myren (Kate McCallister), Meegan King (Mark McCallister), Kevin Brando (Rupert McCallister), Guy Raymond (Ezra McCallister), Elvia Allman (Abigail McCallister), Lynne Lipton (Amber LaRue), Sarah Kennedy (Delight), Robin Strand (Chance), Joe Silver (Max), Roy Brocksmith (Orthwaite Frodo), Herb Kaplowitz (Dark), Robert Short (Hudson), Buddy Douglas (Mrs. Bridges), J.C. Wells (Tashko), Chris Wales (Mary-John), Cynthia Latham (Madame Dumont).

CBS / DRAMA

1639. **Bender.** 60 min. Airdate: 9/12/79. Production Company: Carnan- Becker Productions. Director: Ray Danton. Executive Producers: Carroll O'Connor and Terry Becker. Producer: Sy Gomberg. Writer: Sy Gomberg. Harry Guardino is a 20-year veteran of the New York City police force who retires and moves to the peaceful Southern California desert community of Tamarisk Wells, only to discover that organized crime is gaining a foothold there. So, he signs on as police chief. *Cast:* Harry Guardino (as Bender), Nicholas Coster (Bert Atkins), Joe Burke (Wade Rawlings), Susan Damante Shaw (Joanne Clark), Stephen Elliott (R.J. Phillips), Ben Piazza (Vincent Farragut), Will Hare (Zachary Wilson), Robert Phalen (Raker), Sean Roche (Bill Watson), Chad Roche (Jim Watson), Nancy Bleier (Pat Farragut), James Jeter (Sgt. Johnson), Art Kassul (H.H. Dodd), Joe Bratcher (Doyle), Margaret Cordova (Maid).

1640. **Boston and Kilbride.** 60 min. Airdate: 3/3/79. Production Companies: Universal Television and Stephen J. Cannell Productions. Director: Lou Antonio. Executive Producer: Stephen J. Cannell. Producer: Alex Beaton. Writer: Stephen J. Cannell. Creator: Stephen J. Cannell. This is writer/producer Stephen J. Can- nell's second unsuccessful attempt to sell CBS a series starring Tom Selleck and James Whitmore, Jr. Boston (Selleck) is a former military commando who teams up with a "think-tank" researcher and computer whiz (Whitmore) to tackle dangerous and seemingly impossible missions for anyone with the cash to pay them. In the pilot, they retrieve an airplane from a South American country that's holding it. *Cast:* Tom Selleck (as Tom Boston), James Whitmore, Jr. (Jim Kilbride), Jamie Lyn Bauer (Jill Miller), Don Ameche (Armand Beller), Marlena Amey (Maria Sangria), William Daniels (C. Donald Devlin), Lane Bradbury (Louise), Kathryn Leigh Scott (Toby Nash), David Palmer (Turgeyev), George Fisher (Markov), Walt Davis (Manolito), Elizabeth Halliday (Dianne), Michael Brick (Vince), June Whitley Taylor (Mrs. Beller).

1641. **Captain America.** 2 hours. Airdate: 1/19/79. Production Company: Universal Television. Director: Rod Holcomb. Executive Producer: Allan Balter. Producer: Martin Goldstein. Writer: Don Ingalls, from a story by Chester Krumholz and Don Ingalls, based on the Marvel Comics character. Music: Mike Post and Pete Carpenter. The first of two silly pilots starring Reb Brown as an ex-Marine who follows in his Dad's erimefighting footsteps by swallowing a super-steroid potion and becoming superhero Captain America. As is common in all concepts of this type, this super hero gets his daring-do orders from a government agent (Len Birman) and is kept under the watchful, and wistful, eye of a scientist (Heather Menzies). In the pilot, he battles an evil scientist out to destroy Phoenix with a neutron bomb. *Cast:* Reb Brown (as Steve Rogers), Len Birman (Dr. Simon Mills), Heather Menzies (Dr. Wendy Day), Lance LeGault (Harley), Frank Marth (Charles Barber), Robin Mattson (Tinay Hayden), Joseph Ruskin (Rudy Sandrini), Steve Forrest (Lou Brackett), Nocona Aranada (Throckmorton), Michael McManus (Ortho), Chip Johnson (Jerry), Dan Barton (Jeff Hayden), James Ingersoll (Lester Wiant), Jim Smith (FBI Agent), Ken Chandler (1st Doctor), Jason Wingreen (2nd Doctor), Buster Jones (3rd Doctor), June Dayton (Secretary), Diana Webster (Nurse).

1642. **Captain America II (aka Death Too Soon).** 2 hours. Airdates: 11/23/79 and 11/24/79. Production Company: Universal Television. Director: Ivan Nagy. Executive Producer: Allan Balter. Producer: Martin Goldstein. Writers: Wilton Schiller and Patricia Payne. Music: Mike Post and Peter Carpenter. Captain America (Reb Brown) goes after mad scientist Christopher Lee, who has a dastardly plan for using a serum that advances the aging process. Connie Sellecca replaces Heather Menzies as Dr. Wendy Day, Captain America's love interest—good training for her subsequent role as girlfriend to *The Greatest American Hero*. Cast: Reb Brown (as Steve Rogers), Len Birman (Dr. Simon Mills), Connie Sellecca (Dr. Wendy Day), Katherine Justice (Helen Moore), Christopher Lee (Miquel), William Lucking (Stader), Ken Swofford (Everett Bliss), Lana Wood (Yolanda), Stanley Kamel (Kramer), William Mims (Dr. J. Brenner), John Waldron (Peter Moore), June Dayton (June Cullen), Christopher Cary (Professor Ilson).

1643. The Disciple. 60 min. Airdate: 3/16/79. Production Company: Universal Television. Director: Reza Badiyi. Executive Producer: Ken Johnson. Producers: Nicholas Corea and James Hirsch. Writers: Nicholas Corea and James Hirsch. Aired as an episode of *The Incredible Hulk*. An Irish cop (Rick Springfield) resigns from the force after his father is killed and studies with an ancient Chinese philosopher. The ex-cop uses these new skills of self-discipline as a private eye whose cases often bring him into conflict with his brother (Gerald McRaney), who is still on the force. Guest stars included Mako, Stacey Keach, Sr., and George Loros.

1644. Ebony, Ivory and Jade. 90 min. Airdate: 8/3/79. Production Company: Frankel Films. Director: John Llewellyn Moxey. Executive Producer: Ernie Frankel. Producer: Jimmy Sangster. Writer: Jimmy Sangster, from a story by Ann Beckett and Mike Farrell. Music: Earle Hagen. A *Charlie's Angels* rip-off. On the surface, Ebony Bryant (Debbie Allen) and Ivory David (Martha Smith) are a song-and-dance team, managed by slick guy Nick Jade (Bert Convy)—but they are actually three crack secret agents. Cast: Bert Convy (as Nick Jade), Debbie Allen (Claire "Ebony" Bryant), Martha Smith (Maggie "Ivory" David), Claude Akins (Joe Blair), Donald Moffat (Ian Cabot), Nina Foch (Dr. Adela Teba), Clifford David (Grady), Nicholas Coster (Linderman), Lucille Benson (Mrs. Stone), Ji-Tu Cumbuka (Thurston), David Brenner (Himself), Franki Valli (Himself), Ted Shackelford (Barnes), Bill Lane (Heyman), Ray Guth (Conductor), Cletus Young (Plant Cop).

1645. Flatbed Annie and Sweetiepie: Lady Truckers. 2 hours. Airdate: 2/10/79. Production Companies: Moonlight Productions and Filmways. Director: Robert Greenwald. Producer: Frank Von Zerneck. Writer: Robie Robinson. Music: Don Peake. Annie Potts and Kim Darby are two female truckers—one a tough veteran, the other a naive neophyte—trying to outwit an unscrupulous repossessor. Cast: Annie Potts (as Flatbed Annie), Kim Darby (Ginny La Rosa), Fred

Willard (Jack La Rosa), Arthur Godfrey (Uncle Wally), Harry Dean Stanton (C.W. Douglas), Avery Schreiber (Mr. Munroe), Billy Carter (Deputy Miller), Rory Calhoun (Farmer), Ranee Howard (Mr. Murray), Billy Mannix (Georgina), Don Pike (Al), Robert Herman (Nick).

1646. Hunter's Moon. 60 min. Airdate: 12/1/79. Production Company: Aurora Enterprises. Director: Ken Annakin. Executive Producer: David Dortort. Producer: Ken Annakin. Writer: David Dortort. Creator: David Dortort. Cliff DeYoung stars as a would-be sheep rancher in the old West who, when his father and two brothers are killed by henchmen working for evil cattlemen, becomes a lone avenger fighting injustice during the Wyoming range wars. *Cast:* Cliff DeYoung (as Fayette Randall), Robert DeQui (Isham Hart), Alex Cord (The Captain), Leif Erickson (George Randall), Dan O'Herlihy (Hobble), John Ericson (Johansen), Ty Hardin (Marshall), John Quade (Ora Bowen), Morgan Ramsey (Senator Terry), Morgan Stevens (Peter Randall).

1647. The Jordan Chance. 2 hours. Airdate: 12/12/78. Production Companies: Roy Huggins Productions, R.B. Productions, and Universal Television. Director: Jules Irving. Executive Producer: Roy Huggins. Producer: Jo Swerling, Jr. Writer: Stephen J. Cannell, from a story by John Thomas James (aka Roy Huggins) and Stephen J. Cannell. Music: Pete Rugolo. Raymond Burr stars as Frank Jordan, an attorney who was once wrongly imprisoned and is now dedicated to helping others who are unjustly accused or punished for crimes they did not commit. *Cast:* Raymond Burr (as Frank Jordan), Ted Shackelford (Brian Klosky), James Canning (Jimmy Foster), Jeannie Fitzsimmons (Karen Wagner), Stella Stevens (Virna Stewart), George DiCenzo (Sheriff DeVega), John McIntire (Jasper Colton), Peter Haskell (Lee Southerland), Maria Elena Cordero (Elena Delgado), Gerald McRaney (Sid Burton), John Dennis (Lew Mayfield), Grant Owen (Mike Anderson), Michael Don Wagner (Judge Miller).

1648. M Station: Hawaii. 2 hours. Airdate: 6/10/80. Production Company: Lord and Lady Enterprises. Director: Jack Lord. Executive Producer: Jack Lord. Producer: Fred Baum. Writer: Robert Janes. Music: Morton Stevens. Jared Martin heads an elite oceanic exploration team that tackles tough assignments for the government and even the private sector. It's *Hawaii Five-0* on the high-seas with Jack Lord, director and producer of this pilot, guesting as the Admiral who enlists the team to salvage a sunken Russian submarine. Moe Keale reprises his role as Truck Kealoha from *Hawaii Five-0*. *Cast:* Jared Martin (as Dana Ryan), Jo Ann Harris

(Karen Holt), Andrew Duggan (Andrew McClelland), Elissa Dulce (Luana Sorel), Moe Keale (Truck Kealoha), Jack Lord (Admiral Henderson), Dana Wynter (Maggie Michaels), Tom McDadden (Billy Jim Whitney), Ted Hamilton (Vasily Litvak), Lyle Bettger (Admiral Lincoln), Andrew Prine (Capt. Ben Galloway), Frankie Stevens (Restov), James Reynolds (Barsak), Alan Andrade (Commander Black).

1649. **Momma the Detective aka See China and Die.** 90 min. Airdate: 11/12/81. Production Company: Big Hit Productions. Director: Larry Cohen. Producers: Larry Cohen and Hal Schaffel. Writer: Larry Cohen. Creator: Larry Cohen. Music: Joey Levine and Chris Palmaro. Esther Rolle is a maid who solves mysteries and, in the pilot, she unravels the stabbing death of her boss to the consternation of her son (Kene Holliday), a homicide detective. Shot on location in New York. Syndicated under the title *See China and Die. Cast:* Esther Rolle (as Momma Sykes), Kene Holliday (Sgt. Alvin Sykes), Paul Dooley (Ames Prescott), Andrew Duggan (Edward Forbes), Jean Marsh (Sally Hackman), Frank Converse (Tom Hackman), Laurence Luckinbill (Dr. Glickman), Fritz Weaver (Mr. Foster), Claude Brooks (Jessie Sykes), William Walker, II (Andy Sykes), Jack Straw (Norman), Arthur French (Ribman), Colin Evans (Butler), James Dickson (Sweeny), Gordon Gould (DeSantos), also, Jane Hitchcock and Miguel Pinero.

1650. **A Real American Hero.** 2 hours. Airdate: 12/9/78. Production Company: Bing Crosby Productions. Director: Lou Antonio. Executive Producer: Charles A. Pratt. Producer: Samuel A. Peeples. Writer: Samuel A. Peeples. Music: Walter Sharf. Brian Dennehy assumes the role of real-life Tennessee Sheriff Buford Pusser, portrayed in the motion picture *Walking Tall* by Joe Don Baker and in the two sequels by Bo Svenson. In the pilot, the angry, club-wielding Sheriff takes on moonshiners. Forrest Tucker reprises his movie role (having replaced Noah Beery in the second sequel) as Buford's father. Although this pilot didn't sell, Bo Svenson would later star again as Pusser in the 1981 NBC series *Walking Tall*, which lasted a mere eight episodes. *Cast:* Brian Dennehy (as Sheriff Buford Pusser), Forrest Tucker (Carl Pusser), Brian Kerwin (Til Johnson), Ken Howard (Danny Boy Mitchell), Sheree North (Carrie Todd), Lane Bradbury (Debbie Pride), Brad Davis (Mick Rogers), Ed Call (Grady Coker), W.O. Smith (Obra Eaker), Julie Thrasher (Dana Pusser), Jason Hood (Mike Pusser), Ann Street (Grandma Pusser), George Boyd (Lloyd Tatum), Maureen Burns (Amelia Biggins), Charlie Briggs (Miles Conway), Elizabeth Lane (Sabrina Marlowe).

1651. The Return of Frank Cannon. 2 hours. Airdate: 11/1/80. Production Company: Quinn Martin Productions. Director: Corey Allen. Executive Producer: Quinn Martin. Producer: Michael Rhodes. Writers: James David Buchanan and Ronald Austin. Music: Bruce Broughton. Theme: John Parker. An attempt to revive *Cannon*, the 1971–76 CBS series about overweight private eye Frank Cannon (William Conrad), who tooled around Los Angeles in a Lincoln Continental and had a taste for gourmet food. Now Cannon has opened up his own restaurant and instead of chasing crooks, he hits the high seas to catch fish for his cook (James Hong) to prepare. But Cannon becomes a detective once again (hunting down clues in his Cadillac convertible) when an old C.I.A. buddy's suicide looks more like murder. In the proposed series, Cannon would double as restaurateur and P.I. *People* magazine said the plot of this pilot "lumbers along as heavily as its star." *Cast:* William Conrad (as Frank Cannon), James Hong (Yutong), Diana Muldaur (Sally Bingham), Joanna Pettet (Alana Richardson), Ed Nelson (Mike Danvers), Burr DeBenning (Charles Kirkland), Arthur Hill (Curtis McDonald), Allison Argo (Jessica Bingham), Taylor Lacher (Lew Garland), William Smithers (William Barrett), Hank Brandt (Pearson).

1652. S.H.E. 2 hours. Airdate: 2/23/80. Production Company: Martin Bregman Productions. Director: Robert Michael Lewis. Producer: Martin Bregman. Writer: Richard Maibaum. Music: Michael Kamen. Singer: Linda Gaines. Producer Martin Bregman hired screenwriter Richard Maibaum, coscripter of 14 James Bond films, to bring 007 to television—as a woman. Cornelia Sharpe is Lavinia Kean who, as a crack Securities Hazard Expert (S.H.E.) for a covert agency, tackles megalomaniac villains (Omar Sharif) and handsome men with ease. Shot on location in Italy and Germany. A second pilot was written by Maibaum, but never filmed. *Cast:* Cornelia Sharpe (as Lavinia Kean), William Traylor (Agant Lacey), Robert Lansing (Owen Hooper), Omar Sharif (Cesare Magnasco), Isabella Rye (Fanya), Thom Christopher (Eddie Bronzi), Anita Ekberg (Dr. Else Biebling), Fabio Testi (Rudolph Caserta), Mario Colli (Alfredo Mucci), Claudio Ruffini (Larue), Fortunato Arena (Paesano), Emilio Messina (Zel).

1653. Steeltown. 60 min. Airdate: 5/19/79. Production Companies: Cypress Point Productions and Paramount Television. Director: Robert Collins. Executive Producers: Gerald W. Abrams and Bruce J. Sallan. Producer: Erv Zavada. Writer: Laurence Heath. This pilot focused on the intertwining lives of two families, the blue collar Modgelewskys and the white collar Andersons in a Pennsylvania steeltown in the early 1960s. Frank Converse is Modge Modgelewsky, a widowed steel worker and union leader raising three kids, and Bibi Besch is Janet Anderson, a widow with two sons, one of whom runs the steel mill her late husband founded. Shot on location in Portland, Oregon. *Cast:* Frank Converse (as Modge Modgelewsky), Michael Biehn (Gibby Anderson), Craig Cassity (cq) (Chris Modgelewsky), James Carroll Jordan (Bill Anderson), Mare Winningham (Aggie Modgelewsky), Richard Hill (Coach Szabo), Justin Randi (Steve Modgelewsky), Bibi Besch (Janet Anderson), Wendy Rastatter (Terri), Charles Cooper (Charley Lemke), Ken Washington (Doc Brinjac), Trevor Henley (Ed Lemke), Anna Garduno (Alma), Kevin Geer (Joe Falcone), Gregory Chase (John Carlyle).

1654. Stunt Seven. 2 hours. Airdate: 5/30/79. Production Company: Martin Poll Productions. Director: John Peyser. Producers: Martin Poll and William Craver. Writer: David Shaw. Music: Bill Conti. Christopher Connelly heads a versatile, seven-member Hollywood stunt team who, in this light-hearted pilot, save a movie star (Elke Sommer) held prisoner by a pirate (Patrick MacNnee) in an island fortress. *Cast:* Christopher Connelly (as Hill Singleton), Christopher Lloyd (Skip Hartman), Morgan Brittany (Elena Sweet), Bob Seagren (Wally Ditweiler), Soon Teck Oh (Kenny Uto), Brian Brodsky (Horatio Jennings), Juanin Clay (Dinah Lat-timore), Bill Macy (Frank Wallach), Peter Haskell (Phil Samson), Patrick MacNee (Maximillian Bourdeaux), Elke Sommer (Rebecca Wayne), Morgan Pauli (John Heinlein), Robert Ritchie (Harrison), Lynda Beattie (Monica).

1655. The Ultimate Imposter. 2 hours. Airdate: 5/12/79. Production Company: Universal. Director: Paul Stanley. Producer: Lionel E. Siegel. Writer: Lionel E. Siegel, from the novel *Capricorn Man* by William Zacha, Sr. A secret agent (Joseph Hacker) whose brain is "erased" by bad guys has a computer surgically implant in his skull, allowing him to be programmed with an all-new personality and set of skills. The catch is the programming fades after 72 hours. You can just imagine how each episode in the proposed series would have ended. Keith Andes is the scientist who programs him, Macon McCalman gives him his assignments, and Erin Gray is a fellow agent. This is a reworking of an unsold pilot that aired in 1977 as an episode of *The Six Million Dollar Man*. *Cast:* Joseph Hacker (as Frank Monihan), Keith Andes (Eugene Danziger), Macon McCalman (Jake McKeever), Erin Gray (Beatrice Tate), Tracy Brooks Swope (Danielle Parets), John Van Dreelen (Rueben

Parets), Rosalind Chao (Lai-Ping), Bobby Riggs (Tennis Pro), Norman Burton (Papich), Robert Phillips (Red Cottle), Greg Barnett (Sgt. Williger), Thomas Beilin (Joe Mason), Loren Berman (Dominic), Bill Capizzi (Tony), Cindy Castillo (Esteban), Joseph Hardin (Eddie), Mark Garcia (Felippe), Graydon Gould (Carl Lathrop), Chip Johnson (Martin), Mike Kulcsar (Vaya Makov), Betty Kwan (Ms. Wang), Bob Thomas (Tomas), W.T. Zacha (Weeks).

1656. **Wild Wild West Revisited.** 2 hours. Airdate: 5/9/79. Production Company: CBS Entertainment. Director: Burt Kennedy. Executive Producer: Jay Bernstein. Producer: Robert L. Jacks. Writer: William Bowers. Creator: Michael Garrison. Music: Richard Markowitz. The first of two unsold pilots reuniting secret service agents James West (Robert Conrad) and Artemus Gordon (Ross Martin), who traveled the frontier in the 1860s and the airwaves on CBS from 1965–69. They are brought out of retirement (West owns a border saloon, Gordon is a struggling actor) to battle the son (Paul Williams) of their long-dead, arch-foe Dr. Loveless, who is dabbling in cloning and nuclear power. *Cast:* Robert Conrad (as James West), Ross Martin (Artemus Gordon), Paul Williams (Michelito Loveless), Harry Morgan (C.I.A. Director Robert T. Malone), Rene Auberjonois (Capt. Sir David Edney), Jo Ann Harris (Carmelita Loveless), Trisha Noble (Penelope), Jeff MacKay (Hugo Kaufman), Susan Blu (Gabrielle), Pavla Ustinov (Nadia), Wilford Brimley (President Grover Cleveland), Robert Shields (Alan), Lorene Yarnell (Sonya), Jacqueline Hyde (Queen Victoria), Alberto Morin (Spanish King), Jeff Redford (The Kid), Ted Hartley (Russian Tsar), Skip Homeier (Joseph), John Wheeler (Henry), Mike Wagner (Manager), Joyce Jameson (Lola).

NBC / COMEDY

1657. **The Boss and the Secretary.** 30 min. Production Company: Lorimar Productions. Executive Producers: Lee Rich and Marc Merson. Producers: William Bickley and Michael Warren. Writers: William Bickley and Michael Warren. James Staley is an up-and-coming executive in a St. Louis marketing firm who is promoted to assistant vice president and transferred to New York—where he is saddled with more responsibility, more pressure, and an uninhibited secretary (Ellen Greene) who can't stay out of everyone's personal and professional lives. He'd fire her, but sometimes her meddling always helps him triumph over his slick and scheming office rival (Jeff Maxwell).

1658. But Mother! (aka Mr. Right). 30 min. Airdate: 6/27/79. Production Company: TAT Communications. Director: Jack Shea. Executive Producers: Bob Weiskopf and Bob Schiller. Writers: Bob Weiskopf and Bob Schiller. Creators: Bob Weiskopf and Bob Schiller. The adventures of a widowed, former Madame (Dena Dietrich) and her divorced, would-be actress daughter (Amy Johnson), who are at each other's throats but share a desperate longing to find their own "Mr. Right." This unsold pilot, which originally starred Beverly Archer as the daughter, was described as "odious" by the Associated Press. *Cast:* Dena Dietrich (as Billie Barclay), Amy Johnston (Sharon Barclay), Allan Rich (Dr. Leopold Kaufer), James Callahan (Judge Harrington), Harry Gold (Barney), Robert Alda (Paul Fitzpatrick), Gloria LeRoy (Trixie), Philip Bruns (Harold).

1659. Butterflies. 30 min. Airdate: 8/1/79. Production Company: EMI Television. Director: James Burrows. Executive Producers: Roger Gimbel and Tony Converse. Producers: Milt Josefsberg and Conrad Holzgang. Writer: Carla Lane. Creator: Carla Lane. Based on Lane's bittersweet, British series about a bored housewife (Jennifer Warren) who has a chaste, daytime affair with an infatuated, wealthy playboy (Jim Hutton). Her conservative dentist husband (John McMartin) has no inkling of her secret life, though her two liberal, frequently unemployed sons (Craig Wasson and Robert Doran) notice the change in her and are amused by it.

1660. Crash Island. 60 min. Airdate: 4/11/81. Production Company: Universal Television. Director: Hollingsworth Morse. Producers: Don Nelson and Gino Grimaldi. Writers: Don Nelson and Arthur Alsberg. Yet another in Universal's endless stream of "stranded-on-an-uncharted island" pilots and, by far, the worst of the lot. Greg Mullavey and Meadowlark Lemon are charter airline pilots flying a 15-member Y.M.C.A. coed swim team to Hawaii when, suddenly, the weather started getting rough, the tiny plane was tossed . . . you get the idea. Stranded on an uncharted isle, and aided by a Japanese soldier who has been a castaway there for 30 years, they form their own society and try to cope with their plight. *Variety* called it a cross between *Gilligans Island* and *The Bad News Bears*, and "the resultant silliness was highly unpromising." *Cast:* Greg Mullavey (as Happy Burleson), Meadowlark Lemon (Meadowlark), Jenny Sherman (Ceci), Warren Berlinger (Coach Bundy), Sheila DeWindt (Tina), Pat Morita (Kazi Yamamora), Penelope Sudrow (Sandy), Lisa Lindren (Kris), Heather Hobbs (Heather), Elizabeth Ring-wald (Susan), Paul Jarnagin, Jr. (Chubby), Jeffrey Knootz (Harry), Gregory

Knootz (Larry), Bradley Liberman (Brett), Rusty Gilligan (Fred), Danie Wade Dalton (Mark), Cjon Damitri Patterson (Angie), Jeff Kirkland (Jeff).

1661. **The Further Adventures of Wally Brown.** 30 min. Airdate: 8/21/80. Production Companies: Rothman/Ganz Productions and Paramount Television. Director: Lowell Ganz. Executive Producers: Mark Rothman and Lowell Ganz. Producer: John C. Shulay. Writer: Babaloo Mandel. Based on the 1950s song "Charlie Brown" by The Coasters. The adventures of Wally Brown, a black teenager, and his white friend Dougie, both of whom are on the school track team. Wally lives with his grandfather, but spends most of his time hanging out with Dougie and his family. *Cast:* Clinton Carroll (Wally Brown), Peter Scolari (Dougie Burdett), Arlene Golonka (Mrs. Burdett), Ron Masak (Mr. Burdett), Gilbert Gottfried (Bernstein), Richard Karron (Bruno), Bobby Ellerbee (Kline), Marvin Braverman (Coach).

Gilligan's Island. Three pilots were made aimed at reviving the beloved 1964–67 CBS comedy.

1662. **[#1] Rescue from Gilligan's Island.** 2 hours. Airdates: 10/14/78 and 10/21/78. Production Companies: Redwood Productions and Paramount Television. Director: Leslie H. Martinson. Executive Producer: Sherwood Schwartz. Producer: Lloyd J. Schwartz. Writers: Sherwood Schwartz, Elroy Schwartz, A1 Schwartz, and David P. Harmon. Creator: Sherwood Schwartz. This revival pilot of the beloved 1964–67 CBS series *Gilligan's Island* was the surprise smash hit of the 1979–80 season (30.4 rating/52 share), prompting a rash of series revivals—over 50 in all—that continued virtually unabated through 1986, when the success of *Perry Mason Returns* sparked a whole new wave of resurrections. In this, the first of three *Gilligan's Island* revival pilots, the castaways are swept out to sea by a tidal wave, are rescued, and return home to Hawaii, only to get shipwrecked on the same uncharted island during a reunion cruise a year later. *Cast:* Alan Hale, Jr. (as the Skipper), Bob Denver (Gilligan), Jim Backus (Thurston Howell, III), Natalie Schafer (Lovey Howell), Dawn Wells (Mary Ann Summers), Russell Johnson (the Professor), Judith Baldwin (Ginger Grant), Vincent Schiavelli (Dimitri), June Whitley Taylor (Miss Ainsworth), Martin Ashe (Butler).

1663. **[Pilot #2] [Gilligan's Island] Castaways on Gilligan's Island.** 90 min. Airdate: 5/3/79. Production Companies: Redwood Productions and Paramount

Television. Director: Earl Bellamy. Executive Producer: Sherwood Schwartz. Producer: Lloyd J. Schwartz. Writers: Sherwood Schwartz, Elroy Schwartz, and A1 Schwartz. Creator: Sherwood Schwartz. The hapless castaways find the remains of two planes and (a la *The Flight of the Phoenix*) use the parts from both to make one working aircraft. They once again leave their uncharted island. But this time, they intentionally return once more and, with millionaire Thurston Howell's money, open a resort hotel that purposefully lacks many of the modern amenities. The proposed series would spring, not unlike *The Love Boat*, from the interactions between the castaways and their many guests. *Cast:* Alan Hale, Jr. (as the Skipper), Bob Denver (Gilligan), Jim Backus (Thurston Howell, III), Natalie Schafer (Lovey Howell), Dawn Wells (Mary Ann Summers), Russell Johnson (the Professor), Constance Forslund (Ginger Grant), David Ruprecht (Thurston Howell, IV), Tom Bosley (Henry Elliot), Marcia Wallace (Myra Elliot), Ronnie Scribner (Robbie), Rod Browning (Tom Larsen), Lanna Saunders (Mrs. Sloan), Mokihana (Naheete), Joan Roberts (Laura Larsen).

1664. **[Pilot #3] [Gilligan's Island] Harlem Globetrotters on Gilligan's Island.** 2 hours. Airdate: 5/15/81. Production Company: Paramount Television. Director: Peter Baldwin. Executive Producer: Sherwood Schwartz. Producer: Lloyd J. Schwartz. Writers: Sherwood Schwartz, A1 Schwartz, David P. Harmon, and Gordon Mitchell. Creator: Sherwood Schwartz. The castaways and the Harlem Globetrotters battle an evil scientist (Martin Landau) and his army of robots who are after a rare mineral found only on the island. Originally, this was intended to feature the Dallas Cowboy Cheerleaders. The castaways later reappeared in animated form on the 1982–83 CBS Saturday morning series *Gilligan s Planet*, and showed up in the flesh in 1987 on episodes of *The New Gidget* and *ALF.* A new incarnation, *Gilligan's Island II*, in which the children of the original castaways are themselves stranded on the island, was in the works in 1987 by Sherwood Schwartz for WTBS/The Super Channel. *Cast:* Alan Hale, Jr. (as the Skipper), Bob Denver (Gilligan), Jim Backus (Thurston Howell, III), Natalie Schafer (Lovey Howell), Dawn Wells (Mary Ann Summers), Russell Johnson (the Professor), Constance Forslund (Ginger Grant), David Ruprecht (Thurston Howell, IV), Dreama Denver (Lucinda), Rosalind Chao (Manager), Martin Landau (J.J. Pierson), Barbara Bain (Olga Schmetner), Whitney Rydbeck (George), Scatman Crothers (Dewey Stevens), Chick Hearn (Sportscaster), Bruce Biggs (Referee), Cindy Appleton (Linda), Wendy Hoffman (Jackie).

1665. Gossip. 30 min. Airdate: 6/10/79. Production Company: EMI Television. Executive Producer: Roger Gimbel. Producers: Mort Lachman and Michael Shamberg. Writers: Bernie Kukoff and Jeff Harris. Creator: Michael Shamberg. The first of two pilots about the staff of *The National Gossip*, a weekly scandal sheet. This one focused on a reporter (Charles Levin) and photographer (Jeff Altman) who are desperately in search of jazzy copy that will boost the magazine's sagging circulation. *Cast:* Jeff Altman (as Milton), Charles Levin (Mac), Judy Landers (Goldie), Raymond Singer (Leech), Thomas Hill (Ed Stone), Fern Fitzgerald (Luanda Neester).

1666. [Pilot #2] Gossip. 30 min. Airdate: 7/10/79. Production Company: EMI Television. Director: Peter Baldwin. Executive Producer: Roger Gimbel. Producers: Michael Shamberg and Jerry McPhie. Writer: Roger Gimbel. Creator: Michael Shamberg. Only Jeff Altman and Charles Levin are back, albeit with different names and slightly reworked characters, in this second attempt to sell a scandal sheet sitcom. *Cast:* Charles Levin (as Jeb), Jeff Altman (Flash), John Hiller- man (Mr. Dempster), Dena Dietrich (Mrs. Gallup), Mary Catherine Wright (Mittie), Robbie Rist (Tip).

1667. Heaven on Earth. 30 min. Airdate: 6/28/79. Production Company: Universal Television. Director: Lou Antonio. Executive Producer: Peter Meyerson. Producer: Richard Caffey. Writers: Jim Fritzell and Everett Greenbaum. Creators: Jim Fritzell and Everett Greenbaum. Two roommates (Carol Wayne and Donna Ponterotto) are killed in a car crash and called to heaven "before their time." So, they are sent back to earth on one condition: that they perform a good deed every day. They are given some magical powers and are supervised by spirit Sebastian (William Daniels).

1668. Home Again (aka Not Until Today). 30 min. Airdate: 6/27/79. Production Company: MTM Enterprises. Director: Michael Zinberg. Executive Producers: Michael Zinberg and David Lloyd. Writer: David Lloyd. Music: Patrick Williams. Aired as part of the "Battle of the Generations" compilation of unsold pilots. This pilot depicts what happens when a small town police chief (Darren McGavin) meets a teenage son (Michael Horton) he never knew he had. *Cast:* Darren McGavin (as Jason Swann), Michael Horton (Jake Warren), Lynn Carlin (Mae Henderson), Dick Sargent (Father Dacey), Peter Jurasik (Ned), Raleigh Bond (Harry Henderson), Alexandra Stoddard (Sally), David Cohn (Morton), Parris Buckner (Mr. Fenner).

1669. Jump Street. 30 min. Production Companies: Rollins-Joffe-Bessell Productions and Universal Television. Executive Producers: Charles Joffe and Larry Brezner. Producers: Michael Kagan and Alan Uger. Writers: Michael Kagan and Alan Uger. Creators: Michael Kagan and Alan Uger. When four brothers are orphaned, they stick together in their Bronx home. They live off odd-jobs and their parents' trust fund, hire a wise-cracking black housekeeper named Jazz, and get advice from Uncle Eddie. The cast included Scott Colomby, Ralph Seymour, Glenn Scarpelli, Danny Dayton, and Clarice Taylor.

1670. Love and Learn. 30 min. Airdate: 8/1/79. Production Company: Wayne/Burditt Productions. Director: Jack Shea. Producers: George Burditt and Paul Wayne. Writers: George Burditt and Paul Wayne. Creators: George Burditt and Paul Wayne. Lawrence Pressman is a sedate college English professor who, while on a trip to Las Vegas, falls in love with a showgirl (Candy Clark), marries her, and brings her back home to live with him and his 20-year-old brother (James Van Patten). *Cast:* Lawrence Pressman (as Professor Jason Brewster), Candy Clark (Holly Brewster), James Van Patten (Mark Brewster), Earl Bowen (Harvey), Kelly Bishop (Denise).

1671. McGurk (aka A Dog's Life). 30 min. Airdate: 6/15/79. Production Company: TAT Communications. Director: Peter Bonerz. Producer: Charlie Hauck. Writers: Arthur Julian and Charlie Hauck. Creators: Arthur Julian and Charlie Hauck. A classic unsold pilot, an embarrassing disaster from the company responsible for such landmark shows as *All in the Family* and *Maude*. Barney Martin headed a cast of actors who dressed in dog suits and barked one-liners at each other. The idea, supposedly, was to offer wry observations about man through the eyes of his best friend. *Cast:* Barney Martin (as McGurk), Beej Johnson (Iris), Sherry Lynn (Camille), Charles Martin Smith (Tucker), Hamilton Camp (Spike), Michael Huddleston (Turk).

1672. Me and Ducky. 30 min. Airdate: 6/21/79. Production Company: Lorimar Productions. Director: Bill Persky. Executive Producers: Lee Rich and Marc Merson. Producer: Steve Zacharias. Writer: Steve Zacharias. The misadventures of San Francisco high school student Carol Munday (Linda Cook) and Ducky Hopnagel (Jayne Modean). *Cast:* Linda Cook (as Carol Minday), Jayne Modean (Ducky Hopnagel), Dawn Dunlap (Dawn Duval), Valerie Landsberg (Babs Hulet), Susan Duvall (Toby Walls), Gary Imhoff (Rims), Kathleen Doyle (Mrs. Munday), James Karen (Mr. Munday).

1673. **Mother and Me, M.D.** 30 min. Airdate: 5/14/79. Production Company: MTM Enterprises. Director: Michael Zinberg. Executive Producer: Michael Zinberg. Producers: Jennie Blacton and Charles Raymond. Writers: Jennie Blacton and Charles Raymond. Music: Patrick Williams. The misadventures of a doctor (Leah Ayres) who interns at the hospital where her mother (Rue McClanahan) is the head nurse. "Rue is absolutely great," then-MTM president Grant Tinker told the *Los Angeles Times*, "what ever is wrong with the pilot, she's not it." *Cast:* Leah Ayres (as Barrie Tucker), Rue McClanahan (Lil Brenner), Jack Riley (Evan Murray), Kenneth Gilman (Dr. Mace Oatfield), Howard Witt (Dr. Sam Kanin).

1674. **Piper's Pets.** 30 min. Airdate: 5/21/79. Director: Russ Petranto. Executive Producer: Aaron Ruben. Producer: Gene Marcione. Writer: Aaron Ruben. Don Knotts is Dr. Donald Piper, a bumbling veterinarian who works with a dim- witted assistant (Peter Isacksen). Maggie Roswell is Piper's wife, and Jacque Lynn Colton is his receptionist.

1675. **Sgt. T.K. Yu.** 30 min. Airdate: 4/10/79. Production Company: Hanna- Barbera Productions. Director: Paul Stanley. Executive Producer: Joseph Barbera. Producer: Terry Morse, Jr. Writer: Gordon Dawson. Johnny Yune is a Korean L.A.P.D. detective who works part-time as a stand-up comic. Costars John Lehne and Marty Brill. Writer Dawson would later create and produce *Bret Maverick*.

1676. **Two Guys from Muck.** 30 min. Airdate: 3/29/82. Production Company: Lorimar Productions. Director: John Astin. Executive Producers: Lee Rich and Phil Capice. Producer: Lawrence Kasha. Writer: Steve Zacharias. Somebody at NBC thought scandal sheets would make a good sitcom. Like *Gossip*, also piloted this season, this is the story of two reporters (Adam Arkin and Rick Casorla) who work for a sleazy tabloid. And, like most shows about reporters, these guys often end up solving the wild crimes they are assigned to report. *Cast:* Adam Arkin (as Louie), Rick Casorla (Buzz), Graham Jarvis (Mr. Davis), Gwen Humble (Sybil Sanders), Jill St. John (Miss DeMandt), Victor Buono (Mr. Big), Larry Storch (Casey Muir), Sid Haig (Thug), Beverly Sanders (Bridle Muir), J.J. Barry (Cop).

1677. **Uptown Saturday Night.** 30 min. Airdate: 6/28/79. Production Company: Warner Bros. Television. Director: Bill Davis. Producer: Eric Cohen. Writer: Eric Cohen. Creator: Richard Wesley. Based on the 1974 movie *Uptown Saturday- Night* and its two sequels, all of which starred Sidney Poitier and Bill Cosby as two friends who get involved in wild schemes. Cleavon Little and Adam Wade assay the roles this time. Starletta DuBois, Julius Harris, and Don Bexley guest star.

NBC / DRAMA

1678. **The Aliens (aka Aliens Are Coming; aka The New Invaders).** 2 hours. Airdate: 3/2/80. Production Company: Quinn Martin Productions. Director: Harvey Hart. Executive Producer: Quinn Martin. Producer: Philip Saltzman. Writer: Robert W. Lenski. Music: William Goldstein. A new version of *The Invaders*, Quinn Martin's 1967–68 series about an architect who knows Earth is being invaded by humanoid aliens—but only a handful of people believe him. In this remake/pilot, Dr. Scott Dryden (Tom Mason) tries to stop invading aliens who possess earthlings to achieve their evil ends. But Dr. Dryden isn't fighting alone—he works with the Nero Institute, where he gets help from Leonard Nero (Eric Braeden) and Gwen O'Brien (Melinda Fee). *Cast:* Tom Mason (as Dr. Scott Dryden), Melinda Fee (Gwen O'Brien), Eric Braeden (Leonard Nero), Max Gail (Russ Garner), Caroline McWilliams (Sue Garner), Matthew Laborteaux (Timmy Garner), Fawne Harriman (Joyce Cummings), Ron Masak (Harve Nelson), John Milford (Eldon Gates), Lawrence Haddon (Bert Fowler), Hank Brandt (John Sebastian), Richard Lockmiller (Officer Strong), Sean Griffin (Dr. Conley), Gerald McRaney (Norman), Curtis Credel (Frank Foley).

1679. **And Baby Makes Six.** 2 hours. Airdate: 10/22/79. Production Company: Alan Landsburg Productions. Director: Waria Hussein. Executive Producers: Alan Landsburg and Sonny Fox. Producers: Kay Hoffman and Shelley List. Writer: Shelley List. Music: Fred Karlin. When 46-year-old Anna Cramer (Colleen Dewhurst) discovers she is pregnant and decides to have the baby, she at first faces opposition from her husband (Warren Oates), who was looking forward to retiring and traveling, and her two eldest (A1 Cooley and Timothy Hutton) children. Only her 16-year-old daughter (Maggie Cooper) backs her mother. But when the baby is born, the family has a change of heart—and would face many more changes, some of which were chronicled in a second flop pilot *(Baby Comes Home)* a year later on CBS. *Cast:* Colleen Dewhurst (as Anna Cramer), Warren Oates (Michael Cramer), Maggie Cooper (Elizabeth Winston), Al Corley (Franklyn Cramer), Timothy Hutton (Jason Cramer), Allyn Ann McLerie (Dora), Mildred Dunnock (Serena Fox), Mason Adams (Dr. Eliot Losen), Maria Melendez (Marla Montez), Lee Wallace (Sam Blumenkrantz), Christopher Allport (Jeff Winston), Tamu (Donna), Joshua Glen- rock (Alex).

1680. Buffalo Soldiers. 60 min. Airdate: 5/26/79. Production Company: MGM Television. Director: Vincent McEveety. Executive Producers: Douglas Net- ter and Jim Byrnes. Producer: Les Sheldon. Writer: Jim Byrnes. Creator: Jim Byrnes. Music: Jerrold Immel. The adventures of an all-Black cavalry unit assigned to post-Civil War duty keeping the peace with Apaches and Comanches during the construction of the Texas railroad. *Cast:* John Beck (as Col. Frank "Buckshot" O'Connor), Stan Shaw (Sgt. Joshua Haywood), Richard Lawson (Caleb Holiday), Hilly Hicks (Willie), Ralph Wilcox (Oakley), Charles Robinson (Wright), L.Q. Jones (Renegade), Don Knight (Renegade), Angel Tompkins (Townsperson), Marla Pennington (Girl).

1681. Catalina C-Lab. 60 min. Airdate: 1/3/82. Production Companies: Marty Katz Productions and Paramount Television. Director: Paul Krasny. Executive Producer: Marty Katz. Producers: Jonathan Haze and Michael Lindsay. Writer: Gordon Dawson. Bruce Weitz is the leader of a science team manning an underwater research laboratory off Catalina Island. In the pilot, his daughter becomes accidentally tangled in an old drifting mine that could also destroy the lab, which is the site of a press junket. *Cast:* Bruce Weitz (as Dr. Matt Jennings), Gary Prendergast (Johnny Silver), Jeff Daniels (Rick Guthrie), Steve Vinovitch (Dwight Purdy, III), Nani Asing (Valerie Ono), Melora Hardin (Christy Jennings), Malachy McCourt (Tom Whitehead), Carl Byrd (Lt. Walker), Pearl Sher (Martha Levitz), John O'Leary (Hallet), Sidney Clute (Doctor), Harvey J. Goldenberg (Reporter), William Brian Curran (Photographer), Susan Backline (Diver).

1682. Charleston. 2 hours. Airdate: 1/15/79. Production Company: Robert Stigwood Productions. Director: Karen Arthur. Producer: Beryl Vertue. Writer: Nancy Lynn Schwartz. Music: Elmer Bernstein. A gothic serial about a woman (Delta Burke) fighting to hold onto her family's holdings after the Civil War. *Cast:* Delta Burke (as Stella Farrell), Jordan Clarke (Gregg Morgan), Richard Lawson (James Harris), Lynne Moody (Minerva), Patricia Pearcy (Valerie Criss), Martha Scott (Mrs. Farrell), Mandy Patinkin (Beaudine Croft), Richard Bradford (Cluskey), Lucille Benson (Miss Fay), Ben Hailey, Jr. (Gabriel), Dennis Burkley (Tom Doder), Ancel Cook (Rev. Dr. Palmer), Alan McRae (Lt. Beeson), Rockne Tarkington (Rev. Duchamp), William Norren (Major Day), Sam Cotten (Ned Wilson), Charles Coles (Old Shady), Robert Easton (Rev. Allen), Eddie Hailey (Luke).

1683. Doctor Franken. 2 hours. Airdate: 1/13/80. Production Companies: Titus Productions, Janus Productions, and NBC Productions. Directors: Jeff Lieberman and Marvin J. Chomsky. Executive Producer: Herbert Brodkin. Producer: Robert Berger. Writer: Lee Thomas, from a story by Jeff Lieberman and Lee Thomas, from the book *Frankenstein* by Mary Shelley. Music: John Morris. In the television world, a man with special powers either becomes a secret agent or a fugitive. The latter is the case in this pilot, a weird rehash of *Frankenstein*. Dr. Victor Franken (Robert Vaughn) is a descendant of the infamous Dr. Frankenstein, and creates a creature of his own when he revives a dead accident victim by rebuilding him with organs and limbs from the hospital medical bank. The result is a creature (Robert Perrault) who has a mind of his own—but also has the memories, convictions, and emotions of the people whose "parts" he now has. In the proposed series, he'd seek out those associated with the people who gave him organs to learn more about himself and would inevitably get involved in their lives. He is pursued by police and scientists out to destroy him, but he stays one step ahead of them, thanks to Dr. Franken. Composer John Morris, ironically, did the score for Mel Brooks' spoof *Young Frankenstein*, which costarred Teri Garr, a guest star in this pilot. *Cast:* Robert Vaughn (as Dr. Franken), Robert Perrault (John Doe), David Selby (Dr. Mike Foster), Teri Garr (Kelly Fisher), Josef Sommer (Mr. Parker), Cynthia Harris (Anita Franken), Addison Powell (Dr. Eric Kerwin), Takayo Doran (Claire), Claiborne Carey (Jenny), Nicholas Surovy (Martin Elson), Rudolph Willrich (Arthur Gurnesy), Sam Schracht (Lt. Pearson), Conchetta Tolman (Reporter), Theodore Sorel (Gerald Blake), Sylvia Loew (Mrs. Parker), Penelope Paley (Technician), Roger Til (Anesthesiologist), Myra Stennett (Hello Woman), Ed Van Nuys (Bartender), William Huston (Cop), Ralph Driscoll (Doorman), Norman Parker (Morgue Attendant), Florence Rupert (Woman).

1684. Dracula. 60 min. Production Company: Universal Television. Executive Producer: Kenneth Johnson. Writer: Kenneth Johnson. Creator: Kenneth Johnson. A spin-off from *Cliffhangers*, a short-lived series made up of three continuing 20-minute serials each week, one of which was *Curse of Dracula*. Michael Nouri is Dracula who, in this reworking, teaches a night course in history at a San Francisco college so he can meet chicks. He was a bad guy, and was killed off in the serial, but in the proposed series he's alive and well and wants to be cured. He has fallen in love with a woman (Carol Baxter) whose mother he also loved—and killed—decades ago. The series would follow his efforts to find a cure, withstand the urge to kill his beloved, and avoid those who are chasing him. Three one-hour pilots were being developed but apparently never came to fruition.

1685. **Earthbonnd.** 90 min. Production Company: Schick Sunn Classic Films. Executive Producer: Charles E. Sellier, Jr. Producer: Michael Fisher. Writer: Michael Fisher. The adventures of a kindly grandfather (Burl Ives) and his orphaned grandson (James L. Conway) who befriend an extraterrestrial family (Christopher Connelly, Meredith MacRae, Todd Porter, Marc Gilpin, and Elissa Leeds) when the aliens' flying saucer crashlands into a nearby lake. The alien family does its best to fit into American society, but their super-strength and psychic powers cause problems, and could betray them to the military man (Joseph Campanula) who is searching for them. Burl Ives replaced Ken Curtis as the star early in the making of this pilot, which Leonard Maltin, in his book *TV Movies*, lambasted as "trite, dumb, (and) idiotic." This was released as a feature film before it was broadcast on television.

1686. **Every Stray Dog and Kid.** 60 min. Airdate: 10/21/81. Production Company: MTM Enterprises. Director: James Burrows. Executive Producer: Steven Bochco. Producers: William Phillips and Gregory Hoblit. Writer: James Gunn. Maureen Anderman is a convicted car thief who, upon her release from prison, dabbles as a writer and becomes the court-appointed guardian of four teenage felons (Jackie Earle Haley, Denise Miller, Pat Petersen, and Kris McKeon)—and one stray dog. Bruce Weitz, later to costar in *Hill Street Blues*, is her friend on the police force and Alan Fudge is her literary agent. *Cast:* Maureen Anderman (as Bobbi Marshall), Bruce Weitz (Sgt. Mike Pirelli), Denise Miller (Jenny Baxter), Jackie Earle Haley (Tommy Ryan), Kris McKeon (Cathy Aronson), Pat Petersen (Normie Taylor), Alan Fudge (Lee Hatfield), Rita Taggert (Geri Ballin), Toni Gilman (Mrs. Braverman), Todd Lookinland (Jeff Hatfield), Steve Spencer (Eric Hatfield), Veronica Redd (Mrs. Carson), Linda Hayes (Hooker), Stanley Brock (Trick).

1687. **Father Brown, Detective (aka Sanctuary of Fear).** 2 hours. Airdate: 4/23/79. Production Company: Marble Arch Productions. Director: John Llewellyn Moxey. Executive Producer: Martin Starger. Producer: Phillip Barry. Writers: Don M. Mankiewicz and Gordon Cotter, from the novel *Father Brown*, by G.K. Chesterton. Barnard Hughes is Father Brown, a friendly Manhattan parish priest who solves baffling crimes, leaving his young conservative assistant (Robert Schenkkan) to reluctantly cover for him with the disapproving monsignor (George Hearn). Hughes felt the pilot might have sold had it been an hour or 90 minutes. But at two hours, "it just went on and on and on," he says. "That was a great disappointment, because it would have been a very good series." *Cast:* Barnard Hughes (as Father Brown), Kay Lenz (Carol Bain), Michael McGuire (Lt. Bellamy), George Hearn (Monsignor Kerrigan), Robert Schenkkan (Father Wembley), David Rashe (Jack Collins), Fred Gwynne (Judge Potter), Elizabeth Wilson (Mrs. Glidden), Donald Symington (Russell Heyman), Saul Rubinek (Jerry Stone), Peter Maloney (Eli Clay), Jeffrey DeMunn (Whitney Fowler), Maureen Silliman (Beth Landau), Alice Drummond (Grace Barringer), Thomas Hill (Carl Barringer).

1688. Five Aces (aka Secret War of Jackie's Girls). 2 hours. Airdate: 11/29/80. Production Companies: Penthouse Productions, Public Arts Inc., and Universal Television. Director: Gordon Hessler. Executive Producers: Florence Small and Alan Surgal. Producers: Jo Swerling, Jr. and Dorothy J. Bailey. Writers: Theodore Jonas and D. Guthrie, from a story by Theodore Jonas, from an idea by Jean Ross Kondek and Mary Ann Donahue. Creators: Theodore J. Flicker and Leigh Vance. The adventures of American women pilots—cropdusters, stunt pilots, barnstormers—recruited by the R.A.F. to fight the Germans in the days before the United States entered World War II. Producer Jo Swerling Jr. says this is "the project I would most like to forget." Huggins and Swerling were asked by the studio to supervise the project because the pilot's original producers, Florence Small and Alan Surgal, didn't have enough experience. Swerling was horrified by the script, which he recalls as "not only being terrible in every way, but the premise was totally false. We all hated the project so much." *Cast:* Lee Purcell (as Casey McCann), Ann Dusenberry (Donna), Tracy Brooks Swope (Zimmy), Dee Wallace (Maxine), Caroline Smith (Patti), John Reilly (Russ Hamilton), Sheila MacRae (Phyllis), Mariette Hartley (Jackie Scott), Don Knight (Sgt. McPherson), Ben Murphy (Buck Wheeler), Marilyn Chris (Corporal Mabel Wheaton), Edward Bell (Brewer), Curt Lowens (Dr. Kruger), Henry Olek (Dieter), William Lodge (Kaminsky), Mark Neely (Peter), George DeRoy (Al), Duane Tucker (Sergeant), Nick Mariano (Mechanic), Robert Pierce (Hans).

1689. Follow Me If You Dare (aka The Mysterious Two). 2 hours. Airdate: 5/31/82. Director: Gary Sherman. Executive Producer: Alan Landsburg. Producers: Sonny Fox and Gary Credle. Writer: Gary Sherman. Music: Joe Renzetti. Tim Armstrong (James Stephens) is the only one who knows that two evangelists (John Forsythe and Priscilla Pointer) are actually alien invaders out to brainwash earthlings as the first step towards invasion. In the proposed series, the aliens snatch his girlfriend and he vows to save her, warn society and thwart the aliens' evil plot. *Cast:* James Stephens (as Tim Armstrong), John Forsythe (He), Priscilla Pointer (She), Vic Tayback (Ted Randall), Noah Beery, Jr. (Sheriff Virgil Malloy), Robert Pine (Arnold Brown), Karen Werner (Natalie), Kenny Roker (William), Robert Englund (Boone), Mo Malone (Martha), Candy Mobley (Amanda), Dale Reynolds (Reporter), Georgia Paul (Woman).

1690. **Hotshot Harry and the Rocking Chair Renegades (aka Better Late Than Never; aka Never Too Young).** 2 hours. Airdate: 10/17/79. Production Company: Ten-Four Productions. Director: Richard Crenna. Executive Producers: Greg Strangis and William Hogan. Producer: Peter Katz. Writers: Greg Strangis and John Carpenter. Creators*. Greg Strangis and John Carpenter. Music: Charles Fox. Harold Gould stars as Harry Landers, a young-hearted and feisty senior citizen at the Lost Horizons Retirement Home, whose out-going nature often puts him at odds with the strict administrator (Tyne Daly) and inspires his elderly friends (Strother Marin, Lou Jacobi, Marjorie Bennett, and Paula Truman) to join his crusades, adventures, schemes, and rebellions. Victor Buono costars as the Home's physician. *Cast:* Harold Gould (as Harry Landers), Strother Martin (J.D. Ashcroft), Tyne Daly (Ms. Davis), Harry Morgan (Mr. Scott), Marjorie Bennett (Marjorie Crane), Victor Buono (Dr. Zoltán Polos), George Gobel (Capt. Taylor), Jeanette Nolan (Lavinia Leventhal), Donald Pleasence (Col. Riddle), Larry Storch (Sheriff), Lou Jacobi (Milton Cohen), Paula Truman (Alke Elam), Bill Fiore (Tom Wallace), Joyce Bulifant (Jean Wallace).

1691. **Institute for Revenge.** 90 min. Airdate: 1/22/79. Production Companies: Gold-Driskill Productions and Columbia Television. Director: Ken Annakin. Executive Producers: Bill Driskill and Otto Salamon. Producer: Bert Gold. Writer: Bill Driskill, from a story by Bill Driskill and Otto Salamon. Music: Lalo Schifrin. A "Mission Impossible"-esque adventure about a high-tech, world-wide organization that helps victims of conmen get non-violent revenge and bring the baddies to justice. Sam Groom is the leader who, aided by the sophisticated IFR computer, tackles each case with a hand-picked team of crack agents (T.J. McCavitt, Robert Coote, and Lane Binkley). John Hillerman provided IFR with its voice. Composer Lalo Schifrin, who scored the pilot, created the music for *Mission: Impossible.* *Cast:* Sam Groom (as John Schroeder), Lauren Hutton (Lilah), Lane Binkley (JoAnn), T.K. McCavitt (Bradley), Robert Coote (Wellington), Leslie

Nielsen (Counselor Barnes), Ray Walston (Frank Anders), George Hamilton (Alan Roberto), Robert Emhardt (Senator).

1692. The Last Convertible. 6 hours (3x2 hours). Airdates: 9/24, 25, 26/79. Production Companies: Public Arts Inc. and Universal Television. Directors: Sidney Hayers, Gus Trikonis, and Jo Swerling, Jr. Executive Producer: Jo Swerling, Jr. Producer: Robert F. O'Neill. Writers: Phil DeGuere, Clyde Ware, Stephen McPherson, from the novel by Anton Myrer. Music: Pete Rugolo. A television series based on the six-hour mini-series that traced five young men from their Harvard days in the 1940s (a time symbolized by a Packard convertible they drove and still share) on through 1969. Perry King, Bruce Boxleitner, Edward Albert, Jack Shea, and Michael Nouri star. *Cast:* Bruce Boxleitner (as George Virdon), Perry King (Russ Currier), Michael Nouri (Jean des Barres), John Shea (Terry Garrigan), Edward Albert (Ron Dalrymple), Deborah Raffin (Chris Farris), Sharon Gless (Kay Haddon), Kim Darby (Ann Rowan), Jenna Michaels (Denise), Caroline Smith (Nancy Van Breymer), Stacey Nelkin (Sheila Garrigan), Sam Wiesman (Mel Strasser), Tracy Brooks Swope (Liz), Fred McCarren (Paul McCreed), Stuart Whitman (Col. Elkart), Vic Morrow (Chief Lonborg), Pat Harrington (Major Fred Goodman), Martin Milner (Sgt. Dabric), Lisa Pelikan (Rosamond Ardley), John Houseman (Dr. Wetheral), Shawn Stevens (Bobby Dalrymple), Peggy Foster (Peggy Virdon), David Drucker (Rhino Tannehall), Chip Johnson (Capt. Phillip Burrell), Timothy O'Hagen (Fletcher).

1693. Legend of the Golden Gun. 2 hours. Airdate: 4/10/79. Production Companies: Bennett-Katleman Productions and Columbia Pictures Television. Director: Alan J. Levi. Executive Producers: Harris Katleman and Harve Bennett. Producers: B.W. Sandefur and Dan Cohan. Writer: James D. Parriott. This is "Star Wars" in the old West. After John Colton's (Jeffrey Osterhage) parents are murdered by the evil Quantrill (Robert Davi), he seeks out legendary gunfighter Jim Hammer (Hal Holbrook), who teaches him how to become a master gunslinger—and bequeaths to him his infamous golden, seven-barrelled gun and his white chamois suit. Carl Franklin is Book, a runaway slave, and Colton's companion. *Cast:* Jeffrey Osterhage (as John Colton), Carl Franklin (Joshua Brown), Hal Holbrook (Jim Hammer), Keir Dullea (General Custer), Robert Davi (William Quantrill), Michele Carey (Maggie Oakley), John McLiam (Jake Powell), Elissa Leeds (Sara Powell), R.G. Armstrong (Judge Harrison Harding), R.L. Tolbert

(Buffalo Bill), William Bryant (William Ford), J. Brian Pizer (Capt. Marks), Rex Holman (Sturges).

1694. Murder in Music City (aka Music City Murders; aka Country Music Murders; aka Sonny and Sam). 2 hours. Airdate: 1/16/79. Production Company: Frankel Films/Gank Inc. Director: Leo Penn. Executive Producer: Ernie Frankel. Producer: Jimmy Sangster. Writers: Ernie Frankel and Jimmy Sangster. Music: Earle Hagen. Sonny Bono is a songwriter who buys a detective agency as a tax shelter and ends up taking over the business—with his bride, a model (Lee Purcell)—when the private eye is killed. Country-western singers Charlie Daniels, Larry Gatlin, Barbara Mandrell, Ronnie Milsap, Ray Stevens, and Mel Tillis all made cameo appearances as themselves. *Cast:* Sonny Bono (as Sonny Hunt), Lee Purcell (Samantha Hunt), Lucille Benson (Mrs. Bloom), Claude Akins (Billy West), Belinda J. Montgomery (Peggy Ann West), Morgan Fairchild (Dana Morgan), Michael MacRae (Chigger Wade), Harry Bellaver (Jim Feegan), Jim Owen (Sam Prine), T. Tommy Cutrer (Lt. Culver).

1695. The Nightingales. 60 min. Airdate: 5/19/79. Production Company: Lawrence Gordon Productions. Director: Charles Dubin. Executive Producer: Lawrence Gordon. Producer: Jay Benson. Writer: Richard Christian Danus. Creator: Richard Christian Danus. Music: Barry DeVorzon. The adventures of under-cover cops Jenny Palermo (Marcia Strassman), a street-smart brunette, and Cotton Gardner (Colette Blonigan), a blonde former actress, working the nightbeat in Hollywood. Other regulars include a local DJ (James Spinks), and two officers (Granville Van Dusen and Mark Schneider) who watch out for them. *Cast:* Marcia Strassman (as Jenny Palermo), Colette Blonigan (Cotton Gardner), Mark Schneider (Officer Ray Sikora), Granville Van Dusen (Officer Joe Tussing), James Spinks (Big Duane Lockridge), Dennis Rediield (Ice), Ji-Tu Cumbuka (James), Eugene Butler (Jumbo), Sheree North (Fingernail Dolly), Ivan Wideman (Anthony Walker), Kimberly Woodward (Brigid Walker), Jerry Lacy ("Humphrey Bogart").

1696. Operating Room (aka Doctors and Nurses). 60 min. Airdate: 10/4/78. Production Company: MTM Enterprises. Director: Bruce Paltrow. Producer: Mark Tinker. Writers: Steven Bochco and Bruce Paltrow. Music: Mike Post and Pete Carpenter. This could be considered an early attempt at *St. Elsewhere*, the medical comedy/drama that Tinker and Paltrow mounted in 1982 following the success of Bochco's serialized copshow *Hill Street Blues*. The series would have focused on the professional and personal lives of the surgical section of a fictional Los Angeles Hospital. This pilot actually sold, but Bochco says he turned NBC down because the network only ordered six episodes. "I had learned a lesson from *Richie Brockleman*," he says. "When I came to MTM, I said 'please understand right now, that I'm never going to get involved with taking a six show order on something. When you make six episodes of a series, you get used as corks to plug holes in the schedule. You get stuck on the air at the last minute. You can't keep the morale of your unit up because nobody knows what the hell is going on. And, the reality of TV being what it is today, your odds of doing a show that will succeed are terrible anyway. You need a minimum of 13 to get a run going." *Cast:* David Spielberg (as Dr. Jim Lawrence), Oliver Clark (as Dr. Charles Webster), James Sutorius (Dr. Robert Robinson), Barbara Babcock (Jean Lawrence), also, Bruce Bauer, Janice Kent, Barbara Bosson, Cyb and Tricia Barnstable, Patricia Conklin, Ronne Troup, Barbara Perry.

1697. **The Rivals.** 60 min. Production Company: Lyman Dayton Productions. Executive Producer: Lyman Dayton. Writer: Keith Merrill. The story of what happens when a midwestern farm boy (Stuart Petterson) moves with his widowed mother (Shannon Farnon) and younger sister (Lachelle Price) to Los Angeles—where he's a "fish out of water" and must vie with Clyde (Philip Brown), the "Big Man on Campus," for the affections of beautiful Brooke (Dana Kimmell).

1698. **Salem's Lot.** 60 min. Production Company: Warner Bros. Television. Producers: Richard Kobritz and Douglas Benton. Writers: Robert Bloch and Paul Monash. Five scripts were developed for a proposed series based on the four-hour CBS mini-series of Stephen King's horror tale *Salem's Lot*. David Soul starred as Ben Mears, a novelist on the run with teenager Mark Petrie (Lance Kerwin) from vampires. The prospect of a series didn't thrill King, who wrote in his book *Danse Macabre* that he was relieved "when that rather numbing prospect passed the boards." A two-hour version of the original mini-series is available in home video. A sequel, entitled *Return to Salem's Lot*, was made in 1987 for the home video market by writer/director Larry Cohen.

1699. **Tut and Tuttle (aka Through the Magic Pyramid).** 2 hours (2x60 min.). Airdates: 12/6/81 and 12/13/81. Production Company: Major H. Productions. Director: Ron Howard. Executive Producer: Ron Howard. Producers: Ron Howard and Herbert J. Wright. Writers: Ranee Howard and Herbert J. Wright. Creators: Ranee Howard and Herbert J. Wright. Music: Joe Renzetti. The misadventures of a boy (Christopher Barnes) who gets a toy pyramid for his birthday—a pyramid that is actually a magic device that can transport him back to ancient Egypt, where he befriends young King Tut (Eric Greene) and helps him deal with his problems. This two-hour pilot was sliced in half and broadcast as two hour- long specials, which were nominated for an Emmy as Outstanding Children's Special. *Cast:* Christopher Barnes (as Bobby Tuttle), James Hampton (Sam Tuttle), Betty Beaird (as Eleanor Tuttle), Robbie Rist (Bonkers), Olivia Barash (Princess Baket), Hans Conried (Ay), Vic Tayback (Horembeb), Kario Salem (Akenaten), Eric Greene (Tutankamen), Jo Anne Worley (Mutjnedjmet), Mel Berger (Yuzannout), Mary Carver (Tiye), Daniel Leon (Guard), Gino Conforti (Hotep), Elaine Gif- tos (Neferiti), David Darlow (Taduhk), Sydney Penny (Princess).

1700. **Undercover Girls.** 60 min. Production Companies: Miller-Milkis-Boyett Productions, and Paramount Television. Executive Producer: John Furia, Jr. Producer: Ben Kadish. Writer: Robert Dozier. Creators: Tom Miller and Robert Dozier. A proposed spin-off from *Sweepstakes,* a series which ran for a mere 10 weeks in 1979. This envisioned series would have focused on two undercover female cops, one a veteran who is still sympathetic and gullible, and her partner, a self-assured, ex-beauty parlor operator looking for more excitement in her life

1980–1981

ABC / COMEDY

1701. **Between the Lines.** 30 min. Airdate: 7/7/80. Production Company: Time-Life Television. Director: Charlotte Brown. Executive Producer: Philip Mandelker. Producers: Freyda Rothstein and Russ Petranto. Writer: Fred Barron. Music: Kenny Loggins. Based on the 1977 feature *Between the Lines,* which was also written by Fred Barron. A quirky look at the young staff as they struggle to publish their anti-establishment, alternative Boston weekly. *Cast:* Kristoffer Tabori (as Harry), Susan Krebs (Abbie), Sandy Heiberg (Stanley), Nancy Lane (Lynn), Squire Fridell (Frank), Charley Lang (David), Adam Arkin (Max), Gino Conforti (Teacher), Peggy Pope (Mrs. Boudry), Henry Hoing (Mr. Boudry).

1702. **Blue Jeans (aka Forever Blue Jeans).** 30 min. Airdate: 7/26/80. Director: J.D. Lobue. Executive Producers: Leonard Goldberg and Jerry Wein- traub. Producers: Alan Eisenstock, Larry Mintz, and Gene Marcione. Writers: Alan Eisenstock and Larry Mintz. A comedy centering on the struggle of four young rockers trying to make their group "Blue Jeans" a success. *Cast:* Elissa Leeds (as Vicki Gardner), Paul Provenza (Jimmy Scanlon), Charles Fleischer (Miles Savatini), Jay Fenichel (Beethoven), George S. Irving (Mr. Zwirko), Ruth Manning (Mrs. Zwirko).

1703. **Garbage Is My Life.** 30 min. Production Company: The Kaplan Company. Creator: Gabe Kaplan. A comedy about the relationship between an Italian father and son (Gabe Kaplan) who operate a sanitation truck.

1704. **Ghost of a Chance.** 30 min. Airdate: 7/7/81. Production Companies: Arim Productions and Paramount Television. Director: Nick Havinga. Executive Producers: Austin and Irma Kalish. Producer: Gene Marcione. Writers: Austin and Irma Kalish. A pale imitation of the then-popular feature *Dona Flor and Her Two Husbands.* When Shelley Long marries Barry Van Dyke, the ghost of her dead first husband (Steven Keats) comes back to haunt her. Gretchen Wyler played Long's mother. *Cast:* Shelley Long (as Jenny Clifford), Barry Van Dyke (Wayne Clifford), Steven Keats (Tom Chance), Gretchen Wyler (Frances), Archie Hahn (Michael), Rosalind Kind (Leslie), John O'Leary (Minister).

439

1705. Gypsies. 30 min. Production Company: Herbert Ross Productions. Producer: Herbert Ross. Writer: Liz Coe. The serialized experiences of aspiring Broadway dancers and actors, as they struggle to "make it." The producers intended to go for the feel of the popular play *A Chorus Line* and would base their storylines on real experiences.

1706. Jack Flash. 30 min. Production Company: Warner Bros. Television. Director: Sidney Hayers. Producer: William Phillips. A DMV clerk is given superpowers by a mysterious, dying uncle.

1707. Joan Rivers Project. 30 min. Producer: Edgar Rosenberg. Writers: Joan Rivers and Donald Westlake. Comedienne Joan Rivers and novelist Donald Westlake were preparing a concept that would focus on a group of teenagers.

1708. Katmandu. 30 min. Production Company: Paramount Television. Producer: Garry Marshall. Writer: Jeff Ganz. A teenage prince and princess of an exotic foreign land, and their beautiful female bodyguard Kat, are on-the-run from the country's evil king, and take refuge with a typical American family. Stars include Vicki Lawrence, Victor Buono, Alice Ghostley, and Deborah Pratt. Although the *Katmandu* pilot never aired, the character appeared on the "Happy Days" episode "Fonzie Meets Kat" on 9/25/79. Deborah Pratt, later producer of *Quantum Leap*, starred as Kat.

1709. Mr. and Mrs. Dracula. 30 min. Airdate: 9/5/80. Director: Doug Rogers. Executive Producer: Robert Klane. Producer: Stanley Korey. Writer: Robert Klane. Creator: Robert Klane. Music: Ken Lauber. The Dracula family is forced by a villagers' uprising to move from their Transylvania castle to a New York apartment. The proposed series would have focused on their troubles adjusting to a new way of life. Paula Prentiss replaced Vicki Lawrence as Mrs. Dracula in a second, unaired pilot. *Cast:* Dick Shawn (as Dracula), Carol Lawrence (Sonia Dracula), Gail Mayron (as Minna Dracula), Anthony Battaglia (Sonny Dracula), Johnny Haymer (Gregor the Bat), Barry Gordon (Cousin Anton), Rick Aviles (Mario).

1710. Toga Tales. 30 min. Production Company: Boiney Stoones Productions. Producers: Bernie Kukoff and Jeff Harris. Modern social and political problems would be satirized in this proposed sitcom set in ancient Rome.

1711. Welcome Home. 30 min. Production Company: D'Angelo Productions. Producer: William D'Angelo. Writer: Stu Silver. Yet another take on a recurring pilot concept: a retired couple find themselves having to take care of their children, now adults, once again. The offspring are a low-paid law clerk who can't afford to live alone, a divorcee and her nine-year-old daughter, and a lonely, single woman. The concept would reemerge in this season's *Alone at Last* on NBC and in *And They All Lived Happily Ever After*, a 1981 flop pilot.

ABC / DRAMA

1712. Gabe and Walker. 60 min. Airdate: 7/20/81. Production Company: Paramount Television. Director: Lou Antonio. Executive Producers: Henry Winkler and Allan Manings. Producer: Robert Lovenheim. Writers: Allan Manings, Dan Bockman, and David Peckinpah. The misadventures of Gabe Petersen (Charles Martin Smith) and Marion Walker (Frank Converse), the owners of a struggling California horse ranch. In the pilot, they battle the modern-day version of an unscrupulous western land baron. *Cast*: Frank Converse (as Marion Walker), Charles Martin Smith (Gabe Petersen), Katherine Cannon (Cassie), Jason Harvey (Kevin), John Cunningham (Mr. Watkins), Hugh Gillin (Lee Lawson), Lisa Loring (Girl), Claire Mills (Iris O'Reilly), J.P. Bumstead (Deputy Chief), Stefan Gierasch (Chef).

1713. Ladies in Blue. 60 min. Airdate: 3/19/80. Production Company: Aaron Spelling Productions. Director: Lewis Teague. Executive Producers: Aaron Spelling and Douglas S. Cramer. Producers: Phil Fherle and Larry Forrester. Writer: Larry Forrester. Aired as an episode of *Vega$*. Michelle Phillips and Tanya Roberts are two undercover cops with the San Francisco Police Department who, in the pilot, search for a cop killer. *Cast*: Michelle Phillips (as Casey Hunt), Tanya Roberts (Britt Blackwell), Peter Haskell (Capt. Turner), Bruce Kirby (Sgt. Culley), Natalie Schafer (Mrs. Hunt), Andrew Robinson (Derek), Peggy Cass (Dottie), Peter Mark Richman (Sam), Robert Urich (Dan Tanna), Phyllis Davis (Bea Travis), Bart Braverman (Binzer), Greg Morris (Lt. Dave Nelson).

1714. The Long Days of Summer. 90 min. Airdate: 5/23/80. Production Company: Dan Curtis Associates. Director: Dan Curtis. Executive Producer: Dan Curtis. Producers: Joseph Stern and Lee Hutson. Writer: Lee Hutson, from a story by Hildi Brooks and Lee Hutson. Creator: Dan Curtis. Music: Walter Scharf. A second pilot attempting to sell ABC a series, set in Bridgeport, Connecticut, in the 1930s, about a lawyer (Dean Jones) and his family, as seen through the eyes of his teenage son (Ronnie Scribner). Like the first pilot, *When Every Day Was the Fourth of July*, this pilot is loosely based on Director/Producer Dan Curtis' childhood. Charles Aidman is the narrator, the now-adult boy. *Cast*: Dean Jones (as Ed Cooper), Joan Hackett (Millie Cooper), Ronnie Scribner (Daniel Cooper),

Louanne (Sarah Cooper), Donald Moffat (Josef Kaplan), Andrew Duggan (Sam Wiggins), David Baron (Freddy Landauer, Jr.), Michael McGuire (Lt. O'Hare), Lee DeBroux (Fred Landauer, Sr.), Baruch Lumet (Rabbi), Leigh French (Frances Haley), John Karlen (Duane Haley), Tiger Williams (Charlie Wilson), Stepen Roberts (F.D.R.).

1715. Max Sinclair, M.D. 60 min. Production Company: Blinn/Thorpe Productions. Executive Producers: William Blinn and Jerry Thorpe. Writers: William Blinn and Jerry Thorpe. Creators: William Blinn and Jerry Thorpe. A reworking of the flop series *The Lazarus Syndrome,* which survived a scant six weeks in 1979. Louis Gossett reprises his role as Dr. Max Sinclair, a cardiologist who, in this new concept, becomes teacher and mentor to a group of interns.

1716. Once Upon a Spy. 2 hours. Airdate: 9/19/80. Production Companies: Columbia Pictures Television and David Gerber Productions. Director: Ivan Nagy. Executive Producer: David Gerber. Producer: Jay Daniel. Writer: Jimmy Sangster. Music: John Cacavas. A reworking of last season's flop *Billion Dollar Threat* pilot, which starred Dale Robinette as a spy. This time, Ted Danson is a brainy chess- master and computer expert who is reluctantly drafted into espionage and teamed with Mary Louise Weller, the female answer to James Bond. Christopher Lee, who menaced 007 in *Man with the Golden Gun,* is the mad scientist out to control the world. *Cast:* Ted Danson (as Jack Chenault), Mary Louise Weller (Paige Tannehill), Eleanor Parker (The Lady), Christopher Lee (Marcus Volarium), Burke Byrnes (Berkle), Leonard J. Stone (Dr. Charlie Webster), Terry Lester (Rudy), Jo McDonnell (Susan Webster), Julius Ruval (Christine), Gary Dontzig (Klaus), Bob Hopkins (Hanns), Vicky Perry (Cashier), John R. Hostetter (Chief), Irene Serris (Greta).

1717. Reward. 90 min. Airdate: 5/23/80. Production Companies: Lorimar Productions, Jerry Adler Productions, and Esprit Enterprises. Director: E.W. Swackhamer. Executive Producer: Lee Rich. Producer: Jerry Adler. Writer: Jason Miller. Music: Barry DeVorzon. Michael Parks is a San Francisco cop who quits the force to find his partner's killer, and then becomes a bounty hunter. Shot on location. *Cast:* Michael Parks (as Michael Dolan), Richard Jaeckel (Capt. Randolph), Annie McEnroe (Christine), Andrew Robinson (Frank Morelia), Bridget Hanley (Marie Morelia), Malachy McCourt (Jimmy Moran), David Clennon (Steve Rawlin), Calvin Jung (Melon), Lance LeGault (Van Dyke), James Watson, Jr. (Officer Marley), Martin Cassidy (Zedick), Byron Webster (Sherril), Bill Warren (Krebs).

1718. **Stunts Unlimited.** 90 min. Airdate: 1/4/80. Production Companies: Paramount Television and Lawrence Gordon Productions. Director: Hal Needham. Executive Producer: Lawrence Gordon. Producer: Lionel E. Siegel. Writer: Laurence Heath. Music: Barry DeVorzon. Glenn Corbett is an ex-C.I.A. agent who recruits three stunt experts (Sam Jones, Chip Mayer, Susanna Dalton) to form an elite counter-espionage team which, in the pilot, retrieves a stolen laser. *People* magazine thought "the idea is ingenious; it ought to be a series." Apparently, nobody else did. *Cast:* Chip Mayer (as Matt Lewis), Susanna Dalton (C.C. Brandt), Sam Jones (Bo Carlson), Glenn Corbett (Dirk Macauley), Linda Grovernor (Jody Webber), Alejandro Rey (Fernando Castilla), Vic Mohica (Tallis), Mickey Gilbert (Horse Gilbert), Charles Picerni (Stuntman).

1719. **Toni's Boys (aka Toni's Devils).** 60 min. Airdate: 4/2/80. Production Company: Spelling/Goldberg Productions. Director: Ron Satlof. Executive Producers: Aaron Spelling and Leonard Goldberg. Producer: Robert James. Writer: Kathryn Michael Powers. An obvious reworking of *Charlie's Angels*, the hit show which hosted the pilot episode. Barbara Stanwyck is the matriarchal private eye who solves cases with the help of three hunks (Bob Seagren, Stephen Shortridge, and Bruce Bauer) and her butler (James E. Boardhead). Stanwyck would later star in *The Colbys,* a spin-off of *Dynasty,* which starred *Charlie's Angels* title character John Forsythe. *Cast:* Barbara Stanwyck (as Antonia Blake), Bob Seagren (Bob Sorenson), Stephen Shortridge (Cotton Harper), Bruce Bauer (Matt Parrish), James E. Broadhead (Rolph), Cheryl Ladd (Kris Munroe), Jaclyn Smith (Kelly Garrett), Shelley Hack (Tiffany Wells), David Doyle (John Bosley), John Forsythe (Charlie), Robert Loggia (Michael Durrano).

1720. **Turnover Smith.** 90 min. Airdate: 6/8/80. Production Company: Wellington Productions. Director: Bernard Kowalski. Executive Producer: William Conrad. Producer: Everett Chambers. Writer: Richard Jessup. William Conrad is Professor Thaddeus Smith, a criminologist who teaches at a San Francisco university and uses the latest scientific methods, a host of high-tech gadgetry, his students' exhaustive legwork, and simple elemental deduction to solve baffling cases. In the pilot, he chases a strangler (James Darren). *Cast:* William Conrad (as Prof. Thaddeus Smith), Belinda J. Montgomery (Kelly Kellogg), Hilly Hicks (Eddie), Michael Parks (Lt. Brophy), Nita Talbot (Sgt. McCaUister), James Darren (George Green), Gail Landry (Dr. Rita Downey), Cameron Mitchell (Col. Simmons), Nehemiah Per- soff (Ashmed), Richard Dimitri (Sharif),

Sondra Blake (Victoria Simmons), Tracy Reed (Anini), Ben Wright (Franz Gerhardt).

1721. **Waikiki.** 2 hours. Airdate: 4/21/80. Production Company: Aaron Spelling Productions. Director: Ron Satlof. Executive Producers: Aaron Spelling and Douglas S. Cramer. Producer: Robert Janes. Writers: Curtis Kenyon, Dan Balluck, Robert Janes, and Rod Friedman, from a story by Curtis Kenyon and Robert Janes. Music: Stu Phillips. This jinxed pilot was scrapped midway through production, recast and reshot, though the final product contains some footage salvaged from the original shoot. Californian Ron Browning (Dack Rambo) and New Yorker David King (Steve Marachuk) team up as private eyes who, in the pilot, hunt for a rapist/killer. Richard Serafin directed the first shoot, which costarred Tim McIntyre as David King. Dack Rambo (as Ron Browning), Steve Marachuk (David King), Donna Mills (Officer Cassie Howard), Cal Bellini (Rex), Kack Hisatake (Kahona), Darren McGavin (Capt. McGuire), Robert F. Lyons (Mark Barrington), Mark Slade (Lloyd Barrington), Betty Carvalho (Anne Kahmonhu), Branscombe Richmond (Walter Kahmonhu), Tanya Roberts (Carol), Angus Duncan (Joe Farnsworth).

1722. **Willow B: Women in Prison (aka Cages).** 60 min. Airdate: 6/29/80. Production Company: Lorimar Productions. Director: Jeff Bleckner. Executive Producers: Lee Rich and Michael Filerman. Producer: Lawrence Kasha. Writer: Gerry Day. Kim Cavanaugh is convicted of manslaugther for killing a pedestrian in a drunk driving accident and is sent to an all-female detention center. The proposed series would follow her day-to-day life in prison, and the experiences of her fellow prisoners. Based on the Australian series *Prisoner: Cell Block H*, which was syndicated in America in 1980. *Cast:* Debra Clinger (as Kim Cavanaugh), Trisha Noble (Chris Bricker), Carol Lynley (Claire Hastings), Sally Kirkland (Kate Stewart), Sarah Kennedy (Sabrina Reynolds), Elizabeth Hartman (Helen), Liz Torres (Trini Santos), Susan Tyrrell (T.J.), Lynne Moody (Lynn), Sandra Sharpe (Francine), Virginia Capers (Eloise Baker), Ruth Roman (Sgt. Pritchett), Norma Donaldson (Mrs. McCallister), Jared Martin (Dave Tyree), John P. Ryan (Mr. Canady).

CBS / COMEDY

1723. **Brothers.** 30 min. Airdate: 7/30/80. Production Company: MTM Enterprises. Director: Will MacKenzie. Executive Producers: Rick Podell and Michael

Preminger. Producers: Norman Stiles and Charles Raymond. Writers: Rick Podell and Michael Preminger. The misadventures of two adopted brothers—one Jewish (Charles Levin) and one Irish (James O'Sullivan)—who share an apartment. *Cast:* Charles Levin (as Michael Radford), James O'Sullivan (Allan Radford), Dori Brenner (Sheri), Jeannette Arnette (Rhonda), James Hong (Lee On Wong), Bobby Ramsen (Horatio Beckett), Keye Luke (Mr. Hu), Chip Fields (Ellen).

1724. **Carlton Your Doorman.** 30 min. Airdate: 5/21/80. Production Companies: MTM Enterprises, Murikami, Wolf, and Swenson Productions. Directors: Charles Swenson and Fred Wolf. Producers: Lorenzo Music and Barton Dean. Writers: Lorenzo Music and Barton Dean. Creators: Lorenzo Music and Barton Dean, from characters created by James L. Brooks, Allan Burns, David Davis, and Lorenzo Music. Music: Stephen Cohn. An animated spin-off from *Rhoda*. This cartoon finally showed us Carlton, the lazy, shiftless, irresponsible and unseen doorman at Rhoda's New York apartment building. Had this enjoyable, adult cartoon sold, it would have been the first animated series since *The Flintstones* to appear in primetime. Lorenzo Music, who provided Carlton's voice in *Rhoda*, does it again here—beginning a voice-over career that would soon eclipse his writing and producing efforts. Music is best known now for giving the cartoon cat "Garfield" his voice. Other "voices" in the pilot included Jack Somack, Lucille Meredith, Lurene Tuttle, Kay Cole, Alan Barzman, Bob Arbogast, Charles Woolf, Roy West, and Paul Lichtman. Several scripts were ordered, but a series never materialized.

1725. **The Countess and the Cowboy.** 30 min. Production Company: Columbia Pictures Television. Executive Producers: Harve Bennett and Harris Katleman. Writers: Louise Del Grande and David Barlow. A recently widowed Italian countess (Marilu Tolo) comes to Nevada to sell off her dead husband's ranch, but ends up staying to manage it with a widowed cowhand, and his two teenage kids.

1726. **Did You Hear About Josh and Kelly?** 30 min. Airdate: 10/13/80. Production Company: Elmar Productions. Director: Hal Cooper. Executive Producers: Rod Parker and Hal Cooper. Writer: Rod Parker. Creators: Rod Parker and Hal Cooper. A divorced couple (Dennis Dugan and Jane Daly) fall back in love and decide to live together. Jimmy Samuels and Denise Galik play their best friends, a conservative married couple.

1727. **Ethel Is an Elephant.** 30 min. Airdate: 6/18/80. Production Company: Columbia Pictures Television. Director: John Astin. Executive Producers: Bob Sweeney,

Larry Rosen, and Edward H. Feldman. Producer: Larry Tucker. Writer: Larry Tucker. Todd Susman is a New York photographer who shares his apartment with a baby elephant abandoned by a circus. The proposed series would chronicle this awkward living arrangement and his constant battles with the city and his landlord to keep the animal. *People* called it a "smartly written bit of Aesopian whimsy." *Cast:* Todd Susman (as Eugene Henderson), Steven Peterman (Howard Dimitri), Liberty Godshall (Dr. Diane Taylor), Ed Barth (Harold Brainer), Stephen Pearlman (Prosecutor), John C. Becher (Judge), Bernie McInerney (Cop).

1728. **First Time, Second Time (aka For Better or Worse).** 30 min. Airdate: 10/25/80. Production Company: MTM Enterprises. Director: Asaad Kelada. Executive Producer: Grant Tinker. Producers: Rick Kellard and Bob Comfort. Writers: Rick Kellard and Bob Comfort. When a widowed executive at a "think-tank" (Ronny Cox) marries a writer of children's books (Julie Cobb), his 11-year-old son (David Hollander) has a hard time accepting it. *Cast:* Ronny Cox (as Doug Fitzpatrick), Julie Cobb (Karen Fitzpatrick), David Hollander (David Fitzpatrick), Mary Frann (Joan Armstrong), Sumant (Jhampur Nehrudi), David Clennon (Lester Brot- man), Todd Starke (Brian), Joan Crosby (Mrs. Redack).

1729. **Four in Love.** Producer: Hank Bradford. A sitcom following two married couples (she's a model, he's a medical student/she's a songwriter, he's a book editor) who share a New York apartment.

1730. **The Georgia Peaches.** 2 hours. Airdate: 11/8/80. Director: Daniel Haller. Executive Producer: Roger Corman. Producers: James Sbardellati and Thomas Hammel. Writers: Michael Benderoth, Monte Stettin, and Lois Luger. Music: R. Donovan Fox, sung by Tanya Tucker. Two sisters—a country-western singer (Tanya Tucker) and a mechanic (Terri Nunn)—and a stock car racer (Dirk Benedict) team up as secret agents. *Cast:* Tanya Tucker (as Lorette Peach), Terri Nunn (Sue Lynn Peach), Dirk Benedict (Dusty Tyree), Lane Smith (Randolph Dukane), Sally Kirkland (Vivian Stark), Dennis Patrick (Wade Holt), Noble Willingham (Jarvis Wheeler), Burton Gilliam (Delbart Huggins), David Hayward (Joe Dan Carter), Bob Hannah (Officer Orville), David Treas (Marko), Ed Bakey (Desmond).

1731. **The G.I.'s.** 30 min. Airdate: 7/20/80. Production Company: 20th Century Fox Television. Director: Peter Bonerz. Producers: Bernard Rothman and Jack Wohl.

Writers: Jack Wohl, Bernard Rothman, and Phil Hahn. The misadventures of American soldiers in Italy during World War II. *Cast:* Kenneth Gilman (as Cpl. Peter Buchanon), Jonathon Banks (Sgt. John Vitalla), Gregg Berger (Pvt. T.J. Witherspoon), Michael Binder (Pvt. Leroy Lumskin), Lorry Goldman (Pvt. Harry Freedman), Chick Vennera (Pvt. Joseph Battaglia), Lillian Garrett Bonner (Peasant), Lew Horn (Soldier), Patrick Gorman (Officer).

1732. **Landon, Landon and Landon (aka Gumshoes).** 60 min. Airdate: 6/14/80. Production Company: Quinn Martin Productions. Director: Charles Dubin. Executive Producer: Don Reo. Producers: Bruce Kalish and Philip John Taylor. Writers: Bruce Kalish and Philip John Taylor. A brother (Daren Kelly) and sister (Nancy Dolman) share a detective agency with the ghost of their dead P.I. father (William Windom). *People* said: "William Windom is a private eye who returns from the grave to solve his own murder, but the real zombie is this sitcom pilot." This concept was reworked in 1981 as *Quick and Quiet*, and only Windom as the ghost and Millie Slavin as the agency secretary survived. *Cast:* William Windom (as Ben Landon), Nancy Dolman (Holly Landon), Daren Kelly (Nick Landon), Millie Slavin (Judith Saperstein), Richard O'Brien (Inspector Ulysses Barnes), Norman Bartold (George Rumford), Sudie Bond (Billie), Jason Wingreen (Daryl Goren), Wil Albert (Reggie Ozer), Pat Studstill (Capt. Nestor), Maurice Hill (Cy Vorpal).

1733. **Love at First Sight.** 30 min. Airdate: 10/13/80. Production Company: Filmways. Director: Bill Persky. Executive Producer: Nick Arnold. Producer: Peter Locke. Writer: Nick Arnold. Creator: Nick Arnold. Music: Jose Feliciano. The first of two pilots about a woman (Susan Bigelow) with conservative parents (Robert Rockwell and Peggy McCay) who marries a blind musician (Philip Levien) who writes jingles for an ad agency. *Cast:* Philip Levien (as Jonathon Alexander), Susan Bigelow (Karen Alexander), Pat Copper (Francis Fame), Deborah Baltzell (Genevieve Lamont), Angela Aames (Denise), Robert Rockwell (Mr. Bellamy), Peggy McCay (Mrs. Bellamy).

1734. **[Pilot #2] Love at First Sight.** 30 min. Airdate: 3/29/82. Production Company: Filmways. Director: Nick Havinga. Executive Producer: Nick Arnold. Producer: Peter Locke. Writer: Nick Arnold. Creator: Nick Arnold. Music: Jose Feliciano. The Alexanders think about buying a gun after they are robbed. *Cast:* Philip Levien (as Jonathan Alexander), Susan Bigelow (Karen Alexander), Macon McClanahan (Mr. Sawyer), Reni Santoni (Stan).

1735. Me on the Radio. 30 min. Production Company: Warner Bros. Television. Director: William Asher. Executive Producers: Madelyn Davis and Bob Carroll, Jr. Producer: William Asher. Writers: Fred Freeman and Larry Cohen. CBS bought this concept, set in New York during World War II, but for some reason the series never materialized. Sally Struthers stars as a young girl whose first "big break" in show business is on a radio soap opera. Judy Kaye costars as her roommate. Other characters included her agent, a harried producer, a moody star, and a womanizing sound effects engineer.

1736. The Many Wives of Patrick. 30 min. Production Company: NRW Productions. Producers: Don Nicholl, Mickey Ross, and Bernie West. Writer: Budd Grossman. From the folks behind *Three's Company* comes this adaptation of a BBC sitcom about an insurance agent who has been married and divorced six times. The comedy would arise from myriad complications of life with his six former spouses and his various children.

1737. Mr. and Mrs. and Mr. 30 min. Airdate: 9/1/80. Director: Hal Cooper. Executive Producers: Hal Cooper and Rod Parker. Producers: Rod Dames, Bob Fraser, and Rita Dillon. Writer: Rod Parker. Widow Jenny Collins (Rebecca Baldin) marries Jeff (Patrick Collins) only to discover afterwards that her first husband (Kale Browne)—believed dead in a plane crash—is still alive. She has to pick which husband to keep, and while she thinks about it, they stay in the guest room.

1738. My Wife Next Door. 30 min. Airdate: 9/11/80. Production Company: Marble Arch Productions. Director: Bill Persky. Executive Producer: Martin Starger. Producers: Dick Clement, Ian LeFrenais, and Allan McKeown. Writers: Dick Clement and Ian LaFrenais. Based on BBC sitcom. TV producer Lee Purcell and baseball player Granville Van Dusen just got a divorce—and now they discover they've inadvertently bought condominiums next door to each other. Bill Persky directed a flop pilot, also called *My Wife Next Door*, for NBC in 1975. *Cast:* Lee Purcell (as Lisa Pallick), Granville Van Dusen (Paul Gilmore), Desiree Brochetti (Jan Pallick), Michael Delano (Vinnie Messina), Frank Dant (Lionel), Phil Rubenstein (Artie).

1739. Natural Enemies. 30 min. Production Companies: Metromedia Producers Corp. and Lila Garrett Productions. Director: Lila Garrett. Executive Producer: Lila Garrett. Producers: Sandy Krinski and Chet Dowling. Writers: Sandy Krinski, Chet Dowling, and Lila Garrett. The adventures of a brainy teenage girl and her best friend, the beautiful cheerleader.

1740. Our Place. 30 min. Production Company: O'Connor/Becker Company. Executive Producer: Terry Becker. Writers: Rick Podell and Michael Preminger. The story of three law school students—a rich guy who aspires to be a divorce lawyer, a serious student, and a ladies' man—who manage the San Francisco apartment building they live in.

1741. Two Plus Two. 30 min. Production Company: 20th Century Fox Television. Director: Bill Persky. Executive Producer: Frank Konigsberg. Producers: Eric Cohen and Nick Arnold. Writers: Eric Cohen and Nick Arnold. Chris Barnes is a young boy who has to move from rural Texas to New York City when his mother marries a plastic surgeon—and has to adjust both to a new lifestyle, a new environment, and most of all, to a new stepsister (Andrea McArdle), whom he immediately dislikes.

CBS / DRAMA

1742. Baby Comes Home. 2 hours. Airdate: 10/16/80. Production Company: Alan Landsburg Productions. Director: Waria Hussein. Executive Producer: Alan Landsburg. Producer: Kay Hoffman and Shelley List. Writer: Shelley List. Music: Fred Carlin. A second attempt to sell this concept, first pitched in the 1979 NBC pilot *And Baby Makes Six*, about a middle-aged couple who unexpectedly welcome a newborn child. The pilot was virtually recast, with the exception of stars Colleen Dewhurst and Warren Oates. *Cast:* Colleen Dewhurst (as Anna Cramer), Warren Oates (Michael Cramer), Devon Ericson (Elizabeth Winston), Fredric Lehne (Franklin Cramer), Christopher Marcantel (Jason Cramer), Mildred Dunnock (Serena), Paul McCrane (Bobby Moore), David Huffman (Jeff Winston), Dena Dietrich (Dora), James Noble (Dr. Elliot Losen), Lee Wallace (Sam Blumenkrantz), Floyd Levine (Louis Zambello), Toni Gellman (Loretta Zambello), Maria Melendez (Marta Cramer), Mel Stewart (Mr. Adams), John Medici (Officer Caputo).

1743. Home Front. 60 min. Airdate: 10/9/80. Production Company: Charles Fries Productions. Director: Harry Harris. Executive Producers: Charles Fries and Malcolm Stuart. Producers: Rita Lakin and Buck Houghton. Writer: Rita Lakin. Music: Pete Rugolo. This story, set during World War II, would chronicle the lives of the Travis family, who own a ship-building business, and the Spinellis, who work for the company but dislike the owners. *Cast:* Craig Stevens (as

John Travis), Jean Simmons (Enid Travis), Martinna Diegnan (Kate Travis), Dana Witherspoon (Christopher Travis), Mayo McCaslin (Cynthia Travis), Nicholas Hammond (Jack Travis), Eunice Christopher (Leona Spinelli), Delta Burke (Angela Spinelli), Joe Penny (Rocco Spinelli), Christine DeLisle (Helen Maddox), Ivor Francis (Birch), John Furey (Bradley), Steve Marlo (Stebbins), Mike Stroka (Johnson), Janice Carroll (Housekeeper).

1744. **Jake's Way.** 60 min. Airdate: 6/28/80. Director: Richard Colla. Executive Producer: Richard Lewis. Producer: S. Bryan Hickox. Writer: Richard Fielder. Robert Fuller stars as Jake Rudd, a sheriff in rural Texas who, in the pilot, tries to find out who killed his friend. *Cast:* Robert Fuller (as Sheriff Jake Rudd), Slim Pickens (Sam Hargis), Steve McNaughton (Deputy Daniel Doggett), Ben Lemon (Deputy Steve Cantwell), Lisa LeMole (Christina O'Toole), Andrew Duggan (Mace Kaylor), Kristin Griffith (Luana Kaylor), Michael Jaynes (Tom Ross), Susie Humphreys (Corrine Burke), Chris Godfredson (Billy Jean), Merill Connally (Judge Pettibone), Donna Marie Awtrey (Maybelle).

1745. **Joshua's World.** 60 min. Airdate: 8/21/80. Production Company: Lorimar Productions. Director: Peter Levin. Executive Producers: Lee Rich, Earl Hamner, and Mike Filerman. Producer: Claylene Jones. Writer: Earl Hamner. Creator: Earl Hamner. Music: Leonard Rosenman. Richard Crenna is a widower, raising an 8-year-old daughter and an 11-year-old son with the help of a black housekeeper in a small rural Arkansas town during the 1930s. He's also a strident liberal, and the only doctor and veterinarian in the town, which is torn by racial strife. *Cast:* Richard Crenna (as Dr. Joshua Torrance), Tonya Crowe (Thorpe Torrance), Randy Cray (James Torrance), Mary Alice (Donie), Carol Vogel (Caroline Morgan), Alexandra Pauley (Dawn Starr), LaShana Dandy (Josie), Carl Franklin (Nathaniel), Chez Lester (Thee), Hunter Von Leer (Billy Bob), Brion James (Shug), Roberta Jean Williams (Viola), Sharon Madden (Waitress).

1746. **Kops.** 60 min. Production Company: Metromedia Producers Corp. Writer: Arthur Marks. The adventures of Kavanaugh's Ocean Patrol (K.O.P.), a group of young volunteers who patrol the beaches helping people in trouble.

1747. **Mickey Spillane's Mike Hammer (aka Margin for Murder).** 2 hours. Airdate: 10/15/81. Production Company: Columbia Pictures Television. Director: David Haller. Executive Producers: Robert Hamner, Jay Bernstein, and Larry Thompson. Producers: Biff Johnson and Alex Lucas. Writer: Calvin Clements, Jr., based on characters created by Mickey Spillane. Kevin Dobson starred as rugged private eye Mike Hammer, Cindy Pickett was his secretary Velda, and Charles Hallahan was his friend-on-the-force, Capt. Pat Chambers. Although this pilot film was rejected, CBS had faith in the concept. The stars were replaced (with Stacy Keach, Lindsay Bloom, and Don Stroud), two new pilots were commissioned in 1983, and the series sold in midseason 1984. Like many episodes of the series, this flop pilot had Hammer investigating the death of a close friend. *Cast:* Kevin Dobson (as Mike Hammer), Cindy Pickett (Velda), Charles Hallahan (Capt. Pat Chambers), Donna Dixon (Daisy), Asher Brauner (Jerry Adams), John Considine (Lou Krone), Floyd Levine (Geraldo Marchetti), Erica Wells (Lindsay Brooke), Charles Picerni (Glover), Renata Vanni (Mama DeFelitta), Nicholas Horman (John O'Hare).

1748. More Wild Wild West. 2 hours. Airdate: 10/7/80. Production Company: CBS Entertainment. Director: Burt Kennedy. Executive Producer: Jay Bernstein. Producer: Robert L. Jacks. Writers: William Bowers and Tony Kayden. Creator: Michael Garrison. Music: Richard Markowitz and Jeff Alexander. A sequel to *Wild Wild West Revisited,* and the second attempt to revive the beloved western starring Robert Conrad and Ross Martin as secret agents in the old West. This time, the agents are pitted against mad scientist Jonathan Winters. Guest star Victor Buono was the bad guy in the original *Wild Wild West* pilot, and Harry Morgan and Rene Auberjonois reprise their roles from the first revival. *Cast:* Robert Conrad (as James West), Ross Martin (Artemus Gordon), Harry Morgan (Robert T. Malone), Rene Auberjonois (Sir David Edney), Jonathan Winters (Professor Albert Paradine), Victor Buono (Dr. Messenger), Liz Torres (Juanita), Randi Brough (Yvonne), Candi Brough (Daphne), Emma Samms (Mirabelle), Avery Schreiber (Russian Ambassador), Dr. Joyce Brothers (Bystander), Jack LaLanne (Jack LaStrange), Hector Elias (Spanish Ambassador), Joe Alfasa (Italian Ambassador), Dave Madden (German Ambassador), Gino Conforti (French Ambassador).

1749. The Pony Express (aka Riding for the Pony Express). 60 min. Airdate: 9/3/80. Production Company: O'Connor/Becker Company. Director: Don Chaffey. Executive Producer: Carroll O'Connor. Producer: Terry Becker. Writer: Jim Menzies. Creator: Jim Byrnes. The adventures of two teenage riders (John Hammond and Harry Crosby) working for the Pony Express during the 1860s. *Cast:* John Hammond (as Jed Beechum), Harry Crosby (Albie Foreman), Victor French (Irving G. Peacock), Glenn Withrow (Billy Bloss), Richard Lineback

(Willy Gomes), Susan Myers (Nancy Durfee), Byron Morrow (Rev. Slaughter), Phillip Baker Hall (Mr. Durfee), Alex Kubik (Blue Hawk), Del Hinkley (Seth Coleman).

1750. **Tarkington.** 60 min. Airdate: 4/3/80. Production Company: Quinn Martin Productions. Director: Michael Preece. Executive Producer: Philip Saltzman. Producer: Robert Sherman. Writer: Norman Jolley. Aired as "The Killin' Cousin" episode of *Bamaby Jones*. The misadventures of father-and-son private eyes William Tarkington IV (Kenneth Mars) and William Tarkington V (Thomas Havens). In the pilot, they suspect Barnaby Jones' secretary of murdering her cousins. *Cast:* Kenneth Mars (as William Tarkington, IV), Thomas Havens (William Tarkington, V), Madeline Fisher (Jennifer Hunt), Buddy Ebsen (Barnaby Jones), Lee Meriwether (Betty Jones), Mark Shera (J.R. Jones), Lory Walsh (Karen Bigelow), Mark Goddard (Roger Clark), Lurene Tuttle (Emily Carter), John Carter (Lt. John Biddle), Julie Rogers (Susan Clark).

NBC / COMEDY

1751. **Alone at Last.** 30 min. Airdate: 6/24/80. Production Company: Columbia Pictures Television. Director: Hy Averback. Executive Producers: Bob Sweeney and Edward H. Feldman. Producers: Larry Tucker and Larry Rosen. Writers: Larry Tucker and Larry Rosen. The first of two pilots about a middle-aged couple who, ready to enjoy living alone again, find themselves having to take care of their adult children. At first, the network liked the concept but not the cast. But when it was reshot and recast, the network decided it didn't like the concept either—at least that's the story Larry Tucker was telling *Panorama* magazine in March 1981. *Cast:* Bill Daily (as Gregg Elliott), Virginia Vestoff (Laurie Elliott), Kerry Sherman (Nancy Elliott), Michael Horton (Michael Elliott), Francine Beers (Agnes Bernoski), Martin Garner (Jack Bernoski), Elaine Joyce (Sherry), Melissa Sherman (Lisa), Howard Platt (Harry Elliott).

1752. **[Pilot #2] Alone at Last.** 30 min. Airdate: 9/3/80. Production Company: Columbia Pictures Television. Director: Peter Baldwin. Executive Producers: Larry Rosen and Larry Tucker. Writers: Larry Rosen and Larry Tucker. Only costar Martin Garner survived recasting of this pilot. In this story, Mr. Elliott thinks his son has no sense of responsibility and tries to give him one. *Cast:* Eugene Roche (as Larry Elliott), Susan Bay (Maureen Elliott), Lilibet Stern (Nancy

Elliott), Dana Carvey (Michael Elliott), Florence Halop (Agnes Bernoski), Martin Garner (Jack Bernoski).

1753. **The Broke Family.** 30 min. Production Company: Filmways. Writer: Nick Arnold. How a family copes when the father, a white collar worker, loses his job and everyone has to adjust to a new lifestyle.

1754. **Car Wash.** 30 min. Airdate: 5/24/81. Production Company: Universal Television. Director: Alan Myerson. Executive Producers: Leonard Stern and Arne Sultan. Producer: Bill Dana. Writers: Arne Sultan and Bill Dana. Based on the movie *Car Wash*. The adventure of a car wash owner (Danny Aiello) and his employees, including Rocky, a self-proclaimed ladies' man; Floyd and Lloyd, two aspiring singers; and Fingers, an expert skateboard rider. The other major character is Motor Mouth, a never-seen DJ whose radio show is always playing while they work. *Cast:* Danny Aiello (as Frank Ravelli), Hilary Beane (Charlene Olson), Stuart Pankin (Last Chance), Sheryl Lee Ralph (Melba), Matt Landers (Rocky), John Anthony Bailey (Lloyd), T.K. Carter (Floyd), Lefty Pedroski (Fingers), Pepe Serna (Viva).

1755. **Characters.** 30 min. Airdate: 10/26/80. Production Companies: Levine & Isaacs Productions and 20th Century Fox Television. Director: Will MacKenzie. Executive Producers: Ken Levine and David Isaacs. Producer: Gene Marcione. Writers: Ken Levine and David Isaacs. Creators: Ken Levine and David Isaacs. Jack Elmendorf and Carol Goodman are a stand-up comedy team in Chicago who, in the pilot, must cope with his shyness, her boyfriend, and stardom. *Cast:* Phillip Charles MacKenzie (as Jack Elmendorf), Maggie Roswell (Carol Goodman), Marcia Wallace (Lelia Flynn), Terry Lester (Steve Tucker).

1756. **The Cheap Detective.** 30 min. Airdate: 6/3/80. Production Companies: Rastar Television and Columbia Pictures Television. Producer: Edward H. Feldman. Writer: Richard Powell. Flip Wilson is a cut-rate detective in this sitcom, which began as an adaptation of the Neil Simon movie, a spoof of hard-boiled private eyes starring Peter Falk. This isn't the first time a Simon movie has been adapted with a black cast—the same gimmick was tried unsuccessfully with *Barefoot in the Park* and *The New Odd Couple*. *Cast:* Flip Wilson (as Eddie Krowder), Paula Kelly (Inez Krowder), Richard Beauchamp (Ricky), Murray Hamilton (Ralph), Michael Keenan (Arloe Fairweather), John Quade (Big Sam), Franklyn Ajaye (Elvis), Dave Morick (Fogerty), Daniel Thorpe (Carlton).

1757. Dribble. 30 min. Airdate: 8/21/80. Production Company: Columbia Pictures Television. Director: Charles S. Dubin. Executive Producers: Jim Green and Allen Epstein. Producer: Linda Bloodworth. Writer: Linda Bloodworth. The misadventures of a misfit team of professional basketball players. In the pilot, they have a hard time adjusting when a star player is added to the roster. *Cast:* Dee Wallace (as Anne Harrelson), Dan Frazer (Red Arnold), Joseph Hacker (John Raider), Julius J. Carry, III (Lou Jamison), Larry Anderson (Pete Terry), Edward Edwards (Will Herb), Vernee Watson (Ginny Jamison), Lewis Arguette (Sal), Yulia Gavala (Countess), Basil Hoffman (Fred), Danny Goldman (Bert).

1758. Fisherman's Wharf. 30 min. Airdate: 2/1/81. Production Company: Columbia Pictures Television. Director: Herbert Kenwith. Producers: Roger Shulman and John Baskin. Writers: Roger Shulman and John Baskin. Romeo and Juliet replayed between two Italian-American families—the Barberas and the Funuccis—on the San Francisco waterfront. *Cast:* Tom Quinn (as Vince Barbera), Elaine Giftos (Nina Barbera), Lenny Bari (Johnny Barbera), Glenn Scarpelli (Michael Barbera), Bruce Gordon (Tony Funicci), Louis Gordon (Tom Funicci), Joe Vitalie (Pa Funicci), Rex Everhart (Muldoon), Lola Mason (LaVerne), Helen Page Camp (Elaine Muldoon).

1759. Garbage. 30 min. Production Company: 10-4 Productions. Writers: Peter Lefcourt and Greg Strangis. The adventures of three Los Angeles sanitation workers who work together during the day and hang out at the same bar at night.

1760. The Goodbye Girl (aka Goodbye Doesn't Mean Forever). 30 min. Airdate: 5/28/82. Production Companies: MGM Television, Rastar Television, and Warner Bros. Television. Director: James Burrows. Executive Producer: Allan Katz. Producer: Charles Raymond. Writer: Allan Katz. Creator: Neil Simon. Based on the movie *The Goodbye Girl*, which starred Marsha Mason as a widowed dancer, raising a young girl (Quinn Cummings) who reluctantly shares an apartment with a struggling actor (Richard Dreyfuss) and falls in love with him. Karen Valentine, Lili Haydn (cq) and Michael Lembeck assume the roles in this pilot, which *Variety* felt "came off several niches higher than usual tryouts" and that "as a series, it could be a pleasure."

1761. Goodnight Sweetheart. 30 min. Production Company: Nephi Productions. Executive Producer: Robert Wood. Writer: Ron Blumberg. Four married couples from different backgrounds who get together each week to discuss the personal problems and world events.

1762. Hole 22. 30 min. Production Company: BNB Productions. Executive Producer: Barney Rosenweig. Writer: Dusty Kay. The misadventures of a close-knit group of subway workers.

1763. It Just So Happens. 30 min. Writers: Rick Podell and Michael Preminger. The misadventures of two brothers—one who is recently separated and one who is gay—who share a Venice beach apartment.

1764. Love Island (aka Valentine Magic on Love Island). 2 hours. Airdate: 2/15/80. Production Companies: Dick Clark Productions, RKO Television, and Osmond Television Productions. Director: Earl Bellamy. Executive Producers: Deanne Barkley, Dick Clark, and Paul Klein. Producers: Pat Finnegan and Bill Finnegan. Writers: Madelyn David, Bob Hillyard, and John Kurland. Music: Peter Matz. Janis Paige is a good witch who plays magical match-maker at a tropical resort in this cross between *Love Boat* and *Fantasy Island*. *People* called it a "bubbleheaded brew of *I Dream of Jeannie* and a Club Med vacation." *Cast:* Janis Paige (as Madge), Dominique Dunne (Cheryl), Christopher Knight (Jimmy), Adrienne Barbeau (Beverly McGraw), Bill Daily (Charles), Mary Louise Weller (Denise), Lisa Hartman (Crystal), Howard Duff (A.J. Morgan), Bob Seagren (Billy Colorado), Dody Goodman (Ida Kramer), Rick Hurst (Robert Murphy), Stuart Pankin (Harvey), Ivan Philpot (Bellboy), Rosalyn Joyce (Nurse), Earl Montgomery (The Bishop).

1765. Love, Natalie. 30 min. Airdate: 7/11/81. Production Company: MTM Enterprises. Director: Peter Bonerz. Executive Producer: Judy Kahan. Producer: Patricia Rickey. Writers: Judy Kahan and Merrill Markoe. Music: Patrick Williams. Judy Kahan as a working mother coping with the drudgery, boredom and loneliness of housework, complicated in the pilot by the presence of a houseguest (Kenneth Tigar). Darian Mathias guest stars as a drum majorette selling candy door-to-door. Merrill Markoe later became headwriter on *Late Night with David Letterman*. *Cast:* Judy Kahan (as Natalie Miller), Christopher Allport (Peter Miller), Kenneth Tigar (Mel Orlofsky), Darian Mathias (Majorette), Corey Feldman (Frank Miller), Kimberly Woodward (Nora Miller), Jean DeBaer (Ruth Newman), Becky Michelle (Brownie), Terry Wells (Mover).

1766. The Main Event. Production Company: Warner Bros. Television. Based on the movie, which starred Barbra Streisand as a woman who manages a boxer, played by Ryan O'Neal—though most of the fights happen between them, and not in the ring.

1767. **Reno and White (aka White and Reno).** 30 min. Airdate: 5/3/81. Production Company: Quinn Martin Productions. Director: Dick Martin. Executive Producers: Don Reo and Quinn Martin. Producers: Judith Allison and Charles Raymond. Writer: Don Reo. Music: Keith Allison. The misadventures of a black (William Allen Young) and white (Martin Short) stand-up comedy team who, in the pilot, take a gig not knowing it's a KKK rally. *Cast:* William Allen Young (as Steve White), Martin Short (Danny Reno), Slappy White (Benjamin White), Judy Landers (Bunny Holly), Audrey Landers (Karen Holly), Bobby Remsen (Bernie Starker).

1768. **Rock and a Hard Place.** 30 min. Airdate: 3/8/81. Production Company: Quinn Martin Productions. Director: Rod Daniel. Executive Producer: Don Reo. Producers: Judith Allison and Charles Raymond. Writer: Don Reo. Music: Keith Allison. Jay Kerr is Hunter Crockett, a Ralph Kramden-esque blue collar Texan who schemes to make a quick score so he can live the easy life. Guich Koock is his best friend, who usually gets sucked into Crockett's crazy schemes. *Cast:* Jay Kerr (as Hunter Crockett), Celia Weston (Sherri Crockett), Guich Kooch (R.J. Taggart), Walt Hunter (Bubba), Joan Roberts (Donna Jo), Michael McManus (Len Hooker), Kenneth Kimmins (Larry).

1769. **Saint Peter.** 30 min. Airdate: 3/8/81. Production Company: Warner Bros. Television. Director: Asaad Kelada. Producer: Reinhold Weege. Writer: Reinhold Weege. Creator: Reinhold Weege. Music: Jeff Barry. Fred McCarren is a young, sheltered, Episcopalian priest who's assigned to a church in Manhattan's tough lower east side. *Cast:* Fred McCarren (as Father Peter Mathews), Lou Jacobi (Max), Susan Blanchard (Sheila Haynes), Benson Fong (Hank Chin), Beulah Quo (Martha Chin), Clarice Stellar (Cynthia Kreole), Pearl Shear (Mrs. Grueneuve), Doug Clancy (Officer Eddie Shaw), Curtis Yates (Billy Young).

1770. **Scalpels.** 30 min. Airdate: 10/26/80. Director: John Tracy. Executive Producer: Steve Zacharias. Producers: Bruce Johnson and Robert Keats. Writers: Steve Zacharias and Robert Keats. The misadventures of a zany hospital staff. Had this pilot sold, Charles Haid would have been prevented from appearing in *Hill Street Blues* and Officer Renko would have been killed off—as originally intended—in the first episode. *Cast:* Rene Auberjonois (as Dr. Carl Jarrett), Marilyn Sokol (Dr. Betty Hacker), Livia Denise (Dr. Nicole Tessler), Charles Haid (Dr. Lawrance Hacker), Kimberly Beck (Nurse Connie Primble), Simon MacCorkindale (Dr. Bob Hobart).

NBC / DRAMA

1771. Battles: The Murder That Wouldn't Die (aka Battles). 2 hours. Airdate: 3/9/80. Production Companies: Universal Television and Glen Larson Productions. Director: Ron Satlof. Executive Producer: Glen A. Larson. Producer: Ben Kadish. Writers: Glen A. Larson and Michael Sloan. Music: Stu Phillips and Glen A. Larson. William Conrad as a cop-turned-college security chief and part-time football coach at a Hawaii university who, in his free time, also dabbles in crime-solving. The concept was designed to both provide room for young story-lines (and engender youth appeal) and more traditional action/adventures plots (and appeal to adults). Six scripts were ordered, but a series never materialized. *Cast:* William Conrad (as William Battles), Lane Caudell (Joe Jackson), Robin Mattson (Shelby Battles), Marj Dusay (Dean Mary Phillips), Tommy Aguilar (Tuliosis), Roger Bowen (Jack Spaulding), Edward Binns (Alan Battles), Don Porter (Rocky Jenson), John Hillerman (Paul Harrison), Kenneth Tobey (Chuck Parks), Ben Piazza (Dr. John Spencer), Sharon Acker (Jill Spencer), Mike Kellin (Capt. Ames), Jose Ferrer (Jeff Briggs).

1772. Bourbon Street. Production Company: Paramount Television. Producer: Gerald Abrams. The adventures of a hard-boiled private eye who works out of the New Orleans French Quarter with the help of a wealthy, debonair newspaper reporter. This later evolved into the flop, 1982, ABC pilot *The Big Easy*, which starred William Devane as the private eye and Nicholas Pryor as the reporter.

1773. Culpepper (aka Asphalt Cowboy). 60 min. Airdate: 12/7/80. Production Company: Universal Television. Director: Clifford Bole. Executive Producer: Michael Fisher. Producer: Michael Vejar. Writer: Michael Fisher. Music: Ken Harrison. Max Baer is Culpepper, a widowed private eye raising three teenage daughters who frequently get involved in his action-packed cases. *Cast:* Max Baer (as Max Culpepper), Lory Walsh (Molly Culpepper), Robin Dearden (Rosie Culpepper), Lori Lowe (Meg Culpepper), Noah Beery, Jr. (Sgt. Brown), James Luisi (Lt. Lassiter), Richard Denning (Charles Van Huran), James Sloyan (Candy Man), Cal Bellini (Vincent Bustermonte), Jennifer Holmes (Annie Van Huran), Michael Mullins (Richie Bancroft), Kathy Shea (Rita), Ben Frommer (Fat Man), Russ Marin (Coroner).

The Dobermans. Two efforts were made to sell a series loosely based on the three *Doberman Gang* movies, in which a pack of highly trained dogs were used by various owners to pull off ingenious heists.

1774. **[Pilot #1] Alex and the Dobermans.** 60 min. Airdate: 4/11/80. Production Companies: Bennett-Katleman Productions and Columbia Pictures Television. Director: Byron Chudnow. Executive Producers: Harve Bennett and Harris Katleman. Producer: Ralph Sariego. Writers: James D. Parriott and Richard Chapman. Jack Stauffer is a private eye who inherits five trained dobermans from a carnival and uses them to help him solve cases. In the pilot, the dogs sniff out some stolen art treasures. *Variety* felt this pilot "bordered on being infantile" and "only the well-trained dogs were impressive." Byron Chudnow directed the three *Doberman Gang* feature films. The cast included Taurean Blacque, Lane Binkley, Jerry Orbach, William Lucking, Alan Gibbs, and Martha Smith.

1775. **[Pilot #2] [The Dobermans] Nick and the Dobermans.** 60 min. Airdate: 4/25/80. Production Companies: Bennett-Katleman Productions and Columbia Pictures Television. Director: Bernard L. Kowalski. Executive Producers: Harve Bennett and Harris Katleman. Producers: James D. Parriott and Richard Chapman. Writers: James D. Parriott and Richard Chapman. Michael Nouri is a private eye who uses three dobermans to help him solve crime. *Cast:* Michael Nouri (as Nick), Robert Davi (Lt. Elbone), Judith Chapman (Barbara Gatson), John Cunningham (Roger Vincent), Vivian Bonnell (Speed Queen), Chris Hayward (Speedy Man).

1776. **Dusty.** 60 min. Airdate: 7/24/83. Production Company: Lorimar Productions. Director: Don Medford. Executive Producers: Lee Rich and Marc Mer- son. Producer: Stuart Cohen. Writers: Ron Liebman and Marc Merson. Creator: Ron Liebman. Music: Jerry Goldsmith. Saul Rubinek is a Los Angeles cabbie who dreams of being a private eye—and gets his chance when he picks up a legendary detective (Gerald S. O'Loughlin) and is ordered to "follow that car." An uneasy alliance develops, and the cabbie finds himself moonlighting as a P.I. *Cast:* Saul Rubinek (as Dusty), Gerald S. O'Loughlin (Tim Halloran), Nancy McKeon (Slugger), Hank Garrett (Lt. Harry Beathoven).

1777. **Every Wednesday (aka Day the Women Got Even).** 2 hours. Airdate: 12/4/80. Production Company: Otto Salamon Productions. Director: Burt Brinckerhoff. Executive Producers: Paul Klein and Deanne Barkley. Producer: Otto Salamon. Writers: Clyde Ware, Gloria Gonzalas, and Jud Scott. Music: Brad Fiedel. Four housewives (Jo Ann Pflug, Georgia Engel, Tina Louise, and Barbara Rhoades) become vigilantes to bring neighborhood felons to justice. In the pilot, they went after a blackmailing talent agent. NBC would try a similar pilot a few years later under the title *Suburban Beat*. *Cast:* Jo Ann Pflug (as Evelyn Michaels), Georgia Engel (Kathy Scott), Tina Louise (Martha Jo Alfieri), Barbara Rhoades (Dee Dee Fields), Julie Haggerty (Lisa Harris), Rick Aviles (Pancho Diaz), Gerald Gordon (Marder), Vincent Cobb (Mark Fields), Andrew Duncan (Dr. Bill Scott), Tom Keena (Tony Alfieri), Rex Robbins (Steve Michaels), Harry Madsen (Joey), Ed O'Neill (Ed), Charlie White (Father O'Shea), Ed Wheeler (Cop), Mitchell Greenberg (Groucho), Jerry Maltz (Chico), Stuart Chamo (Harpo).

1778. **Eyes of Texas.** 60 min. Airdate: 11/10/79. Production Companies: Universal Television and Glen Larson Productions. Director: Bruce Bilson. Executive Producers: Glen A. Larson and Michael Sloan. Producer: John Peyser. Writer: Glen A. Larson. Music: Stu Phillips. Aired as an episode of *BJ. and the Bear*. Rebecca Reynolds and Lorrie McChaffey are two southern private eyes for a Texas firm, run by Roger C. Carmel. In the pilot, they try to out-con a conman. *Cast:* Rebecca Reynolds (as Heather Fern), Lorrie McChaffey (Caroline Capoty), Roger C. Carmel (Mort Jarvis), Greg Evigan (B.J. McKay), Peter Haskell (Jay Lawrence), Anna Lee (Laura Forrester), Raymond St. Jacques (Bradley), Mitzi Hoag (Freida), Marcia Morgan (Benji), Lenore Hayward (Verna), David Ankrum (Reporter).

1779. **[Pilot #2] Eyes of Texas.** 60 min. Airdate: 2/23/80. Production Companies: Universal Television and Glen Larson Productions. Director: Bruce Bilson. Executive Producers: Glen A. Larson and Michael Sloan. Producer: Robert F. O'Neill. Writer: Glen A. Larson. Music: Stu Phillips. Aired as an episode of *B.J. and the Bear*. The concept is the same, only this time Heather Thomas (who would later costar in Larson's *The Fall Guy*) replaced Lorrie McChaffey and Eve Arden stepped in for her former *Mothers-in-Law* costar Roger C. Carmel as head of the detective agency. B.J. McKay (Greg Evigan) hires the detectives to help him find his sister. John S. Ragin and Robert Ito make cameo appearances in the pilot as their characters from *Quincy*, another Glen Larson program. *Cast:* Rebecca Reynolds (as Heather Fern), Heather Thomas (Caroline Capoty), Eve Arden (Helen Jarvis), Michael Pataki (Det. Rizzo), Greg Evigan (B.J. McKay), Burr De Benning (Garrett Logan), Craig Stevens (Hank Rogers), John S. Ragin (Dr. Robert Astin), Robert Ito (Dr. Sam Fugiyama), Robin Evans (Terri Collins), Vito Kazann (Vince), Helena Carroll (Doris), Stuart Pankin (Harvey Kreppler), Vito Scotti (Warehouse Man), Leonard Ross (Officer Walker), Sandra Peterson (Boom Boom).

1780. **The Gathering II.** 2 hours. Airdate: 12/17/79. Production Company: Hanna-Barbera Productions. Director: Charles S. Dubin. Executive Producer: Joseph Barbera. Producer: Joel Rogosin. Writers: Harry Longstreet and Renee Longstreet. Music: Robert Prince. Maureen Stapleton reprises her Emmy-winning role from the 1977 ABC pilot *The Gathering*, the Christmas tear-jerker about a dying man (played by Ed Asner) who wanted to see his family together one last time. In this sequel/pilot, Stapleton gathers her family together again—but this time there's a new man in her life, played by Efrem Zimbalist, Jr., whose real-life daughter was in the original movie. Rebecca Balding, Bruce Davison, Veronica Hamel, Lawrence Pressman, and Gail Strickland return in their roles they created. *Cast:* Maureen Stapleton (as Kate Thornton), Rebecca Balding (Julie Pelham), Patricia Conwell (Toni Thornton), Bruce Davison (George Pelham), Veronica Hamel (Helen Thornton), Jameson Parker (Bud Thornton), Lawrence Pressman (Tom Thornton), Efrem Zimbalist, Jr. (Victor Wainwright), Gail Strickland (Peggy Thornton), Dennis Howard (Aaron), Jessica Hill (Tiffany), John Ine (Joey), Norman Goodman (Lee Rifkind), Anita Sangiolo (Lucille Rifkind), Naomi Thornton (Dr. Ellis), Edward C. Higgins (Guard), Rose Weaver (Mary), Frank Toste (Priest).

1781. **Goldie and the Boxer.** 2 hours. Airdate: 12/30/79. Production Companies: Orenthal Productions and Columbia Pictures Television. Director: David Miller. Executive Producer: O.J. Simpson. Producer: Hugh Benson. Writers: David Debin and Douglas Schwartz. Goldie (Melissa Michaelson) is a ten-year-old who, when her father dies, befriends boxer Joe Gallagher (O.J. Simpson) and becomes his manager. A second pilot, *Goldie and the Boxer Go to Hollywood*, was made a year later. *Cast:* O.J. Simpson (as Joe Gallagher), Vincent Gardenia (Sam Diamon), Ned Glass (Al Levinsky), Gordon Jump (Alex Miller), Madelyn Rhue (Marsha Miller), Phil Silvers (Wally), Annazette Chase (Anna Bennington), Melissa Michaelson (as Goldie Kellogg), Fran Ryan (Ethel), Judy Landers (Bonnie Dare), Claude Earl Jones (Willie), Larry Levine (Matty), John Roselius (Paul Kellogg), Don Barry (Announcer), Matthew Tobin (Minister), Tim Rossovich (Billy Buck), Gene LaBelle (Vinnie), Walter Wyatt (Boxcar Man).

1782. **Inspector Perez.** 60 min. Airdate: 1/8/83. Production Company: Warner Bros. Television. Director: Lee Phillips. Executive Producer: Joe Byrne. Producers: Robert Dozier and Daniel H. Blatt. Writer: Robert Dozier. Music: Fred Karlin. Jose Perez is a widowed, New York homicide detective transferred to San Francisco, where he moves in with his mother. *Cast:* Jose Perez (as Inspector Antonio Perez), Betty Carvalho (Mama Perez), Dana Elcar (Capt. Hodges), Michael Corneilson (Sgt. Richards), Cyril O'Reilly (Danny McMahon), Irene Yah Ling Sun (Lisa Soong), James Hong (Benson Liu), Beulah Quo (Mrs. Liu), Mary Jackson (Mrs. Rackwolski), Anne Bloom (Janne Langley), Lew Brown (Capt. Groves), Walter Mathews (Sgt. Grady), Howard Mann (Dr. Mirakin), Eddy C. Dyner (Doctor), Sidney Clute (Officer), Bill Walker (Flower Vendor), W. Scott Devenney (Sgt. Shipley), Lydia Lei (Patricia Liu), Chao Li Chi (Master Fong).

1783. **Just a Coupla Guys.** 60 min. Airdate: 12/14/79. Production Companies: Universal Television and Cherokee Productions. Director: Ivan Dixon. Executive Producer: Meta Rosenberg. Producers: Stephen J. Cannell, Chas. Floyd Johnson, David Chase, and Juanita Bartlett. Writer: David Chase. Music: Mike Post and Pete Carpenter. Aired as an episode of *The Rockford Files.* Greg Antonacci and Eugene Davis are two young, New Jersey punks who "get things done." This time, they stumble into a local mafia war. The characters first appeared in the "The Jersey Bounce" episode on 10/6/78, and were toned down considerably for the pilot. Writer Chase would go on to create the landmark series *The Sopranos* about mobsters in New Jersey. The cast included Gilbert Green, Anthony Ponzini, Arch Johnson, Lisa Donaldson, Robin Riker, Cliff Carnell, Eric St. Clair, Doug Tobey, and Simon Oakland as Beppy Connigliaro.

1784. **Lilies of the Field (aka Christmas Lilies of the Field).** 2 hours. Airdate: 12/16/79. Production Companies: Rainbow Productions and Osmond Television Productions. Director: Ralph Nelson. Executive Producer: Ralph Nelson. Producers: Jack N. Reddish and Toby Martin. Writers: John McGreevey and Ralph Nelson, from characters created by William E. Barrett. Music: George Aliceson Tipton. Billy Dee Williams stars as carpenter Homer Smith, who is conned into building an orphanage adjacent to the Chapel he built before—when he was played with Oscar-winning success by Sidney Poitier in the acclaimed 1963 movie *Lilies of the Field.* Williams wanders off in the end, but not before signing a contract to return if NBC opted for a series. Ralph Nelson directed the original and this sequel, which movie critic Leonard Maltin called a "joyous follow-up." *Cast:* Billy Dee Williams (as Homer Smith), Maria Schell (Mother Maria), Faye Hauser (Janet Owens), Lisa Mann (Sister Gertrude), Hanna Hertelendy (Sister Albertine), Judith Piquet (Sister Agnes), Donna Johnson (Sister Elizabeth), Bob Hastings (Harold Pruitt), Jean Jenkins (Mrs. Constance Everett), Fred Hart

(Father Brian Connor), Sam Di Bello (Dr. Mike Robles), Timmy Arnell (Josh), Oliver Nguyen (Trang), Regina Simons (Pokey), Julie Delgado (Felicia), Rachel Ward (Jenny), Danny Zapien (Joseph Owelfeather), Adolpho Flores (Rafael Serrano).

1785. **Palms (aka Palms Precinct).** 60 min. Airdate: 1/8/82. Production Company: Universal Television. Director: Ivan Dixon. Executive Producer: David Chase. Producers: J. Rickley Dumm and John David. Writer: David Chase. Music: Mike Post and Pete Carpenter. Sharon Gless and Steve Ryan are two cops who are complete opposites, but are forced to work together to solve crimes. James Gallery costars as their boss. This pilot was made by a production team comprised of *Rockford Files* staffers. *Cast:* Sharon Gless (as Inspector Alexandra Brewster), Steve Ryan (Inspector Carmine Monaco), James Gallery (Capt. Edward Hammersman), Tricia O'Neil (Jeanine Monaco), Bruce M. Fischer (Dean Kelsey), Mark Thomas (Barry Wittenberg), Alan Stock (Scotty Gabriel), Jack Kelly (Albert Brunswick), Lenora May (Patti Halliwell), Stanley Brock (Sid Yarrow), Lee Anthony (Detective Nerlinger), also, Stewart Moss, Patricia Smith, and Paul Couros.

1786. **Pleasure Cove.** 2 hours. Airdate: 1/3/79. Production Companies: Lou Shaw Productions, David Gerber Productions, and Columbia Pictures Television. Director: Bruce Bilson. Executive Producer: David Gerber. Producer: Mel Swope. Writer: Lou Shaw. Another *Love Boat* rehash, once again set at a resort hotel, that would focus on the lives of the various guests who pass through. James Murtaugh is the manager, Constance Forslund is the assistant manager, Melody Anderson is the reservations hostess, and Ernest Harada is the desk clerk. *Cast:* James Murtaugh (as Henry Sinclair), Constance Forslund (Kim Parker), Melody Anderson (Julie), Jerry Lacy (Chip Garvey), Ernest Harada (Osaki), Tom Jones (Raymond Gordon), Joan Hackett (Martha Harrison), Harry Guardino (Bert Harrison), Shelley Fabares (Helen Perlmutter), David Hasselhoff (Scott), Ron Masak (Joe), Barbara Luna (Gayle Tyler), Tanya Roberts (Sally), Rhonda Bates (Zelda Golden), Robert Emhardt (Fat Man), David Ankrum (Jack), Sandy Champion (Willard), Wes Parker (Donald).

1787. **Sawyer and Finn.** 60 min. Airdate: 4/22/83. Production Company: Columbia Pictures Television. Director: Peter H. Hunt. Producers: George Schenck and Frank Cardea. Writers: George Schenck and Frank Cardea. Music: Arthur B. Rubinstein. Based on characters created by Mark Twain. Tom Sawyer and

Huckleberry Finn meet again nearly twenty years after their childhood adventures and set out to explore the West together. *Cast:* Peter Horton (as Tom Sawyer), Michael Dudikoff (Huckleberry Finn), P.J. Soles (Goldie Mallory), Don Red Barry (Marshal), Slim Pickens (Sheriff), Jack Elam (Boot McGraw), Robert Tessier (Outlaw), Oliver Clark (Railroad Man), John Chandler (Mase), Stack Pierce (Jim), Fred Lerner (Blacksmith), Dave Willock (Old Man), Larry Basham (Young Boy), Jan Goldstein (Young Girl), Bill Baldwin (Townsman).

1788. **Tom Selleck Project.** 60 min. Airdate: 11/16/79. Production Companies: Universal Television and Cherokee Productions. Director: John Patterson. Executive Producer: Meta Rosenberg. Producers: Stephen J. Cannell, Chas. Floyd Johnson, David Chase, and Juanita Bartlett. Writer: Stephen J. Cannell. Creator: Stephen J. Cannell. Music: Mike Post and Pete Carpenter. Aired as the "Nice Guys Finish Dead" episode of *The Rockford Files.* Tom Selleck starred as mediocre private eye Lance White, who did everything wrong but still got more glory than Jim Rockford (James Garner), who did everything right. Lance White is a spoof of *Mannix* and the epitome of the private eye cliche *The Rockford Files* set out to debunk. The White character first appeared in the "White on White and Nearly Perfect" episode, which was written and directed by Cannell and aired on 10/20/78. *Cast:* Tom Selleck (as Lance White), James Luisi (Lt. Chapman), Simon Oakland (Vernon St. Cloud), Larry Manetti (Larry St. Cloud), James Whitmore, Jr. (Fred Beemer), Joseph Bernard (Carmine DeAngelo), Fritzi Burr (Mrs. DeAngelo), Roscoe Born (TV Commentator), Steve James (Newsman), A1 Berry (Ed Fuller), Gregory Norman Cruz (Attendant), Larry Dunn (Norm Cross), John Lombardo (Police Clerk).

1981–1982

ABC / COMEDY

1789. Border Pals. 30 min. Airdate: 8/17/81. Production Companies: Cottage Industries Inc. and Warner Bros. Television. Director: Bruce Kessler. Executive Producer: Rod Amateau. Producer: Jay Daniel. Writers: Rod Amateau and Gary Hudson. Hugh Gillin and Graham Jarvis are two feuding lawmen on either side of the U.S./Canadian border who, in the pilot, fall over themselves trying to capture an aging gangster with a $100,000 price on his head. *Cast:* Hugh Gillin (as Sheriff Norbert Bibey), Graham Jarvis (Supt. Douglas MacDonald), T.K. Carter (Officer Lucas Jordan), Frank O'Brien (Sgt. Major Radcliffe), Gerard Prendergast (Dusty Griffith), Reid Smith (Sgt. Kelly Morgan), Katherine Baumann (Cpl. Juliet Marais), Ray Middleton (Old John), Marc Lawrence (Joe Cincinnati), Dick Bakalyan (Little Eddie), J.P. Bumstead (Lawyer).

1790. Bulba. 30 min. Airdate: 8/3/81. Production Companies: Churoscuro Productions and Ten-Four Productions. Director: James Frawley. Executive Producer: Greg Strangis. Producer: Peter Lefcourt. Writer: Peter Lefcourt. Music: Arthur B. Rubinstein. The misadventures of a U.S. Embassy in the fictional, island country of Bulba. *Variety* summed it up by saying: "No laughs. No Chance." *Cast:* Joyce Van Patten (as Barbara Thatcher), Miles Chapin (Jackson Conway), Jill Jacobson (Holly Compton), Jeff Altman (Gary Holmes), Roger Bowen (Embassador), Gregory Itzin (V. Ogelthorpe), Armen Shimerman (Charles Medwick), Bill Hicks (Phil), Gallard Sartain (H. Choi-Oh Kavee), Lyle Waggoner (Hampton Frazer).

1791. Byrd's Nest. 30 min. Production Companies: Taffner/Stolfi and West Ross Productions. A proposed spin-off from *Three's Company* about a woman living with a younger man in her father's apartment building.

1792. Harry's Battles. 30 min. Airdate: 6/8/81. Production Company: Marble Arch Productions. Director: Alan Rafkin. Executive Producer: Martin Starger. Producer: Charlie Hauck. Writer: Charlie Hauck. Based on the BBC series *A Sharp Intake of Breath*. Dick Van Dyke is a Pittsburgh supermarket manager who always seems to be embroiled in bureaucracy and red tape, to the consternation of his wife (Connie Stevens). Danny Wells and Marley Sims are their neighbors.

467

Cast: Dick Van Dyke (as Harry Fitzsimmons), Connie Stevens (Mary Carol Fitzsimmons), Danny Wells (Herb), Marley Sims (Diane), Brooke Alderson (Nurse Hewitt), Joe Regalbuto (Dr. Harwood), also, David Ruprecht and Florence Halop.

1793. Homeroom. 30 min. Airdate: 8/10/81. Production Company: Paramount Television. Director: Michael Zinberg. Executive Producer: Dale McRaven. Producers: Nick Theil and David Braff. Writers: Dale McRaven, David Brafif, and Nick Thiel. Michael Spound and Ally Sheedy are a brother and sister trying to adjust to a new high school. Andy Levant is the class bully, Eddie Deezen is the class clown, and Irene Arranga is the ugly duckling. Nicholas Pryor is the teacher. *Cast:* Michael Spound (as Craig Chase), Ally Sheedy (Karen Chase), Andy Levant (Steve), Antony Alda (Crazy Willie), Eddie Deezen (Ron Carp), Irene Arranga (Annette Savinski), Nicholas Pryor (Scott Thomas), Donald Fullilove (Billy Coe), Severn Darden (Mr. Melish), Faye Grant (Tina), David Dumas (Sweeney), Curt Ayres (Truck).

1794. Hot W.A.C.S. (aka Soldier Girls). 30 min. Airdate: 6/1/81. Production Company: Paramount Television. Director: Joel Zwick. Executive Producers: Milt Josefsberg and Joel Zwick. Producers: Bruce Johnson, Jeff Franklin, and Brian Levant. Writers: Jeff Franklin and Brian Levant. One of a slew of pilots inspired by the success of the movie *Private Benjamin.* Julie Payne commands five new female recruits torn between the Army's desire to make "men" of them and their own desire to be "all-woman" to snare good-looking G.I.'s. In the pilot, they vie with the men in a tent raising contest. *Cast:* Julie Payne (as Major Janet Morehead), Ellen Regan (Pvt. Pamela Jordan), Dana Vance (Pvt. Kitty Trump), Richard Jaeckel (Major Phillip Seabrook), Rebecca Holden (Pvt. Heather Cassidy), David James Carroll (Sgt. O'Neal), Sandy Heiberg (Pvt. Duckworth).

1795. I Love Her Anyway. 30 min. Airdate: 8/3/81. Production Company: Viacom Enterprises. Director: John Tracy. Executive Producers: George Burns, Jerry Zeitman, and Irving Fein. Writer: Elliot Shoenman. An updated version of *The George Bums and Grade Allen Show.* Diane Stillwell is the scatterbrained, naive wife of tolerant, understanding, amused Dean Jones. Jones' medical-student brother (Charles Levin) and his wife (Jane Daly) live with them, adding to the chaos. The pilot broke the so-called "fourth wall," with characters speaking directly to the audience and writer Shoenman, behind the camera, was seen getting fitted for a jacket at the end of the show. The pilot was reportedly on the 1981 fall schedule until the network made a last-minute decision to renew *Mork and Mindy* for one more season. This was George Burns' final work as a producer. *Cast:* Dean Jones (as Jerry Martin), Diane Stillwell (Laurie Martin), Elliot Shoenman (Himself), Jane Daley (Mona Martin), Charles Levin (Fred Martin), Peter Boyden (Willie Winslow), Howard Witt (Dr. Peterson), Phil Rubenstein (Moving Man), also, Milt Jamin.

1796. In Trouble. 30 min. Airdate: 8/24/81. Production Company: Kukoff/ Harris Productions. Directors: Bernie Kukoff and Jeff Harris. Producers: Bernie Kukoff and Jeff Harris. Writers: Bernie Kukoff and Jeff Harris. Aired as an episode of *ABC Comedy Theatre.* The misadventures of three teenage girls who, in the pilot, try to make money by throwing a garage sale in the school cafeteria and working as waitresses in a bar. *Cast:* Nancy Cartwright (as Annie Monahan), Deena Freeman (Janey Zerneck), Lisa Freeman (Ivy Miller), Peter Michael Gertz (Mr. Zerneck), Tim Thomerson (Mr. Damrush), Doris Roberts (Irma DeGroot), also, Marvin Katzoff, Charles Bloom, David Greenlee, Sally, Kemp, Roger Price, Cathy Cutler.

1797. Mr. and Mrs. Dracula. 30 min. Production Companies: Marble Arch Productions and ABC Circle Films. Director: Doug Rogers. Executive Producer: Robert Klane. Producer: Stanton Corey. Creators: Dick Clement and Ian LaFranais. A reworking of last year's pilot. Dick Shawn is back as Dracula, who moves with his family from Transylvania to the South Bronx. Paula Prentiss replaces Carol Lawrence as Mrs. Dracula.

1798. Nuts and Bolts. 30 min. Airdate: 8/24/81. Production Companies: David Gerber Productions and Columbia Pictures Television. Director: Peter H. Hunt. Executive Producer: David Gerber. Producers: Gene Marcione, Larry Rhine, and Mel Tolkin. Writers: Rudy DeLuca, Jim Evering, and Gilbert Lee. Rich Little is a widower raising two kids (Tammy Lauren and Justin Dana)— with the help of two robots he designed (Tommy McLoughlin and Mitchell Young Evans). In the pilot, Little doesn't have the money for his daughter's music school, so he sells his older robot to a hamburger stand run by William Daniels and Jo Ann Pflug, Little's love interest. Eve Arden is Little's mother. *Cast:* Rich Little (as Miles Fenton), Tammy Lauren (Lucy Fenton), Justin Dana (Alex Fenton), Eve Arden (Martha Fenton), Jo Ann Pflug (Karen Prescott), Mitchell Young Evans (Primo), Tommy McLoughlin (Victor), William Daniels (Warren Berlinger).

ABC / DRAMA

1799. Crazy Times. 2 hours. Airdate: 4/10/81. Production Companies: Kay- den/Gleason Productions, George Reeves Productions, and Warner Bros. Television. Director: Lee Phillips. Executive Producer: George Reeves. Producer: William Kay den. Writer: George Reeves. The story of three teenagers living in Queens, New York, during the mid-50s. *Cast*: Ray Liotta (as Johnny), Michael Pare (Harry), David Caruso (Bobby), Talia Balsam (Eva), John Aprea (Ralph), Ernie Hudson (Harold Malloy), Annette McCarthy (Carol), Amy Madigan (Marilyn), Joan Lemmo (Mrs. Lazzara), Jack Gregory (Mr. Lazzara), Eddie Egan (Bartender), Sandra Giles (Esther), Bert Remsen (Father Burke), Albert Insinnia (Vinnie), Shannon Presby (Eddie), Sal Lundi (Ricco), Jamie Alba (Mike), Julie Phillips (Mary), Ann Doran (Mrs. Keegan), Howard Mann (Mr. Condosta), Bill Adler (Flash), Alan Oliney (Ray), Carol Capka (Joan).

1800. Fly Away Home. 2 hours. Production Companies: An Lac Productions and Warner Bros. Television. Director: Paul Krasny. Executive Producer: Stirling Silliphant. Writer: Stirling Silliphant. Creator: Stirling Silliphant. Music: Lee Holdridge. Theme: John Stewart. The adventures of Carl Danton (Bruce Box- leitner), a network television cameraman, and Tim Arnold (Brian Dennehy), his weary, cynical boss, as they cover the Vietnam War. Silliphant's wife Tiana Alexandra costarred as Mei, Carl's love interest, a Vietnamese surgeon whose brother is a Viet Cong leader and whose wealthy parents are involved in political corruption. In the original concept, the series would have also examined attitudes and activities back in the states as seen through the eyes of Carl's sister Liz, an activist college student at U.C. Berkeley. This concept was about six years ahead of its time. *Cast*: Bruce Boxleitner (as Carl Danton), Brian Dennehy (Tim Arnold), Michael Fairman (Hap Andrews), Lynne Moody (Mercy), Tiana Alexandra (Mei), Michael Beck (Lt. Mark Wakefield), Laura Johnson (Chickie Wakefield), Randy Brooks (Shenandoah Brookford), Olivia Cole (Sarah Brookford), Edward Winter (Lt. Col. Hannibal Pace), Louis Giambalvo (Vogel), Kieu Chinh (Anh), Keye Luke (Duc), Duc Huy (Wong Lin), Barry Jenner (Sgt. Downs), Michael Alridge (Jed Holston), Teri Copley (Sabrina), John Berwick (Captain), Wayne Heffley (Maloney).

1801. Scruples. 2 hours. Airdate: 5/22/81. Production Company: Warner Bros. Television. Director: Robert Day. Executive Producer: Paul Picard. Producers: Camille Marchetta and Leonard B. Kaufman. Writer: Camille Marchetta, from characters created by Judith Krantz. Music: Charles Bernstein. Based on the Judith Krantz novel and the

1980 CBS miniseries. Shelly Smith steps in for Lindsay Wagner as the owner of a trendy Beverly Hills fashion boutique, the backdrop for soap opera tales of passion and intrigue among the rich and chic. *Cast:* Shelly Smith (as Billy Ikehorn), Priscilla Barnes (Melanie Adams), Dirck Benedict (Spider Elliot), Elisabeth Edwards (Nora Gregson), Olga Karlatos (Valentine O'Neil), Jim McMullan (Greg Dunne), Robert Pierce (Luke), Laraine Stephens (Eliza Dunne), Roy Thinnes (Bennett Hall), Jessica Walter (Maggie MacGregor), James Darren (Vito Orsini), Sandy McPeak (Josh Hillman), Vonetta McGee (Francine), Henry Polic, II (Mark Stiner), Kale Browne (Kenny Higgins), Ted Hartley (Herman Lingwood), Walter Brooke (Dr. Rutgers), Brett Halsey (Derek Wagner), Charles Shull (Andy Lewis), Roger Til (Phillipe), Gregg Enton (Attacker), Gaye Rowan (Denise), Sean Allen (Jerry).

1802. **Travis McGee.** 2 hours. Airdate: 4/18/83. Production Companies: Ha- jeno Productions and Warner Bros. Television. Director: Andrew V. McLaglen. Executive Producer: Stirling Silliphant. Producer: George Eckstein. Writer: Stirling Silliphant, based on the novel *The Empty Copper Sea* by John D. MacDonald. Music: Jerrold Immel. Sam Elliott portrays author John D. MacDonald's philosophical detective hero, a world-weary "salvage expert," whose fee is 50 percent of whatever he recovers. When he's not solving cases, McGee lives aboard the *Busted Flush*, a Florida houseboat he won in a poker game, and passes his time arguing with his economist pal Meyer. Warner Bros, would later mount a series version of *Spenser: For Hire*, adapted from author Robert B. Parker's MacDonald-esque tomes. *Cast:* Sam Elliott (as Travis McGee), Gene Evans (Meyer), Barry Corbin (Sheriff Hack Ames), Katherine Ross (Gretel Howard), Vera Miles (Julie Lawless), Richard Farnsworth (Van Harder), Geoffrey Lewis (John Tuckerman), Amy Madigan (Billy Jean Bailey), Marshall Teague (Nicky Noyes), Walter Olkewicz (Bright Fletcher), Maggie Wellman (Mishy Burns).

1803. **True Life Stories.** 60 min. Airdate: 9/13/81. Production Company: ABC Circle Films. Directors: Mel Shavelson, Jeannot Szwarc, and Larry Einhorn. Producer: Lou Rudolph. Writer: Mel Shavelson. Creator: Lou Rudolph. An anthology of true life fables, hosted by Regis Philbin and Mary Hart. In the first story, directed by Shavelson, Dick Van Dyke is a broke prospector who strikes gold, becomes wealthy, then loses it all 16 years later when the IRS freezes his assets—but he never loses the love of his family, the greatest wealth of all. The second story, directed by Szwarc, follows a woman's (Marion Ross) search to find her long-lost mother. After each fable, the hosts interview the real people the stories are based on. *Cast:* Dick Van Dyke (as Charlie Steen), Marion Ross (Barbara Hallberg), Lisa Blake Richards (Minnie Lee Steen), Sandy Kenyon (John Hallberg), Ryan MacDonald (Emory), Christine Avila (Maria Price), Crystal DeWoody (Michele), also, James Griffith, Lily Valenty, Arlen Dean Snyder, Vincent Gustaferro, David Fresco, Stanley Ralph Ross.

CBS / COMEDY

1804. And They All Lived Happily Ever After (aka Happily Ever After). 30 min. Airdate: 8/4/81. Production Company: Elmar Productions. Director: Hal Cooper. Executive Producers: Rod Parker and Hal Cooper. Producer: Rita Dillon. Writer: Rod Parker. Yet another "parents want to retire but kids come back to roost" story. See if this sounds familiar: Rue McClanahan and Dick Latessa are a married couple who, when their youngest daughter (Wendy Goldman) marries, looked forward to enjoying retirement to Arizona—but then their daughter's marriage sours, their son (Larry Cedar) drops out of law school, and their eldest daughter (Maggie Roswell) can't afford to live alone. Suddenly, the house is full all over again and they are stuck being full-time parents once more. *Cast:* Rue McClanahan (as Liz Wescott), Dick Latessa (Paul Wescott), Maggie Roswell (Loraine Hofstedter), Wendy Goldman (Timmie Gordon), Larry Cedar (Matt Wescott), James Staley (Ted Hofstedter), Sandy Hackett (Ernie Gordon), David Fustiano (Bobby Hofstedter), Anthony Holland (Mr. Wheeler).

1805. Comedy of Terrors (aka Comedy of Horrors). 30 min. Airdate: 9/1/81. Production Company: MTM Enterprises. Director: Bill Persky. Producers: John Boni and Harry Colomby. Writers: John Boni and Harry Colomby. Music: Jonathan Tunick. A comedy/anthology, hosted by Patrick MacNee, that would focus each week on the different guests who visit Beacon House, a haunted hotel on the Carolina coast. *Cast:* Deborah Harmon (as Molly Sutherland), Walter Olkewicz (Danny Logan), Jo De Winter (Eileen Mannings), Vincent Schiavelli (Gregory), Richard Roat (Dr. Landreaux), Ivana Moore (Apparition), Kip Niven (Michael Soames), Patricia Conwell (Pamela Soames).

1806. Fog. 30 min. Airdate: 5/23/81. Production Company: MGM Television. Director: Jay Sandrich. Producers: Lawrence J. Cohen and Fred Freeman. Writers: Lawrence J. Cohen and Fred Freeman. Dick O'Neill is a luxury liner captain who, after an accident at sea, is reduced to helming a tramp steamer until he can prove himself again. *Cast:* Dick O'Neill (as Captain Jack Drummond), Robert Ayres (First Officer Ned Dancer), Scoey Mitchlll (cq) (Navigator Peabody), George Pentecost (Doc Curtis), Steven Peterman (Ken Toomey), G.W. Bailey (Mr. Carrion), Demetre Phillips (Fortunato), Mae Hi (Lin Soo Fu), Christopher McDonald (Simon Carter), Jack Murdock (Lawson).

1807. **Pen 'n' Inc.** 30 min. Airdate: 8/19/81. Production Companies: Limekiln & Templar Productions and Universal Television. Director: Jack Shea. Producer: Jack Shea. Animation Producer: Louis Schwartzberg. Writers: Paul M. Belous and Robert Wolterstorff. The adventures of an adman-turned-political cartoonist on a New England newspaper whose fantasies appear as animated characters. Brianne Leary is his girlfriend, the daughter of the newspaper owner (Peter Hobbs). Andrea Ackers is his landlady and Charles Thomas Murphy is his editor. *Cast:* Matt McCoy (as Alan Ozley), Brianne Leary (Debbie Winson), Peter Hobbs (T.W. Winson), Charles Thomas Murphy (Raymond Babbitt), Doug Cox (Dexter Budd), Andrea Akers (Gretchen Vanderwyck), Fred Willard (Ralph), Richard Karron (Delivery Man).

1808. **Return of the Beverly Hillbillies (aka Beverly Hillbillies Solve the Energy Crisis).** 2 hours. Airdate: 10/6/81. Production Company: CBS Productions. Director: Robert Leeds. Executive Producers: Albert J. Simon and Ron Beckman. Producer: Paul Henning. Writer: Paul Henning. Music: Billy May. The Clampetts, the hillbilly family that struck oil in the Ozarks and moved to Beverly Hills, return pretty much intact to solve the energy crisis for Energy Department Official Jane Hathaway (Nancy Kulp) with Granny's moonshine. Ray Young steps in as the new Jethro, and Imogene Coca guest stars as Granny's 100-year-old mother. *Cast:* Buddy Ebsen (as Jed Clampett), Donna Douglas (Elly May), Nancy Kulp (Jane Hathaway), Ray Young (Jethro Bodine), Imogene Coca (Granny), Werner Klemperer (C.D. Medford), Linda Henning (Linda), King Donovan (Andy Miller), Lurene Tuttle (Mollie Heller), Charles Lane (Chief), Shug Fisher (Judge Gillim), Howard Culver (Veterinarian), also, Heather Locklear, Shad Heller, Earl Scruggs, Nancy Gayle, Dana Kimmell, Fenton Jones, John Hartford, Rodney Dillard, Buddy Van Horn.

1809. **Rise and Shine.** 30 min. Airdate: 8/25/81. Production Companies: Brownstone Productions and 20th Century Fox. Director: Bill Persky. Producer: Marc Merson. Writers: Dan Wilcox and Marc Merson. The adventures of four boys in an eastern prep school where Jayne Meadows is the principal and Art Metrano is the coach. In the pilot, the roomies try to get one of the guys (Scott Schutzman) his first kiss (from Claudia Wells). As *Variety* said, "the kid got kissed, the pilot got kissed off." *Cast:* Christopher Barnes (as Andy Cooper), Joey Green (Richard Moore), Jonah Pesner (Chris Dobbs), Scott Schutzman (Joel Beidermeyer), Art Metrano (Mr. Tillman), Jayne Meadows (Mrs. Moffett), DeCarla Kilpatrick (Carla Franklin), Eric Schiff (Stanley Deerborn), Claudia Wells (Patsy D'Allisandro), Jean- nie Fitzsimmons (Hope Kelly).

1810. **Stephanie.** 30 min. Airdate: 9/8/81. Production Company: MTM Enterprises. Director: Burt Brinckerhoff. Producers: Alan Uger and Michael Kagan. Writers: Alan Uger and Michael Kagan. Stephanie Faracy stars as the naive anchorwoman on a television magazine show who gets the job despite the objections of its polite, but malevolent, creator (Betty White). *Cast:* Stephanie Faracy (as Stephanie), Betty White (Agnes Dewey), Robert Hitt (Harry Babcock), Jeannette Arnette (Rita Melvoin), Alvy Moore (Claude Pomerantz), Kent Perkins (Sonny Brazil), Steve Landesberg (Anatoly Pinsky), Kres Mersky (Hannah Pinsky), Martin Ferraro (Chicken Man), Martin Zagon (Ned Sweeney), Matthew Faison (Dr. Igmar Nord- quist).

1811. **Two the Hard Way.** 30 min. Airdate: 8/11/81. Production Companies: Quinn Martin Productions and Brademan/Self Productions. Director: Hal Cooper. Executive Producers: Bill Brademan and Ed Self. Producer: Bruce Kane. Writer: Bruce Kane. Music: Lee Holdridge. The misadventures of two soap opera writ- ers—one an old hack (Eugene Roche) and the other a bright-eyed neophyte (Fred McCar- ren)—who share an apartment and who, in the pilot, are ordered to write out the hammy, long-time star of the serial (Lyle Waggoner). *Cast:* Eugene Roche (as Walter Chester), Fred McCarren (Richard Mallory), Marlyn Mason (Veronica Moorehead), Mary Jackson (Augusta Sedwell), Loyita Chapel (Penny), Lyle Waggoner (Rodney West).

1812. **Wonderful World of Phillip Malley.** 60 min. Airdate: 5/18/81. Production Companies: David Gerber Productions and Columbia Pictures Television. Director: Harry Falk. Executive Producer: David Gerber. Producer: Charles B. Fitzsimmons. Writers: Rick Kellard and Bob Comfort. Music: Perry Botkin. The age-old story of an absent-minded professor (Stephen Nathan) whose experi- ments often go awry, causing chaos at the small university where he works— and who romances the Dean's (William Daniels) daughter (Lori Lethin). *Cast:* Stephen Nathan (as Prof. Phillip Malley), William Daniels (Dean Frederick Carswell), Lori Lethin (Meredith Carswell), Stubby Kaye (Ben Grady), John

Calvin (Rodney Bronson), Bibi Osterwald (Francine Grady), Stuart Pankin (Lyle Floon), David Knell (Scott Hanson), Alvy Moore (Jonas).

CBS / DRAMA

1813. **Big Bend Country.** 60 min. Airdate: 9/27/81. Production Companies: Norman Rosemont Productions and Viacom Enterprises. Director: Ralph Senensky. Executive Producer: Norman Rosemont. Writer: Blanche Hanalis. Creator: Blanche Hanalis. Music: Allyn Ferguson. Set in 1865, the proposed series would follow the McGregory family as they try to rebuild their lives on their homestead in Eastern Tennessee, a country on both sides in the Civil War and a place where emotions are still smoldering. James Keach is the father, a Confederate soldier recently freed from a Union prison, and Dorothy Fielding is his wife, who thought he was dead. *Cast:* James Keach (as Ian McGregor), Dorothy Fielding (Mary McGregor), Robert MacNaughton (Dave McGregor), Stefan Gierasch (Sam Purdy), Anne Haney (Minerva Purdy), Tamar Howard (Addie McGregor), Nyles Harris (Caleb), Johnny Graves (Donny McGregor), Robert Telford (Reverend Fosser), Andy Robinson (Beau), John Quade (Hart), James McIntire (Dillon), Wendy Fuller (Sarah Marden), Tamara Cooper (Plantation Woman), Vicki Schreck (Plantation Girl).

1814. **Hellinger's Law.** 2 hours. Airdate: 3/10/81. Production Company: Universal Television. Director: Leo Penn. Executive Producers: James McAdams and Jack Laird. Producer: Chas. Floyd Johnson. Writers: Lawrence Vail and Jack Laird. Music: John Cacavas. Telly Savalas is an unorthodox Philadelphia criminal lawyer who, in the pilot, goes to Houston to help an accountant—an undercover Justice Department agent in deep cover with the Mafia—shake a murder rap. Morgan Stevens costarred as Hellinger's young investigative aide. Ja'net Dubois and Roy Poole would also have appeared as regulars in the proposed series. CBS reportedly ordered several scripts, but the series never materialized. *Cast:* Telly Savalas (as Nick Hellinger), Morgan Stevens (Andy Clay), Ja'net Dubois (Dottie Singer), Roy Poole (Judge Carroll), Melinda Dillon (Anne Grenousky), James Sutorius (Lon Braden), Tom McFadden (Detective Roy Donovan), Lisa Blake Richards (Cara Braden), Kyle Richards (Julie Braden), Arlen Dean Snyder (D.A. Fred Whedon), Thom Christopher (Bill Rosetti), M. Emmet Walsh (Graebner), Rod Taylor (Clint Tolliver), Robert Phalen (Dave Fredericks), Jack Ramage (Douglas Langley), Patsy

Rahn (Laura Weire), Don Hamner (D.A. Stevenson), Frank McCarthy (Paul Savage), Cindy Fisher (Jill Gronousky), Bill Cross (Leo), Paul Larson (Judge), Paul Picerni (TV Director), Marcy Pullman (Mrs. Carlson).

1815. J. Digger Doyle. 60 min. Airdate: 4/16/81. Production Company: Universal Television. Director: Winrich Kolbe. Executive Producer: Donald Bellisario. Producers: Reuben Leder, Rick Weaver, and Chris Abbott-Fish. Writer: Donald Bellisario. Music: Mike Post and Pete Carpenter. A spin-off from *Magnum P.I.* Erin Gray stars as a security expert working for a high-tech firm. In the pilot, she's hired to fortify Robin Master's estate for his upcoming visit and she immediately clashes with Magnum. Orson Welles provided the voice of Robin Masters. *Cast:* Erin Gray (as J. Digger Doyle), Tom Selleck (Thomas Magnum), John Hiller- man (Higgins), Larry Manetti (Rick), Roger E. Mosley (T.C.), Rick Marlow (Rene), Dean Wein (Ticket Agent), Philip Bancel (Charles), Patrick Bishop (Attendant), Diane Crowley (Mrs. Blaisdell), J.D. Jones (Pilot), Bruce Atkinson (Robin Masters), Sherly Kaahea (Luana), also, Stewart Moss.

1816. Key Tortuga. 60 min. Airdate: 9/11/81. Production Companies: Paramount Television and Fellows/Keegan Company. Director: William Wiard. Executive Producers: Terry Keegan and Arthur Fellows. Producers: Carl Borack and William Kelley. Writers: Michael Bendix and William Kelley. Music: Tom Simon. John Jack Tyree (Scott Thomas) is an ex-smuggler and ex-mercenary who now runs a charter boat and salvage service with both his marine biologist son and his teenage daughter. They are helped in their exploits by two trained dolphins and a guy named Cyclone (Paul Winfield). *Cast:* Scott Thomas (as John Jack Tyree), Janet Julian (Laura Tyree), Brett Cullen (Matt Tyree), Paul Winfield (Cyclone Williams), Med Flory (Shanklin), Bob Reynolds (Kaiser), Willis Knickerbocker (Brenner), Carole Russo (Kiki), Don Stout (Marvin), Dick Callihan (Durand).

1817. Murder, Ink. 60 min. Airdate: 9/6/83. Production Company: Charles Fries Productions. Director: John Avildson. Executive Producer: Charles Fries. Producer: Alan Sacks. Writers: Gordon Cotler and Don Mankiewicz. Music: Duane Tatro. Daniel Hugh-Kelly is a New York police inspector whose wife (Tovah Feldshuh), owner of a Manhattan bookstore devoted to mystery novels, helps him solve puzzling crimes. *Cast:* Tovah Feldshuh (as Laura Ireland), Daniel Hugh-Kelly (Sgt. Lou Ireland), Ron McLarty (Sgt. Martin Wilkinson), Marcia Jean Kurtz (Claire), Anna Maria Horsford (Hilly), Ellen Barkin (Ellen Gray), Paula Trueman (Greta Stahlmeyer), Harris Laskaway (Ray Stahlmeyer), Brent

Collins (Pinky Musso), Paul D'Amato (Alfred Swallow), Wyman Pendleton (Braunschweig), Matt Russo (Watchman), Tony Vera (Fire Eater).

1818. **One Night Band (aka Band on the Run).** 60 min. Production Company: MTM Enterprises. Director: Robert Butler. Producer: Robert Butler. Writers: Rick Kellard and Bob Comfort. A country/western band hits the road in their battered bus to find their big break—and to keep one step ahead of their evil manager, who is hunting them down for welshing on the bad contract he conned them into signing. Three original songs would have been introduced each week in this comedy-adventure. *Cast:* Brad Maule (as Michael Harrison), Stepfanie Kramer (Vikki Royelle), George Deloy (Tony Glazer), George Cassel (Zack Radford), Monica Parker (Betty), Marji Martin (Claire), Patrika Darbo (Shelly), Deborah Lampel (Helen), Walter Zeri (Pete), Eric Helland (Carlysle), Don Dolan (Cafe Owner), Gil Bowman (Waitress), also, Steve Sandor, Linda Hart, Carl Weintraub, Carmen Filipi, John Steadman, Dennis Haskins, Jay Rasummy, James Petteway.

1819. **Quarrel.** 60 min. Production Company: Lorimar Productions. Director: Ken Hughes. Executive Producer: Lee Rich. Producers: James Brown and Sam Rolfe. Writer: Sam Rolfe. Creator: Sam Rolfe. Anthony Quarrel is a state department special agent who, in the pilot, sniffs out K.G.B. double agents who have infiltrated the highest ranks of American intelligence. Shot on location in Oregon.

1820. **Quick and Quiet.** 30 min. Airdate: 8/18/81. Production Companies: Quinn Martin Productions and Brademan/Self Productions. Director: Don Weis. Executive Producers: Ed Self and Bill Brademan. Producer: Michael Rhodes. Writers: Sam Bobrick, Bruce Kalish, and Philip John Taylor. A reworking of the 1980 pilot *Landon, Landon and Landon*. William Windom returns as the ghost of dead private eye who, this time haunts his fun-loving, irresponsible, irreverent son (Rick Lohman) and helps him reluctantly solve crimes. Millie Slavin once again plays the agency secretary. *Cast:* William Windom (as Thaddeus Clark "T.C." Cooper), Rick Lohman (Elliot Cooper), Millie Slavin (Camille), Lynda Day George (Margo Hilliard), Henry Jones (Walter Hilliard), Warren Berlinger (Leonard Plumb), Lois Areno (Bambi Wilson), Joan Roberts (Trixie Hilliard), Dallas Alinder (Minister), Jerry Marren (Harry Romero), David Pritchard (David), Lee Crawford (Woman).

1821. **Rivkin: Bounty Hunter.** 2 hours. Airdate: 5/20/81. Production Companies: Ten-Four Productions and Chiarascurio Productions. Director: Harry Harris. Executive Producers: Greg Strangis and Peter Lefcourt. Producers: Arthur E.

McLaird and Frank Ballou. Writer: Peter Lefcourt. Music: Arthur B. Rubinstein. Ron Liebman is Stan Rivkin, a New York City bounty hunter who, when he's hunting down bad guys, leaves his crippled, 12-year-old son under the care of his next-door neighbor, a retired priest (Harry Morgan). *Cast:* Ron Liebman (as Stan Rivkin), Glenn Scarpelli (Keith Rivkin), Harry Morgan (Father Everett Kolodny), Verna Bloom (Bertha), Harold Gray (Manny Taylor), Jim Moody (Capt. O'Donnell), Bo Brucker (Nick St. Clair), George DiCenzo (Tony Caruso), John Getz (Lester Derderow), Carl Donn (Gus), Harry Bellaver (Lou Colla), Manuel Martinez (Lupie Manilo), Mort Freeman (Rabbi), Barry Ford (Maitre d'), Tony Tuseo (Foreman), James Aff (Kid).

1822. **Unit Four.** 60 min. Airdate: 9/29/81. Production Companies: Woodruff Productions and Warner Bros. Television. Director: Virgil W. Vogel. Executive Producer: Philip Saltzman. Producer: Cliff Gould. Writer: Cliff Gould. A crack antiterrorist strike force (Ben Murphy, Nick Mancuso, Tori Lysdahl, and William Allen Young)—each person drawn from a different division of the military— try to thwart bad guys who kidnapped a U.S. diplomat and his family from a plane and parachuted out. *Cast:* Nick Mancuso (as Max Catlin), Ben Murphy (Martin Farnum), Tori Lysdahl (Zina Brandt), William Allen Young (Deke Thomas), Michael Zaslow (Tafir Sadek), Keye Luke (Jimmy Yew), Keene Curtis (Jordan Harrower), Dominique Dunne (Tracy Phillips), Lin McCarthy (Dwight Phillips), Jane Merrow (Liz Phillips), Jeff Pomerantz (Bobby Sayers), Than Wyenn (Dr. Yephrani).

NBC / COMEDY

1823. **Almost American (aka Night School).** 30 min. Airdate: 4/1/81. Production Company: Tandem Productions. Director: Garren Keith. Executive Producers: Budd Grossman and Howard Leeds. Producer: John Maxwell Anderson. Writers: Howard Leeds, Ben Starr, Martin Cohan, and Warren Murray. Creators: Bernie Kukoff and Jeff Harris. Music: Alan Thicke, Gloria Loring, and Al Burton. Aired as an episode of *Diff'rent Strokes.* Maureen McNamara is a teacher who teaches immigrants about America so they can pass their naturalization tests. A similar concept, *What A Country!* lasted a season in first-run syndication in 1986. *Cast:* Maureen McNamara (as Catherine Armstrong), Bob Ari (Milosh Dubroski), Rosalind Chao (Ming-Lee Chang), Richard Yniquez (Rudy), Ernie Hudson

(Kwame Botulo), Anne Bjorn (Kristen), Dana Plato (Kimberly Drummond), Gary Coleman (Arnold Jackson), Todd Bridges (Willis Jackson), Brad Trumbull (Detective Simpson).

1824. **Angie (aka The Angie Dickinson Show).** 30 min. Production Company: Carson Productions. Executive Producer: Allan Katz. Writer: Allan Katz. Creator: Allan Katz. NBC gave Johnny Carson a 13 episode commitment for a sitcom starring Angie Dickinson, and this was the result—the story of a recent divorcee who reenters the singles scene and the work force. The sitcom pilot was shot, but neither Dickinson nor the network was happy with it. The troubled development and ultimate rejection of this pilot are described in detail in an interview with Allan Katz in the book *The Sweeps*. Angie Dickinson opted instead for *Cassie and Company*, an ill-fated NBC detective series Carson Productions developed for her—and it survived just long enough to satisfy the remaining 12 episodes of the contract.

1825. **Bungle Abbey.** 30 min. Airdate: 5/31/81. Production Company: Lucille Ball Productions. Director: Lucille Ball. Executive Producers: Gary Morton and Lucille Ball. Writers: Seamon Jacobs and Fred Fox. Creators: Seamon Jacobs and Fred Fox. Aired as an episode of *NBC Comedy Theatre*. Charlie Callas, Graham Jarvis, Antony Alda, Peter Palmer, Guy Marks, and Gino Conforti are among the wacky monks in this zany monastery. Gale Gordon stars as the Abbott. William Lanteau guest starred in the pilot, which had the monks scheming to sell the portrait of monastery founder Brother Bungle to raise money for an orphanage.

1826. **Dear Teacher.** 30 min. Airdate: 7/17/81. Production Companies: Bron- tosauraus Productions, Wooly Mammoth Productions, and Columbia Pictures Television. Director: Herbert Kenwith. Producers: Roger Schulman and John Baskin. Writers: Roger Shulman and John Baskin. Aired as an episode of *NBC Comedy Theatre*. The misadventures of a fifth grade teacher (Melinda Culea) and her class. This pilot was, in *Variety's* estimation, "simply dreadful." Cast: Melinda Culea (as Annie Cooper), Nan Martin (Karen Lipner), Sydney Penny (Gloria), Jim Welsh (Vernon Thorpe), David Hollander (Todd Goodwin), Willie Dejean (Wendell Trupp), LaShanda Dendy (Cece Taft), Bret Shryer (R.J.), Rachel Jacobs (Heidi Prince), Ted Danson (Steve Goodwin).

1827. **Flatfoots.** 30 min. Airdate: 7/3/82. Production Company: Paramount Television. Director: Herbert Kenwith. Executive Producer: A.C. Lyles. Producers: Lowell Ganz and Arthur Silver. Writers: Lowell Ganz and Arthur Silver. Music: David

Frank, theme "Crime Isn't Pretty" sung by Bob Lind. Aired as an episode of *Here's Boomer*. A comedic version of *Adam-12* with Todd Susman and John Reilly as two hapless cops patroling the streets of Los Angeles. In the pilot, they try to find Boomer the dog a home. *Cast:* John Reilly (as Officer Frank Shackleford), Todd Susman (Officer Gabe Fortunato), Jason Bernard (Sgt. Lindsey Andrews), April Clough (Officer April Mukulanitz), Gary Epp (Officer Dave Heinrich), Raymond Singer (Officer George Pesky), Tracie Savage (Sunny), William Bumiller (Paris), James Stanley (Reporter), Eddie Quillan (Arthur), Jim Knaub (Magic), Pan- chito Gomez (Panchito).

1828. **The Goodbye Girl.** 30 min. Production Company: MGM. Director: Charlotte Brown. Executive Producer: Gerald Isenberg. Producers: Charlotte Brown and Pat Nardo. Writers: Charlotte Brown and Pat Nardo. Creator: Neil Simon. A second pilot based on the movie *The Goodbye Girl*, the story of an out-of- work dancer and her nine-year-old daughter, who share their New York apartment with a struggling actor. Although the two adults fight constantly, they are held together by the clear-thinking girl. New characters included the dancer's middle- aged boyfriend and the actor's uptight, executive brother. JoBeth Williams was slated to star, taking over for Karen Valentine, who played the role in last year's pilot.

1829. **The Grady Nutt Show (aka Reverend Grady).** 30 min. Airdate: 7/24/81. Production Companies: Bansley Productions and Yongestreet Productions. Director: Jack Shea. Producer: John Aylesworth. Writers: John Aylesworth, Barry Adelman, and Barry Silver. Real-life minister Grady Nutt portrays a pastor with a wife and teenage daughter and a colorful congregation. In the pilot, he has to eulogize a man he didn't like. *Cast:* Rev. Grady Nutt (as Rev. Grady Williams), Elinor Donahue (Ellie Williams), Debby Lynn (Becky Williams), Ed Marshall (Jeremy), Peggy Pope (Liz), Raleigh Bond (Joe), Candy Azzara (Mona Thompson), Michael Dudikoff (Randy), also, Billie Jackman.

1830. **Irene.** 30 min. Airdate: 8/19/81. Production Companies: Henerson- Hirsch Productions, Carub Productions, Zephir Productions, and 20th Century Fox. Director: John Tracy. Executive Producers: James Henerson and James Hirsch. Producer: Selma Rubin. Writer: Carol Gary. Music: Irene Cara. Aired as an episode of *NBC Comedy Theatre*. Irene Cara is a preacher's daughter and an aspiring singer who moves into a loft above her uncle's (Theodore Wilson) Soho store, an apartment she shares with career-minded Julia Duffy and man-minded Dee Dee Rescher. *Cast:* Irene Cara (Irene), Dee Dee Rescher (DeDe Thomas), Julia

Duffy (Lois Swenson), Theodore Wilson (Lloyd Cannon), Keenan Wayans (Ray Brewster), Kaye Ballard (Dottie Busmill), also, Michael Winslow, Bill Ostrander, Hoolihan Burke, John Shearin, Rose Lewis, Carole Goldman.

1831. **Living in Paradise.** 30 min. Airdate: 6/14/81. Director: Alan Rafkin. Executive Producers: Bob Schiller and Bob Weiskopf. Producer: Rita Dillon. Writers: Bob Schiller and Bob Weiskopf. Aired as an episode of *NBC Comedy Theatre*. Eddie Albert is a widower living in a mobile home. *Cast:* Eddie Albert (as Vincent Slattery), Georgann Johnson (Winnie Coogan), Jerry Houser (Jason Slattery), Debralee Scott (Hazel Adamson), Alan Oppenheimer (Mel Adamson), Patti Townsend (Donna).

1832. **Munster's Revenge.** 90 min. Airdate: 2/27/81. Production Company: Universal Television. Director: Don Weis. Executive Producer: Edward Montagne. Producers: Don Nelson and Arthur Alsberg. Writers: Don Nelson and Arthur Alsberg. A plodding revival of *The Munsters*. The Munster family is wanted for crimes committed by a mad scientist's (Sid Caesar) robots, which look just like them. A new version of the sitcom, entitled *The Munsters Today*, was launched in 1988 with an entirely new cast by Universal Television and the Arthur Company for first- run syndication. *Cast:* Fred Gwynne (as Herman Munster), Yvonne DeCarlo (Lily Munster), Al Lewis (Grandpa), Jo McDonnell (Marilyn Munster), K.C. Martel (Eddie Munster), Sid Caesar (Dr. Diablo/Emil Hornshymier), Bob Hastings (Phantom of the Opera), Howard Morris (Igor), Herbert Voland (Chief Harry Boyle), Peter Fox (Detective Glen Boyle), Charles Macauley (Commissioner McClusky), Colby Chester (Michael), Michael McManus (Ralph), Joseph Ruskin (Pizza Man), Ezra Stone (Dr. Licklider), Billy Sands (Shorty), Billy Sands (Officer Leary), Barry Pearl (Warren Thurston), Al C. White (Prisoner), Tom Newman (Slim), Anita Dangler (Elvira), Dolores Mann (Mrs. Furnston).

1833. **Pals.** 30 min. Airdate: 7/31/81. Production Company: Columbia Pictures Television. Director: Bob Claver. Executive Producers: Larry Tucker and Larry Rosen. Writers: Larry Tucker and Larry Rosen. Creators: Larry Tucker and Larry Rosen. Music: Ken Harrison. The story of two very different men—one a conservative loan officer (Jeffrey Tambor) and the other an eccentric investment counselor (Tony LoBianco)—who are drawn together because their wives are sisters and they live next door to one another. *Cast:* Tony LoBianco (Frank Greene), Jeffrey Tambor (Harry Miller), Linda Carlson (Shirley Miller), Margaret Willock

(Beverly Greene), Nedra Volz (Emily Baines), Luis Avalos (Capt. Durate), Woodrow Parfrey (Prisoner), Ernie Fuentas (Inspector).

1834. The Parkers (aka Brian and Sylvia). 30 min. Airdate: 3/25/81. Production Company: TAT Communications. Director: John Bowab. Executive Producer: Jack Elinson. Producer: Rita Dillon. Writer: Jack Elinson. Aired as an episode of *Facts of Life*. The story of an aggressive, black anchorwoman (Rosanne Katon) at a Buffalo TV station who is married to an easy-going, white, high school coach (Richard Dean Anderson) and the conflicts their different races and aspirations cause in their lives. *Cast:* Rosanne Katon (as Sylvia Parker), Richard Dean Anderson (Brian Parker), Ja'net Dubois (Ethel), Anthony Holland (Ray), Charlotte Rae (Edna Garrett), Kim Fields (Tootie), Mindy Cohn (Natalie), Lisa Whelchel (Blair), Nancy McKeon (Jo).

1835. Stockers. 30 min. Airdate: 4/24/81. Production Company: Carson Productions. Director: Hal Needham. Executive Producer: John J. McMahon. Producer: Albert S. Ruddy. Writer: Brook Yates. From the makers of *Smokey and the Bandit*. Mel Tillis and Terry Bradshaw are two stock car racers traveling the country, seeking adventures and trying to stay one step ahead of a tireless bill collector (Robert Tessier) who's hunting them down. *Cast:* Terry Bradshaw (J.J. Spangler), Mel Tillis (Curtis Witlock), Samantha Harper (Joanie Fisk), Robert Tessier (Crusher), Archie Hahn (Lee Weldon), R.G. Armstrong (Mr. Fisk), Alice Nunn (Gas Station Owner).

1836. Two Reelers (aka National Lampoon's Two Reelers). 30 min. Airdate: 8/28/81. Production Company: National Lampoon Productions. Director: Kenneth C. Gilbert. Executive Producer: Matty Simmons. Producer: Carlyn Snyder. Writers: Matty Simmons and Hugh Snyder. Creators: Matty Simmons and John Hughes. Music: Jeffrey Tipton. This pilot was designed to evoke fond memories of Abbott and Costello and Laurel and Hardy comedies. Roger Bumpass is the smooth-talking charmer, and Stephen Furst is his bumbling, overweight partner and, each week, these two oafs would find themselves in another fix. Guest stars in the pilot included Penny Peyser, Pierrino Mascarino, Victor Brandt, Owen Rush, and Peter Schrum.

1837. Wendy Hooper—U.S. Army. 30 min. Airdate: 8/14/81. Production Companies: Andomar Productions and Columbia Pictures Television. Director: Jack Shea. Executive Producer: Aaron Ruben. Producer: Gene Marcione. Writer: Aaron Ruben. Aired as an episode of *NBC Comedy Theatre*. NBC's *Private Benjamin* clone casts Wendy Holcombe as a female "Gomer Pyle," a naive country girl who enlists in the Army Signal Corps thinking it will spark a career as a country- western singer. Holcombe became a regular that fall on the NBC sitcom *Lewis and Clark*. *Cast:* Wendy Holcombe (as Pvt. Wendy Hooper), Dana Elcar (Colonel Alfred Hubik), Michael Pataki (Sgt. Michael Bruno), Vanessa Clarke (Pvt. Diane Simpson), Carol Ann Susi (Pvt. Theresa Pelligrini), Helen Page Camp (Mrs. Hubik), also, Dana House, Kathryn Shea.

1838. **Whacked Out.** 30 min. Airdate: 9/26/81. Production Company: Filmways. Director: Michael Zinberg. Executive Producers: Nick Arnold and Eric Cohen. Producers: Robert Sertner and Karen Cooper. Writers: Nick Arnold and Eric Cohen. Music: Terri Falconi. What happens when a daring, underground humor magazine is bought out by a stuffy, huge, publishing conglomerate? There's conflict—between the eccentric staff and the straight-laced execs—the kind of conflict that's supposed to cause sparks and laughs. Not this time. *Cast:* Desi Arnaz, Jr. (Jack Ferguson), Richard Dimitri (Hini), Susanna Dalton (Sarah), Howard Witt (Bud Dugan), Melinda Culea (Trish Van Gordon Gordon), Dana Carvey (Simon), Hansford Rowe (Mr. Van Gordon Gordon), Tom Villard (Louis), Helene Winston (Mrs. Dumont).

1839. **Why Us?** 30 min. Airdate: 8/21/81. Production Companies: Why Us Company, B & E Enterprises, Carson Productions. Director: John Bowab. Executive Producer: John J. McMahon. Producers: Brad Buckner and Eugene Ross- Leming. Writers: Brad Buckner and Eugene Ross-Leming. Music: Tom Scott. Aired as an episode of *NBC Comedy Theatre*. The story of a college professor (John Lawlor) who marries an auto mechanic (Joanna Gleason). Their different backgrounds aren't their only problem—his bookish daughter (Lauri Hendler) and her extroverted daughter (Kim Richards) hate each other. In the pilot, the girls vie for the same guy (Lance Guest). *Cast:* John Lawlor (as Prof. Jules Sanborn), Joanna Gleason (Geri Sanborn), Kim Richards (Holly Sanborn), Lauri Hendler (Zoey San- bornn), Lance Guest (Hugh Whittaker).

NBC / DRAMA

1840. **Advice to the Lovelorn.** 2 hours. Airdate: 11/30/81. Production Company: Universal Television. Director: Harry Falk. Executive Producer: Jon Epstein. Writer: Howard Berk. Music: John DiPasquale. Cloris Leachman is a Los

Angeles newspaper's advice columnist who, in each episode, would involve us in the lives of two of her letter-writers and their problems. Walter Brooke is her editor, and Kelly Bishop is her secretary. *Cast:* Cloris Leachman (as Maggie Dale), Kelly Bishop (Rita Borden), Walter Brooke (Walter Sheehan), Melissa Sue Anderson (Maureen Tyler), Desi Arnaz, Jr. (Steve Vernon), Lance Kerwin (Larry Ames), Donna Pescow (Janice Vernon), Rick Lenz (Prof. Jonas Miller), Tina Louise (Diane Marsh), Dennis Patrick (Dave Marsh), Paul Burke (Nicholas Fraser), Danny Dayton (Drape Man), Peter De Anda (Tim Sharp), Dave Aggress (Delivery Man), Ann Doran (Ada Wells), Barbara Block (Alicia), Joe Terry (Eliot Turner), Jeane Byron (Mrs. Crowley), Rico Cattani (Vittorio Mazzini), Bill Dodenhoff (Bobby), Robert Dunlap (Frank Selby), Ben Hammer (Matthew Cutter), Morgan Jones (Security Officer), Gregory Michaels (Dan Coolidge), Michael Mullins (Greg Allen), Eddie Peterson (Director), Karen Philip (Marie Moore), Charles Walker (Prof. Bennett).

1841. **The Archer—Fugitive from the Empire.** 2 hours. Airdate: 4/12/81. Production Companies: Universal Television and Mad Dog Productions. Director: Nicholas Corea. Producers: Nicholas Corea and Stephen Caldwell. Writer: Nicholas Corea. Music: Ian Underwood. Lane Caudell is young Prince Toran, who is forced to flee his mystical empire when the evil Gar the Destroyer (Kabir Bedi) frames him for killing Toran's father the King (George Kennedy). Toran, brandishing his magical bow and arrow, wanders the fantasy world, accompanied by a gambler named Slant (Victor Campos) and the sensuous enchantress named Estra (Belinda Bauer). They are searching for the Wizard who can give him the throne, and they must find him before Gar finds them. Available on video cassette. *Cast:* Lane Caudell (as Prince Toran), Belinda Bauer (Estra), Victor Campos (Slant), Kabir Bedi (Gar), George Kennedy (King Brakus), George Innes (Mak), Marc Alaimo (Sandros), Tony Swartz (Captain Riis), Richard Dix (Rak), Larry Douglas (Lazar Sa), Alan Rich (Yos), Ivan J. Rado (Vors), Frank Pinkard (Merchant), Richard Moll (Ferryman), Priscilla Pointer (Hawk Lady), John Hancock (Blador), Robert Feero (Ria), Sharon Barr (Mandra), Scott Wilder (Dar).

1842. **Coach (aka Coach of the Year).** 2 hours. Airdate: 12/29/80. Production Company: A Shane Co. Director: Don Medford. Executive Producer: Joan Conrad. Producer: John Ashley. Writer: Frank Abatemarco. Music: Mike Post and Pete Carpenter. Robert Conrad is a former football star who returns from Vietnam crippled, depressed, and confined to a wheelchair—but he regains his self-esteem and self-confidence by coaching juvenile delinquents. *Cast:* Robert Conrad (as Jim Brandon), Erin Gray (DeFalco), Red West (Turner), Daphne Maxwell (Merissa Lane), David Hubbard (Sweetlife), Ricky Pauli Goldin (Andy DeFalco), Alex Paez (Hector), Radames Torres (Peanut), Lou Carello (Eddie), Joneal Joplin (Coach Forrester), Dana Hill (McLeash), Kelly Keefe (Cheerleader).

1843. **Hoyt Axton Show.** 60 min. Airdate: 10/28/81. Production Companies: Joseph P. Byrne-Lou Step Productions and Warner Bros. Television. Director: Richard Crenna. Executive Producers: Joseph P. Byrne and Paul R. Picard. Producer: William L. Young. Writer: Robert Foster. Hoyt Axton is a country singer who, after his wife dies, returns from life on the road to raise his three kids. The series would focus on his attempt to understand his kids and become accustomed to staying in one place for a long time. In the pilot, his 16-year-old daughter is dating a divorced man and his son is hitting the road with his rock band. *Cast:* Hoyt Axton (as Del Parsons), John Shepherd (Dean Parsons), Tanja Walker (Jenny Parsons), Tonya Crowe (Norma Sue Parsons), Joy Garrett (Carol Dean), Sally Kemp (Mrs. Carucci), Reid Smith (Walker Lee), Kenny Davis (Billy Dee).

1844. **Joe Dancer (aka The Big Black Pill).** 2 hours. Airdate: 1/29/81. Production Companies: Mickey Productions and Filmways. Director: Reza S. Badiyi. Executive Producer: Robert Blake. Producer: Alan Godfrey. Writer: Michael Butler. Creator: Robert Blake. Music: George Romanus. Robert Blake is private eye Joe Dancer, a modern-day version of Raymond Chandler's Phillip Marlowe, fighting crime and corruption in sundrenched southern California. *Cast:* Robert Blake (as Joe Dancer), Sondra Blake (Charley), James Gammon (Capt. Jake Jacqualone), JoBeth Williams (Tiffany Farrenpour), Kevin Howard (David Farrenpour), Neva Patterson (Eliza Farrenpour), Edward Winter (Jerrold Farrenpour), Carol Wayne (Allegra Farrenpour), Veronica Cartwright (Sister Theresa), Eileen Heckart (Sister Carla), Wilford Brimley (Wally Haskell), Bubba Smith (Big Foot), Robert Phillips (Little Al), Deborah Levine (Sara), Phillip R. Allen (Wilkie).

1845. **[Pilot #2] [Joe Dancer] The Monkey Mission.** 2 hours. Airdate: 3/23/81. Production Companies: Mickey Productions and Filmways. Director: Burt Brinckerhoff. Executive Producer: Robert Blake. Producer: Alan Godfrey. Writer: Robert Crais. Creator: Robert Blake. Music: George Romanus. Joe Dancer uses a monkey to steal back artwork stolen from his client. *Cast:* Robert Blake (as Joe Dancer), Sondra Blake (Charlie), John Fiedler (Jimmy), Pepe Serna (Vito), Clive Revill (Teabag), Keenan Wynn (Stump Harris), Mitchell Ryan (Keyes), Andy

Wood (Benny), Logan Ramsey (Curator), Alan Napier (Briarton), Elizabeth Haliday (Jennifer Athens), also, Laura Jacoby, Jennifer Gordon, Norman Rice.

1846. **[Pilot #3] [Joe Dancer] Murder 1, Dancer 0.** 2 hours. Airdate: 8/5/83. Production Companies: Mickey Productions and Filmways. Director: Reza S. Badiyi. Executive Producer: Robert Blake. Producer: Alan Godfrey. Writer: Ed Waters. Creator: Robert Blake. Music: George Romanus. Joe Dancer is framed for murder while investigating a tinsel town scandal. *Cast:* Robert Blake (as Joe Dancer), Sondra Blake (Charley), Robin Dearden (Jenny Burnell), William Prince (Asa Lamar), Joel Bailey (Jud Hampton), Royal Dano (Cow John), Kenneth McMillan (Lt. Herbie Quinlan), Jane Daley (Carol), Sam Anderson (Paul Iberville), Deborah Geffner (Jackie), Kelly Lange (Newscaster), Gino Conforti (Photographer), Harriet Mathey (Jill), Sydney Lassick (Phil Estin).

1847. **Judgment Day.** 60 min. Airdate: 12/6/81. Production Companies: Ed Friendly Productions and NBC Productions. Director: Alan J. Levi. Executive Producer: Ed Friendly. Writer: William Froug. Music: Morton Stevens. An anthology that features different dead people each week as they face sentencing to heaven or hell by the judge (Barry Sullivan) of the celestial court. Heaven is represented by Victor Buono, who tells us in flashbacks about the person's good deeds, while the Devil, represented by Roddy McDowall, shows us what this person did to deserve hell. This pilot reportedly cost $1.3 million to produce. *Cast:* Barry Sullivan (the Judge), Victor Buono (Mr. Heavener), Roddy McDowall (Mr. Heller), Carol Lynley (Harriet Egan), Beverly Garland (Vicki Connors), Robert Webber (Charles Egan), John Larch (Burton Randolph), Hari Rhodes (Joseph Pierson), Joseph Chapman (Bob Simmons), Priscilla Pointer (Mrs. Miller).

1848. **Nichols and Dymes (aka Iron Cowboys).** 60 min. Production Company: MTM Enterprises. Director: Rod Daniel. Executive Producers: Rick Kellard and Bob Comfort. Producer: Les Sheldon. Writers: Rick Kellard and Bob Comfort. Creators: Rick Kellard and Bob Comfort. Two funloving, outgoing, undercover cops travel around the country on motorcycles helping local law enforcement agencies. *Cast:* Rocky Bauer (as Buck Nichols), Robin Strand (Willis Dymes), George McDaniel (Whitney), Bill Cross (Sgt. Wilkins), Teddi Siddall (Laura Jean), Kate Murtaugh (Aunt Lydia), Don Richard Gibb (Cogsworth), E. Frantz Turner (Bailiff), Esther Sutherland (Cook), E.A. Sirianni (Julius Skidmore).

1849. **Norma Rae.** 60 min. Production Companies: 20th Century Fox and McKeand Productions. Director: Ed Parone. Executive Producers: Alex Rose and Tamara

Assseyev. Producer: Nigel McKeand. Writer: Carol McKeand. Music: David Shire. Based on the movie that earned Sally Field an Academy Award. Cassie Yates takes over the role of Norma Rae, an outspoken millworker, union organizer and mother of two who lives with her father in a small southern town. *Cast:* Cassie Yates (as Norma Rae Webster), Nancy Jarnagin (Willie Webster), Keith Mitchell (Craig Webster), Barry Corbin (Vernon Witchard), Jane Atkins (Alma Woodruff), Jordan Clarke (Frank Osborne), Ernest Hardin, Jr. (William Poole), Gary Frank (Reuben), Mickey Jones (Emery), Richard Dysart (Judge Elvin Allen), James T. Hall (Clay Johnson), Enid Kent (Waitress), Jon Van Ness (Process Server), Ed Call (Boss Man), Jack Garner (Bailiff).

1850. O'Malley. 60 min. Airdate: 1/8/83. Production Company: Columbia Pictures Television. Director: Michael O'Herlihy. Producers: Frank Cardea and George Schenck. Writers: George Schenck and Frank Cardea. Music: Pete Rugolo. Mickey Rooney is an eccentric New York private eye who works out of the backroom of a Soho Gallery, drives a '59 Caddy convertible, wears Hawaiian shirts, and likes to listen to big band music. *Cast:* Mickey Rooney (Mike O'Malley), Anne Francis (Amanda O'Malley), Pete Cofheld (Guy Fleming), Sarah Abrell (Denny), Tom Waits (Paul), Paula Trueman (Mrs. Douglas), Martin Rosenblatt (Bernie), Jeffrey DeMunn (Carl), Richard Clarke (Ian Davis), Robin Mary Paris (Donna), James Dukes (Hagar), Mark Linn-Baker (Public Defender), Ralph Drischell (Fingers), Cherry Jones (Secretary), Jack Marks (Officer), Ed Van Nuys (Judge), J.C. Quinn (Bailiff), Jose Seneca (Professor), Joe Sharkey (Guard).

1851. Revenge of the Gray Gang. 60 min. Airdate: 10/20/81. Production Company: MTM Enterprises. Director: Gary Nelson. Producer: Gary Nelson. Writer: Michael Norell. Five retired, senior citizens led by an ex-cop become a vigilante band of crimefighters. *Cast:* Noah Beery (as Milo Hoots), Scatman Crothers (Rueben), Mike Mazurki (Joe Malcheski), Maxine Stuart (Daisy Duffy), Richard Whiting (Walter Smith), Tony La Torre (Theodore Koestler), Pat McNamara (Officer Francis Hoots), Susan Niven (Charlene), Nicholas Pryor (Harry Feather-stone), Charles Dierkop (Weasel), Stephen Furst (Fats), Adrian Zmed (Jimmy), Peggy Pope (Millie Koestler), Tom Villard (Officer McGrady), Jane Dulo (Mrs. Tansey).

1852. The Seal. 60 min. Airdate: 11/27/81. Production Company: Universal Television. Director: William Wiard. Executive Producers: James D. Parriott and Richard Chapman. Producer: Ralph Sariego. Writers: Richard Chapman and

James D. Parriott. Ron Ely is a mercenary-for-hire who dresses in black and tools around in a Porsche. Known only as "The Seal," he takes on high-risk missions for big paychecks and worthy causes. In the pilot, he is engaged by the C.I.A. to find a kidnapped cryptographer. Guest star Denny Miller, like Ely, is a former Tarzan. *Cast:* Ron Ely (as The Seal), Jenny Sullivan (Stephanie Thayer), Lee DeBroux (Bill Thayer), Kyle Richards (Lily Thayer), Karen Machon (Paula), Denny Miller (Hutchins), Gerald McRaney (Jennings), Richard Dysart (Haskell), Sandy McPeak (Fletcher).

1853. **Skyward Christmas.** 60 min. Airdate: 12/3/81. Production Company: Major H/Anson Productions. Director: Vincent McEveety. Executive Producers: Ron Howard and Anson Williams. Producers: Joe Pope and John Kuri. Writer: Craig Buck. Music: Lee Holdridge. A pilot based on the acclaimed 1980 TV movie *Skyward.* The continuing adventures of 16-year-old paraplegic and amateur pilot Julie Ward (Suzy Gilstrap). Bibi Besch, Christopher Connelly, Kelly Ann Conn, Geoffrey Lewis, and Audra Lindley take over roles originated by Marion Ross, Clu Gulager, Lisa Whelchel, Howard Hesseman, and Bette Davis. *Cast:* Suzy Gilstrap (as Julie Ward), Bibi Besch (Natalie Ward), Christopher Connelly (Steve Ward), Kelly Ann Conn (Lisa Ward), Audra Lindley (Billie Dupree), Geoffrey Lewis (Koup Trenton), Jack Elam (Clay Haller), Justin Dana (Billy Ward), Harold Scruggs (Leo).

1854. **Texas Rangers.** 60 min. Airdate: 5/16/81. Director: George Fenady. Executive Producers: Frank Von Zerneck and Robert Greenwald. Producer: David Garcia. Writers: Stanley Ralph Ross and David Balkin. Music: Jerrold Immel. Jeff Osterhage and Larry Gilman are two Texas Rangers who, in the pilot, hunt down escaped murderers. *People* called this a "witless failed pilot, a sort of sagebrush *Adam-12.*" *Cast:* Jeff Osterhage (as Ranger Andy Bennett), Larry Gilman (Ranger Bill Cavanaugh), Richard Farnsworth (Ranger J.W. Stevens), Arlen Dean Snyder (Capt. Richard Barton), Patricia Barry (Blanche), Michael Cavanaugh (Bobby Joe Ames), Jonathan Gries (Sherman Ames), Marie Lynn Ross (Lois Ames), Paul Brinegar (Old Al), Robert J. Wilke (Train Engineer).

1982–1983

ABC / COMEDY

1855. Callahan. 30 min. Airdate: 9/9/82. Production Company: Carsey/ Werner Productions. Director: Harry Winer. Executive Producers: Marcy Carsey and Tom Werner. Producer: Bill Finnegan. Writers: Ken Finkleman, David Misch. An outlandish, campy, fast-moving spoof of movie serials that bares a striking resemblance to the "Indiana Jones" films. Hart Bochner is Callahan, the adventurous curator of New York's Natural History Museum who, with his naive assistant Rachel (Jaime Lee Curtis), is constantly on the go, traveling all over the globe in search of relics and encountering excitement and danger at every moment. *Cast:* Hart Bochner (as Callahan), Jaime Lee Curtis (Rachel Bartlet), John Harkins (Marcus Vex), Peter Maloney (Mustaf), Herb Braha (Boondaran), Tony Plana (Vostonovich), John Moschitta, Jr. (Phloti).

1856. For Lovers Only (aka Honeymoon Hotel; aka Bliss). 2 hours. Airdate: 10/15/82. Production Companies: Henerson-Hirsch Productions and Caesars Palace Productions. Director: Claudio Guzman. Executive Producers: James S. Henerson and James G. Hirsch. Producer: Jay Daniel. Writer: James G. Hirsch. Music: Pete Rugolo. Yet another "Love Boat" ripoff set at a hotel, this one a honeymoon retreat in the Poconos operated by Andy Griffith. *Cast:* Andy Griffith (as Vernon Bliss), Katherine Helmond (Bea Winchell), Deborah Raffin (Lilah Ward), Robert Hegyes (Frankie Spoleto), Anna Garduno (Candy), Christopher Wells (Flip Leonard), Gary Sandy (Peter Ward), Sally Kellerman (Emmy Pugh), Gordon Jump (Harvey Pugh), Jane Kaczmarek (Margie Spoleto), Alan North (Max).

1857. Heavens. 30 min. Production Company: Spelling/Weintraub Productions. Writer: Iris Rainier. A "Love Boat"-style comedy that follows the lives of the people who shop at Heavens, an ultra-trendy department store, and their relationships with the regular cast of salespeople.

1858. Hitchhiker's Guide to the Galaxy. 30 min. Production Company: D.L. Taffner, Ltd. Director: Theodore Flicker. Executive Producer: Don Taffner. Producer: Bill D'Angelo. Writer: Stu Silver. Creator: Douglas Adams. Based on the book by Douglas Adams, and the subsequent British television and radio series. Just before the Earth is destroyed, an alien saves an American and, together, they hitchhike throughout the galaxy.

1859. **Scared Silly.** 30 min. Airdate: 9/2/82. Production Company: Aaron Spelling Productions. Director: John Astin. Executive Producers: Aaron Spelling and Douglas S. Cramer. Producers: Jim Mulligan and E. Duke Vincent. Writers: Rich Eustis and Michael Elias. Jeff Altman and Donovan Scott are two bumbling investigators of the supernatural working for the renowned parapsychologist Dr. Beardsley (Wilfred Hyde-White) and his Office of Occult Occurrences—which is where people turn when they are threatened by ghosts, vampires, mummies and other spooky things. After the success of the movie *Ghostbusters* several years later, there was talk of reviving this pilot, but nothing ever materialized. *Cast:* Wilfred Hyde-White (as Dr. Beardsley), Jeff Altman (Skip), Donovan Scott (Harold), Lisa Hartman (Darcy Winfield), Steve Franken (Bryce Needles), Fred Stuthman (Edgar).

ABC / DRAMA

1860. **The Big Easy.** 60 min. Airdate: 8/15/82. Production Company: Paramount Television. Director: Jud Taylor. Executive Producer: Dan Curtis. Producer: Joe Stern. Writer: Lee Hutson. Creator: Lee Hutson. Music: J.J. Johnson and the Camellia Jazz Band. This evolved from the "Bourbon Street" concept Paramount and producer Gerald Abrams pitched to NBC in 1980. William Devane stars as Jake Rubidoux, a New Orleans detective who plays clarinet at the Big Easy, a French Quarter jazz club, where his friend Walker Garrett (Nicholas Pryor), a newspaper reporter, hangs out and fishes for story ideas. Together, they solve crimes, which pays Jake's rent and provides the grist for Walker's columns. *Cast:* William Devane (as Jake Rubidoux), Nicholas Pryor (Walker Garrett), Ja'net Dubois (Gloria Shenar), Lane Smith (Lt. Frank Medley), Elliot Keener (Henry), Mary Crosby (Cynthia Hayes), Barbara Babcock (Lorri Fitzgerald), Matt Clark (Dan O'Keefe), Hugh Gillin (Nunally Hayes), Jared Martin (Jeb Walker), Ed Rombola (Shoes), Crofton Hardester (Laveau), Stocker Fontelieu (Walter), Dick Durock (Goggles), Ann Merie (Maid), Shirley Harrison (Witch).

1861. **Farrah Fawcett Project.** Production Companies: The Jozak Company and MGM. Producer: Gerald Isenberg. Writer: Woody Gould. An adventure series starring Farrah Fawcett, as an undercover agent working for a specialized government agency.

1862. Massarati & the Brain. 2 hours. Airdate: 8/26/82. Production Company: Aaron Spelling Productions. Director: Harvey Hart. Executive Producers: Aaron Spelling and Douglas S. Cramer. Producers: Charles B. Fitzsimons and E. Duke Vincent. Writer: George Kirgo. Music: Billy Goldenberg. Daniel Pilon is Massarati, a slick, millionaire adventurer who becomes guardian to his brilliant 10-year-old nephew Christopher (Peter Billingsley), who outfits his 007-ish uncle with an array of gadgets to fight crime. Markie Post is a spy who gives them assignments, and Christopher Hewitt is their butler—a role he played in the ABC series *Fantasy Island* and *Mr. Belvedere*. *Cast:* Daniel Pilon (as Massarati), Peter Billingsley (Christopher), Christopher Hewitt (Anatole), Markie Post (Julie Rams- dale), Ann Turkel (Wilma Hines), Camilla Sparv (Dorothea Martin), Kathryn Witt (Diana Meredith), Christopher Lee (Victor Leopold), Kaz Garas (Nick Henry), Gail Jensen (Camille Henry), Heather O'Rourke (Skye Henry), Ricky Supiran (Rocky Henry), Yukio Collins (Yukio), Jeff Imada (Sushi), Greta Blackburn (Sharon), Chuck Tamburo (Joe Perkins).

1863. Modesty Blaise. 60 min. Airdate: 9/12/82. Production Companies: Paramount Television and Barney Rosenweig Productions. Director: Reza S. Badiyi. Executive Producer: Barney Rosenweig. Producer: Carl Kugel. Writer: Steve Zito, based on characters created by Peter O'Donnell. Based on the books by Peter O'Donnell. Ann Turkel is Modesty Blaise, a former criminal who now uses her beauty and savvy to fight crime. She is aided by the handsome Willie Garvin (Lewis Van Bergen), a man whose life she once saved. Van Bergen would later star in the short-lived, 1987 ABC series *Sable*. *Cast:* Ann Turkel (as Modesty Blaise), Lewis Van Bergen (Willie Garvin), Sab Shimono (Wang), Keene Curtis (Gerald Tarent), Douglas Dirkson (Jack), Sarah Rush (Emma Woodhouse), Carolyn Seymour (Debbie DeFarge), Charles Cioffi (Leo Bazin), Hector Elias (Placido), Jan Van Reenen (Narvick), Lenny Bremen (Sun Bather), Jeff Chayette (Bartender), Pearl Shear (Mrs. Turner), Akira (Prof. Toru Tanaka).

1864. Outlaws. 90 min. Airdate: 7/9/84. Production Companies: Universal Television and Limekiln and Templar Productions. Director: James Frawley. Executive Producers: Robert Wolterstorff and Paul Belous. Producer: Les Sheldon. Writers: Robert Wolterstorff and Paul Belous. Music: Jerrold Immel. Charles Rocket and Chris Lemmon are two plumbing company executives who are arrested for a jewel heist they didn't commit and break out of jail. *Cast:* Christopher Lemmon (Eugene Griswold), Charles Rocket (Stanley Flynn), Joan Sweeny (Cindy Dawson), Charles Napier (Capt. Striker), Robert Mandan (Nicholas Zotanis), Dub Taylor (L.D. Sloane), Panchito Gomez (Raphael), Mel Stewart (Det. Lou Franklin), M. Emmet Walsh (Warden MacDonald), Geoff Edwards (Roger Demerest), John Steadman (Prospector), Joe Montegna (Yuri), Shelly Batt (Mona Griswold), Nathan Roberts (Phil Barnes), Yolanda Marquez (Mother), Frank Lugo (Roberto), Tony Crupi (Chauffeur), Teri Beckerman (Arlene), Martin Azarow (Emil), Carl Strano (Eddie Sawyer), Tao Horino (Fujiyama), Andrew Bloch (Cameraman), Garry Goodrow (Hotel Clerk), Duke Stroud (Prison Guard), Sam Scarber (Bubba), Steve L. Buckingham (Larry).

1865. Rooster. 2 hours. Airdate: 8/19/82. Production Companies: Glen Larson Productions, 20th Century Fox. Director: Russ Mayberry. Executive Producer: Glen Larson. Producer: Harker Wade. Writers: Glen Larson and Paul Williams. Music: Stu Phillips. An attempt to re-capture the charm of the Paul Williams/Pat McCormick partnership from the movie *Smokey and the Bandit*. Williams is Rooster Steele, an ex-police shrink who teams up with ex-cop Sweets McBride (McCormick) to work as insurance investigators. *Cast:* Paul Williams (as Rooster Steele), Pat McCormick (Sweets McBride), J.D. Cannon (Chief Willard T. Coburn), Ed Lauter (Jack Claggert), Jill St. John (Joanna Van Egan), Katherine Baumann (Amy Hammond), Amy Botwinick (B.B.), William Bryant (Fire Chief), Delta Burke (Laura De Vega), Charlie Callas (Francis A. Melville), Henry Darrow (Dr. Sanchez), Pamela Hensley (Bunny Richter), Lara Parker (Janet), William Daniels (Dr. DeVega), John Saxon (Jerome Brademan), Marie Osmond (Sister Mae Davis), Eddie Albert (Reverend Harlan Barnum), Severn Darden (Conway), Ken Lynch (Poker Player), Michele Carey (Policewoman), Betty Bridges (Nurse), Darian Dash (Billy), Cody Jones (Eno), also, Dan Pastorini, Dusty Baker, Jerry Reuss, and Mike Scioscia.

1866. [Pilot #2] Rooster. 60 min. Airdate: 12/15/82. Production Companies: Glen Larson Productions and 20th Century Fox Television. Director: Daniel Haller. Executive Producer: Glen Larson. Producers: Lee Majors and Harry Thomason. Writer: Glen Larson. Music: Stu Phillips. Aired as the "How Do I Kill a Thief— Let Me Count the Ways" episode of *The Fall Guy*. Rooster and Sweets clash with bounty hunter Colt Seavers (Lee Majors). *Cast:* Paul Williams (as Rooster Steele), Pat McCormick (Sweets McBride), Lee Majors (Colt Seavers), Markie Post (Terry

Shannon), Douglas Barr (Howie Munson), Heather Thomas (Jody Banks), Peter Mark Richman (Frank), David S. Sheiner (Durwood), Jack Ging (Johnson), Thomas Albert Clay (Operator), John Shull (Deputy), Barry Bartle (Jackson), Art Kassul (Drunk), Raymond Lynch (Officer), Tom Peters (Director), Charles Ringa (Controller).

1867. **This Is Kate Bennett.** 90 min. Airdate: 5/28/82. Production Company: Lorimar Productions. Director: Harvey Hart. Executive Producers: Lee Rich and Joanne Brough. Producers: James H. Brown and Karen Mack. Writer: Sue Milburn. Music: Lee Holdridge. Janet Eilber is Kate Bennett, a crusading TV reporter and a single mother trying to balance the demands of her career and her child. In the pilot, she becomes the target of the killer she's covering. *Cast:* Janet Eilber (as Kate Bennett), Kyle Richards (Jenny Bennett), David Groh (Jeff Bennett), Greg Mullavey (Ed Fiore), David Haskell (Marv Epstein), Linda P. Stuart (Audrey), Granville Van Dusen (Tim Maxwell), Larry Breeding (Seth Greenwald), Stephanie Blackmore (Melissa Morgan), Nora Heflin (Pat Gans), Beverleigh Banfield (Maura Wilson), Carole Tru Foster (Lisa), Fred Holliday (Larry Hamilton), James Noble (Mr. Fairmont), Garret Pearson (Manny Resino), Helen Page Camp (Margaret Harris), Dick Anthony Williams (Leonard Hayes), Joel Bailey (Bill Harris), William Bogert (Lawson), Royce Wallace (Virginia Watson), Jennifer Berito (Esther O'Donnell), William Callaway (Morris Steinman), Michael Talbott (Gary Harris), Michael Laurence (Fred Barnes), John Stuart West (Stage Manager), Robert Jarvis (Sergeant), Blake Conway (Officer), Tommy Lee Holland (Attorney), Vance Davis (Pool Player), Cheryl Francis (Mary Watson), Rosanna Christian (Nurse), Pam Galloway (Exercise Leader).

CBS / COMEDY

1868. **Adams House.** 30 min. Airdate: 7/14/83. Production Companies: 20th Century Fox Television and Allan Katz Productions. Director: Jay Sandrich. Producer: Allan Katz. Writer: Allan Katz. Creator: Allan Katz. Music: Stuart Katz. The troubled history of this failed pilot is examined in detail in the book *The Sweeps*, which examined the 1983–84 season. Karen Valentine stars as a Chicago social worker and a divorced mother who works out of a refurbished house on Adams Street. The show was shot as a one-hour drama, but was reworked as a half-hour comedy at the network's insistence. Lloyd Nolan guest starred as an elderly widower facing eviction. *Cast:* Karen Valentine (Chris Bennett), Shelby Balik (Jennifer Bennett), Mark Shera (Michael Purcell), Earl Boen (Gilbert Spencer), Byrne Piven (Mr. Webster), T.K. Carter (Ronnie), Lloyd Nolan (Frank Gallagher), Lili Haydn (Lauren Drucker), David Cooper (Mr. Drucker), Shirley Prestia (Mrs. Drucker), Bill Caldert (Barry Drucker), J. Brennan Smith (Harvey Dutton), Georgia Schmidt (Woman).

1869. **After George.** 30 min. Airdate: 6/6/83. Production Companies: MGM and Humble Productions. Director: Linda Day. Producers: Fred Freeman and Lawrence J. Cohen. Writers: Dennis Danizger and Ellen Sandler. Susan Saint James stars as a widow who discovers her late husband, who died in a car accident, programmed his personality into the computer that operates their house. *Cast:* Susan Saint James (as Susan Roberts), Joel Brooks (Cal Sloan), Susan Rattan (Marge), Allyn Ann McLerie (Rose), Richard Schaal (George), John Reilly (Walt), George Pentecost (Frank), Steve Anderson (Charles).

1870. **The Astronauts.** 30 min. Airdate: 8/11/82. Production Company: Elmar Productions. Director: Hal Cooper. Executive Producers: Rod Parker and Hal Cooper. Producer: Rita Dillon. Writer: Rod Parker. Creators: Hal Cooper and Rod Parker. Music: Billy Byers. Based on the BBC sitcom, a "Three's Company" in outer space with two men and a beautiful woman stuck in an orbiting space station, dubbed Scilab. McLean Stevenson is their earthbound commanding officer. *Cast:* Granville Van Dusen (Capt. Roger Canfield), Brianne Leary (Astronaut Jennifer Tate), Bruce Davison (Astronaut David Ackyroyd), McLean Stevenson (Col. Michael C. Booker), Nathan Cook (Scotty).

1871. **Cass Malloy.** 30 min. Airdate: 7/21/82. Production Company: Lorimar Productions. Director: J.D. Lobue. Executive Producers: Karen Mack and Gary Adelson. Producers: Steve Marshall and Dan Guntzelman. Writers: Steve Marshall and Dan Guntzelman. Caroline McWilliams stars as a widow with two children who takes over her late husband's job as sheriff. This pilot served as the basis for a new first-run syndicated series in 1987. The subsequent series was originally billed as *Suddenly Sheriff,* starring Priscilla Barnes, but shortly before production, Barnes was replaced by Suzanne Somers, the character became Hildy Granger, and the title was changed to *She's the Sheriff.* George Wyner returned for the new series, and his character was rechristened "Deputy Max Rubin." *Cast:* Caroline McWilliams (as Cass Malloy), Amanda Wyss (Colleen Malloy),

Heather Hobbs (Nona Malloy), Corey Feldman (Little Big Jim Malloy), George Wyner (Max Rosen- cratz), Dianne Key (Tina Marie Nelson), Lou Richards (Dennis Little), Glynn Turman (Woodrow Freeman), Dick Butkus (Alvin Dimsky), Murphy Dunne (Adam Barrett), Buzz Sapien (Chip Carbin).

1872. In Security. 30 min. Airdate: 7/7/82. Production Company: Lorimar Productions. Director: Peter Bonerz. Executive Producer: Lee Rich. Producer: Bob Ellison. Writers: Bob Ellison and Barry Kemp. Creators: Bob Ellison, Barry Kemp. Music: Patrick Williams. Annie Potts stars as a divorcee who, after years as a housewife, becomes an assistant to the security chief (John Randolph) at a major department store. Her co-workers include a chauvinistic, macho ex-marine (Peter Jurasik); a matronly grandmother and ex-policewoman (Cara Williams); and a lovesick, wanna-be sportscaster (James Keane). At home, she faces the romantic overtures of her next-door neighbor (James Murtaugh), a newspaper columnist, who often uses his daughter (Kari Ann Patterson) to help him snare Annie. *Cast:* Annie Potts (as Annie Leighton), Cara Williams (Doris Gleen), John Randolph (Eldon Radford), James Murtaugh (Garrett Lloyd), Kari Ann Patterson (Jennie Lloyd), James Keane (Rudy DeMayo), Peter Jurasik (Henry), Margaret Wheeler (Shoplifter), Robert Lussier (Man in Draperies), Esther McCarroll (Lady in Cookware), John Dennis (Mr. Bowman), Greg Lewis (Man).

1873. Johnny Garage. 30 min. Airdate: 4/13/83. Production Companies: Grosso-Jacobson Productions and Columbia Pictures Television. Director: Bill Per- sky. Producers: Sonny Grosso and Larry Jacobson. Writer: Gary Gilbert. Music: Bill Persky and Elliot Lawrence. Ron Carey is Johnny "Garage" Antonizzio, the owner of a troubled gas station in Queens. Val Bisoglio is his partner Frankie, Carlin Glynn is his landlord, and Timothy Van Patten is his womanizing, not-too-bright mechanic. *Cast:* Ron Carey (as Johnny Antonizzio), Val Bisoglio (Frankie), Carlin Glynn (Harriet), Timothy Van Patten (Mike), Christina Avis-Krauss (Brenda), William Smitrovich (Steve Enright), Jack Hallett (Paul Enright), Robert Cenedella (Mr. Freeze-It), Tony DiBenedetto (Mailman), Bill Marcus (Battery Man), Carol Levy (Girl).

1874. Kudzu. 30 min. Airdate: 8/13/83. Production Company: Tomorrow Entertainment. Director: Rod Daniel. Executive Producers: Thomas W. Moore and John D. Backe. Producers: Rod Daniel, E. Jack Kaplan. Writer: E. Jack Kaplan, from the comic strip. Music: Tim Simon. Tony Becker stars as a whimsical, ideal-istic 15-year-old who lives in a sleepy North Carolina town and dreams of being a writer. Larry B. Scott is Maurice, his best friend; Teri Landrum is Veranda, his vain, true love; Linda Henning is his abandoned, domineering mother; James Hampton is his uncle, who operates a gas station-come-general store; and John Chappell is the self- centered reverend. *Cast:* Tony Becker (as Roger "Kudzu" DuBose), Linda Henning (Mavis DuBose), James Hampton (Uncle Dub), Larry B. Scott (Maurice), Teri Landrum (Veranda), John Chappell (Preacher Dunn), Mallie Jackson (Betty Jane), Leslie Vallen (Lady), Mickey Cherney (Man).

1875. **Now We're Cookin'.** 30 min. Airdate: 4/19/83. Production Company: Universal Television. Director: Noam Pitlik. Executive Producer: Joel Schumacher. Producer: Noam Pitlik. Writer: Joel Schumacher. Music: Glen Ballard, Mark Mueller. Three ex-cons (Lyman Ward, Cleavon Little, Paul Carafotes) who man-age a down-town diner. Other regulars include a beat cop who models himself after TV characters (Joe Montegna), their parole officer (Lynne Moody), and the owner of the restaurant (Carole Cook). *Cast:* Lyman Ward (as Cookie Porter), Cleavon Little (Rollin Hutton), Paul Carafotes (Anthony Tarzola), Carole Cook (Marge), Lynne Moody (Janine Rogers), Gary Allen (Vern), Joe Montegna (Ernie), Toni Kalem (Roxanne La Tucci).

1876. **One More Try.** 30 min. Airdate: 8/31/82. Production Company: Universal Television. Director: Noam Pitlik. Executive Producer: Jerry Davis. Producer: John E. Quill. Writer: Lynn Grossman. Music: Dan Foliart, Howard Pearl, and Madeline Stone. Sung By: Lucie Arnaz. Real-life couple Lucie Arnaz and Laurence Luckinbill portray two mis-matched, but in-love, divorcees who get married even though they failed at their first marriages. The humor would arise from their conflicting personalities—he's the quiet, scholarly curator of the Natural History Museum, she's a harried, scatterbrained caterer. *Cast:* Lucie Arnaz (as Dede March), Laurence Luckinbill (Adam Margolin), Judy Gibson (Jenny Marlowe), Randall Batinkoff (Paul Margolin), Benjamin Bernouy (Daniel Margolin), Maurice Shrong (Mr. Liebowitz), Jeff Brooks (Dwayne), William LeMessena (Judge), Richard Za- qvaglia (Nick), Antonia Rey (Cabbie).

1877. **She's with Me.** 30 min. Airdate: 8/24/82. Production Company: Alan Landsburg Productions. Director: Will MacKenzie. Executive Producer: Mort Lachman. Producer: Sy Rosen. Writers: Sy Rosen and C.J. Banks. Creators: Sy Rosen and C.J. Banks. The misadventures of two black sisters who move from a small, Illinois town to a houseboat in San Francisco. The mature, older sister (Gloria

Gifford) becomes assistant buyer at a department store, where she works for a tyrannical boss (Greg Mullavey) while her irresponsible, younger sister (Deborah Pratt) goes from job to job. Patrick J. Cronin costars as their landlord. *Cast:* Gloria Gifford (as Ellen Madison), Deborah Pratt (Bonnie Madison), Patrick J. Cronin (Chatfield), Barry Hope (Captain), Greg Mullavey (Mr. Rogers), Howard Morton (Mr. Meltzer), David Paymer (Space Cadet), Toby Hand (Hare Krishna), Joan Dareth (Saleslady), Barbara Hamilton (Bus Official).

1878. Suzie Mahoney (aka The Suzanne Somers Show). 30 min. Production Companies: Embassy Television and Hamel/Somers Entertainment. Director: Doug Rogers. Executive Producers: Dick Bensfield, Perry Grant, and Alan Hamel. Writers: Dick Bensfield and Perry Grant. Suzanne Somers plays a regular in a long- running sitcom who lives in an apartment with her six-year-old (Ryan Janis). William Windom, who runs the building and John Putch, her next-door neighbor, double as surrogate fathers to her son while she is working. Each episode would include scenes from the fictional series that would spotlight Somers in physical comedy.

CBS / DRAMA

1879. Adventures of Pollyanna. 60 min. Airdate: 4/10/82. Production Company: Walt Disney Productions. Director: Robert Day. Executive Producer: William Robert Yates. Producer: Tom Leetch. Writer: Anne Beckett, from the novel by Eleanor Porter. Music: Jerrold Immel. Based on the 1960 Walt Disney film *Pollyanna*. Patsy Kensit takes over for Hayley Mills as the energetic, 12-year-old girl who, after her parents die, emigrates from England to live with her aunt (Shirley Jones) in a small American town, circa 1912. The stories would revolve around the young girl's unique ability to enliven the people around her. Rossie Harris and Rox- anna Zal are her two best friends, kids from the local orphanage. *Cast:* Patsy Kensit (as Pollyanna Harrington), Shirley Jones (Aunt Polly), Edward Winter (Herman Chilton), Roxanna Zal (Mary Lee), Lucille Benson (Mrs. Leveler), Stacey Nelkin (Cora Spencer), Beverly Archer (Angelica), John Putch (Johnny Muller), John Randolph (Mr. Muller), Rossie Harris (Jimmy Bean), Mitzi Hoag (Mrs. Muller), Nicholas Hammond (Reverend Tull), Jay Macintosh (Widow Jenn), James Collins (Thomas Jenn), Anne Hanley (Miss Bess), Gretchen Wyler (Mrs. Tarkell).

1880. Beyond Witch Mountain. 60 min. Airdate: 2/20/82. Production Company: Walt Disney Productions. Director: Robert Day. Executive Producer: William Robert Yates. Producer: Jan Williams. Writers: Robert Malcolm Young, B.W. Sandefur, and Hal Kanter. Music: George Duning. A sequel/pilot based on the movies *Escape from Witch Mountain* and *Return from Witch Mountain*. Tracy Gold and Andy Freeman are alien children with psychic powers who, with their families, crash-landed on Witch Mountain. They become separated from the survivors and befriend a man (Eddie Albert) who helps them elude a millionaire (Efrem Zimbalist, Jr.) who wants to exploit their incredible powers. *Cast:* Eddie Albert (as Jason O'Day), Efrem Zimbalist, Jr. (Aristotle), Tracey Gold (Tia), Andy Freeman (Tony), J.D. Cannon (Deranian), Noah Beery, Jr. (Uncle Ben), Stephanie Blackmore (Dr. Adrian Molina), Peter Hobbs (Dr. Peter Morton), James Luisi (Foreman), William H. Bassett (Lowell Roberts), also, Gene Dynarski, Lola Mason, Eric Aved.

1881. Birds of a Feather. 60 min. Airdate: 3/17/83. Production Company: Universal Television. Director: Virgil Vogel. Executive Producer: Donald Bellisario. Producers: Reuben Leder, Rick Weaver, Chris Abbott-Rish, and Charles Floyd Johnson. Writer: Donald Bellisario. Creator: Donald Bellisario. Music: Mike Post and Pete Carpenter. Aired as an episode of *Magnum PI*. William Lucking stars as a charter airline pilot and soldier-of-fortune who, in the pilot, crashes his plane in the ocean outside Robin Master's estate—where private eye Magnum (Tom Selleck) lives. Richard Roundtree co-stars as Peter Jordan, the owner of the airline.

1882. Cherokee Trail. 60 min. Airdate: 11/28/81. Production Company: Walt Disney Productions. Director: Keith Merrill. Executive Producer: Douglas Netter. Writers: Michael Terrance and Keith Merrill. Creator: Louis L'Amour. Music: Jerrold Immel. The adventures of widow Mary Breydon (Cindy Pickett) and her daughter Peggy (Tina Yothers) on the western frontier operating a stagecoach way station on the Cherokee Trail. The Breydons run the station with the help of a young, Irish cook (Mary Larkin); a grizzled, hired hand (Richard Farnsworth); an orphan boy (Tommy Peterson); and a laconic cowboy (David Hayward). The story, like *Little House on the Prairie* and *The Waltons*, would be told from the perspective of the now-adult daughter. *Cast:* Cindy Pickett (as Mary Breydon), Tina Yothers (Peggy Breydon), Mary Larkin (Matty Maginnis), David Hayward (Temple Boone), Victor French (Scant Luther), Richard Farnsworth (Ridge

Fenton), Tommy Peterson (Walt Tanner), Timothy Scott (Wilbur Pattishal), Buck Taylor (Laird), Gene Russ (Grocer), Whitney Rydbeck (Bob), Ben Miller (Stagedriver), Skeeter Vaughn (Indian).

1883. **Family in Blue.** 60 min. Airdate: 6/10/82. Production Company: Glicksman-Brinkley Productions. Director: Jackie Cooper. Executive Producers: Frank Glicksman and Don Brinkley. Producer: Jack Sontag. Writer: Don Brinkley. Creator: Don Brinkley. Music: Patrick Williams. The proposed series would focus on the good-natured conflict and competition between a retired cop-turned-private eye (Efrem Zimbalist, Jr.), his police sergeant son (Dirk Benedict), his crime lab technician daughter (Nancy Dolman) and his police captain brother (Dick O'Neill). *Cast:* Efrem Zimbalist, Jr. (as Marty Malone), Dirk Benedict (Matt Malone), Nancy Dolman (Julie Malone), Dick O'Neill (Chester Malone), Michael Corneilson (Dabney Malone), Doris Singleton (Bernice Malone), Edward Winter (Barney Hathaway), Cindy Pickett (Tina Royce), Michael McGuire (Edward Wyler), Timothy Brown (Officer Zimmerman), also, Benson Fong, Michael Collins, Hamilton Camp.

1884. **Gib.** 60 min. Production Company: Warner Bros. Television. Director: Jack Smight. Executive Producer: Philip Saltzman. Producer: Douglas Benton. Writer: Tom Lazarus. Gil Gerard is an ex-quarterback who becomes trouble-shooter for the Mayor of New Orleans (George Coe) and ends up helping a lot of people in trouble. Other characters include his friend-on-the-Force (Don Hood) and his attorney/manager (Mimi Rogers), who still manages to land him a television commercial here and there. Reworked in 1983 as *Johnny Blue*. Writer Tom Lazarus and costar Mimi Rogers also worked with Gerard in *Hear No Evil*, another unsold, CBS pilot.

1885. **Hear No Evil.** 2 hours. 11/10/82. Production Companies: Paul Pompian Productions and MGM. Director: Harry Falk. Producer: Paul Pompian. Writer: Tom Lazarus. Music: Lance Rubin. Gil Gerard is a cop who is left deaf by a car bomb and adapts to his new disability with the help of his partner (Bernie Casey), a therapist (Mimi Rogers) and a "hearing" dog. In the pilot, he tracks the PCP- producing motorcycle gang that tried to kill him. *Cast:* Gil Gerard (as Inspector Bill Dragon), Bernie Casey (Inspector Monday), Mimi Rogers (Meg), Ron Karabatsos (Lt. Lew Haley), Robert Dryer (Vinnie Holzer), Christina Hart (Sheila Green), Brion James (Bobby Roy Burns), Wings Hauser (Don Garrard), Emily Heebner (Vicki), Bruce McKay (Capt. Shelhart), Parker Whitman (Riles),

Joe Bellan (Cabbie), Mickey Jones (Blackman), Raven De La Croix (Candy Burns), William Paterson (Minister), John G. Scanlon (Summers), Jana Winters (Hooker), Charles Bouvier (Wilkes), Steve Burton (Cop), Sam Conti (Sonny), W. Scott Devenney (Rachmil), Chuck Dorsett (Dr. Larsen), Paul Drake (T.D.), Julianna Fjeld (Rico), Cab Covay (Hit Man), Gary Pettinger (Wrigley), Janet Raney (Terri).

1886. **Little Lord Faimtleroy.** 60 min. 8/14/82. Production Company: Norman Rosemont Productions. Director: Desmond Davis. Executive Producer: Norman Rosemont. Producer: William Hill. Writer: Blanche Hanalis, from the novel by Hodgson Burnett. Music: Allyn Ferguson. A sequel to the 1980 CBS TV movie which starred Ricky Schroder as the poor, New York child who becomes heir to a British estate owned by his grandfather, played by Alec Guinness. Jerry Supiran and John Mills take over the role for the pilot, which has them helping a poor preacher. *Cast:* John Mills (as Earl of Doricourt), Jerry Supiran (Cedric Erroll/Little Lord Fauntleroy), Caroline Smith (Mrs. Erroll), Godfrey James (McGregor), Dennis Savage (Billy), Avis Bunnage (Mrs. Lemmy), Gerry Cowper (Mellon), David Cook (Hustings), Carmel McSharry (Mary), Kenneth Midwood (Groom), Jim Norton (Tom Mulley), Kate Binchy (Mrs. Mulley), Jeremy Hawk (Doctor).

1887. **Moonlight.** 90 min. Airdate: 9/14/82. Production Company: Universal Television. Directors: Alan Smithee (Jackie Cooper and Rod Holcomb). Executive Producer: David Chase. Producer: Alex Beaton. Writer: David Chase. Music: Patrick Williams. Robert Desiderio is a New York Chinese food deliv-eryman who is recruited as a spy and, while keeping his old job as a cover, is given seemingly innocuous missions that inevitably turn into something big. *Cast:* Robert Desiderio (as Lenny Barbello), Michelle Phillips (Meredith Tyne), William Prince (Mr. White), Anthony Ponzini (Victor Barbella), Carmine Mitore (Pop Barbella), Penny Santon (Josephine Barbella), Benson Fong (Clifford Wu), Sandra Kearns (Judi Becker), Christa Linder (Ulriche Pabst), Christopher Pennock (Bob Smith), Alexander Zale (Anatoli), Rosalind Chao (Daphne Wu), Martin Rudy (Dr. Rex Becker), Hank Brandt (Mr. Green), Evan Richards (Sean), Zitto Kazann (Yusef), Bill Erwin (Dr. Tucker), Pedro Montero (Pulgar), Murray MacLeod (Agent Barhydt), William H. Bassett (Tappan Zee), J.P. Bumstead (Interrogator), Kathryn Reynolds (Joan Barbella), Vince Howard (Chief).

1888. Parole. 2 hours. Airdate: 4/20/82. Production Companies: Parole Productions and RSO Films. Director: Michael Tuchner. Producer: Beryl Vertue. Writer: Edward Hume. Music: George Fenton. The adventures of a caring, Boston parole officer (James Naughton) punctuated by snatches of Bob Dylan's "I Shall Be Released" warbled by Sting. *Cast:* James Naughton (as Andy Driscoll), Lori Dardille (Suzanne Driscoll), Mark Soper (Jimmy McCusick), Barbara Meeks (Mrs. Sawyer), Ted Ross (Barney), Brent Jennings (Marco), Ellen Barkin (Donna), Jay Acavone (Leo), Ann Gillespie (Marie), Jerry Gershman (Augie), Patricia Wettig (Maureen), Stephen Mendillo (Mike), Robert Dean (Cory), John Bottoms (Willy), Brad Jones (Dexter), Peter Siragusa (Louis), John LaGioia (Mathew), Tom Kemp (Frank), Richard Jenkins (Cop), J.J. Wright (Desmond), Brett Smith (Daniel), Charles Werner Moore (McLeod), Bill Winn (Sergeant), Matt Siegel (David), Jon Peters (Doorman), Meg Boden (Marge), John Drabick (Tuttle), Joe Wilkins (Cop on Wharf).

NBC / COMEDY

1889. The Academy. 30 min. Airdate: 3/31/82. Production Company: TAT Communications. Director: Asaad Kelada. Executive Producer: Jack Elinson. Producer: Jerry Mayer. Writer: Jerry Mayer. The flipside of *The Facts of Life*, the sitcom which hosted the pilot as an episode. The adventures of several boys attending the Stone Military Academy (not far from *Facts of Life's* Eastland School for Girls) and their understanding headmaster (David Ackroyd). *Cast:* David Ackroyd (as Major Tim Dorsey), Jimmy Baio (Cadet Buzz Ryan), Peter Frechette (Cadet George Knight), John P. Navin, Jr. (Cadet Alfred Webster), David Hubbard (Cadet Chip Nelson), Lisa Whelchel (Blair Warner), Nancy McKeon (Jo Polniachek), Charlotte Rae (Edna Garrett), Kim Fields (Tootie Ramsey), Mindy Cohn (Natalie Greene).

1890. [Pilot #2] The Academy. 30 min. Airdate: 12/8/82. Production Company: TAT Communications. Director: Asaad Kelada. Executive Producer: Jack Elinson. Producer: Jerry Mayer. Writer: Jerry Mayer. Aired as an episode of *The Facts of Life*. A cadet (John P. Navin, Jr.) enters a boxing match to impress a girl (Mindy Cohn). *Cast:* David Ackroyd (as Major Tim Dorsey), Jimmy Baio (Cadet Buzz Ryan), Peter Frechette (Cadet George Knight), John P. Navin, Jr. (Cadet Alfred Webster), David Rayner (Cadet Chip Nelson), Ben Marley (Cadet

Hank Barton), Charlotte Rae (Edna Garrett), Mindy Cohn (Natalie Greene), Bill Galligan (Michael Mongo Moran), Eddie Deezen (Gursky), Crispin Glover (Cadet), Barbara Stock (Nurse Burton), Kenny Tessel (Chester).

1891. **Dad.** 30 min. Production Companies: Starry Night Productions and Warner Bros. Television. Director: Alan Bergman. Executive Producer: Reinhold Weege. Producer: Jeff Melman. Writer: Reinhold Weege. Creator: Reinhold Weege. The comedic adventures of four generations of men living in the same home. Widower Sid (Eugene Roche) and his son Ken (Martin Short) run the family's New York lady's garments business—and disagree on just about everything. They also live together, with Sid's eccentric father (Charles Lane) and Ken's quick-witted, 10-year-old son (Justin Dana). Rounding out the cast is Selma Diamond as their irascible cook and housekeeper. Weege, Melman and actress Diamond would later reteam for NBC's *Night Court.*

1892. **Fit for a King.** 30 min. Airdate: 6/11/82. Production Company: Metromedia Producers Corp. Director: Robert Moore. Executive Producer: Jay Wolpert. Producers: Eugene Ross-Leming and Brad Buckner. Writers: Eugene Ross-Leming and Brad Buckner. Creators: Eugene Ross-Leming and Brad Buckner. Music: John Addison. The adventures of a royal family in a small, European country. Dick Van Patten is King Alfred, who is bored much of the time; Katherine Helmond is the Queen, who loves being royalty; Adam Redfield is Prince Conrad, who tries hard to be proper and aristocratic, but doesn't quite cut it; Talia Balsam is the Princess, who finds the whole notion of royalty out-dated; and Todd Waring is 10-year-old Prince Maximillian, who just has fun. Leonard Frey costars as the cost-conscious Prime Minister. *Cast:* Dick Van Patten (as King Alfred), Katherine Helmond (Queen Mary), Adam Redfield (Prince Conrad), Talia Balsam (Princess Nicole), Todd Waring (Prince Maximillian), Leonard Frey (Prime Minister Dupree), Maxine Stuart (Grand Duchess Edwina), Gregory Brown (Victor), Audrey Landers (Sandra Bacon), Virginia Cook (Servant), James Elhardt (Reporter), Bruce Winet (Servant).

1893. **High Five.** 30 min. Airdate: 7/22/82. Production Companies: Orenthal Productions and Columbia Pictures Television. Director: Peter Bonerz. Executive Producer: O.J. Simpson. Producers: John Baskin and Roger Schulman. Writers: John Baskin and Roger Schulman. Life at a strapped, low-power, all-black television station in Watts that produces fare like "Dialing for Cash Money" and "Ghetto Gourmet." Ted Ross is the slick, fast-talking station owner and Harrison

Page is the reliable station manager and camera operator. The station boasts two newsanchors, a divorcee with two kids (Clarice Taylor), and an idealist (Wilson Porter) who dreams of landing a network job. *Cast:* Harrison Page (as Al Cook), Franklyn Seales (Wilson Porter), Cindy Haron (Stacey), Ted Ross (Clavin T. Washburn), Clarice Taylor (Velma Williams), Clinton Derricks Carroll (Jamol), Roscoe Lee Browne (Truman Murdock).

1894. **Highway Honeys (aka Towheads).** 60 min. Airdate: 1/13/83. Production Companies: NBC Productions and Rod Amateau Productions. Director: Rod Amateau. Executive Producer: Rod Amateau. Producers: Frank Beetson and Gary Hudson. Writers: Rod Amateau and Gary Hudson. Creators: Rod Amateau and Gary Hudson. Music: Ken Harrison. A "Dukes of Hazzard"-esque comedy about the competition being waged in a small, Texas town between the Good Shepherd Towing Company—run by Cannonball Shepherd (Don Collier) and his two kids (Mary Davis Duncan, Will Bledsoe)—and the dastardly Apocalypse Towing Service, run by corrupt Wolfe Crawley (Matt Clark) and his Four Horsemen (Kirstie Alley, Michael Crabtree, Miquel Rodriquez, and Keenan Wynn.) *Cast:* Mary Davis Duncan (as Carol Lee Shepherd), Will Bledsoe (Daytona Shepherd), Don Collier (Cannonball Shepherd), Glen Ash (Wilber T. Mossburgh), Kirstie Alley (Draggin' Lady), Matt Clark (Wolfe Crawley), Tina Gail Hernandez (Conchita Valdez), Miquel Rodriquez (Amigo), Keenan Wynn (Tattoo Calhoun), Michael Weston Crabtree (Pig Long), Jerry Biggs (Junker), Carla Palmer (Leora Permutter), Rod Amateau (Sweeper), Jessie Lee Fulton (Old Lady), Joe Berryman (Oil Man), Harlan Jordan (FBI Agent).

1895. **James Boys.** 30 min. Airdate: 6/25/82. Production Companies: American Flyer Films and Television, Ltd. and Warner Bros. Television. Director: Michael Zinberg. Executive Producer: Michael Zinberg. Producer: Susan Seeger. Writers: Michael Zinberg and Susan Seeger. Creators: Michael Zinberg and Susan Seeger. Music: Patrick Williams. Brian Kerwin is a widowed construction worker struggling to balance the demands of work with the demands of raising his precocious, seven-year-old son (Eric Coplan). He's helped by his divorced neighbor (Kelly Harmon), who operates a health food lunch wagon, and her daughter (Viveka Davis) and by a burly construction worker (Edward Edwards). *Cast:* Brian Kerwin (as Willie James), Eric Coplan (Sam James), Kelly Harmon (Kate Allgood), Viveka Davis (Emily Allgood), Edward Edwards (Jake), Arthur Rosenberg (Dan Felix), Patricia Cobert (Kathy), Liberty Godshall (Mindy).

1896. Jo's Cousins. 30 min. Airdate: 4/14/82. Production Company: TAT Communications. Director: Asaad Kelada. Executive Producer: Jack Elinson. Producer: Jerry Mayer. Writers: Linda Marsh and Margie Peters. Aired as an episode of *The Facts of Life*. The misadventures of widow Sal Largo (Donnelly Rhodes), who runs a New Jersey gas station, and his three kids. The Largos are the cousins of *Facts of Life* character Jo (Nancy McKeon), who stops by for a visit. *Cast:* Donnelly Rhodes (as Sal Largo), Megan Follows (Terry Largo), John Mengatti (Pauli Largo), D.W. Brown (Bud Largo), Grant Cramer (Tony Valente), Nancy McKeon (Jo), Lisa Whelchel (Blair Warner), Kim Fields (Tootie Ramsey), Charlotte Rae (Edna Garrett).

1897. Kangaroos in the Kitchen. 30 min. Airdate: 7/25/82. Production Company: David Gerber Company. Director: Jack Shea. Executive Producer: David Gerber. Producers: Austin Kalish, Irma Kalish, and Gene Marcione. Writers: Austin Kalish and Irma Kalish, from the book by Lorraine D'Essen. Music: Earle Hagen. The misadventures of the Provosts—he's a struggling attorney (Sam Freed) and she's (Lauralee Bruce) an animal trainer who loans her pets to television shows, circuses and the like. Of course, her pets roam freely through their apartment, to his constant consternation. Other characters include her assistant Lila (Peggy Pope), an aspiring actress, and Kenneth, an 11-year-old street urchin (Meeno Peluce). *Cast:* Lauralee Bruce (as Ginny Provost), Sam Freed (Richard Provost), Peggy Pope (Lila), Meeno Peluce (Kenneth), Nancy Andrews (Mrs. Burgess), Fred Stuthman (Judge), Martin Ferrero (Attorney).

1898. Little Darlings. 30 min. Production Companies: Miller-Milkis-Boyett Productions and Paramount Television. Director: Joel Zwick. Executive Producers: Tom Miller, Ed Milkis, and Bob Boyett. Producers: Stu Silver and Joel Zwick. Writer: Stu Silver. Based on the 1980 motion picture that starred Tatum O'Neal and Kristy McNiehol as two girls at a co-ed summer camp who bet on which of them will lose her virginity first. The sitcom, also set at a summer camp, would focus on teenagers Angel (Pamela Segall), a streetwise girl from the inner-city, and Ferris (Tammy Lauren), a rich girl from Beverly Hills, both of whom have a passion for hatching outlandish schemes. Other characters include flirtatious Lisa (Heather Me Adam) and TV nut Ruthie (LaShana Dendy), and the couple who run the camp (Michael McManus, Anne Schedeen).

1899. Love Birds. 30 min. Production Company: Warner Bros. Television. Director: Marc Daniels, Executive Producers: Bob Carroll, Jr. and Madelyn Davis.

Producers: Linda Morris and Vic Rauseo. Writers: Mark Egan, Mark Soloman, Linda Morris, Vic Rauseo, Bob Carroll, Jr., and Madelyn Davis. David Rounds is Gordon, a good-natured but clumsy fellow who means well, but always gets into trouble. When he loses his job, he and his kind-hearted wife (Stephanie Faracy) move to San Diego, where they inhabit a condominium next-door to her sister (Joyce Van Patten) and her grumpy husband (David Doyle). Gordon goes to work for his brother-in-law's toy factory and, although he earnestly tries to do his best, always causes trouble.

1900. **The Martin Mull Show.** 30 min. Production Companies: Universal Television and Steve Martin Productions. Executive Producer: Alan Rucker. Producer: Peter Torokvei. Writer: Peter Torokvei. Martin Mull would have starred as a car salesman who becomes press secretary to a neophyte Senate candidate who unexpectedly wins the election and is sent to Washington. Mull finds himself constantly covering for his naive boss' blunders. Costars would have included Ray Goulding and Bob Elliot. Universal and Steve Martin Productions later developed the short-lived CBS series *Domestic Life* for Mull.

1901. **Rainbow Girl (aka The Ann Jillian Show).** 30 min. Airdate: 6/4/82. Production Companies: Intermedia Entertainment and MGM. Director: Herbert Kenwith. Executive Producer: Fred Silverman. Producer: Ernest Chambers. Writers: Danny Jacobson and Barry Vigon. Music: Dennis McCarthy. Singer: Ann Jillian. Ann Jillian is a singer who performs on egotistical bandleader Cesar Romero's cheapo local television show. She and her sister (Candy Azzara) still live at home with their Lithuanian immigrant mother (Rae Allen) who, in the pilot, is trying to scratch together enough money to visit the old country. *Cast:* Ann Jillian (as Annie Jordan), Candy Azzara (Natalie Jordan), Cesar Romero (Miles Starling), Rae Allen (Irena Jordan), Robert Alan Browne (Sam), Rick Dean (George), Dallas Alinder (Bert Connolly), Michael Tucci (Armando), John McCook (Ted Black), Peter Brocco (Vitos), Charlie Webb (Short Guy).

1902. **Scamps (aka Three to Six).** 30 min. Airdate: 6/3/82. Production Companies: Redwood Productions and Universal Television. Director: Harry Harris. Executive Producer: Sherwood Schwartz. Producer: Lloyd J. Schwartz. Writers: Sherwood Schwartz and Lloyd J. Schwartz. Creators: Sherwood Schwartz and Lloyd J. Schwartz. Music: George Wyle. Singer: Robert Jason. Bob Denver is a struggling writer who pays his bills by running a daycare center for kids afterschool (hence the original title "Three to Six"). Cliff Pellow is the sarcastic landlord, Alma

Rosa Martinez is the social worker who keeps an eye on the center, and Dreama Denver is the mail carrier who delivers more rejection slips than acceptance letters. Dena Dietrich is the next-door neighbor who, in the pilot, gets splattered with paint when the kids try to paint the fence around Denver's house. *Cast:* Bob Denver (as Oliver Hopkins), Dena Dietrich (Miss Pitts), Joey Lawrence (Sparky), Jennifer George (Princess), Parker Jacobs (Jinx), Matt Connors (Tank), Marissa Medenhall (Daisy), Scooter Cohen (Scooter), Erin Nicole Brown (Crickett), Shannon Izuhara (Buttons), Damon Hines (Casey), Dreama Denver (Mandy), Cliff Pellow (Mr. Grimsley), Alma Martinez (Susan Alvarez).

NBC / DRAMA

1903. **Capture of Grizzly Adams.** 2 hours. Airdate: 2/21/82. Production Companies: Sunn Classic Pictures and Taft International Pictures. Director: Don Kessler. Executive Producer: Charles E. Sellier, Jr. Producer: James L. Conway. Writer: Arthur Heinemann, from the book by Charles E. Sellier, Jr. An attempt to revive the 1978 NBC series *Life and Times of Grizzly Adams*, which was based on the motion picture. Haggerty reprises his role as a man who flees into the mountains after being framed for a crime he didn't commit—and becomes a rugged mountaineer with a unique rapport with wild animals. In this sequel pilot, he risks his freedom to stop his niece from being sent to an orphanage. *Cast:* Dan Haggerty (as James "Grizzly" Adams), Kim Darby (Kate Brady), Noah Beery (Sheriff Hawkins), Keenan Wynn (Bert Woolman), June Lockhart (Liz Hawkins), Sydney Penny (Peg Adams), Chuck Connors (Frank Briggs), G.W. Bailey (Tom Quigley), Peg Stewart (Widow Thompkins), Spencer Austin (Daniel Quigley), Jesse Bennett (Doc), Shephard Sanders (Ranch Foreman).

1904. **Circle Family.** 60 min. Airdate: 7/29/82. Production Companies: Cy Chermack Productions and MGM. Director: Russ Mayberry. Executive Producer: Cy Chermak. Writer: Larry Mollin. Max Baer stars as Hearst Circle, a lovable eccentric who closes his traveling circus when his wife runs off with the strong man. So he gathers up his animals, the three orphans he took in during his travels (and now pretends are his real children so juvenile authorities won't take them) and moves into the family-owned Los Angeles hotel. Besides the tenants, there's also his father (Morgan Woodward), his brother (Granger Hines) and his real daughter (Sara Torgov), a struggling medical student. *Cast:* Max Baer (as Hearst Circle),

Sarah Torgov (Betsy Circle), Sydney Penny (Roxy Circle), Roberto Ramon (Dakota Circle), Granger Hines (Hemi Circle), Barrett Oliver (Q.P. Circle), Morgan Woodward (Grandpa Circle), Ben Piazza (Adrian Tweed), Jineanne Ford (Robbie), Guich Kooch (Carter Boyd), Betty Kennedy (Lili Boyd), William Mims (Gunner), Linda Kaye Henning (Registrar), Lisa Pascal (Teacher), Joan Shawlee (Meter Maid), Eric Walker (Morris), Jack Perkins (Grad).

1905. **The Doctors Brennan.** 60 min. Production Company: Paramount Television. Director: Richard Crenna. Executive Producer: David Victor. Writer: James Lee Barrett. Creator: James Lee Barrett. Andy Griffith is a general practitioner who shares his busy Los Angeles practice with his strong-willed daughter (Cassie Yates), a relationship marked by frequent clashes over how to handle various situations. Meanwhile, his other daughter (Leslie Ackerman) is in medical school, but isn't sure whether she'll join the practice or strike out on her own.

1906. **Farrell: For the People (aka Prosecutor at Law).** 2 hours. Airdate: 10/18/82. Production Companies: MGM and Intermedia Productions. Director: Paul Wendkos. Executive Producers: Fred Silverman and Tony Caccitotti. Producer: Lin Bolen. Writers: Larry Brody and Janice Hendler. Music: Bill Conti. Valerie Harper is an aggressive New York City prosecutor who, in the pilot, goes after an ex-con-turned-author accused of a stabbing (inspired by the real-life story of Norman Mailer protege Jack Abbott). *Cast:* Valerie Harper (as Elizabeth Farrell), Eugene Roche (Patrick J. Malloy), Steve Inwood (Alan Hellinger), Judith Chapman (Victoria Walton Mason), Gregory Sierra (Officer Mike Rodriquez), Ed O'Neill (Officer Jay Brennan), Calvin Jung (Otis), Bob Goldstein (Beansie), Millie Slavin (Mazene), Dennis Lipscomb (Jed Carter), Frank McCarthy (Vince Raliegh), Stacey Dash (Denise Gray), Richard Herd (Randolph Gardner), Cathy Worthington (Shirley Sanders), Alba Oms (Rosa Delgado), East Carlo (Judge Sanchez), Martin Spear (Dr. Cramer), Willie Nye (Fenwick), Chip Johnson (Barron), William Brian Curran (Correlli), Norma Donaldson (Mrs. Gray), Celia Perry (Ann Grady), Bill Capizzi (Christy), William Marquez (Oscar Rivera), M.K. Lewis (Bailiff), Bert Hinchman (Clerk), Fil Formicola (Cop), Sandy Martic (Newswoman).

1907. **The Firm.** 60 min. Airdate: 8/23/83. Production Company: Titus Productions. Director: Elliot Silverstein. Executive Producer: Herbert Brodkin. Producer: Robert Berger. Writer: Ernest Kinoy. Music: John Morris. From the team behind the acclaimed series *The Defenders* comes this potential series about an esteemed trial lawyer (Wilford Brimley) and his estranged daughter, a former congress-woman, who agrees to join his New York firm and rebuild their relationship as they tackle their highly charged, issue-oriented cases. *Cast:* Wilford Brimley (as Martin Barry), Anne Twomey (Grace Harmon), Carolyn Byrd (Francine), Paul Dooley (Dick Albright), Lori Putnam (Jane Albright), Kevin Conway (Peter Blau), Michael Higgins (Judge Whitewood), Mansoor Najee-Ullah (Coker), Tony Turco (Sgt. Albioni), Anna Maria Horsford (Sgt. Johnson), Beth Shorter (Doreen Washburn), Sylvia Short (Shirley Kravitz), Dan Ziskie (Court Officer).

1908. Force Seven. 60 min. Airdate: 5/23/82. Production Company: MGM. Director: Lee H. Katzin. Executive Producers: Cy Chermak and Eric Bercovici. Producer: Paul Rabwin. Writer: Stephen Downing. Music: Alan Silvestri. Aired as an episode of *CHiPS*. Fred Dryer stars as the leader of an elite LAPD squad that uses martial arts to fight crime. His team includes a sumo wrestler (Tony Longo), a female Akido expert (Donna Benz), and an overly enthusiastic but physically agile young officer (Tom Reilly). *Cast:* Fred Dryer (as Lt. John LeGarre), Donna Kei Benz (Cindy Miwa David), Tony Longo (Sly Angelitti), Tom Reilly (Rick Nichols), Steve Franken (Alan Drummond), Larry Wilcox (Jon), Erik Estrada (Ponch), Gene LaBell (Dogface), Sam Yorty (Mayor), Ted White (Ernie), Chuck Hicks (Frank), Alex Sharpe (Gino), Glenn Wilder (Abel), Tony Edder (Baker).

1983–1984

ABC / COMEDY

1909. Bliss. 30 min. Airdate: 6/28/84. Production Company: MTM Enterprises. Director: Gene Reynolds. Producers: Chip Keyes, Doug Keyes, and Beth Hillshafer. Writers: Chip Keyes and Doug Keyes. George Kennedy is Harry Bliss, a widower who retires and hands over the reins of his chocolate factory to his Harvard-educated daughter (Diane Stilwell), who applies the new techniques she learned at business school to the old-fashioned company—a change the employees and her father have a hard time accepting. Other regulars include the union leader (Chris Sarandon), her high school sweetheart who still carries a torch for her but with whom she's always at odds. *Variety* loathed this pilot, "peopled with nice, gentle and bland characters mixed down with material that has all the impact of a powder puff." *Cast:* George Kennedy (as Harry Bliss), Diane Stilwell (Kate Bliss), Chris Sarandon (Bo), Allan Miller (Fritz), Philip Sterling (Marvin Shefter), George D. Wallace (Lyle), Anne Haney (Eleanor), Dan Frischman (Walter), Barbara Babcock (Velma).

1910. Family Business. 30 min. Airdate: 5/5/83. Production Company: D.L. Taffner Productions. Director: Howard Storm. Executive Producers: Don Taffner and Arne Sultan. Producers: Norman Hopps and Earl Barrett. Writers: Phil Doran and Douglas Arango. Music: Johnny Mandel. Aired as an episode of *Too Close for Comfort*. Lainie Kazan is a widow who runs her husband's construction business with the help of her two dimwitted sons (George DeLoy and Jimmy Baio). *Cast:* Lainie Kazan (as Lucille Garibaldi), George DeLoy (Sal Garibaldi), Jimmy Baio (Freddy Garabaldi), Hillary Bailey (Donna Sullivan), Ted Knight (Henry Rush), Nancy Dussault (Muriel Rush), J.J. Bullock (Monroe), Deborah Van Valkenburgh (Jackie Rush), Lydia Cornell (Sarah Rush).

1911. Herndon (aka Herndon and Me). 30 min. Airdate: 8/26/83. Production Companies: Garry Marshall Productions and Paramount Television. Director: Garry Marshall. Executive Producers: Garry Marshall, Ronnie Hallin, and Lowell Ganz. Producer: Bob Brunner. Writers: Lowell Ganz and Babaloo Mandel. The high school nerd Herndon and the high school all-star Shack Shackleford have grown up. Ten years later, Herndon (Michael Richards) is a top computer scientist and still a nerd. Shack (Ted McGinley) still has lots of charisma, but no job—so Herndon hires him as his assistant. But it isn't long before Shack takes over Herndon's life, and people assume Shack is the one running things. *Cast:* Michael Richards (Herndon Stool), Ted McGinley (Shack Shackleford), Randi Brooks (Hilary Swanson), Anne Ramsey (Miss Helter), Robin Riker (Connie Kokoorium), Marla Pennington (Laura), F. William Parker (Mr. Coombe), Tony Longo (Stanley Gabotowski), Owen Bush (Coach), Sharon Thomas (Paula), E.E. Bell (Ralph), Kyle Heffner (Satyajit), Walter Robles (Stuntman).

1912. Side by Side. 30 min. Airdate: 7/6/84. Production Company: 20th Century Fox Television. Director: Jay Sandrich. Executive Producer: Marc Merson. Producers: Bob Schiller and Bob Weiskopf. Writers: Bob Schiller and Bob Weiskopf. Music: Peter Matz. Singers: Charles Durning and Ron Leibman. Charles Durning and Ron Leibman are two guys—one a conservative who plays it safe, the other irreverent and irresponsible—who work together at a restaurant supply plant and live in the same duplex. Durning occupies the bottom unit with his wife (Katherine Helmond) and Leibman lives upstairs—his wife went to visit her mother and never came back. *Cast:* Charles Durning (as Harry Deegan), Ron Leibman (Joey Caruso), Katherine Helmond (Mildred Deegan), Caren Kaye (Deborah Kazinsky), Joseph Mascolo (Peter Wagner), Justin Lord (Moose), Dick Balduzzi (Hernandez), Charles Lane (George McCloskey).

1913. Weekends (aka I Do, I Don't). 30 min. Airdate: 9/2/83. Production Company: Carsey/Werner Productions. Director: Will MacKenzie. Executive Producers: Marcy Carsey and Tom Werner. Producer: Chris Thompson. Writer: Chris Thompson. Everything about Shelley (Linda Purl) and Ivan's (Charles Rocket) divorce was amicable except one thing—they couldn't agree on who would keep their weekend getaway retreat in the mountains, so it remains common property. That arrangement is a problem now that Shelley has married a widower (Bo Sven- son), and become stepmother to his rebellious son Zak (Scott Schutzman). The teen is just as irresponsible as Ivan, who regularly shows up at the retreat when they do, and the two become fast friends—and a constant source of trouble for the newlyweds. *Cast:* Linda Purl (as Shelley Hewitt), Bo Svenson (Earl Hewitt), Martha Byrne (Lisa Hewitt), Scott Schutzman (Zack Hewitt), Charles Rocket (Ivan), Robin Eisen- mann (Taffee McDermott), Sandy Ward (Sheriff McDermott).

ABC / DRAMA

1914. Concrete Beat. 90 min. Airdate: 7/9/84. Production Companies: Pic- ture-maker Productions and Viacom Enterprises. Director: Robert Butler. Executive Producer: Glenn Gordon Caron. Producers: Jay Daniel and Robert Butler. Writer: Glenn Gordon Caron. Creator: Glenn Gordon Caron. Music: Artie Kane. John Getz is a crusading, Jimmy Breslin/Mike Royko-esque New York newspaper columnist who chronicles the lives of average people—and gets intimately involved in their problems. He's still in love with his ex-wife (Darlanne Fluegel), who is his boss' (Kenneth McMillan) daughter. In the pilot, he helps a mother who is blamed for her child's death in a Harlem apartment house fire. *Cast:* John Getz (as Mickey Thompson), Darlanne Fluegel (Stephanie Thompson), Kenneth McMillan (Marion Kaiser), Rhoda Gemignani (Sylvie), Vanessa L. Clarke (Corrie James), Dean Santoro (Davis), Marla Adams (Cathy Lord), Ingrid Anderson (Michelle), Thom Bray (Ralph Gurling), Gerry Gibson (Philip Swanson), Bert Rosario (Jose), Ray Girardin (Phil), Alexandra Johnson (Girl), Terrence McNally (Single Man of the Month), Patricia McPherson (Woman in First Bar), Mary Caron (Woman in Second Bar), Joe Ponazecki (Priest), Henry G. Sanders (Lt. Lucas), Le Tari (Big Black Man), Dave Berman (First Cabbie), David E. Boyle (Maitre d'), Clarence Felder (Police Captain), Fil Formicola (Man in Bus), Jay Fletcher (Factory Foreman), Baxter Harris (Undercover Cop), Alan Koss (Guard), Bob Maroff (Desk Sergeant), Judith Searle (Swanson's Secretary), Marion Yue (Receptionist).

1915. Feel the Heat. 60 min. Airdate: 8/5/83. Production Company: Paramount Television. Director: Ray Danton. Producers: Ronald Cohen and Ed Milkis. Writer: Ronald Cohen. Creator: Ronald Cohen. Nick Mancuso is an unorthodox Key West private eye in love with an idealistic DA (Lisa Eichhorn) he's often professionally pitted against. Producer Barney Rosensweig is credited as a creative consultant on the project. *Cast:* Nick Mancuso (as Andy Thorn), Lisa Eichhorn (Honor Campbell), Robert Hooks (Capt. Barney Hill), Philip Clark (Det. Frank Dawson), Paula Kelly (Sally Long), Mario Marcelino (Angel Moreno), Hector Elizondo (Monkey Moreno), Pepe Serna (Emille Sanchez), Julian Byrd (Skeeter), Bruce McLaughlin (Coogan), Dennis Madlone (Pepe Moreno), Charles Harris (Bobby Dan), Glenn Scherer (Billy Music), Lenny Juliano (Eddie Music), Alberto Martin (Jose Gomez).

1916. The Last Ninja (aka Master of Darkness). 2 hours. Airdate: 7/7/83. Production Company: Paramount Television. Director: William A. Graham. Producer: Anthony Spinner. Writer: Ed Spielman. Music: Robert Cobert. Michael Beck is Ken Sakura, an orphan raised by Japanese-Americans and schooled in the ancient rituals art of "Ninjutsu." Now he's an international art dealer who, unbeknownst to anyone but his sister Nancy Kwan, doubles as a Ninja-master and secret agent. *Cast:* Michael Beck (as Ken Sakura), Nancy Kwan (Noriko), John McMartin (Cosmo), Mako (Mataro Sakura), Richard Lynch (Professor Gustave Norden), John Larroquette (Army Officer), Irene Tedrow (Dr. Stanford), Carmen Argenziano (Rooney), Kevin Brando (Young Ken), Robin Gammell (Dr. McAllister), Shizuko Hoshi (Miyako), Rob Kim (Sasaki), Christopher Mahar (Amin), Rob Narita (Akira), Ivan Saric (Aziz), Henry Slate (Cleaning Man), Curtis Credel (Hauptman), Carolyn Seymour (Lydia), Frank Arno (Operative), Clabe Hartley (Seidler), John Hugh (Bob), Tony Lee (Hiromi), Leigh Walsh (Green Eyes).

1917. Shooting Stars (aka Hawke and O'Keefe). 2 hours. Airdate: 7/28/83. Production Company: Aaron Spelling Productions. Director: Richard Lang. Executive Producers: Aaron Spelling, Douglas S. Cramer, and E. Duke Vincent. Producers: Richard Lang and Michael Fisher. Writer: Michael Fisher, from a story by Michael Fisher and Vernon Zimmerman. Music: Dominic Frontiere. Billy Dee Williams and Parker Stevenson are two costars in a popular detective series who, when they are fired by the jealous star (Efrem Zimbalist, Jr.), become real-life private detectives. They work out of a beachside cafe/bar and utilize the skills of their various entertainment industry cronies (stunt men, make-up men, writers) to help them solve crimes. *Cast:* Billy Dee Williams (as Douglas Hawke), Parker Stevenson (Bill O'Keefe), John P. Ryan (Detective McGee), Edie Adams (Hazel), Fred Travelena (Teddy), Dick Bakalyan (Snuffy), Victoria Spelling (Danny), Frank McRae (Tubbs), Robert Webber (J. Woodrow Norton), Kathleen Lloud (Laura O'Keefe), Denny Miller (Tanner), John Randolph (Stevenson), Efrem Zimbalist, Jr. (Jonathan Lieghton), Herb Edelman (Rex), Don Calfa (Driscoll), Kathryn Daley (Janie), D.D. Howard (Glenda), Lurene Tuttle (Mrs. Brand), Eric Server (Director), David Faustino (Patrick O'Keefe), Paul Tuerpe (Patrolman), Larry McCormick (Newscaster), Cis Rundle (Girl), Elisabeth Foxx (Tracy), Tim Haldeman (Propman), Stephen Miller (Newsman).

1918. Spraggue. 90 min. Airdate: 6/29/84. Production Companies: MF Productions and Lorimar Productions. Director: Larry Elikann. Executive Producer: Michael Filerman. Producer: Joe Wallenstein. Writer: Henry Olek. Creator: Linda Barnes. Music: Lalo Schifrin. Michael Nouri is a Boston biology professor who spurns his family's wealth in favor of living simply in the carriage house of his eccentric Aunt's (Glynis John) mansion and riding his ten-speed to work. He also, as a hobby, solves baffling crimes—despite his Aunt's meddling. In the pilot, he's pitted against Patrick O'Neal, who is inducing heart attacks in his victims. *Cast:* Michael Nouri (as Michael Spraggue), Glynis Johns (Mary Spraggue), James Cromwell (Lt. George Hurley), Mark Herrier (Randy Hern), Andrea Marcovicci (Samara Weller), Patrick O'Neal (Dr. Miles Richards), Hank Garrett (Knuckles), Callann White (Hildegarde), John Savola (Wink), Melissa Ann Green (Melody), Bill Corsair (Attorney), Fritzi Jane Courtney (Judge), Bruce Donaldson (Bike Race Doctor), Alice Fredey (Tiny Lady).

1919. Wishman. 60 min. Airdate: 6/23/83. Director: Viacom Enterprises. Director: James Frawley. Executive Producers: Terry Morse, Jr., Rick Rosenberg, and Robert Christiansen. Producer: Chris Seitz. Writer: John Stern. Music: Fred Karlin. This flop features a creature modeled after *ET* and a timeworn concept that simply refuses to die–the [FILL IN THE BLANK] and his/her friend [FILL IN THE BLANK] pursued by an obsessed [FILL IN THE BLANK] intent on a) dissecting him/her/it or, b) prosecuting him/her/it for a crime he/she/it didn't commit or, c) [FILL IN THE BLANK]. This time, a bioengineer creates a lovable creature in his lab and is forced to flee, along with his fashion-photographer wife (Linda Hamilton), when the evil corporation wants to exploit the cute beastie for profit. James Keach is their obsessed pursuer. *Cast:* Joseph Bottoms (as Dr. Alex MacGregor), Linda Hamilton (Mattie MacGregor), James Keach (Galen Reed), Margarita Fernandez (Wishman), John Reilly (Sam), Jean Bruce Scott (Karen Kaleb), Sam Weisman (Nat Kaleb), Robin Gammell (Dr. Harold Wish), Jason Presson (Bruce Kaleb), Seaman Glass (Gate Guard), Burt Edwards (Ed).

CBS / COMEDY

1920. Author! Author! (aka Full House). 60 min. Airdate: 9/20/83. Production Companies: Brownstone Productions and 20th Century Fox. Director: Tony

Bill. Executive Producer: Marc Merson. Producer: Paul Waigner. Writer: Israel Horovitz. Creator: Israel Horovitz. Music: Fred Karlin. Based on the 1982 motion picture *Author! Author!* Dennis Dugan assumes A1 Pacino's role as a harried New York playwright who has acquired five children—one of which is his, the four others are from his runaway wife's first three failed marriages. The disorganized, financially troubled father often has to rely on his children to keep the chaotic household—and his life—together. *Cast:* Dennis Dugan (as Ivan Travalian), Ari Meyers (Debbie Travalian), Shelby Balik (Bonnie Travalian), Eric Gurry (Igor Travalian), Scott Nemes (Spike Travalian), Danny Ponce (Geraldo Travalian), Kenneth Mars (Arthur Krantz), Miriam Flynn (Bobbie Hall), Roberta Picardo (Mary), James Murtaugh (Eugene), Julie Payne (Mrs. Knopf), Ray Girardin (Ken Adams), Sam J. Cooper (Tony).

1921. Back Together. 30 min. Airdate: 1/25/84. Production Companies: Chagrin Productions and Lorimar Productions. Director: Peter Bonerz. Executive Producer: Charlie Hauck. Writer: Charlie Hauck. Music: David Franko and Willie Wilkerson. Herkie Burke is dead, but an administrative foul-up in heaven prevents him from passing through the Pearly Gates, so he chooses to wait things out with his old college friends, the Harringtons, who aren't wild about having a ghost in the house—especially one who doesn't care how he behaves since there's nothing to lose, he's dead anyway. *Cast:* Paul Provenza (as Herkie Burke), Jamie Widdoes Grace Harrison (Anne Harrington), Lisa Jane Persky (Dora Holloway), Richard Hamilton (Mr. Christopher), Mina Kolb (Mrs. Burke).

1922. Best of Times (aka Changing Times). 30 min. Airdate: 8/29/83. Production Companies: Thunder Road Productions and Lorimar Productions. Director: Bill Bixby. Executive Producer: Stuart Sheslow. Producers: Rick Kellard and Bob Comfort. Writers: Rick Kellard and Bob Comfort. Music: Craig Safan. The misadventures of three boys in a mid-western high school—Pete, the mischievous ringleader (Robert Romanus); Dewey, known as "The Phantom" for his ability to cut classes (Chris Nash), and Neil, the brainy nerd (Leif Green). Their arch foe is the school's security chief (William Schilling). *Cast:* Robert Romanus (Pete Falcone), Krista Errickson (Robin Dupree), Hallie Todd (Patti Eubanks), Chris Nash (Dewey Hooper), Leif Green (Neil Hefernan), Alex Rocco (Gene Falcone), Arlene Golonka (Peggy Falcone), Rosanna Locke (Theresa Falcone), William Schilling (Franklin T. Otto), Kene Holliday (Don Kingman), Denise Galik (Kim Sedgewick), Whitman Mayo (Howlin' Joe), Tony Longo (Garth

Stimolvich), Robert Scott Garrison (Cliff), Felix Nelson (Wheeler), Ron Thomas (Student).

1923. **Branagan and Mapes.** 30 min. Airdate: 8/1/83. Production Companies: Chagrin Productions and Lorimar Productions. Director: Noam Pitlik. Executive Producer: Charlie Hauck. Producer: Faye Oshima. Writer: Charlie Hauck. Creator: Charlie Hauck. Music: Artie Butler. Dan Branagan (Don Murray) is an advertising executive whose wife dies shortly after they are married, leaving this life-long bachelor to raise her three children, who are practically strangers to him. He's helped with his new-found fatherhood by the eldest child, resourceful Gussie Mapes (Dana Hill), and together they try to make the family work. Add to the mix the children's nosey, straight-laced Aunt (Judith Kahan), who disapproves of Branagan, and you have the conflicts that would have driven this sitcom concept. *Cast:* Don Murray (as Dan Branagan), Dana Hill (Gussie Mapes), Brett Johnson (Logan Mapes), Rebecca Sweet (Theresa Mapes), Bruce Kirby (Barney Sutter), Judith Kahan (Cathy), Cyndi James-Reese (Susan), Christine Dickerson (Renee), Earl Bullock (Mr. Barnes), Candi Brough (Blonde), Randi Brough (Brunette).

1924. **Diner.** 30 min. Airdate: 8/8/83. Production Companies: Weintraub/Levinson Productions and MGM/UA Television. Director: Barry Levinson. Executive Producers: Jerry Weintraub and Barry Levinson. Producer: Mark Johnson. Writer: Barry Levinson. Creator: Barry Levinson. Music: Harry Lojewski. Based on writer/director Barry Levinson's 1982 hit movie, set in 1960 Baltimore, that focused on five young men who are making the awkward transition into adulthood and who gather nightly at a local diner to hash out their problems and grapple with their new responsibilities. The characters include a hairdresser with big dreams, an appliance salesman in his first year of marriage, a sports-addicted newlywed, and a college drop-out flirting with alcoholism. Paul Reiser reprises his role as Modell, an insecure man with a motormouth. *Cast:* Paul Reiser (as Modell), James Spader (Fenwick), Michael Binder (Eddie), Max Cantor (Shrevie), Michael Madsen (Boogie), Alison LaPlaca (Elyse), Mandy Kaplan (Beth), Robert Pastorelli (Turko), Arnie Mazer (The Gipper), Ted Bafaloukos (George).

1925. **A Fine Romance.** 30 min. Airdate: 7/20/83. Production Company: D.L. Taffner Productions. Director: Alan Rafkin. Executive Producers: Don Taffner and John Fitzgerald. Producers: George Barino and Robert Stolfi. Writer: Bob Larbey. Music: Joe Raposa. Singers: Julie Kavner and Leo Burmester. Based on the

British sitcom of the same name and shot in New York. This series would chart the awkward romance of Laura (Julie Kavner) and Mike (Leo Burmester), two insecure people desperately afraid of losing their independence and yet in love with one another. *Cast:* Julie Kavner (as Laura Prescott), Leo Burmester (Mike Selway), Kristin Meadows (Helen), Kevin Conroy (Phil), Jeffrey Jones (Harry), Amy Wright (Jean), Bobbi Jo Lathan (Party Guest).

1926. For Members Only. 30 min. Airdate: 7/11/83. Production Companies: Saul Ilson Productions and Columbia Pictures Television. Director: Kim Friedman. Executive Producer: Saul Ilson. Producers: John Baskin and Roger Schulman. Writers: John Baskin and Roger Schulman. On the heels of the hit movie *Caddy- shack* comes this pilot about caddies (Joey Davis, Kevin Hooks, and Stephen Furst) working at a snobbish East Coast country club and constantly scheming against their stuffy employers (Robert Mandan and Earl Boen). *Cast:* Robert Mandan (as Austin Ruggles), Joey Davis (Richie), Kevin Hooks (Eddie), Stephen Furst (Gilbert), Kristine DeBell (Ginger), Gretchen Wyler (Alicia McKnight), Earl Boen (Sherman Ralston), Jamie Gertz (Monica Mitchell), Peggy Pope (Mrs. Ralston).

1927. Great Day. 30 min. Airdate: 11/19/83. Production Companies: Intermedia Entertainment and MGM/UA Television. Director: Michael Preece. Executive Producer: Fred Silverman. Producers: Mark Fink, Stephen Miller, and Edward H. Feldman. Writers: Mark Fink and Stephen Miller. Tim Conway heads a family plagued by small problems that always turn into major catastrophes—and that are usually his fault. These slapstick escapades are narrated by Mason Adams, an omniscient observer. *Cast:* Tim Conway (as Howard Simpson), Joanna Gleason (Jennifer Simpson), Jill Schoelen (Carla Simpson), Corky Pigeon (Ricky Simpson), Gordon Jump (Ralph Maxwell), Philip Bruns (Police Sergeant), Kenneth Tigar (Burglar), Danny Wells (Dog Trainer), Bill Paxton (Rudy), Suzanne Kent (Woman).

1928. Poor Richard (aka The George Hamilton Show). 30 min. Airdate: 1/21/84. Production Company: MGM/UA Television. Director: Rod Daniel. Executive Producer: Jerry Weintraub. Producers: Tim Berry and Hal Dresner. Writer: Hal Dresner. Music: Craig Safan. George Hamilton is a millionaire who squanders his fortune and is forced to fire his servants and sell his mansion. He's standing alone in his mansion when the new owners—a "Beverly Hillbillies"–type family that made a fortune on a new pig feed—arrive and mistake him for the butler.

He plays along, hiding his true identity from his employers and his new iden-
tity from his friends—who think he's still the wealthy master of the house. *Cast:*
George Hamilton (as Rich Manning), Geoffrey Lewis (Rudy Hopper), Alley
Mills (Terry), Cynthia Sikes (Vicki), Nancy Stafford (Randi), John Hunsaker
(Jimmy), Glynn Turman (Jonathan).

1929. Still the Beaver. 2 hours. Airdate: 3/19/83. Production Companies: Bud Austin
Productions and Universal Television. Director: Steven Hiliard Stern. Executive
Producer: Bud Austin. Producer: Nick Abdo. Writer: Brian Levant, from a story
by Brian Levant and Nick Abdo. Creators: Joe Connelly and Bob Mosher. Music:
John Cacavas. Theme: Melvin Lenard, Mort Green, and Dave Kahm. A nostalgic,
bittersweet pilot that reunites the cast of the beloved comedy *Leave It to Beaver.*
Beaver Cleaver, now a divorced father of two kids, returns to Mayfield to raise his
kids with the help of his widowed mother. His brother Wally is now a married
lawyer with a daughter of his own, and his friend Eddie Haskell is married, too,
and has a son that's the mirror image of himself as a kid. Although CBS passed on
it, *Still the Beaver* went on to become (with some cast changes) a successful series
on the Disney Channel cable network. It then jumped to Superstation WTBS,
where it was redubbed *The New Leave It to Beaver* and continued for several seasons before going into syndication. *Cast:* Barbara Billingsley (as June Cleaver),
Tony Dow (Wally Cleaver), Jerry Mathers (Beaver Cleaver), Ken Osmond
(Eddie Haskell), Frank Bank (Clarence "Lumpy" Rutherford), Ed Begley, Jr.
(Whitey Whitney), Corey Feldman (Corey Cleaver), John Snee (Oliver Cleaver),
Richard Correll (Richard Rickover), Rusty Stevens (Larry Mondello), Janice
Kent (Mary Ellen Cleaver), Joanna Gleason (Kimberly Cleaver), Diane Brewster
(Miss Canfield), Luke Fafara (Tooey Brown), Damon Hines (Marcus Garvey),
Eric Osmond (Eddie Haskell, Jr.).

1930. Sutter's Bay. 30 min. Airdate: 8/15/83. Production Companies: Mort
Lachman and Associates and Alan Landsburg Productions. Director: Bill
Persky. Executive Producer: Alan Landsburg. Producers: Mort Lachman
and Sy Rosen. Writers: Mort Lachman and Sy Rosen. Music: Artie Butler.
The comedic adventures of the people who inhabit Sutter's Bay, a small New
England community, as seen through the eyes of Jeff and Barbara Hamner
(Granville Van Dusen and Linda Carlson), who just moved there from
Manhattan to run the local paper and live the simple life. *Cast:* Granville Van
Dusen (as Jeff Hamner), Linda Carlson (Barbara Hamner), Sally Kellerman

(Monnie), Dennis Burkley (Sheriff Ward), Alice Ghostley (Elfreda), Frank Cady (Doc Medford), William Lanteau (Mervyn), Bryan O'Byrne (Leroy), Meg Wyllie (Margaret Pierson), Richard B. Shull (Blake Simmons), Georgann Johnson (Ellen Simmons), Jay Johnson (Edwin Simmons), Dana Kimmell (April Hamner), Brandis Kemp (Emma Frye), Kathleen Freeman (Mildred Janovich), Frank Bonner (Howard).

1931. **Thicker than Water.** 30 min. Production Company: Embassy Television. Executive Producer: Jack Elinson. Writers: Julio Vera and Luis Santeiro. A proposed spin-off from *The Jeffersons* about a Cuban family running a Miami bakery and catering service who take in a Cuban refugee.

1932. **13 13th Avenue.** 30 min. Airdate: 8/15/83. Production Company: Paramount Television. Director: John Bowab. Executive Producer: Chris Thompson. Producers: Lenny Ripps and Don Van Atta. Writer: Lenny Ripps. The misadventures of a widower (A.C. Weary) and his son (Wil Wheaton), who move into a Greenwich Village apartment building inhabited by a model who's a witch (Ilene Graff), a C.P.A. who's a werewolf (Robert Harper), a lawyer who's a vampire (Paul Kreppel), a superintendent who's a troll (Ernie Sabella), and their psychiatrist (Clive Revill). Elisabeth Savage and Stanley Brock guest star.

CBS / DRAMA

1933. **Crossfire.** 20 min. Production Companies: 20th Century Fox Television and Glen Larson Productions. Director: Dan Haller. Executive Producer: Glen Larson. Writer: Gary Michael White. Wayne Massey and Irena Ferris are a brother and sister motorcross racing team who are actually special agents for the Justice Department. They chose this secret vocation after their father, an attorney general, and their entire family were killed in a mysterious explosion, and the two are now always looking for that one clue that will lead to the killers. A short demo film was shot for presentation to network executives.

1934. **Johnny Blue.** 60 min. Airdate: 9/4/83. Production Company: Warner Bros. Television. Directors: Richard Irving and Bernard L. Kowalski. Executive Producer: Robert Carrington. Producer: Richard Irving. Writer: Robert Carrington. Music: Dick De Benedictis. A reworking of last season's flop *Gib.* Gil Gerard is now Johnny Blue, a former mercenary turned proprietor of a New Orleans restaurant who helps people in trouble and solves crimes for his police buddy (Eugene Roche). Writer Jack Sowards was brought on during production to begin writing follow-up scripts. He says: "the pilot had a very good script that was treated very badly. The first executive producer was fired, the second producer (also the director) got as far as New Orleans, and half way through a terrible shoot, before being fired by Gil Gerard. Gil's production company, in association with Warner Brothers, was making it. The pilot was a one-hour episode, which shot for almost four weeks in New Orleans and another two weeks in Los Angeles. We developed six more scripts, but they were sent to Gil in New Orleans, and he kept rewriting them. The inmates had taken over the asylum and I slipped away when my option expired. Nobody called. I breathed a sign of relief. *Cast:* Gil Gerard (as Johnny Blue), Eugene Roche (Deputy Chief Mitchell), George Kee Cheung (Saffron), Delta Burke (Joanne Kruger), Rebecca Holden (Kathy Weatherby), Patricia Klous (Jenny).

1935. Monument County. 60 min. Production Company: Orion Television. Executive Producer: Daron J. Thomas. Writer: David J. Chisholm. The adventures of a big city cop who becomes sheriff of a southwestern county.

1936. Night Partners. 2 hours. Airdate: 10/11/83. Production Company: Moonlight Productions. Director: Noel Nosseck. Executive Producer: Frank Von Zerneck. Producer: Robert M. Sertner. Writers: Judy Merl and Paul Eric Meyers. Music: Fred Karlin. Yvette Mimieux and Diana Canova are two housewives who mount a police-assisted neighborhood patrol, prowling the streets of Bakersfield in a used police car. *Cast:* Yvette Mimieux (as Elizabeth McGuire), Diana Canova (Lauren Hensley), Arlen Dean Snyder (Glen McGuire), M. Emmet Walsh (Joe Kirby), Patricia McCormack (Sophie Metzman), Patricia Davis (Janice Tyler), Michael Cavanaugh (Roy Henderson), Peter Brocco (Zachary Katsulas), Larry Linville (Chief John Wilson), Dick Anthony Williams (Instructor), Nellie Bellflower (Battered Wife), Dee Dee Bridgewater (Gloria), Ed Lottimer (Buzz Cochran), Cynthia Avila (Rita Torres), Patrick Brennan (Sam McGuire), Barbara Barron (Elvira Newton), M.C. Gainey (Rapist), Ron Prince (S.W.A.T. Commander), Mary Gregory (Ms. Larson), John Howard Swain (Andy Hensley), Tricia Cast (Francine McGuire), Michael Evans (Josh Hensley), Kurt Smildsin (Dan), Robert Balderson (Jack), William Vincent Kulak (Officer), Kathleen Coyne (Student), Ed Hooks (Man), Nancy Pearlsberg (Elderly Woman), Grant Owens (Watch Commander), Robert Moberly (Mr. Newton).

1937. **Return of Man from UNCLE: The Fifteen Years Later Affair.**
2 hours. Airdate: 4/5/83. Production Companies: Viacom Enterprises and
Michael Sloan Productions. Director: Ray Austin. Executive Producer: Michael
Sloan. Producer: Nigel Watts. Writer: Michael Sloan. Creators: Norman Felton
and Sam H. Rolfe. Music: Gerald Fried. Theme: Jerry Goldsmith. Superspies
Napoleon Solo, now a computer company chief with a taste for gambling, and Ilya
Kuryakin, now a fashion designer, are called out of retirement by the new boss
of UNCLE (Patrick MacNee) to battle an old THRUSH foe (Anthony Zerbe)
who has escaped from prison. The veteran, albeit rusty, agents are teamed with
a Benjamin Kowalski (Tom Mason), a brash, new UNCLE operative. George
Lazenby, one-time 007, made a cameo appearance as a thinly veiled James Bond.
Michael Sloan would later oversee the unsold pilot revivals of *The Six Million Dollar
Man*, *The Bionic Woman* and *McCloud*. He'd later produce the TV series revival
Kung Fu: The Legend Continues. *Cast:* Robert Vaughn (as Napolean Solo), David
McCallum (Ilya Kuryakin), Patrick MacNee (Sir John Raleigh), Tom Mason
(Benjamin Kowalski), Gayle Hunnicutt (Andrea Markovich), Geoffrey Lewis
(Janus), Anthony Zerbe (Justin Sepheran), Simon Williams (Nigel Pennington
Smythe), John Harkins (Alexi Kemp), Jan Triska (Vaselievitch), Susann Woolen
(Janice Friday), Carolyn Seymour (Actress), George Lazenby (J.B.), Judith
Chapman (Z), Lois De Banzie (Ms. Delquist), Dick Durock (Guido), Randi
Brooks (Model), Jack Somack (Tailor), Eddie Barker (Card Dealer).

1938. **Savage in the Orient.** 60 min. Airdate: 6/21/83. Production Company: Terry
Becker Productions. Director: Sidney Hayers. Executive Producer: Terry Becker.
Producer: Lee Siegel. Writer: Wendell Mayes. Music: Morton Stevens. Joe
Penny is Savage, a rich private eye who owns an antique shop in Manila that runs
with his operative, ex-con "Major" (Leif Erickson), and keeps close tabs on the
orphanage where he was raised, which is managed by Sister Mary Francis (Lotis
Key). Other regulars include Tap Lee (Irene Yah Ling Sun), onetime Queen of
the Manila underworld; Leslie DeLand (Heather McNair), a computer expert
who can plug him into any police databank; and Capt. Saprido (Butz Aquino),
a policeman wary of Savage's activities. *Cast:* Joe Penny (as Peter Savage), Leif
Erickson (Major), John Saxon (Nick Costa), Lew Ayres (Allan Clydesdale),
Irene Yah Ling Sun (Tap Lee), Heather McNair (Leslie DeLand), Butz Aquino
(Captain Saprido), Gayle Hunnicutt (Julian Clydesdale), Anthony Castello
(Clarence Ford).

1939. Uncommon Valor. 2 hours. Airdate: 1/22/83. Production Companies: Brademan-Self Productions and Sunn Classic Pictures. Director: Rod Amateau. Executive Producers: Bill Brademan and Ed Self. Producer: Mark Rodgers. Writer: Mark Rodgers. Mitchell Ryan is a fire chief who, in the pilot, saves the patients at a Salt Lake City hospital that was set aflame by a psycho. *Cast:* Mitchell Ryan (Chief Tom Riordan), Ben Murphy (Jim Merritt), Rick Lohman (Joe Donovan), Barbara Parkins (Dr. Margaret Houghton), Norman Fell (Garvin), Gregory Sierra (George Callender), John Reilly (Hamner), Salome Jens (Nurse Ann Bott), Julie Cobb (Karen Merritt), Chris Lemmon (Reggie), Harold Sylvester (Sergeant), Michael Talbott (Pasco), Belinda J. Montgomery (Joan Donovan), Spencer Alston (Jimmy), Jay Bernard (Corvallis), Nancy Borgenicht (Nurse), Brendan Burns (Pete Grant), Michael Flynn (Dr. Johnson), Nicholas Guest (Johnny Robertson), John Hansen (Dr. Lister).

NBC / COMEDY

1940. Another Jerk (aka The Jerk, Too). 2 hours. Airdate: 1/6/84. Production Companies: 40 Share Productions and Universal Television. Director: Michael Schultz. Executive Producer: Steve Martin. Producers: Ziggy Steinberg and Al Burton. Writers: Ziggy Steinberg and Rocco Urbisci. Creators: Steve Martin and Carl Gottlieb. Theme: John Sebastian. A sequel/adaptation of the Steve Martin movie *The Jerk.* Mark Blankfield is Navin Johnson, a naive, good-natured, clumsy goon, a white orphan raised by a family of black sharecroppers. He leaves his family to go on a cross-country trek to prevent his true-love (Stacey Nelkin) from marrying an unscrupulous, European aristocrat (Barrie Ingham). Along the way, Navin befriends Diesel, a hobo (Ray Walston), who wants to exploit Navin's skill at cards. In the proposed series, Navin would settle with Diesel in Los Angeles, screw up at various odd jobs, and court his true-love, to the consternation of her snobbish parents. *Cast:* Mark Blankfield (as Navin Johnson), Ray Walston (Diesel), Stacey Nelkin (Marie Van Buren), Barrie Ingham (Carl), Jean LeClerc (Count Marco del Belvedere), Thalmus Rasulala (Crossroads), Mabel King (Mama Johnson), A1 Fann (Papa Johnson), Robert Sampson (Gilbert Van Buren), Patricia Barry (Helen Van Buren), Todd Hollowell (Damon Johnson), Larry B. Scott (Harold Johnson), Stacy Harris (Carmen Johnson), Lina Raymond (Cheetah Johnson), Pat McCormick (Dudley), Bill Saluga (Shoes), William Smith (Suicide), Peter

Schrum (Ugly Eddie), Lainie Kazan (Card Player), Martin Mull (Card Player), Jimmie Walker (Card Player), Gwen Verdon (Bag Lady), Jack O'Leary (Porter), Benny Baker (Pop), Frank Birney (Priest).

1941. **A Girl's Life.** 30 min. Airdate: 8/4/83. Production Companies: American Flyer Productions and Warner Bros. Television. Director: Michael Zinberg. Executive Producer: Michael Zinberg. Producer: Susan Seeger. Writer: Susan Seeger. Music: Patrick Williams. Karen Valentine stars as a divorcee who writes advertising jingles and lives in a Manhattan loft. The proposed series would follow her day-to-day life as she dates, fields passes from her baseball player ex-husband (Fred Dryer), mothers her mother (Joan Hackett), consults her alter-ego (played by herself), and directly addresses the viewing audience. The pilot also featured flashbacks and, if it had gone to series, would have employed animation and other effects. Guests included Christopher Allport, Nea Bryant, Lyman Ward, and Phil Rubenstein.

1942. **The Invisible Woman.** 2 hours. Airdate: 2/13/83. Production Companies: Redwood Productions and Universal Television. Director: Alan J. Levi. Executive Producers: Sherwood Schwartz and Lloyd J. Schwartz. Producer: Alan J. Levi. Writers: Sherwood Schwartz and Lloyd J. Schwartz. Music: David Frank. Theme: Sherwood Schwartz, Lloyd J. Schwartz, and David Frank. Chemist Bob Denver creates an invisibility serum that his investigative reporter niece (Alexa Hamilton) uses to help crack stories. Although the pilot scored well in the ratings, no series materialized. *Cast:* Bob Denver (as Dr. Dudley Plunkett), Jonathan Banks (Daren), David Doyle (Neil Gilmore), George Gobel (Dr. Farrington), Anne Haney (Mrs. Van Dam), Harvey Korman (Carlisle Edwards), Art LaFleur (Phil), Garrett Morris (Lt. Greg Larkin), Ron Palillo (Spike Mitchell), Richard Sanders (Orville), Mel Stewart (Guard), Jacques Tate (Lt. Dan Williams), Alexa Hamilton (Sandy Martinson), Scott Nemes (Rodney Sherman), Jake Steinfeld (Attendant), Ken Sansom (Lionel Gilbert), Teri Beckerman (Receptionist), Ronald E. Morgan (First Cop), Joseph Phelan (Second Cop), Don Woren (Gallery Guard), Marsha Warner (Saleslady), Clinton Chase (Officer), David Whitfield (Marvin Carter), Valerie Hall (Miss Tomkins).

1943. **The Ladies.** 30 min. Production Company: Ed Friendly Productions. Director: Jackie Cooper. Executive Producer: Ed Friendly. Producer: Robert Klane. Writer: Robert Klane. When Patricia Elliott is abandoned by her husband after 27 years of marriage, she moves in with her daughter Talia Balsam, a divorced archaeologist who still sees her own ex-husband (Steven Peterman), a man her mother hates.

1944. Littleshots. 30 min. Airdate: 6/25/83. Production Companies: Major H Productions, Anson Productions, and Paramount Television. Director: Ron Howard. Executive Producers: Ron Howard and Anson Williams. Producer: Bruce Johnson. Writer: Bob Dolman. An attempt to update the old *Our Gang/ Little Rascals* comedies about the misadventures of a group of six- to twelve-year-olds in a lower middle-class, big city neighborhood. *Cast:* Joey Lawrence (as Pete), Robbie Kiger (Spitter), Keri Houlihan (Griddy), Maya Akerling (Linda), Jeff Cohen (Ralph), Kevin Burlat (Wiener), Erin Nicole Brown (Iris), Vincent Schiavelli (Smokey Joe), Christopher Kinnear (D'Arcy), Jannice Kawaye (Harley), Soleil Moon Frye (Samantha), Frankie Hill (Mrs. Cooper), Kelly Grogan (Nancy), D.C. Seawell (Bobby), Ken Magee (Man at Party), Louis Perez (Officer), Jennifer B. Edwards (D'Arcy's Mom).

1945. Love for Hire. 30 min. Production Company: EMI Productions. Director: Leonard Stern. Producer: Leonard Stern. Writer: Leonard Stern. Crocker Love (Michael Pritchard) is a Hawaiian private eye who bills himself as the best there is—although he's about as good an investigator as Maxwell Smart was a secret agent. That's no coincidence, since Leonard Stern also produced *Get Smart.* And like Maxwell Smart, he irritates the Chief—in this case, the Chief of Police, who has assigned an officer (Jeanne Mori) to keep an eye on him.

1946. Max (aka The Don Rickles Show). 30 min. Airdate: 4/28/83. Production Company: Alan Landsburg Productions. Director: Oz Scott. Executive Producer: Mort Lachman. Producers: Coleman Mitchell and Geoff Neigher. Writer: Ted Bergman. A spinoff from *Gimme a Break.* Don Rickies stars as Max Sorenson, a grocer who takes in a streetwise orphan (LaShana Dendy) to live with him in the apartment above the store. In the pilot, Nell Carter catches the girl shoplifting. The authors of *The Sweeps* say that "the pilot was of such negligible substance that it collapsed of its own weightlessness." *Cast:* Don Rickles (as Max Sorenson), LaShana Dendy (Danny), Nell Carter (Nell Harper), Dolph Sweet (Carl Kanisky), Lara Jill Miller (Samantha Kanisky), Lauri Hendler (Julie Kanisky), Kari Michaelson (Katie Kanisky), Barbara Hamilton (Shopper).

1947. President of Love. 30 min. Production Company: Paramount Television. Director: Will MacKenzie. Executive Producer: Chris Thompson. Producer: Jeff

Ganz. Writer: Chris Thompson. Van Johnson is an eccentric millionaire who, with the help of his nephew Beany (Robert Peirce), tries to solve people's romantic problems and play matchmaker—and he does both very well.

1948. There Goes the Neighborhood. 30 min. Airdate: 6/4/83. Production Companies: Saul Ilson Productions and Columbia Pictures Television. Director: Dick Martin. Executive Producer: Saul Ilson. Writer: David Duclon. Buddy Hackett, G.W. Bailey, and Patrick Collins are three hobos who inherit the estate of a Bel Air millionaire, and proceed to shock and embarrass the dead man's servants, family, and neighbors. The hobos hire a business manager (Graham Jarvis) who watches out for them, to the dismay of his snobbish wife (Sue Ann Gilfillan). In the book *The Sweeps*, the authors say the pilot was killed by Hackett, who was funny during rehearsals but "froze up" when the cameras started rolling, so that his "screwball attitude congealed into a stilted, painful tightness that brought the entire production down around him." The show was "written off as a $500,000 bath." *Cast:* Buddy Hackett (as Boxcar), Patrick Collins (The Kid), G.W. Bailey (Barney), Graham Jarvis (Milton Crocker), William Glover (Filkins), Sue Ann Gilfillan (Hortense Crocker), Keene Curtis (Charles Hawthorne).

1949. Yazoo (aka Wizzle Falls). 30 min. Airdate: 3/18/84. Production Company: Carson Productions. Director: Perry Rosemond. Executive Producer: April Kelly. Producers: Jim Gentry and Dave Pavelonis. Writers: Jeff Franklin and April Kelly. William Conrad is a widowed journalist who goes fishing one day, falls asleep in the boat, and wakes up in a magical world called Yazoo, populated by the Peppercorn Puppets. Although he can leave, he finds a contentment there. The proposed series would follow him as he learns about their world, and they learn about his. The original concept had him crashing his single-engine plane in the mystery land, then dubbed Wizzle Falls.

1950. Young Hearts. 30 min. Airdate: 3/18/84. Production Company: Carson Productions. Director: Tony Mordente. Executive Producer: Jeff Franklin. Producer: Gary Menteer. Writer: Jeff Franklin. Music: Bennett Salvay. Singer: Donna McDaniel. The misadventures of Doug (Jeffrey Rogers) and Karen (Ann Howard), a brother and sister growing up in a small, mid-western town where the big teen hangout is the local shopping mall. *Cast:* Jeffrey Rogers (as Doug Fraser), Ann Howard (Karen Fraser), Jerry Supiran (Larry Fraser), Patricia Harty (Wendy Fraser), Michael Callan (Carl Fraser), Michelle Downey (Kate),

Anthony Holland (Bernie), Charlie Zucker (Eddie), Michael Zorek (Beef), Janeen Best (Jeanie Grousley), Michael Dudikoff (Keith).

NBC / DRAMA

1951. Allison Sidney Harrison. 60 min. Airdate: 8/19/83. Director: Richard Crenna. Executive Producer: Leon Tokatyan. Producer: John Cutts. Writer: Leon Tokatyan. Ted Danson is a wealthy, San Francisco private eye who solves crimes with the help of his teenage daughter (Katy Kurtzman). According to the book *The Sweeps*, the pilot "grabbed Danson's career momentum like a hydraulic brake" because he was deemed unsympathetic by test audiences. Subsequently, Danson was placed on out-going NBC President Fred Silverman's blacklist. The authors of the book quote an unnamed NBC executive who explains "how could the audience like him? He was sending his little girl out to chase guys with guns!" *Cast:* Katy Kurtzman (as Allison Sidney Harrison), Ted Danson (David Harrison), Don Calfa (Pat Rosetti), Ellen Travolta (Joyce), Clyde Kusatu (Jimmy), James McEachin (Lt. Jesse Herman), Elaine Joyce (Valerie Parker), Granville Van Dusen (Walt Spencer), Hans Conried (Art Appraiser), Cynthia Harris (Clarise Spencer), Charles Hallahan (Sgt. Beatty), Macon McCalman (Dean), Corbin Bernsen (Steve Malloy), Dan Leegant (Detective Davis), Stanley Ralph Ross (Karate Instructor), Billy Swan (Doorman).

1952. Big John (aka Big Bad John). 60 min. Airdate: 12/3/83. Production Companies: Intermedia Entertainment and MGM/UA Television. Director: Paul Wendkos. Executive Producers: George Reeves and Fred Silverman. Producer: Al Godfrey. Writer: James Lee Barrett. Music: Mike Post and Pete Carpenter. The fish-out-of-water tale "McCloud"–style. Dale Robertson stars as a Montana county sheriff who goes to New York to investigate his son's murder and ends up joining the N.Y.P.D., where he's teamed up with a streetwise young officer (Joey Travolta) and assigned to a tough, black captain (Dick Anthony Williams). This pilot was originally set to star Wilford Brimley and was to have been directed by David Anspaugh. *Cast:* Dale Robertson (as Big John Corbin), Joey Travolta (Frank Novaricchi), Dick Anthony Williams (Capt. Hawkins), Karen Lee (Katherine Corbin), Natalie Klinger (Marcia Corbin), Tracy Scoggins (Alicia Bridgeport), Michael Goodwin (Nick North), Richard Bradford (William Bridgeport), Bobby Ellerbee (Harold), Fil Formicola (Busi), Alma Beltran (Maid).

1953. Cocaine and Blue Eyes. 2 hours. Airdate: 1/2/83. Production Companies: Orenthal Productions and Columbia Pictures Television. Director: E.W. Swackhamer. Executive Producer: O.J. Simpson. Producer: Dan Mark. Writer: Kendall J. Blair, from the novel by Fred Zackel. Music: Morton Stevens. O.J. Simpson as a black private eye working in San Francisco. *Cast:* O.J. Simpson (as Michael Brennan), Cliff Gorman (Rikki Anatole), Candy Clark (Ruth Anne Gideon), Eugene Roche (Sgt. Khoury), Maureen Anderman (Lillian Anatole), Cindy Pickett (Catherine), Tracy Reed (Chris Brennan), Leonardo Cimino (Orestes Anatole), Vanessa L. Clarke (Maid), Keye Luke (Tan Ng), Irene Farris (Dani Anatole), John Spencer (Joey Crawford), Evan Kim (Davy Huey), Ted LePlat (Alex Simons), Belita Moreno (Waitress), Dick Balduzzi (Barkeep), Stephen Toblowsky (TV Clerk), Bumper Robinson (Brennan's Son), Micah Morton (Brennan's Daughter), Jessica Biscardi (Nurse), Nigel Butland (Arnold), Stephen Burks (Doc), Beach Dickerson (Bartender), Marc Silver (Morgue Clerk), Sam Vicenzio (Hotel Clerk).

1954. The Cutting Edge. 60 min. Airdate: 5/11/83. Production Companies: Universal Television and Glen Larson Productions. Director: George Fenady. Executive Producer: Glen Larson. Producer: David Moessinger. Writer: Jeri Taylor. Aired as an episode of *Quincy*. Barry Newman is an idealistic doctor who uses the very latest technology to heal the sick and suffering. Costars included John Randolph, Paul Rudd, Mary Louise Weller, Julie Phillips, Allan Fawcett, and Chevi Colton.

1955. Lone Star. 60 min. Airdate: 7/31/83. Production Company: Lorimar Productions. Director: John Flynn. Executive Producers: Lawrence Gordon and Charles Gordon. Producer: R.J. Lewis. Writers: John Flynn and Henry Rosenbaum. Creator: John Flynn. Music: Barry DeVorzon. The story of two brothers who are partnered as Texas Rangers—big, soft-spoken George (Alan Autry), and cocky, fun-loving Ben (Lewis Smith)—and solve crimes with the help of their retired-Ranger Uncle (John McIntire) and an attractive deputy sheriff (Terri Garber). "We were doing a hard-edged thing, like *Wanted: Dead Or Alive*," recalls Lewis Smith. "So we started filming and the network stepped in and said 'the stars gotta smile the whole fucking time.' I started getting directions like 'okay, rolling, smiling with tension. Action.' It was terrible." *Cast:* Alan Autry (as George McCollum), Lewis Smith (Ben McCollum), John McIntire (Uncle Luthor), Terri Garber (Deputy Cissy Wells), Sandy McPeak (Capt. Sam Mellon), Chuck Connors (Jake Farrell), Nancy Stafford (Amanda Talbot), Amanda Wyss

(Maggie Holloway), Claude Earl Jones (Sheriff Pritchett), Brion James (Breyer), Bill Erwin (Ezra Holloway), Frank Schuller (Dandy Jim Candy), Kelly Palzis (Redhead), Jeffrey Josephson (Willard Barnes), Joe Medalis (Lab Technician), Doug McGrath (Amos Caldwell).

1956. The Naturals. 20 min. Production Company: Blinn/Thorpe Productions. Director: Jerry Thorpe. Executive Producers: William Blinn and Jerry Thorpe. Writer: William Blinn. A 20-minute demonstration film was shot about a brash New York cop named Joe Triplett (Michael Brandon) teamed with brooding, native Texan D.W. Pardee (Stephen Parr) on the Houston force. A nearly identical series called *Houston Knights* would premiere on CBS a few seasons later.

1957. Nightingale. 20 min. Production Company: Universal Television. Director: Reza S. Badiyi. Executive Producer: Phil DeGuere. Producer: Richard Chapman. Writers: Phil DeGuere and Richard Chapman. A 20 minute demonstration film about a female Ninja (Robyn Douglass) who works as a secret agent for boss Richard Cox.

1958. Nightmares. 99 min. Production Company: Universal Television. Director: Joe Sargent. Executive Producer: Christopher Crowe. Producers: Andrew Mirisch, Alex Beaton, and Alan Barnette. Writers: Christopher Crowe (segments 1–3) and Jeffrey Bloom (segment 4). Creative Consultant: William Sackheim. Music: Craig Safan. An anthology of horror stories about ordinary people thrust into supernatural situations. "The stories are all contemporary," said Christopher Crowe in Universal publicity materials. "Our emphasis is on the horror to be found in the simplest, most reassuring objects and surroundings." In "Terror of Topanga," a madman is loose in Topanga Canyon, and everyone is advised to stay indoors—but one woman, a chain-smoker, goes out anyway for a pack of cigarettes. "Bishop of Battle" pits Emilio Estevez against a supernatural video game. "The Benediction" follows a priest, who has lost his faith, terrorized by a driverless truck on the Mojave Desert. And "Night of the Rat" follows a suburban family battling a giant rat in their home. This pilot was released as a feature film, rather than broadcast, when NBC failed to pick it up. Universal did this once before when NBC passed on *Buck Rogers in the 25th Century*, but that film ended up doing so well at the box office the network changed its mind and ordered the series. The same didn't happen with *Nightmares*, although Crowe, Mirisch, and Barnette later went on to produce Universal's *Alfred Hitchcock Presents* revival for NBC.

"Terror of Topanga." *Cast:* Cristina Raines (as Wife), Joe Lambie (Husband), Claire Nono (Newswoman), Raleigh Bond (Neighbor), Robert Phelps (Newsman), Dixie Lynn Royce (Little Girl), Lee James Jude (Glazier).

"Bishop of Battle." *Cast:* Emilio Estevez (as J.J.), Mariclare Costello (Mrs. Cooney), Louis Giambalvo (Mr. Cooney), Moon Zappa (Pamela), Billy Jacoby (Zock), Joshua Grenrock (Willie), Gary Cervantes (Mazenza), C. Stewart Burnes (Root), Andre Diaz (Pedro), Rachel Goslins (Phyllis), Joel Holman (Z-Man), Christopher Bubetz (Jeffrey), Rudy Negretl (Emiliano), James Tolkan (Bishop's Voice).

"The Benediction." *Cast:* Lance Henriksen (as MacLeod), Tony Plana (Delamo), Timothy Scott (Sheriff), Robin Gammell (Bishop), Rose Marie Campos (Mother).

"Night of the Rat." *Cast:* Richard Masur (as Steve Houston), Veronica Cartwright (Claire Houston), Bridgette Andersen (Brooke Houston), Albert Hague (Mel Keefer), Howard F. Flynn (Radio Announcer).

1959. Six Pack (aka Brewster's Brood). 60 min. Airdate: 7/24/83. Production Company: 20th Century Fox Television. Director: Rod Amateau. Executive Producer: Gy Waldron. Producers: Rod Amateau and James Heinz. Writer: Gy Waldron. Music: Lance Rubin. Based on the movie *Six Pack,* starring Kenny Rogers as a race car driver who takes in five orphaned kids as his pit crew. Don Johnson takes over the role for the TV version. Mae Marmy is the prim English nanny he hires to teach the kids on the road; Markie Post is his girlfriend. *Cast:* Don Johnson (as Brewster Baker), Markie Post (Sally Leadbetter), Jennifer Runyon (Heather Akins), Billy Warlock (Duffy Akins), Bubba Dean (Rebel Akins), Con Martin (Hank Akins), Leaf Phoenix (Tad Akins), Mae Marmy (Sybil Cadbury), Ralph Pace (Joe Apple), Terry Beaver (Jo Jo), Jerry Campbell (Red Lyles), Cliff Brand (D.C. Dempsey), Julian Bond (Judge), Wallace Wilkinson (Superintendent), C. Pete Munro (Luther), Tad Currie (Policeman), Jim Peck (Man at Gas Station).

1984–1985

ABC / COMEDY

1960. Earthlings. 30 min. Airdate: 7/5/84. Production Companies: Starry Night Productions and Warner Bros. Television. Director: Jay Sandrich. Executive Producer: Reinhold Weege. Producer: William Phillips. Writer: Reinhold Weege. Music: Jack Elliott. A space shuttle carrying a civilian crew malfunctions, leaving them "lost in space." The characters include the straight-arrow pilot (Mike Connors), the impetuous co-pilot (Charlie Hill), an eccentric scientist (Ray Birk), a rich businessman (Dan Hedaya), a psychologist (Ilene Graff), an astronaut-in-training (Robin Dearden) and Jayza (Leonard Frey), an alien they meet along the way. *Cast:* Mike Connors (as Capt. Jim Adams), Dan Hedaya (Cal), Charlie Hill (Noah Greene), Robin Dearden (Sally), Ilene Graff (Jane Lassiter), Michael D. Roberts (D.J. Young), James Cromwell (Simon Ganes), Ray Birk (Vince Martoni), Leonard Frey (Jayza), Debbie Carrington (Zet), Edwin Newman (Newsman), Michael Sheehan (Chuck Richter), G.W. Bailey (Bobo).

1961. Fraud Broads (aka Fraud Squad). 30 min. Airdate: 5/17/85. Production Company: Universal Television. Director: Jim Drake. Executive Producers: Allen Epstein, Jim Green, and Buddy Bregman. Producers: Bill Chapman and Jeff Dial. Writers: Bill Chapman and Jeff Dial. The professional and personal lives of the women who comprise the L.A.P.D.'s all-female bunco squad. *Cast:* Lu Leonard (Fran), Beverly Todd (Carmen), Nana Visitor (Bonnie), Audrie Neenan (Joyce), Ann Dusenberry (Kelly).

1962. Goldie and the Bears. 60 min. Airdate: 5/26/85. Production Companies: Fred Weintraub & Daniel Grodnick Productions and Warner Bros. Television. Director: Russ Mayberry. Executive Producer: Dean Hargrove. Producer: Jeff Peters. Writers: Jeff Reno and Ron Osborn, from a story by David Engelbach. Music: Dick DeBenedictis. Stephanie Faracy is a neophyte private eye, daughter of a beloved football coach, who hires three former football players (Julius J. Carry, III, Terry "Hulk" Hogan, and Ben Davidson) to be the "muscle" behind her brains. In the pilot, the four foil a plot to smuggle military secrets out of the country in toy robots.

1963. Just Married. 30 min. Airdate: 5/10/85. Production Company: Witt-Thomas Productions. Director: Bill Foster. Executive Producers: Paul Witt and Tony Thomas. Writer: Jeff Franklin. Creator: Greg Antonacci. Paul Reiser is a steelworker who marries a rich man's daughter (Barton Hyman), and finds himself constantly under pressure from his father-in-law to work harder and be a better provider. Matt Craven and Kathleen Wilhoite are their newlywed neighbors. *Cast:* Paul Reiser (as Mickey Montana), Gail Edwards (Lynda Montana), Matt Craven (Buddy), Kathleen Wilhoite (Doreen), Barton Hyman (Jake Borassi).

1964. Mr. Mom. 30 min. Airdate: 11/30/84. Production Companies: Sherwood Productions and 20th Century Fox Television. Director: Terry Hughes. Executive Producers: Frank Dungan and Jeff Stein. Producer: Pat Rickey. Writers: Frank Dungan and Jeff Stein. Creator: John Hughes. Music: Dave Fisher. Singers: Gary Portnoy and Judy Hart Angelo. Based on the movie, which starred Michael Keaton as an unemployed auto worker who takes over running the household when his wife, played by Teri Garr, goes to work at an advertising agency. Barry Van Dyke and Rebecca York assume the roles in the TV version. Aaron Spelling, who produced the movie, is billed on the pilot as executive consultant. *Cast:* Barry Van Dyke (as Jack Butler), Rebecca York (Caroline Butler), Brendon Blincoe (Curtis Butler), Sean deVeritch (Kenny Butler), Heidi Zeigler (Megan Butler), Phyllis Davis (Joan Hampton), Howard Honig (Darryl Fetty), Pat McNamara (Vernon Wesley), Sam Scarber (Sgt. Preston), Dimitri Michas (Marine).

1965. Never Again. 30 min. Airdate: 11/30/84. Production Company: Universal Television. Director: Hal Cooper. Executive Producers: Paul Levenback, Wendy Riche, and Sandy Veith. Producer: Terri Guarnieri. Writer: Sandy Veith. Music: Ira Newborn. The comic misadventures of three single yuppies living in neighboring condos. *Cast:* Jamie Rose (as Abby Cartwright), Judge Reinhold (Larry Newman), Allen Garfield (Mitchell Franklin), Margot Rose (Denise), Loyita Chapel (Dawn Stephenson), Dalton Cathey (Allen), Mark Sawyer (Man).

1966. Old Friends. 30 min. Airdate: 7/12/84. Production Company: Paramount Television. Director: Michael Lessac. Executive Producer: Elliot Shoenman. Producer: Tom Cherones. Writer: Elliot Shoenman. Music: Artie Butler. Christopher Lloyd stars as a big-city lawyer who, after his divorce, moves back to his small home town with his 15-year-old son (Grant Forsberg) to help his father (John Randolph) run the family drugstore. His old girlfriend (Jennifer Salt) is now a sexy- voiced DJ married to his old, best friend, now the school football coach (Stanley Kamel). *Cast:* Christopher Lloyd (as Jerry Forbes), Grant Forsberg (Mark Forbes), John Randolph (Phil Forbes), Jennifer Salt (Susan King), Stanley Kamel (Charlie), Steve Ryan (George), Peter Van Norden (Earl).

1967. **100 Centre Street.** 30 min. Airdate: 8/31/84. Production Company: ABC Circle Films. Director: Mark Tinker. Executive Producer: Norman Steinberg. Producer: Bob Sand. Writer: Bob Sand. Music: Artie Butler. The professional and personal lives of the judges working at New York's Hall of Justice. *Cast:* Len Carriou (as Judge Charles Felt), Dee Wallace (Judge Nell Harrigan), J.A. Preston (Judge Earl Doucette), Lela Ivey (Pam Verderamo), Henry Darrow (Judge Ramon Robledo), James Canning (Louis Keck), Ernie Hudson (Leo Kelly), Ernie Sabella (Harry Pike), Christine Belford (Fran Felt), Wright Dorsey (Andre Bussey).

ABC / DRAMA

1968. **Cobra (aka Condor).** 90 min. Airdate: 8/10/86. Production Companies: Orion Television and Jaygee Productions. Director: Virgil Vogel. Executive Producer: Jerry Golod. Producers: Peter Nelson, Arnold Oroglini, Len Janson, and Chuck Menville. Writers: Len Janson and Chuck Menville. Music: Ken Heller. Set in the 1990s, the adventures of an ace secret agent (Ray Wise) and his robot part-ner (Wendy Kilbourne), working for an elite, high-tech espionage agency run by Craig Stevens. *Cast:* Ray Wise (as Chris Proctor), Wendy Kilbourne (Lisa Hampton), Craig Stevens (Cyrus Hampton), Vic Polizos (Commissioner Ward), James Avery (Cass), Cassandra Gava (Sumiko), Carolyn Seymour (Rachel Hawkins), Shawn Michaels (Watch Commander), Mario Roccuzzo (Manny), Catherine Battistone (Lieutenant), Barbara Beckley (Water Controller), Diane Bellamy (Opera Singer), Gene Ricknell (Bartender), Myra Chason (Pirate Pete Waitress), Tony Epper (Cop), Brad Fisher (Man), Phil Fondacaro (Quaid), Mike Freeman (Technician), Karen Montgomery (Monique).

1969. **Command Five.** 2 hours. Airdate: 8/5/85. Production Company: Paramount Television. Director: E.W. Swackhamer. Executive Producer: Tony Ford. Producers: Anthony Spinner and James O'Keefe. Writer: Anthony Spinner. Music: Lalo Schifrin. An elite, paramilitary, anti-crime force that works for the law, but outside the law. In the pilot, they free an entire town taken hostage by escaped convicts. *Variety* labeled this pilot a "repugnant endeavor" and a "shoddy misapplication of talent" for what the reviewer felt was a glorification of official law-breaking that "rings of fascism." *Cast:* Stephen Parr (as Blair Morgan), Wings Hauser (Jack Coburn), John Matuszak (Nick Kowalski), William Russ (J.D. Smith), Sonja Smits (Chris Winslow), Gregory Sierra (Delgado), Bill Forsythe (Hawk), Robert F. Lyons (Vince), Bruce Abbott (Duke Williams), Arthur F. Adams (Joseph Murphy), Marc Alaimo (Businessman), Derek Barton (Corporal), Lynn Benesch (Ann Bryan), Katherine Boyer (Kuza Bryan), Dennis Bowen (Larry Webster), W.T. Zacha (Van Orden), Garry Walberg (Arthur Steur), Ann Walker (Mary Randolph), Chere Bryson (Hooker), Timothy Burns (Sergeant), David Cass (Longshoreman), Rande Deluca (Trooper Pilot), Thomas E. Duffy (Lew), Greg Finley (Col. Henderson), Ken Foree (Air Controller), Hank Garrett (Capt. Ed Draper), Stan Haze (Pimp), Trevor Henley (Jonas), Peter Jason (Warden Bryan), Ted Leplatt (Tony Jones), Scott Lincoln (Highway Patrolman), Morgan Lofting (Nancy Danelli), Alex MacArthur (Deputy), Frank McCarthy (Chicago Police Lieutenant), Robert Miranda (Ricco).

1970. Long Time Gone. 2 hours. Airdate: 5/22/86. Production Companies: Picturemaker Productions and ABC Circle Films. Director: Robert Butler. Executive Producer: Glenn Gordon Caron. Producer: Jay Daniel. Writer: Glenn Gordon Caron. Creator: Glenn Gordon Caron. Music: Artie Kane. From the same team behind *Moonlighting,* only this came first. Paul LeMat is a bad private eye in over- his-head with gambling debts to the mob when his wife, whom he deserted ten years ago, unexpectedly saddles him with his 11-year-old son (Wil Wheaton) and goes away. Richard Sarafian is the bookie. *Cast:* Paul LeMat (as Nick Sandusky), Wil Wheaton (Mitchell), Ann Dusenberry (Marilyn), Ray Giridian (Michael Diablo), Barbara Stock (Georgia Diablo), Richard C. Sarafian (Omar), Deborah Wakeman (Peggy), Eddie Zammit (Carl), Bill Marcus (Associate), Melvin E. Allen (Security), Blake Clark (Bartender), Art Evans (Neighbor), Jessie Lawrence Ferguson (Man), Mary Ann Gibson (Secretary), Michael Laskin (Ray), Ann Pennington (Catherine), Vicky Perry (Flight Attendant), Nicholas Shields (Wise Guy), Beau Starr (Man in Car).

1971. [Marcus Welby] Return of Marcus Welby, M.D. (aka Jennings and Jennings: A Family Practice). 2 hours. Airdate: 5/16/84. Production Companies: Marstar Productions and Universal Television. Director: Alexander Singer. Executive Producer: Martin Starger. Producers: Dennis Doty, Michael Braverman, and Howard Alston. Writers: John McGreevey and Michael Braverman. Creator: David Victor. Music: Leonard Rosenman. A revival of *Marcus Welby, M.D.*

aimed at launching a different, but similarly themed show entitled *Jennings and Jennings: A Family Practice* in which Robert Young might occasionally appear. In the pilot, Marcus Welby fights to retain his accreditation at the hospital where he now works. The proposed series would focus on Dr. David Jennings (Darren McGavin), a doctor who believes, as Dr. Welby does, that he has a responsibility to his patients that extends beyond mere diagnosis and treatment. Jennings opens a practice with his son (Morgan Stevens) and hires Welby's nurse (Elena Verdugo). On some cases, Jennings would work with a husband-and-wife team of pediatricians (Dennis Haysbert and Cyndi James-Reese). In 1989, another sequel, *Marcus Welby: A Holiday Affair*, was broadcast on NBC to lackluster ratings. Cast: Robert Young (as Dr. Marcus Welby), Elena Verdugo (Nurse Consuelo Lopez), Darren McGavin (Dr. David Jennings), Morgan Stevens (Dr. Matt Jennings), Dennis Haybert (Dr. Hoover Beaumont), Cyndi James-Reese (Phaedra Beaumont), Jessica Walter (Astrid Carlisle), Yvonne Wilder (Dr. Nina Velasquez), Cristina Raines (Nikki St. Hilliare), Joanna Kerns (Pamela Saletta), Katherine DeHetre (Francine Parnell), Milt Kogan (Perry Mc- Masters), Robert Carnegie (Dr. Ingram), Milt Oberman (Joel Silvers), Nicholas Hormann (Kevin Saletta), Fran Ryan (Millie Clark), Jacqueline Hyde (Fanny Glickman), Momo Yashima (Angela), James Carroll (Blackie), A1 Christy (Aaron Glickman), Lee Armone (Second Nurse), Chris Kriesa (First Doctor), Linda Hoy (Third Nurse), Richard Marion (Second Doctor), Cynthia Avila (Fourth Nurse), Barbara Mealy (Second ER Nurse).

1972. **Midas Valley.** 2 hours. Airdate: 6/27/85. Production Company: Warner Bros. Television. Director: Gus Trikonis. Executive Producer: Edward H. Feldman and Clyde Phillips. Producer: Robert Lewis. Writer: Ann Beckett. Music: Jerrold Immel. *Dallas/Dynasty/Falcon Crest* in the Silicon Valley. Josh Grumman (James Read) and Brad Dexter (Brett Cullen) are two successful entrepreneurs in the volatile computer industry. Their arch rival is their former mentor, the diabolical Drew Hammond (Robert Stack), who is even more furious at them when his daughter (Shanna Reed) joins their upstart firm. George Grizzard costars as another competitor. Cast: James Reed (as Josh Grumman), Brett Cullen (Brad Dexter), Robert Stack (Drew Hammond), Shanna Reed (Lillian Hammond), George Grizzard (George Carew), Phillip R. Allen (Eric Gregory), Stephen Elliott (Elias Markov), Joseph Hacker (Franklin Hammond), France Nuyen (Mitsi Kawamoto), Linda Purl (Sarah), Catherine Mary Stewart (Betsy), Scott

Paulin (Seth), Kathryn Witt (Donna), Albert Hall (Dr. Aaronson), Richard Kuss (Max), Woody Eney (Mr. Baxter).

1973. **Velvet.** 2 hours. Airdate: 8/27/84. Production Company: Aaron Spelling Productions. Director: Richard Lang. Executive Producers: Aaron Spelling and Douglas S. Cramer. Producers: E. Duke Vincent and Richard Lang. Writers: Ernest Tidyman and Ned Wynn. Music: Dominic Frontiere. Yet another attempt to clone Aaron Spelling's hit *Charlie's Angels*, this time by Spelling himself. Four attractive aerobic dancers (Leah Ayres, Shari Belafonte-Harper, Mary-Margaret Humes, and Sheree Wilson) are actually secret agents using Polly Bergen's Velvet International health spas as a front for their espionage activities. Spelling was developing a new version of *Charlie's Angels* in 1988 for the fledgling Fox Broadcasting Company. *Cast:* Leah Ayres (as Cass Dayton), Shari Belafonte-Harper (Julie Rhodes), Mary- Margaret Humes (Lauren Dawes), Sheree Wilson (Ellen Stockwell), Polly Bergen (Mrs. Vance), Michael Ensign (Stefan), Leigh McCloskey (James Barstow), Bruce Abbott (Breed), Judson Scott (Mats Edholm), Bo Brundin (Prof. Charles Vandemeer), Clyde Kusatsu (Dr. Edward Yashima), William Windom (Government Official), Ellen Geer (Nora Vandemeer), David Faustino (Billy Vandermeer), Bill Quinn (Dr. Harmon), Stanley Bower (Cullom), Stephen Davies (Farrow), Holly Butler (Receptionist), Carrie Rhodes (Instructor), Paul Tuerpe (Contact), Danny Wells (Producer), Anthony DeLongis (Rawls), Tim Haldeman (Sammy), Cis Rundle (Flight Attendant), Alya Swan (Dowager).

CBS / COMEDY

1974. **Another Man's Shoes.** 30 min. Airdate: 5/28/84. Production Company: Embassy Television. Director: Noam Pitlik. Executive Producers: Dick Bensfield and Perry Grant. Producers: Katherine Green and Patricia Fass-Palmer. Writers: Dick Bensfield and Perry Grant. Music: Jeff Barry and Nancy Barry. Aired as the last episode of *One Day at a Time*. Pat Harrington's Schneider character moves to Florida when his brother dies, leaving him to raise his niece (Natalie Klinger) and nephew (Corey Feldman), who are living in an amusement park arcade run by Candice Azzara. *Cast:* Pat Harrington (as Dwayne Schneider), Corey Feldman (Keith Schneider), Natalie Klinger (Lori Schneider), Candice Azzara (Jackie Cahill), Darian Mathias (Cassie), Bill Zuckert (Mr. Tuller), Biff Yeager

(Bernard), Ruth Kobart (Madame Zorina), J. Bill Jones (Clifford), Michael Shea (Pete).

1975. The Bounder. 30 min. Airdate: 7/7/84. Production Companies: Can't Sing, Can't Dance Productions and Columbia Pictures Television. Director: Sam Weisman. Executive Producer: Barbara Corday. Producers: Fred Barron and Andrew Selig. Writer: Fred Barron. Based on the British sitcom. Michael McKeon is a lovable con man who gets out of prison and moves in with his sister (Jeannette Arnette) and her husband (Richard Masur). His schemes get everyone in trouble, but he still manages to endear himself to the woman next door (Francine Tacker). Shot in New York. *Cast:* Michael McKeon (as Howard), Jeannette Arnette (Bonnie), Richard Masur (Charles), Francine Tacker (Laura).

1976. Boys in Blue. 60 min. Airdate: 9/9/84. Production Companies: David Gerber Company and MGM/UA Television. Director: Gary Nelson. Executive Producer: David Gerber. Producer: Stephen Cragg. Writers: Andy Borowitz and Bob Collins. Music: Lee Holdridge. The adventures of police officers, swinging single Danny Harris (Dean Paul Martin) and his older partner Jeff Martin (Gregg Henry), who considers himself more responsible than his irreverent friend. Other characters include a black officer who wants to be Mayor (William Allen Young), the precinct captain with a gambling problem (Murray Hamilton), and an officer who likes to play practical jokes (Maggie Cooper). *Cast:* Dean Paul Martin (as Officer Danny Harris), Gregg Henry (Officer Jeff Martin), Maggie Cooper (Officer Grace Carpenter), Murray Hamilton (Capt. Sid Bender), Luis Avalos (Sgt. Hernandez), Vince McKewin (Officer Don Mutuccie), Gerritt Graham (Lt. Shenk), William Allen Young (Officer Carl Johnson), David Rayner (Mason Bradley), Ruth Britt (Rena), Rhonda Aldrich (Nancy), Patrick J. Cronin (Drunk), Rick Fitts (Detective Miller), John Bloom (Capt. Video), Ben Lum (Chef), P.J. Goodwin (Kid), Art LaFleur (Stanley Singleton), Glen Bowman (Matt Landers), Jonathan Banks (Slick Slim), John DeSantis (Mr. O'Brien).

1977. His and Hers. 30 min. Airdate: 5/15/84. Production Companies: Telepictures and The Brillstein Company. Director: Sam Weisman. Executive Producers: Frank Königsberg and Bernie Brillstein. Producer: Arnold Kane. Writer: Arnold Kane. The story of what happens when a 40-year-old newspaper columnist (Richard Kline) marries a divorced writer of children's books (Shelley Fabares) with two teenage daughters (Dana Kimmell and Shannen Doherty). Kline would later star in *Together Again*, a 1986 flop pilot for first-run syndication that had almost the same concept. *Cast:* Richard Kline (as Jimmy McCabe), Shelley Fabares (Barbara McCabe), Dana Kimmell (Kelly McCabe), Shannen Doherty (Stacy McCabe), Leslie Easterbrook (Sharon), Richard Foronjy (Larry), Terrence McGovern (Pete), Pamela Newman (Inga), John Shepherd (Rick Dana).

1978. Second Edition. 30 min. Airdate: 7/17/84. Production Companies: Leeway Productions and 20th Century Fox Television. Director: Charlotte Brown. Executive Producer: John Rappaport. Producers: David Landsburg and Lauren Dreyfuss. Writer: John Rappaport. Creator: John Rappaport. Music: Chick Corea. Hal Linden is Cliff Penrose, an English professor at a small Ohio college who, when his 20-year marriage breaks up, quits and makes a mid-life change in job and locale. He moves to Columbia, becomes editor of a struggling, regional magazine, and joins a therapy group for newly divorced men. *Cast:* Hal Linden (as Cliff Penrose), Sharon Spelman (Ruth Rigby Rosen Reynolds), Emory Bass (Caron Barrett), Lou Richards (Rick Williams), Gordon Jump (Fred Lewicki), Isabel Grandin (Jaime Scott), Don Diamond (Mr. Antoine), Edie McClurg (Ida Antoine), G.W. Bailey (Howard), Alley Mills (Denise), Jane Hallaren (Dr. Emily Maxwell).

1979. Summer. 30 min. Airdate: 7/14/84. Production Companies: Don Reo Productions and MGM/UA Television. Director: Allan Arkush. Executive Producers: Don Reo and Judith Allison. Producer: Ed Ledding. Writer: Don Reo. The summer adventures of five high school students and the two adults in their lives—the beach lifeguard (Gerard Prendergast) and the woman who owns the disco (Sally Kirkland). *Cast:* Gary Hershberger (as Alex), Tico Wells (Desmond), Johnny Timko (Zack), Jill Carroll (Candy), Peggy Holmes (Karen), Gerard Prendergast (Erik), Sally Kirkland (Mother).

1980. Used Cars. 30 min. Airdate: 8/15/84. Production Companies: Can't Sing, Can't Dance Productions and Columbia Pictures Television. Director: Victor Lobi. Executive Producer: Barbara Corday. Producer: Bob Gale. Writer: Bob Gale. Creators: Robert Zemeckis and Bob Gale. Music: Norman Gimbel and Charles Fox. Singer: Roy Clark. Based on the 1980 movie. Deborah Harmon inherits a struggling Las Vegas used car lot, run by Fred McCarren, who will resort to just about any outlandish scheme to outsell her unscrupulous Uncle Roy (Pat Corley), who owns every other car lot in town. Clayton Landey is McCarren's assistant and Frank McRae is a mechanic learning to be a fast-talking salesman. *Cast:* Deborah Harmon (as Barbara Fuchs), Fred

McCarren (Rudy Russo), Clayton Landey (Jeff Kirkwood), Frank McRae (Jim), Pat Corley (Uncle Roy), Michael Talbott (Mickey), Robert Costanzo (Irving), David Wyley (Claude Wiggins), J.P. Bumstead (Sam), Don Maxwell (Sergeant).

1981. Walter (aka Radar). 30 min. Airdate: 7/17/84. Production Company: 20th Century Fox Television. Director: Bill Bixby. Executive Producers: Michael Zinberg, Bob Schiller, and Bob Weiskopf. Writers: Bob Schiller, Bob Weiskopf, and Everett Greenbaum. Music: Patrick Williams. The continuing adventures of Walter "Radar" O'Reilly, the character Gary Burghoff portrayed in both the movie and television series versions of *M*A *S*H*. Following the war, Radar took over the family farm and married his sweetheart, but the farm went broke and she left him for another man. Radar moves to Kansas City to live with his cousin Wendell (Ray Buktenica), a Hawkeye-like police officer. So Radar joins the Force, too. The proposed series would have chronicled his adventures as a rookie cop and his romance with a warm-hearted, soda-fountain girl (Victoria Jackson). *Cast:* Gary Burghoff (as Walter "Radar" O'Reilly), Ray Buktenica (Wendell Mikeljohn), Victoria Jackson (Victoria Petersen), Noble Willingham (Sgt. Sowell), Lyman Ward (Sgt. Bigelow), Sarah Abrell (Judith Crane), Larry Cedar (Zipkin), Francine Gable (Pretty Girl), Meeno Peluce (Elston Krannick), Clete Roberts (Interviewer), Sam Scraber (Haskell), Victoria Carroll (Bubbles Sincere), June Berry (Dixie Devoe), Bobby Ramsen (Singer), Dick Miller (Theatre Owner).

CBS / DRAMA

1982. Adventures of Alexander Hawkins. 60 min. Production Company: Warner Bros. Television. Director: Lee Katzin. Executive Producers: Bryan Hickox and Jay Daniel. Producer: Leon Tokatyan. Writer: Leon Tokatyan. Duncan Regehr is a wealthy bachelor private eye who lives in a luxurious, Nob Hill penthouse who solves crimes with the help of Chip (Clyde Kusatsu), his Chinese/American chauffeur, and his rich grandmother (Mildred Natwick). Reworked as the 1986 NBC pilot *Champion*.

1983. The Bounty Hunter. 60 min. Airdate: 4/23/84. Production Company: Orion Television. Director: Bill Duke. Executive Producer: Barney Rosenweig. Producer: Peter Lefcourt. Writer: Steve Brown. Aired as an episode of *Cagney* *and Lacey.* Brian Dennehy stars as a brash bounty hunter who, in the pilot, is pursuing a Michigan bail-jumper Cagney and Lacey (Sharon Gless and Tyne Daly) are seeking for a New York armed robbery. *Cast:* Brian Dennehy (as Michael MacGruder), Laurie Prange (Violet Reynolds), Peter Voight (Brudinski), Dennis Pratt (Springer), Sharon Gless (Chris Cagney), Tyne Daly (Mary Beth Lacey).

1984. Cat and Mike. 20 min. Production Company: Paramount Television. Director: Sandor Stern. Executive Producers: Gary Nardino and Sandor Stern. Writer: Sandor Stern. Loretta Swit is an Ivy League-educated, New York cop who's teamed up with a streetwise detective from the Bronx (Jack Scalia). George Dzundza is their boss. A 20-minute demonstration film was all that was shot.

1985. London and Davis in New York. 60 min. Airdate: 9/9/84. Production Company: Columbia Pictures Television. Director: Robert Day. Executive Producers: Linda Bloodworth and Harry Thomason. Producer: Harry Thomason. Writer: Linda Bloodworth. Music: Chuck Mangione. The romance between a wealthy, jet-setting photographer (Season Hubley) and a rumpled, country-born, three-times-married journalist (Richard Crenna), her next-door-neighbor in a Manhattan apartment building. Together, they cover stories and solve crimes, to the dismay of her urban former lover and their chief competitor (James Carroll Jordan). Linda Bloodworth and her husband, Harry Thomason, would later write and produce *Lime Street* and *Designing Women. Cast:* Season Hubley (as Claudia London), Richard Crenna (John Greyson Davis), James Carroll Jordan (Brandon Westphal), Roddy McDowall (Paul Fisk), Vernee Watson (Frances Meyers), Gerald S. O'Loughlin (Sam Gains), Karen Austin (Adrienne Crowe), James Ingersoll (Dan Carr), Jay Githens (Tom Fuccello), Mark Carlson (Captain), Dan Dillon (Peter), Leslie Kawal (Misha), Twink Caplan (Woman), Phylis Cowan (Waitress), Conrad Dunn (Punk Rocker), Bobbie Ferguson (Woman), Mark Harrison (Man in Bar).

1986. Return of Luther Gillis. 60 min. Airdate: 2/16/84. Production Company: Universal Television. Director: John Llewellyn Moxey. Executive Producer: Donald Belisario. Producers: Reuben Leder, Rick Weaver, Chas. Floyd Johnson, and Chris Abbott-Fish. Writer: Reuben Leder. Creator: Reuben Leder. Music: Mike Post and Peter Carpenter. Aired as an episode of *Magnum P.I.* An attempt to spin-off Eugene Roche as Luther Gillis, the anachronistic, St. Louis private eye that first appeared on the "Luther Gillis: File #521" (10/6/83) episode, which was written by Leder and directed by Virgil Vogel. The light-hearted episodes, which verged on outright comedy, worked on the conflict between Magnum's (Tom Selleck) easy-going methods and the hardball approach of Luther Gillis, who modeled himself on old movie P.I.'s of the '30s and '40s. This time, Luther Gillis is lured to Hawaii with his bimbo secretary Blanche (Sheree North) by a vengeful crook from his past (Geoffrey Lewis). Although this didn't sell, Roche reprised his role in several more Leder-written *Magnum P.I.* segments.

1987. Shadow of Sam Penny. 60 min. Airdate: 11/3/83. Production Company: Universal Television. Director: Vincent McEveety. Executive Producer: Phillip DeGuere. Producers: John G. Stephens and Richard Chapman. Writer: Michael Piller. Aired as an episode of *Simon and Simon*. The first of two pilots starring Robert Lansing as private eye Sam Penny, a modern-day throwback to the hard-boiled detectives of the '30s and '40s—and a man Rick (Gerald McRaney) and A.J. Simon (Jameson Parker) idolize. In the pilot, Penny tries to find diamonds that were stolen in the 1950s and never found, even though the thieves were caught. Unlike the similarly themed "Luther Gillis" episodes of *Magnum P.I.*, which were played for laughs, Penny was played fairly straight. *Cast:* Robert Lansing (as Sam Penny), Anne Francis (Angel Barkley), Joan Leslie (Toni Myers), Elisha Cook (Dutch Silver), Dane Clark (Del Mooney), Scott Brady (Alex Kidd), Philip Bruns (Wally Kaper), Clete Roberts (Dennis Markell).

1988. The Sheriff and the Astronaut. 60 min. Airdate: 5/24/84. Production Company: Warner Bros. Television. Director: E.W. Swackhamer. Producers: Gerald DiPego and Robert Lovenheim. Writer: Gerald DiPego. Music: Basil Poledouris. Alec Baldwin is a Florida county sheriff in love with an astronaut (Ann Gillespie) and at odds with the space center's security chief (Kene Holliday). *Cast:* Ann Gillespie (as Dr. Ellen Vale), Alec Baldwin (Sheriff Ed Cassaday), Don Hood (Deputy Tom Cassaday), Kene Holliday (A1 Stark), Gregg Berger (John Fitch), Tuck Milligan (Deputy Billy LaPantier), Scott Paulin (Robert Malfi), Ruth Drago (Felice Winter), John Randolph (Hank Bashaw), Steve Franken (Agent Henley), Bruce Fischer (Axel Soames), Stanley Kamel (Phillip Tabbet), Bill Morey (Charles Tab- bet), Mark Schubb (Tim Hillman).

1989. Welcome to Paradise. 60 min. Airdate: 6/12/84. Production Company: Comworld Productions. Director: Dan Haller. Executive Producer: Stirling Silliphant. Producer: Joel Rogosin. Writer: Stirling Silliphant. Creator: Stirling Silliphant. Music: Mike Post and Pete Carpenter. A sea-faring *Route 66* by Stirling Silliphant, the man behind that classic series. The adventures of three

Americans—a divorcee (Kelbe Nugent) who dropped out of Stanford Medical School, an oceanography school graduate (Woody Brown) yearning to get out on the water, and an ex-con (Jerry Dinome) who learned deep-sea diving in a rehab program—who pooled together their money, bought a ketch, and hit the open seas. The pilot was shot on location in New Zealand. *Cast:* Woody Brown (as Andy Coles), Kelbe Nugent (Felicity Ryan), Jerry Dinome (Bo Wallace), Norman Forsey (Henderson), Carmen Heta (Hunemoa), Wi Kuki Kaa (Kahukura), James Cross (Koro), Jim Hickey (Skipper), Bill Johnson (Official), Bruno Lawrence (Tony Blackwood), Tim Lee (Billy Kemp).

NBC / COMEDY

1990. All Together Now. 30 min. Airdate: 6/30/84. Production Company: Embassy Television. Director: Will MacKenzie. Executive Producers: Stuart Wolpert and Deidre Faye. Producers: Patricia Fass-Palmer and Kimberly Hall. Writers: Stuart Wolpert and Deidre Faye. Still another flop pilot about a couple (Peter Michael Goetz and Barbara Barrie) about to retire when their children (Joan Cusak and Tom Byrd) come back to roost. The twist here is that Grandpa (Don Porter) and their son's gay lover (Robert T. Prescott) are moving in, too. *Cast:* Peter Michael Goetz (as Walt Parker), Barbara Barrie (Ellie Parker), Joan Cusack (Linda Parker), Tom Byrd (Kip Parker), Don Porter (Grandpa Ed), Betty Kean (Viola), Robert T. Prescott (Tony Kunkle).

1991. The Center. 30 min. Airdate: 4/19/84. Production Company: Alan Landsburg Productions. Director: John Bowab. Executive Producer: Mort Lachman. Producer: Jeff Franklin. Writer: Jeff Franklin. Aired as an episode of *Gimme a Break.* The story of what happens when an inner-city's community center, a quiet, long-time haven for the local elderly, opens its doors to kids when the nearby youth center burns down. The older characters include a four-time widow looking for a husband (Gwen Verdon) and a retired songwriter (Whitman Mayo), while the teenagers include an aspiring singer (Donna Wilkes) and a tough gang member (Israel Juarbe). *Cast:* Gwen Verdon (as Lilly), Angelina Estrada (Rosa), Ray Walston (Andy), Whitman Mayo (Poppa Jack), Donna Wilkes (Gina), Israel Juarbe (Humberto), Joey Green (Russell), Ola Ray (Deanna).

1992. Crazy Dan Gatlin. 60 min. Airdate: 7/19/86. Production Companies: Glen Larson Productions and 20th Century Fox Television. Director: Stuart Margolin.

Executive Producer: Glen Larson. Producers: Kim Weiskopf and Michael S. Baser. Writers: Michael S. Baser, Kim Weiskopf, and Glen Larson. Music: Peter Myers. A *Dirty Harry* spoof. John Beck stars as Crazy Dan Gatlin, a single-minded cop—with a tendency towards extreme actions—who is teamed with a female officer (Mary Crosby) assigned by his irked Captain (John Hancock) to make sure he goes "by the book." The *Hollywood Reporter* called the pilot "over- campy" and "listless," while *Variety* praised a "stand-out performance by John Beck." The concept bares a striking resemblance to the subsequent, 1986 ABC sitcom *Sledge Hammer*. *Cast:* John Beck (as Crazy Dan Gatlin), Mary Crosby (Bonnie Raines), Lloyd Bochner (Capt. Ritter), also, John Quade, John Hancock, Shannon Tweed, Robert Hogan, Stuart Margolin, Pat Carroll, Steven Keats, Michael Macrae, Terry Kiser, Vincent Schiavelli, John P. Finnegan, Sid Haig, Debra Pauer, David H. Banks, Ted Gehring, Ed Hooks, Ron Jarvis, William Kerr, Dave Morick, Susie Scott, Myra Turley, Lisa Welch.

1993. Help! (aka At Your Service). 30 min. Airdate: 8/1/84. Production Company: Paramount Television. Director: James Burrows. Executive Producer: Gary Nardino. Producers: David Lloyd and Rich Correll. Writer: David Lloyd. Music: Gary Portnoy and Judy Hart Angelo. The slapstick antics of the staff at a lavish country estate who, at every opportunity, try to exploit their frequently traveling employer's (Barbara Rush) riches—but that means out-smarting the snobbish butler (Josef Maher) and her social secretary (Megan Gallagher). This later served as the basis for the flop 1987, first-run sitcom *Marblehead Manor*, which ran on the NBC owned-and-operated stations. Michael Richards reprised his role as the gardener in the series. *Cast:* Barbara Rush (as Barbara Stonehill), Derek McGrath (Jerry Bianco), Megan Gallagher (Audrey Ritter), Garrett Morris (Dwayne), Joseph Maher (Albert Vogel), Maria Duvall (Theresa), Susan Kellerman (Susan Ottinger), Michael Richards (Rick), Antonio Torres (Jorge), Paul Fielding (Mr. Anderson), Ellen Crawford (Mrs. Anderson).

1994. High School USA. 2 hours. Airdate: 10/16/83. Production Company: Hill/ Mandelker Productions. Director: Rod Amateau. Executive Producers: Leonard Hill and Phil Mandelker. Producers: Alan Eisenstock, Larry Mintz, Robin Clark, and Wolfgang Glattes. Writers: Alan Eisenstock and Larry Mintz. Music: Mike Goodman and Tony Berg. The rivalry between two high school crowds—a fun-loving group led by irreverent J.J. Manners (Michael J. Fox), and the studious children of the town's elite, led by Beau Middleton (Anthony Edwards). First of two pilots banking on the novelty of featuring stars of old, classic sitcoms in key roles. *Cast:* Michael J. Fox (as J.J. Manners), Nancy McKeon (Beth Franklin), Todd Bridges (Otto Lipton), Angela Cartwright (Miss D'Angelo), Bob Denver (Milton Feld), Dwayne Hickman (Mr. Plaza), Lauri Hendler (Nadine), Dana Plato (Cara Ames), Crystal Bernard (Anne Marie Conklin), Anthony Edwards (Beau Middleton), Frank Bank (Mr. Gerardi), Elinor Donahue (Mrs. Franklin), Tony Dow (Pete Kinney), Steve Franken (Dr. Fritz Hauptmann), David Nelson (Mr. Krinsky), Ken Osmond (Baxter Franklin), Dawn Wells (Miss Lorilee Lee), Barry Livingston (Mr. Sirota), Tom Villard (Crazy Leo Bandini), Crispin Glover (Archie Feld), Michael Zorek (Chuck Dipple), Jon Caliri (Jerry), David Packer (Danny), Cathy Silvers (Peggy), Jonathan Gries (Dirty Curt), Kelly Ann Conn (Swoozie), Robin Evans (Girl), Kaley Ward (Chris), Jerry Maren (Otto's Robot), Danny Williams (Clem Pickens).

1995. **[Pilot #2] High School USA.** 60 min. Airdate: 5/26/84. Production Company: Hill/Mandelker Productions. Director: Jack Bender. Executive Producers: Leonard Hill and Phil Mandelker. Producers: Alan Eisenstock, Larry Mintz, and Dori Weiss. Writer: Pat Proft. Music: Brad Fiedel. The second pilot had the same premise, but was marked by many cast changes, with Michael Zorek, Crystal Bernard, and Crispin Glover among the few reprising their roles; Rick Nelson replaces Tony Dow as the principal, Tegan West assumes Anthony Edwards' role as Beau Middleton, and Ben Marley, Anne-Marie Johnson, and Jonathan Gries step in for Michael J. Fox, Nancy McKeon, and Tom Villard, who were busy in NBC series of their own. *Cast:* Rick Nelson (as Pete Kinney), Ben Marley (J.J. Manners), Henry Gibson (Roman Ing), Tegan West (Beau Middleton), Harriet Nelson (Mrs. Crosley), Melody Anderson (Cindy Franklin), Jerry Mathers (Mr. Sirota), Ken Osmond (Biology Teacher), Burt Ward (Teacher), Paul Peterson (Coach), Dick York (Superintendent McCarthy), Barbara Billingsley (Mrs. McCarthy), Michael Zorek (Chuckie), Crystal Bernard (Anne Marie Conklin), Jonathan Gries (Leo Bandini), Crispin Glover (Archie Feld), Anne-Marie Johnson (Beth Franklin), Joann Willett (Nadene), Julie Newmar (Stripper).

1996. **I Gave at the Office.** 30 min. Production Companies: Ten-Four Productions and NBC Productions. Airdate: 8/15/84. Director: Tom Patchett. Executive Producer: Sam Strangis. Producer: Larry Konner. Writers: Danny Jacobson and Barry Vignon. The misadventures of a new employee (Matt DeGanon) at a small, close-knit, advertising agency in Detroit, who falls in love with the receptionist (Kathleen York), who is in love with someone else. Michael Lerner is his boss. *Cast:* Michael Lerner (as Larry Brinker), Matt DeGanon (Michael Boatwright), Kathleen York (K.C. Conklin), Candy Clark (Julie), Janet Carroll (Janet Holloway), Max Wright (Jimbo), Jill Jacobson (Yvonne), George Soloman (Sal), Zelda Rubinstein (Scruffy).

1997. **Mr. Success.** 30 min. Airdate: 6/23/84. Production Company: Viacom Enterprises. Director: Jack Shea. Executive Producers: Howard Gewirtz and Ian Praiser. Producer: Don Van Atta. Writers: Howard Gewirtz and Ian Praiser. This concept, about a lovable shlump who works in a department store and is constantly beset by problems, was tailored for Nick Apollo Forte, who was subsequently replaced by James Coco. *Cast:* James Coco (as Vernon Stilt), Miriam Flynn (Helen Stilt), Viveka Davis (Libby Stilt), Pat Cochran (Andy Stilt), Murphy Dunne (Lonnie Barst), Patsy Pease (Louie), Ivana Moore (Marie), Jake Steinfeld (Officer Winston Simon), Samantha Lewis (Customer), Jennifer Savidge (Lara).

1998. **Not in Front of the Kids.** 30 min. Airdate: 6/16/84. Production Company: Alan Landsburg Productions. Director: Bill Persky. Executive Producers: Mort Lachman and Sy Rosen. Producer: Michael Mount. Writers: Mort Lachman and Sy Rosen. Music: David Garfield. Don Ameche and Katherine Helmond are enjoying their retirement in a small town when they suddenly find themselves caring for their two irrepressible teenage grandchildren (Amanda Herman and Jayson Naylor) when their divorced daughter in the city needs "space" to get her life together.

1999. **P.O.P.** 30 min. Airdate: 8/29/84. Production Company: Embassy Television. Director: James Burrows. Executive Producer: Norman Lear. Producer: Rick Mitz. Writers: Rick Mitz, Jack Elinson, and Norman Lear. Charles Durning stars as P. Oliver Pendergast, a lovable rogue who shows up at home 20 years after deserting his wife (Beatrice Arthur) and two sons (Jim Lashley and Todd Graff) and forces his way back into their lives—but they want nothing to do with him. His wife long-since divorced him, and his sons are the beleaguered publishers of a struggling national magazine that depends on the good graces of their financial backer—so Pendergast ingratiates himself to the wealthy man and gets himself hired on staff. *Cast:* Charles Durning (as P. Oliver Pendergast), Beatrice Arthur (Rosalyn), Todd Graff (Johnny), Jim Lashley (Russell), Fran Drescher (Maggie), Jane Anderson (Dana), Antonio Fargas (Frank), Anthony Holland (Marc), Bert Rosario (George),

Anne Henry (Lily), Beeson Carroll (John Ellsworth), Barrie Ingram (Sir Roger Blakely), Gloria Hayes (Flight Attendant), Bobby Remsen (Salesman).

2000. **Temporary Insanity.** 30 min. Production Company: Paramount Television. Director: Harry Winer. Executive Producers: Chris Thompson and Ed Milkis. Writer: Chris Thompson. Cindy Morgan and David Naughton are a married couple who run an employment agency for the under-privileged. Reni Santoni and Keone Young are the Latino and Chinese-American van drivers who ferry the people the couple find work for to their new jobs.

2001. **T.L.C.** 30 min. Airdate: 8/8/84. Production Company: Embassy Television. Director: Will MacKenzie. Executive Producers: Dick Bensfield and Perry Grant. Producer: Bruce Taylor. Writers: Bob Meyer, Bob Young, and Bruce Taylor. The misadventures of the first two male students (Jonathan Schmock and James Vallely) at a formerly all-girls nursing school. One of them is there with serious career intentions, the other has a photographic memory and is just after fun and girls. They are kept under close watch by the tough Dean (Jessica Walter). *Cast:* Jonathan Schmock (as Danny Martin), James Vallely (Pete Hamlin), Jessica Walter (Dean Craigmont), Cathy Silvers (Liz Hunter), Stacey Nelkin (Debbie Fisher), Rosalind Ingledew (Claudia), Mary Garripoli (Judy), Jere Fields (Beth), Judy Walton (Rhonda), Wendy Levin (Kitty), Rex Ryon (Perry).

NBC / DRAMA

2002. **All That Glitters.** 60 min. Airdate: 4/8/84. Production Companies: Universal Television and Glen Larson Productions. Director: Winrich Kolbe. Executive Producers: Glen Larson and Robert Foster. Producers: Robert Gilmer, Gian Grimaldi, and Tom Greene. Writers: Robert Foster and Robert Gilmer. Aired as an episode of *Knight Rider.* The adventures of a suave undercover agent (Charles Taylor) teamed with a rich socialite (Joanna Pettet) to ferret out crimes among the international jet-set. George Murdock is their boss. *Cast:* Charles Taylor (as David Drew Brighton), Joanna Pettet (Joanna St. John), George Murdock (Archibald Hendley), David Hasselhoff (Michael Knight), William Daniels (KITT), Robert Colbert (Elton Matthews), Patty Kotero (Tiara), Pedro Armendariz, Jr. (Eduardo O'Brien), Emily Banks (Priscilla Ragsdale), Robert Clarke (John Ragsdale), Chuck Lindsly (Stewart), Louis Contreras (Coyote), Areil Blanton (Frank), Tom Gilleron (Arthur Abraham), Todd Martin (Elmo Elliott).

2003. Dreamers (aka Heartbeat). 60 min. Airdate: 8/14/85. Production Company: Lorimar Productions. Director: Michael Lindsey-Hogg. Executive Producers: David Jacobs, Gary Adelson, and Karen Mack. Writer: Dalene Young. Two dancers from Kansas City (Karen Kopins and Whitney Kershaw) go to New York to find fame and fortune. They live in a loft on the New Jersey waterfront, where they meet Carla (Christine Langer), an 18-year-old break-dancer who disguises herself as a man to get work on the docks to support herself until her "big break." *Cast:* Karen Kopins (as Erin), Whitney Kershaw (Monica), Christine Langner (Carla), Michael Sabatino (Kevin), Stephen Shellen (Nick).

2004. Eagle of Encino. Production Company: Universal Television. Executive Producer: James Parriott. Writer: James Parriott. The adventures of a disenchanted NASA scientist who retreats to a suburban, southern California neighborhood and dabbles with strange inventions. The local kids fall in love with him, and soon he crawls out of his shell again. He tackles both government missions and problems for his new-found friends. A 20-minute demonstration film was planned.

2005. The Ferret. Production Company: Centerpoint Productions. Director: Terry Marcel. Executive Producer: Blake Edwards. Writer: Blake Edwards. Creator: Blake Edwards. Steve Guttenberg is Sam Valenti, a professional musician and amateur inventor whom discovers his father (Robert Loggia), whom he believed was dead, is actually alive—and is the legendary, anti-terrorist agent known as The Ferret. He has reappeared because he is getting tired, and wants to train his son to replace him. A demonstration film was shot.

2006. Four Eyes. 60 min. Airdate: 3/6/84. Production Company: Stephen J. Cannell Productions. Director: Bruce Kessler. Executive Producers: Stephen J. Cannell and Frank Lupo. Producer: Babs Greyhosky. Writer: Babs Greyhosky. Music: Mike Post and Pete Carpenter. Aired as an episode of *Riptide*. Stepfanie Kramer and Didi Howard are two southern California private eyes—one an expert in detection methods and technology, the other a firearms expert. Originally developed by writer James Parriott. *Cast:* Stepfanie Kramer (as Tracy), Didi Howard (Jane), Perry King (Cody Allen), Joe Penny (Nick Ryder), Thom Bray (Murray Bozinsky), Jack Ging (Lt. Ted Quinlan), Joan Freeman (Joan Ramsdale), Michael Baselson (Roger Ramsdale), Mary Beth Evans (Ellie), Danny Wells (Myron Bell), Craig Littler (Waters), Margo Kelly (Hostess).

2007. Happy Endings. 2 hours. Airdate: 12/26/83. Production Companies: Blinn/Thorpe Productions and NBC Productions. Director: Jerry Thorpe.

Executive Producers: William Blinn and Jerry Thorpe. Producers: Chris Beaumont and Harvey Frand. Writer: Chris Beaumont. Creator: Chris Beaumont. Music: J.A.C. Redford. From the producers of TV's *Fame*. Lee H. Montgomery is a would-be songwriter who's granted custody of his three younger siblings (Jill Schoelen, Sarah Navin, and Robbie Kiger) when his parents die. Oliver Clark costars as Murray, a struggling writer and close friend of the parents who helps out and Robin Gammell is Uncle John, who disapproves of the arrangement and keeps a watchful eye on them. *Cast:* Lee H. Montgomery (as Jimmy Bartlett), Jill Schoelen (Anne Marie Bartlett), Sarah Navin (Suzanna Bartlett), Robbie Kiger (Bobby Bartlett), Robin Gammell (Uncle John), Oliver Clark (Murray), Joey Gian (Mario), Carol Rossen (Aunt Deborah), Carol Mayo Jenkins (Jan Wilkerson), John Hancock (Judge Randolph), Warren Munson (Lawyer), Laura Dern (Audrey).

2008. Hard Knox. 2 hours. Airdate: 1/13/84. Production Company: A. Shane Productions. Director: Peter Werner. Executive Producer: Joan Conrad. Writer: David Kinghorn, from a story by David Kinghorn and Robert Conrad. Music: Mike Post and Pete Carpenter. Robert Conrad is Joe Knox, a hard-nosed, ex-Marine who takes over a struggling, coed military academy where he was once a student. Red West costars as the athletic supervisor, and Joan Sweeney is the liberal-minded, academic supervisor with whom Knox is frequently at odds. *Cast:* Robert Conrad (as Col. Joe Knox), Red West (Master Sergeant Red Tuttle), Joan Sweeney (Marilyn Cole), Bill Erwin (General Garfield), Dean Hill (Major Benjamin Garfield), Stephen Caffey (Cadet Captain Gary Pascoe), Ricki Pauli Goldin (Cadet Lt. Jeff Bridley), Dianne Shaw (Lela Stallings), Shane Conrad (Erik Shaner), Alan Ruck (Frankie Tyrone), Kathleen Sisk (Jessi Richards), David Saunders (Bobby Sayers), Casey Siemaszko (Aaron Davis), Michael Baselson (General Green), Alex Sterling (Kami), Christian Conrad (Major Whitehouse), John West (Cory Beasley), Frank Howard (David Ambrose).

2009. No Man's Land. 2 hours. Airdate: 5/27/84. Production Companies: Jadda Productions and Warner Bros. Television. Director: Rod Holcomb. Executive Producer: Juanita Bartlett. Producer: Michael J. Maschio. Writer: Juanita Bartlett. Creator: Juanita Bartlett. Music: Mike Post and Pete Carpenter. Stella Stevens is a showgirl-turned-sheriff of a wild frontier town in the old West, who keeps justice with the help of her three daughters—each of whom (a la *Bonanza*) had a different father. Brianne (Terri Garber) is a gambler, Sara (Donna Dixon) is a magician, and Missy (Melissa Michaelson) is an expert cowhand. Other regulars include the town blacksmith (Sam Jones) and the powerful local rancher (Robert Webber) who is the sheriffs secret lover. Bartlett and Maschio later produced Warner Bros. *Spenser: For Hire.* Cast: Stella Stevens (as Nellie Wilder), Terri Garber (Brianne Wilder), Donna Dixon (Sara Wilder), Melissa Michaelson (Missy Wilder), Robert Webber (Will Blackfield), Sam Jones (Eli Howe), Estelle Getty (Euroi Muller), Frank Bonner (Deputy Thad Prouty), John Rhys-Davies (John Grimshaw), Dack Rambo (Pat Connell), Ralph Michael (Doc Havilland), Janis Paige (Maggie Hodiak), John Quade (Henry Lambert), Bryan McGuire (Dandy Wallace), Wil Albert (Wilmot), Tony Swartz (Monroe), Marc Alaimo (Clay Allison), Jack Garner (Simon Claypool), Eldon Quick (Everett Vanders), Roz Witt (Harriet Claypool), Billy Streeter (Holden), Jeremy Ross (Pratt), Buck Taylor (Feeny).

2010. **The Streets (aka Street Heat).** 60 min. Airdate: 9/2/84. Production Company: Lorimar Productions. Director: Gary Sherman. Executive Producers: Lawrence Gordon, Charles Gordon, and Stuart Sheslow. Producer: Jay Benson. Writer: Gary Sherman. The adventures of a cop (Michael Beck) working undercover as a Manhattan cab driver, a street hustler in a souped-up sedan. He gets his assignments from Lt. Grosso (Jerry Orbach), fields passes from his next-door neighbor (Nancy Grigor), and befriends a ten-year-old street kid (Leo O'Brien). *Cast:* Michael Beck (as Roger Wreade), Jerry Orbach (Lt. Max Grosso), Nancy Grigor (Marsha), Leo O'Brien (Willie), Val Avery (Whitcomb), Dana Delany (Jean- nie), Jerry Strivelli (Morrison).

1985–1986

ABC / COMEDY

2011. **Emily.** 30 min. Production Companies: Guber/Peters and Centerpoint Productions. Director: Paul Bogart. Executive Producers: Jon Peters and Peter Guber. Producer: Paul Bogart. An unsuccessful attempt at crafting a sitcom for Ellen Burstyn, whose subsequent ABC sitcom *The Ellen Burstyn Show* in 1986 would be one of the first—and biggest—bombs of the season. Burstyn is an Erma Bombeck-type columnist who, when her son dies, takes in her college student daughter-in-law and her two grandchildren.

2012. **The Faculty.** 30 min. Airdate: 6/20/86. Production Company: You & Me, Kid Productions. Director: Jay Tarses. Executive Producer: Bernie Brillstein. Producer: Gayle S. Maffeo. Writer: Jay Tarses. Creator: Jay Tarses. Music: Patrick Williams. The daily lives of a principal and six teachers at an inner-city school. There was no regular cast of students and most of the story took place in the teacher's lounge—and characters often talked directly into the camera. This unusual pilot, based on the documentary *Save Our Schools, Save Our Children*, elicited strong—and varied—reaction from critics. The *Los Angeles Times* found it a "dark comedy" that was an "enormously intriguing, distinctly unsettling half-hour" while *Variety* felt it "flunked in the laugh department." Even ABC's then-Entertainment President Lewis Erlicht thought it was strange, commenting to *TV Guide* that it's a pilot the network "wouldn't have ordered three years ago." Future episodes would have dealt with competency tests for teachers, faculty romances, teachers on drugs, and racism. The pilot sat on the shelf for over a year before airing. Star Blair Brown would later star in NBC's *The Days and Nights of Molly Dodd* for the same production team. *Cast:* Max Wright (as Principal Leon Pakulski), Blair Brown (Valerie Arnold), Richard McKenzie (George Dent), Allyn Ann McLerie (Edna McCauley), Richard Lawson (Dr. Juluis Pepper), Jason Bernard (Finney Morgan), Albert Macklin (Jonathan Covington).

2013. **Full House.** 30 min. Production Company: Embassy Television. Director: John Bowab. Executive Producers: Blake Hunter and Marty Cohan. Writers: Blake Hunter and Marty Cohan. An extended black family tries to live together under one roof in Chicago. An out-going widow (Della Reese) has to contend with her son (Ernie Hudson), his wife (Beverly Todd), their children, (Akili Prince and Jamila Perry) and her daughter-in-law's widowed father (Paul Winfield), who lost his farm in the South and has come to Chicago to start again. This busted pilot was, itself, trying to start again. This is a recast version of an earlier pilot, from which only Winfield was retained. Lee Chamberlin originally played the widow, William Allen Young was her son, and Lisa Wilkinson was her daughter-in-law. Martin Davis and Ebonie Smith were the grandchildren. *Cast:* Paul Winfield (as Henry Owens), Della Reese (Lucille Grant), Ernie Hudson (Noah Grant), Beverly Todd (Denise Grant), Akili Prince (Jeff Grant), Ebonie Smith (Camille Grant; aka Olivia Grant).

2014. **Goodbye Charlie.** 30 min. Airdate: 6/4/85. Production Company: 20th Century Fox. Director: Charlotte Brown. Executive Producer: Pat Nardo. Writer: Pat Nardo, from the play by George Axelrod and the motion picture screenplay by Harry Kurnitz. Music: Charles Fox. Lyrics: Al Kasha and Joel Hirschorn. Based on the 1964 movie starring Debbie Reynolds and Tony Curtis. In the play and movie, a womanizing mobster named Charlie, killed by a jealous husband, returns to earth as a woman (Reynolds). In the sitcom, a womanizing advertising executive falls to his death—and comes back as Suzanne Somers, a fate worse than death. The reincarnated Charlie...now Charlene...goes to work as the secretary for the guy (Ray Buktenica) who replaced him. But She's still very much He, and best friend John Davidson is the only one who knows the truth. *Cast:* Suzanne Somers (as Charlie/Charlene), John Davidson (George), Ray Buktenica (Ray), Kathleen Wilhoite (Victoria).

2015. **Harry and the Kids.** 30 min. Airdate: 7/5/85. Aired as an episode of *Comedy Factory.* Max Gail is a carefree bachelor who has to raise his brother's two kids. *Cast:* Max Gail (as Harry), Patricia Idette (Mavis), Derek McGrath (Otis).

2016. **Hearts of Steel.** 30 min. Airdate: 6/13/86. Production Companies: Witt-Thomas Productions and Sheldon Bull Productions. Directors: Barry Kemp and Gary Shimokawa. Executive Producers: Tony Thomas and Paul Junger Witt. Writer: Sheldon Bull. Annie Potts runs a Pittsburgh bar where unemployed steel workers hang out. When she decides to turn it into a plush restaurant, the steel workers become her partners. Matt Craven is a steel worker, Tracy Nelson is a teenage chef. *Cast:* Annie Potts (as Annie), Gregory Salata (Tom), Harold Sylvester (Granville), Matt Craven (Eddie), Tracy Nelson (Michelle), Kevin

Scannell (Jake), also, Richard Stahl, Jamil Howell, Jerry Potter, Gary Clarke, and Marina Ferrier.

2017. Joanna. 30 min. Airdate: 4/30/85. Production Companies: Antonacci/ Nardino/ Silver Productions and Paramount Television. Director: Greg Antonacci. Executive Producers: Gary Nardino, Greg Antonacci, and Stu Silver. Writers: Greg Antonacci and Stu Silver. Cindy Williams is a Pasadena girl who moves to New York with her lover—and then gets dumped. She's intent on making it anyway, and hurriedly accepts the first job to come her way: dispatcher for a trucking company based on the Brooklyn docks. Lou Jacobi is the seasoned dock hand who helps her; Ron Karabatsos is the dock supervisor; and Julie Payne is a lady forklift driver. And, of course, there's her male chum (and possible romantic entanglement) who lives next door (Reni Santoni). *Cast:* Cindy Williams (as Joanna Weston), Reni Santoni (Michael Braxton), Lou Jacobi (Harold Rosenthal), Ron Karabatsos (Robert Q. Valentine), John Del Regno (Paulie), Danny Mora (Petey Flowers), Larry Hankin (Little Joe), Larry Joshua (Dean Yount), Julie Payne ("Schultzy's Wife").

2018. Max and Me. 30 min. Airdate: 7/12/85. Directors: Peter Moss, Ari Dikijian. Producer: Al Rogers. Writer: Sam Bobrick. Aired as an episode of *Comedy Factory*. Pat Harrington and Dawn Greenhalgh are a couple who move from the suburbs to Manhattan to add some excitement to their lives. *Cast:* Pat Harrington (Max Brennan), Dawn Greenhalgh (Anne Brennan), Mary Long (Susan), Brian George (Ogden Dust), Derek McGrath (Leo Winter)

2019. Moscow Bureau. 30 min. Airdate: 6/6/86. Production Companies: Witt/ Thomas Productions and Paramount Television. Director: John Rich. Executive Producers: Paul Junger Witt and Tony Thomas. Producer: Susan Palladino. Writer: David Lloyd. Music: George Aliceson Tipton. A much-maligned attempt to recapture the charm of *The Mary Tyler Moore Show,* by examining the life of a woman reporter (Caroline McWilliams) in a wire service newsroom, and of *M*A *S*H* by putting the newsroom in Moscow. The *Hollywood Reporter* lamented that "nyet-thing happens," *Variety* dubbed it "a lame entry," and *USA Today* observed "a dumb Russian joke can only go so far." William Windom is the Lou Grant and Nancy Lane is the Rhoda, a television reporter. Dennis Drake is a reporter in love with McWilliams, and Elya Baskin is the translator. *Cast:* Caroline McWilliams (as Christine Nichols), William Windom (Herb Medlock), Dennis Drake (Tim Carmichael), Nancy Lane (Connie Uecker), Barrie Ingham (Rene Werner), Elya Baskin (Sasha Zhukov).

2020. Sam. 30 min. Airdate: 6/11/85. Production Companies: Allan Katz Productions and 20th Century Fox. Director: Alan Rafkin. Executive Producer: Allan Katz. Writer: Allan Katz. Creator: Erica Jong. Based on a novel by Erica Jong. Loretta Swit is Samantha, a divorcee raising her nine-year-old daughter (Keri Houlihan) and working as an editor at a publishing house, where she works for Barney Martin. *Cast:* Loretta Swit (as Samantha Flynn), Keri Houlihan (Megan Flynn), Barney Martin (George Kosovich), Stephen J. Godwin (Barry Zuckerman), Kit McDonough (Valerie Witzel), Cathy Silvers (Sharon Sticker).

ABC / DRAMA

2021. Arthur Hailey's Airport (aka International Airport). 2 hours. Airdate: 6/25/85. Production Company: Aaron Spelling Productions. Directors: Don Chaffey and Charles Dubin. Executive Producers: Aaron Spelling and Douglas Cramer. Producers: E. Duke Vincent and Robert McCullough. Writer: Robert McCullough. Music: Mark Snow. Loosely inspired by the Arthur Hailey book and subsequent movies. The proposed series would be an anthology of sorts revolving around Gil Gerard, the manager of the busy airport where thousands of people—and presumably thousands of stories—come through everyday. The real stars, like in Spelling's *Arthur Hailey's Hotel* series, would be the big-name guest stars. In the pilot, Gerard must contend with an airplane disaster and patch up a friend's crumbling marriage, among other things. Gerard's then-wife Connie Sellecca, a regular on *Hotel*, guest starred. *Cast:* Gil Gerard (as David Benedict), Belinda Tolbert (Kathy Heatheron), Cliff Potts (Jack Marshall), Pat Crowley (Beverly), Kitty Moffat (Marjorie Lucas), Danny Ponce (Pepe), Robert Vaughn (Captain Powell), Bill Bixby (Flight Controller Harvey Jameson), George Kennedy (Rudy Van Leuven), Vera Miles (Elaine Corley), George Grizzard (Martin Harris), Susan Blakely (Joanne Roberts), Susan Oliver (Mary Van Leuven), Robert Reed (Carl Roberts), Connie Sellecca (Dana Fredericks), Robin Greer (Susan Shephard), Don Knight (Jarvis), Jason Wingreen (Mr. Dornan), Fred Sadoff (Jones), Steven Williams (Frazier), Kurtwood Smith (Gilbert), Don Eitner (Morgan), Paul Tuerpe (Officer Munton), Susan McCullough (Jill), Mary Ellen Dunbar (Julie), Baynia White (Sheila), Diane Ander (Smith), Martin Speer (Holtman), Chris Kriesa (Lambert), David Dangler (Ferguson).

2022. Braker. 90 min. Airdate: 4/28/85. Production Companies: Blatt-Singer Productions and MGM/UA Television. Director: Victor Lobi. Executive Producers: Daniel H. Blatt and Robert Singer. Producer: Joe Stern. Writers: Eric Bercovici and James Carabatsos. Carl Weathers is Harry Braker, the only black lieutenant on the force. An ex-Marine, he sometimes bends the rules in his pursuit of justice. He performs this duty with three other detectives—a guy who stalks criminals like a hunter (Randall "Tex" Cobb), an easy-going neophyte (Joseph Bottoms), and a passionate woman (Anne Schedeen). Although the network passed on this, they did greenlight Weathers in *Fortune Dane*, a midseason failure. *Cast:* Carl Weathers (as Lt. Harry Braker), Joseph Bottoms (Eddie Kelso), Randall "Tex" Cobb (Packard), Anne Schedeen (Polly Peters), Peter Michael Goetz (Capt. Joyce), Dann Florek (Hayes), Tracy Ross (Janice), Shanna Reed (Dede Drummond), Ed O'Neill (Danny Buckner), Kristoffer Tabori (Bruce Wines), Ian McShane (Alan Roswell), Eugenie Ross-Leming (Belsky), Gwen Humble (Kate Taylor), Robert Pastorelli (Tyler), E.J. Castillo (Forensics), Maurice Sneed (Booker), Pamela Matteson (Bernice), Becca C. Ashley (Hostage), Richard Burns (Medic), Dick Durock (Troy), Allan Graf (Jason), Cindi Eyman (Girl).

2023. Brothers-in-Law. 90 min. Airdate: 4/28/85. Production Company: Stephen J. Cannell Productions. Director: E.W. Swackhamer. Executive Producer: Stephen J. Cannell. Producer: Bill Phillips. Writer: Stephen J. Cannell. Creator: Stephen J. Cannell. Music: Mike Post and Pete Carpenter. The first flop pilot Cannell had since forming his own production company. Mac Davis and Joseph Cortese are, respectively, an ex-cop and an ex-trucker, who were once brothers-in-law married to a pair of beautiful twin sisters. Their marriages broke up, but the two guys didn't. They now operate a private eye-cum-salvage business that charges clients 10 percent of whatever the action is. *Cast:* Mac Davis (as T.K. Kenny), Joe Cortese (Mickey Gabiacci), Robert Culp (Winston Goodhue), John Saxon (Royal Cane), Daphne Ashbrook (Barbara Jean), Gerald S. O'Loughlin (Bud Oliver), John S. Ragin (Colton), Candi Brough (Deborah Goodhue), Randi Brough (Gail Goodhue), Dennis Burkley (Frank Lupo), Frank McCarthy (Chief Darcy), Randolph Powell (David DeLoria), Bill Morey (Judge William Greystone), Jack Riley (Freeman), Geno Silva (Alejandro), Dick Balduzzi (Bailiff), Lukas Haas (Luke), Beau Billingslea (Carter), Suzanne Fagan (Nurse), Don Maxwell (Doorman), John Petlock (Calvin), John Roselius (Sgt. Adamson), Bruce Tuthill (Floyd), Mark Voland (Deputy).

2024. Club Med. 2 hours. Airdate: 1/19/86. Production Company: Lorimar Productions. Director: Bob Giraldi. Executive Producer: Karen Mack. Producer: Ervin Zavada. Writers: Judith Paige Mitchell and Jeff Freilich, from a story by Judith Paige Mitchell. Music: Peter Bernstein. Jack Scalia is the manager of a Mexican resort in this would-be "Love Boat"-style anthology. In the pilot, his old fiancée (Linda Hamilton) comes to Club Med for a vacation—and is forced to tell him about a son he never knew he had. *Cast:* Jack Scalia (as O'Shea), Linda Hamilton (Kate), Timothy Williams (Danny), Traci Lin (Simone), Patrick MacNee (Gilbert), Janis Lee Burns (Jodie), Jeff Kaake (Bart), Traci Lin-Tavi (Simone La Fontanne), Bill Maher (Rick), Adam Mills (Gypsy), Sinbad (Himself), Timothy Williams (Danny).

2025. Dark Mansions. 2 hours. Airdate: 7/23/86. Production Company: Aaron Spelling Productions. Director: Jerry London. Executive Producers: Aaron Spelling and Douglas Cramer. Supervising Producer: E. Duke Vincent. Producers: Jerry London and Robert H. Justman. Writer: Robert McCullough. Music: Ken Harrison. Loretta Young was the original star of this proposed serial, set in San Francisco, but was later replaced by Joan Fontaine. Ms. Fontaine is Margaret Drake, matriarch of a family made rich by ship-building, a business now fought over by her two sons, Paul Shenar and Michael York, now that her husband (Dan O'Herlihy) is struck dead by lightning. But there are other problems—her secretary Linda Purl bears a haunting resemblance to her grandson Grant Aleksander's dead wife; her blind granddaughter Melissa Sue Anderson struggles to make it in the world; and her grandson Yves Martin lusts for his cousin Nicolette Sheridan. The family all live on the same block in side-by-side mansions, hence the title. *Cast:* Joan Fontaine (as Margaret Drake), Paul Shenar (Charles Drake), Michael York (Bryan Drake), Melissa Sue Anderson (Noelle), Linda Purl (Shellane), Yves Martin (Cody Drake), Grant Aleksander (Nicholas), Nicolette Sheridan (Banda), Lois Chiles (Jessica), Raymond St. Jacques (Meadows), Dan O'Herlihy (Alexander Drake), Brian Morrow (David Forbes), Steve Inwood (Mills), Vincent Pandoliano (Chef), Lee Corrigan (Capt. Hemmings).

2026. Embassy. 2 hours. Airdate: 4/21/85. Production Companies: Stan Margulies Company and ABC Circle Films. Director: Robert Lewis. Producer: Stan Margulies. Writer: John McGreevey. Music: Gerald Fried. Nick Mancuso is a diplomat at the U.S. Embassy in Rome who helps Americans in trouble and dabbles in espionage and diplomacy. Shot on location in Italy. *Cast:* Nick Mancuso (as Harry Brackett), Mimi Rogers (as Nancy Russell), Richard Masur (Dennis Thorne), Blanche Baker (Megan Hillyer), Richard Gilliland (Ted Davidson), Eli Wallach (Joe Verga), Kim Darby (Sue Davidson), Sam Wanamaker (Ambassador), Lee Curreri (Mike Forte), George Grizzard (Senator Tunnard), Elya Baskin (Alex Serov), Marino Mase (Inspector Casalli).

2027. **Fraud Squad.** 60 min. Production Company: Universal Television. Executive Producers: Jim Green, Allen Epstein, and Buddy Bregman. Producer: Joel Blasberg. Writer: Joel Blasberg. A revamped version of last season's flop, half-hour pilot.

2028. **Generation.** 2 hours. Airdate: 5/24/85. Production Company: Embassy Television. Director: Michael Tuchner. Executive Producer: Gerald DiPego. Producers: Bill Finnegan and Pat Finnegan. Writer: Gerald DiPego. The adventures of a typical American family, The Breeds, in the year 2000. Alan Breed (Richard Beymer) is an inventor for a large corporation, which frequently alters his creations for their own profit. His brother (Drake Hogestyn) is a gladiator in a national sport not unlike *Rollerball*. Alan's wife (Marta Dubois) is the host of a self-help television show. Hanna Kutrona is their daughter. Bert Remsen and Priscilla Pointer are the grandparents, who fight to retain the values of the 1900s. *Cast:* Richard Beymer (as Alan Breed), Marta Dubois (Kate Breed), Drake Hogestyn (Jack Breed), Cristina Raines (Roma Breed), Hannah Cutrona (Bel Breed), Bert Remsen (Tom Breed), Priscilla Pointer (Ellen Breed), Kim Miyori (Teri Tanaka), Reid Sheldon (Raymond Wilke), Lorene Tarnell (Pal), Scott Paulin (Graff), Harrison Page (George Link), Liz Sheridan (Clara), Michael Young (Rick Tolmer), Grand L. Bush (Catt), Nick Corri (Scrad), Beau Richards (Edna), Stephen Lee (Mark Stein), Leigh Lombardi (Ann), Michael Lemon (Henderson), Paige Price (Gila), Bill Erwin (John), Kevin Sifuentes (Gang Boy), Dean Dittman (Taxi Driver).

2029. **In Like Flynn.** 2 hours. Airdate: 9/14/85. Production Companies: Glen Larson Productions, Astral Film Enterprises, and 20th Century Fox Television. Director: Richard Lang. Executive Producer: Glen Larson. Producers: Richard Lang and Harker Wade. Writer: Glen Larson. Creator: Glen Larson. Music: Glen Larson and Stu Phillips. Jenny Seagrove is an editor for a large publishing company who oversees just one best-selling author—the famous, reclusive Daryl E. Raymond, creator of Jason Flynn, the rugged adventurer. She also doubles as his researcher. She's so devoted to him because, unknown to anyone, she *is* Raymond. Shot on location in Montreal. *Cast:* Jenny Seagrove (as Terri Malone), William Gray Espy (Beatty Woodstock), Eddie Albert (Bill White), William Conrad (Sgt. Dominic), Robert Webber (Col. Harper), Murray Cruchley (Fulton), Maury Chaykin (Williams), Chuck Shambata (Dawson), Laura Press (Stephanie Holden), Dennis Strong (Thurman), Barry Greene (Tugger), Page Fletcher (Tim Holden), Alan Jordan (Dover), Phillip Akin (Customs Officer), Lee Broker (Bunco), John Loxley (Sgt. Bunker), Louis Degin (Dr. Howe), Lawrence Dane (Gavin), Ian Deakin (Medical Examiner), Karl Binger (Taxi Driver), Barry Edward Blake (Beals), Jean Raymond Chales (Little Tourist), Harry Hill (Big Tourist), Cathy Levy (Stewardess).

2030. **J.O.E. and the Colonel (aka J.O.E. and Michael).** 2 hours. Airdate: 9/13/85. Production Companies: Mad Dog Productions and Universal Television. Director: Ron Satlof. Executive Producer: Nicholas Corea. Producer: Stephen P. Caldwell. Writer: Nicholas Corea. Creator: Nicholas Corea. Music: Joseph Conlan. The title changes reflect a change in concept. Originally, this was the 90-minute story of liberal, idealistic scientist Michael Moran (Terence Knox), whose genes are used by the government to create a "superhuman" soldier (Gary Kasper) named Joe that's designed to be the ultimate killer. Unfortunately, Joe won't just obey orders—he has to make up his own mind whether to kill or not. So, the government decides to destroy him. Michael fakes his demise, as well as Joe's, and they hit the road to help people in need. Now, in the two-hour version that aired, Michael is killed off and Joe is teamed up with a tough army man (William Lucking). This pilot was rechristened yet again, as *Humanoid Defender,* when it was released on video cassette in 1987. *Cast:* Gary Kasper (as J.O.E.), Terence Knox (Michael Moran), William Lucking (Col. Fleming), Gail Edwards (Dr. Lena Grant), Allan Miller (Lyle), Douglas Alan (Alpha), Christie Houser (Pam), Allan Rich (Pop Roth), Aimee Eccles (Miss Kai), William Riley (Travis), Michael Swan (Pike), Don Swayze (Max Carney), Douglas Alan Shanklin (Alpha), Robert Feero (Mueller), Bruce Corvi (Technician), Frankie Hill (Technician), John Davey (Wilson), Joe Borgese (Agent), Leigh Lombardi (Angelina).

2031. **Looking for Love.** 60 min. Production Company: Universal Television. Executive Producer: Stefanie Kowal. Producer: Renee Taylor. Writer: Renee Taylor. A proposed anthology comprised of different love stories.

2032. **Mr. & Mrs. Ryan.** 60 min. Airdate: 4/11/86. Production Company: Aaron Spelling Productions. Director: Peter H. Hunt. Executive Producers: Aaron

Spelling and Douglas S. Cramer. Supervising Producer: E. Duke Vincent. Producers: Tom Swale, Duane Poole, and Ralph Riskin. Writers: Bill and Jo LaMond. Music: John Davis. The misadventures of a rich Beverly Hills socialite (Sharon Stone) with a cop for a husband (Robert Desiderio). Joseph Mahler is their chauffeur, and if this sounds like *Hart to Hart,* keep in mind it was made by the same people for the same network. *Cast:* Sharon Stone (as Ashley Hamilton Ryan), Robert Desiderio (Lt. Michael Ryan), Joseph Mahler (Stockwell), also, Christine Belford, David Fox-Brenton, Jay Robinson, Nicholas Worth, Frederick Coffin, Walter Dalton, John H. Evans, Garry Goodrow, Frank Birney, Don Pugsley, Scott Lincoln, Victoria Tucker, Michael Misita.

2033. **Northstar.** 90 min. Airdate: 8/10/86. Production Companies: Phillips/ Grodnick Productions and Warner Bros. Television. Director: Peter Levin. Executive Producers: Clyde Phillips and Dan Grodnik. Producer: Howard Lakin. Writer: Howard Lakin. Music: Brad Fiedel. Originally titled *The Einstein Man,* this stars Greg Evigan as an astronaut who, while on a walk outside the spaceship, is zapped by a solar disturbance. When he gets back to earth, he has superhuman powers—and a superhuman mind—that's triggered by sunlight. But if he gets too much direct sunlight—without the protection of special sunglasses—he'll literally explode from overload. So, like his predecessor "The Six Million Dollar Man," he becomes a secret agent. Mitchell Ryan is his boss, Deborah Wakeman is the scientist who works with him. *Cast:* Greg Evigan (as Major Jack North), Deborah Wakeman (Dr. Allison Taylor), Mitchell Ryan (Col. Evan Marshall), Mason Adams (Dr. Karl Janss), David Hayward (Bill Harlow), Sonny Landham (Becker), Robin Curtiss (Jane Harlow), Richard Garrison (Agent), Steven Williams (Agent), Ken Foree (Astronaut).

2034. **[T.J. Hooker] The New T.J. Hooker.** 60 min. Airdate: 5/85. Production Companies: Spelling/Goldberg Productions and Columbia Pictures Television. Director: Michael Lange. Executive Producers: Aaron Spelling and Leonard Goldberg. Producers: Steve Kline, Bernie Kukoff, and Kenneth R. Koch. Writers: Steve Kline and Bernie Kukoff. Music: John E. Davis. Theme: Mark Snow. Aired as the last episode of *T.J. Hooker.* In a last-ditch effort to keep the series alive, the producers crafted this pilot for a proposed "revamped" version of the series. William Shatner's hard-nosed Sgt. T.J. Hooker, who drove a black-and-white for the fictional L.C.P.D., is loaned to the Chicago police force, put into plainclothes, and teamed up with a jive-talking, black undercover cop (Charlie Barnett). Although

ABC wasn't interested, *T.J. Hooker* did come back, in the original format, on CBS' late-night schedule. Another *T.J. Hooker* pilot *(Blood Sport)* was tried in 1986. *Cast:* William Shatner (as T.J. Hooker), Charlie Barnett (Sidney P. Stover), Lynne Moody (Nadine), Richard Briggs (Frawley), J.D. Hall (Bartender), John Mahon (Mr. Zewecki), Nicholas Mele (Freddie Lanier), Frank Wagner (Det. Fryberg), Brooks Gardner (Hogan), Leelan Demoz (Jimmy), Michael Stoyanov (Ray), Nick Kubenko (Detective #1), Ron Bean (Detective #2), Ernest Perry, Jr. (Man in Line), Ronald Carter (Kid), D.V. De Vincentis (Yooch), also, Jesse Wells, Bobby Remsen, Vic Polizos, and Brooke A. Jarchow.

2035. **Triplecross.** 2 hours. Airdate: 3/17/86. Production Companies: Tisch/Avnet Productions and ABC Circle Films. Director: David Greene. Executive Producers: Steve Tisch and Jon Avnet. Producers: Marty Katz and Dusty Kaye. Writer: Dusty Kaye. Elliot, Delia, and Cole were three cops until a rich man, grateful to them for saving his daughter, gave them stock in his company and made them millionaires. They quit, but they still love crime-solving. So they find unsolved crimes, and place bets with each other to see who can solve them first. Each episode a different one would solve the case—and win the big-money wager. *Cast:* Ted Wass (as Elliot Taffle), Markie Post (Delia Langtree), Gary Swanson (Cole Donovan), Shannon Wilcox (Rochelle Wingate), Robert Costanzo (Jack Avalon), Ric Mancini (Lt. Snead), Mike Genovese (Easier), Christopher McDonald (Steve Tyler), Donald Holton (Andrew Wingate), Barbara Horan (Vicki Janus), Mike Genovese (Mike Easier), Tony Longo (Tweetie Pie), Sandy Simpson (James Wingate), Steve Williams (Kyle Banks), Anthony Holland (Curator), Rex Ryan (Marty), John Sanderford (Lannie Novak), Jonathan Goldsmith (Martin Baker), Val Bettin (Winslow), Thomas Beilin (Judge Zowel), John Fujioka (Toshi), Mario Machado (TV Reporter), Nick DeMauro (Eddie Green), Tony O'Neil (Bobby Dee), Cindi Dietrich (Charmayne).

CBS / COMEDY

2036. **Love Long Distance.** 30 min. Airdate: 7/30/85. Production Company: Procter & Gamble Productions. Director: Burt Brinekerhoff. Executive Producer: Jerry Davis. Producer: Sherry Cohen. Writer: Sherry Cohen. Creator: Sherry Cohen. The lives of a married couple (Tricia Pursley and Harley Venton) with a problem: he's got a Philadelphia construction business, she's awarded a grant to conduct research at the Museum of Natural History in New York. They can only get together on weekends. Can they sustain their love, and their marriage? We'll never know. Shot in New York. *Cast:* Tricia Pursley (as Leslie Cummings), Harley Venton (David Cummings), Mike Starr (Stan Cummings), Austin Pendleton (Arthur Ruskin), Christine Rose (Christine).

2037. **No Place Like Home.** 30 min. Airdate: 9/6/85. Production Company: D. L. Taffner Productions. Director: Ellen Chaset Falcon. Executive Producer: D.L. Taffner. Producer: Jeff Harris. Writers: Brian Cooke and Johnnie Mortimer. Creators: Brian Cooke and Johnnie Mortimer. Based on the writers' British series, *Full House,* about two couples—one married (Susan Hess and Jack Blessing) and one that's not (Molly Cheek and Rick Lohman)—who share a house together.

2038. **The Recovery Room.** 30 min. Airdate: 7/16/85. Production Company: Embassy. Director: Peter Bonerz. Executive Producers: Steve Haft, John Lollos, and Bob Ellison. Producer: Rita Dillon. Writer: Neil Cuthbert. Imagine *Cheers,* except with doctors. The result would be *The Recovery Room,* a New York bar across the street from a bustling urban hospital. The bar is run by an ex-nurse (Kelly Bishop) and an ex-doctor who quit during his residency (Mark Linn-Baker). The regular characters are played by Christopher Rich, Adam LeFevre, J. Smith Cameron, Priscilla Lopez, Lynne Thigpen, Yeardley Smith, Charles Kimbrough, and Alvin Lum. Shot in New York.

2039. **Rockhopper.** 30 min. Airdate: 7/9/85. Production Company: Lorimar Productions. Director: Bill Bixby. Executive Producers: Jeff Freilich and Karen Mack. Producer: Jim Brecher. Writer: Jim Brecher. Music: Mark Snow. Nick Larabee (Parker Stevenson) tells everyone he is a bird-watcher for a non-profit organization. His mother (Janis Paige) and his brother (Robert Wuhl), who owns a swinging Manhattan single's bar, think he's wasting his life. He's actually a secret agent, codenamed "Rockhopper," who is trying not to fall in love with his arch enemy, beautiful KGB agent Sonya (Amy Yasbeck). In the pilot, he tries to find a defecting Soviet scientist before the KGB does. *Cast:* Parker Stevenson (as Nick Larabee), Robert Wuhl (Joel), Amy Yasbeck (Sonya), Oliver Clark (Carl), Pat Carroll (Mildred), Janis Paige (Mrs. Larabee), Jessica Nelson (Neighbor).

2040. **Royal Match.** 60 min. Airdate: 8/2/85. Production Companies: Mandy Films and MGM/UA Television. Director: E.W. Swackhamer. Executive Producer: Leonard Goldberg. Supervising Producer: A.J. Carothers. Producer: Michele Rappaport. Writer: Katherine Green. Music: Mark Snow. An American woman

(Haviland Morris), just out of college, travels across Europe and falls in love with a handsome young man (John Moulder Brown) in the tiny kingdom of Cresenda, only to discover he's the king. They get married, captivating the imagination of the country and aggravating the king's mother (Tammy Grimes), who will do anything to sabotage the marriage and return things to what they once were. Shot in the Biltmore Estates, Asheville, North Carolina. *Cast:* Haviland Morris (as Susan), John Moulder Brown (King Edmond), Tammy Grimes (Queen Mother Estelle), Clive Revill (Prime Minister Weyback), Jean Smart (Katerina), Leslie Ackerman (Becky), Ian Abercrombie (Duke Alford), Jim Piddock (Interpreter), Earl Boen (Agent), Ivor Barry (Deevers), Carol Tietel (Mrs. Weyback).

CBS / DRAMA

2041. **Brass.** 2 hours. Airdate: 9/11/85. Production Companies: Jay Gee Productions, Orion Television, and Carnan Inc. Director: Corey Allen. Executive Producer: Jerry Golod. Producer: T.J. Castronova. Writers: Roy Baldwin and Matt Harris, from a story by Roy Baldwin. Music: Joe Sherman. Carroll O'Connor is widower Frank Nolan, a 30-year N.Y.P.D. veteran appointed chief-of-detectives. But Nolan can't just sit behind a desk, he still has to get out on the street where the real police work is done. He has a housekeeper (Pauline Meyers) and a sister who is a nun (Anita Gillette) operating a shelter for the homeless. He's also got a girlfriend (Lois Nettleton) who owns an art gallery and who has a daughter (Marcia Gross) who disapproves of their romance. Vincent Gardenia is his chief-of-operations, Begona Plaza is his driver and protege. Shot in New York. *Cast:* Carroll O'Connor (as Frank Nolan), Lois Nettleton (Claire Willis), Larry Atlas (Capt. Jacobs), Samuel E. Wright (Capt. Shore), Jimmy Baio (Tony Covello), Paul Shenar (Schuyler Ross), Begona Plaza (Rose Garcia), Pauline Meyers (Lucy Ward), Vincent Gardenia (Chief Maldonato), Anita Gillette (Sister Elizabeth), Robert Brown (Chief Shannon), Richard Bright (Philip Stack), Wayne Tippet (P.C. Haines), Hugh O'Connor (James Flynn), Marcia Gross (Victoria Willis), Gary Klare (Leland Brice), A1 Mancini (Gianni Farro), Patricia Kalember (Lori Cartwright), Pat McNamara (Lt. Hanley), Angelo Tiffe (Officer), Louis Guss (Samuel Selig), Jude Ciccolella (Detective Si Levy), David S. Chandler (Bradley Oates), Andrew Davis (Arnold Boone), Dan Lauria (Detective Navarro), Graciela Lecube (Old Woman), Rudolfo Diaz (Mr. Vargas), Susan Rydin (Michaela), Jim

Moody (Medical Examiner), Lori Tan Chinn (Hilda), Barrett Heins (Swidon), Paul Herman (Sergeant), Rita Karin (Mrs. Dietz), Francine Beers (Eileen), Tom Spackman (Doctor), Andrew Clark (Doorman), Tudi Wiggins (Mrs. Amory), Stefan Schnabel (Norman Steingarten), Franklin Scott (Detective), Gerry Bamman (George Whitman), Liam Gannon (Priest), Dennis McMullen (Lt. Mulcahy), Shirley Stoller (Woman), Thomas Ikeda (Butler).

2042. **D5B—Steel Collar Man.** 60 min. Airdate: 8/7/85. Production Companies: Columbia Pictures Television and Cypress Point Productions. Director: James Frawley. Executive Producers: Gerald Abrams and Dave Thomas. Producer: David Latt. Writer: Dave Thomas. Creator: Dave Thomas. Music: Tom Scott. Like ABC's *J.O.E. & The Colonel*, this is the story of a government-created robot soldier (Charles Rocket) which can think for itself—which isn't exactly what the government ordered when it financed the experiments. The government wants it destroyed. The scientist (Dorian LoPinto) who created D5B helps the robot escape and they team up with a truck driver (Hoyt Axton). Together, the robot, trucker, and scientist roam the country, helping people and running from an obsessed government agent (Chuck Connors). The proposed series would mix adventure with comedy. *Cast:* Charles Rocket (as D5B), Dorian LoPinto (Dr. Constance Fletcher), Hoyt Axton (Red), Chuck Connors (J.G. Willis), Paul Dooley (Don Liddle), Chuck Mitchell (Big Jake), David Wohl (Weasel), Robert O'Reilly (Johnny), Jeffrey Josephson (Tino), John Brandon (General), Kevin Scannell (Trooper), Jon Lystine (Trooper #2), John Furlong (Security Guard), Biff Yeager (Truck Driver #1), Scott Perry (Truck Driver #2), John C. Reade (Truck Driver #3), Ebbe Roe Smith (Salesman), John Solari (Cashier), David Dunard (Bob), Kelly Jean Peters (Bob's Wife), Barry Kivel (Attendant), Dan Barrows (Al).

2043. **Dirty Work.** 60 min. Airdate: 6/6/85. Production Company: Lorimar Productions. Director: Jerry Thorpe. Executive Producer: Seth Freeman. Producer: Michelle Gallery. Writer: Seth Freeman. A young woman (Kerrie Keane) is hired as the secretary for a private eye—who disappears two days later. No one knows what happened to him. She finds herself running the agency, and doing her best to solve crimes until the private eye ever returns. *Cast:* Kerrie Keane (as Nadine Leevanhoek), Dorian Harewood (Lt. Hill), Louis Giambalvo (George Wiley), Teresa Ganzel (Secretary).

2044. **Murphy's Law.** 60 min. Production Company: 20th Century Fox Television. Director: Glenn Jordan. Executive Producer: Richard Alan Simmons. Producer:

Stuart Cohan. Writer: Richard Alan Simmons. Barry Newman stars as attorney David Murphy, once a highly paid partner in a prestigious law firm, who chucked it all to become a low-paid prosecutor in the District Attorney's office. Cecille Callan is a D.A. who sometimes helps him out. The twist in this proposed series is that each case would unfold over four to six episodes, following its development from police investigation and arrests, through jury selection and trial. Newman was the star of NBC's short-lived series *Petrocelli*, in which he played a lawyer.

2045. **On Our Way (aka On the Road).** 60 min. Airdate: 6/29/85. Production Companies: Frank Van Zerneck Films and Warner Bros. Television. Director: Michael Pressman. Executive Producer: Frank von Zerneck. Supervising Producer: Jeffrey Lane. Producer: William Beaudine, Jr. Writer: Jeffrey Lane, from a story by Jeffrey Lane and Stan and Carole Cherry. Music: Dennis McCarthy. A retired reporter (Harry Guardino) and his wife (Janet Leigh) set out to discover America in their motor home. They inevitably get involved in people's lives, and more often than not, find themselves solving crimes. In the pilot, they travel to Memphis, which is beset by murder in the midst of an Elvis Presley look-a-like contest. *Cast:* Janet Leigh (as Kate Walsh), Harry Guardino (Sam Walsh), also, Ben Marley, Scott Paulin, Andrew Prine, Gail Strickland, Brenda Lily, Savannah Smith Boucher, Phillip Henderson, John Malloy, Florence Leffler, Joe Woodward, David Page, Richard Papp, Fred Ford, Gris Ellis.

2046. **The Return of Kojak (aka Kojak: The Belarus File).** 2 hours. Airdate: 2/15/85. Production Company: Universal Television. Director: Robert Markowitz. Executive Producer: James McAdams. Producer: Albert Ruben. Writer: Albert Ruben. Creator: Abby Mann, from a novel by Selwin Raab. Music: Joseph Conlan and Barry DeVorzon. An attempt to revive the series *Kojak*, which ran from 1973–1978. He's still a tough N.Y.P.D. detective bucking bureaucrats while baring down on his hard-working staff, which once again includes Stavros (George Savalas), Rizzo (Vince Conti) and Saperstein (Mark B. Russell). Even Capt. McNeil (Dan Frazer) shows up. Notably absent is Crocker, Kojak's young protege, played by Kevin Dobson, who was tied up as a regular on *Knots Landing* when this was made. In the pilot, Kojak's friend (Max Von Sydow) may be involved in the murders of three suspected Nazi war criminals living in New York. Suzanne Pleshette is a concerned State Department official who helps Kojak obtain crucial information—contained in the so-called Belarus file—that the agency won't reveal. John Loftus, author of *The Belarus*

Secret, was technical advisor. A second pilot, *Kojak: The Price of Justice*, was made in 1987, and while it didn't lead to a new series, six more *Kojak* TV movies were made for ABC in 1989 as part of a rotating mystery anthology that also included new *Columbo* movies. Both were shot in New York. *Cast:* Telly Savalas (Lt. Theo Kojak), Max Von Sydow (Peter Barak), Suzanne Pleshette (Dana Sutton), Betsy Aidem (Elissa Barak), Alan Rosenberg (Lustig), Herbert Berghoff (Buchardt), Charles Brown (Julius Gay), David Leary (Chris Kennert), George Savalas (Stavros), Mark B. Russell (Saperstein), Vince Conti (Rizzo), Dan Frazer (Capt. Frank McNeil), Clarence Felder (Kelly), Adam Klugman (Morgan), Rita Karin (Mrs. Fitzev), Harry Davis (Rabbi), Margaret Thomson (Secretary), Otto Von Wernherr (Bodyguard), James Handy (First Federal Agent), Dan Lauria (Second Federal Agent), Martin Shakar (Assistant D.A.), Noberto Kerner (Nicholas Kastenov), Herman Schwedt (Vadim Savatsky), Jose Santana (Ristivo), Adam Klugman (Lane), Michael Long- field (Sergeant), Sal La Pera (Vladimir Fitzev), Brian Keeler (Film Editor), Lydia Prochnicka (Second Mourner).

2047. Sam Penny. 60 min. Airdate: 11/14/85. Production Company: Universal Television. Director: Vincent McEveety. Executive Producer: Philip DeGuere. Writer: Mike Piller. Aired as the "Reunion at Alcatraz" episode of *Simon and Simon*. A second attempt to spin-off Robert Lansing as hard-boiled San Francisco private eye Sam Penny, whom the Simon brothers idolize. In this version, the Simons' cousin Elizabeth (Caren Kaye) is fresh out of college and wants to be a private eye. She ends up, after tracking down the only man ever to escape from Alcatraz, becoming Penny's partner—in detection and love. *Cast:* Robert Lansing (as Sam Penny), Caren Kaye (Elizabeth Charles), Jameson Parker (A.J. Simon), Gerald McRaney (Rick Simon), Mary Carver (Cecilia Simon), Tim Reid (Downtown Brown), Vincent Baggetta (Ron Lottick), Rosemary Forsyth (Ellen Lottick), Barry Jenner (Latham), Jamie Widdoes (Roger), A1 White (Inmate), Virginia Vincent (Toni Myers), Richard Green (Motel Manager), David Frishberg (Piano Man).

2048. Soloman's Universe. 60 min. Production Companies: David Gerber Productions and MGM/UA Television. Director: Lee Katzin. Executive Producer: David Gerber. Producer: Barry Steinberg. Writer: Westbrook Claridge. Telly Savalas is Soloman Roarke, an intellectual who has gathered together the nation's brightest young people to devote their superior intelligence to fighting crime. They are Casey, his personal assistant (Clarence Gilyard, Jr.), Randall, a mathematical genius (Phillip Coccioletti), and Stephany (Cindy Morgan), a woman with degrees in zoology, biology, geophysics, and botany. To further aid them, Roarke has built a supercomputer connected to a complex global communications system so they can process information gleaned from monitoring events all over the world.

2049. **Stark.** 2 hours. Airdate: 4/10/85. Production Company: CBS Productions. Director: Rod Holcomb. Supervising Producers: Sam Strangis and Bill Stratton. Producer: David H. Balkan. Writer: Ernest Tidyman. Creators: Ernest Tidyman and David H. Balkan. Music: Bill Conti. Nicholas Surovy is a Wichita cop who journeys to Las Vegas to find his lost sister and her roommate. A sequel/pilot aired a year later. *Cast:* Nicholas Surovy (as Evan Stark), Marilu Henner (Ashley Walters), Pat Corley (Chief Waldron), Seth Jaffe (A1 Conner), Arthur Rosenberg (Jeff Draper), Dennis Hopper (Lt. Ron Bliss), Norbert Weisser (Powell), Barry Gordon (Lee Vogel), Wendel Meldrum (Laura Stark), Denise Crosby (Kim Parker), Allen Williams (Tom Hefton), Tom Henschel (Bobby Dukes), Bill Cross (Walter Reinhardt), Mike Genovese (Officer Chalmers), Peter Vogt (Todd Seymour), Peter Anthony (Lorenzo), Jane Hallaren (Judge Margaret Hallaren), Michael Champion (Sam), Bob Hopkins (Dino), Charles Hayward (Scurvy), John Bloom (Rhino), Michael Crabtree (Security Guard), Don Hedrick (Biker Buddy), Leo Needham (Night Watchman), Sly-Ali Smith (Patrolman), Perry Sheehan Adair (Frumpy Woman), Billy Ray Sharkey (Brock), Paul Brent (Officer Metz), John Liscio (Booking Sergeant), Stefan Zema (Pit Boss), R. Scott Hamann (Manager Jack), Cameron Milzer (Chorus Girl).

NBC / COMEDY

2050. **Anything for Love (aka Lookin' for Love).** 30 min. Airdate: 8/7/85. Production Companies: Taft Entertainment, Swany Inc., and Danceteam Productions. Director: Jim Drake. Executive Producer: Sy Rosen. Producers: Douglas Arango and Phil Doran. Writers: Douglas Arango, Phil Doran, Sy Rosen, Tom Seeley, and Norman Gunzenhauser. Music: Jack Dorsey and Doug McKeehan. Lauren Tewes and Vicki Lawrence are two single women who run a beauty parlor. Tewes is a divorcee raising two children (Christa Denton and Leaf Phoenix) and Lawrence has never been married. In the pilot, Tewes goes after her old flame

(Paul Gleason) when she hears gossip that his wife (Jennifer Savidge) wants a divorce. Marsha Warfield is a manicurist and Rebecca Arthur is a hairstylist. *Cast:* Lauren Tewes (as Dot), Vicki Lawrence (Elaine), Marsha Warfield (Cleo), also, Jay Johnson, Vanda Barra, Cameron Smith, Peter Parros, Florence Halop.

2051. **Fenster Hall.** 30 min. Airdate: 3/30/85. Production Company: NBC Productions. Director: Art Diehlen. Executive Producer: David Duclon. Supervising Producer: Gary Menteer. Producers: Rick Hawkins and Liz Sage. Writers: David Ducklon, Rick Hawkins, and Liz Sage. Aired as an episode of *Punky Brewster.* T.K. Carter is a counselor for young boys in a home for abandoned kids—the place where he was raised.

2052. **Handsome Harry's.** 60 min. Airdate: 4/25/86. Production Company: Scoey Mitchell Productions. Director: Bill Foster. Producer: Scoey Mitchell. Writers: Calvin Kelly, James Tisdale, Joseph Van Winkle, Scoey Mitchlll, Joe Restivo, and Monty Morris. Creator: Scoey Mitchlll. It took a lot of writers to fashion this flop pilot for a proposed half-hour sitcom. Scoey Mitchlll is a barber working in a St. Louis shop which, like *Cheers,* is the local hang-out frequented by a group of regulars, including Art Evans, Ketty Lester, Don Bexley, Cliff Norton, and Michelle Davison.

2053. **Hearts Island.** 30 min. Airdate: 8/31/85. Production Company: NBC Productions. Director: Art Diehlen. Producers: David Duclon, Rick Hawkins, and Liz Sage. Writers: David Duclon, Rick Hawkins, and Liz Sage. Dorothy Lyman is a widow, trying to raise two kids by working day-and-night as a seamstress and a waitress in 1950s Shreveport, Louisiana. She also takes in an ex-con (Gary Sandy) who gets work as a mechanic. *Cast:* Dorothy Lyman (as Johnnie Baylor), Clarice Taylor (Mattie), Gary Sandy (Ex-Con), Sydney and Christopher Burton (Kids).

2054. **No Complaints (aka Friends).** 30 min. Airdate: 7/17/85. Production Company: Embassy Television. Director: Asaad Kelada. Executive Producers: Linda Marsh and Margie Peters. Producer: Asaad Kelada. Writers: Linda Marsh and Margie Peters. Valerie Anastos (Diana Conova) and Joanne Newman (Anne Twomey) were childhood friends. Valerie got married to a bicycle shop owner (James Sutorius) and raised two kids (Matt Dill and Emily Moultrie) while Joanne went to Manhattan and became a hotshot advertising executive. When Joanne is transferred to Los Angeles, their friendship picks up where it left off—though they never admit they are actually jealous of each other's lives. Harold Gould plays

Jack, Joanne's boss. Brad O'Hare is Michael, a co-worker who has a romantic interest in Joanne.

2055. **Off the Boat (aka Big Shots in America).** 30 min. Airdate: 6/20/85. Production Company: The Brillstein Company. Director: James Burrows. Executive Producers: Bernie Brillstein and Lorne Michaels. Writer: Alan Zweibel. From the creators and writers of the classic *Saturday Night Live.* This sitcom pilot is, not coincidentally, reminiscent of the "two wild and crazy guys" characters created by Dan Aykroyd and Steve Martin on the show. The proposed series would follow the comic misadventures of two immigrants—Jovan (Joe Montegna) and Enci Shegula (Keith Szarabajka)—from an unnamed East-European country who come to America and end up managing a Brooklyn apartment house. *Cast:* Joe Montegna (as Jovan Shegula), Keith Szarabajka (Enci Shegula), Dan Vitale (Dae), Christine Baranksi (Cara).

2056. **Slickers.** 30 min. Airdate: 8/12/87. Production Company: Paramount Television. Director: Tom Trobvich. Executive Producer: Gary Nardino. Producer: Chris Thompson. Writer: Chris Thompson. Creator: Chris Thompson. N.Y.P.D. Officer Mike Blade (Michael Richards) is rough, tough, unconventional and a real pain. So his superiors transfer him to a sleepy little town, where he has to work for easy-going, friendly, rule-abiding Sheriff Elliot Clinton (Dana Carvey). Brandon Call costars as Scooter.

2057. **Tony Orlando Show.** 30 min. Airdate: 5/2/85. Production Companies: Carsey-Werner Co. and Bill Cosby Productions. Director: Jay Sandrich. Executive Producers: Marcy Carsey, Tom Werner, and Bill Cosby. Writer: Emily Tracy. Aired as the "Mr. Quiet" episode of *The Cosby Show.* Tony Orlando stars as Tony Castillo, the director of a New York community center who falls in love with the head counselor. He also becomes very close to an 11-year-old Puerto Rican boy named Enrique (Alexis Cruz), whose father was killed by the police. Cosby was reportedly furious that the pilot didn't get picked up. Grant Tinker, who was running NBC at the time, told columnist Marilyn Beck that "We don't put something on because someone wants it on. Bill Cosby understands that. He knows that spinoffs are very tricky and that almost never do you do one right. The Tony Orlando spin-off didn't work." Cast: Tony Orlando (Tony Castillo), Alexis Crus (Enrique Tarron), Ada Maris (Selena Cruz), Pearl Tama (Sonya Tarron), Angela Bassett (Mrs. Mitchell), Olga Merediz (Mrs. Rodriquez).

NBC / DRAMA

2058. Boston (aka Long Arm). 60 min. Production Company: David Gerber Co. Producer: David Gerber. Writers: E. Jack Neuman and Mark Rodgers. A pilot concept about a tough Boston assistant D.A. named Ben Eagan, who will sometimes bend the rules to prevent wily attorneys from getting guilty clients freed through loopholes in the law. Eagan is also in love with Anne, another assistant D.A., who isn't ready to settle down.

2059. Champion. 60 min. Production Company: Warner Bros. Television. Director: James Goldstone. Executive Producers: Frank Abatemarco and Clyde Phillips. Writers: Frank Abatemarco and Steven De Souza. Duncan Regehr is David Champion, a modern-day "Green Hornet," a rich inventor who tools around town in a chauffeur-driven limo—but who, unknown to all, is a mysterious crime-fighter who always leaves a small figure of the Egyptian Goddess of Justice as his calling card. The only one who knows about his double-life is his chauffeur Tony (Tony Quinn), who drives his gadget-laden supercar. A reworking of the 1984 CBS pilot *Adventures of Alexander Hawkins*.

2060. Covenant. 2 hours. Airdate: 8/5/85. Production Companies: Michael Filerman Productions and 20th Century Fox Television. Director: Walter Grauman. Executive Producer: Michael Filerman. Supervising Producer: J.D. Feigelson and Dan DiStefano. Producer: Joseph B. Wallenstein. Writers: J.D. Feigelson and Dan DiStefano. Music: Charles Bernstein. A supernatural soap opera focusing on the evil Nobles, who use their dark powers against their foes and use their earthly powers, in the form of a San Francisco bank built by Nazi riches, to finance global terrorism and crime. Jose Ferrer is Josef Noble, who knows the future of his family's evil powers rests with his twin daughters—nasty Dana (Jane Badler) and good-hearted Claire (Michelle Phillips), whose nice daughter Angelica (Whitney Kershaw) will inherit the powers someday. Dana would like to see Claire and Angelica vanish. Playing on his family rivalry are the good guys, headed by Barry Morse and Charles Frank, who call themselves the Judges and will do anything to destroy the Nobles. *Cast:* Jose Ferrer (as Josef Noble), Jane Badler (Dana Noble), Whitney Kershaw (Angelica), Michelle Phillips (Claire), Barry Morse (Judge), Charles Frank (David), Bradford Dillman (Eric), Kevin Conroy (Stephen), Judy Parfitt (Renata Beck), Laurence Guittard (Stuart Hall), John Van Dreelen (Heinrich Bosch), Jan Merlin (Constance), Ji-Tu Cumbuka (Duboff), Tia Carrere

(Girl), Will Gerard (Officer), Fred Lerner (Stranger), Mike Runyard (Waiter), James Saito (Cabbie), Jon Sharp (Captain), Erica Todd (Stewardess), Scott Utley (Freddie), Charles Walker (Announcer).

2061. **Dalton: Code of Vengeance.** 2 hours. Airdate: 6/30/85. Production Company: Universal Television. Director: Rick Rosenthal. Executive Producer: Robert Foster. Producer: Stu Cohen. Executive Consultant: William Sackheim. Writer: Robert Foster. Creator: Robert Foster. Music: Don Peake. Charles Taylor is a watered-down Rambo, a Vietnam vet wandering around the country and helping people in trouble. In the pilot, he helps a young ranch-owner (Erin Gray) and her son (Chad Allen) find out who killed her brother and avenge his death. The pilot scored impressively in the ratings and inspired several sequel pilots that didn't, despite changes in the behind-the-scenes production team. *Cast:* Charles Taylor (as David Dalton), Charles Haid (Jim Blanton), Randall "Tex" Cobb (Willard Singleton), Keenan Wynn (Willis), Erin Gray (Nadine Flowers), Chad Allen (A.J.), Lenka Peterson (Ione Flowers), Joe Dorsey (Chief Milford Carsworth), Victor Mohica (Mexican Police Chief), Tiny Welles (Curly), Robert Dryer (Barnes), Leigh Hamilton (Louise), Michael Rider (Driver), Tex Hill (Officer), Terry Seago (Angelo).

2062. **Nick Tattinger.** 60 min. Production Company: MTM Enterprises. Director: Bruce Paltrow. Executive Producer: Bruce Paltrow. Producers: John Masius, Tom Fontana, and Mark Tinker. Writers: John Masius and Tom Fontana. Nick Tattinger runs a Manhattan restaurant and helps people in trouble, which often includes his socialite ex-wife Hilary or his two teenage daughters. This was never cast or shot. The concept, revived in 1988, with Stephen Collins starring, was quickly cancelled, then brought back for 3 episodes as a half-hour sitcom.

2063. **O.S.S. (aka Behind Enemy Lines; aka 72 Grovesner Square).** 2 hours. Airdate: 12/29/85. Production Company: MTM Enterprises. Director: Sheldon Larry. Executive Producer: Steven McPherson. Producers: Judith DePaul and Gareth Davies. Writer: Steven McPherson. Creator: Steven McPherson. The adventures of the Office of Strategic Services unit, an espionage force, in London during World War II. Filmed on location. *Cast:* Hal Holbrook (as Col. Calvin Turner), David McCallum (Major Shelly Flynn), Ray Sharkey (Max Zieman), Tom Isbell (Lt. Phil Bradshaw), Steve Shellen (Lt. David Holland), Anne Twomey (Helen Isaacs), Alan Lewis (Jack Gifford), Peter Whitman (Capt. Jerry Primack), Mirym D'Abo (Claude De Brille), Renee Soutendijk (Ragni Carswell),

Lucy Homak (Peggy Whitmore), Ian Lavender (Col. Lumsden Smith), Julian Glover (Prof. Ivar Thoreson), T.P. McKenna (Sir James Dorsett), Michael J. Shannon (Robert Harwell), William Hope (Lt. Michael Turner), Nick Brimble (Henrik Wergeland), Owen Windhoek (Sgt. Rudolph Rau), Adrian Hough (Corp. Copper), Nancy Crane (Claire), Jean Badin (Major Henri Grisard), Sylvia Coleridge (Mavis).

2064. Private Sessions. 2 hours. Airdate: 3/18/85. Production Companies: Comworld Productions, Raven's Claw Productions, and Seltzer-Gimbel Productions. Director: Michael Pressman. Executive Producers: Deanne Barkley, Philip Capice, and Norman Gimbel. Producer: Thom Thomas. Writers: Thom Thomas and David Seltzer. Music: Lalo Schifrin. Mike Farrell is Joe Braden, a caring New York psychologist who sometimes uses unconventional methods to help people in trouble. He shares an office with his best friend Liz (Maureen Stapleton), and still maintains a strong relationship with his ex-wife (Kathryn Walker), perhaps because they are both so worried about their introverted daughter (Mary Tanner). In the pilot, he helps a cab driver (Tom Bosley) who hears voices (which Braden discovers is due to a chemical in the car's upholstery) and a woman (Kelly McGillis) with marriage problems. *Cast:* Mike Farrell (as Dr. Joe Braden), Maureen Stapleton (Dr. Liz Bolger), Kathryn Walker (Claire Braden), Mary Tanner (Millie Braden), Robert Vaughn (Oliver Coles), Greg Evigan (Rick), David Labiosa (Ramon), Hope Lange (Mrs. Coles), Kim Hunter (Rosemary O'Reilly), Denise Miller (Angie), Kelly McGillis (Jennifer Coles), Tom Bosley (Harry O'Reilly), Victor Garber (Jery Sharma), John Cunningham (Paul Rodgers), Wendie Malick (Tippi), Elias Koteas (Johnny O'Reilly), Paul Land (Delivery Boy), Davenia McFadden (Gail), Edmond Genest (Quentin Byrd), Evin Harisborough (Jennifer—age 9), John Horton (Businessman), Kathryn Dowling (Susan Prescott), Jane Cronin (Miss Finney), Raul Davila (Mr. Fontana), John Capodice (George), Geoffrey Horne (Man).

2065. Streets of Justice (aka Point Blank). 2 hours. Airdate: 11/10/85. Production Company: Universal Television. Director: Christopher Crowe. Executive Producer: Christopher Crowe. Producers: Alex Beaton and Alan Barnette. Writer: Christopher Crowe. Creator: Christopher Crowe. An attempt to capture the success of *Death Wish* and translate it to television. John Laughlin is Hudson James, an auto assembly-line worker who becomes an urban vigilante when his family is murdered by a motorcycle gang—which is released by the courts on a technicality. On top of all this, he's mugged on his way back from court. *Cast:* John Laughlin (as Hudson James), Robert Loggia (Det. Phil Ryan), Jack Thibeau (Zero McKenzie), Paul Shenar (J. Elliot Sloan), Cristina Raines (Carol Neilson), Wayne Anderson (Lee James Smithbeck), Lance Hendriksen (D.A. Jerry Logan), Fred Taylor (Stink), Don Gibb (Road Rodent), Roger Aaron Brown (Det. Crowther), John Hancock (Henry Brewer), Richard Foronjy (Det. Arnold Johnson), Kate Charleson (Madeline James), Pepe Serna (Det. Almos), Robin Grimmell (Judge Phineas Odets), Les Dudek (Bill McDowell), William Sanderson (Weasel), Clyde Kusatsu (Dr. Edwards), Tandy Cronyn (Tina), Douglas Dirkson (Bull), A1 Israel (Colombian), Sam Vlahos (Burt), Susan Powell (Gena), Nancy Grahn (Lawyer), Steve Eastin (P.R. Officer), Joshua Horowitz (Danny James), Casey Sander (Deputy), Walter Klenhard (Officer Peters), Paul Tuerpe (Officer Matthews), Bill Dearth (Officer Rutherford), Claire Nono (TV Anchorwoman), Joel Oliansky (Brent Burrows).

2066. **Suburban Beat.** 60 min. Airdate: 8/17/85. Production Companies: B&E Enterprises and Viacom Television. Director: Mike Vejar. Executive Producers: Brad Buckner and Eugenie Ross-Leming. Producer: Christopher Nelson. Writers: Brad Buckner and Eugene Ross-Leming. Creators: Brad Buckner and Eugene Ross-Leming. Music: Mark J. Hoder. From the producers/creators of *Scarecrow and Mrs. King,* about a suburban housewife who is also a spy, comes this concept about suburban housewives who form a neighborhood watch group and, to the consternation of the police, set out to solve crimes. Dee Wallace, Shelley Fabares, Heather Langenkamp, Patti Austin, and Elena Verdugo star. Guest stars included Stephen Parr, Jeff Pomerantz, Sharon Spelman, Joe Santos, Arthur G. Koustik, Jeff Severson, Ralph Bruneay, San Martin, Jenny Lewis, Troy Eckert, Liz Sheridan, Matthew Faison, Eric Stern, Lew Horn, Carol Lipin, Lowell Gytri, Channing Chase, Howard Stover, and John Bloom.

1986-1987

ABC / COMEDY

2067. Almost Home. 30 min. Production Company: Paramount Television. Director: Joel Zwick. Executive Producers: Madeline and Steve Sunshine. Producer: James O'Keefe. Writers: Madeline and Steve Sunshine. Aired as an episode of *Webster.* Mac Davis is Jake Tyler, a country-western singer living in New York who runs a foster home for kids in trouble.

2068. Arena. 30 min. Airdate: 6/27/86. Production Company: Witt-Thomas Productions. Director: Terry Hughes. Executive Producers: Paul Junger Witt and Tony Thomas. Producers: Barry Fanaro and Mort Nathan. Writers: Barry Fanaro and Mort Nathan. Ted Bessell stars as the owner of a rundown sports arena that hosts everything from bigtime wrestling to rock concerts. His booking agent is a midget (Jimmy Briscoe) and his maintenance man doubles as a human cannonball (Kevin Scannell). *Cast:* Ted Bessell (as Max Harrison), Teresa Ganzel (Loraine Lamelle), Jimmy Briscoe (Gus Leddas), Kevin Scannell (Cannonball Righetti), Mario Lopez (Johnny Vegas).

2069. Carly Mills. 30 min. Production Company: MTM Enterprises. Director: Rod Daniel. Executive Producer: John Steven Owen. Producer: Rod Daniel. Writer: John Steven Owen. Kate Mulgrew is a traditional, old-fashioned mother, married to an overworked college professor (Jack Bannon), who has chosen to be a housewife and raise their four children because she *wants* to. *Cast:* Kate Mulgrew (as Carly Mills), Jack Bannon (Evan Mills), Matt Adler (Pete Mills), Amanda Peterson (Trisha Mills), Hannah Cutrona (Brigid Mills), R.J. Williams (Jeffy Mills), Betsy Randall (Maggie Wallace), Rebecca Bush (Cynthia James).

2070. Casebusters. 60 min. Airdate: 5/25/86. Production Companies: Elsboy Entertainment and Walt Disney Television. Director: Wes Craven. Executive Producers: Erwin Stoff and Paul Aaron. Producer: John Garbett. Writers: George Arthur Bloom and Donald Paul Roos, from a story by Donald Paul Roos. Music: David Frank. Aired as an episode of the *Disney Sunday Movie.* Wes Craven, best known for explicit horror tales like *Nightmare on Elm Street,* directed this story about two kids (Noah Hathaway and Virginia Keehne) who, with the help of their security- guard grandfather (Pat Hingle), solve crimes. *Cast:* Virginia Keehne (as Allie), Noah Hathaway (Jamie), Pat Hingle (Grandpa Sam), Gary Riley (Ski), Ebbe Roe Smith (Joe Bonner), Sharon Barr (Loretta Bonner), Nicholas North (Riker).

2071. **Cathy.** 30 min. Production Company: Universal Television. Producer: Emily Levine. Writer: Cathy Guisewite. A sitcom based on Guisewite's comic strip about the travails of a single woman.

2072. **Chameleon.** 30 min. Airdate: 7/18/86. Production Companies: Gary Nardino Productions and Paramount Television. Director: John Rich. Executive Producer: Gary Nardino. Producer: David Lloyd. Writer: David Lloyd. Madeline Kahn stumbles into a job of an undercover reporter for an egotistical television consumer advocate (George Wyner). Nina Foch is her overbearing mother, and Henry Jones is the understanding owner of the TV station. *Cast:* Madeline Kahn (Violet Kingsley), Nina Foch (Hannah Kingsley), Andrew Prine (Lucas Hanlon), Taliesin Jaffe (Neil Hanlon), George Wyner (Wes Bushnell), Henry Jones (Morton Waterman).

2073. **Charmed Lives.** 30 min. Production Company: Embassy Television. Director: Assad Kelada. Executive Producers: Eve Brandstein and Paul Haggis. Producer: John Anderson. Writer: Paul Haggis. Aired as an episode of *Who's the Boss?* Lauren (Donna Dixon) is a photographer for whom life has always come easy. Joyce (Fran Drescher) is a model who has had to work very hard against many obstacles. The two women are friends, roommates, and compete for the same jobs—and it's from this relationship the laughs were supposedly going to come had anyone bought the series.

2074. **Dick Van Dyke Show.** 30 min. Production Company: New World Television. Producers: Anson Williams and Ron Howard. Dick Van Dyke stars as a widower who marries a woman who is 20 years younger than he is.

2075. **Father's Day (aka The Family Battle).** 30 min. Airdate: 7/25/86. Production Companies: Mort Lachman and Associates and Reeves Entertainment. Director: Hal Cooper. Executive Producers: Mort Lachman and Merrill Grant. Producer: Allen Leicht. Writer: Allen Leicht. Creator: Allen Leicht. Twenty years ago Robert Morgan (Robert Klein)—initially named Calvin Battle when this pilot was in development—was a '60s activist, a liberal free of commitments or responsibilities of any kind. Now he's married, an IRS agent, and is considered a conservative by his 14-year-old daughter Daisy. She constantly argues with him about politics and scolds her mother (Frances Lee McCain) for not challenging herself with more than housework. His young son just sits back and watches it all. The pilot was shot in New York. *Cast:* Robert Klein (as Robert Morgan), Frances Lee McCain (Mary Ellen Morgan), Royana Black (Daisy Morgan), Josh Blake (John Morgan).

2076. **Fuzzbucket.** 60 min. Airdate: 5/16/86. Production Company: Walt Disney Television. Director: Mick Garris. Executive Producer: John Landis. Producer: Mick Garris. Writer: Mick Garris. Aired as an episode of the *Disney Sunday Movie.* The misadventures of an invisible creature and the only person who can see him, a 12-year-old boy. *Cast:* Chris Herbert (as Mickey Gerber), Phil Fondacaro (Fuzzbucket), Joe Regalbuto (Dad), Wendy Phillips (Mom), Robyn Lively (Stevie).

2077. **Just Plain Folks.** 30 min. Production Companies: Mort Lachman and Associates and Reeves Entertainment. Producers: Mort Lachman and Merrill Grant. Consultant: Aaron Spelling. A blue-collar family wins $5 million in the state lottery and it changes their lives.

2078. **Man About Town.** 30 min. Airdate: 7/11/86. Production Company: MTM Enterprises. Director: David Steinberg. Executive Producers: Richard Rosenstock and Roy Teicher. Producer: Ron Frazier. Writers: Richard Rosenstock and Roy Teicher. Music: David Shire. Daniel Stern is Leon Feddick, a lovable neb- bish and klutz who never seems to do anything right. He's the guy who always slips on the banana peel. His friends include Vic, the friendly bookstore owner; Sandy, Vic's clerk; and Terry, the girl-next-door who, unknown to Leon, might be falling in love with him. In the pilot, he meets a woman at a wedding and takes her to a natural history museum—where he accidentally bumps into a dinosaur skeleton and knocks the whole thing down. *Cast:* Daniel Stern (as Leon Feddick), Toni Kalem (Ellen), George Wyner (Mike the Mailman), Jayne Modean (Terry Bishop), Tom Henschel (Vic), Karlene Crockett (Sandy).

2079. **Mr. Boogedy.** 2 hours. Airdate: 4/30/86. Production Company: Walt Disney Television. Director: Oz Scott. Producers: Oz Scott and Michael Janover. Writer: Michael Janover. Aired as an episode of the *Disney Sunday Movie.* The misadventures of the Davis family, who move into a New England house haunted by pilgrim prankster William Hanover, aka "Mr. Boogedy," who had sold his soul to the devil in return for a magic cloak. A second pilot, *The Bride of Boogedy,* was made the following season. *Cast:* Richard Masur (as Carleton Davis), Mimi Kennedy (Eloise Davis), Tammy Lauren (Jennifer), David Faustino (Corwin), Joshua Rudoy (Ahri Davis), Howard Witt (Mr. Boogedy).

2080. **My Fat Friend.** 30 min. Producers: Allan Carr and Fred Gershon. The misadventures of a middle-aged cook with his own cable TV show and his 22-year- old female helper.

2081. **The Rowdies.** 60 min. Airdate: 8/8/86. Production Company: Universal Television. Director: Burt Kennedy. Executive Producers: Richard Chapman and Bill Dial. Writers: Richard Chapman and Bill Dial. Pat Harrington is C.T. "Rowdy" Harlan, an entrepreneur business man who runs a suburban security outfit made up of his misfit friends—played by Sam Anderson, Dennis Burkley, John Scott Clough, Jim Haynie, Kitty Moffat, Tommy Swerdlow, and Michael Wren.

2082. **Two and a Half Dads.** 60 min. Airdate: 4/16/86. Production Companies: Twenty Paws Productions, Intermedia Entertainment, and Walt Disney Television. Director: Tony Bill. Executive Producers: Fred Silverman and Gordon Farr. Producer: Tony Bill. Writer: Gordon Farr. Music: Robert Folk. Aired as an episode of *Disney Sunday Movie*. Three Vietnam veterans live together with their families under one roof. Richard Young is a widower with two kids; George Dzundza is separated and raising his three kids; and Sal Viscuso is single and out of work. Living together isn't easy. Lenore Kasdorf is a concerned neighbor. Mary Kohnert, Billy Warlock, Ricky Stout, Marissa Mendenhall, Shane O'Neil, and Sharon Madden costar.

ABC / DRAMA

2083. **Charley Hannah.** 90 min. Airdate: 4/6/86. Production Companies: A Shane Productions and Telepictures Productions. Director: Peter H. Hunt. Executive Producer: Joan Conrad. Producer: Roger Bacon. Writer: David J. Kinghorn. Music: Jan Hammer. Robert Conrad is a Ft. Lauderdale vice detective who becomes a foster parent to a teenage thief (played by his son Shane Conrad) while investigating cop killings and cocaine smuggling. Red West, who costarred with Conrad in *Black Sheep Squadron*, and Stephen J. Cannell, who produced and created that series, guest starred. *Cast:* Robert Conrad (as Charley Hannah), Red West (Buck), Joan Leslie (Sandy Hannah), Christian Conrad (Officer Andy Simms), Stephen J. Cannell (Roscoe Tanner), Kelly Minter (Tony), Antoni Corone (Marco), B. Miko Machalski (Andre), Mario Sanchez (Pizer), James Deuter (Pope), Alex Paez (Lance), Tracy Holt (Robby Barnes), David Saunders

(Manny Short), Deanna Dunagan (Nurse), Alex Panas (Chief Raleigh Poole), David Darlow (Capt. Ray Albright), Jorge Gil (Willie Jones), Miryam Suarez (Carol Mather).

2084. **The City.** 60 min. Airdate: 8/1/86. Production Company: Lorimar-Telepictures Productions. Director: Jack Bender. Executive Producer: William Blinn. Producer: Frank Fischer. Writer: William Blinn. Music: J.A.C. Redford. The city of Chicago, as seen through the interweaving stories of the mayor (Chris Sarandon), his aide (Gary Swanson), his aide's newspaper-editor girlfriend (Season Hubley), a weary reporter (M. Emmet Walsh), the tyrannical newspaper publisher (Fritz Weaver) and the chief of police (Georg Stanford Brown). *Cast:* Chris Sarandon (as Mayor Chet Lugar), Gary Swanson (Cary Brock), M. Emmet Walsh (Bear Werner), Season Hubley (Chris Racine), Fritz Weaver (Stewart Moffitt), George Stanford Brown (Chief Otis Pittman).

2085. **The Costigans (aka Home).** 60 min. Airdate: 3/6/87. Production Companies: Mandy Films and Paramount Television. Director: Sheldon Larry. Executive Producer: Leonard Goldberg. Executive Supervising Producer: Deborah Aal. Producer: Carroll Newman. Writer: Christopher Knopf. The lives of a blue collar couple (Max Gail and Anne Twcmey) raising their three teenage children in Chicago. The eldest daughter is flexing her independence, their 15-year-old son is going through the awkward stages of manhood, and their 12-year-old kid is a loner. In the pilot, the father loses a construction contract he wanted, the eldest son starves himself to prepare for a wrestling match, and the youngest son worries about his bad grades. *Cast:* Max Gail (as Will Costigan), Anne Twomey (Maggie Costigan), Tracy Nelson (Susan Costigan), Michael Sharrett (Kelly Costigan), Jody Lambert (Brian Costigan), Barbara Baxley (Katherine), Dennis Holahan (Phillip Beaumont), Robert Lipton (Ray), Damon Martin (Bo), Kevin McCarthy (Edison), Kristoffer Tabori (Scott Diamond), Robin Wright (Valerine Kane), Gregory Morgan (Coach), Noon Orsati (Gary), Richard D'Aurelio (Shev), Eric Brown (Arnie), Curtiss Marlowe (Jerry), Jimmy Bridges (Kid #1), Josh Cohen (Kid #2).

2086. **Destination: America.** 2 hours. Airdate: 4/3/87. Production Company: Stephen J. Cannell Productions. Director: Corey Allen. Executive Producer: Stephen J. Cannell. Producer: Patrick Hasburgh. Writer: Patrick Hasburgh. Creator: Patrick Hasburgh. Music: Mike Post. Bruce J. Greenwood is Corey St. James, a loner whose search for the serial killer who murdered his millionaire father sends him wandering through the backroads and small towns of America. *Cast:* Bruce J. Greenwood (as Corey St. James), Rip Torn (Corbet St. James, IV), Joe Pan-toliano (Lt. Mike Amico), Alan Autry (Larry Leathergood), Henry Kingi (Reno Sam), Norman Alden (Beller).

2087. **The Eagle and the Bear.** 90 min. Airdate: 1985. Production Company: Columbia Pictures Television. Director: Lee H. Katzin. Producers: Larry A. Thompson, Mel Swope. Writers: Andrew Britt, Stephen Nathan, Paul B. Price, Jeff Silverman. The misadventures of a private eye (Jeff Allin) who teams up with a former KGB agent (Sherman Howard) to solve crimes. Carroll O'Connor was courted to play the Russian, but he passed. *Cast:* Jeff Allin (Charlie Patterson), Sherman Howard (Ivan Belkovski), Deborah May, Bill Morey, Alan Autry, Daniel Davis, Adam Gregor, Miro Polo.

2088. **Flag.** 90 min. Production Company: Lorimar-Telepictures Productions. Director: Bill Duke. Executive Producers: David Jacobs and Stuart Sheslow. Writer: David Jacobs. Creator: David Jacobs. David Jacobs, creator of *Dallas* and *Knots Landing,* crafted this spoof of his own shows by the same production company that makes them. Tom Isbell is Rudy Flag, a social worker who, much to his chagrin, inherits control of his family's multinational conglomerate. He reluctantly becomes involved, and his naive, compassionate, liberal and homespun approach immediately clashes with his heartless, conservative relatives—who only want to make a profit. *Cast:* Tom Isbell (as Rudy Flag), Moses Gunn (Griffin), Darren McGavin (Brian Flag), Robin Strand (Wilson Flag), Holland Taylor (Aunt Glynnis), Wendy Fulton (Hillary Street), Beau Starr (Malcolm).

2089. **Gladiator.** 2 hours. Airdate: 2/3/86. Production Companies: Walker Bros. Productions and New World Television. Director: Abel Ferrara. Executive Producers: Jeffrey Walker, Michael Chase Walker, and Tom Schulman. Producers: Robert Lovenheim and Bill Bleich. Writer: Bill Bleich, from a story by Tom Schulman and Jeffrey Walker. Creators: Jeffrey Walker and Tom Schulman. Music: David Frank. Rick Benson (Ken Wahl) becomes a secret vigilante who roams the roads of southern California fighting all sorts of vehicular crimes (reckless driving, drunk drivers, etc.) with his souped-up tow truck after his brother is killed by a psychopathic, hit-and-run driver. Nancy Allen is a radio talkshow host who becomes romantically involved with Benson. *Cast:* Ken Wahl (as Rick Benson), Nancy Allen (Susan Neville), Robert Culp (Lt. Frank Mason), Stan Shaw (Joe), Rosemary Forsyth (Dr. Loretta Simpson), Bart Braverman (Man),

Brian Robbins (Jeff Benton), Rick Dees (Garth), Michael Young (Reporter), Harry Beer (Franklin), Garry Goodrow (Cadillac Drunk), Gary Lev (Fast Food Manager), Georgia Paul (Elderly Woman), Mort Sertner (Elderly Man), Jose Flores (Policeman), Royce D. Applegate (Phil), Robert Phalen (Dr. Maxwell), Linda Thorson (Woman in Class), Stephen Anthony Harry (Man in Class), Jim Wilkey (Death Car Driver).

2090. Hardesty House. 60 min. Airdate: 6/5/86. Production Companies: Artists United, ABC Circle Films, Robert Ginty/Phoenix Entertainment Productions. Director: Martin Davidson. Executive Producers: Robert Ginty and Gerald I. Isenberg. Producer: R.W. Goodwin. Writer: Susan Seeger, from a story by Larry Mollin. Music: Fred Karlin. Robert Ginty stars as a lawyer who, with five friends from law school, turns his Victorian house into a law firm that caters half the time to pro bono cases (Ginty played a law student in the first season of *The Paper Chase*). His partners are Charlie (Susan Anton), his former flame; Judy (Melanie Chartoff), a single mother trying to balance her homelife with her career; Max (Harley Ven- ton), who chose not to work for his father's big law firm; Ramon (Paul Rodriquez), who handles entertainment law; and Robbie, (Randy Brooks), who wants to get into politics. Cec Verrell, Kenneth Kimmins, John Anderson, Danny Capri, Hanna Hertelendy, Arnold Johnson, Margaret Nagle, Shari Shattuck, Deanna Claire, Briggette Desper, Tiffany Desper, and Tad Horino guest starred.

2091. Harry's Hong Kong (aka China Hand). 2 hours. Airdate: 5/8/87. Production Company: Aaron Spelling Productions. Director: Jerry London. Executive Producers: Aaron Spelling and Douglas S. Cramer. Executive Supervising Producer: E. Duke Vincent. Writing Producer: Stirling Silliphant. Producers: Jerry London and James L. Conway. Writer: Richard Alan Simmons. Music: Dominic Frontiere. David Soul is Harry Petros, a mystery man who runs a lavish casino on a Chinese junk moored outside Hong Kong. He inevitably gets involved in people's problems and is helped out in his adventures by his Chinese-American secretary, an American journalist and the police superintendent. In the pilot, he investigates the death of an old friend. Shot on location in Hong Kong. *Cast:* David Soul (as Harry Petros), Mike Preston (Police Superintendent Max Trumble), Jan Gan Boyd (Sally Chen), Mel Harris (Fay Salerno), Lisa Lu (Rose), James Hong (Yu), Julia Nickson (Mei Ling), Rosanna Huffman (Mrs. Hamilton), David Hemmings (Jack Roarke), Russell Wong (Sgt. Lee), David

Chow (Bodyguard #1), Mike Harley (Skipper), David Ho (Bodyguard #2), Wilson Lam (Helmsman), Michael Lee (Soothsayer), Cho Lo (Sparrow Man), Mansoor (Salesman), Matthew James McAuley (Sergeant), Mak Yuen Mei (Mamasan), Bill Pak (Mr. Cheng), Wilson N.G. Wing Sam (Tailor).

2092. **Hope Division.** 60 min. Airdate: 7/17/87. Production Company: Aaron Spelling Productions. Director: Mel Damski. Executive Producers: Aaron Spelling and Douglas S. Cramer. Producers: E. Duke Vincent and Mel Damski. Writer: Patricia Green. Music: John E. Davis. The adventures of two cops—a black family man (Dorian Harewood) and a divorced mother (Mimi Kuzyk)—chasing a serial killer. The proposed series would have focused on both their police work and family crises. *Cast:* Dorian Harewood (as James Reynolds), Mimi Kuzyk (Anne Russell), Hayley Carr (Lilah Reynolds), Cliffy Magee (Lewis Reynolds), Saba Shawel (Melissa), H. Richard Greene (Capt. Thorpe), K. Callan (Caroline Braden), Mason Adams (Peter Braden), Mae Hi (Sgt. Nimura), Nat Bernstein (Ackerman), Mindy Seeger (Hooker).

2093. **I-Man.** 60 min. Airdate: 4/6/86. Production Companies: Michael Ovitz Productions and Walt Disney Television. Director: Corey Allen. Executive Producer: Mark Ovitz. Producers: Richard Briggs, Howard Friedlander, and Ken Peragine. Writers: Howard Friedlander and Ken Peragine. Music: Craig Safan. Aired as an episode of the *Disney Sunday Movie*. A single father working as a cabbie (Scott Bakula) is accidentally exposed to a strange gas—while rescuing a truck driver from a wreck—that makes him an "indestructible man." He, of course, becomes a secret agent and, in the pilot, teams up with a sexy female spy (Ellen Bry) to retrieve a stolen laser from an evil madman (John Anderson). Herschel Bernardi plays I-Man's boss. *Cast:* Scott Bakula (as Jeffrey Wilder), Joey Cramer (Eric Wilder), John Anderson (Oliver Holbrook), Ellen Bry (Karen McCorder), Herschel Bernardi (Internal Security Agency Chief), John Bloom (Harry), Dale Wilson (Rudy), Cindy Higgins (Allison), Charles E. Siegel (Cannoe), Joseph Golland (Meek Man), Jan Tracey (Robbery Suspect), Ted Stidder (Dr. Allen), George Josef (Guide Guard), Campbell Lane (General), Terry Moore (Distinguished Man), Lillian Carlson (Emergency Room Nurse), Roger Allford (ISA Agent), Anthony Harrison (Curtain Guard), Don Davis (Surgeon), Rebecca Bush (Sara), Garwin Sanford (Van Driver), Doug Tuck (Paramedic), Brian Arnold (Newscaster), Ralmund Stamm (Norman), Janne Mac-Dougall (Station Nurse), Nicolas Von Zill (Party Guard).

2094. Island Sons. 2 hours. Airdate: 5/15/87. Production Company: Universal Television. Director: Alan J. Levi. Executive Producers: James D. Parriott and Deanne Barkley. Producer: Leonard Kaufman. Writer: James Dott. Music: Basil Poledouris. Tim, Joe, Sam, and Ben Bottoms are four brothers working in Hawaii. Tim runs a charter boat service, Joe owns a hotel, Sam is the assistant district attorney in Honolulu, and Ben manages the family cattle ranch. When their father dies, they have to overcome their personal conflicts and work together when troubles arise—usually in the form of solving crimes. Executive producer James Parriott wrote and produced *Hawaiian Heat*, a short-lived Universal series for ABC starring Robert Ginty the previous season, and producer Leonard Kaufman worked on *Hawaii Five-0*. *Cast:* Timothy Bottoms (as Tim Faraday), Joseph Bottoms (Joe Faraday), Sam Bottoms (Sam Faraday), Ben Bottoms (Ben Faraday), Claire Kirkconnell (Abby Faraday), Richard Narita (Saito), Kim Miyori (Diane Ishimura), David Wohl (Herb Engleman), Romy Windsor (Kate Landis), Mokihana (Malama), Michael Currie (Jess Hamlin), Henry K. Bai (Abraham).

2095. The Last Resort. 60 min. Production Company: Paramount Television. Director: Bill Bixby. Bill Bixby stars as a wealthy, Hawaii-based investigative reporter.

2096. The Man Who Fell to Earth. 2 hours. Airdate: 8/23/87. Production Company: MGM Television. Director: Bobby Roth. Executive Producer: David Gerber. Producers: Lewis Chesler and Richard Kletter. Writer: Richard Kletter, from the screenplay by Paul Mayersberg, based on the book by Walter Tevis. Music: Doug Timm. Lewis Smith takes over the role, originated by David Bowie in director Nicholas Roeg's 1976 movie, of an extraterrestrial from a drought-stricken planet who crashlands on earth. He infiltrates society and, teamed with a shrewd businessman (James Laurenson), uses his advanced knowledge to create inventions and build a successful company. He hopes to use his money to build a craft to take him home—and lead his people back here. But a government agent (Robert Pi- cardo) uncovers him and he flees, forced to find another way to build his craft before his people perish—and before he is caught. Lewis Chesler produced HBO's *Hitchhiker* anthology. *Cast:* Lewis Smith (as Thomas Newton), James Laurenson (Felix Hawthorne), Robert Picardo (Agent Richard Morse), Beverly D'Angelo (Eva), Bruce McGill (Gage), Wil Wheaton (Billy), also, Annie Potts, Bobbi Jo Lathan, Henry Sanders, Chris DeRose, Richard Shydner, Bob Neilsen, Steve Natole, Michael Fontaine, Albert Owens, Anne O'Neill, Amy Sawaya, Carl Parker, Hank Stratton, Carmen Argenziano.

2097. **Reddwhite and Blue.** 60 min. Production Company: Aaron Spelling Productions. Executive Producer: Aaron Spelling. A wealthy widow marries a private eye and they run their agency out of her luxurious Beverly Hills mansion.

2098. **Riviera.** 2 hours. Airdate: 5/31/87. Production Company: MTM Enterprises. Director: Alan Smithee (John Frankenheimer). Executive Producer: Michael Sloan. Producer: Robert L. Rosen. Writer: Michael Sloan. Creator: Michael Sloan. Three adventurers—a former spy (Patrick Bauchan), an ex-mercenary (Ben Masters) and a federal agent (Elyssa Davalos)—tackle difficult undercover missions all over Europe. "Alan Smithee" is the nom-de-plume directors frequently use when they are dissatisfied with how their work has been altered by others. The pilot was shot on location in Europe and North Africa. *Cast:* Patrick Bauchan (as Rykker), Ben Masters (Jonathan Patrick Kelly), Elyssa Davalos (Ashley Stevens), Richard Hamilton (Kennedy), Jon Finch (Jeffers), Daniel Emilfork (Messenger), also, Michael Lonsdale, Shane Rimmer, Lalia Ward, Geoffrey Chater, Patrick Monckton, Jacques Marin, George Murcell, Tony Jay, Danil Torppe, Jason Nardone, Stefan Gryff.

2099. **The Spirit.** 60 min. Airdate: 7/31/87. Production Company: Warner Bros. Television. Director: Michael Schultz. Executive Producers: Frank Von Zerneck and Stu Samuels. Producers: Paul Aratow, Steven De Souza, and William Beaudine, Jr. Writer: Steven DeSouza, from the comic book by Will Eisner. Music: Barry Goldenberg. Sam Jones is Denny Colt, a police officer who was shot and left for dead. But he was saved by a boy named Eubie and now, having taken refuge in a mausoleum, fights crime as the masked crusader known as The Spirit. A high- camp pilot that got a thorough panning from most critics not unlike 1979 movie *Flash Gordon,* which also starred Sam Jones. *Cast:* Sam Jones (as The Spirit), Bumper Robinson (Eubie), Garry Walberg (Commissioner Dolan), Nana Vistor (Ellen Dolan), Les Lannom (Officer King), John Allen (Bruno), McKinlay Robinson (P'Gell), Daniel Davis (Simon Teasdale), also, Sarah Dammann, Janet Rotblatt, Ernestine Mercer, Annibal Llende, Joe Newnow, Robert Pastorelli, Bill Marcus, Edmund Cambridge, Bobby Jacoby.

2100. **Waco and Rhinehart.** 2 hours. Airdate: 3/27/87. Production Company: Walt Disney Television. Director: Christian Nyby. Executive Producers: Lee David Zlotoff and Dan Petrie, Jr. Producer: Richard Briggs. Writers: Lee David Zlotoff and Dan Petrie, Jr. Music: Mark Vieha, Klif Magness, and Tom Bahler. Justin Deas and Charles C. Hill are two U.S. marshals—one a slick New Yorker, the other a country boy—who are accidentally teamed up despite their differences. In the proposed series, they would travel around the country tackling special cases puzzling local police at the behest of their boss in Washington, D.C. *Cast:* Justin Deas (as Milo Rhinehart), Charlie Hill (Waco Wheeler), Bob Tzudiker (Chief Ed Peavey), Bill Hootkins (Mirch), also, Kathleen Lloyd, Daniel Feraldo, Eugene Butler, Justin Lord, Carmen Argenziano, Nancy Stafford.

2101. **The White Knight.** 60 min. Producer: Harve Bennett. Sir Lancelot and Sir Mordred are transported to modern-day Los Angeles.

CBS / COMEDY

2102. **The Alan King Show.** 30 min. Airdate: 7/12/86. Production Company: Universal Television. Director: Jim Drake. Executive Producers: Emily Levine and Deanne Barkley. Writer: Emily Levine. Music: Peter Robinson. Alan King is a successful businessman who leaves Wall Street to become a professor at the Long Island college he graduated from. In the pilot, he is named best new professor on campus by an almost unanimous vote of the student body—save one anonymous student who called him "a bully." King becomes obsessed with finding out who the student is. *Cast:* Alan King (as Alan "Coop" Cooper), Dina Merrill (Nan Cooper), Sarah Jessica Parker (Samantha Cooper), Catherine Keener (Abby), Lisa Reiffel (Casey Cooper), Paxton Whitehead (Dean John Emerson), Max Cantor (Kit Henderson), David Knell (Barton Sommers), Robin Menken (Miss Kemper).

2103. **Bloodbrothers.** 30 min. Production Companies: Viacom Enterprises and Procter & Gamble Productions. Director: Gene Reynolds. Executive Producers: Andy Borowitz and Gene Reynolds. Writer: David Chambers. Creator: David Chambers. Charles Rocket and Joe Regalbuto are Rick and Benny, two bosom buddies in college who lost track of each other after leaving school. Rick became a successful yuppie businessman and is in love with a corporate lawyer woman who wants to marry him. One day Benny, who has been wandering the country aimlessly, shows up on Rick's doorstep ready to try and work in the "materialistic world." Rick takes him in—but his girlfriend is worried Benny will ruin her marriage plans. *Cast:* Charles Rocket (as Rick), Joe Regalbuto (Benny), Kristine Sutherland (Leslie).

2104. **Blue Skies.** 30 min. Production Company: CBS Productions. Director: Glenn Jordan. Executive Producers: Carl and Nigel McKeand. Writers: Carol McKeand

and Mark Nasatir. This pilot is an odd mix between *Green Acres* and *The Brady Bunch*. A divorced man (Beau Bridges) marries a hip, divorced New Yorker (Debra Engle) and they move into his rural Idaho home. Together, with her savvy 12-year-old daughter Zoe, his 12-year-old son T.J., and his 8-year-old daughter Sarah, they try to make the family work. To make things worse, the man's cantankerous father, Grandpa Will, separates from his wife and moves in, too. The comedy would come from the clash of cultures as well as the pressures of making a new family work. This was reworked and recast in 1988 as an hour-long dramatic series starring Tom Wopat and Season Hubley. *Cast:* Beau Bridges (as Frank Clayton), Debra Engle (Anne Pfieffer), John Randolph (Grandpa Will), Barrett Oliver (T.J.), Brandy Gold (Sarah), Kim Hauser (Zoe).

2105. **The Family Martinez.** 30 min. Airdate: 8/2/86. Production Company: Embassy Television. Director: Oz Scott. Executive Producers: Tommy Chong and Howard Brown. Producers: Bob Myer, Bob Young, and Roxie Wenk. Writer: Tommy Chong. Creator: Tommy Chong. Robert Beltran stars as a former gang member who becomes a lawyer and returns to his East L.A. home—where he lives with his mother, who is an off-beat artist (she turns his legal notes into a sculpture) and his 16-year-old sister Rainbow. In the pilot, he frees his funloving friend Romeo from jail. Tommy Chong, of the comedy team of Cheech and Chong, wrote and created this pilot, which was reworked and recast as *Amigos* (aka *Trial and Error*) and became a 1988 sitcom starring Eddie Velez and Paul Rodriquez. *Cast:* Robert Beltran (Hector Martinez), Daniel Faraldo (Romeo Ortega), Anne Betancourt (Anita Martinez), Karla Montana (Rainbow Martinez), Denise Crosby (Rachael McCann), Diana Bellamy (Sister Mary Luke), Will Nye (Officer Daniel Kelly), Joshua Gallegos (Gonzalez), Andy Aybar (Schumwald), Mae E. Campbell (Bailiff), Bob Frank (Denton), James Shigeta (Judge Yamamoto).

2106. **Home Improvements.** 30 min. Production Companies: Scholastic Productions and Universal Television. Director: Linda Day. Executive Producer: John Matoian. Writer: Larry Levin. Creator: Larry Levin. Not unlike *Blue Skies*, this too is a sitcom about adjustments when a widower (Tony Lo Bianco) with three kids married a divorcee (Tricia O'Neill) with one. The widower's oldest daughter is married and lives next door—who doesn't like having her role as surrogate mother snatched away. Shot in New York. *Cast:* Tony Lo Bianco (as Joseph Lopardo), Tricia O'Neill (Joanna), Anthony Rapp (Danny), Lycia Naff (Alice Lopardo).

2107. Lily. 60 min. Production Companies: Viacom Enterprises and Platypus Productions. Director: Rick Wallace. Executive Producers: Shelley Duvall and Andy Borowitz. Supervising Producer: Joel Rogosin. Producers: Edward D. Markley and Fred Fuchs. Writer: Andy Borowitz. Shelley Duvall plays a female Indiana Jones in this series proposal. She's Lily Miniver, an undercover investigator with a private Washington, D.C., museum called The Jeffersonian. Her boss (Donald Moffat) sends her all over the world looking for valuable objects and checking out possible art fraud. *Cast:* Shelley Duvall (as Lily Miniver), Donald Moffat (John Farnsworth), also, Peter Jurasik, Beverly Hope Atkinson, Tom Conti, and Spiros Focus.

2108. Mixed Company. 30 min. Production Company: Lorimar-Telepictures Productions. Director: Joel Zwick. Producers: Tom Miller and Bob Boyett. This sitcom, about the misadventures of New York firefighters, was trying for a "M*A*S*H"-like approach to comedy. The series would focus as much on the six public servants (two of whom are women, one a mother) fighting fires as well as fighting amongst themselves as they share a typical 24-hour shift together.

2109. Rita (aka The Rita Moreno Show). 30 min. Airdate: 8/13/86. Production Companies: Gabe Katzka Productions and 20th Century Fox Television. Director: Dave Powers. Executive Producers: Pat Nardo and Gabe Katzka. Writer: Allen Leicht. Rita Moreno plays a hot-tempered toy puppet designer who rules over a brood that includes her husband (Barry Primus), three children, and a housekeeper (Ruth Jaroslow) who behaves as if she is Rita's mother. Moreno, in press reports, said "the series idea was marvelous. Oh, I did love it. But the chemistry wasn't right." The pilot was shot in New York. *Cast:* Rita Moreno (as Rita Best), Barry Primus (Max Best), April Lehrman (Fernanda "Nandy" Best), Mollie Hall (Adrian Best), Jeremy Schein (Nicky Best), Ruth Jaroslow (Mrs. Gladstone).

2110. Shelley. 30 min. Production Company: Alan Landsburg Productions. Director: Peter Bonerz. Executive Producer: Alan Landsburg. Producers: Michael and Jake Weinberger. Writers: Michael and Jake Weinberger. Shelley Winters and Harry Guardino are a retired couple who, after turning over their appliance business to their son-in-law and touring the country in their motorhome, return to Scottsdale, Arizona, and adopt three children—which comes as a big surprise to the couple's daughter (Lee Garlington), her husband, and their child. *Cast:* Shelley Winters (as Shelley), Harry Guardino (Mike), Leel Garlington (Paula), Brandon Call (Danny), Laura Jacoby (Margy), Christian Hoff (Nick).

2111. Sisters. 30 min. Production Companies: Fries Entertainment and Procter & Gamble Productions. Executive Producers: Paul Belous and Bob Wolterstorff. Producer: George Sunga. Writers: Paul Belous and Bob Wolterstorff. Two sisters in their 40s—Joan and Naomi—have a hard time adjusting when the youngest, left penniless after her third divorce, is forced to move in with her liberal elder sister in Connecticut. Stuck in the middle of their constant bickering is Brian, Naomi's 20-year-old son, who never knows which side he should stand on. The pilot starred Sally Kellerman and Gail Strickland.

2112. We're Putting on the Ritz (aka Puttin' on the Ritz). 60 min. Airdate: 7/26/86. Production Companies: Alan Wagner Productions and Reeves Entertainment. Director: Michael Tuchner. Executive Producers: Merrill Grant and Alan Wagner. Producers: Ira Marvin and Joseph Kane. Writers: Michael Zettler and Shelly Altman. The adventures of Micki and Max (Leah Ayres and Matt McCoy), both of whom work for reclusive millionaire John Wilkes Barry, who is never seen. She's his secretary, he's his chauffeur, they both lead double lives—they also pretend to be wealthy brother-and-sister socialites who are residing with Mr. Barry. Inevitably this leads to trouble (of the crime-solving kind), especially since they must keep their double lives a secret from Mr. Barry, the house staff, and the chic New York society they are hoodwinking. *Cast:* Leah Ayres (as Micki Cline), Matt McCoy (Max Montana), George N. Martin (Mr. Duvall), Kim Chan (Mr. Mao), also, John Horton, John Bedford-Lloyd, Jane Hoffman, Rosalyn Landor, James Cahill, Phillip Benichou, Arthur French.

CBS / DRAMA

2113. Adam's Apple. 60 min. Airdate: 8/23/86. Production Company: CBS Productions. Director: James Frawley. Executive Producer: Frank Abatemarco. Producer: Andrew Gottlieb. Writer: Frank Abatemarco. Creator: Frank Abatemarco. Music: Lee Holdridge. New York private eye Toni Adams (Syndey Walsh) is *too* much—she's a Yale-educated, former district attorney with four years of Army training in weapons, munitions and self-defense. Her boyfriend works for a top-notch law firm and refers cases, her friend Janice gets her information from the D.A.'s office (to the consternation of her old boss Trisha), and Det. Marshall is her friend-on-the-force. In the pilot, shot in New York, she defends a man falsely accused of rape. Frank Abatemarco and CBS would team up in

1987 on the shortlived series *Legwork,* which starred Margaret Colin as a sharp New York private eye. *Cast:* Sydney Walsh (as Toni Adams), John Furey (Jeff Chapman), Cherry Jones (Janice Eaton), Kasi Lemmons (Marcy Potts), Terrence V. Mann (Det. Danny Marshall), Carolyn Seymour (D.A. Trisha Hammond), Lois Smith (Dora Adams), Polly Draper (Bernadette Pascoe), Keith Szarabajka (Garth Russell), Benjamin Hendrickson (Mitlock), John Cunningham (George Markell), Ron Parady (Paul Neumier), Jim Borelli (Richie).

2114. D.C. Cop. 60 min. Airdate: 8/27/86. Production Companies: Stonehenge Productions and Paramount Television. Director: Mel Damski. Executive Producer: Dick Berg. Producers: Allen J. Marcil and Neal Nordlinger. Writers: James Grady and Dick Berg. Music: Tony Berg. Cotter Smith is Lt. John Halsey, a former Washington, D.C. police reporter who becomes a cop. He often collides with Deborah Matthews (Carolyn McCormick), the new police reporter, whom he thinks isn't tough enough. The pilot story, shot on location in Washington, D.C., had Halsey chasing a lawyer (Fritz Weaver) who kills his mistress (Nancy Stafford) before she can testify against him. McCormick costarred during 86–87 on *Spenser: For Hire. Cast:* (in brackets, the original names of the characters as listed in CBS internal reports) Cotter Smith (Det. John Halsey [Michael Halsey]), Robert Hooks (Deputy Chief Peter Jensen [Nathan Jackson]), Carolyn McCormick (Deborah Matthews [Deborah Matheson]), Mario Van Peebles (Det. Cliff Dickerson), Kyle T. Heffner (Det. Lucas Adams).

2115. Kung Fu: The Movie (aka The Return of Kung Fu). 2 hours. Airdate: 2/1/86. Production Companies: Lou-Step Productions and Warner Bros. Television. Director: Richard Lang. Executive Producer: Paul R. Picard. Producers: Skip Ward and David Carradine. Writer: Durrell Royce Crays, from the TV series created by Ed Spielman and developed by Herman Miller. Music: Lalo Schifrin. An attempt to revive *Kung Fu,* the 1972–75 ABC series. David Carradine once again is Kwai Chang Caine, the soft-spoken Shaolin priest who fled China after being forced to kill an Imperial Manchu's son. Caine became a loner, roaming the West, pursued by Chinese assassins and American bounty hunters. He hated violence, but when he had to, he relied on the deadly art of Kung Fu and other teachings of Master Po (Keye Luke), his blind mentor in China. In the pilot, he's framed for murder, accidentally uncovers an opium smuggling ring, and the assassins he's eluded in the series catch up with him—The Manchu Lord and his deadly servant Chung Wang. CBS and producer Paul Picard later updated

Kung Fu to the present day for 1987–88's unsold pilot *Way of the Dragon* (aka *Kung Fu: The Next Generation* and *Warriors*), which focused on Caine's Chinese-American namesake and descendant, played by David Darlow. The two concepts would be combined in *Kung Fu: The Legend Continues*, a 1993-1997 syndicated series that starred Carradine as a modern-day descendent of Caine who teams up with his estranged son, a cop played by Chris Potter, to fight crime. *Cast:* David Carradine (as Kwai Chang Caine), Kerrie Keane (Sarah Perkins), Mako (The Manchu), William Lucking (Wyatt), Luke Askew (Sheriff Mills), Keye Luke (Master Po), Benson Fong (The Old One), Brandon Lee (Chung Wang), Martin Landau (John Martin Perkins), Ellen Geer (Old Wife), Robert Harper (Prosecutor), Paul Rudd (Rev. Lawrence Perkins), John Alderman (Well Dressed Man), Michael Paul Chan (Ching), Patience Cleveland (Maid), Roland Harrah, III (Liu), Jim Haynie (Federal Marshal), Roy Jenson (Foreman).

2116. **Maggie (aka Starting Over).** 60 min. Airdate: 7/19/86. Production Company: Warner Bros. Television. Director: Waris Hussein. Producer: William Hill. Writers: Juanita Bartlett, Katherine Craddock, and Rod Browning. Music: Charles Fox. Stefanie Powers is Maggie Webb, an American in England who is left broke when her journalist-husband dies and leaves her nothing but a big home and a giant tax debt. Her sister-in-law (Ava Gardner) hires her to work in her international public relations firm so she can make some money to keep the government, in the form of tax collector Ian Ogilvy (Simon Templar in *The Return of the Saint*) at bay. Maggie, somehow, always stumbles into trouble—and crimesolving. She's aided by Pidge, her husband's reporter friend and Jeremy, an impoverished young aristocrat who moves into her house as a boarder. Shot on location in London. *Cast:* Stefanie Powers (as Maggie Webb), Ava Gardner (Diane Webb), Ian Ogilvy (Denholm Sinclair), Jeremy Lloyd (Jeremy Ashton-Davis), Herb Edelman (Harry Pidge Pidgeon), Paul Geoffrey (Flintwright), Barry Corbin (Jimmy Scott Farnsworth), Deborah Foreman (Alyce Farnsworth), Alley Mills (Charlotte Farnsworth), Don Fellows (Ralph Booker), Betsy Flair (Eulene Booker), Marshall Colt (Charles McLean), Lucy Aston (Receptionist).

2117. **Power's Play.** 60 min. Airdate: 8/30/86. Production Companies: Furia/Oringer Productions and Proctor & Gamble Productions. Director: Kevin Connor. Executive Producers: Barry Oringer and John Furia, Jr. Producer: Lorin B. Salob. Writers: James David Buchanan and Noreen Stone, from a story by Harry and Renee Longstreet, James David Buchanan, Noreen Stone, and Pamela Chais.

Twenty-five-year-old Rowena Powers (Sheree J. Wilson) inherits a huge multi-national corporation from her recently deceased father—whom she thought had died in a car accident when she was a baby. Not only does she have to learn about the company—and the life her father led—but she has to cope with Daddy's partner, dashing adventurer Lucas Cord (David Birney). Shot on location in Arizona and Canada. *Cast:* David Birney (as Lucas Cord), Sheree J. Wilson (Rowena Powers), Noah Beery (Harry), Thaao Penghlis (Paul), Kurtwood Smith (Major), David Longworth (First Survivalist), Jacob Rupp (Second Survivalist), Alex Green (Third Survivalist), Garwin Sanford (Male Secretary), Campbell Lane (First Executive), Ernie Philips (Shaman), Gabrile George (Indian Boy), Franklin Johnson (Prospector), Buffalo Child (Guide), Leroy Schultz (Geologist), Douglas Tuck (Manager).

2118. **R.E.L.A.X.** 60 min. Production Company: CBS Productions. Director: Paul Michael Glaser. Executive Producers: Barry Beckerman and Floyd Mutrux. Producers: Alan Levin and Bernie Sofronski. Writer: Floyd Mutrux. The adventures of the Regional Enforcement officers at Los Angeles International Airport—a team made up of airport security agents, FBI agents, L.A.P.D. officers, sheriff's deputies and customs agents. The cast includes Scott Colomby, Richard Tyson, Patti D'Arbanville, Pepe Serna, Larry Fishburne, Michael Bowen, Tim Carhart, and Jana Marie Hupp. Glaser, who directed many *Miami Vice* episodes, is perhaps best known as Starsky in *Starsky and Hutch*.

2119. **Stark II (aka Stark: Mirror Image).** 90 min. Airdate: 5/14/86. Production Company: CBS Productions. Director: Noel Nosseck. Producers: David H. Balkan and Sam Strangis. Writer: David H. Balkan. Creators: David H. Balkan and Ernest Tidyman. Music: Peter Myers. Theme: Bill Conti. Nicholas Surovy is once again Wichita police detective Evan Stark, this time dispatched to Las Vegas to find out who killed his former partner (Ben Murphy). Dennis Hopper, Barry Gordon, and Pat Corley reprise their roles from the original pilot. Shot on location. *Cast:* Nicholas Surovy (as Evan Stark), Pat Corley (Chief Waldren), Ben Murphy (Steve Graves), Michelle Phillips (Jennifer Clayton), David Ackroyd (Kenneth Clayton), Barry Gordon (Lee Fogel), Dennis Hopper (Lt. Ron Bliss), Belinda J. Montgomery (Claire Graves), Kirstie Alley (Maggie), Alan Chandler (Baker), Gina Gershon (Allison Cromwell), Peter Boyden (Chester Moonchase), Thomas Ryan (Wade Davis), Jeffrey Josephson (Clement), Diane Delano (Simone Lubchansky), Sly-Ali Smith (Patrolman), Theresa Gilmore (Dance Instructor),

Rick Wagner (Police Officer), Rusty Feuer (Acting Instructor), Stefan Zema (Delvecchio), Jim Owen (Hotel Guard), Maureen Hopkins (Judge), Rose Rivers (Donna), Karyn Sherman (Woman Customer).

2120. **T.J. Hooker: Blood Sport.** 2 hours. Airdate: 5/21/86. Production Companies: Spelling-Goldberg Productions and Columbia Pictures Television. Director: Vincent McEveety. Executive Producer: Leonard Goldberg. Producers: Rick Husky, Kenneth R. Koch, and Don Ingalls. Writers: Rudolph Borchert, Don Ingalls, Stan Berkowitz, Bruce Reisman, and Rick Husky. Creator: Rick Husky. Music: John Davis. Theme: Mark Snow. A pilot for a primetime revival of *T.J. Hooker*, a series that ran on ABC from 1982–85, before becoming a short-lived, first-run, CBS latenight series in 1985. Sgt. T.J. Hooker (William Shatner) goes to Hawaii to protect his Senator friend (Don Murray) and his wife (Kim Miyori) from killers. Hooker clashes with a Hawaiian cop (Henry Darrow), an assassin (James Pax) and a mobster (Soon-Teck Oh). His faithful friends, L.C.P.D. officers Stacy Sheridan (Heather Locklear) and Jim Corrigan (James Darren) are also along for the ride and are joined by newcomer, eager Hawaii police officer Yuji Okumoto. This pilot, and the latenight series, ignored the fact that Sgt. Hooker, in the last episode of the ABC series, jumped to the Chicago police force (on temporary assignment). *Cast:* William Shatner (as T.J. Hooker), Heather Locklear (Stacy Sheridan), James Darren (Jim Corrigan), Don Murray (Senator Stuart Grayle), Kim Miyori (Barbara Grayle), Yuji Okumoto (Howie Kalanuma), Nobu McCarthy (Nikko McAllister), Tim O'Connor (John McAllister), Henry Darrow (Gus Kalioki), Soon-Teck Oh (Ginzo), James Pax (Makio), Keye Luke (Dr. Makimura), Hugh Farrington (Lt. O'Brien), Randy Hamilton (Tim Braddock), Buck Taylor (Officer Phillips), Casey Sander (Ricky), Dana Lee (Fujikawa), Jacquie Koch (Carol Raymond), Branscombe Richmond (Bartender), Tanja Walker (Nancy Bosca).

NBC / COMEDY

2121. **All the Way Home (aka Taking It Home).** 30 min. Airdate: 9/12/86. Production Companies: UBU Productions and Paramount Television. Director: Sam Weisman. Executive Producer: Gary David Goldberg. Producers: Ruth Bennett and Susan Seeger. Writers: Ruth Bennett and Susan Seeger. A spin-off from *Family Ties* built around Nick Morelli (Scott Valentine), Mallory's (Justine

Bateman) boyfriend on the hit sitcom. Nick returns to his hometown of Detroit and helps save his family's struggling toy business following his father's death. Costar Herschel Bernardi died in May 1986, four weeks after completing this pilot. A new format for Valentine was developed in 1987–88, and the subsequent pilot, entitled *The Art of Being Nick*, aired after the *Cosby Show* to big ratings but, alas, no series deal. *Cast:* Scott Valentine (as Nick Morelli), Herschel Bernardi (Papa Joe), Natalia Nogulich (Kitty), Summer Phoenix (Frannie), Ray Baker (Johnny), Harry Basil (Cousin Gino), Lisa Jane Persky (Sheilah), Liz Torres (Lola).

2122. Hotel Hawaii (aka Sylvan in Paradise). 30 min. Airdate: 8/2/86. Production Company: United Artists Television. Director: Terry Hughes. Executive Producers: Robert Illes and James Stein. Producer: Gayle S. Maffeo. Writers: Robert Illes and James Stein. Jim Nabors is a dim-witted, bumbling bell captain at a third-rate Hawaiian resort hotel where his sister Polly runs a gift shop. This pilot managed to crack the Nielsen top 10 the week it aired but still couldn't crack the fall schedule. *Cast:* Jim Nabors (as Sylvan Sprayberry), Ann Wedgeworth (Polly), Brent Spiner (Clinton C. Waddle), Courteney Cox (Lucy), Glenn Withrow (Sparky).

2123. The Line. 30 min. Airdate: 7/29/87. Director: Witt-Thomas Productions. Director: Terry Hughes. Executive Producers: Paul Junger Witt and Tony Thomas. Producer: Marsha Posner Williams. Writers: Katherine Reback and Barbara Benedik, from a story by Katherine Reback, Barbara Benedik, and Marc Sotkin. Creator: Katherine Reback. The lives of four women working on an assembly line in a Houston aerospace plant—Denise (Alfre Woodard), a single mother raising a teenage son; Lucy (Park Overall), who married when she was sixteen; Jo (Lori Petty), a party-going playgirl; and Karen (Dinah Manoff), who recently moved here from New York with her blue collar husband. *Cast:* Dinah Manoff (as Karen Cooper), Alfre Woodard (Denise Powell), C.C.H. Pounder (Anna Mae Demsey), Lori Petty (Jo Lanier), Park Overall (Lucy Kershaw), Brian George (Benno), Andrew Rubin (Ken Morris), Cecilia Garcia (Rachel), Lou Hancock (Alice).

2124. She's with Me. 30 min. Airdate: 7/19/86. Production Company: Embassy Television. Director: John Bowab. Executive Producers: Ron Leavitt and Michael Moye. Producer: John Anderson. Writers: Ron Leavitt and Michael Moye. Creators: Ron Leavitt, Michael Moye, and David W. Duclon. A comedy about an ordinary, bland, New York divorcee (Dinah Manoff) working as a door-to-door cosmetics saleswoman who becomes friends with a rich, flashy, jet-setting European model (Jerry Hall). Together, they set off to explore each other's vastly different social circles. *Cast:* Dinah Manoff (as Edie Gruber), Jerry Hall (Maris McKay), Candy Azzara (Alma Alderman), Christopher Rich (Cubby Lyons), Charles R. Floyd (Mark Denton), Beatrice Cohen (Woman #1), Carol Helvey (Woman #2), Michael Sabatino (Ray), Betty Kean (Wendi), Earl Boen (Waiter), Larry McKay (D.J.).

2125. The Stiller & Meara Show. 30 min. Airdate: 6/9/86. Production Companies: Stiller & Meara Enterprises, Mort Lachman & Associates, and Reeves Entertainment. Director: Hal Cooper. Executive Producer: Mort Lachman. Writers: Jerry Stiller and Anne Meara. Creators: Jerry Stiller and Anne Meara. Music: Artie Butler. The misadventures of Jerry and Anne Bender, a couple celebrating their 30th wedding anniversary. He's a New York City assistant deputy mayor and she's an actress who does commercials. Their oldest boy Daniel, a law school drop-out, plays his Sax on a street corner; their daughter Krissy is a married psychologist who loves to give advice, to her husband and child and to her parents; and their teenage son Max always seems to get into trouble. *Cast:* Jerry Stiller (as Jerry Bender), Anne Meara (Anne Bender), Todd Waring (Daniel Bender), Peter Smith (Max Bender), Laura Innes (Krissy Bender Marino), Bill Cobbs (Lt. Langston).

NBC / DRAMA

2126. The Annihilator. 2 hours. Airdate: 4/6/86. Production Company: Universal Television. Director: Michael Chapman. Executive Producer: Roderick Taylor. Producer: Alex Beaton. Writers: Roderick Taylor and Bruce Taylor. Music: Sylvester Levay. Mark Lindsay Chapman is a newspaper publisher who discovers that his reporter girlfriend (Catherine Mary Stewart), and all the passengers of a commercial jetliner she was on, have been eliminated and replaced by alien-made robots. He kills her in self defense and is hunted by both the police (who want him for murder) and the aliens (who don't want him ruining their plans of world domination). Chapman was to have portrayed John Lennon in the 1985 NBC TV movie *John and Yoko: A Love Story* but was fired because he had the same name as Len- non's killer. Roderick Taylor produced CBS' short-lived

1985 series *Otherworld*. *Cast:* Mark Lindsay Chapman (as Richard Armour), Catherine Mary Stewart (Angela Taylor), Susan Blakely (Layla), Lisa Blount (Cindy), Earl Boen (Sid), Geoffrey Lewis (Alan Jeffries), Nicole Eggert (Elyse), Brion James (Alien), Barry Pearl (Eddie), Paul Brinegar (Pops), Channing Chase (Susan Weiss), Barbara Townsend (Celia Evans), Glen Vernon (Henry Evans), Biff Yeager (F.B.I. Agent), Richard Partlow (F.B.I. Agent #2), Toni Attell (Patti), James Parks (Policeman), Roger LaRue (Man in Coat), Stanley Bennett Clay (Cammie), Gregg Collins (Policeman).

2127. **Blue De Ville.** 2 hours. Airdate: 12/29/86. Production Companies: B&E Enterprises and NBC Productions. Director: Jim Johnston. Executive Producers: Eugene Ross-Leming and Brad Buckner. Producers: Christopher Nelson and Edward D. Markley. Writers: Brad Buckner and Eugene Ross-Leming. Music: Don Felder. The misadventures of two young girls and a musician on a cross country trek in a '59 Cadillac Coupe De Ville. *Cast:* Jennifer Runyon (as J.C. Swift), Kimberley Pistone (Gus Valentine), Mark Thomas Miller (Rod Sandusky), Alan Autry (Sgt. Augie Valentine), Robert T. Prescott (Kevin), Nicole Mercurio (Vee Valentine), William Frankfather (President Fryborg), Noel Conlon (Marshall Swift), Laurel Adams (Mrs. Fryborg), Toni Sawyer (Justine Swift), John Lafayette (Myers), Paul Scheurer (Jeff), Hal Havins (Shoe), Joe Lynn Turner (Eric).

2128. **C.A.T. Squad.** 2 hours. Airdate: 7/27/86. Production Companies: NBC Productions and Filmline International. Director: William Friedkin. Executive Producer: William Friedkin. Producers: David Salven and Bud Smith. Writer: Gerald Petievich. Creator: Gerald Petievich. Music: Ennio Morricone. An odd attempt at crossing the humorless, methodical capering of *Mission Impossible* with the slick, stylish bloodshed of *Miami Vice*. Director/producer Friedkin reteamed with Treasury agent-turned-novelist Gerald Petievich, with whom he made the theatrical film *To Live and Die in L.A.*, to make this hard-edged, violent pilot about the adventures of four federal agents working in the elite Counter Assault Tactical squad. Joseph Cortese is the stone-faced leader of the espionage/anti-terrorist team, which includes a weapons expert (football star Jack Youngblood), a forensics expert (Patricia Charbonneau), and an undercover expert (Steve James). In the pilot, they try to stop the systematic murders of scientists involved in a top-secret government laser project. A sequel/pilot was mounted in 1988. *Cast:* Joseph Cortese (as John "Doc" Burkholder), Steven James (Bud Raines), Jack

Youngblood (John Sommers), Patricia Charbonneau (Nikki Pappas), Bradley Whitford (Leon Trepper), Edwin Velez (Carlos), Thomas Hauff (Nolan), John Novak (Connery), Hans Boggild (Por- zig), Michael Sinelnikoff (Sir Cyril), Sam Gray (Spivak), Ann Curry (Janet), Reg Hanson (Woodhouse), Al Shannon (Irish Johnny), Anna Maria Horsford (Mrs. Raines), Umar Rasberry (Buddy Jr.), Pamela Collyer (Janice).

2129. **Dalton: Code of Vengeance II.** 2 hours. Airdate: 5/11/86. Production Company: Universal Television. Director: Alan Smithee. Executive Producer: Lou Shaw. Producer: Herman Miller. Writers: Luther Murdoch and Aiken Woodruff. Creator: Willard Walpole. Music: Don Peake. Charles Taylor reprises his role as loner David Dalton, a Vietnam Special Forces veteran roaming the country in his motor home with his dog Wichita. The first pilot about this watered-down Rambo aired in June 1985 and scored in the Nielsen top 10. In this sequel, Dalton's former commanding officer (Donnelly Rhodes) has gone crazy and formed his own radical paramilitary organization. The c.o.'s wife asks Dalton for help. (Alan Smithee is the pseudonym used when a director removes his name from a film.) *Cast:* Charles Taylor (as David Dalton), Ed Bruce (Sheriff Johnson), Donnelly Rhodes (Major Bennett), Karen Landry (Jeanne Bennett), Shannon Stein (Tip Bennett), Alex Harvey (Sheriff Willoughby), Belinda J. Montgomery (Libby), Mitch Pileggi (Verbeck), Tony Frank (Honus), William Sanderson (Bobby), Jim Howard (Deputy), Mac Aikenhead (Harry), Thomas Baird (Freddie), Sal Biagini (Surfer), Jerry Biggs (Randy), James Monroe Black (Paramedic), John Allen Brasington (Man), Blue Deckert (Deputy Campbell), Jim Howard (Deputy Morris), Will Knickerbocker (Clerk), Bradley Leland Williams (Deputy Hackett), John Meadows (Minister), James Brett Rice (Sgt. Brown).

2130. **Dalton's Code of Vengeance: Rustler's Moon.** 60 min. Airdate: 7/27/86. Production Company: Universal Television. Director: Winrich Kolbe. Executive Producers: Alex Beaton and Robert F. O'Neil. Producers: Edward K. Dodds and Bruce Bell. Writers: Joe Gannon, Ross Hagen, and Jim Trombetta. Creator: Willard Walpole. Yet another *Dalton* pilot, this time sporting a new production team. Dalton helps a Houston rancher (Susan Walden) harassed by rustlers. Guest stars include Larry Drake, Paul Carr, Mickey Gilley, Brandon Smith, Dave Efrom, Chris Douridas, Harvey H. Christianson, J. David Moeller, and Edward Geldart.

2131. Dalton's Code of Vengeance: The Last Holdout. 60 min. Airdate: 8/24/86 (or 8/10/86). Production Company: Universal Television. Executive Producers: Alex Beaton and Robert F. O'Neil. Producers: Edward K. Dodds and Bruce Bell. Creator: Willard Walpole. Dalton (Charles Taylor) travels to New Orleans, where he helps a produce seller fight an evil real estate tycoon who wants the property.

2132. Popeye Doyle. 2 hours. Airdate: 9/7/86. Production Company: 20th Century Fox Television. Director: Peter Levin. Executive Producer: Robert Singer. Producer: Richard Dilello. Technical Consultant: Eddie Egan. Writer: Richard Dilello. Music: Brad Fiedel. Another attempt to turn the adventures of real-life cop Eddie Egan, popularized in director William Friedkin's 1971 movie *The French Connection*, into a TV series. Gene Hackman portrayed Egan, dubbed Popeye Doyle in the movie, and won an Oscar. He reprised the role in the sequel *French Connection II*. Later, Eugene Roche starred in a half-hour ABC pilot called *Egan*, also based on Eddie Egan's adventures as an N.Y.P.D. detective. In fact, Egan himself became an actor, and costarred in the TV series *Eischied*. Now, Ed O'Neill is Popeye Doyle, a tough narcotics detective absorbed in his job. Matthew Laurance is his partner, and James Handy is his boss. (Later that year, both Ed O'Neill and Matthew Laurance would land starring roles in sitcoms for the new Fox Broadcasting Company: O'Neill in *Married With Children*, Laurance in *Duet*.) *Cast*: Ed O'Neill (as Popeye Doyle), Matthew Laurance (Tony Parese), James Handy (Lt. Gregory Paulus), Audrey Landers (Jill Anneyard), Elias Zarou (Fahoud Nazzin), Candy Clark (Corrine), Nicholas Kadi (The Weasel), George de la Pena (The Shadow), Gary Tacon (Deli Bandit #1), Phil Neilson (Deli Bandit #2), Elizabeth Len- nie (Toni), Richard Monette (Patrick Henley), Peter Virgile (Pretty Boy), S.J. Fellows (Nurse #1), Guy Sanvido (Sammy), Phillip Williams (Patrolman #1), Linda Gambell (Nurse #2), Chick Roberts (Detective Bender), Jonathan Simmons (Park Patrolman), Richard McMillan (Apartment Manager), Joanna Perica (Connie Parese), Alexandria Innes (Maria Rodriquez), Tony Rosato (Wiseass Reporter), Todd Postlethwaite (Club Manager), Susan Diol (The Blonde).

2133. The Return of the Greatest American Hero (aka Another Great American Hero; aka A New Great American Hero; aka Greatest American Heroine). 20 min. Production Company: Stephen J. Cannell Productions. Director: Tony Mordente. Executive Producers: Stephen J. Cannell and Babs Greyhosky.

Producer: Jo Swerling, Jr. Writer: Babs Greyhosky. Creator: Stephen J. Cannell. Music: Mike Post and Pete Carpenter. A demonstration film aimed at sparking a revamped version of the ABC series *The Greatest American Hero* for the Sunday evening, 7–8 p.m. timeslot (that eventually went to *Our House*). The original series followed schoolteacher Ralph Hinkley (William Katt), who was given a superhero suit by benevolent aliens and fought crime with conservative F.B.I. agent Bill Maxwell (Robert Culp). Now, the aliens give the suit to a young woman (Mary Ellen Stuart), also a school teacher and a foster parent (to Mya Akerling), and she, too, fights baddies with Maxwell's help. The demo film was later combined with excerpts from previous episodes, dubbed *Greatest American Heroine*, and added to the syndication package. Jerry Potter and John Zee guest starred.

1987–1988

ABC / COMEDY

2134. Bride of Boogedy. 60 min. Airdate: 4/12/87. Production Company: Walt Disney Television. Director: Oz Scott. Producers: Oz Scott and Michael Janover. Writer: Michael Janover. Aired as an episode of *The Disney Sunday Movie*. This is the second attempt to sell ABC on *Mr. Boogedy* (4/23/86), the misadventures of a New England family haunted by a mischievous pilgrim who sold his soul to the devil 300 years ago. *Cast:* Richard Masur (as Carleton Davis), Mimi Kennedy (Eloise Davis), Tammy Lauren (Jennifer), David Faustino (Corwin), Joshua Rudoy (Ahri), Leonard Frey (Walter Witherspoon), Howard Witt (Mr. Boogedy), Eugene Levy (Tom Lynch).

2135. Canteen Ladies. 30 min. Production Companies: Avnet/Kerner Productions and Disney Productions. Executive Producers: John Avnet and Jordan Kerner. Writers: Gary Jacobs and Harold Kimmel. The misadventures of Viola and May, two opinionated, working class gals who have toiled in the White House cafeteria for 20 years, and readily share their views with the senators, congressmen, and bureaucrats they befriend.

2136. Cowboy Joe. 30 min. Airdate: 9/16/88. Production Company: Imagine Entertainment. Director: Barnet Kellman. Executive Producers: Bob Dolman and Dori Weiss. Writer: Bob Dolman. Music: Ry Cooder. Tom Callaway is "Cowboy" Joe Cutler, who deserted his loving, devoted wife (Patti Lupone) and his daughter (Louanne) 15 years ago and now reappears at their doorstep, wanting to be a part of the family again. The proposed series would depict their efforts at being a family once again. *Cast:* Tom Callaway (as Cowboy Joe Cutler), Patti LuPone (Linda Tud- muck), Louanne (Isabelle), also, J. Michael Flynn.

2137. Doodles. 30 min. Airdate: 8/26/88. Production Companies: Beth Poison Productions and Tristar Television. Director: Robert Scheerer. Executive Producer: Beth Poison. Writer: Emily Tracy. Hoyt Axton is Doodles, the outspoken owner of a small-town general store and surrogate father to an eight-year-old tomboy (Gennie James) who hangs out at his place afterschool because both her parents (Chris Cote and Melanie Jones) work. Shot on location in Houston. Costars included Ryan Beadle and Ann Wedgeworth.

2138. **Mona.** 30 min. Airdate: 5/12/87. Production Company: Embassy Television. Director: Assad Kelada. Producers: Marty Cohan and Blake Hunter. Writers: Marty Cohan and Blake Hunter. Aired as an episode of *Who's the Boss?* An attempt to spin-off series regular Katherine Helmond into a series of her own. Mona moves to New York to operate and renovate a rundown hotel with her stuffy brother Cornelius (James B. Sikking), a retired military man.

2139. **The Oprah Winfrey Show (aka Natalie).** 30 min. Production Companies: Reeves Entertainment and Mort Lachman Productions. Director: Barnet Kellman. Executive Producer: Mort Lachman. Writers: Winifred Hervey and Mort Lachman. ABC hoped to capitalize on the phenomenal success of syndicated talk- show host Oprah Winfrey by giving her a 13-episode commitment for a sitcom loosely based on her own life. However, Winfrey scuttled the deal after filming the pilot, which she publicly decried as horrible, and chose instead to concentrate on her movie career. The pilot died, however, after Helmond decided that she wanted "to stick with a winner" rather than gamble on a spin-off.

2140. **Peggy Sue.** 30 min. Production Companies: Rastar Productions and TriStar Television. Writers: Arlene Sarner and Jerry Leichtling. Based on the 1987 motion picture *Peggy Sue Got Married*, which was written by Sarner and Leichtling. The proposed series would follow Peggy Sue, a 40-year-old woman who travels back in time to 1960, where she begins reliving her life knowing what the future holds for her—unless she changes things.

2141. **Second Stage.** 30 min. Production Companies: Winkler/Rich Productions and Paramount Television. Director: John Rich. Executive Producers: Henry Winkler and John Rich. Writer: Carol Gary. Joanna Cassidy is a divorced mother who, with her 16-year-old son (Kriss Kamm), decides to give up her low-paying L.A. job, move to Boston, and work in her father's public relations firm. It's a chance for her to make more money, for her son to get to know his grandfather, and for her to come to terms with her father's new wife (Cecilia Hart), who is younger than she is.

2142. **Too Many Cooks (aka Home Again).** 30 min. Airdate: 7/2/88. Production Companies: Pillsbury/Sanford Productions, Giggling Goose Productions, and Warner Bros. Television. Director: Art Dielhenn. Executive Producers: Sarah Pillsbury, Midge Sanford, and Gary Gilbert. Producer: Jan Siegelman. Writers: Gary Gilbert and Harvey Miller. Music: Tyrell Mann. The misadventures of

Maureen DeFranco (Betty Thomas) and Estelle Foster (Deborah Rush), two estranged sisters who inherit their mother's restaurant in their small, Ohio hometown. Other characters include their mother's old lover (Henry Gibson), Maureen's 16-year-old daughter (Pam Segall), and a dim-witted, but handsome, busboy (Beau Dremann). *Cast:* Betty Thomas (as Maureen DeFranco), Deborah Rush (Estelle Foster), Pam Segall (Angela DeFranco), Joe Guzaldo (Derek), Beau Dremann (Brian), Henry Gibson (Duke).

2143. **Wayside School.** 30 min. Production Company: Broadcast Arts. Director: Tom Schlamme. Executive Producers: Michael Barker and Peter Rosenthal. Producer: Pam Norris. Writer: Pam Norris. The producers planned to mix live action with animation, puppetry, and other special effects to tell the story of Andy, the new kid in a typical American high school. Other characters include the stern principal, Miss Mangles, whom everyone fears; the beautiful Miss Butterfield, the teacher every child loves; and the strange custodian Van Zandt, who has a mysterious past and a big crush on the kids' favorite teacher. *Cast:* P.J. Ochlon (as Andy), Bobo Lewis (Miss Mangles), J. Smith-Cameron (Miss Butterfield), Conrad McLaren (Van Zandt).

ABC / DRAMA

2144. **After Midnight.** 60 min. Airdate: 4/30/88. Production Company: Orion Television. Director: Tony Richardson. Executive Producer: Richard Kletter. Producer: David Latt. Writer: Richard Kletter. Music: Stewart Copeland. The adventures of four night owls—Donna (Stella Hall), a freelance photographer; Joe (John Goodman), her widowed lover who runs a market; Arthur (Calvin Leavells), a private detective; and Iowa (Kyle Secor), a bartender at the hot nightspot where they all met. Their story, as well as the stories they become involved with, are told to us by an omniscient voice called "The Storyteller"—and whom the characters know as a nameless voice on the radio. *Cast:* Gary Cole (as Gordon), John Goodman (Joe), Dedee Pfeiffer (April), Calvin Leavells (Arthur), Kyle Secor (Iowa), Stella Hall (Donna), Joelle Allen (Lulu), Denis Forest (Chef), George Duza (James), J.J. Stocker (Timmy), also, Kenneth McGregor, Ewart Williams, Jane Brucker, Todd Graff, Barbara Harris, Patrick Myles.

2145. **Best of Times.** Production Companies: Columbia Pictures Television and Aaron Spelling Productions. A proposed "Love Boat"-style anthology about a woman who holds different kinds of reunions (the old Vietnam squadron, the college cheerleading team, the graduating class of '65, etc.) at her home. The stories would have revolved around the different guests who are reunited each week.

2146. **Circus.** 60 min. Airdate: 8/3/87. Production Companies: Khrys One Inc. Productions, Phoenix Entertainment, and New World Television. Director: Fielder Cook. Executive Producer: Judith Palone. Producers: Dennis Turner and Carroll Newman. Writer: Dennis Turner. Music: Morton Stevens. The adventures of Jason (Billy Sullivan), an eight-year-old whose parents were killed performing on the high wire, and his grandfather (Richard Hamilton), and the traveling circus (run by Tony Jay and Margaret Hall) that is their home. Karen Kopins is a runaway the circus takes in and Krista Tesreau is the tutor who teaches the circus kids. "All that is puzzling," *Variety* commented, "is why it was approved for filming." *Cast:* Tony Jay (as Conrad), Michael Gates (Paul), Krista Tesreay (Crissy), Richard Hamilton (Antonio), Gerald Hiken (Kokotchka), Thalmus Rasulala (Clarence), Karen Kopins (Jennifer), also, Margaret Hall, Michael Phenicie, Vincent Irizarry, Kurt Thomas, Billy Sullivan.

2147. **Deadline (aka Deadline: Madrid).** 90 min. Production Company: Universal Television. Director: John Patterson. Executive Producers: Meta Rosenberg and Karen Harris. Producers: Pamela De Maigret and Kevin Donnelly. Writer: Karen Harris, from a story by Pamela De Maigret. Music: Larry Carlton. The adventures of foreign correspondent Erin Wainwright (Leigh Lawson) and her photographer Robert Minelli (Brynn Thayer) working out of Madrid for a Philadelphia newspaper. Also, Joe Santos, J. Kenneth Campbell, Valerie Wildmon, Paul McCrane, Wortham Krimmer, Andrew Rubin, Neva Patterson, George Harris, Marta DuBois, Charles Cioffi, Reggie Montgomery, Miriam Colon, Jorge Bosso, and Isabel Prinz.

2148. **Desperate.** 90 min. Airdate: 9/19/87. Production Companies: Toots Productions and Warner Bros. Television. Director: Peter Markle. Executive Producer: Michael Braverman. Producer: Alex Beaton. Writer: Michael Braverman. Creator: Michael Braverman. Music: Lee Holdridge. John Savage is Noah Sullivan, a tortured man with a troubled past. He earned the scorn of his prestigious, Boston family by choosing a life at sea and becoming Captain of his own vessel. But that was short-lived. In a moment of panic on a doomed ship in stormy seas, he jumped overboard. Many people died in the subsequent shipwreck. Now he's a Key West charter boat Captain, wracked with guilt, and dedicated to helping desperate people to soothe his shame. He's also fallen in love with a tavern owner (Meg Foster) and has befriended her 14-year-old son (Christopher Burke), who suffers from Downs syndrome. In the pilot, he gets involved in a gun-running scheme. *Variety* said "it's never clear whether Noah is playing it cool, or is just plain dumb." *Cast:* John Savage (as Noah Sullivan), Liane Langland (Deirdre), Meg Foster (Dorymai), Christopher Burke (Louis), also, Andrew Robinson, J.A. Preston, George Dickerson, Castulo Guerra, Frances Foster, Byrne Piven, Ned Bellamy, John Patrick Hurley, Susan Chris Stone, Stanley Grover, Alma Beltran, Victor Vidales, Oscar Chavez, Mina Martell, Odalys.

2149. Divided We Stand. 60 min. Airdate: 7/21/88. Production Companies: Don Brinkley Productions and Aaron Spelling Productions. Director: Michael Tuchner. Executive Producer: Aaron Spelling. Producer: Don Brinkley. Writer: Don Brinkley. Music: Artie Kane. This pilot offers an unusual format for telling a traditional story. The proposed series would focus on Cody (Seth Green), a ten-year-old boy whose parents (Michael Brandon and Kerrie Keane) are divorced but share joint custody. In television land, that means Daddy gets Cody for the first half of the show, and Mommy gets him for the second half. In the pilot, Cody tries to reunite his parents on what would have been their 14th wedding anniversary. The "Gibbs" became the "Dobbs" in the final pilot. *Cast:* Michael Brandon (as Bryan Gibbs), Kerrie Keane (Katie Gibbs), Seth Green (Cody Gibbs), Madge Sinclair (Hattie Wickwire), Irena Ferris (Topaze), Diane Stilwell (Rachel).

2150. Free Spirit. 60 min. Production Company: Aaron Spelling Productions. Director: Paul Aaron. Executive Producer: Aaron Spelling. Writer: Richard Shapiro. Yet another failed attempt to sell a series about a widow (Lisa Eilbacher) who remarries (Robin Thomas), only to be haunted by the ghost of her dead first husband (Michael Des Barres).

2151. Old Dogs. 60 min. Airdate: 8/10/87. Production Companies: Beech-wood Productions and Columbia Pictures Television. Director: Gary Nelson. Executive Producer: Seth Freeman. Producer: Michelle Gallery. Writer: Michelle Gallery. Mayo Dunlap (Robert Prosky) is a retired, by-the-book cop, working as an unappreciated volunteer shuffling papers at his old precinct. Robert Loggia is a rogue cop bounced from the force for bending too many rules, who's now toiling as a security guard at a bingo parlor. These two "old dogs" accidentally meet, solve a crime that baffled the police, and end up being appointed as special consultants to the force. *Cast:* Robert Loggia (as Jimmy Bryce), Robert Prosky (Mayo Dunlap),

Franc Luz (Lt. Randy Granville), Cassie Yates (Ginger), Alex Rocco (Rudy Luchese), Les Lannom (Ned Haas), Richard Yniquez (Frankie Polon), David Kagen (Ray Brinkman), J. Michael Flynn (Detective #2), Juney Smith (Detective #1).

2152. **Remo Williams (aka The Destroyer).** 60 min. Airdate: 8/18/88. Production Companies: Dick Clark Productions and Orion Television. Director: Christian I. Nyby, II. Executive Producers: Dick Clark and Dan Paulson. Producers: Larry Speigel and Judy Goldstein. Writers: Steven Hensley and J. Miyoko Hensley. Creators: Warren Murphy and Richard Sapir. Music: Craig Safan. Based on the 1985 movie *Remo Williams* and the popular novels by Warren Murphy, Richard Sapir. Music: Craig Safan. Based on the 1985 movie *Remo Williams* and the popular novels by Warren Murphy, Richard Sapir, and a string of ghostwriters. The ligh-thearted pilot, which picked up where the film left off, moved the action from New York to Los Angeles and starred Jeffrey Meek (taking over for Fred Ward) as a rogue N.Y.P.D. cop who, after his murder is faked and he undergoes extensive plastic surgery, becomes a special government agent trained in the deadly ancient art of Sinanju. He's taught this incredible, mystical skill by Chiun, the elderly and witty master of Sinanju (Roddy McDowall), and works for CURE, a super-secret organization run by Harold Smith (Stephen Elliott). The series would have focused on the relationship between Remo and his mentor Chiun (Joel Grey in the movie), who decries just about everything in American life except soap operas. Only the last 15 minutes of the pilot were seen on the West Coast—the rest were pre-empted by a speech by President Reagan. *Cast:* Jeffrey Meek (as Remo Williams), Roddy McDowall (Chiun), Stephen Elliott (Harold Smith), Andy Romano (Derek Boland), Judy Landers (Taffy), Carmen Argenziano (Tony).

CBS / COMEDY

2153. **Baby on Board.** 30 min. Airdate: 7/12/88. Production Company: Hart/Thomas/Berlin Productions. Director: David Steinberg. Executive Producers: Marlo Thomas, Kathie Berlin, and Carol Hart. Producers: Cathy Cambria and Peter Stone. Writer: Peter Stone. Music: Stephen Lawrence. Aired as an episode of *CBS Summer Playhouse.* Lawrence Pressman and Jane Galloway are a married couple (he's a teacher, she's a travel agent) in their 40s who've just had their first child. In the pilot, they plan their first vacation since having the child. Shot in

New York. *Cast:* Lawrence Pressman (as George Morgan), Jane Galloway (Sally Morgan), Emily/Abigail Simpson (Abigail Morgan), Joan Copeland (Marion), Teri Hatcher (Lauri the Nanny), Larry Haines (George, Sr.).

2154. Changing Patterns. 30 min. Airdate: 6/26/87. Production Companies: Ogiens/Kanne Company, Procter & Gamble Productions, and MGM/UA Television. Director: Linda Day. Executive Producers: Josh Kane, Michael Ogiens, and Arthur Silver. Producers: Joel Stein, Phil Kellard, and Tom Moore. Writers: Arthur Silver, Phil Kellard, and Tom Moore. Aired as an episode of *CBS Summer Playhouse.* Valerie Perrine and Brenda Vaccaro are two sister-in-laws who, after their children go off to college, become small-time dress makers to the delight of their husbands, who think their wives' new jobs can hasten their own early retirement from the tire business. *Cast:* Valerie Perrine (as Molly), Brenda Vaccaro (Maxine), Alex Rocco (Arthur), Robert S. Woods (Skip), Eric Christmas (Edgar), George Deloy (Steve), Deanna Oliver (Female Buyer), Meg Wittner (Alice Ballinger), Hugh Maguire (Jim).

2155. Day to Day. 30 min. Airdate: 8/28/87. Production Companies: Hill-O'Connor Television and Lorimar-Telepictures. Director: Lee Shallat. Executive Producers: Leonard Hill and Robert O'Connor. Producers: Wendy Kout and Judith Zaylor. Writer: Wendy Kout. Aired as a segment of *CBS Summer Playhouse.* The misadventures of three sisters—Shirley (Deborah Harmon), a happy housewife and mother of two; Judith (Linda Purl), a pediatrician who lives with a college professor (Tim Isbell); and Hope (Noelle Parker), a rebellious and impulsive single woman. In the pilot, they gather for their parents' (Darren McGavin and K. Callan) 35th wedding anniversary. Cliff Potts is Shirley's husband. *Cast:* Linda Purl (as Judith Lumley), Darren McGavin (Walter Lumley), K. Callan (Jean Lumley), Deborah Harmon (Shirley Rovitch), Noelle Parker (Hope Lumley), Tom Isbell (Jonathan Geller), Cliff Potts (Mike Rovitch), Jenny Beck (Diane), Jessica Puscas (Carrie), Pat Corley (Uncle Bob), Diane Stilwell (Aunt Sue).

2156. In the Lion's Den. 30 min. Airdate: 9/4/87. Production Company: MTM Enterprises. Director: James Burrows. Executive Producer: Dan Wilcox. Producer: Gayle Maffeo. Writer: Dan Wilcox. Music: Dan Foliart and Howard Pearl. Aired as a segment of *CBS Summer Playhouse.* This pilot is *The Mary Tyler Moore Show* revolving around a Texas children's show rather than a Minneapolis newscast. Wendy Crewson is the soft-spoken, insecure new producer of a kid's show run by an egotistical, manic-depressive puppeteer (Dennis Boutsikaris), who is the voice of Maynard, the lion star of the show. Maynard was designed by Emilie Kong. *Variety* loved the show, praising it as "well structured, rich with quick humor and inventiveness." The fact the pilot wasn't picked up, the critic mused, must mean "all of CBS' upcoming sitcoms are lulus. Or someone's not thinking straight." *Cast:* Wendy Crewson (Dana Woodrow), Dennis Boutsikaris (Keith Warfield), Fred Applegate (Newton Gorse), Brian Backer (Stan Timmerman), Marcia Gay Harden (Kim Fellows), Brad Greenquist (Forrest), Jack Blessing (Jerry Sims), Steven Hansen (Jake), Joshua Grenrock (Stage Manager).

2157. **King of the Building.** 30 min. Airdate: 7/31/87. Production Companies: The Komack Company and Procter & Gamble Productions. Director: James Komack. Executive Producer: James Komack. Producer: Barry Vigon. Writer: Barry Vigon. Aired as a segment of *CBS Summer Playhouse.* Richard Lewis is the doorman of a posh Park Avenue apartment building who tries too hard to please the tenants, usually causing many more problems than his schemes would have solved. *Cast:* Richard Lewis (as Joey), Jose Perezury (Hector), Tiger Haynes (Leon), Simon Jones (Mr. Jamison), Bobby Slayton (Eddie).

2158. **Kingpins.** 30 min. Airdate: 9/18/87. Production Companies: Barton Dean Productions and Paramount Television. Director: Greg Antonacci. Executive Producer: Barton Dean. Producer: Jay Klecker. Writer: Barton Dean. Aired as a segment of *CBS Summer Playhouse.* Dorian Harewood is a widower who buys a struggling Ohio bowling alley and puts his family to work running it. In the pilot, teenage daughter Lindsay (Marie-Alise Recasner), the manager, cuts off credit to her father's four oldest friends, who have run up a $2000 tab—an action that causes problems for everyone. *Cast:* Dorian Harewood (as Hank Whittaker), Marie-Alise Racasner (Lindsay Whittaker), David Alan Grier (Dieter Philbin), Ji-Tu Cumbuka (Sonny Whittaker), Bill Henderson (Vince Haines), Diana Bellamy (Darla Easterwood), Jason Bernard (Vern Puckett), Leonard Garner (Ernie Bunsen), Tommy Hicks (Milt Simmons), Eric Fleeks (Duncan Moss).

2159. **Mabel and Max.** 30 min. Airdate: 7/31/87. Production Companies: Bar- wood Productions and Warner Bros. Television. Director: John Pasquin. Executive Producer: Cis Corman. Producer: Henry Johnson. Writers: Elayne Boosler and Barra Grant. Music: Steve Dorff. Lyrics: John Bettis. Aired as a segment of *CBS Summer Playhouse.* Two actresses with dreams of broadway stardom—one in her sixties (Geraldine Fitzgerald) and the other in her 20s (Mary B. Ward)—who meet at an audition, become friends, and decide to share an apartment together.

Shelley Berman costars as their agent, and Tony Goldwyn plays Mabel's son. Barbra Streisand's production company produced this pilot. *Cast:* Geraldine Fitzgerald (as Mabel), Mary B. Ward (Max), Tony Goldwyn (Paul), Shelley Berman (Harry), Pearl Shear (Betty), Nada Despotovich (Receptionist), Martin Garner (Norman), Robert P. Lieb (Simon), John Wesley (Larry), John Apicella (Casting Director), Tony Perez (Rinaldo), Mitzi Stollery (Adele).

2160. **Mickey and Nora.** 30 min. Airdate: 6/26/87. Production Companies: Lowell-Bergman Productions and Walt Disney Television. Director: Paul Bogart. Executive Producers: Andrew Bergman and Michael Lobell. Producers: Paul Bogart and Marcia Govons. Writer: Andrew Bergman. Aired on *CBS Summer Playhouse.* The misadventures of newlyweds Mickey, a former CIA agent-turned-lawyer, and Nora, the manager of a Manhattan toy store, who try to lead normal lives despite the fact that Mickey's cloak-and-dagger past keeps catching up with them. Florence Stanley is Mickey's mixed-up secretary, Nancy Lenehan is Nora's naive sister and partner, and George Furth is Mickey's neurotic, old CIA boss. *Cast:* Ted Wass (as Mickey), Barbara Treutelaar (Nora), George Furth (Rip), Nancy Lenehan (Vivian), Cleavant Derricks (Marvin), Florence Stanley (Adele), Jesse Lawrence Ferguson (Col. Ntsunge), Miriam Flynn (Betty).

2161. **Morning Maggie.** 30 min. Production Company: Procter & Gamble Productions. Director: Jack Shea. Executive Producer: Nelle Nugent. Producer: Craig Buck. Writer: Craig Buck. The misadventures of a family that owns and operates a small, Schenectady radio station during the 1950s. The mother, Maggie (Ellen Greene), hosts the popular *Morning Maggie* talkshow, while her husband Mack (John Vickery) handles the newscast and the station's books. Daughter Dorothy produces the soap opera while her 15-year-old brother does a bit of everything and elderly Aunt Esther chooses the music. Mack's brother Philly and his Japanese bride also help out. According to *TV Guide,* the pilot impressed CBS executives and sponsors, but flunked with test audiences, who found the show too confusing. *Cast:* Ellen Greene (as Maggie McAllister), John Vickery (Mack McAllister), Marita Geraghty (Dorothy McAllister), Matthew Perry (Bradley McAllister), Eileen Heckart (Esther), Hank Azaria (Philly McAllister), Marilyn Tokuda (Sayoko), Larry Riley (George).

2162. **No, Honestly.** 30 min. Production Company: Procter & Gamble Productions. Director: Ellen Falcon. Executive Producer: Bob Shayne. Writer: Bob Shayne, based on the book by Charlotte Bingham. Based on the BBC series *No, Honestly* and *Yes, Honestly*. The 22 years of marriage lived by C.D. and Clara Douglas, as seen in anecdotal flashbacks narrated by the couple. Although they are both writers—he writes articles, she writes children's books—they came from very different backgrounds. He was an orphan shuffled between various Bronx foster homes while she came from a very wealthy family and went to the finest schools.

2163. **Puppetman.** 30 min. Airdate: 7/3/87. Production Companies: Brillstein Company and Henson Associates. Director: Alan Rafkin. Executive Producers: Bernie Brillstein and Jim Henson. Producers: Mark Reisman and Jeremy Stevens. Writers: Mark Reisman and Jeremy Stevens. Creator: Jim Henson. Music: Phil Ramone. Aired as a segment of *CBS Summer Playhouse*. Fred Newman is a beleaguered puppeteer balancing the demands of his second-rate children's show with the responsibilities of single parenthood. Michael Carter is his six-year-old son and Jack Burns is the egotistical producer. *Cast:* Fred Newman (as Gary), Richard Hunt (Del), Jack Burns (Bud), Julie Payne (Rita), Lisa Waltz (Holly), Michael Carter (Zack), Steve Levitt (Bud Jr.), Ron Fassler (Mitchell), Marianne Jueller (Nurse), Linda Hoy (Dee), Tad Horino (Man in Emergency Room).

2164. **Reno and Yolanda.** 30 min. Airdate: 8/28/87. Production Companies: Dick Berg/Stonehenge Productions and Paramount Television. Director: Joel Zwick. Executive Producers: Dick Berg and Hal Dresner. Producer: Allan Marcil. Writer: Hal Dresner. Music: Patrick Williams. Aired as a segment of *CBS Summer Playhouse*. Reno and Yolanda are a married couple who run an Atlantic City dance studio, perform in a hotel lounge, and dream of stardom. Although Reno's a charming dreamer with no business sense, sensible Yolanda loves him anyway. *Cast:* Louis Giambalvo (as Reno), Suzie Plaksin (Yolanda), Richard Dimitri (Harry Zenko), Cristine (cq) Rose (Raylene Smith), William Christopher (Bill Smith), Leo Rossi (Ricky Barron), Karen Kondazian (Lila Grappas), Joan Rein (Letty Petzler), Zachary Berger (Sam Petzler), David Sargent (Nelson Whittaker).

2165. **Sawdust.** 30 min. Airdate: 7/3/87. Production Companies: MGM/UA Television and Bedford Falls Company. Director: Jeffrey Hornaday. Executive Producers: Marshal Herskovitz and Ed Zwick. Producers: Mark R. Gordon and Gary Markowitz. Writer: Gary Markowitz. Music: Ralph Burns. Aired as a segment of *CBS Summer Playhouse*. James Eckhouse is an unhappy accountant who quits his job and buys a struggling, small-time, traveling circus which he will run with his wife (Marsha Waterbury) and his teenage kids (Kellie Overbey and Bradley Gregg). Elya Baskin is the ringmaster, Ben Slack is the kids' tutor, and Leslie Jordan is the circus' one-man band. *Variety* panned the pilot, dubbing Markowitz's script a "minor league tent show (that) plays more like a carny hustle." Although this flopped, Herskovitz and Zwick went on to produce the critically acclaimed drama *thirtysomething* for ABC that season. *Cast:* James Eckhouse (as Max Galpin), Marsha Waterbury (Dana Galpin), Elya Baskin (Serge), Ben Slack (Halpern), Kellie Overbey (Molly Galpin), Bradley Gregg (Russ Galpin), Leslie Jordan (Worm), Robin Hudis (Gorilla Girl), Colin Hamilton (Priest), Kerry Michaels (Manicurist), Jadeen Barbor (Woman in Salon), Cheri Cameron-Newell (Seamstress), Mousie Garner (Worker), Don Hepner (Worker), Darin Taylor (Worker).

2166. **Sirens.** 30 min. Airdate: 9/4/87. Production Company: Stephen J. Cannell Productions. Director: Michael Pressman. Executive Producers: Stephen J. Cannell and Ian Praiser. Producer: Burt Nodella. Writers: Sara Parriott and Josann McGibbon. Creator: Stephen J. Cannell. Music: Mike Post. Aired as a segment of *CBS Summer Playhouse*. While this is prolific action/adventure producer Stephen J. Cannell's first sitcom pilot, he's mining familiar terrain—the story of two mismatched female cops. Cheryl (Loretta DeVine) is a strong-willed black policewoman married to an anthropology student and partnered with white cop Frannie (Dinah Manoff), a single woman with a daffy, psychic mother (Joyce Van Patten). Shannon Tweed is their snooty boss. Shot in Vancouver. *Cast:* Dinah Manoff (as Franny Aronson), Loretta DeVine (Cheryl Kelly), Shannon Tweed (Beth McCarty), Stephen Godwin (Rick Alberghini), Terry Correll (Mike Graham), Joyce Van Patten (Ilene Ziskind), Randi Brooks (Beau Kelly), Alan Oppenheimer (Reuben Ziskind), Max Reimer (Jonny [cq] Step).

2167. **Sons of Gunz.** 30 min. Airdate: 9/18/87. Production Companies: Brownstone Productions and Paramount Television. Director: Barnet Kellman. Executive Producer: Marc Merson. Producer: Bob Sand. Writer: Bob Sand. Aired as a segment of *CBS Summer Playhouse*. Kenneth McMillan is an over-bearing, strong-willed, widowed car salesman raising an artistically minded 17-year-old son (Corey Parker) and running the business with his other three boys—headstrong Hog (Dirk Blocker), womanizing Charley (Robert Firth) and yuppie Brian (John Walker). *Cast:* Kenneth McMillan (as Harry Gunz), Dirk Blocker (Hog Gunz), John Walker (Brian Gunz), Robert Firth (Charley Gunz), Corey Parker (Michael Gunz), Camille Saviola (Belle Myers).

2168. Sounds Like. Production Company: Orion Television. The life of a widowed commercial special effects man raising a teenage daughter.

CBS / DRAMA

2169. Barrington. 60 min. Airdate: 7/10/87. Production Companies: The Zanuck/ Brown Co. and New World Television. Director: Richard Compton. Executive Producers: Richard Zanuck and David Brown. Producer: Robert Jacks. Writer: Peter Benchley. Creator: Peter Benchley. Music: Patrick Williams. Aired as a segment of CBS Summer Playhouse. This pilot is a strange hybrid of Burke's Law, Matt Houston, and Jaws. Matt Salinger is James Cabot Barrington, a wealthy playboy who becomes the police chief of a small New England coastal village after his Shinnecock Indian wife is killed by a drunk driver. Robert Beltran is his Indian deputy, Barbara Bain is Barrington's widowed mother, William Glover is the butler, and Beah Richards is the housekeeper. In the pilot, a hitman (Ian McShane) comes to King's Bay to murder a relocated government witness. Shot on location in Vancouver. Cast: Matt Salinger (as James Cabot Barrington), Robert Beltran (Howard Thunder), Barbara Bain (Julia Barrington), William Glover (Oliver), Beah Richards (Katherine), Salome Jens (Glenda Davis), Chelsea Field (Kelsey Baker), Madeleine Sherwood (Emily Welles), Bill Morey (Cyrus Welles), Ian McShane (Marbury), Andrea Marcovicci (Ian Parker), D.D. Howard (Tessa Benson).

2170. Doctors Wilde (aka Zoovets). 60 min. Airdate: 7/17/87. Production Companies: Columbia Pictures Television. Director: Noel Black. Executive Producer: Steve Kline. Producers: Andrey Blasdel-Goddard and Dr. Martin R. Dinnes. Writer: Steve Kline. Music: Dana Kaproff. Aired as a segment of CBS Summer Playhouse. The adventures of veterinarians Martin and Melanie Wilde (Joseph Bottoms and Jennifer Hetrick), who travel the world treating exotic animals. They are assisted in their work by veterinarian Tran Loc (Dr. Haing S. Ngor), a Cambodian refugee, and their ten-year-old daughter (Bridgette Andersen). The pilot was initially rejected by CBS, which then changed its mind after the show aired on its summer anthology of flop pilots. The show garnered 120,000 enthusiastic responses from viewers who called a special number to vote on the program, prompting CBS to order seven episodes for midseason. Production was about to begin in November 1987, when CBS unexpectedly reneged on its pick-up, outraging producer Steve

Kline, who publicly accused the network of unethical behavior. *Cast:* Joseph Bottoms (as Dr. Martin Wilde), Jennifer Hetrick (Dr. Melanie Wilde), Dr. Haing S. Ngor (Tran Loc), Kit McDonough (Norma), Bridgette Andersen (Jamie Wilde), Dann Florek (Herb Winthrop), G.W. Bailey (Macklin), Glynn Turman (Roger Donnelly), Rhonda Aldrich (Penny), Branscombe Richmond (Lance), Bruce French (Prosecutor), Andrew Divoff (SWAT Leader), Alex Powers (Mr. Noris), David Sabin (Judge).

2171. **Infiltrator.** 60 min. Airdate: 8/14/87. Production Companies: Ron Samuels Productions and TriStar Television. Director: Corey Allen. Executive Producer: Ron Samuels. Producer: Terry Morris. Writers: Kerry Lenhart and John Sakmar. Music: Barry Goldberg. Aired as a segment of *CBS Summer Playhouse*. Scott Bakula is an irreverent scientist working on a transporter device in the same complex where Deborah Mullowney is working on an ultra-high tech space satellite. Bakula accidentally beams himself into the satellite, which is then absorbed into his molecules. Now, whenever he gets angry, he becomes a neon-and-metal Gobot with an array of deadly weapons. Of course, like most guys who gain an uncontrollable and unpredictable power in a freak accident, he becomes a secret agent. The cute female Doc tags along to keep a watchful eye on her satellite—and on him, though she'd never admit she's got the hots for him. Charles Keating sends them on their missions. *Cast:* Scott Bakula (as Paul Sanderson), Deborah Mullowney (Kerry Langdon), Charles Keating (John J. Stewart), Michael Bell (Markus), Peter Palmer (Minion).

2172. **Kojak: The Price of Justice (aka The Return of Kojak).** 2 hours. Airdate: 2/21/87. Production Company: Universal Television. Director: Alan Metzger. Executive Producer: James McAdams. Producer: Stuart Cohen. Writer: Albert Ruben, from the book by Dorothy Uhnak. Creator: Abby Mann, from the book by Selwin Raab. Music: Patrick Williams. A second attempt to revive *Kojak*. Theo Kojak (Telly Savalas) is now an inspector heading an N.Y.P.D. Major Crime Unit. In the pilot, Kojak investigates charges that a woman (Kate Nelligan) murdered her children while they slept. John Bedford-Lloyd is Kojak's new protege. Shot on location in New York. In 1989, ABC commissioned a series of *Kojak* movies. *Cast:* Telly Savalas (as Inspector Theo Kojak), Kate Nelligan (Kitty Keeler), Pat Hingle (George Keeler), Jack Thompson (Aubrey Dubose), Brian Murray (Tim Neary), John Bedford-Lloyd (Milton Bass), Jeffrey DeMunn (Marsucci), Tony DiBenedetto (Det. Catalano), Ron Frazier (J.T. Williams), Stephen Joyce (Chief

Brisco), Earl Hindman (Danny), James Rebhorn (Quibro), Martin Shakar (Arnold Nadler), Joseph Carberry (Lorenzo), Fausto Bara (Benjamin), Novella Nelson (Mrs. Silverberg), Kenneth Ryan (Johnson), Candace Savalas (Anna).

2173. **Kung Fu: The Next Generation (aka Way of the Dragon; aka Warriors).** 60 min. Airdate: 6/19/87. Production Company: Warner Bros. Television. Director: Tony Wharmby. Executive Producers: Paul Picard and Ralph Riskin. Producers: Paul DiMeo and Danny Bilson. Writers: Paul DiMeo and Danny Bilson, from the series *Kung Fu*, created by Ed Spielman and developed by Herman Miller. Music: Stanley Clarke. Aired as a segment of *CBS Summer Playhouse*. David Darlow stars as the modern-day descendant of the character David Carradine played in the western series *Kung Fu*. Like his ancestor, this Caine is a gentle man who espouses inner peace and lives modestly—he teaches Kung Fu, sells herbs, and helps people in trouble. Perhaps the person who needs his help most is his estranged son Johnny (Brandon Lee), who became a gang member, served a short jail term for burglary, and, in the pilot, hooks up with some dangerous criminals. But thanks to a ghostly visit from the original Caine, Johnny turns away from crime and adopts his father's altruistic lifestyle. *Cast:* David Darlow (as Kwai Chang Caine), Brandon Lee (Johnny Caine), Miguel Ferrer (Mick), Paula Kelly (Lt. Lois Poole), Marcia Christie (Ellen), Victor Brandt (Buckley), Dominic Barto (Carl Levin), John C. Cooke (Cliff), Aaron Hey man (Sid), Eddie Mack (Rob), Michael Walter (Dave), Richard Duran (Raul), Michael Gilles (Security Cop), Neil Flynn (L.A.P.D. Officer), Mark Everett (Student), Oscar Dillon (Darnell).

2174. **The Saint (aka Saint in Manhattan).** 60 min. Airdate: 6/12/87. Production Companies: D.L. Taffner Productions and Television Reports International Ltd. Director: James Frawley. Executive Producers: Dennis E. Doty and Robert S. Baker. Producer: George Manasse. Writers: Peter Gethers and David Handler. Creator: Leslie Charteris. Music: Mark Snow. Aired as a segment of *CBS Summer Playhouse*. Andrew Clark, a mustachioed Australian actor, assumes the role of Simon Templar, the handsome rogue, thief, and dapper adventurer who, in this flop pilot, moves from London to New York, where he and his man-servant Woods (George Rose) reside in a luxurious Waldorf Astoria suite, to the consternation of N.Y.P.D. Inspector Fernack (Kevin Tighe). Clark winked, mugged, and wiggled his eyebrows across Manhattan, but failed to capture the charm of his predecessors in the role. In the pilot, he becomes the prime suspect when the ballerina he's been protecting finds her diamond tiara missing. Robert S. Baker also served as executive producer of the original *Saint* TV series starring Roger Moore and its short-lived sequel, *Return of the Saint*, which starred Ian Oglivy and aired on CBS late-night during the late '70s. Undaunted by CBS' rejection, the producers took the project to syndication for a series of TV movies starring Simon Dutton. *Cast:* Andrew Clarke (as Simon Templar), George Rose (Woods), Kevin Tighe (Inspector John Fernack), Christopher Mercantel (Joey), Holland Taylor (Fran Grogan), Caitlin Clarke (Jessica Hildy), Liliana Komorowska (Margot Layne), Michael Lombard (Wally Grogan), Raymond Serra (Carmine), Robert LuPone (Jeffrey Sinclair), Peter Maloney (The Fixer), Ben Vereen (Nightclub Singer), Kevin O'Rourke (Detective), Kelly Connell (Elevator Man), Brian Evers (Bartender), Mick Muldoon (Doorman), Elyse Knight (Stewardess), Katie Anders (Nanny), Ellis E. Williams (Wilie the Con), Mary Lou Picard (Desk Clerk), Frank Ferrara (Goon #1), Valentino Diaz (Goon #2), A1 Cerullo (Helicopter Pilot), Ray Iannicelli (Toy Store Clerk).

2175. **Shaun Cassidy Project.** 60 min. Airdate: 2/8/87. Production Company: Universal Television. Director: Nick Havinga. Executive Producers: Richard Levinson, William Link, and Peter S. Fischer. Producer: Robert F. O'Neill. Writers: Peter S. Fischer, Arthur Marks, and Gerald K. Siegel. Aired as the "Murder in a Minor Key" episode of *Murder She Wrote.* This pilot is told to us by mystery author Jessica Fletcher (Angela Lansbury), under the guise of her latest novel. A law student (Shaun Cassidy) investigates charges that a student (Paul Clemons) murdered the music professor (Rene Auberjonois) who plagiarized the suspect's compositions. *Cast:* Angela Lansbury (as Jessica), Rene Auberjonois (Prof. Harry Papazian), Shaun Cassidy (Chad Singer), Paul Clemens (Michael Prescott), Herb Edelman (Max Hel- linger), Karen Grassle (Christine Stoneham), George Grizzard (Prof. Tyler Stoneham), Tom Hallick (Vice Chancellor Alexander Simon), Jennifer Holmes (Reagen Miller), Scott Jacoby (Danny Young), Dinah Manoff (Jenny Cooper- smith).

2176. **Times of Their Lives.** 60 min. Airdate: 8/7/87. Production Company: Reeves Entertainment. Director: Hal Cooper. Executive Producers: Hal Cooper, Rod Parker, Fred Silverman, and Perry Lafferty. Producer: Alan C. Blomquist. Writer: Rod Parker, from a story by Hal Cooper and Rod Parker. Music: D'Vaughn Pershing. Aired as a segment of *CBS Summer Playhouse.* Buddy Ebsen is a traveling song-and-dance man who retires to help his estranged, widowed son (Jamie Wid- does), a corporate executive, raise his four daughters. Lionel Stander costars as Buddy's agent. Executive producers Silverman and Lafferty are both former CBS programming executives. *Cast:* Buddy Ebsen (as Buddy Tucker), Jamie Widdoes (Brian Tucker), Karen Bercovici (Greta), Lionel Stander (Sully Carson), Suzanne Snyder (Andrea), Christa Denton (Beth), Tanya Fenmore (Cathy), Jaclyn Bernstein (Denise Tucker), Warren Munson (Gordon Percell).

2177. **Traveling Man.** 60 min. Airdate: 9/11/87. Production Companies: December 3rd Productions and 20th Century Fox Television. Director: Peter H. Hunt. Executive Producers: Robert Singer and Randy Visk. Writer: Robert Singer. Music: Brad Fiedel. Aired as a segment of *CBS Summer Playhouse.* James Naughton is John "Doc" Dockery, a man who made it as a surgeon thanks to the support of his loving wife. But when she dies of a long illness he can't cure, his life loses its significance and he chucks everything, hits the road in his '57 Chevy, and searches for new meaning. In the pilot, he helps a recalcitrant rancher fight evil land barons. *Cast:* James Naughton (as John Dockery), Kay Lenz (Ray), Matt Clark (Matt), Richard Farnsworth (Carl), Dennis Letts (Dudan), Tony Mockus (Dr. Henry Gordon), Leslie Wing (Annie).

NBC / COMEDY

2178. **Act II.** 30 min. Airdate: 9/3/87. Production Company: NBC Productions. Director: Tom Patchett. Executive Producer: Michael Filerman. Producer: Janis Hirsch. Writer: Janis Hirsch. Sandy Duncan stars as a Broadway actress who gives up her career and moves to Sante Fe to become the mother of her new husband's three children. *Variety* panned the pilot, originally scheduled to air July 18, as a "dreadful, old hat sitcom." Although this didn't sell, she assumed a similar role when she replaced Valerie Harper in *Valerie* just a few weeks after this flop pilot aired. *Cast:* Sandy Duncan (as Meg Madison), Charles Frank (Ben Prescott), Cami Cooper (Laura Prescott), Hayley Carr (Zan Prescott), Joel Carlson (Jimmy Prescott), Miriam Byrd-Netherly (Dee Dee McKenna).

2179. **The Art of Being Nick.** 30 min. Airdate: 8/27/87. Production Companies: UBU Productions and Paramount Television. Director: Sam Weisman. Executive Producer: Bruce Helford. Producer: June Galas. Writer: Bruce Helford. A second attempt to spin-off Mallory's boyfriend, Nick Moore (Scott Valentine), from *Family Ties.* In the last pilot (9/12/86), Nick moved to Detroit to take over his family's toy business after his father's death. When that pilot flopped, he returned to *Family Ties* as if nothing had happened. This time, he moves to New York to live with his divorced sister (Kristine Sutherland) and her young son (John Damon) and takes a job at her bookstore, which she co-owns with an intellectual (Julia Louis Dreyfus) who finds him attractive—but dumb. The pilot aired after *Cosby* to enormous ratings (23.3 rating/40 share), becoming the second most-watched show of the week, but NBC still didn't give Valentine his own series. Again, Nick reappeared on *Family Ties* without explanation. *Cast:* Scott Valentine (as Nick Moore), Kristine Sutherland (Marlene Moore), Julia Louis Dreyfus (Rachel), John Damon (Lewis Moore), also, Ray Buktenica, Ellen Crawford, Richard Fancy.

2180. **Bennett Brothers.** 30 min. Airdate: 8/22/87. Production Companies: Double L Productions and NBC Productions. Director: Will MacKenzie. Executive Producer: Lloyd Garver. Producer: Bettina Bennewitz. Writers: Lloyd Garver, Elias Davis, and David Pollock. Music: David Frishberg. An attempt to recapture the charm of *The Odd Couple*. A swinging bachelor (George Clooney), whose live-in girlfriend (Dorothy Parke) just left him, takes in his conservative, philosophical, recently divorced brother (Richard Kind) as a roommate (his wife left him because he was so dull). NBC programming executive Warren Littlefield told *TV Guide* that the pilot failed because "the chemistry of the two leads just wasn't right." *Cast:* George Clooney (as Tom Bennett), Richard Kind (Richard Bennett), Dorothy Parke (Denise), Rosalind Ingledew (Natasha), Alan North (Manny Bennett), Peggy Pope (Shirley Bennett), also, Willard Scott, Robert Costanzo, Barry Cutler.

2181. **Empty Nest.** 30 min. Airdate: 5/16/87. Production Companies: Witt- Thomas-Harris Productions and Walt Disney Television. Director: Jay Sandrich. Executive Producers: Paul Junger Witt, Tony Thomas, and Susan Harris. Writer: Susan Harris. Creator: Susan Harris. Music: George Aliceson Tipton. A spin-off from *The Golden Girls*. When George and Renee Corliss' daughter Jenny goes off to college, Renee is forced to confront her loneliness and nags her physician husband to spend more time at home. When he doesn't, she ends up spending her days with her brother Chuck, who is plagued by multiple personalities and her bachelor neighbor Oliver, a test pilot. Research audiences felt there was no chemistry between the stars, the concept was uninteresting, and that the program relied too heavily on the *Golden Girls* cast for its laughs. *Empty Nest* was subsequently completely retooled and recast (with the exception of David Liesure) and became the hit 1988 sitcom of the same name. *Cast:* Paul Dooley (as George Corliss), Rita Moreno (Renee Corliss), Geoffrey Lewis (Chuck), David Liesure (Oliver), Jane Harnick (Jenny), Beatrice Arthur (Dorothy Zbornak), Betty White (Rose Nylund), Rue McClanahan (Blanche Devereaux), Estelle Getty (Sophia Petrillo).

2182. Glory Days (aka Glory Years; aka Small Victories). 30 min. Airdate: 8/5/87. Production Company: Embassy Television. Director: Eve Brandstein. Executive Producers: Eve Brandstein and Ron Clark. Producer: A1 Lowenstein. Writer: Ron Clark. The misadventures of two working-class buddies—Jack, a sanitary engineer, and Frank, a telephone repairman—who met as kids and are still tied to their high school sweethearts. Jack is married to Kate, a bakery clerk who worries her husband will fall in love with somebody else, and Frank is living with Tracy, a beautician who wants to finally get her lover to marry her. In the pilot, the boys nurse an inferiority complex brought on by the prospect of attending their high school reunion and seeing a classmate who became a multi-millionaire. NBC programming executive Warren Littlefield told *TV Guide* the pilot "had a great cast but couldn't overcome the script." *Cast:* Mike Haggerty (Jack Duffy), John Kapelos (Frank Pappas), Deborah Allison (Katie), Tracy Schaffer (Tracy), also, Ron Dean, James Lashly, Donna DuBain.

2183. Good Morning, Miss Bliss (aka What Now, Mrs. Davis?). 30 min. Airdate: 7/11/87. Production Company: NBC Productions. Director: Peter Bonerz. Executive Producer: Peter Engel. Writer: Sam Bobrick. Originally developed for Sandy Duncan, who opted for *Act II* instead. Hayley Mills stars as a sixth grade teacher who becomes very involved in her students' lives, to the consternation of her new husband (Charles Siebert). Maria O'Brien guest starred. The series later materialized as a short-lived Disney Channel sitcom (canceled in December 1988) and still later was reworked as the NBC Saturday morning show *Saved by the Bell*

2184. Paradise Motel. 30 min. Production Company: MGM/UA Productions. Director: Bud Yorkin. Executive Producers: Bud Yorkin and Sam Simon. Producer: Cheech Marin. Writers: Alan Eisenstock, Larry Mintz, and Sam Simon. A 15-minute demonstration film was shot in front of a live audience. Cheech Marin is Teddy Vargas who, after working as a parking valet at the Beverly Hills Hotel and a waiter at the Beverly Wilshire, thinks he knows everything about the hotel business. So, he buys a rundown East L.A. motel he dreams of turning into the flagship of his own national chain. But first, he's got to make this place work, and that will take a lot of doing. The pilot didn't click with network brass, NBC programmer Warren Littlefield told *TV Guide*, because "the venue wasn't right. The characters, besides Cheech, weren't fresh—the feeling was that they were a downer."

NBC / DRAMA

2185. Austral Downs (aka Harris Down Under; aka Danger Down Under).
2 hours. Airdate: 3/14/88. Production Companies: Weintraub Entertainment
Group and TriStar Television. Director: Russ Mayberry. Executive Producers:
Jerry Weintraub, Reuben Leder, and Lee Majors. Writer: Reuben Leder. Music:
Bruce Rowland. Lee Majors is Reed Harris, an American horse breeder who
travels with his son (William Hughes) to his ex-wife's (Rebecca Gilling) rural
Australia ranch, where she lives with his two estranged, younger sons and her
father (Martin Vaughn). When she is killed by horse thieves, Reed stays on
to manage the ranch and re-establish ties with his sons. Shot on location in
Australia. *Cast:* Lee Majors (as Reed Harris), William Wallace (Brian Harris),
Bruce Hughes (Danny Harris), Morgan Lewis (James Harris), also, Martin
Vaughn, Paul Chubb, Rebecca Gilling, Natalie McCurry, Moya O'Sullivan,
Warwick Moss, Emily Stocker, Mervyn Drake, Ken Radley, Benita Collings,
Robert Taylor, John Hallyday, Richard Boue, Andy Down, Glen Boswell, Zev
Eleftheriou, George Parker, Patsy Stephen, Bruce Rowland.

2186. Bates Motel. 2 hours. Airdate: 7/5/87. Production Company: Universal Television.
Director: Richard Rothstein. Executive Producer: Richard Rothstein. Producers:
Ken Topolsky and George Linder. Writer: Richard Rothstein, from characters created by Robert Bloch. Music: J. Peter Robinson. A sequel to the classic 1960 thriller
Psycho that ignores events portrayed in the two theatrical sequels (released in 1983
and 1986 respectively). Bud Cort is a mental patient who inherits murderer Norman
Bates' crumbling (and haunted) motel and reopens it, with the help of a runaway
girl (Lori Petty) he finds living in the place. The proposed anthology would follow
the guests who stay at the motel and their supernatural experiences. The NBC ad
campaign proclaimed: "Norman Bates may be gone, but his motel lives on!" *Cast:*
Bud Cort (as Alex West), Lori Petty (Willie), Moses Gunn (Henry), Gregg Henry
(Tom), Kerrie Keane (Barbara), Jason Bateman (Tony), also, Khrystyne Haje, Robert
Picardo, Lee DeBroux, Kurt Paul, Marla Frumkin, Rick Liebergman, Timothy
Fall, Kelly Ames, Peter Dobson, Paula Irvine, Scot Saint James, Greg Finley, Nat
Bernstein, Buck Flower, Carmen Filpi, David Wakefield, Gart Ballard, Andy Albin,
Dolores Albin, Hardy Rawls, Peter A. Stelzer, George J. Woods, Jack Ross Obney,
John Kenton Schull, George Skinta, Pedro Gonzales- Gonzales, Robert Axelrod,
Chad Jonas.

2187. Braddock. 60 min. Production Company: Viacom Enterprises. Executive Producers: Fred Silverman and Dean Hargrove. Writer: John McGreevey. Planned as a spin-off from *Matlock*. Hal Holbrook is Sam Braddock, police chief of a seaside California community whose son, an Atlanta cop, is drummed off the Force after being cleared (by Andy Griffith's "Matlock") of a false murder charge. Braddock's son moves west, joins his father's Force and, together, they fight crime in the resort town.

2188. Cameo by Night. 60 min. Airdate: 8/2/87. Production Companies: Lauren Shuler-Donner Productions and Touchstone Pictures. Director: Paul Lynch. Executive Producer: Lauren Shuler-Donner. Producers: Christopher C. Carter and John Ziffren. Writer: Christopher C. Carter. Music: Fay Ferguson. Jennifer Cameo (Sela Ward) is an L.A.P.D. secretary who is, unbeknownst to her colleagues and her cop boyfriend (Justin Deas), the infamous nocturnal crimefighter who leaves behind a black, paper silhouette as her calling card. Her brilliant disguise consists of better make-up, a nicer hairstyle, and trendier clothes than she usually wears. Thomas Ryan is her helper Sorry Eddie and George Kirby is the newspaper vendor who cuts out her silhouettes and gives her "the word and the streets." *Cast:* Sela Ward (as Jennifer Cameo), Thomas Ryan (Sorry Eddie), George Kirby (Grubby), Mary Jo Deschanel (Mrs. Schwinn), Justin Deas (Detective Bellflower), Art LaFleur (Pinky), David Graf (Kraxburger), Stephen Shellen (Larry Willard), Scott Coffey (Gordon Schwinn), Tim Thomerson (Damon Rhodes), Kaz Garas (Red), Christopher Jackson (Dagood), Charles H. Hyman (Large Man), Bert Hinchman (Security Guard), Dennis A. Pratt (First Hood), Brian Brophy (Slick), Jeanine Jackson (Saleswoman), Louis Mauna (Newsstand Boy), Howard Allen (Lab Man), Michael Francis Clarke (First Deputy), Marie Post (Singer), also, Tim Jones, Michael Greene, Russell Curry.

2189. Carly's Web. 2 hours. Airdate: 7/12/87. Production Company: MTM Enterprises. Director: Kevin Inch. Executive Producer: Michael Gleason. Producer: Gareth Davies. Writers: Michael Gleason, Brad Kern, and John Wirth. Music: Richard Lewis Warren. From the creative team behind *Remington Steele* comes this pilot about a Justice Department bureaucrat (Daphne Ashbrook) who sifts through complaints filed by citizens bilked in apparently legal schemes. She also sifts through the department computers to organize a group of operatives— ordinary citizens, specialists, and "shady characters"—to help her bilk the bilkers (a la *Mission: Impossible* and *Masquerade*). *Cast:* Daphne Ashbrook (as Carly Foxe), Robert Symonds (Senator), Ramon Bieri (Union Boss), Bert Rosario (Hector

Figueroa), Cyril O'Reilly (Frankie Bell), Peter Billingsley (Roland Krantz, Jr.), Jennifer Dale (Celeste Hedley), Carole Cook (Myrtle), Robert S. Woods (Donald Stevens), also, John Christy Ewing, Vincent Baggetta, Gary Grubbs, Gregory Itzin, Lewis Collins, Joel Colodner, Norman Parker, K. Callan, Daniel Ziskie, Michael James Horse, Frank Sotonoma Salsedo, Nick Savage, Joe Unger, Nancy Hinman, Fred McGrath, Gene Ross, Ron Kilogie, Linda Hoy, Richard Kelley, Doug Franklin.

2190. **Desperado.** 2 hours. Airdate: 4/27/87. Production Companies: Walter Mirisch Productions, Charles E. Sellier Productions, and Universal Television. Director: Virgil Vogel. Executive Producer: Andrew Mirisch. Producer: Charles E. Sellier, Jr. Writer: Elmore Leonard. Music: Michael Columbier. Alex McArthur is Duell McCall, a wandering cowboy who walks into a mining town and right into the middle of a pitched battle between the corrupt company and a rancher who won't give them his land. By the time it's all over, he's falsely accused of murdering a sheriff and is forced to flee, searching the West for the one man who can clear his name. *Variety* panned this pilot as "a miserable collection of familiar schticks, seemingly written from memory." Shot on location in Tucson, Arizona. *Desperado* scored impressive ratings, and although no series materialized, a succession of *Desperado* pilots followed—*Return of Desperado* on 2/15/88, *Avalanche at Devils Ridge* on 5/24/88, *The Outlaw Years* on 10/10/89 and finally *Badlands Justice* on 12/17/89. Cast: Alex McArthur (as Duell McCall), David Warner (Johnny Ballard), Yaphet Kotto (Bede), Robert Vaughn (Sheriff Whaley), Pernell Roberts (Marshall Dancey), Gladys Knight (Mona Lisa), Dirk Blocker (Grady), Donald Moffat (Malloy), Stephen Davies (Calvin), Lise Cutter (Nora), Sydney Walsh (Sally), Richard Marcus (Emmett), Townsend Cannon (Rollie), Karen Smythe (Jenny).

2191. **Independence.** 2 hours. Airdate: 3/29/87. Production Company: Sunn Classics Pictures. Director: John Patterson. Executive Producer: Gordon Dawson. Producer: Joe Wallenstein. Writer: Gordon Dawson. The adventures of Sam Hatch, sheriff of the small town of Independence, his four daughters, and his second wife. In the pilot, the outlaws who murdered his first wife 15 years ago terrorize the town. Michael Kozoll served as creative consultant on the project. Cast: John Bennett Perry (as Sheriff Sam Hatch), Isabella Hofmann (Bridie Fitzgerald), Anthony Zerbe (General Oral Grey), Stephanie Dunnam (Prudence), Vanessa Vallez (Keelia), R.G. Armstrong (Uriah Creed), Chris Clemenson (Isaiah Creed), Carlo Pettine (Sam Jr.), Sandy McPeak (Sterling

Mott), Macon McCalman (Angus Thurston), Joshua Julian (Fitz), Amanda Wyss (Chastity), Devin Hoelscher (Deputy Tait), Joseph Brutsman (Ezekial Creed), Adam Gregor (Ivo Kanker), Gisli Bjorgvinsson (Deputy Nilsson).

2192. **Jake's M.O. (aka Jake's Beat).** 60 min. Airdate: 7/30/87. Production Companies: Lane Slate Productions and Warner Bros. Television. Director: Harry Winer. Executive Producer: Lane Slate. Producer: Paul Waigner. Writer: Lane Slate. Creator: Lane Slate. Music: Ray Colcord. Fred Gwynne stars as a crusty, eccentric crime reporter for an L.A. wire service who has a knack for solving baffling crimes—though he always gives the credit to the cops. He may have no taste in clothes, drive a horrendous clunker, and do things "the old-fashioned way," but he's also got a photographic memory and a keen eye for details. Jeff McCracken is his eager young apprentice, Caroline McWilliams is his journalistic rival, and Abel Barnes is his "friend-on-the-Force." In the pilot, he catches a serial killer. Based on the real-life exploits of reporter Jake Jacoby. *Cast:* Fred Gwynne (as Jake Tekulve), Caroline McWilliams (Flo Duffy), Jeff McCracken (Tad Hoberman), James Avery (Abel Barnes), James Handy (Danny Bauer), Kenneth Tigar (Saul Goldman), Claudette Nevins (Mrs. Tompkins).

2193. **Kowalski's Way (aka Kowalsky Loves Ya; aka Time Out for Dad).** 60 min. Airdate: 6/22/87. Production Companies: Robert L. McCullough Productions and NBC Productions. Director: Harry Harris. Executive Producer: Robert L. McCullough. Producer: Dick Gallegly. Writer: Robert L. McCullough, from a story by Robert L. McCullough, Janice Hirsch, and Ron Friedman. Music: Robert Kraft. Dick Butkus is Dick Kowalski, a surly, ex-Chicago Bears linebacker who retires and manages his household of three kids while his wife (Sandy Faison) pursues her writing career. Harriet Nelson costars as Kowalski's mother-in-law, who lives with them. *Cast:* Dick Butkus (as Dick Kowalski), Sandy Faison (Pam Kowalski), Harriet Nelson (Mary McLaughlin), Tricia Leigh Fisher (Shelley Kowalski), Miss Crider (Suzanne Kowalski), Johnny Galecki (Matt Kowalski), also, Paul Shenar, Stu Nahan, Beah Richards, Sam Chew, Jr., Jonathan Schmook, Gary Miller, Ken Smolka, Robert King, Tina Junger, Craig Stark.

2194. **On the Edge (aka Dirty Work; aka Shake and Baker).** 60 min. Airdate: 6/5/87. Production Companies: Penumbra Productions and NBC Productions. Director: Robert Butler. Executive Producer: George Geiger. Producer: Douglas Benton. Writer: George Geiger. Music: David Grusin. A crusty, veteran cop (Tom Skerritt) who bucks authority is teamed up with a young, irreverent, over- zealous rookie (Tom O'Brien). Both of them are going to get booted from the Force unless they clean up their act. In the pilot, they catch a serial killer, a newspaper reporter (Robert Curtis Brown). Producer/writer Geiger later worked on NBC's *Miami Vice*, and then switched to *Hunter*. *Cast*: Tom Skerritt (as Jack Shake), Tom O'Brien (Mr. Baker), Robert Curtis Brown (Dean Albrecht), J.T. Walsh (Capt. Quail), Joan Chen (Ellen Yung), Peter Iacangelo (D'Agostion), Shawnee Smith (Gretchen), Howard Sherman (Tommy G.), Miles Davis (Ozzie Whitehouse), also, David Florek, Carlos Cervantes, Richard Duran, Janet Koo, Raymond Oliver, Betty Ann Rees, Dennis Stewart, Robert Schuch.

2195. **Police Story (aka Police Story: The Freeway Killings).** 3 hours. Airdate: 5/3/87. Production Companies: David Gerber Productions, MGM/UA Television, and Columbia Pictures Television. Director: William A. Graham. Executive Producer: David Gerber. Producer: Charles B. Fitzsimons. Writer: Mark Rodgers. Creator: Joseph Wambaugh, developed by E. Jack Neuman. Music: John Cacavas. Theme: Jerry Goldsmith. An attempt to revive the 1973–77 NBC anthology *Police Story*, which continued as a series of TV movies for a season after its cancellation. The pilot mixed internal police politics, the troubled personal lives of police officers, and the hunt for a serial killer. The cast was comprised of frequent *Police Story* guest stars. Several more *Police Story* movies, remakes of the old episodes, were produced for ABC during the 1988 Writers' Strike. *Cast*: Richard Crenna (as Deputy Chief Bob Devers), Angie Dickinson (Officer Anne Cavanaugh), Ben Gazzara (Capt. Tom Wright), Tony Lo Bianco (Detective DiAngelo), Don Meredith (Detective Foley), James B. Sikking (Major Cameron), Gloria Loring (Kate Devers), Vincent Baggetta (Paul Harris), Michael C. Gywnne (Calvin), Joan McMurtrey (Joan Manning), Rob Knepper (Karl Jones), Marc Alaimo (Morello), Sam Vlahos (Diaz), Javier Graieda (Gracia), Ken Hixon (Hallett), Louise Shaffer (Laura Henley), Freddye Chapman (Mary Morris), Michael Griswold (A1 Nader), Julie Ariole (Test Examiner), Carlos Cervantes (Chico), Hawthorn James (Reverend Johnson), Kamala Lopez (Lydia Chacon), Murray Leward (Max), Susie Chan (Kim), Steve Kahan (Paulis), Tony Perez (Capt. Rodriquez), Wendy Cooke (Marna), James Hess (Chairman), Charles Fitzsimons, Jr. (Tony), Lawrence Lott (Businessman), also, Scott Paulin, Francis Lee McCain, Julie Phillips.

2196. **Return of the Six Million Dollar Man and the Bionic Woman.** 2 hours. Airdate: 5/17/87. Production Companies: Michael Sloan Productions and Universal Television. Director: Ray Austin. Executive Producer: Michael Sloan.

Producer: Bruce Lansbury. Writer: Michael Sloan, from a story by Michael Sloan, Bruce Lansbury, from the book *Cyborg* by Martin Caidin. An attempt to mount a spin-off of *The Six Million Dollar Man* (ABC 1973–1978) and *The Bionic Woman* (ABC 1976–77, NBC 1977–78) series off this reunion. The bionic duo of Steve Austin (Lee Majors) and Jaime Sommers (Lindsay Wagner) are called out of retirement and reunited by Oscar Goldman (Richard Anderson) to battle a maniacal villain (Martin Landau). In the midst of it all, they relive (via flashbacks) and rekindle their ill-fated romance. But the real story revolves around Steve's (never before mentioned) estranged son Michael (Tom Schanley), an Air Force test pilot who, like his father, is nearly killed in a castastrophic crash. He's fitted with bionic parts, helped through feelings of freakishness by shrink Jaime, and reconciles with his father—all before being kidnapped by the evil baddie. Although this pilot earned big ratings, a Tom Schanley bionic series didn't happen and a second pilot, *The Bionic Showdown*, featuring a young, female bionic spy, was made in 1989 and starred newcomer Sandra Bullock. A third revival movie, *Bionic Ever After*, the wedding of Steve and Jaime, aired on CBS in 1994. In 2007, NBC attempted to 'reboot' *The Bionic Woman* in a new series with Michelle Ryan in the lead. It was a disaster that lasted a mere eight episodes. *Cast:* Lee Majors (as Steve Austin), Lindsay Wagner (Jaime Sommers), Richard Anderson (Oscar Goldman), Tom Schanley (Michael Austin), Martin E. Brooks (Dr. Rudy Wells), Martin Landau (Charles Stenning), Lee Majors, II (Jim Castillian), Gary Lockwood (John Praiser), Deborah White (Sally), Robert Hoy (Kyle), Patrick Pankhurst (Duke Rennecker), Terry Kiser (Santiago).

2197. **Three on a Match.** 2 hours. Airdate: 8/2/87. Production Company: Belisarious Productions and TriStar Television. Director: Donald Bellisario. Executive Producer: Donald Bellisario. Producer: Stuart Segall. Writer: Donald Bellisario. Creator: Donald Bellisario. Music: Ian Freebairn-Smith. The adventures of three prisoners—a computer expert (Patrick Cassidy) a con man (David Hem- mings) and a tough loner (Bruce A. Young)—who escape from a hellish Louisiana prison and face a life on-the-run. NBC had committed to 13 episodes, but a series never materialized. *Cast:* David Hemmings (as Newt), Bruce A. Young (Ripper), Patrick Cassidy (Scott), also, Lance LeGault, Mitch Pileggi, Deborah Pratt, Diana Bellamy, Raynor Scheine, Dendrie Allyn Taylor, Jim Haynie, Everett McGill, Geraldine Pratt, B.J. Hopper, Elliot Keaner, Jason Saucier, Trelis Septor, Louis Bourgeois, Jeffrey Hays, Duane Bennet, Ken Gerson.

1988–1989

ABC / COMEDY

2198. Cadets. 30 min. Airdate: 9/26/88. Production Company: Viacom Enterprises. Director: Zane Buzby. Executive Producers: Jeff Harris, Arlene Sellers, and Alex Winitsky. Producer: A1 Lowenstein. Writer: Jeff Harris. Music: Jeff Harris. The misadventures of a 12-year-old girl (Soleil Moon Frye) and her friends attending a military academy that only recently went co-ed. Howard Murray was originally tagged to direct this pilot, aimed at the Sunday 7:30 p.m. time slot previously occupied by Frye's *Punky Brewster*. *Cast:* Soleil Moon Frye (as Tyler McKay), Richard Roundtree (Sgt. Matthew Gideon), Barclay DeVeau (Lucy).

2199. The Flamingo Kid. 30 min. Airdate: 6/11/89. Production Companies: Viacom Enterprises, Sweetum Productions, and Mercury Entertainment Corp. Director: Tom Moore. Executive Producers: Michael Phillips, Richard Rosenstock, and Michael Vittes. Writer: Richard Rosenstock, based on a character created by Neal Marshall. Based on the 1984 film. Sasha Mitchell stars as Jeffrey, a 16-year-old whose blue-collar father (Dan Hedaya) expects him to follow in his work-a-day footsteps. But when Jeff takes a job at a beach club, he meets a fun-loving car sales-man who introduces him to a different lifestyle, and another perspective on life. The series would depict Jeffs attempts to reconcile what his father wants with what he is learning about the world. *Cast:* Sasha Mitchell (as Jeffrey Willis), Dan Hedaya (Arthur Willis), Jerry Orbach (Phil Brody), Todd Graff (Hawk), Carol Locatel (Ruth), Patty McCormack (Mrs. Brody), Bobby Costanzo (Angry Man), Carmine Garidi (Harvey), Kellie Martin (Lauren Brody), Taryn Smith (Ellen Brody), Madelyn Cates (Mrs. Gaskin), Jill Klein (Angry Man's Wife), Myra Turley (The Chickenfat Lady).

2200. Heart and Soul. 30 min. Airdate: 5/2/89. Production Companies: Phoenix Entertainment and New World Television. Director: Stan Lathan. Executive Producers: Gerald Isenberg and Jennifer Alward. Writer: Beverly Sawyer. Aired as an unannounced substitution for *Crimes of Passion II*, which was pulled from the schedule due to lack of advertiser support. A black version of *Romeo and Juliet* set amidst the turbulent social change of 1960s Philadelphia. B'Nard Lewis, from working class family, and Rene Jones, from a rich family, team up as songwriters despite their parents' disapproval of their careers and relationship. *Cast:* Rene Jones (as Brenda Kinkaid), B'Nard Lewis (Wesley Harris).

2201. Justin Case. 90 min. Airdate: 5/15/88. Production Companies: Walt Disney Television and Blake Edwards Company. Director: Blake Edwards. Executive Producer: Blake Edwards. Producer: Tony Adams. Writer: Blake Edwards, from a story by Jennifer Edwards and Blake Edwards. Music: Henry Mancini. Aired as an episode of *The Disney Sunday Movie.* An unemployed actress (Molly Hagin) who applies for a secretarial job at a detective agency is haunted by a dead private eye (George Carlin) in search of his killer. *Cast:* George Carlin (as Justin Case), Molly Hagin (Jenny Spaulding), Timothy Stack (Detective), Kevin McClarnon (Detective), Gordon Jump (Psychic), Douglas Sills (Paramedic), Paul Sand (Cab Driver), also, Valerie Wildman, Todd Susman, Ron McCary, Philippe Denham, Richard McGonagle, Jay Thomas, Kenneth Tigar, Kay Perry, John Lavachielli, Dotty Colorso, Reed McCants, Joe Mays, Lily Mariye, Andrew Nadell, Nina Mann, Jerry Martin, Stuart Tanney.

2202. Lanny and Isabelle. 30 min. Production Company: Imagine Entertainment. Executive Producers: Bob Dolman and Dori Weiss. Writer: Bob Dolman. Andrea Martin is a recently divorced woman who shares a Manhattan apartment with her optimistic, 18-year-old niece (Louanne), a budding writer.

2203. Livin' Large. 30 min. Airdate: 5/2/89. Production Company: Stephen J. Cannell Productions. Director: Les Sheldon. Executive Producers: David Burke, Steve Kronish, Tom Mankiewicz, and Quincy Jones. Producer: George Jackson. Writer: Ralph Farquhar. Aired as a last-minute substitution for *Crimes of Passion //,* which was pulled due to lack of advertiser support. The struggles of teenage newlyweds and parents Billy and Marsha, who hang out at the local barbershop with their friends. *Cast:* Eagle-Eye Cherry (as Billy), Alexia Robinson (Marsha), Jon Polito (Sal), Tim Guinee (Kevin), Keith Amos (G.Q.), Tasia Valenza (Luz).

2204. Mutts. 30 min. Production Companies: Ron Howard/Brian Grazer Productions and Imagine Entertainment. Director: Linda Day. Executive Producer: Brian Brazer. Producers: Howard Bendetson and Bob Bendetson. Writers: Howard Bendetson and Bob Bendetson. Music: Alf Clausen. Theme: Harry Nilsson, sung by Rick Riccio. The adventures of a boy (Stephen Dorff) and his telepathic dog. In the pilot, they try to win the affections of the girl next door (Amy Hathaway). *Cast:* Stephen Dorff (as Eric Gillman), Wendy Schaal (Janice Gillman), Geoff Pierson (Stuart Gillman), Amy Hathaway (Chris Hayden), Mike the Dog

(Jeepers), Ray Buktenica (Glen), Jennifer Darling (Michelle), Sam Ballantine (Attendant), Catherine Ann Christianson (Customer).

2205. Nick Derrenger, P.I. 30 min. Airdates: 5/4 and 5/11/88. Production Company: 20th Century Fox. Director: Michael Zinberg. Executive Producers: Robert My man and Rick Kellard. Producers: Phil Kellard and Tom Moore. Writers: Steven Bochco and Rick Kellard. Creators: Steven Bochco and Rick Kellard. Music: Mike Post. Aired as a two-part episode of *Hooperman*. David Rappaport is a dapper, four-foot-tall private eye who barely skates above bankruptcy and whose motto is "no case too small." *Cast:* David Rappaport (as Nick Derrenger), John Ritter (Det. Harry Hooperman), Debrah Farentino (Susan Smith), Jillie Mack (Eva), Sydney Walsh (Officer Maureen DeMott), Joe Gian (Officer Rick Silardi), Clarence Felder (Officer Boris Pritzger), Barbara Bosson (Capt. Celeste Stern), Laura Bassett (Yolanda), Felton Perry (Insp. Clarence McNeil), Michael Crabtree (Drug Dealer), Barbara Rush (Susan's Mother).

2206. Past Imperfect. 30 min. Production Company: Castle Rock Entertainment. Director: Bill Persky. Executive Producer: Gary Gilbert. Writer: Gary Gilbert. Ted is 40, and as he sits in his study, he thumbs through a scrapbook and reflects on his life. And it is from these yellowed pictures that the stories for this series would arise, framed by his narration. Dwight Schultz was supposed to star as Ted. But the day before shooting, ABC decided he wasn't right for the role. Talent agent George Shapiro called Rob Reiner, one of the founders of Castle Rock, and recommended a young comic named Jerry Seinfeld to take Schultz's place. But the network felt that Seinfeld didn't have enough experience and went with Howie Mandel instead. However, Castle Rock liked what they saw in Seinfeld and backed another show for him. The rest, as the cliché goes, is history. *Cast:* Howie Mandel (Ted) Talia Balsam (Jill), Sharon Spelman (Ruth) John Astin (Sam).

2207. Somerset Gardens (aka Primetime). 30 min. Airdate: 7/28/89. Production Companies: Viacom Entertainment and Ready to Wear Productions. Director: John Pasquin. Executive Producer: Jeff Harris. Producer: Al Lowenstein. Writer: Jeff Harris. Music: Peter Matz. A painfully unfunny ensemble comedy built around the homeowners association of a San Diego condo complex for retired folks. *Cast:* June Lockhart (as Debbie Whitmire), Bill Macy (Monroe Shamsky), Betty Garrett (Susannah Somerset), Rebecca Schull (Ada), Warren Frost (Dean), Mary Jackson (Helen), Clifton James (Jack), Al Ruscio (Edd).

ABC / DRAMA

2208. Badlands 2005. 60 min. Airdate: 8/29/88. Production Companies: Lizard Productions, Hoyts Productions, and Columbia Pictures Television. Director: George Miller. Executive Producer: Rueben Leder. Writer: Rueben Leder. Creator: Rueben Leder. Music: Bruce Rowland. The story of a U.S. marshal (Lewis Smith) and his Cyborg partner (*Robocop*'s Miguel Ferrer) who patrol the now- barren American West in a high-tech car for a tough female boss (Sharon Stone). The pilot opened with the crawl: "In 1995, a severe drought forced Americans to flee the West for the cities. Water became more precious than gold. Now, in 2005, settlers are coming back, meeting new challenges, and age-old adversaries." And age-old plots—in the pilot, entitled *Brides of Lizard Gulch* the hero must escort mail order brides through dangerous territory. *Cast:* Lewis Smith (as Garson MacBeth), Miguel Ferrer (Rex), Sharon Stone (Alex Neil), Debra Engle (Joanie Valentine), Caitlin O'Heaney (Sara Gwynne), Lloyd Alan (Johnny Cantrell), Hugh Keays-Byrne (Moondance), Gus Mercurio (Stubbs), Robyn Douglass (Sue Cantrell), Marc Cales (Engineer), Steven Kuhn (Delaney), Justin Mongo (Braggo), Dave Arnett (Technician).

2209. Chain Letter. 60 min. Production Companies: Indie Production Company and Phoenix Entertainment. Director: Tom Wright. Executive Producer: Bruce Sallan. Producer: Irv Zavada. Writer: Bill Bleich. Ian McShane is The Messenger of Death who sends out chain letters to mortals that offer temptation—and those who give in could die. His adversary is Miss Smith (Leslie Bevis), who believes that people are basically good, and who tries to steer people away from tempta-tion—and doom.

2210. Cyberforce. 20 min. Production Company: Warner Bros. Television. Director: Russell Mulcahey. Executive Producer: Peter Wagg. Writers: Danny Bilson and Paul De Meo. Creator: Peter Wagg. The adventures of four Cyborg secret agents. One is an ex-ball player with bullet-proof skin (Bob Hosea), an ex-test pilot with a Titanium spine and arm (Amy Steele), and a teenager with a brain that can be plugged into computers (Scott Grimes). The fourth agent, uncast, has super-resilient skin. The 1988 writers' strike forced producers to shoot a demo film rather than the planned 90-minute pilot.

2211. Dakota's Way. 60 min. Airdate: 8/20/88. Production Company: Phoenix Entertainment. Director: Michael Switzer. Executive Producer: Gerald Isenberg.

Producers: Robert Avrech and Christopher Chulack. Writer: Robert Avrech. Music: Brad Fiedel. Patricia Charbonneau is a wild, eccentric former secret agent turned cop who is partnered with a conservative, by-the-book family man (Bruce Davison). *Cast:* Patricia Charbonneau (as Dakota Goldstein), Bruce Davison (Preston Rafferty), James Avery (Capt. Beckett), Michelle Joyner (Leda), Shawn Modrell (Kimberly), Jonathan McMurtry (Nelson Charlesworth), Louise Claire Clark (Patsy Rafferty), also, Don Amendola, Tommy Hicks, Christine Jones, Stuart Fratkin, Elkarah Burns, Jimmy Skaggs, Lili Haydn (cq), Douglas Mark Kamen, Jimmy Medina-Taggert, Michael Faustino, Lisa Fuller, Anne Marie McEvoy, Clive Rosengren, William Youmans, Brad Burlingame.

2212. **Gang of Four.** 60 min. Airdate: 6/11/89. Production Company: MGM Television. Director: Jan Egelson. Executive Producer: David Manson. Producer: Cyrus Yavneh. Writer: Charlie Haas. Music: John Hiatt. The misadventures of four high school teenagers—Ellen, whose boyfriend just went off to college; Jennifer, who is beautiful but thinks she isn't; Eric, who is into photography at the expense of his grades; and Cary, their easy-going leader—as they enter their senior year. Think of it as *Seventeensomething. Variety* criticized the pilot for inferior writing, inept execution and an abundance of tired cliches. *Cast:* Kris Kamm (as Cary), Laray Flynn Boyle (Ellen), Amber O'Shea (Jennifer), Grant Heslov (Eric), Tom Atkins (Ben Moore), Lindsay Fisher (Denise Cullen), Joseph Hindy (Stan Klein).

2213. **Half and Half.** 60 min. Airdate: 9/1/88. Production Companies: Bonnie Raskin Productions, Echo Cove Productions, and Lorimar Telepictures. Director: Noel Nosseck. Executive Producers: William Blinn, Bonnie Raskin, and Gary Adelson. Producers: Frank Fischer, Ann McCurry, and Louise Hoven. Writer: William Blinn. Creator: William Blinn. Music: James Di Pasquale. A black jazz musician (Dorian Harewood) and a white race car driver (Perry King) discover they are brothers when their mother dies and leaves them a newspaper business. In the pilot, they discover their mother was murdered, and they hunt down the killer. As unsold pilots go, *Variety* dubbed this "a shoo-in for dumbest idea of them all." *Cast:* Dorian Harewood (as Ben Colter), Perry King (Scott Kallen), Walter Olkewicz (Mr. Elmandorf), A1 Fann (Davey), Danielle von Zerneck (Melissa Parachek), Stephen Liska (J. Benson), Diana Bellamy (Receptionist), Charles McDaniel (Weston), Roseanne Katon (Frenchwoman), Christine Avila (Office Worker), Tonya Lee Williams (Young Woman), Bruce

Beatty (Staffer), Larnya Derval (Staffer), Carol Bruce (Voice of Mama Bess), and Ann McCorry.

2214. **If You Knew Sammy.** 60 min. Airdate: 1/30/88. Production Company: Warner Bros. Television. Director: Bruce Bilson. Executive Producers: William Robert Yates and Stephen Hattman. Producer: Michael Maschio. Writers: Lee Goldberg and William Rabkin. Creators: Lee Goldberg and William Rabkin. Music: Steve Dorff and Larry Herbstritt. Aired as the "Play It Again, Sammy" episode of *Spenser: For Hire*, and an attempt to spin-off characters introduced in a previous episode entitled "If You Knew Sammy" (4/15/87). The misadventures of Sammy Backlin (Sal Viscuso), a cowardly conman-turned-pulp novelist who, with his naive, enthusiastic publicist (Kate Burton), inadvertently solves crimes. In the pilot, Sammy is on the run from mob killers and turns to Spenser for help—and ends up becoming a private eye, dedicating his life to ridding the world of crime. Of course, the agency is only a ploy for making a fast buck—by turning his adventures into a stream of lurid paperbacks and bilking vulnerable clients who'd entrust him with ransoms, family heirlooms, and explosive secrets. *Cast:* Sal Viscuso (as Sammy Backlin), Kate Burton (Randy Lofficier), W.H. Macy (Agent Efrem Connors), Jean De Baer (Dorothy Winsome), Edmond Genest (Burl Dodds), John Bell (Max Winsome), James Baffico (Nash Bodine), Robert Urich (Spenser), Barbara Stock (Susan Silverman), Avery Brooks (Hawk), Ron McLarty (Sgt. Frank Belson).

2215. **Kenya.** 60 min. Production Companies: Robert Halmi Productions and Disney Television. Director: Simon Langton. Executive Producers: Robert Halmi and Hal Sitowitz. Writer: Hal Sitowitz. The adventures of a widow, her father, and her two children, living on a wild game preserve in Africa. *Cast:* Lisa Eichhorn (as Jennifer Yates), Kimber Shoop (Terry Yates), Mary Griffin (Chelsea Yates), David Huddleston (Will).

2216. **Loner.** 60 min. Airdate: 8/18/88. Production Company: Aaron Spelling Productions. Director: Abel Ferrar. Executive Producer: Aaron Spelling. Writer: Larry Gross. John Terry is Michael Shane, who rejects the wealthy society he came from in favor of police work, though he isn't entirely comfortable as a cop, either. He's partnered with a policewoman (Vanessa Bell), who is attracted to him, as is the rich art dealer (Clare Kirkconnell) his socialite mother (Constance Towers) tries to set him up with. Shane's closest friend is Abner, an ex-con poet. *Cast:* John Terry (as Michael Shane), Constance Towers (Kate Shane), Vanessa Bell

(Carver), Clare Kirkconnell (Jessica Grenville), Larry Hankin (Abner Gibson), Michael Medeiros (Hadley).

2217. **Longarm.** 90 min. Airdate: 3/6/88. Production Company: Universal Television. Director: Virgil Vogel. Executive Producer: David Chisholm. Producers: Chuck Sellier and Ken Topolsky. Writer: David Chisholm. Music: Richard Stone. A comedy/adventure about a tough deputy marshal (John T. Terlesky) chasing outlaws in 1870s New Mexico—in this case, a ruthless train robber (John Laughlin). *Cast:* John T. Terlesky (as Deputy Marshal Curtis Long), John Laughlin (Codie Branch), Whitney Kershaw (Miss Barnett), Deborah Dawn Slaboda (Tyler), Daphne Ashbrook (Pearl), Malachi Throne (Blalock), Shannon Tweed (Crazy Sally), Rene Auberjonois (Gov. Lew Wallace), also, Lee De Broux, John Dennis Johnston, John Quade, and Noble Willingham.

2218. **McCallister.** 60 min. Airdate: 4/30/88. Production Company: Warner Bros. Television. Director: Harvey Hart. Executive Producers: William Robert Yates and Stephen Hattman. Producers: Michael Maschio and Mark Horowitz. Writers: William Robert Yates and Stephen Hattman. Creators: William Robert Yates and Stephen Hattman. Music: Steve Dorff and Larry Herbstritt. Aired as an episode of *Spenser: For Hire*. McCallister (Steve Inwood) is a Washington, D.C. attorney in love with a ballerina (Andie McDowell), a woman who is slowly going deaf. In the pilot, he goes to Boston to defend a black sailor accused of murdering a white officer's daughter, and enlists Spenser and Hawk, whom he met in Vietnam, to help him. The proposed series would have been shot in Washington, D.C., where the producers later set their 1989 *A Man Called Hawk* spin-off. *Cast:* Steve Inwood (as Tom McCallister), Andie MacDowell (Maggie), Victor Love (Darnell Lewis), John Seitz (Capt. Warren Sears), James Eckhouse (Lt. Cmdr. Carl Westmore), Will Lyman (Lt. Cmdr. Grant), Tom Urich (Judge), Ving Rames (Henry Brown), Tom Brennan (Capt. Kiparski), Stefan Smolen (William Youmans), Peter MacKenzie (Lt. Travis Williams), Susan Gibney (Molly Sears), Robinson Frank Ado (Ralph Lewis), Jane Kleiss (Jeannette), Robert Urich (Spenser), Barbara Stock (Susan Silverman), Avery Brooks (Hawk), Ron McLarty (Sgt. Frank Belson).

2219. **Three of a Kind.** 60 min. Airdate: 5/9/89. Production Company: MTM Enterprises. Director: Herbert Wise. Executive Producer: Jeffrey Lewis. Producers: Gareth Davies and John Litvack. Writers: Jeffrey Lewis and Walon Green. Music: Dave Grusin. Aired as a last-minute substitution for *Scandals II*, which was yanked due to advertiser apathy. Charlie Gordon (Beau Bridges) is a former CIA agent who opens a restaurant in France, which he runs with a former KGB agent (Emrys James) and a womanizing Italian cook, also an ousted spy (Ian Ogilvy). As much as they'd like to bury their cloaks and daggers, they still find themselves drawn into espionage. Stuart Margolin guest starred as a Soviet defector with information on John F. Kennedy's assassination. After viewing the pilot, ABC backed out of its 13-episode commitment. *Cast:* Beau Bridges (as Charlie Gordon), Ian Ogilvy (Giancarlo Rinaldi), Emrys James (Boris Koragin), also, Shelagh McLeod, Kamie Koss, Stuart Margolin, Ian McNeice, Jonathan Hackett, Boris Isarov, Ian East, Marie Elise Grepne, Janet Henfrey, Charlotte Cornwall, Richard LeParmen- tier, Brett Forrest, Richard Kane, Lin Sagivsky, Michael John Paliotti.

2220. **Why On Earth.** 60 min. Airdate: 7/18/88. Production Company: GTG Entertainment. Director: Donald Petrie. Executive Producers: Michael Kozell and Gordon Dawson. Producer: Sascha Schneider. Writer: Gordon Dawson. Creator: Gordon Dawson. The adventures of a group of alien scientists who study earthlings under the guise of being a research company. Although the Ovatians believe it's wrong to "become involved" with the humans, one young scientist (Chris Makepeace) defies the rule despite himself, to the consternation of his partner (Hilary Edson) and his boss (George Coe). ABC backed out of a 13-episode commitment after seeing this disastrous pilot. *Cast:* Chris Makepeace (as Franklin), Hilary Edson (Patricia), George Coe (Henry), Deborah May (Healer Wilson), Merritt Butrick (Oscar), Ed Wiley (McPeak), also, Christian Clemonson, Yvette Nipar, Joe Maher.

CBS / COMEDY

2221. **Dobie Gillis (aka Bring Me the Head of Dobie Gillis).** 2 hours. Airdate: 2/21/88. Production Company: 20th Century Fox Television. Director: Stanley Z. Cherry. Executive Producer: Stanley Z. Cherry. Producers: Dwayne Hickman, Stan Hough, Marc Summers, and Steve Clements. Writers: Deborah Zoe Dawson, Victoria Johns, and Stanley Z. Cherry, from a story by Max Shulman. Creator: Max Shulman. Music: Jimmy Haskell. Theme: Lionel Newman and Max Shulman. A second attempt to revive *Dobie Gillis* as a half-hour comedy. Dobie (Dwayne Hickman) and his wife Zelda (Sheila James) run the family store while their son Georgie follows in his dad's footsteps in high school. *Cast:* Dwayne Hickman (as Dobie Gillis), Sheila James (Zelda Gillis), Bob Denver (Maynard G. Krebs), Steve Franken (Chatsworth Osborne, Jr.), Scott Grimes (Georgie Gillis), Connie Stevens (Thalia Menninger), also, William Schallert, Lisa Cox, Tricia Leigh Fisher, Mike Jolly, Nicholas Worth, Kathleen Freeman, Joey D. Vieira, Dody Goodman, Hank Rolike, James Staley, Lisa Fuller, William Adams, Janet Rotblatt, Molly David, Billy Beck.

2222. Dr. Paradise. 30 min. Airdate: 7/12/88. Production Company: Universal Television. Director: Peter Baldwin. Executive Producers: Neal Isreal and Dennis Klein. Producers: Ron Zimmerman, Linda Nieber, and Marjorie Gross. Writer: Ron Zimmerman. Aired as a segment of *CBS Summer Playhouse.* Frank Langella is a self-centered, millionaire doctor who operates a health clinic and resort on a tropical island. The proposed series would focus on the eccentric doctors—including a burnt-out hippie shrink and a pediatrician who hates kids—and their equally eccentric patients. *Cast:* Frank Langella (as Dr. Paradise/Dr. Peter Roman), Sally Kellerman (Dr. Amy Hunter), Tommy Hinkley (Dr. Casey Hunter), Xander Berkeley (Dr. Fredericks), Hiram Kasten (Dr. Moore), Barry Gordon (Newton), Beverly Brown (Hilary Dupree).

2223. House and Home (aka Rough-House). 30 min. Airdate: 8/16/88. Production Company: Warner Bros. Television. Director: Martha Coolidge. Executive Producer: Ron Taylor. Producers: John Wells and Robert Hargrove. Writer: John Wells. Creator: John Wells. Music: Stephen J. Taylor. Aired as an episode of *CBS Summer Playhouse.* An ensemble comedy about a family of carpenter/contractors, their crew, and their misadventures on and off the job. *Cast:* Ronny Cox (as Walt Karlson), Robert Prescott (Norm Karlson), Ted W. Henning (Jeff Karlson), Michael Bowen (Chris), Karyn Parsons (Lynette), Deborah Richter (Holly).

2224. Jake's Journey. 30 min. Production Companies: Witzend Productions and 20th Century Fox Television. Director: Hal Ashby. Executive Producers: Mark Merson and Alan McKeown. Producer: Graham Chapman. Writers: Graham Chapman and David Sherlock. Originally slated as a series during the 1988 writers' strike, but then aborted before production. The "Time Bandit"-ish story of a teenage boy (Chris T. Young) who discovers a portal into a medieval fantasy world where he befriends an irascible knight (Chapman).

2225. The Johnsons Are Home. 30 min. Airdate: 7/19/88. Production Company: GTG Entertainment. Director: Jay Sandrich. Executive Producer: Sam Bobrick.

Producer: Louie Anderson. Writers: Louie Anderson and Sam Bobrick. Creator: Louie Anderson. Music: David Burke. Aired as a segment of CBS *Summer Playhouse*. Domestic hell with the Johnson family—blue-collar bigot Andy (Geoffrey Lewis), his bubble-headed homemaker wife (Lynn Milgrim), his cranky Aunt (Audrey Meadows), his idiot son (John Zarchen) and his out-spoken daughter (Hanna Cutrona). *Cast:* Geoffrey Lewis (as Andy Sr.), Lynn Milgrim (Ora), John Zarchen (Andrew), Hanny Cutrona (Mary), Audrey Meadows (Aunt Lunar), also, Billy Bird, Frank Buxton, Julia Condra, Patricia Matthew.

2226. Limited Partners. 30 min. Airdate: 7/19/88. Production Company: Viacom Productions. Director: Zane Busby. Executive Producers: Joe Flaherty and Marshall Goldberg. Producer: Michael Stokes. Writers: Joe Flaherty and Marshall Goldberg. Aired as a segment of CBS *Summer Playhouse*. An age-old formula is tried out one more time (and surely not the last)—two buddies (Joe Flaherty and Kevin Meaney) a la Ralph and Norton concoct crazy schemes to get rich quick, but the plans always backfire. The two hapless guys work for a 16-year-old kid (Karl Weidergott) at a British-style fast-food joint owned by a Cockney gent (Anthony Newley). *Cast:* Joe Flaherty (as Regis Rogan), Kevin Meaney (Tim Tiffel), Holly Fulger (Margie), Anthony Newley (Mr. B), Karl Weidergott (Kurt), also, Richard Karron, Ann Ryerson, Eric Fry, Howard Honig, Lana Schwab, Alex Guerrero, Jr., Kirk Scott, Paul Wilson, Robert Ellenstein, Bill Cort.

2227. Mars: Base One. 30 min. Production Company: Mebzor Productions. Director: Jim Drake. Executive Producers: Edward K. Milkis and Dan Aykroyd. Writer: Dan Aykroyd. Creator: Dan Aykroyd. The misadventures, a la *The Jetsons*, of a family adjusting to life on Mars, where they live next door to a Soviet technician and his American-stripper wife. The 1988 Writers' Strike forced production of the pilot—and any serious consideration of it for the network schedule—to be delayed until 1989. *Cast:* Tim Thomerson (Doug Ludlow), Nancy Youngblut (Ellen Ludlow), Jonathan Brandis (Tyrone Ludlow), Linda Thompson-Jenner (Dixie), Stephen Lee (Nikki), Dennis Burkley (Mickie), Marty Polio (B.O.B.)

2228. Miss Pendelton's Point of View. 30 min. Production Companies: Paramount Television and Garry Marshall Productions. Director: Michael Lessac. Executive Producer: Garry Marshall. Producer: John Rappaport. Writer: Grace McKeaney. Suzie Plakson is Miss Aurora Pendelton, a retired teacher who now runs a children's museum. Other characters include a ditzy secretary, a bunch of kids, and a juvenile delinquent assigned to working off his court-ordered hours of public service at the museum.

2229. **Never Go to Sea**. 30 min. Production Company: Paramount Television. Director: John Rich. Executive Producer: Ed Weinberger. Producer: David Lloyd. Writer: David Lloyd. The adventures of an ensign newly assigned to a naval supply carrier, where he must contend with a tyrannical captain, a conman bunkmate, a female chaplain, and a sailor who constantly goes AWOL.

2230. **Old Money**. 30 min. Airdate: 7/28/88. Production Companies: Ogien/Kane Productions and MGM/UA Television. Director: David Trainer. Executive Producers: Michael Ogiens and Josh Kane. Writer: Jim Brecher. Music: John Debney. The serialized story, a la *Soap*, of an incredibly rich Palm Beach family full of back-stabbing, greedy schemers and a "Benson"-like, no-nonsense maid. Characters include the family patriarch, his wife who writes romance novels, and their three daughters—a much-divorced socialite, a well-meaning philanthropist, and a long-lost woman who returns after a 20-year absence. *Cast:* Don Porter (as Charles Palmer), Nan Martin (Arabia Palmer), Carolyn Seymour (Countess Celia), Sandy Faison (Felicity), Terri Treas (Meg), Tom Isbell (Steven), John Dye (Chip), Jim Piddock (Hank), Abraham Alvarez (Roberto), William Thomas, Jr. (Brian), Conchata Ferrell (Kate), Lori Loughlin (Tammy), T.J. Castronovo (Sid).

2231. **Real Life**. 30 min. Airdate: 7/28/88. Production Companies: Charlotte Brown Productions and 20th Century Fox. Director: Charlotte Brown. Executive Producer: Charlotte Brown. Producer: Deborah Mendelsohn. Writer: Charlotte Brown. Music: Carole King. Theme: "One to One" by Cynthia Weil and Carole King, performed by Carole King. Aired as a segment of *CBS Summer Playhouse*. The lives of two Anaheim housewives—blue-collar Wanda (Sandra Dickerson), who is married to a truck driver and has two teenage kids (Jason Late and Ami Foster), and white-collar Marcy (Donna Bullock), a newlywed yuppie who left her job to start a family. The husbands would never be seen in this proposed series, which would focus entirely on the daily lives of these two women. *Cast:* Sandra Dickerson (as Wanda), Donna Bullock (Marcy), Jason Late (Bobby), Amy Foster (Patty), Miriam Flynn (Cookie), Chloe Amateau (Debbie), Alan Blumenfield (Mover 1), Billy Kane (Mover 2), Tom Simmons (Dean Casey), Saar Swartzon (Earl).

2232. **Sniff**. 60 min. Airdate: 8/9/88. Production Companies: Von Zerneck/Samuels Productions and New York Television. Director: James Quinn. Executive

Producers: Stu Samuels, Frank Von Zerneck, and Robert M. Sertner. Producers: Bruce Jay Friedman and Susan Weber-Gold. Writer: Bruce Jay Friedman. Music: Richard Elliot. The adventures of a tabloid reporter (Robert Wuhl) and his bloodhound dog, Sniff, who is forever leading the reluctant hero into trouble. *Cast:* Robert Wuhl (as Sid Barrows), Louie Guss (Nat Barrows), Tracie Lin (Sharon), Rebecca Holden (as Vanessa), Robin Curtis (Barbara), Edward Power (Blaine Sterling), Richard Roat (Gormley), Nancy Fish (Liz Gertz), Michael Zand (Gaza), Christopher Thomas (Morosco), Gerry Black (Detective), P.R. Paul (Intern), Michael McNab (Guard).

2233. **Some Kinda Woman.** 30 min. Airdate: 9/6/88. Production Companies: Victoria/Benro Productions and Columbia Pictures Television. Director: Bill Bixby. Executive Producers: Larry Rosen and Mark Waxman. Writers: Larry Rosen and Mark Waxman. Creators: Larry Rosen and Mark Waxman. Music: William Goldstein. Aired as an episode of *CBS Summer Playhouse*. Morgan Fairchild is a wild and eccentric woman who falls for a mild-mannered commodities broker (Hunt Block). *Cast:* Morgan Fairchild (as Lisa), Hunt Block (Elliot Benton), S.A. Griffin (Frank), also, Luis Avalos, Carmen Zapata, Roseanna Christianson, Jeff Doucette, Kerry Price.

2234. **Tickets, Please.** 30 min. Airdate: 9/6/88. Production Companies: Walt Disney Television and Charlie Peters Films. Director: Art Dielhenn. Executive Producers: Charlie Peters and Bill Dial. Producer: George Sunga. Writer: Charlie Peters. Creator: Charlie Peters. Music: David Benoit. Aired as a segment of *CBS Summer Playhouse*. An ensemble comedy revolving around the regular riders of a New York commuter train "club car." Cleavon Little is the bartender who runs the car, Yeardley Smith is a law student working as a ticket-taker, David Marciano is the conductor, Marcia Strassman is a divorced lawyer with a teenager daughter, Barbara Howard is an actress, and Bill Macy is a pesticide executive. *Cast:* Cleavon Little (as "Bake" Baker), David Marciano (Sal Bernardini), Yeardley Smith (Paula Bennett), Marcia Strassman (Elaine), Bill Macy (Sam), Harold Gould (Jack), Joe Guzaldo (Ted), Barbara Howard (Ginger).

2235. **Whattley by the Bay.** 30 min. Airdate: 8/9/88. Production Companies: Figment Productions and Orion Television. Director: John Pasquin. Executive Producer: Emily Tracy. Producers: David Felser and William Asher. Writers: Emily Tracy and David Felser. Music: Steve Dorff. Aired as a segment of *CBS Summer Playhouse*. The misadventures of Hank (Richard Gilliland), a widowed big-city newspaper editor who returns to his Chesapeake Bay hometown with his teenage son (Aeryk Egan). Hank's bossy, brassy mother (Anne Pitoniak) runs the general store, and often gets into fights with her Vietnamese short-order cook (George Kee Cheung), the town gossip (Enid Saunders), the sassy waitress (Leslie Deane), and the obnoxious Sheriff (Ken Jenkins), among others. Shot on location in Vancouver, B. C. *Cast:* Richard Gilliland (as Hank Peterson), Aeryk Egan (Max Peterson), Anne Pitoniak (Mom), Ken Jenkins (Sheriff Dwayne Pewe), George Kee Cheung (How Dang), Enid Saunders (Effie Beasley), Lezlie Deane (Annie Porter), Rochelle Greenwood (Libby), Adrien Dorval (Elroy Sloth), David H. MacIntyre (Daddy-Bob Sloth), Lorena Gale (Mona Haynes).

CBS / DRAMA

2236. **Elysian Fields.** 60 min. Airdate: 7/11/89. Director: Joan Tewkesbury. Executive Producer: David Manson. Producer: Joan Tewkesbury. Writer: Joan Tewkesbury. Music: A1 Cooper and Charles Calello. Aired as a critically acclaimed episode of *CBS Summer Playhouse.* The adventures of a Red Cross disaster relief worker (Jeffrey Damon) who moves into a New Orleans boarding house run by the Coffin sisters (Judith Hogue, Frances Fisher), two man-hungry single women, and populated by jazz singers, gypsies and others. *Cast:* Jeffrey DeMunn (as Nate Goodman), Frances Fisher (Violet Coffin), Judith Hogue (Gwen Coffin), J. Epatha Merkerson (Jimmy), Jo Harvey Allen (Abolene), Kris Kamm (George Berger).

2237. **Fort Figueroa.** 60 min. Airdate: 8/2/88. Production Company: Warner Bros. Television. Director: Luis Valdez. Executive Producer: Ron Taylor. Producers: Bob Hargrove and C.J. Charles (aka Carla Jean Wagner). Writer: C.J. Charles. Creator: C.J. Charles. Music: Miles Goodman. Aired as a segment of *CBS Summer Playhouse.* The Perrys are an Iowa family who lose their farm to creditors and are forced to move to a Los Angeles apartment complex they inherit. The ramshackle building in a run-down neighborhood is also home to two immigrant families, the Mexican Corderos and the Vietnamese Trans, as well as a flamboyant disc jockey no one ever sees. The conflict would come from the clash of cultures and the difficulties these families have adapting. The name "Fort Figueroa" comes from the mangled sign above the apartments, which once read "Court Figueroa." "The show is a tad contrived, and overloaded with liberal pieties about immigrants that jar after awhile," David Gritten wrote in the *Los Angeles Herald-Examiner*, "(but) it's also sweet, good-natured, tough-minded and above all, relevant." Cast: Charles Haid (as Dwight Perry), Anne E. Curry (Leanne Perry), Anne Haney (Frieda Perry), Kurt Kinder (Kyle Perry), Holly Fields (Michelle Perry), Frasier Smith (J.J. Bell), Pepe Serna (Mateo Cordero), Dennis Phun (Minh Tran), Obba Babatunde (Terrence Quimby), Le Tuan (Trung Yo), Anahuac Valdez (Benny Cordero), Leon Singer (Inocente Lagunez), Julian Reyes (Polo), Huanani Minn (Thao Tran), Michell Nguyen (Tuey Tran), Brian George (Razi Massoudi), Evelyn Guerrero (Lupe Cordero), Marisol Rodriquez (Xoch Cordero), Patti Yasutaki (Shirley Kajimoto), Robert Evan Collins (Contractor), Phyllis Guerrini (Biker), Charles Hayward (Hippie), Daniel Rosen (Musician).

2238. **Further Adventures.** 60 min. Airdate: 8/30/88. Production Companies: B&E Enterprises and Paramount Television. Director: James Frawley. Executive Producers: Eugenie Ross-Leming and Brad Buckner. Producer: Don Franklin. Writers: Eugenie Ross-Leming and Brad Buckner. Creators: Eugenie Ross-Leming and Brad Buckner. Music: Arthur B. Rubinstein. Aired as a segment of *CBS Summer Playhouse*. The international adventures of two photographers (David Bowe and John Scott Clough) who, in the pilot, help a princess (Ada Maris) find her missing parents. Cast: David Bowe (as Jerry), John Scott Clough (Todd), Ada Maris (Princess), Sherman Howard (Gen. Craw), Jennifer Rhodes (Queen II- lizi), Rene Assa (King Kazamir), Michael Greene (Marcel Huston), Peter Elbling (Moshul), Nick Ramus (Wiseman), Mark Lonow (Mr. Rappaport), Frank Salsedo (Indian Chief).

2239. **Higher Ground.** 90 min. Airdate: 9/4/88. Production Companies: TriStar Television and Columbia Pictures Television. Director: Robert Day. Executive Producers: Alan Epstein and John Denver. Producers: Steve Barnett and Jim Green. Writer: Michael Eric Stein. Music: Lee Holdridge. Theme Song: "Higher Ground" by John Denver. John Denver stars as Jim Clayton, a former FBI agent who moves to Alaska to operate an air charter with his old partner (Martin Kove). When his partner is murdered, Clayton finds the killers, and continues operating the charter with his partner's widow (Meg Wittner) and her son (Brandon Marsh). A soundtrack album by Denver was later released. Cast: John Denver (as Jim Clayton), Martin Kove (Rick Loden), John Rhys-Davies (Lt. Smight), Meg Wittner (Ginny Loden), Brandon Marsh (Tommy Loden), David Renan (Line Holmes), Richard Masur (Bill McClain).

2240. Intrigue. 2 hours. Airdate: 8/11/88. Production Companies: Crew Neck Productions, Linnea Productions, and Columbia Pictures Television. Director: David Drury. Executive Producers: John Scheinfeld and Jeff Melvoin. Producer: Nick Gillott. Writers: Jeff Melvoin and Robert Collins, from a story by Robert Collins. Music: Basil Poledouris. Scott Glenn is a laconic secret agent, posing as a cultural attache to the U.S. Embassy in Brussels, who loves the Chicago Cubs and tools around town in a classic Mustang. In the pilot, he is ordered to find his dying former mentor (Robert Loggia), a defector who wants to return to the U.S. The proposed series, like the pilot, would be shot on location in Europe. *Cast:* Scott Glenn (as Crawford), Robert Loggia (Higbie), William Atherton (Doggett), Martin Shaw (Rozhkov), Cherie Lunghi (Adriana), Eleanore Bron (Sophia), also, Paul Maxwell, William Roberts, Don Fellows, Blain Fairman, Philip O'Brien.

2241. Law and Order. 60 min. Production Company: Universal Television. Director: John Patterson. Executive Producer: Dick Wolf. Producer: James McAdams. Writer: Dick Wolf. Creator: Dick Wolf. An attempt to create a format for crime stories. The first half of each episode would follow a team of detectives, an experienced cop with a love for cigars (George Dzundza) and his single partner (Chris North), as they pursue and capture a criminal. The second half would shift to the district attorneys, a two-time divorce with a teenage daughter (Michael Moriarty) and his out-going, single assistant (Richard Brooks), who must prosecute the case. This became the basis of the 1990 NBC series of the same name that would run for nineteen years and spawn multiple series spin-offs, including *Law & Order SVU* and *Law & Order: Criminal Intent.* CBS made a big mistake passing on this one. *Cast:* George Dzundza (as Det. Sgt. MacGreevey), Chris North (Officer Mike Logan), Dann Florek (Captain Cragin), Michael Moriarty (Ben Stone), Richard Brooks (Paul Robinette), Roy Thinnes (District Attorney Alfred Wentworth).

2242. Mad Avenue. 60 min. Airdate: 8/30/88. Production Companies: Orion Television and Bell Entertainment. Director: Karen Arthur. Executive Producers: Bill Bell, Sr., Chris Knopf, and David Simon. Writers: Chris Knopf and David Simon. Aired as a segment of *CBS Summer Playhouse.* This is *Madison Avenue Blues*—the semi-serialized story of the account executives, copywriters, art directors, and others who work at BCD, a national advertising agency. The principal characters are the senior vp (James McDonnell), the senior copywriter (James B. Sikking), a senior art director (Guy Boyd), an art director (Jennifer

Van Dyck), a copywriter (M.A. Nichols), the senior art director (Brad Hall), and the chief copywriter (Elizabeth Ruscio). The script was nominated for a 1989 Writers Guild award, an unusual distinction for an unsold pilot. *Cast:* James McDonnell (as Bruce Randall), James B. Sikking (Ben Lindsay), Guy Boyd (Murph), Jennifer Van Dyck (Mag Kosar), M.A. Nichols (Kirk McNeil), Brad Hall (Dan Montana), Vicky St. Clair (Harley Kozak), Richard Cox (Peter Searls), Elizabeth Ruscio (C.G.).

2243. **Microcops (aka Micronauts; aka Meganauts).** 60 min. Airdate: 6/20/89. Production Companies: MGM/UA Television and Moonglow Productions. Director: David Jackson. Executive Producer: Lewis Chesler. Producers: Charles "Chip" Proser, Rachel Singer, Terry Carr, and Alan Levy. Writers: Charles "Chip" Proser and Rachel Singer. Music: Tim Truman. The adventures of microscopic, alien cops (William Bumiller and Shanti Owen) who come to earth pursuing an inter- galactic criminal (Page Moseley). The aliens, because of their size, attach their tiny spaceships to people, dogs, birds, or whatever creature is convenient. These aliens communicate to their human hosts through holograms or by appearing in any electronic monitors that are around. Special effects by Industrial Light and Magic. *Cast:* William Bumiller (as Nardo), Shanti Owen (Bidra), Page Moseley (Cloyd), Peter Scolari (Morgan), Tony Bill (Travis), Lucinda Jenney (Lucy), also, Lois Bromfield, Rex Ryan, Brian George.

2244. **Off Duty.** 30 min. Airdate: 8/16/88. Production Companies: Lorimar-Telepictures and Jerry Thorpe Productions. Director: Jerry Thorpe. Executive Producer: Jerry Thorpe. Producers: Gary Michael White and Harvey Frand. Writer: Gary Michael White. Music: Patrick Williams. Aired as a segment of *CBS Summer Playhouse. Cheers* meets *Hill Street Blues* in this proposed series set in a Chicago bar frequented by off-duty cops. Eileen Brennan is the cop's widow who runs the joint, Charles Frank is a disabled cop tending bar as he mends, Lisa Blount is his lady partner who comes to visit, and Tony LoBianco is a legendary retired cop who never seems to leave and has been toiling forever on a novel. *Cast:* Eileen Brennan (Siobahan), Charles Frank (Zack), Tony LoBianco (Tom Cooper), Lisa Blount (Pat Yaraslovsky), Charles Stratton (Officer Charlie DiAntha), Ray Abruzzo (Sgt. Vincent "Mother" DiAntha), also, Taureen Blaque, Nicholas Cascone, Mariclare Costello, David McKnight, Jimie F. Skaggs, Jack McGee, Les Collins, Stephanie Shroyer, Jeff Mooring, Victoria Dakil, Rud Davis, Jan Michael Shultz, Michael Haynes, Rick Avery.

2245. Silent Whisper. 60 min. Airdate: 7/26/88. Production Companies: Above the Line Productions, Maderlay Enterprises, and Lorimar-Telepictures. Director: Jonathan Betuel. Executive Producers: Jonathan Betuel and Gary Adelson. Writer: Jonathan Betuel. Creator: Jonathan Betuel. Music: Bill Conti. Aired as a segment of CBS *Summer Playhouse*. David Beecroft is a San Francisco police detective who discovers his family is about to be murdered by a serial killer, arrives too late, and is stabbed in the throat by the assailant. Now, his voice gone, he works as a special police operative and, in the pilot, stalks the killer who murdered his family. He's aided in his quest by a friend-on-the-force, his former partner (Richard Lawson). *Cast:* David Beecroft (as Eric Bolan), Richard Lawson (as Nick Scott), Claudette Nevins (Capt. Bea Landry), Kate Vernon (Ellen Sanders), Rita Wilson (China Seasons), Joseph Kell (Colin Sanders), Steven Keats (Guido the Ghoul), James Greene (Nathan Sanders), Philip Levien (Dr. Mark Ryler), David Tress (Psychiatrist), Nancy Warren (Elvira Stout), John Brandon (Sergeant), Annie Gegen (Pat Bolari), Robert Factor (Serial Killer), Bridgett Helms (Bolan's Daughter), Brandon Stewart (Bolan's Son), Barney McGeary (Elderly Cop), Laurie Drake (Lady Cop), A1 Pugliese (Mover), Robert Lee (Mayor), Gloria Delaney (Nurse), Marie Halton (Mourner), Justin Whelan (Soccer Player), Gregory Deason (David Sanders).

2246. Sterling (aka The Pretenders). 60 min. Airdate: 7/5/88. Production Company: Aaron Spelling Productions. Director: Aaron Lipstadt. Executive Producers: Aaron Spelling and Douglas S. Cramer. Producer: Gordon Greisman. Writer: Gordon Greisman. Aired as a segment of CBS *Summer Playhouse*. Imagine *The Avengers*, John Steed and Emma Peel, secret agents with elegance, flair, and wit. That's what Nick Sterling and Whitney were—and they were in love. When Nick is killed on a mission, his irreverent, rebellious, twin brother Jack is drafted to masquerade as him. The problem is disc jockey Jack, fired from his last nine jobs, isn't anything like his stylish brother—except in the looks department. All of this, of course, means sparks between Jack and Whitney (redubbed "Jack Stewart" and "Alexandra Greer" in the final pilot) as they fight crime. *Cast:* Roger Wilson (as Jack Stewart (Nick/Jack Sterling)), Amanda Pays (Alexandra Greer [Whitney]), Mitchell Laurence (Sam Everett), David Fox-Brenton (Assassin).

2247. Street of Dreams. 2 hours. Airdate: 10/7/88. Production Companies: Bill Stratton/Myrtos Productions and Phoenix Entertainment. Director: William A.

Graham. Executive Producers: Gerald W. Abrams, Timothy Harris, and Herschel Weingrod. Producers: Bill Stratton, William P. Owens, and Robert M. Ravin. Writer: Bill Stratton, based on the book *Goodnight and Good-bye* by Timothy Harris. Creator: Timothy Harris. Music: Laurence Rosenthal. Ben Masters is Los Angeles private eye Thomas Kyd who saves a damsel-in-distress and becomes embroiled in a case involving a stolen script, an insane assassin, Las Vegas mobsters, and movie stuntmen. *Cast:* Ben Masters (as Thomas Kyd), Morgan Fairchild (Laura), Wendall Wellman (Carl Bomberg), Michael Cavanaugh (Lt. Marcus), Diana Salinger (Ann Kepler), also, Alan Autry, Gerald Hiken, Julie Philips, Danny Goldman, John Putch, Mike Moroff, Richard Green, David Marciano, John Hillerman, Willie Gault, Lisa Dinkins, Laura Julian, Pam Rasak, Jack Frey.

2248. **Two Worlds (aka My Africa).** 60 min. Airdate: 6/21/88. Production Companies: Republic Pictures and Rosemont Productions. Director: Peter Hunt. Executive Producer: Norman Rosemont. Producer: David Rosemont. Writer: Blanche Hanalis. Music: Lee Holdridge. Aired as a segment of CBS *Summer Playhouse*. This pilot, set in 1952, stars Carl Weintraub as Dr. Charles Marston, the son of British and American parents, raised in Africa and educated in America, where he marries and raises a family. When his wife dies, he brings his two children (Jaime McEnnan and Gennie James) to Kenya, where he opens a jungle clinic, aided by his Maasai friend (Joseph Mydell) and a woman doctor from an aristocratic British family (Jenifer Landor). Shot on location in Kenya for $2 million. *Cast:* Carl Weintraub (as Dr. Charles Marston), Gennie James (Sarah Marston), Jaime McEnnan (Davey Marston), Jenifer Landor (Dr. Maggie Forsythe), Joseph Mydell (Peter), Louise Latham (Millie), also, Mwai Muigai, Sid Onyullo, Abdullah Sunado, Kenneth Mason, Ann Wanjugu, Martin Okelo, Nicholas Charles, Jayne Karanja, Joy Mboya.

NBC / COMEDY

2249. **The Big Five (aka The Big Five: The End of Something).** 30 min. Airdate: 6/25/88. Production Company: Weintraub Entertainment. Director: Lasse Hallstrom. Executive Producers: Lasse Hallstrom and John Steven Owen. Producer: Harry R. Sherman. Writer: John Steven Owen. Music: Tom Keane and Rick Bowen. From the director of the popular film *My Life As a Dog,* comes this story about a group of fifth-grade boys who are forced to let a tomboy into their fold. The boys' clubhouse was built in a friend's backyard, and when he moved away, the girl's family moved in—so they make friends with her to save their hideaway. *Cast:* Sean Baca (as Gary Wilson), Ryan Cash (Mike Bradley), Corey Danziger (Bobby Kirkland), Maia Brewton (Melinda "Scotty" Scott), Cameron Brown (Randy Kirkland), Gwen Humble (Barbara Scott), David Ankrum (Robert Kirkland).

2250. **Channel 99.** 30 min. Airdate: 8/4/88. Production Company: Imagine Entertainment. Director: James Burrows. Executive Producers: Lowell Ganz and Babaloo Mandel. Writers: Lowell Ganz and Babaloo Mandel. Marilu Henner is a former Los Angeles station manager trying to make a comeback at a small, struggling New York UHF station, where she has to deal with an insulting, sleazy talk show host (Dennis Dugan), a conservative business manager (Mary Gross), and a military - style boss called The General (Kevin McCarthy). Ron Howard, head of Imagine Entertainment, guest starred as himself. NBC backed out of a 13-episode commitment after viewing the pilot. *Cast:* Marilu Henner (as Susan McDowell), Dennis Dugan (Marty Gessler), Mary Gross (Kiki Kurtz), Kevin McCarthy (General), Bill Duell (Ed Hepley).

2251. **Facts of Life Spin-Off.** 30 min. Airdates: 4/30/88 and 5/7/88. Production Companies: Columbia Television and Embassy Television. Director: John Bowab. Executive Producer: Irma Kalish. Writers: Austin Kalish and Irma Kalish. Creators: Dick Clair and Jenna McMahon. Music: Ray Colcord. Aired as the final, two-part episode of the long-running *Diffrent Strokes* spin-off *Facts of Life*. Blair Warner (Lisa Whelchel) buys Eastland to save it from the wrecking ball, becomes the new headmistress, and turns the formerly all-girl academy into a coed institution. Sherrie Krenn reprises her role as Australian student Pippa McKenna. New characters include a faculty secretary (Kathleen Freeman), a science teacher (Sam Behrens) who thinks Blair is all beauty and no brains and a bevy of young students, among them Juliette Lewis, Mayim Bialik, Seth Green, Marissa Mendenhall, Meredith Scott Lynn, and Jason Naylor. *Cast:* Lisa Whelchel (as Blair Warner), Sam Behrens (Wes Mitchell), Kathleen Freeman (Noreen Grisbee), Mayim Bialik (Jennifer Cole), Seth Green (Adam Brinkerhoff), Juliette Lewis (Terry Rankin), Sherrie Krenn (Pippa McKenna), Meredith Scott Lynn (Ashley Payne), Marissa Mendenhall (Sara Bellanger), Nicholas Coster (David Warner), Danny Dayton (Mr. Avery), Patrick O'Brien (Mr. Copeland), Shirley Prestin

(Miss O'Donnell), Sal Viscuso (Frank Payne), John Welsh (Mr. Morehead), Nancy McKeon (Jo Polniaczek), Mindy Cohn (Natalie Green), Kim Fields (Tootie Ramsey), Cloris Leachman (Beverly Ann Stickle), MacKenzie Astin (Andy Moffet).

2252. **Flipside aka Life on the Flipside.** 30 min. Airdate: 8/29/88. Production Companies: Don Johnson Company and Universal Television. Director: Jeff Melman. Executive Producers: Don Johnson, Neal Israel, and Amy Heckerling. Writer: Ron Zimmerman. Yet another project about a rock star who, when his wife leaves him, is forced to return from years "on the road" to raise his estranged kids. Trevor Eve (stepping in at the last minute for Ringo Starr) is the rock star, Dennis Berkeley is his road manager, and Traci Lin, Frank Whaley, and Jarrett Lennon are his kids. The first pilot produced by actor Don Johnson. *Cast:* Trevor Eve (as Tripper Day), Dennis Berkeley (Mr. Jones), Traci Lin (Better), Frank Whaley (Sonny), Jarrett Lennon (Shea).

2253. **Heart and Soul.** 30 min. Airdate: 7/21/88. Production Companies: Grio Entertainment, Doug McHenry Productions, Giggling Goose Productions, and Castle Rock Entertainment. Director: John Pasquin. Executive Producer: Gary Gilbert. Producers: Jan Siegelman, David Nichols, and Doug McHenry. Writer: David Nichols. The misadventures of two friends who own a recording busi-ness—Curtis Rousseau (Morris Day), an aggressive and energetic record pro-ducer, and his partner Richard Bradley (Clark Johnson), who wants to quit and teach music. Tisha Campbell is a wanna-be rock star, Arnetia Walker is an egotis-tical singer, Barry Sobel is the mailboy who idolizes Curtis and Marge Redmond is their secretary. *Cast:* Morris Day (as Curtis Rousseau), Clark Johnson (Richard Bradley), Tisha Campbell (Jamie Sinclair), Arnetia Walker (Dawnelle), Barry Sobel (Jeff), Marge Redmond (Helen), James Avery (Harlan).

2254. **Homecoming Queen.** 30 min. Production Company: Viacom Entertainment. Director: Terry Hughes. Executive Producer: Chris Thompson. Writer: Chris Thompson. Beverly Jean Sparks left the tiny town of Beauville when she was crowned homecoming queen 16 years ago—and now she's back, wreaking havoc for everybody, to run her father's drug store with her brother. Beverly D'Angelo, for whom the part was tailored, opted out of the project. Victoria Principal was among many actresses who read for the part, but were rejected.

2255. **My Two Dads Spin-Off.** 30 min. Production Companies: Columbia Pictures Television and Embassy Television. Director: Matthew Diamond. Executive

Producer: Michael Jacobs. Writer: Michael Jacobs. An attempt to build a series around Ed Klawicki (Dick Butkus), who owns the diner in the building where Joey, Michael, and Nicole live. Nicole's friend Roy Kupkus (Bradley Gregg) borrows Joey's motorcycle and crashes it through the diner window. When the judge orders the boy to work in the diner to pay damages, Ed becomes involved with Roy's mother (Lauren Tewes) and a family of sorts is born—and with it, it was hoped, a new series. *Cast:* Dick Butkus (as Ed Klawicki), Bradley Gregg (Roy Kupkus), Lauren Tewes (Karen Kupkus), Greg Evigan (Joey Harris), Paul Reiser (Michael Taulor), Staci Keanan (Nicole Bradford), Vonni Ribisi (Cory Kupkus).

2256. **Nurse Bob.** 30 min. Production Company: NBC Productions. Director: Nick Havinga. Executive Producer: Tom Patchett. Writer: Valerie Curtin. An ex- con male nurse (Tim Thomerson), on parole, as a last resort agrees to take care of an elderly man (Norman Fell) at his home—and unwillingly becomes sucked into his weird family. *Cast:* Tim Thomerson (as Bob Wykowski), Norman Fell (Ted Palmer), Valerie Curtin (Natalie), Todd Susman (Frank), Andrew Bednarski (Kelly Carl), Moya Kordick (Chloe).

2257. **Smart Guys.** 30 min. Production Company: Imagine Entertainment. Director: Jonathan Lynn. Executive Producers: Ron Howard, Brian Grazer, and Dori Weiss. Writers: Michael DiGaetano and Larry Gay. Ned (Chris Rich) is an ex-con, imprisoned on false charges, who becomes partners with a smooth schemer (Anthony Starke) and his naive, over-weight brother (John Pinette) to help people solve sticky problems. In the pilot, they help a woman out of a forced marriage. *Cast:* Chris Rich (as Ned), Anthony Starke (Tommy), John Pinette (Nick), Constance Shulman (Arlene).

NBC / DRAMA

2258. **C.A.T. Squad II (aka C.A.T. Squad: Python Wolf).** 2 hours. Airdate: 5/23/88. Production Company: NBC Productions. Director: William Friedkin. Executive Producer: William Friedkin. Producer: David Salven. Writer: Robert Ward, from a story by Gerald Petievich, William Friedkin, and Robert Ward. Creators: William Friedkin and Gerald Petievich. Music: Ennio Morricone. "Officially, the C.A.T. Squad does not exist. Unofficially, they may be the free world's last chance," blared the ads for this, the second attempt to sell NBC on the adventures of the elite Counter-Assault Tactical anti-terrorist squad headed by stony Joe Cortese.

This time, the squad investigates South African slave labor, stolen plutonium, and high-tech espionage. Steve James and Jack Youngblood reprise their roles from the original pilot, which aired in 1986. Shot on location in Montreal. *Cast:* Joe Cortese (as Richard Earl "Doc" Burkholder), Jack Youngblood (John Sommers), Steve James (Bud Raines), Deborah Van Valkenburgh (Nikki Pappas), Miguel Ferrer (Paul Kiley), Alan Scarfe (Bekker), Brian Delate (Trask), also, Michael Fletcher, William Mooney, Alan Coates, Christopher Loomis, Neil Hunt, Tedd Dillon, Peter Neptune, William Bell Sullivan, Chris Walker, Russell Wong, James Saito, Vlasta Vrana, David O'Brien, Ron Frazier, Ron Parady, George Seremba, Adoulaye N'Gom, Seth Sibanda, Bruce Young.

2259. **Desert Rats.** 60 min. Production Company: Universal Television. Director: Tony Wharmby. Executive Producers: David Chisholm and Bernie Kowalski. Producer: Ken Topolski. Writer: David Chisholm. Scott Plank is Josh Bodeen, the 26-year-old Arizona Sheriff in the county where he was once a teenage rabble- rouser. He fights crime with laconic Deputy Bones (Scott Paulin) and Officer Mort Ledonka (Dietrich Bader) in a squad car and chopper souped-up by mechanical whiz Owen (Mark Thomas Miller).

2260. **Desperado (aka Return of Desperado).** 2 hours. Airdate: 2/15/88. Production Companies: Universal Television and Walter Mirisch. Director: E.W. Swackhamer. Executive Producer: Andrew Mirisch. Producer: Charles E. Sellier, Jr. Writers: John Mankiewicz, Daniel Pyne, and Charles Grant Craig, from a story by John Mankiewicz and Daniel Pyne. Creator: Elmore Leonard. Music: Michel Colombier. Alex McArthur returns as wanted gunslinger Duell McCall who, in the second of five pilots, rides into Beauty, where a conman has framed a black homesteader for murder. *Cast:* Alex McArthur (as Duell McCall), also, Robert Foxworth, Marcy Walker, Victor Love, Vanessa Bell, Shelby Leverington, Charles Boswell, Billy Dee Williams, Vivian Bonnell, Hal Havins, J.J. Saunders, John Barks, Greg Brinkley, Rahda Delamarte, Rusty Dillen, Jerry Gardner, Darlan Rusch Gathings, Sam Gauny, Dan Kamin, Ivy Price, Adam Taylor, Tommy Townsend, Marvin Walters.

2261. **Desperado: Avalanche at Devil's Ridge.** 2 hours. Airdate: 5/24/88. Production Companies: Universal Television, Walter Mirisch Productions, and Charles E. Sellier, Jr. Productions. Director: Richard Compton, Executive Producer: Andrew Mirisch. Producer: Charles E. Sellier, Jr. Writer: Larry Cohen. Creator: Elmore Leonard. Music: Michel Colombier. Duell McCall, due to be lynched for impersonating a lawman, escapes the noose by volunteering to help a salt-mine baron (Rod Steiger) find his kidnapped daughter and the bad guy who took her–a varmint who has an affinity for blowing things up. Just about everyone dies in this opus, except for Duell, who lives on, roaming the airwaves in search of a series to call his own. *Cast:* Alex McArthur (as Duell McCall), Hoyt Axton (Sheriff Ben Tree), Alice Adair (Rachel Slaten), Lise Cutter (Nora), Rod Steiger (Silas Slaten), also, Dwier Brown, Lee Paul, Arch Archambault, John Barks, Jack Caffrey, Tom Connor, Ben Connors, Blake Conway, Steve Cormier, Cliff Doran, Katherine Engel, John-David Garfield, R.W. Hampton, Laura Martinez Herring, J.M. Jamison, Suzanne Lederer, Chris McCarty, Marc Miles, Leslie Schwartz, Steve Schwartz-Hartley, Tim Scott, Angela Sorrels, Ben Zeller.

2262. **Down Delaware Road.** 60 min. Airdate: 7/20/88. Production Company: Weintraub Entertainment. Director: David Hemmings. Executive Producer: Lawrence Hertzog. Writer: Lawrence Hertzog. Creator: Lawrence Hertzog. The misadventures of three teenage boys—Mark, the aspiring writer/son of a reverend father and an alcoholic mother; Curtis, whose brother Burt is a juvenile delinquent; and Robbie, who has a crush on Mark's sister and whose parents are splitting up. In the pilot, Mark discovers romance while Robbie and Curtis make cherry bombs and accidentally burn down an abandoned gas station—perhaps killing a derelict in the fire. *Cast:* Mark Bellou (as Curtis Rhonda), Adam Carl (Mark Dirksen), Cami Cooper (Marianne Dirksen), Lee Garlington (Janet Rhonda), David Lascher (Robbie Heller), Norman Parker (Ed Heller), Valerie Wildman (Ann Heller), Leon Russom (Peter Dirksen), Donna Mitchell (Liz Dirksen), John McLiam (Granny), Nicole Huntington (Judi Caine), Devon Odessa (Ellen Payter), Michael Palance (Bert Rhonda), Nicki Vannice (Julie Heller).

2263. **Home Free.** 60 min. Airdate: 7/13/88. Production Company: MTM Enterprises. Directors: Mark Tinker and Eric Leaneuville. Executive Producers: David Milch and John Romano. Producers: Kevin Inch and Michael Warren. Writers: David Milch and John Romano. Creators: David Milch and John Romano. Michael Warren is a construction company exec and foster father to five orphaned kids— problem children from abusive families, broken homes, and other bad situations placed in his large home by the juvenile court. He's aided by social worker Tracey (Lonette McKee), Eddie the cook (Trinidad Silva), and his business partner Barry (Charles Levin). The show was already dead by the time it hit the air, so MTM launched an aggressive ad campaign to save the pilot. Newspaper ads read : "You can program the number one network. Tonight, the producers of *The Mary Tyler*

Moore Show, *St. Elsewhere*, and *Hill Street Blues* will bring you a NEW program starring Michael Warren. It's called *Home Free*. NBC will program *Home Free* as a series if enough of you care. The show must win a 25 share. If you want great TV, get involved. WATCH IT! You'll laugh, you'll feel good, and you'll want to live there. We guarantee it! *Home Free*—where dreams really come true." Unfortunately, the dream of a 25 share didn't. The show earned a 14 share. *Cast:* Michael Warren (as Michael Davis), Trinidad Silva (Eddie), Charles Levin (Barry), Teddy Abner (Jerome), Donnie Jeffcoat (Douglas), Jonathan Brandis (Vladimir), Danny Nucci (Dennis), Ben Hoag (Willie), Lonette McKee (Ms. Tracy).

2264. **Incredible Hulk Returns (aka Thor).** 2 hours. Airdate: 5/22/88. Production Companies: New World Television and B&B Productions. Director: Nicholas Corea. Executive Producers: Nicholas Corea and Bill Bixby. Producer: Daniel McPhee. Writer: Nicholas Corea. Creator: Kenneth Johnson, based on the Marvel Comics character. Music: Lance Rubin. New World Pictures and ABC used a revival of *The Incredible Hulk* (CBS 1978–82) as a ploy to launch *Thor*, a proposed series starring Steve Levitt as an anthropology student who discovers a magic hammer which allows him to conjure up Thor (Eric Kramer), a viking warrior, whom he teams with to fight crime. Thor comes crashing into Banner's life just as he, now working for a high tech corporation, is about to cure himself with a new bolt of gamma radiation ("He's been seething for six long years," blared the ads, "tonight, the incredible explosion!"). But bad guys kidnap his girlfriend (Lee Purcell), dogged reporter McGee (Jack Colvin) comes snooping, and Banner finds himself back on the run again. Although this pilot didn't sell, the stellar ratings of this revival prompted NBC to buy several sequel movies also designed to spin-off Marvel Comics characters. A second revival/pilot, *Trial of the Incredible Hulk*, was directed by star Bill Bixby, who costarred with Rex Smith, who portrayed Daredevil, a blind attorney by day who is a crimefighter by night. A third movie, *Death of the Incredible Hulk*, aired on NBC in 1990. *Cast:* Bill Bixby (as David Banner), Lou Ferrigno (Hulk), Jack Colvin (Jack McGee), Steve Levitt (Donald Blake), Eric Kramer (Thor), Lee Purcell (Maggie Shaw), Tim Thomerson (Jack LeBeau), also, Charles Napier, Eric Kramer, William Riley, Tom Finnegan, Donald Willis, Carl Nick Ciafalio, Bobby Travis McLaughlin, Burke Denis, Nick Costa, Peisha McPhee, William Malone, Joanie Allen.

2265. **McClone.** 60 min. Airdate: 4/8/88. Production Company: New West Productions. Director: Allan Holzman. Executive Producer: Glen A. Larson.

Producers: Donald C. Klune, Scott Levita, J.C. Larson, David Garber, and Bruce Kalish. Writers: Glen A. Larson, David Garber, and Bruce Kalish. Creator: Glen A. Larson. Music: Dave Fisher and Rocky Davis. Aired as the "Send in the Clones" episode of *The Highwayman*. The adventures of a genetically engineered soldier (Howie Long) who escapes from the secret military research base where he was created and now roams America, pursued by evil clones and government scientists. The episode doubled as a send-up of producer Glen Larson's famed *McCloud* series, with J.D. Cannon and Terry Carter returning in thinly disguised reprises of their former roles. Cannon has just been released from the loony bin when he encounters McClone, a fish-out-of-water who makes working with McCloud seem positively tranquil. Phoenix badly, and obviously, stood in for New York locations (with palm trees in Central Park!) in this sloppily shot pilot. *Cast:* Howie Long (as Mac), J.D. Cannon (Cmdr. Briggs), Terry Carter (Lieutenant), Pamela Shoop (Dr. Chadway), Gary Lockwood (Col. Westcourt), Greta Blackburn (Prostitute), Michael Pataki (Detective), Mel Young (Reporter), John Wade (Clone), Perry D'Marco (Hood), Sam Jones (Highwayman), Jacko (Jetto), Jane Badler (Miss Winthrop), Tim Russ (D.C. Montana).

2266. **Oakmont (aka A Father's Homecoming).** 2 hours. Airdate: 6/19/88. Production Company: NBC Productions. Director: Rick Wallace. Executive Producers: Gloria Katz and Willard Huyck. Producers: Edwald Milkovich and R.W. Goodwin. Writers: Gloria Katz and Willard Huyck. Creators: Gloria Katz and Willard Huyck. Music: Tom Scott. Michael McKean is a divorced publisher with two teenagers (Jonathan Ward and Marcianne Warman) who becomes headmaster at the Massachusetts preparatory school he once graduated from—and where his kids are now students. The family becomes embroiled in city politics, school politics, and sexual politics in the small factory town of Barrington. Shot on location in Atlanta. *Cast:* Michael McKean (as Michael Fields), Jonathan Ward (David Fields), Marcianne Warman (Rebecca Fields), Byron Thames (Eric), Brandon Douglas (Corry), Nana Visitor (Laura), also, Peter Michael Goetz, Cady McClain, Reginald Vel Johnson, Susan Krebs, Billy Morrissette, Rosemary Dunsmore, Jadrien Steele, Thomas Royan, Brenda Bakke, David Kaufman, Tom O'Rourke, Bill Cwikowski, Ken Letner, John Sanderford, Hope Clarke, Kevin Joseph, Cynthia Stevenson.

2267. **Out of Time.** 2 hours. Airdate: 7/17/88. Production Company: TriStar Television. Director: Robert Butler. Executive Producer: Robert Butler.

Producers: David Latt, Kerry Lenhart, and John J. Sakmer. Writers: Brian Alan Lane, Kerry Lenhart, and John J. Sakmer, from a story by Brian Alan Lane. Music: Andy Summers. Bruce Abbott is a rogue future cop, living in the shadow of his long-dead, famous grandfather, who chases a notorious criminal (Adam Ant) 100 years into the past, to Los Angeles circa 1988. The future cop ends up teaming with his greatgrandfather (Bruce Maher), now an under-appreciated rookie officer, to find the bad guy and fight crime. *Cast:* Bruce Abbott (as Channing Taylor), Bruce Maher (Max Taylor), Adam Ant (Richard Marcus), also, Kristin Alfonso, Leo Rossi, Ray Girardin, Ana Holt, Tony LaGava, Kimberly Sedgewick, Barbara Tabuck, Chuck Lindsly, Arthur Mendoza, Rick Avery, Ashley Brittingham, Don Maxwell, Richard Lavin, Jay Richardson.

2268. **Satin's Touch.** 60 min. Production Companies: NBC Productions and Edgar J. Scherick Associates. Director: Jan Eliasberg. Executive Producers: Edgar J. Scherick and Gary Hoffman. Writer: R.J. Stewart. Satin Carlyle (Lise Cutter) is a retired Interpol agent who marries an internationally known auctioneer (Martyn Stanbridge) and all is well—until her former partner shows up (Tim Carhart) and enlists them as Interpol agents to track down an art thief. The proposed series would follow this unusual threesome as they fight crime across Europe.

2269. **Shooter.** 2 hours. Airdate: 9/11/88. Production Companies: Paramount Television and UBU Productions. Director: Gary Nelson. Executive Producer: Gary David Goldberg. Producers: David Hume Kennerly, Steve Kline, and Barry Berg. Writers: David Hume Kennerly and Steve Kline. Loosely based on the life of Vietnam war photographer David Hume Kennerly (ex-husband of *Thirtysomething*'s Mel Harris). Jeffrey Nordling is Matt Thompson, a combat photographer who works out of the Saigon bureau of a major magazine and gets involved in the lives of the soldiers he meets. Other characters include Ngoc, the Vietnamese photo lab technician; Klause, a German photographer swiping Buddhas; Rene, a French photographer who brandishes an AK-47; Stork O'Connor, Matt's superstitious roommate and fellow photographer; Rizzo, an irascible editor; Lin, an American educated, Vietnamese reporter; and an Embassy worker (Helen Hunt) who is Matt's former flame. *Cast:* Jeffrey Nordling (as Matt Thompson), Noble Willingham (Rizzo), Kario Salem (Rene), Alan Ruck (Stork O'Connor), Jerry Alan Chandler (Klause), Cuba Nguen (Ngoc), Carol Huston (Cat), Rosalind Chao (Lan), also, Helen Hunt.

BIBLIOGRAPHY

Barnouw, Erik. *Tube of Plenty: The Evolution of American Television*, rev. ed. New York: Oxford University Press, 1982.

Bedell, Sally. *Up the Tube: Primetime TV and the Silverman Years*. New York: Viking Press, 1981.

Brooks, Tim, and Earle Marsh. *The Complete Directory of Primetime Network TV Shows 1946-Present*, rev. ed. New York: Ballantine, 1981.

Castleman, Harry, and Walter J. Podrazik. *Watching TV: Four Decades of American Television*. New York: McGraw-Hill, 1982.

Christensen, Mark, and Cameron Stauth. *The Sweeps: Behind the Scenes in Network TV*. New York: William Morrow, 1984.

Cole, Barry S. *Television—Selections from* TV Guide *Magazine*. New York: The Free Press, 1970.

Eisner, Joel, and David Krinsky. *Television Comedy Series: An Episode Guide to 153 TV Sitcoms in Syndication*. Jefferson, N.C.: McFarland, 1984.

Etter, Jonathan. *Gangway, Lord, The Here Comes The Brides Book*, Albany, Georgia. Bear Manor Media, 2010

Feuer, Jane; Paul Kerr and Tise Vahimagi. *MTM—Quality Television*. London: British Film Institute, 1984.

Fireman, Judy. *TV Book*. New York: Workman, 1977.

Gerani, Gary, and Paul S. Schulman. *Fantastic Television*. New York: Harmony Books, 1977.

Gianakos, Larry James. *Television Drama Series Programming: A Comprehensive Chronicle, 1959–1975*. Metuchen, N.J.: Scarecrow Press, 1978.

_____. _____. *1947–1959*. Scarecrow, 1980.

_____. _____. *1975–1980*. Scarecrow, 1981.

_____. _____. *1980–1982*. Scarecrow, 1983.

Gitlin, Todd. *Inside Primetime*. New York: Pantheon, 1983.

Green, Paul. *Roy Huggins*, Jefferson, NC McFarland & Co, 2014.

659

Head, Sydney, with Christopher H. Sterling. *Broadcasting in America*, 4th ed. New York: Houghton Mifflin, 1982.

Irvin, Richard. *George Burns Television Productions: The Series and the Pilots, 1950-1981*. Jefferson, NC. McFarland & Co., 2014

Kelly, Richard. *The Andy Griffith Show*, rev. & exp. ed. Winston-Salem, N.C.: John F. Blair, 1984.

Levinson, Richard, and William Link. *Stay Tuned: An Inside Look at the Making of Primetime Television*. New York: St. Martin's, 1981.

_____, and William Link. *Off Camera: Conversations with the Makers of Prime-Time Television*. New York: New American Library, 1986.

McCarty, John, and Brian Kelleher. *Alfred Hitchcock Presents*. New York: St. Martin's, 1985.

McNeil, Alex. *Total Television—A Comprehensive Guide to Programming from 1948 to the Present*, 2d ed. New York: Penguin Books, 1984.

Maltin, Leonard. *TV Movies and Video Guide*. An annual. New York: New American Library.

Marill, Alvin H. *Movies Made for Television—The Telefeature and the MiniSeries*. New York: New York Zoetrope, 1987.

Meyers, Richard. *TV Detectives*. San Diego, Calif.: A.S. Barnes, 1981.

Miller, Merle, and Evan Rhodes. *Only You, Dick Daring: How to Write One Television Script and Make $50,000,000*. New York: William Sloan Assoc., 1964.

Mitz, Rick. *The Great TV Sitcom Book*, exp. ed. New York: Perigee Books, 1983.

Newcomb, Horace, and Robert S. Alley. *The Producer's Medium*. New York: Oxford University Press, 1983.

Parish, James Robert. *Actors Television Credits 1950–1972*. Metuchen, N.J.: Scarecrow Press, 1973.

_____, and Mark Trost. *Supplement I*. Scarecrow, 1978.

_____, and Vincent Terrace. *Supplement II: 1977–1981*. Scarecrow, 1982.

_____, and _____. _____. *Supplement III: 1982–1985*. *Scarecrow, 1986*.

Perry, Jeb H. *Universal Television: The Studio and Its Programs, 1950–1980*. Metuchen, N.J.: Scarecrow Press, 1983.

Sanders, Steven Coyne & Gilbert, Tom. *Desilu: The Story of Lucille Ball and Desi Arnaz*. New York. Harper Collins, 2011

Scheuer, Steven H. *The Television Annual*. New York: Collier Books, 1978–79.

_____. *Movies on TV*. New York: Bantam, 1982.

Schow, David J., and Jeffrey Frentzen. *The Outer Limits: The Official Companion.* New York: Ace Science Fiction Books, 1986.

Terrace, Vincent. *Encyclopedia of Television—Series, Pilots and Specials 1936–1973.* New York: New York Zoetrope, 1986.

_____. _____. *1974–1984.* New York Zoetrope, 1985.

_____. _____. *The Index: Who's Who in Television 1937–1984.* New York Zoetrope, 1986.

TV Guide Roundup, various authors. New York: Holt, Rinehart and Winston, 1960.

Weissman, Ginny, and Coyne Steven Sanders. *The Dick Van Dyke Show—Anatomy of a Classic.* New York: St. Martin's, 1983.

Wicking, Christopher, and Tise Vahimagi. *The American Vein: Directors and Directions in Television.* New York: E.P. Dutton, 1979.

Woolley, Lynn; Robert W. Malsbary and Robert G. Strange, Jr. *Warner Brothers Television.* Jefferson, N.C.: McFarland, 1985.

Zicree, Marc Scott. *The Twilight Zone Companion.* New York: Bantam, 1982.

ABOUT THE AUTHOR

Lee Goldberg is a two-time Edgar Award and Shamus Award nominee whose many TV writing and/or producing credits include *Martial Law, SeaQuest, Diagnosis Murder, The Cosby Mysteries, Hunter, Spenser: For Hire, Nero Wolfe, The Glades* and *Monk*. His many books include *The Walk, King City, Successful Television Writing, Watch Me Die*, the *Diagnosis Murder* and *Monk* series of original mystery novels, and the internationally bestselling Fox & O'Hare series that he co-authors with Janet Evanovich. As a TV development consultant, he's worked for production companies and broadcasters in Germany, Spain, Sweden, and the Netherlands.

INDEX

Titles of unsold pilots (including alternate titles) are in **bold**; all other titles (series, films, books, etc.) are in *italics*. Entries are cited as they appear in credit listings.

A

A Shane Productions
1842, 2008, 2083
Aal, Deborah 2085
Aames, Angela 1733
Aames, Willie 1093
Aaron, Paul
2070, 2150
Aaron Ruben
Productions 1283,
1434, 1529
Aaron Spelling
Productions 1077,
1079, 1132, 1534,
1539, 1612, 1615,
1713, 1721, 1859,
1862, 1917, 1973,
2021, 2025, 2032,
2091, 2092, 2097,
2145, 2149, 2150,
2216, 2247
Abatemarco, Frank
1842, 2059, 2113
Abbot, Jane 1637
Abbott, Bruce 1969,
1973, 2267
Abbott, Frankie 854
Abbott, John
752, 1567
Abbott, Norman
1431, 1486, 1543
Abbott, Philip
832, 1583

Abbott-Fish, Chris
1815, 1881, 1985
Abbotts 215
ABC Circle Films
1180, 1251, 1309,
1322, 1368, 1438,
1532, 1797, 1803,
1967, 1970, 2026,
2035, *2090*
*ABC Comedy
Theatre 1796*
ABC Productions
450, 1034, 1062
Abdo, Nick 1929
Abel, Rudy E.
21, 764, 886
Abel Marsh 1254
1315, 1503,
1513, 1595
Abercrombie, Ian
1441, 2040
Abner, Teddy 2263
Above the Law 929
Above the Line
Productions 2245
Abraham, F.
Murray 1192
Abrams, Edward
1294
Abrams, Gerald W.
1408, 1490, 1491,
1492, 1653, 1772,
2042, 2246
Abrams, Mort 848

Abrell, Sarah
1850, 1981
Abruzzo, Ray 2244
Academy 1889, 1890
Acavone, Jay 1888
Ace 1405
**Ace of the
Mounties** 865
Aces Up 1262
Acker, Sharon 1235,
1249, 1377, 1771
Ackerman, Bettye
1145, 1246
Ackerman, Harry
22, 25, 26, 497,
627, 743, 761,
864, 863, 942,
969, 1008, 1012,
1025, 1051, 1090,
1095, 1110, 1203
Ackerman, Leonard
J. 1102
Ackerman, Leslie
1413, 1905, 2040
Ackroyd, David
1514, 1569, 1889,
1890, 2119
Acres and Pains 642
Act II 2178, 2182
Actman, Jane 1245,
1468, 1558
A.D.A. 1511
Adair,
Alice 2261

Adair, Perry
Sheehan 2049
Adam McKenzie 695
Adam-12 1292, 1302,
1354, 1467, 1827
Adams, Arthur 957
Adams, Arthur F. 1969
Adams, Beverly 833
Adams, Brooke 1319,
1329, 1361
Adams, Clifford 877
Adams, Don 1393
Adams, Douglas 1858
Adams, Edie 412,
536, 1151, 1917
Adams, Julie 208,
704, 925
Adams, Kate 1520
Adams, Laurel 2127
Adams, Lillian 1446
Adams, Marla 1914
Adams, Marlin 1248
Adams, Mary
268, 319
Adams, Mason 1679,
1927, 2033, 2092
Adams, Maud 1582
Adams, Nick
605, 646
Adams, Richard 1267
Adams, Stanley
717, 834
Adams, Susan 1486,
1487, 1595

Adams, Tony 2201
Adams, William 2221
Adam's Apple 2113
Adam's House 1868
Adams of Eagle Lake 1254, 1315, 1513
Addison, John 1615, 1892
Adelman, Barry 1829
Adelson, Arthur 954
Adelson, Gary 1614, 1871, 2003, 2213, 2245
Adler, Andrea 1461
Adler, Bill 1799
Adler, Ed 1281
Adler, Jay 582, 615
Adler, Jerry 1717
Adler, Luther 478, 1181
Adler, Matt 2069
Ado, Robinson Frank 2218
Adrian, Charles 1215
Adventures in Happiness 517
Adventures in Paradise 94
Adventures of a Model 18
Adventures of Alexander Hawkins 1982, 2059
Adventures of Ali Baba 432
Adventures of Andy Hardy 248
Adventures of Duncan Maitland 433
Adventures of Freddy 1505
Adventures of Fremont 26
Adventures of Hiawatha 222
Adventures of Johnny Dollar 205

Adventures of Nick Carter 1126
Adventures of Pollyanna 1879
Adventures of the Queen 1335
Adventures of the U.S. Secret Service 303
Adventures of Tom Swift 363
Adventurizing with the Chopper 1341
Advice to the Lovelorn 1840
Aero Squad 1347
Aff, James 1821
African Drumbeat 92
African Queen 696, 1466, 1536
After George 1869
After Midnight 2144
After the Honeymoon 1080
Aftermath 470, 841
Aggie 235
Aggress, Dave 1840
Aguilar, Tommy 1771
Ahlers, David 271
Ahn, Phili 1376
Aidem, Betsy 2046
Aidman, Betty 1200
Aidman, Charles 494, 1597
Aiello, Danny 1478, 1754
Aikenhead, Mac 2129
Ainsworth, Helen 475
Airline Hostess 187
Airport 1189
A.J. Fenady Productions 1347, 1474
Ajaye, Franklyn 1756
Akerling, Maya 1944
Akers, Andrea 1807
Akin, Phillip 2029

Akins, Claude 305, 314, 607, 701, 719, 1063, 1103, 1166, 1232, 1369, 1644, 1694
Akira 1863
Al Rogers Productions 1633
Alaimo, Marc 1358, 1525, 1841, 1969, 2009, 2195
Alan, Douglas 2030
Alan, Lloyd 2208
Alan King Productions 1106
Alan King Show 549, 639, 831, 2102
Alan Landsburg Productions 1209, 1679, 1742, 1877, 1930, 1946, 1991, 1998, 2110
Alan Wagner Productions 2112
Alarm 77
Alba, Jamie 1799
Alberghetti, Anna Maria 79
Alberoni, Sherry 870, 1188
Albert, Darlene 156
Albert, Eddie 225, 1082, 1084, 1123, 1201, 1831, 1865, 1880, 2029
Albert, Edward 1566, 1692
Albert, Wil 1732, 2009
Albert S. Ruddy Productions 1407
Albertson, Grace 656
Albertson, Jack 522, 939, 1010, 1103, 1326
Albertson, Mabel 935, 1274
Albin, Andy 2186

Albin, Dolores 2186
Albright, Lola 68, 655, 804, 912, 929, 1526
Alcoa Premiere 155, 630, 713, 715, 718, 719, 757
Alcoa Theatre 265
Alcoa/ Goodyear Theatre 381, 382, 383, 385, 386, 390, 403, 497, 500, 501, 520, 522, 523
Alda, Alan 901, 1109, 1254, 1346, 1502
Alda, Antony 930, 1793, 1825
Alda, Robert 1349, 1658
Alden, Lynn 662
Alden, Norman 704, 1213, 1268, 1270, 1551, 1619, 2086
Alderman, John 1519, 2115
Alderson, Brooke 1792
Alderson, John 1295
Aldo, Ray 558
Aldon, Mari 271
Aldrich, Rhonda 1976, 2170
Alec Tate 808
Alejandro, Miguel 1079
Aleksander, Grant 2025
Alende, Tommy 806
Aletter, Frank 691
Alex and the Dobermans 1774
Alexander, Ben 102
Alexander, David 654
Alexander, Denise 724
Alexander, Jane 1287
Alexander, Jeff 930, 1374, 1534, 1748
Alexander, John, Jr. 1160

Alexander, Nick 845

Alexander, Robert 438

Alexander, Ronald 20, 651

Alexander Botts 57

Alexander the Great 750

Alexandra, Tiana 1800

Alf 1664

Alfasa, Joe 1748

Alfonso, Kristin 2267

Alfra Productions 1395

Alfred Hitchcock Presents 51, 579, 772, 902, 1958

Alfred of the Amazon 949

Alias Sherlock Holmes 1418

Alice, Mary 1469, 1745

Aliens 1678

Aliens Are Coming 1678

Alinder, Dallas 1820, 1901

All About Barbara 728

All in the Family 386, 497, 1671

All My Children 1172

All My Clients Are Innocent 630

All That Glitters 2002

All the Way Home 2121

All Together Now 1990

Allan, Jed 1317, 1350

Allan, Lane 1525

Allan 1091

Allan Carr Enterprises 1631

Allan Katz Productions 1868, 2020

Allbright, Budd 1059

Alldredge, Michael 1617

Allen, Chad 2061

Allen, Corey 1651, 2041, 2086, 2093, 2171

Allen, Debbie 1644

Allen, Gary 1616, 1633, 1875

Allen, Howard 2188

Allen, Irwin 995, 1101, 1335, 1372, 1382

Allen, Jed 1152, 1302

Allen, Jo Harvey 2236

Allen, Joanie 2264

Allen, Joelle 2144

Allen, John 2099

Allen, Jonelle 1568, 1621

Allen, Lee 876

Allen, Lewis 126, 396

Allen, Marty 813, 1039, 1506

Allen, Melvin E. 1970

Allen, Nancy 2089

Allen, Phillip R. 1460, 1844, 1972

Allen, Rae 1203, 1228, 1405, 1901

Allen, Ray 1044, 1112

Allen, Rex, Jr. 954

Allen, Ricky 292

Allen, Sean 1801

Allen, Seth 1192

Allen, Steve 760

Allen, Ta-Ronce 1089, 1248

Allen, Woody 1206

Alley, Kirstie 1894, 2119

Allford, Roger 2093

Allied Artists 1321

Allin, Henry 958

Allin, Jeff 2087

Allison, Deborah 2183

Allison, Jean 503

Allison, Judith 1767, 1768, 1979

Allison, Keith 1767, 1768

Allison Sidney Harrison 1951

Allman, Elvia 646, 647, 1638

Allman, Sheldon 1048, 1315

Allport, Christopher 1389, 1679, 1765, 1941

Allyson, June 1190

Almost American 1823

Almost Home 2067

Alone at Last 1711, 1751, 1752

Along the Barbary Coast 602

Alpern, Susan 1330

Alpha Caper 1183

Alredge, Dawn 1457

Alridge, Michael 1800

Alsberg, Arthur 1660, 1832

Alston, Howard 1971

Alston, Spencer 1939

Altman, Jeff 1665, 1666, 1790, 1859

Altman, Robert 607, 905

Altman, Shelly 2112

Alto, Bobby 1488

Altzman, Walter 1302

Alvarez, Abraham 1525, 2230

Alward, Jennifer 2200

Always April 550

Alzamora, Armand 720

Amanda Fallon 1157, 1226

Amanda's 1527

Amateau, Chloe 2231

Amateau, Rod 115, 292, 663, 835, 915, 1789, 1894, 1939, 1959, 1994

Amateur's Guide to Love 1081

Amazon Trader 2

Ambler, Eric 919

Ameche, Don 114, 1046, 1110, 1640, 1998

Amendola, Don 2211

America 2100 1598

American Flyer Films and Television, Ltd. 1895, 1941

American Gigolo 1359

American in Italy 312

American in Paris 454

American International Pictures 1255

American Zoetrope 1129

Ames, Judith 263

Ames, Kelly 2186

Ames, Leon 115, 444

Ames, Rachel 886

Amey, Marlena 1640

Amigo 378

Amigos 2105

Amos, John 1137, 1154, 1208

Amos, Keith 2203

Amos and Andy 587

Amos Burke 603

Amsterdam, Morey 1437

Amy 690

An Lac Productions 1800

Anchorage 148

And Baby Makes Six 1679, 1742

And Other Things I May Not Be 1226

And They All Lived Happily Ever After 1711

And They All Lived Happily Ever After 1804

Ander, Diane 2021

Anderman, Maureen 1686, 1953

Anders, Chris 1302

Anders, Katie 2174

Anders, Luana 704, 815, 1151

Anders, Merry 268, 598

Andersen, Bridgette 1958, 2170

Anderson, Arline 1124

Anderson, Dame Judith 828, 1301

Anderson, Ernie 1203

Anderson, Harry 1562

Anderson, Herbert 75

Anderson, Howard 539

Anderson, Ingrid 1914

Anderson, Jane 1999

Anderson, John 715, 853, 1159, 1163, 1184, 1210, 1318, 1324, 1352, 1419, 1423, 2073, 2090, 2093, 2124

Anderson, John Maxwell 1823

Anderson, Kyle 1302

Anderson, Larry 1757

Anderson, Loni 1505

Anderson, Louie 2225

Anderson, Mabel 698

Anderson, Melissa Sue 1840, 2025

Anderson, Melody 1786, 1995

Anderson, Michael, Jr. 1075, 1267, 1369

Anderson, R.H. 1377

Anderson, Richard 125, 605, 699, 844, 850, 971, 1229, 1233, 1442, 2196

Anderson, Richard Dean 1834

Anderson, Sam 1846, 2081

Anderson, Steve 1363, 1554, 1869

Anderson, Warner 1004

Anderson, Wayne 2065

Anderson and Company 1022

Andersons: Dear Elaine 1189

Andes, Keith 30, 250, 319, 1655

Andomar Productions 1045, 1304, 1837

Andrade, Alan 1648

Andre, E J. 1250

Andreas, Luke 1636

Andrews, Dana 1316, 1320

Andrews, Edward 519, 642, 657, 665, 952, 965, 971, 1040, 1054, 1090, 1094, 1238, 1406, 1589

Andrews, Nancy 767, 1897

Andrews, Tige 960, 1618

Andrews, Tina 1197

Andrews, Todd 446

Androsky, Carol 1135

Andy Capp 1171

Andy Griffith Show 1546

Andy Williams Show 1149

Angarola, Richard 1090, 1280

Angel's Nest 1395

Angeli, Barbara 1077

Angelo, Judy Hart 1964, 1993

Angie 1824

Angie Dickinson Show 1824

Anhalt, Edna 202

Anhalt, Edward 1519

Aniov, Mario 1004

Anka, Paul 1123

Ankrum, David 1778, 1786, 2249

Ankrum, Morris 93

Ann in Blue 1236

Ann Jillian Show 1901

Ann Sothem Show 550, 556

Annakin, Ken 1646, 1691

Annapolis 90

Annie 1062

Annie Flynn 1540

Annie Oakley 127

Annihilator 2126

Another April 550, **1263**

Another Day,

Another Dollar 381, 385

Another Great American Hero 2133

Another Jerk 1940

Another Man's Shoes 1974

Anov, Gil 1117

Ansara, Edward 1267

Ansara, Michael 695, 1210, 1562

Anson Productions 1944

Anspaugh, David 1952

Ant, Adam 2267

Anthony, Jane 1207

Anthony, Lee 1785

Anthony, Luke 522, 555

Anthony, Peter 2049

Anto, Matthew 1273

Anton, Susan 2090

Antonacci, Greg 1963, 2017, 2158

Antonacci/ Nardino/Silver Productions 2017

Antonio, Jim 1260, 1316, 1443, 1535, 1587

Antonio, Lou 1164, 1224, 1233, 1503, 1564, 1586, 1587, 1640, 1650, 1667, 1712

Anything for Love 2050

Anything, Inc. 278

Apartment House 760

Apartment in Rome 643

Apicella, John 2159

Apjac Productions 1149, 1155

Apo 923 664

Applegate, Fred 2156

Applegate, Royce D. 1317, 1384, 1463, 1567, 2089

Appleton, Cindy 1664

Appointment with Fear 434

Aprea, John 1625, 1799

Apstein, Theodore 1158

Aquarians 1057
Aquino, Butz 1938
Aranada, Nocona
  1641
Arango, Douglas
  1910, 2050
Aratow, Paul 2099
Arbogast, Bob 1724
Arbus, Alan 1424
Archambault,
  Arch 2261
Archer, Anne 1253,
  1295, 1358,
  1373, 1423
Archer, Beverly
  1879
**Archer–Fugitive
  from the
  Empire** 1841
Archibek, Ben 1030
Arcola Productions
  924
Arden, Eve 543,
  761, 811, 927,
  1008, 1125, 1331,
  1779, 1798
Ardisson, Giorgio
  803
Ardley Productions
  543
*Are You Being
  Served?* 1541
Area Code 212 854
Arena, Fortunato
  1652
Arena 2068
Arena Productions
  932, 975, 1158
Areno, Lois
  1620, 1820
Aresco, Joey 1298
Argenziano, Carmen
  1327, 1525,
  1916, 2096,
  2100, 2152
Argo,
  Allison 1651
Argo, Victor 1337
Arguette, Lewis 1757

Ari, Bob 1823
Aries Films 1289
Arim Productions
  1704
Ariole, Julie 2195
Arizona Ames 3
Arkin, Adam 1273,
  1676, 1701
Arkin, Alan 1174
Arkush, Allan 1979
Arland, Rozanne 18
Arlen, Richard 289
Arliss, Dimitria
  1356
Armen, Margaret
  1196, 1374
Armendariz,
  Pedro, Jr. 1077,
  1295, 2002
Armer, Alan A. 1235
Armone, Lee 1971
Arms, Russell 516
Armstrong, Dick
  1477, 1567
Armstrong, John
  499
Armstrong, R.G.
  1447, 1693,
  1835, 2191
Armstrong, Vaughn
  1450, 1557
Arnaz, Desi 311,
  317, 325, 675,
  973, 1289
Arnaz, Desi, Jr.
  1138, 1515, 1584,
  1838, 1840
Arnaz, Lucie
  1138, 1876
Arne, Peter 718,
  1380
Arnell, Timmy 1781
Arnett, Dave 2208
Arnette, Jeannette
  1599, 1723,
  1810, 1975
Arno, Frank
  1229, 1916
Arnold, Brian 2093

Arnold, Danny 390,
  894, 1083, 1091,
  1244, 1262
Arnold, Edward 433
Arnold, Jack 824, 892
Arnold, Jeane 1409
Arnold, Monroe
  893
Arnold, Nick 1465,
  1733, 1734, 1741,
  1753, 1838
Arnold, Phil 18
Arnold Margolin
  Productions 1623
Arnott, Bob 1333
Arquette, Cliff 870
Arquette, Lewis 1363
Arranga, Irene 1793
Arrangement 1573
**Arrowhead
  Productions** 544
Arroyo 68
Art of Being Nick
  2121, 2179
Art of Crime 1356
Arthur, Beatrice
  1527, 1999, 2181
Arthur, Indus 845
Arthur, Karen 1213,
  1682, 2242
Arthur, Maureen
  1045, 1394, 1495
Arthur, Robert
  Alan 712, 748,
  767, 771, 829
**Arthur Among the
  Animals** 1578
Arthur Company
  1832
**Arthur Hailey's
  Airport** 2021
*Arthur Hailey's
  Hotel* 2021
Artists United 2090
Arvan, Jan 561
Arvin Productions
  991
Arwin Productions
  1083, 1088

Asa Maynor
  Enterprises 1631
Ash, Glen 1894
Ashbrook, Daphne
  2023, 2189, 2217
Ashby, Hal 2224
Ashe, Martin 1662
Asher, Inez 251
Asher, William 250,
  463, 518, 553,
  649, 868, 872,
  1015, 1735, 2235
Ashford &
  Simpson 1265
Ashley, Becca C. 2022
Ashley, Ed 1212
Ashley, Elizabeth
  1131, 1569
Ashley, John 1842
Ashley Steiner
  Agency/ Productions
  105, 303, 452, 512,
  519, 545, 639
Ashmont
  Productions 872
Asing, Nani 1681
Asinoff, Eliot 391
Askew, Luke 1358,
  1420, 2115
Askin, Leon
  949, 1212
Aslan, Gregoire 1376
Asner, Edward
  723, 1061, 1294,
  1444, 1780
Aspen Hill 572
Asphalt Cowboy
  1773
Assa, Rene
  1517, 2238
Assassin 559
Asseyev, Tamara 1629
**Assignment:
  Earth** 1000
**Assignment:
  Mexico** 22
Asseyev, Tamara 1849
Astaire, Fred
  155, 1041

Astar, Ben 954
Astin, John 968,
　1151, 1342, 1625,
　1627, 1676, 1727,
　1859, 2206
Astin, MacKenzie
　2251
Aston, Lucy 2116
Astor, David 913
Astor, Suzanne 1330
Astral Film
　Enterprises 2029
Astronaut 294
Astronauts 1870
At Ease 1384
At Your Service
　454, 889, 1993
Ates, Roscoe 290
Atherton, William
　2240
Atkins, Jane 1849
Atkins, Tom
　1339, 2212
Atkinson, Beverly
　Hope 1424, 1471,
　1567, 2107
Atkinson, Bruce
　1815
Atkinson, Buddy
　1354
Atlas, Larry 2041
Atmore, Ann 921
Attack 875
Attell, Toni 2126
Atterbury, Malcolm
　314, 971, 1346
Attmore, William 1240
Attorney General 697
Atwater, Barry 1373
Auberjonois, Rene
　1243, 1378, 1656,
　1748, 1770,
　2175, 2217
Aubrey, Skye 1014,
　1102, 1125
Aubry, Daiele 509
Aubrey, James 820
Aubuchon, Jacques
　479, 833, 1537

Audley, Eleanor
　250, 870
Auer, Mischa 313
Auerbach, Artie 31
August, Tom 1085
Aumont, Jean
　Pierre 1006
Aurora Enterprises
　1646
Austin, Al 561
Austin, Bud
　1551, 1929
Austin, James 1482
Austin, Karen 1986
Austin, Pamela
　896, 948, 1151
Austin, Patti 2066
Austin, Ray
　1937, 2196
Austin, Ronald 1340,
　1609, 1651
Austin, Spencer 1903
Austral Downs 2185
Author! Author!
　1920
Autry, Alan 1955,
　2086, 2087,
　2127, 2246
Autry, Eugene 1324
Autry, Gene 1483
Avalos, Luis 1391,
　1833, 1976, 2233
Aved, Eric 1880
Avedon, Barbara
　805
Avenger 503
Avengers 1563
Averback, Hy 766,
　822, 856, 863,
　880, 952, 1155,
　1171, 1203, 1273,
　1341, 1406, 1408,
　1411, 1415, 1448,
　1495, 1498, 1505,
　1545, 1616, 1751
Avery, James 1968,
　2192, 2211, 2253
Avery, Phyllis
　650, 764

Avery, Rick
　2244, 2267
Avery, Tol 395, 781
Avery, Val 877,
　1429, 2010
Avila, Christine
　1803, 2213
Avila, Cynthia 1594,
　1936, 1971
Avildson, John 1817
Aviles, Rick
　1709, 1777
Avis-Krauss,
　Christina 1873
Avnet, John 2135
Avnet, Jon 2035
Avnet/Kerner
　Productions 2135
Avon, Roger 761
Avrech, Robert 2211
Awtrey, Donna
　Marie 1744
Axelrod, George 2014
Axelrod, Robert 2186
Axton, Hoyt 1843,
　2042, 2137, 2261
Aybar, Andy 2105
Aycee Productions
　1515
Aykroyd, Dan
　2055, 2227
Aylesworth, John
　934, 1389, 1829
Ayres, Curt 1793
Ayres, Gerry 1310
Ayres, Leah 1673,
　1973, 2112
Ayres, Lew 265, 495,
　517, 829, 1073,
　1234, 1235, 1938
Ayres, Robert 1806
Azaria, Hank 2161
Azarow, Martin
　1864
Azzara, Candice
　1334, 1974
Azzara, Candy
　1388, 1454, 1829,
　1901, 2124

B

B&B Productions
　2264
B&E Enterprises
　1839, 2066,
　2127, 2238
Babatunde,
　Obba 2237
Babbin, Jacqueline
　1182
Babcock, Barbara
　1348, 1696,
　1860, 1909
Baby Comes Home
　1679, 1742
Baby Crazy 790
Baby Makes
　Three 790
Baby on Board 2153
Baby Snooks 58
Baca, Sean 2249
Bacall, Lauren 851
Baccaloni 362
Bach, Barbara 1474
Bach, Catherine
　1328, 1518
Bachelor Party 306
Bachelor-at-
　Law 1198
Bachelors'
　Quarters 705
Back Together 1921
Backe, John D. 1874
Backer, Brian 2156
Backes, Alice 306,
　1119, 1465, 1534
Backline, Susan 1681
Backus, Henny 1096
Backus, Jim 445,
　1096, 1662,
　1663, 1664
Bacon, James 1260
Bacon, Roger 2083
Bad Dude 1402
Bad News Bears 1660
Baddeley, Hermione
　872, 1150, 1627
Bader, Dietrich 2259

Badham, John 1104, 1168, 1254, 1338
Badin, Jean 2063
Badiyi, Reza S. 1094, 1122, 1643, 1844, 1846, 1863, 1957
Badlands 2005, 2208
Badler, Jane 2060, 2265
Baehr, Nicholas E. 1420
Baer, Art 935
Baer, Johanna 1129
Baer, John 68
Baer, Max 1773, 1904
Baer, Parley 60, 126, 809, 1041, 1078, 1296, 1536, 1592
Baer, Richard 1222
Baer, Russell 1259
Bafaloukos, Ted 1924
Baff, Reggie 1099
Baffico, James 2214
Baffled 1158
Bagdasarian, Ross 1108
Baggetta, Vincent 1561, 2047, 2189, 2195
Bagley, Fuddie 1418, 1447
Bahler, Tom 2100
Bai, Henry K. 2094
Bail, Chuck 1092
Bailey, David 870
Bailey, Dorothy J. 1688
Bailey, F. Lee 1038
Bailey, G.W. 1355, 1806, 1903, 1948, 1960, 1978, 2170
Bailey, Hillary 1910
Bailey, Joel 1846, 1867
Bailey, John Anthony 1754
Bailey, Raymond 64, 382

Bain, Barbara 825, 1169, 1664, 2169
Bain, Sherry 1539
Baines, Cindy 1634
Baio, Jimmy 1311, 1362, 1889, 1890, 1910, 2041
Baird, Thomas 2129
Bait 1180
Bakalyan, Dick 1522, 1789, 1917
Bakalyan, Richard 582
Baker, Art 139
Baker, Benny 1940
Baker, Belle 693
Baker, Blanche 2026
Baker, Diane 828, 877, 1133, 1299
Baker, Dusty 1865
Baker, Elsie 846
Baker, Fay 115, 555
Baker, Herbert 693
Baker, Joby 925
Baker, Lenny 1479, 1498
Baker, Ray 2121
Baker, Robert S. 2174
Baker, Tom 1075
Bakey, Ed 1730
Bakke, Brenda 2266
Bakshi, Ralph 1458, 1547
Bakula, Scott 2093, 2171
Bal, Jeanne 1021
Balaban, Bob 1098
Baldavin, Barbara 1128
Balderson, Robert 1936
Balding, Rebecca 1444, 1504, 1737, 1780
Balduzzi, Dick 858, 1012, 1274, 1502, 1912, 1953, 2023
Baldwin, Alec 1988
Baldwin, Bill 1787

Baldwin, Janit 1338
Baldwin, Judith 1662
Baldwin, Peter 1137, 1272, 1409, 1434, 1490, 1500, 1630, 1664, 1666, 1752, 2222
Baldwin, Roy 2041
Balik, Shelby 1868, 1920
Balin, Ina 754, 1030, 1210
Balkan, David H. 1854, 2049, 2119
Ball, Lucille 672, 1138, 1825
Ball, Robert E. 1387
Ballad of Andy Crocker 1007
Ballad of the Bad Man 313
Ballantine, Carl 955, 1238, 1599
Ballantine, Sam 2204
Ballard, Garth 2186
Ballard, Glen 1875
Ballard, Kaye 1830
Ballard, Ray 1164, 1245
Ballimore, Maurice 872
Ballou, Frank 1821
Balluck, Dan 1721
Balsam, Martin 1352, 1566
Balsam, Talia 1528, 1566, 1799, 1892, 1943, 2206
Balter, Allan 1073, 1517, 1619, 1641, 1642
Baltzell, Deborah 1733
Balzar, George 967
Bamman, Gerry 2041
Banana Company 1452
Banas, Arlene 1160
Bancel, Philip 1815

Band of Gold 455
Band on the Run 1818
Bandini Brothers 1363
Banfield, Beverleigh 1867
Bang, Joy 1054
Banjo Hackett 1419
Banjo Hackett: Roamin' Free 1419
Bank, Frank 1929, 1994
Banks, C.J. 1877
Banks, David H. 1992
Banks, Emily 906, 2002
Banks, Jonathan 1503, 1544, 1731, 1942, 1976
Banner, Bob 693
Banner, Jill 1157
Banner Productions 944
Bannon, Jack 1368, 1390, 1502, 2069
Bansley Productions 1829
Banta, Gloria 1360
Bar 1106
Bara, Fausto 2172
Barab, Nita 1186
Baranski, Christine 2055
Barash, Olivia 1485, 1699
Barbara and Phillip 1342
Barbara Eden Show 1172
Barbara Rush Show 805
Barbara Stanwyck Theatre **498, 505, 514, 602**
Barbara Warren 805
Barbarians 504
Barbash, Robert 753, 780

Barbeau, Adrienne 1544, 1764

Barbera, Joseph 916, 1112, 1444, 1675, 1780

Barbi, Vincent 450

Barbor, Jadeen 2165

Barclay, Jerry 552, 648

Bare, Richard L. 266, 544, 662, 1026, 1084

Barefoot in the Park 1014, 1756

Bari, Lenny 1758

Bari, Lynn 68

Barino, George 1925

Barker, Cece 816

Barker, Cecil 460 Barker, Eddie 1937

Barker, Michael 2143

Barkin, Ellen 1817, 1888

Barkley, Deanne 1764, 1777, 2064, 2094, 2102

Barks, John 2260, 2261

Barlow, David 1725

Barmak, Ira 1312, 1317, 1332

Bamabee 456

Bamaby 855

Bamaby Jones 1561, 1750

Barnaby Monk 545

Barnes, Bart 1210

Barnes, Chris 1455, 1542, 1741

Barnes, Christopher 1699, 1809

Barnes, Joanna 270, 301, 523, 669, 952

Barnes, Linda 1918

Barnes, Priscilla 1801, 1871

Barnes, Walter 1168, 1258

Barnett, Charlie 2034

Barnett, Greg 1619, 1655

Barnett, Mary Lou 1093

Barnett, Steve 2239

Barnette, Alan 1958, 2065

Barney 856

Barney Miller 1180

Barney Rosenweig Productions 1863

Barney's Bounty 561

Barnstable, Cyb 1696

Barnstable, Tricia 1696

Barnstormers 631

Barnum, H.B. 1199

Baron, Allen 975

Baron, David 1714

Baron Gus 558

Baron of Boston 613

Barr, Douglas 1866

Barr, Sharon 1841, 2070

Barra, Vanda 2050

Barrett, Earl 1222, 1910

Barrett, James Lee 1063, 1173, 1905, 1952

Barrett, Joe 1389

Barrett, June 1562

Barrett, Majel 1212, 1234, 1260, 1524

Barrett, Stan 1347

Barrett, Tony 519, 802, 1010, 1195

Barrett, William E. 1784

Barrie, Barbara 1121, 1218, 1990

Barrington, Lowell 925

Barrington 2169

Barron, Barbara 1936

Barron, Baynes 1382

Barron, Fred 1701, 1975

Barrows, Dan 1437, 2042

Barry, Dave 969

Barry, Don 1781

Barry, Don Red 1787

Barry, Donald 1122, 1167, 1233, 1296

Barry, Gene 603, 1508

Barry, Ivor 1150, 1468, 2040

Barry, J.J. 1676

Barry, Jeff 1054, 1627, 1769, 1974

Barry, John 1444

Barry, Nancy 1974

Barry, Patricia 647, 952, 1854, 1940

Barry, Phillip 249, 969, 1469, 1470, 1471, 1578, 1687

Barry Weitz Productions 1468

Barrymore, John 116

Barrymore, John Drew 828

Bartell, Jack 314

Bartell, Richard 607

Barth, Ed 1314, 1727

Bartle, Barry 1866

Bartlett, Bonnie 1246

Bartlett, Juanita 1260, 1422, 1448, 1783, 1788, 2009

Barto, Dominic 2173

Bartold, Norman 1520, 1628, 1732

Bartoli, Luciano 1596

Barton, Charles 462, 1018

Barton, Dan 263, 1641

Barton, Derek 1969

Barton, Franklin 1497, 1508

Barton, Gary 1267

Barton Dean Productions 2158

Barty, Billy 1296, 1371, 1386, 1434

Barwood Productions 2159

Barzelle, Wolff 758

Barzman, Alan 1724

Basehart, Richard 736, 1101, 1382, 1429, 1587

Baselson, Michael 1147, 1349, 1512, 2006, 2008

Baser, Michael S. 1992

Basham, Larry 1787

Bashful Clipper 679

Basil, Harry 2121

Basinger, Kim 1442a

Baskin, Elya 2019, 2026, 2165

Baskin, John 1554, 1758, 1826, 1893, 1926, 2253

Bass, Emory 1437, 1637, 1978

Bassett, Angela 2057

Bassett, Laura 2205

Bassett, William H. 1441, 1880, 1887

Batanides, Arthur 478, 781

Bateman, Charles 1016

Bateman, Jason 2186

Bates, Jeanne 1155

Bates, Jimmy 382, 743

Bates, Rhonda 1786

Bates Motel 2186

Batinkoff, Randall 1876

Batjac 110, 198

Batjak 305

Batman 1353

Batson, Susan 1004, 1567

Batt, Shelly 1864

Battaglia, Anthony 1709

Battistone, Catherine 1968

Battle of the Generations 1579, 1580, 1668

Battles, Marjorie 1266, 1378

Battles 1771

Battle: The Murder That Wouldn't Die 1771

Bauchan, Patrick 2098

Bauer, Belinda 1841

Bauer, Bruce 1696, 1719

Bauer, Jamie Lyn 1640

Bauer, Rocky 1848

Baum, Fred 1477, 1648

Baum, Lal 1234, 1404

Bauman, Paul 1479

Baumann, Katherine 1352, 1789, 1865

Baumann, Kathy 1190

Baumes, Bud 1111, 1121

Baumes, Wilfred Lloyd 1327, 1352

Baumes, William 1150

Bavier, Frances 263

Baxley, Barbara 1294, 2085

Baxter, Anne 1099

Baxter, Carol 1684

Baxter, Clayton 1637

Baxter, Meredith 1294, 1298

Bay, Susan 1495, 1752

Bay City Amusement Company 1483

Beach, Billie Jean 1296

Beach, James 1316

Beach Front 559

Beach Party 873

Beach Patrol 1609

Beadle, Ryan 2137

Beaird, Betty 1699

Bean, Orson 258, 390, 463, 557

Bean, Ron 2034

Beane, Hilary 1754

Beane's of Boston 1541

Bear and I 1149

Bear Heart 741

Bearde, Chris 1050, 1067, 1149, 1177

Beaton, Alex 1352, 1373, 1426, 1451, 1562, 1564, 1616, 1617, 1640, 1887, 1958, 2065, 2126, 2130, 2131, 2148

Beattie, Lynda 1654

Beatty, Bruce 2213

Beatty, Roger 1438

Beauchamp, Richard 1756

Beaudine, William, Jr. 1535, 2045, 2099

Beaumont, Chris 2007

Beauty Parlor 4

Beauvy, Nick 1022

Beaver, Terry 1959

Becher, John C. 1727

Beck, Billy 2221

Beck, James 876

Beck, Jenny 2155

Beck, John 1103, 1282, 1680, 1992

Beck, Kimberly 1016, 1518, 1580, 1770

Beck, Marilyn 2057

Beck, Michael 1800, 1916, 2010

Beck, Stanley 937, 1123

Becker, Terry 1639, 1740, 1749, 1938

Becker, Tony 1376, 1874

Beckerman, Barry 2118

Beckerman, Teri 1864, 1942

Beckett, Ann 1644, 1879, 1972

Beckley, Barbara 1968

Beckley, William 1383

Beckman, Henry 1159, 1187

Beckman, Ron 1808

Bed 1014

Beddoe, Don 456

Bedelia, Bonnie 1170

Bedeviled 1028

Bedford Falls Company 2165

Bedford-Lloyd, John 2112, 2172

Bedi, Kabir 1841

Bednarski, Andrew 2256

Bee, Molly 290

Beebe, Lucious 431

Beebees Abroad 105

Beechwood Productions 2151

Beecroft, David 2245

Beer, Harry 2089

Beers, Francine 1751, 2041

Beery, Noah, Jr. 561, 721, 1034, 1183, 1689, 1773, 1880, 1903

Beetlejuice 2253

Beetson, Frank 1894

Begg, Jim 871, 1094

Beggs, Hagger 972

Beggs, Russell 199

Begley, Ed 697, 776

Begley, Ed, Jr. 1134, 1250, 1409, 1437, 1929

Begun, Jeff 1567

Behind Enemy Lines 2063

Behind the Lines 1441

Behrens, Frank 478, 665, 670

Behrens, Sam 2251

Bel Air Patrol 952

Belafonte-Harper, Shari 1973

Belarus Secret 2046

Belford, Christine 1502, 1560, 1967, 2032

Belkin, Gary 1553

Bell, Andrea 1622

Bell, Ann 1524

Bell, Bill, Sr. 2242

Bell, Bruce 2130, 2131

Bell, E.E. 1911

Bell, Edward 1073, 1210, 1518, 1688

Bell, Emily 1469

Bell, John 2214

Bell, Michael 767, 1184, 1217, 1345, 2171

Bell, Ralph 766

Bell, Vanessa 2216, 2260

Bell, Book and Candle 1406

Bell Entertainment 2242

Bellah, James Warner 17, 933

Bellamy, Anne 743

Bellamy, Diana 1968, 2105, 2158, 2197, 2213

Bellamy, Earl 519, 646, 1030, 1404, 1663, 1764

Bellamy, Ned 2148

Bellamy, Ralph 124, 515, 603, 1295, 1327, 1335,

1509, 1566,
1585, 1611
Bellan, Joe 1885
Bellaver, Harry 860,
1694, 1821
Belle Star 314
Beller, Kathleen
1336, 1384
**Bellevue Hospital
446**
Bellflower, Nellie
1394, 1486,
1637, 1936
Beilin, Thomas
1655, 2035
Bellini, Cal **1009,
1421, 1426,
1721, 1773**
Bellinis 1407
Bellisario, Donald
1815, 1881,
1985, 2197
Bellisarius
Productions
1815, 2197
Bellou, Mark 2262
Bells Are Ringing
1114
Beloin, Ed 808
Belous, Paul 1807,
1864, **2111**
Belson, Jerry 968,
1014, 1035, 1087,
1113, 1151, 1200,
1274, 1437,
1608
Beltran, Alma
1952, 2148
Beltran, Robert
2105, 2169
**Ben Blue's
Brothers 199**
**Ben Fox Productions
148**
Benaderet, Bea 728
Benchley, Peter 1397,
1588, 2169
**Bend in the
River 842**

Bender, Jack 1169,
1298, 1995, 2084
Bender 1639
Benderoth,
Michael 1730
Bendetson, Bob
2204
Bendetson,
Howard 2204
Bendett, Kathy 1552
Bendix, Michael 1816
Bendix, William
310, 679, 704,
733, 743, 779
Bendixsen, Mia
1086, 1189
Benedetto, Julio
D. 549
Benedict, Dirk 1468,
1730, 1801, 1883
Benedict, William
1108, 1126
Benediction 1958
Benedik, Barbara
2123
Benesch, Lynn 1969
Benet, Brenda
1156, 1214
Benichou, Phillip
2112
Benjamin,
Christopher 1158
Benjamin, Paul
1231, 1321
Benjamin, Richard
815, 1606
Bennet, Duane 2197
Bennett, Bruce 848
Bennett, Constance
550
Bennett, Harve 1183,
1442a, 1445,
1693, 1725, 1774,
1775, 2101
Bennett, Jesse 1903
Bennett, Joan 114,
1110, **1122**
Bennett, Joe 1438,
1537, 1538

Bennett, Marjorie
202, 509,
554, 1690
Bennett, Ruth 2121
Bennett Brothers
2180
Bennett-Katleman
Productions 1445,
1693, 1774, 1775
Bennewitz,
Bettina 2180
Benny, Jack 20
**Benny & Barney:
Las Vegas
Undercover** 1506
Benoit, David 2234
Bensfield, Dick 1199,
1878, 1974, 2001
Benson, Carl 1245
Benson, Hugh 1122,
1293, 1486,
1487, 1781
Benson, Jay 1164,
1384, 1695, 2010
Benson, Leon
925, 959
Benson, Lucille 1074,
1331, 1355, 1376,
1535, 1644, 1682,
1694, 1879
Benson, Norland
1328
Benson, Robbie 1297
Benson, Sally 818
Benson 2230
Bentley, Savannah
1125
Benton, Douglas
932, 1072, 1296,
1430, 1523, 1698,
1884, 2194
Benton, Eddie 1562
Benz, Donna
1213, 1591
Benz, Donna
Kei 1908
Berall, Roxanne 807
Bercovici, Eric 1133,
1588, 1908, 2022

Bercovici, Karen 2176
Beregi, Oscar
696, 738
Berg, Barry 2268
Berg, Dick 512, 757,
843, 1145, 1196,
2114, 2164
Berg, Tony 1994,
2114
Bergan, Judith
Marie 1606
Bergen, Edgar 603,
744, 1140
Bergen, Frances 250
Bergen, Polly 615,
820, 1973
Berger, Anna 1368
Berger, Bob 1269
Berger, Gregg
1731, 1988
Berger, Mel 1699
Berger, Robert 1370,
1398, 1683, 1907
Berger, Robert
Buzz 1130
Berger, Zachary 2164
Bergerac, Jacques 647
Bergere, Lee
383, 1502
Berghoff, Herbert
318, 2046
Bergman, Alan 1891
Bergman, Andrew
2160
Bergman, Ted 1181,
1556, 1577, 1946
Berito, Jennifer 1867
Berk, Howard 1840
Berkeley, Dennis
2252
Berkeley, Xander
2222
Berkowitz, Stan 2120
Berle, Jack 1264
Berle, Milton 252,
488, 1151, 1460
Berlin, Jeannie 1008
Berlin, Kathie 2153
Berlin Affair 1058

Berlinger, Warren 802, 1087, 1154, 1415, 1660, 1820

Berman, Dave 1914

Berman, Loren 1655

Berman, Shelley 2159

Berman, Shelly 856, 1538

Bernard, Barry 1124

Bernard, Crystal 1994, 1995

Bernard, Ed 1213

Bernard, Ian 1050

Bernard, Jason 1827, 2012, 2158

Bernard, Jay 1939

Bernard, Joseph 1788

Bernard, Tommy 67

Bernardi, Herschel 703, 763, 1209, 1411, 2093, 2121

Bernardi, Jack 1147

Bernardo, Al 1482

Bernhardi, Lee H. 1306

Bernouy, Benjamin 1876

Berns, Seymour 460

Bernsen, Corbin 1951

Bernstein, Charles 1539, 1583, 2060

Bernstein, Elmer 1167, 1256, 1525, 1682

Bernstein, Jaclyn 2176

Bernstein, Jay 1656, 1747, 1748

Bernstein, Jonathan 2264

Bernstein, Nat 2092, 2186

Bernstein, Peter 2024

Bernstein, Rick 1626

Bernstein, Walter 1479, 1568

Berry, Al 1788

Berry, June 1981

Berry, Ken 1190, 1240, 1412, 1624

Berry, Lloyd 1259

Berry, Noah 562, 1034, 1282, 1650, 1851, 2117

Berry, Tim 1928

Berryman, Joe 1894

Berti, Dehl 1426, 1594

Bertrand, Jacqueline 1099

Berwick, John 1800

Besch, Bibi 1393, 1569, 1653, 1853

Bessell, Ted 624, 1092, 2068

Besser, Joe 1010

Best, James 165, 340, 392, 470, 479, 611, 1355, 1475

Best, Janeen 1950

Best, Larry 1330

Best Friends 1385, 1453

Best of the Post 16

Best of Times 1922, 2145

Best Years 1023

Best Years of Our Lives 1316

Beswick, Martine 1328, **1336, 1480**

Betancourt, Anne 2105

Beth Poison Productions 2137

Bette Davis Show 791

Better Late Than Never 1690

Bettger, Lyle 94, 1648

Bettin, Val 2035

Bettis, John 2159

Betton, Jacqueline 905

Betts, Jack 604

Betty Hutton Show 60, 66, 257

Betuel, Jonathan 2245

Between the Lines 1701

Betz, Carl 1010, 1047, 1075, 1319

Beverly Hills Is My Beat 539

Beverly Hillbillies 754, 1928

Beverly Hillbillies Solve the Energy Crisis 1808

Bewitched 810

Bexley, Don 1541, 1677, 2052

Beymer, Richard 846, 2028

Beyond from Witch Mountain 1880

Beyond Tomorrow 178

Bezaleel, Khalil Ben 1164

Bezzerides, A.I. 13

Biagini, Sal 2129

Bialik, Mayim 2251

Bible 1610

Bickford, Charles 441, 611, 689, 739, 785, 789

Bickley, William 1657

Biehn, Michael 1653

Bien, Walter 1155, 1177

Bier, Fred 1371

Bieri, Ramon 1048, 1055, 1357, 1520, **1536, 2189**

Big Bad John 1952

Big Bend Country 1813

Big Bob Johnson's Fantastic Speed Circus 1582

Big Brain 689

Big Chill 876

Big City Boys 1542

Big Daddy 1199

Big Easy 1772, 1860

Big Five 2249

Big Five: The End of Something 2249

Big Foot Wallace 5

Big George Diamond 1431

Big Hit Productions 1649

Big Jake 505

Big John 1952

Big Man, Little Lady 1063

Big Prize 992

Big Rose 1277

Big Shots in America 2055

Big Time 111

Big Train 1002

Big Walk 299

Big Wheel 692

Bigelow, Joe 627

Bigelow, Susan 1539, 1733, 1734

Biggers, Earl 1100

Biggs, Bruce 1664

Biggs, Jerry 1894, 2129

Bikel, Theodore 775

Bill, Francesca 1542

Bill, Tony 1920, 2082

Bill Cosby Productions 2057

Bill Stratton/Myrtos Productions 2246

Billie 20

Billingslea, Beau 2023

Billingsley, Barbara 1929, 1995

Billingsley, Jennifer 765

Billingsley, Peter 1862, 2189

Billion Dollar Threat 1611, 1716

Billy Boy! 979

Billy the Kid 280

Bilson, Bruce 1082, 1324, 1374, 1387,

1452, 1778, 1779, 1786, 2214
Bilson, Danny 2173, 2210
Bimini Gal 994
Binchy, Kate 1886
Binder, Michael 1731, 1924
Bing Crosby Productions 568, 645, 790, 797, 876, 884, 1235, 1249, 1650
Binger, Karl 2029
Bingham, Charlotte 2162
Binkley, Lane 1387, 1691, 1774
Binns, Edward 736, 739, 1048, 1078, 1123, 1469, 1471, 1615, 1771
Biography 1115
Bionic Boy 1442
Bionic Ever After 2196
Bionic Woman 1442, 1937
Bird, Billy 2225
Bird, Michael J. 1379
Birds of a Feather 1881
Birk, Ray 1960
Birman, Len 1563, 1641, 1642
Birney, David 1246, 2117
Birney, Frank 1940, 2032
Birney, Meredith 1088
Birsky, Alan 1309
Birth of a Legend 296
Biscardi, Jessica 1953
Biscoglio, Val 1228
Bishoff, Samuel 93
Bishop, Ed 1379
Bishop, Kelly 1670, 1840, 2038

Bishop, Larry 1541
Bishop, Patrick 1815
Bishop, Pete 603
Bishop, William 126, 197, 728
Bishop of Battle 1958
Bisoglio, Val 1094, 1121, 1873
Bissell, Whit 253, 306, 317, 1101, 1592
Bixby, Bill 943, 1168, 1243, 1420, 1496, 1578, 1922, 1981, 2021, 2039, 2095, 2233, 2264
B.J. and the Bear 1778, 1779
Bjorgvinsson, Gisli 2191
Bjorn, Anne 1823
Black, Don 1039
Black, Gerry 2232
Black, James Monroe 2129
Black, John D.F. 1186, 1261, 1585
Black, Karen 1025
Black, Noel 1572, 2170
Black, Royanba 2075
Black Arrow 216
Black Bart 1329
Black Cat 370
Black Cloak 902
Black Gold 315
Black Knight 259
Black Sheep Squadron 1564, 2083
Black Thorn 1478
Blackburn, Greta 1862, 2265
Blackburn, Norman 106
Blackburn, Tom 7
Blackmer, Sidney 932
Blackmore, Stephanie 1867, 1880

Blackstone, Harry, Jr. 1591
Blacque, Taurean 1774
Blacton, Jennie 1673
Blair, Kendall J. 1953
Blair, Patricia 662
Blake, Barry Edward 2029
Blake, Ellen 1504
Blake, Josh 2075
Blake, Larry 806, 1327
Blake, Madge 307, 658, 790, 1025
Blake, Robert 1844, 1845, 1846
Blake, Sondra 1617, 1720, 1844, 1845, 1846
Blake, Timothy 1214, 1390
Blake, Whitney 206, 1316, 1424
Blake Edwards Company 2201
Blakely, Donald 1359
Blakely, Gene 743
Blakely, Susan 2021, 2126
Blakeney, Olive 255
Blanc, Mel 456
Blanch, Jewel 1158, 1162
Blanchard, Mari 317
Blanchard, Susan 1309, 1448, 1505, 1769
Blandings 403
Blank, Tom 1316
Blankfield, Mark 1940
Blanton, Areil 2002
Blaque, Taureen 2244
Blasberg, Joel 2027
Blasdel-Goddard, Audrey 2170
Blatt, Daniel H. 1520, 1594, 1782, 2022

Blatt-Singer Productions **2022**
Blatty, William Peter 864
Blazing Saddles 1329
Bleckner, Jeff 1722, 2264
Bledsoe, Will 1894
Blees, Robert 619, 799, 847, 893
Bleich, Bill 2089, 2209
Bleier, Nancy 1639
Blessing, Jack 2037, 2156
Bletcher, Billy 1067
Blincoe, Brendon 1964
Blinn, William 1052, 1447, 1528, 1613, 1715, 1956, 2007, 2084, 2213
Blinn/Thorpe Productions 1613, 1715, 1956, 2007
Bliss 1856, 1909
Bloch, Andrew 1864
Bloch, Robert 1698, 2186
Block, Andrew 1553
Block, Barbara 1840
Block, Ethelin 1423
Block, Ethelinn 1521
Block, Hunt 2233
Block, Larry 1358, 1500
Blockade Runner 120
Blocker, Dan 318
Blocker, Dirk 1318, 2167, 2190
Blomquist, Alan C. 2176
Blonde 1082
Blondell, Joan 387, 763, 790, 865, 938, 994, 1092

Blonigan, Colette 1695
Blood, Jay 970
Blood, Stephen 1539
Blood Sport 2034
Bloodbrothers 2103
Bloodworth, Linda 1412, 1757, 1986
Bloom, Anne 1782
Bloom, Charles 1796
Bloom, George 1097, 1311
Bloom, George Arthur 2070
Bloom, Harold Jack 804, 1295, 1339
Bloom, Jeffrey 1958
Bloom, John 1976, 2049, 2066, 2093
Bloom, Lindsay 1546, 1747
Bloom, Verna 1303, 1821
Blount, Lisa 2126, 2244
Blow High, Blow Clear 715
Blu, Susan 1656
Blue, Ben 824, 916
Blue and Grey 506
Blue De Ville 2127
Blue Fox 671
Blue Jeans 1702
Blue Skies 2104, 2106
Bluel, Richard 1174, 1294
Blumberg, Ron 1761
Blumenfield, Alan 2231
Blunt, Erin 1404
Blyden, Larry 573, 641, 665, 699, 844, 888
Blye, Allan 1067, 1149, 1177
Blye, Maggie 1255
Blye-Beard Productions 1067

Blyth, Ann 604, 850
BNB Productions 1762
Boa, Bruce 1039
Bob Banner and Associates 693
Bob Crane Show 1152
Bob Cummings Show 243
Bob Hope Chrysler Theatre 774, 775, 843, 846, 851, 852, 906, 912, 917, 918, 920, 922, 974
Bob Hope Enterprises 238, 1415
Bob Newhart Show 1239, 1363
Bobby 1250
Bobby Jo and the Big Apple Good-Time Band 1134
Bobby Parker and Company 1092
Bobrick, Sam 1142, 1143, 1454, 1820, 2018, 2182, 2225
Bochco, Steven 1183, 1621, 1686, 1696, 2205
Bochner, Hart 1855
Bochner, Lloyd 852, 957, 1061, 1168, 1526, 1992
Bockman, Dan 1712
Boden, Meg 1888
Bodwell, Boyd 1471
Boen, Earl 1553, 1868, 1926, 2040, 2124, 2126
Bogart, Humphrey 696, 829, 1466
Bogart, Linda Scruggs 1513
Bogart, Paul 1075, 1286, 2011, 2160
Bogart, Tracy 1252
Bogert, William 1867

Boggild, Hans 2128
Bohan, Jim 1561
Boiney Stoones Productions 1435, 1436, 1710
Boland, Bonnie 1050
Bold Ones 1157, 1226
Bolden, Ronnie 1328
Bole, Clifford 1773
Bolen, Lin 1446, 1906
Bolender, Charles 902
Bolger, Ray 1613
Bolling, Tiffany 1230
Bologna, Joe 1062
Bologna, Joseph 1488, 561
Bolt, Pat 1477
Bonaduce, Danny 1150
Bonaduce, Joseph 1601
Bonanza 503, 607, 2009
Bonar, Ivan 845
Bond, Dennis M. 1579
Bond, Derek 761
Bond, James, III 1582
Bond, Julian 1959
Bond, Raleigh 1668, 1829, 1958
Bond, Sudie 1370, 1732
Bondelli, Phil 1442
Bonerz, Peter 871, 1083, 1306, 1460, 1671, 1731, 1765, 1872, 1893, 1921, 2038, 2110, 2182
Boni, John 1500, 1805
Bonilla-Giannini, Roxanna 1384
Bonnar, Ivan 1583
Bonnell, Vivian 1775, 2260
Bonner, Frank 1930, 2009

Bonner, Lillian Garrett 1731
Bonnie Raskin Productions 2213
Bono, Sonny 1694
Booke, Sorrell 752, 1126, 1278
Boom Town 315, 800
Boomtown Band and Cattle Company 1173
Boon, Robert 703
Boone, Brendon 1249
Boone, Daniel 1318
Boone, Pat 793, 896
Boone, Randy 624
Boone, Richard 994
Boone Bay Harbor 685
Boosler, Elayne 2159
Booth, Connie 1527
Booth, James 1518
Booth, Nelson 607
Borack, Carl 1816
Borchert, Rudolph 2120
Borden, Lynn 1197
Border Pals 1789
Border Patrol 37, 716
Border Town 378, 716
Borelli, Jim 2113
Boretz, Alvin 1165, 1181, 1511, 1595
Borgenicht, Nancy 1939
Borges, Jimmy 1565
Borgese, Joe 2030
Borgnine, Ernest 858, 1105, 1118, 1300, 1583
Born, Roscoe 1788
Born to the Wind 1594
Borowitz, Andy 1976, 2103, 2107
Bosley, Tom 858, 1134, 1618, 1663, 2064

**Boss and the
Secretary** 1657
Bosson, Barbara
1696, 2205
Bostock, Barbara
646
Boston 2058
**Boston and
Kilbride 1640**
Boston Terrier
507, 717
Bostwick, Barbara
1008
Bostwick, Barry
1245, 1275, 1381,
1449, 1608
Boswell, Charles 2260
Boswell, Glen 2185
Botkin, Perry 1812
Bottoms, Ben 2094
Bottoms, John 1888
Bottoms, Joseph
1919, 2022,
2094, 2170
Bottoms, Sam 2094
Bottoms, Timothy
2094
Botwinick, Amy 1865
Boucher, Savannah
Smith 2045
Bouchey, Willis 7
Boue, Richard 2185
Bounder 1975
Bounty Hunter 1983
Bourbon Street
1772, 1860
Bourgeois, Louis
2197
Boutsikaris,
Dennis 2156
Bouvier, Charles 1885
Bova, Ben 1583
Bova, Joe 833, 1459
Bovasso, Julie 1485
Bow, Michael 1072
Bowab, John 1834,
1839, 1932, 1991,
2013, 2124, 2251
Bowe, David 2238

Bowen, Dennis
1423, 1969
Bowen, Earl 1670
Bowen, Michael
2118, 2223
Bowen, Rick 2249
Bowen, Roger 1048,
1238, 1387, 1488,
1771, 1790
Bowen, Sybil 831
Bower, Antoinette
716, 920
Bower, Herbert
W. 679
Bower, Stanley 1973
Bower, Tom 1525
Bowers, Bob 879
Bowers, William
1258, 1282, 1534,
1656, 1748
Bowles, Billy 1124
Bowman, Gil 1818
Bowman, Glen 1976
Bowman, Katherine
1515
Box 13 49
Boxleitner, Bruce
1245, 1369,
1692, 1800
Boyd, George
1587, 1650
Boyd, Guy 2242
Boyd, Jan Gan 2091
Boyd, Jimmy 1500
Boyd, Stephen
1230, 1351
Boyden, Peter
1795, 2119
Boyden, Sally 1535
Boyer, Charles
147, 377, 737
Boyer, Katherine
1969
Boyett, Bob
1898, 2108
Boyett, William 1574
Boyle, David E. 1914
Boyle, Laray
Flynn 2212

Boys 1264
Boys in Blue 1976
Boys' Town 29
Bracken, Eddie 19
Bracken, Jimmy 1015
Bradbury, Lane
1640, 1650
Braddock 957, 2187
Brademan, Bill 1811,
1820, 1939
Brademan-Self
Productions 1811,
1820, 1939
Bradford, Hank 1729
Bradford, Richard
884, 1682, 1952
Bradley, Anne
H. 1560
Bradley, Bart 309
Bradley, Dan 1177
Bradshaw, Terry 1835
Brady, Scott 202,
211, 212, 727,
869, 1322, 1424,
1488, 1597, 1987
Brady Bunch
1240, 2104
Braeden, Eric 1060,
1117, 1164, 1188,
1510, 1615, 1678
Braff, David 1793
Braha, Herb
1621, 1855
Brahm, Roberta 1261
Brahmin 1420
Braithwaite,
E.R. 1207
Braker 2022
Bram, Babett 1567
Bramley, William 756
**Branagan and
Mapes** 1923
Brand, Cliff 1959
Brand, Jolene
253, 890
Brand, Neville 68,
574, 1098, 1103,
1126, 1132, 1163
Brand, Roland 1158

Brande, Tony 1340
Branding Irons 274
Brandis, Jonathan
2263
Brando, Jocelyn 731
Brando, Kevin
1638, 1916
Brandon, Jane
Alice 1319
Brandon, John
2042, 2245
Brandon, Michael
1044, 1104, 1426,
1956, 2149
Brandon, Peter
1446
Brands, X 1318
Brandstein, Eve
2073, 2183
Brandt, Hank 1324,
1516, 1591, 1651,
1678, 1887
Brandt, Janet 1320
Brandt, Victor 1091,
1836, 2173
Brandis, Jonathan
2227
Brasington, John
Allen 2129
Brass 2041
Brasselle, Keefe
392, 460, 559
Bratcher, Joe 1639
Brauner, Asher 1747
Braverman, Bart
1495, 1713, 2089
Braverman,
Marvin 1661
Braverman, Michael
1971, 2148
Bravo, Danny 695
Bravo Duke 827
Bravo Two 1467
Bravos 1072
Brawner, Hilde 849
Bray, Thom
1914, 2006
Brazzi, Rosanno
565, 922

Breakfast at Tiffany's 1006
Brecher, Jim 2039, 2230
Breck, Peter 620
Breeding, Larry 1460, 1867
Bregman, Buddy 1961, 2027
Bregman, Martin 1652
Bremen, Lenny 1863
Bremmer, Lennie 484
Brenda Starr 1317
Brendel, El 307, 457, 658
Brenlin, George 1520
Brennan, Andrew 1041
Brennan, Claire 1260, 1337
Brennan, Eileen 2244
Brennan, Frederick Hazlett 534
Brennan, Patrick 1936
Brennan, Tom 2218
Brennan, Walter 255, 1040, 1043, 1132
Brenner, David 1417, 1644
Brenner, Dori 1326, 1460, 1479, 1545, 1723
Brenner, Ray 1493
Brent, Eve 270
Brent, George 169
Brent, Paul 2049
Breslin, George 1596
Breslin, Pat 623, 732, 966
Brestoff, Richard 1636
Bret Maverick 1448, 1675
Brewer, James 769, 1534
Brewer, Jameson 1040

Brewster, Diane 125, 268, 1929
Brewster's Brood 1959
Brewton, Maia 2249
Brez, Ethel 1413
Brez, Mel 1413
Brezner, Larry 1669
Brian, David 542
Brian and Sylvia 1834
Brice, Fanny 161
Brick, Michael 1640
Brickell, Beth 1159
Bricken, Jules 707
Brickman, Marshall 1236, 1459
Brickman, Paul 1555
Bride of Boogedy 2079, 2134
Brides of Lizard Gulch 2208
Bridge, Lois 656
Bridger, Jim 1318
Bridger 1318
Bridges, Beau 792, 1586, 2104, 2219
Bridges, Betty 1865
Bridges, James 1024
Bridges, Jeff 1075, 1586
Bridges, Jimmy 2085
Bridges, Julie 1586
Bridges, Lloyd 925, 1020, 1146, 1211, 1586, 1587
Bridges, Todd 1314, 1618, 1823. 1994
Bridgewater, Dee Dee 1936
Briefcase 69
Briggs, Charlie 662, 850, 1007, 1650
Briggs, Richard 2034, 2093, 2100
Bright, Richard 1182, 1583, 2041
Brill, Marty 860, 1675

Brill, Richard 746
Brilliant Benjamin Boggs 809, 906
Brillo 1583
Brillstein, Bernie 1221, 1241, 1977, 2012, 2055, 2163
Brillstein Compan 1977, 2055, 2163
Brimble, Nick 2063
Brimley, Wilford 1656, 1844, 1907, 1952
Brinckerhoff, Burt 1309, 1459, 1491, 1492, 1499, 1581, 1777, 1810, 1845, 2036
Brinegar, Paul 1595, 1854, 2126
Bring Me the Head of Dobie Gillis 1465, 2221
Bringing Up Mother 532
Brinkley, Don 1883, 2149
Brinkley, Greg 2260
Briscoe, Jimmy 2068
Briskin, Fred 204
Briskin, Irving 81
Briskin, Mort 973
Bristol-Meyers 934
Britt, Andrew 2087
Britt, Melendy 122
Britt, Ruth 1976
Brittany, Morgan 1443, 1619, 1654
Brittingham, Ashley 2267
Britton, Barbara 308
Broadcast Arts 2143
Broadhead, James E. 1719
Brocco, Peter 1025, 1229, 1279, 1426, 1901, 1936
Brochetti, Desiree 1738

Brock, Stanley 1408, 1686, 1785, 1932
Brock's Last Case 1159
Brocksmith, Roy 1638
Brockwell, Leonard 1207
Brodax, Al 813
Brodie, Kevin 627, 886
Brodie, Steve 396
Brodkin, Herbert 124, 469, 641, 879, 883, 1130, 1165, 1370, 1398, 1683, 1907
Brodsky, Brian 1654
Brody, Larry 1906
Brogger, Frederick 1572
Brogill Productions 546
Broke Family 1753
Broker, Lee 2029
Bromley, Sheila 207, 310, 900
Bron, Eleanore 2240
Bronk 1399
Bronson, Charles 814
Bronson, Lillian 1041
Brontosaurus Productions 1826
Brooke, Sorrell 855, 1252, 1317, 1335, 1366, 1494
Brooke, Walter 1245, 1254, 1801, 1840
Brookes, Ray 1158
Brooks, Avery 2214, 2218
Brooks, Barry 853
Brooks, Claude 1649
Brooks, Geraldine 735, 757, 1161
Brooks, Hildi 1714
Brooks, Hildy 1616

Brooks, James L. 1109, 1152, 1363, 1724
Brooks, Jeff 1876
Brooks, Joel 1869
Brooks, Martin E. 1442, 1442a, 2196
Brooks, Mel 746, 1329, 1684
Brooks, Peter 659
Brooks, Randi 1911, 1937, 2166
Brooks, Randy 741, 1800, 2090
Brooks, Richard 2241
Brooks, Stephen 1132
Brophy, Brian 2188
Brothers, Dr. Joyce 1748
Brothers 1723
Brothers-in-Law 2023
Brotherson, Eric 1124
Brough, Candi 1748, 1923, 2023
Brough, Joanne 1867
Brough, Randi 1748, 1923, 2023
Broughton, Bruce 1651
Browar, Herbert W. 953
Brower, Mitchell 1411
Brown, Barry 1072
Brown, Beverly 2222
Brown, Blair 1381, 1449, 1509, 1525, 2012
Brown, Bob 1452
Brown, Cameron 2249
Brown, Charles 2046
Brown, Charlotte 1432, 1701, 1828, 1978, 2014, 2231
Brown, Courtney 1230
Brown, D.W. 1896

Brown, David 2169
Brown, Doolie 1228
Brown, Dwier 2261
Brown, Earl 1067
Brown, Eric 2085
Brown, Erin Nicole 1902, 1944
Brown, Garrett 1623
Brown, George Stanford 2084
Brown, Gregory 1892
Brown, Harry 801
Brown, Harry Joe 388
Brown, Henry 1148
Brown, Henry, Jr. 1123
Brown, Howard 920, 947, 2105
Brown, J.E. 1076
Brown, James 1505, 1819
Brown, James H. 1320, 1441, 1867
Brown, Jeannine 1247
Brown, Jim 617
Brown, Joe E. 595
Brown, John Moulder 2040
Brown, Johnny 1238
Brown, Judith 1378
Brown, Kenneth 14
Brown, Les, Jr. 921
Brown, Lew 1260, 1585, 1782
Brown, Mark 1016
Brown, Marsha 1472
Brown, Peter 695
Brown, Philip 1697
Brown, R.G. 1549
Brown, Reb 1641
Brown, Red 1642
Brown, Robert 735, 759, 2041
Brown, Robert Curtis 2194
Brown, Roger Aaron 1525, 2065
Brown, Roscoe Lee 1168

Brown, Russ 660, 737
Brown, Sharon 1333
Brown, Steve 1983
Brown, Susan 1296
Brown, Tally 1356
Brown, Timothy 1883
Brown, Tom 1019
Brown, Wally 554
Brown, Woody 1989
Brown Horse 491
Browne, Arthur, Jr. 726
Browne, Howard 845
Browne, Kale 1737, 1801
Browne, Kathie 1058
Browne, Robert Alan 1901
Browne, Roscoe Lee 1451, 1893
Brownell, Barbara 1405
Browning, Rod 1663
Browning, Susan 1381, 1449
Brownstone Productions 1809, 1920, 2167
Brubaker, Robert 253, 268, 521
Bruce, Carol 2213
Bruce, Ed 2129
Bruce, Edwin 115
Bruce, Lauralee 1897
Bruce Lansbury Productions 1419, 1450, 1476
Bruck, Bella 765, 1501
Brucker, Bo 1821
Brucker, Jane 2144
Bruckner, Brad 1635
Brundin, Bo 1973
Bruneay, Ralph 2066
Brunner, Bob 1531, 1911
Bruns, Philip 1231, 1298, 1322, 1349,

1433, 1658, 1927, 1987
Brutsman, Joseph 2191
Bry, Ellen 2093
Bryan, Arthur 67
Bryant, Ben 659
Bryant, John 314
Bryant, Joshua 1590
Bryant, Lee 1535, 1552, 1578
Bryant, Nea 1941
Bryant, William 582, 668, 846, 1101, 1128, 1235, 1249, 1611, 1693, 1865
Bryar, Claudia 1007, 1190
Bryar, Paul 1279
Brydon, William 1185
Brynes, Jim 1559
Bryson, Chere 1969
Bubetz, Christopher 1958
Buchanan, Edgar 607, 626, 814, 1040, 1079
Buchanan, James David 1340, 1609, 1651, 2117
Bucholz, Horst 1250
Buck, Craig 1853, 2161
Buck, David 718
Buck Rogers in the 25th Century 1958
Buckingham, Steve L. 1864
Buckley, Betty 1498
Buckley, Hal 1005
Buckman, Tara 1537
Buckner, Brad 1573, 1839, 1892, 2066, 2127, 2238
Buckner, Parris 1668
Buckner, Susan 1545

Bud Austin
   Productions 1551,
   1623, 1929
Buffalo Soldiers
   1680
Buktenica, Ray 1360,
   1432, 1981, 2014,
   2179, 2204
Bula, Tammi
   1212, 1279
Bulba 1790
Bulifant, Joyce 646,
   1050, 1272, 1690
Bull, Sheldon
   1541, 2016
Bulloch, Jeremy 718
Bullock, Donna 2231
Bullock, Earl 1923
Bullock, Harvey
   1044, 1112
Bullock, J.J. 1910
Bullock, Sandra 2196
Bumiller, William
   1827, 2243
Bumpass, Roger 1836
Bumpers 1432
Bumstead, J.P. 1712,
   1789, 1887, 1980
Bunco 1507
Bundy, Brooke 917,
   1023, 1090, 1126,
   1224, 1240
Bungle Abbey 1825
Bunnage, Avis 1886
Buono, Victor 860,
   1211, 1317, 1383,
   1552, 1618, 1676,
   1690, 1708,
   1748, 1847
Burditt, George
   1670
Bureau 1408
Burghoff, Gary
   1612, 1981
Burke, Charles 1536
Burke, Christopher
   2148
Burke, David
   2203, 2225

Burke, Delta 1682,
   1743, 1865, 1934
Burke, Hoolihan
   1830
Burke, Joseph
   1622, 1639
Burke, Nellie 828
Burke, Paul 785,
   1211, 1539,
   1609, 1840
Burke, Sonny 644
Burke, Walter 654,
   1041, 1213, 1382
Burke's Law
   603, 2169
Burkley, Dennis
   1682, 1930, 2227,
   2023, 2081
Burks, Stephen 1953
Buriat, Kevin 1944
Burleigh, Stephen
   1511
Burleson, Don 1397
Burlingame,
   Brad 2211
Burmester, Leo 1925
Burnes, C. Stewart
   1958
Burnett, Carol
   670, 1274
Burnett, Hodgson
   1886
Burnett, W.R. 802
Burnham, Terry 650
Burnier, Jeanine 1097
Burns, Allan 976,
   1046, 1363, 1724
Burns, Bart 1073
Burns, Brendan 1939
Burns, Catherine
   1099, 1132
Burns, Elkarah 2211
Burns, George 115,
   156, 157, 391,
   679, 870, 1795
Burns, Jack 954,
   1068, 2163
Burns, Janis Lee 2024
Burns, Maureen 1650

Burns, Michael 596,
   893, 1088, 1110,
   1159, 1505
Burns, Paul 322
Burns, Philip 1279 .
Burns, Ralph 2165
Burns, Richard 2022
Burns, Ronnie 20
Burns, Stan 1027
Burns, Timothy
   1969
Burns, William 870
*Burns & Allen
   Show* 156
Burr, Fritzi
   1411, 1788
Burr, Raymond
   6, 212, 1117,
   1425, 1647
Burrafato, George
   1010
Burrows, Abe 162,
   794, 1309
Burrows, Blair 1534
Burrows, James 1432,
   1484, 1551, 1558,
   1659, 1686, 1760,
   1993, 1999, 2055,
   2156, 2250
Burstyn, Ellen 2011
Burton, Al 1823,
   1940
Burton, Christopher
   2053
Burton, Jay 1389
Burton, Kate 2214
Burton, Norman
   1061 1337, 1350,
   1518, 1655
Burton, Richard 434
Burton, Robert 603,
   1319, 1336, 1429
Burton, Steve 1885
Burton, Warren 1557
Burtons Abroad
   1107
Busby, Zane 2226
Bush, Billy Green
   1420

Bush, Grand L. 2028
Bush, Nat 1596
Bush, Owen 1122,
   1222, 1911
Bush, Rebecca
   2069, 2093
Bushkin, James 1564
Busters 1508, 1559
But Mother! 1658
*Butch Cassidy and the
   Sundance Kid* 1257
Butenuth, Claudia
   1202
Butkus, Dick 1358,
   1871, 2193, 2255
Butland, Nigel 1953
Butler, Artie 1261,
   1923, 1930, 1966,
   1967, 2125
Butler, David
   314, 650
Butler, Eugene 1539,
   1695, 2100
Budar, J. 879
Buder, Holly 1973
Butler, Michael 1844
Butler, Robert 722,
   723, 1328, 1329,
   1589, 1818, 1914,
   1970, 2194, 2267
Butrick, Merritt 2220
Butterball Jones 711
Butterflies 1659
Butterworth,
   Donna 869
Butterworth,
   Shane 1423
Buttolph, David 521
Buttons, Red 678,
   1344, 1501
Buttons 686
Buttram, Pat 457
Buxton, Frank 2225
Buzby, Zane
   1432, 2198
Buzzi, Ruth
   1008, 1142
Bybee, Lair 1123
Byers, Billy 1870

Byington, Spring 500, 861
Byner, John 1142, 1435, 1436, 1634
Byrd, Carl 1681
Byrd, Carolyn 1907
Byrd, David 1589
Byrd, Julian 1915
Byrd, Tom 1990
Byrd's Nest 1791
Byrd-Netherly, Miriam 2178
Byrne, Joe 1782
Byrne, Joseph P. 1843
Byrne, Martha 1913
Byrnes, Burke 1110, 1716
Byrnes, Edd 834
Byrnes, Jim 1508, 1680, 1749
Byron, Ed 123
Byron, Jean 663
Byron, Jeane 1840
Byron, Jeffrey 1580

C

C.A.T. Squad 2128
C.A.T. Squad II 2258
C.A.T. Squad: Python Wolf 2259
Caan, James 1275
Caballero 317
Cabin Boy 106
Cable Car Murder 1089
Cabot, Sebastian 827
Cabot Connection 1468
Cacavas, John 1321, 1396, 1477, 1716, 1814, 1929, 2195
Caccitotti, Tony 1906
Caddyshack 1926
Cadets 2198
Cady, Frank 1930
Caen, Herb 569

Caesar, Sid 405, 892, 1515, 1598, 1832
Caesars Palace Productions 1856
Cafe Bravo 591
Caffey, Michael 1249
Caffey, Richard 1667
Caffey, Stephen 2008
Caffrey, Jack 2261
Cages 1722
Cagney and Lacey 1983
Cahan, George 652
Cahill, James 2112
Cahn, Dann 973
Caidin, Martin 1514, 2196
Caillou, Alan 1057, 1124, 1234
Cairny, John 745
Calamity Jane 110, 228
Calder, King 563, 756
Caldert, Bill 1868
Caldwell, Stephen 1841
Caldwell, Stephen P. 2030
Calello, Chane 2236
Cales, Marc 2208
Calfa, Don 1489, 1917, 1951
Calhoun, Rory 190, 594, 738, 842, 973, 1515, 1636, 1645
Calhoun 771
California Girls 1574
California National 547
Caliri, Jon 1994
Call, Brandon 2110
Call, Ed 1316, 1650, 1849
Call Her Mom 1033, 1108
Call Holme 1150
Call Me Annie 498
Call Me First 468

Call To Danger 665, 958, 1210
Callahan, James 667, 1090, 1658
Callahan 1855
Callan, Cecille 2044
Callan, K. 1370, 2092, 2155, 2189
Callan, Michael 1008, 1950
Callas, Charlie 1825, **1865**
Callaway, Tom 2136
Callaway, William 1867
Callihan, Dick 1816
Calling All Cars 141
Calling C.Q. 490
Calling Dr. Storm, M.D. 1484
Calling Terry Conway 59
Calloway, Bill 1052
Calloway, Cheryl 204
Calloway, William 1307
Calnan, Matilda 1468
Calvelli, Joseph 126, 1162, 1290
Calvin, John 1118, 1137, 1254, 1574, 1812
Calvin and Clyde 444
Camacho, Corinne 1110
Cambria, Cathy 2153
Cambridge, Edmund 1151, 2099
Cambridge, Godfrey 889, 1177
Cameo by Night 2188
Cameron, J. Smith **2038**
Cameron, Joanna **1170, 1383**
Cameron, John 1524

Cameron-Newell, Cheri 2165
Camp, Hamilton 896, 1364, 1636, 1671, 1883
Camp, Helen Page 1201, 1535, 1758, 1867
Camp Grizzly 1599
Campanella, Frank 846, 1213, 1511
Campanella, Joseph 775, 1059, 1347, 1685
Campbell, Graham 1100
Campbell, J. Kenneth 1583
Campbell, Jerry 1959
Campbell, Mae E. 2105
Campbell, Norman 1177 Campbell, Tisha 2253
Campbell, William 1280
Campo 44 832
Campos, Rafael 1249, 1618
Campos, Rose Marie 1958
Campos, Victor 1210, 1294, 1427, 1841
Camsler, Larry 1636
Canary, David 1167, 1255
Candid Camera 47, *1081*
Candy Cane 424
Canfield, Mary Grace 657, 812
Cannell, Stephen J. 1422, 1426, 1451, 1564, 1616, 1617, 1640, 1647, 1783, 1788, 2006, 2023, 2083, 2086, 2133, 2166

Canning, James 1385, 1453, 1647, 1967

Cannon, Anthony 1398

Cannon, Glenn 1565

Cannon, J.D. 725, 1105, 1219, 1590, 1865, 1880, 2265

Cannon, Katherine 1712

Cannon, Townsend 2190

Canova, Diana 1407, 1936

Canova, Judy 229, 806, 909, 1035

Can't Sing, Can't Dance Productions 1975, 1980

Canteen Ladies 2135

Cantor, Charles 115

Cantor, Max 1924, 2102

Capers, Virginia 723, 1164, 1624, 1722

Capice, Philip 1467, 1494, 1507, 1571, 1614, 1676, 2064

Capizzi, Bill 1655, 1906

Capka, Carol 1799

Caplan, Twink 1986

Capodice, John 2064

Capp, Al 835, 909, 963, 1067

Capri, Danny 2090

Capricorn Man 1655

Captain Ahab 806

Captain America 1641

Captain America II 1642

Captain Grief 43

Captain Newman, M.D. 1064

Captain Horatio Hornblower 718

Captain Video and his Video Rangers 44

Capture of Grizzly Adams 1903

Capuano, Sam 954

Car Wash 1754

Cara, Irene 1830

Carabatsos, James 2022

Carafotes, Paul 1875

Carberry, Joseph 2172

Carbone, Anthony 723

Cardea, Frank 1787, 1850

Cardinelli, Bart 1348

Carello, Lou 1842

Carey, Christopher 1060

Carey, Claiborne 1683

Carey, Harry, Jr. 1534

Carey, MacDonald 733, 845, 1110

Carey, Michele 1169, 1225, 1232, 1693, 1865

Carey, Olive 117, 203

Carey, Philip 631, 720

Carey, Ron 1873

Carey, Timothy 1180

Carey, Timothy Agoglia 1617

Carhart, Tim 2118, 2268

Caridi, Carmine 1274, 1407, 1488

Carl, Adam 2262

Carl Reiner Productions 1344

Carlin, Fred 1572, 1742

Carlin, George 2201

Carlin, John 1184

Carlin, Lynn 1252, 1351, 1467, 1668

Carliner, Mark 1390, 1410, 1412, 1437, 1466, 1519, 1557, 1637

Carlino, Lewis John 1076, 1303

Carlo, East 1906

Carlson, Charles 931

Carlson, Joel 2178

Carlson, Karen 1160, 1320

Carlson, Lillian 2093

Carlson, Linda 1833, 1930

Carlson, Mark 1986

Carlson, Richard 785

Carlton, David 1355

Carlton, Larry 2147

Carlton Your Doorman 1363, 1724

Carly Mills 2069

Carly's Web 2189

Carmel, Roger C. 960, 1778, 1779

Carmichael, Hoagy 345, 391

Carnan, Inc. 2041

Carnan-Becker Productions 1452, 1639

Carnegie, Robert 1971

Carnell, Cliff 1298, 1783

Carney, Alan 807

Carney, Otis 322

Carney, Robert 322

Carney, Thom 1261

Carol, Cindy 761

Carol, Ronnie 1611

Carol 1082

Carol Channing Show 156, 950

Carolyn 60

Caron, Glenn Gordon 1914, 1970

Caron, Mary 1914

Carothers, A.J. 1139, 1155, 2040

Carpenter, Carleton 814

Carpenter, John 1690

Carpenter, Pete 1420, 1422, 1426, 1451, 1497, 1509, 1564, 1616, 1626, 1641, 1642, 1696, 1783, 1785, 1788, 1815, 1842, 1881, 1952, 1985, 1989, 2006, 2008, 2009, 2023

Carpenter, Peter 1110

Carpenter, Thelma 1108

Carpetbaggers 1353

Carr, Allan 1631, 2080

Carr, Darleen 1245, 1421

Carr, Dick 267

Carr, Geraldine 255

Carr, Hayley 2092, 2178

Carr, Jamie 1054

Carr, Jane 1207

Carr, Michael 1059

Carr, Paul 1335, 1351, 2130

Carr, Richard 396, 733, 1041, 1195, 1612

Carr, Thomas 263, 392, 926

Carradine, David 2115

Carradine, Keith 1147

Carraher, Harlen 1004

Carrere, Tia 2060

Carricart, Robert 1253

Carrier, Albert 670

Carrington, Debbie 1960

Carrington, Robert 1371, 1383, 1934

Carriou, Len 1967

Carrole, Mona 314

Carroll, Beeson 1408, 1638, 1999

Carroll, Bob, Jr. 728, 950, 1735, 1899

Carroll, Clinton 1661

Carroll, Clinton Derricks 1893

Carroll, David James 1794

Carroll, Dee 870

Carroll, Helena 1369, 1779

Carroll, James 1971

Carroll, Janet 1996

Carroll, Janice 1586, 1743

Carroll, Jill 1979

Carroll, Leo G. 1155

Carroll, Nancy 743

Carroll, Pat 555, 1080, 1131, 1141, 1992, 2039

Carroll, Sidney 1381, 1449

Carroll, Victoria 1628, 1981

Carrott, Rick 1549

Carry, Julius J., III 1757, 1962

Carsey, Marcy 1855, 1913, 2057

Carson, Fred 1089

Carson, Jack 62, 68, 381, 603

Carson, John 1035

Carson, John David 1108

Carson, Johnny 573, 1824

Carson Productions 1824, 1835, 1839, 1855, 1913, 1949, 1950, 2057

Carsy, Olive 203

Carter, Beverly 1276

Carter, Billy 1645

Carter, Burnham 271

Carter, Christopher C. 2188

Carter, Conlan 482, 726

Carter, Jack 867

Carter, John 1073, 1750

Carter, Lynda 1261, 1358

Carter, Michael 693, 2163

Carter, Nell 1946

Carter, Ronald 2034

Carter, T.K. 1557, 1754, 1789, 1868, 2051

Carter, Terry 1021, 2265

Carter's Eye 334

Cartoon Jesters 237

Cartwright, Angela 965, 1994

Cartwright, Nancy 1796

Cartwright Veronica 1844, 1958

Carub Productions 1830

Carusico, Enzo 1096

Caruso, Anthony 697, 752, 913, 1030

Caruso, David 1799

Caruso, Dee 936, 940, 1111, 1238, 1505

Carvalho, Betty 1511, 1721, 1782

Carver, Mary 1699, 2047

Carver, Randall 1319, 1374

Carvey, Dana 1752, 1838, 2056

Cary, Christopher 1260, 1642

Cary, Claiborne 1211

Casablanca 318

Cascone, Nicholas 2244

Case, Allen 643, 1489

Casebusters 2070

Casey, Bernie 1885

Casey, Lawrence 1057, 1168, 1423, 1516

Casey, Lee J. 1052

Cash, Ryan 2249

Casino 1612

Cason, Barbara 1348

Casorla, Rick 1676

Cass, Dave 1401, 1969

Cass, Peggy 498, 1713

Cass Malloy 1871

Cassavetes, John 750, 843, 853, 1192

Cassel, George 1818

Cassell, Seymour 1192

Cassell, Wally 388

Cassidy, Jack 1097, 1170, 1224, 1352, 1506

Cassidy, Joanna 2141

Cassidy, Martin 1717

Cassidy, Patrick 2197

Cassidy, Shaun 2175

Cassidy, Ted 1212, 1260, 1506

Cassidy and Torres 1120

Cassie and Company 1824

Cassity, Kraig 1653

Cast, Edward 129

Cast, Tricia 1936

Castaways On Gilligan's Island 1663

Castellano, Richard 1167

Castello, Anthony 1938

Castelnuovo, Nino 930

Castillo, Cindy 1655

Castillo, E.J. 2022

Castle, Peggie 22, 130

Castle Rock Entertainment 2206, 2253

Castleman, Boomer 1054

Castronova, T J. 2041, 2230

C.A.T. Squad 2128

C.A.T. Squad II 2258

C.A.T. Squad: Python Wolf 2259

Cat and Mike 1984

Cat Ballou 1051, 1052

Cat of Many Tales 1102

Catalina C–Lab 1681

Catch 22 1174

Catcher 1099

Catching, Bill 1249

Cates, Joe 1062

Cates, Madelyn 2199

Cathey, Dalton 1965

Cathy 2071

Catlett, Mary Jo 1412, 1457

Cattani, Rico 1840

Cattrall, Kim 1446, 1616

Catusi, Jim 1413

Caudell, Lane 1577, 1771, 1841

Cavallero, Gaylord 647

Cavalry Patrol 23

Cavalry Surgeon 174

Cavanaugh, Jimmy 582

Cavanaugh, Michael 1451, 1854, 1936, 2246

Cave Creek Productions 1205, 1311

Cavell, Marc 772

Cavender Is

Coming 463, 670
Cavenoish, Constance 1124
Cavett, Dick 1192
Cavonis, Paul 1137
Cayuga Productions 463, 670
CBC Productions 996
CBS Comedy Playhouse 1046, 1083
CBS Comedy Showcase 62
CBS Comedy Trio 1137, 1141, 1142
CBS New Comedy Showcase 311, 467
CBS Productions 113, 206, 207, 824, 887, 896, 905, 952, 955, 958, 989, 1018, 1019, 1044, 1048, 1049, 1136, 1138, 1140, 1143, 1144, 1148, 1199, 1204, 1211, 1263, 1278, 1391, 1477, 1656, 1748, 1808, 2049, 2104, 2113, 2118, 2119
CBS Summer Playhouse 2153, 2154, 2155, 2156, 2157, 2158, 2159, 2163, 2164, 2165, 2166, 2167, 2169, 2170, 2171, 2173, 2174, 2176, 2177, 2222, 2223, 2225, 2226, 2231, 2233, 2234, 2235, 2237, 2238, 2242, 2244, 2245, 2247, 2248
CBS Triple Play 1205, 1206
Cecchini, Mimi 1359
Cedar, Larry 1545, 1617, 1804, 1981

Celeste Holm Show 281
Cenedella, Robert 1873
Center 1991
Centerpoint Productions 2005, 2011
Central Intelligence 374
Centurian 364
Cerf, Bennett 10
Cerullo, Al 2174
Cervantes, Carlos 2194, 2195
Cervantes, Gary 1958
Cervera, George 1253
Cesana, Renzo 894
Chad and Jeremy 910
Chadwick Family 1245
Chaffey, Don 1535, 1612, 1749, 2021
Chagrin Productions 1921, 1923
Chain Letter 2209
Chais, Pamela 1496, 1580, 2117
Chales, Jean Raymond **2029**
Chalk One Up For Johnny 632
Challengers 992
Chamber of Horrors 880
Chamberlain, Richard 495, 496, 1116
Chamberlin, Lee 2013
Chambers, David 1634, 2103
Chambers, Ernest 1137, 1208, 1366, 1901
Chambers, Everett 771, 839, 1195, 1368, 1371, 1720
Chambliss, Woody 1463, 1535

Chameleon 2072
Chamo, Stuart 1777
Champion 1982, 2059
Champion, John 23
Champion, Michael 2049
Champion, Sandy 1786
Champions 1246
Chan, Herman 1256
Chan, Kim 2112
Chan, Paul 2115
Chan, Susie 2195
Chance, Naomi 129
Chandler, Alan 2119
Chandler, Chick 113
Chandler, Dan 1057
Chandler, David S. 2041
Chandler, David T. 1039
Chandler, George 264, 817
Chandler, James 1090, 1347
Chandler, Jerry Alan 2269
Chandler, John 1787
Chandler, Ken 1641
Chanel, Lorraine 1353
Chaney, Jan 549
Change at 125th Street 1265
Changing Patterns 2154
Changing Times 1922
Channel 99 2250
Channing, Carol 156, 950
Chantler, Peggy 383, 807
Chao, Rosalind 1655, 1664, 1823, 1887 2269
Chapel, Loyita 1811, 1965

Chapin, Doug 1303
Chapin, Lauren 1486, 1487
Chapin, Miles 1790
Chapman, Ben 1588
Chapman, Bill 1961
Chapman, Freddye 2195
Chapman, Graham 2224
Chapman, Joseph 1847
Chapman, Judith 1775, 1906, 1937
Chapman, Lonny 877, 1048, 1098, 1277, 1489
Chapman, Mark Lindsay 2126
Chapman, Michael 2126
Chapman, Richard 1774, 1775, 1852, 1957, 2081
Chapman, Tom 1592
Chappell, John 1546, 1874
Characters 1755
Charbonneau, Patricia *2128, 2211*
Chariots of the Gods? 1327
Charisse, Cyd 298
Charisse, Zan 1601
Charles, C.J. 2237
Charles, Keith 1391
Charles, Nicholas 2248
Charles, Ray 1454
Charles E. Sellier Productions 2190
Charles Fries Productions 1349, 1371, 1392, 1526, 1743, 1817
Charles Laughton Presents 154
Charleson, Kate 2065

Charleson, Leslie 1263, 1307
Charleston 1682
Charley Hannah 2083
Charley Paradise 469
Charlie Angelo 644
Charlie Chan 1100
Charlie Cobb: Nice Night for a Hanging 1509
Charlies McCarthy Show 744
Charlie Peters Films 2234
Charlie's Angels 1093, 1539, 1644, 1719, 1973
Charlotte Brown Productions 2231
Charmed Lives 2073
Charnota, Anthony 1348
Charo 1304
Charo and the Sergeant 1304
Charter Pilot 168
Charteris, Leslie 2174
Chartoff, Melanie 2090
Chase, Annazette 1098, 1781
Chase, Barry 1124
Chase, Channing 2066, 2126
Chase, Clinton 1942
Chase, David 1422, 1783, 1785, 1788, 1887
Chase, Eric 1226
Chase, Frank 926
Chase, Gregory 1620, 1653
Chase, Stanley 810, 918, 974
Chason, Myra 1968
Chateau Snavely 1527

Chater, Geoffrey 2098
Chattin, Sarah 1260
Chavez, Jose 1077
Chavez, Oscar 2148
Chayefsky, Paddy 858, 1288
Chayette, Jeff 1863
Chaykin, Maury 2029
Cheap Detective 1756
Cheaper by the Dozen 83
Cheatham, Marie 1187
Cheek, Molly 2037
Cheerleaders 1343
Cheers 2038, 2052, 2244
Cheers for Miss Bishop 372, 599
Chelsea D.H.O. 1181
Chen, Joan 2194
Chermak, Cy 1029, 1289, 1904, 1908
Cherney, Mickey 1874
Cherokee Productions 1200, 1426, 1448, 1783, 1788
Cherokee Trail 1882
Cherones, Tom 1966
Cherry, Carole 2045
Cherry, Eagle-Eye 2203
Cherry, Stan 2045
Cherry, Stanley Z. 2221
Chertok, Jack 1, 27, 28, 160, 491, 588, 731, 904, 934
Cheshire, Harry 263
Chesler, Lewis 2096, 2243
Chesney, Diana 1213
Chester, Colby 1168, 1213, 1832

Chesterton, G.K. 1687
Cheung, George Kee 2235
Chevillat, Dick 388, 407, 1026, 1082, 1084, 1201
Chew, Sam 1452
Chew, Sam, Jr. 2193
Cheyenne 296
Chez Rouge 318
Chi, Chao Li 1782
Chiarascurio Productions 1821
Chicago 212, 121
Chicago Beat 242
Chick Bowdrie 330
Chihara, Paul 1338
Child, Buffalo 2117
Chiles, Linden 645, 926, 1335, 1362
Chiles, Lois 2025
China Hand 2091
Chinh, Kieu 1800
Chinn, Mary Ann 1625
Chiou, Nang Sheen 1256
Chips 1347, 1908
Chisholm, David 1935, 2217, 2259
Choderker, George 1391
Choice 1144
Chomsky, Marvin J. 1123, 1257, 1358, 1424, 1683
Chong, Rae Dawn 1545
Chong, Tommy 2105
Chopped Liver Brothers 1433
Chorus Line 1705
Chow, David 1256, 2091
Chrichton, Andrew 1129
Chris, Marilyn 1359, *1688*

Christabel 390
Christian, Leigh 1443
Christian, Linda 733
Christiansen, Robert 1185 1463, 1919
Christianson, Catherine Ann 2204
Christianson, Harvey H. 2130
Christianson, Roseanna 1867, 2233
Christie, Audrey 766, 1015, 1434
Christie, Howard 509, 695, 734, 751, 788, 842, 850, 910
Christie, Marcia 2173
Christmas, Eric 1510, 2154
Christmas Lilies of the Field 1784
Christofer, Michael 1336
Christopher, Eunice 1187, 1743
Christopher, Thom 1652, 1814
Christopher, William 2164
Christy, Al 1971
Chubb, Paul 2185
Chuck Goes to College 243
Chudnow, Byron 1774
Chulack, Christopher 2211
Church, Elaine 1124, 1203
Churoscuro Productions 1790
Ciafalio, Carl Nick 2264
Ciannelli, Eduardo 752
Cibbison, Patti 1234

Ciccolella, Jude 2041
Cimino, Leonardo 1478, 1953
Cimino, Michael 1420
Cinader, Robert A. 1295, 1302, 1522, 1537, 1538
Cindy 107
Cintron, Sharon 1245
Cioffi, Charles 1133, 1281, 1619, 1863
Circle Family 1904
Circus 2146
Circus Is Coming, The Circus Is Coming 1622
Citizen's Band 1555
City 50, 2084
City Beneath the Sea 1001, 1101
Clair, Dick 2251
Claire, Deanna 2090
Claire, Edith 478
Clancy, Doug 1769
Clancy, Tom 1338, 1424
Clappers 1575
Claridge, Westbrook 2048
Clark, Andrew 2041
Clark, Andy 559
Clark, Blake 1970
Clark, Bobby 7
Clark, Candy 1670, 1953, 1996, 2132
Clark, Dane 1430, 1987
Clark, Dick 753, 1764, 2152
Clark, Dort 1382
Clark, Fred 554, 674, 743, 952
Clark, Gary 921
Clark, Jason 1258
Clark, John B. 636
Clark, Ken 316
Clark, Louise Claire 2211

Clark, Mae 6
Clark, Matt 920, 1255, 1322, 1589, 1860, 1894, 2177
Clark, Michael 1197, 1562
Clark, Oliver 1243, 1314, 1696, 1787, 2007, 2039
Clark, Philip 1427, 1523, 1915
Clark, Robin 1994
Clark, Ron 1142, 1143, 2183
Clark, Roy 1026, 1980
Clark, Vernon 449, 539, 830
Clark, William 1615
Clarke, Andrew 2174
Clarke, Caitlin 2174
Clarke, Don 1139
Clarke, Gary 1122, 2016
Clarke, Hope 2266
Clarke, Jordan 1682, 1849
Clarke, Michael Francis 2188
Clarke, Phil 1014
Clarke, Richard 1850
Clarke, Robert 2002
Clarke, Ron 1306
Clarke, Stanley 2173
Clarke, Vanessa L. 1914, 1953
Class of 55 1109
Claudette Colbert Show 251
Clausen, Alf 2204
Clausen, Suzanne 1259
Clavell, James 1207
Claver, Bob 942, 1025, 1052, 1384, 1412, 1485, 1580, 1833
Clay, Juanin 1654
Clay, Roger 462

Clay, Stanley 1098
Clay, Stanley Bennett 2126
Clay, Thomas Albert 1866
Clayburgh, Jill 1152, 1356
Clayton, Jan 491, 588, 599
Cleaves, Robert 901
Cleese, John 1527
Clemens, Brian 1563
Clemens, Paul 1269, 2175
Clemenson, Chris 2191
Clement, Dick 1364, 1461, 1738, 1797
Clements, Calvin, Jr. 1747
Clements, Richard 1157, 1328
Clements, Steve 2221
Clemonson, Christian 2220
Clennon, David 1336, 1717, 1728
Cletro, Timmy 385, 463
Cleveland, Patience 2115
Cliff Dwellers 876
Cliffhangers 1684
Clifton, George 1074
Climb An Angry Mountain 1162
Clinger, Debra 1722
Clinic on Angel Street 1290
Clone Master 1585
Clooney, George 2180
Clooney, Rosemary 737
Clough, April 1827
Clough, John Scott 2081, 2238
Clovis Productions 988

Club Med 2024
Clue 241
Clumbsies 866
Clute, Sidney 1272, 1681, 1782
Coach 1842
Coach of the Year 1842
Coast-to-Coast 1576
Coasters 1661
Coates, Alan 2258
Coates, Phyllis 797
Cobb, Julie 1403, 1476, 1635, 1728, 1939
Cobb, Lee J. 1145, 1278
Cobb, Randall "Tex" 2022, 2061
Cobb, Vincent 1777
Cobbs, Bin 2125
Cobert, Patricia 1895
Cobert, Robert 1009, 1232, 1250, 1255, 1322, 1916
Coblenz, Walter 1248
Cobra 1968
Coburn, James 696, 1377
Coca, Imogene 1627, 1808
Cocaine and Blue Eyes 1953
Coccioletti, Phillip 2048
Cochran, Pat 1997
Cochran, Steve 26, 521
Coco, James 1288, 1997
Code Name Diamond Head 1510
Code of Jonathan West 470
Code 3 1121
Cody, Kathleen 1343
Coe, Fred 1272

Coe, George
1884, 2220
Coe, Liz 1705
Coffey, Scott 2188
Coffield, Pete 1850
Coffield, Peter 1472
Coffin, Frederick
2032
Coffin, Tristram 207
Cohan, Buz 1266
Cohan, Dan 1693
Cohan, Martin
1460, 1823
Cohan, Marty 1390,
2013, 2138
Cohan, Stuart 2044
Cohen, Beatrice 2124
Cohen, Eric 1384,
1626, 1677,
1741, 1838
Cohen, Harold
1131
Cohen, Jeff 1944
Cohen, Josh 2085
Cohen, Larry 872,
1150, 1600, 1649,
1698, 1735, 2261
Cohen, Lawrence
J. 1025, 1095,
1217, 1407, 1439,
1479, 1484, 1550,
1806, 1869
Cohen, Leonard
J. 767, 1093
Cohen, M.
Charles 1228
Cohen, Miriam 1061
Cohen, Ronald 1915
Cohen, Scooter 1902
Cohen, Sherry 2036
Cohen, Stuart 1425,
1776, 2061, 2172
Cohn, Art 25, 281
Cohn, David 1668
Cohn, Mindy 1834,
1889, 1890,
1890, 2251
Cohn, Stephen 1724
Cohoon, Patti 1093

Coit, Stephen
1211, 1525
Colasanto, Nicholas
961, 1418, 1473
Colbea, Claudette
251
Colbert, Robert 849,
1101, 1376, 2002
Colbert, Stanley 1377
Colbys 1719
Colcord, Ray
2192, 2251
Cole, Barry 632
Cole, Dennis 1182
Cole, Gary 2144
Cole, John J. 1100
Cole, Kay 1724
Cole, Michael 1618
Cole, Olivia 1800
Cole, Sidney 262
Cole, Tina 1080
Coleman, Dabney
1169, 1184,
1316, 1369
Coleman, Gary 1823
Coleman, Joey 1599
Coleman, Marlyn
1587
Colen, Beatrice 1270
Coleridge, Sylvia
2063
Coles, Charles 1682
Coles, Stedman 264
Colgate Theatre 18,
74, 251, 255,
263, 267, 271
Colicos, John
1117, 1358
Colin, Margaret 2113
Colla, Richard A.
1234, 1247, 1744
Collasanto,
Nicholas 1550
Collectors Item 206
Colley, Don
Pedro 1089
Colli, Mario 1652
Collier, Don 1230,
1534, 1894

Collier, John 74
Collier, Marian 1058,
1089, 1148, 1424
Collier, Richard 306
Collings, Benita 2185
Collins, Bob 1976
Collins, Brent 1817
Collins, Gary
1042, 1066
Collins, Gregg 2126
Collins, James 1879
Collins, Joan 1059
Collins, Les 2244
Collins, Lewis 2189
Collins, Michael 1883
Collins, Patrick
1543, 1737, 1948
Collins, Ray 65
Collins, Richard
568, 1030
Collins, Robert
1653, 2240
Collins, Robert
Evan 2237
Collins, Russell 507
Collins, Stephen
1272, 2062
Collins, Yukio 1862
Collinson,
Wilson 117
Collyer, Pamela 2128
Colman, Booth 1126,
1224, 1299, 1316,
1382, 1418
Colman, Ronald 245
Colmans, Edward
271
Colodner, Joel 2189
Colodny, Lester 811,
937, 939, 964
Colombier,
Michel 2261
Colomby, Harry
1436, 1805
Colomby, Scott
1531, 1669, 2118
Colon, Alex 1347
Colon, Miriam
1030, 1278

Colonel North 108
Colonel's Lady 543
Color Playhouse 70
Colorado C-I 1560
Colorso, Dotty 2201
Colossus 735
Colt, Marshall 1191,
1560, 2116
Colt, Stephen
1222, 1246
Colton, Chevi 1954
Colton, Jacque Lynn
1334, 1674
Columbia Pictures
Television 985,
1078, 1177, 1181,
1291, 1307, 1310,
1320, 1358, 1369,
1400, 1405, 1406,
1419, 1430, 1441,
1445, 1450, 1468,
1476, 1486, 1487,
1500, 1505, 1511,
1512, 1513, 1523,
1540, 1584, 1595,
1611, 1631, 1691,
1693, 1716, 1725,
1727, 1747, 1751,
1752, 1756, 1757,
1758, 1774, 1775,
1781, 1786, 1787,
1798, 1812, 1826,
1833, 1837, 1850,
1873, 1893, 1926,
1948, 1953, 1975,
1980, 1986, 2034,
2042, 2087, 2120,
2145, 2151,
2170, 2195, 2208,
2233, 2239, 2240,
2251, 2255
Columbier, Michael
2190, 2260
Columbo 1352,
1400
Colvin, Jack 894,
1506, 1514, 2264
Comacho, Corinne
1060, 1260, 1302

Combat Correspondent 179

Come a 'Runnin' 645

Comedy 623

Comedy Factory 2015, 2018

Comedy of Horrors 1805

Comedy of Terrors 1805

Comedy Spot 251, 459, 461, 462, 651, 658

Comer, Anjanette 1250

Comerate, Sheridan 314

Comfort, Bob 1582, 1728, 1812, 1818, 1848, 1922

Comfort, David 1589

Comi, Paul 713, 717, 885

Command Five 1969

Command Performance 6

Commuters 7 06

Como, Perry 530, 531, 611

Company Four 1621

Company of Killers 1021

Compton, Forrest 665

Compton, Richard 2169, 2261

Comworld Productions 1989, 2064

Conan Doyle, Sir Arthur 1124

Conaway, Jan 743

Conaway, Jeff 1443

Concept II Productions 1264, 1285

Concrete Beat 1914

Conde, Rita 1384

Condor 1968

Condra, Julia 2225

Coner, Stan 1417

Confidentially Yours 471

Conforti, Gino 1222, 1429, 1699, 1701, 1748, 1825, 1846

Congressional Investigator 351

Conklin, Patricia 1696

Conlan, Joseph 2030, 2046

Conlon, Noel 1486, 2127

Conn, Didi 1212, 1457

Conn, Kelly Ann 1853, 1994

Connally, Merill 1744

Connaway, Dick 1354

Conne-Stephens Productions 5, 29

Connecticut Yankee in King Arthur's Court 361

Connection 1182

Connell, Gordon 1622

Connell, Jane 1505, 1627

Connell, Jim 871, 1050, 1150

Connell, Kelly 2174

Connelly, Christopher 1008, 1076, 1509, 1518, 1592, 1654, 1685, 1853

Connelly, Joe 587, 966, 978, 1016, 1929

Connelly, Norma 1471

Connie Stevens Show 1033

Connolly, Norma 385, 1280

Connor, Erin 1278

Connor, Kevin 2117

Connor, Tom 2261

Connors, Ben 2261

Connors, Chuck 726, 1419, 1903, 1955, 2042

Connors, Matt 1902

Connors, Mike 219, 541, 634, 789, 1376, 1612, 1960

Conova, Diana 2054

Conrad, Christian 2008, 2083

Conrad, Joan 1842, 2008, 2083

Conrad, Linda 1392

Conrad, Michael 1133, 1320, 1348

Conrad, Robert 1126, 1656, 1748, 1842, 2008, 2083

Conrad, Shane 2008

Conrad, Sid 1617

Conrad, William 1441, 1651, 1720, 1771, 1949, 2029

Conried, Hans 418, 1014, 1699, 1951

Conroy, Kevin 1925, 2060

Considine, John 1600, 1747

Conspiracy of Terror 1350

Constantine, Michael 699, 844, 1104, 1180, 1277, 1350, 1371, 1485

Conte, Richard 845

Conti, Bill 1463, 1654, 1906, 2049, 2119, 2245

Conti, Sam 1885

Conti, Tom 2107

Conti, Vince 1478, 2046

Contreras, Donald 884

Contreras, Louis 2002

Converse, Frank 1148, 1166, 1181, 1649, 1653, 1712

Converse, Tony 1659

Convicting the Innocent 99

Convy, Bert 382, 876, 1136, 1219, 1223, 1291, 1644

Conway, Blake 1867, 2261

Conway, Curt 1198

Conway, Gary 875, 1164

Conway, James L. 1592, 1685, 1903, 2091

Conway, Kevin 1130, 1231, 1907

Conway, Pat 703

Conway, Tim 1264, 1438, 1927

Conwell, Patricia 1780, 1805

Caoder, Ry 2136

Coogan, Jackie 890, 1302

Coogan's Reward 807

Cook, Ancel 1543, 1682

Cook, Carole 570, 890, 1219, 1447, 1637, 1875, 2189

Cook, David 1886

Cook, Doria 1055

Cook, Elisha 870, 1250, 1987

Cook, Fielder 1105, 1242, 1470, 1471, 2146

Cook, Fredric 1536, 1567

Cook, Lawrence 1048, 1089, 1341

Cook, Linda 1672

Cook, Nathan 1870

Cook, Virginia 1892

Cook, Whitfield 251, 252, 825

Cooke, Brian 2037

Cooke, Jennifer 1569

Cooke, John C. 2173

Cooke, Wendy 2195

Cookie Bear 1149

Cool and Lam 207

Cooley, Dennis 1499

Coolidge, Martha 2223

Coolidge, Phillip 306

Coons, Gene 1193

Coons, Gene L. 1234

Coons, Hannibal 762

Cooper, Al 2236

Cooper, Ann 1501

Cooper, Ben 960

Cooper, Cami 2178, 2262

Cooper, Charles 519, 1653

Cooper, David 1868

Cooper, Gary 350, 933, 1321

Cooper, Hal 1085, 1134, 1270, 1362, 1435, 1527, 1549, 1636, 1726, 1737, 1804,1811, 1870, 1965, 2075, 2125, 2176

Cooper, Jackie 644, 771, 985, 1093, 1136, 1203, 1220, 1310, 1416, 1883, 1887, 1943

Cooper, Jeff 792

Cooper, Jim 479

Cooper, June 1039

Cooper, Karen 1838

Cooper, Maggie 1679, 1976

Cooper, Pat 1221

Cooper, Sam J. 1920

Cooper, Tabi 1317

Cooper, Tamara 1813

Cooper-Finkel Productions 1220

Cooperman, Alvin 530, 531, 610, 611, 723

Coopersmith, Jerome 1231, 1294

Coote, Robert 1298, 1691

Copeland, Joan 2153

Copeland, Stewart 2144

Coplan, Eric 1895

Copley, Teri 1800

Copper, Pat 1733

Coppola, Carmine 1129

Coppola, Francis Ford 1129

Coppola, Sam 1231

Cops 1200

Cops and Robin 1583

Corbett, Glenn 624, 848, 1184, 1235, 1295, 1421, 1718

Corbett, Gretchen 1591

Corbin, Barry 1802, 1849, 2116

Corby, Ellen 126, 696, 917

Cord, Alex 1212, 1635, 1646

Cord, Eric 1353

Corday, Barbara 1975, 1980

Cordea, Frank 1570

Corden, Henry 598, 813, 1136

Cordero, Maria Elena 1647

Cordic, Regis J. 1246, 1298, 1336, 1421, 1520

Cordova, Caesar 1278

Cordova, Francisco 1077

Cordova, Margaret 1639

Cordova, Margarita 1164, 1318

Corea, Chick 1978

Corea, Nicholas 1643, 1841, 2030, 2264

Corey, Jeff 927, 1186, 1258, 1326, 1413, 1419

Corey, Joe 792

Corey, Stanton 1797

Corey For The People 1511

Corley, Al 1679

Corley, Pat 1381, 1449, 1473, 1980, 2049, 2119, 2155

Corman, Cis 2159

Corman, Gene 986

Corman, Roger 986, 1567, 1730

Cormier, Steve 2261

Corneilson, Michael 1617, 1782, 1883

Cornell, Lydia 1910

Corner Bar 1106

Cornwall, Charlotte 2219

Corone, Antoni 2083

Corporal Crocker 1007

Correll, Rich 1993

Correll, Richard 1929

Correll, Terry 2166

Corri, Adrienne 262

Corri, Nick 2028

Corridor 400 775

Corrigan, Lee 2025

Corrigan, Lloyd 68, 126

Corsair, Bill 1918

Corsaut, Anita 1016

Cort, Bill 2226

Cort, Bud 2186

Cort, William 871

Cortese, Joe 2023, 2128, 2258

Corvi, Bruce 2030

Cosby, Bill 1530, 1596, 1677, 2057

Cosby Show 2057, 2121, 2179

Cosell, Howard 1182

Cosmo Productions 1620

Costa, Don 1393

Costa, Nick 2264

Costanzo, Robert 1980, 2035, 2180, 2199

Costello, Anthony 1280

Costello, Lou 367

Costello, Mariclare 1350, 1958, 2244

Costello, Ward 1421, 1510

Coster, Nicholas 901, 1639, 1644, 2251

Costigans 2085

Cote, Chris 2137

Cotler, Gordon 1180, 1817

Cotler, Jeff 1403

Cotsworth, Staats 314

Cottage 64 547

Cottage Industries, Inc. 1789

Cotten, Joseph 750, 919, 1019, 1029, 1101, 1612

Cotten, Sam 1682

Cotter, Gordon 1687

Couch, Bill 582

Couch, Chuck 1324

Coulouris, George 1235

Councilman 1135

Count Your Chickens 681

Counter Point 676

Countess and the Cowboy 1725

Country Cousin 623

Country Music
  Murders 1694
Courage 54
Courage and the
  Passion 1584
Couros, Paul 1785
Courtland, Jerome
  1004, 1166
Courtney, Alan
  777, 818, 874
Courtney, Alexander
  1425
Courtney, Fritzi
  Jane 1918
Courtship of Eddie's
  Father 1114
Cousins 1360
Cousteau, Jacques
  1057
Covay, Cab 1885
Covenant 2060
Cover, Frank 1265
Cover Girls 1512
Covsentino,
  Frank 1607
Cowan, Jerome 744
Cowan, Phylis 1986
Cowboy Hall of
  Fame 282
Cowboy Joe 2136
Cowley, William 383
Cowper, Gerry 1886
Cox, Courteney
  2122
Cox, Doug 1617,
  1807
Cox, Lisa 2221
Cox, Richard 1599,
  1957, 2242
Cox, Ronny 1130,
  1182, 1227, 1511,
  1728, 2223
Cox, Wally 949,
  1043, 1096
Cox, William R. 213
Coyne, Kathleen
  1936
Crabtree, Michael
  2049, 2205

Crabtree, Michael
  Weston 1894
Cragg, Stephen 1976
Craig, Carolyn 204
Craig, Charles
  Grant 2260
Craig, John 726, 802
Craig, Yvonne
  202, 203, 729,
  930, 1229
Crain, Jeanne 552,
  648, 733
Crais, Robert 1845
Cramer, Douglas S.
  1108, 1111, 1121,
  1147, 1150, 1154,
  1156, 1166, 1214,
  1238, 1327, 1352,
  1534, 1539, 1615,
  1713, 1721, 1859,
  1862, 1917, 1973,
  2021, 2025, 2032,
  2091, 2092, 2247
Cramer, Grant 1896
Cramer, Joey 2093
Cramer, Suzanne
  848, 850
Crane, Les 972
Crane, Nancy 2063
Crash Island 1660
Craven, Matt
  1963, 2016
Craven, Wes 2070
Craver, William 1654
Crawford, Broderick
  776, 906, 1126
Crawford, Ellen
  1993, 2179
Crawford, Jan 870
Crawford, Joan
  581, 785, 348
Crawford, John 995,
  1537, 1538
Crawford,
  Johnny 726
Crawford, Katherine
  1031
Crawford, Lee
  1549, 1820

Crawley, Kathleen
  827
Cray, Randy 1745
Crays, Durrell
  Royce 2115
Crazy Dan
  Gatlin 1992
Crazy Times 1799
Creasy, John 613
Credel, Curtis 1522,
  1537, 1678, 1916
Credle, Gary 1689
Crenna, Richard
  790, 806, 938,
  1064, 1293, 1343,
  1601, 1690, 1745,
  1843, 1905, 1951,
  1986, 2195
Crenshaw, Pat
  1434, 1489
Crescendo
  Productions 1425
Crest, Jonah 410
Crew Neck
  Productions 2240
Crewson, Wendy
  2156
Crider, Dorothy 381
Crider, Missi 2193
Crime 1183
Crime Classics 48
Crime Club
  1211, 1336
Crimes of Passion?
  2200, 2203
Criscuolo, Lou 846,
  1099, 1493, 1557
Crisis Clinic745
Crisis 1047
Crisis Clinic 1047
Crisis in Sun-valley
  1513, 1595
Critical List
  1586, 1587
Crittenden,
  James 1443
Crockett, Karlene
  2078
Croft, David 1541

Croft, Mary Jane 660
Cro-Magnon 1247
Cromwell, James
  1404, 1416, 1454,
  1503, 1504, 1594,
  1631, 1636,
  1918, 1960
Cronin, Jane 2064
Cronin, Joe 495
Cronin, Patrick J.
  1877, 1976
Cronyn, Hume 1325
Cronyn, Tandy 2065
Crosby, Bing 528,
  645, 1249
Crosby, Cathy Lee
  1261, 1441, 1581
Crosby, Denise
  2049, 2105
Crosby, Dennis 659
Crosby, Gary 20,
  1233, 1354
Crosby, Harry 1749
Crosby, Joan 1260,
  1539, 1728
Crosby, Lindsay 659
Crosby, Mary
  1860, 1992
Crosby, Percy 286
Crosby, Philip 659
Cross, Bill 1814,
  1848, 2049
Cross, James 1989
Cross, Jimmy 18
Crosscurrent 1089
Crosse, Rupert 772
Crossfire 1357, 1933
Crothers, Scatman
  1664, 1851
Crowder, Deena
  1469, 1471
Crowe, Christopher
  1958, 2065
Crowe, Tonya
  1745, 1843
Crowley, Diane 1815
Crowley, Matt 1567
Crowley, Pat 386,
  660, 1566, 2021

Crowley, Patricia
306, 497, 826
Crowley, William 807
Cruchley, Murray
2029
Crunch 1367
Crupi, Tony 1864
Crutcher, Robert
Riley 502, 647
Cruz, Alexis 2057
Cruz, Brandon 1397
Cruz, Gregory
Norman 1788
Cry Fraud 404
Crystal, Linda 1150
Cuckoo Waltz 1556
Cudney, Roger 1353
Culea, Melinda
1826, 1838
Cullen, Brett
1816, 1972
Cully, Zara 1248
Culp, Robert 517,
584, 610, 1524,
1596, 2023,
2089, 2133
Culpepper 1773
Culver, Howard
213, 1808
Culver, Lillian 199
Culzean Corporation
1348, 1583
Cumbuka, Ji-Tu
1591, 1644, 1695,
2060, 2158
Cummings, Bob
156, 493, 733,
1004, 1233
Cummings, Irving,
Jr. 188
Cummings, Quinn
1397, 1760
Cummings, Susan 7
Cunningham, John
1712, 1775,
2064, 2113
Cunningham, Sarah
1279, 1444
Cupito, Suzanne 818

Curran, William
Brian 1681, 1906
Curreri, Lee 2026
Currie, Michael
2094
Currie, Tad 1959
Curry, Ann 2128
Curry, Anne E. 2237
Curry, Russell 2188
Curse of Capistrano
1253
Curse of Dracula
1684
Curtin, Valerie
1438, 2256
Curtis, Barry 325
Curtis, Craig 753
Curtis, Dan 1009,
1232, 1250, 1255,
1322, 1597, 1714
Curtis, Dick 893, 897
Curtis, Jaime
Lee 1855
Curtis, Keene 132,
1505, 1822,
1863, 1948
Curtis, Ken, 1685
Curtis, Lorraine 1595
Curtis, Nathaniel 906
Curtis, Robin 2232
Curtis, Tony 622,
880, 2014
Curtiss, Robin 2033
Cusack, Joan 1990
Cusack, Sinead
1379, 1380
Cuthbert, Neil 2038
Cutler, Barry 2180
Cutler, Brian
1519, 1545
Cutler, Cathy 1796
Cutler, Jon 1598
Cutler, Stan 1553
Cutler, Wendy 1621
Cutrer, T. Tommy
1694
Cutrona, Hannah
2028, 2069, 2225
Cutter 1160

Cutter, Lise 2190,
2261, 2268
Cutter's Trail 1019
Cutter's Edge 1954
Cutts, John 1951
Cwikowski, Bill 2266
Cy Chermack
Productions 1904
Cy Howard
Productions 654
Cyborg 2196
Cyperforce 2210
Cypher, Jon 1121
Cypress Point
Productions
1653, 2042

D

**D5B–Steel Collar
Man** 2042
DA 1368
*D.A. Draws a
Circle* 1061
D'Abo, Mirym 2063
Dad 1891
Dad's Army 1305
Daddy O 551
Daddy's Girl 1201
Dailey, Dan 569,
604, 653, 769,
1218, 1319, 1374
Daily, Bill 1008, 1135,
1637, 1751, 1764
Dainard, Neil 1100
Dainton, Joanne
1039
Dakil, Victoria 2244
Dakota's Way 2211
Dale, Jennifer 2189
Dale, Jimmy 1067
Dales, Arthur 1168
Daley, Jane 1795,
1846
Daley, Kathryn
1917
Dalio, Marcel 454
Dallas 688,
1421, 2088

Dallgren, Jack 1129
Dallimore,
Maurice 670
Dalton 2130
Dalton, Abby 314,
1022, 1096,
1215, 1315
Dalton, Danie
Wade 1660
Dalton, Lezlie 1374
Dalton, Susanna
1718, 1838
Dalton, Walter 2032
**Dalton: Code of
Vengeance** 2061
**Dalton: Code of
Vengeance II** 2129
**Dalton's Code
of Vengeance:
Rustler's
Moon** 2130
**Dalton's Code
of Vengeance:
The Last Hold
House** 2131
Daly, Bill 1094
Daly, Jane 1636,
1726
Daly, Jonathan
978, 1315
Daly, Tyne 1075,
1144, 1145,
1690, 1983
D'Amato, Paul 1817
Dames, Rod 1737
Dammann,
Sarah 2099
Dammett, Blackie
1519
Damn Yankees 770
Damon, Cathryn
1627
Damon, Jeffrey 2236
Damon, John 2179
Damon, Lee 704
Damon, Mark
388, 490
Damser, John 603
Damsker, Gary 1583

Damski, Mel 2092, 2114
Dan Curtis Associates 1714
Dan Curtis Productions 1232, 1250, 1255, 1597
Dana, Bill 1754
Dana, Justin 1798, 1853, 1891
Danahy, Michael 1619
Danceteam Productions 2050
D'Andrea, Tom 388, 1092
Dandy, LaShana 1745
Dane, Lawrence 1377, 2029
D'Angelo, Beverly 2096, 2254
D'Angelo, Bill 1065, 1173, 1179, 1711, 1858
D'Angelo, William P. 1266
D'Angelo Productions 1711
Danger Down Under 2185
Dangerfield, Rodney 1506
Dangerous Dan McGrew 342
Dangerous Days of Kiowa Jones 877
Dangler, Anita 1832
Dangler, David 2021
Daniel, Henry 131
Daniel, Jay 1584, 1611, 1716, 1789, 1856, 1914, 1970, 1982
Daniel, Rod 1768, 1848, 1874, 1928, 2069
Daniel, Stan 1220
Daniel Wilson Productions 1449

Daniels, Jeff 1681
Daniels, Marc 733, 1036, 1260, 1487, 1899
Daniels, Stan 1386
Daniels, William 1185, 1213, 1493, 1582, 1640, 1667, 1798, 1812, 1865, 2002
Dannay, Frederick 1102
Danner, Blythe 1282
Danny and the Mermaid 1543
Danny Thomas Hour 965, 971
Danny Thomas Productions 1131, 1258, 1298, 1383, 1580, 1619, 1624
Danny Wilson Productions 1381
Dano, Linda 1268
Dano, Ric 1519
Dano, Royal 23, 877, 1518, 1846
Danova, Cesare 301, 716, 730, 880, 1358
Danse Macabre 1698
Danson, Ted 1716, 1826, 1951
Dant, Frank 1738
Dante's Inferno 1612
Dantine, Helmut 1150
Danton, Ray 111, 318, 621, 633, 697, 755, 1125, 1377, 1639, 1915
D'Antoni, Philip 1182, 1231, 1359, 1427, 1498
D'Antoni Productions 1182, 1231, 1498
D'Antoni-Weitz Productions 1359, 1427

Danus, Richard Christian 1695
Danza, Tony 1528
Danziger, Corey 2249
Daphne 887
Dapo, Pamela 797, 953
Dapo, Ronnie 385, 790
D'Arbanville, Patti 2118
Darbo, Patrika 1818
Darby, Kim 1129, 1645, 1692, 1903, 2026
Darden, Severn 1567, 1625, 1637, 1793, 1865
Dardille, Lori 1888
Daredevil 2264
Dareth, Joan 1877
Darin, Bobby 927
Darin, Robert 314
Daring Deeds of Johnny Dru 614
Dario, Tony 1129
Daris, James 1347
Dark Intruder 902
Dark Mansions 2025
Dark Shadows 1009
Dark Side 1161
Dark Side of Innocence 1422
Darling, Jennifer 2204
Darlow, David 1516, 1699, 2083, 2115, 2173
Darnell, Linda 304
Darren, James 995, 1101, 1351, 1430, 1720, 1801, 2120
Darro, Frankie 1291
Darrow, Barbara 316
Darrow, Henry 1117, 1159, 1227, 1865, 1967, 2120
Darrow, Paul 1039
Darrow the Defender 592

Darwell, Jane 311
Darwin Family 61
DA's Investigator 1369
Dash, Darian 1865
Dash, Stacey 1906
DaSilva, Howard 1136
Dateline 707
Dating Game 1532
Daugherty, Herschel 1301
Daugherty, Stanley 609
Daughters 1485
Daughters of Joshua Cabe Return 1319
Daughterly, Herschel 751
Dauphin, Claude 1058
D'Aurelio, Richard 2085
Davalos, David 506
Davalos, Dick 630
Davalos, Elyssa 1446, 1539, 2098
Davenport, Bill 679
Davenport, Mavis 204
Davenport, William 553
Davey, John 1347, 2030
Davi, Robert 1693, 1775
David, Brad 1104, 1586
David, Clifford 1644
David, Frank 1198
David, Jeff 1583
David, John 1785
David, Madelyn 1764
David, Molly 2221
David, Nick 1442
David, Thayer 1009
David Gerber Company 1897, 1976, 2058

David Gerber
Productions 1207,
1229, 1291, 1430,
1441, 1505, 1523,
1584, 1611, 1716,
1786, 1798, 1812,
2048, 2195
David Niven Theatre
392, 395, 396
David Wayne
Show 492
David Wolper
Productions 1202,
1256, 1305, 1317
Davidson, Ben 1962
Davidson, Bill
1187, 1356
Davidson, James 1167
Davidson, John
1170, 1339, 1450,
1549, 2014
Davidson, Martin
1361, 2090
Davidson/Verona
Productions 1361
Davies, Gareth 2063,
2189, 2219
Davies, Stephen
1973, 2190
Davila, Raul 2064
Davis, Andrew 2041
Davis, Ann B. 710
Davis, Bette 509,
791, 1127, 1164,
1216, 1233, 1853
Davis, Bill 1677
Davis, Brad
1475, 1650
Davis, Brent 1123
Davis, Bud 1519
Davis, Charles 1126
Davis, Clifton 1177
Davis, Daniel
2087, 2099
Davis, David 915,
1046, 1135, 1239,
1432, 1724
Davis, Desmond
1886

Davis, Don
1386, 2093
Davis, Elias 1288,
1491, 1492, 2180
Davis, Frank 1299
Davis, Gale 127
Davis, Harry 1028,
1104, 2046
Davis, Jeff 669
Davis, Jefferson 819
Davis, Jerry 822, 863,
1035, 1085, 1172,
1285, 1287, 1363,
1405, 1876, 2036
Davis, Jim 217, 686,
1157, 1355, 1421,
1472, 1590
Davis, Joan 253
Davis, Joanne 523
Davis, Joey 1926
Davis, John 2032,
2034, 2092, 2120
Davis, Kathy
1035, 1331
Davis, Kenny 1843
Davis, Leo 960
Davis, Lorri 1098
Davis, Luthor 920
Davis, Mac
2023, 2067
Davis, Madelyn
728, 1735, 1899
Davis, Madelyne
950
Davis, Martin 2013
Davis, Michael
737, 738
Davis, Miles 2194
Davis, Muriel 169
Davis, Ossie 1078
Davis, Patricia 1936
Davis, Phyllis 1264,
1713, 1964
Davis, Phyllis
Elizabeth 1334
Davis, Rocky 2265
Davis, Roger 878,
1043, 1077
Davis, Rud 2244

Davis, Sammy, Jr.
559, 1222
Davis, Susan
1465, 1616
Davis, Tony 850
Davis, Troy 501
Davis, Vance 1867
Davis, Viveka
1895, 1997
Davis, Walt 1640
Davison, Bruce 1200,
1271, 1444, 1780,
1870, 2211
Davison, Davey
970, 927, 1047
Davison, Michelle
2052
Dawber, Pam 1531
Dawn Patrol 291
Dawson, Deborah
Zoe 2221
Dawson, Gordon
1675, 2191, 2220
Dawson, Jim 832
Dawson, Richard 1203
Dawson, Vicki 1370
Day, Doris 693
Day, Gerry 1722
Day, Linda 1869,
2106, 2154, 2204
Day, Lynda 743,
1028, 1078
Day, Morris 2253
Day, Otis 1032
Day, Robert 262,
1371, 1480, 1801,
1879, 1880,
1986, 2239
Day by Day 1175
Day the Earth
Stood Still 995
Day the Women
Got Even 1777
Day to Day 2155
Days and Nights of
Molly Dodd 2012
Daystar Productions
716, 724, 725,
753, 754, 758

Dayton, Danny
1669, 1840, 2251
Dayton, June 456,
1119, 1190,
1641, 1642
Dayton, Lyman 1697
DC Cop 2114
Deacon, Richard
892, 1082
Dead Man on the
Run 1324
Dead of Night 1250
Deadline 2147
Deadline: Madrid
2147
Deadly Game
1254, 1504
Deadly Triangle
1513
Deadrick, Vince 561
Deakin, Ian 2029
Dean, Barton
1724, 2158
Dean, Bubba 1959
Dean, Fabian 912
Dean, Freeman 830
Dean, Gerri 1213
Dean, Jimmy 1007
Dean, Pamela 204
Dean, Phil 1032
Dean, Rick 1901
Dean, Robert 1888
Dean, Ron 2183
Dean Jones Show
783, 808
DeAnda, Peter
1160, 1840
Deane, Lezlie 2235
Dear Maggie 1190
Dear Mom, Dear
Dad 382
Dear Monica 1190
Dear Teacher 1826
Dear Vincent 1190
Dearden, Robin 1574,
1773, 1846, 1960
Dearth, Bill 2065
Deas, Justin
2100, 2188

Deason, Gregory 2245

Death Among Friends 1352

Death of the Incredible Hulk 2264

Death Too Soon 1642

Death Valley Days 32, 483, 484

Death Wish 2065

DeBaer, Jean 1765, 2214

DeBanzie, Lois 1937

DeBell, Kristine 1926

DeBenedictis, Dick 1418, 1934, 1962

DeBenning, Burr 899, 1101, 1335, 1651, 1779

Debin, David 1781

DeBlasio, Ed 1119, 1430, 1523

Debney, John 2230

DeBroux, Lee 1420, 1536, 1714, 1852, 2186, 2217

DeCamp, Rosemary 632, 1150

DeCaprio, Al 466

DeCarlo, Yvonne 1253, 1291, 1832

December 3rd Productions 2177

Decision 262, 266, 268

Deckert, Blue 2129

Decoit, Dick 1590

DeCordova, Fred 805, 860, 936, 1080

DeCordova, Luis 1298

De Corsica, Ted 697

DeCosta, Morton 887

Dee, Ruby 1078, 1181

Deen, Nedra 1332

Deep Lab 1057

Dees, Rick 2089

Deezen, Eddie 1629, 1793, 1890

Defenders 1907

Defiance County 666

DeFoe, Don 530

Defore, Don 551

DeGanon, Matt 1996

Degin, Louis 2029

Deguere, Phil 1031, 1525, 1562, 1564, 1692, 1957, 1987, 2047

DeHart, Judith 1152

DeHaven, Gloria 1108, 1156, 1419, 1468

DeHetre, Katherine 1971

Dehner, John 7, 134, 434, 737, 1086, 1293, 1374

DeJean, Willie 1826

DeKova, Frank 781

DeKova, Fred 1357

De La Croix, Raven 1885

Delamarte, Rahda 2260

DeLancie, John 1617

Delaney Street 1348

Delancy Street: The Crisis Within 1348

Delaney 1349

Delaney, Gloria 2245

Delaney, Larry 1522

Delaney, Pat 1005, 1150

Delano, Diane 2119

Delano, Michael 1148, 1738

Delany, Dana 2010

DelaPena, George 2132

Delate, Brian 2258

DeLaurentis, Robert 1542

Delegall, Bob 1562

Delfino, Frank 1297

Delgado, Emilio 1594

Delgado, John 1275

Delgado, Julie 1784

Delgado, Luis 1059

DelGrande, Louis 1725

Delightful Imposter 55

DeLisle, Christine 1539, 1560, 1609, 1743

Dell, Gabriel 1106, 1160, 1400

Della, Jay 792

Delman, David 1350

DeLongis, Anthony 1973

DeLory, Al 1259

Deloy, George 1818, 1910, 2154

Del Regno, John 2017

Delta County USA 1443

Deluca, Rande 1969

DeLuca, Rudy 1798

DeLuise, Dom 1151

Del Valle, James 577

Del Vando, Amapola 1227

DeMaigret, Pamela 2147

Deman, Robert 1518

Demarest, William 85, 1566

Demas, Carole 935

DeMauro, Nich 2035

DeMeo, Paul 2210

DeMetz, Danielle 832, 960, 1015

Demoz, Leelan 2034

DeMunn, Jeffrey 1687, 1850, 2172

Demyan, Lincoln 1147

Denbeaux, Jacques 1059

Dendy, LaShana 1826, 1898, 1946

Denham, Philippe 2201

Denis, Burke 2264

Denise, Livia 1770

Dennan, John 1508

Dennehy, Brian 1432, 1457, 1650, 1800, 1983

Dennen, Barry 955

Denning, Richard 1773

Dennis, John 1615, 1647, 1872

Dennis, Robert 260

Dennis, Sandy 1113

Dennis the Menace 652, 1140

Denny, Dodo 833

Denoff, Sam 1264, 1285, 1501

Denor, Suzanne 1294

Denton, Christa 2176

Denton, Crahan 482

Denver, Bob 1087, 1465, 1662, 1663, 1664, 1902, 1942, 1994, 2221

Denver, Dreama 1664, 1902

Denver, John 2239

DePaul, Judith 2063

Deputies 1421

Deputy Seraph 365

DeQui, Robert 1248, 1646

Derman, Lou 679

Dern, Bruce 1105

Dern, Laura 2007

DeRochement, Louis 223

DeRose, Chris 2096

DeRoy, Dick 1307, 1387, 1403, 1406, 1518

DeRoy, George 1688

DeRoy, Glorie 1453

Derricks, Cleavant 2160

Derval, Larnya 2213

DeSantis, Joe 211, 319, 1221

DeSantis, John 1976

DesBarres, Michael 2150

Deschanel, Mary Jo 2188

Desert Rats 2259

DeShannon, Jackie 1099

Desiderio, Robert 1887, 2032

Designer Gal 687

Designing Women 1986

Desilu Playhouse 313, 318, 325, 478

Desilu Productions 18, 74, 136, 215, 292, 307, 311, 313, 317, 318, 325, 330, 467, 478, 550, 553, 555, 569, 654, 659, 660, 671, 722, 723, 727, 799, 815, 819, 833, 881, 897, 921, 949, 950, 973, 1000

Desk Space 398, 536

DeSouza, Noel 1517

DeSouza, Steven 2059, 2099

Desper, Briggitte 2090

Desper, Tiffany 2090

Desperado 2190, 2260

Desperado Avalanche at Devil's Ridge 2261

Desperado: Badlands Justice 2190

Desperado: The Outlaw Years 2190

Desperate 2148

Desperate Mission 1030

Despotovich, Nada 2159

D'Essen, Lorraine 1897

Destination America 2086

Destination Anywhere 410

Destroyer 2152

Deuel, Geoffrey 1166

Deuel, Peter 1031, 1043

Deuter, James 2083

Deutsch, Barbara 1628

Deutsch, Patti 1199, 1275

Devane, William 1180, 1211, 1243, 1772, 1860

DeVargas, Val 1061

DeVeau, Barclay 2198

Devenney, W. Scott 1782, 1885

DeVeritch, Sean 1964

Devery, Elaine 602

De Vincentis, D.V. 2034

Devin, Marilyn 951, 1032

Devine, Andy 505, 518, 826, 1040

Devine, Jerry 15

DeVine, Loretta 2166

Devis, Andy 956

Devlin, John 1325

DeVol, Frank 901, 1213, 1230, 1240, 1268, 1378, 1566

Devon, Laura 880

DeVorzon, Barry 1589, 1609, 1695, 1717, 1718, 1955, 2046

DeVries, Peter 1274

Dewey, Brian 1073

Dewey, Martin 23

Dewhurst, Colleen 1118, 1679, 1742

DeWindt, Sheila 1660

DeWinter, Jo 1260, 1805

DeWinter, Joe 1222

DeWitt, Faye 459

DeWitt, Joyce 1400

DeWoody, Crystal 1803

Dexter, Alan 723, 1280

Dexter, Anthony 261

Dexter, Brad 1424

DeYoung, Cliff 1298, 1525, 1646

Dhiegh, Khigh 1251

D.H.O. 1181

Dhooge, Desmond 1227

Diagnosis Danger 772

Dial, Bill 2081, 2234

Dial, Jeff 1961

Dial M for Murder 149

Diamond, Arnold 1127

Diamond, Don 1031, 1164, 1978

Diamond, Matthew 2255

Diamond, Mel 766

Diamond, Selma 1096, 1891

Diamond Jim 801

Diane, Maria 1616

Dias, Rudy 1594

Diaz, Andre 1958

Diaz, Rudolfo 2041

Diaz, Valentino 2174

DiBello, Sam 1784

DiBenedetto, Tony 1873, 2172

DiCenzo, George 1349, 1475, 1647, 1821

Dick Berg/ Stonehenge Productions 2164

Dick Clark Five 879

Dick Clark Productions 1764, 2152

Dick Powell Theatre 507, 603, 696, 697, 699, 703, 704, 733, 735, 736, 737, 738, 739

Dick Tracy 970

Dick Van Dyke Show 33, 308, 2074

Dickerson, Beach 1953

Dickerson, Christine 1923

Dickerson, George 2148

Dickerson, Sandra 2231

Dickinson, Angie 1232, 1824, 2195

Dickson, James 1649

Did You Hear About Josh and Kelly? 1726

Diegnan, Martinna 1743

Diehlen, Art 2051, 2053

Dielhenn, Art 2142, 2234

Dierkop, Charles 871, 1101, 1103, 1213, 1851

Dietrich, Cindi 2035

Dietrich, Dena 1239, 1658, 1666, 1742, 1902

Diff'erent Strokes 1823, 2251

DiGaetano, Michael 2257

Digby 85
Dijoux, Robert 1427
Dikijian, Ari 2018
Dilby 935
Dilello, Richard 2132
Dill, Matt 2054
Dillard, Rodney 1808
Dillen, Rusty 2260
Dillman, Bradford 776, 1028, 1122, 1246, 1335, 1337, 1368, 2060
Dillon, Brendon 1124, 1525, 1621
Dillon, Dan 1986
Dillon, Melinda 1362, 1472, 1586, 1587, 1814
Dillon, Oscar 2173
Dillon, Rita 1168, 1737, 1804, 1831, 1834, 1870, 2038
Dillon, Tedd 2258
DiMaggio, Madeline 1589
Dimas, Ray 1022
DiMeo, Paul 2173
Dimitri, Nick 1232
Dimitri, Richard 1626, 1720, 1838, 2164
Dimsdale, Howard 1292
Diner 1924
Dinkins, Lisa 2246
Dinnes, Dr. Martin R. 2170
Dinome, Jerry 1989
Diol, Susan 2132
Dion, Little 1200
Di Pado, Vince 1519
DiPasquale, James 1337, 1425, 2213
DiPasquale, John 1840
DiPego, Gerald 1578, 1988, 2028
Diplomat 122

DiReda, Joe 1103, 1269
DiReda, Joseph 1316
Dirkson, Douglas 1863, 2065
Dirty Dozen 1337
Dirty Harry 1992
Dirty Work 2043, 2194
Disbury, Ray 1101
Disciple 1643
Discovery at 14 1157
Dishy, Bob 1405
Disney Sunday Movie 2070, 2076, 2079, 2082, 2093, 2134, 2201
DiStefano, Dan 2060
Dittman, Dean 2028
Divided We Stand 2149
Divoff, Andrew 2170
Dix, Richard 1841
Dixon, Donna 1747, 2009, 2073
Dixon, Ernest 1469
Dixon, Franklin W. 971
Dixon, Ivan 1783, 1785
Dizon, Jesse 1587
D.L. Taffner, Ltd. 1858
D.L. Taffner Productions 1910, 1925, 2037, 2174
D'Marco, Perry 2265
Doberman Gang 1774
Dobermans 1774
Dobie, Alan 1127
Dobie Gillis 243, 663, 1465, 2221
Dobkin, Larry 309
Dobkin, Lawrence 733, 1188, 1315
Dobson, Kevin 925, 1404, 1478, 1747
Dobson, Peter 2186
Doc 951

Doc Holliday 208
Doctor Cyrian 508
Doctor Dan 1092, 1093
Dr. Domingo 1289
Doctor Franken 1683
Doctor Grainger 1144
Dr. Kate 540
Dr. Kildare 495, 702, 932
Dr. Max 1278
Doctor Mike 319
Doctor on Horseback 696
Dr. Paradise 2222
Dr. Pygmalian 560
Dr. Scorpion 1451
Dr. Strange 1562
Doctor Was a Lady 250
Doctors 1157
Doctors and Nurses 1696
Doctors Brennan 1905
Doctors Wilde 2170
Dodd, Molly 1240
Dodds, Edward K. 2130, 2131
Dodenhoff, Bill 1840
Dodson, Jack 1365, 1527
Doen, Earl 1579
Dog Face 320
Dog Troop 751
Dog's Life 1671
Doherty, Carla 853
Doherty, Shannen 1977
Dolan, Don 1818
Dolan, Trent 1585
Doleman, Guy 1472
Dolman, Bob 1944, 2136, 2202
Dolman, Nancy 1732, 1883
Domestic Life 1900

Dominic's Dream 1266
Don Brinkley Productions 2149
Don Fedderson Productions 572, 1080, 1213, 1268, 1567
Don Johnson Company 2252
Don Kirshner Productions 1413, 1499
Don Reo Productions 1979
Don Rickles Show 1034, 1946
Don Sharpe Productions 618
Don't Call Us 1386
Don't Wait For Tomorrow 922
Dona Flor and Her Two Husbands 1704
Donahue, Brenda 1569
Donahue, Elinor 501, 1008, 1110, 1269, 1486, 1487, 1829, 1994
Donahue, Mary Ann 1688
Donahue, Troy 1029
Donald O'Connor Show 809
Donaldson, Bruce 1918
Donaldson, Lisa 1783
Donaldson, Martin 1159
Donaldson, Norma 1722, 1906
Donaldson Street 1561
Donat, Peter 1100, 1320, 1349, 1443
Donath, Ludwig 738

Doniger, Walter 703, 957
Donlevy, Brian 78, 472
Donn, Carl 1821
Donna Reed Show 623, 628
Donnell, Jeff 614, 1017, 1637
Donnell, Kate 1589
Donnelly, Jamie 1361
Donnelly, Kevin 2147
Donnelly, Paul 1020, 1058, 1146
Donner, Clive 1524
Donner, Richard 759, 849, 1148, 1192, 1227
Donner, Robert 1257, 1473
Donohue, Eleanor 501
Donohue, Jack 728, 819, 890
Donovan, King 1808
Donovan, Richard 797
Dontzig, Gary 1716
Dooder, Dennis 1599
Doodles 2137
Dooley, Paul 934, 1649, 1907, 2042, 2181
Dooley Brothers 1623
DoQui, Robert 1450
Doran, Ann 93, 1250, 1252, 1799, 1840
Doran, Cliff, 2261
Doran, Phil 1910, 2050
Doran, Robert 1659
Doran, Takayo 1683
Dorff, Stephen 2204
Dorff, Steve 2159, 2214, 2218, 2235
Dorfman, Sid 292, 1498

Doris Day Show 1088
Dorn, Dolores 1289
Dorr, Lester 381
D'Orsay, Fifi 455
Dorsett, Chuck 1885
Dorsey, Jack 2050
Dorsey, Joe 2061
Dorsey, Wright 1967
Dorso, Dick 956
Dortort, David 607, 1646
Dorval, Adrien 2235
Dott, James 2094
Doty, Dennis E. 1971, 2174
Doubet, Steve 1436, 1495
Double Hazard 493
Double Indemnity 776
Double Jeopardy 851
Double L Productions 2180
Double Trouble 1297
Doucette, Jeff 2233
Doucette, John 131, 957, 1378
Doug McHenry Productions 2254
Doug Selby 1061
Dougfair Productions 138, 272
Douglas, Bill Henry 1385, 1453
Douglas, Brandon 2266
Douglas, Buddy 1638
Douglas, Burt 1536
Douglas, Diana 1324
Douglas, Donna 670, 1808
Douglas, Gordon 1353
Douglas, James 656
Douglas, Jerry 723, 1235, 1512
Douglas, Larry 1841

Douglas, Melvyn 1246
Douglas, Phyllis 821
Douglas, Robert 301, 1116, 1234
Douglas Family 1248
Douglas S. Cramer Company 1327, 1352
Douglas S. Cramer Productions 1214
Douglass, Robyn 1585, 1957, 2208
Douridas, Chris 2130
Dow, Tony 915, 1929, 1994
Dowdell, Bob 1101
Dowling, Chet 1739
Dowling, Kathryn 2064
Down, Andy 2185
Down Delaware Road 2262
Down Home 457, 1469, 1471
Downey, Michelle 1950
Downing, Frank 1468
Downing, Stephen 1908
Downs, Frederic 985
Doyle, David 642, 1167, 1320, 1415, 1539, 1719, 1899, 1942
Doyle, Kathleen 1672
Doyle, Peggy 1266
Doyle, Sir Arthur Conan 1124
Doyle, Popeye 1184, 2132
Dozier, Lamont 1353
Dozier, Robert 1076, 1373, 1700, 1782
Dozier, William 812, 826, 919, 970, 1013

Drabick, John 1888
Dracula 1684
Drady, Dorothy 1129
Drago, Ruth 1988
Dragon by the Tail 516
Draine, George 437
Drake, Charles 918, 1233
Drake, Dennis 2019
Drake, Jim 1624, 1961, 2050, 2102, 2227
Drake, Larry 2130
Drake, Laurie 2245
Drake, Mervyn 2185
Drake, Paul 1885
Drake, Tom 582, 1101, 1358
Draper, Polly 2113
Drasnin, Robert 1030, 1061, 1133
Dream for Christmas 1248
Dream Wife 810
Dreamers 2003
Dreelen, John Van 894
Drehen, Stanley 826
Dreier, Alex 1038, 1143, 1213
Drelen, John Van 931
Dremann, Beau 2142
Drescher, Fran 1999, 2073
Dresden, Hal 1174
Dresner, Hal 1270, 1494, 1928, 2164
Dressler, Lieuz 1418
Drew, Barbara 164
Drew, Robert 745
Dreyfus, Julia Louise 2179
Dreyfuss, Lauren 1978
Dreyfuss, Richard 1132, 1174, 1760
Dribble 1757

Drier, Moosie 1153, 1172, 1401, 1588, 1597

Drischell, Ralph 1850

Driscoll, Ralph 1683

Driskill, William 1368, 1400, 1441, 1691

Drivas, Robert 1047, 1605

Drive Hard, Drive Fast 1059

Dru, Joanne 18

Drucker, David 1692

Drumbeat 458

Drummond, Alice 1687

Drury, David 2240

Drury, James 451, 585

Dryer, Fred 1908, 1941

Dryer, Robert 1885, 2061

DuBain, Donna 2183

Dubin, Charles S. 1213, 1513, 1571, 1594, 1620, 1633, 1695, 1732, 1757, 1780, 2021

Dubin, Gary 1189

Dubois, Ja'net 1814, 1834, 1860

Dubois, Marta 2028

DuBois, Starletta 1677

Ducey, Chris 879

Duchowny, Roger 1436

Duclon, David 1948, 2051, 2053, 2124

Dude Ranch 188

Dudek, Les 2065

Dudikoff, Michael 1787, 1829, 1950

Duell, Bill 2250

Duet 2132

Duff, Howard 203, 771, 1764

Duff, Warren 931

Duffin, Shay 1530

Duffy 1387

Duffy, Colin 1398

Duffy, Julia 1830

Duffy, Thomas E. 1969

Dugan, Dennis 1306, 1726, 1920, 2250

Dugan, John T. 1583

Dugg, Howard 1075

Duggan, Andrew 775, 826, 905, 1146, 1252, 1471, 1516, 1522, 1648, 1649, 1714, 1744

Duke, Bill 1402, 1983, 2088

Duke, Daryl 1100, 1228, 1275

Duke, Patty 20, 1342

Dukes, David 1445, 1457, 1578

Dukes, James 1850

Dukes of Hazzard 1894

Dukoff, Edward 92

Dulce, Elissa 1648

Dullea, Keir 1424, 1693

Dulo, Jane 1232, 1387, 1526, 1851

Dumas, David 1793

DuMaurier, Daphne 1168

Dumbrillie, Douglas 64

Dumm, J. Rickley 1616, 1785

Dunagan, Deanna 2083

Dunard, David 2042

Dunaway, Don Carlos 1298

Dunaway, Fay 1116

Dunbar, Mary Ellen 2021

Dunbar, Olive 1131

Duncan, Andrew 1777

Duncan, Angus 969, 1721

Duncan, Kirk 1585

Duncan, Mary Davis 1894

Duncan, Sandy 2178, 2182

Dungan, Frank 1964

Duning, George 1025, 1079, 1880

Dunlap, Dawn 1672

Dunlap, Robert 1840

Dunlop, Dawn 1629

Dunlop, Vic 1622

Dunn, Conrad 1986

Dunn, George 112, 1534

Dunn, Harvey C. 846

Dunn, James 659

Dunn, Kathy 693

Dunn, Larry 1788

Dunn, Liam 1124, 1212, 1218, 1269, 1292, 1299, 1378, 1381, 1393, 1405, 1449

Dunnam, Stephanie 2191

Dunne, Dominique 1764, 1822

Dunne, Irene 83

Dunne, Murphy 1438, 1871, 1997

Dunne, Steve 403, 826

Dunnock, Mildred 1246, 1679, 1742

Dunsmore, Rosemary 2266

Dupont Theatre, 121

DuQui, Robert 1476

Duran, Richard 2173, 2194

Durant 561

Durant, Don 267

Durante, Jimmy 766

Durning, Charles 1130, 1182, 1912, 1999

Durock, Dick 1860, 1937, 2022

Durrell, Michael 1501, 1537, 1538

Durren, John 1336, 1400

Durso, Kim 1245

Duryea, Dan 395, 471, 688, 715

Duryea, Peter 977

Dusay, Marj 1009, 1092, 1162, 1518, 1771

Dusenberry, Ann 1429, 1521, 1688, 1961, 1970

Dussault, Nancy 1205, 1910

Dusty 1776

Duvall, Maria 1993

Duvall, Robert 846

Duvall, Shelley 2107

Duvall, Susan 1580, 1672

Duza, George 2144

D'Vaseau, Loring 740

Dwan, Allan 113

Dye, John 2230

Dyer, Eddy C. 1177

Dylan, Bob 1888

Dymally, Amaentha 1190

Dynarski, Gene 1880

Dynasty 686, 1719

Dyner, Eddy C. 1782

Dysart, Richard 1307, 1849, 1852

Dzundza, George 1984, 2082, 2241

E

Eagle, Jack 1363

Eagle, John War 1327, 1375

Eagle and the
  Bear 2087
Eagle of Encino 2004
Earle, Merle 1008
Earnshaw,
  Fenton 131
Earth II 1073
Earthbound 1685
Earthlings 1960
Easier, Fred 199
East, Ian 2219
Easterbrook,
  Leslie 1977
Eastham, Richard
  602
Eastin, Steve
  1585, 2065
Easton, Jane 655
Easton, Robert 290,
  1125, 1229, 1682
Eastwood, Clint 1401
Eastwood, Jaune
  1482
Ebony, Ivory and
  Jade 1644
Ebsen, Buddy 754,
  1374, 1561, 1586,
  1750, 1808, 2176
Eccles, Aimee 2030
Eccles, Robin 1022
Eccles, Teddy 953,
  1022, 1269
Echo Cove
  Productions
  2213
Eckert, Troy 2066
Eckhouse, James
  2165, 2218
Eckstein, George
  1247, 1338, 1387,
  1414, 1802
Eckstein, Ronnie 985
Ed Friendly
  Productions
  1847, 1943
Edder, Tony 1908
Eddie 952
Eddie Albert
  Show 225

Eddie and
  Herbert 1454
Eddie Hodges
  Show 485
Eddie Skinner 952
Eddington, Paul 1207
Edelman, Herb
  1218, 1264, 1357,
  1917, 2116, 2175
Edelman, Louis F.
  196, 394, 498,
  505, 514, 602
Eden, Barbara 802,
  1172, 1244, 1429
Edgar J. Scherick
  & Associates
  1520, 2270
Edge, Frank 1259
Edie Adams
  Show 536
Edelman, Herb 1008
Edmiston, Walker
  845, 1308
Edmond, Lada,
  Jr. 1024
Edmonds, Don 729
Edmonds, Louis 1009
Edson, Hilary 2220
Edwards, Anthony
  1994
Edwards, Blake
  507, 668, 689,
  717, 1010, 1612,
  2005, 2201
Edwards, Burt 1919
Edwards, Edward
  1757, 1895
Edwards, Elaine
  450, 774
Edwards, Elisabeth
  1801
Edwards, Gail
  1963, 2030
Edwards, Geoff 1864
Edwards, Jennifer
  2201
Edwards, Jennifer
  B. 1944
Edwards, Patti 1578

Edwards, Ralph
  12, 630, 676
Edwards, Ronnie
  Claire 1597
Edwards, Sam 1592
Edwards, Vince
  1512, 1584
Efrom, Dave 2130
Efron, Marshall 1099
EF-OH-EX-EX
  Productions 1431
Egan 1184
Egan, Aeryk 2235
Egan, Eddie
  1799, 2132
Egan, Mark 1899
Egan, Richard 925
Egan 1184, 2132
Egelson, Jan 2212
Egerton, Nancy 1039
Eggar, Samantha
  1376
Eggenweiler,
  Robert 905
Eggert, Nicole 2126
Ehrlich, Jack 1258
Ehrlich, Jake 523
Eichhom, Lisa
  1915, 2215
Eight Is Enough 1614
Eilbacher, Bob 1249
Eilbacher, Cynthia
  1022, 1268
Eilbacher, Lisa 2150
Eilber, Janet 1867
Einhorn, Larry 1803
Einstein, Bob 1037
Einstein Man 2033
Eischied 1184, 2132
Eisenmann, Ike
  1419, 1580
Eisenmann,
  Robin 1913
Eisenstock, Alan
  1702, 1994,
  1995, 2184
Eisner, Will 2099
Eitner, Don
  1123, 2021

Ekberg, Anita 1652
El Coyotes Rides 169
Elam, Jack 325,
  1040, 051, 1282,
  1374,1589,
  1787, 1853
Elbling, Peter
  1551, 2238
Elcar, Dana 1072,
  1123, 1174, 1227,
  1421, 1782, 1837
Elcar, Danny 1619
Elder, Ann 1214
Elder, Lonne 1327
Eleftheriou, Zev
  2185
Elegy 722
Elene, Susie
  1251, 1438
Elerick, John
  1396, 1560
Elhardt, James 1892
Elhardt, Kaye 656
Elias, Alix 1555
Elias, Hector 1348,
  1748, 1863
Elias, Louis 1515
Elias, Michael
  1329, 1859
Eliasberg, Jan 2268
Elic, Joseph 1434
Elikann, Larry
  1918
Elinson, Jack 112,
  965, 1017, 1834,
  1889, 1890, 1896,
  1931, 1999
Elisha Cooper 1162
Elison, Irving 62
Elizabeth McQueeny
  Story 509
Elizalde, John 1480
Elizondo, Hector
  1104, 1915
Elke 1083
Elke Sommer
  Show 1083
Elkington, Peter
  J. 1249

Ellen Burstyn Show 2011
Ellenstein, Robert 1133, 2226
Ellerbee, Bobby 1661, 1952
Ellery Queen 1102
Ellery Queen: Don't Look Behind You 1102
Elliot, Bill 1061
Elliot, Bob 1900
Elliot, David 1600
Elliot, Denholm 1127
Elliot, Jack 1037, 1092, 1180
Elliot, Jane 1185, 1520
Elliot, Marge 1130
Elliot, Nancy 1247
Elliot, Richard 2232
Elliot, Ross 472
Elliot Lewis Productions 48
Elliott, Jack 925, 1505, 1581, 1960
Elliott, Pat 1449
Elliott, Patricia 1381, 1943
Elliott, Sam 1267, 1802
Elliott, Stephen 1420, 1639, 1972, 2152
Ellis, Adrienne 704
Ellis, Gris 2045
Ellis, Louie 1617
Ellis, Monie 1110
Ellis, Ray 1519
Ellison, Bob 1558, 1872, 2038
Ellison, Harlan 994, 1584
Ellison, Robert 1360
Ellsworth, Whitney 537
Elman, Irving 876
Elmar Productions 1636, 1726, 1804, 1870

Elrardt, Horst 125
Elsboy Entertainment 2070
Elysian Fields 2236
Ely, Ron 270, 301, 1852
Embassy 2026
Embassy Pictures 803
Embassy Television 1878, 1931, 1974, 1990, 1999, 2001, 2013, 2028, 2038, 2054, 2073, 2105, 2124, 2138, 2183, 2251, 2255
Emergency 366, 489, 1302
Emergency! 1354
Emergency Ward 352, 354
Emery, John 18, 254, 550
Emhardt, Robert 1103, 1168, 1691, 1786
EMI Television 1659, 1665, 1666, 1945
Emilfork Daniel 2098
Emily 2011
Emmet, Michael 115
Emmet G. Lavery Productions 1348
Emmich, Cliff 1094, 1275, 1339, 1396
Empty Copper Sea 1802
Empty Nest 2181
Enchanted Forest 189
End of the Rainbow 139
Enders, Robert 933
Enders, Robert J. 465
Endo, Harry 1510
Endore, Guy 1028
Eney, Woody 1972
Engel, Charles 1092, 1093
Engel, Georgia 1777

Engel, Katherine 2261
Engel, Peter 1574, 1579, 1626, 2182
Engelbach, David 1962
England, Hal 1486, 1487
Engle, Debra 2104, 2208
English, Jack 1637
English, John 213
Englund, Robert 1689
Enhardt, Robert 1433
Enigma 1472
Enigma People 1472
Enriquez, Rene 1383
Ensign, Michael 1973
Ensign Pulver 112
Enter Horowitz 1350
Enton, Gregg 1801
Entre Nous 633
Entry 38
Ephraim, Lionel 1469
Ephron, Henry 796
Ephron, Phoebe 796
Epicac 1168
Epp, Gary 1385, 1453, 1827
Epper, Tony 1968
Epstein, Alan 2239
Epstein, Allen 1757, 1961, 2027
Epstein, Jon 1052, 1078, 1119, 1233, 1840
Erdman, Richard 76, 211, 260, 955, 1442
Erhart, Thomas 1160
Erich, John 1302
Erickson, Leif 472, 846, 1128, 1337, 1353, 1646, 1938
Ericson, Devon 1355, 1404, 1559, 1742

Ericson, John 341, 605, 822, 863, 1646
Erman, John 1190
Ernest, Dudley 129
Ernestine 307
Ernie and Joan 1388
Ernie, Madge and Artie 1176
Errickson, Krista 1922
Erskine, Howard 608
Ervens, Isabelle 1058
Erwin, Bill 267, 325, 1887, 1955, 2008, 2028
Erwin, Judy 1574
Erwin, Stu 645, 727, 951, 1559, 1586, 1587
Escapade 1563
Escape 1074
Escape from Witch Mountain 1880
Escape to Chaos 521
Espinosa, Jose Angel 1295
Espionage 782
Esprit Enterprises 1717
Espy, William Gray 2029
Estevez, Emilio 1958
Esther Williams Show 414
Estrada, Angelina 1991
Estrada, Erik 1908
ET 1919
Ethel Is an Elephant 21, 1727
Etlienne, Roger 768
Eunson, Dale 455, 966
Eunson, Katherine 455, 966
European Eye 993

Eustis, Rich 1053, 1306, 1546, 1622, 1859

Evans, Art 1314, 1970, 2052

Evans, Colin 1649

Evans, Dame Edith 885

Evans, Gene 510, 751, 1024, 1282, 1534, 1535, 1612, 1802

Evans, John H. 2032

Evans, Linda 686

Evans, Mary Beth 2006

Evans, Michael 1936

Evans, Mike 1108

Evans, Mitchell Young 1798

Evans, Richard 894

Evans, Robin 1779, 1994

Evans, Smith 1338

Eve Arden Show 761, 811

Evel Knieval 1267

Evenson, William 1057

Everett, Chad 777, 849, 874

Everett, Mark 2173

Everhart, Rex 1404, 1632, 1758

Evering, Jim 1798

Evers, Brian 2174

Evers, Jason 931, 944

Every Stray Dog and Kid 1686

Every Wednesday 1777

Everything is Coming Up Roses 1455

Everything Money Can't Buy 1237

Eve, Trevor 2252

Evigan, Greg 1442, 1778, 1779, 2033, 2064, 2255

Evil Roy Slade 968, 1151

Ewell, Tom 137, 674, 748, 1618

Ewing, John Christy 2189

Except for Me and Thee 1321

Exoman 1514

Expendables 541, 634, 1147

Expert Witness 260

Express to Danger 1002

Ex-Secretary 1082

Eyes of Charles Sand 1122

Eyes of Texas 1778, 1779

Eyes of the Night 433

Eyman, Cindi 2022

F

Fabares, Shelley 818, 898, 1132, 1347, 1786, 1977, 2066

Fabiani, Joel 1317, 1374, 1400, 1569

Fabray, Nanette 66, 254, 1096

Fabulous Doctor Fable 1185

Fabulous Oliver Chantry 157

Faceless Man 918

Factor, Robert 2245

Facts of Life 1834, 1889, 1890, 1896, 2251

Facts of Life Spin-off 2251

Faculty 2012

Fafara, Luke 1929

Fagan, Phil 846

Fagan, Suzanne 2023

Fair, A.A. 207

Fair Exchange 979

Fairbairn, Bruce 1467

Fairbanks, Douglas, Sr. 138

Fairchild, Don 303

Fairchild, Morgan 1563, 1570, 1694, 2233, 2247

Fairman, Blain 2240

Fairman, Michael 1800

Faison, Matthew 1810, 2066

Faison, Sandy 1368, 1409, 2193, 2230

Falcon, Ellen 2162

Falconi, Terri 1838

Falk, Harry 1256, 1577, 1591, 1812, 1840, 1885

Falk, Peter 1756

Falk, Tom 1280

Fall, Timothy 2186

Fall Guy 1779, 1866

Fame 2007

Family Battle 2075

Family Business 1910

Family in Blue 1883

Family Kovack 1279

Family Martinez 2105

Family Ties 2121, 2179

Family Tree 27

Famous Artists 222, 691, 692

Fanaro, Barry 2068

Fancy, Richard 2179

Fann, Al 1940, 2213

Fantastic 353

Fantastic Journey 1256, 1419

Fantasy Island 1189, 1764, 1862

Faracy, Stephanie 1432, 1544, 1810, 1899, 1962

Faraldo, Daniel 2105

Faralla, William Dario 472

Farber, Mel 1455

Farentino, Debrah 2205

Farentino, James 1285, 1357, 1521

Fargas, Antonio 1341, 1447, 1999

Farley, Elizabeth 1583

Farley, Morgan 1472, 1541

Farmer, Gene 1177

Farnon, Shannon 1697

Farnsworth, Richard 1328, 1802, 1854, 1882, 2177

Farquhar, Ralph 2203

Farr, Gordon 1154, 2082

Farr, Jamie 582

Farr, Stephen 1484

Farrah Fawcett Project 1861

Farrar, David 699

Farrell, Brioni 1091, 1441

Farrell, Conchata 1631

Farrell, Glenda 126

Farrell, Henry 1122

Farrell, Mike 1157, 1234, 1644, 2064

Farrell, Sharon 690, 809, 961, 1122, 1301

Farrell: For the People 1906

Farrington, Hugh 2120

Farris, Irene 1953

Farrow, Mia 1241

Fass, George 450

Fass, Gertrude 450

Fass-Palmer, Patricia 1974, 1990

Fassler, Ron 2163

Fast Lane Blues 1528

Fat Man 295

Father Brown 1687

Father Brown, Detective 1687

Father Knows Best 101

Father Knows Best: Home for Christmas 1487

Father Knows Best Reunion 1486

Father O Father! 1306

Father of the Bride 445

Father on Trial 1153

Father's Day 2075

Father's Homecoming 2266

Faulkner, Edward 1295

Faulkner, William 249

Faustino, David 1917, 1973, 2079, 2134

Faustino, Michael 2211

Favorite Son 2264

Fawcett, Allan 1954

Fawcett, Farrah 1094, 1861

Fawcett, William 1035

Fawlty Towers 1527

Fax, Jesslyn 115

Fay, Frank 67

Fay, Herbie 1272

Faye, Deidre 1990

Faye, Herbie 1267

Faylen, Frank 809, 952

Fazel, Rick 1543

Fazio, Dino 832

Fear No Evil 1028

Featherstone's Nest 1624

Fedderson, Don 710, 1080, 1213, 1268, 1566

Don Fedderson Productions 573, 1566

Federico, Armando 1425

Fee, Melinda 1678

Feel the Heat 1915

Feero, Robert 1841, 2030

Fehrle, Philip 1609

Feigelson, J.D. 2060

Fein, Irving 1795

Feiner, Ben 278

Feinstein, Alan 1340, 1507, 1516

Feld, Fritz 647, 1108

Feld, Margot 1380

Felder, Clarence 1914, 2046, 2205

Felder, Don 2127

Feldman, Corey 1765, 1871, 1929, 1974

Feldman, Edward H. 769, 1086, 1213, 1259, 1270, 1727, 1751, 1756, 1927, 1972

Feldman, Marty 1344

Feldon, Barbara 1153, 1370, 1496

Feldshuh, Tovah 1482, 1817

Feliciano, Jose 1733, 1734

Fell, Norman 699, 844, 1014, 1152, 1400, 1627, 1939, 2256

Fellows, Arthur 1076, 1090, 1816

Fellows, Don 2116, 2240

Fellows, S.J. 2132

Fellows/Keegan Company 1816

Felser, David 2235

Felton, Norman 592, 687, 688, 699, 732, 844, 898, 932, 975, 1098, 1158, 1937

Feminine Touch 159

La Femme 538

Fenady, Andrew J. 450, 582, 585, 721, 1235, 1249, 1347, 1474

Fenady, George 1854, 1954

Fenady Associates 1249

Fenady/Kowalski Corp. 582

Fenichel, Jay 1599, 1702

Fenmore, Tanya 2176

Fennelly, Parker 466

Fennelly, Vincent 264, 265, 338, 392, 395, 396, 487

Fenneman, George 71, 740

Fenster Hall 2051

Fenton, Frank 776, 877, 922

Fenton, George 1888

Feraldo, Daniel 2100

Ferber, Mel 1585

Ferdin, Pamelyn 790, 964, 1299

Fergus, Lee 1567

Ferguson, Allyn 1037, 1092, 1180, 1505, 1581, 1813, 1886

Ferguson, Bobbie 1986

Ferguson, Frank 510

Ferguson, Jay 2188

Ferguson, Jesse Lawrence 1970, 2160

Ferguson, Ma 406

Ferguson, William 1577

Fernandez, Abel 317, 318

Fernandez, Margarita 1919

Ferrar, Abel 2089, 2216

Ferrara, Frank 2174

Ferraro, Martin 1810

Ferrell, Conchata 1437, 2230

Ferrer, Jose 593, 667, 1057, 1089, 1237, 1356, 1514, 1771, 2060

Ferrer, Miguel 2173, 2208, 2258

Ferrero, Martin 1897

Ferret 717, 2005

Ferrier, Marina 2016

Ferrigno, Lou 2264

Ferris, Irena 1933, 2149

Ferro, Talya 1637

Ferziger, Diana 1117

Fess Parker Show 1268

Fessier, Michael 765, 806

Fetchit, Stepin 1160

Fetty, Darrell 1545

Feuer, Debra 1589

Feuer, Rusty 2119

Feylen, Frank 1465

Fherle, Phil 1713

Fiedel, Brad 1777, 1995, 2033, 2132, 2177, 2211

Fiedler, John 553, 670, 1163, 1480, 1845

Field, Chelsea 2169

Field, Julianna 1885

Field, Sally 1004, 1098, 1103, 1110, 1163, 1318

Field, Virginia 462

Fielder, Richard 1403, 1584, 1744

Fielding, Dorothy 1813, 1962

Fielding, Jerry 1044, 1094, 1102, 1156, 1224, 1293
Fielding, Paul 1993
Fields, Chip 1265, 1561, 1723
Fields, Herman Julian 584
Fields, Holly 2237
Fields, Jere 2001
Fields, Kim 1834, 1889, 1896, 2251
Fields, W.C. 855
15 Blocks 907
Fifty Grand Mystery 71
Fighting Marines 153
Fighting Nightingales 1544
Figment Productions 2235
Figueroa, Reuben 1099
Filerman, Michael 1722, 1745, 1918, 2060, 2178
Files of the Tokyo Police 356
Filipi, Carmen 1818
Film-Masters 334, 575, 678
Filmline International 2128
Filmways 391, 679, 873, 951, 961, 997, 1081, 1082, 1084, 1201, 1259, 1312, 1332, 1454, 1495, 1577, 1581, 1645, 1733, 1734, 1753, 1838, 1844, 1845, 1846
Filpi, Carmen 2186
Fimple, Dennis 1105, 1110
Finch, Jon 2098
Finch Finds a Way 383

Finder of Lost Loves 1189
Fine, Mort 1077
Fine Romance 1925
Fink, John 1155, 1238, 1383
Fink, Mark 1927
Finkel, Bob 869, 1093, 1220
Finklehoff, Fred 713
Finkleman, Ken 1855
Finley, Greg 1969, 2186
Finley, Pat 1154, 1344, 1412
Finley, William 1349
Finnegan, Bill 1181, 1324, 1764, 1855, 2028
Finnegan, John 1350, 1992
Finnegan, Pat 1764, 2028
Finnegan, Tom 2264
Fiore, Bill 1064, 1690
Fireball Forward 1123
Firefighters 123
Fireman's Ball 1238
Firestone, Eddie 1213, 1326, 1358
Firm 1907
First Artists 1360, 1515, 1574, 1579
First Hundred Years 646
First the Tube, and Now You, Darling 1228
First 36 Hours of Dr. Durant 1320, 1395
First Time, Second Time 1728
Firth, George 1509
Firth, Robert 2167

Fischer, Bruce 1785, 1988
Fischer, Frank 2084, 2213
Fischer, Peter S. 1509, 2175
Fish, Nancy 2232
Fishburne, Larry 2118
Fisher, Bob 729
Fisher, Brad 1968
Fisher, Bruce 1546
Fisher, Cindy 1814
Fisher, Dave 1964, 2267
Fisher, Frances 2236
Fisher, George Shug 1019, 1035, 1230, 1525, 1640, 1808
Fisher, Harvey 1451
Fisher, Lindsay 2212
Fisher, Madeline 1433, 1750
Fisher, Michael 1685, 1773, 1917
Fisher, Phil 1398
Fisher, Steve 269, 814
Fisher, Tricia Leigh 2193, **2221**
Fisherman's Wharf 1758
Fit as a Fiddle 357
Fit for a King 1892
Fitch, Robert 954
Fitts, Rick 1976
Fitzgerald 1196
Fitzgerald, Fern 1665
Fitzgerald, Geraldine 1381, 1449, 2159
Fitzgerald, John 1925
Fitzgerald and Pride 1145, 1196
Fitzsimmons, Jeannie 1647, 1809
Fitzsimons, Charles, Jr. 2195
Fitzsimons, Charles B. 1141, 1350,

1512, 1533, 1812, 1862, 2195
Five Aces 1688
Five Hundred Pound Jerk 1202
Five, Six Pick Up Sticks 757
Five's a Family 595
Fix-it City 1625
Flag 2088
Flagg, Fannie 1308
Flaherty, Joe 2226
Flaherty, Joseph X. 1348
Flair, Betsy 2116
Flamingo Kid 2199
Flanagan, Neil 1612
Flanders, Ed 1048, 1187, 1326
Flannery and Quilt 1344
Flash Gordon 2099
Flatbed Annie and Sweetiepie: Lady Truckers 1645
Flatbush Avenue 1361
Flatfoots 1827
Flatley, William 1428
Flavin, James 307, 792, 1424
Fleeks, Eric 2158
Fleet, Jo Van 770
Fleischer, Charles 1702
Fleishman, Larry 1094
Fleming, Rhonda 1349
Flessas, Mimis 960
Fletcher, Bill 1441, 1472
Fletcher, Jack 549, 1536, 1540
Fletcher, Jay 1914
Fletcher, Lester 1074
Fletcher, Michael 2258
Fletcher, Page 2029

Fletcher, William 1213

Flick, Ginger 1554

Flicker, Theodore J. 815, 1688, 1858

Fliers 843

Flight 198, 391

Flight Line 226

Flight of the Phoenix 1663

Flight Plan 46

Flight to Holocaust 1515

Flim-Flam Man 1024

Flint, Shelby 1565

Flintstones 833, 1724

Flippen, Jay C. 189, 392, 808, 1105

Flipside 2252

Flo's Place 1300, 1345

Florea, John 701

Florek, Dann 2022, 2170, 2241

Florek, David 2194

Flores, Adolpho 1784

Flores, Jose 2089

Floria, John 945

Florida Dragnet 180

Flory, Med 886, 1504, 1539, 1816

Flower, Buck 2186

Floyd Gibbons: Reporter 727

Floyd, Charles R. 2124

Fluegel, Darlanne 1914

Fluellen, Joel 1078, 1248

Fluffy 809

Fly Away Home 1800

Flying A Productions 14, 32, 149, 224

Flynn, Howard F. 1958

Flynn, J. Michael 2136, 2151

Flynn, Joe 663, 912, 1018, 1081, 1149, 1172

Flynn, John 1955

Flynn, Michael 1939

Flynn, Miriam 1920, 1997, 2160, 2231

Flynn, Neil 2173

Foch, Nina 667, 895, 1004, 1636, 1644, 2072

Focus, Spiros 2107

Focus on Adventure 784

Fog 1806

Fogel, Jerry 1123, 1142, 1332

Folb, Jay 1581

Foliart, Dan 1876, 2156

Folk, Robert 2082

Follow Me If You Dare 1689

Follow That Man 252

Follow the Sun 632

Follows, Megan 1896

Fonda, Henry 1183

Fonda, James 75, 316, 970

Fonda, Jane 1014

Fonda, Peter 933

Fondacaro, Phil 1968, 2076

Fong, Benson 1769, 1883, 1887, 2115

Fong, Brian 971

Fong, Frances 1251

Fong, Harold 845

Fontaine, Joan 535, 2025

Fontaine, Michael 2096

Fontana, Tom 2062

Fontelieu, Stocker 1324, 1860

Fools, Females & Fun 1224

For Better, For Worse 1283

For Better Or Worse 1728

For Heaven's Sake 1613

For Lovers Only 1856

For Members Only 1926

For the Defense 93

For the Love of Mike 459

Foran, Dick 7, 595, 893

Forbes, Brenda 1496

Force Five 1337

Force Seven 1908

Forced Landing 211

Ford, Anitra 1261

Ford, Barry 1821

Ford, Fred 2045

Ford, Glenn 1229, 1296, 1525

Ford, Harrison 1521

Ford, Jineanne 1904

Ford, John 51

Ford, Paul 114, 935, 1008

Ford, Peter 1296

Ford, Phil 768

Ford, Tony 1969

Forde, Brinsley 1207

Fordyce Productions 143

Foree, Ken 1969, 2033

Forefront 1029

Foreman, Deborah 2116

Forest, Denis 2144

Forest Ranger 7

Forester, C.S. 718

Forever Blue Jeans 1702

Formicola, Fil 1906, 1914, 1952

Forms of Things Unknown 758

Foronjy, Richard 1427, 1428, 1625, 1977, 2065

Forrest, Brett 2219

Forrest, Sally 6

Forrest, Steve 313, 804, 1249, 1257, 1641

Forrester, Larry 803, 1713

Forresters: Dear Karen 1189

Forsberg, Grant 1966

Forsey, Norman 1989

Forslund, Constance 1582, 1663, 1664, 1786

Forster, Robert 1401

Forsyth, Rosemary 1095, 1101, 2047, 2089

Forsythe, Bill 1969

Forsythe, Dawning 1583

Forsythe, John 314, 646, 731, 757, 985, 1189, 1292, 1689, 1719

Fort Figueroa 2237

Forte, Nick Apollo 1997

Fortier, Bob 805

Fortunate Painter 1168

Fortune Dane 2022

Fortus, Danny 1238

Forty-Niners 193

40 Share Productions 1940

Forward, Robert H. 1290

Foster, Amy 2231

Foster, Bill 1027, 1143, 1963, 2052

Foster, Bob 1448

Foster, Carol
  Tru 1867
Foster, Frances 2148
Foster, Gloria 1596
Foster, Harvey 260
Foster, Henry 793
Foster, Jill 1008
Foster, Jodie 1140
Foster, Lewis R. 13
Foster, Lin 825
Foster, Linda
  1289, 1584
Foster, Meg 2148
Foster, Norman 121
Foster, Peggy 1692
Foster, Preston 42
Foster, Robert 1031,
  1348, 1843,
  2002, 2061
Foster, Ron 1477
Foster, Susan 1141
Foulkes, Ted 1015
Fountain of Youth 74
Four Eyes 2006
  416th 1626
Four in Love 1729
Four of Us 1370
Four R Productions
  1633
Four Star 3, 33, 112,
  147, 208, 225, 226,
  227, 265, 267, 337,
  396, 472, 479, 485,
  507, 557, 561, 565,
  577, 603, 625, 626,
  643, 653, 669, 680,
  696, 697, 699, 703,
  704, 717, 726, 733,
  735, 736, 737, 738,
  739, 779, 784, 791,
  802, 808, 839,
  864, 865, 885, 923,
  931, 933, 936,
  940, 976, 1075
Four the Hard
  Way 1409
Fournier, Noel 1519
Fournier, Rift 1519
Fours Company 1306

Fowler, Gene 78
Fox 261
Fox, Ben 7, 148,
  149, 168, 173
Fox, Bernard 978,
  1124, 1188
Fox, Charles 1152,
  1197, 1411, 1496,
  1690, 1980, 2014
Fox, Fred 1825
Fox, Fred S. 563
Fox, Michael
  1132, 1164
Fox, Michael J. 1994
Fox, Nancy 1308
Fox, Paula 164
Fox, Peter 1832
Fox, R. Donovan
  1730
Fox, Sonny
  1679, 1689
Fox, William 1055
Fox, William P. 893
Fox-Brenton, David
  2032, 2247
Foxworth, Robert
  1128, 1234, 1257,
  1502, 2260
Foxx, Elisabeth 1917
Foxx, Redd
  1431, 1604
Foxx, Rhonda 1624
Foy, Eddie, Jr. 357,
  774, 1504, 1549
Foy, Eddie, III 604
Frakes, Jonathan
  1609
Franciosa, Tony
  1073, 1099
Francis, Anne 76,
  1020, 1123, 1146,
  1850, 1987
Francis, Cheryl 1867
Francis, Ivor 1008,
  1122, 1403, 1418,
  1527, 1743
Franciscus, James
  325, 455
Francks, Don 391

Franco, Abel 1059
Francy Goes to
  Washington 251
Frand, Harvey
  2007, 2244
Frank, Bob 2105
Frank, Charles
  1378, 1445, 1448,
  1489, 1540, 2060,
  2178, 2244
Frank, David 1827,
  1942, 2070, 2089
Frank, Frederic 75
Frank, Gary 1849
Frank, Harriet 790
Frank, Milo 380
Frank, Tony 2129
Frank Capra
  Comedy
  Theatre 578
Frank Cooper and
  Associates 134,
  458, 466, 482
Frank Merriwell
  792
Frank Von Zerneck
  Films 2045
Frankel, Ernie 1446,
  1644, 1694
Frankel Films 1644
Frankel Films/
  Gang Inc. 1694
Franken, Steve 811,
  1037, 1214, 1235,
  1347, 1369, 1465,
  1859, 1908, 1988,
  1994, 2221
Frankenheimer,
  John 2098
Frankenstein 1683
Frankfather,
  William 2127
Frankham, David
  1254
Franklin, Carl
  1693, 1745
Franklin, Don 2238
Franklin, Doug
  2189

Franklin, Jeff 1794,
  1949, 1950,
  1963, 1991
Franklin, Pamela
  1084, 1188,
  1189, 1357
Franklin Barton
  Productions 1497
Franklyn, Fredric
  1488
Franko, David 1921
Frankovich, M.J. 1403
Frankovich/Self
  Productions 1367
Frann, Mary 1728
Franz, Arthur
  208, 1246
Franz, Eduard 206
Fraser, Bob 1737
Fraser, Elisabeth 893
Fraser, Jerri Lynn 886
Fraser, Tony 966
Fraternity
  Mother 399
Fratkin, Stuart 2211
Fraud 425, 1290
Fraud Broads 1961
Fraud Squad
  1961, 2027
Frawley, James 1005,
  1006, 1314, 1348,
  1790, 1864, 1919,
  2042, 2113,
  2174, 2238
Frawley, William
  357, 518
Frazer, Dan 1210,
  1478, 1757, 2046
Frazier, Roger 1536
Frazier, Ron 2078,
  2172, 2258
Frechette, Peter
  1889, 1890
Fred Astaire
  Presents 155
Fred Weintraub &
  Daniel Grodnick
  Productions 1962
Frederick, Hal 1004

Frederick, Lynn 1203

Fredericks, Wendy 1493

Fredey, Alice 1918

Free Spirit 2150

Free Wheelers 647

Freebairn-Smith, Ian 2197

Freebooters 960

Freed, Bert 704, 812

Freed, Sam 1897

Freeman 1362

Freeman, Andy 1880

Freeman, Arny 1526

Freeman, Benedict 555

Freeman, Bud 872, 1216

Freeman, David 1099

Freeman, Deena 1796

Freeman, Devry 325, 499, 525

Freeman, Everett 310, 590, 646, 650, 731

Freeman, Fred 767, 1025, 1094, 1150, 1217, 1407, 1439, 1484, 1550, 1735, 1806, 1869

Freeman, Jerrold 1252

Freeman, Joan 2006

Freeman, Joel D. 1186

Freeman, Kathleen 647, 731, 833, 912, 1108, 1163, 1319, 1930, 2221, 2251

Freeman, Larry 1600

Freeman, Leonard 722, 723, 727, 777

Freeman, Lisa 1796

Freeman, Marion 1457

Freeman, Mike 1968

Freeman, Mort 1821

Freeman, Seth 2043, 2151

Frees, Paul 131, 253

Frees, Shari 1199

Freiberger, Fred 265

Freilich, Jeff 2024, 2039

French, Arthur 1649, **2112**

French, Bruce 1637, 2170

French, Leigh 1238, 1348, 1390, 1546, 1714

French, Victor 1019, 1247, 1749, 1882

French Connection 1184, 2132

French Connection II 2132

Fresco, David 1226, 1803

Frey, Jack 2246

Frey, Leonard 1243, 1550, 1892, 1960, 2134

Friday Night Group 1156, 1214

Friday Night Movie 1336

Fridell, Squire 1701

Fried, Gerald 1937, 2026

Friedberg, Billy 458, 766

Friedhofer, Hugo 1040

Friedkin, David 1077

Friedkin, William 2128, 2132, 2258

Friedlander, Howard 2093

Friedman, Bruce Jay 1206, 2232

Friedman, Hy 740

Friedman, Irving 611

Friedman, Kim 1926

Friedman, Rod 1721

Friedman, Ron 1447, 1499, 2193

Friend, Robert L. 465

Friendly, Ed 1027, 1847, 1943

Friendly Persuasion 1321

Friends 1545, 2054

Friends. Romans and Countrymen 867

Fries, Charles 1215, 1232, 1272, 1296, 1303, 1349, 1371, 1392, 1526, 1743, 1817

Fries Entertainment 2111

Frischman, Dan 1909

Frishberg, David 2047, 2180

Fritz, Leslie 1630

Fritzell, James 822, 1667

Frizzell, Lou 1119, 1190, 1316, 1357, 1529, 1560

From Here To Eternity 878

Frome, Milton 250

Fromkess, Leon 9

Frommer, Ben 1773

Front Office 124

Frontier World of Doc Holiday 296

Frontiere, Dominic 754, 758, 1078, 1166, 1571, 1917, 1973, 2091

Frontiersman 510

Frost, Alice 552, 648

Frost, Lauren 1494

Frost, Michael 1473

Frost, Warren 2207

Froug, William 703, 1075, 1847

Frumkin, Marla 2186

Fry, Eric 2226

Frye, Soleil Moon 1944

Frye, William 306, 1226

Fuchs, Fred 2107

Fudge, Alan 1119, 1245, 1369, 1420, 1686

Fuentas, Ernie 1833

Fugitive 913

Fujioka, John 1404, 2035

Fulger, Holly 2226

Full House 1920, 2013, 2037

Full Speed For Anywhere 112

Fuller, Barbara 255

Fuller, Jerry 1134

Fuller, Lisa 2211, 2221

Fuller, Nancy Belle 1337, 1347

Fuller, Penny 1042, 1236

Fuller, Robert 850, 1744

Fuller, Samuel 704

Fuller, Wendy 1813

Fullerton, Melanie 1258

Fullilove, Donald 1793

Fulton, Jessie Lee 1894

Fulton, Wendy 2088

Fun Makers 712

Funai, Helen 1004

Funny Funny Films 740

Funny Thing Happened on the Way to the Forum 867

Furey, John 1743, 2113

Furia, John, Jr. 1292, 1700, 2117

Furia/Oringer Productions 2117

Furlong, John 2042

Furst, Stephen 1836, 1851, 1926

Furst Family of Washington 1177
Furth, George 1006, 1105, 1271, 2160
Further Adventures 2238
Further Adventures of Wally Brown 1661
Fury, Ed 1190
Fustiano, David 1804
Future Cop 1583
Fuzz Brothers 1186
Fuzzbucket 2076

G

Gabe and Walker 1712
Gabe Katzka Productions 2109
Gabel, Martin 667
Gable, Clark 800, 1295
Gable, Francine 1981
Gable, June 1411, 1483
Gabor, Eva 553, 1084
Gabor, Zsa Zsa 63, 443, 851
Gage, Pat 1100
Gail, Ed 1074
Gail, Max 1280, 1678, 2015, 2085
Gaines, Jimmy 552, 648
Gaines, Linda 1652
Gaines, Richard 118
Gaines, Sonny Jim 1469, 1471
Gainey, M.C. 1936
Galas, June 2179
Galaxy 411
Gale, Bob 1980
Gale, Eddra 1030
Gale, Lorena 2235
Galecki, Johnny 2193
Galik, Denise 1435, 1726, 1922

Gallagher, Megan 1993
Gallagher, Mel 1586
Gallagher, Peter 1629
Gallant Men 720, 755
Gallardo, Silvana 1578, 1594
Gallegly, Dick 2193
Gallegos, Joshua 2105
Gallery, Dan 388
Gallery, James 1785
Gallery, Michelle 2043, 2151
Galligan, Bill 1890
Gallison, Joseph 1294
Gallo, Lew 632, 1263, 1389, 1457, 1494, 1589
Gallo, Lillian 1496
Galloway, Don 1117, 1366, 1512
Galloway, Jane 2153
Galloway, Pam 1867
Gallu, Sam 37, 38, 474, 547, 548
Gambell, Linda 2132
Gamble, Ralph 381
Gammell, Robin 1520, 1916, 1919, 1958, 2007
Gammon, James 1844
Gandolf and Fitch 1422
Gang of Four 2212
Gangster Squad 163
Gannaway, Albert 228, 786
Gannes, Gayle 1561
Gannon, Joe 2130
Gannon, Liam 2041
Gantman, Joseph 1582
Ganz, Jeff 1531, 1708, 1947
Ganz, Lowell 1365, 1552, 1598, 1630, 1661, 1827, 1911, 2250

Ganzel, Teresa 2043, 2068
Garas, Kaz 1078, 1261, 1349, 1518, 1862, 2188
Garbage 1759
Garbage Is My Life 1703
Garber, David 2265
Garber, Terri 1955, 2009
Garber, Victor 2064
Garbett, John 2070
Garcia, Cecilia 2123
Garcia, David 611, 1854
Garcia, Mark 1655
Gardenia, Vincent 1200, 1781, 2041
Gardiner, Reginald 19, 418
Gardner, Arthur 726
Gardner, Ava 2116
Gardner, Brooks 2034
Gardner, Christopher 1486, 1487
Gardner, David 666
Gardner, Dee 1266
Gardner, Erle Stanley 207, 1061
Gardner, Gerald 936, 940, 1150, 1238, 1505
Gardner, Gerry 1111
Gardner, Harvey 1092
Gardner, Jerry 2260
Gardner, Reginald 760
Gardner, Stu 1596
Garduno, Anna 1653, 1856
Garfield 1363, 1724
Garfield, Allen 1276, 1965
Garfield, Brian 1477
Garfield, David 1998
Garfield, John-David 2261

Garidi, Carmine 2199
Garland, Beverly 475, 1019, 1197, 1292, 1847
Garland, Judy 818
Garland, Richard 547
Garland, Robert 1349
Garlington, Lee 2110, 2262
Garner, Jack 1403, 1448, 1849, 2009
Garner, James 1254, 1282, 1358, 1426, 1448, 1503
Garner, Leonard 2158
Garner, Lili 768
Garner, Martin 1751, 1752, 2159
Garner, Mousie 2165
Garner, Peggy Ann 722
Garnett, Tay 391
Garr, Teri 1424, 1683, 1964
Garralaga, Martin 169
Garrett, Betty 2207
Garrett, Donna 1261
Garrett, Eliza 1526
Garrett, Hank 1776, 1918, 1969
Garrett, Jimmy 673
Garrett, Joy 1843
Garrett, Lila 1263, 1311, 1392, 1411, 1493, 1526, 1627, 1739
Garrett, Michael 309
Garrett, Steve 803
Garripoli, Mary 2001
Garris, Mick 2076
Garrison, Greg 1097
Garrison, Michael 1656, 1748
Garrison, Richard 2033
Garrison, Robert Scott 1922

Garrison, Sean 903, 1126, 1512, 1637

Garry Marshall Productions 1911, 2228

Garson, Greer 52

Garson, Hank 808

Garvarentz, George 1376

Garver, Lloyd 1491, 1492, 2180

Gary, Carol 1830, 2141

Gary, Lorraine 1233

Gary Nardino Productions 2072

Gast, Harold 722, 723

Gates, Gilbert 1459

Gates, Larry 707, 782

Gates, Michael 2146

Gates, Nancy 67

Gates, Rick 971

Gathering 1444

Gathering II 1780

Gathings, Darlan Rusch 2260

Gatlin, Jerry 1353

Gatteys, Bennye 507

Gaucho 138

Gault, Willie 2246

Gauny, Sam 2260

Gautier, Dick 1017, 1506

Gava, Cassandra 1968

Gavala, Yulia 1757

Gavin, James 271

Gavin, John 1019

Gaviola, Sandy 1261

Gay, John 1245, 1335

Gay, Larry 2257

Gaye, Lisa 925

Gaye, Marvin 1007

Gayle, Nancy 1808

Gayle, Rozelle 1561

Gaynes, George 1503

Gaynor, Jock 604

Gazzaniga, Don 846

Gazzara, Ben 1123, 2195

Gazzo, Michael V. 1609

G.E. Theatre 309, 455, 456, 461, 470, 471, 473, 564, 565, 642, 647, 665, 667, 1470

Gebert, Gordon 200

Geer, Ellen 1973, 2115

Geer, Kevin 1653

Geer, Will 1105, 1159, 1169, 1249, 1293, 1326, 1424, 1507

Geeson, Judy 1105

Geffner, Deborah 1846

Gegen, Annie 2245

Gehring, Ted 1105, 1228, 1452, 1483, 1992

Geiger, George 2194

Geiger, Milton 231

Gelbart, Larry 952, 1086, 1269, 1489

Geldart, Edward 2130

Geller, Bruce 736, 737, 779, 1048, 1340, 1399, 1530

Geller, Harry 1394

Geller, Marian 1184

Gellis, Danny 1633

Gellman, Toni 1742

Gelman, Larry 1110, 1620

Gelman, Milton 6, 264

Gemignani, Rhoda 1914

Gemini 1371

Gene Autry Productions 139

General Artists Corporation 342

General Foods 805, 808, 821, 857, 859, 860, 863, 930, 933, 950, 976

General Teleradio 235

Generation 2028

Genesis II 1212, 1260, 1328

Genest, Edmond 2064, 2214

Genise, Livia 1544

Genovese, Mike 2035, 2049

Gentry, Jim 1949

Gentry, Minnie 1469

Gentry's People 392

Geoffrey, Paul 2116

George, Alan 1353

George, Brian 2123, 2237

George, Christopher 1074, 1147

George, Eben 1245

George, Gabrile 2117

George, George W. 382

George, Howard 1457

George, Jennifer 1902

George, Judith 382

George, Lynda Day 1352, 1371, 1612, 1820

George, Sue 200

George Burns and Grade Allen Show 1795

George Hamilton Show 1928

George Huskin and Associates 356

George Reeves Productions 1799

Georgia Peaches 1730

Georgiade, Nicholas (Nick) 478, 1222

Geraghty, Marita 2161

Gerard, Gil 1508, 1590, 1884, 1885, 1934, 2021

Gerard, Merwin 1318

Gerard, Will 2060

Gerber, Bill 1526

Gerber, David 1036, 1141, 1167, 1176, 1207, 1229, 1291, 1358, 1430, 1441, 1505, 1512, 1523, 1584, 1611, 1716, 1786, 1798, 1812, 1897, 1976, 2048, 2058, 2096, 2195

Gerber, Joan 1050

Gerbert, Gordon 731

Gere, Richard 1181, 1359

Geritol Adventure Showcase 212, 316, 326

Gerritsen, Lisa 390

Gershman, Jerry 1888

Gershon, Fred 2080

Gershon, Gina 2119

Gershwin, George 454

Gerson, Ken 2197

Gersten, Baille 1392

Gerstie, Frank 388, 765

Gertz, Frank 1333

Gertz, Jamie 1926

Gertz, Mitchell 432

Gertz, Peter Michael 1796

Gethers, Peter 2174

Getting There 1627

Getty, Estelle 2009, 2181

Getz, John 1821, 1914

Gewirtz, Howard 1997

Ghost and Mrs. Muir 1036

Ghost Breakers 844
Ghost of a
  Chance 1704
Ghost of Sierra De
  Cobra 830
Ghost Squad of
  Scotland Yard 375
Ghost Story 2253
Ghostbreaker 1009
Ghostbreakers 699
Ghostbusters 1859
Ghostley, Alice
  1708, 1930
GI's 1731
Giambalvo, Louis
  1800, 1958,
  2043, 2164
Gian, Joe 2205
Giannini, Roxanna
  Bonilla 1427
Gib 1884, 1934
Gibb, Don 2065
Gibb, Don
  Richard 1848
Gibbon, Sandy 1592
Gibbs, Alan 1774
Gibbs, John 6,
  423, 442
Gibbs, Michael 1127
Gibney, Susan 2218
Gibson, Beau 1355
Gibson, Gerry 1914
Gibson, Henry 1151,
  1408, 1995, 2142
Gibson, Judy 1876
Gibson, Mary
  Ann 1970
Gidget 1005
Gidget Gets
  Married 1110
Gidget Goes to New
  York 1004
Gidget Grows
  Up 1004
Gierasch, Stefan
  716, 772, 1396,
  1712, 1813
Gifford, Frank
  426, 481

Gifford, Gloria 1877
Giftos, Elaine 1414,
  1429, 1699, 1758
Giggling Goose
  Productions
  2142, 2253
Gigi 158
Gil, Jorge 2083
Gilbert, Billy 169
Gilbert, Edmund
  878, 1232
Gilbert, Gary 1873,
  2142, 2206, 2253
Gilbert, Herschel
  Burke 208, 603,
  699, 726, 733,
  735, 737, 738
Gilbert, Joanne 632
Gilbert, Jody 1229
Gilbert, Kenneth
  C. 1836
Gilbert, Larry 527
Gilbert, Mickey 1718
Gilbert, Millie 816
Gilbert, Morgan 662
Gilbert, Paul 601
Giles, Sandra 1799
Gilfillan, Sue
  Ann 1948
Gilford, Gwynne
  1264, 1433
Gilford, Jack
  1346, 1386
Gilgreen, John 1471
Gill, Beverly 1261
Gill, Elizabeth 1427
Gill, John 129
Gillard, Stuart 1558
Gilleron, Tom 2002
Gilles, Michael 2173
Gillespie, Ann
  1888, 1988
Gillespie, Gina 470
Gillespie, Jean 381
Gillette, Anita
  1358, 2041
Gilley, Mickey 2130
Gilliam, Burton 1297,
  1308, 1582, 1730

Gilliam, David 1467
Gilliam, Stu 1362
Gilligan, Rusty 1660
Gilligan's Island 889,
  1404, 1660, 1662
Gilligan's Island
  II 1664
Gilligan's Planet 1664
Gilliland, Richard
  1279, 1408,
  2026, 2235
Gillin, Hugh 1525,
  1616, 1712,
  1789, 1860
Gillin, Linda 1125
Gilling, Rebecca 2185
Gillis, Jackson 1382
Gillott, Nick 2240
Gilman, Kenneth
  1111, 1384,
  1673, 1731
Gilman, Larry 1854
Gilman, Sam
  781, 1247
Gilman, Toni 1686
Gilmer, Robert 2002
Gilmore, Doug 1634
Gilmore, Theresa 2119
Gilpin, Marc 1685
Gilroy, Frank 603
Gilstrap, Suzy 1853
Gilyard, Clarence,
  Jr. 2048
Gimbel, Norman
  1980, 2064
Gimbel, Roger 1659,
  1665, 1666
Gimignani,
  Rhoda 1413
Gimme a Break
  1946, 1991
Gimmick Man 346
Ging, Jack 852, 1140,
  1185, 1294, 1441,
  1866, 2006
Ginger Rogers
  Show 730
Gingold, Hermione
  158

Ginnes, Abram
  S. 1184
Ginty, Robert
  1584, 2090
Giobus, Dorothy
  J. 1370
Giorgio, Bill 954
Giorgio, Tony
  1092, 1230
Giraldi, Bob 2024
Girard, Bernard
  704, 1185
Girard, Eydse 1234
Girardin, Ray 1914,
  1920, 2267
Giridian, Ray 1970
Girillo, Joe 1231
Girl from UNCLE
  1155
Girl in the Empty
  Grave 1254, 1503
Girl on the Late
  Late Show 1291
Girl's Life 1941
Girls About Town 80
Gish, Lillian
  1371, 1568
Gist, Robert 807
Githens, Jay 1986
Gitlin, Irving 903
Gittings, Richard
  1198
Givney, Kathryn 1036
Gizzard, George
  1351
Gladiator 2089
Glan, Joey 2007
Glaser, Darel 1343
Glaser, Paul Michael
  1262, 1447, 2118
Glass, Ned 267,
  833, 869, 890,
  900, 912, 1126,
  1332, 1357, 1781
Glass, Ron
  1014, 1265
Glass, Seaman
  1275, 1919
Glass, Tod 1140

Glattes, Wolfgang 1994

Gleason, Joanna 1839, 1927, 1929

Gleason, Michael 1224, 1337, 2189

Gleeson, Redmond 1280, 1349, 1424, 1536

Glen Larson Productions 1506, 1565, 1617, 1771, 1778, 1779, 1815, 1865, 1866, 1933, 1954, 1992, 2002, 2029

Glenn, Louise 292

Glenn, Scott 2240

Glenrock, Joshua 1679

Gless, Sharon 1290, 1565, 1692, 1785, 1983

Glickman, Will 114

Glicksman, Frank 1144, 1211, 1395, 1481, 1883

Glicksman-Brinkley Productions 1883

Glory Days 2183

Glory Years 2183

Glover, Bruce 1079, 1294, 1369, 1436

Glover, Crispin 1890, 1994, 1995

Glover, Julian 1380, 2063

Glover, William 1948, 2169

Glynn, Carlin 1873

Go West, Young Girl! 1445

Gobel, George 590, 683, 760, 840, 1506, 1690, 1942

God Bless Mr. Ferguson 1065

Goddard, John 447

Goddard, Mark 654, 1750

Godfather 1407

Godfredson, Chris 1744

Godfrey, Alan 1615, 1844, 1845, 1846, 1952

Godfrey, Anne 1039

Godfrey, Arthur 1645

Godshall, Liberty 1727, 1895

Godwin, Stephen J. 2020, 2166

Goetz, Peter Michael 1990, 2022, 2266

Golf, Ivan 707, 839, 885, 931, 1376

Going Places 1152

Gold, Bert 1691

Gold, Brandy 2104

Gold, Harry 1497, 1658

Gold, Heidi 1636

Gold, Tracey 1880

Gold-Driskill Productions 1691

Goldberg, Marshall, M.D. 1586, 1587

Goldberg, Barry 2171

Goldberg, Gary David 2121, 2269

Goldberg, Lee 2214

Goldberg, Leonard 1180, 1189, 1190, 1195, 1238, 1319, 1325, 1374, 1443, 1447, 1609, 1702, 1719, 2034, 2040, 2085, 2120

Goldberg, Marshall 2226

Goldberg, Rose Leiman 1398

Golden, Bob 1123, 1147, 1224

Golden, Richard 23

Golden Girls 2181

Goldenberg, Barry 2099

Goldenberg, Billy 1028, 1278, 1327, 1383, 1862

Goldenberg, Harvey J. 1681

Goldfinger 1611

Goldie 257

Goldie and the Bears 1962

Goldie and the Boxer 1781

Goldie and the Boxer Go to Hollywood 1782

Goldie 257

Goldin, Ricky Paul 1842, 2008

Goldman, Carole 1830

Goldman, Danny 1384, 1757, 2246

Goldman, Hal 967, 1495

Goldman, Lorry 1731

Goldman, Wendy 1804

Goldoni, Lelia 1446, 1519

Goldsmith, Jerry 1089, 1187, 1254, 1299, 1315, 1776, 1937, 2195

Goldsmith, Jonathan 1518, 2035

Goldstein, Bob 1906

Goldstein, Jan 1787

Goldstein, Judy 2152

Goldstein, Martin 1641, 1642

Goldstein, William 1678, 2233

Goldstone, James 1278, 1326, 2059

Goldstone, Jules 390, 441

Goldstone, Richard 44

Goldstone/Tobias Agency 236

Goldwyn, Tony 2159

Golland, Joseph 2093

Golod, Jerry 1968, 2041

Golonka, Arlene 1150, 1180, 1397, 1661, 1922

Gomberg, Sy 761, 1639

Gomez, Panchito 1278, 1516, 1609, 1827, 1864

Gomez, Thomas 206, 768

Gonneau, Pete 1339

Gonzalas, Gloria 1777

Gonzales, Gonzales 423

Gonzales, Jose 112

Gonzales-Gonzalez, Pedro 653, 2186

Goober and the Trucker's Paradise 1546

Good Against Evil 1446

Good Boy 1228

Good Heavens 383, 670, 1237

Good Morning, America 1205

Good Morning, Miss Bliss 2182

Good News 1628

Good Ol' Boys 1577

Good Old Days 833

Good Penny 1488

Good Time Harry 1206

Goodbye Charlie 2014

Goodbye Doesn't Mean Forever 1760

Goodbye Girl 1760, 1828

Gooden, Robert 1105, 1515
Goodeve, Grant 1421, 1428, 1614
Goodfellow, Joan 1258, 1316
Goodfellow, Kate 1475
Goodman, Dody 1764, 2221
Goodman, George 1231
Goodman, Hal 819, 833
Goodman, John 2144
Goodman, Mike 1994
Goodman, Miles 2237
Goodman, Norman 1780
Goodnight and Good-bye 2246
Goodnight Sweetheart 1761
Goodrow, Garry 1864, 2032, 2089
Goodson, Joseph 1147, 1314, 1331
Goodson, Mark 582
Goodson-Todman Productions 10, 39, 75, 150, 346, 384, 451, 488, 582, 681, 721, 816, 941
Goodwin, Laurel 958
Goodwin, Michael 1952
Goodwin, P.J. 1976
Goodwin, R.W. 1582, 2090, 2266
Goodyear Theatre 75
Gordon, Al 967, 1495, 1553
Gordon, Alex 1159
Gordon, Barry 766, 1394, 1709, 2049, 2119, 2222

Gordon, Bruce 263, 917, 1484, 1758
Gordon, Charles 1955, **2010**
Gordon, Clarke 772
Gordon, Don 912, 1100, 1368, 1479, 1568
Gordon, Gale 292, 459, 628, 672, 1825
Gordon, Gerald 723, 1337, 1777
Gordon, Jennifer 1845
Gordon, Lawrence 1308, 1589, 1695, 1718, 1955, 2010
Gordon, Leo 726
Gordon, Leo V. 1467
Gordon, Louis 1758
Gordon, Mark 1480
Gordon, Mark R. 2165
Gordon, Ruth 1606
Gordon, Susan 390
Gore, Natalie 1441
Gores, Joe 1478
Gorman, Cliff 1238, 1359, 1953
Gorman, Patrick 1731
Gorman, Ray K. 1621
Gorshin, Frank 1347
Gortner, Marjoe 1258
Goslins, Rachel 1958
Gossett, Lou 879, 1137, 1186, 1282, 1329, 1348, 1422, 1587, 1715
Gossip 1665, 1666, 1676
Gottfried, Gilbert 1661
Gottfried, Howard 1288

Gottlieb, Alex 435, 443
Gottlieb, Andrew 2113
Gottlieb, Carl 1336, 1363, 1513, 1595, 1940
Gould, Chester 970
Gould, Cliff 1048, 1246, 1278, 1367, 1376, 1475, 1480, 1822
Gould, Gordon 1649
Gould, Graydon 1655
Gould, Harold 756, 1012, 1198, 1213, 1344, 1690, 2054, 2234
Gould, Heywood 1396
Gould, Morton 1370
Gould, Sandra 670
Gould, Sid 806
Gould, Woody 1861
Goulding, Ray 1900
Govons, Marcia 2160
Gower, Carlene 1245
Goz, Isaac 1446
GP 696
Grabowski, Norman 388, 1141
Grace, Wayne 1539
Grad, Peter 1625
Grad, Sam 264
Grady, Don 1080
Grady, James 2114
Grady Nutt Show 1829
Graf, Allan 2022
Graf, David 2188
Graff, Ilene 1960
Graff, Todd 1999, 2144
Graff, Wilton 253
Graham, Fred 317
Graham, Gerritt 1328, 1329, 1368, 1976
Graham, Gloria 1291

Graham, Joe 264
Graham, Ronald F. 1328
Graham, Stacy 665
Graham, William A. 739, 845, 931, 1096, 1231, 1427, 1916, 2195, 2246
Grahame, Gloria 1074
Grahn, Nancy 2065
Graieda, Javier 2195
Grammer, Gabbie 1015
Grand Hotel 777
Grand Old Opry 234
Grand Slam 688, 732
Grande, Louis Del 1569
Grandin, Isabel 1978
Grandpa Max 1330
Grandpa, Mom, Dad and Richie 1215
Grandparents 400
Grandy, Fred 1238, 1387
Granet, Bert 478
Granger, Farley 1351
Granger, Stewart 486, 1124
Granik, Ted 303
Granstedt, Greta 319
Grant, Barra 1206, 1501, 2159
Grant, Bill 1633
Grant, Faye 1793
Grant, Lee 1164, 1233
Grant, Linda 1212
Grant, Merrill 2075, 2077, 2112
Grant, Perry 1199, 1878, 1974, 2001
Grant, Robert 1178
Grant, Sarina 1248, 1501, 1529
Grant Goodeve Project 1614

Grant's Beat 1196

Granville, Bonita 16

Grassle, Karen 2175

Gratsos, Xenia 1180

Graubart, Judy 1558

Grauman, Walter 381, 385, 717, 847, 1061, 1315, 1337, 1561, 2060

Gravers, Steve 1587

Graves, Johnny 1813

Graves, Peter 582, 665, 754, 925, 958, 1210, 1301, 1303, 1324

Graves, Teresa 1154

Gray, Billy 1486, 1487

Gray, Charles 23

Gray, Charles H. 1059

Gray, Ciney 314

Gray, Coleen 679, 1102

Gray, Eric 2061

Gray, Erin 1655, 1815, 1842

Gray, Harold 1821

Gray, Linda 1518

Gray, Michael 1134

Gray, Norm 1384

Gray, Sam 2128

Grayson, Kathryn 212

Grazer, Brian 2204, 2257

Great Bible Adventures 752

Great Dane 435

Great Day 1434, 1927

Great Detectives 1124

Great Mouthpiece 78

Great Muldoon 283

Greatest American Hero 1642, 2133

Greatest American Heroine 2133

Green, Alex 2117

Green, Clarence 408, 614, 634, 666, 789, 837

Green, David 879

Green, Dorothy 395

Green, Gerald 1252

Green, Gilbert 902, 1783

Green, Grizzly 1623

Green, Jim 1757, 1961, 2027, 2239

Green, Joey 1809, 1991

Green, John 412, 499, 525

Green, Katherine 1974, 2040

Green, Leif 1922

Green, Melissa Ann 1918

Green, Michael 553

Green, Mort 1929

Green, Nigel 718

Green, Patricia 2092

Green, Richard 2047, 2246

Green, Seth 2149, 2251

Green, Shecky 891

Green, Walon 1328, 2219

Green Acres 650, 1026, 1082, 1084, 2104

Green and Stone Productions 787

Green Felt Jungle 845

Green for Action 888

Green for Danger 888

Green Hornet 277, 2059

Green-Rouse Productions **666**

Greenbaum, Everett 306, 822, 1667, 1981

Greenbaum, Fritzell 306

Greenberg, Dan 1284

Greenberg, Mitchell 1777

Greene, Angela 169

Greene, Barry 2029

Greene, Clarence 541, 615

Greene, David 1127, 2035

Greene, Ellen 1657, 2161

Greene, Eric 1594, 1699

Greene, H. Richard 2092

Greene, Harold 211, 319

Greene, James 2245

Greene, Lorne 1168, 1353

Greene, Michael 2188, 2238

Greene, Richard 473, 945

Greene, Shecky 823

Greene, Terry 266

Greene, Tom 1442, 1425, 2002

Greenhalgh, Ted 1100

Greenhalgh, Dawn 2018

Greenhut, Robert 1520

Greenlee, David 1796

Greenquist, Brad 2156

Greenwald, Robert 1443, 1645

Greenway, Ron 164

Greenway, Tom 523, 770

Greenway Productions 919

Greenwood, Bruce J. 2086

Greenwood, Charlotte 189

Greenwood, Katy 761

Greenwood, Rochelle 2235

Greer, Ann 1566

Greer, Dabbs 7, 213, 390, 1017, 1056

Greer, Robin 2021

Gregg, Bradley 2165, 2255

Gregg, Christina 742

Gregg, Julie 819, 1571

Gregg, Virginia 392, 1235, 1403

Gregor, Adam 2087, 2191

Gregory, Jack 1799

Gregory, James 499, 958, 1024, 1085, 1125, 1197, 1244

Gregory, Mary 1461, 1936

Gregory, Michael 1609

Greisman, Gordon 2247

Grenrock, Josh 1540

Grenrock, Joshua 1958, 2156

Grepne, Marie Elise 2219

Grey, Duane 1008

Grey, Joel 815, 1147, 2152

Grey Ghost 209

Greyhosky, Babs 2006, 2133

Griego, Sandra 1594

Grier, David Alan 2158

Grier, Rosie 1030, 1131, 1199, 1402, 1478

Gries, Jonathan 1854, 1994, 1995

Gries, Tom 852, 1073, 1182, 1210, 1292
Griffeth, Simone 1591, 1605
Griffin, Mary 2215
Griffin, Pam 1296
Griffin, Robert 21, 265
Griffin, S.A. 2233
Griffin, Sean 1678
Griffith, Andy 1254, 1315, 1368, 1503, 1504, 1856, 1905, 2187
Griffith, James 751, 1803
Griffith, Kristin 1744
Grigor, Nancy 1581, 2010
Grimaldi, Gian R. 1537, **2002**
Grimaldi, Gino 1522, 1538, 1660
Grimes, Jack 1461
Grimes, Scott 2210, 2221
Grimes, Tammy 2040
Grimm, Maria 1321
Grimmell, Robin 2065
Grio Entertainment 2253
Griswold, Michael 2195
Gritten, David 2237
Grizzard, George 502, 883, 1090, 1187, 1616, 1972, 2021, 2026, 2175
Grodnik, Dan 2033
Grogan, Kelly 1944
Groh, David 1867
Groober Hill 908
Groom, Sam 1382, 1691
Gross, Charles 1159, 1231
Gross, Jack 41

Gross, Larry 2216
Gross, Marcia 2041
Gross, Marjorie 2222
Gross, Mary 2250
Gross-Krasne Productions 41, 436
Grossman, Budd 743, 1543, 1736, 1823
Grossman, Lynn 1876
Grosso, Sonny 1231, 1359, 1498, 1873
Grosso-Jacobson Productions 1873
Group, Mitchell 1608
Grout, James 1207
Grover, Edward 1181, 1359
Grover, Stanley 2148
Grovernor, Linda 1718
Groves, Herman 722, 723
Groves, Robin 1485
Grubbs, Gary 2189
Gruber, Frank 373, 447
Gruber, John 1123
Gruner, Mark 1247
Grusin, Dave 1226, 1560, 2194, 2219
Gryff, Stefan 2098
Gryn, Clintin 1031
GTG Entertainment 2220, 2225
Guardino, Harry 318, 925, 1175, 1187, 1233, 1368, 1639, 1786, 2045, 2110
Guardino, Jerome 1147
Guarnieri, Terri 1965
Guber, Frank 450
Guber, Peter 2011
Guber/Peters Productions 2011
Guedel, John 71, 87
Guerra, Castulo 2148

Guerrasio, John 1491, 1492
Guerrero, Alex, Jr. 2226
Guerrero, Evelyn 2237
Guerrini, Phyllis 2237
Guess What I Did Today? 964
Guess Who's Coming to Dinner? 1307
Guest, Lance 1839, 2264
Guest, Nicholas 1939
Guide for the Married Man 1005
Guilbert, Ann Morgan 1131
Guild Films 43, 151
Guiliani, John 1100
Guillerman, John 235
Guillermo, San Juan 1594
Guilty or Not Guilty 846
Guinee, Tim 2203
Guinness, Alec 1886
Guisewite, Cathy 2071
Guittard, Laurence 2060
Gulager, Clu 926, 1021, 1144, 1210, 1376, 1509, 1853
Gulliver 742
Gumshoes 1732
Gun and the Pulpit 1258
Gun and the Quill 39
Gunfighter 415
Gunkel, Chuck 1355
Gunn, Bill 724
Gunn, James 482, 1686

Gunn, Moses 1078, 2088, 2186
Gunn, Nicholas 1621
Gunn, Rocky 1100
Gunner, Bob 1511
Guns of Destiny 175
Gunsmoke 325
Gunty, Morty 308
Guntzelman, Dan 1871
Gunzenhauser, Norman 2050
Gur, Alizia 1117
Gurry, Eric 1920
Guss, Jack 1030
Guss, Louis 756, 1356, 1540, 2041, 2232
Gustaferro, Vincent 1803
Guth, Ray 1644
Guthrie, D. 1688
Guthrie, Tani Phelps 1247
Guthrie, Walt 1469
Guttenberg, Steve 1494, 2005
Guzaldo, Joe 2142, 2234
Guzman, Claudio 660, 672, 673, 674, 1856
Gwynne, Fred 964, 1022, 1106, 1687, 1832, 2192
Gwynne, Michael C. 1275, 1292, 1294, 2195
Gypsies 1705
Gypsy in Amber 1356
Gypsy Warriors 1564
Gytri, Lowell 2066

H

Haas, Charlie 770, 2212
Haas, Ed 1081

Haas, Lukas 2023
Haase, Rod 1337
Hack, Shelley 1719
Hackabee, Cooper 1467
Hacker, Joseph 1655, 1757, 1972
Hackett, Buddy 1948
Hackett, Joan 1043, 1165, 1250, 1429, 1521, 1714, 1786, 1941
Hackett, Jonathan 2219
Hackett, Sandy 1804
Hackman, Gene 985, 1184, 2132
Haddon, Lawrence 961, 1678
Haden, Sarah 457
Haft, Steve 2038
Hagen, Earle 669, 965, 1010, 1262, 1343, 1536, 1618, 1624, 1644, 1694, 1897
Hagen, Jean 325
Hagen, Kevin 125
Hagen, Ross 2130
Hager, Jim 1371
Hager, Jon 1371
Hagerthy, Ron 465
Haggerty, Dan 1592, 1903
Haggerty, H.B. 1089, 1597
Haggerty, Julie 1777
Haggerty, Mike 2183
Haggis, Paul 2073
Hagin, Molly 2201
Hagman, Larry 1183, 1282, 1418
Hagman, Stuart 1479
Hague, Albert 1958
Hahn, Archie 1239, 1581, 1704, 1835
Hahn, Phil 1731

Haid, Charles 1297, 1770, 2061, 2237
Haig, Sid 1418, 1435, 1436, 1676, 1992
Haile, Marian 1271
Hailey, Arthur 2021
Hailey, Eddie 1682
Hailey, Marian 1104
Hailey, Oliver 1228
Haines, Larry 1309, 1549, 2153
Haines, Lloyd 961
Haje, Khrystyne 2186
Hajeno Productions 1802
Hal Hackett Productions 349
Hal Roach Productions 118, 174, 199, 274, 398
Haldeman, Tim 1917, 1973
Hale, Alan, Jr. 265, 645, 655, 1168, 1662, 1663, 1664
Hale, Chanin 1008
Hale, Jean 851
Hale, John 853
Hale, William 1357, 1376
Haley, Jack 313
Haley, Jackie Earle 1686
Half and Half 2213
Halfway House 1456
Haliday, Elizabeth 1845
Hall, Adam 1379
Hall, Albert 1972
Hall, Brad 2242
Hall, Cynthia 1185
Hall, Harriet 1533
Hall, Huntz, 1074
Hall, J.D. 2034
Hall, James T. 1849
Hall, Jerry 2124
Hall, Jon 9, 171
Hall, Kimberly 1990

Hall, Margaret 2146
Hall, Mollie 2109
Hall, Monty 1584
Hall, Phillip Baker 1619, 1749
Hall, Stella 2144
Hall, Tom T. 1053
Hall, Valerie 1942
Hallahan, Charles 1747, 1951
Hallaren, Jane 1978, 2049
Hallenbeck, Darrell 1435, 1436
Haller, Dan 1933, 1989
Haller, Daniel 1730, 1866
Haller, David 1747
Hallett, Jack 1873
Hailey, Ben, Jr. 1682
Hallick, Tom 1382, 2175
Halliday, Brett 268
Halliday, Clive 758
Halliday, Elizabeth 1558, 1640
Hallin, Ronnie 1911
Hallstrom, Lasse 2249
Hallyday, John 2185
Halmi, Robert 2215
Halop, Billy 769
Halop, Florence 357, 1091, 1752, 1792, 2050
Halsey, Brett 619, 632, 1801
Halton, Marie 2245
Hamann, R. Scott 2049
Hamel, Alan 1878
Hamel, Veronica 1444, 1780
Hamel/Somers Entertainment 1878
Hamer, Rusty 965

Hamill, Mark 1348, 1425
Hamill, Pete 1120, 1192
Hamilton, Alexa 1942
Hamilton, Barbara 1877, 1946
Hamilton, Bernie 926, 966, 1016, 1195
Hamilton, Colin 2165
Hamilton, George 802, 1267, 1691, 1928
Hamilton, Joe 1438, 1600
Hamilton, Kim 966
Hamilton, Kipp 126
Hamilton, Leigh 2061
Hamilton, Linda 1919, 2024
Hamilton, Lynn 1248
Hamilton, Margaret 651, 699, 844, 1095
Hamilton, Murray 732, 1167, 1213, 1756, 1976
Hamilton, Randy 2120
Hamilton, Richard 1921, 2098, 2146
Hamilton, Robert 1476
Hamilton, Ted 1648
Hamlin, Janice 1567
Hamlin, Jerry 1567
Hamlisch, Marvin 1271
Hammel, Thomas 1730
Hammer, Barbara 552
Hammer, Ben 1840
Hammer, Jan 2083
Hammer, Jay 1253

Hammer of C
  Block 1422
Hammett,
  Dashiell 295
Hammond, Bart 755
Hammond,
  John 1749
Hammond, Nicholas
  1421, 1743, 1879
Hamner, Barbara 648
Hamner, Don 1814
Hamner, Earl
  1032, 1745
Hamner, Earl, Jr.
  1194, 1248
Hamner, Robert 1747
Hampshire,
  Susan 1158
Hampton, James
  1337, 1467,
  1699, 1874
Hampton, Orville 94
Hampton, Paul
  1147, 1400
Hampton, R.W. 2261
Hanalis, Blanche
  1299, 1813,
  1886, 2248
Hancock, John
  1010, 1841, 1992,
  2007, 2065
Hancock, Lou 2123
Hancocks 1423
Hand, Toby 1877
Handle With Care
  1457, 1555
Handler, David 2174
Handsome
  Harry's 2052
Handy, James 2046,
  2132, 2192
Haney, Anne 1813,
  1909, 1942, 2237
Hanged Man 1249
Hangin' Out 1547
Hanging Judge 511
Hanging Out 1458
Hankammer,
  Heidren 1058

Hankin, Larry
  1151, 1551, 1567,
  2017, 2216
Hanley, Anne 1879
Hanley, Bridget 871,
  964, 1406, 1717
Hanna, William
  916, 1112
Hanna-Barbera
  Productions
  916, 1112, 1444,
  1675, 1780
Hannah, Bob 1730
Hannibal's Boy 944
Hanold, Marilyn 913
Hansen, John
  1592, 1939
Hansen, Steve 2156
Hansen, William
  1298
Hanson, Reg 2128
Happeners 879
Happily Ever After
  499, 810, 1804
Happiness Is A
  Warm Clue 1100
Happy Endings 2007
Happy Time 358
Harada, Ernest 1100,
  1510, 1786
Harbough,
  Logan 1016
Harbour Productions
  1289
Hard Case 472
Hard Day's Night 868
Hard Knox 2008
Hardcastle and
  McCormick 1131
Harden, Marcia
  Gay 2156
Hardester, Crofton
  1860
Hardesty House
  2090
Hardin, Ernest,
  Jr. 1849
Hardin, Jerry
  1534, 1625

Hardin, Joseph 1655
Hardin, Melora 1681
Hardin, Ty 1646
Harding, John 667
Hardwicke, Sir
  Cedric 758
Hardy, Joel 1299
Hardy, Joseph
  1170, 1349
Harty, Patricia 1950
Hardy Boys 971
Hare, Will 1586,
  1639
Harewood, Dorian
  1520, 2043, 2092,
  2158, 2213
Hargrove, Bob 2237
Hargrove, Dean
  1160, 1219, 1418,
  1527, 1962, 2187
Hargrove, Marion
  199, 836
Hargrove, Robert
  2223
Harisborough,
  Evin 2064
Hariss, Julius 1076
Harkess, Peter 166
Harkins, John 1349,
  1446, 1855, 1937
Harlan, Jeff
  1493, 1535
Harlem
  Globetrotters
  on Gilligan's
  Island 1664
Harley, Mike 2091
Harmon, David P.
  958, 1662, 1664
Harmon, Deborah
  1805, 1980, 2155
Harmon, Drew 912
Harmon, Kelly 1895
Harmon, Mark 1354
Harmon, William
  307, 658
Harmsen, Dina 1061
Harnick, Jane 2181
Haron, Cindy 1893

Harper 1361
Harper, Robert
  1932, 2115
Harper, Samantha
  1835
Harper, Valerie 1906
Harper Valley
  PTA 1053
Harper Valley,
  USA 1053
Harrah, Roland,
  III 2115
Harriman, Fawne
  1515, 1561, 1678
Harrington, Pat, Jr.
  664, 759, 1045,
  1156, 1169, 1214,
  1292, 1506, 1586,
  1587, 1692, 1974,
  2018, 2081
Harrington,
  Vicki 978
Harris, Barbara 2144
Harris, Baxter 1914
Harris, Berkeley
  772, 893
Harris, Charles 1915
Harris, Cynthia
  1683, 1951
Harris, Harry 1743,
  1821, 2193
Harris, Jack 562
Harris, Jeff 1271,
  1341, 1362, 1435,
  1436 1665, 1710,
  1796, 1823, 2037,
  2198, 2207
Harris, Jo Ann 1052,
  1648, 1656
Harris, Jonathan 815
Harris, Julius 1677
Harris, Karen 2147
Harris, Ken 1057
Harris, Leslie 324
Harris, Marc 1207
Harris, Matt 2041
Harris, Mel
  2091, 2271
Harris, Nyles 1813

Harris, Richard
Brian 1162
Harris, Robert 877
Harris, Rossie 1879
Harris, Stacy
396, 1940
Harris, Susan
1485, 2181
Harris, Timothy
2246
**Harris Down
Under** 2185
Harrison, Anthony
2093
Harrison, Grace
1921
Harrison, Gregory
1444
Harrison, Heather
1022
Harrison, Joan 919
Harrison, Ken 1773,
1833, 1894, 2025
Harrison, Mark 1986
Harrison, Noel 1150
Harrison, Rex 1170
Harrison, Shirley
1860
Harrold, Kathryn
1621
Harrower, Elizabeth
1126
Harry, Harvey, Jr. 256
Harry, Stephen
Anthony 2089
**Harry and
David** 987
**Harry and
Maggie** 1331
**Harry and the
Kids** 2015
Harry O 1373
Harry Stoones,
Inc. 1362
Harry's Battles 1792
Harry's Business 596
Harry's Girls 573
**Harry's Hong
Kong** 2091

Harryhausen, Ray 74
Hart, Bill 1489
Hart, Carol 2153
Hart, Cecilia 2141
Hart, Christina
1250, 1319, 1355,
1502, 1885
Hart, Fred 1784
Hart, Harvey 902,
922, 926, 1246,
1280, 1368, 1481,
1678, 1862,
1867, 2218
Hart, Linda 1818
Hart, Mary 1803
Hart, Moss 488
Hart, Stan 1141
Hart, William 562
Hart of Honolulu 24
Hart to Hart 2032
Hart/Thomas/Berlin
Productions 2153
Hartford, John 1808
Hartley, Clabe 1916
Hartley, Mariette
1073, 1212, 1376,
1466, 1605, 1688
Hartley, Ted 1553,
1656, 1801
Hartman, David 972
Hartman, Edmund
207, 1080
Hartman, Elizabeth
1722
Hartman, Lisa
1764, 1859
Hartman, Paul 949
Harvey, Alex 2129
Harvey, Gene 125
Harvey, Harry, Jr.
255, 263, 582
Harvey, Harry,
Sr. 1007
Harvey, Irene
519, 690
Harvey, Jason 1712
Harvey, Michael 704
Harwood, Richard
1488

Hasburgh,
Patrick 2086
Haskell, David 1867
Haskell, Jimmy 2221
Haskell, Peter 937,
1007, 1122, 1400,
1591, 1647, 1654,
1713, 1778
Haskins, Dennis
1818
Haslett, Anthony 262
Hass, Ed 964
Hasselhoff, David
1786, **2002**
Hasso, Signe 1339
Hastings, Bob 1024,
1102, 1125, 1270,
1350, 1784, 1832
Hastings Corner
1025
**Hat of Sergeant
Martin** 719
Hatch, Richard 1211
Hatcher, Teri 2153
Hatfield, Bobby 1007
Hatfield, Hurd 1232
Hathaway, Amy 2204
Hathaway, Noah
2070
Hathaway, Robert
1212
Hattman, Stephen
2214, 2218
Hauck, Charlie 1671,
1792, 1921, 1923
Hauff, Thomas 2128
Haunted 828
Hauser, Faye 1784
Hauser, Kim 2104
Hauser, Wings
1885, 1969
Haven, John 1583
Havens, Thomas
1750
Haveron, John 653
Havinga, Nick 1704,
1734, 2175, 2256
Havins, Hal
2127, 2260

Havoc, June 1192
Hawaii Five-0 1324,
1510, 1648, 2094
Hawaiian Heat 2094
Hawaiian Honeymoon
1084
Hawk, Jeremy 1886
**Hawke and
O'Keefe** 1917
Hawkins, Ira 1469
Hawkins, Jimmy
60, 836
Hawkins, Rick
2051, 2053
Hawkins, Susan 60
Haworth, Jill 1007
Hayakawa,
Sessue 356
Haybert, Dennis
1971
Hayden, Jeffrey 628
Hayden, Russell 302
Haydin, Richard 306
Haydn, Lili (cq)
1760, 1868, 2211
Haydn, Richard
1100
Hayers, Sidney 1039,
1692, 1706, 1938
Hayes, Alison 207
Hayes, Annelle
552, 648
Hayes, Billy 1067
Hayes, Gloria 1999
Hayes, Herbert 93
Hayes, Isaac 1422
Hayes, Jimmy 113
Hayes, John Michael
347, 1254,
1315, 1353
Hayes, Katherine
1079
Hayes, Linda 1686
Hayes, Maggie
403, 651
Hayes, Margaret 19
Hayes, Peter
Lind 201
Hayes, Ron 751, 849

Haymer, Johnny 954, 1709
Haynes, Dick 1282, 1290
Haynes, Michael 2244
Haynes, Tiger 2157
Haynie, Jim 2081, 2115, 2197
Hays, Jeffrey 2197
Hays, Robert 1443
Hayward, Charles 2049, 2237
Hayward, Chris 976, 1046, 1223, 1775
Hayward, Cynthia 1296
Hayward, David 1730, 1882, 2033
Hayward, Jim 317
Hayward, Lenore 1778
Hayward, Lillie 636
Hayward, Louis 262
Hayward, Susan 1145, 1196
Hazard, Richard 1301, 1424
Hazard's People 1396
Haze, Stan 1419, 1969
Head of the Family 308
Healers 1292
Healy, David 1127, 1378
Healy, Mary 201
Healy, Myron 985
Healy, Richard 264
Hear No Evil 1884, 1885
Hearn, Chick 1664
Hearn, Dick 361
Hearn, George 1687
Heart and Soul 2200, 2253
Heartbeat 2003
Hearts Island 2053

Hearts of Steel 2016
Hearts of the West 1489
Heat of Anger 1145, 1196
Heath, Laurence 958, 1210, 1653, 1718
Heatherton, Joey 1007, 1097
Heatter, Merrill 1081
Heave Ho Harrigan 384
Heaven Help Us 812
Heaven on Earth 1667
Heaven's Gate 1420
Heavens 1857
Heberle, Kay 1551
Hecht, Ben 76
Hecht, Harold 858
Hecht, Paul 1294, 1368
Hecht/Hill/ Lancaster Productions 350
Heck's Angels 1389
Heckart, Eileen 1220, 1844, 2161
Heckerling, Amy 2252
Hedaya, Dan 1960, 2199
Hedison, David 1211, 1335, 1351, 1356, 1518, 1560, 1615
Hedrick, Don 2049
Hee Haw 1053, 1546
Heebner, Emily 1885
Heffley, Wayne 1198, 1587, 1595, 1617, 1800
Heffner, Kyle 1911
Heffner, Kyle T. 2114
Heffron, Richard T. 1536
Heflin, Nora 1867
Heflin, Van 231
Hefti, Neal 1202, 1350

Hegyes, Robert 1424, 1856
Heideman, Leonard 391
Heidi 170
Heigh, Helen 497
Heilpern, Steve 1043, 1059
Heilveil, Elayne 1254
Heilweil, David 267
Heinemann, Arthur 1903
Heinemann, Laurie 1542
Heins, Barrett 2041
Heinz, James 1959
Heiberg, Cindy 1497
Helberg, Frank 1497
Helberg, Sandy 1497, 1701, 1794
Held, Carl 780
Held, Karl 756
Helford, Bruce 2179
Helimarines 416
Helix Productions 1346, 1502
Hell Cats 802
Helland, Eric 1818
Heller, Barbara 199
Heller, Joseph 1174
Heller, Ken 1968
Heller, Shad 1808
Hellinger's Law 1814
Hellmore, Tom 129
Hello Dere 813
Hello Dolly 156, 1382
Hello Mother, Goodbye! 1216
Helm, Connie 756
Helm, Peter 836
Helmond, Katherine 1278, 1320, 1428, 1856, 1892, 1912, 1998. 2138
Helmore, Tom 599
Helms, Jim 1352
Helms, Bridgett 2245
Help 889
Help! 1993

Help, Inc. 1111
Helstrom, Gunnar 905
Helton, Jo 756
Helton, Percy 64
HelVeil, Elayne 1228
Helvey, Carol 2124
Hembreck, John 470
Hemingway, Ernest 781
Hemmings, David 2091, 2197, 2262
Henderson, Albert 1218
Henderson, Bill 2158
Henderson, Douglas 772, 853
Henderson, Marcia 597
Henderson, Phillip 2045
Henderson, Zenna 1129
Henderson Productions 1266, 1365
Hendler, Janice 1906
Hendler, Lauri 1839, 1946, 1994
Hendrickson, Benjamin 2113
Hendriksen, Lance 2065
Hendry, Ian 884
Henerson, James 1006, 1202, 1830, 1856
Henerson-Hirsch Productions 1830, 1856
Henfry, Janet 2219
Henley, Trevor 1653, 1969
Henner, Marilu 1459, 1550, 2049, 2250
Henning, Linda 1808, 1874
Henning, Linda Kaye 1904

Henning, Paul 243, 1082, 1808

Henning, Ted W. 2223

Henreid, Monika 1148

Henreid, Paul 1352

Henriksen, Lance 1958

Henrig, Merriana 1074

Henry, Anne 1999

Henry, Buck 1174, 1286

Henry, Emmaline 747, 1082, 1414

Henry, Gloria 65

Henry, Gregg 1976, 2186

Henry, Mike 928, 942, 1094

Henry, Pat 1171

Henry D 494

Henry Jaffe Enterprises 1192

Henschel, Tom 2049, 2078

Hensen, Jim 1313

Hensley, J. Miyoko 2152

Hensley, Pamela 1352, 1442a, 1865

Hensley, Steven 2152

Henson, Jim 1241, 2163

Henson Associates 2163

Hentelhoff, Alex 1320, 1397, 1510

Hepburn, Katherine 696, 1307, 1466

Hepner, Don 2165

Her Honor, The Mayor 347

Her Majesty, The Queen 181

Her Twelve Men 1139

Herbert Brodkin Productions 1130, 1165

Herbert, Charles 67, 189, 390

Herbert, Chris 2076

Herbert, Hugh F. 709

Herbert, Pitt 670, 1397, 1511

Herbert F. Solow Productions 1475

Herbert Leonard Productions 948, 960, 1099, 1120, 1638

Herbert Ross Productions 1705

Herbsleb, John 1387

Herbstritt, Larry 2214, 2218

Hercule Poirot 593, 667

Hercules 803

Herd, Richard 1396, 1451, 1528, 1534, 1906

Here Comes Melinda 500

Here Comes the Judge 1153

Here Comes the Showboat 81

Here Comes Tobor 44

Here's Boomer 1827

Here's Lucy 1138

Here's O'Hare 537

Herlie, Eileen 1116

Herman, Amanda 1998

Herman, Paul 2041

Herman, Randy 1479, 1568

Herman, Robert 1645

Herman Rush and Associates 1181, 1305

Hermione Gingold Show 158

Hernandez 1227

Hernandez, Juan 696

Hernandez, Rogelio 271

Hernandez, Tina Gail 1894

Hernandez: Houston PD 1227

Herndon 1911

Herndon and Me 1911

Herrara, Anthony 1591, 1616

Herrara, Joseph Paul 1229

Herrick, Frederick 1189

Herrier, Mark 1918

Herring, Laura Martinez 2261

Herron, Kevin 966

Hersey, Sherry 1385

Hershberger, Gary 1979

Hershey, Barbara 917

Herskovitz, Marshal 2165

Hertelendy, Hanna 1587, 1784, 2090

Hertzog, Lawrence 2262

Hervey, Winifred 2139

Heslov, Grant 2212

Hess, James 2195

Hess, John 558

Hess, Susan 2037

Hesseman, Howard 1263, 1567, 1853

Hessie, DeWayne 1551

Hessler, Gordon 772, 1688

Heta, Carmen 1989

Heteloff, Alex 1563

Hetrick, Jennifer 2170

Heverly, Robert 1515

Hewitt, Christopher 1862

Hey, Mack 200

Hey Mom 258

Hey Teacher 762

Heyday Productions 1393, 1414, 1416

Heydt, Louis Jean 260

Heyes, Douglas 325, 605, 827, 1059, 1293, 1301

Heyman, Aaron 2173

Heyman, Burt 1266

Heys, Kathryn 826

Hi, Mae 1806, 2092

Hiatt, Michael 1447

Hickey 1346

Hickey, Jim 1989

Hickey vs. Anybody 1346

Hickman, Beau 582

Hickman, Darryl 329, 384, 506, 624, 729, 833, 1391

Hickman, Dwayne 243, 762, 826, 916, 1465, 1994, 2221

Hickox, Bryan 1488, 1744, 1982

Hicks, Bill 1790

Hicks, Catherine 1568

Hicks, Chuck 1074, 1124, 1908

Hicks, Hilly 1500, 1680, 1720

Hicks, Tommy 2158, 2211

Hide and Seek 260

Higgins, Cindy 2093

Higgins, Edward C. 1780

Higgins, Joel 1007, 1051

Higgins, Michael 1907

Higgins, Ron 730
High Five 1893
High Noon 393, 933
High Risk 1383
High School USA 1994, 1995
High Time 460
Higher and Higher 988
Higher Ground 2239
Highway Honeys 1894
Highway Patrol 272
Highway to Heaven 383
Highwayman 262, 2265
Hiken, Gerald 1228, 2146, 2246
Hiken, Nat 116
Hildegarde Withers 1125
Hildegard Withers Makes the Scene 1125
Hill, Arthur 366, 489, *1015, 1651*
Hill, Charlie 1960, 2100
Hill, Craig 1596
Hill, Dana 1579, 1624, 1842, 1923
Hill, Dean 2008
Hill, Frankie 1944, 2030
Hill, Harry 2029
Hill, Jessica 1780
Hill, Jim 1255
Hill, Leonard 1994, 1995, 2155
Hill, Marianna 1477
Hill, Maurice 1732
Hill, Maury 806
Hill, Richard 1158, 1609, 1653
Hill, Robert 301
Hill, Roger 1396
Hill, Tex 2061

Hill, Thomas 1665, 1687
Hill, William 1886
Hill/Mandelker Productions 1994, 1995
Hill-O'Connor Television 2155
Hill Street Blues 1099, 1183, 1621, 1686, *1696,* 1770, 2244, 2265
Hillaire, Marcel 1037, 1441
Hillard, Suzanne 1140
Hiller, Arthur 746, 830
Hillerman, John 1420, 1477, 1541, 1666, 1771, 1815, 2246
Hilliard, Robert 1097, 1415
Hillshafer, Beth 1909
Hillyard, Bob 1764
Hilton, Arthur David 21
Hilton, Arthur O. 1124, 1126
Hilton, Jasmina 1039
Hilton, Robyn 1352, 1447
Hinchman, Bert 1906, 2188
Hindle, Art 1424, 1581, 1585, 1615
Hindman, Earl 1230, 2172
Hindy, Joseph 1100, 1357, 2212
Hindy, Patricia 1566
Hines, Brick 1301
Hines, Connie 522
Hines, Damon 1902, 1929
Hines, Dennis 1248
Hines, Granger 1904
Hines, Mimi 768

Hingle, Pat 824, 1007, 1252, 2070, 2172
Hinkley, Del 1749
Hinkley, Tommy 2222
Hinman, Nancy 2189
Hinn, Michael 169
Hinton, Ed 125
Hirsch, James 1189, 1643, 1830, 1856
Hirsch, Janice 2193
Hirsch, Janis 2178
Hirsch, Judd 1338
Hirschborn, Joel 1355
Hirschman, Herbert 1115, 1168, 1316
Hirschorn, Joel 2014
Hirson, Alice 1534, 1558
Hirson, Roger O. 1359
Hirt, John 1524
His and Hers 1977
His Model Wife 552, 648
His Two Right Arms 1135
Hisatake, Kack 1721
Hitchcock, Alfred 241
Hitchcock, Jane 1649
Hitched 1103, 1163
Hitchhiker 2096
Hitchhiker's Guide to the Galaxy 1858
Hite, Kathleen 482, 1319
Hitt, Robert 1459, 1810
Hitzig, Rupert 1462, 1548, 1632
Hixon, Ken 2195
Ho, David 2091
Hoag, Ben 2263

Hoag, Mitzi 1093, 1180, 1503, 1504, 1778, 1879
Hobbs, Heather 1660, 1871
Hobbs, Mary Gail 1075
Hobbs, Peter 1558, 1807, 1880
Hobin, Bill 1439
Hoblit, Gregory 1621, 1686
Hocson, Ching 1251
Hoder, Mark J. 2066
Hodge, Max 1248
Hodge, Patricia 1380
Hodges, Eddie 328, 766
Hoelscher, Devin 2191
Hoff, Christian 2110
Hoffe, Arthur 550, 555
Hoffman, Basil 1604, 1757
Hoffman, Gary 2268
Hoffman, Herman 814
Hoffman, Jane 2112
Hoffman, Kay 1679, 1742
Hoffman, Wendy 1664
Hofmann, Isabella 2191
Hogan's Heroes 832
Hogan, Hulk 1962
Hogan, Jack 611, 1302
Hogan, Robert 1037, 1157, 1195, 1224, 1484, 1508, 1586, 1587, 1600, 1992
Hogan, Terry 1962
Hogan, William 1690
Hogestyn, Drake 2028
Hogue, Judith 2236
Hoing, Henry 1701

Holahan, Dennis 2085

Holbrook, Hal 876, 1090, 1325, 1693, 2063, 2187

Holcomb, Rod 1641, 1887, 2009, 2049

Holcombe, Wendy 1837

Holden, Rebecca 1794, 1934, 2232

Holding, Bonnie 265

Holdridge, Lee 1224, 1522, 1800, 1811, 1853, 1867, 1976, 2148, 2239, 2248

Hole 22, 1762

Hole, Jonathon 870, 1041

Holiday Abroad 471

Holiday for Hire 786

Holland, Anthony 1111, 1804, 1834, 1950, 1999, 2035

Holland, Buck 1123

Holland, Erik 1321

Holland, Jeff 1479

Holland, John 920

Holland, Tommy Lee 1867

Hollander, David 1591, 1728, 1826

Holliday, Fred 1168, 1184, 1450, 1867

Holliday, Hope 1618

Holliday, Kene 1649, 1922, 1988

Holliman, Earl 1030, 1107

Hollingshead, Lee 1139

Holloway, Jean 169, 1022, 1036

Holloway's Daughters 917

Hollowell, Todd 1940

Holly Golightly 1006

Hollywood Angel 512

Hollywood High 1490, 1491, 1492

Hollywood Police Reporter 401

Hollywood Squares 1081

Hollywood Yesterday 787

Holm, Celeste 60, 818, 1301

Holman, Joel 1958

Holman, Rex 1693

Holme, John Cecil 846

Holmes, Jennifer 1773, 2175

Holmes, Lynne 1314

Holmes, Madeline 758

Holmes, Peggy 1979

Holt, Ana 2267

Holt, Bob 1438

Holt, Charlene 1261

Holt, Tracy 2083

Holton, Donald 2035

Holzgang, Conrad 1659

Holzman, Allan 2265

Homak, Lucy 2063

Home 2085

Home Again 1668, 2142

Home Cookin 1308

Home Free 2263

Home Front 1743

Home Improvements 2106

Homecoming Queen 2254

Homeier, Skip 1132, 1656

Homeroom 1793

Hometown 530

Honer, Jimmy 764

Honeymoon Hotel 1856

Honeymooners 1036

Hong, Dick Kay 515

Hong, James 1251, 1451, 1480, 1520, 1591, 1651, 1723, 1782, 2091

Hong, Pearl 1100

Honig, Howard 1964, 2226

Honky Tonk 1293

Hood, Don 1324, 1884, 1988

Hood, Jason 1650

Hoofer 890

Hook 697

Hooks, David 1562, 1591, 1621

Hooks, Ed 1936, 1992

Hooks, Eric 1469, 1471

Hooks, Kevin 1469, 1471, 1926

Hooks, Robert 876, 1089, 1132, 1195, 1376, 1469, 1470, 1471, 1584, 1915, 2114

Hooperman 2205

Hooray for Hollywood 763

Hooray for Love 729

Hooten, Peter 1562

Hootkins, Bill 2100

Hope, Barry 1877

Hope, Bob 238, 528, 690

Hope, William 2063

Hope Division 2092

Hopkins, Bo 1051, 1322, 1355, 1420, 1481, 1559, 1595, 1612

Hopkins, Bob 1716, 2049

Hopkins, Kenyon 1128

Hopkins, Maureen 2119

Hopkins, Telma 1601

Hopper, B.J. 2197

Hopper, Dennis 2049, 2119

Hopper, Hal 325

Hopper, Jerry 729

Hopps, Norman 1604, 1910

Horan, Barbara 2035

Horino, Tad 1864, 2090, 2163

Horman, Nicholas 1747

Hormann, Nicholas 1971

Horn, Lennie 1199

Horn, Leonard J. 632, 753, 1020, 1029, 1048, 1146, 1162, 1180

Horn, Lew 1731, 2066

Hornaday, Jeffrey 2165

Horne, Geoffrey 2064

Horovitz, Israel 1920

Horowitz, Alan 1407

Horowitz, Howie 1404

Horowitz, Joshua 2065

Horowitz, Mark 2218

Horowitz and Horowitz 1350

Horse, Michael James 2189

Horsford, Anna Maria 1817, 1902, 2128

Horton, Edward 20

Horton, Edward Everett 896

Horton, John 2064, 2112

Horton, Michael 1668, 1751

Horton, Peter 1787

Horton, Robert 829, 877

Horvath, Charles 737, 833, 1030

Hosea, Bob 2210

Hoshi, Shizuko 1916

Hostetter, John R. 1716

Hot Footage 473

Hot W.A.C.S. 1794

Hotchkis, Joan 390, 1626

Hotel 1189

Hotel Hawaii 2122

Hotshot Harry and the Rocking Chair Renegades 1690

Hough, Adrian 2063

Hough, Stan 1257, 2221

Houghton, Buck 463, 667, 670, 1743

Houghton, James 1423

Houlihan, Keri 1944, **2020**

Hound of the Baskervilles 1124

House, Billy 74

House, Dana 1497, 1541

House and Home 2223

House of Four Keys 486

House of Seven 689

House of Seven Garbos 143, 429

House of Wax 194, 880

House on Rue Riviera 605

Houseman, Arthur 787

Houseman, John 1396, 1692

Houser, Christie 2030

Houser, Jerry 1393, 1544, 1831, 1962

Houston Knights 1956

Hovan, Louise 1626

Hoven, Louise 2213

Hovey, Tim 310

Hovis, Larry 1374

How Do I Kill a Thief—Let Me Count the Ways 1866

How to Steal an Airplane 1031

How to Succeed in Business Without Really Trying 1309

How's Business? 385

Howard, Andrea 1414

Howard, Ann 1950

Howard, Barbara 2234

Howard, Cy 63, 328, 553, 570, 654

Howard, D.D. 1917, 2169

Howard, Dennis 1483, 1780

Howard, Didi 2006

Howard, Frank 2008

Howard, Jim 2129

Howard, Ken 1586, 1587, 1650

Howard, Kevin 1844

Howard, Matthew 1059

Howard, Rance 1403, 1645

Howard, Ron 456, 1157, 1699, 1853, 1944, 2074, 2257

Howard, Sherman 2087, 2238

Howard, Susan 1145, 1169, 1187, 1559, 1615

Howard, Tamar 1813

Howard, Trudy 797

Howard, Vince 1887

Howe, Darrell 203

Howe and Hummell 182

Howell, Arlene 424

Howell, Hoke 1025

Howell, Jamil 2016

Howes, Sally Ann 1036, 1124

Howie 649

Howitzer, Bronson 1322

Howland, Beth 1206

Hoxie, Richmond 1451

Hoy, Linda 1971, 2163, 2189

Hoy, Robert 2196

Hoyle, Stuart 1127

Hoyt, John 76, 93, 717

Hoyt Axton Show 1843

Hoyts Productions 2208

Hubbard, David 1842, 1889

Hubbard, John 955, 1444

Hubbert, Corky 1622

Hubley, Season 1134, 1292, 1986, 2084, 2104

Hud 790

Huddleston, David 1150, 1258, 1354, 1427, 1480, 1534, 2215

Huddleston, Michael 1366, 1495, 1671

Huddleston, Robert 741

Hudis, Norman 1610

Hudis, Robin 2165

Hudis, Stephen 1105

Hudson, Bill 1566

Hudson, Deidre 1126

Hudson, Ernie 1799, 1823, 1967, 2013

Hudson, Gary 1789, 1894

Hudson, Hal 208, 213, 563, 572

Hudson, John 370

Hudson, Mark 1566

Hudson, William 472

Hudson Brothers 1371

Huebling, Craig 1026

Huffman, David 1742

Huffman, Rosanna 1164, 1336, 2091

Huggins, Roy 296, 604, 605, 611, 845, 847, 852, 922, 927, 1031, 1043, 1059, 1105, 1299, 1396, 1420, 1448, 1525, 1647, 1688

Huggy Bear and the Turkey 1447

Hugh, John 1916

Hugh-Kelly, Daniel 1817

Hughes, Barnard 1263, 1508, 1572, 1687

Hughes, Bruce 2185

Hughes, John 1836, 1964

Hughes, Ken 1819

Hughes, Terry 1964, 2068, 2122, 2123, 2254

Hull, Henry 497

Hull, Shelley 1010, 1040, 1041

Hulswit, Mart 803

Human Comedy 764

Human Thing To Do 140

Humanoid Defender 2030

Humberstone, Bruce H. 270

Humble, Gwen 1676, 2022, 2249

Humble Productions
1439, 1869
Hume, Doug
1561, 1617
Hume, Edward 1888
Humes, Mary-
Margaret 1973
Humphreys,
Susie 1744
Hundley, Craig
790, 1260
Hunley, Gary 662
Hunnicutt, Arthur
626, 842, 1162,
1257, 1319
Hunnicutt, Gayle
1937, 1938
Hunsaker, John 1928
Hunt, Alan 1591
Hunt, Gareth 1563
Hunt, Helen
1259, 2269
Hunt, Marsha
213, 1028
Hunt, Neil 2258
Hunt, Peter
1632, 2248
Hunt, Peter H.
1437, 1557, 1637,
1787, 1798, 2932,
2083, 2177
Hunt, Richard 2163
Hunted Lady 1516
Hunter, Blake
2013, 2138
Hunter, Jeffrey 919
Hunter, Kim 1075,
1423, 2064
Hunter, Ross
1351, 1388
Hunter, Walt 1768
Hunter 1564, 2194
Hunter's Moon
1646
Hunters 619
**Hunters of the
Reef** 1588
Huntington,
Nicole 2262

Hupp, Jana
Marie 2118
Hurley, John
Patrick 2148
Hurrah for Love 624
**Hurricane
Island** 562
Hursey, Shery 1453
Hursley, Doris 709
Hursley, Frank 709
Hurst, Rick 1461,
1582, 1631, 1764
Hurt, Mary Beth
1236, 1401
Hurwitz, Howie
1234
Hush, Lisabeth 1164
Husky, Rick
1591, 2120
Husman, Ron 900
Hussein, Waria
1679, 1742
Hussey, Olivia 1610
Hussey, Ruth 20, 645
Hussman, Ron 865
Hustable, Vicky 1269
Hustler 981
Huston, Brick 1189
Huston, Carol 2269
Huston, Karen 1059
Huston, William
1683
Hutchins, Will
649, 816
Hutchinson,
Bill 1158
Hutchinson,
Josephine 1090
Hutson, Lee
1597, 1714
Hutton, Betty 66, 257
Hutton, Jim 662,
856, 1061, 1064,
1102, 1108, 1150,
1156, 1301, 1659
Hutton, Lauren
1170, 1691
Hutton, Timothy
1679

Huy, Duc 1800
Huyck, Willard 2266
Hyde, Bruce 792, 935
Hyde, Jacqueline
1656, 1971
Hyde-White, Wilfred
822, 863, 880,
1028, 1859
Hyland, Diana
803, 846
Hyland, Diana 771
Hylands, Scott
1073, 1117, 1320,
1395, 1469
Hyman, Barton 1963
Hyman, Charles
H. 2188
Hyman, Earl 782
Hyman, Mac 290

I

I Am a Lawyer 321
I and Claudie 765
**I Cover the
Waterfront** 84
I Do, I Don't
1600, 1913
I Dream of Jeannie
1764
**I Gave at the
Office** 1996
I Gotta be Me 1224
I Love a Mystery
91, 972
**I Love Her
Anyway** 1795
**I Love My
Doctor** 650
I Married a Bear 976
I Married a Dog 597
I Remember Caviar
386, 497
I Spy 1596
I Was a Bloodhound
309
I, Mickey Spillane 45
I-Man 2093
Iacangelo, Peter 2194

Iannicelli, Ray 2174
**Ida Lupino
Presents** 579
Idelson, Bill
1307, 1541
Idette, Patricia 2015
Idle, Eric 2253
If I Had a Million
1228
**If I Love You,
Am I Trapped
Forever?** 1269
**If You Knew
Sammy** 2214
**If You Knew
Tomorrow** 263
IFA 1241
Ihnat, Steve
921, 1048
Ikeda, Thomas 2041
Illes, Robert 2122
Ilson, Saul 1137,
1366, 1926, 1948
Ilson-Chambers
Productions
1137, 1366
Imada, Jeff, 1862
Imagine
Entertainment
2136, 2202, 2204,
2250, 2257
Imhoff, Gary
1629, 1672
Immel, Jerrold 1445,
1535, 1559, 1680,
1802, 1854, 1864,
1879, 1882, 1972
Impatient Heart
1104
Impostor 1294
Impulse 436
*In Darkness
Waiting* 841
In Like Flint 1377
In Like Flynn 2029
In Name Only 1008
In Old Chicago 1382
**In Search of
America** 1075

In Security 1872
In the Dead of
Night 1250
In the Dead of the
Night 844
In the Lion's
Den 2156
In Trouble 1796
Inch, Kevin
2189, 2263
Incident at 125th
Street 1076
Incident in San
Francisco 1076
Incident on a Dark
Street 1167
Incredible Hulk
1643, 2266
Incredible Hulk
Returns 2264
Incredible Jewel
Robbery 461
Incredible Rocky
Mountain
Race 1592
Indemnity 264
Independence
2191
Independent
Television
Corporation 363
Indian Scout 227
Indiana Jones 1855
Indians 1594
Indict and
Convict 1187
Indictment 846
Indie Production
Company 2209
Ine, John 1780
Infiltrator 2171
Info C-3 1058
Ingalls, Don 1358,
1641, 2120
Ingels, Marty 550
Ingersoll, James
1429, 1641, 1986
Ingham, Barrie
1940, 2019

Ingledew, Rosalind
2001, 2180
Ingram, Barrie 1999
Ingram, Elisa 1057
Innes, Alexandria
2132
Innes, George 1841
Innes, Jean 869
Innes, Laura 2125
Innocent Jones 598
Inquest 437
Inside Danny
Baker 746
Inside Job 1183
Inside O.U.T. 1094
Insider 615, 903
Insinnia, Albert 1799
Inspector
General 376
Inspector Perez 1782
Instant Family 1493
Institute for
Revenge 1691
Intermedia
Entertainment
1901, 1906, 1927,
1952, 2082
International
Airport 2021
International
Television
Corporation 489
International
Theatre 8
Intertect 1188
Intrigue 2240
Invaders 758, 1678
Invasion of Johnson
County 1420
Invisible Woman
1942
Inwood, Steve 1906,
2025, 2218
Iquchi, Yoneo 768
Ireland, John 89,
1291, 1566
Irene 1830
Irizarry, Vincent 2146
Iron Cowboys 1848

Iron Horse 394, 513
Iron Horseman 394
Iron Man 904
Ironside 1029,
1289, 1425
Irvine, Paula 2186
Irving, Amy 1378
Irving, George S.
1627, 1702
Irving, Hollis
292, 595
Irving, Jules
1356, 1647
Irving, Richard 131,
471, 1124, 1160,
1356, 1514, 1934
Irving Brecher
Productions 111
Irwin, Carol 181
Irwin, Wynn 1308,
1465, 1511
Irwin Allen
Productions 1335,
1372, 1382
Is There a Doctor
in the House?
1095, 1224
Isaacs, Charles
112, 389
Isaacs, David
1483, 1755
Isarov, Boris 2219
Isacksen, Peter
1674
Isbell, Tom 2063,
2088, 2155, 2230
Isenberg, Gerald
I. 1129, 1251,
1252, 1303, 1408,
1490, 1491, 1492,
1828, 1861, 2090,
2200, 2211
Isis 1383
Island of the
Lost 945
Island Sons 2094
Islander 1565
Isn't It Shocking? 1254
Israel, Al 2065

Israel, Neal
2222, 2252
Istanbul Express
1002
It Happened One
Night 578
It Just So Happens
1763
It Pays to Be
Ignorant 367
It Takes a Thief 633
It's a Living 405
It's a Man's World 624
It's Always
Sunday 113
ITC Entertainment
993, 1039, 1127,
1158, 1321
Itkin, Paul Henry
1252
Ito, Robert
1256, 1779
Itzin, Gregory
1790, 2189
Ivan Tors
Productions 945,
1032, 1057, 1543
Ives, Burl 428, 529,
794, 1685
Ivey, Lela 1967
Ivy League 310
Izuhara, Shannon
1902

J

J. Digger Doyle
1815
J. Levine Productions
837
J.T. 1178
Jabara, Paul 1252,
1361, 1498
Jack Chertok
Productions
27, 934
Jack Flash 1706
Jack Webb
Productions 820

Jackie and
Darlene 1529
Jackie Cooper
Productions 771
Jackman, Billie 1829
Jacko, 2265
Jacks, Robert L. 733,
930, 1194, 1248,
1367, 1403, 1656,
1748, 2169
Jackson, Anne 642
Jackson, Christopher
2188
Jackson, Colette 957
Jackson, Cornwell
1061
Jackson, Gail
Patrick 207
Jackson, George 2203
Jackson, Gordon
1127, 1524
Jackson, Harry 202
Jackson, Jamie
Smith 1297
Jackson, Jeanine 2188
Jackson, Kate 1128,
1155, 1166, 1620
Jackson, Mallie 1874
Jackson, Mary 1787,
1811, 2207
Jackson, Sammy 470,
909, 941, 963
Jackson, Sherry 645,
1291, 1316, 1317,
1472, 1612
Jackson, Tyrone 1466
Jackson, Victoria
1981
Jackson County
Jail 1567
Jacksons 387
Jacobi, Lou 767, 879,
1091, 1164, 1217,
1690, 1769, 2017
Jacobi, Scott 1284
Jacobs, Arthur P.
1149, 1155
Jacobs, David
2003, 2088

Jacobs, Gary 2135
Jacobs, Michael 2255
Jacobs, Parker 1902
Jacobs, Peter
Morrison 1125
Jacobs, Rachel 1826
Jacobs, Ronald 1010,
1580, 1619, 1624
Jacobs, Seamon 1825
Jacobson, Danny
1901, 1996
Jacobson, Jill
1790,1996
Jacobson, Larry 1873
Jacoby, Billy 1958
Jacoby, Bobby 2099
Jacoby, Coleman 549
Jacoby, Jake 2192
Jacoby, Laura
1845, 2110
Jacoby, Scott
1215, 2175
Jacques and Jill 176
Jadda Productions
2009
Jaeckel, Richard 655,
814, 1233, 1445,
1717, 1794
Jaffe, Sam 1105,
1242, 1326
Jaffe, Seth 2049
Jaffe, Taliesin 2072
Jagger, Dean 474,
564, 1076,
1235, 1249
Jake's Beat 2192
Jake's Journey 2224
Jake's M.O. 2192
Jake's Way 1744
James, Brion 1546,
1745, 1885,
1955, 2126
James, Clifton
1321, 1355
James, Ed 518
James, Emrys 2219
James, Gennie
2137, 2248
James, Godfrey 1886

James, Hawthorn
2195
James, John Thomas
922, 927,
1059, 1647
James, Michael 1020
James, Scot
Saint 2186
James, Sheila 663,
1465, 2221
James, Steve 1788,
2128, 2258
James, Susan Saint
912, 1096,
1426, 1869
James Boys 1895
James Michener
Presents a
South Pacific
Adventure 94
James-Reese, Cyndi
1923, 1971
Jameson, Jerry
1351, 1420
Jameson, Joyce 763,
892, 1021, 1089,
1320, 1656
Jamin, Milt 1795
Jamison, J.M. 2261
Jamison-Olsen,
Mikki 1593
Jan and Dean
Show 868
Jan Clayton
Show 372
Jane, Margot 1004
Jane Ahoy 239
Jane Wyman Theatre
250, 260
Janes, Loren 169
Janes, Robert 1618,
1648, 1719,
1721
Janis, Conrad 112,
1463, 1505, 1543
Janis, Ryan 1878
Janiss, Vivi 520
Janover, Michael
2079, 2134

Jansen, Jim 1309
Janson, Len 1968
Janssen, David 615,
1259, 1373
Janus Productions
1683
Jarbo Pierce Story 842
Jarchow, Brooke
A. 2034
Jaress, Jill 1046
Jarnagin, Nancy 1849
Jarnagin, Paul,
Jr. 1660
Jaroslow, Ruth 2109
Jarrell, Andy 1174
Jarrett, Renne 1075,
1279, 1320, 1374
Jarrett 1229
Jarrett of K
Street 474
Jarvis, Bill 1256
Jarvis, Graham
1448, 1676, 1789,
1825, 1948
Jarvis, Robert 1867
Jarvis, Ron 1992
Jason, Harvey 1050,
1212, 1438
Jason, Peter
1032, 1969
Jason, Rick 74,
1010, 1036
Jason, Robert 1902
Jaws 1397, 2169
Jay, Tony 2098, 2146
Jay Hawkers 604
Jaygee Productions
1968, 2041
Jaynes, Michael 1744
Jayston, Michael
1379, 1380
J. Digger Doyle 1815
Jean Lafitte 1372
Jed Productions 1273
Jeffcoat, Donnie 2265
Jefferson, Herbert,
Jr. 1160
Jefferson, Tony 1595
Jeffersons 1931

Jeffreys, Anne 176, 699, 844, 1155
Jeffries, Herb 1229, 1300
Jellison, Robert D. 18
Jenkins, Allen 7
Jenkins, Carol Mayo 2007
Jenkins, Dan 1103
Jenkins, Gordon 1404
Jenkins, Jean 1784
Jenkins, Ken 2235
Jenkins, Larry 1595
Jenkins, Mark 1091
Jenkins, Paul 1296, 1424
Jenkins, Richard 1888
Jenks, Frank 21
Jenner, Barry 1800, 2047
Jenni Productions 1511
Jennings, Brent 1888
Jennings and Jennings: A Family Practice 1971
Jens, Salome 1939, 2169
Jensen, Dick 1565
Jensen, Eileen 113
Jensen, Gail 1862
Jensen, Karen 920, 926, 972
Jenson, Roy 1210, 1337, 1617, 2115
Jeremiah of Jacob's Neck 1397
Jergens, Diane 113, 388, 502
Jergenson, Randy 1231
Jericho 475
Jeris, Nancy 821
Jerk 1940
Jerk, Too 1940
Jerome, Patti 1421
Jerry 1270
Jerry Adler Productions 1717

Jerry Thorpe Productions 2244
Jerry Tokofsky Productions 1605
Jersey Bounce 1783
Jessel, George 787
Jessie, Dewayne 1177
Jessup, Richard 1720
Jeter, James 1279, 1639
Jetsons 1439, 2227
Jigsaw 918
Jillian, Ann 808, 893, 1901
Jillson, Joyce 1518
Jim Dandy 483
Jim Ireland Meets the Giants 299
Jimmy Durante/ Eddie Hodges Show 580
Jimmy Durante Show 766
Jimmy Rodgers-Campus Show 343
J. Levine Productions 837
Jo's Cousins 1896
Joan Crawford Show 348
Joan Davis Enterprises 253
Joan Davis Show 525, 544
Joan of Arkansas 253
Joan Rivers Project 1707
Joanna 2017
Joaquin Murietta 1003, 1030
Jodelsohn, Anita 1624
J.O.E. and Michael 2030
J.O.E. & The Colonel 2042
J.O.E. and the Colonel 2030

Joe DiMaggio Show 177
Joe Hamilton Productions 1600
Joe Starr 829
Joelson, Ben 935
Joffe, Charles 1206, 1669
Jogadi/Elephant Productions 1459
John, Stephen 971
John and Yoko: A Love Story 2126
John Ford Presents 51
John Payne Show 519
John Rich Productions 1364, 1461
John Wayne Productions 110
Johnny Blue 1884, 1934
Johnny Come Lately 62
Johnny Dollar 668
Johnny Eager 379
Johnny Fletcher 447
Johnny Garage 1873
Johnny Guitar 322
Johnny Hawk 244
Johnny Mayflower 210
Johnny Moccasin 72
Johnny Nighthawk 211
Johnny Pilgrim 197
Johnny Ringo 479
Johnny Risk 265
Johnny Wildlife 275
Johns, Glynis 696, 1918
Johns, Milton 1158
Johns, Victoria 2221
Johnson, Alexandra 1914
Johnson, Amy 1531

Johnson, Anne-Marie 1995
Johnson, Arch 926, 1301, 1783
Johnson, Arnold 2090
Johnson, Arte 310, 1050, 1150, 1300, 1507
Johnson, Beej 1671
Johnson, Biff 1747
Johnson, Bill 1989
Johnson, Brett 1923
Johnson, Bruce 1175, 1221, 1574, 1770, 1794, 1944
Johnson, Charles Floyd 1422, 1783, 1788, 1814, 1881, 1985
Johnson, Chip 1641, 1655, 1692, 1906
Johnson, Clark 2253
Johnson, Coslough 1050, 1067
Johnson, Dale 1295
Johnson, Dennis 1601
Johnson, Don 1421, 1512, 1537, 1538, 1959, 2252
Johnson, Donna 1784
Johnson, Franklin 2117
Johnson, Georgann 390, 693, 1831, 1930
Johnson, Henry 2159
Johnson, J.J. 1186, 1368
Johnson, Jarrod 1387
Johnson, Jason 1595
Johnson, Jay 1930, 2050
Johnson, Keg 743
Johnson, Ken 1546, 1590, 1643, 1684, 2264
Johnson, Kyle 1078

Johnson, Lamont 164, 884, 958, 994
Johnson, Laura 1800
Johnson, Mark 1924
Johnson, Melodie 912, 972, 1472
Johnson, Monica 1551
Johnson, Monica McGowan 1343
Johnson, Rafer 921
Johnson, Reginald Vel 1548, 2266
Johnson, Robert 6
Johnson, Russell 1119, 1335, 1662, 1663, 1664
Johnson, Valorie 1171
Johnson, Van 454, 796, 1021, 1044, 1108, 1133, 1291, 1947
Johnsons Are Home 2225
Johnston, Amy 1658
Johnston, Jim 2127
Johnston, John Dennis 2217
Joker 33
Jolley, Norman 556, 695, 751, 1750
Jolley, Stanford 853
Jolly, Mike 2221
Jonas, Chad 2186
Jonas, Theodore 1688
Jones, Amanda 1384
Jones, Barbara O. 1472
Jones, Brad 1888
Jones, Buster 1641
Jones, Carol 1442
Jones, Carolyn 603
Jones, Cherry 1850, 2113
Jones, Christine 2211
Jones, Claude Earl 1503, 1504, 1781, 1955

Jones, Claylene 1745
Jones, Cody 1865
Jones, Dary 1048
Joens, Dean 380, 472, 603, 783, 808, 907, 1597, 1714, 1795
Jones, Fenton 1808
Jones, Hank 1123
Jones, Henry 463, 1142, 1163, 1189, 1190, 1820, 2072
Jones, J. Bill 1974
Jones, J.D. 1815
Jones, James 878
Jones, James Cellan 1370
Jones, Jeffrey 1925
Jones, Judith Bess 207
Jones, L.Q. 734, 1072, 1123, 1257, 1289, 1419, 1560, 1680
Jones, Melanie 2137
Jones, Mickey 1471, 1546, 1625, 1849, 1885
Jones, Morgan 1840
Jones, Quincy 2203
Jones, Rene 2200
Jones, Sam 1718, 2009, 2099, 2265
Jones, Shirley 459, 810, 955, 1351, 1879
Jones, Simon 2157
Jones, Stanley G. 670
Jones, Tim 2188
Jones, Tom 1786
Jong, Erica 2020
Joplin, Joneal 1355, 1842
Jordan, Alan 2029
Jordan, Beverly 64
Jordan, Christy 774
Jordan, Glenn 1325, 1339, 1443, 2044, 2104
Jordan, Harlan 1894
Jordan, James Carroll 1653, 1986

Jordan, Leslie 2165
Jordan, Richard 756, 1192
Jordan, Susannah 879
Jordan, William 1210, 1322
Jordan Chance 1647
Jorden, Jan 1633
Josef, George 2093
Josefsberg, Milt 62, 457, 1659, 1794
Joseph, Allen 772
Joseph, Kevin 2266
Joseph, Robert 1100, 1278
Joseph P. Byrne-Lou Step Productions 1843
Josephine Little 514
Josephson, Jeffrey 1955, 2042, 2119
Josh 'n' Willie T. 1548
Joshua, Larry 2017
Joshua Tree 1584
Joshua's World 1745
Josie and Joe 625
Joslyn, Allyn 384
Jourdan, Louis 1028
Journey into Fear 919
Joy, Christopher 1604
Joyce, Elaine 1082, 1751, 1951
Joyce, Jimmy 853
Joyce, Rosalyn 1764
Joyce, Stephen 470, 2172
Joyce, Susan 1023
Joyce, William 322, 1586
Joyner, Michelle 2211
Jozak Productions 1303, 1408, 1490, 1491, 1492, 1861
JP 487
J.T. 1178
Juarbe, Israel 1991
Jude, Lee James 1958
Judge 736

Judge and Jake Wyler 1164, 1233
Judge Dee 1251
Judge Dee and the Haunted Monastery 1251
Judge Dee and the Monastery Murders 1251
Judgment Day 1847
Judy Canova Show 229, 337
Jueller, Marianne 2163
Julia, Raul 1262
Julian, Arthur 654, 660, 674, 1305, 1671
Julian, Charles 1623
Julian, Janet 1816
Julian, Joshua 2191
Julian, Laura 2246
Juliano, Lenny 1915
Julie Loves Rome 79
Jump, Gordon 1781, 1856, 1927, 1978, 2201
Jump Street 1669
June 254
June Allyson Show 390, 557, 565
Jung, Calvin 1717, 1906
Junger, Tina 2193
Jungle of Fear 850
Junior Miss 114
Jurado, Katy 933
Jurasik, Peter 1668, 1872, 2107
Jurist, Ed 311, 813, 890
Jury, Richard 955
Just a Coupla Guys 1783
Just an Old Sweet Song 1469
Just Another Polish Wedding 1422
Just Married 1963

Just Plain Folks
63, 2077
Just Us Kids 1629
Justice, Katherine
884, 1324, 1642
Justice of the
Peace 395
Justin Case 2201
Justman, Robert
H. 1260, 2025
Juttner, Christian
1292
Juttner, Shelly 1292
Juvenile Hall 1049

K

K-Nine Patrol 618
Ka'ahea, Ed 1565
Kaahea, Sherly 1815
Kaake, Jeff 2024
Kabott, Frankie 855
Kaczmarek,
Jane 1856
Kadi, Nicholas 2132
Kadish, Ben
1700, 1771
Kadison, Ellis 632
Kagan, Diane 1356
Kagan, Jeremy
Paul 1251
Kagan, Michael
1632, 1669, 1810
Kagan, Steve 1544
Kagen, David 2151
Kahan, Judy
1765, 1923
Kahan, Steve 2195
Kahana, Kim 1544
Kahn, Bernard
1452, 1625
Kahn, Dave 1929
Kahn, Madeline
1533, 2072
Kahn, Norman 771
Kalcheim, Lee 1366
Kalder, Eric 1408
Kalem, Toni 1266,
1875, 2078

Kalember, Patricia
2041
Kaliban, Robert 954
Kalish, Austin 1312,
1340, 1557, 1598,
1603, 1637, 1704,
1897, 2251
Kalish, Bruce 1732,
1820, 2265
Kalish, Irma 1312,
1340, 1557, 1598,
1603, 1637, 1704,
1897, 2251
Kallis, Stanley 737,
824, 1124, 1126,
1369, 1588
Kamekona,
Danny 1565
Kamel, Stanley 1425,
1642, 1966, 1988
Kamen, Douglas
Mark 2211
Kamen, Michael 1652
Kamen, Milt 1164
Kamin, Dan 2261
Kamm, Kris 2141,
2212, 2236
Kamman, Bruce 31
Kan, Victor 1256
Kanaly, Steve 1255
Kandel, Stephen
880
Kane, Arnold
1154, 1977
Kane, Artie 1914,
1970, 2149
Kane, Billy 2231
Kane, Bruce
1579, 1811
Kane, Jackson
D. 1327
Kane, Joel 809
Kane, Joseph 2112
Kane, Josh 2154,
2230
Kane, Richard
2219
Kangaroos in the
Kitchen 1897

Kanin, Fay 1145,
1196
Kanin, Garson
421, 625
Kansas City Massacre
1255, 1322
Kanter, Hal 457,
806, 821, 900,
930, 1533, 1880
Kapelos, John 2183
Kaplan, Brooke 1637
Kaplan, E. Jack 1874
Kaplan, Elliot
1318, 1328
Kaplan, Gabe 1703
Kaplan, Mandy 1924
Kaplan, Marvin
204, 654, 763,
955, 1027
Kaplan, Sol 985
Kaplan Company
1703
Kaplowitz,
Herb 1638
Kapp, Joe 1162
Kaprall, Bo 1626
Kaprall, Robert
1483
Kaproff, Dana
1514, 2170
Karabatsos, Ron
1885, 2017
Karanja, Jayne 2248
Karb, David 1254
Karen, James 1444,
1620, 1672
Karen Valentine
Show 1179, 1239
Karew, Diana 1482
Karin, Rita
2041, 2046
Karlan, Richard 213
Karlatos, Olga 1801
Karlen, John 1255,
1322, 1348, 1560,
1618, 1714
Karlin, Fred 1296,
1475, 1482, 1619,
1620, 1621, 1679,

1782, 1919, 1920,
1936, 2090
Karliski, Steve 877
Karlson, Phil 750
Karman, Janice 1586
Karnes, Robert
164, 1585
Karp, David 486
Karpf, Elinor 1098
Karpf, Stephen 1098
Karr, David 877
Karr, Joan 1047
Karras, Alex 1202
Karron, Richard
1437, 1608, 1661,
1807, 2226
Kascia, Mary
Anne 1620
Kasdorf, Lenore
1277, 2082
Kasha, Al 1355, 2014
Kasha, Lawrence
1263, 1332, 1345,
1676, 1722
Kasner, Jillian 1389
Kasper, Gary 2030
Kass, Jerome 1190
Kassul, Art
1639, 1866
Kasten, Hiram 2222
Kasznar, Kurt 318
Kate and the
Mississippi
Queen 1589
Kate Bliss and the
Ticker Tape
Kid 1534
Kates, Bernard 644
Katkov, Norman 453
Katleman, Harris
1445, 1693, 1725,
1774, 1775
Katmandu 1708
Katon, Roseanne
1834, 2213
Katt, William 2133
Katz, Allan 1458,
1628, 1760,
1824, 1868

Katz, Eugene Ray 1099

Katz, Gloria 2266

Katz, Marty 2035

Katz, Peter 1518, 1690

Katz, Stuart 1868

Katz, William 1281

Katzin, Lee H. 1235, 1347, 1475, 1477, 1619, 1908, 1982, 2048, 2087

Katzka, Gabe 2109

Katzman, Sam 834

Katzman, Sherrill Lynn 1581

Katzoff, Marvin 1796

Katzin, Lee H. 2087

Kauffman, John 1571

Kaufman, Andy 1439

Kaufman, Bob 893

Kaufman, David 2266

Kaufman, Leonard B. 1280, 1466, 1801, 2094

Kaufman, Robert 810, 1215, 1343

Kavner, Julie 1925

Kawal, Leslie 1986

Kawaye, Janice 1944

Kay, Beatrice 726

Kay, Dianne 1871

Kay, Dusty 1762, 2035

Kay, Mary Ellen 156

Kayden, Tony 1748

Kayden, William 1061, 1583, 1799

Kayden/Gleason Productions 1799

Kaye, Caren 1496, 1912, 2047

Kaye, Gordon 567

Kaye, Judy 1735

Kaye, Stubby 112, 460, 908, 1017, 1391, 1812

Kayro Productions 987, 1016

Kazaele, William 1592

Kazan, Elia 1299

Kazan, Lainie 1910, 1940

Kazann, Vito 1779

Kazann, Zitto 1451, 1565, 1887

Keach, James 1589, 1813, 1919

Keach, Stacey, Sr. 1585, 1643

Keach, Stacy 1747

Keale, Moe 1648

Keams, Geraldine 1594

Kean, Betty 1990, 2124

Keanan, Staci 2255

Keane, James 1872

Keane, Kerrie 2043, 2115, 2149, 2186

Keane, Tom 2249

Keaner, Elliot 2197

Kearney, Carolyn 825

Kearney, Gene 1100

Kearney, Mark 1056

Kearns, Sandra 1579, 1887

Keating, Charles 2171

Keating, Fred 20

Keating, Larry 728

Keaton, Buster 627

Keaton, Michael 1964

Keats, Robert 1770

Keats, Steven 1340, 1606, 1704, 1992, 2245

Keays-Byrne, Hugh 2208

Kee Cheung, George 1934

Keefe, Adam 913

Keefe, Kelly 1842

Keefer 1441

Keefer, Don 756, 1180, 1316, 1619

Keegan, Terry 1816

Keegans 1338

Keehne, Virginia 2070

Keeler, Brian 2046

Keeler, Ruby 763

Keena, Tom 1777

Keenan, Michael 1756

Keene, Carolyn 128

Keener, Catherine 2102

Keener, Elliot 1860

Keep, Stephen 1611

Keep an Eye on Denise 1203

Keep the Faith 1136, 1204

Keeping Up with the Joneses 1154

Kehoe, Jack 1339

Keitel, Harvey 1530

Keith, Brian 134, 737, 1131, 1301, 1353

Keith, Garren 1604, 1823

Keith, Lawrence 1370

Keith, Robert 329

Kelada, Asaad 1728, 1769, 1889, 1890, 1896, 2054, 2073, 2138

Kell, Joseph 2245

Kellard, Phil 2154

Kellard, Rick 1582, 1728, 1812, 1818, 1848, 1922, 2205

Keller, Sheldon 763

Kellerman, Sally 878, 1856, 1930, 2222

Kellerman, Susan 1993

Kelley, DeForest 265, 523, 666, 921

Kelley, John T. 1168

Kelley, Richard 2189

Kelley, William 1816

Kellin, Mike 1099, 1182, 1192, 1356, 1771

Kelljan, Bob 1609

Kellman, Barnet 2136, 2139, 2167

Kellman, Rick 915

Kellogg, John 929, 1072

Kellogg, Marjorie 164

Kellogg, Ray 890

Kelly, April 1546, 1949

Kelly, Barry 603, 797

Kelly, Brian 1021, 1059, 1058

Kelly, Calvin 2052

Kelly, Daren 1732

Kelly, Gene 454

Kelly, Jack 247, 776, 851, 920, 974, 1448, 1785

Kelly, John T. 757

Kelly, Margo 2006

Kelly, Nancy 1294

Kelly, Patsy 819

Kelly, Paula 1756, 1915, 2173

Kelly, Roz 1363

Kelly, Sean 718, 1022

Kelly's Kids 1240

Kelly's Kingdom 891

Kelman, Ricky 650

Kelton, Pert 767

Kelton, Richard 1445

Kemmer, Ed 450, 704, 738

Kemmerling, Warren 1468

Kemp, Barry 1872, 2016

Kemp, Brandis 1930

Kemp, Jeremy 1441

Kemp, Sally 1260, 1566, 1796, 1843

Kemp, Tom 1888

Kempeter, Vanessa 1127

Kempley, Walter 1018
Kendis, William 18, 268
Kenin, Alexa 1459
Kennedy, Adam 7
Kennedy, Arthur 76, 782, 1119
Kennedy, Betty 1904
Kennedy, Burt 800, 1282, 1534, 1656, 1748, 2081
Kennedy, George 1633, 1841, 1909, 2021
Kennedy, Jayne 1512
Kennedy, Joseph 308
Kennedy, Leon Isaac 1604
Kennedy, Mimi 2079, 2134
Kennedy, Richard 1477
Kennedy, Sam 1238
Kennedy, Sarah 1198, 1638, 1722
Kennely, David Hume 2269
Kenney, H. Wesley 1332, 1391
Kensit, Patsy 1879
Kent, Enid 1849
Kent, Janice 1696, 1929
Kent, Paul 1183
Kent, Suzanne 1927
Kenwith, Herbert 1032, 1044, 1308, 1758, 1826, 1827, 1901
Kenya 2215
Kenyon, Curtis 1721
Kenyon, Sandy 1803
Keough, Dan 1123
Kepler, Shell 1553
Kerew, Diana 1569
Kerman, Janice 1587
Kern, Brad 2189
Kern, James 534

Kern, James V. 62
Kerner, Jordan 2135
Kerner, Noberto 2046
Kerns, Joanna 1971
Kerns, Sandra 1451
Kerr, Elizabeth 1558
Kerr, Jay 1768
Kerr, John 1079
Kerr, M.E. 1269
Kerr, William 1992
Kerschner, Irvin 451, 585
Kersh, Kathy 957
Kershaw, Whitney 2003, 2060, 2217
Kershner, Irvin 611
Kerwin, Brian 1559, 1650, 1895
Kerwin, Lance 1292, 1698, 1840
Kessler, Bruce 1518, 1537, 1789, 2006
Kessler, Don 1903
Ketchens, Damon 1209
Ketchum, Dave 1150, 1221
Ketchum, David 1238
Key Tortuga 1816
Key West 1230
Keyes, Chip 1909
Keyes, Doug 1909
Keyes, Joe, Jr. 1182
Keys, William 1594
Khambatta, Persis 1517
Khrys One Inc. Productions 2146
Kibbee, Roland 772, 846, 861, 1159, 1418, 1527
Kibbee Hates Fitch 767, 1217
Kicks 912
Kidder, Margot 1293
Kierney, Gene R. 1336
Kiger, Bob 1638

Kiger, Robbie 1944, 2007
Kilbourne, Wendy 1968
Kiley, Richard 264, 1076, 1321
Killer Who Wouldn't Die 1376
Killin' Cousin 1750
Killing Stone 1590
Killmond, Frank 662, 717
Kilogie, Ron 2189
Kilpatrick, DeCarla 1809
Kilpatrick, Lincoln 846, 1060, 1451, 1469, 1471
Kim, Evan 1409, 1953
Kim, Rob 1916
Kim Finally Cuts You-Know-Whos Apron Strings 1138
Kimber, Les 1259
Kimbrough, Charles 2038
Kimbrough, Clint 1096
Kimmel, Bruce 1505, 1633
Kimmel, Harold 2135
Kimmell, Dana 1697, 1808, 1930, 1977
Kimmins, Kenneth 1768, 2090
Kincaid 753
Kincaid, Jason 1617
Kincaird, Aron 1260
Kind, Richard 2180
Kind, Rosalind 1704
Kinder, Kurt 2237
Kinfolks 1470
King, Alan 549, 831, 1106, 1462, 1548, 1632, 2102
King, Brett 208
King, Carole 2231

King, Christopher 701
King, Dennis 182
King, Freeman 1438
King, Louis 482
King, Mabel 1940
King, Mark 1598
King, Meegan 1638
King, Paul 924, 1510
King, Perry 1692, 2006, 2213
King, Robert 2193
King, Stephen 1698
King, Walter Wolf 916
King, Wright 395, 1586, 1587
King, Zalman 877
King Brothers 962
King-Hitzig Productions 1462, 1548, 1632
King of the Building 2157
King of the Road 1549
Kinghorn, David 2008
Kinghorn, David J. 2083
Kingi, Henry 2086
Kingpins 2158
Kings of Broadway 691
Kingskey, Leonid 550
Kingsley, Sidney 133, 329
Kingston Trio 661
Kinnear, Christopher 1944
Kinnear, Roy 1127
Kino, Lloyd 768, 912
Kinon, Richard 643, 8, 1389, 1392
Kinoy, Ernest 681, 879, 1130, 1265, 1907
Kirby, Bill 1310

Kirby, Bruce 1350, 1713, 1923
Kirby, Bruce, Sr. 1435, 1436, 1601
Kirby, George 1332, 1431, 2188
Kirgo, George 1317, 1468, 1526, 1620, 1862
Kirkconnell, Claire 2094, 2216
Kirkland, Jeff 1660
Kirkland, Sally 1322, 1415, 1429, 1722, 1730, 1979
Kirkpatrick, Jess 765
Kirksey, Dianne 1455
Kirshner, Don 1054, 1413, 1499
Kiser, Terry 1265, 1483, 1506, 1583, 1992, 2196
Kiser, Virginia 1230
Kiss Me Again, Stranger 1168
Kiss Me, Kill Me 1369
Kissin' Cousins 834
Kivel, Barry 2042
Kjellin, Alf 1468
Klane, Robert 1262, 1272, 1332, 1452, 1599, 1606, 1709, 1797, 1943
Klare, Gary 2041
Klecker, Jay 2158
Klee, Lawrence 266
Kleeb, Helen 1061
Klein, Dennis 2222
Klein, Jill 2199
Klein, Larry 819, 833
Klein, Paul 1764, 1777
Klein, Robert 2075
Kleinschmitt, Carl 1065, 1274
Kleiser, Randall 1444
Kleiss, Jane 2218

Klemperer, Werner 902, 1808
Klenhard, Walter 2065
Klenman, Norman 1377
Kletter, Richard 2096, 2144
Kleven, Max 1255, 1595
Kline, Richard 1977
Kline, Steve 2034, 2170, 2269
Kling, Woody 1457
Klinger, Natalie 1952, 1974
Klondike Lou 438
Klous, Patricia 1934
Klugman, Adam 2046
Klugman, Jack 853, 974, 1222, 1301
Klune, Donald C. 2265
Knapp, Robert 548
Knaub, Jim 1827
Knell, David 1812, 2102
Knepper, Rob 2195
Kneubuhl, John 129, 319
Knickerbocker, Willis 1816, 2129
Knickley, Alfred 846
Knight, Christopher 1764
Knight, Don 1163, 1213, 1510, 1680, 1688, 2021
Knight, Ed 1616
Knight, Elyse 2174
Knight, Gladys 2190
Knight, Jack 1324, 1400, 1424
Knight, Shirley 829, 918, 1321
Knight, Ted 1238, 1910
Knight of the South Seas 9

Knight Rider 2002
Knight's Gambit 847
Knootz, Gregory 1660
Knootz, Jeffrey 1660
Knopf, Christopher 704, 1072, 1257, 2085, 2242
Knops, Chris 482
Knots Landing 2088
Knotts, Don 972, 1331, 1674
Knowles, Patrick 202
Knox, Mona 115
Knox, Terence 2030
Knudsen, Peggy 649
Knudson, Gunilla 1004
Knudson, Kurt 1568
Kobart, Ruth 1974
Kobritz, Richard 1698
Koch, Howard 1113, 1301
Koch, Jacquie 2120
Koch, Kenneth R. 2034, 2120
Koenig, Walter 1234
Kogan, Arnie 1438
Kogan, Milt 1388, 1507, 1566, 1971
Kohen, Buzz 1334
Kohner, Frederick 1004, **1110**
Kohnert, Mary 2082
Kohoon, Patti 1516
Kojak 1402, 1478, 2046
Kojak: The Belarus File 2046
Kojak: The Price of Justice 2046, 2172
Kolb, Gideon 1380
Kolb, Mina 1921
Kolbe, Winrich 1815, 2002, 2130
Kolber, Larry 877
Kolchak: The Night Stalker 1009

Kolden, Scott 1085
Kolima, Lee 1229
Kolldehoff, Reinhard 1058
Koltenmeyer's Kindergarten 31
Komack, James 528, 644, 1069, 1114, 1219, 1417, 1465, 1553, 1602, 2157
Komack Company 1417, 1465, 1553, 1602, 2157
Komorowska, Liliana 2174
Kona Coast 994
Kondazian, Karen 2164
Kondek, Jean Ross 1688
Kondon, Karen 1124
Konigsberg, Frank 1455, 1484, 1542, 1550, 1741, 1977
Konner, Larry 1996
Konrad, Dorothy 766, 1434, 1506
Koo, Janet 2194
Kooch, Guich 1768, 1904
Koolsber, William K. 1324
Koons, Bob 1259
Kopell, Bernie 821, 1345, 1414
Kopins, Karen 2003, 2146
Kopit, Arthur 1638
Kops 1746
Kordick, Moya 2257
Korey, Stanley 1709
Korman, Harvey 1527, 1942
Korper, Rene 125
Kort, Dennis 1266
Korty, John 1129
Korwin, Devra 1254
Koska and His Family 1218

Koss, Alan 1914
Koss, Kamie 2219
Kotcheff, Ted 1130
Koteas, Elias 2064
Kotero, Patty 2002
Kotto, Yaphet
  1367, 2190
Koustik, Arthur 2066
Kout, Wendy 2155
Kovack, Nancy 893
Kovacs, Ernie
  309, 627
Kove, Martin 2239
Kowal, Stefanie 2031
Kowalski, Bernard
  L. 582, 736, 737,
  779, 1128, 1132,
  1340, 1400, 1515,
  1617, 1720, 1775,
  1934, 2259
Kowalski, Peter 1617
Kowalski's Way 2193
**Kowalsky Loves
  Ya** 2193
Kowboys 1054
Kozak, Elliot 1415
Kozell, Michael 2220
Kozoll, Michael 1621
Kraft, Robert 2193
*Kraft Mystery
  Theatre* 776
Kraft Suspense Theatre
  781, 841, 845, 847,
  848, 850, 853
*Kraft Television
  Theatre* 858
Kragen, Ken 1037
Kramer, Eric 2264
Kramer, George 1222
Kramer, Jeffrey
  1439, 1533
Kramer, Stanley
  149, 393, 1307
Kramer, Stepfanie
  1818, 2006
Krantz, Judith 1801
Krasna, Norman 501
Krasne, Phil 41,
  480, 526

Krasny, Paul 1126,
  1189, 1278, 1476,
  1565, 1800
Kraushaar, Raoul 679
Krebs, Susan
  1701, 2266
Krell, Mac 1036
Krenn, Sherrie
  2251
Kreppel, Paul 1932
Kriesa, Chris
  1971, 2021
Krinski, Sandy 1411,
  1627, 1739
Krone, Fred 7
Kronick, William
  1202
Kronish, Steve 2203
Kronman, Harry
  1013
Kruger, Otto 736
Krumholz, Chester
  1478, 1641
Kruschen, Jack 1006,
  1204, 1295, 1592
Kubenko, Nick 2034
Kubik, Alex 1749
Kudzu 1874
Kugel, Carl 1863
Kuhn, Steven 2208
Kukoff, Bernie 1271,
  1341, 1362, 1435,
  1436, 1665, 1710,
  1796, 1823, 2034
Kukoff/Harris
  Productions 1796
Kulak, William
  Vincent 1936
Kulcsar, Mike 1655
Kulick, Danny 670
Kulik, Buzz 206,
  693, 732, 756,
  832, 1117, 1167,
  1259, 1298, 1511
Kulky, Henry 117
Kulp, Nancy 18,
  74, 307, 647,
  658, 679, 1808
Kuluva, Will 922

Kung Fu 2115
*Kung Fu: The
  Legend Continues*
  1937, 2115
**Kung Fu: The
  Movie** 2115
**King Fu: The Next
  Generation**
  2115, 2173
Kupacek, Linda 1259
Kupperman, Alvin
  1409, 1494
Kuri, John 1853
Kurland, John 1764
Kurnitz, Harry
  2014
Kurtz, Marcia Jean
  1231, 1370, 1817
Kurtz, Swoosie
  1478
Kurtzman, Katy
  1588, 1597, 1951
Kusatsu, Clyde 1366,
  1562, 1951, 1973,
  1982, 2065
Kushida, Beverly
  1251
Kuss, Richard 1972
Kuzyk, Mimi 2092
Kwan, Betty 1655
Kwan, Nancy 1916
Kwasman, Sam 1490
**Kwimpers of New
  Jersey** 748
Kwouk, Burt 1127
Kydd, Sam 262
Kyle, David 1518

L

La Femme 538
LaBell, Gene 1908
LaBelle, Gene 1782
Labiosa, David 2064
Laborteaux, Matthew
  1467, 1590, 1678
Lacher, Taylor 1513,
  1516, 1595,
  1618, 1651

Lachman, Mort
  1493, 1665, 1877,
  1930, 1946, 1991,
  1998, 2075, 2077,
  2125, 2139
Lacy, Jerry 1695,
  1786
Lacy, Tom 1253
**Lacy and the
  Mississippi
  Queen** 1589
Ladd, Alan 310, 1353
Ladd, Cheryl
  1523, 1719
Ladd, David 636
Ladies 1943
Ladies in Blue 1713
La Due, Joe 1447
Lady Law 183
Lady Luck 1219
Laemmle, Nina 213
Lafayette, John 2127
Lafferty, Marcy 1148
Lafferty, Perry 642,
  665, 1454, 1495,
  1577, 1581, 2176
LaFleur, Art 1942,
  1976, 2188
LaFrenais, Ian 1364,
  1461, 1738, 1797
LaGava, Tony 2269
LaGioia, John 1888
LaHendro, Bob 1497
Lahr, Bert 456, 797
Lahti, Christine 1451
Lai, Francis 1058
Laine, Frankie 362
Laird, Jack 774, 781,
  902, 906, 912,
  967, 1100, 1115,
  1157, 1226, 1814
Laird, Michael 1157
Lake, Florence 1268
Lakin, Howard 2033
Lakin, Rita 1743
Lakso, Ed 1615
LaLanne, Jack 1748
LaLoggia, Frank
  1333, 1527

Lam, Wilson 2091

Lamas Corporation 1619

Lamas, Fernando 332, 925, 1619

Lamas, Lorenzo 1465, 1553

Lamb, Guthrie 846

Lambert, Doug 744

Lambert, Jane 1387

Lambert, Jody 2085

Lambert, Paul 1316

Lambie, Joe 1958

Lambrinos, Vassili 894

Lamm, Karen 1615

LaMond, Bill 2032

LaMond, Jo 2032

L'Amour, Louis 1882

Lampel, Deborah 1818

Lampert, Zohra 1182, 1437

Lan, Hsai Ho 1256

Lancaster, Burt 350

Lancaster, Stuart 1487

Lanchester, Elsa 1008, 1606

Land, Judy 818

Land, Paul 2064

Land of Hope 1398

Land's End 973

Landau, Martin 828, 1169, 1664, 2115, 2196

Lander, Diane 1637

Landers, Audrey 1546, 1767, 1892, 2132

Landers, Harry 23, 657

Landers, Judy 1485, 1665, 1767, 1781, 2152

Landers, Matt 1607, 1754

Landers, Muriel 1297

Landesberg, Steve 1329, 1810

Landey, Clayton 1980

Landham, Sonny 2033

Landis, John 2076

Landmark Show 10

Landon, Michael 265, 314, 413, 814, 1081, 1590

Landon, Landon and Landon 1732, 1820

Landor, Jenifer 2248

Landor, Rosalyn 2112

Landrum, Teri 1874

Landry, Gail 1720

Landry, Karen 2129

Landry, Ron 1622

Landsberg, David 1628, 1631, 1978

Landsberg, Valerie 1672

Landsburg, Alan 1209, 1679, 1689, 1742, 1930, 2110

Landsbury, Angela 2175

Landzaat, Andre 1441

Lane, Bill 1644

Lane, Brian Alan 2267

Lane, Campbell 2093, 2117

Lane, Carla 1659

Lane, Charlie 67, 463, 658, 1163, 1808, 1891, 1912 307

Lane, Elizabeth 1650

Lane, Jeffrey 2045

Lane, Jocelyn 920

Lane, Michael 1564

Lane, Nancy 1701, 2019

Lane, Scott 614

Lane Slate Productions 2192

Laneuville, Eric 1177, 1300, 1345

Lanfield, Sidney 309, 554, 652

Lang, Charley 1701

Lang, Doreen 1004, 1326, 1396

Lang, Richard 1451, 1516, 1917, 1973, 2029, 2115

Langdon, Sue Ane 497, 760, 869, 1308

Lange, Hope 1396, 2064

Lange, Kelly 1846

Lange, Michael 2034

Lange, Ted 1177

Langella, Frank 1253, 1372, 2222

Langenkamp, Heather 2066

Langland, Liane 2148

Langner, Christine 2003

Langton, Paul 727

Langton, Simon 2215

Lanier, Susan 1412, 1557, 1626

Lanin, Jay 701

Lankford, Kim 1490

Lanning, Jerry 765, 1055

Lannom, Les 1373, 1397, 1589, 2099, 2151

Lanny and Isabelle 2202

Lansbury, Bruce 1074, 1406, 1419, 1476, 2196

Lansing, Joi 74

Lansing, Robert 628, 881, 1336, 1513, 1652, 1987, 2047

Lanteau, William 819, 1825, 1930

Lantz, Jim 905

LaPage, Kimberly 1531

LaPera, Sal 2046

LaPiere, Georganne 1421

LaPlaca, Alison 1924

Larbey, Bob 1925

Larch, John 520, 722, 1096, 1245, 1254, 1587, 1847

Lardner, Ring 160

Laredo 910, 929

Larkin, John 606, 739, 751

Larkin, Kristin 1553

Larkin, Mary 1882

LaRoche, Mary 1279

La Rouche, Mary 600

LaRoy, Gloria 1488

Larroquette, John 1626, 1916

Larry, Sheldon 2063, 2085

Larry Gordon Productions 1308

Larry White Productions 1400, 1405

Larsen, Darrel 1068

Larson, Charles 1211, 1367, 1481

Larson, Glen A. 1224, 1506, 1565, 1617, 1771, 1778, 1779, 1865, 1866, 1933, 1954, 1992, 2002, 2029, 2265

Larson, J.C. 2265

Larson, Paul 1814

Larson, Robert 1317, 1328

LaRue, Jack 861

LaRue, Roger 2126

La Salle, John 611

La Salle, Richard 1101, 1335

Lascher, David 2262

Lashley, Jim 1999

Lashly, James 2183

Laskaway, Harris 1817
Laskin, Michael 1970
Laslo, Ernest A. 1252
Lasser, Louise 1109, 1273
Lassick, Sydney 1846
Lassie 56, 97, 189
Lassie: A New Beginning 1535
Last, Simon 1100
Last Angry Man 1252
Last Chance 1494
Last Clear Chance 848
Last Convertible 1692
Last Detail 1310
Last Frontier 417
Last Hours Before Morning 1349
Last Marshall 217
Last Ninja 1916
Last of the Private Eyes 733
Last Resort 2095
Last Season 571
LaStarza, Roland 845
Las Vegas Beat 582
Las Vegas File 620
Las Vegas Story 195, 452
Late, Jason 2231
Late Night with David Letterman 1765
Latessa, Dick 1804
Latham, Cynthia 1638
Latham, Louise 1169, 1254, 1325, 1339, 1429, 2248
Lathan, Bobbi Jo 1925, 2096
Lathan, Stan 2200
Latitude Zero 11
LaTorre, Tony 1851
LaTourette, Frank 102, 288, 481

Latt, David 2042, 2144, 2267
Lau, Wesley 1089, 1167, 1210
Lauber, Ken 1709
Laudigan, William 733
Laugh-In 389, 1027, 1050
Laughlin, John 2065, 2217
Laughton, Charles 53, 154
Laurance, Matthew 2132
Lauren, Tammy 1798, 1898, 2079, 2134
Lauren Shuler-Donner Productions 2188
Laurence, Michael 1867
Laurence, Mitchell 2247
Laurenson, James 2096
Lauria, Dan 2041, 2046
Lauter, Ed 1349, 1585, 1865
Lava, William 880
Lavachielli, John 2201
Laven, Arnold 726, 1168
Lavender, Ian 2063
Lavender Hill Mob 860
Lavery, Emmet G., Jr. 1348
Lavin, Linda 1267
Lavin, Richard 2269
Law and Order 1424, 2241
Law & Order: Special Victims Unit 2241
Law & Order: Criminal Intent 2241
Law of the Land 1421

Lawford, Peter 67, 308, 1102
Lawlor, John 1408, 1477, 1550, 1567, 1636, 1839
Lawrence, Anthony 1372, 1404, 1515
Lawrence, Bruno 1989
Lawrence, Carol 1709, 1797
Lawrence, Elizabeth 846
Lawrence, Elliot 1873
Lawrence, Joey 1902, 1944
Lawrence, Linda 1608
Lawrence, Marc 1789
Lawrence, Stephen 1272, 2153
Lawrence, Vicki 1708, 2050
Lawrence Gordon Productions 1695, 1718
Lawson, Lee 1312
Lawson, Leigh 2147
Lawson, Richard 1680, 1682, 2012, 2245
Lawyer 816
Layton, Jerry 379, 433
Lazarre, Adam 737
Lazarus, Tom 1884, 1885
Lazarus Syndrome 1715
Lazenby, George 1512, 1937
Lazer, Peter 870
Leach, Britt 1200, 1567
Leach, Rosemary 1207
Leachman, Cloris 64, 625, 1176, 1211, 1274, 1840, 2251
Leacock, Philip 1158, 1230, 1539, 1594

Leaf, Paul 1596
Leak, Jennifer 1170
Leaneuville, Eric 2263
Lear, Norman 455, 494, 837, 855, 1034, 1549, 1999
Leary, Brianne 1807, 1870
Leary, David 2046
Leathernecks 276, 720
Leave It To Beaver 1016, 1929
Leavells, Calvin 2144
Leavitt, Gene 875
Leavitt, Ron 2124
LeBroux, Lee 1007
LeClair, Michael 1411
LeClerc, Jean 1940
Lecube, Graciela 2041
Ledding, Ed 1979
Leder, Reuben 1815, 1880, 1985, 2185, 2208
Lederer, Charles 144
Lederer, Suzanne 2261
Lee, Anna 1616, 1778
Lee, Brandon 2115, 2173
Lee, Cherylene 729, 769
Lee, Christopher 235, 1222, 1642, 1716, 1862
Lee, Dana 2120
Lee, Gilbert 1798
Lee, James 1351
Lee, Johnny 1036
Lee, Johnny Scott 1101
Lee, Karen 1952
Lee, Manfred 1102
Lee, Michael 2091
Lee, Michele 976, 1142, 1272, 1412

Lee, Peggy 419
Lee, Peter 940
Lee, Pinky 230
Lee, Robbie 1531
Lee, Robert 2245
Lee, Rose 1040
Lee, Rudy 117
Lee, Rusty 1623
Lee, Ruta 563,
   657, 1187
Lee, Ruth 264
Lee, Stan 1562
Lee, Stephen
   2028, 2227
Lee, Tasha 1119
Lee, Tim 1989
Lee, Tommy
   1150, 1251
Lee, Tony 1916
Lee, Virginia 1100
Lee-Sung, Richard
   1251
Leeds, Elissa 1685,
   1693, 1702
Leeds, Howard
   646, 659, 909,
   1240, 1823
Leeds, Phil
   1408, 1624
Leeds, Robert
   322, 1808
Leegant, Dan 1951
Leeson, Michael
   1437, 1463, 1608
Leetch, Tom 1879
Leeway Productions
   1978
Lefcourt, Peter 1759,
   1790, 1821, 1983
LeFevre, Adam 2038
Leffler, Florence 2045
Left Hand of
   David 207
Legal Eagle 816
LeGault, Lance
   1259, 1559, 1641,
   1717, 2197
Legend in Granite
   1118

Legend of Billy
   the Kid 448
Legend of the
   Golden Gun 1693
Legwork 2113
Lehman, Lillian
   1157, 1302
Lehmann, Ted 1329
Lehne, Fredric
   1632, 1742
Lehne, John
   1278, 1675
Lehrman, April
   2109
Lei, Lydia 1782
Leibman, Ron
   1606, 1912
Leicht, Allen
   2075, 2109
Leichtling, Jerry
   2140
Leigh, Barbara 1007
Leigh, Janet 859,
   1010, 1086,
   1213, 2045
Leighton, Ted 1102
Leisen, Mitch 811
LeMat, Paul 1970
LeMay, Alan 34
LeMay, General 75
Lembeck, Harvey
   612, 1014, 1530
Lembeck, Helaine
   1629
Lembeck, Michael
   1004, 1344,
   1628, 1760
LeMessena,
   William 1876
Leming, Eugene
   Ross 1573, 1635
Lemmo, Joan 1799
Lemmon, Chris
   1864, 1939
Lemmon, Jack
   622, 1113
Lemmons, Kasi 2113
LeMole, Lisa 1744
Lemon, Ben 1744

Lemon, Meadowlark
   1660
Lemon, Michael 2028
Len Rosenberg
   Productions 1500
Lenard, Melvin 1929
Lenard, Melvyn 6
Lenehan, Nancy
   2160
Lenhart, Kerry
   2171, 2267
Lennie, Elizabeth
   2132
Lennon, Jarrett 2252
Le Noir, Rosetta
   1307
Lenski, Robert W.
   1399, 1560, 1678
Lenz, Kay 1197,
   1301, 1687, 2177
Lenz, Rick 1840
Leon, Daniel 1699
Leonard 1550
Leonard, Arthur 440
Leonard, Elmore
   2190, 2260, 2261
Leonard, Herbert
   617, 896, 948,
   960, 1099, 1120,
   1192, 1321, 1479,
   1568, 1638
Leonard, Lu 1961
Leonard, Sheldon
   113, 390, 669,
   907, 965, 1142,
   1262, 1565, 1596
Leonard Goldberg
   Productions 1443
Leone, Sergio 1401
Leontovich,
   Eugenie 565
LePartmentier,
   Richard 2219
LePlat, Ted 1953
Leplatt, Ted 1969
LePore, Richard
   1525
Lerner, Fred 1619,
   1787, 2060

Lerner, Michael
   1096, 1098, 1330,
   1426, 1996
LeRoy, Gloria 1385,
   1620, 1658
LeRoy, Mervyn 488
Leslie, Bill 652
Leslie, Joan 1338,
   1987, 2083
Leslie, Phil 40
Lessac, Michael
   1966, 2228
Lesser, Sol 270
Lessey, Ben 31
Lester, Buddy 1222
Lester, Chez 1745
Lester, Jerry 909
Lester, Ketty
   1341, 2052
Lester, Richard 879
Lester, Terry
   1716, 1755
Lester, Tom 1304
Lester Hodges and
   Dr. Fong 1373
Le Tari 1914
Lethin, Lori 1812
Letner, Ken 2266
Let's Make a Hit 439
Letters 1189
Letters from Three
   Lovers 1190
Letters II 1190
Letts, Dennis 2177
Lev, Gary 2089
Levant, Andy 1793
Levant, Brian
   1794, 1929
Levay, Sylvester 2126
Levenback, Paul
   1965
Levene, Sam 328
Leverington,
   Shelby 2260
Leves, Michael 1501
Levi, Alan J. 1050,
   1394, 1445, 1556,
   1693, 1847,
   1942, 2094

Levien, Philip 1733, 1734, 2245
Levin, Alan 2118
Levin, Carl 2173
Levin, Charles 1665, 1666, 1723, 1795, 2263
Levin, Larry 2106
Levin, Peter 1745, 2033, 2132
Levin, Wendy 2001
Levine, Deborah 1844
Levine, Dennis 1506
Levine, Emily 2071, 2102
Levine, Floyd 1742, 1747
Levine, Joey 1649
Levine, Joseph 803
Levine, Ken 1483, 1755
Levine, Larry 1122, 1506, 1781
Levine, Laura 1607, 1631
Levine, Philip 1039
Levine, Richard 114
Levine, Robert 1231
Levine & Isaacs Productions 1755
Levinson, Barry 1924
Levinson, David 1028, 1227, 1228, 1337, 1596
Levinson, Richard 1105, 1164, 1169, 1233, 159, 2175
Levita, Scott 2265
Levitt, Steve 2163, 2264
Levy, Carol 1873
Levy, Cathy 2029
Levy, David 798, 1430
Levy, Eugene 1630, 2134
Levy, Jules 726

Levy, Ralph 20, 212, 953
Lew Archer 1289
Leward, Murray 2195
Lewin, Al 788
Lewis, Al 761, 1832
Lewis, Alan 2063
Lewis, Andrew 1090
Lewis, Andy 1277
Lewis, Arthur 162, 366
Lewis, B'Nard 2200
Lewis, Bobo 1012, 1067, 1632, 2143
Lewis, Cathy 937
Lewis, David 697, 1302
Lewis, Elliot 48, 256, 660, 672, 673, 674, 797
Lewis, Forrest 265, 958
Lewis, Geoffrey 1258, 1293, 1374, 1513, 1516, 1597, 1619, 1802, 1853, 1928, 1937, 1985, 2126, 2181, 2225
Lewis, Gilbert 1178
Lewis, Greg 1872
Lewis, Harvey 1540
Lewis, Jeffrey 2219
Lewis, Jenny 2066
Lewis, Juliette 2251
Lewis, M.K. 1907
Lewis, Morgan 2185
Lewis, Morton 1245
Lewis, Richard 846, 851, 1626, 1744, 2157
Lewis, R.J. 1955
Lewis, Robert 1972, 2026
Lewis, Robert Michael 1183, 1652
Lewis, Rose 1830
Lewis, Samantha 1997

Lewis, Warren 121, 763, 765
Lewis and Clark 1837
Leydig, Greg 1319
Leyteys, Joseph 925
Li, Pat 1245
Li'l Abner 835, 1067
Liberatore, Hugo 803
Liberman, Bradley 1660
Liberman, Richard 1398
Libertini, Richard 1484, 1622
Lichterman, Marvin 1273
Lichtman, Paul 1424, 1724
Lieb, Robert 756
Lieb, Robert P. 2159
Liebergman, Rick 2186
Lieberman, Jeff 1683
Lieberman, Norman 964
Lieberman, Robert 1151
Liebert, Judy 1379
Liebman, Ron 1340, **1356, 1473, 1776, 1821**
Liesure, David 2181
Lieutenant 664
Life and Times of Grizzly Adams 1903
Life Guard 449
Life of Vernon Hathaway 64
Life on the Flipside 2252
Life Story 12
Life with Virginia 651
Light in the Fruit Closet 403
Light of the World 151
Lights Out 1165

Ligon, Tom 1523
Ligudi, Gabriella 1127
Likely Lads 1461
Lil Abner 482, 909, 963
Lila Garrett Productions 1493, 1627, 1739
Lilies of the Field 1784
Lily 1220, 2107
Lily, Brenda 2045
Lim, Kwan Hi 1376
Lim, Pik-Sen 1127
Lime Street 368, 1986
Limekiln & Templar Productions 1807, 1864
Limited Partners 2226
Lin, Traci 2024, 2232, 2252
Lincoln, Scott 1969, 2032
Lind, Bob 1827
Lind, Brit 1522
Linden, Hal 1025, 1231, 1978
Linder, Christa 1887
Linder, George 2186
Lindley, Audra 1853
Lindren, Lisa 1660
Lindsay, Cynthia 454, 588
Lindsay, Laura 957
Lindsay, Margaret 1245
Lindsey, George 1546
Lindsey-Hogg, Michael 2003
Lindsly, Chuck 2002, 2267
Line 2123
Lineback, Richard 1749
Link, William 1105, 1164, 1169, 1233, 1509, 2175

Linke, Richard
O. 1254, 1315,
1503, 1504
Linkroum, Dick 705
Linn-Baker, Mark
1850, 2038
Linnea Productions
2240
Linville, Joanne 1587
Linville, Larry
1484, 1936
Liotta, Ray 1799
Lipin, Carol 2066
Lippe, Jonathon
985, 1070, 1128
Lippin, Rene 1540
Lipscomb, Dennis
1907
Lipscott, Alan 729
Lipsky, Eleanor 756
Lipstadt, Aaron 2247
Lipton, Lynne 1638
Lipton, Peggy 1618
Lipton, Robert 1098,
1278, 2085
Liscio, John 2049
Liska, Stephen 2213
Lison, Saul 1208
Lison-Chambers
Productions 1208
List, Shelley
1679, 1742
Litel, John 763
Little, Cleavon 1329,
1677, 1875, 2234
Little, Rich
1026, 1798
Little America 359
Little Amy 652
Little Darlings 1898
**Little Green
Book** 476
Little Joe 514
Little Kidnappers 987
Little Leatherneck
869
**Little Lord
Fauntleroy** 1886
Little Rascals 1944

Little Trooper 484
Littlefield, Warren
2180, 2183, 2184
Littler, Craig
1121, 2006
Littleshots 1944
Little Sky, Dawn
482
Little Sky, Eddie 1401
Litvack, John 2219
Liu, Frank Michael
1510
Lively, Robyn 2076
**Lives of Jenny
Dolan** 1351
Livin' Large 2203
Living End
1137, 1208
Living in Paradise
1831
Livingston, Barry
660, 1994
Livingston,
Mickey 1595
Lizard Productions
2208
Llende, Annibal 2099
Lloud, Kathleen 1917
Lloyd, Christopher
1589, 1654, 1966
Lloyd, David 1386,
1558, 1668, 1993,
2019, 2072, 2229
Lloyd, Jeremy 761,
1541, 2116
Lloyd, Kathleen
1167, 1589, 2100
Lloyd, Norman
464, 1072
Lo, Cho 2091
Lobell, Michael 2160
Lobi, Victor
1980, 2022
LoBianco, Tony
1231, 1833, 2106,
2195, 2244
Lobue, J.D.
1702, 1871
Local 306 1410

Locatel, Carol 2199
**Lock, Stock and
Barrel** 1103, 1163
Locke, Peter
1733, 1734
Locke, Rosanna 1922
Locke, Sara 554
Locke, Tammy 818
Lockhart, June 1180,
1903, 2207
Locklear, Heather
1808, **2120**
Lockmiller,
Richard 1678
Lockwood, Gary
632, 821, 1073,
2196, 2265
Lodge, William 1688
Loew, Sylvia 1683
Lofting, Morgan 1969
**Log of the Black
Pearl** 1295
Logan, Robert 1593
Logan, Terence 876
Loget, Claudine
1031
Loggers 609
Loggia, Robert 697,
779, 850, 1368,
1425, 1426, 1612,
1719, 2005, 2065,
2151, 2240
Loggins, Kenny 1701
Lohman, Rick 1820,
1939, 2037
Lojewski, Harry 1924
Lollipop Louie 713
Lollos, John 2038
Lom, Herbert 1039
Lombard, Carole 787
Lombard, Michael
1398, 2174
Lombardi, Leigh
2028, 2030
Lombardo, John 1788
London, Frank 1371
London, Jerry 1271,
1482, 1512, 1563,
2025, 2091

London, Julie
267, 396
London, Michael
J. 1525
**London and Davis in
New York**
1986
Lone Sierra 635
Lone Star 1955
Lone Woman 212
Lonely Wizard 125
Loner 2216
Long, Howie 2265
Long, Shelley 1608,
1623, 1704
Long, Sumner
21, 628
Long, William,
Jr. 1008
Long Arm 2058
Long Days of Summer
1597, 1714
Long Green 297
Long Highway 13
**Long Hunt of April
Savage** 881
**Long Time
Gone** 1970
Longarm 2217
Longdon, Terence
718
Longfield, Michael
2046
Longo, Tony 1908,
1911, 1922, 2035
Longstreet, Harry
1780, 2117
Longstreet,
Renee 1780
Longstreet 1429
Longworth,
David 2117
Lonow, Mark 2238
Lonsdale, Michael
2098
Lontoc, Leon
603, 1126
Look Out World
1495

Lookin' for
   Love 2050
Looking for
   Love 2031
Lookinland, Todd
   1240, 1686
Loomis, Christopher
   2258
Loomis, Dayton
   521
Lopez, Kamala 2195
Lopez, Mario 2068
Lopez, Priscilla
   2038
LoPinto, Dorian
   2042
Lor, Denise 549
Lord, Jack 212, 373,
   716, 724, 753,
   918, 929, 1648
Lord, Jeff 130
Lord, Justin 1495,
   1912, 2100
Lord, Marjorie 965
Lord and Lady
   Enterprises 1648
Lord Jack 213
Lord Joe 360
Lords of Flatbush
   1361
Lorenzo and Henrietta
   Music Show 1363
Lorimar Productions
   1194, 1225, 1244,
   1248, 1284, 1316,
   1350, 1355, 1394,
   1409, 1428, 1467,
   1494, 1507,
   1571, 1613, 1657,
   1672, 1676, 1717,
   1722, 1745, 1776,
   1819, 1867, 1871,
   1872, 1918, 1921,
   1922, 1923, 1955,
   2003, 2010, 2024,
   2039, 2043
Lorimar-Telepictures
   Productions
   2084, 2088, 2108,

2155, 2213, 2244,
   2245, 2253
Lorimer, Louise
   518, 656
Loring, Gloria
   1823, 2195
Loring, Lisa
   1540, 1712
Loring, Lynn 790,
   1322, 1618
Lormer, Jon
   1258, 1350
Loros, George 1337,
   1340, 1643
Lorre, Peter 206
LoRusso, Eddie 1447
Losby, Donald 732
Losers 737
Lost Flight 925,
   1020, 1146, 1404
Lost in Space 995
Lost Treasure 960
Lott, Lawrence 2195
Lott, Walter 1425
Lottery 1191
Lottimer, Ed 1936
Lou Shaw
   Productions 1786
Lou-Step
   Productions 2115
Louanne 1714,
   2136, 2202
Louden, Dorothy
   823, 1271
Lough, Jim 1539
Loughlin, Lori 2230
Louise, Tina 1210,
   1386, 1777, 1840
Lound, Tom 806
Love, Victor
   2218, 2260
Love, Natalie 1765
Love Affair Just
   for Three 730
Love American
   Style 738, 1014,
   1065, 1112
Love and Kisses 553
Love and Learn 1670

Love and the Good
   Deal 1014
Love and the Private
   Eye 1112
Love and the Young
   Unmarrieds 1065
Love and Wahr 473
Love at First Sight
   1733, 1734
Love Birds
   1630, 1899
Love Boat 192,
   738, 1189, 1612,
   1637, 1663, 1764,
   1786, 1856, 1857,
   2024, 2145
Love for Hire 1945
Love for Ransom
   1450
Love Island 1764
Love Long
   Distance 2036
Love That Jill 176
Lovejoy, Frank 121
Lovenheim, Robert
   1411, 1712,
   1988, 2089
Lovers and
   Madmen 758
Lovsky, Celia 772
Low Man on the
   Totem Pole 653
Lowe, Lori 1773
Lowell-Bergman
   Productions 2160
Lowens, Curt 1057,
   1123, 1468,
   1616, 1688
Lowenstein, Al
   2183, 2198
Lowry, Marcella 1309
Lowy, Otto 1100
Loxley, John 2029
Loy, Myrna
   181, 1187
Lu, Lisa 2091
Lubin, Arthur
   311, 679
Lucas, Alex 1747

Lucas, John
   Meredyth 1101
Lucas, Jonathan
   1053, 1097
Lucille Ball
   Productions
   1138, 1825
Luckinbill, Laurence
   1165, 1287,
   1649, 1876
Lucking, William
   1337, 1425, 1560,
   1642, 1774, 1880,
   2030, 2115
Lucy Arnaz
   Show 1138
Lucy Show 672
Ludwig, Edwin 117
Ludwig, Jerry 1133,
   1507, 1619
Luger, Lois 1730
Lugo, Frank 1864
Luisi, James 1052,
   1119, 1386, 1468,
   1773, 1788, 1881
Luke, Jorge
   1077, 1353
Luke, Keye 1251,
   1373, 1723, 1800,
   1822, 1953,
   2115, 2120
Luke and the
   Tenderfoot 814
Lukens, Linda 1578
Lulu 1039
Lum, Alvin 2038
Lum, Ben 1976
Lum and Abner
   626
Lumet, Baruch
   1279, 1714
Lumley, Joanna 1563
Luna, Barbara 771,
   1249, 1317, 1334,
   1391, 1786
Lund, Art 635, 1349
Lund, Deanna 972
Lundi, Sal 1799
Lunghi, Cherie 2240

Lupino, Ida 95, 143, 203, 917, 972, 1189
Lupo, Frank 2006
Lupo, Tom 1619
Lupone, Patti 2136
LuPone, Robert 2174
Lupton, John 618, 757, 966, 1164
Lussier, Robert 1411, 1457, 1872
Luther Gillis 1987
Luther Gillis: File #521 1985
Luxury Liner 738
Luz, Franc 2151
Lydon, James 1374
Lyles, A.C. 1515, 1827
Lyman, Dorothy 2053
Lyman, Will 2218
Lyman Dayton Productions 1697
Lyn, Dawn 1268
Lynch, Ken 845, 1076, 1222, 1865
Lynch, Paul 2188
Lynch, Peg 105
Lynch, Raymond 1866
Lynch, Richard 1446, 1450, 1621, 1916
Lynde, Janice 1413, 1563, 1617
Lynde, Paul 649, 798, 872, 936, 1004, 1110
Lyndon, Barre 902
Lynley, Carol 114, 843, 985, 1089, 1583, 1722, 1847
Lynn, Debby 1829
Lynn, Diana 114, 653
Lynn, Jonathan 2257
Lynn, Meredith Scott 2251
Lynn, Sherry 1671

Lyons, Gene 724
Lyons, Richard E. 1534
Lyons, Robert F. 1310, 1319, 1721, 1969
Lysdahl, Tori 1822
Lystine, Jon 2042

M

M Station: Hawaii 1648
Ma and Pa 1271
Ma and Pa Kettle 788
Mabe, Byron 1257
Mabel and Max 2159
Mac 1311
MacArthur, Alex 1969
MacArthur, Douglas 484
MacArthur, James 329, 721, 961
Macauley, Charles 957, 1418, 1832
MacCloskey, Isabell 1615
MacCorkindale, Simon 1770
MacDonald, Casey 1096, 1148
MacDonald, John D. 994, 1802
MacDonald, Ross 1301
MacDonald, Ryan 1429, 1803
MacDonnell, Norman 482
MacDougall, Burke Jamie 1096
MacDougall, Janne 2093
MacDougall, Randall 1096
MacDougall, Ruth Doan 1343

MacDowell, Andie 2218
Macero, Teo 1596
MacFarland, Louella 203
MacGibbon, Harriet E. 1164
MacGruder and Loud 1280
Machado, Mario 2035
Machalski, B. Miko 2083
Machon, Karen 1339, 1852
Macht, Stephen 1442a, 1588
MacIntosh, Jay 1879
MacIntyre, David H. 2235
Mack, Eddie 2173
Mack, Jillie 2205
Mack, Karen 1867, 1871, 2003, 2024, 2039
MacKay, Jeff 1656
MacKenzie, Allison 1518
MacKenzie, Gisele 731
MacKenzie, Patch 1617
MacKenzie, Peter 2218
MacKenzie, Phillip Charles 1755
MacKenzie, Will 1263, 1723, 1755, 1877, 1913, 1947, 1990, 2001, 2180
Macklin, Albert 2012
Macklin, David 753
MacLachlan, Janet 1135
MacLeod, Catherine 499
MacLeod, Gavin 790, 1508

MacLeod, Murray 1007, 1350, 1421, 1887
MacMichael, Florence 310, 463
MacMurray, Fred 760, 1245
MacNaughton, Robert 1813
MacNee, Patrick 1039, 1116, 1250, 1563, 1611, 1654, 1805, 1937, 2024
Macon, Sara 1355
MacRae, Gordon 518
MacRae, Heather 1182, 1370
MacRae, Meredith 1557, 1685
MacRae, Michael 1496, 1580, 1694, 1962, 1992
MacRae, Sheila 518, 1688
Macy, Bill 1654, 2234, 2207
Macy, W.H. 2017, 2214
Mad Avenue 2242
Mad Dog Productions 1841, 2030
Mad Mad Scientist 964
Madame Sheriff 1631
Madame Sin 1127, 1164
Madden, Bill 1284
Madden, Dave 1748
Madden, Sharon 1745, 2082
Maddows, Ben 1147
Maddox, Lester 1322
Maderlay Enterprises 2245
Madigan, Amy 1799, 1802

Madison, Guy 475

Madlone, Dennis 1915

Madsen, Harry 1777

Madsen, Michael 1924

Maffeo, Gayle S. 2012, 2122, 2156

Magee, Cliffy 2092

Magee, Ken 1944

Maggie 115, 2116

Maggie Brown 654

Maggie Malone 267, 396

Magic Carpet 1096

Magistretti, Paul 1473

Magness, Klif 2100

Magnificent Magical Magnet of Santa Mesa 1505

Magnificent Montague 116

Magnum PI 1507, 1564, 1815, 1880, 1985, 1987

Maguire, Hugh 2154

Maguire, Kathleen 1245

Maguire, Mady 1132

Mahar, Christopher 1916

Maharis, George 1010

Maher, Bill 2024

Maher, Bruce 2267

Maher, John 1348

Maher, Joseph 1993, **2220**

Mahin, John Lee 29, 504, 521

Mahin-Rackin Productions 504, 521

Mahler, Joseph 2032

Mahlin, Richard 504

Mahon, John 2034

Mahoney, Jock 450

Mahoney, Maggie 207, 211, 582

Mahoney, Trish 1189

Maibaum, Richard 117, 380, 1229, 1652

Main, Laurie 1051

Main Event 1766

Maisie 117

Major H Productions 1699, 1944

Major H/Anson Productions 1853

Majors, Lee 1007, 1442, 1866, 2185, 2196

Majors, Lee, II 2196

Make Room for Daddy 965

Make Room for Grand-daddy 965

Makepeace, Chris 2220

Making It 1409

Mako 949, 1251, 1643, 1916, 2115

Makoui, Rudy 169

Malave, ChuChu 1366

Malet, Arthur 1124, 1298

Malick, Wendie 2064

Mallory 1425

Mallory, Carole 1450

Mallory, Edward 497

Mallory: Circumstantial Evidence 1425

Malloy, John 2045

Malloy, William 1566

Malmbourg, Mike 1108

Malolo of the South Seas 171

Malone, Dorothy 727, 1518

Malone, Joel 770

Malone, Mo 1577, 1689

Malone, Nancy 1044, 1130, 1299, 1457

Malone, William 2264

Maloney, James 117

Maloney, Patty 1296, 1386

Maloney, Peter 1370, 1687, 1855, 2174

Malooly, Maggie 1476

Maltin, Leonard 902, 1685, 1781

Maltz, Maxwell 560

Maltz, Jerry 1777

Mamakos, Peter 781

Man About Town 2078

Man Against Crime 267

Man Called Hawk 2218

Man from Denver 213

Man from Everywhere 563

Man from Independence 1119

Man from Lloyds 368

Man from Telegraph Hill 569

Man from the 25th Century 995

Man from UNCLE 1155

Man in the House 526

Man in the Middle 616, 1044

Man in the Square Suit 934

Man Named McGee 857

Man of Fear 209

Man of Many Faces 331

Man of the World 640

Man on a String 1147

Man on Raft 268

Man on the Beach 477

Man on the Road 483

Man Who Fell to Earth 2096

Man Who Never Was 881

Man Whose Name Was John 1117

Man with the Golden Gun 1716

Man with the Power 1517, 1615

Manasse, George 2174

Mancini, Al 1127, 1158, 2041

Mancini, Henry 717, 1122, 2201

Mancini, Michael 1525

Mancini, Ric 1633, 2035

Mancuso 2264

Mancuso, Nick 1451, 1822, 1915, 2026

Mandan, Robert 1232, 1864, 1926

Mandel, Alan 1200, 1407

Mandel, Alex 1219

Mandel, Babaloo 1661, 1911, 2250

Mandel, Howie 2206

Mandel, Johnny 1012, 1150, 1910

Mandel, Loring 1569

Mandelker, Philip 1423, 1521, 1701, 1994, 1995

Mandrake 1591

Mandrake the Magician 1591

Manduke, Joe 1281

Mandy Films
2040, 2085
Manet, Jeanne 202
Manetta, Joe 1273
Manetti, Larry
1788, 1815
Mangione, Chuck
1986
Manheim,
Manny 492
Manheim, Michael
1465
Manhoff, Bill 115,
250, 653, 654, 953
Manings, Allan 1712
Mankiewicz, Don
M. 146, 1029,
1180, 1687, 1817
Mankiewicz,
John 2260
Mankiewicz, Tom
1530, 2203
Manley, Stephen
1387, 1388
**Manley and the
Mob** 936
Mann, Abby
2046, 2172
Mann, Alan 740
Mann, Delbert 1569
Mann, Dolores 1832
Mann, Howard
1784, 1799
Mann, Lisa 1784
Mann, Nina 2201
Mann, Terrence
V. 2113
Mann, Tyrell 2142
Manners, Mickey 726
Manners, Sam 1479
Manning, Ruth
1405, 1414, 1702
Mannings, Allan
1413
Mannix 1057, 1788
Mannix, Billy 1645
Manoff, Dinah
1521, 2123, 2124,
2166, 2175

Mansfield, Jayne 605
Manson, Alan
1222, 1346
Manson, David
2212, 2236
Manson, Maurice 207
Mansoor 2091
Mantee, Paul 752,
1210, 1277
Mantell, Joe 204
Mantley, John
325, 1019
Mantooth, Randolph
1072, 1098
Manulis, Martin 784
**Many Loves of
Arthur** 1578
**Many Wives of
Patrick** 1736
Manza, Ralph 713,
1526, 1619
Mapes, Jacques
1351, 1388
Marable, Mary
Bradley 1444
Marachuk, Steve
1721
Marble Arch
Productions 1687,
1738, 1792, 1797
Marblehead
Manor 1993
Marcantel,
Christopher 1742
Marcel, Terry 2005
Marcelino, Mario
1915
March, Alex 877
March, Fredric 1316
March, Hal 306,
597
March, Judy 1093
March, Linda 1136
Marchetta,
Camille 1801
Marcia, Denise
1365, 1440
Marciano, David
2234, 2246

Marcil, Allen J.
2114, 2164
Marcione, Gene 1394,
1434, 1499, 1529,
1631, 1636, 1674,
1702, 1704, 1755,
1798, 1837, 1897
Marcovicci, Andrea
1918, 2169
Marcus, Ann
1172, 1190
Marcus, Bill 1873,
1970, 2099
Marcus, Ellis 255,
1049, 1189
Marcus, Joe, Jr. 1327
Marcus, Joe
David 1327
Marcus, Larry
429, 430, 431,
495, 853, 925
Marcus, Richard
2190
Marcus, Sparky
1321, 1493
**Marcus Welby:
A Holiday
Affair** 1971
*Marcus Welby
MD* 1971
Marden, Adrienne
670, 1008
Maren, Jerry 1994
**Margin for
Murder** 1747
Margolin, Arnold
1015, 1042, 1056,
1107, 1135, 1152,
1314, 1331, 1365,
1440, 1623
Margolin, Janet
1260, 1473, 1518
Margolin, Stuart
969, 1007, 1151,
1200, 1407, 1608,
1992, 2219
Margotta, Michael
985, 1252
Marguilies, Stan 1202

Margulies, Stan
1256, 2026
Mariano, Nick 1688
Marie 1601
Marie, Rose
978, 1081
Marin, Cheech 2184
Marin, Jacques 2098
Marin, Russ 1773
Marineland 14
Marion, Richard
1971
Maris, Ada
2057, 2238
Mariye, Lily 2201
Mark, Dan 1953
Mark, Flip 381
Mark, Stevens
50, 269
Mark Carliner
Productions
1437, 1637
Mark Dolphin 829
**Mark Hellinger
Theatre** 440
Mark of Zorro 1253
Mark VII
Productions
102, 153, 370,
586, 1290, 1295,
1302, 1354
**Mark Twain's
America** 1592
**Marked Down for
Connie** 501
Markell, Robert
1162, 1281
Markes, Larry 916
Markham, Monte
1144, 1477
Markland, Ted 1477
Markle, Fletcher
136, 271, 825
Markle, Peter 2148
Markley, Edward
D. 2107, 2127
Markoe, Merrill 1765
Markowitz,
Gary 2165

Markowitz, Richard 582, 1235, 1249, 1291, 1369, 1588, 1656, 1748

Markowitz, Robert 2046

Marks, Arthur 1746, 2175

Marks, Guy 1434, 1825

Marks, Jack 1850

Marks, Lawrence 309, 912, 1262, 1394

Marks, Marianne 1611

Marks, Sherman 456, 647, 769, 955

Marks, Walter 1153

Marley, Ben 1890, 1995, 2045

Marley, John 507, 1076, 1078, 1183, 1215

Marlo, Steven 1249, 1347, 1743

Marlow, Rick 1815

Marlowe, Curtiss 2085

Marlowe, Nora 952, 1086, 1139

Marlowe, Scott 758, 1090, 1586

Marmer, Mike 1027

Marmy, Mae 1959

Maroff, Bob 1914

Maross, Joseph 1126

Marquez, William 1907

Marquez, Yolanda 1864

Marquis, Kristopher 1423

Marriage Broker 126

Marriage: Year One 1098

Marren, Jerry 1820

Married With Children 2132

Marrow, Merlene 673

Mars, Kenneth 1046, 1085, 1131, 1216, 1228, 1544, 1750, 1920

Mars: Base One 2227

Marsac, Maurice 6

Marsh, Brandon 2239

Marsh, Ellen 1620

Marsh, Jean 1649

Marsh, John 213

Marsh, Linda 1010, 1896, 2054

Marsh, Marion 200

Marsh, Tiger Joe 912

Marshal of Manitoba 190

Marshall, Ann 553

Marshall, Don 957, 1506

Marshall, E.G. 1102, 1621

Marshall, Ed 1829

Marshall, Garry 968, 1014, 1035, 1087, 1113, 1151, 1156, 1214, 1266, 1334, 1365, 1440, 1541, 1708, 1911, 2228

Marshall, Jack 994

Marshall, Nancy 825

Marshall, Penny 1151, 1334

Marshall, Peter 601, 1081

Marshall, Sarah 674, 753

Marshall, Shari 652

Marshall, Steve 1871

Marshall, Tony 1266, 1334, 1365, 1541

Marshall, William 1060

Marstar Productions 1971

Marta, Lynne 1212

Martel, Arlene 1126, 1187, 1350

Martel, K.C. 1832

Martell, Mina 2148

Marth, Frank 1211, 1335, 1641

Martic, Sandy 1907

Martin, Alberto 1915

Martin, Andrea 2202

Martin, Anthony S. 1230

Martin, Barney 1671, **2020**

Martin, Con 1959

Martin, Damon 2085

Martin, Dean 1097

Martin, Dean Paul 1976

Martin, Dewey 23, 208, 477, 1133

Martin, Dick 570, 1081, 1767, 1948

Martin, George 1039

Martin, George N. 2112

Martin, Helen 1199

Martin, Irene A. 772

Martin, Jared 1256, 1648, 1722, 1860

Martin, Jerry 2201

Martin, Kelley 2199

Martin, Kiel 1099, 1295

Martin, Lewis 319

Martin, Lorie 915

Martin, Marji 1818

Martin, Nan 1297, 1567, 1826, 2230

Martin, Pamela Sue 1258

Martin, Pepper 1041, 1473

Martin, Peter 303

Martin, Quinn 728, 804, 1047, 1076, 1090, 1188, 1246, 1357, 1421, 1480, 1510, 1516, 1561, 1563, 1628, 1634, 1651, 1678, 1767

Martin, Randi 1368

Martin, Ross 765, 1078, 1100, 1539, 1618, 1656, 1748

Martin, Russ 1586

Martin, San 2066

Martin, Steve 1940

Martin, Strother 1690

Martin, Toby 1784

Martin, Todd 1059, 2002

Martin, Tony 298

Martin, Yves 2025

Martin Bregman Productions 1652

Martin Mull Show 1900

Martin Poll Productions 1654

Martin Rackin Productions 1300

Martinelli: The Outside Man 1473

Martinez, A. 1352, 1425, 1514, 1594

Martinez, Alma 1902

Martinez, Claudio 1318, 1594

Martinez, Joaquin 1072

Martinez, Kenneth 1384

Martinez, Manuel 1821

Martinson, Leslie H. 296, 1031, 1100, 1662

Marty 858

Marty Katz Productions 1681

Marvin 40

Marvin, Ira 2112

Marvin, Lee 242, 737

Marvin Worth Productions 1606

Marx, Arthur 492

Marx, Chico 365, 461

Marx, Groucho 941

Marx, Harpo 365, 461

Marx Brothers 940

Mary Tyler Moore Show 1135, 1198, 1386, 2019, 2156, 2265

Masak, Ron 1145, 1397, 1452, 1661, 1678, 1786

Mascarino, Pierrino 1836

Maschio, Michael J. 2009, 2214, 2218

Mascolo, Joseph 1266, 1429, 1912

Mase, Marino 2026

M*A*S*H 1269, 1484, 1544, 1626, 1981, 2019, 2108

Masius, John 2062

Mask, Don 905

Mask of Alexander 1474

Mask of Sheba 1061

Maslansky, Paul 1258

Mason 1313

Mason, Donna 1599

Mason, F. Van Wyck 504

Mason, Kay 1099

Mason, Kenneth 2248

Mason, Laura 846

Mason, Lola 1758, 1881

Mason, Marlyn 839, 1074, 1457, 1811

Mason, Marsha 1760

Mason, Pamela 1604

Mason, Paul 1169, 1317, 1465

Mason, Perry 666

Mason, Tom 1678, 1937

Masquerade 665, 958, 2189

Massarati & the Brain 1862

Massey, Gene 1519

Massey, Raymond 495

Massey, Wayne 1933

Master of Darkness 1916

Masters, Ben 1409, 1476, 2098, 2246

Masters, Michael 1249

Masterson, Peter 1381, 1443, 1449

Masur, Richard 1432, 1578, 1958, 1975, 2026, 2079, 2134, 2239

Mate, Rudolph 504, 521

Mathers, Jerry 1929, 1995

Matheson, Don 1467

Matheson, Murray 847, 1116, 1139

Matheson, Richard 611, 974, 1250

Matheson, Tim 797, 915, 971, 1103, 1163, 1297, 1355

Mathews, Carmen 1061, 1105, 1509

Mathews, Walter 1782

Mathey, Harriet 1846

Mathias, Darian 1765, 1974

Matinee Theatre 70, 164

Matlock 2187

Matlovsky, Samuel 877

Matoian, John 2106

Matson, Robin 1771

Matt Houston 2169

Matter of Wife and Death 1358

Matteson, Pamela 2022

Matthau, Walter 642, 1274

Matthew, Patricia 2225

Matthews, Kerwin 75, 699, 742, 844, 1009, 1232

Matthews, Sheila 1101, 1335

Mattingly, Hedley 1612

Mattson, Robin 945, 1343, 1641

Matuszak, John 1969

Matz, Peter 1280, 1408, 1412, 1423, 1434, 1438, 1455, 1469, 1526, 1552, 1630, 1764, 1912

Maude 1671

Maude-Roxby, Roddy 1207

Maugham, Somerset 1168

Maule, Brad 1818

Mauna, Louis 2188

Maureen 1045, 1390

Maury, Derrel 1536

Maverick 325, 611, 737, 1282, 1293, 1420, 1448

Max 1946

Max and Me 2018

Max Sinclair, M.D. 1715

Maxwell, Daphne 1842

Maxwell, Don 1525, 1980, 2023, 2267

Maxwell, Jeff 1657

Maxwell, Paul 1127, 2240

Maxwell, Reed 43

Maxwell, Robert 21, 97, 189, 686

Maxx 1602

May, Billy 267, 970, 1007, 1808

May, Deborah 2087, 2220

May, Donald 810

May, Lenora 1785

Mayama, Miko 1226

Mayberry, Rus 1125, 1429, 1473, 1525, 1865, 1904, 1962, 2185

Mayberry, RFD 1546

Mayday 344

Mayehoff, Eddie 57, 906, 967

Mayer, Chip 1718

Mayer, Dorothy 1279

Mayer, Hans 1380

Mayer, Jerry 1342, 1889, 1890, 1896

Mayer, Ken 970

Mayersberg, Paul 2096

Mayes, Wendell 1938

Maynard, Mimi 1609

Maynor, Asa 1631

Mayo, Virginia 118

Mayo, Whitman 1922, 1991

Mayor 849

Mayron, Gail 1709

Mays, Joe 2201

Mazer, Arnie 1924

Mazurki, Mike 737, 1851

Mazursky, Paul 665

Mboya, Joy 2248

MCA/Revue 12, 49, 100, 125, 129, 154, 200, 241, 250, 310, 372, 454, 455, 471, 473, 491, 587, 638, 647, 668, 683, 695, 698, 700, 702, 711, 734, 757, 788

McAdam, Heather 1898

McAdams, James 1228, 1336, 1402,

1814, 2046, 2172, 2241

McAndrew, Marianne 1280

McArdle, Andrea 1741

McArthur, Alex 2190, 2260, 2261

McAuley, Matthew James 2091

McBain, Diane 808, 851

McBride 1038

McBride, Dan 1590

McBride, Harlee 1543

McBroom, Amanda 1579

McCabe, Jud 1249

McCadden Productions 54, 115, 156, 374

McCain, Frances Lee 2075, 2195

McCall, Mary 117, 236

McCall, Mitzi 1214

McCallion, James 1126, 1190, 1211, 1480

McCallister 2218

McCallum, David 758, 1937, 2063

McCalman, Macon 1554, 1620, 1655, 1951, 2191

McCambridge, Mercedes 825, 1132

McCann, Chuck 767, 1050, 1217

McCann, Marie 1569

McCann, Shawn 1482

McCants, Reed 2201

McCardle, Andrea 1273

McCarey, Leo 67

McCarren, Fred 1439, 1692, 1769, 1811, 1980

McCarroll, Esther 1872

McCarthy, Annette 1799

McCarthy, Dennis 1901, 2045

McCarthy, Frank 1005, 1123, 1814, 1907, 1969, 2023

McCarthy, Kevin 699, 844, 1514, 2085, 2250

McCarthy, Lin 117, 179, 1822

McCarthy, Mary 1395

McCarthy, Nobu 851, 2120

McCarthy, Winwood 1586, 1587

McCarty, Chris 2261

McCary, Rod 1384, 1502, 1530, 1544

McCary, Ron 2201

McCashin, Constance 1578

McCaslin, Mayo 1743

McCavitt, T.J. 1691

McCay, Peggy 164, 1446, 1733

McChaffey, Lorrie 1778

McClain, Cady 2266

McClanahan, Macon 1734

McClanahan, Rue 1620, 1673, 1804, 2181

McClarnon, Kevin 2201

McClean, Bill 1190

McCleery, Albert 164, 750

McClone 2265

McClory, Sean 267, 1374

McClosket, Yale 1511

McCloskey, Leigh 1973

McCloud 1159, 1952, 2267

McClure, Doug 310, 1164, 1233, 1243, 1539, 1617

McClurg, Edie 1636, 1978

McCook, John 1901

McCord, Kent 1522

McCord, Megan 1522

McCormack 1104

McCormack, Patricia 1936, 2199

McCormick, Carolyn 2114

McCormick, Frank 121

McCormick, Larry 1213, 1917

McCormick, Myron 384

McCormick, Pat 1415, 1483, 1865, 1866, 1940

McCourt, Malachy 1681, 1717

McCowan, George 1041, 1618

McCoy, Matt 1807, 2112

McCracken, Jeff 2192

McCrane, Paul 1742

McCrea, Ann 450

McCrea, Jody 72, 243, 900

McCrea, Joel 72, 232

McCready, Ed 1261

McCulley, Johnston 1253

McCullough, Andrew 502

McCullough, Robert 2021, 2025

McCullough, Robert L. 2193

McCullough, Susan 2021

McCurry, Ann 2213

McCurry, Natalie 2185

McDadden, Tom 1648

McDaniel, Charles 2213

McDaniel, Donna 1950

McDaniel, George 1224, 1471, 1848

McDermott, Brian 129

McDermott, Tom 854, 885, 1535

McDermott/Wrather Productions 1535

McDevitt, Ruth 200, 1044, 1075, 1228, 1244, 1254, 1343

McDonald, Christopher 1806, 2035

McDonnell, James 2242

McDonnell, Jo 1619, 1716, 1832

McDonnell, Ray 970

McDonough, Eileen 1316, 1428

McDonough, Kit 1388, 1526, 1552, 2020, 2170

McDougall, Don 265, 395, 487, 1057

McDowall, Roddy 1155, 1847, 1986, 2152

McDuff, Jeff 1229

McEachin, James 1089, 1164, 1183, 1619, 1951

McElroy, J.C. 1162

McEnnan, Jaime 2248

McEnroe, Annie 1717

McEveety, Bernard 721, 1474

McEveety, Vincent 921, 1019, 1261, 1559, 1680, 1853, 1987, 2047, 2120

McEvoy, Anne Marie 2211

McFadden, Davenia 2064

McFadden, Tom 1582, 1814

McGarry and His Mouse 118

McGarry and Me 118

McGavin, Darren 266, 878, 1058, 1153, 1232, 1424, 1668, 1721, 1971, 2088, 2155

McGeary, Barney 2245

McGee, Jack 2244

McGee, Vonetta 1232, 1801

McGerr, Patricia 820

McGhee 817

McGibbon, Josann 2166

McGill, Bruce 2096

McGill, Everett 2197

McGillis, Kelly 2064

McGinley, Ted 1911

McGinn, Walter 1348

McGiver, John 507, 653, 731, 1105

McGonagle, Richard 2201

McGonigle 388

McGovern, Terrence 1977

McGowan, Debbie 652

McGowan, Don 1255

McGowan, George 1007, 1010

McGowan, Jane 199

McGowan Productions 56

McGrath, Derek 1993, 2015

McGrath, Doug 1955

McGrath, Frank 509, 695

McGrath, Fred 2189

McGraw, Charles 772

McGreedy's Woman 267, 396

McGreevey, John 850, 1004, 1110, 1116, 1117, 1248, 1268, 1296, 1316, 1971, 2026, 2187, 1566, 1784

McGregor, Kenneth 2144

McGugan, Stuart 1127

McGuire, Barry 646

McGuire, Biff 1301, 1336, 1424, 1450

McGuire, Bryan 2009

McGuire, Don 644, 817, 857, 859

McGuire, Dorothy 1321

McGuire, Michael 1165, 1338, 1516, 1687, 1714, 1883

McGuire, Phyllis 1332

McGurk 1671

McHattie, Stephen 1327

McHenry, Doug 2253

McHugh, Frank 629, 746

McInerney, Bernie 1727

McIntire, James 1813

McIntire, John 451, 695, 766, 861, 923, 951, 1292, 1374, 1535, 1595, 1647, 1955

McIntyre, Tim 1721

McKay, Brian 905

McKay, Bruce 1885

McKay, Gardner 94, 730

McKay, Larry 2124

McKean, Michael 2266

McKeand, Carol 1849, 2104

McKeand, Nigel 1849, 2104

McKeand Productions 1849

McKeaney, Grace 2228

McKee, John 1353

McKee, Lonette 2263

McKee, Tom 125

McKeehan, Doug 2050

McKenna, Colin 1569

McKenna, T.P. 2063

McKennon, Dale 726

McKenzie, Richard 2012

McKenzie, Will 1494

McKeon, Kris 1686

McKeon, Mary Ellen 1571

McKeon, Michael 1975

McKeon, Nancy 1776, 1834, 1889, 1896, 1994, 2251

McKeown, Alan 2224

McKeown, Allan 1738

McKeown, Kate 1072

McKewin, Vince 1976

McKinney, Bill 1292, 1301, 1328

McKinsey, Beverlee 876

McKnight, David 2244

McKnight, Tom 117, 508

McKrell, Jim 1607

McLaglen, Andrew V. 1419, 1802

McLain, Duncan 671

McLaird, Arthur E. 1821

McLaren, Conrad 2143

McLaren's Riders 1475

McLarty, Ron 1817, 2214, 2218

McLaughlin, Bobby Travis 2264

McLaughlin, Bruce 1915

McLean, Bill 1308

McLean, David 704

McLeod, Murray 1151

McLeod, Norman 64, 199, 499, 525, 730

McLeod, Shelagh 2219

McLerie, Allyn Ann 1299, 1531, 1679, 1869, 2012

McLiam, John 1118, 1163, 1443, 1693, 2262

McLoughlin, Tommy 1798

McMahon, Horace 463

McMahon, Jenna 2251

McMahon, John J. 1835, 1839

McMahon, Karen 1400

McManus, Michael 1432, 1628, 1641, 1768, 1832, 1898

McMartin, John 955, 1065, 1659, 1916

745

McMaster, Mary
Rose 1129
McMillan, Kenneth
1498, 1846,
1914, 2167
McMillan, Richard
2132
McMillan, Will 1370
*McMillan and
Wife* 407
McMullan, Jim 884,
1486, 1487, 1801
McMullen,
Dennis 2041
McMullen, Jim 975,
1030, 1121
McMurtrey,
Joan 2195
McMurtry,
Jonathan 2211
McNab, Michael
2232
McNab's Lab
870, 964
McNair, Heather
1938
McNally, Bill 846
McNally, Stephen
957, 1210, 1351
McNally, Terrence
1914
McNamara,
Maureen 1823
McNamara, Pat
1324, 1851, 1964
McNamara, Paul 172
McNamara's Band
1435, 1436
McNaughton,
Steve 1744
McNear, Howard
156, 204
McNeice, Ian 2219
McNeely, Jerry
1586, 1587
McNeil, Claudia
1076
McNeill 1254, 1315

**McNeill – Winter
Kill** 1513
McNichol, Jimmy
1404
McNichol, Kristy
1898
McPeak, Sandy
1522, 1537, 1801,
1852, 1955, 2191
McPhee, Daniel 2264
McPhee, Peisha 2264
McPherson,
Patricia 1914
McPherson, Steven
1692, 2063
McPhie, Jerry 1666
McQueen, Justice 305
McQueen, Steve
1353
McRae, Alan
1450, 1682
McRae, Ellen 691
McRae, Frank 1314,
1917, 1980
McRaney, Gerald
1643, 1647, 1678,
1852, 2047
McRaven, Dale
1558, 1793
McReady, Ed 1347
McShane, Ian 1351,
1510, 2022, 2169
McSharry, Carmel
1886
McVey, Tyler 1282
McWilliams, Caroline
1533, 1578, 1678,
1871, 2019, 2192
Me and Benjie 1016
Me and Ducky 1672
Me and Joe 1085
Me and Maxx 1602
Me on the Radio
1735
Mead, Selena 820
Meaden, Dan 1158
Meadow, Herb
206, 266

Meadows, Audrey
2225
Meadows, Herb 475
Meadows, Jayne 1809
Meadows, John 2129
Meadows, Kristin
1925
Mealy, Barbara 1971
Meaney, Kevin 2226
Meara, Anne 1062,
1106, 1114,
1392, 2125
Mebzor Productions
2227
Med-Ex 1128
Medalis, Joe 1436,
1500, 1955
Medaris, Theresa
1343
Medeiros, Michael
2216
Medenhall,
Marissa 1902
Medford, Don 697,
735, 844, 1076,
1186, 1585,
1776, 1842
Medford, Kay 1083
Medical Center
1144, 1395
Medical Detective
583
Medici, John 1742
Medicine Lance 700
Medicine Men
627, 937
Medina-Taggert,
Jimmy 2211
Medley, Bill 1546
Meek, Jeffrey 2152
Meeker, Ralph
903, 1020, 1146,
1289, 1291
Meeks, Barbara 1888
**Meet Maggie
Mulligan** 859
**Meet Me in St.
Louis** 818

Meet the Girls 462
**Meeting in
Appalachia** 478
Meganauts 2243
Megna, John 1490
Megowan,
Debbie 456
Megowan, Don 207
Mei, Mak Yuen 2091
Mel Ferber
Productions 1585
Melchoir, Lauritz 435
Meldrum, Wendel
2049
Mele, Nicholes 2034
Melendez, Maria
1679, 1742
Meier, Gustave 271
Mell, Joseph 309,
509, 1435
Melle, Gil 1164,
1233, 1234, 1267,
1296, 1336, 1356
Mellin, Sherman 699
Melman, Jeff
1891, 2252
Melnick, Don 977
Melody Ranch 127
Melton, Sid
965, 1017
Melton, Troy 1036
Melville, Sam 1224
Melvin, Allan 855,
916, 949, 1044
**Melvin Danger,
Private Eye** 1112
**Melvin Purvis,
G-Man** 1255
Melvoin, Jeff 2240
Men in White 329
**Men of the
Dragon** 1256
Mendelker,
Phillip 1271
Mendelsohn,
Deborah 2231
Mendelsohn,
Jack 1553

Mendenhall, Marissa 2082, 2251

Mendillo, Stephen 1230, 1888

Mendoza, Arthur 2267

Mengatti, John 1896

Menjou, Adolphe 557

Menken, Robin 2102

Menteer, Gary 1598, 1950, 2051

Menville, Chuck 1968

Menzies, Heather 1044, 1093, 1338, 1641

Menzies, Jim 1749

Merande, Doro 466

Mercantel, Christopher 2174

Mercer, Agatha 1259

Mercer, Ernestine 2099

Mercer, Louis 647

Mercer, Marian 1484, 1549

Mercurio, Gus 2208

Mercurio, Nicole 2127

Mercury Entertainment Corp. 2199

Mercy or Murder 1246

Meredith, Burgess 463, 1103, 1128, 1534

Meredith, Don 1347, 1419, 1534, 1584, 2195

Meredith, Judi 454, 902

Meredith, Lucille 1724

Merediz, Olga 2057

Meridian Productions 6

Merie, Ann 1860

Meriwether, Lee 819, 851, 1536, 1561, 1750

Merkel, Una 59

Merkerson, J. Epatha 2236

Merl, Judy 1936

Merlin, Barbara 64

Merlin, Jan 2060

Merlin the Magician 361

Merlini, Marisa 1596

Merman, Ethel 654, 1455, 1542

Merrill, Dina 634, 747, 1189, 2102

Merrill, Gary 201, 877, 1073, 1482

Merrill, Keith 1697, 1882

Merrill, Larry 659, 818

Merrily We Go 412

Merritt, Theresa 1177

Merrow, Jane 1124, 1822

Mersky, Kres 1810

Merson, Marc 935, 1273, 1346, 1489, 1502, 1657, 1672, 1776, 1809, 1912, 1920, 2167, 2224

Messick, Dale 1317

Messina, Emilio 1652

Metalious, Grace 1518

Metcalfe, Burt 459, 1409, 1428

Metrano, Art 659, 1008, 1345, 1809

Metromedia Producers Corp. 1129, 1131, 1145, 1196, 1215, 1231, 1232, 1250, 1262, 1272, 1296, 1303, 1627, 1739, 1746, 1892

Mettey, Lynnette 1145, 1157, 1580

Metzger, Alan 2172

Meurer, Manfred 1058

Meyer, Bob 2001

Meyer, Dorothy 1248, 1333, 1480

Meyer, Emile 971

Meyer, Nancy 1629

Meyer, Nicholas 1251

Meyers, Ari 1920

Meyers, Marilyn 1454

Meyers, Paul Eric 1936

Meyers, Pauline 2041

Meyerson, Peter 1385, 1453, 1465, 1667

MF Productions 1918

MGM Television 117, 159, 248, 378, 388, 495, 591, 667, 685, 732, 749, 752, 777, 778, 800, 810, 818, 834, 836, 844, 849, 874, 877, 898, 932, 954, 962, 1038, 1061, 1069, 1073, 1114, 1139, 1186, 1216, 1243, 1254, 1275, 1293, 1314, 1331, 1340, 1345, 1349, 1353, 1383, 1395, 1399, 1474, 1489, 1501, 1503, 1504, 1680, 1760, 1806, 1828, 1861, 1869, 1885, 1901, 1904, 1907, 1908, 2096, 2212

MGM Theatre 249

MGM/UA Television 1060, 1924, 1927, 1928, 1952, 1976, 1979, 2022, 2040, 2048, 2154, 2165, 2184, 2195, 2230, 2243

Miami Vice 111, 1421, 2118, 2128, 2194

Miano, Robert 1318

Michael, Ralph 2009

Michael Filerman Productions 2060

Michael Ovitz Productions 2093

Michael Sloan Productions 1937, 2196

Michael Stoner, M.D. 1520

Michael-Liu, Frank 1245

Michaels, Corinne 1590

Michaels, Gregory 1840

Michaels, Jenna 1692

Michaels, Kerry 2165

Michaels, Lorne 2055

Michaels, Nicola 131

Michaels, Richard 1240, 1509

Michaels, Shawn 1968

Michaels of Africa 152

Michaelson, Kari 1946

Michaelson, Melissa 1602, 1781, 2009

Michas, Dimitri 1964

Michele Lee Show 1272

Michelle, Becky 1765

Michenaud, Gerald 959

Michener, James 94, 784

Mickey and Nora 2160

Mickey and the Contessa 553

Mickey Productions 1844, 1845, 1846
Mickey Rooney Show 747
Mickey Spillane's Mike Hammer 1747
Microcops 2243
Micronauts 2243
Midas Valley 1972
Middlemass, Frank 1127
Middleton, Ray 1789
Middleton, Robert 804, 808, 913, 1021, 1253, 1297
Middleton, Tom 1318
Midnight Mystery 164
Midwood, Kenneth 1886
Mighty O 655
Mike and the Mermaid 886
Mike Angel 576
Mike Shayne 268
Mike the Dog 2204
Milan, Lita 271
Milburn, Sue 1594, 1867
Milch, David 2263
Miles, Joanna 1443
Miles, Marc 2261
Miles, Rosalind 1506
Miles, Sylvia 308
Miles, Vera 255, 758, 994, 1075, 1158, 1301, 1403, 1802, 2021
Milford, John 2678
Milgrim, Lynn 2225
Milius, John 1255
Milkis, Ed 1184, 1197, 1365, 1898, 1915, 2000, 2227
Milkovich, Edwald 2266
Millan, Robyn 808, 1023, 1025

Millan, Victor 1104
Milland, Ray 686, 941, 1021, 1077
Millard, Oscar 129
Millay, Diana 507, 582
Mille, Gil 1169
Miller, Allan 129, 1386, 1489, 1606, 1909, 2030
Miller, Allen F. 792
Miller, Ben 1882
Miller, David 1781
Miller, Dean 831
Miller, Denise 1686, 2064
Miller, Denny 270, 301, 1451, 1852, 1917
Miller, Dick 1981
Miller, Doreen 901
Miller, Gary 2193
Miller, George 2208
Miller, Harvey 1575, 1629, 2142
Miller, Herman 1089, 1327, 2115, 2129, 2173
Miller, Ira 1567
Miller, Jack 1535
Miller, James 1316
Miller, James M. 1129
Miller, Jason 1621, 1717
Miller, Jason M. 960
Miller, Joseph 1398
Miller, Kathleen 1328
Miller, Lara Jill 1946
Miller, Lee 792, 1361, 1415, 1633
Miller, Mark 213, 1516
Miller, Mark Thomas 2127, 2259
Miller, Marvin 1566
Miller, Max 84
Miller, Merle 771
Miller, Michael 1567
Miller, Okay 1457

Miller, Robert Ellis 383, 603, 757, 764, 920, 1469
Miller, Roger 1549
Miller, Sam 521
Miller, Sidney 760, 1302
Miller, Stephen 1917, 1927
Miller, Thomas L. 1365
Miller, Tom 1184, 1197, 1700, 1898, 2108
Miller, Walter Driscoll 1043
Miller, Winston 1057, 1187
Miller-Milkis-Boyett Productions 1700, 1898
Miller Milkis Productions 1365
Milligan, Spencer 1338
Milligan, Tuck 1988
Mills, Adam 2024
Mills, Alley 1928, 1978, 2116
Mills, Claire 1712
Mills, Donna 1180, 1481, 1507, 1516, 1721
Mills, Hayley 1879, 2182
Mills, John 1562, 1886
Mills, Juliet 922, 974, 1168, 1190
Milner, Jesamine 1346
Milner, Martin 830, 852, 926, 973, 1692
Milton Berle Show 694
Milzer, Cameron 2049
Mimi 768

Mimieux, Yvette 1406, 1508, 1567, 1936
Mimieuz, Amparo 1567
Mims, William 695, 1315, 1642, 1904
Minardos, Nico 920
Mineo, Sal 877, 1031, 1075
Miner, Allen H. 267, 509, 1099
Miner, Jan 1636
Miner, Tony 69
Minkus, Barbara 1027, 1530
Minn, Huanani 2237
Minnie Pearl Show 1017
Minoff, Phyllis 1381, 1449
Minor, Bob 1321, 1451, 1619
Minor, Michael 1080, 1566
Minter, Kelly 2083
Mintz, Larry 1702, 1994, 1995, 2184
Mintz, Robert 1468
Miraculous Journey of Tadpole Chan 515
Miranda, Robert 1969
Miranda, Susanna 1101
Mirisch, Andrew 1958, 2190, 2260, 2261
Mirisch, Walter 394, 510, 2260
Mirisch-Rich Productions 968
Misch, David 1855
Mishkin, Phil 1276
Misita, Michael 2032
Mislov, Michael 940

Miss and the
   Missiles 731
Miss Bishop 599
Miss Brewster's
   Millions 546
Miss Pendelton's
   Point of
   View 2228
Miss Peters
   Speaking 501
Miss Stewart,
   Sir 1139
Mission Impossible
   958, 1210, 1691,
   2128, 2189
Missy's Men 989
Mr. Adams &
   Eve 203
Mr. and Mrs.
   Cop 1280
Mr. and Mrs. and
   Mr. 1737
Mr. and Mrs.
   Dracula
   1709, 1797
Mr. & Mrs.
   Ryan 2032
Mr. Belvedere 19,
   418, 860, 1862
Mr. Bevis 463, 670
Mr. Big 28, 172
Mr. Boogedy
   2079, 2134
Mr. Doc 564
Mr. Ed 679
Mr. In-Between 678
Mr. Inside/Mr.
   Outside 1231
Mister Jericho 1039
Mr. Kingston 754
Mr. Lucky 1612
Mr. Mom 1964
Mr. O'Malley 456
Mr. Paracelsus, Who
   Are You? 882
Mr. Quiet 2057
Mr. Right 1658
Mr. Success 1997
Mr. Tutt 256

Misty 636
Mitchell, Bobbie
   1501, 1637
Mitchell, Cameron
   321, 478, 961,
   1160, 1235, 1249,
   1291, 1720
Mitchell, Chuck
   2042
Mitchell, Coleman
   1540, 1607, 1946
Mitchell, Donna 2262
Mitchell, Gordon
   1664
Mitchell, Guy 555
Mitchell, Judith
   Paige 2024
Mitchell, Keith 1849
Mitchell, Mary 649
Mitchell, Sasha 2199
Mitchell, Shirley
   250, 309, 728,
   836, 1552
Mitchlll, Scoey 1200,
   1806, 2052
Mitchell, Steve 268
Mitchell, Thomas 41
Mitchum, Chris
   1170, 1515
Mitchum, John
   207, 1249
Mitera Target 1450
Mitore, Carmine
   1887
Mitz, Rick 1999
Mixed Company
   2108
Mixed Nuts 1437
Miyori, Kim 2028,
   2094, 2120
Mizzy, Vic 1026,
   1082, 1125, 1201
Moberly, Robert 1936
Mobile Medics 1476
Mobley, Candy 1689
Mobley, Mary Ann
   1065, 1291
Mobley, Roger 746
Mockridge, Cyril 843

Mockus, Tony 2177
Mod Squad 1193,
   1337, 1396
Modean, Jayne
   1672, 2078
Model and the
   Marriage
   Broker 126
Modesty Blaise
   1863
Modrell, Shawn
   2211
Moe, Douglas 769
Moe and Joe 1273
Moeller, J. David
   2130
Moessinger,
   David 1954
Moffat, Donald
   1168, 1644, 1714,
   2107, 2190
Moffat, Kitty
   2021, 2081
Moffitt, Susan 1128
Mohica, Vic 1425,
   1718, 2061
Mohr, Gerald 96,
   786, 827
Mohre, Kelly 1627
Moio, John 1514
Mokihana 1663, 2094
Molinario, Al 1434
Moll, Richard 1841
Mollin, Larry
   1904, 2090
Molloy, William 1176
Mom Is the
   Governor of
   Texas 406
Momma the
   Detective 1649
Mona 2138
Monash, Paul
   125, 379, 496,
   957, 1698
Monaster, Nate 381,
   385, 386, 497
Monckton,
   Patrick 2098

Mond, Stephen
   1545, 1627
Monette, Richard
   2132
Mongo, Justin 2208
Monica, Corbett
   1108
Monk 1010
Monkees 1054
Monkey Mission
   1845
Montagne, Ed 458,
   698, 861, 891, 913,
   1102, 1125, 1832
Montalban, Ricardo
   136, 271, 558,
   1030, 1057, 1123,
   1253, 1261
Montalban
   Enterprises 1030
Montana, Karla 2105
Monte, Mary
   Elaine 1236
Monte Carlo 605
Montegna, Joe 1864,
   1875, 2055
Montero, Pedro
   1887
Montgomery, Belinda
   J. 1072, 1103,
   1163, 1190, 1211,
   1694, 1720,
   1939, 2119, 2129
Montgomery,
   Bryan 1052
Montgomery,
   Earl 1764
Montgomery,
   Elizabeth
   717, 1257
Montgomery, Eliot
   129, 1245
Montgomery,
   Karen 1968
Montgomery, Lee
   H. 1093, 1250,
   1536, 2007
Montgomery, Tanis
   1173, 1269

Monument County 1935
Moody, David 1314, 1348
Moody, Jim 1821, 2041
Moody, Lynne 1682, 1722, 1800, 1875, 2034
Moody, Ralph 582
Mookie and Sheryl 1603
Moon Frye, Soleil 2198
Moon Is Blue 709
Mooney, Hal 912, 1160, 1219, 1245, 1247
Mooney, Maureen 1500
Mooney, Paul 1362
Mooney, William 2258
Moonjean, Hank 877
Moonlight 1887
Moonlight Productions 1645, 1936
Moonlighting 1970
Moore, Alvy 62, 603, 729, 1589, 1810, 1812
Moore, Archie 1160
Moore, Bob 1494
Moore, Candy 651
Moore, Charles Werner 1888
Moore, Del 614
Moore, H. Curley 1567
Moore, Ivana 1805, 1997
Moore, Joanna 704, 705, 751, 812, 930
Moore, Juanita 1248
Moore, Lisa 1074
Moore, Mary Tyler 310

Moore, Robert 1386, 1414, 1463, 1496, 1501, 1540, 1892
Moore, Roger 262, 1448, 2174
Moore, Terry 2093
Moore, Thomas W. 1874
Moore, Tom 140, 629, 879, 2154, 2199, 2205
Moorehead, Agnes 657, 1007, 1098, 1168
Mooring, Jeff 2244
Moose 1284
Mora, Danny 1501, 2017
Moran, Monica 900
Moray, Dean 833
Mordente, Lisa 1360
Mordente, Tony 1360, 1363, 1552, 1607, 1950, 2133
More Wild Wild West 1748
Moreland, Barry 1127
Moreland, Mantan 1098
Moreno, Belita 1953
Moreno, George 169
Moreno, Rita 1266, 1552, 2109, 2181
Moreno, Reuben 1329
Morey, Bill 1988, 2023, 2087, 2169
Morgan, Christopher 1291, 1560
Morgan, Cindy 2000, 2048
Morgan, Gary 308
Morgan, Gregory 2085
Morgan, Harry 126, 1052, 1282, 1475, 1505, 1514,

1534, 1656, 1690, 1748, 1821
Morgan, Jaye P. 806, 1126
Morgan, Judson 1245, 1301
Morgan, Marcia 1778
Morgan, Read 447, 1229, 1296, 1611
Morgan, Ronald E. 1942
Morgan, Stafford 1519
Morgan, Tracy 62
Morheim, Lou 211, 1127
Mori, Jeanne 1945
Moriarty, Michael 2241
Morick, Dave 1213, 1756.1992 Morin, Alberto 1656
Morita, Pat 1125, 1151, 1159, 1172, 1200, 1296, 1334, 1608, 1660
Morning Maggie 2161
Moroff, Mike 2246
Morricone, Ennio 2128, 2258
Morrill, Priscilla 1302, 1487, 1518
Morris, Ben 451
Morris, Chester 843, 847
Morris, Garrett 1265, 1942.1993
Morris, Greg 1515, 1713
Morris, Haviland 2040
Morris, Howard 833, 1832
Morris, Jeff 1419
Morris, John 1683, 1906
Morris, Linda 1899

Morris, Michael 916, 1131
Morris, Monty 2052
Morris, Terry 2171
Morris, Wayne 219, 465
Morrison, Barbara 670
Morrison, Shelley 1350
Morrissette, Billy 2266
Morrow, Brian 2025
Morrow, Byron 1126, 1147, 1224, 1340, 1503, 1561, 1749
Morrow, Doug 682
Morrow, Karen 1390
Morrow, Patricia 60
Morrow, Scott 385
Morrow, Susan 64
Morrow, Vic 503, 986, 1090, 1197, 1399, 1517, 1539, 1692
Morse, Barry 630, 2060
Morse, Carleton 91, 972
Morse, Hollingsworth 1660
Morse, Robert 164, 293
Morse, Terry, Jr. 1675, 1919
Morsell, Fred 1624
Mort Lachman and Associates 1930, 2075, 2077, 2125
Mort Lachman Productions 2139
Mortimer, Henry 1057
Mortimer, Johnnie 2037
Morton, Gary 1138, 1825
Morton, Howard 1190, 1877

Morton, Louisa 1165
Morton, Micah 1953
Morton, Mickey 1447
Moschitta, John,
Jr. 1855
Moscow Bureau
2019
Moseley, Page 2243
Moser, Jim 452
Moses, David 1078
Moses, Harry 1403
Moses, Marion 917
Mosher, Bob 587,
1016, 1929
Mosher, James 288
Mosley, Roger 1137
Mosley, Roger
E. 1815
Moss, David 815
Moss, Peter 2018
Moss, Stewart 1174,
1247, 1350, 1412,
1785, 1815
Moss, Warwick 2185
Mostel, Josh 1459
Mother and Me,
M.D. 1673
Mother Climbs
Trees 588
Mother Goose 254
Mother Is a
Freshman 279
Mother, Juggs and
Speed 1530
Mothers-in-Law 1779
Motorcycle Cop 100
Moulton, Charles
1261
Moultrie, Emily 2054
Mount, Michael 1998
Mountain Man 482
Mouse That
Roared 892
Movies on TV 880
Movin' On
1166, 1427
Movita 207
Moxey, John
Llewellyn 1074,

1212, 1303, 1350,
1520, 1584, 1615,
1644, 1687, 1985
Moye, Michael 2124
Mrs. G. Goes to
College 694
Mrs. R. 1352
Mrs. Sundance 1257
Mrs. Thursday 938
MTM Enterprises
1135, 1152, 1198,
1363, 1386, 1401,
1432, 1433, 1469,
1470, 1471, 1472,
1496, 1558, 1559,
1578, 1586, 1587,
1621, 1668, 1673,
1686, 1696, 1723,
1724, 1728, 1765,
1805, 1810, 1818,
1848, 1851, 1909,
2062, 2063, 2069,
2078, 2098, 2156,
2189, 2219, 2263
Mueller, Mark 1875
Muigai, Mwai 2248
Mulcahey, Russell
2210
Muldaur, Diana
1210, 1260, 1513,
1522, 1651
Muldoon, Mick
2174
Mulgrew, Kate 2069
Mulhare, Edward
1004
Mull, Martin
1900, 1940
Mullaney, Jack 1415
Mullaney, Kieran
1153
Mullavey, Greg
1156, 1557, 1660,
1867, 1877
Mullavey, Jack
552, 648
Mullendore,
Joseph 603
Mulligan, Jim 1622

Mulligan, Richard
1225
Mullikin, Bill
596, 743
Mullins, Michael
1773, 1840
Mullowney,
Deborah 2171
Mumy, Billy 660
Muni, Paul 1252
Munker, Ariane
1398
Munne, Maria 271
Munro, C. Pete 1959
Munson, Warren
2007, 2176
Munsters 1832
Munster's Revenge
1832
Munsters Today 1832
Muntner, Simon
1441, 1498
Muppet Show 1241
Muppets 1241
Muppets
No-Nonsense
Show 1313
Murcell, George
2098
Murder in a Minor
Key 2175
Murder in Music
City 1694
Murder in Peyton
Place 1518
Murder, Ink 1817
Murder 1, Dancer
0 **1846**
Murder, She
Wrote 2175
Murdoch, Luther
2129
Murdock, George
720, 1072, 1294,
1349, 1537,
1538, 2002
Murdock, Jack 1806
Murdocks and the
McClays 1035

Murdock's
Gang 1213
Murikami, Wolf,
Swenson
Productions 1724
Murney, Christopher
1636
Murphy, Alma 497
Murphy, Ben 1189,
1191, 1318, 1688,
1822, 1939, 2119
Murphy, Charles
Thomas 1461,
1807
Murphy, George
311, 467
Murphy, Joan 1057
Murphy, Martin 1054
Murphy, Mary 736
Murphy, Michael 905,
1134, 1406, 1480
Murphy, Ralph
Francis 388
Murphy, Richard
796, 971
Murphy, Warren
2152
Murphy, William 448
Murphy's Law 2044
Murphy's Romance
790
Murray, Brian 2172
Murray, Don 1293,
1921, 2120
Murray, Howard
2198
Murray, Jan 907, 1419
Murray, John
Fenton 556
Murray, Ken 169
Murray, Lyn
772, 1096
Murray, Mike 1158
Murray, Warren
1081, 1823
Murrell, John 1259
Murtaugh, James
1451, 1612, 1786,
1872, 1920

Murtaugh, John 1182, 1359, 1466

Murtaugh, Kate 1436, 1848

Musante, Tony 1519, 1610

Muse, Clarence 1248

Music, Henrietta 1363

Music, Lorenzo 1239, 1363, 1545, 1724

Music City Murders 1694

Music Maker 757

Music Man 328

Mustin, Burt 871, 1041

Mutrux, Floyd 2118

Mutts 2204

Muzurki, Mike 1592

My Africa 2248

My Boy Googie 953

My Brother's Keeper 1632

My Buddy 1604

My Cousin Davey 679

My Darling Judge 554

My Fat Friend 2080

My Favorite Love Story 568

My Favorite Son 201

My Friend Irma 307

My Husbands, Tom and John 977

My Island Family 793

My Life as a Dog 2249

My Love Affair with the State of Maine 119

My Lucky Penny 815

My Man St. John 794

My Old Man 109

My Sister Hank 1140

My Son, the Doctor 819

My Three Sons 1080

My Two Dads Spin-Off 2255

My Wife Next Door 1285, 1738

My Wife's Brother 570

My Wives Jane 1086

My World and Welcome To It 390, 557

Mydell, Joseph 2248

Myer, Bob 2105

Myers, Paulene 1098

Myers, Peter 1992, 2119

Myers, Susan 1749

Myerson, Alan 1622, 1754

Myhers, John 1623

Myles, Patrick 2144

Myman, Robert 2205

Myren, Tania 1638

Myrer, Anton 1692

Myrow, Fred 1075

Mysterious Island 86

Mysterious Two 1689

Mystery Movie 1160

Mystery Writer's Theatre 73

N

Naar, Joseph T. 1447

Nabors, Jim 2122

Nadell, Andrew 2201

Nadler, Regis 647

Naff, Lycia 2106

Nagle, Margaret 2090

Nagy, Ivan 1642, 1716

Nahan, Stu 2193

Nail, Joanne 1530

Naish, J. Carrol 1019

Najee-Ullah, Mansoor 1906

Name of the Game 1336

Nancy Drew 128

Nancy Dussault Show 1205

Nancy Walker Show 407

Napier, Alan 805, 1211, 1845

Napier, Charles 1508, 1582, 1864, 2264

Napier, John 995

Napolean, Titus 1447

Napoleon, Art 417, 680

Nardini, Tom 878, 1051, 1076

Nardino, Gary 1984, 1993, 2017, 2056, 2072

Nardo, Pat 1360, 1575, 1828, 2014, 2109

Nardone, Jason 2098

Narita, Richard 1386, 1514, 1519, 2094

Narita, Rob 1916

Nasatir, Mark 2104

Nash, Bob 1010

Nash, Chris 1922

Nash, Robert 309, 829

Natalie 2139

Nathan, Mort 2068

Nathan, Robert 1516

Nathan, Stephen 1245, 1367, 1426, 1812, 2087

National Lampoon Productions 1836

National Lampoon's Two Reelers 1836

Natole, Steve 2096

Natural Enemies 1739

Natural Look 1496

Naturals 1956

Natwick, Mildred 1982

Natwick, Myron 1057, 1164

Naud, Melinda 1617

Naughton, David 2000

Naughton, James 1320, 1888, 2177

Navarro, Anna 1104, 1160, 1338

Navin, John P., Jr. 1889, 1890

Navin, Sarah 2007

Naylor, Jayson 1633, 1998

NBC Comedy Hour 61

NBC Comedy Theatre 1825, 1826, 1830, 1831, 1837, 1839

NBC Productions 57, 72, 254, 582, 832, 914, 963, 1161, 1683, 1847, 1894, 1996, 2007, 2051, 2053, 2127, 2128, 2178, 2180, 2182, 2193, 2194, 2256, 2258, 2264, 2266, 2268

Neal, Navis 1190

Neal, Richard 925

Near, Holly 1280

Needham, Hal 1718, 1835

Needham, Leo 2049

Neeley, Ted 1475

Neely, Mark 1688

Neenan, Audrie 1961

Neff, Elsie 125

Negretl, Rudy 1958

Neighbors 767, 1068

Neigher, Geoffrey 1540, 1607, 1946

Neill, Bob 1517

Neilsen, Bob 2096

Neilson, Barry 299

Neilson, James 916

Neilson, John 1055
Neilson, Phil 2132
Neiman, Irving
  Gaynor 1466
Nelkin, Stacey 1692,
  1879, 1940, 2001
Nelligan, Kate 2172
Nelson, Barry 423,
  812, 1086, 1162,
  1224, 1312, 1463
Nelson, Carolyn 1147
Nelson, Chris 1518
Nelson, Christopher
  2066, 2127
Nelson, Craig
  Richard 1439
Nelson, Craig T. 1198
Nelson, David 1994
Nelson, Dick
  925, 1029
Nelson, Don 307,
  658, 1660, 1832
Nelson, Ed 698,
  1290, 1518, 1651
Nelson, Erik 1101
Nelson, Felix 1922
Nelson, Gary 1150,
  1291, 1378, 1405,
  1851, 1976,
  2151, 2269
Nelson, Gene 204,
  765, 901, 1189
Nelson, Harriet
  1995, 2193
Nelson, Herbert 1073
Nelson, Jessica 2039
Nelson, Kris 1040
Nelson, Noble 1093
Nelson, Novella
  2172
Nelson, Oliver
  972, 1183
Nelson, Peter
  1180, 1968
Nelson, Portia 971
Nelson, Ralph
  114, 1781
Nelson, Rick
  1040, 1995

Nelson, Tracy
  2016, 2085
Nemes, Scott
  1920, 1942
Nepenthe
  Productions 938
Nephi Productions
  1551, 1761
Neptune, Peter
  2258
Nervik, Leig 1022
Nesbitt, Derren
  1058
Nethery, Miriam-
  Byrd 1410, 1504
Netter, Douglas
  1680, 1882
Nettleton, Lois
  925, 2041
Neufeld, Marc 1286
Neufield, Stanley
  1099
Neuman, Dorothy
  463
Neuman, E. Jack 334,
  849, 1021, 1058,
  1089, 1148, 1167,
  1424, 2058, 2195
Neuman, Sam 391
Neumann, Jenny
  1549
Nevada Smith 1353
Never Again 1965
Never Cry Wolf 1421
Never Go to
  Sea 2229
Never Plead
  Guilty 523
Never Say Never
  1635
Never Too
  Young 1690
Nevins, Claudette
  1257, 1423, 1521,
  2192, 2245
New, Nancy 1439
New Avengers 1563
New Comedy
  Showcase 465, 466

New Daughters of
  Joshua Cabe 1374
New Doctor in
  Town 932
New Doctors 1029
New Gidget 1664
New Great American
  Hero 2133
New Healers 1128
New Invaders 1678
New Kind of
  Love 1158
New Leave It to
  Beaver 1929
New Lorenzo Music
  Show 1363
New Maverick 1448
New Millionaire
  1566
New Odd Couple
  1014, 1756
New Orleans
  Force 1324
New Robinson
  Crusoe 284
New T.J. Hooker
  2034
New Tightrope
  541, 1147
New West
  Productions 2265
New World
  Productions 1567
New World
  Television 2074,
  2089, 2146, 2169,
  2200, 2232, 2264
New York's
  Finest 214
Newborn, Ira 1965
Newell, Karen 1617
Newland, John
  653, 718
Newley, Anthony
  2226
Newman, Barry
  1954, 2044
Newman, Carroll
  2085, 2146

Newman, Edwin
  1960
Newman, Fred
  2163
Newman, Joseph
  301, 478
Newman, Lionel
  1123, 2221
Newman, Melissa
  1077
Newman, Pamela
  1977
Newman, Paul 1301
Newman, Roger 954
Newman, Tom 1832
Newman, Walter 39
Newman's
  Drugstore 1411
Newmar, Julie 900,
  1125, 1224,
  1526, 1995
Newnow, Joe 2099
Newton, Richard 603
Newton, Sandi 1546
Newton, Theodore
  164
Ney, Richard
  521, 844
N'Gom, Adoulaye
  2258
Ngor, Dr. Haing
  2170
Nguen, Cuba 2269
Nguyen, Michell
  2237
Nguyen, Oliver 1784
Nice Guys Finish
  Dead 1788
Nicholl, Don 1171,
  1554, 1736
Nichols, Barbara
  586, 728, 757
Nichols, Bob 1131
Nichols, David 2253
Nichols, M.A. 2242
Nichols, Michelle
  1063
Nichols, Mike 1174
Nichols, Robert 292

Nichols and
  Dymes 1848
Nicholson, Jack 1310
Nick and Hillary
  2062
Nick and the
  Dobermans 1775
Nick Derrenger,
  P.I. 2205
Nick Quarry 982
Nick Tattinger 2062
Nick Vanoff
  Productions 1599
Nickerson, Denise
  1269, 1423
Nickson, Julia 2091
Nicky's World 1281
Nieber, Linda 2222
Nielsen, James 93
Nielsen, Leslie 845,
  846, 902, 1057,
  1061, 1076, 1100,
  1189, 1226, 1691
Nielson, Christine
  760
Niese, George 691
Night Court 1891
Night in Havana 136
Night of the
  Father 1380
Night of the Rat 1958
Night Partners 1936
Night People 298
Night Rider 1616
Night School 1823
Night Stalker 1009,
  1232, 1621
Night Stick 299
Night Strangler 1009
Nightingale 1957
Nightingales 1695
Nightmare in
  Chicago 905
*Nightmare on Elm
  Street* 2070
Nightmares 1958
Nightside 1192, 1617
Nightwatch 905
Nilsson, Harry 2204

Nimoy, Leonard
  925, 1158, 1168,
  1183 905
905-WILD 1354
William Street 88
Nipar, Yvette 2220
Nisbet, Stuart 1098,
  1164, 1616
Niven, David 147
Niven, Kip 1187,
  1416, 1511, 1805
Niven, Susan 1851
No Complaints 2054
*No Facilities for
  Women* 281
No, Honestly 2162
No Man's Land 2009
No Place Like
  Home 518, 2037
*No Such Thing As A
  Vampire* 1250
Noble, James
  1742, 1867
Noble, Melanie 1635
Noble, Nancy 1567
Noble, Trish 1584
Noble, Trisha
  1656, 1722
Nodella, Burt
  1254, 2166
Noel, Chris 816, 833
Noel, Hubert 1564
Nogulich, Natalia
  2121
Nolan, Jeanette 60,
  392, 734, 861, 880,
  923, 974, 1374,
  1424, 1535, 1690
Nolan, Katherine
  1226
Nolan, Kathleen
  1156
Nolan, Lloyd
  325, 592, 665,
  1515, 1868
Nolan, William
  F. 1232, 1255,
  1322, 1347
Noland, Ann 1189

Nolte, Nick 1254,
  1315, 1355
Nono, Claire
  1958, 2065
Noonan, Tommy 647
Nordling, Jeffrey
  2269
Nordlinger,
  Neal 2114
Norell, Michael
  1533, 1624, 1851
Norliss Tapes
  1009, 1232
Norma Rae 1849
Norman Rosemont
  Productions 1299,
  1813, 1886
Norman, B.G. 743
Norman, Gerard
  1127
Norman, Maidie
  1248, 1634
Norman Tokar
  Productions 1199
Norren, William
  1682
Norris. Pam 2143
North, Alan
  1856, 2180
North, Chris 2241
North, Edmund
  H. 1123, 1213
North, Nicholas 2070
North, Sheree 537,
  723, 1230, 1254,
  1650, 1695, 1985
Northon, Cliff 2052
Northstar 2033
Norton, Cliff 653,
  819, 890, 1018,
  1082, 1439
Norton, Jim
  1380, 1886
Norway Productions
  1524
Nosey and the
  Kid 1634
Nosseck, Noel 1936,
  2119, 2213

Not As a Crocodile
  492
Not in Front of
  the Kids 1998
Not Until Today
  1668
Nothing Is Easy
  1240
Nouri, Michael 1684,
  1692, 1775, 1918
Novack, Shelly 1189
Novak, John 2128
Novello, Jay 64,
  765, 827, 1407
Now Is Tomorrow
  611
Now We're
  Cookin' 1875
Nowhere Boys 144
Nowhere to
  Hide 1519
NRW Productions
  1554, 1736
Nucci, Danny 2263
Nugent, Kelbe 1989
Nugent, Nelle 2161
Nunn, Alice
  1434, 1835
Nunn, Terri 1730
Nunn, William
  1100
Nunundaga 1375
Nurse Bob 2256
Nurses 1457
Nurses in Korea
  1457
Nuts and Bolts
  1798
Nutt, Grady 1829
Nuyen, France
  1510, 1972
Nyby, Christian
  670, 2100, 2152
Nyby, Christian,
  II 1522
Nye, Louis 1552
Nye, Willie
  1907, 2105
Nype, Russell 685

O

Oakes, Randy 1371
Oakland, Simon 76, 750, 756, 1089, 1230, 1783, 1788
Oakmont 2266
Oates, Warren 852, 875, 1466, 1536, 1679, 1742
Oath 1325, 1326
Oatman, Doney 1443
Ober, Philip 59, 667
Oberman, Milt 1971
Oblong, Harold 1317
Obney, Jack Ross 2186
Oboler, Arch 1165
O'Brien, Clay 1162
O'Brien, David 2258
O'Brien, Edmond 523, **666**
O'Brien, Frank 1789
O'Brien, Hugh 752, 1506
O'Brien, Kenneth 1419
O'Brien, Leo 2010
O'Brien, Liam 1168
O'Brien, Margaret 115
O'Brien, Maria 1438, 2183
O'Brien, Marie 1339
O'Brien, Melody 504
O'Brien, Pat 323, 1040, 1041, 1126, 1226, 1369
O'Brien, Patrick 2251
O'Brien, Philip 2240
O'Brien, Richard 1076, 1537, 1732
O'Brien, Robert 62
O'Brien, Rory 670
O'Brien, Tom 2194
O'Byrne, Bryan 1930
Ochlon, P.J. 2143
O'Connell, Arthur 390, 557, 636, 764

O'Connell, David J. 1116, 1117, 1245, 1429
O'Connell, James 1450, 1585
O'Connell, John 1368
O'Connell, William 670
O'Conner, Darren 1491, 1492
O'Conner, Frank 765
O'Conner, Carroll 615, 738, 759, 905, 1028, 1452, 1639, 1749, 2041, 2087
O'Conner's Ocean 519
O'Connor, Donald 809, 890, 906
O'Connor, Hugh 2041
O'Connor, Robert 2155
O'Connor, Tim 1076, 1130, 1235, 1254, 1403, 1517, 1518, 2120
O'Connor/Becker Company 1740, 1749
Octavius and Me 656
Odalys 2148
O'Daniel, Michael 1604
Odd Couple 1014, 1142, 1344, 2180
Oden, Susan 949
Odessa, Devon 2262
Odley, Eleanor 21
Odney, Douglas 75
O'Donnell, Peter 1863
Odyssey Productions 272
Off Campus 1459
Off Duty 2244
Off the Boat 2055
Off the Wall 1459, 1497

Off to See the Wizard *301*, 750, 802, 886, 945
Off We Go 893
Officer and a Gentleman 1359
Official Detective Story 218
Official Films 166, 356
Official Productions 893
Ogg, Sammy 125
Ogiens, Michael 2154, 2230
Ogiens/Kane Productions 2154, 2230
Ogilvy, Ian 2116, 2174, 2219
Oh, Johnny 573
Oh, Nurse 1141
Oh, Soon-Teck 1100, 1168, 1251, 1472, 1654, 2120
O'Hagen, Timothy 1692
Ohanion 1376
O'Hanlon, George 65, 656, 1284, 1636
O'Hanlon, George, Jr. 1303, 1541
O'Hanlon, Phillip 662
O'Hara, Jenny 1418, 1445, 1516
O'Hara, Maureen 327, 887
O'Hara, Shirley 1515
O'Hare, Brad 2054
O'Hare, Michael 1441
O'Heaney, Caitlin 2208
O'Henry Playhouse 41
O'Herlihy, Dan 8, 284, 1129, 1419,

1446, 1481, 1504, 1646, 2025
O'Herlihy, Michael 1267, 1369, 1469, 1850
O'Keefe, Dennis 17, 113, 241
O'Keefe, James 1969, 2067
O'Keefe, Kevin 1321
O'Keefe, Michael 1321, 1325, 1378
O'Keefe, Winston 255, 382, 386, 497, 743, 807
O'Keefer, Paul 746
O'Kelley, Tim 894
Okelo, Martin 2248
Okon, Tim 1569
Okumoto, Yuji 2120
Olafson, Ken 1413
Old Dogs 2151
Old Friends 1966
Old Man and the City 739
Old Man Coffee 34
Old Money 2230
Oldknow, John 1158
O'Leary, Jack 16f37, 1940
O'Leary, John 1419, 1681, 1704
Olek, Henry 1537, 1688, 1918
Oliansky, Joel 1425, 2065
Oliney, Alan 1799
Oliphant, Peter 600
Oliver, Barrett 1904, 2104
Oliver, Deanna 2154
Oliver, Gordon 774
Oliver, Henry 1116
Oliver, Raymond 2194
Oliver, Susan 643, 2021

Olkewicz, Walter 1802, 1805, 2213
O'Loughlin, Gerald S. 1568, 1776, 1986, 2023
Olson, Eric 1350
Olson, James 1118, 1167, 1299, 1328, 1424
O'Malley 1850
O'Malley, David 1592
O'Malley, J. Pat 13, 455, 526, 1032, 1238
O'Malley, Kathleen 1198
O'Malley, Princess 1609
O'Moore, Patrick 1424
Oms, Alba 1907
On Ice 1635
On Our Way 2045
On the Edge 2194
On the Road 2045
On the Rocks 1364
On the Waterfront 173
Once Upon a Spy 1611, 1716
One Day at a Time 1974
One Embezzlement and Two Margaritas 920
One False Step 87
100 Centre Street 1967
110 in the Shade 829
One Man's Family 101
One More Try 1876
One Night Band 1818
One Performance Only 488
One-Eyed Jacks Are Wild 883
O'Neal, Kevin 766

O'Neal, Patrick 880, 1357, 1371, 1376, 1918
O'Neal, Ryan 1012, 1518, 1533, 1766
O'Neal, Tatum 1898
O'Neil, Shane 2082
O'Neil, Tony 2035
O'Neil, Tricia 1509, 1785
O'Neill, Anne 2096
O'Neill, Dick 1137, 1340, 1491, 1492, 1806, 1883
O'Neill, Ed 1184, 1777, 1907, 2022, 2132
O'Neill, Johnny 612
O'Neill, Richard 1384
O'Neill, Robert F. 1298, 1692, 1779, 2130, 2131, 2175
O'Neill, Tricia 2106
Only in America 1242
Only One Day Left Before Tomorrow 1031
Only You, Dick Daring! 771
Onyullo, Sid 2248
Opatoshu, David 266, 780, 1076, 1117, 1350, 1481
Operating Room 1696
Operation Greasepaint 954
Operation Hang-Ten 1193
Operation Razzle-Dazzle 894
Operation Red 996
Operation Secret 755
Operation: Runaway 1188

Oppenheimer, Alan 1025, 1037, 1094, 1138, 1201, 1217, 1243, 1390, 1502, 1831, 2166
Oppenheimer, Jess 58, 66, 76, 254, 257, 387, 556, 691, 1351
Oprah Winfrey Show 2139
Oquendo, Luis 271
Orbach, Jerry 1774, 2010, 2199
Orchard, John 1127
O'Reilly, Cyril 1782, 2189
O'Reilly, Robert 2042
Orenstein, Bernie 1143, 1576
Orenthal Productions 1781, 1893, 1953
Oringer, Barry 1127, 2117
Orion Television 1935, 1968, 1983, 2041, 2144, 2152, 2168, 2235, 2242
Orlandi, Felice 1291
Orlando, Tony 2057
Oroglini, Arnold 1968
O'Rourke, Heather 1862
O'Rourke, Kevin 2174
O'Rourke, Tom 2266
Orphan and the Dude 1314
Orr, William 756
Orrinson, Jack 457
Orsati, Noon 2085
Orson Welles Show 74
Osborn, Ron 1962
O'Shea, Amber 2212
O'Shea, Michael 118
Oshima, Faye 1923
Osmond, Alan 774

Osmond, Cliff 750, 1356, 1385
Osmond, Donny 774
Osmond, Eric 1929
Osmond, Jay 774
Osmond, Ken 1929, 1994, 1995
Osmond, Marie 1601, 1865
Osmond, Merrill 774
Osmond, Wayne 774
Osmond Company 1601
Osmond Television Productions 1764, 1781
O.S.S. 2063
O'Steen, Sam 1383
Osteloh, Robert 93
Osterhage, Jeff 1536, 1570, 1693, 1854
Osterwald, Bibi 757, 884, 939, 1812
Ostrander, Bill 1830
O'Sullivan, Colleen 463
O'Sullivan, James 1723
O'Sullivan, Moya 2185
O'Sullivan, Richard 262
Oswald, Gerd 758
Otherworld 2126
Otto Salamon Productions 1777
Our Gang 1944
Our House 2133
Our Man Flint 1377
Our Man Flint: Dead on Target 1377
Our Man in Rome 565
Our Miss Brooks 23
Our Place 1740
Our Town 428
Our Two Hundred Children 534

Our Very Own 430
Ousley, Dina 1403
Out of the Blue
670, 955
Out of Time 2267
Out-of-Towners
1113
Outer Limits 758
Outlaws 701,
734, 1864
Outpost 402, 701
Outpost of
Space 397
Outrider 338
Outside Chance
1567
Outside Man 946
Outward Bound
1513, 1595
Over and Out 1412
Over-the-Hill
Gang 1040
Over-the-Hill Gang
Rides Again 1041
Overall, Park 2123
Overbey, Kellie 2165
Overstreet,
Dion 1173
Overton, Bill
1307, 1512
Overton, Frank
666, 735, 775
Ovitz, Mark 2093
Owen, Beverly 776
Owen, Bud 1230
Owen, Grant 1647
Owen, Jim 1694,
2119
Owen, John Steven
2069, 2249
Owen, Reginald
1155
Owen, Shanti 2243
Owen, Tony 552,
623, 628, 805
Owens, Albert 2096
Owens, Gary 870
Owens, Grant
1595, 1936

Owens, William
P. 2246
Owl and the Pussy
Cat 1286
Owns, Alan 1106

P

Pace, Judy 1141
Pace, Ralph 1959
Pace, Tom 1212
Pacino, Al 1920
Packard, John 1249
Packer, David 1994
Packer, Peter 126
Padilla, Manuel,
Jr. 1019
Paez, Alex 1842,
2083
Pagan, Anna 1529
Page, David 2045
Page, Harrison 1341,
1893, 2028
Page, LaWanda
1429, 1447
Page, Patti 538
Pagett, Gary 1339
Paige, Janis 117,
318, 733, 1764,
2009, 2039
Paine, Debbie 860
Paisano Productions
207
Paiva, Nestor 6, 813
Pak, Bill 2091
Palance, Jack 504
Palance, Michael
2262
Paleface 910
Paley, Penelope 1683
Paliotti, Michael
John 2219
Palish, Thelma 1108
Pall, Gloria 653
Palladino, Susan 2019
Pallilo, Ron 1942
Palmaro, Chris 1649
Palmer, Anthony
1589

Palmer, Carla 1894
Palmer, David 1640
Palmer, Gregg
1445, 1536
Palmer, Leland
1386, 1463
Palmer, Maria 436
Palmer, Peter 482,
1825, 2171
Palmer, Stuart 1125
Palmer, Tom 1397
Palmer, Tony 1231
Palms 1785
Palms Precinct
1785
Palomar Productions
1191, 1236,
1375, 1397
Palone, Judith 2146
Pals 1833
Paltrow, Bruce 1243,
1455, 1542,
1696, 2062
Paluzzi, Luciana 533
Palzis, Kelly 1955
Pam 1084
Panache 1378
Panama 606, 850
Panas, Alex 2083
Pandoliano,
Vincent 2025
Pandora 555
Pandora and
Friends 555
Panic in Echo
Park 1520
Pankhurst,
Patrick 2196
Pankin, Stuart 1754,
1764, 1779, 1812
Pantoliano, Joe
1436, 2086
Papa G.I. 769
Papa Said No 202
Papazian, Robert
A. 1620
Paper Chase
1396, 2090
Papp, Richard 2045

Paradise Kid 496
Paradise Motel 2184
Parady, Ron
2113, 2258
Paramount Television
499, 525, 599, 740,
805, 838, 869,
999, 1014, 1015,
1035, 1042, 1056,
1065, 1070, 1074,
1085, 1087, 1113,
1128, 1133, 1170,
1174, 1184, 1197,
1210, 1217, 1222,
1240, 1301, 1334,
1341, 1348, 1365,
1376, 1384, 1388,
1411, 1424, 1440,
1460, 1481, 1490,
1491, 1492, 1531,
1536, 1541, 1551,
1552, 1555, 1570,
1582, 1583, 1585,
1588, 1589, 1598,
1603, 1630, 1653,
1661, 1662, 1663,
1664, 1681, 1700,
1704, 1708, 1712,
1718, 1772, 1793,
1794, 1816, 1827,
1860, 1863, 1898,
1905, 1911, 1915,
1916, 1932, 1944,
1947, 1966, 1969,
1984, 1993, 2000,
2017, 2019, 2056,
2067, 2072, 2085,
2095, 2114, 2121,
2141, 2158, 2164,
2167, 2179, 2228,
2229, 2238, 2269
Pare, Michael 1799
Parent, Gail 1108,
1460, 1555
Parfitt, Judy 2060
Parfrey, Woodrow
760, 974, 1025,
1048, 1105, 1125,
1133, 1183, 1255,

1268, 1418, 1471, 1597, 1833
Paris, Jerry 968, 1014, 1051, 1108, 1151, 1154, 1156, 1176, 1214, 1238, 1385, 1453, 1531, 1541
Paris, Robin Mary 1850
Park, Charles Lloyd 1127
Parke, Dorothy 2180
Parker, Bret 1131
Parker, Carl 2096
Parker, Corey 2167
Parker, Eleanor 847, 1307, 1716
Parker, F. William 1911
Parker, Fess 470, 567, 1162, 1268
Parker, George 2185
Parker, James 1015, 1042, 1056, 1331, 1457
Parker, Jameson 1780, 2047
Parker, Janet 20
Parker, Jim 1107, 1135, 1152, 1314, 1623
Parker, John 1019, 1421, 1507, 1651
Parker, Lara 1245, 1335, 1404, 1865
Parker, Monica 1818
Parker, Noelle 2155
Parker, Norman 1683, 2189, 2262
Parker, Robert B. 1802
Parker, Rod 1097, 1549, 1636, 1726, 1737, 1804, 1870, 2176
Parker, Sarah Jessica 2102
Parker, Suzy 822, 862, 880

Parker, Warren 1126, 1246
Parker, Wes 1584, 1786
Parkers 1834
Parkingtons: Dear Penelope 1189
Parkins, Barbara 1586, 1939
Parkinson, Dian 1270
Parkinson, Nancee 1067
Parks, James 2126
Parks, Michael 704, 724, 772, 1401, 1588, 1717, 1720
Parnell, Emory 21
Parole 1888
Parole Productions 1888
Parone, Ed 1849
Parr, Larry 1547
Parr, Stephen 1956, 1969, 2066
Parriott, James D. 1693, 1774, 1775, 1852, 2004, 2006, 2094
Parriott, Sara 2166
Parros, Peter 2050
Parry, Harvey 206
Parslow, Phillip 1301
Parsons 1258
Parsons, E.M. 756
Parsons, Estelle 1258
Parsons, Julie 1595
Parsons, Karyn 2223
Parsons, Lindsay 120, 209, 490
Parsons, Milton 1410
Parsons, Nicholas 761
Partington, John 1519
Partlow, Richard 2126
Partners 1092
Partners in Crime 1164, 1233
Parton, Reg 322

Partridge Family 1134
Pascal, Ernest 471
Pascal, Lisa 1904
Pascal, Milton 309
Pasquin, John 2159, 2207, 2235, 2253
Passarella, Art 870
Past Imperfect 2206
Pastorelli, Robert 1924, 2022, 2099
Pastorini, Dan 1865
Pataki, Michael 743, 1061, 1433, 1506, 1597, 1619, 1779, 1837, 2265
Patchett, Tom 1433, 1996, 2178, 2256
Pate, Michael 845
Pateraude, Hugette 1519
Paterson, William 1885
Patinkin, Mandy 1682
Patrick, Alain 1441, 1480
Patrick, Dennis 1320, 1510, 1561, 1730, 1840
Patrick, James 776
Patrick, Lee 126, 253, 768
Patrick Stone 669
Patsy 1221
Patten, Robert 1515
Patterson, Cjon Damitri 1593, 1660
Patterson, Dick 819, 897
Patterson, John 1788, 2147, 2191, 2241
Patterson, Kari Ann 1872
Patterson, Lee 925
Patterson, Lorna 1541, 1630
Patterson, Neva 464, 1533, 1844

Patton 1123
Patton, Robert 1123
Pauer, Debra 1992
Paul, Byron 1205, 1311
Paul, Georgia 1689, 2089
Paul, Kurt 2186
Paul, Lee 1298, 1337, 2261, 1301
Paul, Norman 870, 965, 1017, 1601
Paul, P.R. 1566, 2232
Paul, Richard 1500
Paul, Roderick 1253
Paul, Steven 1465
Paul Pine 947
Paul Pompian Productions 1885
Paul Williams Show 1579
Pauley, Alexandra 1745
Paulin, Scott 1621, 1972, 1988, 2028, 2045, 2195, 2259
Pauline 948
Paull, Morgan 1123, 1322, 1369, 1654
Paulsen, Albert 905, 958, 1436, 1466, 1564
Paulson, Dan 2152
Pavan, Marisa 1019
Pavelonis, Dave 1949
Pax, James 2120
Paxton, Bill 1927
Paxton, John 470
Pay the Piper 851, 920
Paymer, David 1877
Payne, John 246, 519
Payne, Julie 1794, 1920, 2017, 2163
Payne, Patricia 1642
Pays, Amanda 2247
Payton, Jo Marie 1551
Peabody, Dick 1282

Peace in the Family 939

Peake, Don 1531, 1541, 1645, 2061, 2129

Peaker, E.J. 937

Pearce, Alice 642, 953

Pearcy, Patricia 1682

Pearl, Barry 1385, 1453, 1832, 2126

Pearl, Howard 1876, 2156

Pearl, Minnie 1017

Pearlman, Stephen 1727

Pearlman, Steve 1511

Pearlsberg, Nancy 1936

Pearson, Billy 207

Pearson, Garret 1867

Peary, Harold 871

Pease, Patsy 1997

Peck, Ed 665

Peck, Gregory 718, 1064

Peck, Jim 1959

Peck, Stanley 266

Peck, Steve 523

Peck, Steven 1164

Peckinpah, David 1712

Peckinpah, Sam 737

Pedi, Tom 1266

Pedrosa, Inez 845

Pedroski, Lefty 1435, 1754

Pedroza, Inez 1562

Peeples, Samuel A. 1524, 1650

Peerce, Larry 971

Peggy Cass Show 498

Peggy Lee Show 419

Peggy Sue 2140

Peirce, Robert 1623, 1947

Pelikan, Lisa 1536, 1692

Pelletier, Louis 456

Pellow, Cliff 1601, 1902

Peluce, Meeno 1897, 1981

Pen 'n Inc. 1807

Pendergast, Gary 1528

Pendleton, Austin 1455, 1542, 2036

Pendleton, David 1477

Pendleton, Wyman 1817

Penelope Beware 895

Penghlis, Thaao 2117

Penn, Leo 1610, 1694, 1814

Pennell, Larry 845, 931, 1101

Pennington, Ann 1970

Pennington, Marla 1680, 1911

Pennock, Christopher 1887

Penny, Jennifer 1145

Penny, Joe 1443, 1530, 1619, 1743, 1938, 2006

Penny, Sydney 1616, 1699, 1826, 1903, 1904, 2053

Pentecost, George 1527, 1550, 1558, 1806, 1869

Penthouse Productions 1688

Penumbra Productions 2194

People 102, 1129

People Like Us 1428

Peppard, George 1072

Pepper, Barbara 657, 1015

Pepper, Cynthia 821, 930

Peppiatt, Frank 1389

Pera, Lisa 813

Pera, Rademas 1110

Peragine, Ken 2093

Perak, John 1504, 1536

Perelman, S.J. 642

Perez, Inez 1253

Perez, Jose 1262, 1782

Perez, Louis 1944

Perez, Tony 1621, 2159, 2195

Perezury, Jose 2157

Perica, Joanna 2132

Perils of Pauline 527, 637, 896, 948, 998

Perils of Pinky 230

Perine, Parke 1190

Perito, Jennifer 1600

Perkins, Barbara 1421

Perkins, Jack 737, 1904

Perkins, Kent 1810

Perkins, Leslie 916

Perl, Arnold 1078

Perrault, Robert 1683

Perreau, Gigi 632

Perrin, Nat 483, 484

Perrin, Vic 93

Perrine, Valerie 1219, 2154

Perry Mason 666

Perry, Barbara 1554, 1696

Perry, Celia 1907

Perry, Elizabeth 1419

Perry, Ernest, Jr. 2034

Perry, Felton 1186, 1561, 1586, 1587, 1588, 2205

Perry, John Bennett 1134, 2191

Perry, Joseph 1123

Perry, Kay 2201

Perry, Matthew 2161

Perry, Roger 311, 467, 646, 719, 1047, 1110, 1172, 1350, 1517

Perry, Scott 2042

Perry, Vicky 1716, 1970

Perry, Vincent 1008

Pershing, D'Vaughn 2176

Persky, Bill 1037, 1092, 1264, 1285, 1462, 1542, 1672, 1733, 1738, 1741, 1805, 1809, 1873, 1930, 1998, 2206

Persky, Lisa Jane 1921, **2121**

Persoff, Nehemiah 802, 877, 1019, 1244, 1590, 1610, 1720

Personal Report 219

Pescow, Donna 1840

Pesner, Jonah 1809

Pet Set 911

Petch, David 1129

Pete 'n' Tillie 1274

Peter Benchley's Mysteries of the Deep 1588

Peter Gunn 717

Peter Novak's America 453

Peterman, Steven 1727, 1806, 1943

Peters, Bernadette 1286, 1565

Peters, Brock 1194, 1248

Peters, Charlie 2234

Peters, Erika 847

Peters, House, Jr. 463

Peters, Jeff 1962

Peters, Jon 1888, 2011

Peters, Kelly Jean 956, 2042

Peters, Margie 1896, 2054
Peters, Mary 1620
Peters, Tom 1866
Petersen, Pat 1686
Peterson, Amanda 2069
Peterson, Arthur 1126
Peterson, Chris 1597
Peterson, Eddie 1840
Peterson, Eugene 1211, 1586, 1587
Peterson, Lenka 1316, 2061
Peterson, Nan 213
Peterson, Paul 1004, 1083, 1995
Peterson, Sandra 1779
Peterson, Tommy 1882
Peterson, Warren 1007
Petievich, Gerald 2128, 2258
Petit, Michael 595
Petit, Pascale 1058
Petitclerc, Denne Bart 1230, 1256
Petlock, John 1587, 2023
Petrakis, Harry Mark 736
Petranto, Russ 1493, 1529, 1674, 1701
Petrie, Dan, Jr. 2100
Petrie, Daniel 1258, 1316, 1381, 1449
Petrie, Donald 1626, **2220**
Petrocelli 2044
Petterson, Stuart 1697
Pettet, Joanna 931, 1139, 1197, 1259, 1423, 1480, 1651, 2002
Petteway, James 1818

Pettine, Carlo 2191
Pettinger, Gary 1885
Pettus, Ken 1126, 134, 1327
Petty, Lori 2123, 2186
Peyser, John 1654, 1778
Peyser, Penny 1381, 1836
Peyton Place: The Next Generation 1518
Pfeiffer, Dedee 2144
Pflug, Jo Ann 1061, 1223, 1301, 1600, 1777, 1798
Phalen, Robert 1639, 1814, 2089
Phelan, Joseph 1942
Phelps, Lee 839
Phelps, Robert 1958
Phenicie, Michael 2146
Phil Silvers Show 956
Philbin, Phil 1057
Philbin, Regis 1803
Philip, Karen 1267, 1840
Phillips, Barney 1094, 1203, 1421
Phillips, Bill 2023
Phillips, Carmen 737
Phillips, Clyde 1972, 2033, 2059
Phillips, Demetre 1553, 1599, 1806
Phillips, Ernie 2117
Phillips, James 1526
Phillips, Julie 1799, 1954, 2195, 2246
Phillips, Lee 770, 842, 1152, 1489, 1782, 1799
Phillips, Michael 2199

Phillips, Michelle 1713, 1887, 2060, 2119
Phillips, Phil 125
Phillips, Robert 1079, 1258, 1655, 1844
Phillips, Roger 1057
Phillips, Stu 743, 1506, 1721, 1771, 1778, 1779, 1865, 1866, 2029
Phillips, Wendy 1489, 2076
Phillips, William 1686, 1706, 1960
Phillips, William Edward 845
Phillips, William F. 1616
Phillips, William T. 1473
Phillips/Grodnick Productions 2033
Philpot, Ivan 1764
Philpots, Ambrosia 761
Phipps, William 470
Phipps, William Edward 1500
Phoenix, Leaf 1959
Phoenix, Summer 2121
Phoenix Entertainment 2146, 2200, 2209, 2211, 2246
Phun, Dennis 2237
P.I. 1399
Piazza, Ben 1587, 1597, 1639, 1771, 1904
Picard, Mary Lou 2174
Picard, Paul 1255, 1801, 1843, 2115, 2173
Picardo, Robert 2096, 2186

Picardo, Roberta 1920
Picerni, Charles 388, 1189, 1358, 1718, 1747
Picerni, Paul 1277, 1814
Pickard, John 23, 739
Pickens, Slim 609, 610, 1030, 1163, 1258, 1300, 1301, 1419, 1559, 1744, 1787
Pickering, Robert 923
Pickett, Cindy 1747, 1882, 1883, 1953
Pickle Brothers 940
Picture Window 600
Picturemaker Productions 1914, 1970
Piddock, Jim 2040, 2230
Pidgeon, Walter 400, 754, 1060, 1291
Piece, Maggie 509
Pierce, Robert 1688, 1801
Pierce, Stack 1094, 1229, 1428, 1787
Pierce, Webb 234, 845
Piernas, Lynette 1078
Pieroni, Leonardo 1039
Pierson, Frank 1226
Pierson, Geoff 2204
Pigeon, Corky 1927
Pikard, John 1476
Pike, Don 1645
Pilaven, Barbara 1096
Pileggi, Mitch 2129, 2197
Pilgrimage 1129
Piller, Michael 1987, 2047
Pillsbury, Sarah 2142
Pillsbury/Sanford Productions 2142

Pilon, Daniel 1862
Pilot Showcase 708
Pina, Chris 1490
Pinassi, Dominique
1247, 1411
Pincus, Irving 952
Pine, Lester 507
Pine, Philip 1585
Pine, Robert
1167, 1689
**Pine Canyon Is
Burning** 1522
Pine Lake Lodge 679
Pinero, Miguel 1649
Pinette, John 2257
Pingitore, Carl 1031,
1043, 1059
Pink Panther 717
Pinkard, Frank 1841
Pinkard, Ron 1093
Pinsent, Gordon
1167
Pinson, Allen 1030
Pintoff, Ernest
1054, 1467
**Pioneer Go
Home** 748
Pioneer Spirit 1026
Pioneer Woman
1259
Piper's Pets 1674
Piquet, Judith 1781
**Pirates of Flounder
Bay** 871
Pirosh, Robert
750, 1300
Pirrone, George 306
Pistone, Kimberley
2127
Pitlik, Noam 769,
1092, 1180, 1304,
1394, 1875, 1876,
1923, 1974
Pitman, Frank 661
Pitoniak, Anne 2235
Pittman,
Montgomery
645, 814
Pitts, ZaSu 19

Piven, Byrne
1868, 2148
Pizer, J. Brian 1693
Place, Mary Kay 1343
Plainsman 638
Plaksin, Suzie 2164
Plakson, Suzie 2228
Plana, Tony
1855, 1958
Plane-for-Hire 25
Planet Earth 1212,
1260, 1328
*Planet of the
Apes* 1212
Plank, Scott 2259
Plant Family 1551
Plato, Dana
1823, 1994
Platt, Edward 603
Platt, Howard
1280, 1751
Platypus Productions
2107
Plautus Productions
879, 883
*Play it Again,
Sammy* 2214
Play of the Month 531
Playboy Productions
1279, 1287,
1411, 1582
Playdon, Paul
1074, 1474
Playhouse 90 213
Playten, Alice 1412
Plaza, Begona 2041
Pleasence, Donald
1690
Pleasure Cove 1786
Pleshette, John
1243, 1406
Pleshette, Suzanne
455, 775, 1077,
1424, 1534, 2046
**Plotkin Prison, We
Love You** 914
Plowden, Julian 718
Plowman,
Melinda 554

Plumb, Eve 970
Plumb, Susan 1617
**Plumber and his
Daughters** 156
Plumley, Don 1355
Podell, Rick 1433,
1579, 1633, 1723,
1740, 1763
Poe, James 1444
Poe, Jerome 645
Point Blank 2065
Pointer, Priscilla
1338, 1525, 1689,
1841, 1847, 2028
Poitier, Sidney 1207,
1307, 1677, 1781
Poledouris, Basil
1988, 2094, 2240
Polic, Henry, II 1389,
1435, 1801
Police Boat 272
**Police Hall of
Fame** 238
Police Station
353, 354
Police Story 523,
921, 1184, 2195
**Police Story:
The Freeway
Killings** 2195
Police Woman
1430, 1523
Polio, Marty 2227
Polito, Jon 2203
Polizos, Vic
1968, 2034
Polizzi, Joseph 1425,
1537, 1538
Poll, Martin 1654
Poll, Marty 308
Pollack, Dee 885
Pollack, Sydney 611,
772, 781, 843, 848
Pollard, Michael
J. 731
Pollick, Steve 1599
Pollock, David 1177,
1288, 1392, 1491,
1492, 2180

**Polly Bergen
Show** 820
Polo, Miro 2087
Polonsky, Abraham
848
Polson, Beth 2137
Pomerantz, Jeff
1822, 2066
Pompian, Paul 1885
Pomroy's People
1194, 1248
Ponazecki, Joe 1914
Ponce, Danny
1920, 2021
Ponterotto, Donna
1433, 1667
Pony Express
165, 1749
Ponzini, Anthony
1477, 1783, 1887
Poole, Duane 2032
Poole, Roy 1398,
1814
Poor Devil 1222
**Poor Mr.
Campbell** 657
Poor Richard 1928
P.O.P. 1999
Pope, Joe 1853
Pope, Peggy 1391,
1701, 1829, 1851,
1897, 1926, 2180
Popwell, Albert 1354
Popwell, Johnny
1469
Port of Call 89
Porter, Don 555,
650, 806, 1084,
1186, 1232, 1246,
1349, 1533, 1771,
1990, 2230
Porter, Eleanor 1879
Porter, Robert 1261
Porter, Todd 1685
Portillo, Rose 1594
Portis, Charles 1536
Portnoy, Gary
1964, 1993
Portrait 245

Portrait: DuPont Cavalcade of Television 1115
Possessed 1521
Post, Marie 2188
Post, Markie 1862, 1866, 1959, 2035
Post, Mike 1110, 1420, 1422, 1426, 1451, 1497, 1509, 1564, 1616, 1626, 1641, 1642, 1696, 1783, 1785, 1788, 1815, 1842, 1880, 1952, 1985, 1989, 2006, 2008, 2009, 2023, 2086, 2133, 2166, 2205
Post, Ted 1072, 1079
Postlethwaite, Todd 2132
Postmark: Jim Adam 721
Postmark: Jim Fletcher 721
Poston, Tom 642, 851, 1092, 1331, 1505, 1541
Potter, Carol 1540
Potter, Chris 2115
Potter, Jerry 2016, 2133
Potts, Annie 1490, 1491, 1492, 1645, 1872, 2016, 2096
Potts, Cliff 1096, 1353, 2021, 2155
Pottsville 1636
Pounder, C.C.H. 2123
POW 852
Powder Room 1097
Powell, Addison 1684
Powell, Dick 507, 565, 603, 696, 697, 699, 703, 704, 735, 737, 738, 739, 779

Powell, Jane 147, 1133, 1189
Powell, Norman S. 1581
Powell, Randolph 1560, 2023
Powell, Richard 1756
Powell, Richard M. 673
Powell, Ricky 1242, 1350
Powell, Susan 2065
Power 1615
Power, Edward 2232
Power, Tyrone 787
Power, Udana 1125
Power Man 1615
Power Within 1615
Powers, Alex 2170
Powers, Constance 521
Powers, Dave 2109
Powers, Katharyn Michael 1719
Powers, Stefanie 659, 1006, 1102, 1155, 1347, 2116
Power's Play 2117
Prager, Stanley 767
Praiser, Ian 1997, 2166
Prange, Laurie 1226, 1508, 1983
Prather, Joan 1614
Pratt, Charles A. 1650
Pratt, Deborah 1708, 1877, 2197
Pratt, Dennis 1983
Pratt, Dennis A. 2188
Pratt, Geraldine 2197
Pratt, Judson 1197
Pratt, Robert 1096, 1098
Precht, Robert 1265, 1276
Preece, Michael 1750, 1927

Premiere 905, 960
Preminger, Michael 1723, 1740, 1763
Prendergast, Gary 1681
Prendergast, Gerard 1789, 1979
Prentiss, Ann 1008, 1085
Prentiss, Paula 1709, 1797
Presby, Shannon 1799
Prescott, Robert 2223
Prescott, Robert T. 1990, 2127
President of Love 1947
Presley, Elvis 834
Press, Barbara 1091
Press, Laura 2029
Pressman, Lawrence 1205, 1254, 1320, 1444, 1670, 1780, 2153
Pressman, Michael 2045, 2064, 2166
Presson, Jason 1919
Prestia, Shirley 1868
Prestin, Shirley 2251
Preston, J.A. 1967, 2148
Preston, Mike 2091
Preston, Wayde 391
Pretenders 2247
Preview Tonight 752, 884
Price, Allen 1316
Price, Frank 840, 925, 926, 972, 1020, 1066, 1146
Price, Ivy 2260
Price, Kerry 2233
Price, Lachelle 1697
Price, Paige 2028
Price, Paul B. 2087
Price, Roger 1218, 1796

Price, Sherwood 325, 1294
Price, Vincent 206, 212
Price Gabriel Productions 1488
Price of Peace 231
Prickett, Maudie 250, 314
Primary English Class 1438
Primetime 2207
Primrose 288
Primus, Barry 1277, 1450, 2109
Prince, Akili 2013
Prince, Robert 1100, 1277, 1780
Prince, Ron 1936
Prince, Ronald 940
Prince, William 1230, 1846, 1887, 1962
Prince Valiant 240
Princess and Me 980
Principal, Victoria 1349, 2254
Prine, Andrew 645, 861, 1020, 1261, 1421, 1648, 2045, 2072
Prine, Jack 655
Pringle, Joan 1511
Prisoner: Cell Block H 1722
Pritchard, David 1820
Pritchard, Michael 1945
Pritzker, Steve 1066, 1545
Private Benjamin 1794, 1837
Private Sessions 2064
Privateer 332
Privney, Chuck 953
Prochnicka, Lydia 2046

Proctor, Bernie 128, 132, 214

Procter & Gamble Productions 710, 901, 916, 973, 2036, 2103, 2111, 2117, 2154, 2157, 2161, 2162

Professor and the Kids 31

Prof. Huberty Abernathy 826

Profile 420

Proft, Pat 1995

Prohaska, Janos 1149

Prosecutor at Law 1907

Prosecutors 1167

Proser, Chip 2243

Prosky, Robert 2151

Protectors 1021

Proud Earth 520

Proval, David 1519

Provenza, Paul 1702, 1921

Provine, Dorothy 637, 662

Prowse, Juliet 1131

Prudence and the Chief 1036

Pryor, Nicholas 1337, 1473, 1772, 1793, 1851, 1860

Psycho 2186

Public Arts 927, 1031, 1043, 1105, 1422, 1525, 1688, 1692

Public Enemies 426

Publicity Girl 1

Puedes, Salvatore C. 1077

Puglia, Frank 894

Pugliese, Al 2245

Pugsley, Don 2032

Pullman, Marcy 1814

Pulson, Una 1259

Punch and Jody 1296

Punky Brewster 2051, 2198

Puppetman 2163

Purcell, Lee 1688, 1694, 1738, 2264

Purl, Linda 1403, 1913, 1972, 2025, 2155

Pursley, Tricia 2036

Pursue and Destroy 885

Pursuit 922

Puscas, Jessica 2155

Pushman, Terence 1124

Pusser, Buford 1650

Putch, John 1878, 1879, 2246

Putnam, Lori 1906

Puttin' on the Ritz 2112

Pyle, Denver 1246, 1282, 1352

Pyle, Gomer 1837

Pyne, Daniel 2260

Q

Quabuis, Faith 1419

Quade, John 1260, 1349, 1646, 1756, 1813, 1992, 2009, 2217

Quail Lake 1522

Qualen, John 505, 821, 1156

Quarrel 1819

Quarry, Robert 1567

Quayle, Anthony 1229

Queen, Ellery 1102

Quentin Method 1450

Quest 1061

Questor 1234

Questor Tapes 1234

Quick, Eldon 951, 1315, 2009

Quick, Susan 1343

Quick and Quiet 1732, 1820

Quiet Man 373

Quigley, Robert 1081

Quill, John E. 1876

Quillan, Eddie 806, 1164, 1255, 1331, 1452, 1827

Quiller 1379

Quiller: Price of Violence 1379

Quincy 1779, 1954

Quine, Don 926

Quine, Richard 1174, 1302

Quinlan, Dolores 1336

Quinlan, Eddie 765

Quinlan, Kathleen 1303

Quinn, Bill 561, 1078, 1224, 1511, 1595, 1973

Quinn, J.C. 1850

Quinn, James 2232

Quinn, Louis 1275

Quinn, Teddy 1036

Quinn, Tom 1758

Quinn, Tony 2059

Quinn, Valentina 1590

Quinn Martin Productions 800, 946, 947, 1047, 1075, 1090, 1188, 1246, 1357, 1421, 1480, 1510, 1516, 1560, 1561, 1563, 1622, 1628, 1633, 1651, 1678, 1732, 1750, 1767, 1768, 1811, 1820

Quinns 1381, 1449

Quinton, Dolores 1302

Quo, Beulah 1212, 1619, 1769, 1782

R

Raab, Selwin 2046, 2172

Rabkin, William 2214

Rabwin, Paul 1908

Racasner, Marie-Alise 2158

Racimo, Victoria 1327

Racket Squad 1523

Rackin, Martin 504, 521, 1300, 1345, 1353

Rackmil, Lewis 651

Radar 1981

Radley, Ken 2185

Radnitz, Brad 1583

Radnitz, Robert 636, 1328

Rado, Ivan J. 1841

Rae, Charlotte 1541, 1834, 1889, 1890, 1896

Rae, John 1158

Rafelson, Bob 943

Rafferty, Chips 994

Rafferty's Angels 134

Raffill, Stuart 1593

Raffin, Deborah 1692, 1856

Rafkin, Alan 1024, 1065, 1201, 1263, 1410, 1457, 1548, 1792, 1831, 1925, 2020, 2163

Ragin, John S. 1348, 1565, 1779, 2023

Rahn, Patsy 1814

Rails 173

Rainbow Girl 1901

Rainbow Productions 1781

Rainer, Joe 1539

Raines, Cristina 1958, 1971, 2028, 2065

Rainey, Ford 607, 724, 995, 1230, 1328, 1374
Rainier, Iris 1857
Raitt, John 483
Raksin, David 1041
Ralph, Sheryl Lee 1754
Ralph Bakshi Productions 1458, 1547
Ralph Edwards Productions 31, 139, 572, 676
Ralston, Gilbert 994
Ramage, Jack 1814
Ramar of the Jungle 9
Rambeau, Marc 772
Rambling Wreck from Discotheque 934
Rambo, Dack 1077, 1446, 1721, 2009
Rames, Ving 2218
Ramirez, Frank 1059
Ramirez, Tony 1601
Ramon, Roberto 1904
Ramone, Phil 2163
Ramrus, Al 1323
Ramsen, Bobby 1723, 1981
Ramsey, Anne 1911
Ramsey, Logan 1190, 1350, 1535, 1845
Ramsey, Morgan 1646
Ramus, Nick 1594, 2238
Rance, Tia 1469, 1471
Rand-Brooks Productions 741
Randall, Betsy 2069
Randall, Bob 1273
Randall, Sue 311, 467, 770, 812
Randall, Tony 291, 458, 807, 1534

Randell, Ron 469, 589
Randi, Justin 1653
Randolph, Amanda 965
Randolph, John 1089, 1155, 1164, 1233, 1236, 1335, 1444, 1519, 1872, 1879, 1917, 1954, 1966, 1988, 2104
Random, Robert 1019
Raney, Janet 1885
Ranier, Jeanne 953
Rannow, Jerry 1179
Ransom for Alice 1508
Ransom in Diamonds 1561
Rapf, Matthew 878, 985, 1336, 1402, 1478
Rapoport, I.C. 1375, 1594
Raposa, Joe 1313, 1925
Rapp, Anthony 2106
Rapp, Phil 253, 365, 526, 768
Rappaport, David 2205
Rappaport, John 1393, 1978, 2228
Rappaport, Michele 2040
Rasak, Pam 2246
Rasberry, Umar 2128
Rasey, Jean 1629
Rashe, David 1687
Raskin, Bonnie 2213
Raskin, Carolyn 1050
Raskin, Damon 1495
Rassulo, Joe 1615
Rastar Productions 2140
Rastar Television 1756, 1760

Rastatter, Wendy 1653
Rasulala, Thalmus 1180, 1349, 1940, 2146
Rasummy, Jay 1818
Rathbone, Basil 391, 871
Ratoff, Gregory 28, 172, 328
Rattan, Susan 1869
Rattray, Heather 1593
Raucher, Herman 1297
Rauseo, Vic 1899
Raven's Claw Productions 2064
Ravetch, Irving 790
Ravin, Robert M. 2246
Rawhide Riley 289
Rawls, Hardy 2186
Ray, Aldo 556, 710, 713, 837
Ray, Gerald 1280
Ray, Marsha 1620
Ray, Ola 1991
Raybould, Harry 1212
Raye, Martha 58, 161
Raye, Tisch 1443
Rayfield, David 781, 843
Raymond, Charles 1673, 1723, 1760, 1767, 1768
Raymond, Gene 739
Raymond, Guy 1024, 1638
Raymond, Lina 1564, 1940
Raymond, Robin 199
Raymond, Sid 383
Rayner, David 1890, 1976
Raynor, William 813
R.B. and Mymalene 710
R.B. Productions 1425, 1647

Rea, Peggy 1148, 1340
Read, James 1972
Reade, John C. 2042
Readinger, Maureen 1444
Readinger, Ronald 1444
Ready and Willing 912, 1092
Ready for the People 756
Ready, Willing, and Pamela 912
Reagan, Maureen 1302
Reagan, Ronald 603, 2152
Real American Hero 1650
Real George 65
Real Life 2231
Real McCoys 337
Reardon, Don 787
Reason, Rhodes 900, 1036
Reback, Katherine 2123
Rebhorn, James 2172
Recovery Room 2038
Recruiters 897
Red, Piano 1099
Red Skeleton Productions 955
Redbill Productions 609
Redcross, Bebe 1248
Redd, Mary Robin 1503
Redd, Veronica 1686
Reddecker, Quinn 541, 1516
Reddish, Jack N. 1784
Reddwhite and Blue 2097
Redfearn, Linda 1594
Redfield, Adam 1892

Redfield, Dennis 1403, 1695

Redfield, William 18, 456, 1395

Redford, J.A.C. 1608, 2007, 2084

Redford, Jeff J. 1637, 1656

Redford, Robert 1014

Redmond, Liam 872

Redmond, Marge 1204, 1283, 2253

Redwood Productions 1662, 1663, 1902, 1942

Reed, Alan 704, 1008

Reed, Jerry 1053, 1577

Reed, Kathy 382

Reed, Marshall 741

Reed, Napoleon 1057

Reed, Paul 383

Reed, Robert 894, 909, 977, 1188, 1424, 1516, 1591, 1612, 2021

Reed, Roland 78, 79

Reed, Shanna 1972, **2022**

Reed, Tracy 1076, 1195, 1596, 1720, 1953

Reed, Walter 1010

Rees, Angharad 1158

Rees, Betty Ann 2194

Reese, Della 1201, 1300, 1345, 2013

Reese, Mason 1312

Reese, Tom 723, 957

Reeves, Dick 62

Reeves, George 1799, 1952

Reeves Entertainment 2075, 2077, 2112, 2125, 2139, 2176

Regalbuto, Joe 1792, 2076, 2103

Regan, Ellen 1630, 1794

Regehr, Duncan 1982, 2059

Regimo, Victoria 1375

Reichert, Nancy 1222

Reid, Britt 277

Reid, Elliot 306, 386, 897

Reid, Kate 1352

Reid, Tim 1432, 2047

Reiffel, Lisa 2102

Reigert, Peter 1459

Reilly, Charles Nelson 1108

Reilly, John 1452, 1478, 1535, 1688, 1827, 1869, 1919, 1939

Reilly, Tom 1908

Reimer, Max 2166

Rein, Joan 2164

Reiner, Carl 308, 1143, 1205, 1225, 1237, 1344

Reiner, Rob 1276, 2206

Reinhold, Judge 1965

Reiser, Paul 1924, 1963, 2255

Reiser, Robert 1093

Reisman, Bruce 2120

Reisman, Del 1594

Reisman, Mark 2163

Reisman, Philip, Jr. 1125

Reisner, Allen 1583

Reisner, Dean 1011, 1020, 1146

R.E.L.A.X. 2118

Relentless 1477

Reluctant Eye 160

Relyea, Robert E. 1230, 1267, 1378, 1383

Relyea-Petitclerk Productions 1230

Remember When 1297

Remington Steele 2189

Remo Williams 2152

Remsen, Bert 1326, 1799, 2028

Remsen, Bobby 1767, 1999, 2034

Renan, David 2239

Rendezvous Hotel 1637

Renegade 521

Rennie, Michael 829, 882, 920

Reno, Jeff 1962

Reno and White 1767

Reno and Yolanda 2164

Reno Brothers 479

Renzetti, Joe 1689, 1699

Reo, Don 1458, 1628, 1732, 1767, 1768, 1979

Report to the Commissioner 1367

Republic Pictures 82, 2248

Rescher, Dee Dee 1360, 1830

Rescue 95, 145

Rescue from Gilligan's Island 1662

Resin, Alan 1309

Resnick, Muriel 1225

Restivo, Joe 2052

Rettig, Tommy 836

Return from Witch Mountain 1881

Return of Charlie Chan 1100

Return of Desperado 2190, 2260

Return of Frank Cannon 1651

Return of Kojak 2046, 2172

Return of Kung Fu 2115

Return of Luthor Gillis 1985

Return of Man from UNCLE: The Fifteen Years Later Affair 1937

Return of Marcus Welby, M.D. 1971

Return of Melvin Purvis, G-Man 1322

Return of the Beverly Hillbillies 1808

Return of the Greatest American Hero 2133

Return of the Mod Squad 1618

Return of the Original Yellow Tornado 967

Return of The Saint 2116, 2174

Return of the Six Million Dollar Man and the Bionic Woman 2196

Return of the World's Greatest Detective 1418

Return to Salem's Lot 1698

Return to the City 707

Returning Home 1316

Reunion at Alcatraz 2047

Reuss, Jerry 1865

Revenge of the Gray Gang 1851

Rever, Ann 1132

Reverend Grady 1829

Revill, Clive 1480, 1845, 1932, 2040

Reward 1717

Rex Harrison
  Presents Short
  Stories of
  Love 1168
Rex Morgan,
  M.D. 135
Rey, Alejandro
  931, 1718
Rey, Antonia 1876
Rey, Araceli 1519
Reyes, Julian 2237
Reynolds, Carroll
  1477
Reynolds, Bob 1816
Reynolds, Burt
  563, 961, 1358
Reynolds, Dale 1689
Reynolds, Debbie 2014
Reynolds, Gene
  659, 1022, 1055,
  1068, 1269, 1428,
  1909, 2103
Reynolds, George
  1587
Reynolds, James 1648
Reynolds, Kathryn
  1887
Reynolds, Rebecca
  1778, 1779
Reynolds, Sheldon 8,
  252, 259, 434, 854
Reynolds,
  William 609
RFD USA 15
Rhine, Larry 1798
Rhoades, Barbara
  1164
Rhoda 407,
  1363, 1724
Rhoades, Barbara
  1048, 1296, 1336,
  1350, 1371,
  1408, 1777
Rhodes, Carrie
  1973
Rhodes, Donnelly
  922, 1377,
  1896, 2129
Rhodes, Evan 771

Rhodes, Hari 1073,
  1207, 1248, 1847
Rhodes, Jennifer
  2238
Rhodes, Jordan
  1261
Rhodes, Michael
  1651, 1820
Rhubarb 941
Rhue, Madelyn
  1781
Rhys-Davies, John
  2009, 2239
Riano, Renie 1022
Ribisi, Vonni 2255
Riccio, Rick 2204
Rice, Alan 1177
Rice, James
  Brett 2129
Rice, Norman 1845
Rich, Allan 1359,
  1411, 1425, 1426,
  1526, 1566, 1628,
  1658, 1841, 2030
Rich, Christopher
  2038, 2124, 2257
Rich, David Lowell
  776, 846, 853,
  1058, 1060, 1078,
  1159, 1164, 1211,
  1245, 1318, 1319,
  1335, 1403, 1508
Rich, John 464,
  679, 870, 1304,
  1330, 1364, 1461,
  1530, 2019, 2072,
  2141, 2229
Rich, Lee 968, 1194,
  1225, 1244, 1248,
  1316, 1350, 1355,
  1394, 1409, 1428,
  1467, 1494, 1507,
  1571, 1614, 1657,
  1672, 1676, 1717,
  1722, 1745, 1776,
  1819, 1867, 1872
Rich, Ron 976
Rich, Ted 1218
Rich, Vernon 67

Rich Eustin
  Productions 1546
Rich-Ruben
  Productions 1330
Richard, Daryl 766
Richard Crenna
  Productions 938
Richard Diamond 6
Richards, Beah 1248,
  1469, 1470, 1471,
  2169, 2193
Richards, Beau 2028
Richards, Blake 1814
Richards, Christine
  1599
Richards, Evan 1887
Richards, Grant 723
Richards, Kim 1839
Richards, Kyle
  1486, 1487, 1814,
  1852, 1867
Richards, Lisa
  Blake 1803
Richards, Lloyd
  1021, 1089
Richards, Lou
  1871, 1978
Richards, Michael
  1911, 1993, 2056
Richards, Paul
  23, 169, 1041,
  1169, 1247
Richards, Rick 955
Richards, Sally
  Ann 1005
Richardson, Don
  819
Richardson, Jay 2267
Richardson,
  Tony 2144
Riche, Wendy 1965
Richelin, Rochelle
  1633
Richie Brockleman
  1696
Richlin, Maurice 118
Richman, Peter Mark
  902, 1713, 1079,
  1425, 1565, 1866

Richmond,
  Branscombe 1721,
  2120, 2170
Richter, Caroline 607
Richter, Deborah
  2223
Richter, W.D. 1275
Rickey, Patricia
  1765, 1964
Rickles, Don 767,
  914, 1217, 1946
Rickman, Tom
  1308, 1443
Ricknell, Gene 1968
Ricky of the
  Islands 220
Riddle, Nelson 722,
  723, 727, 1355
Riddle at 24,
  000 1289
Ride the Bugle 17
Ride the High Iron 6
Rider, Michael 2061
Ridgely, Ralph 1578
Ridgely, Robert 607
Riding High 1489
Riesner, Dean 1338
Rifkin, Ron 1198
Rifleman 726
Riger, John 1409
Rigg, Diana 1563
Riggs, Bobby 1655
Riker, Robin
  1783, 1911
Riley, Gary 2070
Riley, Jack 1432,
  1673, 2023
Riley, Jeannine
  909, 968
Riley, Larry 2161
Riley, Norman 662
Riley, Rex 1579
Riley, William
  2030, 2264
Rimmer, Shane
  1158, 2098
Ringa, Charles 1866
Ringwald, Elizabeth
  1660

Rintels, David W. 876

Rio 611

Riopelle, Jerry 1151

Ripps, Lenny 1932

Riptide 2006

Rise and Shine 1809

Risel, Robert 1231

Rising Damp 1462

Riskin, Ralph
2032, 2173

Risko 1400

Risley, Ann 1459

Rissien, Edward
L. 1279, 1582

Rist, Robbie 1493,
1555, 1666, 1699

Rita 2109

Rita Moreno Show
1364, 1552, 2109

Ritchie, Robert 1654

Ritelis, Viktors 1380

Ritter, John 1151,
1198, 2205

Ritter, Tex 494

Ritter, Thelma 126

Ritual of Evil 1028

Ritz Brothers 98

**Rivak the
Barbarian** 504

Rivals 1697

Rivas, Carlos 781

River Men 1355

River of Gold 1077

Rivers, Joan 1707

Rivers, Rose 2119

Riviera 2098

Rivkin, Allen 202

**Rivkin: Bounty
Hunter** 1821

R.J. Reynolds 977

RKO 168, 169, 170,
171, 172, 173

RKO Television 1764

Roach, Hal 107

Roach, Hal, Jr. 7, 118

Road, Mike 524, 620

Roaring Camp 884

Roat, Richard
1805, 2232

Robbins, Brian 2089

Ribbins, Gale 462

Robbins, Harold
1353

Robbins, Marty 234

Robbins, Rex 1777

Robert, Malcolm
Young 1881

Robert Ginty/
Phoenix
Entertainment
Productions 2090

Robert Halmi
Productions 2215

Robert L.
McCullough
Productions
2193

Robert Maxwell
Productions 886

Robert Papazian
Productions 1620

Robert Radnitz-
Mattel
Productions 1328

Robert Stigwood
Productions
1682

Robert Taylor Show
704, 779

**Roberta Sherwood
Show** 628

Roberts, Anthony
1005

Roberts, Arthur 1317

Roberts, Ben
707, 839, 885,
931, 1376

Roberts, Chick 2132

Roberts, Christian
1058

Roberts, Clete 1117,
1981, 1987

Roberts, Conrad
1612

Roberts, Davis 1320

Roberts, Doris 1325,
1406, 1796

Roberts, Ewan 1158

Roberts, Joan 1522,
1560, 1663,
1768, 1820

Roberts, Juarez 696

Roberts, Lois 695

Roberts, Michael
D. 1617, 1960

Roberts, Nathan
1864

Roberts, Pernell
1072, 1126, 1324,
1351, 1509,
1616, 2190

Roberts, Rachel 1158

Roberts, Randolph
1619

Roberts, Roy 126,
654, 743

Roberts, Stanley
543, 1203

Roberts, Stephen
1714

Roberts, Tanya 1713,
1721, 1786

Roberts, Tony 1416

Roberts, William
2240

Robertson, Chuck 7

Robertson, Cliff 1299

Robertson, Dale 46,
394, 801, 1255,
1322, 1952

Robertson,
William 1498

Robinette, Dale 1447,
1513, 1595, 1611

Robinson, Alexia
2203

Robinson, Andrew
1713, 1717, 2148

Robinson, Andy
1099, 1279, 1813

Robinson, Ann 299

Robinson, Bartlett
310, 756

Robinson, Betty
Lou 1585

Robinson, Bumper
1953, 2099

Robinson, Carol 1050

Robinson, Casey 402

Robinson, Charles
1310, 1519, 1680

Robinson, Chris 715,
751, 1057, 1090,
1468, 1559, 1571

Robinson, Edward
G., Jr. 93,
1010, 1101

Robinson, Frances
552, 648

Robinson,
Hubbell 684

Robinson, J.
Peter 2186

Robinson, Jay 2032

Robinson, John
392, 395, 396

Robinson, McKinlay
2099

Robinson, Peter 2102

Robinson, Robie
1645

Robinson, Roger
1402, 1425

Robinson, Ruthie 250

Robinson, Sugar
Ray 1101

Robles, Walter 1911

Rocco, Alex 1118,
1392, 1922,
2151, 2154

Roccuzzo, Mario
1186, 1516,
1585, 1968

Roche, Chad 1639

Roche, Eugene 1106,
1184, 1254, 1336,
1356, 1410, 1425,
1428, 1448, 1511,
1521, 1752, 1811,
1891, 1907, 1934,
1953, 1985

Roche, Sean
1497, 1639

Rock 556

**Rock and a Hard
Place** 1768

Rockabye the
    Infantry 743
Rocket, Charles 1864,
    1913, 2042, 2103
Rockford Files 1358,
    1422, 1426, 1564,
    1783, 1785, 1788
Rockhopper 2039
Rockwell, Robert
    797, 1733
Rod Amateau
    Productions 1894
Rodann, Ziva 750
Rodd, Marcia
    1026, 1555
Roddenberry, Gene
    299, 523, 664,
    666, 881, 921,
    1212, 1234, 1260,
    1323, 1524
Rodgers, Mark 1169,
    1293, 1512, 1939,
    2058, 2195
Rodgers, Pamela
    1017
Roditsky, Barney 163
Rodman, Howard
    381, 385, 1132,
    1280, 1350,
    1428, 1514
Rodney, Gene 793
Rodriques,
    Percy 1212
Rodriquez,
    Alice 1278
Rodriquez,
    Johnny 1355
Rodriquez,
    Marisol 2237
Rodriquez,
    Miquel 1894
Rodriquez, Paul
    2090, 2105
Rodriquez, Percy
    1351, 1472, 1616
Roesch, Timothy
    1599
**Roger and
    Harry** 1450

Roger Corman
    Productions 985
Rogers, Al 1053,
    1306, 1634, 2018
Rogers, Doug 1709,
    1797, 1878
Rogers, Elizabeth
    1335, 1589
Rogers, Ginger 730
Rogers, Jeffrey 1950
Rogers, Julie 1750
Rogers, Kenny 1959
Rogers, Mark 1226
Rogers, Melody
    1584
Rogers, Mimi 1884,
    1885, 2026
Rogers, Shorty 301,
    1004, 1618
Rogers, Stephen
    1197
Rogers, Will 354
Rogosin, Joel 1277,
    1780, 1989, 2107
Rogue for Hire 480
Rojas, Eduardo
    Lopez 1077
Roker, Kenny 1689
Roker, Roxie 1265
Roland Reed
    Productions 77
Roland, Gilbert
    378, 924, 973,
    1167, 1253
Roland, Jeffrey 383
Rolfe, Guy 504
Rolfe, Sam H. 211,
    520, 562, 881,
    1060, 1061, 1162,
    1421, 1472, 1477,
    1819, 1937
Rolike, Hank 2221
Rolle, Esther 1649
Rollerball 2028
Rolley, Sutton 1195
Rollins, Jack 1206
Rollins-Joffe-Bessell
    Productions
    1206, 1669

Roman, Ruth 1047,
    1076, 1200,
    1296, 1722
Roman Grey 1356
Romanis, George
    1211, 1427
Romano, Andy
    1498, 2152
Romano, John 2263
Romanus, George
    1844, 1845, 1846
Romanus, Richard
    1447
Romanus, Robert
    1922
Rombola, Ed 1860
**Rome, Sweet
    Rome** 990
Romero, Cesar 103,
    317, 563, 1901
Romero, Ned
    1375, 1594
Ron Howard/
    Brian Grazer
    Productions 2204
Ron Samuels
    Productions 2171
Roncom 530, 611
Rondeau, Charles
    R. 949, 1035
Rooney, Elaine 110
Rooney, Mickey 248,
    603, 757, 764,
    774, 829, 912,
    967, 1151, 1850
Rooney, Teddy
    526, 629
Rooney, Timmy
    747, 764
Roope, Faye 125
Roos, Donald
    Paul 2070
Roosevelt, Teddy
    1539
Rooster 1865, 1866
Rooster Cogbum 1536
Roots 27
Rorke, Hayden
    307, 1351

Rosario, Bert 1552,
    1914, 1999, 2189
Rosato, Tony 2132
Rose, Alex 1629,
    1849
Rose, Alison 1098
Rose, Christine 2036
Rose, Cristine 2164
Rose, David 607,
    1248, 1508, 1590
Rose, George 2174
Rose, Jamie 1965
Rose, John 1253
Rose, Margot 1965
Rose, Reginald 1370
Rose, Reva 1414
Rose, Si 1018
Roselius, John
    1781, 2023
Rosemond,
    Perry 1949
Rosemont, David
    2248
Rosemont, Norman
    1300, 1813,
    1886, 2248
Rosemont
    Productions 2248
Rosen, Arnie 549,
    949, 1416
Rosen, Daniel 2237
Rosen, Larry 1156,
    1727, 1751, 1752,
    1833, 2233
Rosen, Neil
    1497, 1553
Rosen, Robert
    L. 2098
Rosen, Sy 1877,
    1930, 1998, 2050
Rosenbaum,
    Henry 1955
Rosenberg, Aaron
    924, 1030
Rosenberg,
    Alan 2046
Rosenberg, Arthur
    1895, 2049

Rosenberg, Edgar 1707
Rosenberg, Frank P. 925
Rosenberg, Frank 125, 202, 314, 853, 866, 920
Rosenberg, Leonard A. 1633
Rosenberg, Manny 704
Rosenberg, Meta 1200, 1422, 1426, 1448, 1783, 1788, 2147
Rosenberg, Rick 1185, 1463, 1919
Rosenberg, Stuart 308, 771, 918
Rosenblatt, Martin 1850
Rosenbloom, Richard M. 1075, 1259, 1368, 1454, 1495
Rosengren, Clive 2211
Rosenman, Leonard 1072, 1251, 1320, 1347, 1521, 1745, 1971
Rosenstock, Richard 2078, 2199
Rosenthal, Laurence 1210, 1403, 1516, 1518, 2246
Rosenthal, Peter 2143
Rosenthal, Rick 2061
Rosenthal and Jones 1332
Rosenweig, Barney 1256, 1762, 1863, 1915, 1983
Rosetti, Richard 1424
Rosner, Rick 1347
Rosqui, Tom 1182, 1324, 1366
Ross, Arthur 1287
Ross, Caroline 1074
Ross, Don 1222

Ross, Gene 2189
Ross, Herbert 1705
Ross, Jeremy 2009
Ross, Jerry 1431
Ross, John 1567
Ross, Katherine 752, 1257, 1802
Ross, Leonard 1779
Ross, Marie Lynn 1854
Rosse, Marion 1197, 1803, 1853
Ross, Michael 1554
Ross, Mickey 1736
Ross, Sammy 962
Ross, Stanley Ralph 1177, 1345, 1347, 1352, 1385, 1410, 1453, 1803, 1854, 1951
Ross, Ted 1888, 1893
Ross, Tracy 2022
Ross Hunter Productions 1351
Ross of the Everglades 566
Ross-Leming, Eugenie 1839, 1892, 2022, 2066, 2127, 2238
Rossen, Carol 876, 1325, 1511, 2007
Rossi 1357
Rossi, Leo 2164, 2267
Rossi, Steve 813
Rossillon, Gabrielle 758
Rossovich, Tim 1781
Rostram, Byron 1596
Roswell, Maggie 1674, 1755, 1804
Rotblatt, Janet 2099, 2221
Roth, Bobby 2096
Roth, Lynn 1392
Roth, Phil 1433
Roth, Ron 1145, 1279

Roth, Wolf 1383, 1466
Rothman, Bernard 1053, 1625, 1731
Rothman, Mark 1365, 1552, 1598, 1630, 1661
Rothman/Ganz Productions 1598, 1661
Rothman/Wohl Productions 1625
Rothschild, Harry S. 9
Rothstein, Freyda 1701
Rothstein, Richard 2186
Roueche, Burton 583
Rough-House 2223
Rough Sketch 96
Rounds, David 1899
Roundtree, Richard 1880, 2198
Rourke, Adam 1338
Rouse, Russell 408, 541, 614, 634, 666, 789, 837
Route 66 1166, 1989
Rowan, Dan 570
Rowan, Gaye 1377, 1801
Rowan and Martin Show 389
Rowdies 2081
Rowe, Hansford 1838
Rowe, Vern 1239
Rowland, Bruce 2185, 2208
Rowlands, Gena 853
Rowles, Polly 1309
Roxy 1413
Roxy Page 1413
Roy, David 1252
Roy, Ronald 1343, 1390
Roy Huggins Productions 1298, 1647

Roy Huggins-Public Arts 1396, 1420
Royal Bay 785
Royal Match 2040
Royan, Thomas 2266
Royce 1401
Royce, Dixie Lynn 1958
RSO Films 1888
Rubber Gun Squad 1498
Ruben, Aaron 466, 1045, 1051, 1283, 1304, 1330, 1434, 1529, 1674, 1837
Ruben, Albert 883, 1182, 2046, 2172
Rubenstein, Phil 1738, 1795, 1941
Rubin, Andrew 2123
Rubin, Benny 1418
Rubin, Lance 1885, 1959, 2264
Rubin, Ronald 1207, 1452
Rubin, Selma 1830
Rubin, Stanley 456, 647
Rubinek, Saul 1687, 1776
Rubinstein, Arthur B. 1390, 1787, 1790, 1821, 2238
Rubinstein, John 1511
Rubinstein, Zelda 1996
Ruck, Alan 2008, 2269
Rucker, Alan 1900
Rucker, Dennis 1125, 1224, 1563
Rudd, Paul 1954, 2115
Ruddy, Albert S. 1070, 1407, 1835
Rudie, Evelyn 107
Rudley, Herbert 1108
Rudolph, Lou 1803

Rudolph, Oscar 204, 211, 319, 497
Rudoy, Joshua 2079, 2134
Rudy, Martin 1887
Rue, Madlyn 1222
Ruffini, Claudio 1652
Ruggles, Charles 307, 500, 658, 730, 739
Rugolo, Pete 1031, 1043, 1059, 1105, 1189, 1190, 1349, 1647, 1692, 1743, 1850, 1856
Rule, Janice 985
Ruiz, Isaac 1519
Rumor 306
Run, Buddy, Run 913
Run for Your Life 927
Run, Jack, Run 913
Runacre, Jenny 1524
Runaway Barge 1355
Rundle, Cis 1917, 1973
Runyard, Mike 2060
Runyon, Jennifer 1959, 2127
Rupert, Florence 1683
Rupp, Jacob 2117
Ruprecht, David 1663, 1664, 1792
Ruscio, Al 772, 1473, 2207
Ruscio, Elizabeth 2242
Rush, Barbara 707, 758, 805, 911, 1122, 1160, 1211, 1224, 1993, 2205
Rush, Deborah 2142
Rush, Dennis 790
Rush, Herman 1181, 1305
Rush, Owen 1836
Rush, Sarah 1863
Ruskin, Coby 909, 1017

Ruskin, Joseph 1378, 1451, 1641, 1832
Ruskin, Shimen 1330
Russ, Gene 1882
Russ, Tim 2265
Russ, William 1969
Russell 567
Russell, Bing 23, 609
Russell, Brian 484, 629
Russell, Charles 1479
Russell, Del 1187
Russell, Forbesy 1532, 1607, 1614
Russell, Fran 1377
Russell, Harold 1316
Russell, Jackie 1007
Russell, Jane 267, 313
Russell, Kurt 1327
Russell, Mark 1478, 2046
Russell, Neil 1079
Russell, Nipsey 978
Russo, Carole 1816
Russo, Gianni 1180
Russo, J. Duke 1147, 1190
Russo, Matt 1231, 1817
Russom, Leon 2262
Rutherford, Gene 1583
Ruval, Julius 1716
Ruyman, Ayn 1393
RX for the Defense 1130
Ryan, Deborah 1511, 1553, 1779
Ryan, Dick 206, 263
Ryan, Fran 1504, 1607, 1781, 1971
Ryan, Irene 204
Ryan, John P. 1299, 1722, 1917
Ryan, Kenneth 2172
Ryan, Michelle 2196
Ryan, Mitchell 1120, 1186, 1845, 1939, 2033

Ryan, Natasha 1446, 1583
Ryan, Rex 2035
Ryan, Robert 846
Ryan, Steve 1785, 1966
Ryan, Thomas 2119, 2188
Ryans Hope 1172
Rydbeck, Whitney 1664, 1882
Rydell, Bobby 659, 743
Ryder, Alfred 843, 1187, 1302
Rydin, Susan 2041
Rye, Isabella 1652
Ryerson, Ann 2226
Ryon, Rex 2001

S

Sabatino, Michael 2003, 2124
Sabella, Ernie 1932, 1967
Sabin, David 2170
Sable 1863
Sabol, Dick 1230
Sachs, Eddie 785
Sachs, Sol 643, 812
Sackheim, Tom 858
Sackheim, William 381, 383, 385, 405, 616, 657, 664, 823, 969, 1104, 1168, 1425, 1958, 2061
Sacks, Alan 1385, 1453, 1817
Sacks, Michael 1507
Sad and Lonely Sundays 1326
Sad Sack 137
Sadang, Robert 1251
Sadler, Karl 954
Sadlier, Michael 235
Sadoff, Fred 1213, 1234, 1368, 2021
Safaer, Abraham 962

Safan, Craig 1922, 1928, 1958, 2093
Safari 696
Sagal, Boris 876, 1163, 1187, 1355, 1425
Sagan, Craig 2152
Sage, Liz 2051, 2053
Sagivsky, Lin 2219
Sahl, Mort 625
Sailor, Charles 1408
Saint 262, 2174
St. Clair, Eric 1783
St. Clair, Michael 920, 1124
St. Clair, Vicky 2242
St. Jacques, Raymond 1010, 1173, 1327, 1626, 1778, 2025 St. John, Bill 553
St. John, Christoff 1365, 1440
St. John, Howard 643
St. John, Jill 114, 1317, 1676, 1865
St. Elsewhere 1326, 1696, 2265
Saint in Manhattan 2174
St. Louis Man 333
Saint Peter 1769
Saints Girl Friday 262
Saito, James 2060, 2258
Sakata, Harold 850
Sakmar, John 2171
Sakmer, John J. 2267
Saks, Sol 383, 958
Salamon, Otto 1691, 1777
Salata, Gregory 2016
Salathiel Harms 1402, 1478
Sale, Richard 476, 860
Salem, Kario 1610, 1699, 2269
Salem's Lot 1698

Sales, Soupy 292, 890, 1149

Salinger, Diana 2246

Salinger, Matt 2169

Salkow, Sidney 307, 450, 658

Salkowitz, Sy 756, 1029

Sallan, Bruce J. 1653, 2209

Sally and Sam 821

Salmi, Albert 732

Salob, Lorin B. 2117

Salsedo, Frank Sotonoma 2189, 2238

Salt, Jennifer 1966

Salt and Pepe 1333

Saltzman, Philip 1188, 1357, 1560, 1561, 1563, 1678, 1750, 1822, 1884

Saluga, Bill 1940

Salvage Master 35

Salvay, Bennett 1950

Salven, David 2128, 2258

Sam 2020

S.A.M. 1069

Sam Benedict 523, 666

Sam Gallu Productions 37

Sam Hill 607

Sam Hill: Who Killed the Mysterious Mr. Foster? 1105

Sam Jaffe Productions 45

Sam Penny 2047

Same, Old World 236

Samish, Adrian 1047, 1076, 1090, 1246

Samms, Emma 1748

Sampson, Robert 957, 1156, 1243, 1339, 1423, 1940

Sampson, Will 1477, 1516, 1594

Samuel Goldwyn Productions 1316

Samuels, Jimmy 1636, 1726

Samuels, Ron 2171

Samuels, Stu 2099, 2232

Samurai 1619

San Francisco Beat 707

Sanchez, Mario 2083

Sanchez, Ref 1059

Sanctuary of Fear 1687

Sand, Barry 1544

Sand, Bob 1436, 1967, 2167

Sand, Bruce 1088

Sand, Paul 1069, 1219, 1556, 2201

Sandefur, B.W. 1693, 1881

Sander, Casey 2065, 2120

Sander, Ian 1184

Sanderford, John 2035, 2266

Sanders, Beverly 1346, 1362, 1479, 1491, 1492, 1676

Sanders, George 73, 157, 263

Sanders, Henry G. 1914, 2096

Sanders, Hugh 125

Sanders, Richard 1441, 1446, 1942

Sanders, Shephard 1903

Sanderson, Gerald 1234

Sanderson, William 2065, 2129

Sandor, Steve 1043, 1818

Sandrich, Jay 1135, 1198, 1207, 1331, 1334, 1390, 1393, 1502, 1806, 1868, 1912, 1960, 2057, 2181, 2225

Sands, Billy 1334, 1832

Sands, Diana 1137, 1208

Sands, Tommy 715

Sande, Walter 450

Sandulescu, Jacques 1231

Sandy, Gary 1339, 1856, 2053

Sandy Howard and Associates 351

Sanford, Garwin 2093, 2117

Sanford, Gerald 1235, 1561

Sanford, Midge 2142

Sanford and Son 837, 1365

Sanford Arms 1365

Sangiolo, Anita 1780

Sangster, Jimmy 1446, 1611, 1644, 1694, 1716

Sansom, Ken 1303, 1350, 1942

Santana, Jose 2046

Santangelo, Melody 1231

Santeiro, Luis 1931

Santon, Penny 1104, 1117, 1221, 1252, 1887

Santoni, Reni 1120, 1187, 1734, 2000, 2017

Santoro, Dean 1914

Santos, Joe 1192, 1291, 1358, 1602, 2066

Sanvido, Guy 2132

Sapien, Buzz 1871

Sapir, Richard 2152

Sarafian, Richard 960, 1466

Sarafian, Richard C. 988, 1970

Sarandon, Chris 1909, 2084

Sargent, Alvin 1104

Sargent, Bill 722

Sargent, David 2164

Sargent, Dick 906, 1214, 1224, 1255, 1615, 1668

Sargent, Joseph 1133, 1147, 1321, 1958

Saric, Ivan 1916

Sariego, Ralph 1774, 1852

Sarner, Arlene 2140

Saroyan, Lucy 1467

Saroyan, William 358, 764, 1108

Sarracino, Ernest 62

Sartain, Gallard 1452

Sartain, Gallard 1790

Satan's Waitin' 770

Satin's Touch 2268

Satlof, Ron 1506, 1719, 1721, 1771, 2030

Saturday Evening Post 829

Saturday Night Live 2055

Sauber, Harry 462

Saucier, Jason 2197

Saucier, Luke 846

Saul Ilson Productions 1926, 1948

Saunders, David 2008, 2083

Saunders, Enid 2235

Saunders, Gloria 267, 396

Saunders, Herman 1024

Saunders, J.J. 2260

Saunders, Lanna 1663

Saunders, Lori 1141

Saurel, George 1010
Savadore, Laurence
  D. 1209
Savage 1169
Savage, Brad 1131,
  1180, 1263,
  1330, 1605
Savage, Dennis 1886
Savage, Elisabeth
  1932
Savage, John 2148
Savage, Nick 2189
Savage, Paul 1019,
  1319, 1374
Savage, Tracie 1321
**Savage in the
  Orient** 1938
**Savage Is the
  Name** 323
Savages 923
Savalas, Candace
  2172
Savalas, George
  1478, 2046
Savalas, Telly 781,
  922, 1478, 1814,
  2046, 2048, 2172
*Save Our Schools, Save
  Our Children* 2012
Saved by the Bell 2182
Savidge, Jennifer 1997
Saviola, Camille 2167
Savola, John 1918
Sawaya, Amy 2096
Sawdust 2165
Sawtell, Paul 270
Sawyer, Beverly 2200
Sawyer, Connie
  817, 1091
Sawyer, Joe 117
Sawyer, Mark 1965
Sawyer, Toni 2127
**Sawyer and
  Finn** 1787
Saxon, John 1021,
  1212, 1260, 1328,
  1357, 1865,
  1938, 2023
Say Uncle 1499

Saylor, Katie 1256
Saylor, Shannon 1593
Sbardellati,
  James 1731
Scalia, Jack
  1984, 2024
Scalici, Jack 1247
Scalpels 1770
Scalpone, Al 476, 477
Scamps 1902
Scandals II 2219
Scanlon 1519
Scanlon, John
  G. 1885
Scanlon, Joseph 1377
Scannell, Kevin
  2016, 2042, 2068
Scarber, Sam
  1864, 1964
Scardino, Don 1024,
  1391, 1498
*Scarecrow and Mrs.
  King* 2066
Scared Silly 1859
Scared Stiff 1087
Scarfe, Alan 2258
Scarlet Blade 285
Scarpelli, Glenn
  1669, 1758, 1821
Scarwid, Diana 1521
Scavengers 1031
Schaal, Richard
  1198, 1869
Schaal, Wendy 2204
Schacht, Sam 1370
Schaefer, George
  1398
Schaefer, Jack 465
Schafer, Jerry 448
Schafer, Natalie
  1662, 1663, 1664
Schaffel, Hal 1649
Schaffer, Tracy
  2183
Schaffner, Frank 883
Schallert, William
  68, 213, 463,
  1056, 1074, 1233,
  1297, 2221

Schallter-Friendly
  Productions 1027
Schanley, Tom 2196
Scharf, Sabrina 1048
Scharf, Walter 673,
  674, 1714
Schary, Dore 488
Schedeen, Anne
  1514, 1515, 1556,
  1633, 1898, 2022
Scheerer, Robert
  1222, 2137
Scheff, Michael 1620
Schein, Jeremy 2109
Scheme, Raynor 2197
Scheinfeld, John 2240
Schell, Catherine
  1127
Schell, Maria 1784
Schell, Ronnie 1294
Schemmel,
  Steve 1477
Schenck, Aubrey
  1183
Schenck, George
  1570, 1787, 1850
Schenkkan,
  Robert 1687
Scherer, Glenn 1915
Scherick, Ed 1191,
  1236, 1375, 1397,
  1520, 1594
Scherick, Edgar
  J. 2268
Scheuer, Steven 880
Scheurer, Paul 2127
Schiavelli, Vincent
  1617, 1662, 1805,
  1944, 1992
Schick Sun Classic
  Films 1685
Schiff, Eric 1809
Schifrin, Lalo 781,
  876, 1048, 1057,
  1060, 1073, 1074,
  1144, 1184, 1317,
  1348, 1446,
  1691, 1918, 1969,
  2064, 2115

Schiller, Bob 311,
  1658, 1831,
  1912, 1981
Schiller, Frederick
  495
Schiller, Wilton 1642
Schilling, William
  1922
Schlamme, Tom 2143
Schlatter, George
  1027, 1050
Schlatter-Friendly
  Productions 1050
*Schlitz Playhouse of
  the Stars* 114, 125,
  129, 131, 201, 203,
  306, 310, 314
Schmidt, Georgia
  1266, 1868
Schmock, Jonathan
  2001, 2193
Schnabel, Stefan
  1231, 2041
Schneer, Charles 742
Schneider, Burt 943
Schneider, Mark
  1695
Schneider, Sascha
  2220
Schock, Harriet 1403
Schoelen, Jill
  1927, 2007
Schoenman,
  Elliot 1605
Scholastic
  Productions 2106
Scholl, Danny 738
Schott, Bob
  1229, 1232
Schracht, Sam 1683
Schreck, Vicki 1813
Schreiber, Avery
  954, 1074, 1111,
  1131, 1645, 1748
Schroder, Ricky 1886
Schrum, Pete 1635
Schrum, Peter 1623,
  1836, 1940
Schubb, Mark 1988

Schubert, Gitta 1058
Schuch, Robert 2194
Schuck, John
1048, 1228
Schukin, Phil 612
Schulberg, Budd 566
Schull, John
Kenton 2186
Schull, Rebecca 2207
Schuller, Frank
1466, 1955
Shulman, Max 551,
831, 1465, 2221
Schulman, Roger
1554, 1826, 1893,
1926, 2253
Schulman, Tom 2089
Schultz, Dwight 2206
Schultz, Leroy 2117
Schultz, Michael
1940, 2099
Schumacher,
Joel 1875
Schuster, Frank
460, 867, 954
Schutzman, Scott
1809, 1913
Schwab, Lana 2226
Schwartz, Al 1662,
1663, 1664
Schwartz, Dave 642
Schwartz, Douglas
1781
Schwartz, Elroy
1183, 1662, 1663
Schwartz, Leslie 2261
Schwartz, Lloyd J.
1240, 1662, 1663,
1664, 1902, 1942
Schwartz, Nancy
Lynn 1682
Schwartz, Neil
1123
Schwartz, Sherwood
889, 1240, 1662,
1663, 1664,
1902, 1942
Schwartz, Stephen
1391

Schwartz-Hartley,
Steve 2261
Schwartzberg,
Louis 1807
Schwedt, Herman
2046
Scioscia, Mike 1865
Scoey Mitchlll
Productions 2052
Scofield, Rehn 1099
Scoggins, Tracy 1952
Scolari, Peter 1661
Scotford, Sybil 1586
Scott, Bryan 1599
Scott, Debralee 1831
Scott, Donovan
1859
Scott, Franklin 2041
Scott, Geoffrey 1423
Scott, Gordon 270,
803, 1524
Scott, Jean Bruce
1919
Scott, Jim 1483
Scott, John 1259,
1381, 1449
Scott, Jud 1777
Scott, Judson 1973
Scott, Kathryn Leigh
1564, 1640
Scott, Kendell 278
Scott, Kirk 2226
Scott, Larry B.
1874, 1940
Scott, Linda
1027, 1583
Scott, Martha
311, 467, 599,
1119, 1682
Scott, Oz 1946,
2079, 2105, 2134
Scott, Peter Graham
1379, 1380
Scott, Pippa 559,
702, 846, 1140
Scott, Simon 611,
756, 1618
Scott, Susie 1992
Scott, Tim 2261

Scott, Timothy 1103,
1471, 1882, 1958
Scott, Tom 1302,
1371, 1447, 1473,
1839, 2042, 2266
Scott, Willard 2180
Scott, Zachary 634
Scott Free 1426
Scotti, Vito 463,
726, 832, 847,
1015, 1300, 1335,
1523, 1779
Scraber, Sam 1981
Screen Director's
Playhouse 64,
67, 68, 113
Screen Gems 4, 73,
80, 109, 178, 204,
205, 211, 275, 290,
294, 295, 297, 299,
300, 382, 383, 390,
403, 459, 497, 500,
501, 520, 522, 523,
532, 552, 601, 613,
623, 627, 628, 634,
664, 666, 742, 743,
789, 823, 856, 858,
863, 878, 882, 892,
894, 899, 901, 908,
937, 939, 942, 943,
964, 969, 979,
980, 985, 1004,
1008, 1012, 1025,
1033, 1037, 1051,
1052, 1071, 1078,
1094, 1095, 1097,
1099, 1108, 1110,
1111, 1121, 1134,
1147, 1150, 1154,
1156, 1166, 1176,
1177, 1203, 1207,
1214, 1229, 1237,
1252, 1286, 1291
Scribner, Ronnie
1663, 1714
Scruggs, Earl 1808
Scruggs, Harold 1853
Scruples 1801
Sea Gypsies 1593

Sea Rover 680
Seaforth, Susan 645
Seago, Terry 2061
Seagram, Lisa 582
Seagren, Bob 1654,
1719, 1764
Seagrove, Jenny 2029
Seal 1852
Seales, Franklyn 1893
Search 701, 993
Search for a Dead
Man 723
Search for the
Gods 1327
Search, Pursue,
Destroy 885
Searchers 1228
Searle, Judith 1914
Sears, Fran
1381, 1449
Seawell, D.C. 1944
Sebastian, John 1940
Second Chance 1131
Second Chance 1250
Second Edition 1978
Second Stage 2141
Second Start 1152
Second Time
Around 1414,
1605
Secor, Kyle 2144
Secrest, James 1123
Secret Life of James
Thurber 390, 557
Secret Life of John
Monroe 390, 557
Secret Room 184
Secret War of
Jackie's Girls 1688
Secrets of the Old
Bailey 129
Sedgeley, Karen 1479
Sedgewick,
Kimberly 2267
Sedgewick Hawk-
Styles: Prince
of Danger 872
See China and
Die 1649

See Here, Private Hargrove 836
Seeger, Mindy 2092
Seeger, Susan 1895, 1941, 2090, 2121
Seekers 722
Seeley, Tom 2050
Segal, George 704, 1286, 1379, 1606
Segal, Jonathan 1514
Segal, Lee 1144
Segall, Pam 2142
Segall, Pamela 1898
Segall, Stuart 2197
Seinfeld, Jerry 2206
Seitz, Chris 1919
Seitz, John 2218
Sekka, Johnny 1466
Selby, David 1340, 1616, 1683
Selena Mead 820
Self, Ed 1811, 1820, 1939
Self, William 6, 604, 730, 1367, 1403
Selig, Andrew 1975
Seligman, Selig 759
Sell, Janie 1334, 1391, 1580
Selleca, Connie , Connie 1642, 2021
Selleck, Tom 1316, 1507, 1564, 1640, 1788, 1815, 1880, 1985
Seller, Tom 704
Sellers, Arlene 2198
Sellers, Peter 892, 1405
Sellier, Charles E., Jr. 1592, 1685, 1903, 2190, 2217, 2260, 2261
Selmur Productions 747, 750, 759, 801, 871, 875, 935
Seltzer, David 2064
Seltzer-Gimbel Productions 2064

Selzer, Milton 559, 1105, 1130, 1136, 1213, 1230
Semple, Lorenzo, Jr. 797, 826, 843, 847
Send in the Clones 2265
Seneca, Jose 1850
Senensky, Ralph 1249, 1279, 1397, 1813
Sennett, Susan 1176, 1410
Separate Lives 898
September Jones 714
Septor, Trelis 2197
Serafin, Richard 1721
Seremba, George 2258
Sergeant and the Lady 130
Sgt. Bilko 239
Sgt. T.K. Yu 1675
Sergent, Glenna 1101
Series I 371
Serling, Rod 463, 670, 1209, 1326, 1382
Serna, Pepe 1252, 1395, 1754, 1845, 1915, 2065, 2118, 2237
Sernas, Jacques 131
Serra, Raymond 2174
Serrano, Socorro 1059
Serris, Irene 1716
Sertner, Mort 2089
Sertner, Robert M. 1838, 1936, 2232
Server, Eric 1451, 1917
Service, Robert 342
Sesame Street 1241, 1313
Sessions, Elmira 550, 673
Seven, Johnny 478, 617

Seven Arts 994
Seven Cannery Row 548
Seven Little Foys 774
Seven Rich Years and Seven Lean 752 17
Battery Place 589 72
Grovesner Square 2063
Severson, Jeff 2066
Sevorg, Jon 1294
Seymour, Anne 1299, 1469, 1471
Seymour, Carolyn 1863, 1916, 1937, 1968, 2113, 2230
Seymour, Jane 1506
Seymour, Ralph 1669
Sgarro, Nicholas 1517
Shack 1451
Shackelford, Ted 1556, 1644, 1647
Shadow Man 1011
Shadow of a Man 776
Shadow of Sam Penny 1987
Shadow Over the Land 986
Shady Acres Mob 861
Schafer, Natalie 1713
Shaffer, Louise 2195
Shaftel, Joseph 471, 540, 760
Shakar, Martin 2046, 2172
Shake and Baker 2194
Shallat, Lee 2155
Shallert, William 1147
Shambata, Chuck 2029
Shamberg, Michael 1665, 1666

Shameful Secrets of Hastings Corner 1025
Shampoo 1417
Shamus 1358
Shanklin, Douglas Alan 2030
Shannon, Al 2128
Shannon, Billy 1282
Shannon, Harry 482
Shannon, Michael 1583, 2063
Shannon, Richard 299, 316
Shapiro, George 2206
Shapiro, Richard 2150
Shapiro, Stanley 118, 459, 1242
Sharf, Walter 1650
Sharif, Omar 1652
Shark Kill 1427
Shark Street 335
Sharkey, Billy Ray 2049
Sharkey, Joe 1850
Sharkey, Ray 1385, 2063
Sharma, Barbara 1271, 1400
Sharp, Jon 2060
Sharp, Phil 956
Sharp Intake of Breath 1792
Sharpe, Alex 207, 1908
Sharpe, Cornelia 1512, 1652
Sharpe, Don 11, 121, 502, 1371
Sharpe, Karen 313, 925
Sharpe, Sandra 1722
Sharrett, Michael 1616, 2085
Shatner, William 704, 735, 750, 1124, 1129, 1167, 1187, 1259, 2034, 2120

Shattuc, Norma 670
Shattuck, Shari 2090
Shaughnessey 1415
Shaughnessy, Mickey 388, 553, 1018
Shaun Cassidy Project 2175
Shavelson, Mel 390, 930, 1083, 1091, 1153, 1803
Shaw, Adriana 1247
Shaw, David 693, 883, 1191, 1233, 1654
Shaw, Dianne 2008
Shaw, Frank 1329
Shaw, Jennifer 1124, 1336
Shaw, Lou 1786, 2129
Shaw, Martin 2240
Shaw, Reta 645, 818, 964, 1150
Shaw, Stan 1368, 1447, 1680, 2089
Shaw, Susan Damante 1639
Shaw, Victoria 781
Shawel, Saba 2092
Shawlee, Joan 235, 1904
Shawn, Dick 968, 1151, 1394, 1709, 1797
Shay, Don 744
Shayne, Bob 1384, 2162
S.H.E. 1652
She's the Sheriff 1871
She's with Me 1877, 2124
Shea, Eric 1092, 1597
Shea, Jack 1275, 1284, 1313, 1333, 1366, 1413, 1554, 1658, 1670, 1807, 1829, 1837, 1897, 1997, 2161

Shea, John 1692
Shea, Kathy 1773
Shea, Michael 1974
Shear, Barry 763, 873, 914, 1102, 1127, 1229, 1296, 1359, 1441, 1611
Shear, Pearl 1408, 1769, 1863, 2159
Shearer, Hannah L. 1522, 1537
Shearin, John 1830
Sheedy, Ally 1793
Sheehan, Michael 1960
Sheen, Martin 1190, 1211
Sheerer, Robert 1298, 1454
Sheila 1460
Sheila Levine Is Dead and Living in New York 1460
Sheinberg, Sid 1169
Sheiner, David 1168, 1278, 1866
Sheldon, Jack 913, 1012
Sheldon, James 208, 390, 1004
Sheldon, John 1387
Sheldon, Les 1680, 1848, 1864, 2203
Sheldon, Reid 2028
Sheldon, Sidney 18, 730
Sheldon Bull Productions 2016
Sheldon Leonard Productions 1142, 1262, 1596
Shelhorse, Todd 1257
Shell Game 1339
Shellen, Stephen 2003, 2188
Shellen, Steve 2063
Shelley, Barbara 894
Shelley, Joshua 896, 1203, 1276

Shelley, Mary 1683
Shelley 2110
Shelton, Abigail 858
Shelton, Don 255
Shenar, Paul 1338, 1474, 1584, 2025, 2041, 2065, 2193
Shenson, Walter 761
Shepard, Gerald S. 1092
Shepherd, John 1843, 1977
Shepherd's Flock 1046
Sheppard, Anthony 129
Sher, Jack 1216
Sher, Pearl 1681
Shera, Mark 1281, 1561, 1750, 1868
Sherdeman, Ted 96, 294
Sheridan, Ann 59
Sheridan, Liz 2028, 2066
Sheridan, Nicolette 2025
Sheriff, Sydney 1178
Sheriff 924, 1078, 1089
Sheriff and the Astronaut 1988
Sheriff USA 30
Sheriff Who 968, 1151
Sherlock, David 2224
Sherlock Holmes 1124
Sherman, Deborah 1339
Sherman, Don 1137
Sherman, Ellen 1218
Sherman, Gary 1689, 2010
Sherman, George 75, 664
Sherman, Harry R. 1444, 2249

Sherman, Howard 2194
Sherman, Jenny 1660
Sherman, Joe 2041
Sherman, Karyn 2119
Sherman, Kerry 1442, 1751
Sherman, Larry 1231
Sherman, Leo 842
Sherman, Melissa 1751
Sherman, Orville 1189
Sherman, Robert 1750
Sherman, Vincent 795, 821, 900
Shermer, Jules 620
Shermet, Hazel 204
Sherry, Diane 934
Sherwood, Madeline 1093, 2169
Sherwood, Robin 1567
Sherwood Productions 1964
Sheslow, Stuart 1922, 2010, 2088
Shields, Nicholas 1970
Shields, Robert 1656
Shigeta, James 971, 1234, 1376, 1619, 2105
Shimerman, Armen 1790
Shimoda, Yuki 1251
Shimokawa, Gary 1465, 1553, 2016
Shimono, Sab 1863
Ship-Shape 1553
Shipman, Nina 813
Shire, David 1093, 1098, 1104, 1282, 1292, 1392, 1849, 2078
Shirley, Peg 1384

Shirley Temple Show 795
Shirriff, Catherine 1468
Shirts/Skins 1243
Shockley, Sallie 1219
Shoenman, Elliot 1388, 1633, 1795, 1966
Shoestring Safari 956
Sholdar, Mickey 985
Sholen, Lee 219
Shoop, Kimber 2215
Shoop, Pamela 2265
Shooter 2269
Shooting Stars 1917
Shore, Roberta 500, 651
Shore Leave 601
Shores, Richard 1358, 1512, 1584, 1611
Shorr, Lonnie 1557
Short, Luke 288, 472
Short, Martin 1767, 1891
Short, Robert 1638
Short, Sylvia 1906
Short Circuit 1168
Short Story 1168
Shorter, Beth 1906
Shortridge, Stephen 1601, 1719
Show Wagon 522
Showalter, Max 1309
Showboat 81
Shower of Stars 20
Shpetner, Stan 812, 826, 1013, 1038
Shrong, Maurice 1876
Shroyer, Stephanie 2244
Shryer, Bret 1826
Shuken, Phil 499, 525
Shulay, John C. 1661
Shuler-Donner, Lauren 2188

Shull, Charles 1298, 1801
Shull, John 1866
Shull, Richard B. 1499, 1930
Shulman, Constance 2257
Shulman, Roger 1758
Shultz, Chip 1178
Shultz, Jan Michael 2244
Shutan, Jan 855, 934, 1530
Shutan, Liz 970
Shydner, Richard 2096
Shyer, Charles 1014, 1200, 1219, 1407
Sibanda, Seth 2258
Sicari, Joseph R. 1307
Sicarri, Joseph 1435
Sickner, Roy 670
Siddall, Teddi 1848
Side by Side 1391, 1554, 1912
Side of the Angels 670
Sidekicks 899, 1282
Sidney, George 763
Sidney, Susanne 114
Sidney, Sylvia 1390
Siebert, Charles 1378, 1518, 1539, 1620, 2182
Siegel, Charles E. 2093
Siegel, Don 316
Siegel, Gerald K. 2175
Siegel, Larry 1141
Siegel, Lee 1938
Siegel, Lionel E. 1228, 1442, 1442a 1514, 1655, 1718
Siegel, Matt 1888
Siegelman, Jan 2142, 2253
Siemaszko, Casey 2008

Sierra, Gregory 1238, 1293, 1907, 1939, 1969
Sifuentes, Kevin 2028
Siggins, Jeff 1075
Signed: Anxious 969
Signorelli, Tom 1498
Sikes, Cynthia 1430, 1928
Sikking, James B. 1094, 1147, 1183, 1484, 2138, 2195, 2242
Silent Kill 316
Silent Saber 324
Silent Whisper 2245
Silky Chamberlain 1523
Silliman, Maureen 1687
Silliphant, Stirling 316, 1128, 1166, 1170, 1320, 1484, 1800, 1802, 1989, 2091
Silliphant/ Konigsberg Productions 1484, 1542, 1550
Sills, Douglas 2201
Sills, Stephanie 1542
Silo, Susan 550, 906, 1098, 1389
Silva, Geno 1475, 2023
Silva, Henry 725, 1059
Silva, Trinidad 2263
Silver, Arthur 1531, 1827, 2154
Silver, Barry 1829
Silver, Borah 1539
Silver, David 1030
Silver, Jeff 243
Silver, Johnny 1345
Silver, Joseph 1030, 1638
Silver, Marc 1953
Silver, Ron 1418

Silver, Stu 1711, 1858, 1898, 2017
Silver Springs 886
Silverheels, Jay 1052
Silverman, Fred 1901, 1907, 1927, 1951, 1952, 2082, 2176, 2187
Silverman, Jeff 2087
Silverman, Treva 1141
Silvers, Cathy 1994, 2001, 2020 Silvers, Phil 889, 952, 1781
Silverstein, Elliot 1906
Silvestre, Armando 1030
Silvestri, Alan 1908
Simcha Productions 1288
Simcox, Tom 842, 843, 904, 957, 1057
Simmons, Ed 901, 908, 937, 939, 1081, 1136, 1204
Simmons, Floyd 244
Simmons, Jean 1743
Simmons, Johnathan 2132
Simmons, Matty 1836
Simmons, Richard Alan 735, 785, 899, 961, 1028, 1058, 1103, 1163, 1282, 1351, 2044, 2091
Simmons, Tom 2231
Simon, Al 391, 873
Simon, Albert J. 1808
Simon, Danny 679
Simon, David 2242
Simon, Neil 767, 1113, 1217, 1501, 1756, 1760, 1828

Simon, Robert F. 1503
Simon, Sam 2184
Simon, Tim 1874
Simon, Tom 1816
Simon and Gluckstein 1333
Simon and Simon 1987, *2047*
Simon Lash 450
Simone, Gigi 1368
Simons, Regina 1784
Simoun, Henri 1514
Simpson, Abigail 2153
Simpson, Emily 2153
Simpson, Frank 1498
Simpson, Mickey 325, 607
Simpson, O.J. 1781, 1893, 1953
Simpson, Peter 1593
Simpson, Sandy 2035
Simpson-Raffil Productions 1593
Sims, Marley 1792
Sims, Ray 1145
Simson, Mark 1595
Sin, American Style 1224
Sinatra, Frank, Jr. 1290
Sinbad 2024
Sinbad the Sailor 962
Sindbad 962
Sinclair, Madge 1307, 1365, 1470, 1471, 2149
Sinelnikoff, Michael 2128
Singer, Alexander 1320, 1382, 1507, 1588, 1971
Singer, Leon 2237
Singer, Rachel 2243
Singer, Ray 388, 407
Singer, Raymond 1368, 1665, 1827
Singer, Reuben 1234

Singer, Robert 1322, 1589, 2022, 2132, 2177
Singles 1142
Singleton, Doris 1883
Sinutko, Shane 1522, 1535, 1619, 1624
Sion, Robert F. 1254
Siragusa, Peter 1888
Sirens 2166
Sirianni, E.A. 1848
Sirianni, R.A. 1396
Sirico, Anthony 1551
Sirola, Joseph 1383
Sis 60, 66
Sisk, Kathleen 2008
Sissy 290
Sister Terri 1531
Sisters 2111
Sitowitz, Hal 1189, 1325, 2215
Sitter's Baby 500
Six Guns for Donegan 325
Six Million Dollar Man 1442, 1442a, 1514, 1937, 2033
Six Pack 1959 6
Rms Riv Vu 1273
Six Shooter 246
Six Star Playhouse 339
Sixth Sense 166, 1028 *$64, 000 Question* 191
S/K Productions 1455
Skaff, George 1298, 1338, 1383
Skaggs, Jimmie F. 2244
Skaggs, Jimmy 2211
Skagway 336
Skala, Lilia 1029
Skeletons 1586, 1587
Skelton, Red 488, 956
Skerritt, Tom 2194
Skin Game 1282

Skinta, George 2186
Skippy 286
Skorpios Productions 1622
Skulnik, Menasha 182
Sky, Dawn Little 482
Sky, Eddie Little 1401
Sky Hei$t 1347
Skyward 1853
Skyward Christmas 1853
Slaboda, Deborah Dawn 2217
Slack, Ben 2165
Slade, Bernard 1008, 1012, 1071, 1095, 1134, 1176, 1237
Slade, Betsy 1457
Slade, Mark 1618, 1721
Sladstone, Gale 1518
Slate, Barney 211
Slate, Henry 1916
Slate, Jeremy 702, 817, 857, 874, 1089
Slate, Lane 1247, 1254, 1315, 1503, 1504, 2192
Slattery, Richard X. 1080, 1261, 1335
Slavid, John 1127
Slavin, Millie 1329, 1732, 1820, 1907
Slayton, Bobby 2157
Sledge Hammer 1992
Slezak, Walter 28, 383, 464
Slezak and Son 464
Slickers 2056
Slightly Fallen Angel 383
Slither 1275
Sloan, Michael 1158, 1771, 1778, 1779, 1937, 2098, 2196
Sloan, Rickey 549

Sloane, Allan 465, 704
Sloane, Everett 260, 756, 803
Sloyan, James 1279, 1773
Small, Florence 1688
Small, Marya 1622
Small Step Forward 1320
Small Victories 2182
Smart, Jean 2040
Smart, Patsy 1158
Smart Guys 2257
Smight, Jack 76, 1119, 1233, 1884
Smildsin, Kurt 1936
Smilie, Bill 1539
Smith, Alexis 1192
Smith, Betty 1299
Smith, Bill 716
Smith, Brandon 2130
Smith, Brett 1888
Smith, Bubba 1844
Smith, Bud 2128
Smith, Cameron 2050
Smith, Carl 233
Smith, Caroline 1688, 1692, 1886
Smith, Charles 7
Smith, Charles Martin 1421, 1671, 1712
Smith, Cotter 2114
Smith, Craig 879
Smith, Dean 1257
Smith, Deirdre 1199
Smith, Dwan 1125
Smith, Earl 1477
Smith, Ebbe Roe 2042, 2070
Smith, Ebonie 2013
Smith, Essex 1098
Smith, F.D. 728
Smith, Frasier 2237
Smith, H. Allen 941
Smith, Hal 968

Smith, Howard 466, 670, 761

Smith, J. Brennan 1868

Smith, Jaclyn 1224, 1719

Smith, Jim 1641

Smith, Jim B. 1427

Smith, Juney 2151

Smith, Justin 921

Smith, K.L. 314

Smith, Kelly 518

Smith, Kent 994, 1164, 1246

Smith, Kurtwood 2021, 2117

Smith, Lane 1730, 1860

Smith, Lewis 1955, 2096, 2208

Smith, Lois 2113

Smith, Martha 1644, 1774

Smith, Martin 1356

Smith, Mary Ellen 455

Smith, O.C. 1199

Smith, Pam 636

Smith, Patricia 855, 901, 1260, 1289, 1316, 1785

Smith, Paul 870, 1094, 1350

Smith, Peter 2125

Smith, Reid 1789, 1843

Smith, Rex 2264

Smith, Richard Kimmel 1391

Smith, Roger 847

Smith, Sam 1309

Smith, Shawnee 2194

Smith, Shelly 1801

Smith, Sly-Ali 2049, 2119

Smith, Taryn 2199

Smith, Thorne 1620

Smith, W.O. 1650

Smith, William 1040, 1186, 1352, 1940

Smith, Yeardley 2038, 2234

Smith-Cameron, J. 2143

Smithee, Alan 1887, 2098, 2129

Smithers, William 958, 1010, 1651

Smitrovich, William 1873

Smits, Sonja 1969

Smokey and the Bandit 1835, 1865

Smolen, Stefan 2218

Smolka, Ken 2193

Smoot, Fred 832, 937, 1050

Smothers Brothers 862

Smythe, Karen 2190

Smythe, Marcus 1530

Smythe, Reg 1171

Snafu 1416

Snavely 1527

Sneak Preview, 59, 60

Snee, John 1929

Sneed, Maurice 1502, **2022**

Snider, Barry 1478

Sniff 2232

Snip! 1417

Snodgress, Carrie 1104

Snooks 161

Snow, Mark 1582, 1612, 1618, 2021, 2034, 2039, 2040, 2120, 2174

Snow Fire 56

Snyder, Arlen Dean 1803, 1814, 1854, 1936

Snyder, Carlyn 1836

Snyder, Howard 20

Snyder, Hugh 1836

Snyder, Suzanne 2176

Soap 2230

Soares, Sylvia 1348

Sobel, Barry 2253

Soble, Ron 1436

Soboloff, Arnold 1231, 1389, 1495, 1511

Soderberg, Robert 1011

Sofronski, Bernie 2118

Soft Touch 307, 658

Sohmer, Steve 2264

Sokol, Marilyn 1770

Solari, John 2042

Sold, Jack 1568

Soldier Girls 1794

Soles, P.J. 1484, 1521, 1574, 1787

Solin, Harvey 1378

Solitaire 621

Solms, Kenny 1108, 1460

Soloman, George 1996

Soloman, Kim 1417

Soloman, Mark 1899

Soloman's Universe 2048

Solow, Herbert 949, 1162, 1193, 1475

Somack, Jack 1724, 1937

Some Kinda Woman 2233

Some Like It Hot 622

Some People We Know 1428

Someone to Watch Over Me 1287

Somers, Brett 1228, 1627

Somers, Suzanne 1871, 1878, 2014

Somerset Gardens 2207

Somerville, Karen 1425

Somewhere in Italy, Company B 894

Sommars, Julie 977, 1031, 1071, 1168, 1224, 1285

Sommer, Josef 1683

Sommerfield, Diane 1333

Sommer, Elke 1083, 1654

Sommers, Jay 307, 658, 951, 1026, 1082, 1084, 1201

Sommers, Yale 704

Sonny and Sam 1694

Sonny Boy 1276

Sons of Gunz 2167

Sontag, Jack 1883

Soo, Jack 871, 1010

Soper, Mark 1888

Sopranos, The 1783

Sorel, Louise 1100, 1253, 1597

Sorel, Theodore 1683

Sorenson, Paul 1183

Sorenson, Rickie 270

Soreny, Eva 922

Sorko-Ram, R.B. 1347

Sorrells, Bill 1585

Sorrels, Angela 2261

Sothern, Ann 117, 550, 555, 1197

Sotkin, Marc 1574, 2123

Soul, David 1166, 1188, 1447, 1698, 2091

Soule, Olan 253

Sound and the Fidelity 674

Sounder 1328

Sounds Like 2168

Soutendijk, Renee 2063

Southern Fried 1055

Southill Productions 705

Sowards, Jack 1934

Space, Arthur 44, 1271

Space Force 1500

Spackman, Tom 2041

Spader, James 1924

Spain, Fay 76, 322

Spardlin, G.D. 1105

Sparks, Robert 523

Sparrow 1479, 1568

Sparv, Camilla 1862

Spear, Martin 1907

Specht, Beth 1549, 1611

Specht, Karen 1549, 1611

Specht, Robert 1371

Special Agent 269

Specialists 983, 1302

Spectre 1524

Speer, Martin 2021

Speigel, Larry 2152

Spell, George 1248

Spellbound 355

Spelling, Aaron 208, 479, 603, 733, 738, 791, 802, 862, 1007, 1010, 1040, 1041, 1077, 1079, 1132, 1180, 1189, 1190, 1195, 1238, 1280, 1319, 1325, 1374, 1447, 1534, 1539, 1609, 1612, 1615, 1618, 1713, 1719, 1721, 1857, 1859, 1862, 1917, 1964, 1973, 2021, 2025, 2032, 2034, 2077, 2091, 2092, 2097, 2149, 2150, 2216, 2247

Spelling, Dan 1280

Spelling, Victoria 1917

Spelling/Goldberg Productions 1189, 1190, 1195, 1238, 1319, 1325, 1374, 1447, 1609, 1719, 2034, 2120

Spelling/Thomas Productions 1040, 1041, 1618

Spelling/Weintraub Productions 1857

Spelman, Sharon 1484, 1503, 1504, 1978, 2066, 2206

Spence, Johnnie 1520

Spencer, Dom 1536

Spencer, John 1953

Spencer, Nevada 1093

Spencer, Steve 1686

Spenser: For Hire 1507, 1802, 2009, 2114, 2214, 2218

Sperdakos, George 1414

Sperling, Milton 1452

Spielberg, David 1337, 1525, 1696

Spielberg, Steven 1169

Spielman, Ed 1916, 2115, 2173

Spies, Adrian 478, 1279, 1400

Spillane, Mickey 45, 1747

Spinell, Joe 1359, 1617, 1621

Spiner, Brent 2122

Spinks, James 1695

Spinner, Anthony 756, 1047, 1916, 1969

Spirit 2099

Split Second to Epitaph 1029

Spo-De-Odee 1365, 1434

Spound, Michael 1793

Spradlin, G.D. 1227

Spraggue 1918

Sprang, Laurette 1436, 1560

Spratley, Tom 1620

Springfield, Rick 1643

Sprung, Sandy 1496

Squad Car 141

Squadron 703

Staahl, Jim 1605

Stacey, James 664, 924, 1196

Stack, Lenny 1339

Stack, Robert 410, 722, 723, 727, 1335, 1972

Stack, Timothy 2201

Stacy, James 790, 960, 1145

Stacy, Michelle 1268

Stader, Paul 737

Stafford, Nancy 1928, 1955, 2100

Stage Coach 185

Stage Father 256

Stagecoach 340

Stagg, Jerry 199, 410, 411, 412, 413, 428

Stagg Productions 410

Stahl, Richard 968, 1264, 1306, 1446, 2016

Stake Out 47

Staley, James 1657, 1804, 2221

Staley, Joan 603, 630, 735, 866

Stambler, Robert 767, 1217, 1222, 1294, 1400, 1467, 1513, 1592, 1595

Stamm, Ralmund 2093

Stan Margulies Company 2026

Stanbridge, Martyn 2268

Stander, Artie 398

Stander, Lionel 1501, 2176

Stang, Arnold 733, 1408

Stanley, Florence 1276, 2160

Stanley, James 1827

Stanley, Paul 691, 1442a, 1595, 1655, 1675

Stanley Against the System 991

Stanley Kallis Productions 1369

Stanley Kramer Presents 149

Stanton, Harry Dean 673, 721, 792, 877, 1645

Stanton, Robert 1088

Stanwyck, Barbara 183, 514, 515, 516, 517, 603, 722, 723, 771, 1145, 1189, 1719

Stapleton, Maureen 1444, 1463, 1780, 2064

Star Trek 523, 750, 921, 1000, 1183, 1234, 1328

Star Trek: The Next Generation 1234

Star Wars 1693

Starfire 1594

Starger, Martin 1687, 1738, 1792, 1971

Stark, Craig 2193

Stark, Wilbur 379, 433, 635

Stark, William 1295, 1354

Stark 2049

Stark: Mirror Image 2119

Stark II 2119

Starke, Anthony 2257

Starke, Todd 1728

Starr, Adam 1621

Starr, Beau 1970, 2088

Starr, Ben 204, 1140, 1409, 1823

Starr, Don 1477
Starr, Mike 2036
Starr, Ricki 679
Starr, Ringo 2252
Starr, First
Baseman 830
Starr of the
Yankees 829
Starrett, Claude
Ennis, Jr. 1447
Starrett, Jack
1519, 1582
Starring: Nancy
Clancy 1205
Starry Night
Productions
1891, 1960
Stars and the
State 36
Starsky and Hutch
1447, 2118
Starstruck 1638
Starting Fresh 1580
Starting Over 2116
Stat! 1148
State Fair 1403
Stauffer, Jack
1476, 1774
Stauffer, Teddy 1077
Steadman, John
1818, 1864
Stearns, Michael
1349
Stedman 1315,
1513, 1595
Stedman, Joel 1403
Steel, Charles 1098
Steele, Amy 2210
Steele, Bob 68
Steele, Jadrien 2266
Steele, Karen
817, 957
Steeltown 1653
Steenberg, Richard
423, 442
Stefani, Michael 962
Stefano, John 1519
Stefano, Joseph
758, 828

Steiger, Rod 125,
857, 2261
Stein, James 2122
Stein, Jeff 1964
Stein, Joel 2154
Stein, Michael
Eric 2239
Stein, Shannon
2129
Steinberg, Barry 2048
Steinberg, David
2078
Steinberg, Melissa
1607
Steinberg, Norman
1236, 1341, 1388,
1483, 1967
Steinberg, Ziggy
1940
Steiner, Fred
803, 1077
Steinfeld, Jake
1942, 1997
Steinmetz,
Dennis 1579
Stellar, Clarice 1769
Stelzer, Peter A. 2186
Stennett, Myra 1683
Stephanie 1810
Stephen, Patsy 2185
Stephen J. Cannell
Productions 1451,
1616, 1617, 1640,
2006, 2023, 2086,
2133, 2166, 2203
Stephens, James
1536, 1689
Stephens, John G.
1261, 1987
Stephens, Laraine
1126, 1229, 1291,
1400, 1584, 1801
Steptoe and Son 837
Sterling 2247
Sterling, Alex 2008
Sterling, Jan 1,
454, 738
Sterling, Philip 1451,
1562, 1909

Sterling, Robert 176,
616, 1155, 1190
Sterling, Tisha
792, 1369
Stern, Daniel 2078
Stern, Eric 2066
Stern, John 1919
Stern, Joseph 114,
1714, **2022**
Stern, Leonard
838, 977, 1046,
1159, 1218, 1342,
1393, 1414, 1416,
1754, 1945
Stern, Lilibet 1752
Stern, Martin 235
Stern, Sandor 1303,
1427, 1536, 1984
Stern, Steven 1599
Stern, Steven
Hiliard 1929
Sterne, Morgan 1102
Stetson, Lee 1510
Stettin, Monte 1730
Steubenville 1461
Steve Martin
Productions 1900
Stevens, Andrew
1155, 1620
Stevens, Connie
1039, 1108,
1792, 2221
Stevens, Craig 640,
655, 1023, 1468,
1743, 1779, 1968
Stevens, Frankie
1648
Stevens, George 102
Stevens, Inger 1060
Stevens, Jeremy 2163
Stevens, K.T. 849
Stevens, Kaye 908
Stevens, Leah 482
Stevens, Leslie 716,
724, 725, 754,
773, 792, 972,
1057, 1429
Stevens, Mark
268, 487

Stevens, Morgan
1646, 1814, 1971
Stevens, Morton
1222, 1382, 1419,
1468, 1510, 1591,
1610, 1648, 1847,
1938, 1953, 2146
Stevens, Naomi 774
Stevens, Paul
803, 1421
Stevens, Ray 1546
Stevens, Robert 828
Stevens, Rory 1490
Stevens, Rusty 1929
Stevens, Sally 1166
Stevens, Shawn
1692
Stevens, Stella 1162,
1293, 1369, 1509,
1518, 1647, 2009
Stevens, Warren 24,
450, 850, 923
Stevenson,
Cynthia 2266
Stevenson, McLean
1086, 1243, 1870
Stevenson, Parker
1917, 2039
Steward, Nick 1199
Steward, Paul 468
Stewart, Anne
Randall 1450
Stewart, Brandon
2245
Stewart, Byron 1618
Stewart, Catherine
Mary 1972, 2126
Stewart, Charles
600, 1315
Stewart, Charlotte
1294, 1518, 1530
Stewart, Chuck 916
Stewart, Dennis
2194
Stewart, Donald 1567
Stewart, Douglas
Day 1246
Stewart, Fred
Mustard 1232

Stewart, Jimmy 246, 738, 796
Stewart, John 1800
Stewart, Kay 825
Stewart, Maxine 1233
Stewart, Mel 1296, 1577, 1742, 1864, 1942
Stewart, Milton 1089
Stewart, Paul 1101
Stewart, Peg 1903
Stewart, R.J. 2268
Stewart, Randy 316
Stewart, Roy 1410
Stewart, Trish 1382
Stick Around 1439
Stidder, Ted 2093
Stiers, David Ogden 1360, 1363
Stiles, Norman 1500, 1723
Stiles, Robert 1275
Still the Beaver 1929
Stiller, Jerry 642, 1114, 2125
Stiller & Meara Enterprises 2125
Stiller & Meara Show 2125
Stillman, Robert 253
Stillwell, Diane 1795
Stilwell, Diane 1391, 1909, 2149, 2155
Sting 1888
Stingray 1451
Stock, Alan 1785
Stock, Barbara 1890, 1970, 2214, 2218
Stocker, Emily 2185
Stocker, J.J. 2144
Stocker, Walter 656, 1048, 1302
Stockers 1835
Stockwell, Guy 619
Stoddard, Alexandra 1668
Stoff, Erwin 2070
Stoker, Austin 1057
Stokes, Michael 2226

Stolfi, Robert 1925
Stoller, Shirley 2041
Stollery, Mitzi 2159
Stolnitz, Art 1397
Stone 1195
Stone, Christopher 1133, 1193
Stone, Ezra 1125, 1832
Stone, Harold J. 894, 912
Stone, Leonard J. 1119, 1503, 1716
Stone, Madeline 1876
Stone, Martin 439
Stone, Noreen 2117
Stone, Peter 699, 844, 1462, 1464, 2153
Stone, Richard 2217
Stone, Sharon 2032, 2208
Stone, Susan Chris 2148
Stoneham, Russell 1421
Stonehenge Productions 1145, 1196, 1296, 2114
Stoneman, Robert 1582
Stonestreet 1429
Stonestreet: Who Killed the Centerfold Model? 1492
Stoney Burke 378, 716, 724, 725, 753
Storch, Larry 644, 815, 1592, 1676, 1690
Storer, Lynn 1468
Storer Company 744
Stories About Men 1069
Storm, Debi 1083
Storm, Howard 1344, 1910
Storm, James 1322
Story of a Star 232

Stout, Bill 1301
Stout, Don 1816
Stout, Ricky 2082
Stover, Howard 2066
Stoyanov, Michael 2034
Straight, Beatrice 1482
Strand, Robin 1609, 1638, 1848, 2088
Stranded 925, 1404
Strange, Mark 985
Strange Counsel 255
Strange New World 1212, 1328
Stranger 1235
Strangis, Greg 1179, 1614, 1690, 1759, 1790, 1821
Strangis, Sam 1996, 2049, 2119
Strano, Carl 1864
Strasberg, Susan 1047
Strassman, Marcia 1156, 1317, 1695, 2234
Strategic Air Command 75
Stratton, Bill 2049, 2246
Stratton, Charles 2244
Stratton, Chet 125
Stratton, Gil 21
Stratton, Hank 2096
Strauss, Robert 473, 509
Straw, Jack 307, 1649
Street, Ann 1650
Street, Elliot 1322, 1397
Street Heat 2010
Street Killing 1368
Street of Dreams 2246
Streeter, Bess 599
Streeter, Billy 2009
Streeter, Edward 445

Streets 2010
Streets of Justice 2065
Streets of San Francisco 1089
Streisand, Barbra 1286, 1533, 1766
Stribling, Hugh 129
Strickland, Amzie 1397
Strickland, Gail 1423, 1444, 1780, 2045
Striglos, Bill 1212
Strike Force 1359
Stringer, Marcia 1595
Stritch, Elaine 1097
Strivelli, Jerry 2010
Strode, Woody 1230, 1473
Stroka, Mike 1743
Stromberg, Hunt, Jr. 1219
Strong, Dennis 2029
Strong, Jay 821
Strong, John 1267
Strong, Michael 1090
Strong, Phillip 1403
Stroock, Gloria 1414
Strosier, Henry 1278
Stroud, Claude 307
Stroud, Don 1383, 1430, 1747
Stroud, Duke 1864
Struthers, Sally 1735
Stuart, Barbara 765, 1093, 1312
Stuart, Gil 1189
Stuart, Linda P. 1867
Stuart, Malcolm 1349, 1743
Stuart, Mary 2133
Stuart, Maxine 1224, 1301, 1851, 1892
Stuart, Mel 1317, 1333
Studio 994
Studio City Productions 82

Studstill, Pat 1732
Stumpf, Randy 1544
Stunt Seven 1654
Stunts Unlimited
1718
Sturdevant,
Dennis 549
Sturgess, Olive 243
Sturgis, Alice 499
Sturgis, Olive 413
Stuthman, Fred
1473, 1859, 1897
Styler, Adele 1175
Styler, Bud 788
Styler, Burt 1175
Suarez, Miryam 2083
Suburban Beat
1777, 2066
Suddenly Sheriff 1871
Sudrow, Penelope
1660
Sues, Alan 893, 1541
Sukman, Frances
1032
Sukman, Harry
1032, 1212, 1260,
1279, 1397, 1472
Sullivan, Barry 323,
698, 777, 848,
1079, 1169, 1190,
1612, 1847
Sullivan, Billy 2146
Sullivan, Ian 1585
Sullivan, Jenny 1852
Sullivan, Joe 266, 478
Sullivan, Susan 1406,
1448, 1450, 1505
Sullivan, William
Bell 2258
Sullivan Productions
1265, 1276
Sullivan's Empire
926
Sullivan's Place 926
Sultan, Arne 815,
874, 895, 1222,
1754, 1910
Sumant 1728
Summer 1979

Summer Fun 869, 870
Summer of '42 1298
Summer Playhouse
643
Summers, Andy 2267
Summers, Ann 1197
Summers, Hope 1024
Summers, Marc
2221
Summers, Yale 1277
Sun Valley 682
Sunado, Abdullah
2248
Sunday Man 472
Sundstrum,
Florence 743
Sunga, George
2111, 2234
Sunn Classic Pictures
1592, 1903,
1939, 2191
Sunset Strip 353
Sunshine, Madeline
2067
Sunshine, Steve 2067
Sunshine Boys 1501
Supercops 1340
Supiran, Jerry 1886,
1950
Supiran, Ricky 1862
Surfers 873
Surgal, Alan 1688
Surovy, Nicholas
1683, 2049, 2119
Susan and Sam 1502
**Susan Hayward
Show** 1196
Susskind, David
895, 977, 1482,
1569, 1572
Susman, Todd
1152, 1204, 1497,
1627, 1727, 1827,
2201, 2256
Sutherland, Esther
1264, 1848
Sutherland, John 283
Sutherland, Kristine
2103, 2179

Sutorius, James
1696, 1814, 2054
Sutter's Bay 1930
Sutton, Dudley 1127
Sutton, Frank 1176
Sutton, Henry 1450
Sutton, John 2
Sutton, Raymond
1260
**Suzanne Somers
Show** 1878
Suzie Mahoney
1878
Suzuki Beane 673
Svanoe, Bill 1316
Svenson, Bo 960,
1072, 1163, 1298,
1525, 1650, 1913
Swackhamer, E.W.
1008, 1012, 1037,
1110, 1166, 1468,
1533, 1621, 1717,
1953, 1969, 1988,
2023, 2040
Swain, John
Howard 1936
Swale, Tom 2032
Swan, Alya 1973
Swan, Billy 1951
Swan, Michael 2030
Swanson, Audrey
772
Swanson, Gary
2035, 2084
Swanson, Ted 1057
Swanton, Harold 255
Swany Inc. 2050
Swartz, Tony
1841, 2009
Swartzon, Saar 2231
Swayze, Don 2030
Sweeney, Bob 762,
867, 956, 1141,
1324, 1727, 1751
Sweeney, Joan 2008
Sweeney-Finnegan
Productions 1324
Sweeny, Ann 1511
Sweeny, Joan 1864

Sweeps 1824, 1868,
1946, 1948, 1951
Sweepstakes 1700
Sweet, Dolph 1568,
1637, 1946
Sweet, Katie 673
Sweet, Rebecca 1923
Sweet Life 927
Sweetum
Productions 2199
Swenson, Carol
1032, 1098
Swenson, Charles
1724
Swenson, Inga 1073
Swenson, Karl
125, 651, 905,
1128, 1258
Swerdlow, Tommy
2081
Swerling, Jo, Jr. 845,
922, 927, 1031,
1059, 1105, 1298,
1396, 1420, 1525,
1647, 1688,
1692, 2133
Swerling, Tanya 1525
Swetland, William
1381, 1449
Swift, David 657, 807
Swift, Jonathan 742
Swift, Susan 1624
Swingin' Together
659
Swingles 1027
*Swiss Family
Robinson* 1372
Swit, Loretta
1984, 2020
Switzer, Michael
2211
Swofford, Ken 985,
1019, 1347, 1426,
1595, 1642
Swoger, Harry 912
Swope, Mel 1786
Swope, Tracy Brooks
1595, 1655,
1688, 1692

Sword 131
Sybil 822
Sybil and Lionel 863
Syck, Ken 1075
Sykes, Brenda 1078
Sylvan, Paul 1361
Sylvan in Paradise 2122
Sylvester, Harold 1328, 1939, 2016
Symington, Donald 1004, 1687
Symonds, Robert 1339, 2189
Szarabajka, Keith 2055, 2113
Szwarc, Jeannot 1197, 1336, 1396, 1510, 1803

T

Tabat, Jordan 1551
Tabori, Kristoffer 1701, 2022, 2085
Tabuck, Barbara 2267
Tack Reynolds 724
Tackaberry, Jack 20
Tacker, Francine 1975
Tackett, Steve 1258
Tacon, Gary 2132
Taeger, Ralph 664
Taffner, Don 1858, 1910, 1925, 2037
Taffner/Stolfi 1791
Tafoya, Alfonso 1253
Taft Broadcasting 1475
Taft Entertainment 2050
Taft International Pictures 1903
Tagert, Brian 1253
Taggert, Rita 1686
Taka, Miiko 1251
Take Five 838
Take Her, She's Mine 796

Take Him – He's Yours 761
Taking It Home 2121
Talbot, Nita 1012, 1061, 1415, 1720
Talbot, Stephen 518
Talbott, Michael 1269, 1867, 1939, 1980
Talent Associates 895, 977, 1046, 1053, 1218, 1342, 1482
Tales of Broadway 421
Tales of the Barbary Coast 103
Tales of the Unknown 984
Tall Man 698
Talmadge, Richard 169
Tama, Pearl 2057
Tambor, Jeffrey 1454, 1833
Tamburo, Chuck 1862
Tamu 1520, 1679
Tan Chinn, Lori 2041
Tandem Productions 1573, 1823
Tangiers 594
Tannen, Charles 292
Tanner, Clay 1519
Tanner, Mary 2064
Tanney, Stuart 2201
Tanza, John Ian 1301
Tanzini, Philip 1501
Tapper 300
Tapscott, Mark 1074
Taradash, Daniel 1301
Target Risk 1525
Tarkington, Rockne 1682
Tarkington 1750
Tarloff, Frank 1005, 1064

Tarnell, Lorene 2028
Tarses, Jay 1433, 2012
Tartaglia, John Andrew 1126, 1565, 1617
Tarzan 270, 301, 928, 942, 978
Tarzan and the Trappers 270
Tarzan's Fight for Life 270
Tasco, Rai 1260
Task Force 1430
TAT Communications 1413, 1439, 1635, 1658, 1671, 1834, 1889, 1890, 1896
Tata, Joe E. 1324
Tate, Jacques 1942
Tatelman, Harry 645
Tatro, Duane 1441, 1817
Tattelman, Harry 925
Tattingers 2062
Tattleman, Harry 470
Tatum, Jeanne 115
Taurins, Ilze 1123
Tayback, Vic 1061, 1150, 1183, 1200, 1689, 1699
Tay-Gar 942
Taylor, Adam 2260
Taylor, Bruce 2001, 2126
Taylor, Buck 1534, 1559, 1882, 2009, 2120
Taylor, Charles 2002, 2061, 2129, 2130, 2131
Taylor, Clarice 1333, 1669, 1892, 2053
Taylor, Darin 2165
Taylor, Dendrie Allyn 2197
Taylor, Don 6, 112, 382, 386, 656, 743,

761, 802, 807, 810, 826, 885, 1145, 1157, 1293
Taylor, Dub 656, 737, 968, 1024, 1035, 1105, 1319, 1434, 1623, 1627, 1864
Taylor, Fred 2065
Taylor, Glen Hall 784
Taylor, Holland 2088, 2174
Taylor, Jana 965
Taylor, Jeri 1954
Taylor, Joan 697
Taylor, Josh 1509
Taylor, Jud 1184, 1254, 1327
Taylor, June Whitley 1640, 1662
Taylor, June Whitly 1487, 1525
Taylor, Lance, Sr. 1339
Taylor, Nathaniel, Jr. 1529
Taylor, Philip John 1732, 1820
Taylor, Renee 1062, 1488, 2031
Taylor, Robert 231, 379, 779
Taylor, Rod 665, 707, 958, 1358, 1814
Taylor, Roderick 2126
Taylor, Rommey 1224
Taylor, Ron 2223, 2237
Taylor, Sam 691
Taylor, Stephen J. 2223
Taylor, Valeria 1158
Taylor, Vaughn 1061, 1254
Taylor, Wally 1183
Taylor-Bologna Productions 1456

Taylor-Young, Leigh 1012

TCF Television Productions 206

Teacher 52

Teague, Lewis 1713

Teague, Marshall 1620, 1802

Teal, Ray 1249

Ted Bessell Show 1206

Tedrow, Irene 653, 968, 1428, 1633, 1916

Teenage Idol 204

Teicher, Roy 2078

Teichman, Howard 464

Teigh, Lila 1222, 1488

Telepictures Productions 1977, 2083

Television Reports International, Ltd. 2174

Telford, Frank 264

Telford, Robert 1813

Tell Aggie 839

Temple, Shirley 795

Tempo 757

Temporary Insanity 2000

Ten Commandments 76

Ten Little Fingers 693

Ten-Four Productions 1690, 1759, 1790, 1821, 1996

Tender Years 413

Tenney, Christopher 1504

Tension 149

Tepper, William 1108

Terhune, Shannon 1555

Terlesky, John T. 2217

Terraces 1526

Terrance, Michael 1882

Terrell, Tommy 44

Terror of Topanga 1958

Terry, Joe 1840

Terry, John 2216

Terry Becker Productions 1938

Terry-Thomas 896, 972

Tesreay, Krista 2146

Tessel, Kenny 1890

Tessier, Robert 1787, 1835

Test Pilot 42

Testi, Fabio 1652

Tevis, Walter 2096

Tewes, Lauren 2050, 2255

Tewkesbury, Joan 2236

Tewksbury, Peter 731, 798, 882, 899, 1046, 1131, 1139

Texan 317, 330, 373

Texas Rangers 1854

Thames, Byron 2266

That's My Mama 1177

That's My Mama Now! 1177

That's My Mom 257

Thatcher, Torin 752, 1317

Thaxter, Phyllis 1076

Thayer, Brynn 2147

Thayer, Lorna 1257

Thayer, Norma 1279

There Goes Calvin 258

There Goes the Neighborhood 1948

There's a Small Motel 345

There's Always Room 1463

They Call It Murder 1061

They Drive By Night 13

They Only Kill Their Masters 1254, 1315, 1503

They Went Thataway 465

Thibeau, Jack 2065

Thicke, Alan 1823

Thicker Than Water 1931

Thiel, Nick 1793

Thigpen, Lynn 1636, 2038

Thin Man 216, 988

Thinnes, Roy 121, 1232, 1510, 1618, 1801, 2241

13 13th Avenue 1932

13th Day: The Story of Esther 1610

13th Gate 780

Thirtysomething 2165, 2271

33rd 441

33 Hours in the Life of God 1325

This Better Be It 1392

This Gun for Hire 929

This House Is Haunted 186

This Is a Hospital 823

This Is Kate Bennett 1867

This Is Your Life 12

This Week in Nemtim 1143

Thomas, Betty 1566, 2142

Thomas, Bob 1655

Thomas, Christopher 2232

Thomas, Clarence 1466

Thomas, Danny 965, 1007, 1010, 1040, 1041, 1064, 1131, 1297, 1580, 1618, 1619, 1624

Thomas, Daron J. 1935

Thomas, Dave 2042

Thomas, Della 1278

Thomas, Heather 1779, 1866

Thomas, Jay 2201

Thomas, Kurt 2146

Thomas, Lee 1683

Thomas, Lorrie 552, 648

Thomas, Mark 1785

Thomas, Marlo 2153

Thomas, Phillip Michael 1395

Thomas, Ron 1922

Thomas, Scott 985, 1336, 1816

Thomas, Sharon 1561, 1911

Thomas, Thom 2064

Thomas, Tony 1189, 1258, 1485, 1963, 2016, 2019, 2068, 2123, 2181

Thomas, William, Jr. 2230

Thomas/Crenna Productions 1064

Thomas/Spelling Productions 1007, 1010

Thomason, Harry 1866, 1986

Thomerson, Tim 1506, 1526, 1602, 1627, 1796, 2188, 2227, 2256, 2264

Thompson, Chris 1574, 1913, 1932,

1947, 2000, 2056, 2254

Thompson, Dee J. 772

Thompson, Hilary 1400, 1475, 1599

Thompson, Jack 2172

Thompson, Kay 603

Thompson, Larry 1747, 2087

Thompson, Linda 1577, 2227

Thompson, Mark 1238

Thompson, Palmer 264

Thompson, Robert C. 1253

Thompson, Robert E. 877, 1124, 1369

Thompson, Sada 1271

Thompson's Ghost 797

Thomson, Margaret 2046

Thor 2264

Thor, Jerome 602

Thor, Jerry 480

Thordsen, Kelly 737

Thornton, Naomi 1099, 1780

Thoroughbred Productions 1339

Thoroughbreds 304

Thorpe, Daniel 1756

Thorpe, David 885

Thorpe, Jerry 255, 654, 659, 673, 674, 722, 836, 874, 1021, 1089, 1103, 1292, 1373, 1423, 1521, 1528, 1613, 1715, 1956, 2007, 2043, 2244

Thorsen, Russell 218

Thorson, Linda 1563, 2089

Thrasher, Julie 1650

Three 1228

Three Coins in the Fountain 930

Three Faces of Love 1168

Three for Danger 931

Three for Tahiti 1037 330

Independence Southwest 704, 779

333 Montgomery Street 523, 666

Three in One 912, 1092

Three Men and a Girl 608

Three of a Kind 291, 2219

Three on a Date 1532

Three on a Match 2197

Three on an Island 900

Three Star Theatre 581

Three Thousand Mile Chase 1298, 1525

Three Times Daley 1393

Three to Six 1902

Three Wishes 502

Three Wives of David Wheeler 1581

Three Worlds of Gulliver 741

Three's a Crowd 943

Three's Company 1736, 1791, 1870

Three-Way Love 1555

Throne, Malachi 921, 1170, 2217

Through the Magic Pyramid 1699

Thuna, Leonora 1496, 1580

Thunder Road Productions 1922

Thurber, James 390, 557

Thurshy, David 830

Thurston, Tomi 121

Thy Neighbor Loves Thee 1114

Tiano, Lou 1340

Tibbles, George 656, 760, 855, 1268

Tibbs, Casey 227, 1162

Tick, Tick, Tick 1078

Ticket of Fate 142

Tickets, Please 2234

Tidy man, Ernest 1973, 2049, 2119

Tietel, Carol 2040

Tiffe, Angelo 2041

Tiffin, Pamela 900

Tigar, Kenneth 1564, 1765, 1927, 2192, 2201

Tiger of Sonora 302

Tiger, Tiger 1032

Tigero 584

Tighe, Kevin 2174

Tightrope 634, 1147

Til, Roger 1190, 1683, 1801

Tillis, Mel 1053, 1835

Timber Hill 635

Timber Lake 635

Timberlake, Dee 1332, 1402

Time Bandit 2224

Time for Love 1170

Time-Life Productions 745

Time-Life Television 1701

Time-Life/David Susskind Productions 1569

Time of Flight 974

Time of the Devil 1446

Time Out for Dad 2193

Time Out for Ginger 20, 651

Time Travelers 1382

Time Tunnel 1101, 1382

Times of Their Lives 2176

Timko, Johnny 1979

Timm, Doug 2096

Tin Pan Sally 196

Tinker, Grant 1152, 1728, 2057

Tinker, Mark 1696, 1967, 2062, 2263

Tiomkin, Dimitri 1321

Tippet, Wayne 2041

Tippette, Giles 1298

Tipton, George Aliceson 1258, 1297, 1784, 2019, 2181

Tipton, Jeffrey 1836

Tirelli, Jaime 1476, 1625

Tisch, Steve 2035

Tisch/Avnet Productions 2035

Tisdale, James 2052

Titus Productions 1370, 1398, 1683, 1906

T.J. Hooker 2034, 2120

T.J. Hooker: Blood Sport 2120

Tjan, Willie 1551

T.L.C. 2001

To, Bobby 1256

To Catch a Thief 633

To Live and Die in L.A. 2128

To Sir, With Love 1207

Tobey, Doug 1783
Tobey, Kenneth 739, 1123, 1183, 1290, 1539, 1771
Tobias, George 774
Tobin, Dan 768, 1190
Tobin, Matthew 1781
Tobin, Michelle 1622
Toblowsky, Stephen 1953
Tobor The Great 44
Todd, Beverly 1178, 1961, 2013
Todd, Erica 2060
Todd, Hallie 1922
Todd, Lisa 1007
Todd, Melvin 1477
Todd, Michael 25
Todman, Bill 583
Toga Tales 1710
Together Again 1977
Together We Stand 1240
Togetherness 497
Tokar, Norman 18, 118, 251, 311, 386, 497, 552, 648, 1016, 1088, 1140, 1199
Tokatyan, Leon 1478, 1951, 1982
Tokofsky, Jerry 1605
Tokuda, Marilyn 2161
Tokyo Police 104
Tolan, Michael 1273, 1396
Tolbert, Belinda 2021
Tolbert, R.L. 1693
Toliver, Bill 1348
Tolkan, James 1958
Tolkin, Mel 766, 948, 1798
Toll, Pamela 846, 1566
Tolman, Conchetta 1683
Tolo, Marilu 1725

Tolsky, Susan 1138, 1581
Tom and Jerry 67
Tom and Joanne 1569
Tom, Dick and Harry 204
Tom Selleck Project 1788
Tomlinson, Tom 770
Tomorrow Entertainment 1171, 1185, 1209, 1281, 1874
Tompkins, Angel 1680
Tompkins, Dan 886
Tompkins, Joan 1153, 1211, 1586
Toni's Boys 1719
Toni's Devils 1719
Tonight in Havana 271
Tony Orlando Show 2057
Tony Rome 982
Too Close for Comfort 1205, 1910
Too Many Cooks 2142
Toomey, Regis 76, 396
Toots Productions 2148
Top Secret 1596
Topol 1242
Topolsky, Ken 2186, 2217, 2259
Topper 1620
Topper Returns 1155
Torgov, Sarah 1904
Tori Productions 1479, 1568
Torn, Rip 2086
Torokvei, Peter 1900
Torppe, Danil 2098
Torres, Antonio 1993

Torres, Liz 1722, 1748, 2121
Torres, Radames 1842
Torrid Zone 427
Tors, Ivan 759, 945, 1032, 1057, 1543
Toste, Frank 1780
Tosti and Son 362
Totten, Robert 1019
Totter, Audrey 554, 932
Touchstone Pictures 2188
Tourneur, Jacques 207, 470
Towers, Constance 2216
Towers, Robert 1546
Towheads 1894
Townes, Harry 1061, 1302, 1612
Towns, Harry 325
Townsend, Barbara 2126
Townsend, Patti 1831
Townsend, Tommy 2260
T.O.Y. Productions 1576
Toy Game 1244
TPA 85, 187
T.R. McCoy 1464
Tracey, Jan 2093
Tracy, Emily 2057, 2137, 2235
Tracy, John 1770, 1795, 1830, 2253
Tracy, Lee 632, 837
Tracy, Marlene 1103
Tracy, Spencer 800, 1307
Trade Winds 442
Trailblazer 26
Trailman 341
Trainer, David 2230
Tramp Ship 273, 574
Transatlantic 192
Trask, Diana 605

Traubel, Helen 406, 546
Travanti, Daniel J. 958
Travel Agency 147
Travelena, Fred 1917
Traveling Man 2177
Travis, Richard 1121
Travis Logan, D.A. 1090
Travis McGee 1802
Travolta, Ellen 1512, 1584, 1601, 1951
Travolta, Joey 1952
Traylor, William 1652
Trayne, John 1059
Treas, David 1730
Treas, Terri 2230
Treasury Agent 369
Tree Grows in Brooklyn 1299
Tregaskis, Richard 416, 664
Trellis Productions 1612
Tremayne, Les 118
Trendle/Campbell Productions 277
Trent, John 1181
Trentham, Barbara 1460
Tress, David 2245
Treutelaar, Barbara 2160
Trevey, Ken 1197, 1249, 1419
Treviglio, Leonard 1596
Trial and Error 2105
Trial of the Incredible Hulk 2264
Tribe 1247
Trice, Ron 1586
Tricker, George 1497, 1553
Trikonis, Gus 772, 1692, 1972

Triple Play '72 1150, *1154*

Triple Play '73 1152

Triplecross 2035

Triska, Jan 1937

Tristan, Dorothy 1326

Tristar Television 2137, 2140, 2171, 2185, 2197, 2239, 2267

Trobvich, Tom 2056

Trombetta, Jim 2130

Troobnick, Eugene 1068

Trouble in Paradise 754

Trouble Shooter and Gunga Din 247

Trouble with Richard 465

Troubleshooters 1383

Troup, Bobby 763, 1506

Troup, Ronne 1119, 1319, 1383, 1696

Troupe, Tom 1183

Troy, Louise 860

True Detective Stories 82

True Grit 1063, 1536

True Grit: A Further Adventure 1536

True Life Stories 1802

Trueblood, Guerdon 1467

Trueman, Paula 1817, 1850

Truex, Ernest 748

Truman, Harry 430

Truman, Pamela 860

Truman, Paula 1690

Trumbell, Robert 382

Trumbull, Brad 958, 1823

Trump, Gerald 753

Truth or Consequences 139

Tsang, Willie 554

Tsu, Irene 1251

TTC Productions 1556

Tuan, Le 2237

Tucci, Maria 1398

Tucci, Michael 1545, 1901

Tuchner, Michael 1888, 2028, 2112, 2149

Tuck, Doug 2093, 2117

Tucker, Duane 1688

Tucker, Forrest 1024, 1052, 1134, 1229, 1592, 1636, 1650

Tucker, Larry 1727, 1751, 1752, 1833

Tucker, Michael 1621

Tucker, Tanya 1730

Tucker, Victoria 2032

Tuddenham, Peter 1379

Tuerpe, Paul 1917, 1973, 2021, 2065

Tufts, Sonny 973

Tugend, Harry 309, 492

Tully, Andrew 369

Tunick, Jonathan 1637, 1805

Tupou, Manu 1594

Turco, Paolo 1596

Turco, Tony 1906

Turkel, Ann 1862, 1863

Turley, Myra 1992, 2199

Turman, Glynn 1075, 1871, 1928, 2170

Turman, Lawrence 1024

Turnbull, Glen 112

Turner, Arnold 1183

Turner, Barbara 713, 1423

Turner, Clay 1582

Turner, Dennis 2146

Turner, E. Frantz 1848

Turner, Joe Lynn 2127

Turner, Lana 1295

Turning Point 191, 789

Turnover Smith 1720

Turnpike 167, 481

Turteltaub, Saul 1143, 1576

Tuseo, Tony 1821

Tut and Tuttle 1699

Tuthill, Bruce 2023

Tuttle, Lurene 386, 497, 643, 1257, 1724, 1750, 1808, 1917

Tuttle, Mark 1329

TV Movies 1685

Twain, Arthur 255

Twain, Mark 361

Tweed, Shannon 1992, 2166, 2217

20th Century Fox Television 7, 19, 83, 126, 192, 278, 414, 418, 457, 533, 604, 605, 619, 636, 663, 706, 793, 795, 796, 812, 821, 826, 860, 868, 930, 957, 970, 971, 981, 982, 984, 993, 995, 1001, 1003, 1005, 1006, 1017, 1022, 1024, 1030, 1036, 1054, 1055, 1061, 1068, 1101, 1109, 1123, 1130, 1141, 1149, 1152, 1155, 1165, 1167, 1172, 1173, 1179, 1239, 1242, 1253, 1257, 1269, 1278, 1299, 1335, 1343, 1372, 1375, 1377, 1382, 1397, 1403, 1457, 1472, 1493, 1518, 1524, 1530, 1544, 1605, 1731, 1741, 1755, 1809, 1830, 1849, 1865, 1866, 1868, 1912, 1920, 1933, 1959, 1964, 1978, 1981, 1992, 2014, 2020, 2029, 2044, 2060, 2109, 2132, 2177, 2205, 2221, 2224, 2231

20th Century Fox Hour 19

21st Precinct 132, 215

Twenty Paws Productions 2082

27 Joy Street 1462, 1463

Twice in a Lifetime 1300, 1345

Twigg, Simon 770

Twigs 1271

Twilight Zone 463, 670

Twin Detectives 1371

Two and a Half Dads 2082

Two Boys 1056

Two-Five 1537, 1538

Two for the Money 1132

Two for the Road 528, 612

Two Guys from Muck 1676

Two of Us 660

Two Plus Two 1741

Two Reelers 1836

Two the Hard Way 1811

Two Worlds 2248

Two Young Men and a Girl in a Meat Grinder 975

Two's Company 798, 1137, 1208
Twomey, Anne 1906, 2054, 2063, 2085
Ty Cooper 666
Tyme, Simon 1536
Tyne, Buddy 1626
Tyne, George 1544
Tyner, Charles 1254, 1535, 1608
Tyrrell, Susan 1722
Tyson, Cicely 1098, 1156, 1469, 1470
Tyson, Richard 2118
Tzudiker, Bob 2100

U

UBU Productions 2121, 2179, 2269
Uger, Alan 1236, 1632, 1669, 1810
Uhnak, Dorothy 1180, 1424, 2172
Ullrick, Sharon 1528
Ultimate Imposter 1442a, 1655
Uncalled for Three 940
Uncle Charley's Showboat 81
Uncle Elroy 590, 683
Uncle Harry 531
Uncommon Valor 1939
Under the Yum Yum Tree 1012
Undercover Girls 1700
Underground Man 1301
Underwood, Ian 1841
Underworld 408
Unger, Alan 1544
Unger, Joe 2189
Uninvited 902
Unit Four 1822

United Artists 423, 708, 746, 754, 767, 771, 828, 829, 835, 857, 859, 867, 870, 903, 915
United Artists Television 2122
United States – It Can't Happen Here 985
Universal Television 509, 772, 774, 775, 776, 798, 809, 811, 831, 840, 841, 842, 843, 845, 846, 847, 848, 850, 851, 852, 853, 861, 866, 888, 889, 891, 902, 906, 910, 912, 913, 918, 920, 922, 925, 926, 927, 929, 966, 967, 972, 974, 978, 987, 992, 998, 1002, 1011, 1013, 1016, 1020, 1021, 1028, 1029, 1031, 1043, 1057, 1059, 1060, 1066, 1072, 1092, 1093, 1096, 1098, 1100, 1102, 1103, 1104, 1105, 1107, 1115, 1124, 1146, 1151, 1157, 1159, 1160, 1163, 1164, 1168, 1169, 1183, 1187, 1211, 1219, 1226, 1227, 1228, 1233, 1234, 1245, 1247, 1274, 1289, 1290, 1295, 1298, 1302, 1318, 1336, 1337, 1338, 1342, 1354, 1356, 1387, 1393, 1396, 1402, 1404, 1407, 1414, 1416, 1418, 1420, 1422, 1425, 1426, 1429, 1442, 1442a, 1478, 1483, 1497, 1506, 1508, 1509, 1514, 1517, 1522, 1525, 1537, 1538, 1545, 1562, 1564, 1565, 1590, 1591, 1610, 1616, 1617, 1619, 1625, 1629, 1640, 1641, 1642, 1643, 1647, 1655, 1660, 1667, 1669, 1684, 1688, 1692, 1754, 1771, 1773, 1778, 1779, 1783, 1785, 1788, 1807, 1814, 1815, 1832, 1840, 1841, 1852, 1864, 1875, 1876, 1880, 1887, 1900, 1902, 1929, 1940, 1942, 1954, 1957, 1958, *1961*, 1965, 1971, 1985, 1987, 2002, 2004, 2027, 2030, 2031, 2046, 2047, 2061, 2065, 2071, 2081, 2094, 2102, 2106, 2126, 2129, 2130, 2131, 2147, 2172, 2175, 2186, 2190, 2196, 2217, 2222, 2241, 2252, 2259, 2260, 2261
Unknown 758
Unpardonables 914
Unsolved 542
Until Proven Guilty 1013
Untitled 533
Untouchables 722, 727, 874
UP A Pictures 390
Uptown Saturday Night 1677
Urbisci, Rocco 1940
Urbont, Jack 1340
Urich, Robert 452, 1302, 1507, 1713, 2214, 2218

Urich, Tom 2218
Used Cars 1980
Ustinov, Pavla 1656
Utley, Scott 2060

V

Vacation Playhouse 765, 893
Vacation With Pay 799
Vaccaro, Brenda 815, 1090, 1220, 2154
Vail, Lawrence 1814
Valdez, Anahuac 2237
Valdez, Luis 2237
Valente, Michael 1407
Valente, Rene 1487
Valentine, Chris 1129
Valentine, Dick 1123
Valentine, Karen 1004, 1239, 1445, 1598, 1760, 1828, 1868, 1941
Valentine, Scott 2121, 2179
Valentine, Stephanie 1129
Valentine Magic on Love Island 1764
Valenty, Lily 922, 1803
Valenza, Tasia 2203
Valerie 2178
Vallely, James 2001
Vallen, Leslie 1874
Valley of Blue Mountain 16
Valley of Mystery 925
Vallez, Vanessa 2191
Valli, Franki 1644
Vampire 1621
Van, Bobby 160, 1020, 1146, 1507, 1630

Van Ark, Joan 1064,
1164, 1277,
1339, 1442
Van Atta, Don 1053,
1308, 1932, 1997
Van Bergen,
Lewis 1863
Van Bernard
Productions 956
Van Bridge,
Tony 1048
Van Cleef, Lee 1519
Van Dam, Gwen
1535
Van Der Vlis,
Diana 699, 844
Van Doren,
Charles 76
Van Doren,
Mamie 462
Van Dreelen, John
621, 1585,
1655, 2060
Van Druten,
John 1406
Van Dusen, Granville
1278, 1451, 1482,
1563, 1572,
1695,1738, 1867,
1870, 1930, 1951
Van Dyck, Jennifer
2242
Van Dyke, Barry
1533, 1612, 1704
Van Dyke, Dick
466, 1205, 1311,
1792, 1803, 2074
Van Dyke, Jerry
826, 953
Van Evers, Jan 1572
Van Fleet, Richard
1043, 1070
Van Gulick,
Robert 1251
Van Horn,
Buddy 1808
Van Keuren,
Sidney 113
Van Ness, Jon 1849

Van Norden,
Peter 1966
Van Nuys, Ed 1231,
1683, 1850
Van Patten, Dick
1176, 1304, 1330,
1405, 1442, 1892
Van Patten,
James 1670
Van Patten, Joyce
1254, 1390, 1551,
1790, 1899, 2166
Van Patten,
Timothy 1873
Van Patten, Vincent
1072, 1442
Van Peebles, Mario
1089, 2114
Van Peebles, Melvin
1469, 1470, 1471
Van Reenen, Jan 1863
Van Scoyk, Robert
550, 1227, 1228
Van Valkenburgh,
Deborah
1910, 2258
Van Winkle,
Joseph 2052
Van-Bernard
Productions 955
Vance, Dana 1794
Vance, Leigh
1399, 1688
Vanders, Warren 611,
1247, 1300, 1353
Vandever, Michael
1119
Vandis, Titos 1212,
1450, 1525
Vanishing Kind
1513, 1595
Vanni, Renata 1747
Vannice, Nicki 2262
Vanoff, Nick 1599
Varela, Jay 1301
Varsi, Diane 1129
Vaughn, Martin 2185
Vaughn, Robert 507,
717, 1119, 1369,

1565, 1683, 1937,
2021, 2064, 2190
Vaughn, Skeeter
1318, 1882
Vector 1302
Vega$ 452, 1507,
1612, 1713
Veith, Sandy 1965
Vejar, Michael
1773, 2066
Velez, Eddie 2105
Velez, Edwin 2128
Velvet 1973
Veney, Gary 1553
Vennera, Chick 1731
Venora, Diane 1627
Venton, Harley
2036, 2090
Ventura, Clyde
1222
Venture, Richard
846, 1367, 1511
Venturers 617
Ventures 970
Venuta, Benay 207
Vera, Julio 1931
Vera, Rick 220
Vera, Tony 1817
Vera Cruz 350
Verbit, Helen 1418
Verdon, Gwen
1940, 1991
Verdugo, Elena 531,
596, 1024, 1183,
1971, 2066
Vereen, Ben 2174
Vernan, Ron 1552
Verne, Jules 86
Vernon, Glen
93, 2126
Vernon, John 1048,
1074, 1234, 1294
Vernon, Kate 2245
Vernon's Volunteers
1018
Verona, Stephen
1361
Verrell, Cec 2090
Vertel, Peter 312

Vertue, Beryl
1682, 1888
Very Missing
Person 1125
Vestoff, Virginia
1381, 1449, 1751
Viacom Enterprises
1178, 1193, 1221,
1267, 1280, 1390,
1410, 1412, 1437,
1466, 1519, 1527,
1528, 1557, 1608,
1613, 1795,
1813, 1914, 1919,
1937, 1997, 2066,
2103, 2107, 2187,
2198, 2199, 2207,
2226, 2254
Vicenzio, Sam 1953
Vickers, Martha
526
Vickers, Yvette 199
Vickery, John 2161
Victor, David 844,
1072, 1115, 1187,
1245, 1404, 1610,
1905, 1971
Victor, James
1371, 1437
Victor Borge
Comedy
Theatre 672
Victoria/Benro
Productions 2233
Vidales, Victor 2148
Vieha, Mark 2100
Vieira, Joey D. 2221
Vigilante 1399
Vignon, Barry 1996
Vigon, Barry
1901, 2157
Vigran, Herb 64,
263, 1094
Villard, Tom 1838,
1851, 1994
Villiers, James 1524
Vincent, E. Duke
1175, 1221, 1333,
1378, 1454, 1495,

1534, 1539, 1612, 1615, 1862, 1917, 1973, 2021, 2025, 2032, 2091, 2092
Vincent, Jan-Michael 1099
Vincent, Virginia 1290, 2047
Vinovich, Steve 1108, 1681
Vinson, Gary 363, 1139
Viola, Al 1638
Virela, Jay 1119
Virgile, Peter 2132
Virginia City 431
Viscuso, Sal 2082, 2214, 2251
Visitor, Nana 1961, 2266
Visk, Randy 2177
Vistor, Nana 2099
Vitale, Dan 2055
Vitale, Milly 504
Vitalie, Joe 1758
Vitte, Ray 1347, 1530
Vivian Blaine/ George London Show 287
Vivyan, John 552, 648
Vlahos, Sam 2065, 2195
Vogel, Carol 1745
Vogel, Mitch 1056, 1403
Vogel, Virgil 1421, 1560, 1822, 1880, 1968, 1985, 2190, 2217
Vogt, Peter 2049
Voight, Peter 1983
Voland, Herbert 1008, 1832
Voland, Mark 2023
Volz, Nedra 1549, 1833
Von Däniken, Erich 1326

Von Furstenburg, Betsy 1198
Von Leer, Hunter 1503, 1504, 1745
Vonnegut, Kurt, Jr. 1168
Von Sydow, Max 2046
Von Wernherr, Otto 2046
Von Zerneck, Danielle 2213
Von Zerneck, Frank 1443, 1645, 1936, 2045, 2099, 2232
Von Zerneck, Peter 1117
Von Zerneck/ Samuels Productions 2232
Von Zill, Nicholas 2093
Voskovec, George 1281
Voyage to the Bottom of the Sea 1101
V-R Productions 1030
Vrana, Vlasta 2258
Vye, Murvyn 450, 792

W

Waco and Rhinehart 2100
Wade, Adam 1368, 1677
Wade, Harker 1865, 2029
Wade, John 2265
Wagg, Peter 2210
Waggenheim, Charles 18
Waggoner, George 68
Waggoner, Lyle 1172, 1190, 1261, 1790, 1811

Wagner, Alan 2112
Wagner, Carla Jean 2237
Wagner, Frank 2034
Wagner, Jane 1178
Wagner, Lindsay 1801, 2196
Wagner, Michael Don 1525, 1647
Wagner, Mike 884, 1656
Wagner, Raymond 841, 853, 905
Wagner, Rick 2119
Wagner, Robert 368, 784, 854, 1089, 1101, 1127, 1586
Wagon Train 509, 695, 700, 734, 751, 842
Wahl, Ken 2089
Waigner, Paul 1920, 2192
Waikiki 1721
Wainwright, James 1318
Wait Until Dark 1122
Waitman, Bernie 571
Waits, Tom 1850
Wake Up, Stupid 641
Wakefield, David 2186
Wakefield, Jack 308
Wakeman, Deborah 1970, 2033
Walberg, Garry 1147, 1239, 1969, 2099
Walcott, George 450
Walcott, Gregory 1563
Walden, Robert 1134, 1243, 1270, 1322
Walden, Susan 1521, 2130
Waldis, Otto 6
Waldman, Frank 717
Waldman, Tom 717
Waldman, Tony 717

Waldo 21
Waldron, Gy 1959
Waldron, John 1642
Wales, Chris 1638
Walk in the Night 905
Walker Brothers Productions 2089
Walker, Ann 1969
Walker, Arnetia 2253
Walker, Bill 985, 1099, 1782
Walker, Charles 1840, 2060
Walker, Chris 2258
Walker, Clint 1079
Walker, Elaine 737
Walker, Eric 1904
Walker, Helen 126
Walker, Jack David 1218
Walker, Jason 1494
Walker, Jeffrey 2089
Walker, Jimmie 1940
Walker, John 2167
Walker, Kathryn 1130, 1165, 2064
Walker, Kay 60
Walker, Lou 1469
Walker, Marcy 2260
Walker, Michael Chase 2089
Walker, Nancy 1136, 1631
Walker, Tanja 1843, 2120
Walker, William, II 1649
Walkin' Walter 1365
Walking Tall 1650
Wallace, Art 1482, 1572
Wallace, Charles 472, 1079
Wallace, Chris 1615
Wallace, Dee 1688, 1757, 1967, 2066
Wallace, Earl W. 1539

Wallace, George 1075, 1343
Wallace, George D. 1560, 1909
Wallace, Helen 717
Wallace, Jack 1479
Wallace, Lee 1679, 1742
Wallace, Marcia 1663, 1755
Wallace, Rick 2107, 2266
Wallace, Royce 1200, 1867
Wallace, William 2185
Wallach, Eli 1187, 2026
Wallach, Roberta 1398, 1491, 1492
Wallenberg, Linda 905
Wallenstein, Joe 1918, 2191
Wallenstein, Joseph B. 2060
Wallerstein, Herb 1108
Wallingham, Noble 1267
Walpole, Willard 2129, 2130, 2131
Walsh, Arthur 441
Walsh, J.T. 2194
Walsh, Joey 743
Walsh, Leigh 1916
Walsh, Lory 1750, 1773
Walsh, M. Emmet 1093, 1336, 1420, 1814, 1864, 1936, 2084
Walsh, Sydney 2113, 2190, 2205
Walston, Ray 531, 596, 770, 1543, 1691, 1940, 1991
Walt Disney Productions 1879, 1881, 1882

Walt Disney Television 2070, 2076, 2079, 2082, 2093, 2100, 2134, 2135, 2160, 2181, 2201, 2215, 2234
Walter, Jessica 885, 1061, 1539, 1562, 1621, 1801, 1971, 2001
Walter, Michael 2173
Walter Mirisch Productions 2190, 2261, 2262
Walter 1981
Walter of the Jungle 978
Walters, Anne 1129
Walters, Laurie 1129, 1316
Walters, Marvin 2260
Walton, Jess 1168, 1618
Walton, Judy 2001
Walton, Peggy 1274, 1378
Walt's Girls 999
Waltz, Lisa 2163
Wambaugh, Joseph 2195
Wanamaker, Sam 961, 2026
Wanger, Walter 185
Wanjugu, Ann 2248
Wanted Dead or Alive 340, 338, 561, 1955
Wanted: The Sundance Woman 1257
War, Lee Tit 1256
War and Eric Kurtz 852
War Correspondent 326
War of the Silver Kings 1420

War of the Worlds 1570
Warbirds, 291
Ward, Al C. 212, 1144, 1395
Ward, Burt 1995
Ward, Evelyn 691
Ward, Fred 2152
Ward, Janet 1278
Ward, Jonathan 2266
Ward, Kaley 1994
Ward, Lalia 2098
Ward, Larry 1258
Ward, Lyman 1875, 1941, 1981
Ward, Mary B. 2159
Ward, Rachel 1784
Ward, Robert 2258
Ward, Sandy 1446, 1589, 1913
Ward, Sela 2188
Ward, Skip 812, 2115
Warde, Harlan 1057
Warden, Jack 781, 1133, 1147, 1297, 1620
Warder, Cari Anne 1486, 1487
Ware, Clyde 1692, 1777
Ware, Midge 523
Warfield, Chris 598
Warfield, Donald 1398
Warfield, Marlene 1160, 1194
Warfield, Marsha 2050
Warga, Robert 395
Waring, Richard 1414
Waring, Todd 1892, 2125
Warlock, Billy 1959, 2082
Warman, Marcianne 2266
Warner, David 2190
Warner, Jody 156

Warner, Marsha 1942
Warner, Sandra 812
Warner Bros. Television 2, 13, 88, 193, 280, 296, 315, 424, 631, 637, 755, 756, 880, 911, 959, 994, 1063, 1083, 1089, 1091, 1122, 1153, 1162, 1175, 1212, 1223, 1230, 1260, 1261, 1270, 1271, 1282, 1292, 1294, 1327, 1328, 1329, 1333, 1347, 1352, 1373, 1378, 1385, 1423, 1448, 1455, 1484, 1521, 1533, 1542, 1550, 1593, 1594, 1626, 1633, 1677, 1698, 1706, 1735, 1760, 1766, 1769, 1782, 1789, 1799, 1800, 1801, 1802, 1822, 1843, 1884, 1891, 1895, 1899, 1934, 1941, 1960, 1962, 1972, 1982, 1988, 2009, 2033, 2045, 2059, 2099, 2115, 2116, 2142, 2148, 2159, 2173, 2192, 2210, 2214, 2218, 2223, 2237
Warren, Bill 1717
Warren, Bob 349
Warren, Charles Marquis 23
Warren, Jennifer 1419, 1427, 1659
Warren, Kathleen 310
Warren, Lesley Ann 1051, 1189, 1417
Warren, Michael 1657, 2263
Warren, Nancy 2245

Warren, Richard Lewis 2189
Warren, Stefani 1025
Warriors 2115, 2173
Warwick, Robert 482
Washington, Ken 1653
Washington, Kenneth 1162
Washington, Vernon 1265
Wass, Ted 1457, 1610, 2035, 2160
Wassil, Chuck 330
Wasson, Craig 1659
Watchman 781
Waterbury, Masha 2165
Waterman, Willard 728, 797
Waters, Ed 1846
Waters, Ethel 826
Waterson, Harry 1622
Waterways 677
Watkin, Lawrence Edward 704
Watkins, Carlene 1537
Watkins, James Louis 1338
Watson, Irwin C. 1604
Watson, James 1430
Watson, James, Jr. 1316, 1717
Watson, Larry 912, 1126
Watson, Mills 1103, 1145, 1211, 1322, 1324, 1335, 1420, 1508
Watson, Moray 1379, 1380
Watson, Susan 654
Watson, Vernee 1757, 1986
Watson, William 1471

Watt, Charles 825
Watts, Elizabeth 383
Watts, Nigel 1937
Waxman, Mark 2233
Waxman, Stanley 961
Way of the Dragon 2115, 2173
Way of the West 314
Wayans, Keenan 1830
Wayne, Carol 1667, 1844
Wayne, David 114, 144, 492, 693, 917, 1099, 1102, 1161, 1535
Wayne, Fred 131, 1424
Wayne, John 305, 1536
Wayne, Johnny 460, 867, 954
Wayne, Patrick 203, 1166, 1515
Wayne, Paul 1670
Wayne and Schuster 867
Wayne/Burditt Productions 1670
Ways of Love 535
Ways of the Peacemaker 524
Wayside School 2143
We Love Annie 1114
We Love You, Miss Merkle 1071
We Two 1209
We'll Take Manhattan 916
We're Putting on the Ritz 2112
Weapon 529
Weapons Man 725
Weary, A.C. 1932
Weathers, Carl 2022
Weaver, Dennis 1565

Weaver, Fritz 960, 1048, 1058, 1130, 1145, 1649, 2084
Weaver, Lee 1008, 1307
Weaver, Rick 1815, 1880, 1985
Weaver, Rose 1780
Webb, Charlie 1901
Webb, Clifton 19, 860
Webb, Dick 490
Webb, Gordon A. 1503, 1504
Webb, Jack 102, 153, 335, 370, 371, 444, 586, 603, 820, 1290, 1295, 1354
Webber, Robert 512, 1160, 1246, 1847, 1917, 2009, 2029
Weber-Gold, Susan 2232
Webster 2067
Webster, Byron 1222, 1621, 1717
Webster, Chuck 264
Webster, Diana 1073, 1168, 1562, 1619, 1641
Weddle, Vernon 1131, 1520, 1585
Wedgeworth, Ann 1555, 2122, 2137
Wedlock, Hugh 20
Wednesday Night Group 1214
Wednesday Night Out 1156
Weege, Reinhold 1769, 1891, 1960
Weekend 915
Weekend Nun 1197
Weekends 1913
Weeks, Alan 1498
Weidergott, Karl 2226
Weil, Cynthia 2231
Wein, Dean 1815

Weinberger, Ed 1093, 1198, 1220, 1386, 2229
Weinberger, Jake 2110
Weinberger, Michael 1490, 2110
Weingrod, Herschel 2246
Weinrib, Lennie 1199
Weinstock, Jack 816
Weintraub, Carl 1561, 1818, 2248
Weintraub, Jerry 1306, 1549, 1702, 1857, 1924, 1928, 2185
Weintraub, Sy 944
Weintraub Entertainment Group 2185, 2249, 2262
Weintraub/Levinson Productions 1924
Weintraub Productions 928
Weir, Jack 1127
Weis, Don 129, 202, 308, 690, 713, 834, 888, 893, 1268, 1289, 1345, 1566, 1820, 1832
Weise, George 255
Weiskopf, Bob 311, 1658, 1831, 1912, 1981
Weiskopf, Kim 1992
Weisman, Sam 1561, 1919, 1975, 1977, 2121, 2179
Weiss, Dori 1995, 2136, 2202, 2257
Weisser, Norbert 1441, 2049
Weitman, Robert M. 1358
Weitz, Barry 1359, 1427, 1468, 1595

Weitz, Bruce 1513, 1681, 1686
Welch, Douglas 85
Welch, Lisa 1992
Welch, Louis 1630
Welch, Raquel 1530
Welch, Robert 502
Welcome Home 1711
Welcome to Paradise 1989
Welcome to Washington 251
Weld, Tuesday 675
Weldon, Charles 1369, 1402
Welker, Frank 1050, 1054, 1174
Weller, Mary Louise 1484, 1588, 1716, 1764, 1954
Welles, Halsted 847
Welles, Jesse 1396
Welles, Orson 74, 919, 1815
Welles, Tiny 2061
Wellington Productions 1720
Wellman, Maggie 1513, 1802
Wellman, Wendall 2247
Wellman, William 391
Wells, Christopher 1856
Wells, Claudia 1809
Wells, Danny 1345, 1617, 1633, 1792, 1927, 1973, 2006
Wells, Dawn 1662, 1663, 1664, 1994
Wells, Erica 1747
Wells, George 1185
Wells, H.G. 74
Wells, J.C. 1638
Wells, Jesse 2034
Wells, John 2223
Wells, Terry 1765

Wells, Tico 1979
Wells, Virginia 21
Wells Fargo 373
Welsh, Jim 1826
Welsh, John 2251
Wende, Phillip 1469
Wendell, Howard 607, 772
Wendkos, Paul 523, 1028, 1047, 1090, 1116, 1301, 1352, 1446, 1907, 1952
Wendy Hooper– U.S. Army 1837
Wenk, Roxie 2105
Werle, Barbara 1197
Werner, Karen 1689
Werner, Peter 2008
Werner, Tom 1855, 1913, 2057
Wertimer, Ned 1534
Wescott, Helen 772
Wesley, John 2159
Wesley, Richard 1548, 1677
Wesson, Dick 809, 912
West, Adam 296, 497, 611, 750, 1122, 1222, 1353
West, Bernie 1554, 1736
West, Brooks 543
West, Elliot 1058
West, Jessamyn 1321
West, John 2008
West, John Stuart 1867
West, Mae 438
West, Paul 805, 818, 1486, 1487, 1571
West, Rebecca 249
West, Red 1842, 2008, 2083
West, Roy 1724
West, Tegan 1995
Westburg, David 1212

Westerfield, James 260, 465, 1035
Western Musketeers 233
Westerner 737
Westheimer, David 832
Westinghouse Preview Theatre 384
Westlake, Donald 1707
Westley, William 1564
Westman, Nydia 955, 1035
Weston, Celia 1768
Weston, Dick 831
Weston, Ellen 1190, 1234, 1292, 1335, 1476
Weston, Jack 76, 292, 455, 459, 482, 521, 912, 918, 972, 1181, 1283, 1346
Westwood Productions 1096
Wettig, Patricia 1888
Whacked Out 1838
Whaley, Frank 2252
Wharmby, Tony 2173, 2259
What a Country! 1823
What About That One? 1224
What Are Friends For? 1556
What Are the Odds? 349
What Do You Feel Like Doing Tonight? 1288
What Is a Man? 223
What Is Harry's Business? 531
What Now, Mrs. Davis? 2182
What's Happening Now! **1177**

What's in It for Harry? 986
What's Up, Doc? 1533
Whatever Happened to Dobie Gillis? 1465
Whatever You Do, Don't Panic 684
Whattley by the Bay 2235
Wheaton, Wil 1932, 1970, 2096
Wheeler, Ed 1777
Wheeler, John 1656
Wheeler, Margaret 1872
Wheeler and Murdock 1133
Whelan, Justin 2245
Whelchel, Lisa 1834, 1853, 1889, 1896, 2251
When Every Day Was the Fourth of July 1597, 1714
When Widows Weep 1165
Where Have All the People Gone? 1303
Where There's Smokey 292
Where's Everett? 901
Where's Momma? 1225
Where's Poppa? 1606
Where's the Fire? 1238
Which Way Did They Go? 726
Which Way to the Mecca, Jack? 864
Whistler 73
Whistling Shrimp 782
Whitaker, Johnnie 790

White, Al C. 1832, 2047
White, Andy 661, 801, 1032, 1571
White, Baynia 2021
White, Betty 1527, 1810, 2181
White, Callann 1918
White, Charlie 1777
White, Christine 808
White, Dan 1061
White, David 383, 1371
White, Deborah 1368, 2196
White, Gary Michael 1933
White, Jamina D. 1566
White, Jesse 126, 381, 463, 618, 670, 1551
White, Larry 1400, 1405
White, Michael Gary 2244
White, Sam 289
White, Slappy 1604, 1767
White, Ted 1229, 1908
White, Will J. 164, 603
White, Yvonne 309
White and Reno 1767
White Knight 2101
White on White and Nearly Perfect 1788
Whitefield, Anne 554
Whitehead, Paxton 2102
Whiteman, Frank 1190, 1544
Whiteman, George 1544
Whitfield, Anne 1302
Whitfield, David 1942

Whitford, Bradley 2128
Whiting, Arch 1235
Whiting, Richard 1851
Whitman, Parker 1885
Whitman, Peter 2063
Whitman, Stuart 830, 1101, 1188, 1445, 1692
Whitmore, James 213
Whitmore, James, Jr. 1396, 1424, 1564, 1586, 1587, 1640, 1788
Whitmore, Stanford 1122, 1355
Whitney, Grace Lee 665, 921
Whitney, Mike 904
Whitney, Peter 563, 726
Whittaker, Dori 1406
Whittle, John 1627
Who Goes There? 824
Who Killed Julie Greer? 603
Who's On Call? 1607
Who's the Boss? 2073, 2138
Who's Watching the Fleshpot? 927
Whodunit 422
Whorf, Richard 310, 550, 555, 812
Why on Earth 2220
Why Us? 1839
Why Us Company 1839
Wyler, Gretchen 1704
Whyte, Patrick 1059
Wi Kuki Kaa 1989
Wiard, William 1422, 1426, 1816, 1852
Wibberly, Leonard 892

Wichita Town 510, 511
Wickes, Mary 20, 1010, 1271
Wickwire, Nancy 782
Widdoes, Jamie 1921, 2047, 2176
Widdoes, Kathleen 1100, 1242, 1296
Wideman, Ivan 1695
Widener, Earl 1230
Widmark, Richard 1159
Wiesman, Sam 1692
Wiggins, Tudi 2041
Wilbanks, Don 1041
Wilber Wiggins 629
Wilbur, George 1324
Wilcox, Dan 1809, 2156
Wilcox, Frank 250
Wilcox, Larry 1347, 1477, 1908
Wilcox, Mary 1008
Wilcox, Nina 1273
Wilcox, Ralph 1415, 1548, 1625, 1680
Wilcox, Shannon 2035
Wilcox-Horne, Collin 1351
Wilcoxon, Henry 885, 1247, 1295, 1597
Wild About Harry 1414
Wild and Wooly 1539
Wild Wild West 1748
Wild Wild West Revisited 1656, 1748
Wildcatters 221, 305
Wilder, Gene 1329
Wilder, Glenn 1468, 1908
Wilder, John 396, 509, 1421, 1480
Wilder, Myles 813

Wilder, Scott 1841
Wilder, Yvonne 1276, 1364, 1971
Wilding, Michael 442
Wildman, Valerie 2201, 2262
Wilds of Ten Thousand Islands 1571
Wiles, Gordon 1067, 1081
Wiley, Ed 2220
Wileys 1042
Wilhite, Charlie 1599
Wilhoite, Kathleen 1963, 2014
Wilke, Robert J. 507, 1030, 1061, 1854
Wilkerson, Willie 1921
Wilkes, Donna 1584, 1991
Wilkey, Jim 2089
Wilkie, Robert L. 1539
Wilkin, Brad 1493
Wilkins, Joe 1888
Wilkinson, Lisa 2013
Wilkinson, Wallace 1959
Will, Sandra 1445
Will Banner 804
Willard, Fred 954, 1500, 1645, 1807
Willett, Joann 1995
William Bendix Show 679
William Broidy Productions 17
William Morris Agency 61, 281, 308, 428
Williams, Allen 2049
Williams, Andy 528
Williams, Anson 1853, 1944, 2074
Williams, Barry 1025
Williams, Big Boy 686

Williams, Billy Dee 1020, 1047, 1784, 1917, 2260

Williams, Bradley Leland 2129

Williams, Cara 478, 1872

Williams, Cindy 1068, 2017

Williams, Clarence, III 1618

Williams, Danny 1994

Williams, David 1099

Williams, Dick Anthony 1867, 1936, 1952

Williams, Eddy 781

Williams, Ellis E. 2174

Williams, Esther 414

Williams, Ewart 2144

Williams, Frances E. 1248

Williams, Guy 394, 513

Williams, Hal 1282, 1497

Williams, Hank, Jr. 877

Williams, Jack 1257

Williams, Jan 1881

Williams, JoBeth 1572, 1828, 1844

Williams, John 847, 1124

Williams, Liberty 1346, 1374, 1439

Williams, Marsha Posner 2123

Williams, Patrick 1076, 1090, 1103, 1135, 1155, 1163, 1170, 1246, 1257, 1351, 1357, 1386, 1405, 1429, 1433, 1472, 1517, 1563, 1578, 1668, 1673, 1765, 1872, 1883,

1887, 1895, 1941, 1981, 2012, 2164, 2169, 2172, 2244

Williams, Paul 1515, 1568, 1579, 1656, 1865, 1866

Williams, Phillip 2132

Williams, R.J. 2069

Williams, Rhys 540

Williams, Robert 1332

Williams, Roberta Jean 1745

Williams, Sandra 846

Williams, Simon 1937

Williams, Steve 2035

Williams, Steven 2021, 2033

Williams, Thad 885

Williams, Tiger 1110, 1423, 1597, 1714

Williams, Timothy 2024

Williams, Tonya Lee 2213

Williams, Van 720, 885, 1560, 1616

Williams, Walter 1596

Williard, Carol 1398

Willie, Austin 504

Willie 293

Willies 840

Willingham, Noble 1303, 1329, 1587, 1730, 1981, 2217, 2269

Willis, Ann 1025

Willis, Austin 1078, 1612

Willis, Beverly 729

Willis, Donald 2266

Willock, Dave 819, 893, 1787

Willock, Margaret 1297, 1833

Willow B: Women in Prison 1722

Willrich, Rudolph 1684

Wills, Chill 34, 1040

Wills, Terry 1212

Wilson, Alex 1264

Wilson, Anthony 1348, 1583

Wilson, Dale 2093

Wilson, Daniel 1449

Wilson, Danny 1381

Wilson, Demond 1014

Wilson, Donald 718

Wilson, Elizabeth 1263, 1687

Wilson, Flip 1756

Wilson, Gaby 1567

Wilson, Grant 1631

Wilson, Hugh 1433

Wilson, Iron Jaw 1604

Wilson, Irv 1221

Wilson, Jeannie 1457

Wilson, Marie 307, 658

Wilson, Paul 2226

Wilson, Rita 2245

Wilson, Roger 2247

Wilson, Sheree 1973, 2117

Wilson, Terry 509, 1319

Wilson, Theodore 1177, 1365, 1440, 1637, 1830

Winchell, Paul 1018, 1315

Windhoek, Owen 2063

Windom, William 390, 557, 623, 1074, 1095, 1098, 1128, 1131, 1318, 1389, 1523, 1588, 1732, 1820, 1878, 1973, 2019

Windsor, Marie 62, 67, 643, 880, 1404

Windsor, Romy 2094

Windust, Penelope 1338

Winer, Harry 1855, 2000, 2192

Winet, Bruce 1892

Winfield, Paul 1816, 2013

Winfrey, Oprah 2139

Wing, Leslie 2177

Wing Sam, Wilson N.G. 2091

Wingreen, Jason 1339, 1517, 1641, 1732, 2021

Winitsky, Alex 2198

Winkleman, Wendy 250

Winkler, Harry 762

Winkler, Henry 1712, 2141

Winkler, William 1632

Winkler/Rich Productions 2141

Winn, Bill 1888

Winn, Kitty 1147

Winner Take All 1480

Winning of the West 32, 224

Winningham, Mare 1653

Winslow, Dick 206

Winslow, Michael 1617, 1830

Winslow, Paula 744

Winston, Hattie 1236

Winston, Helene 1838

Winter, Edward 1199, 1420, 1444, 1481, 1503, 1605, 1637, 1800, 1844, 1879, 1883

Winter Kill 1254

Winters, David 753
Winters, Deborah 1595
Winters, Jana 1885
Winters, Jonathan 57, 1748
Winters, Marc 1539
Winters, Marian 1398
Winters, Roland 18, 813
Winters, Shelley 1126, 1277, 2110
Wintersole, William 1473
Wintle, Julian 1039, 1127
Wirth, John 2189
Wisbar, Frank 16
Wise, Alfie 1108, 1608
Wise, Ray 1968
Wiseguy 408
Wiseman, Joseph 752, 1060, 1192, 1228, 1256
Wish You Were Here 146
Wishman 1919
Witch's Milk 1274
Withers, Grant 113
Withers, Jane 760
Witherspoon, Dana 1743
Withrow, Glenn 1749, 2122
Witney, Michael 1099, 1139
Witt, Howard 1673, 1795, 1838, 2079, 2134
Witt, Kathryn 1637, 1862, 1972
Witt, Paul Junger 1071, 1134, 1189, 1190, 1258, 1297, 1383, 1485, 1963, 2016, 2019, 2068, 2123, 2181

Witt, Roz 2009
Witt-Thomas-Harris Productions 1485, 2181
Witt-Thomas Productions 1963, 2016, 2019, 2068, 2123
Wittner, Meg 2154, 2239
Witzend Productions 2224
Wives 1334
Wixted, Michael James 1299, 1303
Wize, Tom 1222
Wizzle Falls 1949
Wohl, David 2042, 2094
Wohl, Jack 1625, 1731
Wolf, Dick 2241
Wolf, Emmanuel 1321
Wolf, Fred 1724
Wolfe, George 466
Wolfe, Winifred 202
Wolfington, Iggie 1306, 1315
Wolper, David 1202
Wolpert, Jay 1892
Wolpert, Stuart 1990
Wolterstorff, Robert 1807, 1864, 2111
Woman I Love 1116
Woman in the Case 327
Woman on the Run 1481, 1516
Women 377
Won't It Ever Be Morning? 853
Wonder Woman 1261
Wonderful World of Little Julius 328
Wonderful World of Phillip Malley 1812

Wonderful World of Sin 1224
Wonderful Years 932
Wong, Anna May 516
Wong, Carey 1240
Wong, Jarroo 1089
Wong, Russell 2091, 2258
Wood, Allen 1567, 1623
Wood, Andy 1845
Wood, Cynthia 1328
Wood, Jane 1620
Wood, Janet 1491, 1492
Wood, Jeane 381, 555
Wood, Lana 1041, 1511, 1642
Wood, Preston 1302
Wood, Robert 1551, 1761
Wood, Teri Lynn 1401
Wood, Ward 885
Wood, William 1321
Woodard, Alfre 2123
Woodfield, William Read 1073
Woodruff Productions 1822
Woods, Donald 690
Woods, George J. 2186
Woods, Jeri 1348
Woods, Lesley 1210
Woods, Robert S. 2154, 2189
Woods, William 1068
Woodville, Kate 1028, 1057, 1292, 1441
Woodward, Joe 2045
Woodward, Kimberly 1695, 1765
Woodward, Morgan 734, 1079, 1904

Woofruff, Aiken 2129
Woolen, Susann 1937
Wooley, Monty 116
Wooley, Sheb 23
Woolf, Charles 1724
Woolman, Claude 1168
Wooly Mammoth Productions 1826
Wopat, Tom 2104
Worden, Hank 1249
Woren, Don 1942
Working Girls 675
Workman, Lindsay 1008, 1246
World Beyond 1572
World of Darkness 1482, 1572
World of Floyd Gibbons 727
World of White 133, 329
World Premiere 1092
World's Greatest Letters 53
Worldvision 1526
Worley, Jo Anne 1699
Worth, Marvin 815, 1078, 1606
Worth, Nicholas 2032, **2221**
Worthington, Cathy 1907
Wrather, Jack 363, 364, 365, 367, 368, 369, 489
Wray, Fay 113
Wren, Michael 2081
Wright, Amy 1925
Wright, Ben 253, 482, 716, 848, 1435, 1720
Wright, Dan 611
Wright, Eboney 1328
Wright, Herbert 1228, 1699
Wright, J.J. 1888
Wright, Judith 1317

Wright, Mary
Catherine 1666
Wright, Max
1996, 2012
Wright, Robin 2085
Wright, Samuel
E. 2041
Wright, Tom 2209
Wright, William
679, 871
**Writer's Guild
Theatre** 409
Writers Company
Productions
1588
Wuhl, Robert
2039, 2232
Wyatt, Jane 572,
715, 1014, 1486,
1487, 1566
Wyatt, Walter 1781
Wyenn, Than 1102,
1335, 1822
Wyle, George 1902
Wyler, David 1980
Wyler, Gretchen
1879, 1926
Wyler, Richard 504
Wyllie, Meg 509, 917,
1166, 1247, 1930
Wyman, Jane 540,
1157, 1226
Wymore, Patrice 880
Wynant, H.M. 1235
Wyner, George
1387, 1460, 1501,
1545, 1565, 1871,
2072, 2078
Wynn, Ed 109,
256, 826
Wynn, Keenan 669,
737, 871, 1298,
1397, 1611, 1845,
1894, 1903, 2061
Wynn, Ned 1973
Wynter, Dana 684,
1182, 1351, 1648
Wyss, Amanda 1871,
1955, 2191

Y

Yah-Ling Sun, Irene
1584, 1782, 1938
Yamashita,
Tadashi 1251
Yancy, Emily 1131,
1222, 1447
Yanez, David
1365, 1542
Yangha, Thomas
301
Yank 451, 585
**Yankee Stay
Here** 874
Yanok, George
1349, 1445
Yapp, Peter 1039
Yarbrough, Jean
391, 813, 1040
Yarmy, Dick 1387,
1408, 1414, 1457
Yarmy, Richard 1238
Yarnall, Bruce 833
Yarnall, Celeste
1008, 1164
Yarnell, Lorene 1656
Yasbeck, Amy 2039
Yashima, Momo 1971
Yasutaki, Patti 2237
Yates, Brook 1835
Yates, Cassie 1849,
1905, 2151
Yates, Curtis 1769
Yates, John
Robert 1599
Yates, William Robert
750, 1516, 1879,
1881, 2214, 2218
Yazoo 1949
Yeager, Biff 1974,
2042, 2126
Yeager, Bill 1519
Year One 1098
Yelland, Sherman
844
Yellow Bird 759
Yes, Honestly 2162
Yiro, Robert 1338

Yniquez, Richard
1123, 1147, 1427,
1516, 1823, 2151
Yohn, Erica 1446,
1544, 1610
Yongestreet
Productions
1389, 1829
York, Dick 162,
329, 1995
York, Francine 806,
1026, 1335, 1382
York, James 1583
York, Kathleen 1996
York, Michael 2025
York, Rebecca 1964
Yorkin, Bud 455,
494, 837, 855, 954,
1034, 1576, 2184
Yorkin, Harvey 642
Yorkin, Lear 855
Yorty, Sam 1908
Yoshioda, Adele 1100
Yothers, Tina 1882
You & Me, Kid
Productions 2012
**You Can't Win
Them All** 571
**You Know Me,
Al** 162
Youmans, William
2211
Young, Alan 64
Young, Bob
2001, 2105
Young, Bruce 2258
Young, Bruce A. 2197
Young, Buck
1061, 1235
Young, Carlton 353
Young, Charles 1566
Young, Chris T. 2224
Young, Cletus 1644
Young, Collier 95,
429, 430, 431, 495,
535, 653, 718, 923
Young, Dalene
1520, 2003
Young, Darryl 1328

Young, David
1222, 1419
Young, Dennis 1212
Young, Donna
Jean 1026
Young, Ericha 1328
Young, Faron 234
Young, Gig 1524
Young, Heather
1008, 1141
Young, John
Sacret 1521
Young, Keone
1270, **2000**
Young, Loretta
377, 2025
Young, Mel 2265
Young, Michael
2028, 2089
Young, Nedrick 985
Young, Otis 925,
1310, 1371
Young, Paul 1127
Young, Ray 1067,
1212, 1808
Young, Richard
1419, 1574, 2082
Young, Robert 917,
1486, 1487, 1971
Young, Robert
Malcolm
1157, 1226
Young, Skip 1043
Young, Stephen
976, 1060, 1141
Young, William
Allen 1767, 1822,
1976, 2013
Young, William
L. 1843
Young & Marcus
Productions 429
Young at Heart 825
Young Country 1043
Young Dr. Kildare 495
Young Frankenstein
1684
**Young Guy
Christian** 1608

Young Hearts 1950
Young Love 1088
Young Maverick 1448
Young Men in a
 Hurry 661
Young Reverend 97
Young Sheriff 234
Youngblood, Jack
 2128, 2258
Youngblut,
 Nancy 2227
Younger, Jack 670
Youngfellow, Barrie
 1483, 1540, 1621
Youngstein, Max
 E. 877
Your Place or
 Mine 1558
You're Gonna Love It
 Here 1455, 1542
You're Just Like Your
 Father 1394
You're Only Young
 Once 380, 662
You're Only
 Young Twice
 311, 467, 826
Yue, Marion 1914
Yulin, Harris 1255,
 1322, 1450, 1508,
 1597, 1610, 1616
Yuma 1079
Yune, Johnny 1675

Z

Zacha, W.T. 1403,
 1442, 1655, 1969

Zacha, William,
 Sr. 1655
Zacharias, Steve
 1441, 1504, 1672,
 1676, 1770
Zackel, Fred 1953
Zagon, Martin
 1537, 1810
Zagor, Michael
 1152, 1207
Zal, Roxanna 1879
Zale, Alexander
 1887
Zammit, Eddie
 1970
Zand, Michael 2232
Zane Grey Theatre
 23, 209, 214,
 472, 475, 563
Zanuck, Richard
 2169
Zanuck/Brown
 Co. 2169
Zapata, Carmen
 1203, 1427, 2233
Zapien, Danny 1249,
 1477, 1784
Zappa, Moon 1958
Zaqvaglia, Richard
 1876
Zarchen, John 2225
Zaremba, John 912
Zarou, Elias 2132
Zaslow, Michael 1822
Zavada, Ervin
 1653, 2024
Zavada, Irv 2209
Zaylor, Judith 2155

Zecher, Roseanne
 1354
Zee, John 2133
Zeigler, Heidi 1964
Zeigler, Ted 1067
Zeitman, Jerry
 1343, 1795
Zelda 663
Zeller, Ben 2261
Zema, Stefan
 2049, 2119
Zemeckis, Robert
 1980
Zenda, John 1525
Zenor, Susan 1174
Zentall, Kate 1624
Zephir Productions
 1830
Zerbe, Anthony
 1124, 1292,
 1937, 2191
Zeri, Walter 1818
Zero Intelligence
 1366 007
 1611, 1652
Zettler, Michael
 2112
Zien, Chip 1389,
 1459, 1625
Ziffren, John 2188
Zimbalist, Al 301
Zimbalist,
 Donald 301
Zimbalist, Efrem,
 Jr. 1414, 1780,
 1880, 1883, 1917
Zimbalist, Stephanie
 1414, 1444

Zimmerman, Ron
 2222, 2252
Zimmerman,
 Vernon 1917
Zinberg, Michael
 1433, 1668, 1673,
 1793, 1838, 1895,
 1941, 1981, 2205
Zipp, Debbie
 1343, 1463
Ziskie, Dan
 1906, 2189
Zito, Steve 1863
ZIV 90, 850
ZIV/UA 622, 642
Zizkind, Trudi 472
Zlotoff, Lee
 David 2100
Zmed, Adrian 1851
Zon, Deborah 1527
Zoovets 2170
Zorek, Michael
 1950, 1994, 1995
Zorich, Louis 1228
Zorro 1616
Zsa Zsa in Paris 443
Zuber, Marc 1379
Zucker, Charlie 1950
Zuckert, Bill 846,
 1102, 1198,
 1592, 1974
Zulu 1510
Zweibel, Alan 2055
Zwerling, Darryl 1447
Zwick, Ed 2165
Zwick, Joel 1598,
 1794, 1898, 2067,
 2108, 2164